A Bronze Age Landscape
in the Russian Steppes
The Samara Valley Project

UCLA COTSEN INSTITUTE OF ARCHAEOLOGY PRESS
Monumenta Archaeologica

MA 36

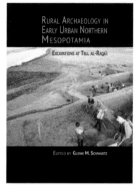

Rural Archaeology in Early Urban Northern
Mesopotamia: Excavations at Tell al-Raqa'i
Edited by Glenn M. Schwartz

MA 35

New Insights into the Iron Age Archaeology
of Edom, Southern Jordan
By Thomas E. Levy, Mohammad Najjar,
and Erez Ben-Yosef

MA 34

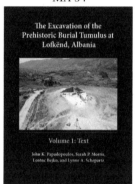

The Excavation of the Prehistoric Burial
Tumulus at Lofkënd, Albania
By John K. Papadopoulos, Sarah P. Morris,
Lorenc Bejko, and Lynne A. Schepartz

MA 33

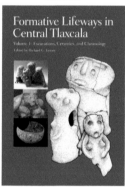

Formative Lifeways in Central Tlaxcala Vol. 1:
Excavations, Ceramics, and Chronology
Edited by Richard Lesure

MA 32

Integrating Çatalhöyük: Themes
from the 2000-2008 Seasons
Volume 10
Edited by Ian Hodder

MA 31

Substantive Technologies at Çatalhöyük:
Reports from the 2000-2008 Seasons
Volume 9
Edited by Ian Hodder

MA 30

Humans and Landscapes of Çatalhöyük:
Reports from the 2000-2008 Seasons
Volume 8
Edited by Ian Hodder

See page 512 for a complete list of Cotsen Institute of Archaeology Press Monumenta Archaeologica volumes.

A Bronze Age Landscape
in the Russian Steppes
The Samara Valley Project

Edited by **David W. Anthony, Dorcas R. Brown, Oleg D. Mochalov,
Aleksandr A. Khokhlov,** and **Pavel F. Kuznetsov**

UCLA COTSEN INSTITUTE OF ARCHAEOLOGY PRESS

Library of Congress Cataloging-in-Publication Data
A Bronze Age landscape in the Russian steppes: the Samara Valley Project / edited by David W. Anthony, Dorcas R. Brown, Oleg D. Mochalov, Aleksandr Khokhlov, Pavel Kuznetsov.
    pages cm. -- (Monumenta archaeologica ; volume 37)
Includes bibliographical references and index.
ISBN 978-1-938770-05-0 (hardback)
1. Bronze age--Russia (Federation)--Samara Region. 2. Samara Valley Project. 3. Srubna culture--Russia (Federation)--Samara Region. 4. Andronovo culture--Russia (Federation)--Samara Region. 5. Steppe archaeology--Russia (Federation)--Samara Region. 6. Pastoral systems--Russia (Federation)--Samara Region--History--To 1500. 7. Landscape archaeology--Russia (Federation)--Samara Region. 8. Excavations (Archaeology)--Russia (Federation)--Samara Region. 9. Samara Region (Russia)--Antiquities. 10. Volga River Region (Russia)--Antiquities. I. Anthony, David W. II. Brown, Dorcas R. III. Mochalov, Oleg D.

GN778.22.R9B76 2015
947).01--dc23

2015030266

Table of Contents

Author Affiliations   ix
List of Figures   xi
List of Tables   xv
Acknowledgments   xix

Part I   Introduction and Overview of the Samara Valley Project 1995–2002   1

Chapter 1
The Samara Valley Project and the Evolution of Pastoral Economies in the Western Eurasian Steppes   3
  David W. Anthony

Chapter 2
Archaeological Field Operations in the Lower Samara Valley, 1995–2001, with Observations   37
  on Srubnaya Pastoralism
  David W. Anthony, Dorcas R. Brown, and Pavel F. Kuznetsov

Part II   History, Ecology, and Settlement Patterns in the Samara Oblast   61

Chapter 3
Historic Records of the Economy and Ethnic History of the Samara Region   63
  Oleg D. Mochalov, Dmitriy V. Romanov, and David W. Anthony

Chapter 4
The Samara Valley in the Bronze Age: A Review of Archaeological Discoveries   71
  Pavel F. Kuznetsov and Oleg D. Mochalov (Translated from Russian by David W. Anthony)

Chapter 5
Paleoecological Evidence for Vegetation, Climate, and Land-Use Change in the Lower Samara River Valley   91
  Laura M. Popova

Part III   Human Skeletal Studies   **103**

Chapter 6
Demographic and Cranial Characteristics of the Volga-Ural Population in the Eneolithic and Bronze Age   105
Aleksandr A. Khokhlov

Chapter 7
Stable Isotope Analysis of Neolithic to Late Bronze Age Populations in the Samara Valley   127
Rick J. Schulting and Michael P. Richards

Chapter 8
A Bioarchaeological Study of Prehistoric Populations from the Volga Region   149
Eileen M. Murphy and Aleksandr A. Khokhlov

**Part IV   Excavation and Specialist Reports for the Krasnosamarskoe Kurgan Cemetery
and Settlement and the Herding Camps in Peschanyi Dol**   **217**

Chapter 9
The Geoarchaeology of the Krasnosamarskoe Sites   219
Arlene Miller Rosen

Chapter 10
Excavations at the LBA Settlement at Krasnosamarskoe   227
David W. Anthony, Dorcas R. Brown, Pavel F. Kuznetsov, and Oleg D. Mochalov

Chapter 11
Bronze Age Metallurgy in the Middle Volga   291
David L. Peterson, Peter Northover, Chris Salter, Blanca Maldonado, and David W. Anthony

Chapter 12
Floral Data Analysis: Report on the Pollen and Macrobotanical Remains from the
Krasnosamarskoe Settlement   333
Laura M. Popova

Chapter 13
Phytoliths from the Krasnosamarskoe Settlement and Its Environment   351
Alison Weisskopf and Arlene Miller Rosen

Chapter 14
Dog Days of Winter: Seasonal Activities in a Srubnaya Landscape   373
Anne Pike-Tay and David W. Anthony

Chapter 15
Archaeozoological Report on the Animal Bones from the Krasnosamarskoe Settlement   385
Pavel A. Kosintsev

Chapter 16

Human-Animal Relations at Krasnosamarskoe   421

Nerissa Russell, Audrey Brown, and Emmett Brown

Chapter 17

The Bronze Age Kurgan Cemetery at Krasnosamarskoe IV   443

Pavel F. Kuznetsov, Oleg D. Mochalov, and David W. Anthony

Chapter 18

Bronze Age Herding Camps: Survey and Excavations in Peschanyi Dol   471

David W. Anthony, Dorcas R. Brown, Pavel F. Kuznetsov, and Oleg D. Mochalov

Index   497

Author Affiliations

David W. Anthony, Hartwick College, Oneonta, New York

Dorcas R. Brown, Hartwick College, Oneonta, New York

Audrey Brown, Knoxville, Tennessee

Emmett Brown, AMEC Foster Wheeler, Knoxville, Tennessee

Aleksandr A. Khokhlov, Volga State Academy of Social Sciences and Humanities, and the Samara State Technical University, Samara, Russia

Pavel A. Kosintsev, Institute of Plant and Animal Ecology, Urals Branch of the Russian Academy of Sciences, Ekaterinburg, Russia

Pavel F. Kuznetsov, Volga State Academy of Social Sciences and Humanities, Samara, Russia

Blanca Maldonado, Eberhard Karls Universität Tübingen, Curt-Engelhorn-Zentrum Archäometrie, Tübingen, Germany

Oleg D. Mochalov, Volga State Academy of Social Sciences and Humanities, Samara, Russia

Eileen M. Murphy, School of Geography, Archaeology and Palaeoecology, Queen's University Belfast, Belfast, Ireland

Peter Northover, Department of Materials, Oxford University, Oxford, United Kingdom

David L. Peterson, Idaho State University, Pocatello, Idaho

Anne Pike-Tay, Department of Anthropology, Vassar College, Poughkeepsie, New York

Laura M. Popova, Barrett Honors College, Arizona State University, Phoenix, Arizona

Michael P. Richards, Department of Human Evolution, Max Planck Institute for Evolutionary Anthropology, Leipzig, Germany, and Department of Anthropology, University of British Columbia, Vancouver, Canada

Dmitriy V. Romanov, Samara State Agricultural Academy, Samara, Russia

Arlene Miller Rosen, Department of Anthropology, University of Texas at Austin, Austin, Texas

Nerissa Russell, Department of Anthropology, Cornell University, Ithaca, New York

Chris Salter, Department of Materials, University of Oxford, Oxford, United Kingdom

Rick J. Schulting, School of Archaeology, University of Oxford, Oxford, United Kingdom

Alison Weisskopf, University College London, Institute of Archaeology, London, United Kingdom

List of Figures

Acknowledgments Figure 1. Igor Borisovich Vasiliev.

Figure 1.1 Eastern part of the Pontic-Caspian steppes.

Figure 1.2 Site distributions in the Samara oblast.

Figure 1.3 Language map of the Middle Volga-Ural region.

Figure 1.4 The Srubnaya-Andronovo horizon around 1800 BC.

Figure 1.5 Late Middle Bronze Age cultures.

Figure 1.6 Frequency of cultivated seeds in LBA, Final Bronze, and Iron Age sites.

Figure 2.1 Survey area in the lower Samara Valley.

Figure 2.2 Samara River marshes and oxbow lakes near Krasnosamarskoe.

Figure 2.3 Samara River floodplain forests.

Figure 2.4 Map of vegetation types in the lower Samara Valley.

Figure 2.5 Recording the GPS location of a Yamnaya kurgan at Pokrovka.

Figure 2.6 Excavations at PD1 in 2000.

Figure 2.7 Decline in artifact densities with distance from the Samara River, for Peschanyi Dol herding camps.

Figure 2.8 Malachite and azurite in iron-rich sandstone at Mikhailovka Ovsianka.

Figure 2.9 Barinovka settlement (SVP 5) excavation 1996.

Figure 2.10 Overview of Krasnosamarskoe.

Figure 2.11 A carving of Gorposemog, god of archaeology.

Figure 2.12 Excavation at Krasnosamarskoe in 1999.

Figure 2.13 Kurgan I, central grave 3 under excavation.

Figure 2.14 Known and probable LBA Srubnaya settlements in the project area.

Figure 3.1 Map of Samara oblast.

Figure 4.1 Map of Srubnaya (Late Bronze Age) settlement sites.

Figure 4.2 Map of Yamnaya (Early Bronze Age) sites.

Figure 4.3 Map of Middle Bronze Age sites, all types.

Figure 4.4 Map of Srubnaya (Late Bronze Age) cemetery sites in the Samara oblast.

Figure 5.1 Location of the coring location at Sharlyk near Krasnosamarskoe.

Figure 5.2 (a) Percentage pollen diagram from Sharlyk swamp.

Figure 5.2 (b) Percentage pollen diagram from Sharlyk swamp

Figure 6.1 Graves by age class: Khvalynsk I and II (Eneolithic).

Figure 6.2 Gender by age class: Khvalynsk II (Eneolithic).

Figure 6.3 Facial Reconstructions based on skulls.

Figure 6.4 Graves by age class: Yamnaya (EBA).

Figure 6.5 Gender by age class: Yamnaya (EBA).

Figure 6.6 Gender by age class: Yamna-Poltavka (EBA/MBA).

Figure 6.7 Graves by age class: Yamna-Poltavka (EBA/MBA) and Potapovka-Sintashta (Late MBA).

Figure 6.8 Gender by age class: Potapovka-Sintashta (Late MBA).

Figure 6.9. Gender by age class: Early Srubnaya (Early LBA).

Figure 6.10. Graves by age class: Potapovka-Sintashta (Late MBA), Early Srubnaya (Early LBA), and Late Srubnaya (LBA).

Figure 6.11. Gender by age class: all Srubnaya (LBA).

Figure 6.12. Graves by age class: all cultures.

Figure 7.1. Map of sites sampled in Schulting and Richards' isotope study (Chapter 7) and Murphy's bioarchaeological study (Chapter 8).

Figure 7.2. Bivariate plot of δ¹³C and δ¹⁵N values for pooled Neolithic/Eneolithic and Bronze Age humans from the Samara Valley.

Figure 7.3. Bivariate plot of δ¹³C and δ¹⁵N values humans from the Samara Valley by period.

Figure 7.4. Bivariate plot of δ¹³C and δ¹⁵N values for Neolithic and Bronze Age males and females from the Samara Valley.

Figure 7.5. Bivariate plot of δ¹³C and δ¹⁵N values humans and fauna from selected Central Eurasian sites.

Figure 8.1 Crude prevalence rates (percentage) based on the numbers of affected individuals for developmental defects.

Figure 8.2 Posterior view of a probable case of slipped femoral capital epiphysis of the right femur.

Figure 8.3 Male and female average greatest femoral lengths (mm) across the different time periods.

Figure 8.4 Caries prevalences (percentage) among the adult teeth of the Volga populations.

Figure 8.5 Prevalence rates (percentage) of extraspinal osteoarthritis.

Figure 8.6 Details of the prevalences (percentage) of degenerative joint disease among the main extraspinal joints.

Figure 8.7 Lateral view of a probable case of slipped femoral capital epiphysis of the right femur.

Figure 8.8 Perimortem gouge or scrape marks apparent on the posterolateral aspect of the right parietal and occipital.

Figure 8.9 Perimortem gouge or scrape marks apparent on the posterolateral aspect of the right parietal and the superior aspect of the occipital.

Figure 8.10 Probable longstanding depressed fracture on the right side of the frontal bone.

Figure 8.11 In situ view of skeleton K1 G4, a newborn to 0.5-year-old infant of Poltavka date.

Figure 8.12 Green discoloration due to association with copper or bronze objects on the left maxilla.

Figure 8.13 In situ view of the disarticulated bundle burial.

Figure 8.14 Disarticulation cut marks on the proximal right femur.

Figure 8.15 Disarticulation cut marks on the right distal humerus.

Figure 8.16 Summary of the prevalence rates (percentage) of cribra orbitalia (by bone), enamel hypoplasia (by individual), reactive new bone formation (crude), and violence (crude).

Figure 8.17 Summary of the dental palaeopathological lesions among the Volga adults.

Figure 8.18 Summary prevalence rates of the potential indicators of physical activity.

Figure 8.19 Summary of the prevalence rates for association with ochre and metal artifacts and evidence for disarticulation and/or defleshing.

Figure 9.1 Google Earth image of Krasnosamarskoe site.

Figure 9.2 Two geological test pits (GS-I and GS-II) were dug in the archaeologically sterile section of the shovel test transect.

Figure 10.1 The Samara River and its oxbow lakes and marshes in the vicinity of Krasnosamarskoe.

Figure 10.2 Plan of the excavated area at the Krasnosamarskoe settlement.

Figure 10.3 Krasnosamarskoe radiocarbon chronology by level (left) and weight of ceramics, separated by chronological type (right).

Figure 10.4 Srubnaya residential architecture in the Samara oblast at the settlements of Shelekhmet, Shigonskoe 1, and Russkaya Selit'ba.

Figure 10.5 1998 aerial photo of Krasnosamarskoe with overlay indicating the archaeological operations at Krasnosamarskoe.

Figure 10.6 (a) Flotation tank and (b) natural stratigraphy at Krasnosamarskoe.

Figure 10.7 ¹⁴C dates from Krasnosamarskoe settlement.

Figure 10.8 The broken Marshalltown trowel, a clear testament to the hardness of the baked steppe soils.

Figure 10.9 N-S profile through the excavated structure including Pit 10 (bottom) and the external occupation surface (top) at Krasnosamarskoe.

Figure 10.10 Artifacts from the Iron Age Gorodetskaya culture component.

Figure 10.11 The excavation grid with inside-the-structure units distinguished from outside-the-structure units.

Figure 10.12 Pottery styles by weight by level inside the structure.

Figure 10.13 Pottery styles by weight by level outside the structure.

Figure 10.14 Top: Central part of excavated structure: units N2-4 and O2-4 with features 10 (the well) and 14 through 20. Lower left: plan showing the same area with adjoining units containing additional features 21 to 22. Lower right: photograph of the semi-circular line of pits between Pit 14 and Pit 10 (the well).

Figure 10.15 Feature 1 in Unit L3, a probable posthole.

Figure 10.16 View south across the 2001 excavation area with the bases of pit features dug into the *materik* subsoil.

Figure 10.17 Feature 2, a probable posthole in Unit L4.

Figure 10.18 Features 3 and 4 in Units K1 and K2 at the base of level 7, 80 cm deep.

Figure 10.19 Feature 5, a depression at the edge of Unit L4/4.

Figure 10.20 Feature 6, a deep disposal pit.

Figure 10.21 The anomalously high proportion of *Chenopodium* pollen in Pit 8 shows that this plant was manipulated.

Figure 10.22 Profile of Pit 10: the well.

Figure 10.23 Pit 10, the well, under excavation near the bottom of the feature.

Figure 10.24 Uppermost wooden artifacts from Pit 10.

Figure 10.25 Ceramics found in Pit 10.

Figure 10.26 Wood and bark from the 210-cm b.s. depth.

Figure 10.27 Wood and bark from the 220- to 230-cm b.s. depth.

Figure 10.28 Wood and bark from the 230- to 240-cm b.s. depth.

Figure 10.29 Wood from the 240- to 250-cm b.s. depth.

Figure 10.30 Animal bones found in Pit 10.

Figure 10.31 Wood from the 260- to 270-cm b.s. depth.

Figure 10.32 Feature 12 was a small pit, possibly a posthole base.

Figure 10.33 Feature 25 was the largest concentration of ash found inside the structure.

Figure 10.34 Semi-complete crushed Vessels 1 to 4 and 6 to 7.

Figure 10.35 Ceramic densities measured by total weight in grams in each 1-m × 1-m unit.

Figure 10.36 Pokrovka-style ceramics.

Figure 10.37 Developed (or mature) Srubnaya style ceramics.

Figure 10.38 Middle Bronze Age ceramics.

Figure 10.39 Chipped stone and metal artifacts.

Figure 10.40 Ground stone artifacts.

Figure 10.41 Worked bone artifacts.

Figure 11.1 Map of sites discussed in the chapter.

Figure 11.2 The copper club from Kutuluk I, Kurgan 4, Grave 1.

Figure 11.3 Above: the copper blade from Kutuluk III. Below: the copper awl from Kutuluk III.

Figure 11.4 Arsenic bronze rings from Nur.

Figure 11.5 Arsenic values from the WDS results.

Figure 11.6 Tin values from the WDS results.

Figure 11.7 Bivariate plot of nickel and arsenic values from the WDS results.

Figure 11.8 Bivariate plot of iron and antimony values in copper and bronze artifacts from Utevka VI and Potpovka I.

Figure 11.9 Work patterns in Bronze Age metalwork from the Middle Volga based on metallographic observations.

Figure 11.10 The tin bronze blade from Grachevka II, Kurgan 8, Grave 8.

Figure 11.11 Comparison of work patterns present in metalwork from Utevka VI and Potapovka I.

Figure 11.12 Top: pendants from Nizhny Orleansky, Bottom: the Spiridonovka II pendant.

Figure 11.13 SEM-EDS element map of the Spiridonovka II girl's pendant.

Figure 11.14 Plan of the location of metal finds at Krasnosamarskoe.

Figure 11.15 The sites identified in Kamyshla.

Figure 11.16 Plan of Kibit I.

Figure 12.1 Plan map of the structure at Krasnosamarskoe highlighting some of the types of pollen collected from the floor.

Figure 13.1 Common phytolith morphotypes (from Weisskopf, 2010).

Figure 13.2 Reference samples.

Figure 13.3 Phytolith weight percentage per gram sediment per sample.

Figure 13.4 Phytoliths per gram sediment.

Figure 13.5 KS-02-01: Unit M2, 220 cm b.s., Pit 10 well: wet with preserved organics.

Figure 13.6 KS-02-02: Unit M3/2, 80 cm b.s., Pit 10 well: small ash lens in pit fill.

Figure 13.7 KS-02-03: Unit L2/ 4, 40 to 50 cm b.s., sticky black soil on top of structure.

Figure 13.8 KS-02-04: Unit K3/3, 70 to 80 cm b.s., Feature 25 ash lens.

Figure 13.9 KS-02-05: Unit L4/1, 30 to 40 cm b.s., sticky black soil on top of structure.

Figure 13.10 KS-02-06: Unit K2/3, 80 to 90 cm b.s., Pit 3.

Figure 13.11 KS-02-07: Unit M2, 240 cm b.s., Pit 10 ash lens.

Figure 13.12 KS-02-08: Unit K3/4, 80 cm b.s., Feature 25, ash lens.

Figure 13.13 KS-02-09: Unit L2/4, 80 to 92 cm b.s., Pit 7 fill.

Figure 13.14 KS-02-10: Unit M2, 200 to 210 cm b.s., Pit 10.

Figure 13.15 KS-02-11: off-site natural buried A horizon dated to 8000 BC.

Figure 13.16 KS-02-12: Unit K2/4 50 to 110 cm b.s., Pit 9.

Figure 13.17 KS-02-13: Unit K2/2, 60 to 70 cm b.s., crushed ceramic vessel 7.

Figure 13.18 KS-02-14: Unit I3/3, 80 to 90 cm b.s., Pit 12.

Figure 13.19 KS-02-15: Unit K5/2, 80 to 90 cm b.s., Pit 11.

Figure 13.20 KS-02-16: Unit L3/3, 80 to 90 cm b.s., Pit 1 ashy soil.

Figure 13.21 KS-02-17: Unit L2/4, 80 to 90 cm b.s., Pit 8.

Figure 13.22 KS-02-18: Unit L4/4, 80 to 90 cm b.s., Pit 22.

Figure 13.23 KS-02-19: Unit M2/4, 94 cm b.s., Pit 10.

Figure 13.24 KS-02-20: Unit L3/2, 70 to 80 cm b.s., Pit 1.

Figure 13.25 Correspondence analysis.

Figure 16.1 Animal bone density by weight.

Figure 16.2 Distribution of taxa outside the structure and in the upper and lower levels of the structure.

Figure 16.3 Percentage of dog bones by NISP in each unit.

Figure 16.4 Body part distributions for major taxa outside the structure and in the upper and lower levels of the structure, with distribution in intact animal for comparison.

Figure 16.5 Chopped dog skull pieces.

Figure 16.6 Size distribution of chopped dog skulls (not including mandibles) in centimeters.

Figure 16.7 Location of chops on dog skulls.

Figure 16.8 Dog atlases chopped longitudinally.

Figure 16.9 Distribution of unchopped and chopped dog skull fragments (not including mandibles or loose teeth) by level.

Figure 16.10 Placement of roasting traces on sheep/goat, cattle, horse, and dog.

Figure 16.11 Rates of roasting per NISP for cattle and dog in the structure.

Figure 16.12 Size range of digested bones.

Figure 16.13 Dog age stages.

Figure 16.14 Dog tibia with ossified hematoma.

Figure 16.15 Cattle femur with osteoarthritis on caput.

Figure 16.16 Cattle posterior first phalanx with exostosis.

Figure 16.17 Horse first phalanx with osteoarthritis.

Figure 16.18 Horse second phalanx with exostosis.

Figure 17.1 Krasnosamarskoe kurgan cemeteries I to VI.

Figure 17.2 Left: aerial photo of Krasnosamarskoe IV Kurgans 1 to 7 and settlement location. Right: drawing of field operations at KS IV.

Figure 17.3 Aerial photo of Krasnosamarskoe Kurgans 1 to 3 and settlement site.

Figure 17.4 Top: bulldozer beginning excavation of Kurgan 1. Bottom: bulldozer exposed strips.

Figure 17.5 Kurgan 1 plan and profile.

Figure 17.6 Kurgan 1, Graves 1 to 4.

Figure 17.7 Kurgan 1, Grave 3, central grave, MBA Poltavka culture.

Figure 17.8 Kurgan 2 plan and profile.

Figure 17.9 Kurgan 2, Graves 1 to 3.

Figure 17.10 Kurgan 2 photographs: (a) measuring and mapping square trench around the kurgan; (b) Grave 1, a bundle burial; (c) Catacomb-type ceramic found in kurgan fill.

Figure 17.11 Kurgan 3 plan and profile.

Figure 17.12 Kurgan 3, Graves 8, 9 and sacrificial deposit 1.

Figure 17.13 Kurgan 3 excavations were very complex with 24 graves.

Figure 17.14 Kurgan 3, Graves 1 to 7 and 10.

Figure 17.15 Kurgan 3, Graves 11 to 16.

Figure 17.16 Kurgan 3, Graves 17 to 19.

Figure 17.17 Kurgan 3, Grave 17. As in Figure 17.7, the floors of the deepest graves were flooded by the 1-m rise in the water table when local fishponds were filled.

Figure 17.18 Kurgan 3, Graves 20 to 24.

Figure 17.19 Kurgan 3, ceramics found in graves.

Figure 18.1 The lower Peschanyi Dol valley looking southwest across the floodplain marshes.

Figure 18.2 Peschanyi Dol, Barinovka, and Krasnosamarskoe.

Figure 18.3 Excavations at PD1 in 2000.

Figure 18.4 The Peschanyi Dol valley with locations of selected test sites (Locations) and archaeological sites discovered (PD1 to PD6).

Figure 18.5 PD1 in 1996 looking west from a high point in the meadow.

Figure 18.6 PD1 in its topographic setting (below) and the PD1 north and south excavation grids (above).

Figure 18.7 PD5 in 1996, looking northwest over the wooded side valley. Crews are 15 m apart.

Figure 18.8 PD1 North plan and profile on the Zh transect.

Figure 18.9 PD1 South artifact densities in Levels 1 to 4, per m^2, by weight.

Figure 18.10 Artifacts from PD1.

Figure 18.11 Excavations at PD2 in 2000.

Figure 18.12 Plan and profile of PD2.

Figure 18.13 Artifacts from PD2, including a mortar and copper casting waste.

Figure 18.14 Percentage of stone, ceramic, and bone finds by count at three sites.

List of Tables

Table 1.1 Chronology for Bronze Ages in the Volga-Ural and surrounding steppe region.

Table 1.2 Domesticated animals by percentage of MNI in LBA Andronovo settlements by region.

Table 2.1 All ^{14}C dates from the Samara Valley Project.

Table 3.1 1864 Herd populations in Buzuluk District, Samara oblast.

Table 4.1 Srubnaya settlements in the Samara River drainage.

Table 4.2 Multicomponent Bronze Age cemetery sites.

Table 4.3 Srubnaya cemeteries in the Samara River drainage.

Table 5.1 Archaeological periods covered in the text for the Middle Volga region.

Table 6.1. Distribution of demographic traits by age class and chronological period.

Table 6.2 Distribution of sexes by age classes of anthropological materials from the Volga-Ural, Eneolithic through the Bronze Ages.

Table 6.3a Craniometric indices of male skulls from the steppe and steppe areas of the Volga-Ural Eneolithic-Bronze Ages.

Table 6.3b Craniometric indices of female skulls from the steppe and steppe areas of the Volga-Ural Eneolithic-Bronze Ages.

Table 6.4 Potapovka-Sintashta burial data.

Table 7.1 Samara Valley Project stable isotope results.

Table 7.2 Stable carbon and nitrogen isotope averages and standard deviations (±1 SD) for Neolithic/Eneolithic to Late Bronze Age human samples from the Samara Valley.

Table 7.3 Mann-Whitney U Test Results for Stable Carbon and Nitrogen Isotope Averages and Standard Deviations (±1 SD) Assessing Locational and/or Period Differences

Table 7.4 Stable carbon and nitrogen isotope averages and standard deviations (±1 SD) for Neolithic/Eneolithic to Middle Bronze Age fauna from Central Eurasia.

Table 7.5 Stable carbon and nitrogen isotope averages and standard deviations (±1 SD) for Bronze Age adolescent/adult humans from selected regions of Central Eurasia.

Table 8.1 Details of the numbers of individuals from each site included in the study.

Table 8.2 Details of the number of individuals from each period included in the study.

Table 8.3 Details of the breakdown of adults and nonadults in the data set included in the current study.

Table 8.4 Details of individuals with defects of the blastemal desmocranium developmental field.

Table 8.5 Details of individuals with defects of the paraxial mesoderm developmental field.

Table 8.6 Details of individuals with defects of the sternal developmental field.

Table 8.7 Summary of male and female femoral greatest lengths for the different cultures.

Table 8.8 Prevalence rates (percentage) of the adults with cribra orbitalia for each culture.

Table 8.9 Numbers of Srubnaya individuals with cribra orbitalia broken down by age and sex ($n = 25$).

Table 8.10 Prevalences (percentage) of adults with porotic hyperostosis based on the numbers of individuals with observable parietals and/or occipitals.

Table 8.11 Prevalence (percentage) of adult individuals with dental enamel hypoplasia.

Table 8.12 Numbers of Srubnaya individuals with enamel hypoplasia broken down by age (years) and sex ($n = 40$).

Table 8.13 Crude prevalence rates (percentage) of individuals with infectious lesions.

Table 8.14 Frequencies of reactive new bone formation by bone.

Table 8.15 Details of the frequencies (percentage) of adults with dentitions and numbers of teeth and sockets by culture.

Table 8.16 Details of the numbers of teeth and tooth socket positions by age and sex for the adults of the different populations.

Table 8.17 Details of the frequencies (percentage) of non-adults with dentitions and numbers of teeth and sockets by culture.

Table 8.18 Details of the caries apparent in the population groups.

Table 8.19 Details of the adult prevalences (percentage) of abscesses by tooth socket position for each population group.

Table 8.20 Details of the prevalences (percentage) of periodontal disease by individual in each adult population group.

Table 8.21 Details of the prevalences (percentage) of calculus deposits by teeth for each adult population group.

Table 8.22 Details of the prevalences (percentage) of calculus deposits by teeth for each nonadult population group.

Table 8.23 Details of individuals with heavy deposits of calculus on one or more teeth.

Table 8.24 Details of the adult prevalences (percentage) of antemortem tooth loss by tooth socket position for each population group.

Table 8.25 Details of the frequencies of adult teeth (percentage) with evidence of secondary dentine or pulp cavity exposure from the different periods.

Table 8.26 Crude prevalence rates (percentage) of non-violence-related fractures based on the numbers of individuals affected in each population group.

Table 8.27 Details of the fractures of the appendicular skeleton apparent in the population groups.

Table 8.28 Prevalence (percentage) of the different fractured long bones based on the numbers of right and left bones for each population group.

Table 8.29 Frequencies (percentage) of fractured appendicular bones as a proportion of the total number of adult long bones across the different time periods.

Table 8.30 Details of spondylolysis in the populations.

Table 8.31 Details of the cases of myositis ossificans traumatica among the Volga populations.

Table 8.32 Frequencies (percentage) of myositis ossificans traumatica as a proportion of the total number of adult long bones across the different time periods.

Table 8.33 Details of osteochondritis dissecans in the Srubnaya population.

Table 8.34 A summary of the prevalences of osteochondritis dissecans in the affected bones of the Srubnaya population (both right and left bones are included).

Table 8.35 Prevalences of enthesophytes in the Srubnaya population.

Table 8.36 Crude prevalence rates (percentage) of non-violence-related injuries.

Table 8.37 Crude prevalence rates (percentage) of extraspinal osteoarthritis based on the numbers of individuals present in each population group.

Table 8.38 Prevalence rates of extraspinal osteoarthritis.

Table 8.39 Details of the prevalences (percentage) of osteoarthritis among the main extraspinal joints for Srubnaya males and females.

Table 8.40 Summary of the prevalences of spinal osteoarthritis (percentage) based on the number of individuals, apophyseal joints (excluding costal and transverse facets), and body surfaces.

Table 8.41 Prevalence (percentage) of osteoarthritis in the apophyseal joints (excluding costal and transverse process facets) of each vertebra.

Table 8.42 Prevalence (percentage) of osteoarthritis in the vertebral body surfaces.

Table 8.43 Summary of the prevalences (percentage) of Schmorl's nodes based on the number of individuals and body surfaces.

Table 8.44 Prevalence (percentage) of Schmorl's nodes in the vertebral body surfaces.

Table 8.45 Yamnaya individual: details of the cranial injuries apparent in the individual recovered from Flat Grave 5 of the Leshevskoe I burial ground.

Table 8.46 Details of individuals with fractured nasal bones in the population groups.

Table 8.47 Crude prevalence rates (percentage) of probable violence-induced trauma based on the numbers of individuals present in the each population group.

Table 8.48 Details of the individuals with red ochre staining from the different cultures.

Table 8.49 The prevalence rates of individuals (percentage) associated with ochre.

Table 8.50 Details of the individuals with green discoloration on bones indicative of association with metal artifacts.

Table 8.51 The prevalence rates (percentage) of individuals with green discoloration due to their association with metal objects.

Table 8.52 Details of individuals with evidence of defleshing and/or disarticulation as part of the funerary process.

Table 8.53 The prevalence rates (percentage) of individuals with evidence of defleshing and/or disarticulation.

Table 9.1 Sediment description of a typical *lugovo'e* meadow soil at Krasnosamarskoe.

Table 9.2 Description of a *solenetz* saline soil.

Table 9.3 Environmental dates from the Samara riverbank and the lake bottom.

Table 9.4a Description of alluvial section on the bank of the Samara River, "Samara 1"; middle of section.

Table 9.4b Description of alluvial section on the bank of the Samara River, "Samara 1"; north portion of section.

Table 9.5 Description of *solenetz* soil formed on old alluvial channel from Geological Section GS-II.

Table 9.6 Description of sediments from section in Kurgan 1.

Table 10.1 Krasnosamarskoe 1998–2001 material culture by level whole settlement area.

Table 10.2. Finds inside the Krasnosamarskoe settlement structure.

Table 10.3 Finds outside the Krasnosamarskoe settlement structure.

Table 10.4 Bone finds in Pit 10 by level.

Table 10.5 Bone finds in Pit 14 by level.

Table 10.6 Percentage of domestic animal NISP in all levels of Pit 10 and Pit 14.

Table 11.1 List of sampled objects.

Table 11.2 EPMA-WDS results.

Table 11.3 Metal groups based on WDS results for major elements.

Table 11.4 Metal finds recovered from Krasnosamarskoe by unit and level.

Table 12.1 Overall pollen concentrations from all samples.

Table 12.2 Count, percent, and concentration of arboreal pollen from Feature 10.

Table 12.3 Count, percent, and concentration of nonarboreal pollen and spores (herbs/shrubs) from Feature 10.

Table 12.4 Count, percent, and concentration of NA pollen and spores (wetlands) from Feature 10 samples.

Table 12.5 Count, percent, and concentration of NA pollen (wetlands) found in samples from inside structure.

Table 12.6 Count, percent, and concentration of NA pollen (wetlands) found in sample outside the structure.

Table 12.7 Count, percent, and concentration of NA pollen (herbs/shrubs) from contexts inside the structure.

Table 12.8 Count, percent, and concentration of NA pollen (herbs/shrubs) from contexts outside the structure.

Table12.9 Arboreal pollen from contexts inside the structure.

Table 12.10 Arboreal pollen from contexts outside the structure.

Table 12.11 Density of macrobotanical remains at Krasnosamarskoe, comparing Pit 10 and all other features.

Table 12.12 List of the count for each taxa represented by macrobotanical remains at Krasnosamarskoe for the features excluding Pit 10.

Table 12.13 List of the count for each taxa represented by macrobotanical remains from Feature 10.

Table 12.14 Macrobotanical remains from 1999 excavations, sorted and analyzed at the Institute of Ecology of Plants and Animals, Russian Academy of Sciences, Ekaterinburg, Russia.

Table 13.1 Krasnosamarskoe phytolith samples grouped by feature.

Table 14.1 Krasnosamarskoe seasonal indicators.

Table 14.2 Bos and sheep-goat ages for Krasnosamarskoe and Mikhailovka Ovsianka.

Table 14.3 Bos and sheep-goat seasonality for Krasnosamarskoe and Mikhailovka Ovsianka.

Table 14.4 Krasnosamarskoe dogs: season of death.

Table 14.5 Dog ages.

Table 15.1 Species present in the fauna excavated in 1999, NISP/MNI.

Table 15.2 Skeletal elements of cattle (*Bos taurus*) in 1999.

Table 15.3 Body parts (percentage) of cattle (*Bos taurus*) and ovicaprid (*Ovis aries, Capra hircus*) in 1999 and 2001 (with isolated teeth/without).

Table 15.4 Age structure of cattle (*Bos taurus*) from maxilla in 1999 and 2001.

Table 15.5 Age structure of cattle (*Bos taurus*) from mandible in 1999 and 2001.

Table 15.6 Skeletal elements ovicaprid (*Ovis aries, Capra hircus*) in 1999.

Table 15.7 Age structure of ovicaprid (*Ovis aries, Capra hircus*) maxilla in 1999 and 2001.

Table 15.8 Age structure of ovicaprid (*Ovis aries, Capra hircus*) mandible in 1999 and 2001.

Table 15.9 Skeletal elements horse (*Equus caballus*) in 1999.

Table 15.10 Skeletal elements pig (*Sus scrofa domestica*) in 1999.

Table 15.11 Skeletal elements dog (*Canis familiaris*) in 1999.

Table 15.12 Body parts (percentage) of dog (*Canis familiaris*) in 1999 and 2001 (with isolated teeth/without).

Table 15.13 Bird (*Aves*) species in 1999.

Table 15.14 Percent of all domesticated animals for each domestic species in 1999 and 2001.

Table 15.15 Percent of indeterminate mammal (Mammalia indet.) bones in 1999 and 2001.

Table 15.16 Species present in the fauna excavated in 2001, NISP/MNI.

Table 15.17 Skeletal elements of cattle (*Bos taurus*) in 2001.

Table 15.18 Skeletal element of ovicaprids (*Ovis aries, Capra hircus*) in 2001.

Table 15.19 Skeletal element of horse (*Equus caballus*) in 2001.

Table 15.20 Skeletal elements of pig (*Sus scrofa domestica*) in 2001.

Table 15.21 Skeletal elements of dog (*Canis familiaris*) in 2001.

Table 15.22 Percent of all domesticated animal bones, by species, 2001.

Table 15.23 Percent of indeterminate mammal (Mammalia indet.) bones 2001.

Table 15.24 Comparison of percentages of domesticated animal bones in Srubnaya settlements in the Middle Volga region (Krasnosamarskoe, Site 1, without/with dogs).

Table 15.25 Body parts (percentage) of cattle (*Bos taurus*) in Srubnaya settlements in the Middle Volga region.

Table 15.26 Age structure (percentage) of cattle (*Bos taurus*) in Srubnaya settlements in the Middle Volga region.

Table 15.27 Measurements of cattle (*Bos taurus*) bones from Krasnosamarskoe settlement.

Table 15.28 Body parts (percentage) ovicaprid (*Ovis aries, Capra hircus*) in Srubnaya settlements in the Middle Volga region.

Table 15.29 Age structure (percentage) of ovicaprid (*Ovis aries, Capra hircus*) in Srubnaya settlements in the Middle Volga region.

Table 15.30 Measurements of sheep (*Ovis aries*) bones from Krasnosamarskoe settlement.

Table 15.31 Measurements of goat (*Capra hircus*) bones from Krasnosamarskoe settlement.

Table 15.32 Measurements of cattle (*Bos taurus*) bones in other LBA sites in Middle Volga region.

Table 15.33 Measurements of sheep (*Ovis aries*) bones in other LBA sites in Middle Volga region.

Table 15.34 Measurements of goats (*Capra hircus*) bones in other LBA sites in Middle Volga region.

Table 15.35 Measurements of horse (*Equus caballus*) bones from Krasnosamarskoe settlement.

Table 15.36 Measurements of horse (*Equus caballus*) bones in other LBA sites of the Middle Volga region.

Table 15.37 Measurements of pig (*Sus scrofa domestica*) bones from Krasnosamarskoe settlement.

Table 15.38 Species identified at Peschanyi Dol 1 and 2.

Table 16.1 Identified macro-mammalian bones from Operation 2 by number of identified specimens (NISP) and diagnostic zones (DZ).

Table 16.2 Proportions of major taxa outside structure vs. upper and lower structure, by diagnostic zones.

Table 16.3 Cut/chop types by taxon, with row percentages.

Table 16.4 Pathologies.

Table 16.5 Identified macro-mammalian bones from Area Y by number of identified specimens (NISP) and diagnostic zones (DZ).

Table 17.1 Krasnosamarskoe IV, Kurgan 3, ages of Srubnaya individuals.

Table 17.2 Dated graves at Krasnosamarskoe IV with typed ceramics.

Table 18.1 Radiocarbon dates from PD1.

Table 18.2 Peschanyi Dol 1 ceramic sources.

Acknowledgments

The Samara Valley Project (SVP) was supported by grants from many different sources. The National Geographic Society supported the initial survey of the lower Samara Valley in 1995 and the Peschanyi Dol survey in 1996. The U.S. National Science Foundation (NSF Project BCS-9818527) supported field excavations from 1999 to 2002 at Krasnosamarskoe and Peschanyi Dol. Support was also provided by the Institute of Archaeology of the Russian Academy of Sciences (RFBR №15-06-01916 and RFH№15-11-63008), a state grant from the Ministry of Education and Science of Russia Federation (33.1195.2014/k), and the facilities at the Institute for the History and Archaeology of the Volga (IHAV) in Samara. Professor C. C. Lamberg-Karlovsky and the American School for Prehistoric Research provided funds for this publication, twenty years after helping to fund a formative field conference in Petropavlovsk, Kazakhstan, in 1995, also supported by a grant from the Wenner-Gren Foundation. Judy and Allen Freedman of the Fortis and Freedman Foundations provided seed funding for the Krasnosamarskoe reconnaissance in 1998, which made the NSF proposal possible. Hartwick College, Oneonta, New York, provided anthropology laboratory facilities and institutional support.

The project probably would not have happened if not for Victor Shnirelman, then an archaeologist and ethnologist at the Institute of Ethnography in Moscow, who visited the United States to attend a historic symposium at the American Anthropological Association (AAA) conference in Chicago in 1991, organized by Antonio Gilman and others. A group of prominent Russian archaeologists was invited to talk about the politics of archaeology in what was then a new Russia full of possibilities (Kohl and Fawcett 1995). Dr. Shnirelman spoke at Hartwick College and visited Anthony and Brown on his way to the AAA conference. In return, he became their guide in Moscow in 1992 when they were awarded a grant by the NSF to study bit-related pathologies on ancient horse teeth in museum collections in Kazakhstan, Russia, and Hungary (Brown and Anthony 1998; Anthony and Brown 2014). Dr. Shnirelman directed Anthony and Brown to the city of Samara and introduced them to Igor B. Vasiliev, the dynamic leader of prehistoric archaeology at the Samara State Pedagogical Institute. They studied Vasiliev's large collections of ancient horse bones at the Institute for the History and Archaeology of the Volga (IHAV), which Vasiliev had founded.

Igor Borisovich Vasiliev was an energetic leader of fieldwork and a perceptive synthesizer of archaeological data. His dissertation advisor was N. I. Merpert, an archaeological giant of the previous generation. After finishing his graduate studies in 1979, Vasiliev's fieldwork and publications revolutionized the prehistoric archaeology of the Volga steppes. His excavations at Khvalynsk and S'yezzhee in the middle Volga region and at Kara Khuduk and other desert sites in the lower Volga region defined a new Eneolithic cultural phase that was clearly ancestral to the Yamnaya culture of the Early Bronze Age. His excavations at Potapovka revealed a sister culture related to the Middle Bronze Age (MBA) II Sintashta culture. (For a Vasiliev bibliography, see Chapter 4.) He made Samara a central place to go to understand steppe archaeology. Vasiliev and his wife Irina (also a highly respected archaeologist) were kind and generous hosts to us during our first visit to Samara in 1992, and their daughter Dasha helped us in the field in 1999. Unfortunately, his health failed just as we started the Samara Valley Project, but he placed it in the hands of three of his former students, now coeditors and authors of this report.

Igor Borisovich Vasiliev
September 15, 1948–August 4, 2004
Photo taken near the site of Potapovka July 1993.

Codirectors, coeditors, and authors Pavel Kuznetsov, Oleg Mochalov, and Aleksandr Khokhlov did most of the work organizing field operations and cataloguing and storing the resulting finds. In 1995, Anatoly Plaksin, a history teacher in the village of Utyevka, shared his home, wooden banya, well-tended garden, and local archaeological knowledge during our initial survey of the lower Samara River valley. Plaksin's cottage had often been a base for Vasiliev during archaeological projects near Utyevka. Plaksin coauthored an illustrated prehistory of the Samara Valley with Kuznetsov (Kuznetsov and Plaksin 2004) not long before his death in 2011.

The 1996 survey of Peschanyi Dol and test excavation at the Late Bronze Age (LBA) Barinovka settlement was conducted by a field team consisting of the coeditors of this volume, university students from Samara, Samara high school students, and U.S. archaeologists Petar Glumac, Charles McNutt, and Christopher Gette, whose familiarity with Cultural Resource Management archaeology in the United States and good humored energy made this initial field operation the success that it was.

In 1998, Boris A. Aguzarov of Samara flew a light-air vehicle 400 m above Krasnosamarskoe to obtain the aerial photos of the site used in this report. Nerissa Russell of Cornell accompanied the coauthors of this volume on the 1998 reconnaissance excavation at Krasnosamarskoe that provided the foundation for the NSF grant proposal.

Between 1999 and 2001, the central part of the SVP occurred, with the NSF-funded excavations at the LBA Krasnosamarskoe settlement, complete excavation of the Krasnosamarskoe IV kurgan cemetery, and significant excavations at two of the Peschanyi Dol LBA herding camps. During the 1999 season at Krasnosamarskoe, more than 100 people were in the field for six weeks, needing food, latrines, tents, equipment, and transportation. The Russian team that made most of this happen included our three Russian coauthors, plus Ala Semonova directing the field laboratory (washing, labeling, cataloguing), Boris Aguzarov as photographer, and graduate students Dmitry Kormilitsyn and Anatoly Pozhidaev as crew-chief field assistants. Dimitry (Dima) was particularly skilled at excavating carefully in muddy conditions beneath the water table, a difficulty we faced because the water table was raised by the creation of a manmade lake just a few meters from our excavation. Mikhail Puchko, Director of Public Schools in Mirnyi (Mirnyy in Google-Earth), provided our project transportation vehicle, a school bus, and supervised a summer archaeological camp for his school students who worked on our excavations each summer between 1999-2001. These local supervisors each contributed essential skills to the project.

Graduate students from the University of Chicago included Laura Popova (then Soikkeli), whose dissertation research produced our paleobotanical reports; and David Peterson, whose dissertation research produced our metallurgy report. Graduate students Elizabeth Beaver and Kay Grennan from Cornell University also assisted in the 1999 season.

Visiting Western specialists included Nerissa Russell of Cornell, assisted from 1999 to 2001 by Emmett Brown and Audrey Brown then of the University of Alabama for archaeozoology, Arlene Rosen then of the London Institute of Archaeology in 1999 for geomorphology; Eileen Murphy of Queen's University Belfast in 1999 for human skeletal pathology and demography; and Suzanne LeRoy, then of the Centre for Palaeoecology, Queen's University Belfast, in 1999 for geomorphological coring in the lake covering the Bronze Age marshes near the settlement.

Pavel Kosintsev from the Institute of Plant and Animal Ecology in Ekaterinburg was present each season from 1999 to 2001 to process the animal bones in the field and afterward, if necessary. His good cheer, familiarity with the regional fauna, and professional zoological expertise identifying species from small bone fragments were invaluable. We also benefited from the advice of Igor V. Ivanov of the Pushtchino Institute of Soil Science on soil geomorphology and G. I. Matveeva for contemporary plant ecology. I. N. Vasilieva and N. P. Salugina analyzed the clays and tempers in our ceramics using microscopic methods developed by A. A. Bobrinskiy. Dimitri Romanov of the Samara State Academy of Agricultural Economics researched the ethnohistory of pastoral production in the region. The IHAV support staff in Samara produced annual reports after each excavation season, including line drawings of artifacts, profile and plan drawings of excavation units, and descriptions and counts of recovered artifacts and features. They also stored and curated the artifacts from all of our excavations.

Students and former students from Hartwick College also assisted in the excavations. These included undergraduate students Russell Becker, Sean Babcock, Ben White-Hammerslough, Alex (AJ) Noury, Eric Regnell, Jeanette LeClaire, and Kate Bachner, as well as graduates Kirstie Haertel and Christopher Gette. In 1999, Joe Anthony-Brown (then 17 years old) and Keith Anthony-Brown (13), sons of authors Anthony and Brown, also assisted.

Finally we thank the Cotsen Institute of Archaeology at UCLA for publishing this monograph, especially Randi Danforth and Gillian Dickens who oversaw the transformation of this long complicated report into a coherent volume. We are especially grateful to our esteemed reviewers, Professors Gregory Areshian (UCLA) and Jim Mallory (Queen's University Belfast), for their thoughtful and useful suggestions for revisions, to say nothing of their time. As with any archaeological study as complex and long term as this one, there are too many people involved to name every individual. We are deeply grateful to all who contributed.

References

Anthony, D. W., and D. Brown

2014   Horseback Riding and Bronze Age Pastoralism in the Eurasian Steppes. In *Reconfiguring the Silk Road: New Research on East-West Exchange in Antiquity*, edited by Victor Mair and J. Hickman, pp. 55–71. University of Pennsylvania Museum, Philadelphia.

Brown, D. R., and D. W. Anthony

1998   Bit Wear, Horseback Riding, and the Botai Site in Kazakhstan. *Journal of Archaeological Science* 25:331–347.

Kohl, Philip L., and Clare Fawcett (editors)

1995   *Nationalism, Politics, and the Practice of Archaeology*. Cambridge University Press, Cambridge.

Kuznetsov, P. F., and A. V. Plaksin

2004   *Drevnosti Neftegorskogo Raiona*. Samarskii Gosudarstvennyi Pedagogicheskii Universitet, Samara.

Part I

Introduction and Overview of the Samara Valley Project 1995–2002

The Samara Valley Project and the Evolution of Pastoral Economies in the Western Eurasian Steppes

David W. Anthony

The Samara Valley Project (SVP) was a collaborative archaeological project conducted in the steppes southeast of the Russian city of Samara between 1995 and 2002. Samara is a river-port and railway hub on the middle Volga River. The city grew around a fort built by Ivan the Terrible in 1586 at the junction of the Volga and Samara Rivers to control the newly conquered middle Volga region, wrested from Bulgar and Kalmyk pastoralists. The fort overlooked a majestic curve in the Volga where the mile-wide river flows against white limestone cliffs on its west bank that divert it into a U-shaped switchback around a high mountain, a curve known as the Samarskaya Luka. The Luka marks the transition between the arid steppes to the south, occupied by pastoralists until the eighteenth century, and the forests to the north, occupied by farmers since the Iron Age. The Samara River, flowing into the Luka from the east, drains the western slopes of the southern Ural Mountains through an ecological borderland between steppe and forest-steppe, contrasting environments exploited by contrasting human social organizations (Figure 1.1), making this region a cultural as well as an ecological border zone. Today, Samara is somewhat like a Russian Chicago, a rail hub that links the Russian east and west, and an industrial center where cattle-raising regions are linked with big meat-importing cities. Chicago, however, has no local oil fields, while the rural landscape east of Samara, where we worked, can resemble Texas, with tall black oil derricks overlooking herds of grazing cattle.

The SVP was conceived and led by David Anthony and Dorcas Brown of Hartwick College on the U.S. side and by Pavel Kuznetsov, Oleg Mochalov, and Aleksandr Khokhlov of the (then) Samara State Pedagogical University (now the Volga State Academy of Social Sciences and Humanities) on the Russian side. Fieldwork continued for seven years, beginning in 1995 with a survey of a 100-km-long segment of the lower Samara River valley above the Bolshoi Kinel' tributary and ending in 2002 with sustained excavations at four sites, including a permanent settlement, a kurgan cemetery, and two herding camps of the Late Bronze Age (LBA) Srubnaya culture, dated 1900 to 1700 BC. A preliminary report was published in 2005 (Anthony et al. 2005), and ancillary reports have appeared occasionally (Popova 2006, 2007; Anthony and Brown 2007; Peterson 2006, 2009; Kuznetsov and Mochalov 1999). This is the final report.

The goal of the SVP was to investigate a striking change in settlement patterns that occurred in the middle Volga region during the opening centuries of the LBA, or between 1900 and 1700 BC (Figure 1.2). At this time, the formerly mobile steppe pastoralists of the Early and Middle Bronze Ages (EBA and MBA, 3300–1900 BC) settled in permanent, archaeologically visible homes, abandoning their old nomadic habits. Settlement sites leaped into view across the middle Volga-Ural region. The pastoral nomads of the EBA and MBA made very visible burial mounds or kurgans for a select few of their dead, creating 50 known

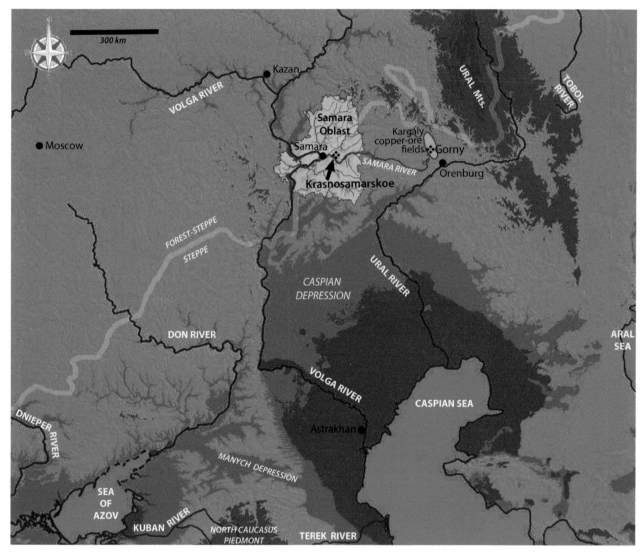

Figure 1.1 Eastern part of the Pontic-Caspian steppes. Samara oblast is highlighted.

kurgan cemeteries in the Samara oblast (Figure 1.2, left), but seem to have lived in wagons (which were buried in some exceptional EBA graves) and tent camps that left almost no archaeological traces. The LBA (1900–1200 BC) saw the creation of 150 new settlements in the Samara oblast (Figure 1.2, right), but only a small increase in the number of cemeteries, from 50 to 60. Cemeteries did not grow enough between the MBA and LBA to account for the explosion in settlements among the living; rather, becoming sedentary probably made the entire population visible archaeologically. The LBA population might also have grown at a moderately higher rate than the EBA/MBA population because sedentary life made it possible to keep a larger number of cows in LBA herds, and this increased the supply of milk and dairy foods (because cows produce six times more milk than goats do), which could have

supported a somewhat larger LBA population. Even so, the huge increase in settlement numbers at the MBA/LBA transition is probably largely due to a sudden change in the permanence and archaeological visibility of settlements rather than a sudden and steep rise in population. Why the early LBA people suddenly settled in permanent homes and what this implied about changes in the LBA pastoral economy was an unresolved problem. It was a significant problem beyond the middle Volga steppes because a similar change affected a much larger area.

Settlements appeared around 1900 to 1700 BC not only in the middle Volga region but across most of the steppe zone from western Ukraine to the borders of China. This LBA "settling-down" process is often assumed to have been caused by the widespread adoption of agriculture and the maturation of a settled agropastoral economy

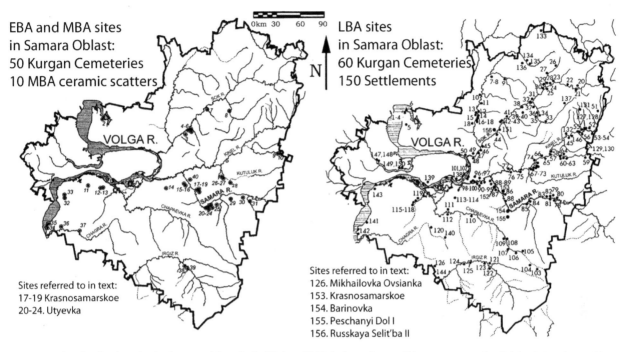

Figure 1.2 Site distributions in the Samara oblast. Left: EBA and MBA sites, almost all kurgan cemeteries. Right: LBA sites, with 150 new LBA settlements. *After Kolev, Mamonov, Turetsky (2000 pp.183 and 227).*

that spread with the Srubnaya (or Timber Grave) culture across the western part of the Eurasian steppes and with the Andronovo horizon across the eastern steppes, between 1900 and 1200 BC (Ostroshchenko 2003; Kuzmina 1994, 2008; Koryakova and Epimakhov 2007:111–160).

The appearance of the Srubnaya-Andronovo horizon was the first time in human history that a bridge of related cultures extended across the Eurasian steppes from the borders of China and Central Asia to the eastern edge of Europe. Unlike later and more familiar steppe-wide revolutions, the first one, at the MBA/LBA transition, was not created by pastoral nomads. Its archaeological signature was many small (agricultural?) settlements, with neighboring cemeteries, dispersed through river valley lowlands near marshes, concentrated particularly in the northern margins of the steppes. This settled river valley economy disintegrated in 1200 to 800 BC (Final Bronze Age) and was replaced by mobile pastoral nomadism of the Scythian-Saka type, generally regarded as a dependent or "non-autarkic" economy (Khazanov's 1984 title, *Nomads and the Outside World*, refers directly to this condition of dependence) that could not exist before the Iron Age. It was only then that centralized agricultural states—China, Persia, and Greece—arose on the margins of the steppe zone, and their economic surplus encouraged the evolution of nomadism by enriching mobile troops of steppe archers

with unprecedented quantities of loot, agricultural products, and iron tools and weapons. The nomads needed these things, it is thought, but did not produce them, unlike their simpler but more independent, sedentary LBA agropastoral ancestors.

Agricultural products are an important part of the theory of pastoral dependency, as it was christened by Nicola Di Cosmo (Di Cosmo 1994:1093; 2002:168–169). Food made from domesticated cereals is considered by Khazanov (1984:70–75) essential for the long-term survival of all pastoralists in the challenging climate of the Eurasian steppes, whether they were sedentary, as in the LBA, or nomadic, like the Iron Age Scythians, Saka, and Hsiung-Nu. In the northern Eurasian steppes, Khazanov observed, regularly recurring episodes of high herd mortality and high annual variability in pasture productivity combined to make it impossible to survive on pastoral production alone; a storable nonpastoral food resource like barley or millet was required to avoid periodic famines. Other influential scholars agreed that Iron Age nomads abandoned LBA agriculture only by outsourcing it to sedentary states bordering the steppes (Golden 2001; Barfield 2006; Jagchid and Symons 1989). At least occasional access to agricultural foods is widely regarded as a prerequisite for steppe pastoralism. This, together with an evolutionary model in which agropastoralism preceded specialized nomadism, has limited the way that archaeologists interpret the economies of the pre–Iron Age steppes. Truly nomadic pastoral economies are confined to the relatively recent eras when nomads who grew no grain could depend on state economies that produced surpluses of grain. As Koryakova and Epimakhov (2007:210) observed, "Eurasian nomadism as an economic and sociocultural phenomenon could not appear earlier [than the Iron Age] because in many respects it depends on economic and sociopolitical relations with settled statehood societies."

One awkward effect of this theoretical model was to require that the mobile pastoralists of the EBA and MBA must have depended on their own agriculture, even in areas like the Volga-Ural steppes, where evidence for agriculture is lacking entirely and where there are no known EBA or MBA settlements and no grain impressions in the EBA or MBA pottery from graves. The tension between the expectations of dependency theory and the actual archaeological evidence from the EBA Yamnaya culture was summarized best by K. P. Bunyatyan, an expert on the Bronze Age in the Ukrainian steppes (Bunyatyan 2003:269): "In this way the population of the Yamnaya culture evolved into a classic nomadic society. However, the basic technological and social foundations for the emergence of such a true society had not yet come about."

The contradiction contained in that assessment was relieved by redefining "true" nomadism, as Bunyatyan proceeded to do. Dependency theory provided a theoretical foundation for expanding a small and regionally defined body of evidence for the presence of occasional agriculture in Yamnaya societies in the westernmost steppe region, west of the Dnieper River, to apply to all of the steppes, including the large region between the Don and Ural Rivers that lacks any such evidence. Here EBA/MBA nomadism seems to have operated without agriculture. The accepted model for the evolution of steppe pastoralism, from settled agropastoralism in the Bronze Age to a parasitical dependency on agricultural states in the Iron Age, assumed that bread was necessary for the survival of steppe pastoralism even in places where we can't see it. Most archaeologists, whether American (Kohl 2007; Frachetti 2011:7) or Russian and Ukrainian (Sedova 2000; Kotova 2003; Bunyatyan 2003), have emphasized the role of agriculture in Bronze Age steppe economies because we believe that it must have been present (we entered this project with the same belief), although the archaeological evidence for grain cultivation in the steppes has always been patchy at best.

Neither Scythian-Saka nor LBA sites were examined by Soviet-era archaeologists specifically to recover botanical remains to determine the presence or absence of agriculture. Impressions of cultivated grains in pottery were studied and still are today (Yanushevich 1989; Pashkevich 2003), but these are relatively rarely found. Pollen studies were undertaken near a limited number of LBA sites (Lavrushin and Spiridonova 1995), but wild grass and cultivated cereal pollen grains differ only in size, and variation in pollen grain size can be caused by other factors (Vicent et al. 2006). Macrobotanical confirmation from charred seeds is desirable to certify the presence of cultivation, and seed recovery depends on flotation, a method not used in Soviet-era settlement excavations. Recently, flotation and various other botanical recovery methods have been used to detect Bronze Age domesticated cereals in the eastern margins of the Eurasian steppes, in eastern Kazakhstan and Mongolia (Frachetti et al. 2010; Spengler et al. 2014; Houle and Broderick 2011), but in the 1990s, the SVP and the multinational Gorny project (Chernykh 2004b) were the first two excavations at LBA settlements in the Russian steppes to use a full suite of botanical recovery methods.

The SVP was the only Russian-American collaborative project targeted specifically on the role of agriculture in a settlement system of the Srubnaya culture, then thought to represent the classic example of an LBA agropastoral economy. We examined permanent Srubnaya settlements and seasonal Srubnaya herding camps. We discovered not a single trace of LBA agriculture, not in seeds, phytoliths, or pollen. A large skeletal sample showed no heightened caries or stable isotope evidence of a diet that included a significant quantity of domesticated grains. If Eurasian steppe pastoralists needed a storable nonpastoral food resource to serve as a buffer against periodic famines, as Khazanov suggested, it is possible that they found what they needed in wild seeds collected from *Chenopodium*, *Amaranthus*, and *Polygonum* plants, which are common weeds in steppe pastures disturbed by cattle. What we discovered was an entirely unexpected past, a surprising pastoral economy that was quite settled, but included no agriculture, breaking the assumed linkage between sedentism and agriculture and showing that agriculture was not necessary in the diet of Eurasian steppe pastoralists, neither settled, as in the sites described here, nor nomadic, by implication. The consumption of barley or millet was a cultural choice in the Eurasian steppes, not an ecological imperative. We can now cast a new eye on the mobile pastoralists of the EBA and MBA and see them for what they were; in many steppe regions, they were nomads, thriving without agriculture and free of any dependence on states. Why they settled and adopted permanent homes at the MBA/LBA transition is one of the subjects of this book.

This chapter briefly introduces the SVP but then looks beyond the Samara Valley to incorporate some of our principal discoveries into an analysis of the role of agriculture in Bronze Age pastoral economies in the Eurasian steppes. Chapter 2 provides a brief summary of the field operations of the SVP and ends with a description of a model of the LBA pastoral economy in the lower Samara Valley that seems compatible with what we found. Chapters 3 to 8 describe the ethnohistory and prehistory, climate and ecology, and changing human populations of the Samara Valley through time, from the Eneolithic to the LBA, and Chapters 9 to 18 focus specifically on our archaeological investigations at LBA sites. Minor components dated to the MBA and Iron Age within our LBA sites are also described briefly in these chapters. Unparalleled ritual winter-season dog and wolf sacrifices were discovered at Krasnosamarskoe, quite surprisingly, but these were not part of our economic research design, so are merely summarized in this essay. They are fully described in the zoological Chapters 14 to 16 and are interpreted most completely at the ends of Chapters 14 and 16. Funding sources and personnel for the project are identified and thanked in the Acknowledgments.

Why Samara?

The Samara *oblast* is an administrative unit in the middle Volga region larger in area (53,600 km²) than Denmark, with open steppe grassland in its southern part and forests in its northern part. The Samara River flows from east to west through the steppe/forest-steppe ecotone, so any shifts in climate or environment were likely to be visible here. The Samara Valley also was a natural conduit for east-west trade and migrations between the Asian steppes and the western Russian steppes. People moving east or west tended to go south of the Ural Mountains and north of the North Caspian Depression, which contains the northernmost sand desert in the world (the Ryn Peski), and these natural brackets tended to funnel trade and migrations into a corridor drained by the Samara Valley. The Samara Valley was a border zone between large external regions or hinterlands. Moreover, educational institutions in Samara had produced an excellent group of archaeologists whose accomplishments provided a strong foundation for a successful collaboration.

An ambitious program of field archaeology was conducted at Samara State University and the Samara State Pedagogical Institute from the 1970s through the 1980s (Vasiliev and Matveeva 1979; Vasiliev 1981; Agapov et al. 1990; Agapov 2010), briefly interrupted by the crisis in state funding that accompanied the political transition of 1991–92. We were fortunate to meet Igor B. Vasiliev (see Acknowledgments), the dynamic leader of prehistoric archaeology at the Samara State Pedagogical Institute, when Dorcas Brown and I first visited Samara in 1992 during a multimuseum study of riding-related pathologies on ancient horse teeth (Brown and Anthony 1998; Anthony and Brown 2011). In that year, we studied collections of ancient horse remains at the Institute for the History and Archaeology of the Volga (IHAV), which Vasiliev had founded, while staying with Vasiliev in his apartment. Vasiliev's energetic direction of fieldwork at many sites, particularly at the Khvalynsk Eneolithic cemetery (Vasiliev 1981; now see Agapov 2010), at the Sintashta-related Potapovka MBA II cemetery (Vasiliev et al. 1994), and in Eneolithic camps in the North Caspian desert (Barynkin et al. 1998), filled an enormous gap in the archaeology of the middle Volga region, making it one of the most dynamic centers of prehistoric archaeology in the former Soviet Union.

Vasiliev's failing health required him to pass the baton to his former students in Samara just as our fieldwork began in 1995, but we were again lucky to work with the triumvirate of Kuznetsov, Mochalov, and Khokhlov during our project, with the lab directed by A. Semenova and the Russian faunal analysis conducted by S. Kosintsev of Ekaterinburg (see, e.g., Vasiliev et al. 1994; Vasiliev et al. 2000; Semenova 2001; Kuznetsov 2006; Mochalov 2008; Khokhlov 2010). One important benefit of choosing Samara for our project was the potential to build on Vasiliev's fieldwork and to collaborate with the well-trained archaeologists he inspired and encouraged.

Overview of the Samara Valley Project

With our Samara colleagues, in 1995, we discovered the permanent Srubnaya settlement north of the Russian village of Krasnosamarskoe (pronounced Krasno-sa-MAR-sko-yeh). In 1999 and 2001 at Krasnosamarskoe, we exposed a structure and part of the occupation surface around it on the edge of a manmade lake that had flooded the remainder of the settlement but, under shallow water, permitted us to define the edge of the site by wading and collecting artifacts that covered the bottom of the lake out to about 30 m from the land's edge. The entire settlement measured about 40 × 60 m, probably containing only one or two structures in addition to the one we excavated on dry land. A well (Pit 10) found inside the excavated structure at Krasnosamarskoe contained a sealed deposit of LBA artifacts, including wooden tools, animal bones, and waterlogged organics with excellent preservation of charred and uncharred LBA seeds and pollen. Smaller excavations were pursued briefly at two other Srubnaya settlements: (1) Barinovka, also located in the floodplain marshes of the Samara River, a Srubnaya settlement site we discovered in 1995, tested in 1996, and rejected (Chapter 2) because of extensive disturbance of the LBA site by an early historic Cossack-period occupation, and (2), Kibit, located in the forest-steppe zone in the northern Samara oblast, investigated independently by Peterson and Popova as an outgrowth of the SVP (Chapter 11). Two seasonal Srubnaya herding camps (Peschanyi Dol [PD] 1 and PD2) were discovered during a 1995–96 systematic shovel-testing survey designed to find low-density seasonal sites, conducted in a tributary stream valley called Peschanyi Dol (PD). PD1 and PD2 were fully excavated during the summer of 2000 (Chapter 18). The PD camps were the first Srubnaya herding camps specifically targeted and made the focus of a season-long excavation with a sizable staff, yielding radiocarbon dates that were contemporary with the Krasnosamarskoe settlement, about 20 km distant, between 1900 and 1700 BC. An overview of our field surveys and excavations at these sites is the principal subject of Chapter 2.

We also recovered two pollen cores from bogs nearby to track anthropogenic and climate-driven changes in vegetation (Chapters 5 and 12). Krasnosamarskoe, Kibit, and the PD camps were systematically sampled for pollen, phytoliths, charcoal, and seeds (Chapters 5, 12, and 13).

We recovered geomorphological soil samples from dated soil horizons (Chapter 9) to investigate the origins and growth of the local marsh and terrestrial sediments near Krasnosamarskoe. We recovered zoological data from more than 22,000 animal bones, more than 8,000 identifiable to species (Chapters 14–16); seasonality data from plant remains (Chapters 12 and 13) and incremental banding on animal teeth (Chapter 14); and behavioral data from a large assemblage of LBA artifacts (Chapters 10 and 18).

Also, we excavated a cemetery of three kurgans (Krasnosamarskoe IV) located beside the Krasnosamarskoe settlement, erected by mobile pastoralists in quick succession during the early MBA, around 2900 to 2800 BC (Chapter 17). Kurgan 3, located 65 m northeast of the LBA settlement, was reused as a cemetery for 27 Srubnaya individuals found in 23 graves dated by radiocarbon to 1900 to 1700 BC, contemporary with the settlement. Murphy (Chapter 8) examined pathologies (particularly diet related but all types), Schulting and Richards (Chapter 7) studied stable isotopes, and Khokhlov provided demographic statistics and craniofacial types (Chapter 6) for a regional skeletal sample that reached 1,350 individuals in the largest study, by Khokhlov; the other studies were on subsets of Khokhlov's sample. Khokhlov

described almost all of the Eneolithic to Bronze Age human skeletons excavated by archaeologists in the Samara oblast up to 2002, when funding for the SVP ended (although analysis continued). The Human Genetics laboratory of David Reich at Harvard University has examined the bones of 66 individuals, largely overlapping with the Schulting and Richards isotope sample (Chapter 6), and has recovered ancient DNA from more than 40 individuals dated 5600 to 1200 BC (Haak et al. 2015). In addition to these targeted discoveries, we also found by accident a small, low-density Iron Age settlement component on top of the LBA Krasnosamarskoe settlement. The Iron Age occupation seems to have been a temporary frontier trading post where people of the Gorodetskaya culture, whose fortified agricultural towns were located west of the Volga, visited the steppe margins to make and repair iron tools and weapons (a Gorodetskaya iron bloom was found) for Sauromatian nomads (an arrowhead of Sauromatian type was found; see Chapter 10), bringing with them a little millet (two charred domesticated millet seeds were found in the Iron Age features). In addition, we found two very rare but light, low-density scatters of MBA pottery at Krasnosamarskoe and at PD1. Both MBA components were so low density that they likely would not have been found if an LBA site had not been situated in the same place, providing an insight into why EBA/MBA pastoral occupation sites are largely absent from the regional archaeological record. And finally, we stumbled across a unique winter-season sacrificial ritual involving dog and wolf sacrifices conducted at Krasnosamarskoe, summarized below.

The combined data from ecological studies, settlements, herding camps, artifacts, floral and faunal remains, and human pathologies and demography provide a multisided view into Bronze Age steppe pastoralism that has not formerly been available in the middle Volga region. The SVP discovered at least three new, unexpected, and surprising facts about Srubnaya settlements, rituals, and economies:

1. The Krasnosamarskoe settlement was not supported by agriculture, and the skeletons and teeth of the Srubnaya people from Krasnosamarskoe and across the Volga-Ural steppes do not contain indications of an agricultural diet, in dental pathologies or in stable isotopes. The settlement, was, however, occupied year-round, indicated by plant phytoliths, pollen, and incremental banding on animal teeth, and the buildup of floor deposits, pit features within them, and dated sediments at the bottom of the well, Pit 10, together

indicate that the structure was occupied without an observable stratigraphic break over a period probably measured in decades or generations rather than years. The fauna indicates a diet based largely on cattle, sheep, and goats for meat and dairy products (and an occasional pig), and very few hunted wild animals with the peculiar exception of wolves, the most frequent wild species hunted at the site (see number 2 below). Seeds and pollen preserved in anaerobic mud in the bottom of the well, Pit 10, dated by three radiocarbon dates from the same depths, show that three genera of wild seeds (*Chenopodium, Amaranthus, Polygonum*) were selectively collected (much more than other wild seed–bearing plants) and selectively charred (the other 28 genera of wild seeds, together providing almost half the total seed count, were not charred). Charring is a step in preparing these three edible and nutritious seed species for human consumption. Wild seeds could have been the storable dietary buffer that we imagined was supplied by agriculture. Increasing reliance on agriculture was not the reason for the LBA "settling-down" process, and the Srubnaya economy in this region was not agropastoral, but rather seems to have been based on herding and gathering.

2. A previously unknown Srubnaya winter ritual occurred at Krasnosamarskoe, featuring the winter-season sacrifices of numerous dogs (51 minimum number of individuals [MNI]) and some wolves (7 MNI), which together accounted for an unprecedented 30 to 40 percent of the faunal remains, by different counting methods, at the settlement (Chapters 14–16). The dog and wolf bones and teeth exhibit signs indicating that the canids were killed almost exclusively during the winter, when they were roasted, filleted, apparently consumed, and chopped into very small and regular pieces, with particular attention to the heads, which were chopped with an axe into 10 to 16 regular segments, certainly a ritual rather than a practical act. Eating dogs and wolves seems to have been for them, as for us today, a transgressive act not seen in any other Srubnaya settlement, a kind of behavior that would normally be permitted only by actors in a liminal state, often associated with rites of passage. In this case, the passage was a winter-season transition to a status symbolized by becoming a dog/wolf through the consumption of its flesh. In Indo-European mythology, boys were initiated at a young age, often in the winter, into roaming warbands of youths (Germanic *männerbünde*, Italic *sodales* or *luperci*, Celtic *fiana*, Greek *ephebes*, and Vedic *Vrātyas* and *Maruts*) who

wore animal skins, appeared as if they were wolves or dogs, and bore names containing the words *wolf* or *dog*, prominent symbols of death and war in Indo-European (IE) mythologies (Lincoln 1991:134; McCone 1987; Bremer 1982:141; West 2007:448-452). After a number of years living "in the wild," raiding, and learning songs, they returned home to become mature men (Falk 1986; McCone 1987; Lincoln 1991; Kershaw 2000; Das and Meiser 2003). The Krasnosamarskoe settlement probably was part of the early Iranian-speaking linguistic world (detailed argument follows later in this chapter), and elements from the dog-wolf-midwinter-youthful-warband complex were present in Iranian and Vedic traditions. This cultural model would explain the otherwise inexplicable dog/wolf-linked, wintertime rites of passage conducted at Krasnosamarskoe. This is the first archaeological site where this ritual has been discovered, so it seems to have been practiced at few places. Participants must have traveled to Krasnosamarskoe from the surrounding region.

3. Srubnaya settlements in the Samara Valley were linked to each other in different ways at different regional scales. This multiscalar regional organization is represented archaeologically by three distinct but overlapping circles of relationship, referred to here as *obligation* (for copper mining), *cooperation* (for herding), and *affiliation* (for shared rituals). The widest-scale set of relationships probably was represented by the apparent obligation of ordinary producers to support specialized Srubnaya copper mining settlements like that at Gorny, excavated by Chernykh (2004a, 2004b) near the headwaters of the Samara River. At Gorny, food and labor apparently were provisioned by surrounding Srubnaya pastoral communities, indicated by the standardized cuts and limited age range of cattle bones provisioned to the Gorny miners (Morales and Antipina 2003:344). Some of the ore smelting was distributed from the almost treeless copper mine site to surrounding communities that had more firewood (Diaz del Río et al. 2006). Similar obligations could have applied also to the support of other known LBA Srubnaya mining settlements in the region. At the scale of the local region, cooperative summer herding probably joined a few neighboring settlements into joint-herding units, perceived archaeologically through the diversity of ceramic paste sources at the Srubnaya herding camps excavated in Peschanyi Dol, PD1 and PD2. The potting clays in the PD camps were three to four times more

diverse than the clays in the much larger ceramic sample from Krasnosamarskoe, suggesting that herders from three to four permanent Srubnaya settlements occupied the same seasonal herding camp and even used the same seasonal trash pit. A modern herding cooperative of three nearby villages uses the PD valley this way today, pooling their cattle under a shared herder. If the LBA herder rotated from different settlements in different months, it would produce such a diverse pattern of clays. Cooperative herding could have been linked to copper mining because the diversion of labor to support mining could have compelled households in neighboring areas to settle near each other to pool their herds to be overseen by a shared herder, permitting a reduction in the number of herders to compensate for the labor lost to mining and metallurgy. Labor sharing is most efficient with cooperating communities that are close to each other, and sustained proximity is easiest to maintain with a settled lifestyle, so cooperative herding, specialized copper mining, and sedentism can be linked. At an even smaller scale than the cooperative herding unit, the third regional organization was the affiliated ritual community that assembled at Krasnosamarskoe for winter initiation rituals featuring dog and wolf sacrifices. These three circles of obligation, cooperation, and affiliation integrated local Srubnaya communities into networks of varying size and meaning, which operated at different scales and seasons, linking overlapping sets of people. Srubnaya societies are often described as hierarchical, dominated by tribal chiefs who were buried with exceptional weapons (socketed spears, daggers, projectile points) and ornaments (imported faience beads, pendants and beads of copper, gold and silver). But the SVP revealed the heterarchical relationships that were equally important in Srubnaya social life.

Archaeological discoveries achieved during the SVP, combined with other recent projects (Chang et al. 2003; Chernykh 2004a, 2004b; Honeychurch and Amartuvshin 2006; Hanks 2010; Houle and Broderick 2011; Frachetti et al. 2010, Frachetti 2011; Freire et al. 2012), have upended established ideas about the evolution of Eurasian steppe pastoralism in the Bronze Age. The settled pastoralists of LBA Krasnosamarskoe and other Srubnaya settlements reviewed here seem to have raised cattle, sheep, goats, and horses and collected wild seeds for food. Agriculture, paradoxically, seems to have been an innovation of the Final Bronze and Iron Ages, when pastoral nomadism

flourished. Pastoral nomadism actually had appeared in the western steppes earlier, during the EBA and MBA, when it was truly utterly independent of agriculture. The reappearance of mobile pastoralism in the Iron Age was not the end point of a linear process but a late phase in a cyclical process of alternation between sedentism and mobility, with neither residential choice being tied to agriculture, at least not during the Bronze Age. We have been fitting the sparse botanical data available previously into a presumed developmental pattern that is not supported by new evidence.

In the remainder of this essay, I explore the role of the SVP in changing explanations for the evolution of steppe pastoral economies during the Bronze Age (3300–800 BC) in the middle Volga steppes, incorporating and briefly summarizing some of the discoveries described in later chapters. The principal focus is on the role of agriculture in both mobile and settled Bronze Age pastoral economies.

The Samara River Valley and Its Region Within the Eurasian Steppes

The Eurasian steppes might seem monotonous but are actually quite varied botanically and geologically, not to mention culturally. The steppes can be divided into regions in several different ways. Here I will use elevation above sea level, with regions defined by elevation separated by mountain ranges that act as borders, to define three regions: the western, central, and eastern steppes. The Ural Mountains form the border between the western and central steppes. The western steppes are the Pontic-Caspian steppes located north of the Black and Caspian Seas and west of the Ural Mountains. The Samara River lies near the eastern border of the western steppes. The western steppes are surprisingly low in average elevation; the mouth of the Samara River is less than 40 m above sea level. They also receive more precipitation than the central steppes, in most places 300 to 500 mm annually. East of the Ural Mountains, in the rocky plains of central Kazakhstan, the central steppes are more elevated, with the heart of the steppe belt lying above 200 m, frequently at 300 m, with many granitic rock outcrops, and with less annual precipitation than the western steppes, often 300 mm or less. The central steppes rise gradually to the mountainous eastern steppes in the Tien Shan foothills of eastern Kazakhstan and the Altai Mountains of Russia, where vertical transhumant pastoralism was practiced. The peaks of the Tien Shan and Altai, substantial mountain ranges, separate the eastern Eurasian steppes from the high plateau of Mongolia, where pastoralists live permanently at subalpine altitudes (average 1400–1500 m), visited only in the summer by transhumant steppe pastoralists in eastern Kazakhstan and never experienced in most of the central and western Eurasian steppes (Russia, Ukraine, and western and central Kazakhstan). The high Mongolian plateau remained a different world culturally and ecologically through much of the Bronze Age.

The western or Pontic-Caspian steppes are generally lower in elevation, have more productive grass cover, and have larger and more diverse riverine woodlands than the central or eastern Eurasian steppes. The mouth of the Samara River receives 550 mm of precipitation annually, and the hills near its source tributaries get about 400 mm annually, significantly drier but still moister than the central steppes of Kazakhstan. The Pontic-Caspian steppes also received cultural influences from southeastern Europe, where Neolithic farmers were established before 6000 BC, and from the North Caucasus Mountains, where Neolithic farmers arrived after 6000 BC (Kotova 2003; Motuzaite-Matuzeviciute 2012). Domesticated cattle and sheep-goat were adopted before 5500 BC in the Ukrainian

steppes at sites between the Dnieper and Don Rivers, long before any other part of the Eurasian steppes, where domesticated animals generally appeared after 3000 BC, in the western Altai and Tien Shan, or even after 2500 BC, over much of central Kazakhstan.

The Samara Valley links the central steppes with the western steppes and is a north-south ecotone between the pastoral steppes to the south and the forest-steppe zone to the north (Figure 1.3). The economic contrast between pastoral steppe subsistence, with its associated social organizations, and forest-zone hunting and fishing economies probably explains the shifting but persistent linguistic border between forest-zone Uralic languages to the north (today largely displaced by Russian) and a sequence of steppe languages to the south, recently Turkic, before that Iranian, and before that probably an eastern dialect of Proto-Indo-European (Anthony 2007). The Samara Valley represents several kinds of borders, linguistic, cultural, and ecological, and it is centrally located in the Eurasian steppes, making it a critical place to examine the development of Eurasian steppe pastoralism.

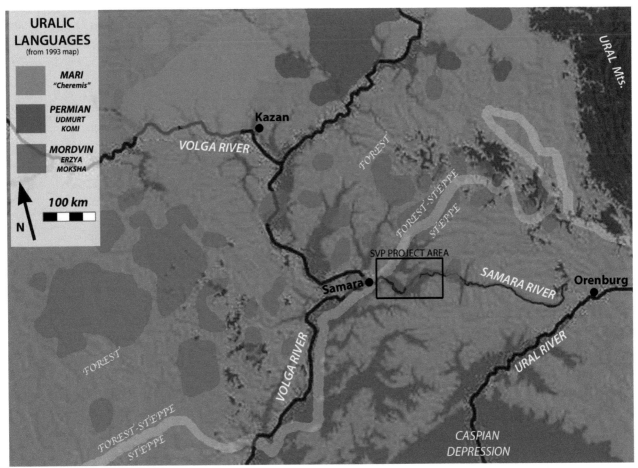

Figure 1.3 Language map of the middle Volga-Ural region. *After "Geographical Distribution of the Uralic Languages" by Finno-Ugrian Society, Helsinki, 1993.*

The Srubnaya-Andronovo Horizon: Typology, Ethnicity, Agriculture, and Mining

In the established literature on the LBA in the Eurasian steppes, the thin evidence for Srubnaya agriculture contrasts with the robust evidence for the Srubnaya cultural-typological sequence. The typological-stratigraphic approach to material culture is highly developed in the region. This LBA cultural-typological-chronological sequence, the backbone of any archaeological interpretation, requires a review. Also, to establish a context for our studies in the SVP, and recognizing that much of the Russian literature is unavailable to many readers, I will review current interpretations of Srubnaya ethnicity, agriculture, and copper mining.

The Regional and Typological Origins of the Srubnaya-Andronovo Horizon

The LBA is dated in the Eurasian steppes ca. 1900 to 1200 BC. In older accounts of the LBA, a beginning date of 1600 BC was often cited (Chernykh 1992; Kuzmina 1994), but calibration of radiocarbon dates and many new dates, including those from LBA Krasnosamarskoe in this report, has shifted the opening

of the LBA back to 1900 to 1800 BC, contemporary with the Únětice culture of the central European EBA and with the Middle Helladic cultures of the Aegean MBA. In the Eurasian steppes, this period has traditionally been interpreted to begin with the rapid appearance of a settled form of agropastoralism that spread suddenly over a vast area between the western Tien Shan and Altai Mountains on the east and the Danube River on the west (Kuzmina 1994, 2003, 2008; Chernykh 1992) (Figure 1.4). The western branch of this pan-continental horizon, west of the Ural Mountains, is called the Timber Grave or Srubnaya culture (or horizon), and the eastern branch, east of the Ural Mountains, is termed the Andronovo culture (or cultural-historical community, or horizon). The border zone between these two macro-cultural entities was located in the southern Ural steppes and included our excavated settlement of Krasnosamarskoe, a Srubnaya settlement that contained imported Andronovo (Alakul-type) pottery sherds. In fact, Andronovo sherds are frequently found in Srubnaya settlements in the Samara Valley, and on the easternmost headwaters of the Samara, there are two thoroughly mixed Andronovo-Srubnaya settlements (see Chapter 4).

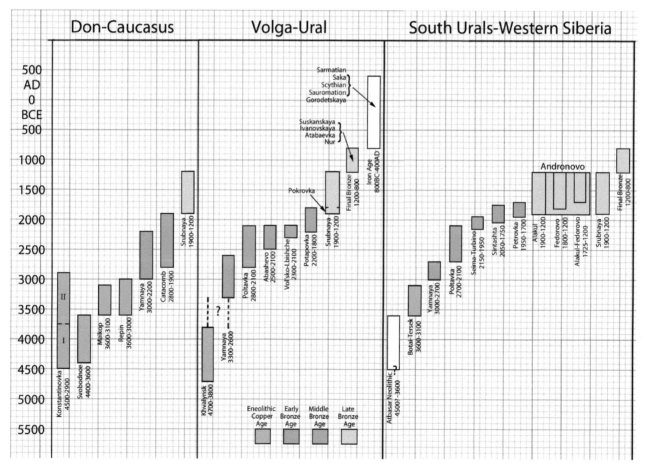

Table 1.1 Chronology for Bronze Ages in the Volga-Ural and Surrounding Steppe Region
The SVP focused on the Bronze Age cultures of the Volga-Ural region.

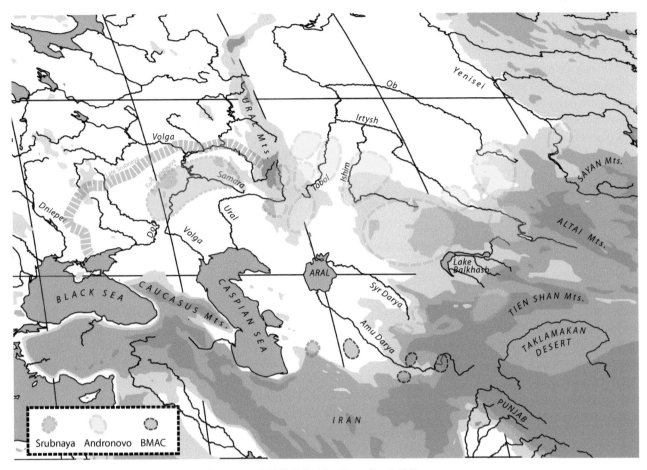

Figure 1.4 The Srubnaya-Andronovo horizon around 1800 BC. After Kuzmina (1994).

The regional origins of the typological traits that define Srubnaya and Andronovo are debated. But in the past two decades, since the publication of the Sintashta site, dated around 2100 to 1800 BC in the southeastern Ural steppes south of Chelyabinsk (Gening et al. 1992; Hanks 2010), most experts agree that Sintashta styles of pottery, weapons, bone cheek-pieces for chariot driving, and graves evolved into Petrovka styles (this sequence is documented stratigraphically at the Ust'ye settlement); that Petrovka ceramics, weapons, and ornaments were the origin of Alakul styles, the earliest typological phase in Andronovo; and that Alakul was soon followed in the Andronovo period by (possibly unrelated) Fedorovo ceramic and grave types, which could be considered an eastern or northern style within the Andronovo horizon, with which the Alakul style interacted contemporaneously in many Andronovo regions (Zdanovich 1988; Chernykh 1992; Kuzmina 1994, 2008). The underlying ceramic sequence has stratigraphic support in vertically sequenced Petrovka > Alakul > Fedorovo deposits at Petrovka II, Pavlovka, and Novonikol'skoe I in northern Kazakhstan, and the Alakul

> Fedorovo stratigraphic sequence is repeated at Atasu in central Kazakhstan (Maliutina 1991). In many Andronovo settlements, Alakul and Fedorovo ceramics are mixed in the same deposits, occasionally in the same features, and there are even Alakul pots that exhibit Fedorovo traits, so they can be mixed in the same artifact. It was in death that they differed the most: typical Alakul and Fedorovo graves and funeral customs differed in many ritual details, including inhumation beneath earth kurgans for the Alakul dead versus cremation graves with stone constructions for the Fedorovo dead. But the Alakul style in ceramic shapes and decorations seems to have appeared earlier.

This typological-stratigraphic sequence shows that Sintashta-Petrovka ceramic and weapon styles are typologically antecedent to Andronovo styles. The violent and transformative Sintashta period, 2100 to 1800 BC, saw the concentration of dispersed MBA mobile herder populations into MBA II fortified settlements east of the Urals, and this settled Sintashta phase ushered in the settled Petrovka-Alakul economy as well as the artifact and grave types of the early LBA Andronovo horizon. The Sintashta transformation was accompanied by an unprecedented level of population mixing and interregional north-south movement across the steppe/forest-steppe border in the middle Volga steppes, visible in craniometrics (described in Chapter 6) and in material culture in shared projectile point styles, ceramic styles, and bronze weapons (Carpelan and Parpola 2001). Given our new skeletal evidence for dietary stress in this period (Chapter 8), and considering the significant technical innovations in weaponry at this time, including the invention of the chariot, these interactions across the steppe/forest-steppe in the late MBA apparently were accompanied by increased stress and warfare. Warfare, as Vehik (2002) has shown in the American Southwest, can lead to increased long-distance trade, caused by war chiefs' competition for exotic goods to distribute as gifts, a necessary part of forging alliances against enemies. Sintashta-Petrovka chariot-driving chiefs contacted the irrigated civilizations of Central Asia (Bactria-Margiana Archaeological Complex [BMAC]), shown at the Petrovka settlement of Tugai near Sarazm and Petrovka-style ceramics inside the walled BMAC town of Gonur (Kuzmina 2003; Salvatori 2003, 2008; Anthony 2009). Perhaps Ural copper and steppe horses were exchanged for Asian luxury goods (textiles?) for distribution to local steppe allies. The geographic expansion of Petrovka-style sites from the southeastern Ural steppes into the Zeravshan Valley in Central Asia was the foundation for the later development of Andronovo styles across Kazakhstan.

Frachetti (2008, 2011) and others argued that the Andronovo horizon included many regional and local populations that had varied local origins, particularly in the Tien Shan piedmont of eastern Kazakhstan. This is undoubtedly true. But the post-Botai, pre-Andronovo phase, between 3000 and 2000 BC, is almost an archaeological blank over most of central and eastern Kazakhstan, even with the welcome discovery by Frachetti of pre-Andronovo settlement components in eastern Kazakhstan at Begash Ia and Tasbas in the Dzungarian Mountains, a foothill range of the northern Tien Shan (Frachetti and Mar'yashev 2007; Frachetti 2011). The pre-Andronovo mortuary custom of cremation documented at Tasbas and Begash continued into the Andronovo period as a distinctive trait of Fedorovo mortuary rituals in the Tien Shan region but with the addition of a kurgan, stone fences, and other Andronovo traits absent from the Begash Ia and Tasbas level 1 mortuary customs. At both sites, the earlier pre-Andronovo phase was followed in 1800 to 1500 BC by Andronovo styles of material culture. As the evidence now stands, it seems that the local pre-Andronovo cultures of the northern Tien Shan were absorbed into the Andronovo cultural interaction

sphere after 1800 BC, adopting many Andronovo customs but retaining many indigenous behaviors as well.

West of the Urals, the Srubnaya culture is similarly derived from the Potapovka culture, dated around 2100 to 1800 BC, a western chronological and typological variant of Sintashta (Vasiliev et al. 1994). Fortified settlements like those of the Sintashta culture have not been found in the Volga-Ural steppes, so Potapovka groups remained mobile, probably living in wagon camps. But Potapovka and Sintashta cemeteries contained almost identical ceramics and very similar weapons, graves, horse cheek-pieces, paired horse sacrifices, and ornaments (Vasiliev et al. 1994). Potapovka cemeteries are found southwest of the Urals, including our project area, while the Sintashta core area was 800 km to the east, southeast of the Urals. In both areas, the period after around 2400 to 2300 BC saw sharply increased interaction between mobile steppe herders, represented by the MBA Poltavka culture in both regions, and the MBA forest-steppe cultures of the Abashevo type. This interaction accounts for the ceramic shapes and decorations of the novel Sintashta-Potapovka ceramic style (derived largely from Abashevo) as well as the kurgan burial customs (derived from Poltavka).

The material traits of the Srubnaya culture appeared earliest in the middle Volga steppe/forest-steppe borderlands in our project area. An exhaustive analysis by Mochalov (2008) of ceramic shapes, fabrics, and decorative motifs characterizing the Potapovka > Srubnaya transition in the middle Volga region established that early Srubnaya pottery-making habits (17 types, nine construction variants, and 84 decorative motifs) were derived principally from Potapovka potters. Srubnaya pottery and bronze weapon styles and grave types then spread from the Volga-Ural steppes westward across the Don River into the Ukrainian steppes around 1800 to 1700 BC, perhaps following the influence of militarily successful chariot warriors who were enriched by the Ural region copper trade (Otroshchenko 2003:319) and who secured their elite positions through the intermarriages that Mochalov (2008:238) emphasized are strongly implied by shared Srubnaya pottery-making customs.

After the formation of the almost pan-continental Srubnaya-Andronovo cultural horizon, beginning around 1900 to 1800 BC, innovations that included bronze casting, chariotry, and some aspects of pastoral subsistence and settlement types began to diffuse between regions that had formerly appeared materially isolated, encouraging the movement of commodities such as copper, tin, and horses and enabling the more patchy diffusion of cultural traits, including language, rituals, and packages of distinctive elite behaviors (Kohl 2007; Koryakova and Epimakhov

2007; Anthony 2007; Kuzmina 2008; Frachetti 2008). At its eastern end, the Andronovo network interacted across the Tien Shan with what is today northwestern China during the rise of the earliest Chinese state in the late Quijia, Erlitou, and early Shang periods (Linduff 2004) and with Central Asia during the declining centuries (1800–1600 BC) of the BMAC and Namazga VI cultures (Lamberg-Karlovsky 2002; Anthony 2007:433–435; Salvatori 2008; Rouse and Cerasetti 2014).

Srubnaya Ethnicity

Russian archaeological traditions permit archaeologists to discuss the linguistic affiliations of prehistoric populations without much apology. Such a relaxed attitude toward language identity and material culture perhaps is facilitated by the steppe/forest ecological border that runs across southern Russia, which was a persistent cultural and linguistic border for millennia. Language and ecology are easily seen as associated in this region because they actually were associated historically at this persistent economic-cultural-linguistic border. Most experts agree that the languages spoken by the Scythians and Sarmatians across the western steppes, north of the Caspian and Black Seas, were Iranian, specifically from the eastern Iranian subgroup ("eastern" in relation to west Iranian within Iran), judging from roots contained in personal names, god names, and occasional other words noted by Greeks and Persians after 500 BC, and from toponyms in the steppes, as well as from archaeological remains that correlate with rituals specified in later Persian texts (Kuzmina 2007; Parpola 2002; Sims-Williams 2002). Continuity in skeletal traits and artifact styles between the LBA and the Iron Age suggests that the LBA (Srubnaya-Andronovo) population was ancestral to the Scythian-Saka population, so almost all Russian archaeologists accept that the languages of the LBA steppes were an archaic form of Iranian, ancestral to the Iranian languages spoken later in the same steppe regions (Koryakova and Epimakhov 2007:150). Western archaeologists tend to be dubious (Lamberg-Karlovsky 2002). The late MBA or MBA II Sintashta-Potapovka-Filatovka chain of cultures (Figure 1.5) between the upper Tobol River in the east (Sintashta) and the upper Don in the west (Filatovka) was ancestral to the LBA Srubnaya-Andronovo cultures, so is often interpreted as the material residue of the common Indo-Iranian ancestral community.

Finno-Ugric, the prehistoric ancestor of the Uralic languages spoken today in the forest zone north of the Samara Valley, borrowed vocabulary from both common Indo-Iranian and early Iranian (Koivulehto 2001), proving that these ancient languages bordered each other, so the forest-zone Volosovo and Garin-Bor cultures are often assumed to represent Finno-Ugric speakers. The Indo-Iranian ethnonym *Arya/Ārya* appeared as a loanword in ancestral Finno-Ugric as *orya, denoting "slave" (Carpelan and Parpola 2001:112), implying that Indo-Iranian Aryans were captured and enslaved by people in the forest zone. *Arya/Ārya* was a self-applied ethnonym of the composers of the oldest hymns in Sanskrit (in the *Rig Veda*) and early Iranian (in the *Avesta*), both compiled before 1000 BC, so it probably was a self-applied ethnonym of the speakers of common Indo-Iranian (Filatovka-Potapovka-Sintashta). Finno-Ugric *orya, "slave," therefore implies hostilities between forest-zone Uralic and steppe-zone Indo-Iranian speakers. But another loan into common Finno-Ugric during the same period was common Indo-Iranian *asura, "lord," borrowed into Finno-Ugric as *asera, "lord" or "prince," implying alliance or integration between Uralic speakers and Indo-Iranian chiefs, testifying to the complexity of the relationships between Finno-Ugric speakers and Indo-Iranian speakers. Finno-Ugric later borrowed phonologically early Iranian terms for *hundred*, *bee*, *honey*, *tribe/troop*, *wheel*, *spindle*, *bridge*, and *boat* (Koivulehto 2001), probably during the Srubnaya period.

Srubnaya Agropastoralism?

Srubnaya and Andronovo communities occupied small settlements that were reoccupied multiple times, creating substantial occupation middens, usually stratigraphically complex. Srubnaya settlements in the Volga-Ural region were usually small and unplanned, containing fewer than five unaligned structures, while Andronovo settlements in Kazakhstan seem to have been larger and more organized, with 5 to 15 houses aligned in rows. Ceramics from settlements usually show multiple ceramic phases, interpreted as indicating a cyclical pattern of abandonment and reoccupation (Kuzmina 2008:62–63; Sedova 2000). The small Srubnaya settlements in the Volga-Ural region suggest an extended family at each site, much like a cattle ranch of the American West. (*Ranch* is used here descriptively, not in Ingold's 1980 sense of commodified pastoralism.) Most settlements were located like Krasnosamarskoe, in the riverine bottomlands near marshes, either on the floodplain itself or on the first terrace.

Srubnaya settlements have traditionally been interpreted as permanent habitations supported partly by agriculture (Kuzmina 2008:60; Chernykh 1992:206; Sedova 2000:218). Botanical evidence for agriculture depends largely on grain impressions in pottery (Yanushevich 1989; Pashkevich 2003), which can be difficult to identify accurately. Generalization from a few sites with evidence

Figure 1.5 Late Middle Bronze Age cultures with the Sintashta-Potapovka-Filatovka group (shaded).*After Anthony (2007 Figure 15.5).*

of agriculture to the entire western steppe region helps to maintain this broad agropastoral stereotype of the LBA economy. But agriculture was most important in the western part of the Pontic-Caspian steppes, around the lower Dnieper, and our excavations combined with the studies of Lebedeva (2005) suggest that it faded out of the pastoral economy almost entirely in the east, in the Don-Volga-Ural steppes.

This west-to-east decline in LBA steppe agriculture can be seen clearly if we begin with the westernmost LBA steppe culture. At the western edge of the Pontic steppes, northwest of the Black Sea in the Bug-Dniester coastal lowlands, settlements of the LBA Noua-

Sabatinovka culture were fully agropastoral, featuring a wide variety of cultivated grains, including three kinds of wheat, two varieties of barley, millet, peas, cannabis, and other cultivated plants (Pashkevich 2003:Table 8.7), during a period contemporary with the fully developed or mature stage of the Srubnaya culture, around 1800 to 1200 BC (Gershkovich 2003). Farther east, east of the Dnieper River in the northern Azov steppes and on the Donets River, some western Srubnaya settlements were agropastoral and even had buildings with stone foundations, but the number and diversity of domestic grains were lower than that of the Sabatinovka culture, with more than two-thirds of the domestic grains being millet (*Panicum miliaceum*) (Pashkevich 2003:Table 8.6). Wheat and barley were rarely found. East of the Don River, between the Volga and Ural Rivers, botanical evidence for agriculture in Srubnaya settlements is almost absent, and the little positive evidence is debated (Lebedeva 2005). Yet this eastern region, including our project area, is where the Srubnaya culture is thought to have originated, as described above (Mochalov 2008). Until recently, most archaeologists emphasized the positive evidence for agriculture in Srubnaya settlements everywhere, including eastern Srubnaya sites in the Samara Valley (Sedova 2000:218), although the evidence there was thin.

A palynological study by Lavrushin and Spiridonova (1995) conducted near the Srubnaya settlement of Tokskoe on the upper Samara River, 180 km east of Krasnosamarskoe, identified some pollen of cultivated cereals, as well as weed pollen typical of arable fields (Lavrushin and Spiridonova 1995:194), and this was interpreted as indicating the presence of agriculture. But the pollen-grain sizes of wild and cultivated grasses can be regionally variable (Vicent et al. 2006), and *Chenopodium* is a weed typical of both arable fields and pastures—it invades opportunistically any disturbed area. No seeds or seed impressions of domesticated grain were found at Tokskoe or at any other LBA Srubnaya settlement in the Volga-Ural steppes (Lebedeva 2005; Ryabogina and Ivanov 2011). Charred seeds of wheat are found in the Volga-Ural region only in settlements of the Final Bronze Age (FBA), after 1200 BC, such as Russkaya Sel'itba on the Sok River (Pashkevich 2003:295). This seems to be when agriculture is first clearly documented, during a period of aridity, when settled pastoralism was declining. FBA sites moved north, away from the steppe border and from the Samara River.

Srubnaya settlements in the Volga-Ural steppes are regarded as agropastoral largely because they exhibit a sedentary settlement pattern indicated by substantial occupation middens, and sedentism is associated in settlement typologies with agriculture (Khazanov 1994:18–24). Other clues taken as indicating the presence of agriculture are the preponderance of cattle in Srubnaya herds; cattle are thought to be unsuited to long-distance seasonal migrations, so indicate a somewhat settled residential pattern consistent with agriculture (Kuzmina 2008:61). Also, curved bronze blades interpreted as sickles are thought to indicate agriculture, but they could have had other uses (carpet knives?). Stone mortars are said to indicate agriculture, but we found a stone mortar at a seasonal herding camp (PD2), and small grinding stones are found frequently in the ditches of EBA and MBA kurgans raised by mobile pastoralists, used for grinding ochre.

The SVP was expected to provide better evidence for Srubnaya agriculture, but instead we found no agriculture at Krasnosamarskoe or at Kibit, two Srubnaya settlements excavated using flotation on systematically sampled constant-volume units of soil taken from every excavation square and level. At Krasnosamarskoe, palynology and phytolith analysis provided additional support for the absence of agriculture. The flotation studies of Lebedeva (2005) at 12 other Volga-Ural Srubnaya settlements, described in more detail below, also detected no cultivated grain, making a total of 14 Srubnaya settlements tested with flotation in the Volga-Ural region and no cultivated grain found. The Srubnaya people in the Volga-Ural region had no dental caries, unlike bread eaters (see Murphy, Chapter 8), and the stable isotopes in their bones showed no positive evidence of millet consumption (see Schulting and Richards, Chapter 7). Seeds found in Pit 10 at Krasnosamarskoe (Chapters 10 and 12) suggest that their seed foods were gathered from wild plants: *Chenopodium*, *Amaranthus*, and *Polygonum*.

Surprisingly, Srubnaya settlements in the Volga-Ural region were not agropastoral, the normal LBA diet did not contain cultivated grain, and the adoption of agriculture was not the cause of the LBA "settling-down" process in the Volga-Ural steppes.

Cultivated cereals appeared in some settlement contexts after 4500 BC in the Ukrainian steppes, west of the Don (Motuzaite-Matuzeviciute 2012), but not in the Don-Volga-Ural steppes. Cultivated cereals also were used earlier far to the east, in the northern piedmont of the Tien Shan, as early as 2800 BC. Charred wheat and millet grains accompanied a human cremation in a stone cist at Begash Ia in eastern Kazakhstan dated 2400 to 2200 BC, and a few grains of wheat or barley were included in another cremation cist grave at Tasbas dated 2800 to 2500 BC (Frachetti et al. 2010; Spengler et al. 2014). Hearths associated with the occupation levels at both sites also produced a handful of charred wheat and barley grains, but the graves contained the majority of the discovered grains, so the economic and dietary importance of wheat cultivation is not clear for these third-millennium BC sites in the northern Tien Shan piedmont. The ceramics have not yet been formally described, but from the published illustrations, they seem unlike the ceramics of Sarazm or Kelteminar or other known third millennium BC complexes in Central Asia to the south, although Central Asian cultures like Sarazm probably were the source of the wheat and barley (Spengler et al. 2014). Unlike these eastern herders, the pastoralists of the Don-Volga-Ural steppes retained the long-established EBA/MBA regional disinterest in agriculture and resisted a diet based on exotic cultivated grains until relatively late, long after this diet had appeared both east and west of their region.

18   David W. Anthony

Srubnaya Copper Mining and the Copper Trade

The Srubnaya economy included mining and metallurgy on a surprisingly large scale. Large copper ore fields exist in and at the edges of the Eurasian steppes, and copper smelting can be accomplished at relatively low temperatures in simple kilns, using the timber available in many steppe river valleys. In the Bronze Age, mining and metallurgical industries were highly productive specializations within the largely pastoral economy of the Volga-Ural steppes. A pastoral economy can, under the right circumstances, support significant specialized industries. A similar copper-mining specialization occurred among the Edomites, Iron Age pastoralists in the Near East (Levy 2009).

E. N. Chernykh directed a multiyear project in the southern Ural steppes at the giant copper mining complex of Kargaly, north of Orenburg just beyond the headwaters of the Samara River (Chernykh 2004a, 2004b). The Kargaly copper ore field, around 500 km² in extent, was located on the headwaters of small rivers flowing both south into the Ural River and west into the Samara River. The area is an elevated, rolling steppe grassland where forests grow only in protected valleys. The large malachite copper oxide sandstone deposit at Kargaly was exploited beginning in the EBA by Yamnaya miners, one of whom was buried in a mining pit around 3000 BC. But the peak of Bronze Age mining occurred in the LBA, when 20 Srubnaya mining settlements exploited the copper ores (Koryakova and Epimakhov 2007:32–33; Kohl 2007:170–178; Chernykh 1997, 2004a, 2004b). Chernykh (2004b:224) estimated that the Bronze Age workings at Kargaly produced 2 to 5 million tons of ore, of which 55,000 to 120,000 tons of ore were smelted at the site. Abundant casting molds (3 whole, 194 fragments) and piles of slag (4,539 pieces weighing more than 20 kg) at the Gorny settlement testify to substantial mine-side ore-processing and casting operations (Chernykh 2004a:101). Kargaly might be the largest mining complex yet found in second millennium BC Europe. Srubnaya mining on this scale implies the operation of a substantial export trade.

Gorny is a Srubnaya mining settlement that exploited the Kargaly ore field and was the focus of a multiseason excavation program directed by E. N. Chernykh. The Srubnaya occupation at Gorny is dated 1700 to 1400 BC by 16 radiocarbon dates. Pollen studies by a Spanish botanical team (López et al. 2003; Diaz del Río et al. 2006; Vicent at al. 2006; Friere et al. 2012) showed that forest resources near the ore field first declined during the EBA, apparently as the result of the first mining and smelting by Yamnaya miners around 3000 BC. Not enough timber remained near Gorny in the LBA to provide sufficient fuel to smelt the amount of copper ore that the mined area produced in the LBA. The botanical team calculated the timber resources

needed and concluded that a significant portion of the LBA copper ore must have been exported for smelting elsewhere (Diaz del Río et al. 2006). This conclusion suggests that the mining operation was organized at a scale larger than the mining site itself, a suggestion also supported by the faunal remains.

Gorny produced over 2.5 million animal bone fragments, compared to 22,000 from Krasnosamarskoe from about one-fifth the area excavated at Gorny (about 200 m² for Krasnosamarskoe and about 1,000 m² for Gorny). Even correcting for the area excavated, Gorny had more than 25 times more animal bones per square meter, an astonishing number. Gorny was more heavily used and longer occupied than Krasnosamarskoe, or, which seems more likely, the area excavated at Gorny was a specialized dump for a neighboring residential zone of the mining settlement. (The features interpreted as residential pit-houses in the Gorny excavation were only 1–3 m long in their longest dimension, unlike Srubnaya residential structures, which are usually more than 20 m long; therefore, the excavated area at Gorny seems to contain refuse pits rather than houses.) Of the more than 300,000 identifiable animal bones, 83 percent were cattle, an unusually high percentage, and half of the cattle were culled at two to four years of age, a narrow age range not typical for a local subsistence cattle herd. Also, the cattle bones were butchered and sawed in standard ways. The high percentage of cattle bones, the age structure of the slaughtered animals, and the standardized cuts indicated to Morales and Antipina that the Gorny copper miners were provisioned with beef by other settlements (Morales and Antipina 2003:344; Chernykh 2004a:223). Provisioning of specialized mining settlements suggests the existence of political integration and the organization of settlement functions on a regional scale, while the scale of metallurgical production at Gorny, combined with the smaller Srubnaya mining settlements known in the Samara oblast, suggests a regional export trade, supported by a settled pastoral economy *without* agriculture. Gorny was examined systematically for botanical remains (Freire et al. 2012) but contained no seeds, pollen, or phytoliths of domesticated plants.

At least two other Srubnaya mining settlements are known in the Samara oblast, and others probably existed. A small copper mine and Srubnaya mining settlement was excavated south of the Samara Valley at Mikhailovka Ovsianka, in the southern Samara oblast, by a Samara Pedagogical University field school from 1996 to 2000 (Chapters 2 and 18). Excavations in 2001, connected with the SVP, at Kibit in the northern Samara oblast revealed a copper-smelting Srubnaya settlement located near local copper outcrops north of the Samara Valley (Peterson 2006, 2009; see Chapter 11). These two Srubnaya copper mines were exploited on a small scale, and most Srubnaya settlements in the Samara oblast show evidence for copper metallurgy at varying scales of intensity.

East of the Urals, Andronovo miners established large copper mines in Kazakhstan near Karaganda at the LBA site of Atasu (Kadyrbaev and Kurmankulov 1992) and near Dzhezkazgan (Zhauymbaev 1984; see also Chernykh et al. 2004). Tin mines were exploited by Andronovo miners in the Zeravshan Valley at Karnab in Uzbekistan (Boroffka et al. 2002; Parzinger and Boroffka 2003) and on the middle Irtysh River southeast of Ust-Kamenogorsk in the western Altai piedmont, where there are rich tin-bearing mineral outcrops (Stöllner et al. 2011). The lead isotope ratio in the tin from these Irtysh sources coincides with the isotope ratio in the tin from Troy IIg, dated around 2300 to 2200 BC, possibly suggesting an east-west trade in tin across the steppes during the late MBA.

More than 90 percent of Andronovo metal objects were made of tin-bronze, while only 20 to 25 percent of Srubnaya metal artifacts were tin-bronze, and 75 percent were made of copper or arsenical bronze (Chernykh 1992:213). Apparently tin, a valuable and rare metal in the Bronze Age, was available principally in the east. However, as Peterson shows in Chapter 11, the wealthiest Srubnaya graves in the Samara Valley, at the Spiridonovka cemetery, contained many ornaments made of tin-bronze, so this alloy was certainly available to the Srubnaya elite in the Samara region.

The scale of copper and tin mining in the steppes during the LBA is difficult to reconcile with the standard image of simple LBA farmer-herders. How the metal trade was articulated with Srubnaya-Andronovo subsistence economies and settlement systems in the mining regions is poorly understood. The ubiquity of copper working of differing intensities at many Srubnaya settlements in the Samara valley is interpreted as indicating a chain of metal-working communities extending from Kargaly down the Samara Valley to the Volga River (Chapter 4).

Some of the Krasnosamarskoe cattle showed leg and hoof pathologies caused by heavy hauling (Chapter 16). Because plowing for cultivation was apparently never practiced, these weight-pulling pathologies probably reflect wagon hauling. Perhaps local cattle were loaned or supplied occasionally to transport the copper ore that Diaz del Río (Diaz del Río et al. 2006) concluded must have left the mines at Kargaly. They probably shifted the load from wagons to rafts or boats either on the Samara River or at the mouth of the Samara, where watercraft could ride the Volga current either to the Caspian or portage to the Don and the Black Sea. Kargaly copper could have been traded up the Danube or through Troy V to VI to the Aegean during the Minoan-Mycenaean age. The monotonously similar and rather plain material culture styles of the Srubnaya culture spread westward into Ukraine from a Volga-Ural core region (Mochalov 2008:238–240), and perhaps this cultural influence followed the copper trade.

The End of the Bronze Age

The settled way of life represented by the Srubnaya-Andronovo horizon was interrupted at the end of the Late Bronze Age, during the Final Bronze Age, around 1200 to 800 BC, by a crisis usually ascribed to increasing climatic aridity. Kuzmina (2008:64–66) argued that the transition to Iron Age nomadism happened slowly over the course of several centuries during the Final Bronze Age, caused by the gradual extension of seasonal herding movements, originally an adjustment to a drier climate, but then trade and warfare encouraged an accelerating trend toward residential mobility. Recent climate studies have documented a similar drying event, a significant increase in aridity, beginning around 1200 BC in the eastern Mediterranean (Kaniewski et al. 2013). The decline of forests in steppe river valleys, combined with the rise of iron making, which required huge quantities of charcoal, moved most metal production into the forested zones during the Iron Age. The most powerful Scythians were able to support iron working on a large scale at their fortified "capital" of Bel'sk (Grakov 1958), but in general, the volume of mining and metal production declined in the steppes during the Iron Age.

In the FBA, the number of settlements in the Samara Valley declined and became concentrated in the lower valley near the Volga, and some (Suskanskoe) were fortified. Oddly, this is when the best evidence for Bronze Age agriculture appeared in the Samara region, in a settlement of the FBA at Russkaya Sel'itba on the Sok River, north of the Samara Valley, where 3 liters of charred grain included two varieties of wheat, two of barley, and one type of millet. The ceramic assemblage from Russkaya Sel'itba is assigned to the FBA Suskanskoe type, although a radiocarbon date of around 1650 to 1400 BC on one animal bone is approximately 200 to 400 years earlier than the ceramic assemblage would suggest, so probably dates an earlier Srubnaya component.

By around 1400 to 1200 BC, steppe herders were cultivating grain not just in the Samara oblast but in many places, from the Don to the Altai and Tien Shan. In the semi-alpine pastures of the western Altai, pastoralists of the Karasuk culture exhibited the earliest elevated stable isotopes attributed to millet consumption, a pattern continued through the Iron Age (Svyatko et al. 2013). Iron Age pastoralists in the Altai ate bread and suffered from caries in their teeth (Murphy 2003), and Iron Age settlements in the Altai contain large stone mortars more than 50 cm across, interpreted as evidence of agriculture (Shul'ga 2012). At Tasbas in the Dzhungarian Mountains of eastern Kazakhstan, a diversified seasonal agriculture was conducted from 1400 to 1200 BC (Spengler et al. 2014), the oldest clear evidence for Andronovo agriculture, and in the northern Tien Shan, there were other sites of this period with abundant domesticated seeds (Jia et al. 2011; Ryabogina and Ivanov 2011).

At the beginning of the Iron Age, around 850 BC, a rapid cooling and humidification of the steppes seems to have provided a fertile medium for an increasingly mobile pastoral organization to expand into steppe regions that formerly had been too arid to exploit, including the Tuva steppes where the earliest Scythian or Saka assemblages are found (van Geel et al. 2004). A new militarily aggressive form of nomadic pastoralism based on cavalry was widely adopted from the Tien Shan and Altai Mountains to the Dnieper River and with it broadly shared artistic styles (the "Animal Style"), styles of horse trappings, and weapon types. Steppe pastoral tribes combined into large, confederated cavalry forces armed with new recurve bows and new kinds of mass-produced socketed arrowheads, and this novel cavalry-based warfare was used to extract unprecedented wealth from sedentary neighbors.

Agriculture and Dependency in the Eurasian Steppes

A central pillar of the preceding summary is the assumption that almost all humans in Eurasia depended on agriculture before they developed such specializations as pastoral nomadism. Since Lees and Bates (1974), pastoralism has been interpreted by Western anthropologists as a specialized subsistence strategy that evolved from a broader agropastoral economy and at least initially retained a partial reliance on agriculture. People who lived in the steppes had to adopt a sedentary existence and grow grain for themselves (in the Bronze Age) or had to obtain grain by trading or raiding (in the Iron Age). Khazanov's (1984) formulation of the dependent and nonautarkic nature of the Iron Age pastoral nomadic economy, which solidified a view of pastoral economies widely held at least since Lattimore (1940 [1988]), was based partly on the dual assumptions that bread was necessary for the long-term survival of steppe pastoralism and that nomads did not make their own bread.

The first assumption is contradicted by the results of the SVP. We found that cultivated grain was not eaten in significant quantities by the supposed agropastoralists of LBA Krasnosamarskoe or Kibit, a result repeated at Gorny (Friere et al. 2012; Diaz del Río et al. 2006) and in Lebedeva's (2005) flotation studies (see below) at other Srubnaya settlements in the Volga-Ural region. The seeds of *Chenopodium*, *Polygonum*, and *Amaranthus* might have been consumed. This novel subsistence economy is not only surprising but also heavy with implications. If LBA communities in the middle Volga steppes were able to live permanently, year-round, in log houses with herds of sheep, cattle, and horses but without agriculture, then steppe pastoralism was not inherently dependent on agriculture. Permanent residence in year-round settlements also was not dependent on agriculture. Sedentism and agriculture were decoupled in the LBA in the Volga-Ural steppes.

Furthermore, if Iron Age nomads chose to eat bread, that choice was cultural and culinary, not inherited passively from Bronze Age ancestors and not imposed by an imagined inherent biological need for cultivated grain in the steppe diet. Bread was neither a nutritional need nor an inherited tradition. In the Volga-Ural steppes, it was a Final Bronze Age/Iron Age novelty that only became widespread with the rise of pastoral nomadism, an economy thought to represent the antithesis of settled agriculture. This apparent paradox—that the consumption of cultivated grain might have become common in many parts of the Eurasian steppes only during the age of pastoral nomadism—raises important questions about how Iron Age pastoral nomadism originated and how it functioned as a part of a differentiated economy that integrated nomadism with local agriculture in or at the edge of the steppe zone.

Dependency Theory in the Study of Eurasian Steppe Pastoralism

Dependency theory was given this name by Nicola Di Cosmo (Di Cosmo 1994:1093; 2002:168–69) in a thoughtful criticism of the attitude toward nomadism articulated by the great Central Asian scholar Owen Lattimore in perhaps his most famous expression (Lattimore 1940 [1988]:73–75): "It is the poor nomad who is the pure nomad." Lattimore's original phrase has been rearranged in popular usage, usually: "The only pure nomad is a poor nomad." Historian and linguist Peter Golden accepted this reversed order to reinforce Lattimore's central point. Golden (2001:86–87) observed that

the situation might best be understood by reversing it: it is the pure nomad who is the poor nomad. . . . [Nomads] had to interact with the sedentary world to gain access to essential goods, such as certain foodstuffs (grains) and manufactures (silk and other fabrics, and weapons). . . .Although sedentary society could do without nomads, nomads would have lived greatly impoverished lives if deprived of contact with sedentary society.

Pastoral nomads, in this view, had to trade with farmers, whether they held the advantage in the exchange or not. Conflict between the steppe and the sown came not from a desire to conquer and hold land but from the nomads' real need for the products of agricultural societies, without which they could barely survive. Even the ability of nomads to unite in threatening confederations depended ultimately on farmers. In the standard view of political organization among steppe pastoralists, nomads are thought to have been so easily fissionable and uncontrollable at the local level that any political alliance was unavoidably unstable. Over the long run, nomadic political leaders had to depend on a settled population if they were to persist in their positions of power (Kradin 2002; Barfield 2001, 2006; Salzman 2004; Mulder et al. 2010).

Anatoly Khazanov's (1984, 1994, 2009) magisterial elaboration of dependency theory gave it the weight of dogma. Khazanov disagreed with Lattimore only in his insistence that a poor (or impoverished) nomad was even *more* dependent on sedentary societies, not less so, and in fact was likely to become sedentary himself: "The well-known aphorism of Lattimore is scarcely true. It so happens that impoverished nomads have been forced more often than other nomads to seek supplementary sources of subsistence and in the process not infrequently have become sedentary" (Khazanov 1984:70).

These ideas taken together imply that pastoral nomadism could exist without agriculture only in a condition of desperate poverty. The weaknesses of Eurasian steppe pastoralism came principally from three sources.

First, steppe pastoral subsistence was inherently prone to famine when winter blizzards or spring ice storms froze or starved entire herds. Free-ranging herds in the steppes of Kazakhstan regularly lost half or more of their numbers (Khazanov 1984:73) during severe ice and snow storms: "large-scale losses occurred every 6–11 years and local ones almost annually." Khazanov (1984:72–75) argued that high annual variation in the severity of the steppe winters and in the productivity of wild steppe pastures meant that steppe herds regularly suffered steep declines, so pastoralists could never depend on livestock alone and therefore supplemented their diet with agricultural foods, even during periods when they were nomadic. Second,

pastoralists detached from state economies had no market for their surplus animals, and in Khazanov's analysis, colored by historic sources on Iron Age and later nomads, there was no other specialization or internal division of labor within pastoral societies. Prestate pastoralists had no incentive to accumulate herds significantly larger than what they needed for subsistence and occasional tribal feasts, imposing a natural limit on pastoral wealth. Finally, lacking internal economic specializations, pastoralism was not able to grow through intensification. To accumulate surplus wealth, the nomadic economy had to either expand into new territory, growing in the only way it could, by simply adding more pasture, or had to be articulated with the economy of an agricultural hinterland. Because of these conditions, Khazanov (2009:120) warned,

> Under these conditions, pastoral nomadic economies were never self-sufficient and could never be so. . . . Pastoral nomadic societies always needed sedentary farming and urban societies for their efficient functioning and their very existence. Cereals and other farm products always formed an important part of their dietary systems.

Dependency theory leads us to posit the existence of prestate, Bronze Age steppe agriculture, even where the archaeological evidence for it is lacking, and to deny the existence of prestate, Bronze Age steppe nomadism, even when the archaeological evidence for it is compelling, as in the EBA and MBA in the western steppes (Merpert 1974). Recently, a second element has been added to the agropastoral stereotype of Bronze Age pastoralism in the *western* steppes: cattle. According to Kohl (2007:78, 162–164), Frachetti (2008, 2011), Kaiser (2010), and Bendrey (2011), cattle were the preferred, numerically dominant domesticated animal in the western Eurasian steppes during the Bronze Age. Cattle are said to be unsuited to long-distance migrations, so their importance implies a somewhat settled residential pattern (Kuzmina 2008:61–62), consistent with occasional agriculture. A steppe-wide Iron Age shift to sheepherding was the signal, in Kuzmina's interpretation, of a shift to mobile pastoralism. Frachetti (2011) argued that sheepherding developed independently in eastern Kazakhstan as a regional adaptation in the Bronze Age and then spread westward with pastoral nomadism in the Iron Age.

This stereotype of *western* steppe pastoralism prior to the Iron Age as agropastoral, with cattle-dominant herds, has been encouraged by the acceptance of dependency theory and by selective readings of the archaeological evidence.

Debating the Cattle-Centered Stereotype

Cattle predominated in Srubnaya herds in the western steppes, but this was a herding strategy specific to the LBA in the western steppes. Srubnaya settlements in the middle Volga region usually had over 50 percent cattle; at the copper-mining settlement of Gorny, cattle reached 83 percent of the fauna. In 21 Srubnaya settlements located across the western steppes between the Dnieper and Ural Rivers compared by Morales and Antipina (2003:Table 22.2), the lowest percentage of cattle was 50 percent, and most LBA Srubnaya settlements contained percentages of cattle bones in the 60 to 70 percent range.

East of the Ural Mountains, the herding strategy of the LBA Andronovo horizon was centered on sheep and goats, with fewer cattle. The eastern and central steppes of Kazakhstan are drier and more elevated than the western steppes of Russia and Ukraine, and stocking rates are lower, favoring sheep, which can subsist on one-sixth of the plant food needed for a cow (Bendrey 2011). In Andronovo settlements between the southern Ural steppes and the Tien Shan piedmont compiled by Kuzmina (1994) (Table 1.2), sheep-goat averaged 41 percent of domesticated fauna (MNI); cattle, 33 percent; and horses, almost 19 percent. The driest region, the central Kazakh steppes, showed the highest reliance on sheep. Sheep were not an Iron Age innovation here.

So in the LBA, cattle dominated Srubnaya herds in the steppes west of the Ural Mountains, and sheep-goat were preferred in most (but not all) Andronovo herds in the central and eastern steppes. Both economies were sedentary, based on year-round residence in timber houses. But the cattle-dominant herds of the LBA Srubnaya culture were not an inherent or necessary part of western steppe herding. Earlier, more mobile pastoralists in the western steppes relied much more on sheep and goats.

Table 1.2 Domesticated Animals by Percentage of MNI in LBA Andronovo Settlements by Region

Region	Cattle	Sheep-Goat	Horse
Southwest Ural steppes	42.8	44.5	12.7
South Ural steppes	33.9	50.5	14.8
Upper Tobol	32.2	40.3	27.5
North Kazakh steppes	37.4	36.5	23.6
Central Kazakh steppes	26	63	23
East Kazakh steppes	25.9	35.1	11.9
Total averages	33.1	41.1	18.9

Source: Kuzmina (1994:Table 6).

The first domesticated animals in the western steppes appeared by 5500 BC in Ukraine, in Late Neolithic/Eneolithic sites in the Dnieper-Azov steppes, and reached the Volga-Ural steppes by 5000 to 4500 BC at sites such as the Khvalynsk cemetery and the Ivanovka settlement (Kotova 2008; Anthony 2007; Agapov 2010; Morgunova 1988). At Eneolithic Khvalynsk, a cemetery of more than 200 graves dated 4500 BC on the Volga, and at the contemporary Nikol'skoe-Mariupol cemeteries between the lower Dnieper and the Sea of Azov, domesticated sheep, goats, and cattle appeared in funerary sacrifices connected with a sharp increase in the number and diversity of new types of body ornaments in graves, some made of exotic materials, including copper, and polished stone maces. Sheep-goats were sacrificed more than any other species in ochre-stained ritual deposits at Khvalynsk, while cattle seem to have predominated in sacrifices at Nikol'skoe on the lower Dnieper. Horse bones, not cattle, dominated the settlement faunas at Ivanovka and Varfolomievka (Anthony and Brown 2014). In this volume, Schulting and Richards's analysis of stable isotopes in the bones of Khvalynsk individuals (Chapter 7) show that their diet depended to a large extent on fish. Eneolithic domesticated cattle and sheep-goats might have been reserved for use as a ritual and feasting currency associated with the elevation of a new social rank of leadership (Anthony 2007:186; Anthony and Brown 2011:138).

In the fourth millennium BC, domesticated sheep-goat and cattle and their dairy products became more important in the daily diet. Mikhailovka level I on the Dnieper, dated around 3800 to 3300 BC, had 65 percent sheep-goat; Konstantinovka on the Don, occupied around 3500 BC, had 30 percent red deer and 25 percent sheep-goat in second place; and Sredni Stog II on the Dnieper, occupied around 3800 BC, had 60 percent sheep-goat (Telegin 1986:88).

In the EBA, after 3300 BC, wagons were adopted and were combined with horse-aided herding, and a highly mobile form of nomadic pastoralism spread across the western steppes with Yamnaya kurgan cemeteries (Anthony 2007; Shishlina 2008). Wagons revolutionized pastoral economies by providing bulk transport for tents, water, and supplies in combination with horseback riding, for which there is clear evidence at contemporary Botai in Kazakhstan (Anthony 2007:Chapter 13; Anthony and Brown 2011). Riding doubled the number of animals a single herder could watch and control and in other ways greatly facilitated a wagon-based mobile way of life. Mobile Yamnaya pastoralists had 65 percent sheep-goat and only 15 percent cattle in their grave sacrifices, according to a survey of 263 Yamnaya graves in the Don-Volga-Ural steppes (Shilov 1985:25–27). Sheep also predominated as sacrifices in Yamnaya graves in the

North Caucasian–Caspian steppes (Shishlina 2008), as well as in MBA Poltavka graves on the middle Volga (Kosintsev and Roslyakova 2000), and they were 58 percent and 76 percent of the fauna at two EBA Usatovo settlements in the northwestern Pontic steppes (Anthony 2007:351). After the EBA, cattle bones predominated in MBA Catacomb-culture sites on the forest-steppe border, but this was a local pattern showing the variability of herding practices prior to the LBA (Kaiser 2010).

These sites show that western steppe pastoralism was not limited to cattle-dominant herds by nature or culture before the LBA, so the LBA preference for cattle was a cultural choice of that period, linked to local conditions. Sheep-dominant herds appeared in many places and times across the western steppes before the LBA and were typical of Andronovo herds in the central Kazakh steppes during the LBA. Frachetti's (2011) suggestion that cattle-dominant western steppe pastoralism could not have been the source of sheep-dominant eastern steppe LBA pastoralism was based on a stereotype of pastoral strategies in the western steppes. Kohl's (2007:236) suggestion that the cattle-centered economy of the agricultural Tripol'ye culture was carried into the steppes in the fourth millennium BC by Tripol'ye farmers who migrated into the western steppes, a hypothesis first advanced by Ukrainian archaeologist Rassamakin (1999:97–100), misrepresents both the chronology of early steppe pastoralism, which was much older than this, and its herding strategies, which often included sheep and goats, and ancient human DNA now shows (Haak et al. 2015) that Neolithic farmer genes did not appear among steppe pastoralists in the fourth millennium BC. The sheep-herding Afanasievo culture of the western Altai, which appeared suddenly around 3300 BC, and introduced pastoral economies to the Altai, exhibited abundant material similarities to EBA Yamnaya metal types, graves and typical grave gifts, and ceramic types (Bobrov 1988; Evdokimov and Loman 1989; Mallory and Mair 2000; Anthony 2007:307–11; Kuzmina 2008:97; Merts and Merts 2010), and ancient human DNA shows that Afanasievo and Yamnaya individuals were genetically the same (Allentoft et al. 2015). The Yamnaya-Afanasievo connection transferred regionally variable EBA western-steppe pastoral economies to the western Altai, where herding strategies were again modified to suit local conditions.

Debating the Agropastoral Stereotype

The second, agropastoral stereotype of Bronze Age economies in the western steppes was the broad subject of our project. Kotova (2003) argued that many Eneolithic settlements in Ukraine, dated 5500 to 3300 BC between the Dnieper and Don Rivers, contained a few pottery sherds with seed impressions of emmer wheat, einkorn wheat, spelt wheat, barley, and millet. A reexamination of these impressions by Motuzaite-Matuzeviciute (2012) confirmed cultivated grain impressions only after 4500 BC, the Late Eneolithic, but that is still much earlier than the appearance of cereals in the Volga-Ural region.

A laboratory at Samara State University specializes in the microscopic analysis of ceramic inclusions and impressions, but no cultivated grain impressions have been found in Eneolithic, EBA, or MBA pottery (Salugina 2011). There is a good possibility that domesticated cattle, sheep, and goats were adopted in the Volga-Ural steppes, possibly for use as feasting foods in an emerging field of political competition between local elites, without any grain cultivation (Anthony and Brown 2011). Direct transitions from foraging economies to pastoral economies, without an intervening agricultural phase, have been identified also in parts of the Negev desert (Rosen 2009) and in North Africa (Linseele 2010). In the Samara Valley, a well-surveyed area, no Yamnaya and little Poltavka settlement evidence has been found in a landscape with 39 known EBA and MBA Yamnaya and Poltavka cemeteries, including the richest Yamnaya-Poltavka grave in the Don-Ural steppes at Utyevka I. The invisibility of settlements in the EBA and MBA suggests a nomadic residential pattern. Shishlina found charred *Amaranthus albus* seeds and *Chenopodium* pollen in EBA Yamnaya graves and MBA Catacomb graves, as well as recovered *Chenopodium* pollen from EBA-MBA pot residues and dental plaques in the Manych steppes north of the North Caucasus Mountains, but found no evidence of cultivated grain in any EBA or MBA context (Shishlina 2008; Shishlina et al. 2008). She suggested that Yamnaya pastoralists ate wild seeds.

Now it appears that even in the LBA, when the Srubnaya population of the Volga-Ural steppes settled in permanent homesteads such as Krasnosamarskoe, cultivated grain was not eaten in any significant quantity, but perhaps *Chenopodium* and *Amaranthus* were. Some cultivation was practiced in the western steppes west of the Don River, both in the Eneolithic and in the Bronze Age, but in the steppes east of the Don, neither the mobile pastoralists of the EBA and MBA nor the settled pastoralists of the LBA ate bread. Their pastoral economies thrived for 2,000 years or more, in both mobile and settled forms, without a trace of agriculture. Pastoral economies in the western steppes did not need agriculture to survive and even thrive.

Recently, the dependency model has been challenged in other ways in other parts of the Eurasian steppes, particularly in Mongolia. Honeychurch (Honeychurch and Amartuvshin 2006) and Houle (Houle 2009; Houle and Broderick 2011) have shown that local settlement types and patterns changed in ways consistent with a local growth of hierarchy that reached down to local herding groups and affected their spatial organization. These changes appeared first in the Late Bronze Age, before any regular contact between Mongolian pastoralists and state-level societies, suggesting that pastoral elites could arise in the steppes and extract sufficient wealth from the internal pastoral economy to maintain themselves, changing the spatial organization of seasonal activities in the process. Here the rise of pastoral political elites, at least on a small scale, occurred independently of contact with state societies. This is also evident in rich Yamnaya graves such as Utyevka I. Neither the steppe subsistence economy nor the hierarchical pastoral political economy depended on states or on agriculture.

LBA Settled Pastoralism in the Volga-Ural Steppes

Why did the pastoralists of the Volga-Ural steppes settle down and become sedentary in the LBA if it wasn't because of agriculture? A markedly cooler, more arid climate began in the Eurasian steppes after around 2500 BC, reaching its coldest and driest peak late in the millennium, around 2250 to 2000 BCE. This event is recorded in pollen cores across the Eurasian continent, from western Russia across Kazakhstan and into the Altai (Blyakharchuk et al. 2004; Kremenetskii 1997, 2002). The same episode is documented in botanical studies in Anatolia, the Caucasus, and Mesopotamia, as well as in East Africa and India (Weiss 2000). Climate scientists Perry and Hsu (2000:12436) called it the most influential Little Ice Age in recorded history. In the Samara Valley, forests, lakes, and marshes declined in area and steppes expanded (Chapter 5).

Increased competition for winter access to declining marshes during these colder, drier centuries might have encouraged mobile herding groups across the steppes to settle near their most vital resource—*Phragmites* marshes composed of reed beds that can grow up to 25 feet (7.6 m) tall and that remained standing above the ice all winter. Tall reeds were good fodder for cattle and sheep and provided shelter from winter winds. Rather than fight with their neighbors over the best winter camping sites near the largest marshes, LBA pastoralists settled permanently in those locations. Rosenberg (1998) proposed this model, which he compared to the child's game of musical chairs, as an explanation for why mobile hunter-gatherers settled down under conditions of declining resources and increasing competition during the Mesolithic-Neolithic transition in the Near East. I borrowed Rosenberg's insight to explain sedentarization in the LBA (Anthony and Brown 2007; Anthony et al. 2005).

In northern steppe pastoralism, the most critical resource was winter fodder/grazing and protection from winter ice and snow. Ethnohistorically, Eurasian steppe pastoralists have favored marshy regions as winter refuges because stands of *Phragmites* reeds offered not only winter grazing and protection from the wind but also roofing and mat-making materials for the exteriors and interiors of log-walled houses. Marshes are rather bleak places, but *Phragmites* reeds are readily eaten by cattle and sheep, and oxbow lakes also support fish, waterfowl, and roe deer. *Phragmites* roots are sweet. When dried, they make a traditional Russian folk candy, like the roots of another marsh plant, *Althaea officinalis* or marshmallow, after which the popular marshmallow candy is named. Grazing can eliminate *Phragmites* reed beds (summer grazing is used in North America to control invasive *Phragmites* stands), so areas grazed in winter would have to be left ungrazed to promote recovery of the reeds, encouraging regular but possibly short-distance shifts in preferred winter residences.

The first cultures to settle in permanent locations near marshes were the Sintashta culture, east of the Urals, and the Mnogovalikovaya culture (now also called the Babino culture) in Ukraine, both east and west of the middle Volga steppes, beginning around 2100 to 2000 BC. All Sintashta settlements were built on the first terrace of a marshy, meandering stream close to winter grazing, rather than on a more easily defended elevation, despite the clear concern with defense implied by Sintashta earth-and-palisade fortification walls. The settling-down trend affected the middle Volga steppes somewhat later, beginning around 1900 BC, but the preferred location for settlements was the same: low terraces beside the wet floodplain, preferably beside a large marsh composed of high, dense stands of *Phragmites* and *Typha* reeds, as at Krasnosamarskoe.

Given the absence of evidence for agriculture in Srubnaya settlements, a climatic cause seems a more likely explanation for the settling-down event of 2100 to 1900 BC than the adoption of agriculture. When the climate in the Northern Hemisphere became colder and more arid after 2500 BCE, previously mobile herders in the northern steppes adopted a defensive resource-claiming reaction in response to an unfolding chain of such claims nearby, as in the game of musical chairs, and settled permanently near the shrinking marshes that were vital for wintering their herds.

At the same time, the increase in copper mining during the MBA/LBA transition might have stabilized the new settlements when additional seasonal labor was diverted from the household economy to support specialized mining settlements such as Gorny and Mikhailovka Ovsianka. As the labor dedicated to copper working increased during the LBA, sedentism might have been encouraged among the families who remained at home. Mobile pastoralism requires substantial labor just to keep moving. House-making and house-breaking tasks are required at frequent intervals, and herds of different species are usually kept in separate pastures by different herders at some distance from the home. Cooperative herding, with herds from several communities combined under a shared herder, would permit a reduction in the number of herders but required sustained geographic proximity, encouraging sedentary settlements. In Peschanyi Dol (Chapter 18), ceramic paste diversity in seasonal herding camps indicates that Srubnaya herders from several different permanent settlements occupied the same seasonal herding camp and even used the same trash pit. This suggests that several Srubnaya communities with different clays combined herds in PD, like the herding cooperative of three nearby villages that uses the PD valley this way today. Cooperative herding might have been adopted to reduce herding labor to compensate for labor lost to copper mining, but it also encouraged and intensified sedentism.

Wild and Cultivated Seeds at Krasnosamarskoe and Other Srubnaya Settlements

As the reports of Popova, Weisskopf, and Murphy in this volume demonstrate, the Srubnaya diet at Krasnosamarskoe and Kibit included no documented cultivated grain (see also Anthony et al. 2005; Anthony and Brown 2007; Popova 2007). Archaeozoological studies (Chapters 15 and 16) show that fishing and hunting were insignificant to the Srubnaya diet.

Popova (Chapter 12) identified 306 charred seeds of *Chenopodium* in the anaerobic mud in the bottom three levels of Pit 10 at Krasnosamarskoe, interpreted as a well. The same bottom sediments contained charred *Polygonum* (74 seeds) and *Amaranthus* (11 seeds). All 391 seeds in these three genera were charred. Seeds of these three species were selectively collected (much more than other seed types) and selectively charred (no other seeds were charred). Charring is a necessary step in removing the bitter pericarp from *Chenopodium* seeds prior to eating them (López et al. 2011). An additional 28 genera were represented among 310 other seeds (701 total) in the anaerobic sediments of the three deepest levels in the well bottom. None of the 310 seeds from these 28 other genera were charred; they were preserved by anaerobic conditions. It is not likely that the charred seeds were included in animal dung that was burned, another possible cause of seed charring, because Weisskopf's analysis of phytoliths from ash deposits at Krasnosamarskoe (Chapter 13) found wood ash, not dung

ash. Also, the uncharred seeds in the well bottom include prime animal fodder species such as ryegrass, bluegrass, and sedges, which should also have been included in animal dung if that was the source of the charring. Another pit feature in the floor of the Krasnosamarskoe structure, Pit 8, contained a uniquely high concentration of *Chenopodium-Amaranthus* pollen, more than 40 percent, while the background level of *Chenopodium-Amaranthus* pollen appears to have been around 24 percent, again suggesting that *Chenopodium-Amaranthus* plants were manipulated selectively. Popova noted that the combination of (1) high levels of *Chenopodium* and *Amaranthus* pollen found concentrated in Pit 8, (2) hundreds of charred seeds of these plants found in Pit 10, and (3) the absence of charring on other seed genera has been interpreted elsewhere as indicating intentional use of wild seeds (also Popova 2006, 2007). But what were they used for? Were they eaten by humans?

In North America, *Chenopodium belandieri* was eaten and eventually domesticated by Native American foragers. Field studies have shown that this wild chenopod grows naturally in dense stands that can produce 500- to 1,000-kg seeds per hectare, comparable to einkorn wheat, which yields 645 to 835 kg/ha (Smith 1989:1569). The seeds are as nutritious as rice or maize (Gremillion 2004). *Chenopodium* seeds are covered with a bitter-tasting skin or pericarp that requires substantial labor to remove. The first step in removing the pericarp is to char the seeds (López et al. 2011). In Neolithic settlements of the Linearbandkeramik (LBK) or Linear Pottery culture in Germany (Bogaard et al. 2011:396), as well as in Swiss lakeside villages and Bronze Age settlements, thousands of charred *Chenopodium* seeds are found occasionally in caches. These finds are regarded by paleobotanists as indicating dietary usage (Behre 2008). In northern Europe, *Chenopodium* seeds were found in the stomachs of bog bodies dated to the late Iron Age. *Chenopodium* is thought to have been used for food in the Gumelniţsa culture Morteni settlement in Romania (Cârciumaru 1996:196). There is no question that *Chenopodium* seeds were consumed as a food at least occasionally in prehistoric Europe.

Charred *Chenopodium*, *Polygonum*, and *Amaranthus* seeds were recovered by flotation at the LBA Srubnaya settlements of Kibit, Krasnosamarskoe, and Gorny in the Volga-Ural region. At the Kibit settlement, charred *Chenopodium album* seeds constituted 55 percent of the macrobotanical remains, with lesser amounts of *Polygonum* and *Amaranthus*. The *Chenopodium* percentage is far higher than its occurrence in the background vegetation. At Gorny, charred *Chenopodium* seeds were the most frequent charred seed species found, and 63 percent of the charred

Chenopodium came from one pit feature containing 146 charred seeds, perhaps the remains of a storage cache, but the excavators concluded that this was a ritual, not an economic feature, and are reluctant to consider *Chenopodium* as a food (López et al. 2003; Vicent et al. 2006; Diaz del Río et al. 2005). Shishlina (2008:Table 30) found *Chenopodium-Amaranthus* pollen in the interdental calculus of mobile Catacomb culture pastoralists of the MBA in the North Caspian steppes. She also found *Chenopodium-Amaranthus* pollen in organic residues on Catacomb culture pottery. She interprets this evidence as indicating dietary use.

Are any seeds of domestic species such as millet or wheat found in the Volga-Ural steppes? In a flotation experiment that began in 1989, Lebedeva and Chernykh took 10-liter soil samples from cores inserted into the cultural levels at 49 Bronze Age settlements in the steppes, including Gorny (Lebedeva 2005). Unlike Gorny, at most sites, the coring happened after archaeological excavations were concluded, so most of the soil samples came from unexcavated sections of known settlements. These multiple 10-liter soil samples were then floated and seeds were recovered. The sampled sites extended from the Danube delta to western Kazakhstan. Of the 36 Srubnaya settlements cored, only seven (20 percent) yielded charred cultivated grain, most consisting of one or two charred grains of millet (*Panicum miliaceum*). All of the Srubnaya settlements with grain were located west of the Volga River in the moister western part of the western steppes. Six of the seven were located west of the Don, emphasizing the western bias of Srubnaya sites with millet. Twelve Srubnaya settlements were cored in the Volga-Ural steppes, the region that contains Krasnosamarskoe. Not one of the 12 yielded a cultivated grain.

Lebedeva's (2005) conclusions were tentative because of the limited number of soil samples taken at 11 of these 12 sites. But the much more intensive excavation and flotation program at the Srubnaya settlement of Gorny also yielded no cultivated grain, and intensive palynological studies around Gorny confirmed the absence of cultivation. Now we can add Kibit and Krasnosamarskoe to the list of intensively studied Srubnaya sites, making it zero for 14: zero cultivated grains in 14 Srubnaya settlements examined with flotation in the Volga-Ural region.

The specialist reports in this volume provide an array of evidence that supports this conclusion in other ways. Paleopathological analysis by Murphy (Chapter 8) of 1,792 Srubnaya teeth from at least 88 individuals excavated from 16 Srubnaya cemeteries across the Samara region showed just three teeth with caries, a rate of 0.2 percent, typical of the teeth of hunter-gatherers, not farmers (Figure 8.3). Caries frequency worldwide is significantly higher among populations that regularly eat starchy cultivated grains. Caries were also absent from earlier Bronze Age populations in the Samara Valley. According to their teeth, the Bronze Age occupants of the Samara Valley, whether settled or mobile, did not eat significant amounts of cultivated grain at any time during the Bronze Age. Also, the study of stable isotopes by Schulting and Richards in Chapter 7 suggests that the isotopic signature of the EBA Yamnaya diet was significantly different from the Eneolithic diet, which was largely based on fish, but after the fully pastoral Yamnaya diet was established in the EBA, it did not change in isotopic signature throughout the Bronze Age (Figure 7.3), not even in the LBA when populations settled. The LBA settling-down event is invisible isotopically and dentally. None of the Bronze Age populations examined in the middle Volga region ate bread in significant amounts.

Agriculture in the Transition to Iron Age Pastoral Nomadism

Lebedeva's (2005) flotation data suggested that the cultivation of grain became widespread at the edges of the western steppes during the Final Bronze Age, 1200 to 800 BC, when the number of settlements in the steppes declined and their distribution contracted, and that cultivation really became an established part of the regional economy only when pastoral nomadism appeared in the steppes in the early Iron Age after 800 BC, a surprising result completely at odds with the standard narrative. In Lebedeva's flotation experiments, the average frequency of charred cultivated grains in flotation samples from 36 Srubnaya settlements was 0.06 grains per 10 liters of floated soil. In Final Bronze Age samples, it was 2.7 grains, a significant increase, and the grains included wheat (emmer, *Triticum dicoccum*, and bread wheat, *Triticum aestivum*) and barley, not just millet (Lebedeva 2005:66). In the Iron Age settlements she sampled, located principally in the Kuban piedmont of the North Caucasus Mountains, the agricultural zone of the southern Crimea, and the upper Don forest-steppe zone, the average frequency was 40 grains per 10 liters of soil, an increase of almost 15 times over the Final Bronze Age and 80 times over the Srubnaya samples from the steppes (Figure 1.6).

The Iron Age settlements sampled by Lebedeva were located not in the steppe itself but on its edges: in piedmont regions on the Crimean peninsula or north of the North Caucasus Mountains, or in the forest-steppe zone of the middle and upper Don River. A similar ecotone was exploited by agricultural communities in steppe-edge settlements far to the east, in the lower piedmont of the Tien

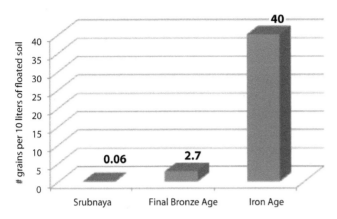

Figure 1.6 Frequency of cultivated seeds in LBA, Final Bronze, and Iron Age sites sampled by Lebedeva. After Lebedeva (2005).

Shan Mountains in eastern Kazakhstan, and in the Talgar River delta south of Lake Balkash. Chang et al. (2003; Chang 2008) conducted multiyear excavations at three Iron Age settlement sites in this region. The charred seeds of wheat, barley, and millet were recovered from levels dated 700 BC through the Iron Age, just a few kilometers distant from kurgan cemeteries containing classic Saka pastoral nomadic artifact assemblages. Other excavations in the same region confirmed that the Scythian-Saka societies of eastern Kazakhstan were not exclusively nomadic but interacted with numerous small agricultural settlements containing stone-built houses (Baipakov 2008). Murphy (2003, 2011), analyzing Iron Age skeletons at the cemetery of Aymyrlyg in Tuva in the Altai Mountains, found significantly more caries among Saka and Hunnic nomads in the Altai, who almost certainly regularly ate bread, than she found among the settled Late Bronze Age herders of the Samara Valley, who didn't. The western Altai, where Scythian tombs frozen in permafrost preserved the bodies of spectacularly outfitted nomadic chiefs, also contained numerous small Iron Age agricultural settlements of stone-built houses, well known to Russian archaeologists (Shul'ga 2012) but not in the Western literature. The Scythian-Saka, portrayed by archaeologists and historians as the stereotype of "nomads," were supported by an agropastoral economy that seems to have been widely adopted in the forest and forest-steppe zones during the Final Bronze and early Iron Ages, while the Srubnaya culture, the classic archaeological example of supposed Eurasian steppe "agropastoralism," actually depended on a novel mixture of settled pastoralism, copper mining, and wild seed gathering.

In the middle Volga steppes, recent flotation campaigns connected with the excavation of Medieval nomadic sites found that the pastoral nomads of the Golden Horde cultivated millet, rye, and wheat (Nedashkovskii 2009), unlike the LBA

sedentary pastoralists of the same region, and Scythian-era pits dated 300 to 200 BC on the lower Donets, in the Black Sea steppes, contained the seeds of cultivated hulled barley (*Hordeum vulgare*) and broomcorn millet (*Panicum miliaceum*), together with seeds of *Chenopodium album*, which the authors noted could have been a food, not a weed (Motuzaite-Matuzeviciute et al. 2012). The authors suggested that Scythian pastoral nomads occasionally cultivated plots of grain in the riverine floodplains of Ukraine.

Iron Age pastoral nomadism was not the antithesis of farming but was articulated with it systematically in and at the edge of the steppe, as Di Cosmo argued long ago (Di Cosmo 1994). At the edges of the steppes, the same people might sometimes appear archaeologically in Iron Age settlements as a part of a seemingly distinct settled population and in graves as nomads. If Iron Age pastoral nomads were dependent on agriculture, that dependence was fed by communities in and at the edges of the steppes, communities that could have included people who regarded themselves as nomads. Ethnographic studies among the Maasai of East Africa (Spear and Waller 1993), who also are often portrayed as "pure" nomadic pastoralists, showed that Maasai nomadism was an ideal state, aspired to by all who regarded themselves as Maasai but actually attained only by the strongest and most powerful Maasai tribes, because only the strongest could actually control large enough pastures to subsist entirely on pastoralism. Most other Maasai engaged in occasional farming or even hunting and gathering while aspiring to nomadism. Far from the "poor nomad" of Lattimore, the "pure nomad" of the Iron Age steppes might have been an ideal that only the most militarily powerful tribes attained, although they ate bread (as their teeth reveal) raised by local agricultural clients.

One notable contrast between Iron Age and Bronze Age pastoralism was the decline of steppe-zone copper mining and the shift of metallurgical production to forested locations where the enormous fuel requirements of iron smelting could be satisfied. The upper level at Krasnosamarskoe contained evidence of this new relationship. An iron bloom and iron slag were associated with a scatter of Gorodetskaya culture forest-zone Iron Age pottery; in the same level was a Sauromatian bronze arrowhead, typical of the regional Iron Age pastoral nomads. Our Samara colleagues suggested that this brief occupation represented a camp of Iron Age iron workers and traders venturing out of their fortified, agricultural Gorodetskaya settlements west of the Volga to a temporary trading post in the steppe margins at Krasnosamarskoe, where they might have forged iron into the kinds of goods that steppe nomads typically obtained from the forest zone during the Iron Age: horse buckles, horse bits, spearheads, swords, and knives. They might also have traded some grain. Two charred seeds of millet, the only cultivated grain recovered at Krasnosamarskoe, originated in this level (Chapter 10).

Conclusions

Many of the assumptions that we carried into the SVP, models that initially guided our fieldwork, turned out to be surprisingly wrong. Archaeologists are now collectively discovering a Bronze Age that we never expected, a bundle of idiosyncratic economic and social practices unlike any known to historians. One achievement of the SVP was the recovery of a multiscalar set of social networks that integrated Srubnaya families into several communities that operated at different scales, with different sets of people, at different seasons. The hierarchical political organization implied by differences in mortuary wealth was just one aspect of a series of overlapping social relationships, many of which were heterarchical, that I have termed relationships of obligation (supporting the mining industry and metals trade), cooperation (communal herding), and affiliation (communal rituals).

One outstanding aspect of the Bronze Age economy in the western steppes was its variability. Agriculture played an important role in the steppes west of the Dnieper and was practiced occasionally in the Dnieper-Don steppes but was absent from the Volga-Ural steppes from the beginning of domesticated food production right up to the end of the Bronze Age. The cattle-dominant herds of the LBA were preceded by much more variable herd compositions in the EBA and MBA. The seeds of wild plants apparently were collected and probably consumed throughout the Bronze Age, contributing to the resilience and persistence of pastoral economies. Copper mining and the copper trade provided an alternate source of wealth and technological specialization that diversified Bronze Age pastoral economies, particularly during the LBA, when copper mining reached a peak after the population became sedentary.

The LBA phase of sedentary pastoralism in the Samara Valley probably started because a colder, drier climate at the end of the third millennium BC encouraged a series of defensive claims to marsh resources, expressed materially in the establishment of permanent settlements near marshes. The new, sedentary way of living was then reinforced by the removal of some people for obligated labor related to the emergence of industrial-scale copper mining. The reduced labor force available for herding increased its efficiency by pooling herds under a shared herder, which worked best if the cooperating communities were sedentary

and maintained their spatial proximity (Chapter 18). Sedentary pastoralism made it possible to raise more cows, meaning more milk, and more dairy food than was possible with the sheep-dominant herds of Yamnaya and Poltavka mobile pastoralists, which probably increased the size of the LBA population. But settled (LBA) and mobile (EBA/MBA) pastoralists in the middle Volga region showed the same isotopic dietary signature and the same diet-related dental pathologies. The difference between nomadic and sedentary residential patterns, a distinction that looms large for sedentary scholars, had surprisingly little effect on daily diet. Whether they lived in mobile wagon camps or permanent houses, Bronze Age pastoralists seem to have eaten much the same foods. Family herding units might have even used the same geographic range of seasonal pastures, changing only the residential mode within those pastures in the settling-down process of the early LBA.

Bread, so central to our definition of civilization, seems in the Volga-Ural steppes to have been a Final Bronze Age/Iron Age novelty that became widespread at the same time as the rise of pastoral nomadism. Nomadic pastoralism of a very different kind prospered independently of agriculture during the EBA and MBA, beginning before 3000 BC. Iron Age pastoral nomadism was closely articulated with agricultural communities at the edges of the steppes, from the upper Don and the Kuban piedmont to the Tien Shan and the western Altai. It appears that Iron Age nomads chose to eat bread, not because they needed it—their Bronze Age ancestors had prospered without it—but because farming was adopted as a major source of food in and at the edges of the steppes only in the Final Bronze Age (1200–800 BC) and Iron Age (after 800 BC), making cultivated grain easily available. Why and how this happened is a major research question. We had thought that Iron Age pastoral nomads depended on China and Persia for their grain. But Iron Age nomads obtained bread from small local settlements like those tested by Lebedeva in the forest-steppe zone of the upper Don and by Chang et al. in eastern Kazakhstan, or they grew it themselves. In doing so, they differed significantly from many of their Bronze Age ancestors, particularly in the Volga-Ural steppes, where the regional resistance to agriculture might paradoxically have been regarded, as it was among the Maasai, as a visible and even edible sign of enduring power and prestige.

Note

Figures in this chapter were prepared by D.Brown using resources noted in the captions. Figures 1.1 and 1.3 were prepared on background maps from the Ancient World Mapping Center (AWMC), www.unc.edu/awmc.

References

Agapov, S. A.
2010   *Khvalynskie Eneoliticheskie Mogil'niki I Khvalynskaya Eneoliticheskaya Kul'tura*. Samarskaya Regional'naya Obshchestvennaya Organizatsiya Istoriko-Eko-Kul'turnaya Assotsiatsiya "Povolzh'e," Samara.

Agapov, S. A., I. B. Vasiliev, and V. I. Pestrikova
1990   *Khvalynskii Eneoliticheskii Mogil'nik*. Saratovskogo Universiteta, Saratov.

Allentoft, Morten E., Martin Sikora, Karl-Göran Sjögren, Simon Rasmussen, Morten Rasmussen, Jesper Stenderup, Peter B. Damgaard, Hannes Schroeder, Torbjörn Ahlström, Lasse Vinner, Anna-Sapfo Malaspinas, Ashot Margaryan, Tom Higham, David Chivall, Niels Lynnerup, Lise Harvig, Justyna Baron, Philippe Della Casa, Paweł Dąbrowski, Paul R. Duffy, Alexander V. Ebel, Andrey Epimakhov, Karin Frei, Mirosław Furmanek, Tomasz Gralak, Andrey Gromov, Stanisław Gronkiewicz, Gisela Grupe, Tamás Hajdu, Radosław Jarysz, Valeri Khartanovich, Alexandr Khokhlov, Viktória Kiss, Jan Kolář, Aivar Kriiska, Irena Lasak, Cristina Longhi, George McGlynn, Algimantas Merkevicius, Inga Merkyte, Mait Metspalu, Ruzan Mkrtchyan, Vyacheslav Moiseyev, László Paja, György Pálfi, Dalia Pokutta, Łukasz Pospieszny, T. Douglas Price, Lehti Saag, Mikhail Sablin, Natalia Shishlina, Václav Smrčka, Vasilii I. Soenov, Vajk Szeverényi, Gusztáv Tóth, Synaru V. Trifanova, Liivi Varul, Magdolna Vicze, Levon Yepiskoposyan, Vladislav Zhitenev, Ludovic Orlando, Thomas Sicheritz-Pontén, Søren Brunak, Rasmus Nielsen, Kristian Kristiansen, and Eske Willerslev
2015   Population Genomics of Bronze Age Eurasia. *Nature* 522:167–172.

Anthony, David W.
2007   *The Horse, the Wheel, and Language: How Bronze Age Riders from the Eurasian Steppes Shaped the Modern World*. Princeton University Press, Princeton, New Jersey.
2009   The Sintashta Genesis: The Roles of Climate Change, Warfare, and Long-Distance Trade. In *Social Complexity in Prehistoric Eurasia: Monuments, Metals and Mobility*, edited by Bryan K. Hanks and Katheryn M. Linduff, pp. 47–73. Cambridge University Press, Cambridge.

Anthony, D. W., and D. Brown
2007   Herding and Gathering during the Late Bronze Age at Krasnosamarskoe, Russia, and the End of the Dependency Model of Steppe Pastoralism. In *Social Orders and Social Landscapes*, edited by L. M. Popova, C. W. Hartley, and A. T. Smith, pp. 393–415. Cambridge Scholars Publishing, Newcastle.
2011   The Secondary Products Revolution, Horse-Riding, and Mounted Warfare. *Journal of World Prehistory* 24(2):131–160.

2014   Horseback Riding and Bronze Age Pastoralism in the Eurasian Steppes. In *Reconfiguring the Silk Road: New Research on East-West Exchange in Antiquity*, edited by Victor Mair and J. Hickman, pp. 55–71. University of Pennsylvania Museum, Philadelphia.

Anthony, D. W., D. Brown, E. Brown, A. Goodman, A. Khokhlov, P. Kuznetsov, P. Kosintsev, O. Mochalov, E. Murphy, A. Pike-Tay, L. Popova, A. Rosen, N. Russell, and A. Weisskopf
2005   The Samara Valley Project: Late Bronze Age Economy and Ritual in the Russian Steppes. *Eurasia Antiqua* (Berlin) 11:395–417.

Baipakov, K.M.
2008   Gorod i step' v drevnosti: osedlost' i zemledelie u Sakov i Usunei Zhetysu. *Khabarlary Izvestiya* 1(254):3–25.

Barfield, Thomas J.
2001   The Shadow Empires: Imperial State Formation along the Chinese-Nomad Frontier. In *Empires: Perspectives from Archaeology and History*, edited by Susan E. Alcock, Terence N. D'Altroy, Kathleen D. Morrison, and Carla M. Sinopoli, pp. 10–41. Cambridge University Press, Cambridge.
2006   Steppe Nomadic Culture and Political Organization. In *The Golden Deer of Eurasia: Perspectives on the Nomads of the Ancient World*, edited by Joan Aruz, Ann Farkas, and Elisabetta Valtz Fino, pp. 12–17. Yale University Press, New Haven, Connecticut.

Barynkin, P. P., I. B. Vasiliev, and A. A. Vybornov
1998   Stoianka Kyzyl-Khak II—Pamyatnik epokhi rannei Bronzy severnogo prikaspiya. In *Problemy Drevnei Istorii Severnogo Prikaspiya*, edited by V. S. Gorbunov, pp. 179–192. Samarskogo Gosudarstvennogo Pedagogicheskogo Universiteta, Samara.

Behre, Karl-Ernst
2008   Collected Seeds and Fruit from Herbs as Prehistoric Food. *Vegetation History and Archaeobotany* 17:65–73.

Bendrey, Robin
2011   Some Like It Hot: Environmental Determinism and the Pastoral Economies of the Later Prehistoric Eurasian Steppe. *Pastoralism: Research, Policy and Practice* 1(8):1–16.

Blyakharchuk, T. A., H. E. Wright, P. S. Borodavko, W. O. van der Knaap, and B. Ammann.
2004 Late Glacial and Holocene Vegetational Changes on the Ulagan High-Mountain Plateau, Altai Mts., Southern Siberia. *Palaeogeography, Paleoclimatology and Paleoecology* 209:259–279.

Bobrov, V. V
1988 On the Problem of Interethnic Relations in South Siberia in the Third and Second Millennia BC. *Arctic Anthropology* 25(2):30–46.

Bogaard, Amy, Rüdiger Krause, and Hans-Christoph Strien
2011   Towards a Social Geography of Cultivation and Plant Use in an Early Farming Community: Vaihingen an der Enz, South-West Germany. *Antiquity* 85:395–416.

Boroffka, Nikolaus, Jan Cierny, Joachim Lutz, Hermann Parzinger, Ernst Pernicka, and Gerd Weisberger
2002   Bronze Age Tin from Central Asia: Preliminary Notes. In *Ancient Interactions: East and West in Eurasia*, edited by Boyle, Katie, Colin Renfrew, and Marsha Levine, pp. 135–159. McDonald Institute, Cambridge.

Bremer, J.
1982   The Suodales of Poplios Valesios. *Zeitschrift für Papyrologie und Epigraphik* 47:133–147.

Brown, D. R., and D. W. Anthony
1998   Bit Wear, Horseback Riding, and the Botai Site in Kazakhstan. *Journal of Archaeological Science* 25:331–347.

Bunyatyan, K.
2003   Correlations between Agriculture and Pastoralism in the North Pontic Steppe Area during the Bronze Age. In *Prehistoric Steppe Adaptation and the Horse*, edited by M. Levine, C. Renfrew, and K. Boyle, pp. 269–286. McDonald Institute, Cambridge.

Cârciumaru, Marin
1996   *Paleoetnobotanica. Studii ín Preistoria şi Protoistoria României*. Glasul Bucovinei Helios, Iasi.

Carpelan, C., and A. Parpola
2001   Emergence, Contacts and Dispersal of Proto-Indo-European, Proto-Uralic and Proto-Aryan in Archaeological Perspective. In *Early Contacts between Uralic and Indo-European: Linguistic and Archaeological Considerations*, edited by C. Carpelan, A. Parpola, and P. Koskikallio, pp. 55–150. Suomalais-Ugrilainen Seura (Memoires de la Société Finno-Ugrienne) 242, Helsinki.

Chang, Claudia.
2008   Mobility and Sedentism of the Iron Age Agropastoralists of Southeast Kazakhstan. In *The Archaeology of Mobility: Old World and New World nomadism*, edited by Hans Barnard and Willeke Wendrich, pp. 329–342. Cotsen Advanced Seminars 4. University of California Press, Los Angeles.

Chang, Claudia, N. Benecke, F. P. Grigoriev, A. P. Rosen, and P. A. Tourtellotte
2003   Iron Age Society and Chronology in South-East Kazakhstan. *Antiquity* 77(296):298–312.

Chernykh, E. N.
1992   *Ancient Metallurgy in the USSR*. Cambridge University Press, Cambridge.

Chernykh, E. N. (editor)
1997   *Kargaly, Zabytni Mir*. NOKS, Moscow.

2004a. *Kargaly, Tom III: Selishche Gornyi: Arkheologicheskie Materialyi: Tekhnologiya Gorno-Metallurgicheskogo Proizvodstva i Arkheobiologicheskie Issledovaniya.* Yazyki Slavyanskoi Kul'tury, Moskva.

2004b. Kargaly: The Largest and Most Ancient Metallurgical Complex on the Border of Europe and Asia. In *Metallurgy in Ancient Eastern Eurasia from the Urals to the Yellow River*, edited by Katheryn M. Linduff, Chinese Studies 31, pp. 223–279. Edwin Mellen, Lewiston.

Chernykh, E. N., S. V. Kuz'minykh, and L. B. Orlovskata
2004   Ancient Metallurgy in Northeast Asia: From the Urals to the Saiano-Altai. In *Metallurgy in Ancient Eastern Eurasia from the Urals to the Yellow River*, edited by Katheryn M. Linduff, Chinese Studies 31, pp. 15–36. Edwin Mellen, Lewiston.

Das, R. P., and G. Meiser (editors)
2003   *Geregeltes Ungestüm. Brüderschaften und Jugendbünde bei altindogermanischen Völkern*. Hempen, Bremen.

Diaz del Río, P., P. L. García, J. A. López Sáez, M. I. Martina Navarette, A. L. Rodrígues Alcalde, S. Rovira-Llorens, J. M. Vicent García, and I. de Zavala Morencos
2006   Understanding the Productive Economy during the Bronze Age through Archaeometallurgical and Paleo-Environmental Research at Kargaly. In *Beyond the Steppe and the Sown: Proceedings of the 2002 University of Chicago Conference on Eurasian Archaeology*, edited by D. L. Peterson, L. M. Popova, and A. T. Smith, pp. 343–357. Brill, Leiden.

Di Cosmo, Nicola
1994   Ancient Inner Asian Nomads: Their Economic Basis and Its Significance in Chinese History. *Journal of Asian Studies* 53(4):1092–1126.

2002   *Ancient China and Its Enemies: The Rise of Nomadic Power in East Asian History*. Cambridge University Press, Cambridge.

Evdokimov, V. V., and V. G. Loman
1989   Raskopi Yamnogo kurgana v Karagandinskoi Oblasti. In *Voprosy Arkheologii Tsestral'nogo i Severnogo Kazakhstana*, edited by K. M. Baipakov, pp. 34–46. Karagandinskii Gosudarstvennyi Universitet, Karaganda.

Falk, Harry
1986   *Bruderschaft und Wülferspiel*. Hedwig Falk, Freiburg.

Frachetti, Michael D.
2008   *Pastoralist Landscapes and Social Interaction in Bronze Age Eurasia*. University of California Press, Berkeley.

2011   Multi-Regional Emergence of Mobile Pastoralism and Non-Uniform Institutional Complexity across Eurasia. *Current Anthropology* 53(1):2–38.

Frachetti, Michael D., and A. N. Mar'yashev

2007   Long-Term Occupation and Seasonal Settlement of Eastern Eurasian Pastoralists at Begash, Kazakhstan. *Journal of Field Archaeology* 32(3):221–242.

Frachetti, Michael D., Robert S. Spengler, Gayle J. Fritz, and Alexei N. Mar'yashev

2010   Earliest Evidence of Broomcorn Millet and Wheat in the Central Eurasian Steppe Region. *Antiquity* 84(326):993–1010.

Freire, Carlos Fernández, A. U. González, J. M. Vicent García, and M. I. Martínez Navarrete

2012   Bronze Age Economies and Landscape Resources in the Kargaly Steppe (Orenburg, Russia): Remote Sensing and Palynological Data for Ancient Landscape Resources Modeling. *EARSeL eProceedings* 11(1):87–97.

Gening, V. F., G. B. Zdanovich, and V. V. Gening

1992   *Sintashta*. Iuzhno-Ural'skoe Knizhnoe Izdatel'stvo, Chelyabinsk.

Gershkovich, Y. P.

2003   Farmers and Pastoralists of the Pontic Lowland during the Late Bronze Age. In *Prehistoric Steppe Adaptation and the Horse*, edited by M. Levine, C. Renfrew, and K. Boyle, pp. 319–328. McDonald Institute, Cambridge.

Golden, Peter B.

2001   Nomads and Sedentary Societies in Medieval Eurasia. In *Agricultural and Pastoral Societies in Ancient and Classical History*, edited by Michael Adas, pp. 71–115. Temple University Press, Philadelphia.

Grakov, B. N.

1958   Stareishiye nakhodki zheleznykh veschei v Evropeiskoi chasti SSR. *Sovetskaya Arkheologiya* 4:3–9.

Gremillion, Kristen

2004   Seed Processing and the Origins of Food Production in Eastern North America. *American Antiquity* 69:215–234.

Haak, Wolfgang, Iosif Lazaridis, Nick Patterson, Nadin Rohland, Swapan Mallick, Bastien Llamas, Guido Brandt, Susanne Nordenfelt, Eadaoin Harney, Kristin Stewardson, Qiaomei Fu, Alissa Mittnik, Eszter Bánffy, Christos Economou, Michael Francken, Susanne Friederich, Rafael Garrido Pena, Fredrik Hallgren, Valery Khartanovich, Aleksandr Khokhlov, Michael Kunst, Pavel Kuznetsov, Harald Meller, Oleg Mochalov, Vayacheslav Moiseyev, Nicole Nicklisch, Sandra L. Pichler, Roberto Risch, Manuel A. Rojo Guerra, Christina Roth, Anna Szécsényi-Nagy, Joachim Wahl, Matthias Meyer, Johannes Krause, Dorcas Brown, David Anthony, Alan Cooper, Kurt Werner Alt, and David Reich

2015   Massive Migration from the Steppe Was a Source for Indo-European Languages in Europe. *Nature* 522(7555):207–211.

Hanks, Bryan

2010   Archaeology of the Eurasian steppes and Mongolia. *Annual Review of Anthropology* 39:469–486.

Honeychurch, William, and C. Amartuvshin

2006   Survey and Settlement in Northern Mongolia: The Structure of Intra-Regional Nomadic Organization. In *Beyond the Steppe and the Sown: Proceedings of the 2002 University of Chicago Conference on Eurasian Archaeology*, edited by D. L. Peterson, L. M. Popova, and A. T. Smith, pp. 183–201. Brill, Leiden.

Houle, Jean-Luc

2009   Socially Integrative Facilities and the Emergence of Societal Complexity on the Mongolian Steppe. In *Social Complexity in Prehistoric Eurasia: Monuments, Metals, and Mobility*, edited by B. K. Hanks and K. M. Linduff, pp. 358–377. Cambridge University Press, Cambridge.

Houle, Jean-Luc, and Lee Broderick

2011   Settlement Patterns and Domestic Economy of the Xiongnu in Khanuy Valley, Mongolia. In *Xiongnu Archaeology: Multidisciplinary Perspectives of the First Steppe Empire of Inner Asia*, edited by U. Brosseder and B. K. Miller, pp. 137–152. Bonn Contributions to Asian Archaeology 5. Bonn University Press, Bonn.

Ingold, Tim

1980   *Hunters, Ranchers, and Pastoralists: Reindeer Economies and Their Transformations*. Cambridge University Press, Cambridge.

Jagchid, Sechin, and V. J. Symons

1989   *Peace, War, and Trade along the Great Wall*. Indiana University Press, Bloomington.

Jia, Peter W., Alison Betts, and Xinhua Wu

2011   New Evidence for Bronze Age Agricultural Settlements in the Zhunge'er (Junggar) Basin, China. *Journal of Field Archaeology* 36(4):269–280.

Kadyrbaev, M. K., and Z. Kurmankulov

1992   *Kul'tura Drevnikh Skotovodov i Metallurgov Sary-Arki*. Gylym, Alma-Ata.

Kaiser, Elke

2010   "Der Übergang zur Rinderzucht im nördlichen Schwarzmeerraum," *Godišnjak Centar za Balkanološka Ispitivanja* (Sarajevo) 39: 23-34.

Kaniewski, D., E. Van Campo, J. Guiot, S. Le Burel, and T. Otto

2013   Environmental Roots of the Late Bronze Age Crisis. *PLoS ONE* 8(8):e71004.

Khazanov, A.

1984   *Nomads and the Outside World*. University of Wisconsin Press, Madison.

1994   *Nomads and the Outside World*. 2nd ed. University of Wisconsin Press, Madison.

2009   Specific Characteristics of Chalcolithic and Bronze Age pastoralism in the Near East. In *Nomads, Tribes, and the State in the Ancient Near East: Cross-Disciplinary Perspectives*, edited by Jeffrey Szuchman, pp. 119–128. Oriental Institute Seminars 5, Chicago.

Kershaw, Kris
2000   *The One-Eyed God: Odin and the Indo-Germanic Männerbünde*. Journal of Indo-European Studies Monograph 36, Washington, D.C.

Khokhlov, A. A.
2010   Demograficheskie protsessy v Volgo-Ural'e v epokhi Eneolita-Bronzy. In *Koni i kolesnichie v stepei Evrazii*, pp. 133–166. Rifei, Ekaterinburg.

Kohl, Philip L.
2007   *The Making of Bronze Age Eurasia*. Cambridge University Press, Cambridge.

Koivulehto, J.
2001   The Earliest Contacts between Indo-European and Uralic Speakers in the Light of Lexical Loans. In *Early Contacts between Uralic and Indo-European: Linguistic and Archaeological Considerations*, edited by C. Carpelan, A. Parpola, and P. Koskikallio, pp. 235–63. Suomalais-Ugrilainen Seura (Memoires de la Société Finno-Ugrienne) 242, Helsinki.

Koryakova, Ludmila, and Andrie Epimakhov
2007   *The Urals and Western Siberia in the Bronze and Iron Ages*. Cambridge University Press, Cambridge.

Kosintsev, P. A., and N. V. Roslyakova
2000   Skotovodstvo neseleniya Samarskogo Pobolzhya, In *Istoriya Samarskogo Povolzh'ya c Drevneishikh Vremen do Nashikh Dnei: Bronzovy Vek*, edited by Iu. I. Kolev, P. F. Kuznetsov, and O. D. Mochalov, pp. 302–308. Integratsiya, Samara.

Kotova, N.
2003   *Neolithization in Ukraine*, translated by V. N. Stepanchuk and N. S. Makhortyk. British Archaeological Reports (International Series) 1109, Oxford.
2008   *Early Eneolithic in the Pontic Steppes*, translated by N. S. Makhortykh. British Archaeological Reports (International Series) 1735, Oxford.

Kradin, Nikolay N.
2002   Nomadism, Evolution, and World-Systems: Pastoral Societies in Theories of Historical Development. *Journal of World-System Research* 8(3):368–388.

Kremenetski, C.
1997   The Late Holocene Environment and Climate Shift in Russia and Surrounding Lands. In *Climate Change in the Third Millennium BC*, edited by H. Dalfes, G. Kukla, and H. Weiss, pp. 351–370. Springer Verlag/NATO ASI Series, Berlin.

2002   Steppe and Forest-Steppe Belt of Eurasia: Holocene Environmental History. In *Prehistoric Steppe Adaptation and the Horse*, edited by M. Levine, C. Renfrew, and K. Boyle, pp. 11–27. McDonald Institute, Cambridge.

Kuzmina, Elena E.
1994   *Otkuda Prishli Indoarii?* M.G.P. "Kalina" VINITI R.A.N., Moskva.
2003   Origins of Pastoralism in the Eurasian Steppes. In *Prehistoric Steppe Adaptation and the Horse*, edited by Marsha Levine, Colin Renfrew, and Katie Boyle, pp. 203–232. McDonald Institute, Cambridge.
2007   *The Origin of the Indo-Iranians*. Brill, Leiden.
2008   *The Prehistory of the Silk Road*. Edited by Victor H. Mair. University of Pennsylvania Press, Philadelphia.

Kuznetsov, P. F.
2006   The Emergence of Bronze Age Chariots in Eastern Europe. *Antiquity* 80(2006):638–645.

Kuznetsov, P. F., and Oleg Mochalov
1999   Nestandartnyi rannesrubnyi kurgannyi kompleks Iuga lesostepnogo Povolzh'ya. In *Okhrana i Izuchenie Pamyatnikov Istorii i Kul'tury v Samarskoi Oblasti*, vol. 1, pp. 59–92. Samarskii Oblastnoi Istoriko-Kraevedcheskii Muzei im. P.V. Alabina, Samara.

Lamberg-Karlovsky, C. C.
2002   Archaeology and Language: The Indo-Iranians. *Current Anthropology* 43(1):63–88.

Lattimore, Owen
1940 [1988]. *The Inner Asian Frontiers of China*. Reprint, Oxford University Press, Hong Kong.

Lavrushin, Y. A., and E. A. Spiridonova
1995   Rezul'taty paleomorfologicheskikh issledovanii na stoyankakh Neolita-Bronzy v basseine R. Samara. In *Neolit i Eneolit Iuga Lesostepi Volgo-Ural'skogo mezhdurech'ya*, edited by N. L. Morgunova. Nauka, Orenburg.

Lebedeva, E. Y.
2005   Archaeobotany and Study of the Bronze Age Agriculture in Eastern Europe. *Opus: Mezhdistsiplinarnye Issledovaniya v Arkheologii* (Moscow) 4:50–68.

Lees, S. H., and D. G. Bates
1974   The Origins of Specialised Nomadic Pastoralism: A Systematic Model. *American Antiquity* 39:187–193.

Levy, Thomas E.
2009   Pastoral Nomads and Iron Age Metal Production in Ancient Edom. In *Nomads, Tribes, and the State in the Ancient Near East: Cross-Disciplinary Perspectives*, edited by Jeffrey Szuchman, pp. 147–177. Oriental Institute Seminars 5, Chicago.

Lincoln, B.
1991   Warriors and Non-Herdsmen: A Response to Mary Boyce. In *Death, War, and Sacrifice: Studies in*

Ideology and Practice, edited by B. Lincoln, pp. 145–166. Chicago: University of Chicago Press.

Linduff, Katheryn (editor)
2004   *Metallurgy in Ancient Eastern Eurasia from the Urals to the Yellow River*, Chinese Studies, v. 31. Edwin Mellen, Lewiston.

Linseele, Veerle
2010   Did Specialized Pastoralism Develop Differently in Africa Than in the Near East? An Example from the West African Sahel. *Journal of World Prehistory* 23:43–77.

López, Laura M., A. Capparelli, and A. E. Nielsen
2011   Traditional Post-Harvest Processing to Make Quinoa Grains (*Chenopodium quinoa* var. quinoa) Apt for Consumption in Northern Lipez (Potosí, Bolivia): Ethnoarchaeological and Archaeobotanical Analyses. *The Journal of Archaeological and Anthropological Sciences* 3:49–70.

López, Pilar, Jose Antonio Lópes-Sáez, Evgeny N. Chernykh, and Pavel Tarasov
2003   Late Holocene Vegetation History and Human Activity Shown by Pollen Analysis of Novienki Peat Bog (Kargaly region, Orenburg oblast, Russia). *Vegetation History/ Archaeobotany* 12:75–82.

Maliutina, T. S.
1991   Stratigraficheskaya pozitsiya materilaov Fedeorovskoi kul'tury na mnogosloinikh poseleniyakh Kazakhstanskikh stepei. In *Drevnosti Vostochno-Evropeiskoi Lesostepi*, edited by V. V. Nikitin, pp. 141–162. Samarskii Gosudarstvennyi Pedagogicheskii Institut, Samara.

Mallory, J. P., and Victor H. Mair
2000   *The Tarim Mummies: Ancient China and the Mystery of the Earliest Peoples from the West.* Thames and Hudson, London.

McCone, Kim
1987,   Hund, Wolf, und Krieger bei den Indogermanen. In *Studien zum Indogermanischen Wortschatz*, edited by W. Meid, pp. 101–154. Institut für Sprachwissenschaft der Universität Innsbruck, Innsbruck.

Merpert, N. Y.
1974   *Drevneishie Skotovody Volzhsko-Uralskogo Mezhdurechya.* Nauka, Moskva.

Merts, V. K., and I. V. Merts
2010   Pogrebeniya 'Yamnogo' tipa vostochnogo i severnogo-vostochnogo Kazakhstana (k postanovke problem). In *Afana s'evskii Sbornik*, pp. 134–144. R.A.N. Sibirskoe Otdelenie, Institut Arkheologii i Etnografii, Barnaul.

Mochalov, Oleg D.
2008   *Keramika Pogrebal'nykh Pamiatnikov Epokhi Bronzy Lesostepi Volgo-Ural'skogo Mezhdurech'ya.* Samarskii Gosudarstvennyi Pedagogicheskii Universitet, Samara.

Morales Muniz, Arturo, and Ekaterina Antipina
2003   Srubnaya Faunas and Beyond: A Critical Assessment of the Archaeozoological Information from the East European Steppe. In *Prehistoric Steppe Adaptation and the Horse*, edited by M. Levine, C. Renfrew, and K. Boyle, pp. 329–351. McDonald Institute, Cambridge.

Morgunova, N. L.
1988   Ivanovskaya stoianka v Orenburgskoi oblasti. In *Arkheologocheskie Kul'tury Severnogo Prikaspiya*, edited by R. S. Bagautdinov, pp. 106–122. Samarskii Gosudarstvennyi Pedagogicheskii Universitet, Kuibyshev.

Motuzaite-Matuzeviciute, Giedre
2012   The Earliest Appearance of Domesticated Plant Species and Their Origins on the Western Fringes of the Eurasian Steppe. *Documenta Praehistorica* 39:1–21.

Motuzaite-Matuzeviciute, Giedre, S. Telizhenko, and M. K. Jones
2012   Archaeobotanical Investigation of Two Scythian-Sarmatian Period Pits in Eastern Ukraine: Implications for Floodplain Cereal Cultivation. *Journal of Field Archaeology* 37(1):51–61.

Mulder, Monique B., I. Fazzio, W. Irons, R. L. McElreath, S. Bowles, A. Bell, T. Hertz, and L. Hazzah
2010   Pastoralism and Wealth Inequality: Revisiting an Old Question. *Current Anthropology* 51(1):35–48.

Murphy, E. M.
2003   *Iron Age Archaeology and Trauma from Aymyrlyg, South Siberia.* BAR International Series 1152. Archaeopress, Oxford.

2011   A Bioarchaeological Study of Xiongnu Expansion in Iron Age Tuva, South Siberia. In *Regimes and Revolutions: Power, Violence, and Labor in Eurasia from the Ancient to the Modern*, edited by C. W. Hartley, B. Yazicioglu, and A. Smith, pp. 240–261. Cambridge University Press, Cambridge.

Nedashkovskii, L. S.
2009   Economy of the Golden Horde Population. *Anthropology & Archeology of Eurasia* 48(2):35–50.

Ostroshchenko, V.
2003   The Economic Peculiarities of the Srubnaya Cultural-Historical Entity. In *Prehistoric Steppe Adaptation and the Horse*, edited by M. Levine, C. Renfrew, and K. Boyle, pp. 319–328. McDonald Institute, Cambridge.

Parpola, Asko
2002   From the Dialects of Old Indo-Aryan to Proto-Indo-Aryan and Proto-Iranian. In *Indo-Iranian Languages and Peoples*, edited by N. Sims-Williams, pp. 43–102. Oxford University Press, London.

Parzinger, Hermann, and Nikolaus Boroffka

2003   *Das Zinn der Bronzezeit in Mittelasien I: Die siedlungsarchäologischen Forschgungen im Umfeld der Zinnlagerstätten.* Archäologie in Iran und Turan, Band 5. Philipp von Zabern, Mainz am Rhein.

Pashkevich, G.

2003   Paleoethnobotanical Evidence of Agriculture in the Steppe and the Forest-Steppe of East Europe in the Late Neolithic and Bronze Age. In *Prehistoric Steppe Adaptation and the Horse*, edited by M. Levine, C. Renfrew, and K. Boyle, pp. 287–297. McDonald Institute, Cambridge.

Perry, C. A., and K. J. Hsu

2000   Geophysical, Archaeological, and Historical Evidence Support a Solar-Output Model for Climate Change. *Proceedings of the National Academy of Sciences* 7(23):12433–12438.

Peterson, David

2009   Production and Social Complexity: Bronze Age Metalworking in the Middle Volga. In *Social Complexity in Prehistoric Eurasia: Monuments, Metal, and Mobility*, edited by Bryan Hanks and Kathryn Linduff, pp. 222–261. Cambridge University Press, Cambridge.

Peterson, David, P. F. Kuznetsov, and O. D. Mochalov

2006   The Samara Bronze Age Metals Project: Investigating Changing Technologies and Transformations of Value in the Western Eurasian Steppes. In *Beyond the Steppe and the Sown*, edited by David Peterson, Laura Popova, and Adam T. Smith, pp. 322–342. Brill, Leiden.

Popova, Laura M.

2006   Political Pastures: Navigating the Steppe in the Middle Volga Region (Russia) during the Bronze Age. Unpublished Ph.D. dissertation, University of Chicago.

2007   A New Historical Legend: Tracing the Long-Term Landscape History of the Samara River Valley. In *Social Orders and Social Landscapes: Proceedings of the 2005 University of Chicago Conference on Eurasian Archaeology*, edited by Laura M. Popova, Charles Hartley, and Adam T. Smith. Cambridge Scholars Press, Newcastle.

Rassamakin, Yuri

1999   The Eneolithic of the Black Sea Steppe: Dynamics of Cultural and Economic Development 4500–2300 BC. In *Late Prehistoric Exploitation of the Eurasian Steppe*, edited by Marsha Levine, Yuri Rassamakin, Aleksandr Kislenko and Nataliya Tatarintseva, pp. 59–182. McDonald Institute for Archaeological Research, Cambridge.

Rosen, Steven A.

2009   History Does Not Repeat Itself: Cyclicity and Particularism in Nomad-Sedentary Relations in the Negev in the Long Term. In *Nomads, Tribes, and the State in the Ancient Near East: Cross-Disciplinary Perspectives*, edited by Jeffrey Szuchman, pp. 57–86. Oriental Institute Seminars 5, Chicago.

Rosenberg, Michael

1998   Cheating at Musical Chairs: Territoriality and Sedentism in an Evolutionary Context. *Current Anthropology* 39(5):653–681.

Rouse, L., and B. Cerasetti

2014   Ojakly: A Late Bronze Age Mobile Pastoralist Site in the Murghab Region, Turkmenistan. *Journal of Field Archaeology* 39(10):32–50.

Ryabogina, N.E. and S. Ivanov

2011   Ancient Agriculture in Western Siberia: Problems of Argumentation, Paleoethnobotanic Methods, and Analysis of Data," *Archaeology, Ethnography and Anthropology of Eurasia* 39(4): 96-106.

Salugina, Natalya P.

2011   The Technology of the Yamnaya (Pit Grave) Ceramic Production and Its Relevance to the Population History of the Volga-Ural Region in the Early Bronze Age. *Archaeology, Ethnology and Anthropology of Eurasia* 39(2):82–94.

Salvatori, Sandro.

2003   Pots and Peoples: The "Pandora's Jar" of Central Asian Archaeological Research; on Two Recent Books on Gonur Graveyard Excavations. *Rivista di Archeologia* 27:5–20.

2008   Cultural Variability in the Bronze Age Oxus Civilization and Its Relations with the Surrounding Regions of Central Asia and Iran. In *The Bronze Age and Early Iron Age in the Margiana Lowlands*, edited by Sandro Salvatori, Maurizio Tosi, and Barbara Cerasetti, pp. 75–98. British Archaeological Reports 1806. Archaeopress, Oxford.

Salzman, P. C.

1974   Tribal Chiefs as Middlemen: The Politics of Encapsulation in the Middle East. *Anthropological Quarterly* 47(2):203–210.

2004   *Pastoralists: Equality, Hierarchy, and the State.* Westview Press, Boulder, Colorado.

Sedova, M. S.

2000   Poseleniya Srubnoi kul'tury. In *Istoriya Samarskogo Povolzh'ya c Drevneishikh Vremen do Nashikh Dnei: Bronzovy Vek*, edited by Iu. I. Kolev, A. E. Mamonov, and M. A. Turetskii, pp. 209–241. Integratsiya, Samara.

Semenova, A. P.
2001   Osnovnye tendentsii razvitiya kermiki Pokrovskogo i razvitogo etapov Srubnoi kul'tury lesostepnogo Povolzh'ya (po dannym pogrebal'nykh pamyatnikov). In *Bronzovyi Vek Vostochnoi Evropy: Kharakteristika Kul'tur, Khronologiya I Periodatsiya*, edited by Iu. I. Kolev, P. F. Kuznetsov, O. V. Kuzmina, A. P. Semenova, M. A. Turetskii, and B. A. Agapov, pp. 273–279. Samarskii Gosudarstvennyi Pedagogicheskii Universitet, Samara.

Shilov, V. P.
1985   Problemy proiskhozhdeniya kochevogo skotovodstva v vostochnoi Evrope. In *Drevnosti Kalmykii*, edited by K. N. Maksimov, pp. 23–33. Kalmytskii Nauchno-Issledovatel'skii Institut Istorii, Filogii i Ekonomiki, Elista.

Shishlina, N. I.
2008   *Reconstruction of the Bronze Age of the Caspian Steppes: Life Styles and Life Ways of Pastoral Nomads*. British Archaeological Reports International Series 1876, Oxford.

Shishlina, N. I., E. I. Gak, and A. V. Borisov
2008   Nomadic Sites of the South Yergueni Hills on the Eurasian steppes. In *The Archaeology of Mobility: Old World and New World Nomadism*, edited by Hans Barnard and Willeke Wendrich, pp. 230–249. Cotsen Advanced Seminars 4. University of California Press, Los Angeles.

Shul'ga, P. I.
2012   O drevnem zemledelii v Gornom Altae. In *Kul'turny Stepnoi Evrazii i Ikh Vzaimodeeistvie s Drevnimi Tsivilizatsiyami*, Vol. 2, pp. 242–248. Institut Istorii Material'noi Kul'tury RAN, "Periferia," St. Petersburg.

Sims-Williams, Nicholas (editor)
2002   *Indo-Iranian Languages and Peoples*. Oxford University Press, Oxford.

Smith, Bruce 1989
        Origins of Agriculture in Eastern North America. *Science* 246(4937):1566–1571.

Spear, Thomas, and R. Waller (editors)
1993   *Being Maasai: Ethnicity and Identity in East Africa*. James Currey, Oxford.

Spengler, R., M. Frachetti, P. Doumani, L. Rouse, B. Cerasetti, E. Bullion, and A. Mar'yashev
2014   Early Agriculture and Crop Transmission among Bronze Age Mobile Pastoralists of Central Eurasia. *Proceedings of the Royal Society, Series B* 281(1783):20133382; 1–7.

Stöllner, Thomas, Z. Samashev, S. Berdenov, J. Cierny, M. Doll, J. Garner, A. Gontscharov, A. Gorelik, A. Hauptmann, R. Herd, G. A. Kusch, V. Merz, T. Riese, B. Sikorski, and B. Zickgraf

2011   Tin from Kazakhstan—Steppe Tin for the West? In *Anatolian Metal V*, edited by Ünsal Yalçin, pp. 231–251. Deutsches Bergbau Museum, Bochum.

Svyatko, S. V., R. J. Schulting, J. Mallory, E. M. Murphy, P. J. Reimer, V. I. Khartanovich, Y. K. Chistov, and M. V. Sablin
2013   Stable Isotope Dietary Analysis of Prehistoric Populations from the Minusinsk Basin, Southern Siberia, Russia: A New Chronological Framework for the Introduction of Millet to the Eastern Eurasian steppe. *Journal of Archaeological Science* 40:3936–3945.

Telegin, D. Y.
1986   *Dereivka: A Settlement and Cemetery of Copper Age Horse Keepers on the Middle Dnieper*. Vol. 287. Edited by J. P. Mallory, translated by V. K. Pyatkovskiy. British Archaeological Reports, I.S., Oxford.

van Geel, B., N. A. Bokovenko, N. D. Burova, K. V. Chgunov, V. A. Dergachev, V. G. Dirksen, M. Kulkova, A. Nagler, H. Parzinger, J. van der Plicht, S. Vasiliev, and G. Zaitseva
2004   Climate Change and the Expansion of the Scythian Culture after 850 BC: A Hypothesis. *Journal of Archaeological Science* 31:1735–1742.

Vasiliev, I. B.
1981   *Eneolit Povolzh'ya*. Kuibyshevskii Gosudarstvenyi Pedagogicheskii Institut, Kuibyshev.

Vasiliev, I. B., P. F. Kuznetsov, and A. P. Semenova
1994   *Potapovskii Kurgannyi Mogil'nik Indoiranskikh Plemen na Volge*. Samarskii Universitet, Samara.

Vasiliev, I. B., and G. I. Matveeva
1979   Mogil'nik u s. S'yezhee na R. Samare. *Sovietskaya Arkheologiia* 4:147–166.

Vasiliev, I. G., P. F. Kuznetsov, and M. A. Turetskii
2000   Yamnaya i Poltavkinskaya kul'tura. In *Istoriya Samarskogo PoVolzh'ya s Drevneishikh Vremen do Nashikh Dnei: Bronzovyi Vek*, edited by Y. I. Kolev, A. E. Mamontov, and M. A. Turetskii, pp. 6–64. Samarskogo Nauchnogo Tsentra R.A.N., Samara.

Vehik, Susan
2002   Conflict, Trade, and Political Development on the Southern Plains. *American Antiquity* 67(1):37–64.

Vicent, Juan, S. Ormeño, M. Martinez-Navarette, and J. Delgado
2006   The Kargaly Project: Modeling Bronze Age Landscapes in the Steppe. In *From Space to Place*, edited by S. Campano and M. Forte, pp. 279–284. BAR International Series 1568, Oxford.

Weiss, Harvey
2000   Beyond the Younger Dryas: Collapse as Adaptation to Abrupt Climate Change in Ancient West Asia and the Eastern Mediterranean. In *Environmental Disaster and the Archaeology of Human Response*, edited by Garth Bawden and Richard M. Reycraft, pp. 75–98. Maxwell Museum of Anthropology, Albuquerque, New Mexico.

West, M. L.

2007   *Indo-European Poetry and Myth.* Oxford University Press, Oxford.

Yanushevich, Zoya V.

1989   Agricultural Evolution North of the Black Sea from the Neolithic to the Iron Age. In *Foraging and Farming: The Evolution of Plant Exploitation,* edited by David R. Harris and Gordon C. Hillman, pp. 607–619. Unwin Hyman, London.

Zdanovich, G. B.

1988   *Bronzovyi Vek Uralo-Kazakhstanskikh Stepei.* Ural'skogo Universiteta, Sverdlovsk.

Zhauymbaev, S. U.

1984   Drevnie mednye rudniki tsentral'nogo Kazakhstana. In *Bronzovyi Vek Uralo-Irtyshskogo Mezhdurech'ya,* pp. 113–120. Chelyabinskii Gosudarst-vennyi Universitet, Chelyabinsk.

Chapter 2

Archaeological Field Operations in the Lower Samara Valley, 1995–2001, with Observations on Srubnaya Pastoralism

David W. Anthony • Dorcas R. Brown • Pavel F. Kuznetsov

This chapter briefly describes the archaeological field operations of the Samara Valley Project (SVP) from the first reconnaissance survey in 1995 (Figure 2.1) to the last excavations at the Srubnaya settlement of Krasnosamarskoe in 2001, closing with a brief overview of how they together contributed to our understanding of Srubnaya pastoralism in this part of the Samara Valley. The Late Bronze Age (LBA) sites where we conducted field excavations, introduced and briefly summarized here, are analyzed in greater detail in Chapters 9 to 18.

The central focus of the SVP was the shift from mobile to settled pastoralism at the beginning of the LBA with the appearance of the Srubnaya culture (Anthony 1998; Anthony et al. 2005). Our goal was to excavate a Srubnaya settlement system with all of its occupation components, including a permanent settlement and seasonal herding camps; to determine the seasons when they were occupied; to recover botanical data that would inform us about the role of agriculture in the LBA economy; to discover and document anthropogenic and natural changes in botanical communities that might be linked to the shift to sedentism; and to excavate a cemetery near the excavated settlements so that we could examine the diet, health, and pathologies of the pre-Srubnaya and Srubnaya populations, particularly those traits related to an agricultural diet.

Local Environment and Survey Region in the Samara River Valley

Our initial archaeological survey was conducted in the lower Samara Valley above the junction with the Kinel' River. In our study area, the Samara River loops through marshes of *Phragmites* and *Typha* reeds up to 8 km wide, populated by flocks of ducks, swans, and cranes (Figure 2.2). The reeds are good forage for cattle, particularly in the winter. The dead winter reed also is harvested by people for use in domestic crafts, flooring, and construction, and the roots are edible through the winter. When the winter ice breaks on the river, it can collect in ice dams that flood 6 to 8 km, refreshing the myriad oxbow lakes, forests, and marshes with new water. Because of the danger of spring floods, in many places, the river is bordered by a zone of unoccupied pastures and seasonally inundated forests, crossed by numerous dirt trails.

When our fieldwork was under way, most of the automobile bridges over the Samara River were approached on those unpaved rutted dirt trails, constantly widened by traffic swerving off road around particularly deep mudholes. The Utyevka bridge, frequently used by our vehicles, was a temporary structure made of metal plates laid over floating barrels held together by steel cables, and the wreckage of the previous cable bridge was visible just downstream, wrapped around the trees, testifying to the strength of the spring floods.

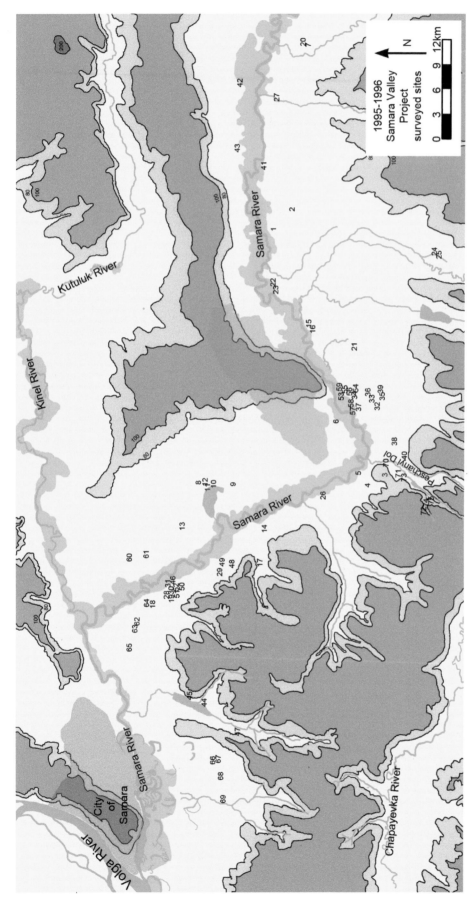

Figure 2.1 Survey area in the lower Samara Valley. Sites 8 to 13 are the Krasnosamarskoe cluster. Peschanyi Dol is at the bottom of the map. 1. Andreevskaya Dune, 2. Andreevka I, 3. Barinovka I, 4. Barinovka II, 5. Barinovka settlement, 6. Chelovech'ya Golova, 7. Gvardeitsi, 8. Krasnosamarskoe Adin Kurgan, 9. Krasnosamarskoe II, 10. Krasnosamarskoe V, 11. Krasnosamarskoe settlement, 12. Krasnosamarskoe IV, 13. Krasnosamarskoe VI, 14. Kristianskii, 15. Maksimovka I, 16. Maksimovka II, 17. Nizhne Nikol'skoe, 18. Nur I, 19. Nur settlement, 20. Odonochnii, 21. Pokrovka, 22. S'yezzhee I, 23. S'yezzhee cemetery, 24. Semenovka settlement, 26. Shirakinskii, 27. Shirochenka, 28. Spiridonovka Adin K.1, 29. Spiridonovka Adin K.2, 30. Spiridonovka I, 31. Spiridonovka stoianka, 32. Utyevka I, 33. Utyevka II, 34. Utyevka IV, 35. Utyevka IX, 36. Utyevka V, 37. Utyevka VI, 38. Utyevka VII, 39. Utyevka VIII, 40. Utyevka X, 41. Vilovatoye Dune, 42. Zakhar-Kal'ma Dune, 43. Zalivnaya Dune, 44. Chernorechensky I, 45. Chernorechensky II, 46. Spiridonovka settlement, 47. Chernaja Rechka, 48. Spiridonovka IV, 49. Spiridonovka III, 49. Spiridonovka Adin K.3, 52. Leshevskoe settlement, 54. Utyevka settlement, 55. Leshevskoe II, 56. Leshevskoe I, 57. Leshevskoe Adin K.1, 58. Leshevskoe III settlement, 59. Leshevskoe II settlement, 60. Gorny I, 61. Bobrovka I, 62. Belosersky II, 63. Belosersky I, 64. Podlesnoe I, 65. Chernovsky I, 66. Nikolaevka II, 67. Nikolaevka III, 68. Nikolaevka IV, 70. Peschanyi Dol 1, 71. Peschanyi Dol 2, 72. Peschanyi Dol 1, 73. Peschanyi Dol 3, 74. Peschanyi Dol 4, 75. Peschanyi Dol 5.

Figure 2.2 Samara River marshes and oxbow lakes near Krasnosamarskoe.

Although the Samara River regularly overflows its banks in the spring season, they can be quite steep, in places forming eroded bluffs 20 to 30 feet or 6 to 9 m high (Figure 2.3). At one such steeply eroded river bank, Arlene Rosen, then of University College London, clambered up a 30-foot profile and extracted a soil sample from a buried A-horizon located just 1 m beneath the modern surface on the north bank of the Samara River 4.7 km west of Krasnosamarskoe. The buried A-horizon was dated 8140 to 7970 BC calibrated (AA41033 8922 ± 59 BP) (see Table 2.1 at the end of the chapter). Such an old date so near the top of the bank suggests that the main bed of the Samara had almost stopped building up sediment in this area on the northern floodplain by around 8000 BC (Chapter 9). The marshes and oxbow lakes south and west of Krasnosamarskoe are probably that old as well. Dates of around 9000 BC for the gray gleys at the bottom of the marsh sediment nearest the Krasnosamarskoe settlement indicate that it was already a marsh, not an active channel of the Samara River, after around 9000 BC (Chapter 9). Between around 9000 and 8000 BC, the Samara River abandoned the channels that now constitute the 4 km of

oxbow lakes and marshes separating the Krasnosamarskoe settlement from the incised modern riverbed. We can safely conclude that the lakes and marshes are millennia old and were present in the Bronze Age (see also Chapters 5 and 12), an important factor in attracting settlement because of their crucial roles supplying animal fodder and protection from the wind in winter.

The south side of the Samara River in our project area is known as the "steppe" side and the north as the "forest-steppe" side, but these labels refer to the landscapes *beyond* the valley. Above the junction with the Bolshoi Kinel' River, in the area where we worked, the north bank is characterized as a "moderately dry" fescue-and-feather-grass steppe and the south bank as a "dry" fescue-and-feather-grass steppe, so both sides exhibit steppe ecologies beyond the riverside marshes, meadows, and forests (Figure 2.4). The north bank has a slightly more herbaceous steppe, and the north bank contains broad patches of forest that are absent on the south bank except in narrow ravines. In our project area, the north bank has flatter landforms and is wider, while the south bank is steeper and is dissected by incised tributary stream valleys.

Figure 2.3 Samara River floodplain forests and eroded cliff on the northern bank (top). (photo by Boris Aguzarov)

The forests on the north side of the Samara are the southernmost fingers of the closed pine-birch-oak broadleaf forest that opens into forest-steppe about 200 km to the northwest. These fingers do not extend to the southern side of the Samara Valley (Figure 2.4). The forests in our study area seemed to prefer the sandy soils and alluvial dunes also found principally on the north side of the river. A large oak-pine forest 22 x 10 km in extent occupies alluvial sand dunes south of Krasnosamarskoe (green tone on Figure 2.1, mapped also on Figure 2.4). Buzuluk forest is even bigger, located around 65 km upstream from Krasnosamarskoe on the north bank. It has existed according to pollen cores continuously since the Bronze Age (Chapter 5). These substantial patches of forest, the last large forests north of the steppes, were a valuable resource on the north bank of the Samara. But forests could be easily logged, hunted, and otherwise exploited from both sides of the river, so Bronze Age settlements were not attracted uniquely to the north bank by the presence of occasional forests.

Surface visibility was better in dune-covered areas on the north side of the river than in most other parts of the valley, because wind erosion has exposed many archaeological sites in clearings in the pine forests that grow on the dunes. These dune sites range in age from Eneolithic through Bronze Age, including Chelovech'ya Golova (SVP 6) and Vilovatoye (SVP 41) in our survey area. Unfortunately, forested dune sites are eroded and deflated, and sandy soils also attract burrowing rodents, *susliks*, very common in the area, whose burrows can erase stratigraphy. The most easily found sites were not necessarily the best for archaeological study.

The Samara Valley Survey, 1995

To understand the spatial distribution of LBA settlements and cemeteries in the lower Samara Valley, we first had to map them. Our initial goal in the summer of 1995 was to visit, walk over, and obtain GPS coordinates for every prehistoric site known to Samara archaeologists, as well as any additional sites we could discover, in a section of the lower Samara River valley about 100 km long above the junction with the Bolshoi Kinel' River. The survey crew consisted of the five coauthors of this report. The survey was partially funded by a grant from the National Geographic Society.

In 1995, operating out of Anatoly Plaxin's cottage in Utyevka, we conducted a nonsystematic walking and windshield survey (Figure 2.5), with occasional surface collecting, coring, and a few shovel test excavations, between the kurgan cemetery of Gvardeitsi (SVP 7) on the east and the junction of the Samara and Bolshoi Kinel' Rivers on the west. We used an early GPS unit, primitive by today's standards, to locate 75 sites (Figure 2.1), many discovered during the survey but most already known but not mapped using geo-coordinates. Google Earth did not exist until three years after the project ended, so we initially mapped the sites by hand on recently declassified Russian military

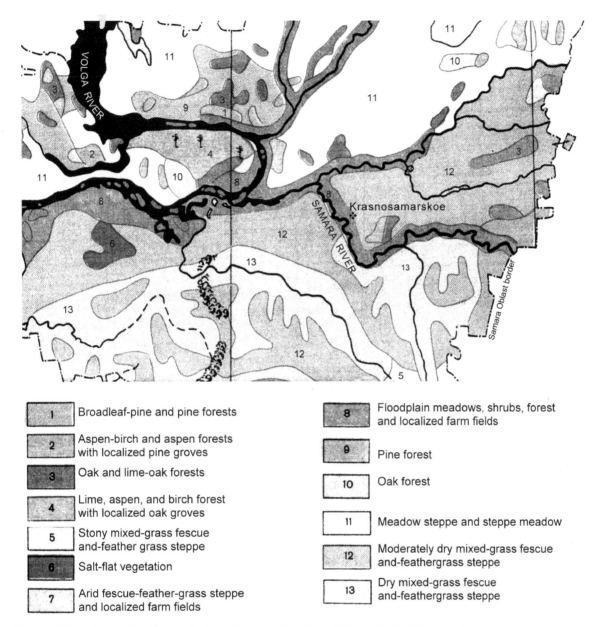

1	Broadleaf-pine and pine forests	
2	Aspen-birch and aspen forests with localized pine groves	
3	Oak and lime-oak forests	
4	Lime, aspen, and birch forest with localized oak groves	
5	Stony mixed-grass fescue and-feather grass steppe	
6	Salt-flat vegetation	
7	Arid fescue-feather-grass steppe and localized farm fields	
8	Floodplain meadows, shrubs, forest and localized farm fields	
9	Pine forest	
10	Oak forest	
11	Meadow steppe and steppe meadow	
12	Moderately dry mixed-grass fescue and-feathergrass steppe	
13	Dry mixed-grass fescue and-feathergrass steppe	

Figure 2.4 Map of vegetation types in the lower Samara Valley. Types 8, 12, and 13 typify our study area.

topographic maps at 1:50,000. Each site also was entered on a data sheet that noted latitude/longitude coordinates, vegetation type, current land use, distance to water, topographic situation, and visible artifacts or features.

Two LBA Srubnaya culture settlements were discovered during the 1995 survey, one located near the modern Russian village of Barinovka (SVP 5) and the other near Krasnosamarskoe (SVP 11). Both contained pottery suggesting occupation during the earliest (Pokrovka) phase of the Srubnaya culture, when the LBA shift to permanent settlements began, so were good candidates to reveal the Srubnaya economy just after the transition to sedentism.

At Barinovka, a Srubnaya kurgan cemetery had already been found and partly excavated by Samara archaeologists (SVP 3), so finding an LBA settlement at SVP 5 was not a big surprise. In contrast, the three unexcavated kurgans at the Krasnosamarskoe IV kurgan cemetery (SVP 12) were thought to be Middle Bronze Age (MBA) in age, so the LBA settlement we found there (SVP 11) was unexpected. Later, we excavated at both Barinovka and Krasnosamarskoe. Near Barinovka, the 1995 survey team also explored a tributary stream valley, Peschanyi Dol ("sandy valley"), with a view to conducting a systematic survey designed to find LBA herding camps possibly connected with LBA

Figure 2.5 Recording the GPS location of a Yamnaya kurgan at Pokrovka, SVP 21 in Figure 2.1, looking north over the Samara Valley. The dark green Samara River gallery forest is on the horizon.

Barinovka, to see how far herds were taken from the settlement, and whether each settlement simply used the nearest pastures or if multiple settlements made a more complicated use of the LBA landscape.

The Peschanyi Dol Survey, 1996, and Excavations, 2000

Peschanyi Dol is a 16-km-long tributary stream valley containing a small stream that originates in a spring at Filipovka and flows north into the Samara River on its southern, "steppe" side about 24 km upstream from the LBA Krasnosamarskoe settlement and 3 to 4 km upstream from the LBA Barinovka settlement (Figures 2.1 and 2.14). A cluster of Early Bronze Age (EBA), MBA, and LBA kurgans is concentrated around Utyevka east of the mouth of the valley, and other, unexcavated, kurgans crown the watershed ridgetop just above the Filipovka springs where the Peschanyi Dol stream originates (see Figures 18.2 and 18.4 for more detailed maps).

Bronze Age herding camps had never been specifically targeted for survey and excavation in the middle Volga

region. Neither the Srubnaya herding economy nor the settlement system could be fully understood until we knew how seasonal Srubnaya herding camps were articulated with permanent settlements. We wanted to know how an LBA herding camp artifact assemblage differed from a permanent settlement, hoped to identify the season of use and the differing density of artifacts as a measure of intensity of occupation at each camp site, and hoped to define the diversity of groups using camps by examining the diversity of the potting clays.

Finding stratigraphically intact Bronze Age herding camps probably was easier in a valley like Peschanyi Dol that constrained and concentrated camp sites than it was in the intensely cultivated fields on the north side of the river, where sites were unconstrained by topography and disturbed by plowing. This was the initial reason for choosing a tributary stream valley to survey for herding camps. Peschanyi Dol (PD) was chosen on Plaxin's advice because it flowed into a part of the Samara Valley that was particularly rich in Bronze Age sites, near the Srubnaya settlement we found at Barinovka. During the 1995

Figure 2.6 Excavations at PD1 in 2000, looking east over cattle grazing in the floodplain meadow, which extends to the dark tree line.

walkover of PD, we intuitively selected 12 locations for testing in the lower and middle valley. We encountered a local cattle herder who grazed his herds, totaling almost 600 cattle, in PD each summer. We asked him why and where he grazed his cattle in the valley, and his responses prompted us to include several places in our archaeological survey. Most of the 12 locations chosen for shovel testing were low, level terraces good for camping overlooking the PD stream and its *Typha/Phragmites* meadows, good for cattle grazing; these also were the places most frequented by the modern herder. Other tested locations were near a forested ravine or on heights overlooking the PD valley (see Chapter 18).

During the 1996 survey, each of the 12 locations chosen in 1995 was tested by excavating 50 cm x 50 cm shovel test pits (STPs) on a grid at 15-m intervals. We dug 78 shovel test pits, or an average of seven STPs per location. We found less than one artifact per STP, or 63 catalogued artifacts. These came from five sites, designated PD1 to PD5, that produced between 2 and 41 artifacts per site. Diagnostic ceramic sherds of the MBA Poltavka type, the LBA Srubnaya type (the majority), Iron Age, and medieval

periods were recovered at depths of 10 to 40 cm beneath the modern surface. Only one site, the largest, PD1, was visible on the surface. One of the accomplishments of the SVP was to demonstrate that ephemeral seasonal camps can be found in feather-grass steppe if shovel-test methods are used.

LBA Srubnaya pottery was discovered at four sites; later, in 2000, an additional Srubnaya camp was found, making five recorded Srubnaya sites. One site (PD4) produced only Iron Age pottery. Subsurface Mesolithic/Neolithic flint tools were found at PD1 and PD2. MBA pottery also was found, but in much smaller quantities, at PD1. The archaeological signature of the MBA camp was lighter by an order of magnitude than the much more intensely used LBA camp in the same location. No EBA Yamnaya pottery was found. We also found sherds of pottery dated to the Golden Horde period (thirteenth to fourteenth century AD) at PD1 and PD2, and one sherd at PD2 probably was an early Russian product of the fourteenth to fifteenth centuries. Seasonal camps were used in Peschanyi Dol through all chronological periods, but the LBA usage left many more artifacts than any other period.

The density of artifacts per cubic meter was greatest at the two sites (PD1 and PD2) nearest the Samara River, in the lower and lower-middle parts of the PD valley. Upstream of PD2, in the middle valley, PD5 and PD6 produced just two Srubnaya sherds each from 24 test units (Figure 2.7). The steep decline in artifact densities between 3 and 5 km from the Samara River suggests that LBA camps located more than 3 to 5 km away from the river were used less frequently or by fewer herders than those camps located closest to the river and floodplain. Much of the decline is accounted for by decreasing counts of animal bone upstream (Chapter 18), suggesting that food was prepared and consumed most often at the lower-valley camps, PD1 and PD2.

In 2000, we returned to excavate the two highest-density campsites, at PD1 in the lower valley (Figure 2.6), overlooking the floodplain meadows, 2 to 3 km wide, and at PD2, overlooking the middle valley, with narrower but still substantial marsh meadows, .5 to .75 km wide (Figures 18.11 and 18.12). The excavations of 2000 showed that 99 percent of the artifacts at PD1 and PD2 were from Srubnaya occupations dated by radiocarbon to around 1900 to 1750 BC at PD1 (Table 2.1). The Srubnaya pottery at the two

camps was made of clays that originated from at least 15 different sources, in contrast to the much larger sample of pottery from the permanent settlement at Krasnosamarskoe, which came from just five clay sources. The diversity of clays at PD1 and PD2 suggests that the herders camping there came not from the nearest Srubnaya settlement, the simplest herding pattern, but from many different Srubnaya settlements with different potting clays, suggesting a more complex and negotiated use of the PD pastures and of the landscape generally. This shared use of the same camp sites by herders from multiple Srubnaya settlements might suggest that cooperative herding arrangements extended across a substantial region around Peschanyi Dol. Today, three nearby Russian villages pool their cattle in the summer and have them watched by a shared herder in Peschanyi Dol. A similar system, with the herder alternating between settlements with different potting clays, could explain the diversity of clays we discovered in the Srubnaya herding camps in Peschanyi Dol. It is significant that these LBA herders, who came from different settlements, used the same two campsites and even the same refuse disposal pits within them, suggesting that they were part of the same extended social group.

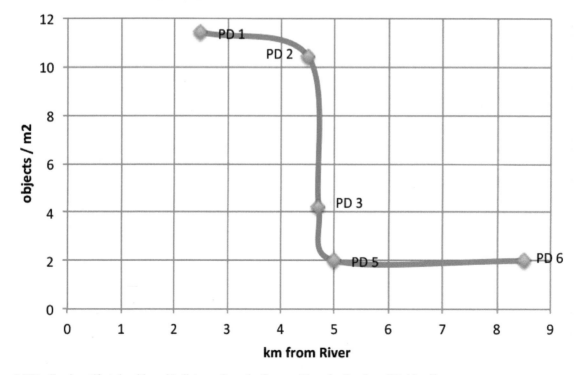

Figure 2.7 Decline in artifact densities with distance from the Samara River for Peschanyi Dol herding camps.

What is the archaeological signature of a herding camp, and how does it differ from a permanent settlement? First, they differ in density. The average count of artifacts per square meter of excavated soil was $10.3/m^2$ at PD1 and $11.9/m^2$ at PD2, while inside the Srubnaya structure at the permanent settlement of Krasnosamarskoe, it was $230.4/m^2$, and even outside the structure, it was $31.3/m^2$, three times greater than PD1. The great difference in artifact density between the *densest* PD site and the *periphery* of the Krasnosamarskoe settlement suggests that the PD sites were fundamentally different kinds of sites. In addition, both PD1 and PD2 had many lithics and relatively few animal bones by weight, while the settlement at Krasnosamarskoe yielded more animal bone by weight than ceramic sherds and actually had fewer stone tools in absolute numbers than PD1 and PD2 combined. Features such as pits or fireplaces were almost absent at the herding camps, and much of the animal bone was discarded, gnawed by dog-sized carnivores, occasionally digested and excreted, and weathered on the surface rather than being preserved unweathered and ungnawed in formal disposal pits, as at Krasnosamarskoe. So the PD sites were not just smaller versions of the year-round settlement; they were different *kinds* of sites with functionally distinct artifact and feature assemblages. These contrasts suggest that PD1 and PD2 were temporary, seasonal Srubnaya camps located in the same places where today cattle are grazed in the summer. PD1 and PD2 are interpreted here as seasonal herding camps tethered to permanent Srubnaya settlements in the Samara Valley (Chapter 18).

The Srubnaya Copper Mining Site of Mikhailovka Ovsianka

In 2000, while excavating at PD1 and PD2, we visited a Srubnaya copper mining/production site at Mikhailovka Ovsianka in the steppes south of the Samara Valley (mapped on Figure 11.1). The mining site was located 100 km south of the Samara River and 115 km northwest of the border with western Kazakhstan at E 49.37.48/N 52.23.06, about 8.2 km west-northwest of the modern Russian village of Mikhailovka Ovsianka (Mihaylo-Ovsyanka on Google Earth). A small seasonal stream had eroded a gully into the sandstone in a grassy, rolling landscape almost devoid of trees, near the top of a south-facing ridge overlooking a western tributary of the minor Bolshaya Irgiz River. The gully was about 4 to 5 m deep and 50 to 60 m wide, and exposed veins of blue azurite, green malachite, and even pure brown copper nuggets fingered through a cream-colored sandstone splotched with red iron ore, giving the copper ore mined here a distinctive Christmas-like set of hues: green and red on a cream-colored background (Figure 2.8). Overlooking the exposure was a Srubnaya mining settlement.

When the SVP began, the biggest comparable archaeological project in the region was led by E. Chernykh, assisted by a Spanish team of landscape ecology specialists (Diaz del Rio et al. 2006), who were just finishing their excavations at the Srubnaya copper-mining site of Gorny (Chernykh 1997, 2004a, 2004b), located in the Kargaly copper ore field, 350 km east of Mikhailovka Ovsianka (see Chapters 1 and 11). The size and complexity of the Gorny settlement and the mine workings near it raised our curiosity about the size and density of the Srubnaya mining settlement at Mikhailovka Ovsianka, located in the southern part of the Samara oblast. SVP members D. Peterson and L. Popova later obtained a grant to investigate another copper-mining site, Kibit, in the northern part of the Samara oblast (Peterson et al. 2006; Popova 2007).

Excavation units from the recently concluded Samara State Pedagogical University Field School excavation at Mikhailovka Ovsianka were still open in 2000, so we had the opportunity to inspect and scrape back several nicely sectioned Srubnaya mining features, including several deep V-shaped pits with brightly banded, brown/red/black stratified fills containing thick bands of charcoal (roasting pits for ore preparation?). Srubnaya pottery and very dense scatters of animal bone were evident for at least 100 m along the valley, principally on its eastern side but also on its western side. The occupation area was at least two times larger than the settlement at Krasnosamarskoe, and the density of pottery and animal bone in sections and even on backdirt piles seemed greater than the artifact density at Krasnosamarskoe, more comparable to the artifact densities at Gorny. At Gorny, Chernykh recovered more than 25 times more animal bones per square meter than we found at Krasnosamarskoe—the Gorny copper miners' settlement was much more heavily used and longer occupied than Krasnosamarskoe. The restricted age structure and standard cuts in the Gorny fauna indicate that the Gorny copper miners were provisioned with beef contributed from other Srubnaya sites (Morales and Antipina 2003:344). Mikhailovka Ovsianka was smaller than Gorny but significantly larger than Krasnosamarskoe. If it also was provisioned with labor and food from surrounding communities like Krasnosamarskoe, mining would have reduced the labor available for herding, leading families to pool their labor as suggested in the section on Peschanyi Dol above and in Chapter 18. Another possibility is that whole Srubnaya family groups moved together from places like Krasnosamarskoe to use the mine when they wished, but specialized provisioning at Gorny would argue against undifferentiated, whole-family groups accessing ores individually.

Table 2.1 All ^{14}C Dates from the Samara Valley Project

Site	Kurgan or Unit	Grave No. or Unit Quadrant	Level	Arizona Lab No.	AZ ^{14}C Age BP	Cal BC Lower	Cal BC Upper	Probability (Percent)	Material
Geomorphological Samples									
KS2 lake core	Lake mud	Basal mud		AA41034a	9895 ± 58	9653	9254	95.40	Soil
KS2 lake core	Plant remains			AA41034b	9534 ± 95	9218	8691	91.20	Plant remains
Samara River	River bed	A-horizon		AA41033	8922 ± 59	8281	7938	94.70	Soil
Peschanyi Dol									
PD1	A16	3	3	AA47798	3480 ± 52	1936	1682	94.60	Animal bone
PD1	I18	2	2	AA47799	$3,565 \pm 55$	2038	1748	94.10	Animal bone
PD1	K18	1	2	AA47800	3440 ± 56	1895	1621	95.40	Animal bone
PD2	A3	3	4	AA47801	514 ± 42	1315AD	1450AD	95.40	Animal bone
Other Sites in the Samara Region									
Grachevka II	Kurgan 5	gr 1	0	AA53804	4179 ± 55	2896	2619	95	Human bone
Grachevka II	Kurgan 5	gr 2	0	AA53805	4342 ± 56	3106	2877	93.10	Human bone
Grachevka II	Kurgan 5	gr 3	0	AA53806	3752 ± 52	2340	2018	94.60	Human bone
Grachevka II	Kurgan 7	gr 1	0	AA53807	4361 ± 55	3317	2885	95.50	Human bone
Grachevka II	Kurgan 7	gr 2	0	AA53808	4419 ± 56	3335	2912	95.40	Human bone
Khvalynsk II	Flat grave	gr 18		AA12572	5985 ± 85	5080	4868	92.40	Human bone
Khvalynsk II	Flat grave	gr 30		AA12571	6200 ± 85	5353	4936	95.40	Human bone
Kurmanaevka III	Kurgan 3	gr 1	0	AA47805	$4,234 \pm 60$	3010	2981	93.60	Human bone
Kutuluk I	Kurgan 4	gr 1		AA12570	4370 ± 75	3335	2881	95.40	Human bone
Kutuluk III	Kurgan 1	gr 2	0	AA53803	4081 ± 54	2867	2486	95.40	Human bone
Lopatino 1	Kurgan 30	gr 1	0	AA47804	4432 ± 66	3339	2918	95.40	Human bone
Luzhki 1	Flat grave	5	0	AA47807	4254 ± 61	3021	2635	95.5	Human bone
Mikhailovka Ovsianka			1.5 m below the modern surface	AA41035	3076 ± 68	1497	1157	93.60	Charcoal
Nizhny Orleansky	Kurgan 4	gr 2		AA12573	4520 ± 75	3497	2933	95.40	Human bone
Nur III	Kurgan 1	gr 4	0	AA53801	4009 ± 54	2850	2347	95.30	Human bone
Nur III	Kurgan 1	gr 5	0	AA47810	4127 ± 59	2882	2569	93.70	Human bone
Potapovka 1	Kurgan 3	gr 1	0	AA47802	3536 ± 57	2025	1740	93.80	Horse bone
Potapovka 1	Kurgan 3	gr 1	0	AA47803	4153 ± 59	2886	2580	95.40	Human bone
Potapovka 1	Kurgan 5	gr 6		AA12569	4180 ± 85	2925	2536	92.50	Ovicaprid bone
Spiridonovka IV	Kurgan 1	gr 15	0	AA47809	3517 ± 56	2014	1692	95.40	Human bone
Spiridonovka IV	Kurgan 2	gr 1	0	AA47808	3455 ± 56	1906	1631	95.40	Human bone
Tanabergin II	Kurgan 7	gr 23	0	AA47806	4020 ± 55	2858	2350	95.30	Human bone
Utyevka VI	Kurgan 6	gr 4		AA12568	3760 ± 100	2469	1928	95.40	Human bone
Utyevka V	Kurgan 4	gr 1	0	AA53802	3583 ± 52	2044	1769	91.70	Human bone

Site	Kurgan or Unit	Grave No. or Unit Quadrant	Level	Arizona Lab No.	AZ ^{14}C Age BP	Cal BC Lower	Cal BC Upper	Probability (Percent)	Material
Krasnosamarskoe IV Kurgan Cemetery									
KS1	Kurgan 1	1	0	AA37031	4284 ± 79	3105	2622	93.90	Human bone
KS1	Kurgan 1	2	0	AA37032	3837 ± 62	2472	2135	95.20	Human bone
KS1	Kurgan 1	3	0	AA37033	4241 ± 70	3021	2620	95.40	Human bone
KS1	Kurgan 1	4	0	AA37034	4306 ± 53	3092	2867	93.10	Human bone
KS1	Kurgan 2	1	0	AA37035	3820 ± 52	2462	2138	95.40	Human bone
KS1	Kurgan 2	2	0	AA37036	4327 ± 59	3106	2867	92.30	Human bone
KS1	Kurgan 2	3	0	AA37037	4207 ± 52	2908	2631	95.40	Human bone
KS1	Kurgan 3	1	0	AA37038	3490 ± 57	1952	1664	95.40	Human bone
KS1	Kurgan 3	6	0	AA37039	3411 ± 46	1879	1615	95.40	Human bone
KS1	Kurgan 3	8	0	AA37040	4239 ± 49	2928	2636	95.40	Human bone
KS1	Kurgan 3	9	0	AA37041	4236 ± 47	2922	2666	95.40	Human bone
KS1	Kurgan 3	10	0	AA37042	3594 ± 45	2129	1777	95.40	Human bone
KS1	Kurgan 3	11	0	AA37043	3416 ± 57	1888	1608	94	Human bone
KS1	Kurgan 3	13	0	AA37044	3358 ± 48	1754	1514	95.40	Human bone
KS1	Kurgan 3	16	0	AA37045	3407 ± 46	1879	1612	95.40	Human bone
KS1	Kurgan 3	17	0	AA37046	3545 ± 65	2039	1732	91.70	Human bone
KS1	Kurgan 3	23	0	AA37047	3425 ± 52	1883	1621	95.40	Human bone
Krasnosamarskoe Settlement Related									
KS2	L5	2	3	AA41022	3531 ± 43	2009	1744	95.40	Animal bone
KS2	M2	4	−276	AA47793	3615 ± 41	2132	1883	95.40	Plant remains
KS2	M2	4	−280	AA47794	3492 ± 55	1953	1682	94.90	Plant remains
KS2	M2	4	−300	AA47795	3550 ± 54	2031	1744	95.40	Plant remains
KS2	M5	1	7	AA41023	3445 ± 51	1899	1643	95.40	Animal bone
KS2	M6	3	7	AA41024	3453 ± 43	1887	1662	95.40	Animal bone
KS2	N2	2	4	AA41032	3448 ± 37	1882	1682	94	Animal bone
KS2	N3	3	7	AA41025	3469 ± 45	1906	1681	94.50	Animal bone
KS2	N4	2	6	AA41026	3491 ± 52	1946	1686	95.40	Animal bone
KS2	O4	1	7	AA41027	3460 ± 52	1905	1641	95.40	Animal bone
KS2	O4	2	5	AA41028	3450 ± 57	1905	1626	95.40	Animal bone
KS2	O5	3	3	AA47790	3311 ± 54	1738	1456	95.40	Animal bone
KS2	P1	4	6	AA41029	3470 ± 43	1904	1683	95.40	Animal bone
KS2	R1	2	5	AA41031	3476 ± 38	1892	1692	95.40	Animal bone
KS2	S2	3	4	AA41030	3477 ± 39	1894	1691	95.40	Animal bone
Lake Finds Next to the Structure									
KS2	Lake find 1		0	AA47791	3494 ± 56	1957	1681	94.70	Animal bone
KS2	Lake find 2		0	AA47792	3492 ± 55	1953	1682	94.90	Animal bone
Ya excavations									
KS2	Y1	3	5	AA47797	3450 ± 50	1891	1638	95.40	Animal bone
KS2	Y2	2	4	AA47796	3416 ± 59	1889	1607	93.60	Animal bone

Figure 2.8 Malachite and azurite in iron-rich sandstone at Mikhailovka Ovsianka.

A sample of charcoal taken from a concentration at the base of a V-shaped, stratified roasting pit exposed in a sidewall yielded a single radiocarbon date (AA 41035, 3076 ± 68 BP) of 1500 to 1130 BC, which overlaps the late Srubnaya phase at Gorny but not the early Srubnaya sites around Krasnosamarskoe. Other parts of the Srubnaya mining settlement at Mikhailovka Ovsianka were not dated, so the actual period of exploitation is not known.

An adult cow tooth and a subadult sheep/goat tooth were collected from the exposed Srubnaya deposits. Pike-Tay (Chapter 14) analyzed the season of death for these two individuals based on incremental banding in their roots and determined that they show a late fall season of slaughter (Table 14.3). This is surprising, as the site is located in open steppe, today almost devoid of forest, and would have been exposed to cold winds. Ore-roasting pits were clearly visible in excavation pit profiles, so perhaps the hot work conducted here was more comfortable in cool weather. The fuel used to heat the ore probably was hauled to the ore source from the nearest floodplain forest in the Bolshaya Irgiz river valley 16 km to the east, as no large patch of forest exists closer to the mine. This again argues against independent family groups operating the

mine and supports the hypothesis of a more specialized mining operation supported by obligated labor from the surrounding community.

The Barinovka Settlement Excavations, 1996

The survey of 1995 discovered Srubnaya ceramic sherds on the surface of a flat-topped ridge near the modern village of Barinovka (SVP 5, Figure 2.1). A Srubnaya kurgan cemetery had already been identified on the other side of the village (SVP 3). The settlement seemed a good candidate for the community that created the cemetery. The sherds were found on an elevated sandy-silt ridge about 1 km south of the modern Samara riverbank and just 3 to 4 km west of the PD valley, so could also have been articulated with the PD herding camps. In 1996, a team consisting of the coauthors of this volume, university students from Samara, local high school students, and U.S. archaeologists Petar Glumac, Charles McNutt, and Chris Gette excavated an area of 72 m² at Barinovka around the 1995 find-spot (Figure 2.9). The excavation was partly supported by the National Geographic Society.

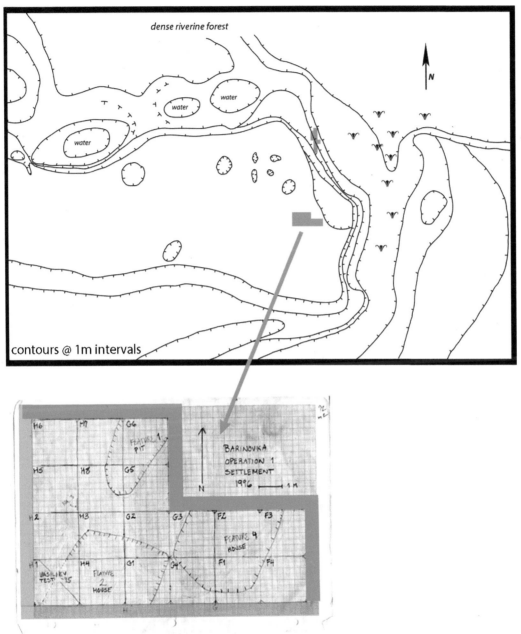

Figure 2.9 Barinovka settlement (SVP 5) excavation 1996. Feature outlines in lower field drawing are early historic.

The LBA Srubnaya occupation was found to be thoroughly disturbed by the pits and houses of an early historic Russian Cossack village. Unfortunately, the site was so disturbed by historic features that its utility for Bronze Age research was limited.

A fairly clean Srubnaya component was confined to the northwestern corner of the excavation, in three 2 m x 2 m squares, H5, H6, and H8 (Figure 2.9). This area of 12 m³ produced 502 ceramic sherds, 99 percent of which exhibited Srubnaya and early Srubnaya (Povkrovka phase) shapes, colors, and fabric. These three units also produced three MBA Poltavka sherds, two MBA Abashevo sherds, and 539 animal bone fragments. We recovered a flat, ovoid bronze perforated pendant from 30 to 40 cm depth in H5, a more refined ornament than any found at Krasnosamarskoe. The LBA artifact densities from this area were similar to those found on the periphery of the Krasnosamarskoe settlement, so perhaps our excavation intersected the periphery of a permanent Srubnaya settlement like Krasnosamarskoe. But the Barinovka site was riddled with *suslik* burrows and early historic Cossack features, so it was not a good candidate for larger-scale excavation.

After finishing at Barinovka in 1996, we revisited the Srubnaya settlement that we had found in 1995 around 24 km to the northwest at Krasnosamarskoe. We found it still eroding into a manmade fish-farming pond beside the Krasnosamarskoe IV kurgan cemetery. The shallow water had swallowed and sectioned part of a Srubnaya feature packed with artifacts. We picked up large Srubnaya rim sherds, a bone weaving tool, and a piece of copper slag. We decided that Krasnosamarskoe was a better candidate than Barinovka for the year-round Srubnaya settlement we needed as a complement for the Peschanyi Dol herding camps in the complete Srubnaya settlement system that was the target of our field operations.

The Krasnosamarskoe Settlement Reconnaissance, 1998

In 1998, we performed an archaeological reconnaissance at Krasnosamarskoe with small grants from the Freedman Foundation and Hartwick College. Our base was a small wooden house with attached wooden banya built in the 1970s as a rural fishing lodge for the First Secretary of the Communist Party of the Samara oblast. The house overlooked manmade ponds stocked commercially with carp by the collective farm (*kolkhoz*) that still managed the fields and marshes in the vicinity (Figure 2.10). (The First Secretary was guaranteed to catch something here.) The fish ponds were created in 1966 by erecting dams across the oxbow lakes and marshes of the Samara River floodplain and filling them, raising the water level by about 1 m within the dams. The raised water level in one fish pond swamped part of the LBA settlement that had been located less than 1 m above the edge of the former oxbow lake.

The Srubnaya settlement site was 1.3 km southeast of the fishing lodge, on the reedy shore of an overgrazed steppe pasture. In July 1998, a single herder, Aleksandr K'nyazev, assisted by two German Shepherd dogs, supervised 314 cattle in the lake-edge pastures in this area. His cattle were daily observers and occasionally invaders of our excavations.

The drowned edge of the former oxbow lake described a long curve between the eroded site and the lodge (Figure 2.10). We found a feature about 8 m wide eroding into the fish pond. Cleaning the bank with shovels for 100 m north and south of the eroding feature, we found only isolated Srubnaya sherds in the exposed 200-m section. The feature was spatially isolated. An exploratory 2 m x 2 m square 7 m back from the water's edge yielded dense Srubnaya sherds and animal bones in a stratified cultural level that began about 20 to 30 cm beneath the surface and continued down to about 70 to 80 cm. It seemed to be a large subsurface

structure. Artifacts covered the shallow lake bottom for an unknown distance out from the shoreline.

Boris A. Aguzarov of Samara flew a light-air vehicle 400 m above the site. His photographs revealed a rectangular cropmark feature that looked like a subsurface rectangular trench enclosing the structure. We excavated another 2 m x 2 m square in 1998 in this apparent rectangular trench and found a shallow subsurface ditch but recovered no diagnostic artifacts associated with it and were therefore unable to date it. In retrospect, the shallow (probably symbolic) enclosing ditch seems stratigraphically linked most closely with the Iron Age activity that we later found near the surface of this site.

The Krasnosamarskoe Settlement Excavations, 1999 and 2001

The Srubnaya settlement at Krasnosamarskoe was excavated in two seasons, 1999 and 2001, partly supported by a grant from the National Science Foundation. Chapter 10 describes the excavations at the site in detail. Each season culminated in an elaborate outdoor initiation of first-time excavators in the Samara Valley, a category that included all foreigners, including directors, in a nighttime introduction to the god of Russian archaeology, Gorposemog, a name derived from the three common types of archaeological sites: fortified towns (*gorodishche*), settlements (*poselenie*), and cemeteries (*mogila*) (Figure 2.11). The initiation was planned and overseen by Russian graduate students who cut dramatic figures around a bonfire as leaping, commanding, and comically insulting shamans. The institution of elaborately staged end-of-season initiations was an entertaining and memorable retention from the field traditions of Soviet-era archaeology, but it also echoed unexpectedly the archaeological discoveries at the site, which included the remains of a Srubnaya initiation ritual (Chapter 14).

In six weeks in 1999, we excavated the southern two-thirds of the Srubnaya settlement. In 2001, we returned for another six weeks with a smaller crew and excavated the northern third of the Srubnaya settlement, opening a total of 207 m² (Figure 10.02), within a triangular 26 m x 12 m grid along the lake edge; most of this area was excavated down to about 70 to 90 cm beneath the surface (Figure 2.12). A contemporary Srubnaya activity area (Area Y) with significantly lower artifact density, probably a garbage dump, was found 160 m south of the structure and was examined with a transect of test pits and a 4 m x 2 m excavation.

Excavation revealed that the feature cut by the fish pond was a Srubnaya structure about 8 x 12 m in preserved

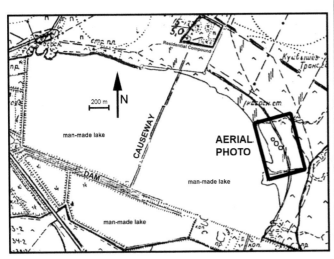
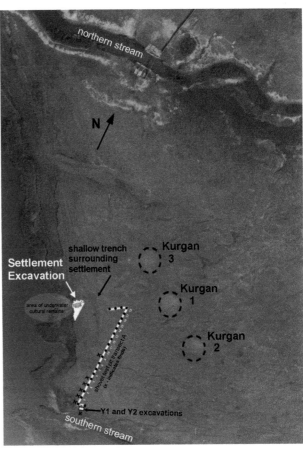

Figure 2.10 Overview of Krasnosamarskoe. Left, the dams and lakes near the site with the fishing lodge located in the top polygon; right, the three kurgans, settlement excavation, shovel test transect, and activity area (Area Y) excavation. (photo by Boris Aguzarov)

dimensions (originally longer, perhaps 8 x 16–20 m), with a post-supported roof probably made of *Phragmites* reed thatch, constructed over a dug-out floor. Most excavated Srubnaya structures in the Samara oblast were more than 20 m long, with dug-out floors and irregular patterns of postholes indicating clusters of roof support posts (Sedova 2000), like our structure at Krasnosamarskoe. The structure and the occupation surface around it contained 4,500 ceramic sherds and 22,000 pieces of animal bone, with more than 8,000 identifiable to species. Kosintsev (Chapter 15) noted that it was unusual to find so many animal bones discarded inside rather than outside the structure at Krasnosamarskoe. The other artifacts on the structure floor indicated craft activities, including ceramic pottery decoration and copper working, rawhide thong smoothing, thread spinning (spindle whorls), a variety of grinding tasks using small handheld grinding tools made on cobbles, and piercing/punching tasks using a bronze awl and a bone awl. This wide variety of domestic tasks and activities suggests a domestic household. Pit 10, a deep feature containing waterlogged organic remains, probably was a Srubnaya well. It yielded wooden artifacts, including long notched poles and rich botanical deposits.

No hearth or oven was found in the structure, perhaps suggesting that it was not a domestic house but an A-frame outbuilding containing a well, used for various crafts and also for rubbish disposal.

The size of the settlement was determined by wading across the shallow pond on transects, collecting Srubnaya artifacts and animal bones from the deflated part of the site underwater, to map the edge of their distribution. The artifact deposit under the pond extended out from the shore no more than 40 m, indicating that the entire settlement was perhaps 60 x 40 m in size, sufficient space for just one or two additional buildings. The principal residence at the site probably is now eroded and deflated on the lake bottom.

Both the excavated and lake-collected parts of the settlement were occupied during two ceramic-style phases within the early Srubnaya period: Pokrovka (early Srubnaya) phase and developed Srubnaya phase (Ostroshchenko 2003; Semenova 2001). Radiocarbon dates on burned animal bones recovered underwater correlated with those from the excavated part of the settlement. They indicated occupation within a fairly tight time range, around 1900 to 1700 BC, when the transition from mobile pastoralism to settled life occurred.

Figure 2.11 A carving of Gorposemog, god of archaeology, dominates the arena chosen for initiations, as a thunderstorm rolls past on the horizon.

Sedova (2000) hypothesized a model for Srubnaya settlement patterns in the Samara oblast in which extended families occupied a sequence of short-lived, small pastoral settlements, with each settlement occupied no more than 10 to 20 years. New settlements were close to old ones, occasionally reusing the same site. It's not clear if the Krasnosamarskoe settlement fits this model. The sequence of pits in the stratified occupation deposits within the excavated structure seem to have developed without an obvious break or period of abandonment, so the structure seems to have been occupied continuously through two ceramic stylistic phases over a period of decades rather than years (see Chapter 10).

Constant-volume 2-liter soil samples were taken for flotation from 274 measured locations representing every 10-cm level (excluding level 1) of every 2 m x 2 m square in the excavation grid; additional samples were taken from 12 pit features, a few of which were intensively studied from a botanical perspective, with Pit 10, the well, receiving the most study. We established through several lines of evidence—from pollen, seeds, and phytoliths, age at death of immature animals less than a year old, and from incremental banding on animal teeth—that the structure was used through all seasons, so was occupied year-round. We found no evidence for agriculture, but we did find evidence for the selective collection and selective charring of *Chenopodium*, *Amaranthus*, and *Polygynum* seeds.

The animal bones from Krasnosamarskoe included cattle, sheep, goats, horses, and a few pigs but very few wild animals, suggesting almost no hunting. Incremental banding on cattle teeth showed that older cattle were culled from the herd in the spring before movement to the summer pastures, and younger animals were butchered in the fall, before the onset of winter (see Chapter 14). Such patterns indicate the maximization of animal products for both meat and milk in normal pastoral production and show that part of the bone assemblage at Krasnosamarskoe was derived from the seasonal management of cattle for food.

But another part of the animal bone assemblage revealed an unexpected surprise: a previously undocumented ritual, conducted in midwinter, involving the sacrifice, burning, and chopping up of at least 51 dogs and at least seven wolves, 98 percent of them killed in the winter (Chapter 12). The remains were discarded in the excavated structure. Most of the dogs were old, 7 to 12 years, and were probably

Figure 2.12 Excavation at Krasnosamarskoe in 1999. The unexcavated square in the center (unit P2/1) was the backfilled 2 m x 2 m square dug in 1998. The LBA structure was north and west of that square, where the students are excavating. The marsh is on the left and our camp tents can be seen as white dots against the tree line, behind which was our fishing cabin HQ.

familiar companions at the end of their useful lives. They were burned or roasted, and then each head was chopped into the same 10 to 16 small squares by well-placed and accurate axe cuts, clearly a ritual act, followed by disposal of the burned and properly chopped pieces among other animal bones, including possibly sacrificed calves, in pits in the floor of an outbuilding. The ritualized burning and intense chopping of the dogs' heads and bodies perhaps was meant to de-sacralize them before they were discarded. Heavily chopped and segmented dog bones accounted for 36 percent of the specimens (number of identifiable specimens [NISP]) and 18 percent of individuals (minimum number of individuals [MNI]) from bones identified to species by Kosintsev (Chapter 15) and also 40 percent of specimens (NISP) as counted by the U.S. archaeozoologists (Chapter 16). The difference between the two counts, 36 percent and 40 percent, is small. Either percentage of canids is unprecedented in Srubnaya settlements, where more than 2 percent dog bones would be unusually high.

Dog or wolf sacrifices and pelts are associated in Indo-European mythology with mid-winter rituals designed to restore light and vigor to the sun, cattle, and humans (Falk 1986; Heesterman 1962; White 1991) and with a mid-winter male initiation ceremony at the transition to becoming a wolf-like warrior and a member of a raiding band of youths, the widely distributed Indo-European institution of the *männerbünde* (Germanic) or *kourios* (Greek) (Kershaw 2000:133–179). In archaic, arguably pre-Brahmanic traditions referenced in the Sanskrit Vedas, the *Vrātyas* were dog-priests of a warrior brotherhood who sacrificed a cow in mid-winter, the leanest time of year, offering the victim to reinvigorate nature, prior to initiating boys into warriorhood and sending them out for years of raiding (Kershaw 2000:133–179; White 1991:96). At the same time of year, European myths suggest, boys were initiated in ceremonies suffused with dog and wolf symbolism, becoming dogs or wolves themselves. We might have evidence for such a mid-winter ritual at Krasnosamarskoe (see Chapter 14).

Interestingly, this ritual was found only at Krasnosamarskoe, out of seven Srubnaya settlements in the middle Volga region with studied fauna compared by Kosintsev (Chapter 15, Table 15.24). If people from other settlements participated in this ritual, they came to this place to do so. Krasnosamarskoe, which seems to have been a rather plain and ordinary Srubnaya settlement in many other ways, was a central place for the performance of this ritual. Perhaps other settlements specialized in hosting other rituals in other seasons.

The Krasnosamarskoe IV Kurgan Cemetery

In six weeks in 1999, we completely excavated all three kurgans at the Krasnosamarskoe IV cemetery. They were about 1 m high and ranged from 40 to 27 m in diameter. We mapped and removed 33 individuals from 30 graves. Eight of these were MBA graves of the mobile Poltavka culture, which erected the three kurgans around 2800 to 2900 BC, but Kurgan 3 also contained 27 LBA Srubnaya individuals buried in 23 graves inserted into this kurgan, on the north side facing away from the settlement. This operation was directed and overseen by Kuznetsov, Mochalov, and Khokhlov and is described in Chapter 17.

The cemetery was designated Krasnosamarskoe IV in the 1980s by Vasiliev and Kuznetsov (1988). They mapped four distinct clusters of kurgans numbered Krasnosamarskoe I through IV, distributed along the eastern and northern edge of the oxbow lakes and marshes near Krasnosamarskoe at intervals of around 1.5 to 2 km between kurgan clusters (see Figure 17.1). Krasnosamarskoe I was a cluster of four kurgans, II also contained four kurgans, III had six kurgans, and IV, excavated in 1999, originally was designated as three kurgans. Additional kurgans 500 m to the south were added to Krasnosamarskoe IV in later site lists (see Figure 17.2). At least two more kurgans were located about 500 m northwest of the fishing lodge in the agricultural fields of the kolkhoz; these were eventually designated Krasnosamarskoe VI and are unexcavated.

Excavations in the 1980s at Krasnosamarskoe I and III, respectively around 4.5 and 1.5 km southeast of Krasnosamarskoe IV, determined that both kurgan cemeteries were created in the MBA by mobile pastoralists of the Poltavka culture. Their modest graves contained pottery, a stone pestle, a bifacial flint tool, a copper awl, and a bone ring (Vasiliev and Kuznetsov 1988). The three kurgans we excavated at Krasnosamarskoe IV also were built in the MBA, at the earliest EBA/MBA transition around 2900 to 2800 BC, by Poltavka pastoralists who also left quite modest funerary gifts (spindle whorls and small ceramic cups). The marsh-side pastures within 4 km of our excavation seem to have been intensively occupied and exploited during the MBA.

Kurgan cemeteries are enduringly visible monuments, and perhaps because of that, they tend to be interpreted as landscape features that people lived with and used repeatedly over long periods of time. Complete excavation and radiocarbon dating of Kurgans 1 to 3 at Krasnosamarskoe IV, however, showed that these three kurgans were erected in a surprisingly short time, probably between 2900 and 2800 BC. Dates on human bone from the three central graves were largely overlapping, suggesting that the three deaths happened in a brief time, three kurgans were raised, and then they were left behind. If the brief usage of this cemetery was reflected in land-use patterns, then early MBA herding groups might have used a particular set of local pastures intensively and then left them fallow for generations.

Two adult women and an adult man were found in the three central graves of the three kurgans (Figure 2.13). The two women were unusual, since more than 80 percent of EBA-MBA kurgans excavated in the middle Volga steppes have an adult man in the central grave (see Chapter 6). Perhaps there were circumstances in which some Bronze Age women could behave as men. This could possibly even be a Bronze Age social antecedent for the Iron Age warrior-equipped women's graves found in the Don-Volga steppes ("Amazons," in popular usage) (Guliaev 2003).

Regardless of how the exceptional people afforded kurgan burial were selected in the EBA and MBA, the function of kurgan burial had changed dramatically by the LBA. Instead of marking the grave of a single important individual, kurgans were used in the LBA to bury the whole population—infants, juveniles, women, and men. The population admitted to kurgan burial first grew wider in the violent and innovative final centuries of the MBA II, 2100 to 1800 BC, when entire elite families, including many children, were buried in cemeteries of the Sintashta and Potapovka type, and then it widened again to include everyone at the start of the LBA, around 1900 to 1700 BC, in Srubnaya cemeteries. Srubnaya kurgan burial practices were much more socially inclusive than kurgan funerals during the era of mobile pastoralism.

Kurgan 3 at Krasnosamarskoe IV, and only Kurgan 3, was used as a cemetery during the Srubnaya period, probably by the family residing at the Krasnosamarskoe settlement. The 27 Srubnaya individuals inserted into this kurgan in 23 Srubnaya graves were uniformly poor—only a few pottery vessels and spindle whorls were included as gifts. Most of the graves that contained pottery had Pokrovka (early Srubnaya) pots, and fewer graves contained the developed Srubnaya type, which was the

Figure 2.13 Kurgan 1, central grave 3 under excavation. A cover of bundled reeds is being cleared by Gette and Kormilitsyn as it dips down into grave 3, following the collapse of the grave roof. A robust MBA female adult, 17 to 20 years old, was buried here.

majority style in the settlement. Possibly, the "early" style was retained primarily for grave gifts during the style shift, so the two types were made side by side for a period but used for different purposes.

The most unusual feature of the Srubnaya cemetery in Kurgan 3 was the high percentage, 82 percent of the Srubnaya individuals, attributed to infants, children, and adolescents. Only four well-preserved adults were buried in the LBA: two men and two women. Another adult was partial and of indeterminate sex. There was little pathological evidence suggesting an unusual level of disease among the 22 children at Krasnosamarskoe. However, it is obvious that either disease or injury was responsible for the deaths of so many infants and juveniles.

One possibility is that ill or injured children were brought to this place for healing, and those who failed to recuperate were buried here. A practiced ritual specialist was required to chop the dog heads at Krasnosamarskoe into such standardized, small pieces, and it is possible

that the same ritual specialist, perhaps a shaman or healer, resided at the site and tended to sick children. Pollen from the herb *Seseli* sp. was found in one pit within the structure at Krasnosamarskoe; this plant grows on chalk hills on the other side of the Volga, 160 km to the west, and has various medicinal uses, including sedation and muscle relaxation. Herb importation from such a distance suggests the presence of an herbalist. Perhaps this individual was the reason so many children were buried at Krasnosamarskoe.

Observations on the Srubnaya Pastoral System

Combined with the cemetery excavations conducted independently by Samara archaeologists at LBA Spiridonovka and Barinovka, and a rescue excavation conducted at the settlement of Poplavskoe after our project concluded, our fieldwork delineated a Srubnaya landscape in one 30-km-long section of the lower Samara Valley. Krasnosamarskoe is the settlement with the largest excavated area, but other Srubnaya settlement components have been sampled at Spiridonovka, Poplavskoe, and Barinovka, and Srubnaya surface scatters suggesting a settlement have been found at Utyevka and S'yezzhee, and a large Srubnaya cemetery at Spiridonovka III and IV (south) suggests that a settlement mij structures) also suggests a family-sized or extended family-sized population. We can suggest a Srubnaya settlement system consistent with the available evidence.

Srubnaya settlements probably were extended-family herding-and-gathering communities consisting of a few long, A-framed, thatched-roofed buildings surrounded by activity areas and dumps (like our Area Y at Krasnosamarskoe, Chapter 10). They were occupied through the entire year. Most of their cattle, sheep, and horse herds probably grazed within 3 to 5 km of the Samara River valley floodplain, if the declining artifact densities in herding camps in Peschanyi Dol with increasing distance from the Samara River are a reliable guide. At Krasnosamarskoe, there was little or no

cultivation of grain. The teeth of Srubnaya people here and throughout the middle Volga steppes were almost free of caries, similar to the teeth of hunter-gatherers, and neither their caries frequency nor their stable isotopes showed any significant change from the mobile herder diet of the MBA to the settled herder diet of the LBA.

We are uncertain if settlements moved at short intervals (10–20 years) or at longer intervals (several generations). The occurrence of both Pokrovka (earliest Srubnaya) and classic Srubnaya ceramic types at the Krasnosamarskoe settlement is typical of Srubnaya sites in the region and would normally be seen as evidence for a cyclical reuse of the site during two chronologically separate ceramic-stylistic phases (Sedova 2000). The same interpretation applies to the appearance of both ceramic types in kurgan cemeteries at Barinovka, Krasnosamarskoe IV, and Spiridonovka (north and south), suggesting more than one phase of kurgan usage. However, in Chapter 10, we

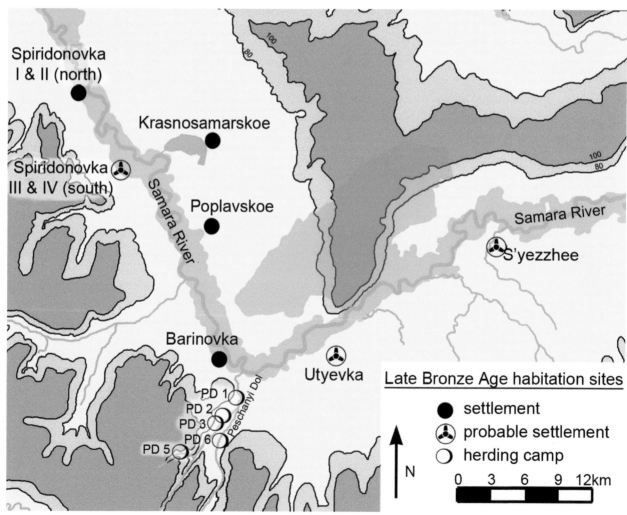

Figure 2.14 Known and probable LBA Srubnaya settlements in the project area.

suggest that Pokrovka and developed Srubnaya styles were contemporary, differing in frequency through time but never chronologically separated throughout the occupation at Krasnosamarskoe. The settlement at Krasnosamarskoe was occupied continuously through a phase transition in ceramic styles, supporting a hypothesis of longer-lasting residential stability. In the excavated structure at Krasnosamarskoe, multiple layers of floor deposits, intercut pit features within the floor deposits, and the range of radiocarbon dates from sediments at the bottom of the well, Pit 10, indicate that the structure was occupied without an observable stratigraphic break over multiple decades, with the oldest phase falling in the century 1900 to 1800 BC and the latest phase falling in the century 1800 to 1700 BC, probably principally between 1850 and 1750 BC, suggesting a settlement period of two or more generations.

Most Srubnaya settlements in the region had an associated cemetery. Settlement-and-cemetery pairs were found in the study area at Spiridonovka, Barinovka, Krasnosamarskoe, and Poplavskoe and probably existed at S'yezzhee and Utyevka. Many of these sites are around 10 km apart: Spiridonovka I and II (north) is about 10 km from Spiridonovka III and IV (south), as are Krasnosamarskoe and Poplavskoe, as well as Barinovka and Utyevka. This spatial distribution suggests that each extended-family herding unit used a herding and grazing territory with around 10 km of frontage on the riverine marshes and, if the Peschanyi Dol pattern is used, less than 10 km of pastures behind the riverfront, making each extended-family territory a maximum of around 100 km². This is obviously an idealized allotment, but it is linked to the mapped archaeological sites in this section of the Samara Valley, and it is useful for the purposes of calculating the herding potential of the catchment around each mapped LBA cemetery-and-settlement unit. A square this size, 10 x 10 km, suggested here as the *maximum* area used in the early LBA Samara Valley by a coresident herding group, would contain 10,000 ha of woodland, marsh, and pasture, mostly feather-grass-and-flowering-herb pasture. This much grazing land would be sufficient for 10,000 sheep at a conservative stocking rate of one sheep per hectare (1.5–2 sheep is possible in this environment) (see tables in Miller 2005 and Boonman and Mikhalev 2005). If the stocking rate for cattle is counted at a conservative six sheep per cow, then 1,667 cattle could graze in the same area.

Looking at herd sizes from an available-labor perspective, one extended Srubnaya family from a settlement like Krasnosamarskoe (with perhaps just one residential structure) might be able to put a *maximum* of four horse-mounted herders into the field, divided between horse, cattle, and sheep herds, usually kept in separate pastures. More than 800 sheep are difficult to manage as a single herd, so the extended family could manage *no more than* 1,600 sheep watched by two herders (probably far less, as there was no urban market) needing 1,600 ha, 150 horses (about the maximum for a single Kalmuck or Mongol herder) needing 900 ha, and up to 600 head of cattle (maximum for a traditional Argentine gaucho) needing 3,600 ha (Khazanov 1994 [1983]:31–32) for a *maximum* usable area of 6,100 ha. Working at maximum capacity with four full-time herders, a difficult pace to maintain, somewhat more than half of the hypothesized 10 km x 10 km extended-family territory could have been used.

In practice, an actual Srubnaya extended family would have had no way to use so many sheep or cattle, although the provisioning of the Kargaly miners with beef, as hypothesized at Gorny (Muñiz and Antipina 2003), might have created a small local market for beef cattle, and the need for ore hauling between Kargaly and effective river transport might have created an occasional market for strong oxen. Even with these incentives, only a tenth of the available pasture, or 1,000 ha, could have provided a significant surplus for each extended-family group. An extended family might have counted itself wealthy with, for example, 200 sheep (1 ha per sheep), 100 cattle (6 ha per cow), and 30 horses (5 ha per horse), easily fed with 1,000 ha of feather-grass-and-leguminous-herb pasture, *not counting* the riverfront marsh resources. With 10 years of fallow, even cultivated steppe can return almost to virgin steppe (Boonman and Mikhalev 2005:389–390), making a one-tenth level of pasture usage sustainable within the allotted 10,000-ha territory over the long term.

If Srubnaya communities in the Samara Valley were distributed over the landscape in this idealized way, then they could have generated a substantial surplus of wool, oxen, horses, leather, or any other animal commodity that might have been valuable in trade on a sustainable basis without overgrazing their pastures. It is not clear if or how the grazing and herding territories of Srubnaya sedentary extended-family herding units were related to the family grazing territories of the preceding era of mobile nomadic pastoralism, but the isotopic signatures of their diets were surprisingly similar. It is possible that mobile and settled pastoralism differed mainly in where the family lived rather than in the size of the territory exploited. The underlying MBA-LBA land-use patterns might not have been as different as the contrasting MBA-LBA residential patterns seem to suggest.

Mining and exchange linked these small Srubnaya communities to a much wider world. The small-scale Srubnaya copper mine at Mikhailovka Ovsianka, south of the Samara Valley, was contemporary with another small mine exploited seasonally at Kibit, north of the Samara Valley (Chapter 11), and with the huge copper mines at Kargaly, intensively exploited from multiple Srubnaya settlements, including a year-round mining settlement at Gorny 350 km to the east (Chernykh 2004a, 2004b). Srubnaya cattle from Krasnosamarskoe had pathologies indicating that they were used to pull heavy loads, probably in wagons, perhaps carrying ore from these sources to the Volga River for export. Beef cattle seem to have been provisioned to the Gorny miners (Muñiz and Antipina 2003), and those provisions probably came partly from cattle herds in the Samara Valley, obtained from Srubnaya settlements like Barinovka, Krasnosamarskoe, and Spiridonovka. Small-scale, repair-type metalworking was practiced at Krasnosamarskoe and even at PD2, a herding camp, and copper smelting occurred in a warm-season settlement near cuprous outcrops at Kibit. In the Samara Valley, many seasonal activities probably were linked to the demand for copper, including production at local mines, transport of the ore, production within settlements, and the provision of surplus beef cattle for the miners at Kargaly. Social and economic integration and articulation between local family-based communities might have depended on the requirements and obligations of copper mining as much as pastoral production.

The elite family in the region appears to have lived near the kurgan cemeteries at Spiridonovka I and II (north). At Spiridonovka II, kurgan 1 contained 17 graves and kurgan 2, 37 graves; several individuals yielded preserved ancient DNA (Mathiesen et al. 2015) Spiridonovka II, kurgan 1, contained four rich Srubnaya graves. Grave 1 a male age 17-25 with weapons—a metal dagger, 12 lanceolate projectile points, and a bone clasp or belt ornament. Grave 2 an adolescent age 13-16, probably female, and a juvenile age 6-8 years, decorated with faience beads probably imported from south of the steppes and numerous tin-bronze bracelets, beads, and pendants, including a pair of long, dangling earrings made of leaf-like sets of pendants arranged in three rows. Grave 7 contained a bronze bracelet, ring, and bead, while Grave 13 an adult female age 25-35 with 16 tubular bronze beads and eight bronze medallions. Gold-covered pendants decorated by depletion gilding were worn by a 12-year-old girl in Grave 29 under Kurgan 2, a few meters from Kurgan 1. Depletion gilding, a complex kind of gilding procedure, has previously been detected only in the Near East (see Chapter 11 for this discovery by Peterson et al.). The faience beads and depletion-gilded pendants both point toward the southern external trade connections enjoyed by the Srubnaya elite in the region, artifacts not seen in more humble communities

such as Krasnosamarskoe. But "hierarchical" describes only one aspect of Srubnaya society.

Three overlapping circles of regional integration can be seen at different scales in the LBA in this part of the Samara Valley: a circle of obligation, for the feeding and maintenance of the copper miners at Gorny (see Chapters 1 and 11); a circle of cooperation for arranging summer herding in Peschanyi Dol (above and Chapter 18); and a third circle of ritual affiliation for the regionally centralized winter initiation and dog sacrifice ritual held at Krasnosamarskoe (above and Chapter 14). Heterarchy is a good description for this multiscalar kind of organization, because different kinds of authority and affiliation—related to mining and trade, summer herding, and winter initiation rituals—were engaged in each of these relationships. It is possible that a loose oversight of some of these regional activities was exercised by the local Srubnaya gentry buried at Spiridonovka (north), representing yet another circle of authority and affiliation, related to patron-client obligations.

It is unusual to be able to describe an ancient landscape at such a well-defined moment in time (thanks to many radiocarbon dates from many sites), with such a well-articulated and semi-complete set of settlement types and a related set of human remains from the same sites and from the greater region, for comparison. In the following chapters, after brief introductions to the ethnohistory, Bronze Age archaeology, and climate history of the Samara Valley (Chapters 3–5), the human remains from the Samara Valley and the middle Volga steppes are analyzed (Chapters 6–8), followed by reports on the field operations of the Samara Valley Project (Chapters 9–18).

Notes

Figures and tables in this chapter were prepared by D.Brown, photographs were taken by D. Brown or D. Anthony unless otherwise noted in captions.

References

Anthony, David W.
1998 The Opening of the Eurasian Steppes at 2000 BC. In *The Bronze Age and Early Iron Age Peoples of Eastern Central Asia*, Vol. 1, edited by Victor H. Mair, pp. 94–113. University of Pennsylvania Museum, Philadelphia.

Anthony, David W., Dorcas Brown, Emmett Brown, Audrey Goodman, Aleksandr Kokhlov, Pavel Kuznetsov, Pavel Kosintsev, Oleg Mochalov, Eileen Murphy, Anne Pike-Tay, Laura Popova, Arlene Rosen, Nerissa Russell, and Alison Weisskopf
2005 The Samara Valley Project: Late Bronze Age Economy and Ritual in the Russian Steppes. *Eurasia Antiqua (Berlin)* 11:395–417.

Boonman, J. G., and S. S. Mikhalev

2005   The Russian Steppe. In *Grasslands of the World*, edited by J. M. Suttie, S. G. Reynolds, and C. Batelo, Vol. 34, pp. 381–416. Food and Agriculture Organization of the United Nations, Rome.

Bunyatyan, Kateryna P.

2002   Correlations between Agriculture and Pastoralism in the North Pontic Steppe Area during the Bronze Age. In *Prehistoric Steppe Adaptation and the Horse*, edited by Marsha Levine, Colin Renfrew, and Katie Boyle, pp. 269–286. McDonald Institute, Cambridge.

Chernykh, Evgenii N.

1997   *Kargaly. Zabytni Mir* [Kargaly, the Forgotten World]. NOX, Moscow.

Chernykh, E. N. (editor)

2004a   *Kargaly, Tom III: Selishche Gornyi: Arkheologicheskie Materialyi: Tekhnologiya Gorno-Metallurgicheskogo Proizvodstva i Arkheobiologicheskie Issledovaniya.* Yazyki Slavyanskoi Kul'tury, Moskva.

2004b   Kargaly: The Largest and Most Ancient Metallurgical Complex on the Border of Europe and Asia. In *Metallurgy in Ancient Eastern Eurasia from the Urals to the Yellow River*, edited by Katheryn M. Linduff, Chinese Studies 31, pp. 223–279. Edwin Mellen, Lewiston.

Diaz del Río, P., P. L. García, J. A. López Sáez, M. I. Martina Navarette, A. L. Rodrígues Alcalde, S. Rovira-Llorens, J. M. Vicent García, and I. de Zavala Morencos

2006   Understanding the Productive Economy during the Bronze Age through Archaeometallurgical and Paleo-Environmental Research at Kargaly. In *Beyond the Steppe and the Sown: Proceedings of the 2002 University of Chicago Conference on Eurasian Archaeology*, edited by D. L. Peterson, L. M. Popova, and A. T. Smith, pp. 343–357. Brill, Leiden.

Falk, Harry

1986   *Bruderschaft und Würfelspiel*. Hedwige Falk, Freiburg.

Guliaev, V. I.

2003   Amazons in the Scythia: New Finds at the Middle Don, Southern Russia. *World Archaeology* 35(1):112–125.

Heesterman, Jan

1962   Vrâtyas and Sacrifice. *Indo-Iranian Journal* 6:3–37.

Kershaw, Kris

2000   *The One-Eyed God: Odin and the (Indo-) Germanic Männerbünde*. Journal of Indo-European Studies Monograph 36. Institute for the Study of Man, Washington, D.C.

Khazanov, Anatoly

1994   [1983]. *Nomads and the Outside World*, revised edition. University of Wisconsin Press, Madison.

Khokhlov, Aleksandr A.

1999a   Kraniologicheskie materialy Spiridonovskogo II mogilnika (kurgan 1). In *Okhrana i Izuchenie Pamyatnikov Istorii i Kul'tury v Samarskoi Oblasti, v.1*: 93–97. Samarskii Oblastnoi Istoriko-Kraevedcheskii Muzei im. P.V. Alabina, Samara.

1999b   Antropologicheskiya kurganov 1 i 2 mogil'nika Spiridonovka IV. In *Voposy Arkheologii Povolzh'ya*, edited by R. S. Bagautdinov and L. V. Kuznetsova, pp. 2227–2230. Samarskii Gosudarstvennyi Pedagogicheskii Universitet, Samara.

2002   Paleoantropologiya mogil'nika Srubnoi kul'tury Barinovka I. In *Voprosy Arkhelologii Povolzh'ya*, pp. 134–144. Samarskii Gosudarstvennyi Pedagogicheskii Universitet, Samara.

Mathieson, Iain, I. Lazaridis, N. Rohland, S. Mallick, N. Patterson, S. A. Roodenberg, E. Harney, K. Stewardson, D. Fernandes, M. Novak, K. Sirak, C. Gamba, E. R. Jones, B. Llama9, S. Dryomov, J. Pickrell, J. L. Arsuaga, J. M. Bermúdez de Castro, E. Carbonell, F. Gerritsen, A. Khokhlov, P. Kuznetsov, M. Lozano, H. Meller, O. Mochalov, V. Moiseyev, M. A. Rojo Guerra, J. Roodenberg, J. M. Vergès, J. Krause, A. Cooper, K. W. Alt, D. Brown, D. Anthony, C. Lalueza-Fox, W. Haak, R. Pinhasi & D. Reich

2015   Genome-wide Patterns of Selection in 230 Ancient Eurasians. *Nature* 528: 499-503.

Miller, Daniel J.

2005   "The Tibetan Steppe." In *Grasslands of the World*, edited by J. M. Suttie, S. G. Reynolds, and C. Batelo, Vol. 34, pp. 305–342. Food and Agriculture Organization of the United Nations, Rome.

Muñiz, Arturo Morales, and Ekaterina Antipina

2003   Srubnaya Faunas and beyond: A Critical Assessment of the Archaeozoological Information from the East European Steppe. In *Prehistoric Steppe Adaptation and the Horse*, edited by Marsha Levine, Colin Renfrew, and Katie Boyle, pp. 329–351. McDonald Institute, Cambridge.

Ostroshchenko, Vitaliy V.

2003   The Economic Peculiarities of the Srubnaya Cultural-Historical Entity. In *Prehistoric Steppe Adaptation and the Horse*, edited by Marsha Levine, Colin Renfrew, and Katie Boyle, pp. 319–328. McDonald Institute, Cambridge.

Peterson, D. L., P. F. Kuznetsov, and O. D. Mochalov

2006   The Samara Bronze Age Metals Project: Investigating Changing Technologies and Transformations of Value in the Western Eurasian Steppes. In *Beyond the Steppe and the Sown: Proceedings of the 2002 University of Chicago Conference on Eurasian Archaeology*, edited by D. L. Peterson, L. Popova and A. T. Smith, pp. 322–339. Colloquia Pontica Series. Brill, Leiden.

Popova, Laura M.

2007   A New Historical Legend: Tracing the LongTerm Landscape History of the Samara River Valley. In *Social Orders and Social Landscapes: Proceedings of the 2005 University of Chicago Conference on Eurasian Archaeology*, edited by Laura M. Popova, Charles Hartley, and Adam T. Smith. Cambridge Scholars Press, Newcastle.

Sedova, M. S.

2000   Poseleniya Srubnoi kul'tury [Settlements of the Srubnaya culture]. In *Istoriya Samarskogo Povolzh'ya c Drevneishikh Vremen do Nashikh Dnei: Bronzovy Vek* [History of the Samara Region from the Most Ancient Times to the Modern Day. Bronze Age], edited by I. Y. Kolev, A. E. Mamonov, and M. A. Turetskii, pp. 209–241. Integratsiya, Samara.

Semenova, A. P.

2001   Osnovnye tendentsii razvitiya keramiki Pokrovskogo i razvitogo etapov Srubnoi kultury lesostepnogo povolzh'ya. In *Bronzovyi Vek Vostochnoi Evropy: Kharakteristika kul'tur, Khronologiya i Periodizatsiya*, edited by Y. I. Kolev, pp. 273–279. Samarskii Gosudarstvennyi Universitet, Samara.

Vasiliev, I. B., and Pavel Kuznetsov

1988   Poltavkinskie mogil'niki u s. Krasnosamarskoe v lesostepnom zavolzh'e. In *Issledovanie Pamyatnikov Arkheologii Vostochnoi Evropy*, edited by A.T. Siniuk, pp. 39–59. Voronezhskii Gosudarstvennyi Pedagogicheskii Institut, Voronezh.

White, David Gordon.

1991   *Myths of the Dog-Man*. University of Chicago Press, Chicago.

Part II

History, Ecology, and Settlement Patterns in the Samara Oblast

Chapter 3

Historic Records of the Economy and Ethnic History of the Samara Region

Oleg D. Mochalov • Dmitriy V. Romanov • David W. Anthony

Ecological and Historic Setting

The headwaters of the Samara River lie in the southwestern piedmont of the Ural Mountains. The Samara is the last significant tributary of the Volga; past the Samara, the rivers that feed the Volga in the steppe zone are shallow and have narrow valleys (Figures 1.1 and 3.1). The Samara Valley, in contrast, is a broad plain up to 10 km wide, overlooked by eroded ridges more than 300 m high, while the mouth of the Samara River is only 25 m above sea level. The valley today supports interspersed pockets of steppe, forest, agricultural fields, and marshland crossed by the sinuous Samara River.

The borderland or frontier function of the Samara River valley is evident in human geography as well as in ecology. The border between Uralic (Finno-Ugric in this region) and Indo-European languages ran through today's Samara oblast (administrative region) for millennia, more or less corresponding with the border between steppe and forest-steppe but moving north or south in response to changes in politics and environment. The word *Volga* could be based on the Proto-Uralic *valkita*, meaning "white" or "bright," and the northern part of the oblast contains significant populations of Finno-Ugric-speaking Mari and Mordvin people. The drier southern part of the oblast, south of the Samara River, was occupied by Iranian-speaking nomadic Scythian tribes in the first millennium BC; they referred to the Volga as the *Rha* River, as it was still known to Ptolemy in about 150 AD. *Rha* possibly was derived from an Indo-Iranian root that also appeared in the ancient Avestan and Sanskrit names *Rañha* and *Rasah* for a mythical river supposed to flow around the earth (Lebedynsky 2002). The westward migrations and military campaigns of, first, the Turkic-speaking Bulgars and, later, the Mongol-speaking nomads drove the Iranian languages out of the western steppes and left the Samara oblast with a patchwork of Turkic, Mongol, and Uralic languages in the era before the rise of the Russian state.

Before the Crusades, an important branch of the Silk Road brought a significant portion of the trade between Europe and Asia through the Bulgar state in the Samara region. Ibn-Fadlan's journey in 921 to 922 AD to the Bulgar Khan at the city of Bulghar, north of Samara, provides the earliest written description of the region. The chronicler's attention was drawn first to the active trade between the Uralic-speaking forest people and the Turkic-speaking Bulgar khan and second to the presence of Scandinavian Vikings who had voyaged down the Volga to trade and raid; this ethnic mix was described by an Arabic-speaking visitor. The Russian state built a fort at the present site of Samara in 1586, and this began the Slavic settlement of the region. When the Russian state expanded eastward in the eighteenth century, it began by building a line of forts along the Samara River to Orenburg, then the eastern gateway of Russia, to protect the agricultural lands north of the Samara Valley.

This brief review of ethnic and ecological history shows that the Samara Valley frontier can be defined in three

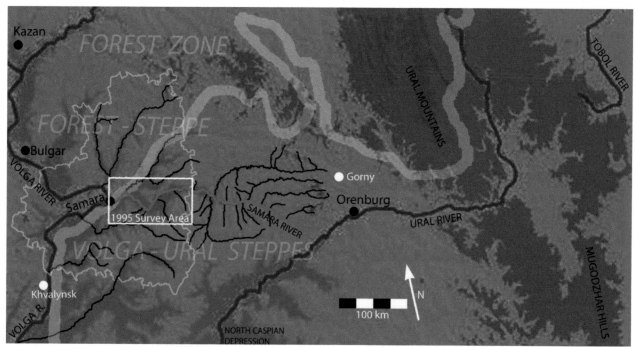

Figure 3.1 Map of Samara oblast. White square encloses the SVP survey area. Background map by the Ancient World Mapping Center (AWMC) *(www.unc.edu/awmc).*

different ways: it is an ecological border where different ecological zones meet, it is a communication corridor that controls east-west movements between Europe and Siberia, and it is a cultural frontier where very different languages, ethnicities, and economies interact. The archaeology of the Samara Valley is important partly because it reveals the interaction of cultural and ecological factors at a major Eurasian frontier.

The Samara River flows into the Volga at the Samara Bend, or Samarskaya Luka, a unique and visually stunning U-curve in the Volga River where the river encounters a massive limestone ridge 370 m (1,200 feet) high, Zhiguly Mountain. Before the construction of modern dams, the Volga flowed eastward for 65 km along the base of sheer white cliffs, cut its way south for 30 km, and then turned back west for another 65 km around the southern margin of Zhiguly Mountain before resuming its southward course. The city of Samara occupies a high ridge, a continuation of the Zhiguly promontory, on the southeastern end of the loop just before the river turns west, overlooking the estuary where the Samara River flows into the Volga. Here on the downstream side of the Luka, very extensive marshes created a rich environment for birds and fish and a useful source of fodder for livestock. The Volga River at Samara is 1,200 m wide, but its associated marshes and islands continue for another 10 to 12 km before Zhiguly Mountain is reached. The first Russian occupants of the Luka were

fishermen who appeared seasonally in the fourteenth and fifteenth centuries to catch sturgeon (beluga and sterlet) and whitefish.

The Samarskaya Luka illustrates another environmental contrast that characterizes the region: the western bank of the Volga is generally high and rocky, while the eastern bank is a low, undulating plain. The high western bank catches westerly winds that drop precipitation on the heights, nurturing forests that grow in the western Volga uplands, while the east bank is deprived of this moisture and exhibits a much more arid steppe landscape. Cultures that occupied the western Volga uplands could at some times have practiced a more settled economy, while cultures occupying the lowlands east of the river tended to depend more on pastoralism. The Volga River, more than 1,500 m (almost a mile) wide below Samara, separated two quite different environments.

Samara began as a military outpost that was intended to secure communications between Kazan, the last capital of the Turkic Bulgars 300 km upriver on the Volga, and Astrakhan, the last capital of the Mongol-descended Nogai nomads 700 km downriver, after both were conquered by Ivan the Terrible in 1552 and 1556. The fort at Samara, built in 1586, developed into a river port, but nomads from the southern steppes still used the Samara Valley as a favored summer grazing territory, and their raids on farming communities discouraged the agricultural settlement of the region through the mid-seventeenth century. Nevertheless, the fort attracted enough Russian settlers to designate Samara a town in 1688. Security improved when a line of forts was built up the Samara Valley to Orenburg in the 1730s. The archaeological remains of one of these forts, Krasni Yar, occupies a high ridge overlooking part of our project area north of the modern village of Utyevka. Catherine the Great invited foreigners, especially Germans, to settle in this frontier territory in 1762, and many Russian immigrants also took advantage of the improved security. By the late eighteenth century, Samara was an important center for trade. It was organized as a city with its own government in 1851. By 1892, it was an important railroad center where agricultural and livestock products were accumulated and shipped westward to Moscow and St. Petersburg. The city's population in 1890 was more than 60,000, and that of the Samara oblast (administrative province) was more than 2 million. Today, the city alone has a population of more than one million.

The middle Volga region, including the Samara Valley, was known as a pastoral region rich in herds and pastures when its economic products were first mentioned in written records, under the Volga Bulgar khans. According to the historian G. I. Peretkovich, the Volga Bulgars paid their tribute to the Golden Horde in leather and livestock, not in agricultural products, in the fourteenth century (Peretyatkovich 1877). From that time until the nineteenth century, livestock was the principal economic resource of the middle Volga region. However, after Russian settlement in the nineteenth century, Samara became an important grain-processing and exporting region. Agriculture yielded wheat, rye, oats, and millet, with enough surplus to export 50,000 tons of grain per year in some years by 1890. These surplus years were interrupted by serious droughts that caused crop failures and widespread famines in the late nineteenth century. Droughts were a constant danger because annual precipitation in the city of Samara is only about 550 mm (21 inches) per year, about the same as Jerusalem and significantly less than Rome. Still, agriculture produced an exportable surplus of grain in the Samara oblast in most years, even using the agricultural tools of the nineteenth century. The decision to depend primarily on agriculture or livestock was not dictated solely by the natural ecology of the region but was also a cultural choice.

The Sauromatians and Sarmatians

The earliest recorded inhabitants of the Samara region were the Sauromatians, who were related to the Scythians. Both names referred to early Iron Age nomadic cultures that lived in the Pontic-Caspian steppes after around the

eighth century BC. The names *Scythian*, *Sauromatian*, and *Sarmatian* seem to refer not to specific ethnic groups but to broad, shifting coalitions of various tribes. In archaeological terminology, the term *Sauromatian* is used for early Iron Age sites located east of the Don River, including the Samara oblast, dated between about 800 and 300 BC, while *Sarmatian* refers generally to the later Iron Age pastoral nomads of all of the Pontic-Caspian steppes between around 200 BC and the fifth century AD. All three groups—Scythians, Sauromatians, and Sarmatians—exhibited place names, personal names, and ethnonyms derived from Iranian languages of the East Iranian type, like Avestan Iranian. Sarmatian tribes such as the Thisomatae, Laxomatae, and the term *Sarmatian* itself are characterized by the suffix *-matae*, apparently meaning something like "tribe, people, men" in East Iranian. The first element of the name is compared to Avestan *zar-*, "old," by Lubotsky (2002:189–202).

The Sarmatians were also known as Alans in the west. They were described by the Roman historian Ammianus Marcellinus in this way in about 380 AD:

> They have no houses, and never use the plough, but live solely on meat and plenty of milk, mounted on their wagons which they cover with a curved awning made of the bark of trees, and then drive them through their boundless deserts. And when they come to any pasture land, they pitch their wagons in a circle, and live like a herd of beasts, eating up all the forage—carrying, as it were, their cities with them in their wagons. In them the husbands sleep with their wives—in them their children are born and brought up; these wagons, in short, are their perpetual habitation, and, wherever they fix them, that place they look upon as their home [Ammianus Marcellinus 1939:391].

In this description, we see the prototypical view that settled civilizations have always had about the Scythians, Sauromatians, and Sarmatians as the epitome of pastoral nomads. Their Bronze Age ancestors, however, never were described, so we do not know to what degree this stereotype, even if partly true, can be projected into the past. Bronze Age archaeological evidence presents quite a different picture, actually a sequence of shifting lifestyles, none of which are usually accepted as the equivalent of Iron Age pastoral nomadism. The forest cultures north of the Samara steppes, with whom the steppe people interacted, also were quite differently organized in the Iron Age from those in the Bronze Age. Iron Age forest communities occupied large timber-built, fortified settlements, supported by agriculture and stockbreeding (Koryakova and Epimakhov 2007:Chapter 7). The forest and steppe communities evolved together through a complex dialectic that produced different results in different ecological zones but nevertheless was mutually transforming.

The Bulgar Khanate of Kazan

The Bulgars originated among the Turkic-speaking tribes that swept over the western steppes in the sixth century AD. One branch of the Bulgars settled in the lower Danube Valley, giving modern Bulgaria its name. In the middle Volga region, another branch of the Bulgars established a state that included the agricultural northern part of the Samara oblast. By the tenth century AD, a multiethnic city, Bulgar, had been built 160 km south of modern Kazan; its archaeological remains are today found just north of the Samara oblast. This fortified city controlled a significant portion of the trade between Europe and Asia before the Crusades. Raids by Russian knights weakened Bulgar, and then in 1223, an advance guard of Genghis Khan's army under Uran, son of the great Mongol general Subutai Bahadur, attacked the Samara Valley and was defeated by a Bashkir and Bulgar army in a battle at Samarskaya Luka. From 1235 to 1236, Batu, son of Genghis Khan, returned with Subutai himself and subjugated the whole country, and from 1237 to 1240, they moved on to conquer the Kievan Rus in what is today Ukraine and much of Russia.

The capital of Batu's Golden Horde was on the lower Volga. But by the fifteenth century, the Golden Horde had broken into six independent khanates, the most important of which was the Kazan khanate on the middle Volga. From the mid-fifteenth to the mid-sixteenth centuries, the northern part of the Samara region was included in the territory of the multinational Kazan khanate, consisting of Turkic (Bulgar and Kipchak) and Uralic (Mordvin, Mari, Udmurt) peoples who were engaged in pastoralism, agriculture on arable lands, lumbering, hunting, fishing, crafts, and trade.

Agricultural settlements were established by the Bulgars in the middle Samara Valley during the tenth century and lasted until the Mongol conquest. Archaeological sites representing these agricultural settlements have been excavated on a northern tributary of the Samara, the Kinel' River, near the modern village Sukhaya Reka, and near Proletaryi, in the northern Samara oblast (Khalikova 1986; Kochkina and Stashenkov 1999).

The Bashkirs

The Magyars who conquered Hungary and imposed their Uralic language on that country in the ninth century AD were linguistic relatives of the Bashkirs of the tenth century. In the tenth century AD, when the Turkic Bulgars ruled the northern part of what is today the Samara oblast and the nomadic Turkic Pechenegs occupied the steppes to the south of the Samara River, between them lived another ethnic group, the Bashkirs, who claimed the territory on the north side of the Samara River. The Bashkirs first appeared as a pastoral Uralic-speaking population that practiced an economy of cattle herding and hunting in the forest-steppe zone. They used the territory on the north side of the Samara River as a summer grazing area for their herds and for hunting and trapping beavers. The principal hunting and herding territories of the Bashkirs were in the forest-steppe zone to the north and east, between the Samara and Ural Rivers; modern Bashkortostan is located on the upper Ural River. There were no permanent Bashkir settlements or towns in the Samara Valley, but their seasonal use of the valley for summer grazing was essential to their economy.

In 1236, the Mongols conquered the Bashkirs, who were already beginning to practice Islam and speak the Turkic language of the Kipchak Turks, who had moved into the forest zone on the Belaya River north of Samara oblast two centuries earlier. In the thirteenth and fourteenth centuries, Islam was widely adopted by the Bashkirs, seen archaeologically in the reduction in the number of pagan kurgan graves. The influence of the khanate of Kazan in the fourteenth and fifteenth centuries probably completed their linguistic conversion to the Turkic language. Peter the Great and Catherine the Great confirmed the now-Turkic-speaking Bashkirs in their possession of hunting and grazing lands in the Samara Valley in an effort to prevent the warfare that broke out frequently in the late seventeenth and early eighteenth centuries with incoming agricultural Russian settlers.

Between 1735 and 1740, the Russian state conquered the Bashkirs in the Samara and Orenburg regions. Indemnities imposed on the Bashkirs included the payment of 12,283 horses and 6,076 cattle and sheep. The suppression of the Pugachev Rebellion (1773–1775) finalized the inclusion of the Bashkirs in the Russian state. Today, there is a Turkic-speaking Bashkir minority population in the Samara oblast.

The Nogai Horde

After the Mongol conquest of 1236 to 1241, the western steppes of Russia and Ukraine were ruled by the sons of Batu, who was the son of Jochi, son of Genghis Khan. Batu's horde is sometimes called the Jochid Ulus but is usually known as the Golden Horde. One part of the Golden Horde, the Nogai, eventually gave their name to many of the nomads who lived in the Pontic-Caspian steppes. From the mid-sixteenth through the early seventeenth centuries, the south side of the Samara Valley was the border between the nomadic and hunting lands of the Nogai nomads, who occupied the steppes to the south, and the Bashkirs, who occupied the forest-steppe to the north. The extensive steppe lands south of the Samara River were referred to by Russian immigrants as the "wild field." For the Nogai horde, the Samara Valley was a rich and important summer pasture for their herds, quite distant from their winter refuges in the marshlands of the lower Volga in the Caspian Depression. Each summer, the Nogai would migrate with their herds over 600 km each way, from the lower Volga to the Bolshoi Irgiz (south of the Samara Valley), the Samara Valley, and the Kinel' River valley north of the Samara River, and then return to the marshlands around the lower Volga for the winter.

The steppes between the Volga and Ural Rivers were the central pastures for the Nogai horde, while the Bashkirs occupied the forest-steppe zone to the north. The steppe in this region was divided into pasture allotments that were tens of thousands of square kilometers in size. In the 1580s, the Englishman Anthony Jenkinson described the Nogai in this way: "Among the Nogai there are neither cities nor houses, they live in the open steppes. When the livestock eat all the grass in one place, they remove to another place. They are a pastoral people, their livestock make their wealth. They eat principally meat, mainly horse, and drink *koumiss* [mare's milk]" (Seredonin 1884:38). For the Nogai, wealth was measured in horses, sheep, cattle, and camels but particularly in horses. The Nogai never engaged in agriculture. A leading man or chief (called a *murza*) had on average 40,000 head of livestock of all kinds (Safargaliev 1949:49).

Livestock breeding produced the basic products for all other branches of the economy down to domestic crafts, including leather and wool for clothes and footwear, skins and felt for houses, and commodities for trade and exchange. The importance of horses among the Nogai, noted by Anthony Jenkinson, was confirmed by trade statistics: G. I. Peretyatkovich (1877) cited a document from 1534 that recorded that the Nogai supplied up to 50,000 horses to Moscow each year.

In 1552, the Kazan khanate was conquered by Ivan the Terrible, and the Samara region became part of the growing Russian state. Russian immigrants began to move on to the free lands and brought with them more effective types of agriculture and new crafts and industries.

The Kalmyks

In 1618, many thousands of Mongolian Oirats, led by the Torghut tribe, migrated from the upper Irtysh River westward across the steppes of Kazakhstan and the southern Ural steppes, raiding Russian agricultural settlements and Kazakh and Bashkir pastoral encampments as they went. They settled in 1630 in the lower Volga region on both sides of the river, conquering and expelling or absorbing the Nogai horde. They were called Kalmyks by their Muslim and Russian neighbors, a name they slowly adopted for themselves. The Kalmyk confederation at its peak around 1700 AD numbered approximately 280,000 persons, many of them probably formerly Nogai. Like the Nogai, the Kalmyks grazed horses, sheep, cattle, and camels, and even fishing and hunting were widely practiced. A small part of Kalmyks, those who converted to Christianity, engaged in agriculture on the north side of the Samara River, but its role was insignificant.

The Russian state settled more and more German and Russian colonists on lands and pastures that had formerly belonged to the Kalmyks, particularly after the line of forts was built in the 1730s up the Samara Valley as far east as Orenburg. In 1767, many thousands of German colonists were invited into the region by Catherine II; they created 57 agricultural colonies on the eastern tributaries of the Volga, including the Samara River. They were engaged in agriculture and trade (Dubman 1999). The Kalmyks came under increasing pressure to convert to Christianity and lost many of the pastures that had formerly been their summer grazing lands; they were also expected to supply cavalry to the armies of Russia. Unhappy with this increasing loss of autonomy, in the winter of 1770 to 1771, between 170,000 and 200,000 Kalmyks migrated across Kazakhstan back to Dzungaria, the homeland of the Oirats, to rejoin their relatives there. It was a disastrous journey; attacks by Kazakh and Kyrgyz enemies caused the enslavement of most of the migrants and the loss of their animals. Only one-third of those who began the trip arrived in Dzungaria. After failing to stop this migration, Catherine the Great abolished the Kalmyk khanate, and the Kalmyks remaining in the Volga steppes became subjects of the Russian government. Kalmykia today is an autonomous republic within Russia, centered on Astrakhan and the west side of the lower Volga.

The Cossacks

From the mid-sixteenth century, Russians began to settle in the Samara Volga region. At first, they built homes on islands and forested peninsulas where the water defended them. Agriculture, their former way of life, could not be practiced in the same way in the new circumstances because of the threat of attacks by nomads. Moreover, the people who were attracted to this dangerous frontier were themselves often prepared to use violence. They lived by fishing in the rich Volga fishery, hunting in the forests and steppes, and attacking and plundering their neighbors and any ships or trading caravans that might pass by. The earliest Cossack communities appeared in the steppe frontier regions of the Dnieper, Don, Volga, and Ural Rivers. They became a cultural and economic network; Cossacks of different areas communicated and had similar goals (Pronshtejn 1967:168, 172). Ukrainian Cossacks visited the Samara Volga region.

After the construction of the Russian government fort at Samara in 1586, the Cossacks disappeared from the Samara Valley, but they remained active on the Ural River steppe frontier and in the region. In the eighteenth century, the expansionist ambitions of the Russian empire relied on the loyalty of Cossacks, causing tension with their traditional independence. Rebellions instigated by Cossack leaders against the Russian state were led by Stenka Razin from 1670 to 1671 and Yemelyan Pugachev from 1774 to 1775. Both rebellions recruited heavily from Bashkir, Turkic, and Kalmyk populations around Samara, and both included important military engagements at the Samara fort in the present city of Samara. After the Pugachev rebellion, many Cossack hosts were dissolved, and the remaining Cossacks became a special social estate, often used to police borders and to provide cavalry units in wars in the Caucasus against the Ottoman Empire.

The Samara Economy in the Seventeenth to the Nineteenth Centuries

During the seventeenth century, the territory of the Samara Valley was divided between two quite distinct economies. Over the steppe part, mainly south of the Samara River and in parts of its middle and upper valley, extensive animal industries dominated, while in the lower river valley around Samarskaya Luka, agriculture prevailed (Kabytova 2000). The development of agriculture was caused by activities on the frontier by Russian, Mordvin, and Chuvash settlers, the latter Uralic speakers. The first written mention of agriculture in the Samara Valley dates to the 1620s. However, already earlier in the sixteenth century, Mordvin and Chuvash communities cultivated the lands around the Samarskaya Luka. Their system of agriculture was a shifting three-field system. But drought caused by the dry climate led to frequent poor harvests. Climate studies have shown that the thirteenth to eighteenth centuries witnessed a Little Ice Age, a climate much colder than today's on all of the European plain. The snow cover stayed longer, summer was colder, and rivers froze over earlier (Borisenkov et al. 1988). The main crops were rye and oats. Commercial crops included flax and hemp. The basic instruments were a plough, a harrow, a hand sickle, and a scythe. They had a special type of plow for plowing new ground called a *saban*.

During the eighteenth century, most agricultural activities in the Samara region were directed toward providing vegetables for local markets, or "truck" farming. Each inhabitant of the typical village had a fenced kitchen garden. In these gardens, they grew melons, watermelons, cucumbers, pumpkins, radishes, carrots, beets, cabbages, horseradish, turnips, green peppers, and tobacco. This kind of gardening has hardly changed to the present day. Syzran, on the west side of the Volga, was known for its apple orchards, and the Mordvin communities were famous as beekeepers (Lepekhin 1795:148).

In 1769, the German naturalist and explorer Peter Simon Pallas traveled through the region. He witnessed how the Russian population managed livestock breeding differently from the nomads who had ruled the region earlier and still lived in the steppe zone to the south. Referring specifically to communities north of the Samara River in Kinel'-Cherkassk, he observed,

> For cattle breeding they [local residents who were immigrants from Ukraine] have constructed cattle corrals in the steppe. The corrals hold many cattle, and in agricultural activity they generally use the bulls, though some men own by themselves 20 to 30 horses. Also there are many flocks of sheep, some farms having up to 400 sheep. However they say that their sheep in this country have become rather primitive and the wool on them grows already longer and thicker [probably the result of acclimatization of the Ukrainian stock, accustomed to a warmer climate] [Pallas 1773].

In this description, we find an alteration of the economy practiced by the nomads. Horses, apparently the most important export commodity and the basic source of meat and milk for the Nogai nomads, were much less important for the Russian-speaking population, although horse breeding remained an important industry in Samara. From 1850 to 1890, the most numerous animal in the herds around Samara was sheep. Of the 49 oblasts in European Russia, the Samara oblast ranked fourth place for its quantity of sheep, while the number of cattle in Samara oblast ranked only 33rd out of 49 oblasts. This can be illustrated with statistics taken from the year 1864 (Table 3.1).

In 1862, the Samara oblast imported commodities worth 886,315 rubles and exported commodities worth 13,806,280 rubles, for a profit of more than 12 million rubles. The value of wheat exports was 8.3 million rubles, and the value of animal products, principally lard packed in barrels, was 3.3 million rubles. After the railroad was

Table 3.1 1864 Herd Populations in Samara Oblast

	Horses	Cattle	Sheep (Ordinary)	Sheep (Thinfleece)	Pigs	Goats
Buzuluk District, Samara Oblast						
Number	180,800	69,900	383,700	19,900	24,100	2,500
Percentage	26.55	10.26	56.35	2.92	3.54	0.37
Samara District, Samara Oblast						
Number	109,300	46,900	33,500	15,700	16,900	800
Percentage	48.99	21.02	15.02	7.04	7.57	0.36
Samara Oblast All Together						
Number	824,900	467,900	1,514,100	1,285,000	235,900	571,000
Percentage	16.83	9.55	30.91	26.23	4.81	11.66

built between 1885 and 1895, linking Samara to the eastern provinces, the city became an important center for shipping grain from Siberia to central Russia.

Fishing always had a special value in the region because of the productivity of fishing on the Samarskaya Luka. The first Russian settlers in the region were fishermen who appeared on the Volga in the fourteenth and fifteenth centuries. Some monasteries, especially Savvo-Storozhevskii, were particularly engaged in the fishing industry.

In the seventeenth and the first half of the eighteenth centuries, hydrochloric acid and sulfur factories had special economic value in the Samara oblast. From the end of the sixteenth century on the Sok River north of the Samara River, sulfur mines began to operate; this led to a large manufacture of gunpowder in the eighteenth century, with three gunpowder factories eventually being established. Salt was mined in the Samarskaya Luka region for many millennia, beginning in the Bronze Age or earlier, but it greatly increased in the 1730s when it was also obtained from the drier southeastern part of the oblast. On the right bank of the Sok River near the village of Baitugan, Lepekhin (1795) and Pallas (1773) observed copper ores in the form of cupric sandstones and copper veins. These were exploited in the eighteenth century. Evidence was found during excavations connected with the Samara Valley project for Late Bronze Age copper working in the area of Bajtugan, at the site of Kibit. A well-known Late Bronze Age copper quarry and processing site has been excavated at Mikhailovka Ovsianka near the southeastern border of the Samara oblast, not far from the modern territory of Kazakhstan. The Samara region contained important deposits of copper, salt, and sulfur in addition to its wealth in animal and plant products.

Summary

This brief account of the historically known tribal confederations, states, and economies of the Samara region shows, above all, the diversity that has characterized this ecological and cultural frontier through all of recorded history. One underlying obvious pattern is that, before the rise of the Russian state, groups whose center of power was in the steppes were generally able to recruit more followers and enjoyed greater military power than those whose center of operation was in the northern forests. The Russian empire decisively reversed this trend, but it was evident in the military preeminence of the Sarmatians, the Turks, the Mongols, and even the pastoral Bashkirs and Cossacks over the forest-zone population. The military effectiveness of cavalry and the defensive advantage of a mobile population combined to maintain this inequality for millennia, an advantage ended only by guns and the organizational power of the Russian state.

Another clear pattern is the separation and interchangeable nature of language, ethnonyms, and populations. After the Mongol conquest, the steppe population remained Turkic speaking but changed to a Mongol ethnonym and Mongol political leadership. After the Turkic conquest, whatever Iranian population survived shifted its language, ethnonyms, and political leadership to the Turks, perhaps with a significant change in the basic population. The Bashkirs shifted from Uralic to Turkic speakers while retaining substantial political independence and continuity in population, while the Cossacks retained a Russian language and identity even after moving into the steppes and intermingling with many other pastoral groups. Equally interesting against all of these shifts in various kinds of identity is the survival of a major language frontier more or less at the steppe/forest-steppe ecotone, with occasional expansions and contractions across the transitional forest-steppe zone, between Uralic languages in the forests to the north and Turkic or Indo-European languages in the steppe zone to the south. This pattern also was disrupted only by the expansion of the Russian state and the spread of the Russian language. Because this linguistic contrast at the ecotone survived through various conquests, we can expect that the steppe and forest populations were linguistically distinct in the Bronze Age as well, with Uralic speakers to the north and Indo-European speakers to the south, the latter probably belonging to the Iranian branch.

Finally, we can see from this account that although extensive stockbreeding tended to dominate the economy of the Samara region in the historic past and that horses in particular were for a long time raised in great numbers here, agriculture and stockbreeding were both possible and actually quite productive in the Samara River valley, even with relatively primitive cultivation methods. Hunting was still productive and important to the Bashkirs well into the eighteenth century, and fishing is the greatest constant in the local economy. Climate change seems to have reduced the feasibility of agriculture in the Samara Valley during the Little Ice Age, 1300 to 1750 AD, although even then agriculture was conducted successfully. We do not know, however, precisely when agriculture first became a regular or expected part of the human geography in the Samara Valley or exactly how it was combined with stockbreeding in the Bronze Age. While the historically recorded past can give guidance to our interpretation of Bronze Age cultures and economies, the archaeological evidence clearly shows that those of the Bronze Age were different.

References

Ammianus Marcellinus.
1939   *History of Rome from Constantine to Valens.* Vol. III. Loeb Classical Library, London.

Borisenkov, E. P., V. M. Paseckij, and M. E. Lyakhov
1988   Ekstremal'nyye klimaticheskiye yavleniia v Evropeiskoi chasti Rossii [Extreme climatic features of the European part of Russia]. In *Klimaticheskiye Izmeneniya za 1000 Let* [Climate Change during the Last Millennium], edited by E. P. Borisenkov, pp. 205–209. Gidrometeoizdat, Leningrad.

Dubman, E. L.
1999   Promyslovoe predprinimatel'stvo i osvoenie ponizovogo Povolzh'ja v konce XVI–XVII vv. Samara.

Kabytova, P. S. (editor)
2000   *Istoriia Samarskogo Povolzh'ia s drevneishih vremen do nashih dnei. XVI – pervaja polovina XIX veka.* Nauka, Moskva.

Khalikova, E. A.
1986   *Musul'manskie nekropoli Volzhskoi Bulgarii X-nachal XIIIvv.* Kazanskogo Universiteta, Kazan.

Kochkina, A. F., and D. A. Stashenkov
1999   Issledovanie musul'manskogo mogil'nika u d. Proletarii. In *Okhrana I Izuchenie Pamyatnikov Istorii I Kul'tury v Samarskoi Oblasti*, Vol. 1, edited by I. N. Vasil'eva and M. A. Turetskii, pp. 179–200. Samarskii oblastnoi istoriko-kraevedcheskii muzei im. P.V. Alabina, Samara.

Koryakova, L., and A. V. Epimakhov
2007   *The Urals and Western Siberia in the Bronze and Iron Ages.* Cambridge University Press, Cambridge.

Lebedynsky, Iaroslav
2002   *Les Sarmates: Amazones et lanciers cuirassés entre Oural et Danube.* Editions Errance, Paris.

Lepekhin, I. I.
1795   *Dnevnye zapiski puteshestvija po raznym provincijam Rossijskogo gosudarstva.* SPb. Ch.1 S.148. RGDA. F. 237. Op.1. D.35. 1684 g. L.140, 143 F.237.Op.1. Ch.II D.255.1702 g. L.2 ob. Russian Academy of Sciences, Saint-Petersburg.

Lubotsky, Alexander
2002   Scythian Elements in Old Iranian. In *Indo-Iranian Languages and Peoples* (Proceedings of the British Academy 116), edited by N. Sims-Williams, pp. 189–202. Oxford University Press, Oxford.

Pallas P. S.
1773   *Puteshestvie po razlichnym provintsiyam Rossiyskoy imperii.* Sankt-Peterburg.

Peretyatkovich, G. I.
1877   *The Samara Volga Region in the XV–XVI Cen.* Moscow.

Pronshtejn, A. P.
1967   K istorii vozniknovenija kazach'ih poselenij i obrazovanija soslovija kazakov na Donu // Novoe o proshlom strany. M., S. 168, 172. Institute of Russian History, Moscow.

Safargaliev, M. G.
1949   Nogajskaja Orda vo vtoroj polovine XVI veka // Sbornik nauchnyh rabot Mordovskogo gosudarstvennogo pedagogicheskogo instituta. Saransk. S.49. Mordovian State Pedagogical Institute, Saransk.

Seredonin, S. M.
1884   Izvestija anglichan o Rossii v XVI v. *Cheteniya v Obshschestve Istorii I Drevnestei Rossiskikh pri Moskovskom Universitete* 4:1–105.

Chapter 4

The Samara Valley in the Bronze Age: A Review of Archaeological Discoveries

Pavel F. Kuznetsov • Oleg D. Mochalov

(Translated from Russian by David W. Anthony)

The Samara River is an eastern tributary of the Volga River, connecting the Volga with the Ural region, which is to say that it connects Europe with Asia. It flows through an ecological border between the steppe and forest-steppe zones. The northernmost point of the Eurasian steppe zone occurs north of the Samara Valley, a salient of grassland surrounded by mixed forest and meadow steppe. The border ecology of the area is unique and strongly affected its cultural and economic development. Although today the Samara Valley is intensively farmed, during the Bronze Age, the focus of this chapter, the ecological resources within the Samara drainage were exploited more often through pastoralism. In the Early Bronze Age (EBA) and Middle Bronze Age (MBA), we can see a mobile form of pastoralism with almost no archaeological evidence of settlements, and in the Late Bronze Age (LBA), many new settlements indicate the beginning of a sedentary form of pastoralism perhaps with some agriculture. The Bronze Age cultures were preceded in the Samara Valley by a variety of archaeological sites dated to the Mesolithic (hunter-fishers without ceramics), Neolithic (hunter-fisher cultures possessing ceramics), and Eneolithic (early domesticated animals and copper) periods, with substantial continuity and evolution between eras. This review is concerned only with Bronze Age sites.

During the Samara Valley Project (SVP), Russian-U.S. teams cooperated in conducting site surveys that continued a long-term goal among Samara archaeologists to collect information on the locations and contents of prehistoric monuments in the Samara Valley. Today, we have sufficient material data to permit generalizations about the chronology of human activities in the Samara River valley, the diverse cultural patterns that distinguished different Bronze Age phases, and the economic activities of the Bronze Age populations. Such information can be obtained, recorded, and synthesized only through collaboration between related fields of science in an integrated approach. In this chapter, our purpose is to publish as much information as possible about the sites and site literature, amounting to a catalogue of the prehistoric monuments of the Samara River drainage.

History of Archaeological Investigations in the Samara Valley

The first exploration of ancient sites and kurgans in the Samara drainage occurred in the upper reaches of the Samara Valley, in the Orenburg oblast near the Urals, where F. D. Nefedov conducted exploratory expeditions in 1887 (Nefedov 1899), which continued under K. V. Gland and other researchers. The first archaeological survey in the lower reaches of the Samara Valley, in the Samara oblast, was undertaken by A. Miller in 1907. Seven years later, in 1914, F. T. Yakovlev examined archaeological deposits, including the remains of a Srubnaya settlement, found eroding out of the sand dune at Zakhar-Kal'ma (Figure 4.1: Site 82). In the 1920s, Vera V.Golmsten (1925) and M. G. Matkin conducted largely exploratory investigations in the lower Samara Valley, recording many sites, for example, Monasheskii Khutor and Kirpichni Sarai (Figure 4.1: Sites 98, 99), two more sites containing LBA Srubnaya settlement components. After a hiatus of many decades, N. Y. Merpert, later a chief scientific officer at the Institute of Archaeology in the Russian Academy of Sciences, excavated many Srubnaya sites in the lower Samara Valley as a leader of the Kuibyshev Expedition (Merpert 1958).

The most intensive and extensive work undertaken by archaeologists began in the 1970s, under the direction of archaeologists from Samara. The most prominent director of fieldwork in the 1970s and 1980s was Igor B. Vasiliev, deputy director of the Institute of History and Archaeology of the Urals Branch of the Academy of Sciences in Ekaterinburg and professor at Samara State Pedagogical Institute, today the Volga State Academy of Social Sciences and Humanities. Vasiliev directed excavations at many sites and conducted the first surveys to create maps of all sites, excavated and unexcavated, in the Samara Valley. Particularly important were his excavations at the Eneolithic cemeteries of S'yezzhee (Vasiliev and Matveeva 1979) and Khvalynsk (Agapov et al. 1990), his exploration of the Sintashta-related Potapovka and Utyevka cemeteries (Vasiliev et al. 1994) and his discovery of Eneolithic and Bronze Age settlements in the semi-deserts of the lower Volga (Vasiliev 1998). In 1987, Vasiliev directed the survey that mapped the kurgan cemeteries around Krasnosamarskoe (153 on Figure 4.1), including Krasnosamarskoe IV, the site that first attracted the joint U.S.-Russian team to the location where the Srubnaya settlement was found in 1995 (Vasiliev and Kuznetsov 1988).

The surveys and excavations of the 1970s and 1980s showed that Bronze Age sites in the Samara Valley were more numerous, and richer in terms of grave gifts, than the sites of any other ancient period. Cultures centered in the steppes and the northern forest-steppe zones met and interpenetrated here during the Bronze Age, when both ecological zones were home to very active, well-defined, and innovative cultures. All the cultures and cultural types that archaeologists have defined for the Bronze Age of the Volga-Ural region can be found in the Samara Valley. These cultures are briefly described below.

Archaeological Cultures of the Bronze Age in the Samara Valley

In Russian archaeology, the concept of the archaeological culture is the subject of many-sided debates. Different points of view on this subject are connected to larger disagreements about the evolution of society, the possibility or even the desirability of deriving ethnocultural meanings and significance from material archaeological remains, and about how to categorize different kinds and degrees of cultural or historical relations (discussed in English by Guliaev 1993; Klejn 1993; and Yablonsky 2002; for a history of concepts in the early Soviet period, see Shnirelman 1995). This is a particularly acute problem in an ecological border region where a shared material adaptation to the steppe or the forest-steppe environment might obscure differences between people with distinct ethnocultural origins. We will not choose here between the various theoretical positions on the relationship between archaeological artifacts/monuments and ethnic cultures. In just one English-language source, the Srubnaya phenomenon is named a cultural-historical region by Malov (1994, 2002) or a horizon by Yablonsky (2002). Here we use Srubnaya culture as a neutral archaeological term. Nevertheless, we accept multidisciplinary arguments derived from historical sources, linguistics, toponyms, and archaeology (Kuzmina 2007) that the Srubnaya, Andronovo, and probably Abashevo archaeological cultures were connected in some way with languages of the Indo-Iranian group.

The earliest culture of the Bronze Age was the EBA Yamnaya culture, a pastoral culture defined only by burial mounds (kurgans) (Figure 4.2). (Again, the Yamnaya phenomenon is called a horizon, an economic-historical region, a cultural-historical region, and other descriptions. Here we use *culture* as an archaeological term.) No Yamnaya settlements have been discovered in the Volga-Ural region. The oldest Yamnaya graves are dated between around 3300 to 3000 BC in the lower Volga and lower Don steppes as well as in the Samara oblast. For example, two Yamnaya graves in the Samara oblast are dated before 3000 BC at Nizhny Orleansky cemetery I, Kurgan 4, Grave 2, 4520 ± 75 BP, calibrated 3497 to 2933 BC, and at Kutuluk, Kurgan 4, Grave 1, (OxA-4306) 4400 ± 70 BP and (AA-12570) 4370 ± 75 BP, calibrated 3100 to 2800 BC. Two Yamnaya wagon graves were excavated at Shumaevo in Kurgans 2 and 6, in the Orenburg region just east of the Samara oblast (Morgunova and Khokhlova 2006; Morgunova and Turetskii 2003). It is probable that Yamnaya people lived in wagon camps, kept herds of sheep and cattle, and moved their place of residence frequently. They also mined copper at Kargaly and made metal tools and weapons. The dated Yamnaya grave at Kutuluk contained a 48-cm-long solid copper mace, weighing 770 g. See Chapter 11 for an analysis of this object by Peterson.

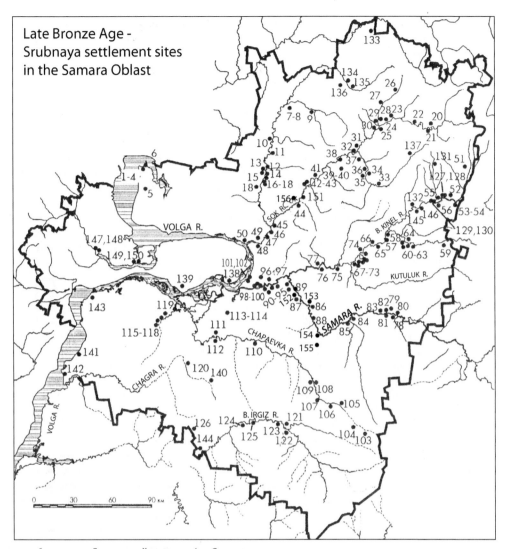

Figure 4.1 Map of all Srubnaya (Late Bronze Age) settlement sites in the Samara oblast. Sites mentioned in chapter 4: 79. Konovalovka, 80. Nemchanka, 81. Vilovatoye, 82. Zakhar-Kal'ma, 84. S'yezzhee, 85. Maksimovka, 87. Nur, 88. Poplavskoe, 98. Monasheskii Khutor, 99. Kirpichni Sarai, 100. Grachev Sad, 152. Spiridonovka Settlement, 153. Krasnosamarskoe, 154. Barinovka, 155. Peschanyi Dol I, 156. Russkaya Selit'ba II. (After Kolev et al. 2000-227)

1-4 - Хрящевка; 5 - дорога Ягодное - Хрящевка; 6 - Сускан; 7,8 - Лузановка; 9 - Мазуровка; 10 - Красное Поселение; 11 - Горностаевка; 12 - Шабановка;13 - Елховка; 14 - Чесноковка; 15 - Булькуновка; 16 - Алмазовка; 17 - Константиновка-Алмазовка; 18 - Высокая Грива; 19 - Калиновка (Кобельма); 20 - II Старое Вечканово; 21 - I Старое Вечканово; 22 - Валентиновка; 23 - Исаклы; 24 - Заря; 25 - Ново-Обошино; 26 - Суруш; 27 - Ключи; 28 - II Чесноковское; 29 - I Чесноковское; 30 - Подгоры; 31 - Рогатка; 32 - Сергиевск; 33 - Умет; 34 - I Калиновское; 35 - II Калиновское; 36 - III Серноводское; 38 - Павловка; 39,40 - Нероновка; 41 - Чесноковка-Чекалино; 42,43 - Раковские; 44 - Лужковские; 45 - Нижне-Солонцовка; 46 - Красный Яр; 47 - Белозерка; 48 - Старо-Семейкино; 49 - Вислая Дубрава; 50 - Волжский (Царевщина); 51 - Терегелевка; 52 - Нугай; 53, 54 - Венера I, II; 55 - Осиновые Ямы; 56 - Чувашская Поляна; 57 - Винная Багановка; 58 - Сопляки; 59 - Березняки; 60 - хут.-Микулино; 61 - Лозовка; 62 - I Лозовское; 63 - II Лозовское; 64 - Полуденка; 65 - Толкай; 66 - Кинель-Черкассы; 67,70 - II Осиновские; 71,72 - I,II Алексеевские; 73 - II Федоровское; 74 - Ключи; 75 - Георгиевка; 76 - Тургеневка; 77 - Кривая Лука; 78 - Широченка; 79 - Коноваловка; 80 - Немчанка; 81 - Виловатое; 82 - Захар-Калма; 83 - Марычевка; 84 - Съезжее; 85 - Максимовка; 86 - Мочи; 87 - Нур; 88 — Поплавское; 89-90 — Подлесное I, II; 91 - Бажаниха; 92,93 - I, II Белозерские; 94-95 - I,II Черновские; 96 - Алексеевка; 97 - Черноречье; 98 - Монашеский Хутор; 99 - Кирпичные Сараи; 100 - Грачев Сад; 101 - Постников Овраг; 102 - Барбашина Поляна; 103 - Пушкарка; 104 - Горяиновка; 105 - Летниково; 106 - I Ивановское; 107 - II Ивановское; 108 - Озерное; 109 - Знамя Труда; 110 - Сухая Вязовка; 111 - Воздвиженка; 112 - совхоз Чапаева; 113,114 - I,II Воскресенское; 115,118 - I-IV Сосновские; 119 - Григорьевское; 120 - Криволучье; 121 - Каралык; 122 - Большая Глушица; 123 - Малая Глушица; 124,125 - I,II Высоковское; 126 - Михайло-Овсянка; 127 - Точка; 128 - Красные Пески; 129-130 - Сухая Речка III, IV; 131 - Новый Аманак; 132 - Дальне-Азинск; 133 - Тимашево; 134 - Токмакла; 135 - Красный Строитель; 136 - Озерки; 137 - Малое Микушкино; 138 - Шелехметь I; 139 - Севрюкаево; 140 - Кировское; 141 - Федоровка; 142 - Екатериновка; 143 - Сачково; 144 - Ялта; 145 - Лагеревка; 145 - Остроумовка; 147,148 - I ,II Шигонские; 149 - Моечное Озеро; 150 — Комаровка; 151 - Лебяжинка V.

152. Spiridonovka Settlement, 153. Krasnosamarskoe, 154. Barinovka, 155. Peschanyi Dol I, 156. Russkaya Selitba II

(Map from Kolev, Mamonov, Turetsky, 2000 p. 227)

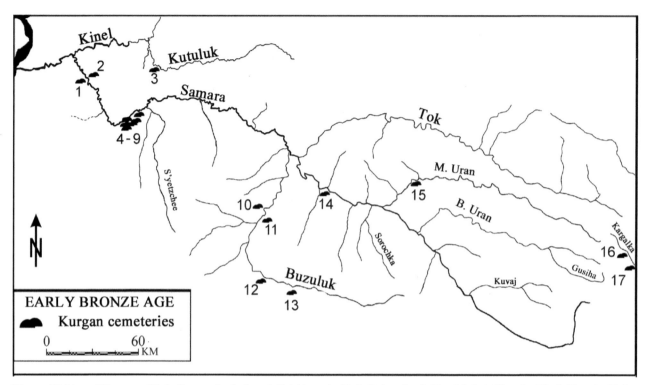

Figure 4.2 Map of Yamnaya (Early Bronze Age) sites: 1. Spiridonovka II, 2. Bobrovka, 3. Kutuluk I, 4. Utyevka III, 5. Utyevka V, 6. Utyevka IX, 7. Leshevskoe I, 8. Pokrovka I, 9. Andreevka, 10. Kurmanaevka III, 11. Petrovskii, 12. Ephimovka, 13. Sverdlovo V, 14. Medvedka, 15. Grachevka, 16, Pershin, and 17. Uranbash. (map by Kuznetsov)

This mobile form of pastoral economy continued into the MBA, dated around 2800 to 2200 BC, with the Poltavka culture (Figure 4.3). The Poltavka culture was an MBA pastoral culture quite similar to Yamnaya, also known almost exclusively through its graves, but with a distinctive style of pottery and changes in the shape of the grave pit and in details of the mortuary rituals, as well as in metal tools and weapon styles. Poltavka cemeteries are distributed from the Ural River steppes on the northeast to the lower Volga-Don steppes on the southwest, in the same geographic region as the northeastern group of the early Yamnaya culture. In the Volga-Don steppes, Poltavka cemeteries overlap geographically and chronologically with cemeteries of the MBA Catacomb culture, typical of the lower Don, Caspian, North Caucasian, and Pontic steppes. Some Poltavka graves in the region of contact with the Catacomb culture have a small side chamber or catacomb for the body off the bottom of the grave shaft, similar to the grave feature that gives the Catacomb culture its name, but Catacomb culture side chambers usually are T-shaped, with a side chamber approached by a straight tunnel, while Poltavka side chambers on the lower Volga usually are shallow hollows that are undercut into the side

of the grave. Typically, Poltavka graves in the Volga-Ural region and in the Samara Valley have no side chamber.

Another MBA culture seen in the Samara Valley, more settled than Poltavka, is known as the Vol'sko-Lbishche group. These sites are located on the elevated, forested height west of the Volga, within the curve of the Samarskaya Luka (Figure 4.3). Some pottery of this type is found in several sites in the Samara Valley, including at the Krasnosamarskoe settlement. These Samara Valley sites represent the eastern extension of this culture from its localized center on the west side of the Volga and belong to the second half of the third millennium BC.

Sites of the Abashevo culture, dated to the middle and second half of the third millennium BC, also appeared in the Samara Valley. Abashevo was connected materially with Fatyanovo and other Corded Ware cultures of eastern and central Europe (Pryakhin 1980). It originated in the forest-steppe ecological zone between the upper Don and the southern Ural Mountains, but a limited number of settlements and cemeteries extended into the Samara Valley from the north, as far south as Barinovka (Figure 4.1: Site 154). Abashevo was a forest-steppe culture of cattle-herding pastoralists who developed a varied material

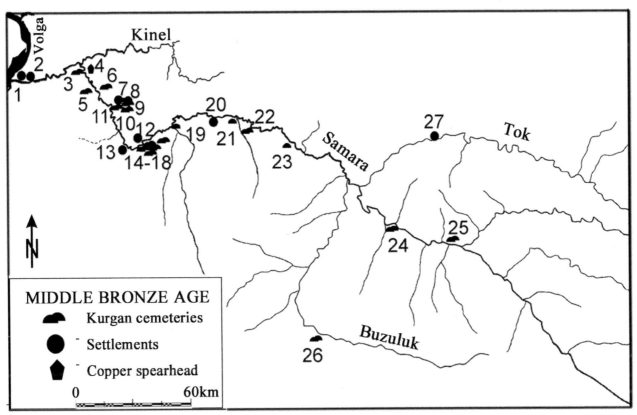

Figure 4.3 Map of Middle Bronze Age sites, all types: Poltavka, Abashevo, Vol'sko-Lbishche, and Potapovka. 1. Grachev Sad—Abashevo, 2. Kirpichni Sarai—Abashevo, Vol'sko-Lbishche, 3. Nikolaevka III—Poltavka, 4. Uste' Reki Kinel'. Nakonechnik kopya—Abashevo, 5. Nur III—Poltavka, 6. Bobrovka—Poltavka, 7. Krasnosamarskoe settlement—Vol'sko-Lbishche, 8. Krasnosamarskoe IV—Poltavka, 9. Krasnosamarskoe III—Poltavka, 10. Krasnosamarskoe II—Poltavka, Abashevo, 11. Krasnosamarskoe I—Poltavka, 12. Chelovech'ya Golova—Abashevo, Vol'sko-Lbishche, 13. Barinovka—Abashevo, Potapovka, 14. Utyevka I—Poltavka, 15. Utyevka III –Poltavka, 16. Utyevka V—Poltavka, 17. Utyevka VI—Poltavka, Potapovka, 18. Pokrovka I—Poltavka, 19. S'yezzhee—Abashevo(?), 20. Vilovatoye—Abashevo, 21. Shirochenka—Poltavka, 22. Gvardeitsi II—Poltavka, 23. Koltuban—Poltavka, 24, Medvedka—Poltavka, 25. Nikiforovskoe Lesnichestvo—Abashevo, 26. Ephimovka—Poltavka, 27. Ivanovka—Abashevo. (map by Kuznetsov)

culture that included copper mining and bronze casting on a significant scale. Abashevo bronze work included very large cast bronze shaft-hole axes and small distinctive copper or bronze ornaments worn around the head and face by women. A mass grave of 28 violently killed Abashevo men at Pepkino in the middle Volga forest-steppe zone attests to large-scale battles between forces armed with bronze axes and daggers, dated by radiocarbon to around 2200 to 2100 BC (3850 ± 95 BP).

Between around 2100 and 1800 BC, the final centuries of the MBA (MBA II in this volume), kurgan cemeteries of the innovative Potapovka type appeared on the Sok and Samara Rivers (Figure 4.3). The Potapovka graves at Utyevka VI in the Samara Valley were far richer and contained many more weapons than the graves of any earlier culture. Grave contents included paired horse burials, warrior equipment related to chariots such as cheekpieces for bits, socketed

bronze spearheads, daggers, and ornaments, including one gold ornament. Potapovka was contemporary with and related to the Sintashta culture, located in the steppes southeast of the Ural Mountains. Potapovka and Sintashta ceramic vessels were very similar, and in other categories of material culture, the two cultural groups were clearly related. Both displayed some customs that were similar to Abashevo (particularly in ceramics) and others that were similar to Poltavka (particularly in graves). Potapovka people remained mobile, while Sintashta people lived in fortified settlements. Potapovka was the last Bronze Age culture that practiced mobile pastoralism in the Samara Valley.

Around 1900 to 1800 BC, Potapovka ceramic styles evolved into the simpler ceramic types of the first LBA culture of the Samara Valley, the Srubnaya culture, which exhibited the first permanent settlements. This transition to sedentary life was the principal focus of the Samara Valley

Project. Srubnaya cemeteries were the first that contain entire social groups. In the EBA and MBA, only a few individuals, usually adult men, were selected for kurgan burial; in the Potapovka period, it seems that some families were admitted to kurgans; and in the LBA, the whole social group, with children, was buried, providing many more individuals for demographic and skeletal studies.

The mature Srubnaya phase, around 1800 to 1200 BC, evolved after 1200 BC into several Final Bronze Age variants such as Suskanskaya; sites were concentrated near the mouth of the Samara. By the early Iron Age, around 800 BC, the Samara Valley returned to a territory of mobile nomads, and settlements were again in wagon camps, making them invisible archaeologically. Iron Age–fortified settlements of the Gorodetskaya culture were located in the forest-steppe zone north and west of the Volga. Level 1 of the LBA Krasnosamarskoe settlement contained a low-density iron-working camp of the Gorodetskaya culture. This site probably was an excursion into the Samara Valley by Gorodetskaya iron makers, who deposited their typical pottery and a bloom of iron in a hearth at Krasnosamarskoe (Figure 10.10).

The Samara Valley is represented by a unique material culture formed through the contact and syncretism of steppe and forest-steppe cultures. Moreover, some individual sites in the Samara drainage, such as Kutuluk (the Yamnaya grave with the largest metal artifact in any Yamnaya grave), Utyevka I (the richest single Yamnaya-Poltavka grave in the Volga-Ural steppes), and Utyevka VI (the richest Potapovka cemetery) are crucial for any understanding of the archaeology of the Bronze Age in the Volga-Ural steppes. These sites are described in almost 50 publications that discuss the Bronze Age archaeology of the Samara Valley, some of them as a part of a larger topic (see, e.g., Korenevsky 1980:59–66).

In recent years, active field research in the Samara Valley resulted in many publications (Demkin 1999; Ivanov et al. 2001; Kosintsev and Roslyakova 2000; Lavrushin and Spiridonov 1995; Petrenko 1995). We have obtained many new absolute dates on Bronze Age sites (Kuznetsov 1996:56–59). Radiocarbon dating confirms the previously identified chronological sequence of cultures and permits an estimation of the length of each phase of the Bronze Age (Kuznetsov 2003).

Bronze Age Sites in the Samara Valley

The Samara River valley, in 2002, contained 131 known and mapped Bronze Age sites, counting all settlements, camps, hoards, chance surface finds, and cemeteries as separate sites. Around 95 of these were tested with some kind of excavation. Most are located in the middle and lower reaches of the river valley, in the Samara oblast, with two strong concentrations, one near the mouth of the Samara on the Volga and the other near the confluence of the Bolshoi Kinel' River with the Samara. In the upper Samara Valley, in the Orenburg oblast, a smaller number of sites are excavated and the region is still incompletely investigated. Much of the known and excavated Bronze Age material from the Samara Valley is not fully published. It is interesting that the majority of Bronze Age cemeteries are located on the left bank, the side of the valley that adjoins the steppe zone. However, many settlements are located on the right (northern) bank of the river, closer to the forest-steppe. Sites in the lower valley are mainly located directly on the Samara floodplain. In the middle and upper reaches, there is a tendency for sites to be located on tributary streams, for example, on the rivers Tok, Buzuluk, and Bol'shoi Uran.

Of the 70 recorded Bronze Age settlements in the Samara Valley, 35 have been investigated by modern archaeologists, and of these, 19 were described in a publication. Most of the known Bronze Age settlements are dated to the LBA. Of the 61 known Bronze Age cemeteries, 32 were described in a publication. Most of the cemeteries were first created in the EBA and MBA, although many were reused in the LBA. Here we consider 29 of the 35 excavated settlements and 50 of the 61 known Bronze Age cemeteries.

Bronze Age Settlements
The MBA: Abashevo, Vol'sko-Lbishche, Potapovka, and Poltavka

The earliest Bronze Age settlement sites in the Samara Valley belong to the MBA. The preceding population of the EBA, 3300 to 2800 BC, is represented by Yamnaya kurgan cemeteries (see Bronze Age Cemeteries below) but produced no detectable settlements.

Probably the first MBA settlement sites that were established in the Samara Valley can be ascribed to the Abashevo culture. These sites defined the southern border of the Abashevo occupation zone. A typologically early Abashevo settlement was established in the lower Samara Valley in our project area at Vilovatoye (Figure 4.3: Site 20; Figure 2.1: SVP 41). This phase is dated at other Abashevo sites between 2500 and 2100 BC. A few Abashevo sherds were found at Barinovka during the SVP survey in 1995 and during the excavation at Barinovka in 1996 (Figure 4.3: Site 13; Figure 2.9), and Abashevo settlement components occur near the mouth of the Samara River at Kirpichni Sarai and Grachev Sad (Figure 4.3: Sites 1, 2). Other Abashevo and "Abashevoid" ceramic assemblages are recorded at six settlements in the upper Samara Valley, including Ivanovka on the Tok tributary almost in the forest-steppe zone (Figure 4.3: Site 27). In all six of the Abashevo settlement sites in the Tok drainage, Abashevo materials are covered by Srubnaya occupations of the LBA. However, there was a chronological and cultural gap between these occupations, and the earliest Srubnaya phase is usually absent, as at Ivanovka. This separation is an important archaeological indication of the absence of direct evolutionary development between the Abashevo culture and the Srubnaya culture.

Another settled culture of the MBA, the Vol'sko-Lbishche culture, was centered on the west side of the Volga. Small assemblages of ceramics of Vol'sko-Lbishche type are found at three settlements in the Samara Valley: Kirpichni Sarai (Figure 4.3: Site 2), Chelovech'ya Golova (Figure 4.3: Site 12), and the Krasnosamarskoe settlement (Figure 4.3: Site 7). These sites represent the easternmost extension of that culture.

The Potapovka culture appeared in the middle Volga steppes at the end of the MBA (MBA II, 2100–1800 BC). A very rich Potapovka cemetery was excavated in the Samara Valley at Utyevka VI (Figure 4.3: Site 17). But Potapovka settlements are not known in the Samara Valley or in the Sok River valley to the north, where Potapovka cemeteries are principally concentrated. Potapovka ceramics are found at only one possible settlement site in the Samara Valley, Barinovka (Figure 4.3: Site 13; Figure 2.1: SVP 5), and even there only a few sherds were found at a site that contained mostly LBA materials.

MBA settlements and seasonal camps occurred in only 12 known sites in the Samara Valley, and 8 contained Abashevo components. Three others contained components of Vol'sko-Lbishche pottery derived from another settled forest-steppe MBA culture. Only two, overlapping with the last three, contained Poltavka pottery derived from mobile MBA pastoralists. Poltavka sherds were mixed with Srubnaya materials at Krasnosamarskoe (Figure 4.3: Site 7) and at the seasonal camp at Peschanyi Dol (PD) 1 (Figure 2.1: Sites 70–75). But at PD1, the MBA seasonal camp was 10 times lower in artifact density than the LBA seasonal camp, suggesting higher mobility in Poltavka seasonal camps. All 12 MBA settlement sites in the Samara Valley were reoccupied in the LBA.

The LBA: Srubnaya and Andronovo

The majority of the Bronze Age settlements in the Samara Valley are dated to the LBA, after 1900/1800 BC, like Krasnosamarskoe (Figure 4.1: Site 153), or to the Final Bronze Age, after about 1200 BC, like Nur and Poplavskoe (Figure 4.1: Sites 87, 88). LBA settlements usually are located on the floodplain or on lowest terrace above the floodplain,

often near oxbow lakes. In addition to these floodplain-oriented settlements, other LBA settlements were located on dune formations that supported pine forests. The best known of these dune sites are the following eight: Nur (Figure 4.1: Site 87), Zakhar-Kal'ma (Site 82), Vilovatoye (Site 81), Andreevskaya Dune (Figure 2.1: SVP 1), Chelovech'ya Golova (Figure 4.3: Site 12), Nemchanka (Figure 4.1: Site 80), and Konovalovka (Figure 4.1: Site 79).

There are 29 archaeologically explored Srubnaya settlement sites in the Samara Valley. Table 4.1, derived from our Samara Valley survey (see Chapter 2), lists 29 Srubnaya settlements located on the main branch of the Samara River and in a few other places. Seventeen settlements contain only a single LBA cultural component, usually the mature phase of the Srubnaya culture. In five settlements in Table 4.1, the Srubnaya occupation is covered by a Final Bronze Age (FBA) settlement. LBA/FBA-stratified settlements are concentrated outside the Samara Valley, in the northern Samara oblast on the Sok River, or near the Samarskaya Luka, on the west side of the Volga. At five settlements in Table 4.1, the Srubnaya occupation was preceded by MBA occupation. MBA/LBA settlements were more widely distributed than FBA settlements. The decline in permanent settlements was particularly steep on the main branch of the Samara River and in the steppes to the south (Figure 4.3), although a few favored locations remained occupied and contained materials of four or even five archaeological cultures: Maksimovka (Figure 4.1: Site 85), Kirpichni Sarai (Site 99), Grachev Sad (Site 100), Vilovatoye (Site 81), and Nur (Site 87).

The Srubnaya culture created the most widely distributed and most numerous Bronze Age settlements in the Samara Valley, suggesting that the LBA settled population in the Samara Valley was particularly dense. Srubnaya settlements extended from the upper Samara tributaries in Orenburg (Gabelko 1977) to the mouth of the Samara near the present city. Larger LBA cemetery populations, discussed below and by Khokhlov (Chapter 6), confirm the increase in the LBA population.

The oldest phase of Srubnaya, initiating the first transition to settled life, can be recognized by its Pokrovka-type ceramics. The Pokrovka phase is named after a kurgan cemetery on the lower Volga where many warrior graves with weapons were found (Malov 2002). Pokrovka phase ceramics occur at nine settlements in the Samara Valley, probably dated around 1950 to 1750 BC, based on the radiocarbon dates for this phase at the Krasnosamarskoe settlement. All Pokrovka settlements were occupied also in the mature Srubnaya period. Krasnosamarskoe is a good example of such a two-phase Srubnaya settlement. However,

Table 4.1 Srubnaya Settlements in the Samara River Drainage

Site Name	SVP No. (see Figure 2.1)	Chronological Period	Type of Site
Barinovka Pos.	5	Potapovka/Abashevo/early Srubnaya disturbed by medieval pits	Settlement
Belosersky I	63	Srubnaya	Settlement
Bezimyanka		Srubnaya	Settlement
Chernorechensky I	44	Srubnaya	Settlement
Grachev Sad		Abashevo/Srubnaya	Settlement multicomponent mixed
Ivanovka		Abashevo, developed Srubnaya	Settlement
Kirpichni Sarai		Vol'sko-Lbishche/Abashevo/Srubnaya	Settlement multicomponent
Krasnosamarskoe settlement	11	Vol'sko-Lbishche/early Srubnaya/developed Srubnaya	Settlement multicomponent
Leshevskoe single grave and settlement	53	Grave dates to Yamnaya. Settlement is developed Srubnaya LBA	Settlement of a short time
Maksimovka I	15	Srubnaya/early	Settlement
Maksimovka II	16	Srubnaya/Atabaevka	Settlement multicomponent
Monasheskii Khutor		Srubnaya/Suskanskaya	Settlement multicomponent
N. Belogorka		Srubnaya/Alakul	Settlement
Nur settlement	19	Srubnaya	Settlement
Peschanyi Dol I	70	Srubnaya/Suskanskaya	Low-density settlement
Peschanyi Dol II	71	Srubnaya	Low-density settlement
Pokrovka		Srubno-Alakul	Settlement
Poplavskoe		Srubnaya/Suskanskaya/Atabaevka/Ivanovskaya	Settlement multicomponent
S'yezzhee I	22	Settlements cultures: Srubnaya/Nur	Settlement
S'yezzhee II		Early Srubnaya	Settlement
Shirakinskii	26	Srubnaya	Undefined activity area
Sorochinsky		Srubnaya	Settlement
Spiridonovka II pos.	52	Srubnaya	Small settlement
Spiridonovka settlement	46	Srubnaya	Small settlement
Suhorechensky II		Srubnaya	Settlement
Tokskoe		Srubnaya	Settlement
Utyevka settlement	54	Srubnaya	Settlement
Zakhar-Kal'ma Dune	42	Srubnaya	Settlement on sand dune
Zalivnaya Dune	43	Srubnaya	Settlement on sand dune

Materials	GPS I Latitude N	GPS I Longitude E
Ceramics, bronze plaque	52.55.22	50.50.36
Materials published	53.10.41	50.32.15
Two vessels, 1 spiral ring		
	53.06.05	50.24.27
Materials partially published		
Two dwellings, 4 pits with slag, 1 pit with ore, 1 terochnik, 2 sickles, 2 awls, adze, hook, 2 stone pestles, 1 clay sinker. Materials are published.		
Bone: awl, "deadlock," a handle, a figure of a small fish, a fragment of a cheekpiece. Stone: casting mold for sickles, 3 hammers for ore crushing, a mortar. Bronze: a chisel, a sickle, a knife. Materials are partially published.		
Bronze: awl, plate. Copper: dross and slag. Stone: 3 stone pestles, 3 quartzite scrapers, 3 flint flakes, stone beads, 3 clay objects, 1 spindle.	53.05.39	50.48.14
Srubnaya pot sherds	52.56.12	50.59.02
	52.58.39	51.06.28
Materials are partially published	52.58.29	51.06.01
Materials are partially published		
Ceramics	53.08.02	50.35.31
See Chapter 18	52.53.32	50.52.10
See Chapter 18	52.52.30	50.51.03
Dwelling and an economic structure. Materials are partially published.		
Srubnaya dwelling. Bronze knife, bone tubule, 3 pestles. Materials are partially published.	52.59.20	50.50.50
Pestle, bone sickle, 2 bone tubes. Materials are partially published.	53.01.07	51.10.34
Bronze needle, 2 spindles, bone tools		
Ceramic sherds	52.57.45	50.48.00
One adze, clay sinker fragment, copper slag, 2 stone objects, charred grains, flint scraper. Materials are partially published.		
Sherds of pottery and flint	53.7.57	50.37.45
Earliest Srubnaya, ceramic sherds from surface of settlement	53.8.8	50.36.46
One pebble hammer, 1 grinding stone, 1 dog canine tooth bead. Materials are partially published.		
One building stone, copper slag, cheekpiece with 2 holes. Materials are partially published.		
Ceramic sherds	52.55.29	50.59.02
Bifacial flints, ceramics	53.03.19	51.32.20
Two ceramic sherds, flint flake?	53.03.31	51.25.16

there is little or no stratigraphic separation between early and mature Srubnaya phases at most settlement sites, and later mixing of materials due to rodent activity makes it difficult to determine the phase of many Srubnaya finds in settlements. Pokrovka ceramics usually range from 2 to 10 percent of the LBA ceramics in settlements.

Excavations in Srubnaya settlements in the Samara Valley have revealed plans of houses at four sites. At Ivanovka and Pokrovka in the upper Samara Valley, Orenburg oblast, both settlements contained one or two residential structures and a large utility structure. One house was revealed in the Srubnaya settlement at Poplavskoe, near Krasnosamarskoe, which contained one structure on land and probably one more flooded under the lake. Most Srubnaya settlements were small and unfortified.

A settled form of life appeared also east of the Ural Mountains in the Kazakh steppes at the same time as mature Srubnaya, where it took the form of the Andronovo culture, 1800 to 1200 BC. Alakul is the earliest phase in the development of Andronovo, and in the eastern part of the Samara drainage, in the Orenburg oblast, two settlements (N. Belogorka and Pokrovka) contain mixed Srubnaya-Alakul components. Alakul ceramic sherds are often found in other Srubnaya settlements in the Samara Valley, including the Krasnosamarskoe settlement.

The FBA

In Table 4.1, which includes sites concentrated on the main branch of the Samara River and in the Samara oblast, there are five settlements of the FBA, normally dated around 1200 to 800 BC. This is a significant reduction from the 29 Srubnaya occupation sites listed in the same table. If we add settlements located farther north, on the Bolshoi Kinel' branch, the number of FBA settlements within the Samara drainage increases to 18 settlement sites. All but one of these 18 was located on a Srubnaya occupation site, so there was no expansion of settlement into new areas; on the contrary, the FBA shows a reduction of the settled area, toward the lower Samara and Volga floodplains and toward the forest-steppe border on the north side of the Samara Valley. The FBA is divided into several quite localized ceramic culture types, including Suskanskaya (three sites), Ivanovskaya (three sites), Atabaevka (four sites), and Nur (eight sites).

Bronze Age Cemeteries

Bronze Age kurgan cemeteries are typical elements of the steppe landscape. The biggest concentration of kurgans in the Samara Valley is near the village of Utyevka, where the Samara River makes a wide curve to the south. Here are found at least 11 separate kurgan cemeteries containing some of the richest graves of the Bronze Age. The second concentration of kurgan cemeteries is located downstream, near the confluence of the Samara and Bolshoi Kinel'. Most kurgans are monocultural in terms of construction, but some contain later graves inserted into the older mound. Some kurgan cemeteries contain burial mounds raised during multiple periods (e.g., EBA and LBA), although most kurgan cemeteries contain mounds built in a single period.

Bronze Age cemeteries took two different forms—kurgans, defined by a burial mound, and flat graves (also called ground graves), with no preserved indicator above the ground. Understandably, flat grave cemeteries are rarely found, usually by accident, while kurgans are easily located. The kurgans of the EBA and MBA could not possibly contain the graves of the whole population or even a significant percentage of it, since most EBA and MBA kurgans contain only one to two graves. But we have found very few Yamnaya or Poltavka flat graves, so the funeral ritual for the majority of the EBA and MBA pastoral population is unknown.

Three flat-grave cemeteries are attributed to the Bronze Age in the Samara Valley. They are Nikiforovskoe Lesnichestvo (MBA Abashevo culture, Figure 4.3: Site 25), S'yezzhee (LBA Srubnaya culture, Figure 4.1: Site 84), and Utyevka VI (Final LBA Ivanovskaya culture, Figure 4.3: Site 17). The tradition of burial in cemeteries without mounds had been practiced in the Samara Valley at least since the late Neolithic/Eneolithic, the most important cemetery of this period being at S'yezzhee, the type site for the Eneolithic Samara culture, located only a few meters from where the Srubnaya flat-grave cemetery was later established. The large Srubnaya flat-grave cemetery at S'yezzhee (76 graves) is surprising, because the normal Srubnaya rite was kurgan burial, and it raises the question of how many flat-grave Srubnaya cemeteries might exist. Perhaps we should include in the list of flat cemeteries those places where graves and artifacts, mostly eroded and found out of context, are exposed in sand dunes. These places include Bor, Leshevskoe (Figure 2.1: SVP 6), and Chelovech'ya Golova (Figure 4.3: Site 12). However, data on the type of burial and the spatial arrangement of the material were destroyed by dune erosion.

Multicomponent Bronze Age cemeteries, exhibiting more than one Bronze Age culture, are identified at 13 sites in the Samara Valley, summarized in Table 4.2 (see also Figure 4.2).

In addition, we should also mention two kurgan cemeteries located in the Ural region between the upper Samara and the Ural drainage near the Kargaly copper mines. These two sites, Uranbash and Pershin, are not in the Samara oblast, but they are associated with the upper Samara River. Of these 15 multicomponent kurgan cemeteries, all but 4 were established in the EBA by the Yamnaya culture.

The EBA: Yamnaya

Archaeologists by 2002 had identified 17 Yamnaya cemeteries in the Samara Valley containing 45 kurgans and 51 graves (Figure 4.2). Thirteen of these were multicomponent, reused as burial sites by later cultures. The average Yamnaya cemetery contained about three kurgans, and each kurgan usually covered a single central grave, sometimes with an additional peripheral grave under the mound. Almost all of the Yamnaya kurgan cemeteries in the Samara Valley are located on the left bank of the river adjoining the steppe zone, so the drier, more open side of the valley was favored. The Samara drainage is almost the northern boundary of the Yamnaya culture; north of the Samara there is only one known Yamnaya cemetery, at Lopatino on the Sok River.

Four of the 17 Yamnaya cemeteries were single component, used only during the EBA by the Yamnaya population. But during the immediately following period, the MBA, only four Yamnaya cemeteries were reused by the Poltavka culture, so it seems that most Yamnaya cemeteries were used in the EBA and then were not reused for many hundreds of years. Therefore,

Yamnaya kurgan cemeteries probably point to a specific period of funeral activity by a specific family group. If the Yamnaya period in the Samara Valley is assigned 500 years, 3300 to 2800 BC, then there were only three to four Yamnaya cemeteries and about 15 kurgans per century in the surveyed area. One of the authors computed this same average, about 15 kurgans per century, using combined EBA and MBA data from well-surveyed local regions such as the area near Utyevka (Kuznetsov 2003). Only one to two people were buried under each kurgan, most of them adult men but about 20% of them adult women. Probably they were important leaders in the family herding unit or in wider clan affairs.[1] From the perspective of the others in the community, each person who helped to build a Yamnaya kurgan probably experienced this ritual only once or twice in his or her lifetime. When ordinary members of the community died, including almost all children and females and the majority of males, their bodies were disposed of in an unknown manner.

The MBA: Poltavka, Catacomb, Abashevo, and Potapovka

In the MBA, there were 22 Poltavka kurgan cemeteries in the Samara Valley containing 32 kurgans and 56 graves. If the Poltavka period is assigned 700 years, 2800 to 2100 BC, then there were three to four kurgan cemeteries per century, about the same as during the EBA, but with the addition of

Table 4.2 Multicomponent Bronze Age Cemetery Sites

Site Name	Culture Group 1	Culture Group 2	Culture Group 3
Grachevka	Yamnaya	Srubnaya	
Spiridonovka II	Yamnaya	Srubnaya	
Pokrovka I	Yamnaya	Srubnaya	
Utyevka III	Yamnaya	Poltavka	Srubnaya
Sverdlovo V	Yamnaya	Srubnaya	
Utyevka I	Poltavka	Srubnaya	
Krasnosamarskoe IV	Poltavka	Srubnaya	
Gvardeitsi II	Poltavka	Srubnaya	
Utyevka VI	Poltavka	Potapovka	Ivanovskaya
Utyevka V	Yamnaya	Poltavka	
Utyevka XI	Yamnaya	Srubnaya	
Ephimovka IV	Yamnaya	Poltavka	Srubnaya
Medvedka	Yamnaya	Poltavka	
Uranbash	Yamnaya	Srubno-Alakul	
Pershin	Yamnaya	Srubnaya	

forest-zone MBA cultures (Abashevo, Vol'sko-Lbishche) that occupied part of the Samara Valley in the MBA. Of 17 studied cemeteries, 5 contained exclusively Poltavka graves, so were new funeral monuments and never were reused. In the Poltavka cemetery at Krasnosamarskoe IV, excavated as part of the Samara Valley Project (see Chapter 17), the three central graves from three adjoining kurgans had largely overlapping radiocarbon dates that range between 2900 and 2700 BC, with very similar means. These three kurgans were created and used in a brief period, followed by the cessation of funeral rituals and apparent abandoning of the cemetery for many centuries. One kurgan was reused as a cemetery later in the MBA and again 1,000 years later in the LBA.[2]

The MBA Catacomb culture, centered in the Dnieper-Azov-Don-Caspian steppes to the south and west of the Volga, is distinguished by graves with a side chamber in which the deceased was placed. Just five Catacomb-style graves have been found in the Samara Valley, always as isolated additions to earlier kurgans, at Krasnosamarskoe II, Krasnosamarskoe IV, Utyevka VI, S'yezzhee, and Utyevka I. These unusual graves might indicate some form of contact or exchange between the Samara Valley and regions far to the south during the MBA. The Catacomb grave at Krasnosamarskoe IV is dated around 2750 BC, very early in the Catacomb period, so might have been among the earliest of such visitors.

The only cemetery of the Abashevo culture in the Samara Valley was found on the upper Samara, on its northern or forest-steppe side, at Nikiforovskoe Lesnichestvo (Figure 4.3: Site 25). This cemetery contained nine Abashevo flat graves. The majority of Abashevo settlements are found substantially farther north, on the Tok River and north of it, so the settlement that created this cemetery is not known. Another site discussed as an Abashevo cemetery is Chelovech'ya Golova (Figure 4.3: Site 12). Copper and bronze ornaments found with human bones in mixed deposits at the eroded dune cemetery were assigned by O. Kuzmina to the Abashevo culture (Kuzmina 2000:96, 121). However, a systematic survey of the dune failed to reveal any pottery of the Abashevo type, only pottery of the Vol'sko-Lbishche type (Vasiliev 1999:103). The metal ornaments were types that were widely used in the MBA. It is doubtful that this cemetery can be assigned unambiguously to a specific funerary culture.

The final MBA II Potapovka culture created one kurgan cemetery in the Samara Valley, at Utyevka VI. The graves here included those of chariot warriors, containing paired horse sacrifices, typical antler or bone cheekpieces of circular or "shield" shapes, bone whip handles, metal-

waisted daggers, shaft-hole axes, long flat axes, socketed spears, and projectile points of bone and flint in both long (10 cm) and short (5 cm) sizes. One grave at Utyevka VI (Kurgan 6, Grave 2) contained a 15-year-old and 17-year-old couple buried with their arms around each other, their faces turned together, with the bodies of four subadult children, which could not have been the children of the couple, who were too young to have such a family but must represent a tragic event.

The LBA: Srubnaya Cemeteries in the Samara River Valley

The Samara Valley contains 37 LBA cemeteries assigned to the Srubnaya culture or to the transitional cultures at the beginning and end of Srubnaya, with 70 kurgans and more than 700 graves. In Table 4.3, which concentrates on sites in the main branch of the Samara River within the Samara oblast, 31 of these Srubnaya cemeteries are listed. Many of the 37 cemeteries are mapped in Figure 4.4. The number of Srubnaya cemeteries (37) is about the same as the total for the EBA and MBA combined (39) and represented a 40% increase in cemeteries compared with the MBA. This points to significant population growth in the LBA. Srubnaya communities usually reused existing kurgan cemeteries: 23 of the 37 LBA cemeteries contained older kurgans (Table 4.2). However, some Srubnaya cemeteries had no kurgans but were flat cemeteries without surface markers that survive, such as the large Srubnaya flat cemetery of 76 graves at S'yezzhee II (Kolev 2003). Srubnaya burial mounds are distributed through the Samara Valley more evenly than earlier kurgan cemeteries, with no apparent concentration in specific areas. Early Srubnaya cemeteries were located in the same low, floodplain-oriented locations as EBA and MBA cemeteries.

The early phase of Srubnaya, also known as the Pokrovka phase, is very strongly represented in the studied sample of cemeteries in the Samara Valley. In only six cemeteries was a Pokrovka phase of activity followed by a mature Srubnaya phase (Krasnosamarskoe IV, Spiridonovka IV, Nikolaevka I, Chisty Yar, Sverdlovo IV, and Burdyginski). In 18 Pokrovka-phase cemeteries, there was no succeeding usage during the mature Srubnaya phase. The most notable difference between the two phases was the total number of cemeteries and graves assigned to each phase. About 400 graves are attributed to Pokrovka-type communities (early Srubnaya) and only about 150 graves to the mature Srubnaya culture. Thus, the number of graves in the relatively short early Srubnaya phase was almost three times greater than the number of graves assigned to the much longer, mature stage of culture and

К карте памятников срубной культуры (могильники).

1 - Хрящевка; 2 - Вислая Дубрава; 3 - Верхние Белозерки; 4 - Золотая Нива; 5 - Луначарский; 6,7 - Ягодное I и один.курган; 8 - Подстепкинский I, II; 9 - Каменный Овраг; 10 - Лузановка; 11 - Четыровка; 12 - Старая Ивановка; 13 - Киевка; 14 - Мазуровка; 15 - Васильевка; 16 - Борма; 17 - Суруш; 18 - Суходол; 19 - Неприк; 20 - Гвардейцы; 21 - Широченка; 22 - Съезжее; 23 - Утевка II,III,IV; 24 - Черновский; 25 - Волчанка; 26 - Кировский I,III; 27 - Андросовка II; 28 - Новопавловка; 29 - Соляниха; 30 - Звенигородка; 31 - Песочное; 32 - Осинки; 33 - Сосновка; 34 - Александровка IV; 35 - Солнечный; 36 - Кашпир I,II,IV; 37 - Нижнеозерецкий; 38 - Федоровка I,II; 39 - Давыдовка; 40 - Владимировка; 41 — Чулпан; 42 - Шигоны; 43 - Новый Ризадей I; 44 - Верхнепечерское; 45 - Виловатое I; 46 - Выселки III; 47 - Красноселки; 48 - Красносамарское; 49 — Кряж; 50 — Лопатино II; 51 — Нижняя Орлянка; 52 — Осиновка; 53 — Бол.Рязань; 54 — Преполовенка; 55 — Студенцы; 56 — Спиридоновка; 57 — Красный Ключ; 58 — Кривая Лука; 59 — Масленниково; 60 —Иоганнесфельд.

Figure 4.4 Map of Srubnaya (Late Bronze Age) cemetery sites in the Samara oblast. (after Kolev et al., 2000 p.183)

Table 4.3 Srubnaya Cemeteries in the Samara River Drainage

Site Name	SVP Survey No. (Fig. 2.1)	Type of Site	Materials
Barinovka I	3	Kurgan, 3 visible	
Chernaja Rechka	47	Three kurgans	Knife, bracelet, timber grave
Chisty Yar I	50	Two kurgans, 12 early burials, 16 late burials	Thirty-one vessels, 1 bronze needle, 2 bone bead necklaces
Domashka		One destroyed early burial	One bracelet, 1 plaque
Ephimovka IV	Site 26 in Figure 4.2 on the Buzuluk River	One kurgan, 2 secondary burials	Two vessels
Gvardetsi I	7	Six kurgans, 13 burials of developed Srubnaya	Nineteen vessels, a bronze plaque, a knife, 2 pendants with 1.5 turns, a cylindrical bone bead
Kinel' I			
Kinzelsky		One kurgan, 1 early burial	Two vessels
Kirsanovka		One destroyed early burial	Two vessels, 1 bracelet, 1 ring of wire
Krasnosamarskoe ADIN.K.	8	One kurgan, 4 burials	Four vessels
Krasnosamarskoe IV	12	One mound, 22 inserted burials	Thirteen vessels, 2 ornamented bone whorls
Leshevskoe		Dune site, some destroyed burials of developed Srubnaya culture	One vessel
Neprik		Seven kurgans, 14 early burials	Seventeen vessels, 2 bronze knives, 1 pendant with 1.5 turns, flint blade, 2 bone buckles
Nikolaevka I		Two kurgans, 7 early burials, 2 late burials	Earliest timber grave culture, pots and tins (9 vessels)
Novoberezovskii		One kurgan, 1 later burial	
Pershin		One destroyed kurgan, 2 burials	Two vessels
Pokrovka I	21	One destroyed burial	One vessel, "Y" bone pin
Proletarskii II		One kurgan, 7 early burials	Six vessels, 1 necklace of faience beads, 1 bronze pendant in gold foil
S'yezzhee II	22	Flat-grave burials with 80 early stage burials	Eighty vessels, ceramic fragments, carved bone tool, cow astragali, 2 silver pendants with 1.5 turns, 3 blade tools, a backed blade, a blade-scraper
Shirochenka	27	Srubnaya	
Spiridonovka I	30	At least 36 burials under one kurgan. Earliest phase of Srubnaya culture	
Spiridonovka II	52	Five kurgans, 105 early burials	One hundred three vessels, 2 bronze knives, 14 fluted bracelets, 5 spiral pendants with 1.5 turns, 22 awls, 1 needle, 7 metal plates, 3 piercers, 4 spiral pendants with 1.5 turns in gold foil, 2 spiral pendants with 1.5 turns in silver foil, 3 bone buckles, 1 piercer, 2 tubules, 5 rings, 1 necklace of canine teeth, 6 flint arrow tips, 8 processed otshepov, 35 nastovix beads, 2 bowls, 2 sandstones
Spiridonovka IV	49	Two kurgans, 23 early burials, 15 late burials	Twenty vessels, 3 grooved bronze bracelets, 1 needle with an eye
Sverdlovo IV		One kurgan, 38 late burials	Twenty vessels, 2 bronze bracelets, 3 bronze pendants with 1.5 turns in gold foil, 3 necklaces of faience beads, 1 disk from sandstone, 1 stone object, 1 pestle, 1 shell buckle, 1 piece of black resin
Sverdlovo V		Five kurgans, 15 early burials, 9 late burials	Nineteen vessels, 5 necklaces of faience beads, 2 bronze pendants with 1.5 turns in gold foil, 2 bone rings, 1 bronze plate, fragments of bronze wire
Utyevka II	33	Kurgan, 4–6 visible	Ceramics
Utyevka III		Three kurgans, 23 early burials	Two pendants in gold foil, 2 bronze knives, 4 fluted bracelets, 2 pendants with 1.5 turns, a necklace of faience beads, a necklace of silver beads, a wolf canine, 1 bowl
Utyevka V	36	Kurgan, 3 known	
Utyevka IX		One kurgan	One vessel
Uvarovka I			
Vilovatoye I		One kurgan, 2 late burials	Two vessels

10 times the number of graves dated to the MBA! For example, in the well-studied area near Spiridonovka, four Srubnaya cemeteries (Spiridonovka II and IV, Nur I, and Chisty Yar) yielded 140 Pokrovka-style Srubnaya graves and only 31 mature-style Srubnaya graves, according to ceramic vessels. In contrast, in most settlements, the mature Srubnaya ceramics greatly predominate (90%).[3]

Bronze Age Metal and Ceramic Artifacts in the Samara Valley

The artifacts obtained in the course of many years of field research can create a solid foundation for historical and cultural reconstruction. Excavations in the Samara Valley have produced hundreds of Bronze Age artifacts, including more than 660 completely reconstructed ceramic vessels.

Few artifacts were deposited in the EBA graves of the Yamnaya culture. In 45 kurgans containing just 51 Yamnaya graves, there were nine copper or bronze objects, nine made of stone, and eight of bone or shell. Only seven whole pots and eight ceramic sherds were found, so ceramics appeared in one of four graves. A copper or bronze knife of EBA type was found as a chance find near the village of Bobrovka, probably from a disturbed EBA grave. The richest Yamnaya grave was at the cemetery of Kutuluk I on the Bolshoi Kinel' River, where under Kurgan 4, Grave 1 contained a robust adult man with a solid copper mace almost 50 cm long, weighing 770 g, with traces of a leather handle. The grave is dated (OxA-4306) 4400 ± 70 BP and (AA-12570) 4370 ± 75 BP, calibrated to 3100 to 2800 BC (Kuznetsov 2005). The mace is discussed in Chapter 11.

The MBA is better documented, with sites attributed to three different cultures: mobile Poltavka pastoralists, settled Abashevo cattle herders, and settled Vol'sko-Lbishche people, who together occupied 26 known cemeteries and 12 settlements in the Samara Valley. The Poltavka culture, genetically related to Yamnaya, is represented at 22 kurgan cemeteries and some additional chance finds. Settlements are almost unknown. In 56 Poltavka graves, the catalogued artifacts consist of 23 metal items, including 2 of gold, 11 made of bone, 11 of stone, and 24 ceramic vessels. Many of these were found in a single grave, the richest Poltavka grave in the Samara Valley, in Kurgan 1 at Utyevka I. In this early Poltavka kurgan, 100 m in diameter, an adult man in Grave 1 had two golden rings with granulated decoration, with analogies in Anatolia; a tanged copper dagger; a copper pin with a forged iron head (a very early use of iron); a flat copper axe; a copper awl; a copper sleeved axe of Volga-Ural type IIa; and a polished stone pestle (Kuznetsov 2005; Vasiliev 1980). Kurgan 2 at Utyevka I contained a Poltavka grave with a bead of carnelian, beads of silver, and an unshaped mass of glass-like material, all probably obtained from the North Caucasus (Vasiliev 1980: 41).

The only known Abashevo cemetery, at Nikiforovskoe Lesnichestvo on the headwaters of the Samara, contained nine MBA burials. They were accompanied by 44 articles of copper and bronze, 2 of stone, 1 of bone, 8 whole ceramic vessels, and a few sherds. The numerous metal objects show the engagement of the Abashevo culture in copper mining and manufacture in the southern Ural forest-steppe piedmont. Traces of Abashevo settlements are known in the lower Samara Valley far to the west of this cemetery, represented by small collections of ceramics at settlements named earlier (see above). Vol'sko-Lbishche sites are represented mostly by small collections of ceramics. However, at Chelovech'ya Golova dune, eroded graves perhaps of this culture contained a collection of 17 metal ornaments, including three silver pendants, located a significant distance east of the center of this culture on the west side of the Volga.

The final centuries of the MBA, 2100 to 1800 BC (MBA II), witnessed a very specific fusion of Abashevo and Poltavka traditions that resulted in the appearance of the Sintashta culture east of the Urals and a very similar variant, the Potapovka culture, west of the Urals, with evidence of chariots and chariot driving gear, new weapon types, and new ceramic types. The type site of Potapovka is located north of the Samara on the Sok River; the only Potapovka kurgan cemetery in the Samara Valley is at Utyevka VI. This is the most complex cemetery of the Bronze Age in the Samara Valley. The number of grave artifacts is much higher than Yamnaya or Poltavka. Utyevka VI contained 46 items of copper and bronze; 40 pottery vessels; 35 flint artifacts, mostly projectile points; 13 bone tools; and 1 gold ornament. A few fragments of Potapovka pottery were found mixed with a nearby Srubnaya settlement at Barinovka, but significant Potapovka settlements are not known.

More than 700 graves are attributed to the LBA Srubnaya culture in the Samara Valley. Most of the excavated graves contain ceramics of the early Pokrovka stage of the Srubnaya culture (but see note 3 above). Particularly striking monuments of the early stage of Srubnaya in the lower Samara Valley are the Spiridonovka II, Utyevka III, Neprik, and Shirochenka kurgan cemeteries, as well as the S'yezzhee flat-grave cemetery, with 76 graves. The richest Srubnaya graves in the Samara Valley were excavated at Spiridonovka II; they contained multiple bronze bracelets and earrings, flint and bone projectile points, imported faience beads, and one bronze bracelet plated with gold (see Chapter 11). The Srubnaya graves in the Samara Valley contained 119 articles of copper and bronze, 7 of gold and 5 of silver, 39 of stone or faience, and 29 of bone and shell.

The Samara Valley contains 29 Srubnaya settlements. Taken together, they produced artifact inventories that include 20 copper and arsenical bronze objects (sickles, knives, awls, hooks, adzes, chisels, ornaments), around 25 stone items (pestles, hammers, worked flint), 16 bone artifacts (spindles, bone bridle cheekpieces, etc.), and 2 clay items (loom weights). It should be noted that in reality, of course, many more objects of these materials existed during the LBA.

Bronze Age Economic Adaptations in the Samara Valley

This volume contains specialist studies of the fauna and flora of the Krasnosamarskoe settlement and of other sites in the Samara Valley. We will make just a few comments from our perspective as Samara archaeologists. First, it is obvious from the domesticated animal bones found on altars and in ritual deposits connected with graves, as well as from bones in LBA settlements, that the pastoral side of the economy was very significant in the Bronze Age subsistence economy in the lower Samara Valley. On the important issues of the particular type of livestock and especially the type of economic structure, the studies of Kosintsev are most important (see Chapter 15). At present, we have only tentative conclusions on this issue (Petrenko 1984:12, 1995:205–221; Kosintsev and Roslyakova 1999, 2000).

Faunal material for the EBA and MBA Yamnaya-Poltavka cultures comes entirely from the excavation of kurgans, as settlements are unknown. This small sample of animal bones is dominated by ovicaprids. The breeding and care of large cattle require a more stationary base and settled residence pattern. The dominance of the bones of sheep in Yamnaya and Poltavka kurgans (Kosintsev and Roslyakova 1999:50) is a typical feature of a mobile form of pastoralism in an ecology of arid steppes. It is no accident that Yamnaya cemeteries are mainly located on the left bank of the Samara Valley, adjacent to the middle Volga steppes. According to soil morphological studies, the EBA and MBA climate in the middle Volga region was markedly continental and dry (Ivanov et al. 2001:379). The MBA, in particular, had a very arid climate, according to pollen studies (Lavrushin and Spiridonova 1995:193). Thus, ovicaprid herding was the basis of a mobile residential pattern for the Yamnaya-Poltavka tribes, who probably lived in wagons and moved with their herds. Cattle apparently were used as draft animals. Beginning in the MBA II, around 2100 BC, the role of cattle increased. Ovicaprids fell to second place.

Horses played a special role in the household economy. Horse bones have not been found in Yamnaya graves in the Samara Valley but did appear in Poltavka graves. Horses were actively used to pull chariots in the MBA II. The process of domestication is a separate topic, requiring in-depth study by specialists. But a reflection of this process can be seen in the Samara Valley, beginning with the first images and symbolic representations of horses, as well as the first horse head-and-hoof sacrifices, in the S'yezzhee Eneolithic cemetery; progressing to the appearance of the heads and hooves of sacrificial horses in MBA graves; and culminating in the appearance of horse bridle cheekpieces and paired horse sacrifices in MBA II Potapovka graves (at Utyevka I, Kurgan 2 and Utyevka VI).

In the LBA, sedentary populations indicate the existence of a settled economy, based on a form of pastoralism in which cattle were clearly the most important animals. Chapter 15 by Kosintsev in this volume confirms the dominance of cattle in the Srubnaya economy in the Samara Valley. Cattle similarly dominated the fauna of Srubnaya communities on the middle Don and farther west in Ukraine, in the Azov-Dnieper steppes.

We should not forget the Srubnaya settlement of Gorny, a mining settlement associated with the giant Kargaly copper mines. The osteological material was published by Antipina (Antipina 1999:103–116; Morales and Antipina 2003). This site in the western Ural piedmont is directly adjacent to the upper tributaries of the Samara River, although geographically it lies within the Ural River drainage. At the Gorny mining settlement, admittedly an unusual place, the bones of cattle account for 83 percent of the fauna, sheep and goat are only 15 percent, and the horse is less than 2 percent. Intense studies of pollen and flotation of seed remains yielded no evidence of agriculture.

The existence of agriculture in the LBA remains an open question. Numerous flotation tests on Srubnaya culture settlements produced no credible evidence of agriculture. However, in the Samara Valley, natural conditions could favor the development of this sector of the economy, without irrigation. The LBA had a favorable climate—a more humid and warmer climate than today (Ivanov et al. 2001:382). Lavrushin and Spiridonova (1995:194) studied pollen at the LBA settlement of Tokskoe on the headwaters of the Samara River, 180 km east of Krasnosamarskoe, and stated that they recorded the pollen of cultivated cereals, as well as weed pollen typical of arable fields. They explicitly suggest the presence of agriculture at this developed Srubnaya settlement. According to them, during the Srubnaya period in the Samara Valley, forests increased. This increase occurred only in the river valley, while the rest of the territory was dominated by a grass-forb steppe. The later palynological studies at Gorny, not far from Tokskoe, yielded no pollen of domesticated cereals, so these two studies of neighboring sites are contradictory. We should also mention the discovery of pollen of cultivated cereals at the Srubnaya settlement of Mosolovskoe on the middle Don (Spiridonova 1989:100), and the discovery of charred grains at other Srubnaya settlements between the Don and the Dnieper in southern Russia and Ukraine.

Archaeological finds, unfortunately, do not directly indicate the practice of agriculture. However, there is indirect evidence: metal and bone sickles, stone pestles, stone mortars, and antler hoes. The interpretation of artifacts as hoes at Sukhorechenskoe II is very controversial and requires more reliable evidence. Sickles could be used to collect grass or fodder for livestock, that is, for gathering and herding. Five bronze sickles (a hoard?) were recorded near the village of Ovsianka in Buzuluk district. But the discussion of agricultural artifacts really centers on the function of stone mortars and pestles.

These comments do not dispute the existence of agriculture in the Srubnaya period; however, we suggest that we need more reliable evidence for its existence. Artifacts may well reflect a certain level of gathering, perhaps a transition to farming or agriculture in the early stages. To discuss the specific type of farming with such contradictory data is not possible.

Bronze Age Metallurgy and Mining in the Samara Valley

Artifactual evidence for the conduct of metallurgy is found in 10 sites in the Samara Valley. Most of them are LBA settlements. However, some evidence appears in two MBA cemeteries: Utyevka I (early stage of the Poltavka culture)—copper slag and Utyevka VI (Potapovka culture)—a copper splash, vitrified clay, and two ceramic nozzles. The LBA settlements with evidence for metallurgy are S'yezzhee Srubnaya settlement (early Srubnaya)—ceramic crucible; Barinovka (Abashevo and Srubnaya)—copper slag, splashed copper; Krasnosamarskoe (Srubnaya culture)—copper slag, splashed copper; Tokskoe (mature Srubnaya culture)—copper slag; Ivanovka (Abashevo and Srubnaya)—four pits containing copper slag, one pit with copper ore, ceramic vessels splashed with copper (probably of the Srubnaya culture) (Morgunova and Porokhova 1989:169); Sorochinsky (Srubnaya culture)—

copper slag; Kirpichni Sarai (Final Bronze Age)—a mold for a sickle, three hammers for crushing ore, and a mortar; and Nur (Final Bronze Age)—fragments of crucibles. In addition, copper ingots were reported as chance finds in the nineteenth century near the villages Kuntuzutamak and Kyzyl-Mechet on the Buzuluk River, and circular ingots were reported from near the village Almaly on the upper Bolshoi Uran River (Nefedov 1899:39).

According to K. V. Sal'nikov, between the upper Samara River and its tributary, the Tok River, are rich cuprous sandstones—a western extension of the same formations mined at Kargaly. The ore here is 3.5 to 5.5 percent copper, while copper ore on the Don, which also was worked in the LBA, yielded only 1 percent copper (Sal'nikov 1967:182). Most of the LBA settlements with evidence of metallurgy are located on the right bank of the Samara, and most date to the mature Srubnaya or Final Bronze Age periods. The westernmost Srubnaya settlement with evidence of metallurgy is Kirpichni Sarai, located near the confluence of the Samara and the Volga, in the modern city of Samara.

We should interpret the copper metallurgy of the Samara Valley in the context of the well-known Srubnaya mining sites around Kargaly, located very close to the tributaries of the Samara. According to E. N. Chernykh, the principal investigator of the Kargaly mining sites, the upper tributaries of the Samara, particularly the M. Uran, the Tochek, and the Tok Rivers, define a part of the Kargaly copper ore field, where many clusters of ancient workings have been discovered (Chernykh 1997:10). These tributaries of the Samara are interwoven with tributaries of the Ural, particularly the upper Usolki River, where the excavated settlement of Gorny is located. Geographically, the upper Samara is a region of contact between the Samara and Ural River drainages.

In the Samara Valley, we can see a long chain of sites with substantial evidence of copper working between Kirpichni Sarai near the Volga confluence and Ivanovka on the Tok. The Gorny mining settlement can be regarded as the beginning of this chain. In the LBA, Gorny might have been a place from which copper ore or smelted copper was transported down the Samara River to the west in exchange for weapons, tools, or other trade items. In addition to traditional methods of ground transportation in wagons, copper ore could be transported by water on rafts. Historical and ethnographic accounts from the late Middle Ages and to modern times confirm that, during floods and high water, the Samara and Ural basins were connected, temporarily forming a single giant water system. These waterways were well known to local people. For example, the Ural Cossacks used these waterways as the shortest route from the Urals to the Volga and then to the Don. Traveling up the tributaries of the lower Samara, it was possible to transfer to the Bolshoi Irgiz and connect with the waters of the Volga south of the Samara confluence (Myakutin 1911:53). In the winter, using sleds, it was possible to transport heavy material such as copper ore over the divide between the Ural and Samara basins with relative ease. The population of the Bronze Age could easily use the tributaries of the Samara, Ural, and Volga Rivers to establish rapid communication with neighboring regions.

Conclusion

In conclusion, we note that the border-zone ecological characteristics of the Samara River valley are crucial preconditions that affected cultural development throughout the Bronze Age. The Samara Valley was directly connected with both the steppe world and the cultures of the forest-steppe zone, reflected in the concentration here of all of the different archaeological cultures of the Volga-Ural region. The archaeological material relates to every stage of the Bronze Age, showing the process of development from mobile, purely stockbreeding cultures in the EBA to contact between settled and mobile populations in the MBA and integration between these traditions in the final MBA, leading to the appearance of settled pastoralists throughout the valley in the LBA. Many materials attest to linkages and interaction between the stockbreeders of the Samara Valley not only with the other cultures of the Volga-Ural region but also with the cultures beyond the Urals (Sintashta, Andronovo), as well as with the Caucasus and the Don basin. The unique and strategic advantages of the region are also demonstrated in the repeated appearance of elite, socially important individuals and groups in the Samara Valley, represented during the Bronze Age by the extraordinarily wealthy and widely connected individuals buried at Kutuluk (Yamnaya), Utyevka I (Poltavka), Utyevka VI (Potapovka), Nikiforovskoe Lesnichestvo (Abashevo), and Spiridonovka II (Srubnaya).

Notes

1   Editor's note: Khokhlov, in Chapter 6 of this volume, described the Yamnaya crania as the most homogeneous in the prehistory of the Samara Valley and Yamnaya bodies as the tallest and most robust, suggesting that the EBA criteria for kurgan burial might have included physical traits such as size, strength, and appearance.

2   Editor's note: Khokhlov's anthropological collection contained three times more skeletons dated to the MBA than the EBA. He suggested a significant increase in population during the MBA. His suggestion is not supported by the small increase in the number of MBA kurgan cemeteries noted here.

3   Editor's note: At Krasnosamarskoe IV cemetery, two graves containing Pokrovka-style ceramics were dated by radiocarbon to 1650 to 1750 BC, making them contemporary with the mature Srubnaya occupation phase at the nearby settlement. In Chapter 10, we argue that the Pokrovka style was retained as a funerary ceramic style during the mature Srubnaya period. A custom such as this could help to explain the predominance of Pokrovka-style pots in Srubnaya graves. The majority of Pokrovka-style ceramics are stratified beneath the majority of mature-Srubnaya-phase ceramics at the Krasnosamarskoe settlement, but both styles co-occur in every level, so seem to have been made at the same time (see Chapter 10, Figure 10.3). The Pokrovka style might have been retained during the mature Srubnaya phase for specialized use in funeral rituals. Of course, this possibility can only be tested by many more radiocarbon dates from graves containing Pokrovka-style ceramics.

References

Agapov, S. A., I. B. Vasiliev, and V. I. Pestrikova
1990   *Khvalynskii Eneoliticheskii Mogil'nik*. Saratovskogo Universiteta, Saratov.

Antipina, Y. Y.
1999   Kostyne ostatki zhivotnikh s poseleniya Gorny. *Rosiiskaya Arkheologiya* 1:106–116.

Chernykh, E. N.
1997   *Kargaly. Zabytnyi Mir*. NOX, Moskva.

Demkin, V. A.
1999   Rekonstruktsiya soderzhimogo glinyanykh sosudov iz kurgannykh zakhoronenii, in *Voprosy Arkheologii Povolzh'ya*, vol. I, pp. 243–248. Samaraskii Gosudarstvennyi Pedagogicheskii Universitet, Samara.

Gabelko, N. L.
1977   Poselenie Srubnoi kul'tury na R. Samare v Orenburgskoi oblasti. In *Neolit i Bronzogo Vek Povolzhya i Priurala*. Kuibyshevskii Gosudarstvennyi Pedagogicheskii Universitet, Kuibyshev.

Golmsten, Vera V.
1925   Materiali po arkheologii Samarskoi gub., *Obshchestva Arkheologii, Istorii, Etnografii Estestvoznaniya pri Samarskom Gosudartsvennom Universitete 1*. SGU, Samara.

Guliaev, V. I.
1993   The Theoretical Archaeology in the USSR. In *Theory and Practice of Prehistory: Views from the Edge of*

Europe, edited by M. Isabel Martinez Navarette, pp. 333–345. Universidad de Cantabria, Santander.

Ivanov, I. V., L. N. Plekhanova, O. A. Chichagova, S. S. Chernyanskii, and D. V. Makhanov

2001 Paleopochvy Arkaimskoi doliny i basseina Samary— indicator ekologichskii uslovii v epokhu Bronzy. In *Bronzovyi Vek Vostochnoi Evropy: Kharakteristika Kul'tur, Khronologiya i Periodatsiy*, pp. 375–384. Samaraskii Gosudarstvennyi Pedagogicheskii Universitet, Samara.

Klejn, Leo S.

1993 To Separate a Centaur: On the Relationship of Archaeology and History in Soviet Tradition. *Antiquity* 67(255):339–348.

Kolev, Iu. I.

2003 Gruntovoyi mogil'nik Srubnoi kul'tury S'ezzhee II (materialy raskopok). In *Material'naya Kul'tura Naseleniya basseina reki Samary v Bronzovom Veke*, edited by Iu. I. Kolev, P. F. Kuznetsov, and O. D. Mochalov, pp. 88–111. Samarskogo Gosudarstvennogo Pedagogicheskogo Universiteta, Samara.

Kolev, Iu. I., A. E. Mamonov, and M. A. Turetskii (editors)

2000 *Istoriya Samarskogo Povolzh'ya c Drevneishikh Vremen do Nashikh Dnei: Bronzovy Vek.* Integratsiya, Samara.

Korenevskii, S. N.

1980 O metallicheskikh veshchakh I Utevskogo mogil'nika, In *Arkheolohiya Vostocjnogo-Evropeiskoi Lesostepi*, pp. 59–66. Voronezhskogo Universiteta, Voronezh.

Kosintsev, P. A., and N. V. Roslyakova

1999 Ostatki zhivotnykh is Kalinovskogo mogil'nika. In *Okhrana i Izuchenie Pamyatnikov Istorii i Kul'tury v Samarskoi Oblasti*, Vol. 1, edited by I. N. Vasil'eva and M. A. Turetskii, pp. 48–58. Samarskii Oblastnoi Istoriko-Kraevedcheskii Muzei im. P.V. Alabina, Samara.

2000 Skotovodstvo neseleniya Samarskogo Pobolzhya. In *Istoriya Samarskogo Povolzh'ya c Drevneishikh Vremen do Nashikh Dnei: Bronzovy Vek*, edited by Iu. I. Kolev, P. F. Kuznetsov, and O. D. Mochalov, pp. 302–308. Integratsiya, Samara.

Kuzmina, Elena E.

2007 *The Origin of the Indo-Iranians*. Brill, Leiden.

Kuzmina, Olga

2000 Abashevskaya kul'tura v Samarskom Povolzh'e. In *Istoriya Samarskogo Povolzh'ya s Drevnesihikh Vremen do Nashikh Dnei*, pp. 85–121. Samaraskii Gosudarstvennyi Pedagogicheskii Universitet, Samara.

Kuznetsov, P. F.

1996 Novye radiouglerodnye daty dlya khronologii kul'tur Eneolita-Bronzogo veka iuga lesostepnogo Povolzhya. *Arkheologiya I Radiouglerod* 1:56–60.

2003 Osobennosti kurgannykh obryadov naseleniya Samraskoi doliny v pervoi polovine Bronzogo Veka. In *Material'naya Kul'tura Naseleniya basseina reki Samary v Bronzovom Veke*, edited by Iu. I. Kolev, P. F. Kuznetsov, and O. D. Mochalov, pp. 43–51. Samarskogo Gosudarstvennogo Pedagogicheskogo Universiteta, Samara.

2005 An Indo-European Symbol of Power in the Earliest Steppe Kurgans. *Journal of Indo-European Studies* 33(3–4):325–338.

Lavrushin, Iu. A., and E. A. Spriridonova

1995 Rezul'taty paleomorfologicheskikh issledovanii na stoiankakh Neolita-Bronzy v basseine r. Samary. In *Neolit i Eneolit Iuga Lesostepi Volgo-Ural'skogo Mezhdurehiya*, edited by N. L. Morgunova, pp. 177–200. OGPU, Orenburg.

Malov, N. M.

1994 Kulturnye tipy pamyatnikov srubnoy kulturno-istoricheskoy oblasti. In *Srubnaya Kulturno-Istoricheskaya Oblast*, edited by N. M. Malov, pp. 8–13. Saratovsky Gosudarstvenny Universitet, Sarato.

2002 Spears—Signs of Archaic Leaders of the Pokrovsk Archaeological Culture. In *Complex Societies of Central Eurasia from the 3rd to the 1st Millennium BC*, Vol. I, edited by Karlene Jones-Bley and D. G. Zdanovich, pp. 314–336. Journal of Indo-European Studies Monograph 45. Institute for the Study of Man, Washington, D.C.

Merpert, N. Y.

1958 Iz drevneishei istorii Srednogo Povozh'ya. *Materiali i Issledovaniya Arkheologiya SSSR* 61:45–157.

Morales Muniz, Arturo, and Antipina, Ekaterina

2003 Srubnaya Faunas and Beyond: A Critical Assessment of the Archaeozoological Information from the East European Steppe. In *Prehistoric Steppe Adaptation and the Horse*, edited by M. Levine, C. Renfrew, and K. Boyle, pp. 329–351. McDonald Institute, Cambridge.

Morgunova, N. L., and O. S. Khokhlova

2006 Kurgans and Nomads: New Investigations of Mound Burials in the Southern Urals. *Antiquity* 80:303–317.

Morgunova, N. L., and O. I. Porokhova

1989 Poseleniya Srubnoi kul'tury v Orenburgskoi oblasti. In *Poseleniya Srubnoi Obshchnosti*, edited by A. D. Pryakhin, pp. 160–172. VGU, Voronezh.

Morgunova, N. L., and M. A. Turetskii

2003 Yamnye pamyatniki u s. Shumaevo: novye dannye o kolesnom transporte u naseleniya zapadnogo Orenburzh'ya v epokha rannego metalla. In *Voprosy Arkheologii Povozh'ya vyp.3*, pp. 144–159. Samarskii Nauchnyi Tsentr RAN, Samara.

Myakutin, A.

1911 *Gnezo Samarskikh Kazakov: Ocherk is istorii Orenburgskogo kazachestva. Voenno-Istoricheskikk Sbornik 4.* SPb, Orenburg.

Nefedov, F. D.

1899   Otchet ob arkheologicheskikh issledovaniyakh v Iuzhnom Priural'e proizvedennykh letom 1887 i 1888 gg. *Материалы по археологии восточных губерний* 3. Императорское Московское Археологическое Общество, Moskva.

Petrenko, A. G.

1984   *Drevnee i Srednevekovoe Zhivotnovodstvo Srednego Povolzh'ya i Predural'ya.* Nauka, Moskva.

1995   Rezultaty opredeleniya arkheologicheskikh materialov iz raskopok Ivanovskoi stoianki. In *Неолит и энеолит юга лесостепи Волго-Уральского междуречья*, edited by N. L. Morgunova, pp. 205–220. OGPU, Orenburg.

Pryakhin, A. D.

1980   Abashevskaya kul'turno-istoricheskaya obshchnost' epokhi bronzy i lesostepe. In *Arkheologiya Vostochno-Evropeiskoi Lesostepi*, edited by A. D. Pryakhin, pp. 7–32. Voronezhskogo Universiteta, Voronezh.

Sal'nikov, K. V.

1967   *Ocherki Drevnei Istorii Iuzhnogo Urala.* Akad. Nauka, Moskva.

Shnirelman, V. A.

1995   From Internationalism to Nationalism: Forgotten Pages of Soviet Archaeology in the 1930s and 1940s. In *Nationalism, Politics, and the Practice of Archaeology*, edited by P. L. Kohl, and C. Fawcett, pp. 120–138. Cambridge University Press, Cambridge.

Spiridonova, E. A.

1989   Rezultati izucheniya kul'turnogo sloya Mosolovskogo poseleniya epokhi pozdnei bronzey metodom sporo-pyl'tsevogo analiza, In *Poseleniya Srubnoi obshnosti—Mezhvuzovskii Sbornik Nauchnikh Trudov*, edited by A. D. Pryakhin, pp. 53–55. Voronezhskogo Univesitet, Voronezh.

Vasiliev, I. B.

1980   Mogil'nik Yamno-Poltavkinslogo vremnei u s. Utyevka v srednem Povolzh'e. In *Arkheologiya Vostochno-Evropeiskoi Lesostepi*, edited by A. D. Pryakhin and N. Y. Merpert, pp. 32–58. Voronezhskogo Universiteta, Voronezh.

1999   Poselenie Lbishche na Samarskoi Luke i nekotorye problem Bronzogo Veka Srednogo Povolzh'ya. In *Voprosy Arkheologii Urala I Povolzh'ya*. Samarskogo Gosudarstvennogo Pedagogicheskogo Universiteta, Samara.

Vasiliev, I. B. (editor)

1998   *Problemy Drevnei Istorii Severnogo Prikaspiya.* Samarskii Gosudarstvennyi Pedagogicheskii Universitet, Samara.

Vasiliev, I. B., and P. F. Kuznetsov

1988   Poltavkinskie mogil'niki u s. Krasnosamarskoe v lesostepnom zavolzh'e. In *Issledovanie Pamyatnikov Arkheologii Vostochnoi Evropy*, edited by A. T. Siniuk, pp. 39–59. Voronezhskii Gosudarstvennyi Pedagogicheskii Institut, Voronezh.

Vasiliev, I. B., P. F. Kuznetsov, and A. P. Semenova

1994   *Potapovskii Kurgannyi Mogil'nik Indoiranskikh Plemen na Volge*. Samarskii Universitet, Samara.

Vasiliev, I. B., and G. I. Matveeva

1979   Mogil'nik u s. S'yezhee na R. Samare. *Sovietskaya Arkheologiia* 4:147–166.

Yablonsky, L. T.

2002   Archaeological Mythology and Some Real Problems of the Current Archaeology. In *Complex Societies of Central Eurasia from the 3rd to the 1st Millennium BC*, Vol. I, edited by Karlene Jones-Bley and D. G. Zdanovich, pp. 82–94. Journal of Indo-European Studies Monograph 45. Institute for the Study of Man, Washington, D.C.

Chapter 5

Paleoecological Evidence for Vegetation, Climate, and Land-Use Change in the Lower Samara River Valley

Laura M. Popova

It is not uncommon in Russian archaeology for climate data to be used to help reconstruct human history (see Mitusov et al. 2009). The two methods most commonly used to reconstruct past climates are the morphological and chemical analysis of buried soils under archaeological monuments (particularly burial mounds) and the palynological analysis of cores from lakes and swamps. In this chapter, the results of this previous research are briefly discussed to demonstrate that most of these studies are aimed at charting major climatic shifts and vegetation changes over large regions. Recently, however, there has been a call to look at the ways in which these broad climatic changes affected local environments, since the steppe regions of Russia are more geologically and botanically diverse than scholars tend to recognize (see Klimenko 1998, 2000, 2003; Koryakova and Epimakhov 2007). From the standpoint of archaeological research, locally oriented paleoecological research is often more helpful for interpreting the remains of a particular place. Thus, the majority of this chapter is devoted to discussing how the local vegetation history of the lower Samara River valley region both reflects larger climatic trends and demonstrates important deviations from the larger picture.

Buried Soil Studies

Although paleosols uncovered under burial mounds in Russia have been studied since the beginning of the twentieth century, this aspect of geological research did not

really develop until after the 1980s (Mitusov et al. 2009). Since then, researchers of the Eurasian Steppe have used a number of soil science methods to better understand past climates. Traditionally, soil scientists have examined "the thickness of soil horizons, the distribution of organic carbon as well as carbonate, soluble salts and gypsum" to reconstruct paleoenvironments (Mitusov et al. 2009:1155). For the purpose of determining paleoclimates, soil scientists prefer to look at buried soils from archaeological monuments in the region between the Caspian and Aral Seas, because salts are transported from the Caspian Sea into the local soils during periods of aridity (Ivanov and Vasiliev 1995). For the most part, however, qualitative changes in climate (with an emphasis on humidity) have been inferred based on carbonate content and distribution in paleosols (Demkin, Borisov, et al. 2004; Morgunova and Khokhlova 2006). Based on this type of research, the climate for the Bronze Age in the Aral-Caspian region has been reconstructed in the following way: there was a period of aridity beginning around 3000 BC and reaching its maximum around 2000 BC, becoming a period of relative humidity by about 1000 BC (e.g., Khokhlova et al. 2001). Ivanov (1992, 1996) and Demkin et al. (1997) place the period of maximum aridity between 2000 and 1700 BC based on paleosols from southern Russia and Ukraine.

Recently, a study was conducted to look at the magnetic property of paleosols from the lower Volga region in an effort to provide a more nuanced precipitation history (see

Alekseeva et al. 2007). The researchers discovered that the level of precipitation was similar to today around 4000 BC, with the lowest levels of precipitation around 3000 to 2000 BC (a 15 percent reduction compared to the present day). There was a modest increase in rainfall around 1800 to 1600 BC, which seemed to continue until about 100 AD (see Alekseeva et al. 2007; Demkin, El'tsov, et al. 2004). This type of research looks promising, but as Mitusov et al. (2009:1157) warn, "Soil magnetic properties strongly depend on the hydrological regime and hence the landscape position." Thus, it is important that the exact position of the archaeological site on the landscape be given. Unfortunately, site descriptions are often missing from archaeological publications from this region. It should be noted in both of these cases that the end result of both forms of research is a description of climatic trends that are supposed to affect a very large area of Eurasia.

Palynological Studies

Although the Siberian portion of the Eurasian steppe is more often the site of palynological research, there have been quite a few pollen studies in the Eastern European section as well (e.g., Bolikhovskaya 1990; Kremenetski 1995, 1997; Kremenetski et al. 1997; Kremenetski, Chichagova, et al. 1999; Spiridonova 1991; Velichko et al. 1997). Studies dealing with the Volga-Ural region in particular have focused on the Pobochnoe swamp (Buzuluk forest) in the Samara oblast (Fedorova 1951; Kremenetski, Bittger, et al. 1999; Piavchenko and Kozlovskaya 1958). In this palynological research, there is always a tension between larger trends in climate change and the way in which these shifts affect subregions. This can be seen in a discussion of the recent palynological research of the Eastern European steppe. There is strong agreement that from 6000 to 4000 BC, the climate in the region was warm and continental with the precipitation levels like today (see Kremenetski 1995). From around 4000 to 2500 BC, the climate was colder and wetter than today. Then, around 2500 BC, the climate started to become drier in the Eastern European steppe region, including Samara oblast. The climate was most arid between 2200 and 1700 BC in the lower Don and Dniepr regions (see Kremenetski 1995; Kremenetski et al. 1997). Spiridonova (1991) and Bolikhovsaya (1990) found similar results in the middle Don and lower Volga regions, respectively. Palynologists have noted that in this region, there was an arid climate phase between 2500 and 1500 BC. This period of aridity, recorded in many regions of Eastern Europe, western Siberia, and Kazakhstan, coincides with the end of the Middle Bronze Age and the beginning of the Late Bronze Age (Kremenetski 1997; Velichko et al. 1997).

The climate started to become wetter and cooler around 1300 to 800 BC for the lower Don and Dniepr region according to Kremenetski, Chichagova, et al. (1999). In the lower Volga region, however, Bolikhovskaya (1990) argued that this moist climatic phase occurred between 1500 and 700 BC.

Based on paleosol research and the palynological studies of swamp and lake cores, it is clear that major climatic events affected the lives of people during the Bronze Age in the Volga-Ural region. The next section, however, is devoted to looking at how the palynological analysis of a core from the Sharlyk swamp in Samara, compared against the regional data, can provide insight into local vegetation shifts.

The Study Region: The Lower Samara River Valley[1]

The Sharlyk swamp is situated in the middle Volga region within the administrative borders of the Samara province of Russia (Figure 5.1). More specifically, it is located in the basin of the Samara River (a left tributary of the Volga River) in the center of the Samara region. It is near the village of Krasnosamarskoe and borders a series of recently created lakes. The forests in the region consist primarily of *Pinus*, *Betula*, and *Populus*. The swamp itself formed from an oxbow lake, a former channel of the Samara River. The coordinates for the extraction point are 53°02'06.5"N, 50°50'17.4"E.

The Samara River, which is about 575 km in length, is one of the longest rivers in Eastern Europe. Connecting the Volga and Ural regions of Russia, this river is also considered to be the dividing line (or ecotone) between the steppe and the forest-steppe. An ecotone is a transitional area between two provincial (zonal) boundaries, which usually has a mixture of vegetation from both provinces. The shifting position of ecotones through time, representing both climate change and human impact, can be easily mapped in a pollen core. For this reason, palynologists often take cores from ecotonal contexts, where the shifting vegetation patterns will be clearest.

The Sharlyk swamp is also located near many places of archaeological significance. During the Bronze Age (~3300–800 BC), the Samara River valley was consistently used as a location for burials and later settlements in the Late and Final Bronze Ages. It was also an important source of pasture, with the lush reeds growing along the abundant marshes of the region providing fodder throughout the year. Archaeologists have discovered more than one hundred Bronze Age sites, both kurgan cemeteries and settlements, in this valley alone.[2] In the immediate vicinity

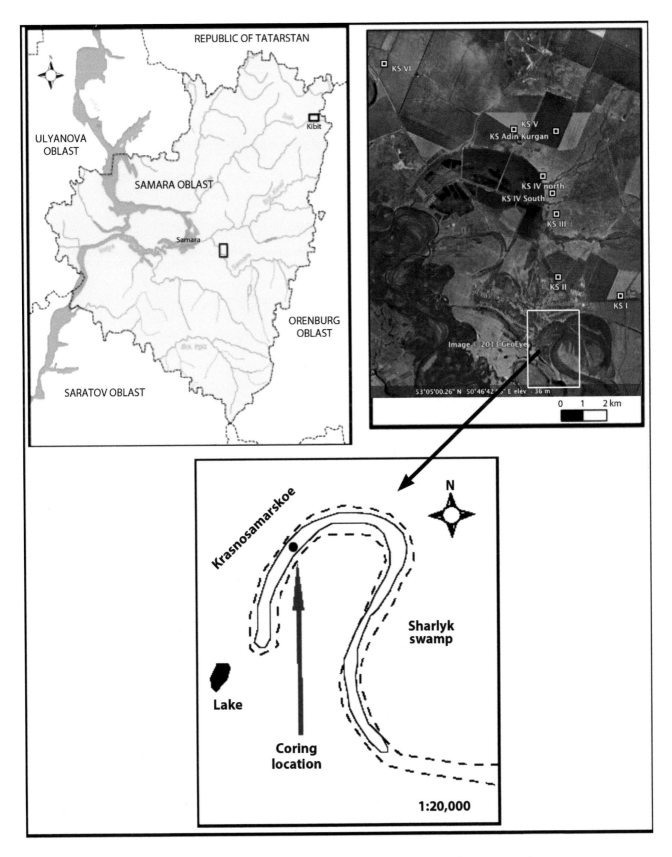

Figure 5.1 Location of the coring location at Sharlyk near Krasnosamarskoe. KS I to VI are kurgan cemeteries. (Top Right: Google Earth; Image © 2013 GeoEye)

of the coring site at Sharlyk, a series of Bronze Age burial and settlement sites were located at Krasnosamarskoe, where the first kurgan burial was established at the very beginning of the Middle Bronze Age. In the next section as I explain each pollen assemblage zone, I will also describe what was happening at Krasnosamarskoe and other areas in the lower Samara River region. In this way, it will be possible to directly address the role of human activity in environmental change in each period.

The pollen sequence from the Sharlyk core can also be related to another pollen core extracted from Pobochnoe swamp in the Buzuluk forest located farther east in the upper Samara River region. Analyzed by Kremenetski, Bittger, et al. (1999), this core was used to establish the basic climatic shifts that affected the region during the Holocene. By comparing Sharlyk and Pobochnoe, it is possible to see both the changes in vegetation that are common to both, reflecting a regional change, and those that are unique to each core, representing local change (Table 5.1).

Sampling and Pollen Analysis

The swamp at Sharlyk was cored with a Russian sediment sampler to the depth of 475 cm.[3] Radiocarbon dates were obtained for the whole length of the core from the University of Arizona AMS laboratory. Here I will present the results from the first 160 cm sampled at 10-cm intervals. The stratigraphy of the peat for the first segment of the core is as follows:

0–15 cm: Brown fibrous herbaceous sediments (Cyperaceae, *Equisetum*, *Phragmites*)

15–88 cm: Dark brown poorly humidified peat

88–160 cm: Dark brown mostly humidified peat

Samples were treated following standard procedures described in detail elsewhere (see Popova 2006:Appendix A). For each sample, a minimum of 300 pollen grains were counted (Maher 1972). Pollen identification was carried out using the standard keys of Moore et al. (1991), Reille

Table 5.1 Archaeological Periods Covered in the Text for the Middle Volga Region

Time Period	Dates
Eneolithic	4500–3300 BC
Early Bronze Age	3300–2800 BC
Middle Bronze Age	2800–1800 BC
Late Bronze Age	1800–1300 BC
Final Bronze Age	1300–800 BC
Iron Age	800 BC–400 AD
Middle Age	400–1500 AD

(1992, 1995, 1998), and Andrew (1984) together with the reference collection at the Paleoecology Laboratory at the University of Chicago and at the Institute of Geography, Russian Academy of Sciences in Moscow. The plant nomenclature used in this text follows Czerepanov (1995). A present-day pollen rain study conducted in the southern Urals designed to establish the relation between pollen production and dispersal of different vegetation types in this particular region was used as an aid in interpreting vegetation patterns in the fossil pollen data (Diaz-del-Rio et al. 2006; Lopez et al. 2003).

Pollen Diagram

Pollen percentages were calculated as percentages of the total pollen sum (arboreal pollen [AP] + nonarboreal pollen [NAP]). The percentages of other microfossils (e.g., pollen of aquatic plants and spores) were calculated as a percentage of the pollen sum plus the microfossil count. To highlight changes in rare taxa, those that regularly constituted less than 5 percent of the total pollen sum, the signature was enhanced three times on the chart (represented by the white as opposed to the black filled lines). The diagram is divided into six local pollen assemblage zones (PAZ) indicating a change in vegetation (Figure 5.2). Calibrated radiocarbon dates, showing the calendric age, are provided on the left side of the diagram to make the chart more accessible to archaeologists. The uncalibrated dates BP are also provided on the right side of the chart to make this pollen diagram comparable to other pollen studies that have been conducted in the region (especially Kremenetski, Bittger, et al. 1999; Lopez et al. 2003). The diagram was plotted using the C2 computer program (Juggins 2006).

Vegetation History

The starting point for the chronology of the Sharlyk pollen record presented here is based on a single radiocarbon date of 5508 ± 45 BP (4380 ± 46 cal BC) (AA60511) from the depth of 163 cm. The pollen assemblage phases presented here are in agreement with the known pollen sequence from the Samara River valley (Kremenetski, Bittger, et al. 1999).

Pollen Assemblage Zone 1 (ca. 5500–4500 BP/4300–3000 cal BC)

PAZ 1 (Figure 5.2) is established at the depth of 160 to 140 cm. It corresponds to the time between 4300 and 3000 BC and thus encompasses much of the Eneolithic in the middle Volga region and the beginning of the Early Bronze Age. At this time, the paleolake at Pobochnoe (Buzuluk forest) was transformed into a peat eutrophic swamp (Krementski, Bittger, et al. 1999). Based on the stratigraphic data, it

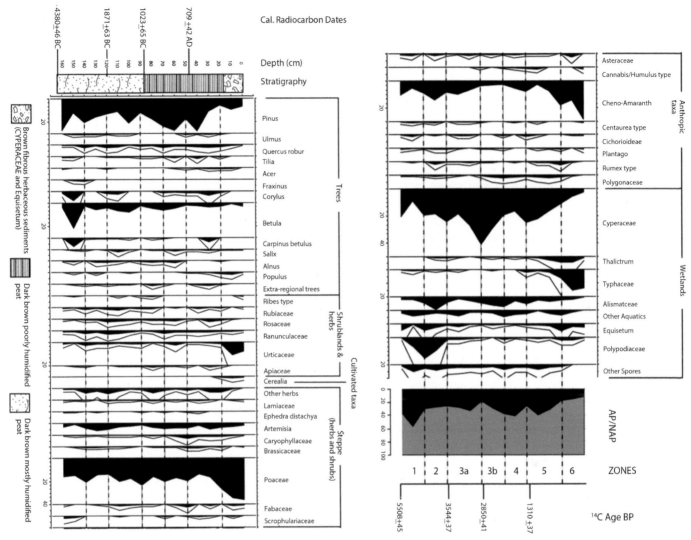

Figure 5.2 (a) Percentage pollen diagram from Sharlyk swamp.   **Figure 5.2 (b)** Percentage pollen diagram from Sharlyk swamp.

seems that the old oxbow lake at Sharlyk became a swamp at an earlier date.

Although the more northern Sok River was the preferred location for most settlements and cemeteries in the Samara oblast in the Eneolithic, the Samara River valley was home to a particularly rich burial ground at S'yezzhee and a settlement further upstream at Vilovatoe. Two of the locations that Early Bronze Age groups preferred were Utyevka and Pokrovka. Burial mounds were built at these locations near major bends in the Samara River. Both were located on the left bank of the river, the zone that is traditionally considered the steppe zone (Kolev et al. 2000).

In PAZ 1, the arboreal pollen is characterized at first by high levels of *Pinus* (28 percent), later followed by a reduction in *Pinus* but an increase in *Betula* (22 percent), *Corylus* (8 percent), and *Carpinus betulus* (7 percent), with *Fraxinus*,

Ulmus, Quercus robur, Tilia, and *Alnus,* among the other tree taxa.[4] The relatively high percentage of *Betula* suggests the development of a riparian forest around the Sharlyk swamp, where birch plays a less significant role at present. Vicent et al. (2000) have confirmed that *Betula* pollen values over 10 percent are only registered in the region when a birch forest grows at a distance of less than 100 m from the sampling point.

Rapid changes in the percentage content between *Pinus* and *Betula* in pollen diagrams often reflect shifts due to periodic forest fires (Kremenetski, Bittger, et al. 1999). Small fragments of charcoal were common in the sample from the 150-cm depth, corresponding to the shift to *Betula* in the pollen diagram during this phase. Rysin (1975) has shown that pine forests, which are sensitive to forest fire, tend to be initially colonized by birch after a fire in European Russia.

In PAZ 1, arboreal pollen constitutes 56 percent of the total terrestrial pollen sum. At no other time period encompassed in this section of the core does the arboreal pollen dominate the pollen assemblage. Among the herbaceous taxa, the presence of Poaceae and Chenopodiaceae/Amaranthaceae pollen indicate the existence of natural steppe communities in the region. It is interesting to note that at the end of this phase, the percentage of aquatic pollen and spores, primarily Polypodiaceae (15 percent), increases considerably, making up 23 percent of the total pollen sum. Polypody, thriving in moist shady conditions, spread throughout the wet swamp. From a paleoclimatic point of view, this 1,300-year phase is usually interpreted as a cool humid period (Kremenetski, Bittger, et al. 1999:1201). Such a climate allowed for the expansion of pine and birch forests, as well as groves of alder (*Alnus*). Moreover, the swamp was more consistently wet, allowing for the spread of Polypodiaceae. However, it did not allow for the expansion of steppe vegetation, which remained relatively stable during this time period.

Pollen Assemblage Zone 2 (ca. 4500–3500 BP/3000–1800 cal BC)

PAZ 2 (Figure 5.2) is established at the depth of 120 to 140 cm. The radiocarbon dates that bracket this zone are 3000 and 1800 BC. The central 600 years within this period represent the Middle Bronze Age, but the earliest two centuries represent the Early Bronze Age, and the last 400 years include the transitional era at the end of the Middle Bronze Age as well as the opening century of the Late Bronze Age. Quite a lot happened in the Samara Valley during these important periods. In the Middle Bronze Age, after around 2800 BC, the number of cemeteries and settlements increased significantly in the Samara Valley. Twenty-one sites are assigned to the Middle Bronze Age Poltavka culture, distributed largely across the steppe zone to the south, with the Samara River valley forming its northern border. Settlements began to increase in size and number in the final transitional centuries of the Middle Bronze Age, around 2200 to 1800 BC, but most occurred north of the Samara River near the Zhiguli Mountains, where they are assigned to the local Vol'sko-Lbishche culture, and in the forest-steppe zone, where they are assigned to the Abashevo culture. In the southern, steppe part of the Samara oblast, the Potapovka culture appeared during this critical era of change but is represented only by cemeteries. Potapovka cemeteries show very close stylistic and ritual similarities to the cemeteries of the Sintashta culture to the east. Potapovka and Sintashta graves had very similar pottery, weapons, paired horse sacrifices, and bone or antler cheekpieces. Late Bronze Age types of graves, pottery, and weapons grew out of Sintashta and Potapovka types.

In the Middle Bronze Age, the Samara River no doubt served as a vital link between the Urals in the east and the Volga River and Zhiguli Mountains in the west. It seems likely that abundant marshes in this river valley were attractive pastures for the pastoralists during this time period (Kolev et al. 2000). At Krasnosamarskoe IV, the archaeological site closest to the Sharlyk swamp, three burials mounds were built at the beginning of this phase around 2900 to 2800 BC. One of the burial mounds, Kurgan 3, was later partially reconstructed and reused around 1950 BC (Anthony et al. 2003).

In PAZ 2, among the terrestrial pollen, the frequency of arboreal pollen decreased and herbs increased during this phase. In particular, this phase is characterized by lower values of *Pinus* (15 percent) and *Betula* (5 percent) pollen. Other tree taxa are *Quercus robur*, *Alnus*, and *Populus*. The low *Betula* values and the increased *Alnus* and, to some extent, *Populus* suggest the decline of birch forests in the region and the spreading of pioneer species (e.g., *Alnus* and *Populus*). A similar signature has been reported at Kargaly in the southern Urals (Lopez et al. 2003).

Although the percentage of Poaceae (14 percent) pollen remains the same throughout this period, there is a significant increase in the percentage of pollen from other herbaceous taxa. For example, the high values of *Artemisia*, Asteraceae, and Chenopodiaceae/Amaranthaceae suggest that steppe vegetation expanded during this phase. A similarly dramatic increase in *Artemisia* has been noted in the Pobochnoe bog for the same time period (Kremenetski, Bittger, et al. 1999).

Throughout this phase, the share of spores in the total percentage values decreased due to a reduction in the frequency of Polypodiaceae and *Equisetum*. However, this decrease in nonpollen palynomorphs is matched by an increase in Cyperaceae (sedges) and Alismataceae. Sedges prefer open moist conditions, in contrast to ferns, such as polypody, which prefer moist shady conditions. Both the reduction in arboreal pollen and a decrease in Polypodiaceae indicate that the forests were receding from the swamp during this phase. The presence of Alismataceae, however, suggests the presence of shallow water somewhere in the vicinity of Sharlyk. Plant species in the family Alismataceae (such as *Alisma* and *Sagittaria*) prefer to grow in shallow water or on the muddy shores of lakes and rivers.

Indicators of human activity, such as *Plantago*, *Rumex*, and Asteraceae (including *Centurea* type), increase slightly during this time period, indicating that this region was used more intensively during the late Early Bronze Age and Middle Bronze Age. The presence of Early and

Middle Bronze Age kurgans at Krasnosamarskoe in the immediate vicinity of Sharlyk swamp further supports the possibility that this region was used for pasture during this phase. Similar signatures of disturbance have been linked to a slightly later period at Kargaly (Lopez et al. 2003).

In this phase, the forest area in the Sharlyk region was reduced and the area of the steppe increased. These changes, similar to those that happened at the Pobochnoe bog further upstream, may be related to a dry and warm climatic phase recorded throughout much of Eurasia (Kremenetski 1997; Kremenetski et al. 1997; Velichko et al. 1997).

Pollen Assemblage Zone 3 (ca. 3500–2200 BP/1800–270 cal BC)

PAZ 3 (Figure 5.2), established at the depth of 70 to 120 m, can be dated to 1800 to 270 BC, which includes the Late and Final Bronze Ages and part of the Iron Age. Generally, this long phase is defined by a rapid increase in Cyperaceae and an increase in herbaceous plants, especially Poaceae, and fluctuating levels of arboreal pollen. This zone has been visually subdivided into two subzones, described below.

Subzone 3a (ca. 3500–2800 BP/1800–1000 cal BC)

Pollen assemblage subzone 3a covers the entire Late Bronze Age. This phase also corresponds with some of the most intense activity in the region recorded in prehistory. During this time, hundreds of new kurgans and settlements were established in the Volga-Ural region, usually on high terraces. It is interesting to note, however, that many of the burial mounds constructed on the lower terraces of the Samara River during the Early and Middle Bronze Ages were reused during the Late and Final Bronze Ages, something that was not normally practiced elsewhere (Kuznetsov and Mochalov 2003). At least 26 long-term settlements were also established in the Samara River valley at this time.

A structure was built at Krasnosamarskoe, 100 m to the west of the kurgan cemetery, at the beginning of this phase in approximately 1850 BC. Moreover, additional burials were added to Kurgan 3, which had been extended about 100 years earlier. Later, around 1750 BC, a larger structure was built in the same location as the first structure. At the same time, Kurgan 3 continued to serve as the local cemetery (Anthony et al. 2005). All of these activities affected the local environment, especially the construction of large semi-subterranean wooden structures.

In pollen assemblage subzone 3a, the percentage of arboreal pollen remains the same as that in the preceding period. This signature stands in contrast to the one found in the Pobochnoe marsh in which total arboreal pollen increased during this time period (Kremenetski, Bittger, et al. 1999). *Pinus* and *Betula* continue to dominate the forests of the region, although the other trees and shrubs represented in the pollen record change. At the beginning of this phase, the percentage of *Corylus* and *Salix* pollen increases, while the percentage of *Alnus* and *Populus* pollen declines. The decrease in *Alnus* pollen could be the result of alder exploitation during the Late Bronze Age. Alder makes good steady burning charcoal, and there is some indication that metalworking was practiced in the region during this time. By removing alder from the region near the Sharlyk swamp, it would have opened the forest up for colonization by other species such as *Salix* and *Corylus*. Based on the presence of charcoal in the samples from the beginning of this phase (120 cm depth), it is possible that a fire in the predominately pine forest allowed for the expansion of these colonizing species. There is also an expansion of shrubs and herbs that favor forests with light cover, including *Ribes*, Rubiaceae, and Rosaceae. It seems likely that pine wood was also used for constructing the large semi-subterranean wooden pit structures in the region, and this no doubt contributed to the decline of pine in the region. The increase in *Corylus* (hazelnut) pollen during this time period could also be linked to human activity, with the inhabitants of the region actively protecting these particular trees for their nutritious seeds.

The sharp decline in arboreal pollen indicated at the end of this phase (ca. 1000 BC) is more a reflection of the higher values of some hydrophyte and hygrophyte palynomorphs, especially Cyperaceae (40 percent), which are likely to be overrepresented in swamp samples. It should be noted that at the same time, there is a reduction in the pollen from aquatic plants, which suggests that the swamp was drier during this time period. It seems likely that at the end of this period, the Sharlyk swamp was expanding, perhaps as lakes in the region dried up.

High percentages of Poaceae, Chenopodiaceae/ Amaranthaceae, and *Artemisia* during this time period indicate the continued dominance of steppe vegetation in the region. It should be noted that Chenopodiaceae/ Amaranthaceae is more dominant at the beginning of this subphase, perhaps because the domesticated animals in the region (including at Krasnosamarskoe) helped to maintain and spread this type of plant as they grazed around the steppe surrounding Sharlyk. Once the settlement nearby was abandoned, grasses (Poaceae) begin to be the dominant plant in the steppe lands of the region. The presence of Asteraceae, *Cichorium*-type, *Rumex*, and *Plantago* pollen (all characteristic indicators of human activity) denote the continued transformation of the vegetation near Sharlyk by humans and animals. It should be noted, however, that the level of disturbance cannot be considered enough to constitute overgrazing.[5] Much higher levels of vegetation transformation have been noted at Gorny, a mining and metalworking settlement in the southern Urals, where palynologists have uncovered signatures of 20 percent *Cichorium*-type and 4 percent *Plantago* pollen (Lopez-Garcia et al. 2000). In the samples from Sharlyk, *Cichorium* and *Plantago* only made up 2 percent of the total terrestrial pollen sum together.[6]

In Russian studies (e.g., Khotinsky 1984), the Late Subboreal (roughly 3200–2500 BP) is characterized by cool climatic event that continues into the Sub-Atlantic (ca. 2500 BP to the present). Still, other pollen studies in the region (see Lopez et al. 2003) have demonstrated that there was a short warming period from 3200 to 3100 BP (1600–1400 BC). The warming period can be seen in this phase by the expansion of *Corylus*, which prefers warmer conditions (Finsinger et al. 2005). Similarly, the expansion of the steppe during the middle of this phase could indicate a short warm, dry period.

Subzone 3b (ca. 2800–2200 BP/1000–270 cal BC)
Pollen assemblage subzone 3b covers the end of the Final Bronze Age and the beginning of the Iron Age. During this time period, most settlements are farther north in the forest-steppe zone of the middle Volga region, particularly in the Sok River valley. There were, however, settlements at Poplavskoe and Maksimovka in the Samara River valley. In both instances, these settlements were first inhabited during the Late Bronze Age but continued to be important throughout the Final Bronze Age (Kolev et al. 2000). During the very beginning of the Iron Age (800–600 BC), local groups used kurgans that were constructed during the Bronze Age as the resting place for their dead (Mishkin and Skarbovenko 2000). Toward the end of this phase, people associated with the early Sarmatian culture continued to use older kurgans, but occasionally they would construct new kurgans in the region as well, including one at Krasnosamarskoe I. They preferred the Samara River valley over the other river valleys in the region in terms of burial locations.

During this phase, the percentage of Cyperaceae (sedges) represented in the terrestrial pollen sum dramatically decreased, and the percentage of aquatic pollen increased, especially Alismataceae. This signature suggests that the Sharlyk swamp was wetter than it was in the previous period, with pockets of standing water.

Although an increase in arboreal pollen is indicated in the pollen diagram for this phase, it seems that this pattern represents more the decrease in Cyperaceae rather than change in the character of forests at this time. The forests are still primarily composed of *Pinus* and *Betula*, with some *Quercus robur* and *Alnus*. *Corylus* and *Salix* are no longer represented in the pollen record during this time period. Pollen from herbaceous plants remains relatively stable, but during the middle of this phase, there is a reduction in Poaceae pollen that is related to an increase in other herbaceous plants such as *Artemisia*, *Campanula*, Liliaceae, and *Convolvulus* type. There are few anthropogenic indicators in this particular pollen assemblage zone, which perhaps shows that humans and animals had less of an impact on the environment of the region during this time period than in the proceeding period.

**Pollen Assemblage Zone 4
(ca. 2200–1300 BP/270 BC–700 AD)**
PAZ 4 (Figure 5.2), established at the depth of 50 to 70 cm, includes the remainder of the Iron Age. During the Middle Sarmatian period of the Iron Age (ca. 200 BC–200 AD), there were few burials in the Samara region. It is interesting to note, however, that one of the most important sites that we know of from this time period is a kurgan cemetery located in the Samara River valley near the Ural Mountain foothills at Gvardetsi (Mishkin and Skarbovenko 2000). This site is particularly interesting in that it has kurgans from the Bronze Age, Iron Age, up to the Middle Ages. The Samara River valley was also the preferred river valley for burials during the Late Sarmatian period (200–500 AD), although they started building their own small kurgans rather than relying on previously built burial mounds.

The percentage of arboreal pollen increases during this time period, as does the diversity of trees represented in the pollen record. *Pinus* is overwhelmingly the most common tree type, with *Quercus*, *Tilia*, *Acer*, *Corylus*, *Betula*, *Salix*, and *Alnus* represented as well. The swamp vegetation is still defined by Cyperaceae, although there is still an element of aquatic plants such as *Alisma* and *Sagittaria*. At the end of this period, *Typha* becomes more common in the region, perhaps growing at the edge of ponds. Plants from Rosaceae and Ranunculaceae families, as well as *Urtica*, composed the understory of the forests. The dominant vegetation in the region was still herbaceous plants, primarily Poaceae, Chenopodiaceae/Amaranthaceae, and *Artemisia*, but also Caryophyllaceae, Fabaceae, and, at the end of the phase, *Brassica*. This phase is marked by increased plant diversity in all environmental settings.

Pollen Assemblage Zone 5
(ca. 1300–500 BP/700–1100 AD)

PAZ 5 (Figure 5.2), established at the depth of 20 to 50 cm and includes most of the Middle Ages. During the early Middle Ages (ca. 400–900 AD), the first large permanent wooden towns were constructed in the region, although not in the Samara River valley. Instead, farmers and pastoralists constructed settlements in more defensible locations, such as the Zhiguli Mountains west of the Volga River. During the second period of the Middle Ages (1000–1300 AD), before the Mongol invasion, pastoralists (Pechenegs) established several kurgan cemeteries in the Samara River valley. For example, at Pokrovka, they established five kurgans. Settlements at this time were still clustered much farther to the north in the more forested region and in the Zhiguli Mountains (Vasiliev and Matveeva 1986).

The percentage of arboreal pollen remained high in this period but decreased substantially in the second half of this phase. This decrease in arboreal pollen is no doubt related to the rapid decrease in pine pollen. The presence of large quantities of charcoal in the pollen sample from a 40-cm depth suggests that this decline could have been related to a forest fire. This perhaps explains the increase in *Corylus*, which can be a colonizer after a fire. However, a fire cannot explain all of the change indicated in the pollen record. *Betula* was relatively unaffected through the period. *Quercus* and *Carpinus betulus*, which are relatively slow-growing trees, both increased during the second half of this phase. It seems that the clearance of forests by humans during this time period led to this particular signature in the pollen record. The percentage of arboreal pollen in the total terrestrial pollen sum never increased after this phase. Other indications of human activity can be found in the pollen record, as the percentage of *Rumex* and *Plantago* pollen increased during this phase.

Steppe vegetation still defined the landscape in the region, dominated by Poaceae, Chenopodiaceae/Amaranthaceae, *Artemisia*, and other herbs such as *Hypericum* and Caprifoliaceae. On the other hand, the vegetation that characterized the swamp changed considerably during this time. The percentage of Cyperaceae pollen continued to decline, replaced in part by an increase in *Thalictrum*. Although the percentage of pollen from Alismataceae and other aquatics decreased during this time period, the percentage of *Typha* increased. *Typha* prefers to grow in shallow ponds up to 15 cm in depth. Similarly, although the amount of nonpollen palynomorphs decreased during this time period in general, there is an increase in the percentage of Polypodiaceae and *Equisetum* spores.

Pollen Assemblage Zone 6 (the Last 500 Years BP)

PAZ 6 (Figure 5.2) is established at the depth of 0 to 20 cm, representing a period extending from the Middle Ages to the present (1100 AD–present). This time was a period of increased activity in the region. During the Golden Horde period (ca. 1236–1500 AD), kurgans continued to be established in the Samara River valley in the same locations where pastoral groups in the previous period had established kurgan cemeteries (Vasiliev and Matveeva 1986). A Russian Imperial presence was established in the region in 1586, when a wooden fort was built at the site of the present-day city of Samara. The region was first defined by cattle trading and later became a major grain-trading center. During the Soviet period, a collective farm (*sovhoz*) was established at Krasnosamarskoe and, at the time, irrigation agriculture was introduced to the region. Settled stock breeding was also an important part of the collective farm. Both wheat (with the addition of barley and sunflower) farming and cattle breeding continue to this day. Many fisheries were also created in the region as well by flooding former channels of the Samara River. Indeed, part of the Sharlyk swamp was flooded to make one of these lakes.

There is continued evidence of deforestation during this period, as the percentage of arboreal pollen steadily declined. *Pinus* and *Betula* pollen still dominated the arboreal pollen sum, while *Ulmus*, *Carpinus betulus*, *Corylus*, *Tilia*, and *Alnus* pollen disappeared from the record. Moreover, there was a decline of both oak (*Quercus*) and maple (*Acer*) pollen throughout this final phase. Only *Populus* slightly increased during this time period. This signature may actually be related to the fact that *Populus* pollen has a thin exine and tends to degrade easily over time (Cushing 1967), thus making it less likely for this pollen type to preserve in the deeper sections of the core. The increase could also be related to the fact that fast-growing Poplar trees are planted for windbreaks in the region to protect the agricultural fields from ravages of steppe winds.

The increase in herbaceous pollen, especially Poaceae and Chenopodiaceae/Amaranthaceae, is another clear indication that the land was used in different ways during this time period. The forests were cleared for wood and for agriculture, which led to an expansion in steppe vegetation. It should be noted that this is the only time period that we have evidence for agriculture in the form of *Cerealia*-type pollen. This signature matches well with the known history of the region, in which large-scale farming was only established sometime in the Russian Imperial period. The significant increase in *Urtica* pollen during this phase clearly demonstrates that the region around the swamp was heavily disturbed, which is not surprising given that a village was established at Krasnosamarskoe during this phase, as was a collective farm and fisheries. The large increase in aquatic pollen, dominated by *Typha*, is no doubt directly related to creation of the artificial fishery ponds that are drained and filled every few years and are all of a relatively uniform depth.

Conclusion

Based on the vegetation history for the lower Samara River valley presented above, it is clear that there were many periods of human activity represented in the pollen profile, from the early Middle Bronze Age to the present. There is evidence that the region around Sharlyk was used as pasture during the Middle Bronze Age, based on the increase in the percentage of *Plantago*, *Rumex*, and *Cannabis/Humulus* in the pollen record. Archaeologists have long assumed that kurgan cemeteries marked seasonal pastures (e.g., Shishlina 2000). It seems that these data support this argument, especially considering that several kurgan cemeteries were constructed in the region during this time period.

A shift in climate was detected for the beginning of the Late Bronze Age from arid and hot to moist and cool, but it should be noted that there were several small climatic oscillations during this time period. The forests of the region would have probably increased in size, as they did further upstream at Pobochnoe, but it seems that people were actively harvesting the forest for fuel, building material, and also perhaps for seeds. Indeed, several large wooden structures were built at Krasnosamarskoe during this time period.

Archaeologists of the region have long interpreted the building of permanent dwellings as a sign that farming cultivated grains became increasingly important during the Late Bronze Age (e.g., Vasiliev and Matveeva 1986). Based on the Sharlyk core, however, there was no evidence of cereal-type pollen in the pollen record until the Late Medieval/early Russian Imperial period. Thus, it seems unlikely that these structures were built at Krasnosamarskoe as farmsteads.

It also been suggested that the pastoralists of the Late Bronze Age, once settled, quickly overgrazed the pastures closest to the settlements, causing widespread environmental degradation and ultimately the migration of people (Kuzmina 2000). Although archaeological evidence from the settlement at Krasnosamarskoe IV suggests that the settlement was inhabited for only a short time (see Anthony et al. 2005), it is clear from the pollen record that people were not driven away from the region due to overgrazing. The presence of moderate percentages of Asteraceae, *Cichorium*-type, *Rumex*, and *Plantago* pollen in the Sharlyk core from this time period suggest that the area around Krasnosamarskoe

was only lightly used as pasture, with the quantity of edible herbaceous plants in the region remaining fairly high.

In conclusion, knowing how the climate broadly changed over time can answer only some archaeological questions. What is needed to fill out the picture is a local vegetation history that shows the way in which both the climate and the actions of human and animals affect the botanical diversity of a locale over time and how these changes create different botanical possibilities for each time period.

Notes

1 It should be noted that all of these data can be found in Popova (2006, 2007) as well.
2 Although most of the known monuments tend to cluster around the middle and lower part of the Samara River, the upper region of the river (in the current day oblast of Orenburg) has been poorly researched.
3 I am indebted to Dr. Kremenetski for his help in extracting the core during the summer of 2002.
4 See Popova (2006:Appendix B) for a more detailed list of the botanical terms used in this text, including common names and habitat.
5 By overgrazing, I mean the overuse of a particular region to the point that the botanical diversity cannot easily recover.
6 It should be noted that these data are not entirely comparable. The Gorny 1 pollen core was taken from a Late Bronze Age settlement context, which is better related to the pollen samples taken from the LBA settlement at Krasnosamarskoe. It should be noted at this point that the pollen percentages for *Plantago* and *Cichorium* are higher at this site than they are for Sharlyk 1, although they still cannot compare with the level of vegetation transformation offered for Gorny 1.
• Figures and tables in this chapter were prepared by L. Popova.

References

Alekseeva, T., A. Alekseev, B. A. Maher, and V. Demkin
2007   Late Holocene Climate Reconstructions for the Russian Steppe Based on Mineralogical and Magnetic Properties of Buried Palaeosols. *Palaeogeography, Palaeoclimatology, Palaeoecology* 249:103–127.
Andrew, R.
1984   *A Practical Pollen Guide to the British Flora*. Quaternary Research Association, Cambridge.
Anthony, D., D. Brown, P. Kuznetsov, O. Mochalov, and A. Khokhlov
2003   The Samara Valley Project: Bronze Age Landscape Archaeology in the Russian Steppes. Presented paper in a symposium entitled *Landscape Archaeology of Late Bronze Age Steppe Pastoralists*, Society for American Archaeology Annual Meeting in Milwaukee, Wisconsin.

Anthony, David W., D. Brown, E. Brown, A. Goodman, A. Khokh-lov, P. Kuznetsov, P. Kosintsev, O. Mochalov, E. Murphy, A. Pike-Tay, A. Rosen, N. Russell, D. Peterson, L. Popova, and A. Weisskopf
2005 The Samara Valley Project: Late Bronze Age Economy and Ritual in the Russian Steppes. *Eurasia Antiqua* 11:395–417.

Bolikhovskaya, N. S.
1990 Paleoindikatskaya izmeniya landshaftov Nizhnego Povolz-hya v poslednie 10 tysiach let. In *Kaspiiskoe More. Voprosy geologii i geomorfologii*, edited by L. I. Lebedev and E. G. Maev, pp. 52–68. Nauka, Moscow.

Cushing, E. J.
1967 Evidence for Differential Pollen Preservation in Late Quaternary Sediments in Minnesota. *Review of Palaeobotany and Palynology* 4:87–101.

Czerepanov, S. K.
1995 *Vascular Plants of Russia and Adjacent States (the Former USSR)*. Cambridge University Press, Cambridge.

Demkin, V. A., A. V. Borisov, A. O. Alekseev, T. S. Demkina, T. V. Alekseeva, and T. E. Khomutova.
2004 Integration of Paleopedology and Archaeology in Studying the Evolution of Soils, Environment, and Human Society. *Eurasian Soil Science* 37(Suppl. 1):1–13.

Demkin, V. A., Y. G. Ryskov, T. S. Demkina, and R. F. Khakimov
1997 Palaeosoils and Palaeoenvironment of the Ural Steppe Region during the Bronze and Early Iron Ages. *ISKOS (Finska Fornminnesfor)* 11:266–270.

Demkin, V. A., M. V. El'tsov, A. O. Alekseev, T. S. Demkina, T. V. Alekseeva, and A. V. Borisov
2004 Soil Development in the Lower Volga Area during the Historical Period. *Eurasian Soil Science* 37:1324–1333.

Diaz-del-Rio, P., P. Lopez, J. A. Lopez-Saez, I. Martinez-Navarette, S. Rovira, J. M. Vincent-Garcia, and I. Zavala-Morencos
2006 Understanding the Productive Economy during the Bronze Age through Archaeometallurgical and Paleoenvironmental Research at Kargaly (Southern Urals, Orenburg, Russia). In *Beyond the Steppe and the Sown: Proceedings of the 2002 University of Chicago Conference on Eurasian Archaeology*, edited by D. Peterson, L. Popova, and A. Smith. Colloquia Pontica Series. Brill, Leiden.

Fedorova, R. V.
1951 The History of the Buzuluk Pine Forest after Pollen Analysis of the "Pobochnoye" Peat Swamp. *Proceedings of the Institute of Geography of the USSR Academy of Sciences* 50:123–141. (In Russian)

Finsinger, W., W. Tinner, W. O. van der Knaap, and B. Ammann
2005 The Expansion of Hazel (*Corylus avellana L.*) in the Southern Alps: A Key for Understanding Its Early Holocene history in Europe? *Quaternary Science Reviews* 25:612–631.

Ivanov, I. V.
1992 *Evolutsiya pochv stepnoi zony v golotsene*. Nauka, Moscow.
1996 Bronzovii vek evraziiskikh stepei. Ego mesto v sisteme landshaftno-klimaticheskhikh ismenenii golotsena i v istoricheskom protsesse. In *Drevnosti Volga-Donskhikh stepei v sisteme vostochno-evropeiskogo bronzogo veka*. Volgagrad.

Ivanov, Igor V., and Igor B. Vasiliev
1995 *Chelovek, priroda i pochvy Ryn-peskov Volgo-Uralskogo meshdurechya v golocene*. Intellect, Moscow.

Juggins, Steve
2006 *C2 version 1.4.2. Software for Ecological and Paleoecological Data Analysis and Visualization*. University of Newcastle, Newcastle upon Tyne.

Khokhlova, O. S., I. S. Kovalevskaya, and S. A. Oleynik
2001 Records of Climatic Change in the Carbonate Profiles of Russian Chernozems. *Catena* 43:203–215.

Khotinsky, N. A.
1984 Holocene Vegetation History. In *Late Quaternary Environments of the Soviet Union*, edited by A. A. Velichko, pp. 179–200. Longman, London.

Klimenko, V. V.
1998 Klimat i istoriya v epokhu pervykh vysokikh kultur (3500–500 gg. do n.e.). *Vostok* 1:5–41.
2000 Klimat i istoriya ot Konfutsiya do Mukhammeda. *Vostok* 1:5–32.
2003 Klimat i istoriya v sredniye veka. *Vostok* 1:5–41.

Kolev, Yuri I., Andrei E. Mamonov, and Mikhail A. Turestskii (editors)
2000 *Istoria Samarskogo Povolzh'e s Drevneishikh Vremen do Nashikh dnei: bronzovii vek*. Tsentr Integratsiia, Samara.

Koryakova, L., and A. V. Epimakhov
2007 *The Urals and Western Siberia in the Bronze and Iron Ages*. Cambridge University Press, Cambridge.

Kremenetski, C. V.
1995 Holocene Vegetation and Climate History of the Southwestern Ukraine. *Review of Palaeobotany and Palynology* 85:289–301.
1997 The Late Holocene Environment and Climate Shift in Russia and Surrounding Lands. In *Climate Change in the Third Millennium BC*, edited by H. N. Dalfes, G. Kukla, and H. Weiss, pp. 351–370. Springer, Berlin.

Kremenetski, C. V., T. Bittger, F. W. Junge, and A. G. Tarasov
1999 Late and Postglacial Environment of the Buzuluk Area, Middle Volga Region, Russia. *Quaternary Science Reviews* 18:1185–1203.

Kremenetski, C. V., O. A. Chichagova, and N. I. Shishlina
1999 Palaeoecological Evidence for Holocene Vegetation, Climate and Land-Use Change in the Low Don Basin and Kalmuk Area, Southern Russia. *Vegetation History and Archaeobotany* 8:233–246.

Kremenetski, C. V., P. E. Tarasov, and A. E. Cherkinsky
1997 Postglacial Development of Kazakhstan Pine Forests. *Geographie Physique et Quaternaire* 51:391–404.

Kuzmina, Elena E.
2000 The Eurasian Steppes: The Transition from Early Urbanism to Nomadism. In *Kurgans, Ritual Sites, and Settlements: Eurasian Bronze and Iron Age*, edited by J. Davis-Kimball, E.M. Murphy, L. Koryakova, and L. T. Yablonsky, pp. 118–125. Bar International Series 890. Archaeopress, Oxford.

Kuznetsov, Pavel F., and Oleg D. Mochalov
2003 Samarskaya Dolina v Bronzovom Veke. In *Material'naya Kul'tura Naseleniya Basseina Reki Samari v Bronzovom Veke*, edited by Yu. I. Kolev, P. F. Kuznetsov, and O. D. Mochalov, pp. 5–29. Izdatel'stvo SGPU, Samara.

Lopez, Pilar, J. A. Lopez-Saez, E. N. Chernykh, and P. Tarasov
2003 Late Holocene Vegetation History and Human Activity Shown by Pollen Analysis of Novienki Peat Bog (Kargaly Region, Orenburg Oblast, Russia). *Vegetation History and Archaeobotany* 12:75–82.

Lopez-Garcia, P., E. N. Chernykh, and J. A. Lopez-Saez
2000 Palynological Analysis at the Gorny Site (Kargaly Region): The Earliest Metallurgical Center in Northern Eurasia (Russia). In *Proceedings of the IX International Palynological Congress, Houston, Texas 1996*, edited by D. K. Goodman, pp. 347–355. American Association of Stratigraphic Palynologists Foundation, Houston, Texas.

Maher, L. J.
1972 Nomograms for Computing 95% Limits of Pollen Data. *Review of Palaeobotany and Palynology* 13:85–93.

Mishkin, N. V., and V. A. Skarbovenko
2000 Kochevniki Samarskogo Povolzh'ya v rannem zheleznom veke. In *Istoria Samarskogo Povolzh'e s Drevneishikh Vremen do Nashikh dnei: Rannii zheleznii vek I srednevekov'ye*, edited by P. S. Kabitov, pp. 9–81. Tsentr Integratsiia, Samara.

Mitusov, A. V., O. E. Mitusova, K. Pustovoytov, C.C.-M. Lubos, S. Dreibrodt, and H.-R. Bork
2009 Paleoclimatic Indicators in Soils Buried under Archaeological Monuments in the Eurasian Steppe: A Review. *The Holocene* 19(8):1153–1160.

Moore, P. D., J. A. Webb, and M. E. Collinson
1991 *Pollen Analysis*. 2nd ed. Blackwell, London.

Morgunova, N. L., and O. S. Khokhlova
2006 Kurgans and Nomads: New Investigations of Mound Burials in the Southern Urals. *Antiquity* 80:303–317.

Piavchenko, N. I., and L. S. Kozlovskaya
1958 On the History of the Buzuluk Pine Forest. *Proceedings of the Forest Institute of the USSR Academy of Sciences* 37:149–162. (In Russian)

Popova, Laura M.
2006 Political Pastures: Navigating the Steppe in the Middle Volga Region (Russia) during the Bronze Age. Unpublished Ph.D. dissertation, University of Chicago.
2007 A New Historical Legend: Tracing the Long-Term Landscape History of the Samara River Valley. In *Social Orders and Social Landscapes: Proceedings of the 2005 University of Chicago Conference on Eurasian Archaeology*, edited by Laura M. Popova, Charles Hartley and Adam T. Smith. Cambridge Scholars Press, Newcastle.

Reille, Maurice.
1992 *Pollen et Spores d'Europe et d'Afrique du Nord*. Laboratoire de Botanique historique et Palynologie, Marseille.
1995 *Pollen et Spores d'Europe et d'Afrique du Nord*. Supplement 1. Laboratoire de Botanique historique et Palynologie, Marseille.
1998 *Pollen et Spores d'Europe et d'Afrique du Nord*. Supplement 2. Laboratoire de Botanique historique et Palynologie, Marseille.

Rysin, L. P.
1975 *Sosnovye lesa Evropeiskoi chasti SSSR*. Nauka, Moskva.

Shishlina, Natalya I.
2000 *Sesonni Economicheskii Tsikl Naseleniia Severa-Zapadnovo Prikaspiya v Bronzovom Veke*. Trydi Gosydarstvennovo Istoricheskovo Muzeya, Vinusk 120, Moscow.

Spiridonova, E. A.
1991 *Evolutsiya rastitelnogo pokrova basseina Dona v verkhnem pleistotsene–golotsene*. Nauka, Moscow.

Vasiliev, Igor B., and Galina I. Matveeva
1986 *Istokov istorii Samarskogo Povolzh'ya*. Kuibyshevskoe Knizhnoe Izdatel'stvo, Kuibyshev.

Velichko, Andrei A., A. A. Andrev, and V. A. Klimanov
1997 Climate and Vegetation Dynamics in the Tundra and Forest Zone during the Late Glacial and Holocene. *Quaternary International* 41/42:71–96.

Vincent, J. M., A. L. Rodriguez-Alcalde, J. A. Lopez-Saez, I. de Zavala-Morencos, P. Lopez-Garcia, and I. Martinez-Navarette
2000 ¿Catastrofes ecologicas en la estepa? Arqueologia del Paisaje en el complejo minero-metalurgico de Kargaly (Region de Orenburg, Rusia). *Trabajos de Prehistoria* 57:29–74. (Translated into English by Antonio Gilman)

Part III

Human Skeletal Studies

Demographic and Cranial Characteristics of the Volga-Ural Population in the Eneolithic and Bronze Age

Aleksandr A. Khokhlov

D emography is concerned with various factors that affect the complex physical and social dimensions of populations. These factors include, first of all, the social mechanisms of reproduction and the determinants of fertility, mortality, and especially marriage. Demography also takes into account the likely impact on these processes of various kinds of human migration, including the penetration into the local population of small foreign populations, which may accelerate, slow down, or reverse the regional reproduction of social groups. Palaeodemographic studies are most productive when conducted with an integrated approach, aggregating data from anthropology, archaeology, archaeozoology, soil science, and ethnology. The core data, however, come from anthropological analysis, which in Eastern Europe refers to the methods of biological anthropology, which provide demographic information on the age and sex composition of the population and its pathological features. Craniometric studies cannot be neglected, as the results may show the process of development of the autochthonous population or indicate the arrival of migrants.

Previously, the author (Khokhlov 1999, 2002, 2003a, 2010a, 2012a) focused on the latter aspect of anthropological analysis, craniometrics. This chapter deals with demographic aspects in a broader perspective—relating various demographic and craniometric indicators to the different archaeological cultures of the Eneolithic to Bronze Age in the Volga-Ural region. This analysis uses the results

of gender and age determinations from 1,350 individuals derived from Eneolithic to Bronze Age cemeteries in the region, mainly in the Samara oblast, but also including data from the Orenburg and Saratov oblasts, located to the east and south of Samara. These individuals represent almost all of the Eneolithic to Bronze Age human skeletons excavated by archaeologists in the Samara oblast as of 2002, when the Samara Valley Project ended.

When studying age groups, demographers might use age intervals consisting of a seven-year span, a decade, or smaller or larger intervals of unequal length. Based on the experience of aging in human history, what people themselves saw as important was not so much their calendar age but their overall physical ability and place in society, which was dependent on biological age. The following intervals were therefore employed for age classes: 0 to 7 years, child; 7 to 14 years, adolescent; 14 to 18 years, junior adult; 18 to 30 years, young adult; 30 to 45 years, mature adult; 45 to 55 years, elderly adult; older than 55 years, senile adult.

Khvalynsk-Eneolithic

The Eneolithic was the period in the middle Volga region when domesticated sheep, goats, and cattle first appeared in the economy, alongside hunting and fishing; it was also when copper ornaments began to be traded over long distances (Agapov et al. 1990; Petrenko 2000). It is represented by burial complexes with various cultural affiliations, such as S'yezzhee 1 and Lipovy Ovrag (Samara culture); Lebyazhinka V (with graves similar to Mariupol in the Dnieper-Azov region); Khvalynsk I, Khvalynsk II, and Khlopkov Bugor (Khvalynsk culture); and Gundorovka (with graves that show both Samara and Volosovo traits, a mixture of steppe and forest cultures). These sites are associated with different stages of the Eneolithic and are thought to date between 5200 and 4000 BC.

The most complete data, including craniometrics, are from the Eneolithic cemeteries Khvalynsk I and II. Cemeteries of this culture, including Khvalynsk itself, are located on the right bank of the middle Volga and on the lower Volga. The Khvalynsk culture or its related variants was prevalent during the Eneolithic in the Volga-Ural steppes, so results of this study might reflect the overall demographic structure of the Eneolithic population.

The designations Khvalynsk I and II refer to separate excavation campaigns conducted at different times in the same general Eneolithic cemetery area on the western bank of the Volga River, 170 km southwest of the city of Samara in the Saratov oblast. The Khvalynsk I and II excavations were about 150 m apart. The study sample from Khvalynsk I (Mkrtchyan 1988a, 1988b) contained 145 individuals with age and/or gender definitions (out of 158 excavated),

Table 6.1 Distribution of Demographic Traits by Age Class and Chronological Period

	Eneolithic			Bronze Age: First Half			Bronze Age: Second Half		
	Khvalynsk I	Khvalynsk II	Khvalynsk Total	Yamnaya	Yamnaya-Poltavka	Total	Potapovka	Early Srubnaya	Late Srubnaya
Number of specimens	145	41	186	30	134	164	103	118	454
Children: 0–7 years	22.1 (32)	26.8 (11)	23.12 (43)	10.7 (3)	13.7 (18)	13.2 (21)	51.48 (52)	32.20 (38)	30.6 (137)
Adolescents: 7–14 years	11.7 (17)	9.8 (4)	11.29 (21)	3.6 (1)	3.9 (5)	3.8 (6)	9.90 (10)	22.88 (27)	14.9 (67)
Juniors: 14–18 years	4.8 (7)	2.4 (1)	4.30 (8)	3.6 (1)	5.3 (7)	5.0 (8)	5.95 (6)	6.78 (8)	5.8 (26)
Young: 18–30 years	13.8 (20)	26.8 (11)	16.67 (31)	25.0 (7)	16.1 (21)	17.6 (28)	13.86 (14)	12.71 (15)	20.2 (90)
Mature: 30–45 years	14.5 (21)	14.6 (6)	14.52 (27)	32.1 (9)	32.8 (43)	32.7 (52)	8.91 (9)	12.71 (15)	16.8 (75)
Elderly: 45–55 years	13.8 (20)	17.2 (7)	14.52 (27)	17.9 (5)	15.3 (20)	15.7 (25)	8.91 (9)	11.03 (13)	9.5 (42)
Senile: ≥55 years	12.4 (18)	2.4 (1)	10.21 (19)	7.1 (2)	12.9 (17)	11.9 (19)	0.99 (1)	1.69 (2)	2.2 (10)
Male/female (n)	44/38	19/6	63/44	17/7/1 undefined	71/33	88/40/1 undefined	23/11	24/21	113/107
Average age	32.0[a]	24.45 (41)	30.34 (186)	33.2 (28)	33.6 (130)	33.5 (158)	14.66 (99)	19.71 (118)	21.29 (438)
Average age male	43.9[a]	38.33 (18)	42.22 (63)	39.9 (15)	42.5 (71)	42.01 (86)	33.55 (22)	38.79 (24)	37.00 (110)
Average age female	34.8[a]	33.25 (6)	34.58 (44)	36.9 (7)	37.8 (29)	37.7 (36)	36.47 (10)	37.43 (21)	33.44 (104)
Unknown	6.9 (10)		5.37 (10)	+2 males	+2 males and 2 females				

Note: Values are presented as "percentage (number)" unless otherwise indicated.
[a]Data from Mkrtchyan (1988a).

and Khvalynsk II (author's data) contained 41 (all of those excavated), for a total of 186 individuals studied. The two excavated components of the Eneolithic cemetery, however, revealed differences of several kinds. Many more copper rings and beads as well as other kinds of ornaments were found in the Khvalynsk II graves. These graves also contained a much higher proportion of males and relatively few females. Also, the age characteristics of the two excavated areas differed, as described below. The Khvalynsk II burial plot might reflect some special episode associated with some kind of separate social group within the society. It is also possible that the two excavations revealed related, but separate groups, or belonged to slightly different time intervals within the overall chronology of the Khvalynsk culture.

The distribution of age categories from the two excavations is presented in Table 6.1 and Figure 6.1. Both excavated plots revealed similar percentages of mortality in childhood (0–7), adolescence (8–14), and junior adult (14–18) age groups, as well as among the mature adults (30–45 years). In Khvalynsk II, there were more children (0–7 years) and young adults (18–30 years), with a significantly higher mortality in the young adults (26.8 percent) than seen in Khvalynsk I (13.8 percent). Mkrtchyan (1988a) noted that most of the young adults in Khvalynsk I were females and attributed their high mortality to the active childbirth period, but at Khvalynsk II the young adults were mainly males (Table 6.2). Also, in Khvalynsk II there were almost no old people (over 55), while in Khvalynsk I the over-55 age category had 12.4 percent of the graves, a significant number. If they survived young adulthood, many men and women in both excavations reached their elder years (45–55 years), but very old people and females were found principally in Khvalynsk I.

The overall percentage of children aged 0 to 7 years (22–27 percent) could be considered normal. For example, in a large sample of 400 graves in the Kuban steppes, derived from the Early Bronze Age Novotitorovskaya culture, Gei (2000) found between 33 and 37 percent of the dead were children in coastal steppe graves, where the residence pattern was more stable, and 17 to 26 percent of the dead were children in the interior steppe graves, where a more pastoral, mobile economy was practiced. The age and gender structure of the people buried in Khvalynsk II (Figure 6.2) corresponds to a more mobile group.

At Khvalynsk I, average life expectancy was 32.0 years, separately 43.9 years for men and 34.8 years for women. In contrast, in Khvalynsk II, the average life span was only 24.5 years, separately 38.3 years for men and 33.3 years for women. The Khvalynsk II burials contained three times more males than females. Perhaps the high mortality of young males in the Khvalynsk II excavation reflected a stressful situation involving, for example, social tensions, including armed conflicts. Distinct injuries on the skeletons, leading to death, are little evidenced. However, their absence may not always testify in favor of peaceful relations.

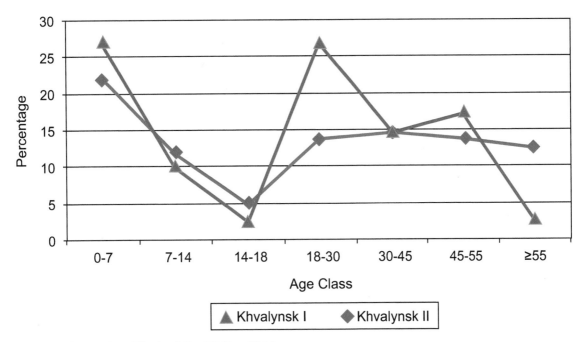

Figure 6.1 Graves by age class: Khvalynsk I and II (Eneolithic).

Table 6.2 Distribution of Sexes by Age Classes of Anthropological Materials from the Volga-Ural, Eneolithic through the Bronze Ages

	Khvalynsk I		Khvalynsk II		Khvalynsk Total	
Sex	Male	Female	Male	Female	Male	Female
Number of specimens	45	38	20	6	65	44
Junior: 14–18 y	3.6 (3)	3.6 (3)	3.08 (1)		3.67 (4)	2.70 (3)
Young: 18–30 y	2.4 (2)	20.50 (17)	26.9 (7)	15.4 (4)	8.28 (9)	19.26 (21)
Mature: 30–45 y	19.3 (16)	4.80 (4)	19.3 (5)	3.9 (1)	19.26 (21)	4.59 (5)
Elderly: 45–55 y	13.3 (11)	10.80 (9)	26.9 (7)		16.51 (18)	8.28 (9)
Senile: >55 y	15.7 (13)	6.00 (5)		3.8 (1)	11.93 (13)	5.51 (6)
	Yamnaya		Yamnaya-Poltavka		Yamnaya-Poltavka Total	
Sex	Male	Female	Male	Female	Male	Female
Number of specimens	18	5	71	36	89	43
Junior: 14–18 y	4.4 (1)	0.0	0.9 (1)	4.7 (5)	1.51 (2)	3.79 (5)
Young: 18–30 y	26.1 (6)	4.3 (1)	6.56 (7)	13.14 (14)	9.94 (13)	11.46 (15)
Mature: 30–45 y	30.5 (7)	4.3 (1)	33.57 (36)	6.53 (7)	32.83 (43)	6.87 (9)
Elderly: 45–55 y	8.7 (2)	13.1 (3)	15.89 (17)	2.81 (3)	14.52 (19)	4.58 (6)
Senile: >55 y	8.7 (2)	0.0	9.35 (10)	6.55 (7)	9.16 (12)	5.34 (7)
	Potapovka – Sintashta		Early Srubnaya		Late Srubnaya	
Sex	Male	Female	Male	Female	Male	Female
Number of specimens	23	14	25	24	120	126
Junior: 14–18 y	2.7 (1)	10.8 (4)	2.04 (1)	6.1 (3)	4.05 (10)	4.85 (12)
Young: 18–30 y	27 (10)	10.8 (4)	14.29 (7)	16.32 (8)	13.9 (37)	26.3 (62)
Mature: 30–45 y	18.9 (7)	2.7 (1)	18.37 (9)	12.24 (6)	17.08 (42)	13.02 (32)
Elderly: 45–55 y	13.56 (5)	10.84 (4)	16.33 (8)	10.2 (5)	10.59 (26)	6.11 (15)
Senile: >55 y		2.7 (1)		4.1 (2)	2.05 (5)	2.05 (5)

Note: Values are presented as "percentage (number)" unless otherwise indicated.

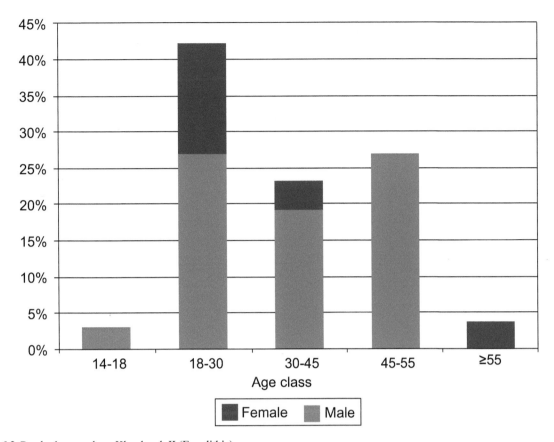

Figure 6.2 Gender by age class: Khvalynsk II (Eneolithic).

In the Khvalynsk cemeteries, there was a custom of ritual scraping of the skulls of some adults, exhibited in particular by striations on the skull consisting of one to seven gouges about 2 to 3 cm in length into the surface of the parietal bone (Khokhlov 2012b; Mkrtchyan 1988a). These marks had a cultural, not pathogenic, origin and are not considered to affect the demographic situation. Skull scraping was a ceremonial act largely limited to mature adults in the 35- to 45-year age range and almost did not touch the young.

The crania from the Khvalynsk II cemetery are characterized by high craniological polymorphism (Khokhlov 1998; Khokhlov and Yablonsky 2000). Some of the skulls can be defined as a typical northern Europeoid structure with a slightly flattened face, known as Uraloid. The other aspect of the Europeoid series was dolichocranial and mesomorphic, with a sharply profiled face, and this form is usually considered typical of the southern branch of the Europeoids. Apparently, the Khvalynsk population was formed as a result of contacts between local people and newcomer groups that came perhaps from the south (Khokhlov 2010a, 2012a; Khokhlov and Yablonsky 2000). The physical appearance of some individuals in the Khvalynsk culture can be obtained by facial reconstruction (Figure 6.3a).

Early Bronze Age

The Early Bronze Age (EBA), 3300 to 2800 BC, witnessed the development of a highly mobile form of pastoralism entirely dependent on domesticated animals, with much reduced hunting and fishing. A new burial ritual, single burial under a kurgan or tumulus, appeared, and settlements disappeared. It should be noted that each EBA kurgan contained only one to three individuals, rarely including children, so the majority of the population must have been excluded from kurgan ceremonies, but we don't know what was done with their bodies after death. The principal EBA culture in the middle Volga steppes is the Yamnaya, or Pit-Grave culture. After the Early Yamnaya period, it evolved into the Middle Bronze Age (MBA) Poltavka culture, so all Yamnaya data from the middle Volga region refer to Early Yamnaya of the EBA.

The Early Yamnaya series, unfortunately, is defined by a small number of skeletons in the middle Volga region—30 individuals, of which only 28 have age data. Because we have not yet found the graves of most of the EBA people who were buried outside of kurgans, we should not think that this number reflects an equivalent actual decline in population. In fact, we know nothing about relative population size in the Eneolithic and the EBA because of the marked change in burial customs.

Figure 6.3 Facial reconstructions based on skulls from (a) Khvalynsk II Grave 24, a young adult male; (b) Poludin Grave 6, Yamnaya culture, a mature male (both by A. I. Nechvaloda); and (c) Luzanovsky cemetery, Srubnaya culture (by L. T. Yablonsky).

The age and sex categories are presented in Figures 6.4 and 6.5 and Tables 6.1 and 6.2. The average life span was 33.2 years: 39.9 years for males and 36.9 years for females. This represented a slight decline in life expectancy for males and a slight increase for females, compared with the Eneolithic, but the comparison is skewed by the introduction of a new, apparently less inclusive burial ritual in the EBA. The Yamnaya age expectancies for the middle Volga are almost identical to those previously published (Alekseev 1972) for Yamnaya graves on the lower Volga and the southern part of the middle Volga: 39.7 years for males and 35.0 years for females. They are also similar to the life expectancy of Yamnaya people on the lower Dnieper: 41.0 for males and 33.1 years for females (Kreutz 1984).

Children and adolescents together (0–14 years) composed only 14 percent of the Early Yamnaya population buried under kurgans in the middle Volga steppes, approximately the same as on the lower Dnieper (16.3 percent). Men in the age category 30 to 45 years were buried more frequently than any other age or sex category (32.1 percent of all graves in the middle Volga and 34 percent in the lower Dnieper steppes). Males made up 78 percent of the burial population in the middle Volga steppes and 67 percent in the lower Dnieper steppes. However, in the Kuban steppes north of the Northern Caucasus Mountains and in the northwest Caspian steppes, children and females were included in Yamnaya kurgan burial rituals much

more frequently than in the Dnieper and Volga steppes (Romanova 1989; Shevchenko 1986).

The average adult of the Yamnaya period in the middle Volga region was quite tall and very powerfully built. Females were only slightly less robust than men, so robust that sometimes, when examining individual parts of the postcranial skeleton, it is not easy to identify the sex of the individual. Apparently, this was due to a high level of physical loading on the musculoskeletal system, indicating a physically active life for both sexes. The small size of Yamnaya mortuary groups, their moderate fertility, their strong bias toward males, and their strong physical development are traits that are generally associated more with mobile populations than sedentary groups. The archaeological characterization of the Yamnaya population as mobile pastoralists of the steppes has been known for a long time (e.g., Danilenko 1974; Kozhin 1997; Kuzmina 1997; Merpert 1974; Morgunova and Kravtsov 1994; Shilov 1975; Shishlina and Bulatov 2000; Vasiliev et al. 2000). Their mobility, demographic composition, and rather complex diet probably provided a positive hardening of the body that limited the negative effects of adverse natural factors.

The Yamnaya population of the Volga-Urals differed craniologically from the previous population of the Khvalynsk Eneolithic culture (Table 6.3a and b). In general, most local groups displayed the properties of a mesocranial, hypermorphic Europeoid type (Figure 6.3b).

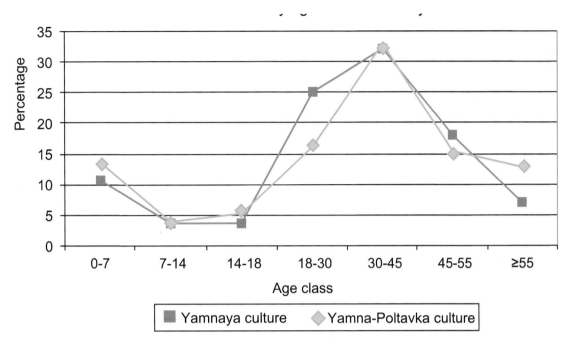

Figure 6.4 Graves by age class: Yamnaya (EBA).

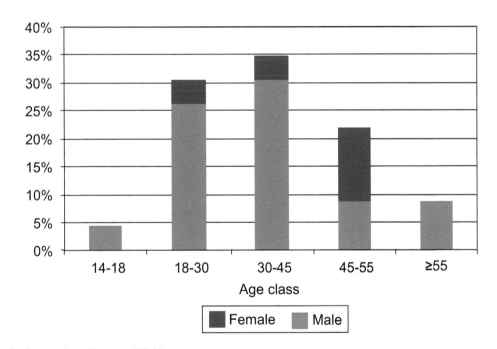

Figure 6.5 Gender by age class: Yamnaya (EBA).

Some mesomorphic Europeoids, similar to Khvalynsk, continued to appear in the Yamnaya population but rarely. Special craniological studies have shown that the principal elements in the craniological combination defining the Yamnaya population could be explained best as resulting from mating between the carriers of a mesomorphic, dolichocranial population, in particular middle Volga Khvalynsk, and a hypermorphic, mesocranial Europeoid population, in particular the descendants of the Dnieper-Donets Neolithic cultural community. The craniological appearance of the Volga Yamnaya population was associated with the migration and infiltration of mobile populations from the west, primarily the Volga-Don steppes (Khokhlov 1999, 2000a). This was accompanied by assimilation of the descendants of local Eneolithic traditions, which contributed to the origin of the middle Volga Yamnaya population.

Table 6.3a Craniometric Indices of Male Skulls from the Steppe and Steppe Areas of the Volga-Ural Eneolithic to Bronze Ages

Standard Cranial Measurements		Eneolithic	EBA	MBA		LBA	
No. according to Martin and Saller 1957	Description	Khvalynsk	Yamnaya	Yamna-Poltavka	Potapovka	Srubnaya	
						Early	Late
1	Maximum cranial length	187.1 (27)	193.6 (11)	191.9 (29)	185.6 (15)	190.8 (19)	189.9 (63)
8	Maximum cranial breadth	138.0 (26)	145.0 (12)	142.0 (27)	141.4 (14)	134.9 (18)	138.8 (62)
17	Basion-bregma height	141.1 (15)	136.5 (8)	139.6 (16)	137.4 (14)	141.1 (11)	139.3 (53)
20	Ear height	116.3 (15)	116.5 (12)	118.2 (20)	116.2 (11)	117.4 (18)	117.8 (57)
9	Minimum frontal breadth	98.1 (29)	101.5 (12)	98.0 (27)	98.6 (14)	98.7 (18)	97.7 (64)
45	Bizygomatic breadth	135.0 (21)	141.3 (12)	138.7 (19)	137.6 (12)	130.3 (16)	135.5 (59)
48	Upper face height	69.5 (20)	73.3 (12)	72.8 (22)	71.2 (12)	72.5 (17)	71.2 (59)
51	Orbital breadth	43.4 (23)	44.3 (12)	44.1 (24)	44.3 (12)	42.9 (14)	42.9 (59)
52	Orbital height	31.4 (24)	32.1 (12)	31.8 (24)	32.2 (13)	32.6 (13)	32.2 (60)
54	Nose breadth	24.3 (20)	25.3 (12)	25.4 (26)	23.8 (13)	23.5 (16)	24.9 (58)
55	Nose height	51.0 (22)	53.6 (12)	52.3 (25)	51.6 (12)	51.9 (17)	51.9 (61)
32	Frontal angle from nasion	81.3° (22)	79.4° (11)	79.4° (19)	81.3° (10)	80.3° (17)	81.5° (57)
72	Total facial angle	84.7° (19)	85.5° (12)	86.2° (18)	84.7° (10)	86.4° (16)	84.7° (52)
75 (1)	Nose protrusion angle	30.7° (11)	37.2° (9)	36.1° (20)	35.7° (10)	31.7° (16)	34.0° (53)
77	Naso-malar angle	137.8° (22)	137.8° (12)	137.8° (24)	139.2° (12)	134.1° (18)	135.3° (62)
Zm	Zygo-maxillary angle	124.5° (24)	123.9° (12)	123.1° (20)	126.1° (10)	120.6° (16)	124.1° (54)
8.1	Cranial index	73.5 (27)	75.1 (11)	74.3 (27)	76.5 (14)	70.8 (18)	73.0 (62)
48/45	Upper facial index	51.4 (18)	51.9 (12)	52.0 (16)	51.7 (10)	55.2 (16)	52.6 (58)
52/51	Orbit index	71.7 (24)	72.3 (12)	72.2 (24)	73.1 (12)	75.8 (17)	75.2 (59)
54/55	Nasal index	48.8 (17)	47.3 (12)	48.5 (24)	46.4 (12)	45.6 (16)	48.5 (59)
Symotic height/ Symotic breadth or SS/SC	Symotic index	53.1 (16)	62.2 (10)	61.8 (24)	60.8 (13)	55.2 (18)	59.6 (61)

Note: Bone measurements are in mm and angles in degrees.

Table 6.3b Craniometric Indices of Female Skulls from the Steppe and Steppe Areas of the Volga-Ural Eneolithic to Bronze Ages

Standard Cranial Measurement		Eneolithic	EBA	MBA		LBA	
No. according to Martin and Saller 1957	Description	Khvalynsk	Yamnaya	Yamna-Poltavka	Potapovka	Srubnaya	
						Early	Late
1	Maximum cranial length	180.8 (13)	178.2 (6)	181.2 (6)	177.7 (7)	183.9 (18)	179.9 (44)
8	Maximum cranial breadth	135.1 (14)	139.2 (6)	137.2 (6)	139.6 (7)	135.3 (17)	135.9 (43)
17	Basion-bregma height	132.0 (6)	130.2 (6)	132.3 (4)	133.7 (6)	135.7 (15)	133.7 (36)
20	Ear height	113.6 (6)	110.7 (6)	111.0 (4)	113.7 (6)	115.2 (17)	113.9 (36)
9	Minimum frontal breadth	94.0 (12)	94.3 (6)	95.8 (6)	97.1 (7)	94.3 (17)	94.1 (43)
45	Bizygomatic breadth	126.0 (7)	128.2 (6)	128.0 (4)	129.3 (6)	122.9 (12)	125.6 (39)
48	Upper face height	64.4 (7)	69.7 (5)	66.5 (4)	67.0 (5)	67.9 (17)	66.8 (41)
51	Orbital breadth	41.5 (8)	41.3 (6)	42.7 (5)	42.4 (6)	41.6 (13)	41.1 (34)
52	Orbital height	30.9 (9)	32.5 (6)	31.5 (5)	33.2 (6)	33.2 (14)	32.4 (40)
54	Nose breadth	25.4 (10)	24.1 (6)	24.3 (4)	23.4 (5)	23.8 (17)	23.9 (40)
55	Nose height	47.1 (10)	49.5 (6)	48.6 (4)	49.2 (5)	49.6 (17)	49.3 (41)
32	Frontal angle from nasion	82.1° (7)	80.2° (6)	81.8° (4)	85.3° (6)	83.0° (17)	83.2° (37)
72	Total facial angle	83.6° (5)	84.2° (6)	87.0° (4)	85.9° (5)	85.2° (17)	84.0° (35)
75 (1)	Nose protrusion angle	22.0° (1)	31.8° (6)	26.0° (2)	26.8° (5)	32.1° (16)	29.5° (35)
77	Naso-malar angle	136.9° (10)	140.3° (6)	138.8° (5)	138.6° (6)	135.5° (17)	137.0° (38)
Zm	Zygo-maxillary angle	124.6° (8)	122.3° (6)	126.0° (4)	130.7° (5)	120.9° (12)	124.8° (31)
8.1	Cranial index	75.1 (13)	78.1 (6)	75.7 (6)	78.7 (7)	73.7 (17)	75.6 (44)
48/45	Upper facial index	50.9 (7)	54.5 (5)	52.4 (3)	52.0 (5)	54.7 (13)	53.3 (39)
52/51	Orbit index	75.5 (9)	78.7 (6)	73.8 (5)	78.5 (6)	78.8 (17)	79.4 (35)
54/55	Nasal index	54.1 (9)	48.9 (6)	49.2 (3)	47.7 (5)	47.9 (16)	48.2 (35)
Symotic height/ Symotic breadth or SS/SC	Symotic index	46.9 (2)	57.4 (6)	51.1 (3)	49.9 (6)	58.9 (15)	53.4 (30)

Note: Bone measurements are in mm and angles in degrees.

Within the Yamnaya cranial series in the middle Volga region, craniological polymorphism is small, in contrast to the Eneolithic period or really any other period. Yamnaya crania in the middle Volga region exhibit more homogeneity than the earlier or later populations, perhaps because of cultural selection and bias affecting those who received a burial under a kurgan, rather than any actual change in the heterogeneity of the regional population as a whole. Where polymorphic cranial series are found, they are defined at the intersite level, not usually within Yamnaya kurgan cemeteries.

Biological contacts between Yamnaya and the forest-zone population remain poorly recognized or not recognized. Groups of forest origin, designated archaeologically as the Volosovo, Garin-Bor, and other northern cultures, lived within the present-day Samara oblast in the forest-steppe zone of the Volga-Ural region. Craniologically, this population is quite specific. It varies, of course, at the statistical level, presenting robust and gracile complexes but almost always with its own morphological characteristics related to the so-called Ural-Lappoid group (Debets 1953). Apparently, this group did not interbreed with the Yamnaya individuals selected for kurgan burial. The Volga-Ural Early Yamnaya population was prevented from genetic mixing with these forest populations, who for the most part remained hunter-fisher-gatherers during the late fourth and early third millennia BC, in contrast to the Yamnaya pastoralists. This avoidance could have been encouraged both by cultural traditions that restricted the marriage community and, of course, by the cultural foreignness of the forest-zone forager population with all its attendant social barriers.

Middle Bronze Age

The Middle Bronze Age in the Volga-Ural region, 2800 to 2100 BC, witnessed the evolution of the Poltavka culture. In the southern Ural steppes, an independent variant called the Tamar-Utkul type has been defined (Bogdanov 2004), also called the Pre-Ural variant of the Late Yamnaya culture. All of these cultures were derived to one degree or another from Early Yamnaya, and their pastoral economy and kurgan burial rituals were generally similar to Early Yamnaya.

For the Middle Bronze Age, in this study, we have 137 individuals with defined sex and/or age, compared to just 30 for the EBA. It could be that the increase in burials in the MBA reflects an increase in the size of the average social community or cultural network, and therefore an increase in the labor pool available to build kurgans, not a simple increase in overall population size or density. Although the sample is much larger than the Early Yamnaya sample, generally speaking, the demographic statistics differ only slightly (see Tables 6.1 and 6.2). There is still a small percentage of child-to-adolescent (0–14 years) mortality (17.6 percent), as well as a virtually unchanged average life span (33.6 years), and many more males than females are found in the recovered mortuary population, although the sex ratio became somewhat more balanced (generally 2 to 1 males over females rather than 3 to 1).

Differences also emerged in the MBA demographic profile. Child and adolescent mortality increased slightly (or more children were accepted into the kurgan burial ritual), female survival improved significantly in the young adult stage (18–30 years; Figure 6.6), and the average age at death increased for women and especially for men. One gets the impression of a somewhat higher fertility among females, with a better probability of surviving to old age. Among males, compared with EBA Early Yamnaya, the MBA males exhibit a much reduced mortality in the 18- to 30-year age category (6.6 percent compared to EBA 26.1 percent), only slightly higher mortality in middle age (33.6 percent compared to EBA 30.5 percent), and a much larger proportion of males surviving to old age (15.9 percent compared to EBA 8.7 percent). In general, we can assume that MBA groups, mostly Poltavka in this sample, were better adapted than EBA herders to the economic and cultural activities of pastoralism, were more favored by local resources, and, accordingly, had a slightly lower mobility.

Middle Bronze Age crania showed more diversity than Early Yamnaya crania. One component, typically hypermorphic and mesocranial, demonstrated continuity with the EBA Yamnaya type, embodied in the anthropological materials of the middle Volga Poltavka culture. Another type, typically dolichocranial and mesomorphic, was found in the more arid lower Volga steppes in both the EBA and the MBA but was almost absent from the middle Volga Poltavka population. Instead a third, new craniofacial conformation appeared, usually dolichocranial, with a moderately wide, wedge-shaped face. The overall preponderance of traits would place this type within the southern Europeoids. At the Poltavka cemetery of Krasnosamarskoe IV, excavated as part of the Samara Valley Project, the male (aged 18–30 years) in the central grave (9) of Kurgan 3 had a northern Europeoid wide-faced, brachycephalic craniofacial conformation, like the regional EBA Yamnaya population, but a female buried in the central grave of Kurgan 2, an unusual distinction for Poltavka females, had a narrow-faced, almost dolichocranial southern Europeoid conformation, a good example of the heterogeneity of the MBA Poltavka population.

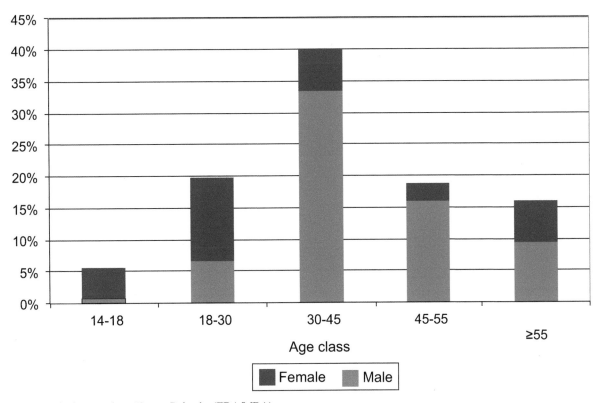

Figure 6.6 Gender by age class: Yamna-Poltavka (EBA/MBA).

Craniological type is fairly highly positively correlated with the position of the skeleton in Poltavka graves. People buried supine with raised knees, the classic position of the Early Yamnaya culture, often had typical middle Volga Early Yamnaya craniofacial types characterized as mesocranial and very wide-faced. People buried contracted on the right or left side were mostly dolichocranial and had relatively narrow, sharply profiled faces. At Krasnosamarskoe IV, however, all three Poltavka individuals in the central graves seem to have been positioned semi-contracted on the side, regardless of skull type, so there are exceptions. But the same correlation of body position and physical type was recorded in the Late Yamnaya graves of the North Pontic steppes north of the Black Sea (Kreutz 1977). The correlation is also documented through indirect parameters—people of southern Europeoid appearance are found frequently in burials with more complex design, often with richer mortuary artifact inventories. These facts argue in favor of the influx of new populations, mainly southern Europeoid in appearance, possibly from the North Caucasus steppes (Khokhlov 1998, 2003b; Kreutz 1977).

It should be emphasized that we are not talking about a direct immigration from Central Asia, the Trans-Caucasus,

or southwestern Europe, where these craniofacial traits can also be found. We are talking about a complex of southern Europeoid traits that often is associated with the well-known Mediterranean craniofacial type in southern Europe. However, already in the Mesolithic era, before the migrations from the Mediterranean parts of southeastern Europe associated with the Early Neolithic, there were narrow-faced, dolichocranial people living in the Caucasus, the Crimea, and the southern parts of Eastern Europe, where there was some mixing with the indigenous population of the steppe, leading to the emergence of heterogeneous later populations in these regions. The Mediterranean-type Neolithic population of southeastern Europe, mixing with this local element, produced what can be called the southern Europeoid type. The high-faced variant of southern Europeoid, for example, typified the Kemi-Oba culture of the EBA in the Crimea. This was also the craniofacial type of the Maikop culture, dated to the later fourth millennium BC in the North Caucasus, which had connections with Kemi-Oba and is known to have strongly influenced cultural and ethnogenetic processes in the steppe world to the north, including direct contact with mesomorphic steppe Early Yamnaya groups.

The appearance of people with new craniofacial types in the MBA between the northern Black Sea steppes and the Urals can be attributed to various causes. In the southern Ural region, some MBA individuals probably represent remnants of the ancient local population of the Khvalynsk Eneolithic. Some MBA individuals also exhibited direct genetic continuity with the local Early Yamnaya population, although the specific graves that contained them (Ishkinovka I, 3/7; Pidlisne, 3/3) occurred in cemeteries and kurgans where people with mature southern Europeoid traits also were buried. It is likely that the mixture of burial ritual customs and craniofacial types that appeared in the MBA between the Black Sea and the Ural steppes represented the radial spread of new elements into the general population (Khokhlov 1999, 2003b). At present, the source of this diffusion could potentially be found in the Novotitarovskaya culture, an EBA Yamnaya variant that developed before 3000 BC in the steppes of the Kuban delta north of the North Caucasus piedmont, some elements of which seem to be visible in the cultural traditions of the MBA of the Volga-Ural steppes (Kuznetsov 1996, 2003; Mochalov 2008; Tkachev and Gutsalov 2000). There are some similarities also between the Novotitarovskaya and the Late Yamnaya mortuary and ornament traditions of the Black Sea steppes. Unfortunately, no craniometric data are published for Novotitarovskaya cemeteries.

The MBA in the Volga-Ural region witnessed the appearance of other archaeological cultures centered outside the steppe zone, including Abashevo (in the forest-steppe) and Vol'sko-Lbishche (in the Zhiguli Hills west of the Volga). Skeletal material for these groups is very scanty and fragmented. They were partly contemporary with Poltavka in the steppes and influenced local historical processes particularly the Final Middle Bronze Age (see below). To the southwest of the middle Volga, the Catacomb culture of the North Caucasus and North Pontic steppes was another MBA steppe culture that also had a definite influence on the development of the Volga-Ural populations during the MBA. Some Catacomb cultural practices diffused to the Volga-Ural region, including occasional artificial deformation of the head. Most of the MBA contacts were within the steppe pastoralist environment and not with the cultures of the forest-steppe and forest.

The MBA population in the Volga-Ural steppes seems to have been much more numerous than that of the EBA. This could have caused conflicts over territory, increasing military activity and intensifying interregional contacts, including peaceful trade and exchange activities. Among the skeletons of Early Yamnaya and Poltavka individuals in the Volga-Ural steppes, 31 percent were described as showing signs of traumatic injury (Kuznetsov and Khokhlov 1998). There are no significant differences in the frequency of injuries on the skulls belonging to these two cultures.[1]

Final MBA Sintashta-Potapovka

In the final stage of the Middle Bronze Age (2100–1800 BC) in the Volga-Ural steppes, the southern Ural steppes, and northwestern Kazakhstan, a series of sites appeared with brilliant archaeological attributes, including chariots, chariot-driving gear such as bone cheekpieces, elaborate horse sacrifices including whole horses, many metal weapons such as socketed spearpoints and waisted-blade daggers, and some new ornament types. They are designated as Potapovka in the middle Volga region and Sintashta in the southeastern Ural steppes. Sintashta sites included more than 20 fortified settlements, while no settlements are known for Potapovka, but the mortuary rituals, metal objects, and ceramics are almost the same (Kuznetsov and Semenova 2000).

The Potapovka individuals in this study came from three cemeteries: Potapovka I, Utyevka VI, and Grachevka II (Table 6.4). In addition, individuals from a Sintashta cemetery at Bulanova (Kurgan 2) in the Ural steppes are described here. There are 194 individuals with age data, including just 68 with gender data. Among the buried adults, there were a little less than two males for each female. The small number of skeletons that can be assigned a gender, compared with the total number studied, is explained by the very large number of children, in which gender cannot be distinguished. Children aged 0 to 7 years averaged 51.48 percent of the burials, varying from 36.8 percent to 80 percent (Tables 6.1 and 6.3, Figure 6.7). This noticeably reduces the average life expectancy to 14.66 years. Also, only one grave of this period (less than 1 percent) contained a person older than 55 years, a sharp decrease from 13 percent in Poltavka graves. If you build these demographics into the dynamics of a real population, it creates a "demographic hole." The children had little chance to survive to adulthood, as 62 percent of the dead were aged 0 to 14 years, and if they survived, males particularly tended to die between 18 and 30 years. Females, unusually, showed no particular peak in mortality in any single age category (Figure 6.8).

This age structure has previously been observed as characteristic for Sintashta burial sites of the Ural-Kazakhstan steppes (Razhev and Epimakhov 2004; Rykushina 2003; Zdanovich 1997, 2002), and it is equally anomalous there. Different hypotheses have attempted to explain the origin of this structure—the random result of finding mostly children's graves or an increased infectious

Table 6.4 Potapovka-Sintashta Burial Data

	Potapovka I	Utyevka VI	Grachevka II
Kurgan number	1, 2, 3, 5	6, 7	3, 8
Number of specimens	43	19	25
Children: 0–7 y	54.5 (24)	36.8 (7)	80.0 (20)
Adolescents: 7–14 y	9.1 (4)	15.8 (3)	12.0 (3)
Juniors: 14–18 y	4.5 (2)	1.8 (3)	0
Male/female	1/1	1/2	
Young adult: 18–30 y	6.8 (3)	10.5 (2)	4.0 (1)
Mature adult: 30–45 y	11.4 (5)	5.3 (1)	0
Elderly: 45–55 y	4.5 (4)	15.8 (3)	4.0 (1)
Senile: ≥55 y	2.3 (1)	0	0
Male/female	7/6	5/1	0/2
Average age	12.05(43)	18.1 (19)	5.8 (25)
Average age, men	38.1 (6)	34.3 (5)	
Average age, women	34.6 (6)	50.0 (1)	39.25 (2)
Adults of indeterminate sex	6.9 percent uncertain		

Note: Values are presented as percentage (number) unless otherwise indicated.

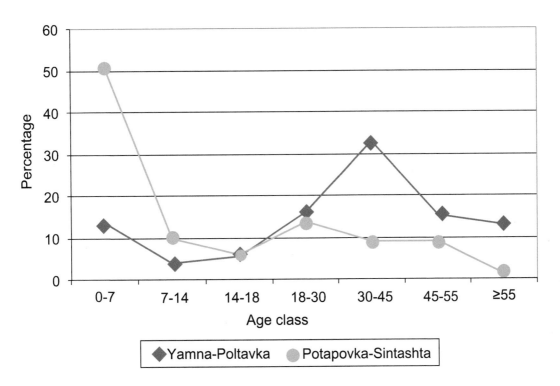

Figure 6.7 Graves by age class: Yamna-Poltavka (EBA/MBA) and Potapovka-Sintashta (Late MBA).

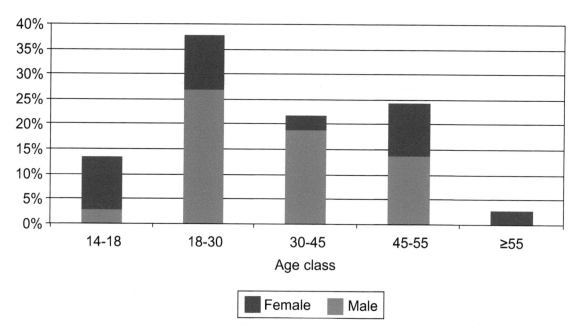

Figure 6.8 Gender by age class: Potapovka-Sintashta (Late MBA).

background because of unsanitary conditions. Such conditions, first and foremost, adversely affect children, childbirth, and the whole family cycle. Perhaps internal and external social tensions also affected survival, including the existence of specific rituals—human sacrifices. Some hypothesize a "sacred" epidemic (Razhev and Epimakhov, 2004), an outbreak of infectious diseases that arose from domestic animals. Kupriyanova (2004) pointed out that Sintashta cemeteries, mostly dominated by children, particularly contain infants. A disease such as scarlet fever affecting mainly children could be indicated. More detailed reflections on this theme are presented in Khokhlov (2010b). Of course, it is also possible that the increase in children occurred partly because this was the first time in the Bronze Age when children were regularly admitted to burial in a kurgan, a cultural change rather than a demographic one.

The origin of the craniofacial type of the Potapovka-Sintashta population is quite difficult to define. The crania (Khokhlov 1996, 1998, 2000b, 2004; Yablonsky and Khokhlov 1994) reveal at least two components. On one hand are Europeoids, probably descendants of Poltavka and Yamnaya steppe populations; on the other hand are people who are derived from the ancient Ural and Trans-Ural (east of the Ural Mountains) populations. Among the Europeoid type are variants recorded as hypermorphic, mesocranial, and relatively dolichocranial. The second craniofacial component, tentatively called Old Uraloid, often is present in the females in Potapovka graves. Moreover, while the Europeoid element predominates among adults, the Old Uraloid aspect is frequently found in the children (Khokhlov 2001). Foreign children might have been captured to use in ritual burial practices. Or children might have been adopted from subjugated peoples to improve the demographic situation, which is a frequent form of human relations (Khokhlov 2010b).

Among all cranial series in the Volga-Ural region, the Potapovka population represents the clearest example of race mixing and probably ethnic mixing as well. The cultural advancements seen in this period might perhaps have been the result of the mixing of heterogeneous groups. Such a craniometric observation is to some extent consistent with the view of some archaeologists that the Sintashta monuments represent a combination of various cultures (principally Abashevo and Poltavka, but with other influences) and therefore do not correspond to the basic concept of an archaeological culture (Kuzmina 2003:76). Under this option, the Potapovka-Sintashta burial rite may be considered, first, a combination of traits to guarantee the afterlife of a selected part of a heterogeneous population. Second, it reflected a kind of social "caste" rather than a single population. In our view, the decisive element in shaping the ethnic structure of the Potapovka-Sintashta monuments was their extensive mobility over a fairly large geographic area. They obtained knowledge of various cultures from the populations with whom they interacted.

The socially dominant anthropological component was Europeoid, possibly the descendants of Yamnaya. The association of craniofacial types with archaeological cultures in this period is difficult, primarily because of the small amount of published anthropological material of the cultures of steppe and forest belt (Balanbash, Vol'sko-Lbishche) and the eastern and southern steppes (Botai-Tersek). The crania associated with late MBA western Abashevo groups in the Don-Volga forest zone were different from eastern Abashevo in the Urals, where the expression of the Old Uraloid craniological complex was increased. Old Uraloid is found also on a single skull of Vol'sko-Lbishche culture (Tamar Utkul VII, Kurgan 4). Potentially related variants, including Mongoloid features, could be found among the Seima-Turbino tribes of the forest-steppe zone, who mixed with Sintashta and Abashevo. In the Sintashta Bulanova cemetery from the western Urals, some individuals were buried with implements of Seima-Turbino type (Khalyapin 2001; Khokhlov 2009; Khokhlov and Kitov 2009). Previously, similarities were noted between some individual skulls from Potapovka I and burials of the much older Botai culture in northern Kazakhstan (Khokhlov 2000a). Botai-Tersek is, in fact, a growing contender for the source of some "eastern" cranial features.

Late Bronze Age

The Late Bronze Age (LBA) in the Volga-Ural region, 1800 to 1200 BC, was represented archaeologically by the Timber-Grave or Srubnaya culture. This culture produced not only burial monuments but also many settlements such as Krasnosamarskoe, an innovation that is usually ascribed to the adoption of agriculture. The number of graves found in both kurgan and flat-grave cemeteries increased markedly compared to previous generations. The number of LBA individuals in this study with gender and/or age determinations is 572, much higher than for the mortuary populations of earlier periods. While one reason for this increase was certainly that almost the whole population was now admitted into cemeteries, rather than only a selected part of the population, also probably there was a real increase in the number of people living in the middle Volga region.

The percentage of children (age 0–7 years) in LBA cemeteries declined to more normal levels, only 30 to 32 percent compared to 51 percent for Potapovka-Sintashta (Tables 6.1 and 6.2, Figure 6.9). The LBA population enjoyed a high survivorship to adolescence (7–14 years), particularly in the developed Srubnaya period. Women's mortality in the childbearing years, 18 to 30 years, was much higher than that of men, again particularly in the developed Srubnaya period. This pattern is expected and helps us to believe that the LBA data might be a more accurate indicator of the living population than can be said for earlier periods. The LBA also shows a nearly equal balance of males and females. The average life span increased by up to 19.71 years and was longer for both men and women (38.79 years and 37.43 years, respectively). In general, we can observe population stabilization during the LBA.

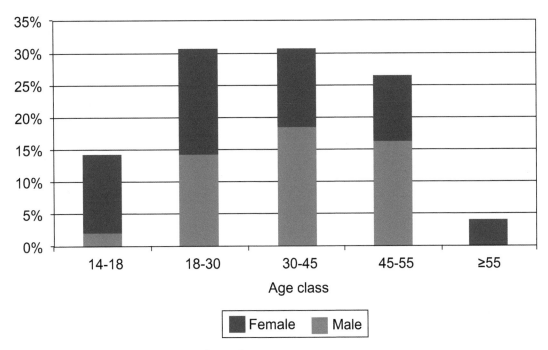

Figure 6.9 Gender by age class: Early Srubnaya (Early LBA).

The Early Srubnaya (Pokrovka) period was the transitional phase between the Final Middle Bronze Age and the Late Bronze Age, dated by radiocarbon at Krasnosamarskoe to about 1900 to 1800 BC. Pokrovka cultural traditions evolved directly from the preceding Potapovka-Sintashta culture (Kuznetsov and Semenova 2000; Mochalov 2008). Based on age and gender characteristics and on archaeological data, the population in the middle Volga region was less mobile than the preceding Potapovka population. Srubnaya burials also contained fewer military artifacts, as well as less evidence of combat injuries. The overall situation probably was more peaceful.

The Early Srubnaya craniofacial type was heterogeneous, similar in this trait to Potapovka-Sintashta, but this heterogeneity is expressed less strongly (Khokhlov 2000a, 2000b). One of the Early Srubnaya anthropological components can be genetically linked with the native Potapovka-Sintashta culture. The dominant component was characterized by dolichocrania and a high and sharply profiled face. This type was morphologically distinct from the southern Europeoid craniological type typical for the local Poltavka MBA population, but it was similar to the lower Volga Pokrovka type. A recent study showed the relationship of the Potapovka component to the so-called Krivoluchi culture of the lower Volga and MBA populations in the North Caucasus steppes (Khokhlov and Mimokhod 2008). Formation of the LBA physical type of the Samara

population east of the Volga was complicated.

The developed or classic Srubnaya phase is dated in the middle Volga region between 1800 and 1200 BC. It is represented by material from 20 cemeteries, 11 of which can be used for intragroup review. In general, the age and sex structure of the developed Srubnaya phase was close to that of Early Srubnaya. The developed Srubnaya phase displayed some of its own trends (Figure 6.10). The slight decline in overall child mortality was due to better survival of adolescent girls and the young (Table 6.1, Figure 6.10). However, there was an increase in the proportion of deaths during childbearing ages for women and a decrease in the number of deaths in the senile period (Figure 6.11). The average life span increased to 21.29 years, due to lower infant mortality.

In general, the sex ratio remained near parity. In the age-specific classes, males and females were almost equal in the adolescent category, but females died much more often than did males in the mature childbearing years, 18 to 30 years. It is likely that in the developed Srubnaya period, females married and began having children later, since girls aged 14 to 18 years had a very low mortality. This could have had a positive impact on the population through higher-quality and more experienced reproduction. Male mortality exceeded female mortality in the older age categories, 30 to 55 years, but they were equal in the senile age category, over 55 years. Some cemeteries contained

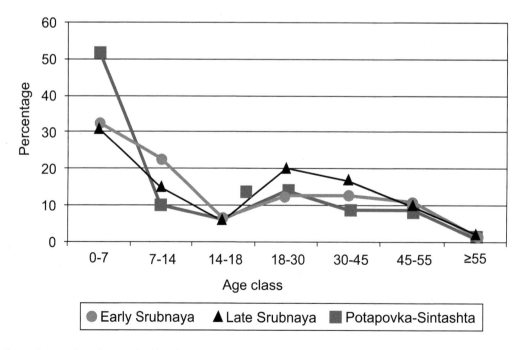

Figure 6.10 Graves by age class: Potapovka-Sintashta (Late MBA) and Early Srubnaya (Early LBA) and Late Srubnaya (LBA).

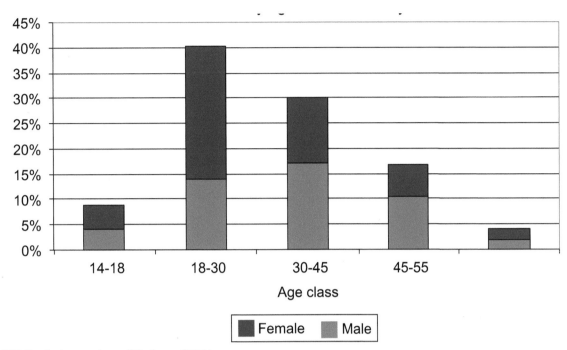

Figure 6.11 Gender by age class: all Srubnaya (LBA).

no individuals in the over-55 category, but where they appeared, they varied from 1.9 percent to 4.8 percent. For sedentary tribal groups, this number is close to normal.

The general demographics of the developed Srubnaya population as well as the suggestion that females married later in life suggest that the population was sedentary. This correlates well with archaeological data about the appearance of settlements and the archaeozoological composition of herds of domesticated animals. In particular, for Srubnaya settlements in the Samara Valley, we see the characteristic traits of permanent occupation such as the transhumance of livestock, with a trend toward a more complex system of managing cattle for dairy products and sheep-goat for wool (Kosintsev 2003:135–136).

The physical type of the developed Srubnaya period in its main features was similar to the Pokrovka type of the earliest LBA, characterized by, first of all, dolichocrania and a sharply profiled face. However, the average skull was larger in transverse diameter. This is a consequence of cross-breeding between the predominantly dolichocranial narrow-faced Europeoid complex and the more ancient local broad-faced meso-dolichocranial complex (Khokhlov 1998). There was a tendency to reduce polytypes within groups, so there was practically no in-site craniological polymorphism (Khokhlov 2004).

One remarkable aspect of Srubnaya kurgan cemeteries was the presence of some kurgans and even cemeteries with an overwhelming dominance of children's burials,

amounting to 100 percent (Taydakovo I, Kurgan 2). Some cemeteries can be identified as "children's fields," where children's burial was practiced, accompanied by a few adults, mostly women. At Spiridonovka II, a developed Srubnaya cemetery not far from Krasnosamarskoe, in Kurgan 2, among the 36 individuals buried, 80.6 percent were children younger than 14 years. In the center of the kurgan was an older woman (Grave 25) and, near the southern edge of the mound, a girl 17 to 19 years (Grave 20). Kurgan 10 at Spiridonovka II could be regarded as a female kurgan (sex ratio 5:1), dominated by women of mature age. In the remaining three mounds at Spiridonovka II (1, 10, 14), the ratio of ages and genders was fairly balanced. Similar children's mounds included Kurgan 3 at Barinovka I, Kurgan 4 at Nizhny Orleansky II, and Kurgan 3 at Krasnosel'skii. Such features occurred in Early Srubnaya also—Kurgans 3 and 8 at Grachevka II. In this context, the fact that 66 percent of the 22 Srubnaya burials that we excavated at the cemetery of Krasnosamarskoe IV were aged 0 to 14 years is part of a recognizable pattern.

It is highly likely that some cemeteries and kurgans of the LBA Srubnaya culture and, even more distinctly, of the Final MBA Potapovka-Sintashta culture were arranged not according to kinship but according to specific social and religious customs related to particular notions of death, burial, and the afterlife. People were segregated by age and by gender in some kurgans. Socially stratified kurgans have been found in a number of cemeteries of the MBA and LBA also in the southern Urals and Kazakhstan: Petrovka, Alakul, and Atasu (Gryaznov 1956; Molodin 1984; Matiushchenko 1994; Tkachev and Tkacheva 2004).

The Final Bronze Age

The Final Bronze Age, 1200 to 900 BC, in the Volga-Ural region was associated with the Suskanskaya, Ivanovo, and Maklasheevka cultures, which developed out of Srubnaya. Few well-preserved skeletons date to this period, so it is impossible to discuss the demographic structure of the population. After this came the Iron Age and the dominance of nomadic pastoralists.

Summary

Several important trends can be seen in the craniometric data that provide a context for the interpretation of population structure and demographics. First, the Eneolithic population of the middle Volga, typified at the Khvalynsk cemetery, was heterogeneous and probably included both southern narrow-faced elements, perhaps from the lower Volga and North Caucasus regions, and a northern element more related to the Uraloid forest-zone population. Second, at the end of the Eneolithic and the opening of the Bronze Age, this middle Volga population absorbed a migration of people who probably came to the middle Volga from the Don steppes in the southwest. This mixture produced the typical cranial characteristics of the middle Volga Yamnaya population. The Repin variety of Early Yamnaya ceramic styles might have entered the middle Volga region with this movement of people from the Don. The Middle Bronze Age Poltavka

population was more heterogeneous than the Early Yamnaya population, perhaps showing the arrival of some new people from the North Caucasus steppes. The Final Middle Bronze Age Potapovka-Sintashta population of the middle Volga region was the most heterogeneous population of the Bronze Age, with many new population elements from the forest zone, from the steppes east of the Ural Mountains, and perhaps from the North Caucasus or the lower Volga regions. This diversity carried through into the Late Bronze Age population, although to a lesser degree.

Demographically, the Early Bronze Age seems to have been a period of high mobility, relatively low population density, and very high muscular activity, producing a quite robust population. The Middle Bronze Age showed an increase in population and in female fertility and perhaps a more successful adaptation to the demands of mobile pastoralism. Both Early and Middle Bronze Age mortuary populations were strongly biased in favor of adult males, but the sex and age ratio was somewhat more balanced in the Middle Bronze Age. The Potapovka-Sintashta population showed a marked increase in child graves (Figure 6.12), partly the result of a new social or cultural system of belief and perhaps partly also caused by an actual increase in child mortality. The Late Bronze Age was a period of population stabilization with a sedentary settlement pattern and a mortuary population that approached normal statistics for gender and age structure, although some individual kurgans still seem to have been reserved almost entirely for children or for females, while others showed a balanced proportion of ages and sexes.

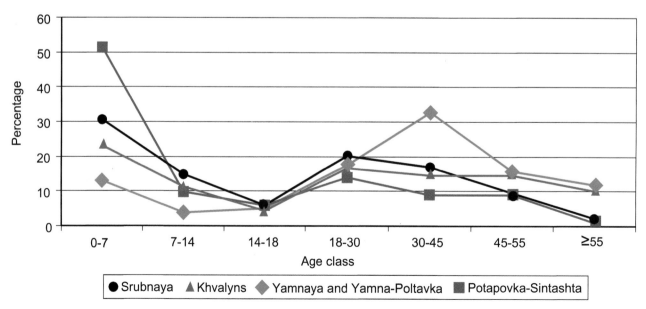

Figure 6.12 Graves by age class: all cultures.

Notes

1   Editor's note: See the report by Murphy for a different interpretation of EBA and MBA violence-related pathologies. She found weapon-related trauma on 18.8 percent of Yamnaya and 2.9 percent of Poltavka skeletons.

•   Figures and tables in this chapter were prepared by A. Khokhlov.

References

Agapov, S. A., I. B. Vasiliev, and V. I. Pestrikova.
1990   *Hvalynskij jeneoliticheskij mogil'nik.* Saratov.

Alekseev, V. P.
1972   *Paleodemografija SSSR // SA.* Vyp.1.

Bogdanov, S. V.
2004   *Jepoha medi stepnogo priural'ja.* Tipografija UrO RAN, Ekaterinburg.

Danilenko, V. N.
1974   *Eneolit Ukrainy.* Kiev.

Debets, G. F.
1953   *K paleoantropologii Urala // KSIJe,* vyp. 18.

Gei, A. N.
2000   *Novotitorovskaya culture.* Russian Academy of Sciences Institute of Archaeology, Moscow.

Gryaznov, M. P.
1956   *Istorija drevnih plemen Verhnej Obi po materialam raskopok bliz s.Bol'shaja Rechka // MIA.* #48.

Khalyapin, M. V.
2001   *Pervyj beskurgannyj mogil'nik sintashtinskoj kul'tury v stepnom Priural'e // Bronzovyj vek Vostochnoj Evropy: harakteristika kul'tur, hronologija i periodizacija.* Samara.

Khokhlov, A. A.
1996   *Kraniologija mogil'nikov potapovskogo tipa v Povolzh'e, sintashtinskogo i petrovskogo - v Kazahstane // Drevnosti Volgo-Donskih stepej v sisteme vostochnoevropejskogo bronzovogo veka (Materialy mezhdunarodnoj nauchnoj konferencii).* Volgograd.

1998   *Paleoantropologija pogranich'ja lesostepi i stepi Volgo-Ural'ja v jepohi neolita-bronzy // avtoref. dis... kand. ist. nauk.* Moscow.

1999   *Kraniologicheskie materialy rannej i nachala srednej bronzy Samarskogo Zavolzh'ja i Orenburzh'ja // Vestnik antropologii.* Vyp.6. Moscow.

2000a   *Paleoantropologija jepohi bronzy Samarskogo Povolzh'ja // Istorija Samarskogo Povolzh'ja s drevnejshih vremen do nashih dnej.* Bronzovyj vek. Samara.

2000b   *Kraniologicheskie materialy srubnoj kul'tury juga Srednego Povolzh'ja // Narody Rossii. Antropologija.* Chast' 2. Moscow.

2001   *Paleoantropologicheskie rekonstrukcii kak istochnik izuchenija jetnogeneticheskih processov (po materialam jepohi bronzy Volgo-Ural'ja).* Samara.

2002   *Paleoantropologija mogil'nika srubnoj kul'tury Barinovka I // Voprosy arheologii Povolzh'ja.* Vyp.2. Samara.

2003a   *Demograficheskie osobennosti naselenija jepohi bronzy bassejna reki Samara // Material'naja kul'tura naselenija bassejna reki Samara v bronzovom veke.* Samara.

2003b   *O specifike antropologicheskogo tipa naselenija Juzhnogo Priural'ja v jepohu rannej i srednej bronzy. Chtenija, posvjashhennye dejatel'nosti V.A.Gorodcova v Gosudarstvennom Istoricheskom muzee.* Chast' II. Moscow.

2004   *Antropologicheskij sostav Volgo-Ural'skogo regiona v jepohu bronzy // Jekologija i demografija cheloveka v proshlom i nastojashhem. Materialy tret'ih antropologicheskih chtenij k 75-letiju so dnja rozhdenija akademika V.P.Alekseeva.* Moscow.

2009   *K voprosu o mongoloidnyh cherepah jepohi bronzy Volgo-Ural'ja // Vestnik Cheljabinskogo gosudarstvennogo universiteta.* #6 (144). Istorija. Vyp.30.

2010a   *Naselenie hvalynskoj jeneoliticheskoj kul'tury. Po antropologicheskim materialam gruntovyh mogil'nikov Hvalynsk I, Hvalynsk II, Hlopkov Bugor // Hvalynskie jeneoliticheskie mogil'niki i hvalynskaja jeneoliticheskaja kul'tura.* Samara. S407-517.

2010b   *O proiskhozhdenii i dal'neyshem razvitii fizicheskogo tipa nositeley sintashtinsko-potapovskogo kruga kul'tur // Arkaim–Sintashta: drevneye naslediye Yuzhnogo Urala.* ChelGU, CH. 2. S. 112–132, Chelyabinsk.

2012a   *Paleoantropologija Volgo-Ural'ja v jepohi neolita i jeneolita. Obzor istochnika i podrobnyj analiz.* LAP LAMBERT Academic Publishing.

2012b   *Ritual'nye travmy na cherepah u nositelej hvalynskoj jeneoliticheskoj kul'tury Povolzh'ja // JeO. - M: Nauka.* Vyp. #2. S.118–125.

Khokhlov, A. A., and E. P. Kitov
2009   *Predvaritel'noe soobshhenie o paleoantropologicheskom materiale jepohi srednej bronzy mogil'nika Bulanovo I Vestnik Cheljabinskogo gosudarstvennogo universiteta.* #6 (144). Istorija. Vyp.30.

Khokhlov, A. A., and R. A. Mimokhod
2008   *Kraniologija naselenija stepnogo Predkavkaz'ja i Povolzh'ja v postkatakombnoe vremja // Vestnik antropologii.* #16. Moscow.

Khokhlov, A. A., and L. T. Yablonsky
2000   *Paleoantropologija Volgo-Ural'skogo regiona jepohi neolita-jeneolita // Istorija Samarskogo Povolzh'ja s drevnejshih vremen do nashih dnej. Kamennyj vek.* Samara.

Kosintsev, P. A.
2003   *Zhivotnovodstvo u naselenija Samarskogo Povolzh'ja v jepohu pozdnej bronzy // Material'naja kul'tura bassejna reki Samara v bronzovom veke.* Samara.

Kozhin, P. M.

1997   *Pokazateli kochevogo byta kul'tur prichernomorsko-prikaspijskih stepej jepohi bronzy // Step' i Kavkaz (kul'turnye tradicii)*. Moscow.

Kozlovskaja, M. V.

1996   *Jekologija drevnih plemen lesnoj polosy Vostochnoj Evropy*. Moscow.

Kreutz, S. I.

1977   *Naselenie stepnoj Ukrainy v jepohu-jeneolita-bronzy /po antropologicheskim dannym/ // avtoref. dis... kand. ist. nauk*. Moskva.

1984 *Paleoantropologicheskie issledovanija stepnogo Podneprov'ja*. Kiev.

Kupriyanova, E. V.

2004   *K voprosu o prichinah detskih kollektivnyh zahoronenij v nekropoljah bronzovogo veka Juzhnogo Zaural'ja // Jetnicheskie vzaimodejstvija na Juzhnom Urale*. Cheljabinsk.

Kuzmina, E. E.

1997   *Ekologija stepej Evrazii i problema proishozhdenija nomadizma Ch.II. Vozniknovenie kochevogo skotovodstva // Vestnik drevnej istorii. #2*. Moscow.

2003   *Abashevo, sintashta i proishozhdenie indoirancev // Abashevskaja kul'turno-istoricheskaja obshhnost': istoki, razvitie, nasledie*. Cheboksary.

Kuznetsov, P. F.

1996   *Kavkazskij ochag i kul'tury bronzovogo veka Volgo-Ural'ja // Mezhdu Aziej i evropoj*. Spb.

2003   *K istokam proishozhdenija poltavkinskoj kul'tury // Chtenija, posvjashhennye 100-letiju dejatel'nosti Vasilija Alekseevicha Gorodcova v Gosudarstvennom Istoricheskom Muzee. Tezisy konferencii*. Moscow.

Kuznetsov, P. F., and A. A. Khokhlov

1998   *Sledy travmaticheskih povrezhdenij ljudej po materialam pogrebenij jepohi bronzy Volgo-Ural'skogo regiona // Voennaja arheologija. Oruzhie i voennoe delo v istoricheskoj i social'noj perspektive*. Sankt-Peterburg.

Kuznetsov, P. F., and A. P. Semenova

2000   *Pamjatniki potapovskogo tipa // Istorija Samarskogo Povolzh'ja s drevnejshih vremen do nashih dnej. Bronzovyj vek*. Samara.

Martin, R., and K. Saller

1957   *Lehrbuch der Anthropologie in Systematischer Darstellung*. 3rd ed. Gustav Fischer Verlag, Stuttgart.

Matiushchenko, V. I.

1994   *Jepoha bronzy. Lesnaja i lesostepnaja polosa //Ocherki kul'turogeneza narodov Zapadnoj Sibiri*. Tomsk.

Merpert, N. Ja.

1974   *Drevnejshie skotovody Volzhsko-Ural'skogo mezhdurech'ja*. Moscow.

Mkrtchyan, R. A.

1988a   *Paleoantropologija neoliticheskogo i jeneoliticheskogo naselenija juga Evropejskoj chasti SSSR (po materialam mogil'nikov "Gospital'nyj holm i Hvalynskij") // dis... kand. ist. nauk*. Moscow.

1988b   *Paleoantropologija neoliticheskogo i jeneoliticheskogo naselenija juga Evropejskoj chasti SSSR (po materialam mogil'nikov "Gospital'nyj holm i Hvalynskij") // avtoref... dis... kand. ist. nauk*. Moscow.

Mochalov, O. D.

2008.   *Keramika pogrebal'nyh pamjatnikov jepohi bronzy lesostepi Volgo-Ural'skogo mezhdurech'ja*. Samara.

Molodin, V. I.

1984   *Osobennosti pogrebal'nogo obrjada detskih zahoronenij andronovcev Barabinskoj lesostepi (po materialam mogil'nika Preobrazhenka-3) // Bronzovyj vek Uralo-Irtyshskogo mezhdurech'ja*. Cheljabinsk.

Morgunova, N. L., and A. Ju. Kravtsov

1994   *Pamjatniki drevnejamnoj kul'tury na Ileke*. Ekaterinburg.

Petrenko, A. G.

2000   *Sledy ritual'nyh zhivotnyh v mogil'nikah drevnego i srednevekovogo naselenija Srednego Povolzh'ja i Predural'ja*. Kazan'.

Razhev, D. I., and A. V. Epimakhov

2004   *Fenomen mnogochislennosti detskih pogrebenij v mogil'nikah jepohi bronzy // Vestnik arheologii, antropologii i jetnografii. Vyp.5*. Tjumen'.

Romanova, G. P.

1989   *Opyt paleodemograficheskogo analiza uslovij zhizni naselenija stepnyh rajonov stavropol'ja v jepohu rannej bronzy // Voprosy Antropologii. Vyp.82*. Moscow.

Rykushina, G. V.

2003   *Antropologicheskaja harakteristika naselenija jepohi bronzy Juzhnogo Urala po materialam mogil'nika Krivoe Ozero // N. B. Vinogradov. Mogil'nik bronzovogo veka Krivoe Ozero v Juzhnom Zaural'e*. Cheljabinsk.

Shevchenko, A. V.

1986   *Antropologija naselenija juzhno-russkih stepej v jepohu bronzy // Antropologija sovremennogo i drevnego naselenija evropejskoj chasti SSSR*. Leningrad.

Shilov, V. P.

1975   *Ocherki po istorii drevnih plemen Nizhnego Povolzh'ja*. Leningrad.

Shishlina, N. I., and V. E. Bulatov

2000   *K voprosu o sezonnoj sisteme ispol'zovanija pastbishh nositeljami jamnoj kul'tury Prikaspijskih stepej v III tys. do n. je. // Sezonnyj jekonomicheskij cikl naselenija severo-zapadnogo Prikaspija v bronzovom veke*. Moscow.

Tkachev, V. V., and S. Ju. Gutsalov

2000   *Novye pogrebenija jeneolita – srednej bronzy iz Vostochnogo Orenburzh'ja i Severnogo Kazahstana // Arheologicheskie pamjatniki Orenburzh'ja.* Orenburg.

Tkachev, A. A., and N. A. Tkacheva

2004   *K voprosu o demograficheskoj situacii v stepjah Central'nogo Kazahstana v jepohu srednej bronzy // Vestnik arheologii, antropologii i jetnografii.* Vyp.5. Tjumen'.

Vasiliev, I. B., P. F. Kuznetsov, and M. A. Turetskii

2000   *Jamnaja i poltavkinskaja kul'tury // Istorija Samarskogo Povolzh'ja s drevnejshih vremen do nashih dnej. Bronzovyj vek.* Samara.

Yablonsky, L. T., and A. A. Khokhlov

1994   Novye kraniologicheskie materialy jepohi bronzy Samarskogo Zavolzh'ja // I. B. Vasil'ev, P. F. Kuznecov, A. P. Semjonova. *Potapovskij kurgannyj mogil'nik indoiranskih plemjon na Volge.* Samarskij universitet.

Zdanovich, G. B.

1997   *Sintashtinskoe obshhestvo: social'nye osnovy «kvazigorodskoj» kul'tury Juzhnogo Zaural'ja v jepohu srednej bronzy.* Cheljabinsk.

2002   *Uralo-Kazahstanskie stepi v jepohu srednej bronzy // Dis. V vide nauch.dokl. ... d-ra ist.nauk.* Cheljabinsk.

Chapter 7

Stable Isotope Analysis of Neolithic to Late Bronze Age Populations in the Samara Valley

Rick J. Schulting • Michael P. Richards

The Samara Valley is located in what is today the steppe/forest-steppe zone of the middle Volga region of Russia. The region forms an important communication route between the Central Eurasian steppes and Europe, particularly from the Bronze Age onward, when the domestication of the horse greatly increased the effective mobility of the steppe peoples (Anthony 2007; Anthony and Brown 2000; Outram et al. 2009). The later prehistoric subsistence economy of the region, and the Eurasian steppes in general, is widely thought to have emphasized sheep and cattle pastoralism, with some contribution from agriculture (Khazanov 1994; Koryakova and Epimakhov 2006; Levine 1999; Frachetti 2008), although the degree to which spatial and diachronic variability may have featured is not well understood (Chapter 1). Stable isotope analysis is increasingly being used to investigate the diets of Eurasian steppe populations, providing direct insights into the diets of individuals and the communities to which they belonged (Hollund et al. 2010; Murphy et al. 2013; Privat 2004; Shishlina et al. 2007, 2009, 2012; Shishlina 2008; Svyatko 2009; Svyatko et al. 2013; Ventrusca Miller et al. 2014). This chapter presents and discusses stable carbon and nitrogen isotope analyses on the bone collagen of 58 individuals from the Samara Valley, ranging in date from the Neolithic to the Late Bronze Age, with one outlier from the Iron Age. Evidence for domestic cattle and sheep appears in the Samara Valley in the Eneolithic, from as early as 4700/4500 BC (Anthony

2007:182; Anthony and Brown 2011). Cereals are not documented in the region until the Late Bronze Age and even then are rare, although visibility and recovery biases remain possible (Anthony et al. 2005). Specific research questions addressed in this chapter include whether dietary shifts can be detected isotopically between the Neolithic/ Eneolithic and Early Bronze Age (EBA), as well as with the beginning of the Late Bronze Age, when a shift toward greater sedentism is attested archaeologically (Chapter 4).

Stable Carbon and Nitrogen Isotopes

Stable carbon and nitrogen isotope analysis has seen application in many parts of the world over the past few decades and is now a standard technique used in the investigation of past human and animal diets. Stable carbon ($\delta^{13}C$) isotopes distinguish between terrestrial and marine-based food webs, as well as between terrestrial systems based on C_3 versus C_4 plants, the most economically important of which are maize (*Zea mays*) and millet (especially *Panicum* spp. and *Secaria* spp.) (Schoeninger 1989). Broadly speaking, human consumers reliant on terrestrial C_3 systems will have bone collagen $\delta^{13}C$ values of approximately –21‰, while those reliant on purely C_4 systems will have values as high as around –7‰. Marine systems are intermediate between these two extremes but can be largely excluded from the present study (Caspian Sea sturgeon were present in the Volga River system [Khodorevskaya et al. 2009] and likely exhibit elevated

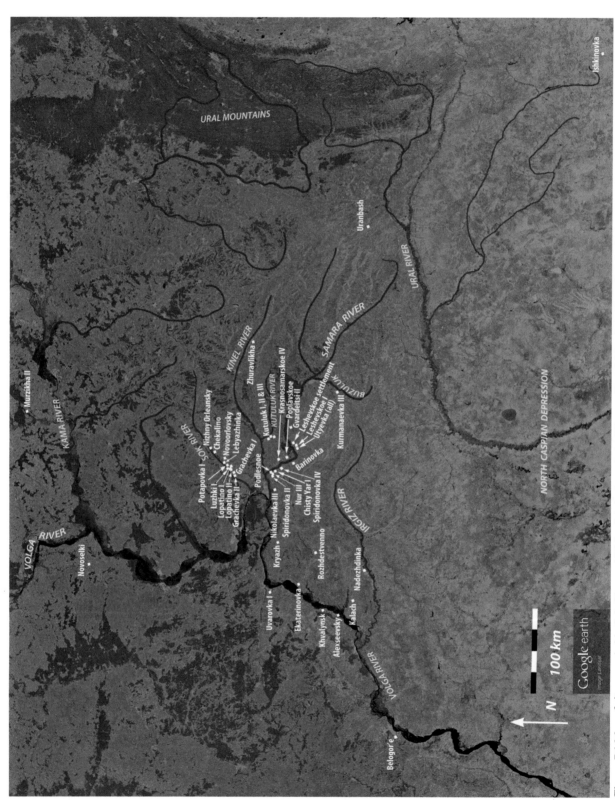

Figure 7.1 Map of sites sampled in Schulting and Richards's isotope study (Chapter 7) and Murphy's bioarchaeological study (Chapter 8). *Background map by Tom Elliott for the Ancient World Mapping Center, University of North Carolina at Chapel Hill.*

$\delta^{13}C$ values, although the isotope ecology of the Caspian is poorly known.) Freshwater aquatic isotopic systems are complex and may be similar to terrestrial C_3 systems or may be either depleted or enriched in ^{13}C (Dufour et al. 1999; Fry 1991; Katzenberg and Weber 1999). They are best dealt with empirically on a regional or even local basis. There are a number of additional sources of variation in plant $\delta^{13}C$ values, such as a depleting "canopy effect" found in the understory of dense woodlands and elevation under conditions of water stress (Bonafini et al. 2013; Tieszen 1991). These are comparatively minor relative to the differences between photosynthetic pathways and C_3 terrestrial/marine systems noted above but can contribute significant variation at finer-scale resolutions.

Stable nitrogen ($\delta^{15}N$) isotopes broadly inform on an organism's trophic level (Schoeninger and DeNiro 1984), although there are other factors involved (Hedges and Reynard 2007). The number of trophic levels is generally limited in the terrestrial ecosystems in which humans generally engage to three: primary producers (plants) and first-order (herbivores) and second-order (carnivores) consumers. Leaving aside aquatic foods, humans, being omnivorous, will generally consume some balance of plants and herbivores. Herbivore $\delta^{15}N$ values can themselves vary widely depending on the values of the plants they consume but are generally in the range 3 to 7‰. Humans are enriched by 3 to 5‰ relative to their protein source (they are also enriched by about 1‰ in $\delta^{13}C$) (Bocherens and Drucker 2003). Thus, adult humans with values higher than approximately 12‰ are likely to have consumed a significant proportion of their protein from higher trophic levels than usually represented by herbivores, such as can be found in freshwater and marine ecosystems (i.e., fish and piscivorous waterfowl). If plants—which usually exhibit relatively low $\delta^{15}N$ values (but see below)—contributed to the diet, the consumption of high trophic-level foods would need to have been proportionately greater to result in the observed high human values.

As with $\delta^{13}C$, however, a number of additional factors affect $\delta^{15}N$ values. One of these is the enrichment seen in nursing individuals, since they are effectively raised by one trophic level above their mothers (Schurr 1998). Measurements on human infants, therefore, should be excluded from an analysis of diet at the population level, since they will artificially raise the average and introduce considerable additional variation. This is not a factor in the present study, as only adults were measured. More relevant here is this same effect in domestic animals, as the consumption of young males is a common practice in herding societies, particularly those emphasizing milk

production. These animals will be significantly elevated above the adults of the same species that are often used to provide baseline $\delta^{15}N$ values. With the single exception of a horse, no faunal isotope values have yet been obtained from the Samara Valley specifically, but comparative data from the wider region are discussed below. Leguminous plants fix nitrogen directly from the air and so exhibit considerably lower $\delta^{15}N$ values than non-nitrogen-fixing plants; however, legumes are not thought to have been a factor in the study area.

Another source of variation involves $\delta^{15}N$ enrichment in animals and humans under arid conditions. While the effect itself is well documented, there remains some debate over whether it is the result of changes in soil and plant values due to aridity, to the animal's physiological response to water stress, or to some combination of the two (Ambrose 1991; Gröcke et al. 1997; Heaton 1987; Heaton et al. 1986; Pate and Anson 2008; Sealy et al. 1987; Vanderklift and Ponsard 2003). This is potentially a factor in the present study, since what is today forest-steppe may have been more arid grassland steppe in the Subboreal. Even today, annual rainfall is low in the Samara Valley, averaging around 400 mm, which is classed as semi-arid (Kremenetski et al. 1999). Saltmarshes—the result of soil salinization in noncoastal environments—can also exhibit $\delta^{15}N$ enrichment (Britton et al. 2008; Heaton 1987; Karamanos et al. 1981; Page 1995; Schwarcz et al. 1999; van Groenigen and Kessel 2002). Finally, the practice of manuring has been shown to increase $\delta^{15}N$ values in cereals, which would in turn affect the animals fed either the grain or chaff, or grazing the stubble (Bogaard et al. 2007; Fraser et al. 2011) (although straw is low in protein and would therefore contribute little nitrogen). While a similar but diluted effect can be envisaged for intensively grazed pastures with high stocking rates, this is unlikely to describe the more extensive pastoral systems characteristic of the steppes, although this warrants further research (cf. Makarewicz 2014).

Stable isotope measurements on adult human bone collagen reflect an averaged dietary signal over a period of approximately the last decade of an individual's life. There is a bias toward the protein component of the diet in collagen $\delta^{13}C$ measurements ($\delta^{15}N$ measurements refer exclusively to protein sources), particularly with moderate to high protein consumption (Ambrose and Norr 1993; Jim et al. 2006). Thus, most plant foods will be underrepresented relative to animal protein, the latter including milk and blood as well as meat. Fish and terrestrial mammals provide similar amounts by weight of high-quality protein.

Materials and Methods

A total of 58 adult human bone (mainly tibia and femur) samples were obtained from Neolithic to Late Bronze Age individuals from a series of sites centering on the Samara Valley (Figure 7.1). In addition, one horse was sampled, from the Bronze Age site of Potapovka. Cultural attributions and their concomitant chronological spans are based on archaeological data and, in 23 cases (including the horse), on direct accelerator mass spectrometry (AMS) ^{14}C dating (Chapter 2). A small number of samples derive from individuals outside the main study area: Belogor'e on the Volga some 300 km to the south of the Samara confluence; Ishkinovka on a tributary of the Ural River to the east; and Tanabergin in Kazakhstan. Despite its later date (contemporary with the EBA in the Samara Valley proper), the single sample from Murzikha II is included in the Eneolithic group, as it derives from the forests further to the north, where communities long retained a fishing-hunting-gathering lifestyle (Piezonka et al. 2013; Wood et al. 2013). Age and sex data were determined by Khokhlov (Chapter 6) according to standard osteological criteria. A number of individuals were reassigned sex on the basis of the results of an ancient DNA study (Table 7.1).

Bone collagen was extracted at the Department of Archaeological Science, University of Bradford using the methods outlined in Richards and Hedges (1999) with the addition of an ultrafiltration step (Brown et al. 1988). Isotope measurements were made using a Thermo Finnigan EA coupled to a Delta XP isotope ratio mass spectrometer. δ^{13}C values are measured relative to the VPDB (Vienna Pee Dee Belemnite) standard and δ^{15}N values relative to the AIR (Ambient Inhalable Reservoir) standard, and they are reported in parts per mil (‰). Errors on both measurements are better than ± 0.2 per mil.

As most of the results are not normally distributed, nonparametric Mann-Whitney U tests and Kruskal-Wallis ANOVA tests are used for statistical analyses of paired and multiple groups, respectively.

Results

Results are shown in Table 7.1. Most samples demonstrated well-preserved collagen, with C:N values falling between 3.1 and 3.4, with only one marginal result of 3.7 falling just outside the accepted range of 2.9 to 3.6 (DeNiro 1985). The yield for this sample (an adult female from Tanabergin II, Kazakhstan) was also very low (0.1 percent), although lower yields are expected for ultrafiltered collagen. The δ^{13}C and δ^{15}N results are entirely in line with other Middle Bronze Age samples; this sample also yielded an acceptable AMS determination (AA47806, 4020 ± 55 BP).

In any case, this individual derives from well outside the Samara Valley and so is excluded from further discussion. The single Bronze Age individuals from Belogor'e and Ishkinovka are also excluded due to their distance from the Samara Valley. Radiocarbon dating placed an individual from Nadezhdinka—initially thought to belong to the Early Bronze Age—in the Iron Age (Beta-392493; 2220 ± 30 BP); this sample is also excluded from the analysis.

The two Neolithic samples from the Sok River are nearly identical to one another, sharing relatively low δ^{13}C values and δ^{15}N values relative to the individuals attributed to the Eneolithic (Tables 7.2 and 7.3). While it must be seen as tentative given the small sample size and uncertainties over dating, this observation is of some interest in that the Eneolithic sees the introduction of domestic animals. However, dating of human bones in both periods is subject to suspected freshwater reservoir effects (Anthony 2007:127), making this division a tentative one based on the present evidence. Not in question, despite some overlap in regards to specific individuals, is the clear division observed between the Eneolithic and Bronze Age groups in both isotopes (Figure 7.2). The δ^{13}C values are significantly lower (Mann-Whitney U test, $Z = 4.43$, $p = 0.000$) in the Eneolithic group, while δ^{15}N values are significantly higher ($Z = 3.73$, $p = 0.000$). This combination of relatively depleted δ^{13}C values and, more importantly, elevated δ^{15}N values, may be attributed to the significant consumption of freshwater fish. As discussed further below, there are three probable outliers (retained in the above statistical comparison) in the Eneolithic data set—all from the site of Lebyazhinka V—with values for both isotopes more similar to those of the Bronze Age group. With these included, there is no correlation between δ^{13}C and δ^{15}N for the combined Neolithic/Eneolithic group ($r^2 = 0.10$, $p = 0.260$); when they are excluded, however, there is a moderate positive linear correlation ($r^2 = 0.38$, $p = 0.034$). The removal of the single result from Murzikha II, arguably another outlier (and from the northern forest, a different ecological zone), improves the correlation in the Neolithic/Eneolithic group significantly ($r^2 = 0.79$, $p = 0.000$). A similar trend is seen in the combined Bronze Age group ($r^2 = 0.32$, $p = 0.000$), but on a substantially different trajectory with differing beginning and end points.

If fish are the main source of protein responsible for this pattern in both cases, they must have been at least slightly elevated in δ^{13}C relative to other sources of protein and significantly so in δ^{15}N. The protein sources in the Neolithic/Eneolithic must have been considerably depleted in δ^{13}C relative to later periods. This could be the result of taking game from C_3 habitats (forests) rather than the

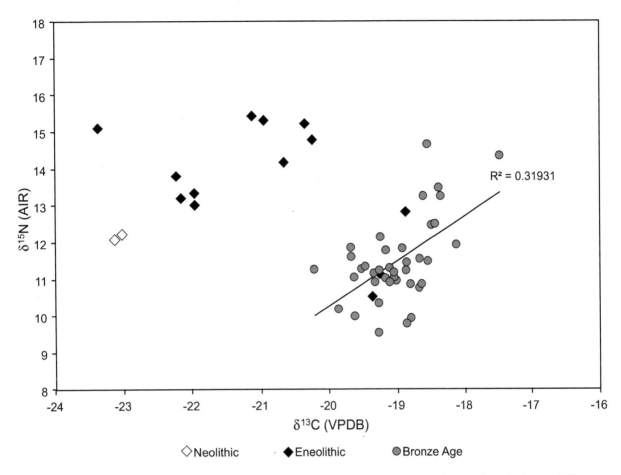

Figure 7.2 Bivariate plot of $\delta^{13}C$ and $\delta^{15}N$ values for pooled Neolithic/Eneolithic and Bronze Age humans from the Samara Valley.

steppe or that avoided C_4 plants if they did graze on the latter. While no fish values are available from the Samara Valley, a single pike (*Esox lucius*) sample from a Bronze Age Caspian site provides values of –16.5‰ and 15.0‰ for $\delta^{13}C$ and $\delta^{15}N$, respectively (Shishlina et al. 2007). Although the $\delta^{15}N$ would be consistent with the observed Neolithic/Eneolithic human values, the $\delta^{13}C$ value is too high. As noted above, however, freshwater ecosystems can demonstrate considerable isotopic variability, and values for fish may have differed along the waterways of the middle Volga region. In fact, the Caspian pike itself seems to be something of an outlier (perhaps reflecting time spent feeding in the brackish Caspian Sea), with other fish $\delta^{13}C$ values from Central Eurasia being significantly lower relative to terrestrial fauna (Privat 2004). This presents something of a conundrum in terms of the significant positive correlation observed between $\delta^{13}C$ and $\delta^{15}N$ values for the Neolithic/Eneolithic (with four outliers excluded) and Bronze Age periods. Given the different trajectories noted above, isotopically distinct foods must be responsible for this pattern in each period. Because the region is itself

so varied, with a geology divided between chalk/limestone uplands on the west bank of the Volga and sandstone bedrock lowlands east of the Volga, overlaid on a botanical divide between southern steppes and northern forest-steppes, the freshwater fauna might also have varied isotopically in the two drainages, Samara/Sok and Volga, that produced most of the human bones sampled. The problem here is the lack of floral and faunal data for the region, particularly the full range of fish/waterfowl. As discussed further below, another possible explanation for the Bronze Age pattern in particular relates to the isotope ecology of the terrestrial flora and fauna of the Samara Valley.

No significant isotopic differences are apparent between the Early, Middle, and Late Bronze Ages (Kruskal-Wallis ANOVA, $\delta^{13}C$: $p = 0.89$; $\delta^{15}N$: $p = 0.25$; Table 7.2, Figure 7.3), nor is there any difference between the earlier and later phases of the MBA, a transition marked by significant developments in many aspects of society (Chapters 1 and 4). Nor are there any significant changes seen in the LBA compared to earlier phases. While $\delta^{15}N$ values are considerably lower than for the preceding Eneolithic period

Table 7.1. Stable Carbon and Nitrogen Isotope Results on Human Bone Collagen from the Samara Valley Project

Isotope Sample #	Sex	Age Group	Era	Site Name	Provenience	Culture Name	Region	$\delta^{13}C$ ‰	$\delta^{15}N$ ‰	%C	%N	C:N	Yield
44	M	Maturus	NEOL	Lebyanzhinka IV	Settlement Grave 1	Samara hunter-gatherer	Sok River	−23.0	12.2	46.4	16.9	3.2	4.7
43	F	Maturus	NEOL	Chekalino IV	Settlement Grave 2	Elshanka	Sok River	−23.1	12.1	44.9	16.3	3.2	5.8
34	M	Adultus	ENEOL	Murzikha II	Grave 94, skeleton a	Garin-Bor	Northern forest	−23.4	15.1	45.2	16.6	3.2	3.6
18	M	Adult	ENEOL	Lebyazhinka V	Settlement Grave 9	Eneolithic	Sok River	−18.9	12.8	44.7	16.8	3.1	8.0
19	F?	Juvenis	ENEOL	Lebyazhinka V	Settlement Grave 8	Eneolithic	Sok River	−19.2	11.2	45.5	16.9	3.1	11.0
20	F	Adult	ENEOL	Lebyazhinka V	Settlement Grave 12 (collective burial, skeleton 2)	Early Eneolithic	Sok River	−22.2	13.2	45.4	16.8	3.2	6.0
21	M	Adultus-Maturus	ENEOL	Lebyazhinka V	Settlement Grave 12 (collective burial, skeleton 3)	Early Eneolithic	Sok River	−21.9	13.3	45.4	16.9	3.1	8.0
22	F	Maturus	ENEOL	Lebyazhinka V	Settlement Grave12 (collective burial, skeleton 1)	Early Eneolithic	Sok River	−22.0	13.0	45.1	16.6	3.2	6.0
23	F	Adultus	ENEOL	Lebyazhinka V	Settlement Grave 12 (collective burial, skeleton 4 or 5)	Eneolithic	Sok River	−19.4	10.5	46.6	16.8	3.2	8.0
33	F	Maturus	ENEOL	Khvalynsk II	Grave 32	Khvalynsk	Volga River west bank	−21.1	15.4	45.9	17	3.1	8.5
35	M	Adultus	ENEOL	Khvalynsk II	Grave 12	Khvalynsk	Volga River west bank	−20.4	15.2	45.6	17.2	3.1	10.0
45	M	Adultus	ENEOL	Khvalynsk II	Grave 23	Khvalynsk	Volga River west bank	−20.6	14.2	46.4	17.3	3.1	10.0
46	M	Maturus	ENEOL	Khvalynsk II	Grave 1	Khvalynsk	Volga River west bank	−20.2	14.8	46.1	17.1	3.1	9.8
47	M	Maturus	ENEOL	Khvalynsk II	Grave 17	Khvalynsk	Volga River west bank	−22.2	13.8	46.4	17.2	3.1	5.4

Isotope Sample #	Sex	Age Group	Era	Site Name	Provenience	Culture Name	Region	$\delta^{13}C$ ‰	$\delta^{15}N$ ‰	%C	%N	C:N	Yield
48	M	Adultus	ENEOL	Khvalynsk II	Grave 7	Khvalynsk	Volga River west bank	−20.9	15.3	46.4	17.6	3.1	9.8
3	M	Maturus-Senilis	EBA	Ekaterinovka	Unit 1, Grave 1	Yamnaya	Southern steppe	−19.6	10.0	41.4	14.5	3.3	14.4
38	M	Maturus	EBA	Lopatino I	Kurgan 31, Grave 1	Yamnaya-Repin	Sok River	−18.5	12.5	45.4	17.1	3.1	11.1
54	F	Maturus	EBA	Kurmanaevka III	Kurgan 3, Grave 2	Yamnaya	Buzuluk River	−18.4	12.5	45.5	16.8	3.2	7.2
5, 37	F	Maturus-Senilis	EBA	Lopatino I	Kurgan 35, Grave 1 (sample #5 is the same as #37 as per ancient DNA analysis)	Yamnaya	Sok River	−18.9	11.4	44.2	16.3	3.2	13.9
52	M	Adultus	EBA	Lopatino I	Kurgan 1, Grave 1	Yamnaya	Sok River	−19.7	11.6	46.4	17.5	3.1	14.8
57	M	Juvenis	EBA	Lopatino II	Kurgan 3, Grave 1	Yamnaya	Sok River	−19.0	11.0	44.5	15.6	3.3	8.3
58	M	Maturus	EBA	Kutuluk I	Kurgan 4 Grave 1	Yamnaya	Kutuluk River	−18.8	10.8	44.9	15.6	3.4	8.4
2	F	Adultus	EBA	Belogor'e I	Kurgan 4, Grave 3	Yamnaya	Volga River west bank	−18.5	13.4	53.2	18.7	3.3	11.8
10	M	Maturus	EBA	Ishkinovka I	Kurgan 3, Grave 7	Yamnaya	Ural steppe	−18.3	10.9	41.2	15.3	3.1	14.1
50	M	Adultus	EBA/MBA	Luzhki I	Flat Grave 5 (bound)	Yamnaya/Poltavka	Samara River	−19.8	10.2	45.4	16.9	3.1	13.2
49	F	Adultus	MBA	Potapovka I	Kurgan 3, Burial 1	Poltavka	Sok River	−19.2	11.8	47	17.5	3.1	9.2
15	M	Maturus	MBA	Nur III	Single kurgan, Grave 5	Poltavka	Samara River	−19.0	11.2	45.7	17.1	3.1	12.0
4	F	Adultus	MBA	Gvardetsi II	Kurgan 1, Grave 2	Poltavka	Samara River	−18.6	13.2	42.3	14.6	3.4	6.2
14	F	Adultus	MBA	Nur III	Single kurgan, Grave 4	Poltavka	Samara River	−18.4	13.5	45.3	17.1	3.1	13.0

Table 7.1. Stable Carbon and Nitrogen Isotope Results on Human Bone Collagen from the Samara Valley Project (*continued*)

Isotope Sample #	Sex	Age Group	Era	Site Name	Provenience	Culture Name	Region	δ¹³C ‰	δ¹⁵N ‰	%C	%N	C:N	Yield
11	M	Adultus	MBA	Grachevka II	Kurgan 1, Grave 1	Poltavka	Sok River	−19.0	11.1	45.0	17.0	3.1	16.0
16	M	Maturus	MBA	Nikolaevka III	Kurgan 5, Grave 1	Poltavka	Samara River	−19.3	10.9	46.9	17.5	3.1	12.0
17	M	Maturus	MBA	Nikolaevka III	Kurgan 1, Grave 3	Poltavka	Samara River	−18.9	11.8	45.1	16.7	3.2	5.0
42	M	Maturus	MBA	Potapovka I	Kurgan 5, Grave 6	Poltavka	Sok River	−18.1	11.9	46.2	17.3	3.1	12.9
53	M	Adultus	MBA	Lopatino II	Kurgan 1, Grave 1	Poltavka	Sok River	−19.3	11.2	46.7	17.8	3.1	13.5
51	M	Adultus	MBA	Kutuluk III	Kurgan 1 Grave 2	Poltavka	Kutuluk River	−19.4	11.3	46.8	17.4	3.1	14.8
55	M	Adultus	MBA	Zhuravlikha I	Burial 16	Poltavka	Kinel' River	−18.5	14.6	46.8	17.4	3.1	8.3
60	F	Adultus	MBA	Tanabergin II	Kurgan 7, Grave 23	Poltavka	West Kazakhstan	−18.7	12.0	42.1	13.3	3.7	0.1
24	F	Adultus	Late MBA	Utyevka IV	Kurgan 4, Grave 1	Potapovka	Samara River	−19.2	11.0	44.4	16.3	3.2	4.0
36	F	Adultus	Late MBA	Potapovka I	Kurgan 5, Grave 2	Potapovka	Sok River	−20.2	11.2	44.1	16.4	3.1	12.3
41	M	Adultus	Late MBA	Utyevka VI	Kurgan 6, Grave 2 (skeleton 1)	Potapovka	Samara River	−18.6	10.7	45.5	16.9	3.1	3.6
27	M	Maturus	Late MBA	Utyevka VI	Kurgan 7, Grave 1	Potapovka	Samara River	−18.5	11.5	46.0	17.5	3.1	15.0
59		HORSE	Late MBA	Potapovka I	Kurgan 3, Grave 1	Potapovka	Sok River	−20.6	3.8	44.7	15.6	3.4	3.4
1	F	Maturus	LBA	Spiridonovka IV	Kurgan 1, Grave 15	Early Srubnaya	Samara River	−18.7	11.6	44.9	16.9	3.1	13.0
25	F	Adultus	LBA	Rozhdestvenno I	Kurgan 5, Grave 7	Early Srubnaya	Samara/Volga steppes	−19.5	11.3	46.3	17.2	3.1	12.0
28	F	Maturus	LBA	Spiridonovka II	Kurgan 11, Grave 7	Early Srubnaya	Samara River	−19.1	11.3	45.8	17.0	3.1	15.0

Isotope Sample #	Sex	Age Group	Era	Site Name	Provenience	Culture Name	Region	$\delta^{13}C$ ‰	$\delta^{15}N$ ‰	%C	%N	C:N	Yield
40	F	Juvenis	LBA	Spiridonovka II	Kurgan 1, Grave 2	Early Srubnaya	Samara River	−18.4	13.2	46.2	17.4	3.1	13.6
26	F	Adultus	LBA	Rozhdestvenno I	Kurgan 4, Grave 4 (skeleton 2)	Early Srubnaya	Samara/Volga steppes	−19.6	11.1	45.6	16.8	3.2	3.0
29	F	Adultus	LBA	Spiridonovka II	Kurgan 11, Grave 12	Early Srubnaya	Samara River	−19.3	11.1	45.1	15.7	3.4	4.6
39	M	Adultus	LBA	Spiridonovka II	Kurgan 1, Grave 1	Early Srubnaya	Samara River	−19.3	10.4	46.5	17.4	3.1	12.5
6	F	Adultus	LBA	Spiridonovka IV	Kurgan 2, Grave 1	Srubnaya	Samara River	−18.6	10.8	41.4	14.8	3.3	4.3
9	M	Juvenis	LBA	Spiridonovka IV	Kurgan 2, Grave 5	Srubnaya	Samara River	−18.8	9.8	41.9	15	3.3	12.2
7	F	Adultus	LBA	Spiridonovka IV	Kurgan 1, Grave 6	Srubnaya	Samara River	−19.3	9.6	38.9	13.9	3.3	15.0
30	F	Maturus	LBA	Barinovka I	Kurgan 2, Grave 24	Srubnaya	Samara River	−17.5	14.3	44.2	15.5	3.3	7.6
8	M	Maturus	LBA	Spiridonovka IV	Kurgan 1, Grave 11	Srubnaya	Samara River	−18.8	9.9	42.9	15.5	3.2	9.5
12	M	Maturus	LBA	Novoselki	Kurgan 6, Grave 1	Srubnaya	Northern forest	−19.2	12.1	45.6	17.1	3.1	13.0
13	M	Adultus	LBA	Novoselki	Kurgan 2, Grave 4	Srubnaya	Northern forest	−19.7	11.8	45	16.2	3.2	6.0
31	M	Maturus	LBA	Barinovka I	Kurgan 2, Grave 17	Srubnaya	Samara River	−18.9	11.2	44.8	16.8	3.1	13.1
32	M	Adultus	LBA	Uvarovka I	Kurgan 2, Grave 1	Srubnaya	Samara River	−19.1	10.9	45.3	16.5	3.2	2.3
56	M	Juvenis	Iron Age	Nadezhdinka	Kurgan 1, Grave 6	Scythian/Iron Age	Volga steppe	−18.0	13.2	45.5	17.1	3.1	13.9

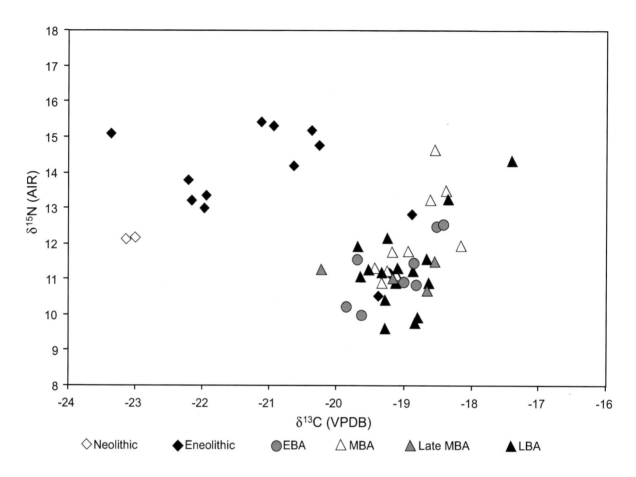

Figure 7.3 Bivariate plot of δ^{13}C and δ^{15}N values humans from the Samara Valley by period.

(ca. 11.5‰ vs. ca. 13.7‰), they remain high in absolute terms (compared to most inland Neolithic/Bronze Age European values [Schulting 2011]), and so freshwater fish may have still featured in the diet, although considerably less so than in the Eneolithic. Nor is there any clear indication of the uptake of millet agriculture in the Samara data—as a C_4 plant, the consumption of millet in any quantity would have a marked impact of human δ^{13}C values and would be clearly detectable if present (cf. Murphy et al. 2013; Privat 2004; Svyatko 2009; Svyatko et al. 2013). While it could be argued that the δ^{13}C values are in fact slightly elevated, the positive correlation with δ^{15}N for the Bronze Age group makes it unlikely that millet consumption is the explanation for this. Steppe grasslands typically include various wild C_4 plants (Pyankov et al. 2000; Wang 2003, 2004, 2005), and so domestic and wild grazing animals could introduce elevated δ^{13}C values into the human food chain.

While faunal isotope values from the Samara Valley itself are at present limited to a single horse, Eneolithic to Iron Age faunal data are available from the surrounding area, including the northwest Caspian region (Shishlina

2008; Shishlina et al. 2007, 2009), the Ukraine (O'Connell et al. 2003; Privat 2004), the Don River region (Iacumin et al. 2004), the North Caucasus (Hollund et al. 2010), the southern Urals/western Siberia (Privat 2004), and, more distantly, the Altai region (Privat 2004). Unfortunately, none of these locations could be said to be near the present study area; however, while some interesting regional variation is subsumed in the averages shown in Table 7.4, the values overall are quite consistent within each species/group, which does suggest a certain degree of confidence in their general validity and applicability to the Samara Valley. One important trend in terms of the interpretation of the human values is that ovicaprids (mainly sheep) are significantly elevated (at the 0.05 level) in both δ^{13}C and δ^{15}N compared to cattle, and both are elevated compared to horse. While there is some variation, sheep are often significantly enriched in δ^{13}C relative to the expectation of around –22‰ for herbivores in a purely C_3 ecosystem (e.g., the averages observed for horse and red/roe deer in Table 7.4). Measurements on 28 Bronze Age sheep from the northwest Caspian, for example, average –18.1 ± 2.1‰ (Shishlina 2008; Shishlina et al. 2007, 2009),

Table 7.2 Stable Carbon and Nitrogen Isotope Averages and Standard Deviations (±1 SD) for Neolithic/Eneolithic to Late Bronze Age Human Samples from the Samara Valley

Period	$\delta^{13}C\%_0$	±	$\delta^{15}N\%_0$	±	n
Neolithic	−23.1	0.1	12.1	0.1	2
Eneolithic	−21.0	1.3	13.7	1.6	13
Early Bronze Age	−19.1	0.6	11.2	0.9	8
Early/Mid Middle Bronze Age	−18.9	0.4	12.0	1.2	11
Late Middle Bronze Age	−19.1	0.6	11.1	0.3	4
Late Bronze Age	−19.0	0.6	11.3	1.2	16
Samara Bronze Age total	−19.0	0.5	11.5	1.1	39

Table 7.3 Mann-Whitney U Test Results for Stable Carbon and Nitrogen Isotope Averages and Standard Deviations (±1 SD) Assessing Locational and/or Period Differences

Period/Site	$\delta^{13}C\%_0$	±	$\delta^{15}N\%_0$	±	n	Comparison	iso	Z	p
Neolithic	-23.1	0.1	12.1	0.1	2	Neo.–Eneo.	$\delta^{13}C$	1.86	0.062
Eneolithic	-21.0	1.3	13.7	1.6	13	Neo.–Eneo.	$\delta^{15}N$	1.53	0.126
Sok River Eneolithic	-20.6	1.6	12.4	1.2	6	Sok–Volga	$\delta^{13}C$		n/s
Volga River Eneolithic	-20.9	0.7	14.8	0.7	6	Sok–Volga	$\delta^{15}N$	2.88	0.004
Bronze Age	-19.0	0.5	11.5	1.1	39	Eneo.–BA	$\delta^{13}C$	4.43	0.000
						Eneo.–BA	$\delta^{15}N$	3.73	0.000
Late Bronze Age, Spiridonovka									
Spiridonovka II	-19.0	0.5	11.5	1.2	4	Spiri II–IV	$\delta^{13}C$		n/s
Spiridonovka IV	-18.8	0.3	10.3	0.8	5	Spiri II–IV	$\delta^{15}N$	1.47	0.142

Note: n/s = not significant.

while 15 sheep from the North Caucasus average −18.1 ± 1.6‰ (Hollund et al. 2010). Within Privat's (2004:Appendix 1) larger data set, nine sheep from sites of the Middle Bronze Age Sintashta culture average −18.1 ± 0.7‰, and five sheep from the Early Bronze Age component at Abganerovo on the Don River average −18.3 ± 1.2‰ (Iacumin et al. 2004). This suggests that sheep and horse in particular were grazing on different parts of the landscape, favoring different plants within the same landscape, and/or were being managed differently (e.g., through foddering).

Another possibility involves physiological differences between species, as these demonstrate marked differences in $\delta^{15}N$ results, with significantly decreasing averages from sheep to cattle to horse in the combined data set. Nearly one-third of the sheep values reported by Privat (2004) are above 8‰, and no young animals were included in her study (so that this cannot reflect a nursing signal). These results are unusually elevated for herbivores, although to a lesser extent, many of the cattle values are also high. Values for horse are generally low in all regions for which data are available, including the single measurement from the Samara Valley itself (Table 7.4). These interspecies differences may be due to differences in grazing/browsing preferences (and the associated $\delta^{15}N$ values of the plants), as noted above, and/or to physiological differences. Regarding the latter, it is worth noting that sheep and cattle are ruminants, in which ingested plant matter is broken down and fermented by gut organisms, with some of the by-products being digested by the animal: isotopic fractionation can potentially occur at each of these steps. By contrast, the hindgut fermentation found in horses, while analogous in function to the rumen, does not permit the absorptions of proteins (Alexander 2009). Therefore, ruminants and nonruminants should be considered separately in isotopic studies.

Table 7.4 Stable Carbon and Nitrogen Isotope Averages and Standard Deviations (±1 SD) for Neolithic/Eneolithic to Middle Bronze Age Fauna from Central Eurasia

Region	Period	Species	δ¹³C‰	δ¹⁵N‰	n
Samara	MBA	Horse	−20.6	3.8	1
Northwest Caspian	Eneolithic–MBA	Sheep	−18.1 ± 2.1	9.9 ± 2.2	28
Northwest Caspian	EBA/MBA	Cattle	−18.6 ± 1.7	9.3 ± 2.1	4
Northwest Caspian	EBA/MBA	Horse	−20.6 ± 0.6	5.5 ± 0.8	3
Northwest Caspian	EBA/MBA	Pike	−16.5	15.0	1
North Caucasus	Eneolithic, EBA	Sheep/goat	−18.1 ± 1.6	8.3 ± 2.2	15
North Caucasus	Eneolithic, EBA	Cattle	−19.7 ± 0.7	7.4 ± 1.0	15
North Caucasus	Eneolithic, EBA	Horse	−20.0 ± 0.5	8.2 ± 1.8	3
North Caucasus	Eneolithic, EBA	Pig	−19.3 ± 0.3	7.6 ± 2.6	2
North Caucasus	Eneolithic, EBA	Dog	−19.4 ± 0.1	9.6 ± 0.5	2
Abganerovo	EBA	Cattle	−19.5 ± 0.4	6.9 ± 1.8	2
Abganerovo	EBA	Sheep	−18.3 ± 1.3	9.2 ± 1.9	5
Ukraine and Kazakhstan	Neolithic to EBA	Horse	−20.7 ± 0.7	3.9 ± 1.3	15
Ukraine	EBA	Cattle	−19.6 ± 0.8	5.7 ± 0.1	2
Central Eurasia	Eneolithic to IA	Dog	−19.8 ± 1.8	10.9 ± 1.5	16
Central Eurasia	Eneolithic to IA	Cattle	−19.9 ± 0.7	6.6 ± 1.1	88
Central Eurasia	Eneolithic to IA	Sheep/goat	−19.4 ± 0.9	7.2 ± 1.2	85
Central Eurasia	Eneolithic to IA	Horse	−20.5 ± 0.5	5.0 ± 1.2	63
Central Eurasia	Eneolithic to IA	Red/roe deer	−21.5 ± 2.2	6.4 ± 1.5	19
Central Eurasia	Eneolithic to IA	Pig	−20.8 ± 0.6	7.7 ± 1.3	25
Central Eurasia	Eneolithic to IA	Fish, various	−22.8 ± 1.6	10.6 ± 1.7	29

Note: Only Privat (2004) specifies that only adult animals were analyzed.

Sources: This study; Hollund et al. (2010); Iacumin et al. (2004); O'Connell et al. (2003); Privat (2004); Shishlina (2008); Shishlina et al. (2007, 2009).

If these faunal values can be applied to the Samara Valley, then the combination of elevated human δ¹³C and δ¹⁵N values is more consistent with sheep and cattle being the major mammalian sources of protein, rather than horse or deer. Their low δ¹⁵N values mean that horse in particular was unlikely to have played an important role in human diet. This raises an interesting issue for the Eneolithic group, given that horse comprises 40 percent of large mammal remains on many steppe sites of this period in the Volga-Ural region (Anthony and Brown 2014:59). It is difficult to reconcile the regular consumption of horse with the high δ¹⁵N values found in humans, unless high-trophic-level fish featured very strongly. However, the mammalian fauna at the Eneolithic cemetery of Khvalynsk, from which came most of the tested Eneolithic human sample,

is dominated by sheep/goat (61 percent) and cattle (27 percent), with horse making a relatively small contribution (13 percent) (Anthony and Brown 2011:Fig. 1). There is less of a discrepancy with the Bronze Age, when faunal assemblages are dominated by sheep and cattle (Chapter 15, this volume), although two Late Bronze Age Srubnaya sites in the valley, Moeknoe Ozero I and Suskanskoe I, are dominated by cattle but with horse being as abundant as sheep (Morales and Antipina 2003:Table 22.2).

No differences are apparent between the sexes (Figure 7.4), although female sample size is limited to only two or three individuals for each period, with the exception of the Late Bronze Age, comprising nine females and seven males exhibiting similar average δ¹³C and δ¹⁵N values. This is a sufficient sample size to detect any consistent differences should they exist, and their absence indicates that male and female diets were not isotopically distinct. The same result is obtained when the Bronze Age sample as a whole is considered. As only adults were sampled, it is not possible to consider age-based differences in diet.

The large number of sites involved makes it difficult to investigate meaningful intersite differences, but there are indications that this might be a factor. The clearest example relates to the small number of Eneolithic individuals from the Sok and Volga Rivers, from the sites of Lebyazhinka V and Khvalynsk II, respectively, with the latter exhibiting significantly higher $\delta^{15}N$ values (Mann-Whitney U test, $p = 0.004$)—indeed, the ranges for the two groups are completely non-overlapping (Tables 7.1, 7.3). This difference may relate to the consumption of different dietary items and/or to differing isotope ecologies in the two rivers. Confusing the interpretation somewhat is the fact that the lower $\delta^{13}C$ values from the tributary Sok River are associated with lower, rather than higher, $\delta^{15}N$ values: if fish were depleted in $\delta^{13}C$, then it would be expected that lower values were associated with enriched $\delta^{15}N$. Nevertheless, the best hypothesis available at

present is that freshwater fish are largely responsible for the overall high $\delta^{15}N$ values seen in both groups. The observed difference, then, may relate to differing proportions and/or types of fish in the diet or to baseline differences in the fish themselves. Interestingly, while they do differ significantly in both isotopes, the two Neolithic individuals from the Sok River, who died before domesticated animals appeared in the region, are more similar to the Eneolithic group from the same area than they are to the Volga River group. The addition of a small percentage of domesticated animals to the Eneolithic diet was masked by continuity in the majority of the local diet on the Sok River, which continued to draw on local wild resources.

There is also an intriguing hint of a difference in $\delta^{15}N$ between individuals from the Late Bronze Age sites of Spiridonovka II and Spiridonovka IV, on the Samara River, although, given the low numbers involved, this does not attain statistical significance ($p = 0.142$; Table 7.3). Because the sites are found very close together, presumably the same foods were available in the general environment of each, and so cultural choice and/or access

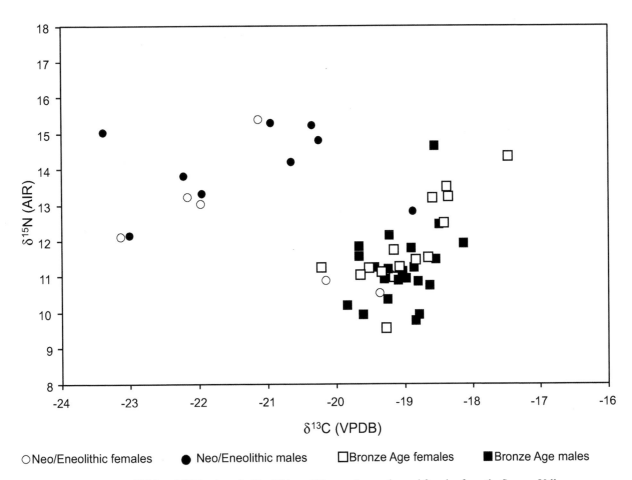

○ Neo/Eneolithic females   ● Neo/Eneolithic males   □ Bronze Age females   ■ Bronze Age males

Figure 7.4 Bivariate plot of $\delta^{13}C$ and $\delta^{15}N$ values for Neolithic and Bronze Age males and females from the Samara Valley.

to different technologies can be envisaged as a possibility. Spiridonovka II probably contains the bodies of the local elite group, as the graves at this cemetery contain a unique assemblage of weapons, faience beads, gilded pendants, and bronze ornaments, while Spiridonovka IV was a more ordinary Srubnaya cemetery, containing just a few bronze ornaments. This raises the possibility that the elite Srubnaya diet differed in some way from that of ordinary people in this area.

Discussion

The clearest trend to emerge from the Samara Valley stable isotope data is the marked difference between the Eneolithic and the Bronze Age. This is interpreted as indicating a substantially greater contribution of freshwater fish and no detectable C_4 input in the diet of most individuals in the earlier population, in contrast to a lower contribution of fish and a greater influence of wild C_4 plants, primarily via grazing stock, in the later population. The timing of this shift can only be viewed in broad terms at this stage, pending a program of further AMS ^{14}C dating. The earliest Bronze Age individual comes from the site of Lopatino I, dating to 3339 to 2918 cal BC (95.4 percent confidence, AA47804), with stable isotope values already typical of the Bronze Age group as a whole. The latest Eneolithic individuals attributed to the Eneolithic lack direct radiocarbon dates but are placed in the period around 4000 to 3500 cal BC, with stable isotope values typical of that period as a whole. Thus, there may be an intervening period of up to a millennium between the two groups, so that it is not possible to address the speed with which the dietary change occurred. The shift could have involved a greater commitment to a specialized pastoral economy, with much reduced use of wild resources, particularly fish. This is not surprising given that the Early Bronze Age in the western steppes is thought to have opened with a shift to a much more mobile form of pastoralism practiced by the Yamnaya or Pit-Grave culture. The use of the steppe grasslands would have played an increasingly important role in the pastoral component of the economy (Shishlina 2001).

Interestingly, there is no suggestion of any dietary change across the later phases of the Bronze Age, including the archaeologically observed shift to greater sedentism at the end of the Middle Bronze Age (Potapovka) and the beginning of the Late Bronze Age, which was the principal focus of the Samara Valley Project. This must have involved significant changes in the subsistence economy, although of course these would not necessarily be detectable isotopically. They may, for example, have more to do with animal management practices than with any change in the

foods eaten. A similar lack of isotopic evidence for dietary change across this period has been reported in a recent study in northern Kazakhstan (Ventresca Miller et al. 2014)

A more precise interpretation of Samaran Bronze Age human diets will require the analysis of associated floral and faunal samples, ideally including contemporary fish remains. In the absence of these, comparisons must be drawn more widely, although this is problematic given variation, first, in the natural environment (the ratio of C_3:C_4 plants, aridity, nitrogen balance, etc.) and, second, in animal management practices (e.g., stocking rates, foddering). With this caveat firmly in place, it can be noted that sheep across the Central Eurasian steppes do show enriched $\delta^{15}N$ values (averaging ca. 7–10‰) that, if the comparison is warranted, would go some way to accounting for the Samara Valley Bronze Age data. The latter's average of 11.5 ± 1.1‰ is elevated by approximately 2‰ compared to other human averages commonly seen in mixed farming groups across prehistoric Europe (Richards 2000; Schulting 2011). It is slightly higher than the average of 10.9 ± 1.7‰ for Neolithic individuals in the Dnieper Rapids region of the Ukraine, who are thought to have incorporated substantial amounts of fish in their diets (Lillie and Jacobs 2006; Lillie and Richards 2000). Other inland human groups inferred to have had an important dietary contribution from fish include those of the Mesolithic and Early Neolithic Iron Gates (averaging ca. 14‰) to the west and those of the Mesolithic to Early Bronze Age Lake Baikal region to the east (showing greater spatial and temporal variability, with averages ranging 10–14‰) (Bonsall et al. 1997; Borić et al. 2004; Katzenberg and Weber 1999; Katzenberg et al. 2009, 2010). Finally, the Late Bronze Age site of Chicha in the Altai region also exhibits high human values (14.5 ± 1.0‰) that have been attributed to fish consumption (Privat 2004).

The above comparisons, however, are rather distant from the Samara Valley both spatially and temporally. As has already been intimated with the fauna, more appropriate comparisons are available, from the Early Bronze Age cultures of the Caspian, spanning the period around 3300 to 2000 cal BC (or 2600–2000 cal BC if a reservoir effect is taken into account) (Shishlina et al. 2007; van der Plicht et al. 2007), and from the Middle Bronze Age Sintashta culture of the southern Urals (Privat 2004). These groups, then, are broadly contemporary with those of the Bronze Age Samara Valley and occupy a not too dissimilar steppe environment (albeit still distant, with the Caspian lying some 500 km to the south and the Sintashta sites some 500 km to the east). The argument that a reservoir effect needs to be taken into account in the Caspian study derives from the paired ^{14}C dating of human/herbivore and human/plant samples from the same graves, in association with elevated human δ¹⁵N values that are difficult to explain without inferring the consumption of considerable quantities of fish (van der Plicht et al. 2007). A comparison of the Caspian and Samaran data sets, however, clearly shows that the δ¹⁵N values for the former are on average substantially higher (15.2 ± 1.8‰) than those for both the Eneolithic and Bronze Age of the Samara Valley (Table 7.5, Figure 7.5). The data from Bronze Age sites in the North Caucasus, the southern Urals, and western Siberia, on the other hand, are very similar to those for the Samara Valley (Table 7.5). In relation to the terrestrial fauna from the same region, the human values are not markedly elevated above what might be expected, particularly if sheep are assumed to have provided the major source of protein (cf. Privat 2004:74).

Thus, while fishing may have played some role in the Samaran Bronze Age, it is unlikely on present evidence to have been a major part of the subsistence economy. This, incidentally, suggests that the radiocarbon dated human remains in the Samara Valley are probably not subject to a large reservoir effect, at least for the Bronze Age, although this would merit testing. No reservoir effect was found in a recent study using paired human/faunal dates from the Early Bronze Age of the North Caucasus (Hollund et al. 2010). Further east, no clear relationship was found between δ¹⁵N values and AMS determinations on Bronze Age humans from the Minusinsk Basin, suggesting, although admittedly not proving, the lack of a substantial reservoir effect there (Svyatko et al. 2009). That a significant reservoir effect has been demonstrated for the Catacomb cultures of the northwest Caspian region (Shishlina et al. 2007, 2009; van

der Plicht et al. 2007) points to regional variability in the use of fish and/or in their reservoir effects (see also Higham et al. 2010). Estimating the potential contribution of freshwater aquatic resources from δ¹³C values is problematic, as these can vary significantly between different drainages (Dufour et al. 1999; Katzenberg and Weber 1999). Thus, for example, the elevated value of –16.5‰ seen for the single pike from the Caspian study may not be applicable to the Samara Valley.

A number of recent isotopic studies have drawn attention to the apparent importance of fish in the diets of Central Eurasian steppe populations, with estimates ranging as high as 50 percent of protein consumption (O'Connell et al. 2003; Privat 2004; Privat et al. 2005; Shishlina et al. 2007, 2009; Svyatko et al. 2013; van der Plicht et al. 2007). This is only partly supported in the present study, primarily for the Neolithic/Eneolithic period, in keeping with the results of other isotopic studies on sites in the upper Volga forest zone to the north (Piezonka et al. 2013; Wood et al. 2013). For the Samaran Bronze Age, other explanations should be considered. First among these is that the high δ¹⁵N values seen for sheep and cattle suggest that the range of faunal variability may be underestimated, particularly as the bulk of these data derive from adult animals, and young animals would exhibit even more enriched values (some of which are likely represented in the data, although this is not specified). Furthermore, grazing of animals in wetland pastures—inferred from the locations of many Samara Valley settlements—might also be expected to result in elevated δ¹⁵N values (Britton et al. 2008), although this remains to be tested specifically for this region. Highly variable δ¹⁵N values have been reported for C₃ reed matting

Table 7.5 Stable Carbon and Nitrogen Isotope Averages and Standard Deviations (±1 SD) for Bronze Age Adolescent/Adult Humans from Selected Regions of Central Eurasia

Region	Period	δ¹³C‰	δ¹⁵N‰	n	Source
Samara Valley	EBA to LBA	−19.0 ± 0.5	11.5 ± 1.1	47	This study
Ukraine	EBA to LBA	−18.9 ± 1.2	12.4 ± 0.9	29	Privat 2004
Northwest Caspian	EBA to MBA	−17.7 ± 1.0	14.9 ± 1.7	74	Shishlina 2008; Shishlina et al. 2007, 2009
North Caucasus	EBA	−18.8 ± 0.9	12.0 ± 1.4	46	Hollund et al. 2010
Abganerovo, Don River	EBA	−17.7 ± 0.9	14.1 ± 1.7	7	Iacumin et al. 2004
Southern Urals/western Siberia steppe	MBA to LBA	−18.9 ± 0.5	11.1 ± 0.8	37	Privat 2004
Southern Urals/western Siberia forest-steppe	MBA	−18.1 ± 0.5	12.8 ± 1.1	19	Privat 2004
Chicha, Altai	LBA	−19.5 ± 0.6	14.5 ± 1.0	11	Privat 2004

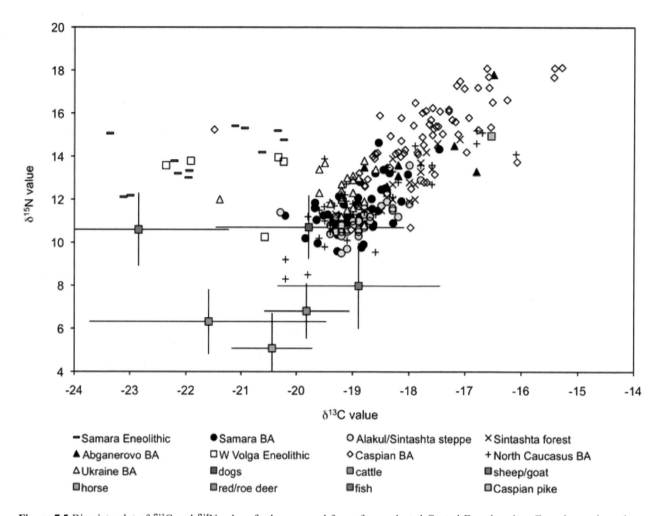

Figure 7.5 Bivariate plot of δ¹³C and δ¹⁵N values for humans and fauna from selected Central Eurasian sites. Faunal error bars show 1σ. For sources of faunal and human data, see Tables 7.4 and 7.5. The "W Volga Eneolithic" measurements derive from the site of Khalynsk II (Shishlina et al. 2009), which also features in the Samara data set; with the exception of one outlier low in δ¹⁵N, there is good correspondence between the two studies.

found in Caspian kurgans, with a number of results >10‰, with the highest being 21‰ (Shishlina et al. 2012:Table 5)—well above any of the human or faunal values that have so far been found in the same region. As noted by Shishlina et al. (2012:184), winter foddering with even a small amount of such material could certainly introduce elevated ¹⁵N into the human food chain.

Particularly interesting is the positive correlation between δ¹³C and δ¹⁵N values seen in Central Eurasian ovicaprids ($r^2 = 0.34$; $df = 84$, $t = 6.5$, $p = 0.000$), with an even stronger correlation seen in humans ($r^2 = 0.68$; $df = 55$, $t = 10.8$, $p = 0.000$) (data from Privat 2004). Hollund et al. (2010) report comparable findings for Early Bronze Age ovicaprids ($r^2 = 0.31$) and humans ($r^2 = 0.65$) in the North Caucasus. A moderate positive correlation ($r^2 = 0.32$) was noted above for Bronze Age humans from the Samara Valley. More widely, a strong correlation between δ¹³C and

δ¹⁵N for the Bronze Age across the overall region can be clearly seen ($n = 264$, $r^2 = 0.38$, increasing to $r^2 = 0.51$ when four outliers are excluded, $p = 0.000$; Figure 7.5). The explanation for this most likely relates to environmental factors (Hollund et al. 2010; Shishlina et al. 2009). Specifically, as was noted above, increasing aridity results in higher δ¹⁵N values in plants and animals. In addition, aridity favors the proportion of C_4 plants in the environment and leads to enriched ¹³C values in C_3 plants (Castañeda et al. 2009; Pyankov et al. 2000; Wang 2004, 2005; Winter 1981), both of which would elevate the δ¹³C values of grazing herbivores. In this regard, it should be noted that the period around 2500 to 1700 BC in the study area has been characterized as particularly arid (Kremenetski et al. 1999; Chapter 5, this volume). Finally, δ¹⁵N values are often elevated in wetland and saltmarsh habitats, which may be a factor locally cf. Shishlina et al. 2012). If it is assumed that sheep milk and meat contributed the majority of the protein in Bronze Age human diets in the Samara Valley, and applying a 4‰ trophic level shift in δ^{15}N, there may be no need to invoke any significant degree of fish consumption to account both for the δ^{15}N values in Bronze Age humans and for the correlation between δ^{13}C and δ^{15}N. It might be mentioned here that dogs, being omnivorous, also typically exhibit elevated δ^{15}N values and, if they were regularly consumed, would affect human values (Table 7.4, Figure 7.5). This recalls the (so far) unique finding of the butchered remains of many dogs at the Srubnaya settlement of Krasnosamarskoe IV, although this appears to have taken place in a ritual context and may not have been a regular occurrence (Anthony et al. 2005; Chapters 14 and 16, this volume). Of course, none of this is to say that fish were not consumed in the Bronze Age Samara Valley but rather that their contribution to the overall diet may be exaggerated if these other potential sources are not considered. At the least, as noted by Privat (2004:83), the importance of fish is likely to have varied through space and time.

The isotopic data from the Samara Valley provide no evidence for the presence of millet, or, if it was present, for its consumption in any significant quantity. The Central Asian "gap" between the early (pre-5000 cal BC) presence of millet both to the west and to the east (Hunt et al. 2008; Zohary and Hopf 2000) has been recently called into question by the direct AMS dating of 10 examples of millet putatively from early contexts in Europe, all of which proved to date to postdate ca. 1500 cal BC, although it is acknowledged that records from the mid-fourth millennium onward are probably reliable (Motuzaite-Matuzaviciute et al. 2013). Millet does not appear in Central Asia until the mid-second millennium, so that something of a gap may still remain, although a reduced one. Carbonized broomcorn millet (*Panicum miliaceum*) recently discovered at Begash Ia in eastern Kazakhstan has been directly dated to 3840 ± 40 BP (Beta-266458: 2462–2154 cal BC at 95.4 percent confidence). While a single fragmentary wheat grain had to be added to the sample of seven millet grain fragments giving this result to achieve the required weight for AMS ^{14}C analysis, other dates on charcoal from the same archaeological context produced comparable results, and so it should be reliable (Frachetti et al. 2010:1003–1004). Millet dating to the late third/early second millennium BC has also been claimed for two sites in the "Country of Towns"—Arkaim and Alandskoe (Gaiduchenko 2002)—somewhat nearer the Samara Valley, although Frachetti et al. (2010:1005) express caution in the acceptance of this evidence without further morphological information and direct dating.

The nearest sites to Samara with claimed early evidence of millet, in both cases by the fifth millennium, are in the Ukraine to the west and in Georgia to the south (Hunt et al. 2008; Séfériadès 2000), although these can now be called into question in the absence of direct dating of the grains themselves (Motuzaite-Matuzeviciute et al. 2013). Despite the wide date ranges associated with some of the human remains in the present study, attributed only to a broad cultural-chronological phase, it seems likely that none fall later than ca. 1500 BC, which would be consistent with those individuals that have been directly radiocarbon dated. In addition, there is the absence of any cultivated cereals of any kind in Eneolithic and Bronze Age sites in the Samara Valley despite a program of sampling and flotation (Chapter 5, this volume; Anthony et al. 2005); indeed, this applies to the Pokrovskaya Srubnaya culture area as a whole (Otroshchenko 2003). The dental palaeopathological evidence also supports the scarcity of sugars and carbohydrates in the diet, with very low caries prevalence, although the etiology of caries is complex, and there are other factors to consider (Chapter 8). Interestingly, the wild plant seeds identified in the Samara Valley Project include the genus *Amaranthus* (Chapter 12), which is composed of C_4 species (Willis 1973). Their consumption could have made some direct contribution to the elevated human δ^{13}C values.

The general absence of sex-based differences is mirrored in other studies of steppe populations (Svyatko et al. 2013), although it should be kept in mind that this does not mean that no such distinctions were present but only that, if they did exist, they did not involve foods that differed isotopically. The simple fact that the burial population contains so many more males than females for all periods in the Samara Valley, with the exception of the Late Bronze Age, would suggest the existence of some social distinctions based on gender (Chapter 8). Indeed, data from the Bronze Age Catacomb culture of the northwest Caspian region may offer an exception, with males showing slightly more depleted δ^{13}C values than females (−17.8 ± 1.0‰ vs. −17.2 ± 0.8‰; df = 54, t = 2.55, p = 0.01) (data from Shishlina 2008; Shishlina et al. 2007). As only adults were analyzed in the present study, it is not possible to investigate subadult–adult differences, and the sample size is too small to compare adults in different age classes, for which any dietary distinctions would be expected to be very minor. Limited data are available on archaeological associations for the Samara Valley sample analyzed here, and possible dietary differences linked to socioeconomic status have not yet been investigated.

Conclusions

The stable isotope data reported here for Neolithic to Late Bronze Age populations from the Samara Valley contribute toward our expanding knowledge of the subsistence adaptations of prehistoric Central Eurasian steppe populations. What isotopic differences are found in the small Neolithic/Eneolithic group appear to relate first and foremost to site location, although considerable variability was also noted within the cemetery at Lebyazhinka V. A much clearer isotopic distinction is seen between the Neolithic/Eneolithic and Bronze Age periods, apparently involving a substantial decrease in—although not necessarily an abandonment of—the consumption of freshwater fish (and perhaps other freshwater aquatic resources such as migratory birds). There is no evidence for any (isotopically visible) dietary change between the Middle and Late Bronze Ages, a key transition period being investigated by the Samara Valley Project. Nor is there any evidence for the uptake of millet agriculture in the early and middle stages of the Late Bronze Age represented here.

Given the small sample sizes available for any single site, consideration of the possibility of finer-scale spatial variability is limited; nevertheless, there is some evidence for the existence of isotopic differences between sites along the Sok and Volga Rivers in the Neolithic/Eneolithic period and perhaps between two Samara River sites, Spiridonovka II and IV, in the Late Bronze Age. The underlying bases for both temporal and spatial distinctions remain unclear and require further investigation, specifically the analysis of additional humans and, equally, of a range of associated faunal remains. Possible explanations include climate change (Hollund et al. 2010; Kremenetski et al. 1999; Shishlina et al. 2009; 2012) and varying animal management practices (stocking rates, shifts in the time spent on different pastures, foddering, etc.) as well as actual differences in the foods consumed.

Subsistence adaptations of the Bronze and Iron Age steppe peoples are of considerable interest, given the dynamic expansions of various nomadic groups at this time and their far-reaching influences. Equally, there are opposing, or complementary, processes of sedentarization—with or possibly without the concomitant uptake of agriculture—in some areas at this time. In the midst of these debates, a number of recent studies have suggested the previously unexpected importance of freshwater fish in steppe diets. The data presented here provide limited support for the latter position, most convincingly for the Eneolithic period, and less so for the Bronze Age that has been a focus of most other Central Eurasian studies. This is seen most clearly in a comparison of the Bronze Age $\delta^{15}N$ values from the Samara Valley to those from the Caspian. This finding is important in that it begins to address the local and regional variability that must have been present in both Neolithic and Bronze Age subsistence economies. During initial isotopic research on the steppes, it was concluded that "there appears to be little change in human diet from the Mesolithic period to the Iron Age" (O'Connell et al. 2003:261). This view has changed substantially in more recent years, further reinforced by the results from the Samara Valley presented here. As more isotopic data become available from the Central Eurasian steppes, it is becoming increasingly clear that significant variation was present, both spatially and chronologically. Understanding this variation is the task that now presents itself.

Acknowledgments

The authors thank Karen Privat for permission to cite data from her DPhil thesis. Thanks are also extended to David Anthony, Dorcas Brown, and Andrzej Weber for their very helpful comments on earlier drafts of the chapter.

References

Alexander, R. M.

2009   The Relative Merits of Foregut and Hindgut Fermentation. *Journal of Zoology* 231:391–401.

Ambrose, S. H.

1991   Effects of Diet, Climate and Physiology on Nitrogen Isotope Abundances in Terrestrial Foodwebs. *Journal of Archaeological Sciences* 18:293–317.

Ambrose, S. H., and L. Norr

1993   Experimental Evidence for the Relationship of the Carbon Isotope Ratios of Whole Diet and Dietary Protein to Those of Bone Collagen and Carbonate. In *Prehistoric Human Bone: Archaeology at the Molecular Level*, edited by J. B. Lambert and G. Grupe, pp. 1–37. Springer-Verlag, New York.

Anthony, D. W., D. Brown, E. Brown, A. Goodman, A. Khokhlov, P. Kosintsev, P. Kuznetsov, O. Mochalov, E. Murphy, D. Peterson, A. Pike-Tay, L. Popova, A. Rosen, N. Russell, and A. Weisskopf

2005   The Samara Valley Project: Late Bronze Age Economy and Ritual in the Russian Steppes. *Eurasia Antiqua* 11:395–417.

Anthony, D. W., and D. R. Brown

2000   Eneolithic Horse Exploitation in the Eurasian Steppes: Diet, Ritual and Riding. *Antiquity* 74:75–86.

2014   Horseback Riding and Bronze Age Pastoralism in the Eurasian Steppes. In *Reconfiguring the Silk Road: New Research on East-West Exchange in Antiquity*, edited by Victor Mair and Jane Hickman, pp. 55–71. University of Pennsylvania Press, Philadelphia.

Bocherens, H., and D. Drucker

2003   Trophic Level Isotopic Enrichments for Carbon and Nitrogen in Collagen: Case Studies from Recent and Ancient Terrestrial Ecosystems. *International Journal of Osteoarchaeology* 13:46–53.

Bogaard, A., T. H. E. Heaton, P. Poulton, and I. Merbach

2007   The Impact of Manuring on Nitrogen Isotope Ratios in Cereals: Archaeological Implications for Reconstruction of Diet and Crop Management Practices. *Journal of Archaeological Science* 34:335–343.

Bonsall, C., R. Lennon, K. McSweeney, D. Harkness, V. Boroneant, L. Bartosiewicz, R. Payton, and J. Chapman

1997   Mesolithic and Early Neolithic in the Iron Gates: A Palaeodietary Perspective. *Journal of European Archaeology* 5:50–92.

Borić, D., G. Grupe, J. Peters, and Z. Mikic

2004   Is the Mesolithic-Neolithic Subsistence Dichotomy Real? New Stable Isotope Evidence from the Danube Gorges. *Journal of European Archaeology* 7:221–248.

Britton, K., G. Müldner, and M. Bell

2008   Stable Isotope Evidence for Salt-Marsh Grazing in the Bronze Age Severn Estuary, UK: Implications for Palaeodietary Analysis at Coastal Sites. *Journal of Archaeological Science* 35:2111–2118.

Brown, T. A., D. E. Nelson, and J. R. Southon

1988   Improved Collagen Extraction by Modified Longin Method. *Radiocarbon* 30:171–177.

Castañeda, I. S., J. P. Werne, T. C. Johnson, and T. R. Filley

2009   Late Quaternary Vegetation History of Southeast Africa: The Molecular Isotope Record from Lake Malawi. *Palaeogeography, Palaeoclimatology, Palaeoecology* 275:100–112.

DeNiro, M. J.

1985   Post-Mortem Preservation and Alteration of In Vivo Bone Collagen Isotope Ratios in Relation to Palaeodietary Reconstruction. *Nature* 317:806–809.

Dufour, E., H. Bocherens, and A. Mariotti

1999   Palaeodietary Implications of Isotopic Variability in Eurasian Lacustrine Fish. *Journal of Archaeological Science* 26:617–627.

Frachetti, M. D.

2008   *Pastoralist Landscapes and Social Interaction in Bronze Age Eurasia.* University of California Press, Berkeley.

Frachetti, M. D., R. N. Spengler, G. J. Fritz, and A. N. Mar'yashev

2010   Earliest Direct Evidence for Broomcorn Millet and Wheat in the Central Eurasian steppe region. *Antiquity* 84:993–1010.

Fraser, R. A., A. Bogaard, T. H. E. Heaton, M. Charles, G. Jones, B. T. Christensen, P. Halstead, I. Merbach, P. R. Poulton, D. Sparkes, and A. K. Styring

2011   Manuring and Stable Nitrogen Isotope Ratios in Cereals and Pulses: Towards a New Archaeobotanical Approach to the Inference of Land Use and Dietary Practices. *Journal of Archaeological Science* 38(10):2790–2804.

Fry, B.

1991   Stable Isotope Diagrams of Freshwater Food Webs. *Ecology* 72:2293–2297.

Gaiduchenko, L. L.

2002   Organic Remains from Fortified Settlements and Necropoli of the 'Country of Towns'. In *Regional Specifics in Light of Global Models BC Complex Societies of Central Eurasia from the 3rd to the 1st Millennium. Volume 2: The Iron Age; Archaeoecology, Geoarchaeology, and Palaeogeography; Beyond Central Eurasia,* edited by K. Jones-Bley and D. G. Zdanovich, pp. 400–418. Institute of Man, Washington, D.C.

Gröcke, D. R., H. Bocherens, and A. Mariotti.

1997   Annual Rainfall and Nitrogen-Isotope Correlation in Macropod Collagen: Application as a Palaeoprecipitation Indicator. *Earth and Planetary Science Letters* 153:279–286.

Heaton, T. H. E.

1987   The ^{15}N/^{14}N Ratios of Plants in South Africa and Namibia: Relationship to Climate and Coastal/Saline Environments. *Oecologia* 74:236–246.

Heaton, T. H. E., J. C. Vogel, G. von la Chevallerie, and G. Collett

1986   Climatic Influence on the Isotopic Composition of Bone Nitrogen. *Nature* 322:822–823.

Hedges, R. E. M., and L. M. Reynard

2007   Nitrogen Isotopes and the Trophic Level of Humans in Archaeology. *Journal of Archaeological Science* 34:1240–1251.

Higham, T. F. G., R. Warren, A. Belinskij, H. Härke, and R. Wood

2010   Radiocarbon Dating, Stable Isotope Analysis and Diet-Derived Offsets in Ages from the Klin Yar Site, Russian North Caucasus. *Radiocarbon* 52:653–670.

Hollund, H. I., T. Higham, A. Belinskij, and S. Korenevskij

2010   Investigation of Palaeodiet in the North Caucasus (South Russia) Bronze Age Using Stable Isotope Analysis and AMS Dating of Human and Animal Bones. *Journal of Archaeological Science* 37:2971–2983.

Hunt, H. V., M. Vander Linden, X. Liu, G. Motuzaite-Matuzeicuite, S. Colledge, and M. K. Jones

2008   Millets across Eurasia: Chronology and Context of Early Records of the Genera *Panicum* and *Setaria* from Archaeological Sites in the Old World. *Vegetation History and Archaeobotany* 17:5–18.

Iacumin, P., V. Nikolaev, L. Genoni, M. Ramigni, Y. G. Ryskov, and A. Longinelli

2004   Stable Isotope Analyses of Mammal Skeletal Remains of Holocene Age from European Russia: A Way to Trace Dietary and Environmental Change. *Geobios* 37:37–47.

Jim, S., V. Jones, S. H. Ambrose, and R. P. Evershed

2006   Quantifying Dietary Macronutrient Sources of Carbon for Bone Collagen Biosynthesis Using Natural Abundance Stable Carbon Isotope Analysis. *British Journal of Nutrition* 95:1055–1062.

Karamanos, R. E., R. P. Voroney, and D. A. Rennie

1981   Variation Natural N^{15} Abundance of Central Saskatchewan Soils. *Soil Science of American Journal* 45:826–828.

Katzenberg, M. A., V. I. Bazaliiskii, O. I. Goriunova, N. Savel'ev, and A. W. Weber

2010   Diet Reconstruction of Prehistoric Hunter-Gatherers in the Lake Baikal Region. In *Prehistoric Hunter-Gatherers of the Baikal Region, Siberia,* edited by A. W. Weber, M. A. Katzenberg, and T. G. Schurr, pp. 175–191. University of Pennsylvania Press, Philadelphia.

Katzenberg, M. A., O. I. Goriunova, and A. Weber

2009   Paleodiet Reconstruction of Early Bronze Age Siberians from the Site of Khuzhir-Nuge XIV, Lake Baikal. *Journal of Archaeological Science* 36:663–674.

Katzenberg, M. A., and A. Weber

1999   Stable Isotope Ecology and Palaeodiet in the Lake Baikal Region of Siberia. *Journal of Archaeological Science* 26:651–659.

Khazanov, A. M.

1994   *Nomads and the Outside World.* 2nd ed. University of Wisconsin Press, Madison.

Khodorevskaya, R. P., G. J. Ruban, and D. S. Pavlov

2009   *Behaviour, Migrations, Distribution, and Stocks of Sturgeons in the Volga-Caspian Basin.* World Sturgeon Conservation Society, Special Publication No. 3, Norderstedt.

Koryakova, L. N., and A. V. Epimakhov

2006   *The Urals and Western Siberian in the Bronze and Iron Ages.* Cambridge University Press, Cambridge.

Kremenetski, C. V., T. Böttger, F. W. Junge, and A. G. Tarasov

1999   Late- and Postglacial Environment of the Buzuluk Area, Middle Volga Region, Russia. *Quaternary Science Reviews* 18:1185–1203.

Levine, M.

1999   The Origins of Horse Husbandry on the Eurasian Steppe. In *Late Prehistoric Exploitation of the Eurasian Steppe,* edited by M. Levine, Y. Rassamakin, A. Kislenko, and N. Tatarintseva, pp. 5–58. McDonald Institute, Cambridge.

Lillie, M., and K. Jacobs

2006   Stable Isotope Analysis of 14 Individuals from the Mesolithic Cemetery of Vasilyevka II, Dnieper Rapids Region, Ukraine. *Journal of Archaeological Science* 33:880–886.

Lillie, M. C., and M. Richards

2000   Stable Isotope Analysis and Dental Evidence of Diet at the Mesolithic-Neolithic Transition in Ukraine. *Journal of Archaeological Science* 27:965–972.

Makarewicz, C. A.

2014   Winter Pasturing Practices and Variable Fodder Provisioning Detected in Nitrogen (δ^{15}N) and Carbon (δ^{13}C) Isotopes in Sheep Dentinal Collagen. *Journal of Archaeological Science* 41:502–510.

Morales, A., and E. Antipina

2003   Srubnaya Faunas and Beyond: A Critical Assessment of the Archaeozoological Information from the East European Steppe. In *Prehistoric Steppe Adaptation and the Horse,* edited by M. A. Levine, C. Renfrew, and K. Boyle, pp. 329–351. McDonald Institute for Archaeological Research, Cambridge.

Motuzaite-Matuzeviciute, G., R. A. Staff, H. V. Hunt, X. Liu, and M. K. Jones

2013   The Early Chronology of Broomcorn Millet (*Panicum miliaceum*) in Europe. *Antiquity* 87:1073–1085.

Murphy, E. M., R. J. Schulting, N. Beer, A. Kasparov, and M. Pshenitsyna

2013   Iron Age Diet in Southern Siberia: Information from Stable Carbon and Nitrogen Isotopes and Dental Palaeopathology. *Journal of Archaeological Science* 40(5):2547–2560.

O'Connell, T. C., M. A. Levine, and R. E. M. Hedges

2003   The Importance of Fish in the Diet of Central Eurasian Peoples from the Mesolithic to the Early Iron Age. In *Prehistoric Steppe Adaptation and the Horse,* edited by M. A. Levine, C. Renfrew, and K. Boyle, pp. 253–268. McDonald Institute for Archaeological Research, Cambridge.

Otroshchenko, V. V.

2003   The Economic Peculiarities of the Srubnaya Cultural-Historical Entity. In *Prehistoric Steppe Adaptation and the Horse,* edited by M. A. Levine, C. Renfrew, and K. Boyle, pp. 319–328. McDonald Institute for Archaeological Research, Cambridge.

Outram, A. K., N. A. Stear, R. Bendrey, S. Olsen, A. Kasparov, V. Zaibert, N. Thorpe, and R. Evershed

2009   The Earliest Horse Harnessing and Milking. *Science* 323:1332–1335.

Page, H. M.

1995   Variation in the Natural Abundance of ^{15}N in the Halophyte, *Silicornia virginica,* Associated with Groundwater Subsidies of Nitrogen in a Southern California Salt-Marsh. *Oecologia* 104:181–188.

Pate, F. D., and T. J. Anson

2008   Stable Nitrogen Isotope Values in Arid-Land Kangaroos Correlated with Mean Annual Rainfall: Potential as a Palaeoclimatic Indicator. *International Journal of Osteoarchaeology* 18:317–326.

Piezonka, H., E. Kostyleva, M. G. Zhilin, D. Maria, and T. Terberger

2013   Flesh or Fish? First Results of Archaeometric Research of Prehistoric Burials from Sakhtysh IIa, Upper Volga Region, Russia. *Documenta Praehistorica* 40:57–73.

Privat, K.

2004   Palaeoeconomy of the Eurasian Steppe: Biomolecular Studies. Unpublished D.Phil. thesis, University of Oxford, Oxford.

Privat, K., T. O'Connell, K. Neal, and R. Hedges

2005   Fermented Dairy Product Analysis and Palaeodietary Repercussions: Is Stable Isotope Analysis Not Cheesy Enough? In *The Zooarchaeology of Fats, Oils, Milk and Dairying*, edited by Jacqui Mulville and Alan K. Outram, pp. 60–66. Oxbow, Oxford.

Pyankov, V. I., P. D. Gunin, S. Tsoog, and C. C. Black

2000 C_4 Plants in the Vegetation of Mongolia: Their Natural Occurrence and Geographical Distribution in Relation to Climate. *Oecologia* 123:15–31.

Richards, M. P.

2000   Human Consumption of Plant Foods in the British Neolithic: Direct Evidence from Bone Stable Isotopes. In *Plants in Neolithic Britain and Beyond*, edited by A. S. Fairbairn, pp. 123–135. Oxbow, Oxford.

Richards, M. P., and R. E. M. Hedges

1999   Stable Isotope Evidence for Similarities in the Types of Marine Foods Used by Late Mesolithic Humans on the Atlantic Coast of Europe. *Journal of Archaeological Science* 26:717–722.

Schoeninger, M. J.

1989   Reconstructing Prehistoric Human Diet. In *The Chemistry of Prehistoric Human Bone*, edited by T. D. Price, pp. 38–67. Academic Press, Cambridge.

Schoeninger, M. J., and M. J. DeNiro

1984   Nitrogen and Carbon Isotopic Composition of Bone Collagen from Marine and Terrestrial Animals. *Geochimica et Cosmochimica Acta* 48:625–639.

Schulting, R. J.

2011   Mesolithic-Neolithic Transitions: An Isotopic Tour through Europe. In *The Bioarchaeology of the Transition to Agriculture*, edited by Ron Pinhasi and Jay Stock, pp. 17–44. Wiley-Liss, New York.

Schurr, M. R.

1998   Using Stable Nitrogen Isotope Ratios to Study Weaning Behavior in Past Populations. *World Archaeology* 30:327–342.

Schwarcz, H. P., T. L. Dupras, and S. I. Fargrieve

1999 ^{15}N Enrichment in the Sahara: In Search of a Global Relationship. *Journal of Archaeological Science* 26:651–659.

Sealy, J. C., N. J. van der Merwe, J. A. Lee Thorp, and J. L. Lanham

1987   Nitrogen Isotopic Ecology in Southern Africa: Implications for Environmental and Dietary Tracing. *Geochimica et Cosmochimica Acta* 51:2707–2717.

Séfériadès, M.

2000   In the Heart of the Eurasian Steppe: Ancient Hunter-Gatherers, First Sedentary Farmers and Nomad Stock Herders of Mongolia (8000–3000 BC). In *Late Prehistoric Exploitation of the Eurasian Steppe*, Vol. 2, edited by Y. Rassamakin, A. Kislenko, and N. Tatarintseva, pp. 141–159. McDonald Institute, Cambridge.

Shishlina, N. I.

2001   The Seasonal Cycle of Grassland Use in the Caspian Sea Steppe during the Bronze Age: A New Approach to an Old Problem. *European Journal of Archaeology* 4:346–366.

2008   *Reconstruction of the Bronze Age of the Caspian Steppes*. Archaeopress, BAR International Series 1876, Oxford.

Shishlina, N. I., V. Sevastyanov, and R. E. M. Hedges

2012   Isotope Ratio Study of Bronze Age Samples from the Eurasian Caspian Steppes. In *Population Dynamics in Prehistory and Early History. New Approaches by Using Stable Isotopes and Genetics*, edited by E. Kaiser, J. Burger and W. Schier, pp. 177–197. De Gruyter, Berlin.

Shishlina, N. I., J. Van der Plicht, R. E. M. Hedges, E. P. Zazovskaya, V. S. Sevastyanov, and O. A. Chichagova

2007   The Catacomb Cultures of the North-West Caspian Steppe: ^{14}C Chronology, Reservoir Effect, and Paleodiet. *Radiocarbon* 49:713–726.

Shishlina, N. I., E. P. Zazovskaya, J. van der Plicht, R. E. M. Hedges, V. S. Sevastyanov, and O. A. Chichagova

2009   Paleoecology, Subsistence, and ^{14}C Chronology of the Eurasian Caspian Steppe Bronze Age. *Radiocarbon* 51:481–499.

Svyatko, S. V.

2009   Palaeodietary Analysis of Prehistoric Populations from the Minusinsk Basin, Southern Siberia. Unpublished Ph.D. thesis, Queen's University Belfast.

Svyatko, S. V., J. P. Mallory, E. M. Murphy, A. V. Polyakov, P. J. Reimer, and R. J. Schulting

2009   New Radiocarbon Dates and a Review of the Chronology of Prehistoric Populations from the Minusinsk Basin, Southern Siberia, Russia. *Radiocarbon* 51:243–273.

Svyatko, S. V., R. J. Schulting, J. Mallory, E. M. Murphy, P. Reimer, V. I. Khartanovich, Y. K. Chistov, N. V. Leontyev, and M. V. Sablin

2013   Stable Isotope Dietary Analysis of Bronze to Early Iron Age Populations in the Minusinsk Basin, Southern Siberia, Russia. *Journal of Archaeological Science* 40(11):3936–3945.

Tieszen, L. L.

1991   Natural Variations in the Carbon Isotope Values of Plants: Implications for Archaeology, Ecology, and Paleoecology. *Journal of Archaeological Science* 18:261–275.

Vanderklift, M. A., and S. Ponsard

2003   Sources of Variation in Consumer-Diet δ15N Enrichment: A Meta-Analysis. *Oecologia* 136:169–182.

van der Plicht, J., N. I. Shishlina, R. E. M. Hedges, E. P. Zazovskaya, V. S. Sevastianov, and O. A. Chichagova

2007   Reservoir Effect and Results of ¹⁴C dating of Catacomb Cultures of the North-West Caspian Steppe Area: A Case Study. *Rossijskaâ arheologiâ* 2:39–47.

van Groenigen, J.-W., and C. Kessel

2002   Salinity-Induced Patterns of Natural Abundance Carbon-13 and Nitrogen-15 in Plant and Soil. *Soil Science Society of America Journal* 66:489–498.

Ventresca Miller, A., E. Usmanova, V. Logvin, S. Kalieva, I. Shevnina, A. Logvin, A. Kolbina, A. Suslov, K. Privat, K. Haas, and M. Rosenmeier

2014   Subsistence and Social Change in Central Eurasia: Stable Isotope Analysis of Populations Spanning the Bronze Age Transition. *Journal of Archaeological Science* 42:525–538.

Wang, G. H.

2003   Differences in Leaf δ¹³C among Four Dominant Species in a Secondary Succession Sere on the Loess Plateau of China. *Photosynthetica* 41:525–531.

Wang, R. Z.

2004 C_4 Species and Their Response to Large-Scale Longitudinal Climate Variables along the Northeast China Transect (NECT). *Photosynthetica* 42:71–79.

2005 C_3 and C_4 Photosynthetic Pathways and Life Form Types for Native Species from Agro-Forestry Region, Northeastern China. *Photosynthetica* 43:535–549.

Willis, J. C.

1973   *A Dictionary of the Flowering Plants and Ferns.* Cambridge University Press, Cambridge.

Winter, K.

1981   C4 Plants of High Biomass in Arid Regions of Asia— Occurrence of C4 Photosynthesis in Chenopodiaceae and Polygonaceae from the Middle East and USSR. *Oecologia* 48:100–106.

Wood, R. E., T. F. G. Higham, A. Buzilhova, A. Surorov, J. Heinemeier, and J. Olsen

2013   Freshwater Radiocarbon Reservoir Effects at the Burial Ground of Minino, Northwest Russia. *Radiocarbon* 55(1):163–177.

Zohary, D., and M. Hopf

2000   *Domestication of Plants in the Old World.* 3rd ed. Clarendon, Oxford.

Chapter 8

A Bioarchaeological Study of Prehistoric Populations from the Volga Region

Eileen M. Murphy and Aleksandr A. Khokhlov

Bioarchaeological research is a valuable methodology for studying the impact that large-scale sociopolitical, environmental, and economic processes may have had on the health and well-being of past populations (Perry 2007:486). This chapter presents the results of a detailed osteological and paleopathological examination of a corpus of 297 Eneolithic to Late Bronze Age human skeletons from the Samara oblast and the neighboring oblasts of the middle Volga-Ural region (Table 8.1, Figure 7.1).

The 297 skeletons included in the analysis were assigned to five cultural groups (Table 8.2). Syntheses of previous research have indicated that, in broad terms, Eneolithic (5200–3500 BC) steppe populations were largely hunters, gatherers, and fishers but had adopted sheep and cattle herding as an adjunct to their foraging-centered economy. Much of the information from this period in the middle Volga region has derived from the cemeteries of Khvalynsk I and II. Grave goods of a variety of materials were commonly associated with the burials and, of particular note, some 286 copper objects were recovered from the approximately 43 burials of the Khvalynsk II cemetery. Animal sacrifices and red ochre were also a feature of Khvalynsk burials (Anthony 2007:182–185). All members of society are considered represented in Khvalynsk cemeteries (Vasiliev et al. 2000, as quoted in Popova 2009:301).

A transition to mobile pastoralism occurred during the Early Bronze Age (3500–2700 BC). Yamnaya culture individuals (Pit Grave) were generally buried lying on organic mats in grave pits beneath kurgans of a diameter of 15 to 60 m. The central burial was usually that of an adult, frequently a male. During the Middle Bronze Age (2700–2200 BC), this mobile economy was continued. Poltavka culture burials generally involved the body having been placed in a single chamber, with a wide step, positioned beneath a kurgan surrounded by a circular ditch. The kurgan was usually erected for an adult male, although adult female central burials are also known from this horizon.

At the end of the Middle Bronze Age, Potapovka burials (2200–1800 BC) were also made beneath kurgans. It is thought that these kurgans may have been reserved for the ruling elite and their families (Popova 2009:310). A rich array of grave goods, which generally comprised weaponry, vehicles, and animal sacrifices, has been discovered within these burials (Anthony 2007:372, 386). The Sintashta and Potapovka cultures are generally characterized by a major increase in demand for metal, and they are believed to have been largely warrior societies (Anthony 2007:391; see also Anthony 2009 and Chernykh 2009).

The transition from the Middle Bronze Age to the Late Bronze Age Srubnaya culture witnessed a great increase in settlement sites as the population of the region generally became more settled at the beginning of the Srubnaya period, around 1900 to 1700 BC. The Srubnaya, or Timber Grave, culture is characterized by more modest burials within timber-lined pits beneath kurgans. The kurgans contain the remains of numerous individuals of all ages and

Table 8.1 Details of the Numbers of Individuals from Each Site Included in the Study

Site Name	Number of Individuals	Percentage of Individuals	Site Name	Number of Individuals	Percentage of Individuals
Alexseevsky	1	0.3	Nikolaevka III	9	3.1
Barinovka I	21	7.1	Nizhny Orleansky I	6	2
Chisty Yar I	11	3.7	Nizhny Orleansky II	6	2
Ekaterinovka	3	1	Nizhny Orleansky IV	6	2
Grachevka I	2	0.7	Nizhny Orleansky V	2	0.7
Grachevka II	5	1.7	Nizhny Orleansky ?	1	0.3
Kalach	1	0.3	Novoorlovsky	1	0.3
Kalinovka	5	1.7	Novoselki	8	2.7
Khvalynsk II	26	8.8	Osinsky II	1	0.3
Kinel' I	4	1.4	Podlesnoe	2	0.7
Krasnosamarskoe IV	31	10.4	Poplavskoe	2	0.7
Krutyenkova	1	0.3	Potapovka I	6	2
Kryazh	1	0.3	Rozhdestvenno I	17	5.7
Kurmanaevka III	2	0.7	Spiridonovka II	28	9.4
Kutuluk I	4	1.4	Spiridonovka IV	26	8.8
Kutuluk II	1	0.3	Studenzy I	9	3.1
Kutuluk III	3	1	Svezhensky	14	4.7
Leshevskoe I	2	0.7	Tryasinovka	1	0.3
Leshevskoe settlement with grave	2	0.7	Uranbash	1	0.3
Lopatino I	8	2.7	Uren II	2	0.7
Lopatino II	4	1.4	Utyevka II	2	0.7
Murzikha	1	0.3	Utyevka IV	1	0.3
Nadezhdinka	1	0.3	Utyevka VI	6	2

Table 8.2 Details of the Number of Individuals from Each Period Included in the Study

Period	Culture	Date	Number of Individuals	Percentage of Individuals
Eneolithic	Khvalynsk	5200–3500 BC	27	9.1
Early Bronze Age	Yamnaya	3500–2700 BC	19	6.4
Middle Bronze Age	Poltavka	2700–2200 BC	41	13.8
Middle Bronze Age	Potapovka	2200–1900/1800 BC	18	6.1
Late Bronze Age	Srubnaya	1900/1800–1300/1200 BC	192	64.6

both sexes, and grave goods generally comprise domestic items or objects of adornment (Anthony et al. 2005:410; Popova 2009:315). It is considered that the Late Bronze Age is characterized by a lack of intersocietal conflict due to the acquisition of new resources. This is believed to have resulted in a change in societal structure from one that focused on status to one that may have had an emphasis on horizontal differentiation, such as kinship (Epimakhov 2009:87).

The key objective of the human skeletal analysis was to gain information pertaining to the health, diet, and lifestyle of these populations, thereby providing a background context that might help explain the development of the Late Bronze Age populations that were central to the overall Samara Valley Project. The distribution of disease over ecological and socioeconomic landscapes has been increasingly recognized as a vital component in the understanding of the human condition, past and present (Goodman 1991:280). So that this might be achieved for the Volga populations, a biocultural approach was adopted for the current study. Using this method, emphasis is placed on the role of health in the interaction between a population, their associated culture, and their local environment. The information obtained from this form of analysis can then be used to gain an understanding of the effect that diseases would have had on the lives of both the overall population and individuals within the population. Previously, a detailed osteological report that included full descriptions of all lesions was produced (Murphy and Khokhlov 2004), and this chapter represents an overview of the main findings of that research. One of the main limitations of the current study is a lack of comparative data for other prehistoric Eurasian populations, but it is hoped that the current study will go some way toward addressing this lacuna.

Materials

Osteological and paleopathological analysis of the 297 individuals was undertaken in June to August 1999. The skeletons had originated from approximately 34 different sites and had been retrieved during the course of some 46 different excavations at these sites (Table 8.1).

The numbers of individuals recovered from each excavation ranged from just 1 (0.3 percent) at 13 sites to 31 (10.4 percent) individuals recovered from three kurgans at Krasnosamarskoe IV excavated as part of the Samara Valley Project in 1999. Full records of the excavations at the majority of sites are unavailable, however, so it is not possible to know if all individuals recovered from a single site have been included in the study. As such, detailed

analysis at site level will not be undertaken. The skeletons were assigned to five chronological phases as described in Table 8.2.

It is clear that the Srubnaya corpus of individuals was substantially larger than all of the other assemblages, representing 64.6 percent (192/297) of the individuals available for study. The remaining five corpuses were relatively small and ranged in size from 18 individuals (6.1 percent) for the Potapovka culture to 41 (13.8 percent) for the Poltavka group. The variations in sample size make comparison between the different population groups difficult, and it is often not possible to be certain if trends are genuine or are simply a reflection of the small sample sizes of the earlier populations. In many cases, the results derived from the smaller assemblages, however, were found to mirror those obtained from the analysis of the substantial Srubnaya corpus of material.

Methods

All skeletons were curated in the Physical Anthropology Laboratory of the Institute for the History and Archaeology of the Volga, Samara. The cranial and postcranial remains of the majority of individuals were not curated together, and it was often necessary to analyze these two components of the body separately and then amalgamate the data at a later date. The sex, age at death, and basic postcranial metrics were recorded for all adult individuals in the corpus. The only osteological feature of the nonadults to be methodically determined was the age at death. If an individual displayed an unusual or a prominent nonmetric trait, this was also recorded. All individuals were subjected to a rigorous macroscopic paleopathological examination of both skeletal and dental remains. Cultural modifications, such as discoloration due to association with metal artifacts or ochre, or cut marks due to secondary burial practices were also recorded for all individuals. The paleopathological analysis of the Eneolithic Khvalynsk II individuals was restricted to the study of metabolic diseases and dental paleopathology.

Sex was determined on the basis of a morphological analysis of the pelvis and skull following the recommendations of Ferembach et al. (1980) and Buikstra and Ubelaker (1994). In cases where neither the skull nor pelvis was present, an attempt was made to determine sex using metrical data obtained from the long bones (Berrizbeita 1989; Krogman and Işcan 1986; Pearson 1917–1919; Stewart 1979).

The age at death of nonadults was determined from the state of epiphyseal fusion (Brothwell 1981:66;

Ferembach et al. 1980:530–531), the diaphyseal lengths of the long bones, dental eruption (Ubelaker 1989:64, 70–71), and dental calcification (Moorrees et al. 1963; Smith 1991:161). It is thought that the tooth calcification method is the most accurate of the nonadult aging techniques, and most weight was given to the values derived from this method (Ferembach et al. 1980:530). Age at death estimates for fetal and perinatal infants were determined using the linear regression equations of Scheuer et al. (1980). Each nonadult was allocated to one of the following age categories: infant (< 2 years), child (2–6 years), juvenile (6–12 years), and adolescent (12–18 years). Adult age atdeath estimates were largely determined from an examination of the morphology of the pubic symphysis (Brooks and Suchey 1990), the auricular surface (Lovejoy et al. 1985), and the sternal rib ends (Işcan et al. 1984, 1985). In cases where these bones were not present, age at death was determined on the basis of the state of dental attrition (Brothwell 1981:71). For younger adults, the state of fusion of the sternal ends of the clavicles and the first and second sacral vertebrae was also observed in addition to an assessment of the state of eruption of the third molars (McKern 1970). Each adult was assigned to one of the following age categories: 18 to 35 years (young adult), 35 to 50 years (middle adult), and 50+ years (old adult). Khokhlov's age categories (this volume) were defined differently.

The research of Trotter and Gleser (1958:121) has indicated significant differences between the relationship of stature to bone length between Europeans, Asians, and blacks. They considered the differences significant enough to warrant the development of different regression equations for each of the three major races. The application of inappropriate stature equations has been demonstrated to have the potential to over- or underestimate living stature (Feldesman and Fountain 1996). Since the population groups from the Volga region may have included some

Asians after the Middle Bronze Age, the estimation of stature could be problematic (see Chapter 6). Krogman and Işcan (1986:302–351) have demonstrated that the maximum length of the femur is related to living stature more closely than the maximum lengths of any of the other long bones. As such, the maximum length of the femur was used as a means of assessing growth for the Volga population groups (cf. Buzon and Judd 2008:95).

When discussing the paleopathological lesions, the prevalence rates are reported based on the number of individuals with the appropriate element present as well as on the actual number of bone elements present. More weight is placed on the latter figures since they are considered to provide the most accurate prevalence rates. In instances where different types of lesions were amalgamated for the purposes of revealing general trends, crude prevalence rates based on the total number of individuals in each population group are used.

Results and Discussion
In the following sections, the results of the osteological and paleopathological analyses will be presented as a series of themes. This approach is considered to have the most potential to provide information on different social and cultural aspects of the populations through time.

Population Profiles
Details of the age and sex profiles of the data set used for the paleopathological study are provided in Table 8.3.

It is clear that nonadults and adult females are generally underrepresented in the data set. Khokhlov's analysis (Chapter 6) of 1,350 individuals from the region revealed a different set of trends and, since his analysis has been based on a more representative sample, no further comment will be made concerning the paleodemographic characteristics of the 297 individuals included in the current study.

Table 8.3 Details of the Breakdown of Adults and Nonadults in the Data Set Included in the Current Study

Culture	Percentage (No./Total No.)			
	Total	Adult Male	Adult Female	Nonadult Total
Khvalynsk	92.6 (25/27)	80 (20/25)	20 (5/25)	7.4 (2/27)
Yamnaya	84.2 (16/19)	75 (12/16)	25 (4/16)	15.8 (3/19)
Poltavka	82.9 (34/41)	85.3 (29/34)	14.7 (5/34)	17.1 (7/41)
Potapovka	77.8 (14/18)	78.6 (11/14)	21.4 (3/14)	22.2 (4/18)
Srubnaya	67.2 (129/192)	52.3 (67/128)	47.7 (61/128)	32.8 (63/128)

Note: It was not possible to determine the sex of one of the Srubnaya adults.

Developmental Defects
Axial Skeleton

Developmental defects of the axial skeleton—skull, vertebral column, ribs, and sternum—were recorded following the morphogenic approach advocated by Barnes (1994). Using this approach, each defect can be traced and described as a consequence of disturbances that occurred during morphogenesis in the specific embryonic developmental fields (Barnes 1994:3). Developmental malformations can arise from genetic or chromosomal abnormalities; as a consequence of environmental disturbances, such as maternal disease (e.g., diabetes mellitus or infection); or, in some instances, by the occurrence of rogue genes that only manifest themselves in particular environmental conditions (Potter and Craig 1975:168).

It is usually the case that the majority of developmental disturbances evident in the skeleton are inherited defects (Potter and Craig 1975:552). As such, similar patterns of developmental defects among skeletal populations from different sites may be an indication of population homogeneity, while dissimilar patterns of defects are suggestive of the occurrence of different gene pools (Barnes 1994:5). The detailed recording of developmental defects is therefore of great importance for gaining an understanding of the genetic trends of a particular population. This, in turn, has significance for the study of past migration as well as kinship and marriage patterns (Barnes 2008:331).

Some 81 different developmental defects of the axial skeletons were recorded in 64 individuals from the Yamnaya to Srubnaya populations. The majority of defects had affected the blastemal desmocranium (53.1 percent; 43/81) and paraxial mesoderm fields (39.5 percent; 32/81), with the sternal (6.2 percent; 5/81) and first branchial arch (1.2 percent; 1/81) developmental fields having only been sporadically affected. A summary of the crude prevalence rates of individuals to display developmental defects of the different fields is provided in Figure 8.1.

The preponderance of defects of the blastemal desmocranium or paraxial mesoderm appears to have been a common trait among all Yamnaya to Srubnaya population groups. The small sample sizes of the earlier groups make it difficult to be certain that the results are reflecting genuine trends. Since this trend was clearly apparent for the larger Srubnaya population, however, the validity of the results is possible.

Blastemal Desmocranium

The blastemal desmocranium is responsible for the development of the calvarium—the frontal, the parietals, the interparietal of the occipital, the squamosa of the temporals, the greater wings of the sphenoid, and the lamina of the pterygoid processes (Barnes 1994:14). Some 33 individuals of the Khvalynsk to Srubnaya cultures displayed a total of 43 various developmental defects of the blastemal desmocranium (Table 8.4).

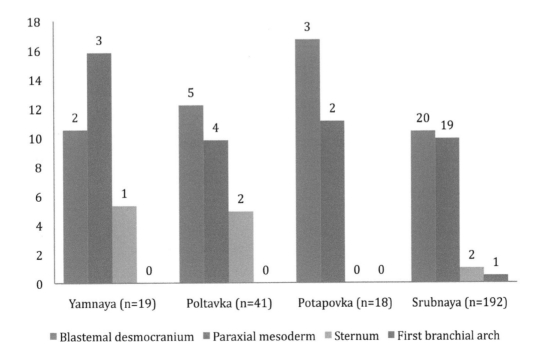

Figure 8.1 Crude prevalence rates (percentage) based on the numbers of affected individuals for developmental defects in the different fields for the Yamnaya to Srubnaya populations (adult and nonadult). The Khvalynsk population group was not included in the analysis.

Table 8.4 Details of Individuals with Defects of the Blastemal Desmocranium Developmental Field

Culture	Site	Context	Age, y	Sex	Lesion	Adult Prevalence by Bone, Percentage (No./ Total No.)
Khvalynsk	Khvalynsk	G22	35–50	M	Retention of the mendosa suture	4.3 (1/23)
Khvalynsk	Khvalynsk	G24	18–35	M	Multiple interparietal bones	4.3 (1/23)
Khvalynsk	Khvalynsk	G25	7–9		Obelion bone	
Yamnaya	Kutuluk I	K3, G4	35–50	M	Metopic suture	11.1 (1/9)
Yamnaya	Lopatino II	K3, G1	15–17	M	Metopic suture	
Yamnaya	Lopatino II	K3, G1	15–17	M	Multiple interparietal bones	
Poltavka	Krasnosamarskoe IV	K1, G3	18–35	F	Metopic suture	5 (1/20)
Poltavka	Krasnosamarskoe IV	K3, G8	35–50	M	Ossicle at lambda	11.1 (2/18)
Poltavka	Lopatino I	K30, G2	35–50	M	Ossicle at lambda	11.1 (2/18)
					Multiple interparietal bones	11.1 (2/18)
Poltavka	Nikolaevka III	K1, G3	35–50	M	Multiple interparietal bones	11.1 (2/18)
Poltavka	Nikolaevka III	K3, G1	6–8		Multiple interparietal bones	
Potapovka	Grachevka II	K3, G9a	50+	F	Multiple interparietal bones	25 (3/12)
Potapovka	Utyevka VI	K6, G1	35–50	F	Metopic suture	16.7 (2/12)
					Multiple interparietal bones	25 (3/12)
Potapovka	Utyevka VI	K6, G5, Sk2	18–35	M	Metopic suture	16.7 (2/12)
					Retention of the mendosa suture	8.3 (1/12)
					Multiple interparietal bones	25 (3/12)
Srubnaya	Barinovka I	K2, G41	18–35	M	Retention of the mendosa suture	11.6 (1/86)
					Multiple interparietal bones	12.8 (11/86)
Srubnaya	Chisty Yar I	K1, G2	35–50	F	Metopic suture	4.5 (4/89)
					Ossicle at lambda	5.8 (5/86)
Srubnaya	Kinel' I	K5, G2	18–35	F	Coronal suture ossicles	1.1 (1/88)
					Multiple interparietal bones	12.8 (11/86)
Srubnaya	Krasnosamarskoe IV	K3, G1	18–35	F	Metopic suture	4.5 (4/89)
Srubnaya	Krasnosamarskoe IV	K3, G14	15–17	M	Multiple interparietal bones	12.8 (11/86)
Srubnaya	Krasnosamarskoe IV	K3, G17	35–50	M	Lambdoid suture ossicles	1.2 (1/86)

Culture	Site	Context	Age, y	Sex	Lesion	Adult Prevalence by Bone, Percentage (No./ Total No.)
Srubnaya	Nizhny Orleansky I	K13, G1	35–50	M	Metopic suture	4.5 (4/89)
					Multiple interparietal bones	12.8 (11/86)
Srubnaya	Nizhny Orleansky II	K4, G14	5–7		Ossicle at lambda	5.8 (5/86)
Srubnaya	Nizhny Orleansky?	K1, G7	18–35	M	Multiple interparietal bones	12.8 (11/86)
Srubnaya	Novoorlovsky	K4, G1	18–35	M	Multiple interparietal bones	12.8 (11/86)
Srubnaya	Poplavskoe	K1	18–35	F	Premature fusion of sagittal suture	1.1 (1/88)
Srubnaya	Poplavskoe	K2	50+	M	Ossicle at lambda	5.8 (5/86)
Srubnaya	Rozhdestvenno I	K5, G11	18–35	F	Ossicles at asterions	1.2 (1/86)
Srubnaya	Spiridonovka II	K10, G3	18–35	F	Multiple interparietal bones	12.8 (11/86)
Srubnaya	Spiridonovka II	K11, G6	18–35	F	Multiple interparietal bones	12.8 (11/86)
Srubnaya	Spiridonovka IV	K2, G13	18–35	F	Ossicle at lambda	5.8 (5/86)
					Multiple interparietal bones	12.8 (11/86)
Srubnaya	Studenzy I	K2, G3	18–35	F	Ossicle at lambda	5.8 (5/86)
Srubnaya	Svezhensky	G73	35–50	F	Multiple interparietal bones	12.8 (11/86)
Srubnaya	Svezhensky	Sk 74	6–7		Multiple interparietal bones	12.8 (11/86)
Srubnaya	Svezhensky	G77	50+	F	Metopic suture	4.5 (4/89)

Note: F = female; G = grave; K = kurgan; M = male; Sk = skeleton.

Nine different defects were evident, the most common of which were multiple interparietal bones (44.2 percent; 19/43), metopic sutures (20.9 percent; 9/43), the presence of a solitary ossicle at the lambda (16.3 percent; 7/43), and the retention of the mendosa suture (7 percent; 3/43)—all of which were caused by the failure of the elements to coalesce. Multiple interparietal bones can arise along any parts of its border as they fail to coalesce, and they are thought to be associated with retention of the mendosa suture (Barnes 1994:143). All five of the populations had individuals with multiple interparietal bones. Again, the small sample sizes of the earlier groups hinders the analysis since it is not possible to reliably compare the frequencies of the lesions for the purposes of gaining insights about the gene pools in operation. Retention of the metopic suture arises as a result of developmental delay in the precursors of the frontal bone during the blastemal stage (Barnes 1994:148). Metopism

was observed among the Yamnaya, Poltavka, Potapovka, and Srubnaya population groups. Research has indicated that in some cases, metopism is hereditary, while in other instances it occurs sporadically (Torgersen 1951:204). The presence of two Potapovka individuals from Kurgan 6 at Utyevka VI with both multiple interparietal bones and metopic sutures might provide a tantalizing glimpse of familial relatedness at that site.

A number of the less frequent defects of the blastemal desmocranium are worthy of comment. Skeleton G25, a 7- to 9-year-old juvenile from the Khvalynsk II cemetery, displayed an obelion bone in the posterior aspect of the sagittal suture. The ossicle is associated with the fetal sagittal fontanelle, which normally closes prior to birth, and is considered a relatively rare occurrence (Barnes 1994:139, 142). Skeleton K5, G2, an 18- to 35-year-old Srubnaya female recovered from the Kinel' I burial ground, displayed two accessory ossicles in the right side of the coronal suture. The individual also displayed multiple interparietal bones as well as defects of the paraxial mesoderm developmental field.

The only field defect of the blastemal desmocranium present among the populations that was not due to a failure of the elements to coalesce was a case of sutural agenesis, which is due to a failure of the elements to differentiate. If opposing cranial bone precursors fail to differentiate, they become partially or completely coalesced into a single bone, and the suture between them fails to develop (Barnes 1994:152). Sutural agenesis can occur within family groups, thereby indicating a genetic relationship, but external factors, such as birth trauma and metabolic disorders, can also result in craniosynostosis (Barnes 1994:152). The posterior aspect of the sagittal suture in Skeleton K1 retrieved from the Srubnaya culture Poplavskoe burial ground had been completely obliterated. The individual was an 18- to 35-year-old female, and the remainder of her sutures were clear and unfused. Unfortunately, only the skull of the individual was available for analysis, and it is not possible to ascertain if the premature suture fusion had occurred as a result of a developmental or external factor.

Paraxial Mesoderm

The paraxial mesoderm results in the production of the vertebral column, the ribs, the exoccipitals (lateral sections of the base of the occipital containing the condyles), and the supraoccipital (Barnes 1994:13). A total of 28 individuals of Yamnaya to Srubnaya culture date displayed some 32 defects of the paraxial mesoderm developmental field (Table 8.5). The overwhelming majority of defects involved clefting or bifurcation of the sacral neural arches, and a bifurcated LV5 was also evident (65.6 percent; 21/32). Sacralization was the next most frequent lesion (18.8 percent; 6/32), followed by the occurrence of block vertebrae (6.3 percent; 2/32) and supernumerary vertebrae (6.2 percent; 2/32). A single individual displayed a rib defect (3.1 percent; 1/32).

If developmental delay results in hypoplasia or aplasia of either or both parts of the precursors of the pedicles, laminae, or spinous process, it can result in the failure of the two halves of the vertebrae to coalesce and the formation of a bifid or cleft neural arch (Barnes 1994:119). Bifid neural arches occur as a result of minor delay during growth, while completely cleft neural arches are caused by major delays. Clefting as a result of developmental delay is a relatively common phenomenon. In cases where the neural arch is cleft, the underlying spinal cord would be exposed. Since the cleft area is bridged by cartilage or

membrane, however, the lesion is clinically insignificant (Roberts and Manchester 2005:55). Cleft neural arches are generally found in the border areas of the vertebral column, especially at the unstable lumbosacral border. The defects were observed in all of the Yamnaya to Srubnaya culture populations. Of particular interest was the occurrence of two Srubnaya individuals from Kurgan 1 at the Spiridonovka IV burial ground (G10 and G13) and a further two Srubnaya individuals with the defect at the Svezhensky burial ground (G71a and G71b). As was the case for the blastemal desmocranium field defects, the presence of multiple individuals with the same developmental defects in the same burial grounds may provide evidence of relatedness.

The number of regional vertebrae can vary as a result of the shifting of differentiating features in border vertebrae. The most common sites for these shifts to occur are in the unstable occipitocervical and lumbosacral borders—in the latter instance, cranial shifting results in sacralization. The etiology for the defect is uncertain, but it is thought to relate to a delay in the formation of the intervertebral disk space and the adjacent vertebral segments of the two bordering regions (Barnes 1994:79–80). Studies have indicated that both cranial and caudal shifting at the lumbosacral border show variable frequencies between populations (Schmorl and Junghanns 1971:61). All six cases of sacralization were observed in individuals from the Srubnaya culture (see Table 8.5).

Skeleton K6, G6, an 18- to 35-year-old Potapovka male recovered from the Utyevka VI burial ground, displayed possible evidence for the irregular segmentation of a rib (Barnes 1994:71). An oval-shaped facet, which measured 26.1 mm mediolaterally by 18 mm anteroposteriorly and had a depth of approximately 4 mm, was apparent on the superior margin of the right eighth rib at the point where the rib curves in an anterior direction. The corresponding seventh rib was not available for analysis. It is possible that the facet had been due to the partial articulation or bridging of the seventh and eighth right ribs. Only a small number of rib segmentation errors have been reported in the paleopathological literature (Barnes 1994:72).

Sternum

The sternebrae, part of the manubrium and the xiphoid process, develop from the sternal plates (Barnes 1994:14). A variety of defects of the sternal developmental field were evident (Table 8.6). Of particular note was the occurrence of a relatively rare defect in the form of a cleft at the distal third of the body in a 50+-year-old Poltavka male (K1, G4) recovered from the Kalinovka burial ground. This defect arises as a consequence of incomplete cohesion of the sternal bands.

Table 8.5 Details of Individuals with Defects of the Paraxial Mesoderm Developmental Field

Culture	Site	Context	Age, y	Sex	Lesion	Adult Prevalence by Bone, Percentage (No./Total No.)
Yamnaya	Leshevskoe I	Flat Grave 5	18–35	M	Cleft neural arch (S)	33.3 (3/9)
Yamnaya	Nizhny Orleansky I	K1, G5	35–50	M	Bifurcated neural arch (S)	33.3 (3/9)
Yamnaya	Nizhny Orleansky I	K4, G2	18–35	M	Cleft neural arch (S)	33.3 (3/9)
Poltavka	Kalinovka	K1, G4	50+	M	Bifurcated neural arch (S)	25 (3/12)
Poltavka	Kryazh	K2, G1	18–35	M	Cleft neural arch (S)	25 (3/12)
Poltavka	Nizhny Orleansky I	K1, G4	35–50	M	Bifurcated and cleft neural arches (S)	25 (3/12)
Poltavka	Lopatino I	K33	18–35	M	Block vertebra (CV7/TV1) (Type II Klippel-Feil syndrome)	12.5 (1/8)
Potapovka	Lopatino II	K1, G1 Sk2	18–35	M	Cleft neural arch (S)	20 (1/5)
Potapovka	Utyevka VI	K6, G6	18–35	M	irregular segmentation of a rib	
Srubnaya	Chisty Yar I	K1, G2	35–50	F	Bifurcated (LV5) Cleft neural arch (S) Sacralization	2.8 (1/36) 28.3 (13/46) 13 (6/46)
Srubnaya	Ekaterinovka	K2, G1	18–35	M	Bifurcated and cleft neural arches (S)	28.3 (13/46)
Srubnaya	Kinel' I	K5, G2	18–35	F	Cleft neural arch (S)	28.3 (13/46)
Srubnaya	Nadezhdinka	G9	18–35	M	Bifurcated neural arch (S)	28.3 (13/46)
Srubnaya	Nizhny Orleansky I	K1, G8	18–35	F	Bifurcated neural arch (S) Sacralization	28.3 (13/46) 13 (6/46)
Srubnaya	Rozhdestvenno I	K5, G10	35–50	M	Cleft neural arch (S)	28.3 (13/46)
Srubnaya	Spiridonovka II	K1, G10	18–35	M	Cleft neural arch (S)	28.3 (13/46)
Srubnaya	Spiridonovka II	K10, G7	18–35	M	Bifurcated neural arch (S)	28.3 (13/46)
Srubnaya	Spiridonovka II	K14, G10	18–35	F	Sacralization	13 (6/46)
Srubnaya	Spiridonovka IV	K1, G8	35–50	M	Sacralization	13 (6/46)
Srubnaya	Spiridonovka IV	K1, G6	18–35	F	Six lumbar vertebrae	6.9 (2/29)
Srubnaya	Spiridonovka IV	K1, G10	35–50	F	Cleft neural arch (S)	28.3 (13/46)
Srubnaya	Spiridonovka IV	K1, G13	35–50	M	Cleft neural arch (S)	28.3 (13/46)
Srubnaya	Spiridonovka IV	K2, G1a	35–50	F	Block vertebra (CV2/3)	5.3 (1/19)
Srubnaya	Spiridonovka IV	K2, G12	50+	M	Sacralization	13 (6/46)
Srubnaya	Studenzy I	K1, G2	18–35	M	Sacralization Six lumbar vertebrae	13 (6/46) 6.9 (2/29)
Srubnaya	Svezhensky	G71a	18–35	M	Cleft neural arch (S)	28.3 (13/46)
Srubnaya	Svezhensky	G71b	35–50	M	Cleft neural arch (S)	28.3 (13/46)
Srubnaya	Uren II	K2 G2	50+	F	Cleft neural arch (S)	28.3 (13/46)

Note: CV = cervical vertebra; F = female; G = grave; K = kurgan; LV = lumbar vertebra; M = male; S = sacrum; Sk = skeleton; TV = thoracic vertebra.

Table 8.6 Details of Individuals with Defects of the Sternal Developmental Field

Culture	Site	Context	Age, y	Sex	Lesion	Adult Prevalence by Bone, Percentage (No./Total No.)
Yamnaya	Nizhny Orleansky I	K4, G2	18–35	M	Aplastic sternebra	20 (1/5)
Poltavka	Kalinovka	K1, G4	50+	M	Cleft of sternal body	11.1 (1/9)
Poltavka	Lopatino I	K33	18–35	M	Hyperplastic body (Type II mesosternum)	11.1 (1/9)
Srubnaya	Studenzy I	K1, G2	18–35	M	Fusion of xiphoid to body	6.2 (1/16)
Srubnaya	Studenzy I	K2, G4	35–50	F	Fusion of manubrio-mesosternal joint	6.2 (1/16)

Note: F = female; G = grave; K = kurgan; M = male.

In this case, since the cleft was quite substantial, it was probably due to the complete failure of fusion of the last sternebra (Barnes 1994:225). Another Poltavka individual, an 18- to 35-year-old male (K33) recovered from the Lopatino I burial ground, had a sternal body with an abnormally large caudal end. It is probable that delayed fusion had resulted in the development of bilateral ossification centers in the lower sternebrae. This type of mesosternum has been classed as Type II, and it is relatively common (Barnes 1994:218). Interestingly, the individual also displayed Type II Klippel-Feil syndrome, and it is possible that the two defects were connected. Likewise, in an 18- to 35-year-old Srubnaya male (K1, G2) recovered from the Studenzy I burial ground, the xiphoid was fused to the sternal body. This defect arises as a consequence of a failure of the fibrous lamina that separates the xiphoid process from the sternum to develop properly (Barnes 1994:213). The individual also displayed an extra lumbar vertebra and sacralization, and again it is possible that the defects were somehow connected.

First Branchial Arch
The branchial arches become apparent in the embryo during the fourth week of gestation, with differentiation completed by the sixth to eighth weeks. The cartilage of the first branchial arch divides into two sections, forming a maxillary and a mandibular part. The former develops into the maxilla and the zygomatic, the lateral area of the upper lip and cheek, and the inferior parts of the helix and the tragus of the ear (Feingold and Gellis 1968:30).

Only a single individual in the corpus displayed a possible developmental defect of the first branchial arch. Skeleton K1, G3, an 18- to 35-year-old Srubnaya male recovered from the Chisty Yar I cemetery, displayed a possible developmental fissural cyst. An oval perforation with smooth margins, which measured 8 mm

anteroposteriorly by 4 mm mediolaterally, was situated immediately posterior to the right maxillary second incisor, canine and first premolar. The location of the cyst would tend to suggest that it was a globulomaxillary cyst. This type of cyst generally arises at the lateral junction of the premaxilla and the maxilla between the second incisor and the canine (Barnes 1994:178). Its origin is uncertain, and it has been suggested that it is due either to the entrapment of epithelial tissue or derived from later odontogenic tissue (Barnes 1994:178). The lesion had a prevalence rate of 1.2 percent (1/83) for the Srubnaya population.

Appendicular Skeleton
Only four of the prehistoric Volga individuals displayed developmental defects of the appendicular skeleton. These comprised a single Yamnaya individual and three individuals from the Srubnaya culture. In all four cases, the lesions had affected the hips—in three cases, only one joint was affected, while in a single case, the lesions were bilateral. All four of the individuals are likely to have suffered from gait disturbances, some of which may have been severe, and would have undoubtedly placed them at some disadvantage relative to unaffected members of their societies.

Slipped Femoral Capital Epiphysis
An 18- to 35-year-old adult male recovered from Flat Grave 5 of the Yamnaya culture Leshevskoe I burial ground displayed probable slipped femoral capital epiphysis of his right femur (Figure 8.2). Both the right femur and acetabulum displayed extensive postmortem damage, but the abnormalities of the hip were clearly apparent. The right femoral head had a flattened appearance with inferior displacement of the capital epiphysis so that it was positioned below the greater trochanter. It was difficult to assess the nature of the depression for the attachment

of the ligamentum teres. Porosity and eburnation were visible on the head, while extensive marginal lipping was apparent, particularly at the margins of its inferior surface. The right acetabulum was hypertrophied and very shallow, and its articular surface displayed extensive porosity and eburnation. The secondary degenerative joint disease is indicative of the long-standing nature of the abnormalities.

The proximal half of the shaft of the right femur had a notably flattened anteroposterior appearance compared to its left counterpart. This flattening was clearly apparent in the metrical analyses of the femora—the anteroposterior diameter of the midshaft of the affected right femur was 21.8 mm compared with 31.1 mm in its normal left counterpart. The midshaft mediolateral diameters were both similar, with the right femur measuring 29 mm and the left femur having a diameter of 29.2 mm. The subtrochanteric anteroposterior diameter of the right femur was approximately 25 mm, while that for the normal left femur was 26.2 mm. The subtrochanteric mediolateral diameters were 35.2 mm and 34.6 mm for the right and left femora, respectively. The abnormal anteroposterior flattening may have been due to the abnormal gait that would have been induced by the femoral head deformities. It was not possible to ascertain the greatest length of the right femur due to postmortem damage.

Slipped femoral capital epiphysis most typically occurs in children and adolescents, with a greater incidence among males. A number of factors have been proposed as possible etiologies of the condition, and a link is generally accepted between it and adolescent growth spurts, as the growth plate is particularly vulnerable to shearing stresses during this period (Resnick et al. 1995:2646). Associated with the adolescent growth period are the influences of a variety of sex hormones. The condition is common in adolescents who are overweight and have delayed sexual maturation. A greater amount of growth hormones relative to sex hormones is present in these individuals, and this may increase the period of time when the proximal epiphysis is vulnerable to slippage (Gruebel Lee 1983:176). In some families, there may be a notable history of slipped epiphysis, and the condition has been observed in monozygotic twins (Resnick et al. 1995:2646).

There are a number of main characteristics of slipped femoral capital epiphysis. These include the crumbling of inadequately ossified metaphyseal bone positioned just inferior to the epiphyseal plate. This results in a chronic slippage in which the bones of the femoral neck gradually bend and deform. Acute slippage occurs as a result of sudden shearing separation of the epiphysis from the metaphysis (Gruebel Lee 1983:175). Chronic slippage occurs in approximately 70 percent of cases, with acute slippage present among 30 percent of affected individuals (Apley and Solomon 1988:172). The sequelae of the condition include severe varus deformity, broadening and shortening of the femoral neck, flattening of the femoral head, osteonecrosis, chondrolysis, and degenerative changes

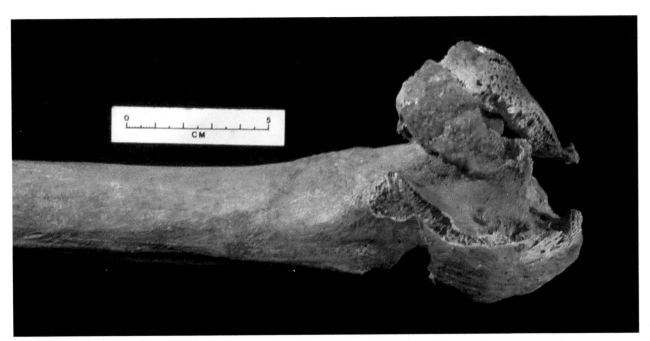

Figure 8.2 Posterior view of a probable case of slipped femoral capital epiphysis of the right femur apparent in an 18- to 35-year-old male of Yamnaya date recovered from Flat Grave 5 of the Leshevskoe I burial ground.

(Resnick et al. 1995:2647). In an individual with slipped femoral epiphysis, the affected leg will be shortened and externally rotated. A loss of abduction, associated with increased adduction due to coxa vara, will be apparent. In addition, there is loss of internal rotation, increased external rotation, and hyperextension with loss of flexion of the hip. The individual may also experience pain upon certain movements (Gruebel Lee 1983:181).

The main differential diagnosis for the abnormalities apparent in the individual from Leshevskoe I is Perthes disease. In Perthes disease, however, one would expect the femoral head to have a mushroom-shaped appearance with notable porosity and a poorly defined depression for the attachment of the ligamentum teres. In addition, in Perthes disease, the center of the femoral head is not markedly dislocated from the femoral neck, and the neck has a generally normal appearance (Ortner 2003:347), and no slippage of the head is expected (Aufderheide and Rodríguez-Martín 1998:90). Other possible etiologies for the abnormalities include dysplasia of the hip or developmental coxa vara.

This disabled adult male from the Leshevskoe I cemetery appeared to have suffered a violent death—his right thigh had been crushed by a heavy blow, and his left leg and skull had been gouged to the bone (see below for full discussion). His body was reported to have been excavated not under the nearby Yamnaya culture kurgan but rather beside it in a grave (Grave 5) without a mound covering. He was reportedly buried in a prone position, face down and contorted, and was referred to as "the prisoner" in casual conversation by the archaeologists, a speculation that is only one among many possible interpretations of this grave. A radiocarbon date on bone from the individual measured by the Arizona laboratory gave an age of approximately 2900 to 2800 BCE (AA47807 4254 ± 61 BP, 2909–2786 cal BC, midline 2883 cal BC), possibly contemporary with the burial of two Yamnaya individuals in one grave (1a and 1b) in the nearby kurgan. These comprised a young adult female (1a) and the poorly preserved remains of a perinatal infant. Presumably, the woman was the mother of the baby, but it is not possible to know if they had died during or after birth. No radiocarbon date is available for Grave 1. There is nothing to indicate any relationship between the individuals buried within Grave 1 and Grave 5, although evidence for the presence of ochre in both burials is suggestive that the mortuary rituals were similar. It seems likely that the male in Grave 5 was either killed in a violent encounter or that he had been intentionally tortured. It is interesting to speculate that this unusual treatment may have arisen because of his physical disabilities, but this will be discussed later in the text.

Developmental Dysplasia and Congenital Dislocation of the Hip

Two Srubnaya individuals displayed possible cases of developmental dysplasia and dislocation of their hip joints. By the eleventh week in utero, the basic morphology of the developed hip joint has been established. Consequently, dislocation of the hip is possible from this stage onward. As such, any defect that acts upon the embryo prior to the eleventh week will not cause a dislocation but will cause the occurrence of a malformation that results in abnormal and misshapen joints. At birth, the hip joint is still cartilaginous in composition, but its associated ligaments are fully developed (Ferrer-Torrelles and Ceballos 1982:21). Genetic, mechanical, hormonal, and social factors have all been implicated as possible factors that are responsible for susceptibility to dislocation of the hip in the embryo. In the majority of cases, the dysplasia arises as a result of abnormalities in the developmental processes, indicating that the abnormality is genetically controlled (Carter 1964:308; Inman 1963:250; Sartoris 1995:4067). There is a marked preponderance of congenital dislocation of the hip in females, with a sex ratio of approximately 6:1 (Carter 1964:308). Most congenital dislocations of the hip occur during the first 2 weeks following birth, although occasionally, a dislocation will occur in individuals of up to 1 year of age. In general, however, late initial dislocations occur rarely during childhood (Sartoris 1995:4068).

Cases of developmental dysplasia of the hip also occur sporadically, however, and it has been suggested that these cases arise due to an intrauterine position of the fetus in which either the hips are flexed or the knees are incompletely flexed and the feet are externally rotated. This posture commonly occurs in breech births, especially among the first born. The practice of swaddling a baby with his or her hips extended and adducted probably also contributes to the occurrence of congenital dislocation of the hip and prevents the spontaneous recovery of some of the milder forms of the defect (Carter 1964:308). Developmental dysplasia of the hip is most common in Native Americans who swaddle their babies tightly with the hips fully extended, but it is uncommon in African tribes where the babies are carried across the back with the hips widely abducted (Apley and Solomon 1988:163). Murphy (2000b:63–65) described two cases of developmental dysplasia of the hip in the semi-nomadic Scythian period population from Aymyrlyg, South Siberia.

Clinical studies have indicated that approximately 0.3 to 1 percent of a population is born with a dysplastic hip (Gruebel Lee 1983:102–103), with the defect bilateral in over 50 percent of cases (Inman 1963:251). Individuals with congenital dislocation of the hip will generally display the Trendelenburg gait, a limp that is characterized by an even timing of the two legs but with a tilt toward the normal hip. From a distance, unilateral examples of the limp are observed as a lateral movement of the shoulders toward the normal side or as a movement of the shoulders from side to side if the condition is bilateral (Gruebel Lee 1983:78). If the dysplasia of the hip has not been treated in individuals older than 3 years, then the femoral head will become deformed and the acetabulum will have a triangular morphology (Inman 1963:252).

In Skeleton K1, G8, a 35- to 50-year-old male recovered from the Spiridonovka IV burial ground, the bones of the left leg had a markedly atrophied appearance and abnormal morphologies. Unfortunately, the left innominate was not available for analysis, and the femoral head had been subject to extensive postmortem damage. The femoral neck was very thin, and a large articular facet, which displayed osteophytes and porosity, was visible in the region of the intertrochanteric line. The mediolateral breadth of the shaft was notably atrophied (subtrochanteric diameter 16.4 mm [L], 33.6 mm [R]; midshaft 17.6 mm [L], 30.7 mm [R]), although its anteroposterior dimensions were similar to its normal right counterpart (subtrochanteric diameter 21.1 mm [L], 26.1 mm [R]; midshaft 26.9 mm [L], 24.9 mm [R]). The muscle markings on the posterior aspect of the femur were unpronounced. Only the proximal third of the left tibia was preserved, but it also had a generally atrophied appearance relative to its normal right counterpart (bicondylar width ca. 74 mm [L], 80.9 mm [R]). The left knee joint did not display any evidence for degenerative changes.

The abnormal morphology of the bones and the lack of secondary degenerative joint disease suggests that the left leg, and presumably hip, was dysfunctional. The right innominate displayed slight marginal osteophytes of the acetabulum, and enthesopathies of the gluteus medius and the tensor fasciae latae were apparent. The right femur was markedly robust with notable enthesopathies of the gluteal tuberosity (gluteus maximus), the lesser trochanter (psoas major and iliacus), and the greater trochanter (gluteus minimus, iliofemoral ligament, and vastus lateralus). In addition, its anteroposterior dimensions were reduced, giving it a notably flattened appearance. The right tibia had a normal appearance, although slight marginal osteophytes were apparent at its proximal articular surface.

It is possible that the robusticity of the right femur and the occurrence of enthesopathies had arisen as a consequence of the individual compensating for the loss of power in his atrophied left leg by developing an unusually strong right leg. Extensive degenerative joint disease was apparent in the lower thoracic and lumbar vertebrae, which may also

have been secondary to the gait disturbance. Differential diagnosis for the abnormal left leg would include a fracture of the femoral neck and head region when the individual was a nonadult.

In Skeleton G1, a possible female adult recovered from the Novoselki cemetery, the right femur had an atrophied appearance. Unfortunately, the right innominate and the remainder of the bones of the right leg were not available for analysis. The femoral head was notably atrophied and had a very flattened macroporotic appearance with marginal osteophytes at its posterior aspect. The mediolateral breadth of the shaft was notably atrophied (subtrochanteric diameter 21.1 mm [R], 27.5 mm [L]) at the proximal end, although it was more similar to its left counterpart at the midshaft (midshaft 24.5 mm [R], 25.4 mm [L]). The right proximal anteroposterior dimensions were slightly greater than those of the left bone (subtrochanteric diameter 28.1 mm [R], 24.5 mm [L]), although the midshaft dimensions were similar to its normal left counterpart (26.1 mm [R], 27 mm [L]). It was difficult to ascertain further information about this case due to the very incomplete nature of the skeleton.

Dysplastic Proximal Femur
In Skeleton K2, G37, an 18- to 35-year-old Srubnaya male retrieved from the Late Bronze Age (LBA) Spiridonovka II burial ground, both femora had abnormal morphologies. The femoral necks were markedly short, with neck-shaft angles of approximately 90°. In addition, the proximal aspects of the femoral heads were positioned at the same level as the superior aspects of the greatest trochanters.

The term *coxa vara* is applied to any condition in which the neck-shaft angle of the femur is less than the normal figure of approximately 125° when viewed anteroposteriorly (Adams and Hamblen 1990:313). In children, coxa vara can be secondary and develop as a result of rickets, bone dystrophies, or Perthes disease (Gruebel Lee 1983:163). A primary developmental form of coxa vara also exists, however, although this is rare and is considered a manifestation of an autosomal dominant gene. The defect affects the neck of the femur. In infantile coxa vara, a triangular portion of metaphyseal bone separates from the inferior aspect of the metaphysis just inferior to the growth plate, and this causes the epiphyseal plate to be positioned vertically. In developmental coxa vara, both hips are generally affected (Gruebel Lee 1983:166), as in Spiridonovka II K2, G37.

It does not seem likely that this individual suffered from proximal femoral focal deficiency (PFFD), also referred to as congenital hypoplasia of the upper femur and femoral hypoplasia with coxa vara. In these congenital conditions, the proximal part of the femur is shortened or partially absent, but they are generally unilateral (Resnick 1995a:4284), as opposed to bilateral, which is the case for the individual from Spiridonovka II.

Health

Wood et al. (1992) warned that less healthy individuals die younger, while healthier individuals live for a longer period of time and therefore have a greater chance of developing paleopathological lesions. To avoid being misled by this osteological paradox, it is necessary to combine paleopathological and paleodemographical data with contextual information (Steckel and Rose 2002a:586). Goodman and colleagues have emphasized the key role that the environment plays in the factors responsible for physiological stress (Goodman 1991; Goodman and Armelagos 1988; Goodman et al. 1984; Goodman et al. 1988). Cultural systems can help buffer a society against stressors, but some stressors can also be culturally induced. Depending on host resistance, the stressors can then cause physiological disruption to the skeleton, which is manifested in disruption to growth and the development of disease. Physiological stress can result in a decreased level of health, a reduced ability to undertake work, a suppressed reproductive capacity, and general sociocultural disruption. The potential indicators of physiological stressors recorded for the Volga populations were growth disturbances, cribra orbitalia, dental enamel hypoplasia, and reactive new bone formation. All lesions were observed macroscopically and were generally recorded following the methods advocated by Buikstra and Ubelaker (1994) and Steckel and Rose (2002b).

Growth and Stature

Growth is controlled by a mixture of environmental and genetic factors (although see Goodman 1991:33–35 for discussion). Stunting of growth can arise as a consequence of both nutritional deficiency and infectious disease processes (Pinhasi 2008:365), and studies of living populations have demonstrated a clear relationship between physiological stress and stature (Larsen 1997:14). Details of the greatest femoral lengths for each population group are provided in Table 8.7 and Figure 8.3.

During the Early Bronze Age (EBA) Yamnaya period, the average femoral greatest length for males was 472.1 mm, which then rose to 478 mm during Middle Bronze Age (MBA) Poltavka times, declined to 469.3 mm during the late MBA Potapovka period, and declined even further to 457.7 mm for the Late Bronze Age (LBA) Srubnaya adult males. A different trend is apparent for females—their average greatest femoral length values were very similar (ca. 442 mm) between the Yamnaya and Potapovka periods but then decreased notably to 422.1 mm during Srubnaya times. The most obvious similarity between the two sexes is the decrease in femoral length, and therefore in stature, during the Srubnaya period. This decrease was markedly more dramatic for females than for males. Steckel (1995) and Larsen (1997:14) have shown that a person's stature is directly related to the quality of his or her diet and disease history, although the latter is of less importance. It appears to be the case that individuals with an adequate diet attain their genetic growth potential, but not individuals with a poor diet. The male trend would appear to indicate that there was a slight improvement in health from the Yamnaya to Poltavka periods followed by a gradual decline in health from the Poltavka to the Srubnaya periods. Female health appears to have been more static between Yamnaya and Potapovka times but then deteriorated during the time of the Srubnaya culture.

If Asian people composed a significant percentage of the Potapovka population (see Chapter 6), this could account for part of the decline in stature during that period. Recent genetic studies have clearly demonstrated that adult height is significantly different for the three main geographical "races": Asian, white, and black (Feldesman and Fountain 1996; Lettre et al. 2008). As such, it is possible that racial differences, as well as health, had an influence on stature among Potapovka populations. But Khokhlov

Table 8.7 Summary of Male and Female Femoral Greatest Lengths (mm) for the Different Cultures

Culture	Male			Female		
	n	Mean	Range	*n*	Mean	Range
Yamnaya	7	472.1	466–480	2	442.5	417–468
Poltavka	16	478	443–516	4	442	424–458
Potapovka	11	469.3	440–520	2	442	441–443
Srubnaya	67	457.7	160–187.5	63	422.1	373–463

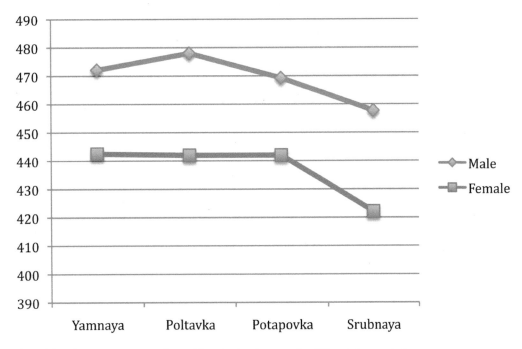

Figure 8.3 Male and female average greatest femoral lengths (mm) across the different time periods.

*(this volume) found only a small influence of Asian cranial types in the Potapovka population and no Asian skull traits in Srubnaya individuals.

Cribra Orbitalia and Porotic Hyperostosis

Cribra orbitalia is the term used to refer to generally symmetrical lesions, with the morphology of small perforations of varying size and density, apparent in the cortical bone of the superior aspects of the orbit. The occurrence of lesions of similar morphology in the skull vault is referred to as porotic hyperostosis (Stuart-Macadam 1991:101). The lesions have traditionally been interpreted as an indicator of iron deficiency anemia acquired during childhood (e.g., Stuart-Macadam 1985). A more recent study by Walker and colleagues (2009) has demonstrated that neither lesion can be physiologically caused by iron deficiency anemia. They have suggested that porotic hyperostosis is due to hemolytic and megaloblastic anemias, which most commonly arise from deficiencies of vitamin B_{12} and vitamin B_9 (folic acid) (Walker et al. 2009:6). They indicate the situation concerning cribra orbitalia is less clear-cut, and the lesions may have been caused by a multitude of conditions, which include chronic infections and deficiencies of vitamins B_{12}, C, and D (Walker et al. 2009:7, 11). They propose that a combination of poor diet, a lack of hygiene, infectious diseases, and cultural practices associated with pregnancy and breastfeeding might explain

the high levels of these lesions in many past populations (Walker et al. 2009:Figure 4). The degree of severity and extent of the surface affected were recorded (cf. Stuart-Macadam 1991:109).

Cribra orbitalia occurred most frequently for the Yamnaya group, both in terms of numbers of individuals and numbers of orbits affected (Table 8.8). The reliability of this result is reduced, however, by the small number of Yamnaya individuals with observable orbits.

The prevalence of cribra orbitalia for the remaining groups was not dissimilar, with values ranging from 9.1 percent for the Poltavka population to 15.7 percent for Srubnaya. Except for the Yamnaya figure, the results from the Volga populations are lower than those obtained in a study of two Iron Age semi-nomadic populations from Aymyrlyg, South Siberia, in which it was found that cribra orbitalia had a prevalence of 18 percent by bone in the observable adult orbits of the Uyuk culture and 28 percent in the Shurmak culture (Murphy 2012:253). Due to the small sample sizes of the earlier populations, it was only possible to compare male and female prevalence rates for the Srubnaya population. Some 12.2 percent of males and 25 percent of females with orbits present displayed cribra orbitalia. This finding would tend to suggest that Srubnaya females were more susceptible to low health and nutritional status during childhood than males, although the results were not statistically significant ($\chi^2 = 2.322$; $p = 0.127$; $df = 1$).

Table 8.8 Prevalence Rates (Percentage) of the Adults with Cribra Orbitalia for Each Culture

| Culture | Prevalence by Individual, Percentage (No./Total No.) | | | Prevalence by Bone, Percentage (No./Total No.) |
	Overall	Male	Female	Overall
Khvalynsk	13 (3/23)	5.3 (1/19)	50 (2/4)	11.1 (5/45)
Yamnaya	37.5 (3/8)	28.6 (2/7)	100 (1/1)	35.7 (5/14)
Poltavka	5.6 (1/18)	6.3 (1/16)	0 (0/2)	9.1 (2/22)
Transitional	0 (0/4)	0 (0/3)	0 (0/1)	0 (0/8)
Potapovka	18.2 (2/11)	25 (2/8)	0 (0/3)	13.6 (3/22)
Srubnaya	17.6 (15/85)	13.6 (6/44)	22 (9/41)	15.7 (26/166)

Among the nonadults, only the Poltavka and Srubnaya populations contained individuals with evidence for cribra orbitalia. The affected Poltavka individuals comprised a 0.5- to 1.5-year-old infant retrieved from the Kalinovka cemetery and a 6- to 8-year-old juvenile recovered from the Nikolaevka III burial ground. It was possible to examine one or both orbits in the crania of 26 Srubnaya nonadults, 38.5 percent (10/26) of which displayed cribra orbitalia. In total, 45 nonadult orbits were examined, 31.1 percent (14/45) of which displayed cribra orbitalia. This is a notably higher prevalence rate than the value of 15.7 percent (26/166) obtained for Srubnaya adult orbits. This finding would tend to suggest that a significantly lower proportion of children who developed cribra orbitalia survived to adulthood ($\chi^2 = 5.499$; $p = 0.019$; $df = 1$). Details of the Srubnaya individuals with cribra orbitalia broken down by age and sex are provided in Table 8.9.

Most of the Srubnaya nonadults with cribra orbitalia had died at the age of 6 to 12 years, and a number of adolescents had also been affected. The majority of affected adults had an age at death of 18 to 35 years (60 percent; 9/15), a finding that would tend to suggest that adults with cribra orbitalia were more likely to die at a younger age. It is also interesting that the majority of affected adults were female

(60 percent; 9/15). This finding may again indicate that female individuals were more susceptible to poor health and vitamin deficiencies during childhood than their male counterparts.

At a number of Srubnaya sites, particular kurgans contained multiple individuals with cribra orbitalia— Krasnosamarskoe IV (K3: G1, G12b, G16, G20), Nizhny Orleansky IV (K1: G2, G3, G8), Spiridonovka II (K11: G15, G21), Spiridonovka IV (K1: G4, G10, G16), and Svezhensky (G52, G55, G71a). These findings may indicate that a more comprehensive study, which analyzes all individuals from particular kurgans, has the potential to yield information about differential health statuses at site level.

As noted above, porotic hyperostosis probably arose from deficiencies of vitamins B_{12} and B_9 (folic acid). The numbers of individuals with porotic hyperostosis in each group were low (Table 8.10). Only single individuals were affected in the Poltavka, Potapovka, and Srubnaya adult populations, with the prevalence ranging from 1.6 percent for the Srubnaya group to 5 percent for the Poltavka population and 8.3 percent for the Potapovka corpus. The spread of results from the Volga populations is not too dissimilar to those obtained from the Iron Age Uyuk culture from Aymyrlyg, South Siberia, where the lesions had a prevalence of 8 percent. They are notably lower than the results obtained for the later Shurmak culture from the same cemetery, however, where a prevalence of 16 percent was recorded (Murphy 2012:253). When the prevalences are examined on the basis of sex for the substantial Srubnaya population, it would appear to be the case that females (2.3 percent) were more susceptible to the development of porotic hyperostosis than males (0 percent). This finding corresponds to the results obtained for cribra orbitalia discussed above.

Table 8.9 Numbers of Srubnaya Individuals with Cribra Orbitalia Broken Down by Age (Years) and Sex ($n = 25$)

	<2	2–6	6–12	12–18	18–35	35–50	50+
Male					3	2	1
Female				2	6	3	
Unknown		1	6	1			
Total	0	1	6	3	9	5	1

Table 8.10 Prevalences (Percentage) of Adults with Porotic Hyperostosis Based on the Numbers of Individuals with Observable Parietals and/or Occipitals

Culture	Overall	Male	Female
	Prevalence by Individual, Percentage (No./Total No.)		
Khvalynsk	0 (0/24)	0 (0/19)	0 (0/5)
Yamnaya	0 (0/8)	0 (0/7)	0 (0/1)
Poltavka	5 (1/20)	5.6 (1/18)	0 (0/2)
Potapovka	8.3 (1/12)	0 (0/9)	33.3 (1/3)
Srubnaya	1.6 (1/88)	0 (0/45)	2.3 (1/43)

Among nonadults, Skeleton K1, G5, a 0.5- to 1.5-year-old infant retrieved from the Poltavka culture Kalinovka burial ground, displayed both porotic hyperostosis and cribra orbitalia. Two Srubnaya nonadults displayed evidence of porotic hyperostosis, both of whom were recovered from the Nizhny Orleansky IV burial ground—Skeleton K1, G8, a 6- to 7-year-old juvenile, and Skeleton K4, G3, a 15- to 17-year-old male adolescent. In the former case, cribra orbitalia was also observable, but the lesions were unobservable in the latter individual.

Dental Enamel Hypoplasia

Dental enamel hypoplasia is one of the most common developmental defects of the tooth enamel. It arises as a consequence of ameloblast disturbance during enamel matrix production. The most common form of hypoplasia is linear enamel hypoplasia, in which the defect has the appearance of a groove, although the defects may also take the form of a sharp line, or as a band of pit-type defects (Hillson 1996:166–167). Once a hypoplastic defect has occurred in the enamel, it cannot be removed since enamel does not have the ability to remodel. Consequently, a hypoplastic defect on a permanent tooth acts as a memory to an incident of physiological stress, which affected the ameloblast activity during childhood (Dobney and Goodman 1991:81; Goodman and Armelagos 1988:90; Goodman and Martin 2002:23). This kind of stress can arise as a consequence of nutritional deficiencies and many childhood illnesses (Roberts and Manchester 2005:75). Enamel hypoplastic defects were recorded on the basis of the methodology advocated by Goodman and colleagues (1980:518–519). The severity of the hypoplastic lesions was categorized on the basis of the grading system of Brothwell (1981:156). Details of the prevalence of adults to display enamel hypoplasia are shown in Table 8.11.

The overall prevalence rates ranged from 37.5 percent for the Poltavka population to 71.4 percent for the Yamnaya population, but again the small sample sizes may be skewing the results. The spread of results from the Volga populations is not too dissimilar to those obtained from two Iron Age semi-nomadic populations from Aymyrlyg, South Siberia, in which it was found that dental enamel hypoplasia occurred among Uyuk culture adult dentitions with a prevalence of 28 percent, while the dentitions of Shurmak culture adults displayed hypoplastic lesions with a frequency of 42 percent (Murphy 2012:254). Lillie (1996:Table 4) reported that 16.7 percent of Ukrainian Mesolithic individuals with teeth displayed hypoplastic lesions, while 11.4 percent of the corresponding Neolithic individuals were affected. These results are notably lower that those derived from the Volga or Aymyrlyg populations. The Ukrainian populations are considered to have followed a hunter-gatherer-fisher economy, which was modified to include a pastoral component during Neolithic times (Lillie 1996:137). It can be tentatively proposed that the more pastoral component of the economies of the Volga and Aymyrlyg populations had resulted in these groups being more susceptible to physiological stress. A major problem with this thesis, however, is that the Khvalynsk population would probably have followed a similar economy to the Ukrainian populations, and it displayed relatively high levels of the lesions (57 percent). When the results for the substantial Srubnaya population are analyzed by sex, it is clear that females (45.9 percent) displayed hypoplastic lesions with a greater prevalence than did males (31.1 percent), although the results were not statistically significant ($\chi^2 = 1.900$; $p = 0.168$; $df = 1$).

Among the nonadults, only the Khvalynsk, Poltavka, and Srubnaya populations contained individuals with evidence for dental enamel hypoplasia. The Khvalynsk individual comprised Skeleton G23, a 13- to 15-year-old

Table 8.11 Prevalence (Percentage) of Adult Individuals with Dental Enamel Hypoplasia

Culture	Overall	Male	Female
	Prevalence by Individuals, Percentage (No./Total No.)		
Khvalynsk	57 (12/21)	52.6 (10/19)	100 (2/2)
Yamnaya	71.4 (5/7)	66.7 (4/6)	100 (1/1)
Poltavka	37.5 (6/16)	42.9 (6/14)	0 (0/2)
Potapovka	50 (5/10)	62.5 (5/8)	0 (0/2)
Srubnaya	37.8 (31/82)	31.1 (14/45)	45.9 (17/37)

possible female, while the affected Poltavka nonadult was Skeleton K2, G3, a 12- to 15-year-old adolescent, recovered from Krasnosamarskoe IV. It was possible to examine the permanent dentitions of 32 Srubnaya nonadults for hypoplastic defects, 28.1 percent (9/32) of which displayed evidence of having been subject to one or more incidents of childhood physiological stress. Although this is a lower prevalence rate than the value of 37.8 percent (31/82) obtained from the Srubnaya adults, the difference was not statistically significant ($\chi^2 = 0.947$; $p = 0.330$; $df = 1$). Details of the Srubnaya individuals with dental enamel hypoplasia broken down by age and sex are provided in Table 8.12.

Most of the nonadults with enamel hypoplasia died between the ages of 12 and 18 years, and a number of juveniles also were affected. The relative paucity of younger children with the defects is probably due to a combination of two factors—the incomplete development of the teeth as well as the likelihood that younger individuals were generally less likely to survive an event that was severe enough to result in the development of a hypoplastic lesion. The majority of affected adults had an age at death of 18 to 35 years (55 percent; 22/40), a finding that would tend to suggest that adults with hypoplastic defects were more likely to die at a younger age.

In addition to the results included in Table 8.12, Skeleton K2, G2b, an 8- to 9-year-old Srubnaya juvenile recovered from the Spiridonovka IV burial ground, displayed crinkling on the tips of the crowns of the mandibular deciduous molars. It is possible that the crinkled appearance was due to hypoplasia and that the individual had been subject to an incident of physiological stress when he or she was a fetus of approximately 5 to 9 months of age (cf. Ubelaker 1989:64). The individual also displayed additional hypoplastic defects, which indicated that he or she had also been subject to physiological stress at an older age.

Nonspecific Infectious Disease

Reactive new bone formation (periostitis) can occur as a result of inflammation in specific and nonspecific infectious processes; it can arise as a result of direct trauma (Ortner 2003:106) or can occur as a consequence of other disease processes that cause physiological stress (Ribot and Roberts 1996:70). Nonspecific pathological bone changes are virtually identical to one another and result from infection by a variety of pyogenic bacteria, including staphylococci, streptococci, pneumococci, and the typhoid bacillus. In the modern world, *Staphylococcus aureus* is responsible for over 75 percent of cases of infection (Finch and Ball 1991:208). The paleopathological changes can involve the development of pits, striations, and plaques of bone formation (Ortner 2003:206–207). Following the guidelines of Lovell (2000:237), the extent and location of the lesions were recorded, as was their state of healing (see Goodman and Martin 2002:34). Details of the crude prevalence rates of individuals with infectious lesions are provided in Table 8.13.

No cases of infection were apparent among the Potapovka group. The crude prevalence rates ranged from 1.6 percent for the Srubnaya culture to 6.3 percent for the Yamnaya group and 8.8 percent for the Poltavka culture. Among the substantial Srubnaya group, males and females appear to have been equally susceptible to the development of infections. Details of the frequencies of reactive new bone formation among adult bones for the Yamnaya, Poltavka, and Srubnaya periods are provided in Table 8.14.

When the total numbers of long bones affected are examined, it is evident that the Poltavka population was affected to the greatest extent (7.9 percent), followed in frequency by the Yamnaya population (2.3 percent) and the Srubnaya group (0.5 percent). It is possible that the Poltavka individuals were genuinely subject to the development of lesions as a result of infectious disease processes with a greater frequency than the other groups. It also needs to be considered, however, that the results have been skewed by the occurrence of Skeleton K3, G9 of Poltavka date from the Krasnosamarskoe IV burial ground (see below). The majority of this individual's bones displayed evidence for

Table 8.12 Numbers of Srubnaya Individuals with Enamel Hypoplasia Broken Down by Age (Years) and Sex ($n = 40$)

	6–12	12–18	18–35	35–50	50+
Male		2	10	4	
Female		2	12	3	2
Unknown	3	2			
Total	3	6	22	7	2

Table 8.13 Crude Prevalence Rates (Percentage) of Individuals with Infectious Lesions

Culture	Prevalence by Individuals, Percentage (No./Total No.)		
	Overall	Male	Female
Yamnaya	6.3 (1/16)	8.3 (1/12)	0 (0/4)
Poltavka	8.8 (3/34)	6.9 (2/29)	20 (1/5)
Potapovka	0 (0/14)	0 (0/11)	0 (0/3)
Srubnaya	1.6 (2/129)	1.5 (1/67)	1.6 (1/61)

Note: One of the Srubnaya individuals was of indeterminable sex. The Khvalynsk population was not included in the study of infectious lesions.

Table 8.14 Frequencies of Reactive New Bone Formation by Bone

	Percentage (No./Total No.) Affected		
	Yamnaya	Poltavka	Srubnaya
Mandible (body)	(0/7)	6.3 (1/16)	(0/78)
Humerus (shaft)	(0/22)	5 (2/40)	(0/157)
Ulna (shaft)	(0/19)	8.3 (3/36)	(0/143)
Radius (shaft)	(0/23)	7.9 (3/38)	(0/142)
Femur (shaft)	(0/20)	4.9 (2/41)	1.1 (2/175)
Tibia (shaft)	8.7 (2/23)	12.8 (5/39)	1.1 (2/174)
Fibula (shaft)	4.8 (1/21)	8.8 (3/34)	0.7 (1/135)
Ribs	(0/70)	5.1 (9/177)	(0/197)
Total	**1.5 (3/205)**	**6 (25/420)**	**0.4 (5/1,201)**
Total long bones only	**2.3 (3/128)**	**7.9 (18/228)**	**0.5 (5/926)**

reactive new bone formation, and it is considered probable that he had been suffering from an overwhelming systemic infection at the time of his death.

The frequency of infection is generally expected to rise in archaeological populations where there has been an intensification of sedentary agriculture, leading to a concomitant increase in population density and levels of nutritional stress. These subsistence factors are considered to provide an environment in which infectious diseases can flourish (Roosevelt 1984:572). Analysis of the frequencies of infectious lesions at the Dickson Mounds, Illinois (AD 950–1300), revealed an increase in levels of infectious lesions from a frequency of 31 percent during periods of low-intensity agriculture to 67 percent during periods when more intensified agriculture was practiced (Goodman et al. 1984:291). Among prehistoric populations from the Ohio River valley, prevalence rates for periostitis of 10.8 percent were recorded for the later part of the Archaic period (8000–1000 BC), with a rate of 28.6 percent noted for the Middle Woodland period (1000–100 BC) and 13 percent by the time of the Mississippian Fort Ancient culture (AD 700–1600) (Perzigian et al. 1984:357). The earliest population group would have been hunter-gatherers, while the later groups would have been involved in gradually intensifying agriculture (Perzigian et al. 1984:348–349).

A study of the frequencies of nonspecific lesions among Japanese hunter-gatherer populations from the Neolithic period (unknown to third century BC) up until the Early Modern period revealed frequencies of lesions ranging from 9.6 to 12.3 percent (Suzuki 1991:133). It is therefore evident that the frequencies of nonspecific lesions among the Volga populations are generally lower than

those recorded for either hunter-gatherer or agricultural population groups from different periods and various geographical locations throughout the world. Murphy (1998:474) observed generally low levels of infection among the Iron Age populations from Aymyrlyg, South Siberia. Despite this fact, evidence for tuberculosis, including the first definitive evidence for the bovine form of the disease in the archaeological record, was identified (Murphy et al. 2009; Taylor et al. 2007). No evidence for specific infective diseases was identified among any of the Volga populations.

The infectious lesions apparent in each individual were rather diverse, and each case will now be described. An 18- to 35-year-old male (K22) recovered from the Yamnaya culture Lopatino I burial ground displayed tibiofibular periostitis. Both tibiae and the left fibula displayed plaques of woven bone, in the process of remodeling, on their midshafts. The medial surfaces were affected in the tibiae, while the lateral surface was affected in the fibula.

Three Poltavka individuals displayed evidence of nonspecific infectious disease, which in all cases took the form of reactive new bone formation. In all three cases, the infectious processes appear to have been systemic since multiple skeletal elements were involved. Skeleton K33, an 18- to 35-year-old male recovered from the Lopatino I burial site, displayed tibiofibular periostitis and rib lesions. Plaques of striated bone in the process of remodeling were apparent on the lateral surfaces of the midshaft regions of the tibiae. Pitted woven bone was also visible on the medial surface of the right tibia. Plaques of gray, pitted woven bone were also evident on the medial surface of the midshaft of the right fibula. Thick plaques of gray woven bone were present on the visceral surfaces of the necks of the left second to tenth ribs. The right ribs were unaffected. The nature of the lesions was indicative that the individual would have had an active chest infection when he died. Skeleton K2, G2, a 35- to 50-year-old female recovered from the Kalach burial site, displayed plaques of woven bone on a number of her bones. Thick plaques of gray woven bone in the early stages of remodeling were apparent on the medial and lateral surfaces of the distal third of the left tibia, while similar lesions were evident on all surfaces of the distal third of the left fibula. The right tibia was not available for analysis, but the right fibula appeared normal. Plaques of gray woven bone in the early stages of remodeling were also visible on the anterolateral surfaces of the distal thirds of the right ulnae and on the medial surface of the distal third of the left radius. The left fifth metatarsal displayed thick plaques of woven bone on all of its surfaces. Skeleton K3, G9, an 18- to 35-year-old male recovered from the Krasnosamarskoe IV burial ground, displayed thick plaques of gray woven bone on practically all of the bones of his skeleton—mandibular bodies, clavicles, scapulae, humeri, radii, ulnae, metacarpals, hand phalanges, ilia, femora, tibiae, fibulae, calcanei, and metatarsals. The nature of the woven bone deposits would tend to suggest that the individual had been suffering from an active systemic infection when he died. Given the extent of the skeletal involvement in the infection in addition to the individual's young age, it is highly feasible that the infection had contributed to his death.

Two Srubnaya individuals displayed evidence of possible nonspecific infectious disease. Skeleton K1, G1, an 18- to 35-year-old male recovered from the Krutyenkova burial site, displayed reactive new bone formation on his femora, tibiae, and right fibula. Plaques of pitted and striated bone in the process of remodeling were apparent on the anterior surfaces of the proximal halves of the femora. The distal half of the left femur also displayed pitting of its cortical surface. Plaques of woven bone were present on the medial surface of the distal third of the right tibia, and the remainder of the medial surface displayed striations. The cortex of the entire medial surface of the left tibia displayed pitting and striations, while plaques of striated bone were evident on the lateral surface of the midshaft of the right fibula. The nature of the lesions would tend to suggest that, although the infection was still active when the individual had died, it was in the process of healing.

Skeleton K2, G36, a 50+-year-old female recovered from the Barinovka I cemetery, displayed a possible case of extensive osteomyelitis on a metatarsal. In osteomyelitis, the pathological process involves bone destruction and pus formation with concomitant bone repair. The bone may become enlarged, and bone destruction is apparent in the form of pitting on the bone surface and, in some cases, the formation of a cavity within the bone. The cavity, which is an abscess and contains pus, may penetrate the cortex and discharge the pus into the adjacent body tissues (Roberts and Manchester 2005:169). In addition, in osteomyelitis, a sequestra may develop, which is a segment of necrotic bone separated from the living tissue by granulation tissue. In the process of bone repair, an involucrum may develop, which is a layer of living bone formed around the dead bone. An opening in the involucrum is referred to as a cloaca, and granulation tissue and sequestra are discharged through this opening via sinuses to the surface of the bone (Resnick and Niwayama 1995a:2326). The skeleton was in a poor state of preservation, with the small number of bones present in a fragmentary and eroded condition. It was not possible to identify which metatarsal was affected since the bone had been so extensively eroded as a consequence of the pathological processes. The proximal and distal ends and the shaft were all extensively eroded, and the bone surface displayed a series of indentations and circular lytic lesions. It is difficult to be certain about the specific etiology of the lesions. Osteomyelitis is considered a feasible interpretation, although it is also possible that a seronegative arthropathy could have caused such bone changes. The latter interpretation is considered less likely, however, since none of the other metatarsals present displayed any pathological changes. The poor state of preservation of the skeleton also makes it feasible that the erosive activity was a pseudo-paleopathology and due to unusual taphonomic processes.

Osteoporosis

The remains of a 35- to 50-year-old female (K1, G6) recovered from the Poltavka Kalinovka burial ground were considered abnormally light (osteopenic). Other lesions apparent in her remains included spondylolysis and extraspinal and spinal degenerative joint disease. The skeletal remains of a 50+-year-old female (K3, G9a), recovered from the Poltavka period Grachevka II burial ground, were also considered osteopenic. The remains were in a poor state of preservation, and the only other lesions apparent were spinal degenerative joint disease and Schmorl's nodes. Given the ages and sex of both individuals, it is considered feasible that they had suffered from osteoporosis.

The metabolic condition of osteoporosis is recognizable by the occurrence of qualitatively normal but quantitatively lacking bone. The cortex of the bone is thinner than usual, and there are fewer trabeculae than normal (Apley and Solomon 1988:52). The condition is arbitrarily identified when the skeleton has lost at least 30 percent of its bone mass (Ortner 2003:411). An individual with the condition will display diffuse osteopenia. In generalized osteoporosis, the axial skeleton and the proximal areas of the long bones are predominantly affected. This form of osteoporosis can arise as a result of a variety of factors, including old age, menopause, nutritional deficiencies, a high number of pregnancies, prolonged periods of lactation, and hormonal conditions such as hyperparathyroidism (Brickley and Ives 2008:152–158; Roberts and Manchester 2005:243). In modern populations, osteoporosis is diagnosed in the majority of cases when the individual sustains a fracture, particularly in the wrist, hip, or spine (Adams and Hamblen 1990:63). Senile and postmenopausal osteoporosis are the most common etiologies of generalized osteoporosis. In modern populations, male skeletons begin to decrease in mass in the fifth or sixth decade of life, while those of females start to decrease in bone mass when the woman is in her 30s (Resnick and Niwayama 1995b:1786). In archaeological cases, the first sign that osteoporosis is present is the occurrence of bones of abnormally low mass (Ortner 2003:413). Diagnosis of osteoporosis on the sole basis of the occurrence of abnormally light bone mass is hazardous, however, since diagenetic factors can affect the density of archaeological bone when it has been buried in the ground. As such, the identification of osteoporosis in these two individuals can only be considered tentative.

Diet

Teeth recovered from archaeological population groups can provide valuable information about diet and subsistence economy. The frequencies of adults with dentitions and numbers of teeth and sockets by culture are provided in

Table 8.15, while the frequencies by age and sex are listed in Table 8.16.

Teeth that were unerupted, or in the early stages of eruption, were excluded from the overall counts of teeth since it is unlikely that they would have been affected by the disease processes under study. In addition, impacted teeth were also excluded since they would have been retained within the jaw and not susceptible to disease processes, such as caries and calculus deposition. The positions of teeth that were unerupted, partially erupted, or genetically absent were excluded from the counts of tooth sockets since these would not have been susceptible to disease processes, such as dental abscesses and periodontal disease. Sockets for impacted teeth, however, were included since impaction can contribute to the development of dental abscesses. Details of the frequencies for nonadult dentitions are provided in Table 8.17.

Table 8.15 Details of the Frequencies (Percentage) of Adults with Dentitions and Numbers of Teeth and Sockets by Culture

Culture	Percentage (No./Total No.)		
	Individuals	Teeth	Sockets
Khvalynsk	92 (23/25)	66.7 (491/736)	88.5 (651/736)
Yamnaya	50 (8/16)	66 (169/256)	77.7 (199/256)
Poltavka	60 (18/30)	56.3 (324/576)	83.9 (483/576)
Potapovka	75 (12/16)	67.7 (260/384)	87.2 (335/384)
Srubnaya	68.2 (88/129)	61.5 (1,732/2,816)	90 (2,536/2,816)

Table 8.16 Details of the Numbers of Teeth and Tooth Socket Positions by Age and Sex for the Adults of the Different Populations

	Khvalynsk		Yamnaya		Poltavka		Potapovka		Srubnaya	
	Male	Female	Male	Female	Male	Female	Male	Female	Male	Female
	Teeth/ Sockets	Teeth/ Sockets	Teeth/ Sockets	Teeth/ Sockets	Teeth/ Sockets	Teeth/ Sockets	Teeth/ Sockets	Teeth/ Sockets	Teeth/ Sockets	Teeth/ Sockets
18–35	265/313	28/44	25/29	22/31	117/159	27/32	137/164	22/28	497/625	470/663
35–50	49/62	0/0	104/122	18/17	112/155	29/32	27/32	25/32	364/565	258/347
50+	135/199	14/33	0/0	0/0	29/105	0/0	31/47	18/32	63/171	80/165
Adult	0/0	0/0	0/0	0/0	0/0	10/0	0/0	0/0	0/0	0/0
Total	*449/574*	*42/77*	*129/151*	*40/48*	*258/419*	*66/64*	*195/243*	*65/92*	*924/1361*	*808/1175*

Table 8.17 Details of the Frequencies (Percentage) of Nonadults with Dentitions and Numbers of Teeth and Sockets by Culture

Culture	Percentage (No./Total No.)		
	Individuals with Dentitions	Deciduous Teeth	Permanent Teeth
Khvalynsk	100 (2/2)	100 (12/12)	87.5 (35/40)
Yamnaya	100 (2/2)	18.8 (3/16)	100 (28/28)
Poltavka	57.1 (4/7)	15.6 (5/32)	65.7 (44/67)
Potapovka	0 (0/3)	0 (0/0)	0 (0/0)
Srubnaya	50.8 (32/63)	42.2 (159/377)	64 (278/434)

Caries

Dental caries arise as a consequence of the destruction of the enamel, dentine, and cement of a tooth as a result of acid production by the bacteria that live in dental plaque. The end result of the destructive action of the bacteria is the development of a cavity in the crown or root surface of the tooth (Hillson 1996:269). The cariogenic qualities of a particular diet are determined by the proportion of readily metabolized carbohydrates it contains. Other variables involved in dietary cariogenicity include the textures of the foods and the population's daily pattern of consumption. Clinical studies have indicated that the most cariogenic foodstuffs are those that are sticky in texture, contain high levels of simple sugars, and are consumed frequently throughout the day. The presence of foods that have a rough texture or the existence of abrasive particles in the diet does not readily promote the development of caries since natural oral cleaning is stimulated (Powell 1985:314).

Caries were notably rare among all of the Volga populations, occurring with a frequency of 0.2 percent (1/491) for the Khvalynsk group and 0.2 percent (3/1732) for the Srubnaya population, while the lesions were absent among the adult teeth of all other cultures. The only nonadult to display caries was a member of the Srubnaya population (Table 8.18).

Cereal grains and starchy tubers can be cariogenic when consumed in large quantities, especially if prepared in soft, sticky porridge-like forms. Natural sugars present in honey, sugarcane, fruit, and some vegetables are, however, also cariogenic (Powell 1985:320). Agriculturists generally display greater frequencies of carious teeth than nonagriculturists or those relying on mixed economies (Leigh 1925:195). In prehistoric South Asia, hunter-gather populations displayed carious teeth with a frequency of 0 percent to 5.3 percent (mean = 1.3 percent), individuals practicing a mixed economy had a frequency of 0.4 percent to 10.3 percent (mean = 4.8 percent), and agricultural populations had a frequency of 2.3 percent to 26.9 percent (mean = 10.4 percent) (Lukacs 1989:281). A large number of other studies have agreed that the frequencies of caries increased as agriculture was adopted. Perzigian et al.

(1984:355–356) found that the frequency of carious teeth in hunter-gatherer populations of the Ohio River valley in North America was 2.5 percent, for example, while the frequencies of carious teeth in the same region's early agricultural groups were approximately 12.5 percent and 24.8 percent for populations of developed agriculturists. In a study of a series of European populations, Meiklejohn et al. (1984:85) found that carious teeth occurred with a frequency of 1.9 percent among Mesolithic hunter-gatherer populations and 4.2 percent among Neolithic agriculturists. In India, Iron Age sites revealed a frequency of 2.5 to 7.7 percent in a period thought to be characterized by a mixed economy of hunting-gathering and agriculture (Lukacs 1989:279–280). Similarly, in two Iron Age semi-nomadic pastoralist populations from Aymyrlyg, South Siberia, carious teeth occurred with a frequency of 6.4 percent among the Uyuk culture adult dentitions and 5.5 percent among the Shurmak culture adults (Murphy 1998:498; Murphy et al. 2013:2551). These frequencies were similar to the range expected for a mixed economy of agriculture and pastoralism. Interestingly, a small group of Hsiung-nu individuals from the cemetery of Naima Tolgoy, Mongolia, displayed no caries, a result said to be expected because the diet of nomads would not have been cariogenic (Regöly-Mérei 1967:407). In his study of Mesolithic (hunter-gatherer-fisher economy) and Neolithic (hunter-gatherer-fisher-pastoralist economy) Ukrainian populations, Lillie (1996:138) reported that caries were universally absent, similar to the Volga populations. The very low frequency rates for all Volga populations across the different periods are not indicative of populations that practiced crop-based agriculture (Figure 8.4).

Abscesses

The development of infection as a consequence of dental abscesses was one of the main potential causes of death among past societies (Rugg-Gunn 1993:1). Dental caries, deposits of calculus, extensive attrition, and periodontal disease can all predispose to the development of dental abscesses (Roberts and Manchester 2005:70). Since the dentitions had not been subject to radiographic analysis, dental abscesses were clas-

Table 8.18 Details of the Caries Apparent in the Population Groups

Culture	Site	Context	Age, y	Sex	Tooth	Size	Position
Khvalynsk	Khvalynsk	G21	50+	M	right mandibular second molar	Medium	Buccal
Srubnaya	Nizhny Orleansky I	K13, G1	35–50	M	right mandibular canine	Medium	Buccal
Srubnaya	Rozhdestvenno I	K4, G4, Sk2	15–17	F	left mandibular second premolar	Small	Distal
Srubnaya	Spiridonovka II	K14, G4	50+	F	left maxillary first premolar	Medium	Mesial
Srubnaya	Spiridonovka IV	K1, G8	35–50	M	right mandibular first molar	Medium	Distal

Note: F = female; G = grave; K = kurgan; M = male; Sk = skeleton.

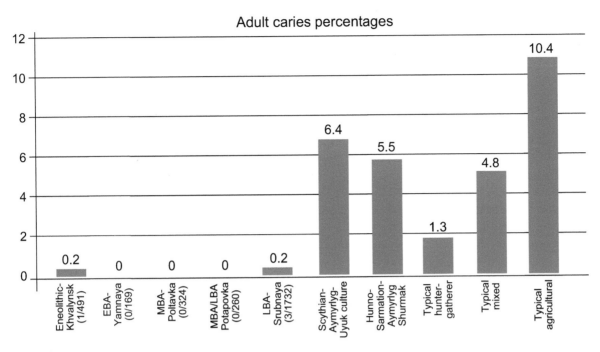

Figure 8.4 Caries prevalences (percentage) among the adult teeth of the Volga populations. Also included in the graph are the prevalences for two Iron Age populations from Aymyrlyg, South Siberia (Murphy: 1998 498; Murphy et al. 2013:2551), and mean typical caries frequencies for groups practicing hunter-gatherer, mixed, or agricultural economies (cf. Lukacs 1989:281).

sified as present only when the abscess fistula had produced a clearly discernible cavity in the alveolar bone, nasal cavity, or maxillary sinus. The size of each abscess cavity was categorized as small (0–3 mm), medium (3–5 mm), or large (5+ mm). Details of the prevalences of abscesses apparent in the different adult population groups are presented in Table 8.19.

The middle Volga populations do not appear to have been particularly susceptible to the development of dental abscesses. The overall prevalences ranged from 0.5 percent (Yamnaya) to 3.3 percent (Potapovka). In general, the prevalences were markedly similar, with the only exception being the value of 3.3 percent attained for the Potapovka group. This figure appears to be notably higher than those of earlier or later groups, and it is possible that individuals in this group

Table 8.19 Details of the Adult Prevalences (Percentage) of Abscesses by Tooth Socket Position for Each Population Group

Culture	Percentage (No./Total No.)		
	Overall	Male	Female
Khvalynsk	1.1 (7/651)	0.9 (5/574)	2.6 (2/77)
Yamnaya	0.5 (1/199)	0.7 (1/151)	0 (0/48)
Poltavka	0.8 (4/483)	1 (4/419)	0 (0/64)
Potapovka	3.3 (11/335)	4.1 (10/243)	1.1 (1/92)
Srubnaya	0.9 (24/2,536)	1.4 (19/1,361)	0.4 (5/1,175)

were more susceptible to the development of abscesses. Dental abscesses occurred among Iron Age semi-nomadic adult individuals recovered from Aymyrlyg, South Siberia, with a frequency of 4.7 percent for the Uyuk culture group and 4.6 percent among the Shurmak culture population (Murphy 1998:501; Murphy et al. 2013:2551). It is difficult to reliably study the prevalence of abscesses over time by sex due to the small sample sizes. The results for the large Srubnaya corpus, however, would tend to suggest that males in this group were significantly more susceptible to the development of abscesses than females ($\chi^2 = 6.336$; $p = 0.012$; $df = 1$).

Periodontal Disease

Periodontal disease generally develops as a consequence of the bacteria contained in dental plaque-producing substances, such as enzymes, which inappropriately trigger an immune response. Initially, the periodontal disease involves the gingivae only and is referred to as gingivitis, but this can eventually develop into periodontitis in which the bone becomes involved (Hillson 1996:262). Clinical studies have indicated that males are generally more frequently affected by the disease than females, but this may be related to habits of oral hygiene rather than biological factors (Hillson 1986:312). In general, however, periodontal disease is multifactorial in origin and related to genetic predisposition, environment, diet, and oral hygiene

(Hillson 1996:269). The identification of periodontal disease in archaeological skeletal remains is problematic, since the distance between the cemento-enamel junction and the alveolar crest increases in periodontal disease but can also increase as a result of the teeth continuously erupting to compensate for extensive attrition (Hillson 1986:312). Bearing these limitations in mind, the system for recording the extent of resorption of the alveolar bone devised by Brothwell (1981:155) was followed during the current analysis (Table 8.20).

Periodontal disease, predominantly of slight severity, appears to have been common in the middle Volga region, with the adult frequencies ranging from 50 percent for the Potapovka population to 87 percent for the Khvalynsk group. It is possible that the preponderance of younger adults in the Potapovka group has contributed to the relatively low level of periodontal disease in this group. Murphy (1998:501) found that periodontal disease occurred in 74 percent of Uyuk culture adult individuals and 77.5 percent of Shurmak culture adults from the Siberian Iron Age site of Aymyrlyg. As stated before, it is difficult to compare the frequencies of affected males and females in each population group due to the small sample sizes. The results for the substantial Srubnaya group, however, would tend to suggest that males were statistically more susceptible to the development of periodontal disease than females ($\chi^2 = 7.271$; $p = 0.007$; $df = 1$).

Calculus

The bacteria that live on the surfaces of teeth are embedded into a matrix, partly developed by the bacteria themselves and partly formed from the proteins that occur in saliva. Together, the matrix and the bacterial community form dental plaque (Hillson 1986:284). Calculus may be defined as mineralized plaque that forms at the base of a living deposit of plaque. The mineral that forms calculus is derived from saliva, and consequently the surfaces of the teeth located nearest the salivary glands are most susceptible to plaque

formation (Hillson 1996:255). Calculus formation arises as a consequence of the factors that are responsible for the accumulation of plaque, including poor standards of oral hygiene and high levels of carbohydrate and/or protein consumption, which result in the creation of an alkaline oral environment (Hillson 1996:259; Roberts and Manchester 2005:71). Details of the prevalence of calculus deposits for the adult teeth of each group are provided in Table 8.21.

Calculus occurred in relatively high frequencies among the Volga adult teeth of all periods, with a range of 74.5 percent in the Khvalynsk population to 87 percent for Poltavka. The prevalence among nonadults was similar to adults (Table 8.22).

No statistically significant differences were observed in the levels of calculus on the teeth of Srubnaya males and females ($\chi^2 = 0.991$; $p = 0.319$; $df = 1$). In the absence of caries, the high levels of calculus among the Volga populations would tend to suggest that all of the groups consumed high levels of protein (cf. Roberts and Manchester 2005:71).

Similarly, deposits of calculus were evident in 77.4 percent of Uyuk culture adult teeth and 78.2 percent of Shurmak culture adult teeth from the Siberian Iron Age site of Aymyrlyg (Murphy 1998:501; Murphy et al. 2013:2551). Lillie (1996:Table 3) reported a prevalence of 36.5 percent (299/820) for Ukrainian Mesolithic populations and 62.5 percent (915/1464) for Ukrainian Neolithic groups.

Table 8.21 Details of the Prevalences (Percentage) of Calculus Deposits by Teeth for Each Adult Population Group

Culture	Percentage (No./Total No.)		
	Overall	Male	Female
Khvalynsk	74.5 (366/491)	75.5 (339/449)	64.3 (27/42)
Yamnaya	82.8 (140/169)	79.1 (102/129)	95 (38/40)
Poltavka	87 (282/324)	84.5 (218/258)	97 (64/66)
Potapovka	85.4 (222/260)	89.2 (174/195)	73.8 (48/65)
Srubnaya	77.3 (1,339/1,732)	78.2 (723/924)	76.2 (616/808)

Table 8.20 Details of the Prevalences (Percentage) of Periodontal Disease by Individual in Each Adult Population Group

Culture	Percentage (No./Total No.)		
	Overall	Males	Females
Khvalynsk	87 (20/23)	89.5 (17/19)	75 (3/4)
Yamnaya	75 (6/8)	83.3 (5/6)	50 (1/2)
Poltavka	76.5 (13/17)	80 (12/15)	50 (1/2)
Potapovka	50 (6/12)	55.6 (5/9)	66.7 (2/3)
Srubnaya	70.1 (61/87)	82.6 (38/46)	56.1 (23/41)

Table 8.22 Details of the Prevalences (Percentage) of Calculus Deposits by Teeth for Each Nonadult Population Group

Culture	Percentage (No./Total No.)	
	Deciduous Teeth	Permanent Teeth
Khvalynsk	50 (6/12)	82.8 (29/35)
Yamnaya	0 (0/3)	100 (28/28)
Poltavka	60 (3/5)	38.6 (17/44)
Potapovka	0 (0/0)	0 (0/0)
Srubnaya	71.1 (113/159)	59 (164/278)

Calculus deposits for both adults and nonadults were invariably of slight or medium severity (cf. Brothwell 1981:155). Details of the individuals to display heavy levels of calculus deposition on one or more teeth are presented in Table 8.23. The prevalence of heavy deposits of calculus by tooth over time was 0 percent for the Khvalynsk and Yamnaya cultures, 0.9 percent (3/324) for the Poltavka individuals, 1.2 percent (3/260) for the Potapovka corpus, and 0.8 percent (13/1732) for the Srubnaya population. It can generally be concluded that, while calculus had a frequent occurrence among all the populations, usually the

deposits were not heavy in nature. Pathological reasons can be found to account for the presence of the heavy deposits for 9 of the 14 (64.3 percent) affected individuals, thereby further supporting this assertion. None of the nonadult teeth displayed heavy deposits of calculus, and in the majority of cases, their teeth displayed only flecks or slight deposits (77.4 percent; 24/31).

Antemortem Tooth Loss
Antemortem tooth loss generally arises as a consequence of periodontal disease—as the loss of alveolar bone and tissue

Table 8.23 Details of Individuals with Heavy Deposits of Calculus on One or More Teeth

Culture	Site	Context	Age, y	Sex	Teeth	Cause
Poltavka	Lopatino I	K30, G2	35–50	M	maxillary second molars	-
Poltavka	Lopatino I	K33	18–35	M	left maxillary third molar	Malalignment of tooth
Potapovka	Grachevka II	K3, G9a	50+	F	maxillary third molars; right mandibular second molar	-
Potapovka	Utyevka VI	K6, G6	18–35	M	left mandibular third molar	-
Srubnaya	Barinovka I	K3, G7	35–50	F	left maxillary second molar	AM loss of left maxillary third molar and left mandibular second and third molars; left maxillary first molar - abscesses
Srubnaya	Krasnosamarskoe IV	K1, G2	35–50	M	left maxillary second and third molars; left mandibular third molar	-
Srubnaya	Nizhny Orleansky I	K13, G1	35–50	M	left mandibular third molar	AM loss of left maxillary third molar
Srubnaya	Poplavskoe	Sk2	50+	M	left maxillary third molar	Right maxillary first molar and right mandibular second premolar and first molar - abscesses
Srubnaya	Spiridonovka II	K14, G4	50+	F	left mandibular second molar	AM loss of left maxillary second premolar, first molar and second molar, and left mandibular second premolar; left maxillary first premolar - caries
Srubnaya	Spiridonovka II	K14, G5	35–50	M	left mandibular third molar	AM loss of left mandibular second molar
Srubnaya	Spiridonovka IV	K1, G8	35–50	M	left mandibular second premolar	AM loss of left maxillary third molar and left mandibular third molar
Srubnaya	Spiridonovka IV	K2, G1a	35–50	F	left maxillary second molar	-
Srubnaya	Studenzy I	K2, G4	35–50	F	left mandibular first premolar	AM loss of left mandibular second premolar
Srubnaya	Svezhensky	G71b	35–50	M	right maxillary third molar left maxillary third molar	AM loss of right mandibular second and third molars and abscess AM loss of left mandibular second and third molars; left mandibular second molar - abscess

Note: F = female; G = grave; K = kurgan; M = male; Sk = skeleton; AMTL = antemortem tooth loss.

Table 8.24 Details of the Adult Prevalences (Percentage) of Antemortem Tooth Loss by Tooth Socket Position for Each Population Group

	Percentage (No./Total No.)		
Culture	Overall	Male	Female
Khvalynsk	4 (26/651)	2.4 (14/574)	15.6 (12/77)
Yamnaya	0.5 (1/199)	0.7 (1/151)	0 (0/48)
Poltavka	12.8 (62/483)	14.6 (61/419)	1.6 (1/64)
Potapovka	4.5 (15/335)	0.4 (1/243)	15.2 (14/92)
Srubnaya	5.2 (131/2,536)	6.2 (84/1,361)	4 (47/1,175)

surrounding the tooth increases, the tooth becomes loosened and is eventually avulsed (Hillson 1986:309). Individuals with extensive antemortem tooth loss would have been at a disadvantage relative to those with more complete dentitions, since it would have been more difficult for edentulous, or near-edentulous, individuals to chew coarser foodstuffs. In addition, clinical studies have indicated that tooth loss predisposes some individuals to death from choking on inadequately masticated pieces of food (Rugg-Gunn 1993:325). Details of the prevalence of antemortem tooth loss for the adults of each group are provided in Table 8.24.

Antemortem tooth loss ranged in frequency from 0.5 percent for the Yamnaya group to 12.8 percent for Poltavka. The rates were similar for the Khvalynsk (4 percent), Potapovka (4.5 percent), and Srubnaya (5.2 percent) cultures. Rates were notably higher for the Poltavka corpus, but this group contained a number of older adult males who were almost edentulous. Antemortem loss was associated with 8.9 percent of Uyuk culture adult tooth positions and 7.9 percent among their Shurmak culture counterparts at the Iron Age cemetery of Aymyrlyg, South Siberia (Murphy 1998:501; Murphy et al. 2013:2551). The results for the large Srubnaya corpus would tend to suggest that males were statistically more susceptible to antemortem tooth loss than females ($\chi^2 = 6.072$; $p = 0.014$; $df = 1$).

Table 8.25 Details of the Frequencies (Percentage) of Adult Teeth with Evidence of Secondary Dentine or Pulp Cavity Exposure from the Different Periods

	Percentage (No./Total No.)		
Culture	Overall	Male	Female
Khvalynsk	16.7 (82/491)	15.6 (70/449)	28.6 (12/42)
Yamnaya	4.7 (8/169)	6.2 (8/129)	0 (0/40)
Poltavka	26.2 (85/324)	28.7 (74/258)	16.7 (11/66)
Potapovka	25 (65/260)	20.5 (40/195)	38.5 (25/65)
Srubnaya	11 (190/1732)	14.9 (138/924)	6.4 (52/808)

Extensive Attrition

Dental attrition generally arises as a result of neighboring, or opposing, teeth coming into contact with one another, and wear facets may develop on the occlusal surfaces or at points of contact between the teeth (Hillson 1996:231). Attrition of the occlusal surfaces may initially destroy the enamel and expose the underlying dentine, and further attrition may then expose the pulp cavity (Ortner 2003:604). The study of tooth attrition can reveal a considerable amount of information on the use of teeth as tools in craftworking, diet, and food preparation techniques (Molnar 1972:511). Details of the frequencies of adult teeth with evidence of secondary dentine or pulp cavity exposure (classed as extensive attrition) from the different periods are provided in Table 8.25.

The frequencies of adult teeth with extensive attrition across the different periods ranged from 4.7 percent for Yamnaya to 26.2 percent for Poltavka. Adults appear to have been most susceptible to extensive attrition during the Poltavka and Potapovka periods. Extensive tooth attrition was associated with 13.8 percent of Uyuk culture adult teeth and 11.2 percent of Shurmak culture teeth at the Iron Age cemetery of Aymyrlyg, comparable to the Srubnaya frequency in the middle Volga (Murphy 1998:499: Murphy et al. 2013:2551). The results for the large Srubnaya corpus would tend to suggest that males were statistically more susceptible to extensive tooth attrition than females ($\chi^2 = 31.884$; $p = 0.000$; $df = 1$). All teeth in the dental arc for all populations appear to have been susceptible to the development of extensive attrition, and it is thought that it was probably mostly related to diet as opposed to the use of teeth as tools.

Correlations between dental attrition, diet, and food preparation techniques have been observed in prehistoric population groups throughout the world (Larsen 1997:248). The occurrence of heavy wear on both deciduous and permanent teeth has often been attributed to the use of stone grinders in the preparation of cereal grains into coarse flour (Powell 1985:309), while research on early modern and modern Inuit populations has attributed the occurrence of heavy wear to occupational activities, including hide processing, and the consumption of large quantities of frozen meat (Powell 1985:326). Larsen (1997:250–251) reported that hunter-gatherers in prehistoric North America displayed more extensive wear patterns than later agriculturalists in the same region. The decrease in wear was explained by the shift in reliance from nondomesticated to domesticated plants or the more intensified use of domesticated plants, which was associated with changes in food-processing techniques. A similar difference has also been reported for hunter-gatherer and agricultural populations in Europe. It has also been suggested that the most important etiological factor relating to dental wear is not the occurrence of a coarse gritty diet but rather the need to chew long and strongly on tough food (Wells 1975:741). Consequently, although fewer abrasive components are contained in meat relative to vegetable foods (Hillson 1979:156), it is possible that tough meat, possibly dried, has the potential to result in the development of extensive dental attrition.

Activity Patterns

Paleopathological lesions can provide insights concerning lifestyles and day-to-day activities. These can occur as skeletal trauma, thought to be more characteristic of everyday accidents than deliberate violence, and as traits associated with joint disease.

Non-Violence-Related Trauma

Fractures of the Appendicular Skeleton

Crude prevalence rates of adults with one or more fractured appendicular bones are provided in Table 8.26. The frequencies of individuals who displayed one or more fractured appendicular bones ranged from 4.6

Table 8.26 Crude Prevalence Rates (Percentage) of Non-Violence-Related Fractures Based on the Numbers of Individuals Affected in Each Population Group

Culture	Percentage (No./Total No.)		
	Adult	Male	Female
Yamnaya	6.3 (1/16)	8.3 (1/12)	0 (0/4)
Poltavka	14.7 (5/34)	17.2 (5/29)	0 (0/5)
Potapovka	7.1 (1/14)	9.1 (1/11)	0 (0/3)
Srubnaya	4.6 (6/129)	4.5 (3/67)	4.9 (3/61)

Note: It was not possible to determine sex for one of the Srubnaya adults or to examine the Khvalynsk group for trauma.

percent (6/129) for the Srubnaya adults to 14.7 percent (5/34) for the Poltavka group. The high prevalence for the Poltavka group is of interest, although it is difficult to be certain if this is a genuine trend or simply an artifact of the relatively small sample size. Although the numbers are small, it is clear that for the Yamnaya to Potapovka populations, males were more susceptible to non-violence-related appendicular fractures than females. The

Table 8.27 Details of the Fractures of the Appendicular Skeleton Apparent in the Population Groups

Culture	Site	Context	Age, y	Sex	Bone	Type	Healing	Cause
Yamnaya	Lopatino I	K29, G1	35–50	M	R radius distal third	Simple oblique	Advanced	Fall on outstretched hand/direct blow
Poltavka	Grachevka	K1, G2	50+	M	L radius proximal third	Simple oblique	Advanced	Fall on outstretched hand/direct blow
Poltavka	Kalinovka	K1, G3	35–50	M	Tibia shaft	Simple oblique	Early-mid	
					R fourth MT distal third			
Poltavka	Lopatino I	K1, G1	18–35	M	L ulna proximal third	Simple oblique	Advanced	Fall on outstretched hand
Poltavka	Tryasinovka	K2, G3	50+	M	R tibia distal third	Simple oblique	Advanced	
Potapovka	Grachevka II	K2, G1	35–50	M	Proximal hand phalanx	Simple oblique	Advanced	
Potapovka	Utyevka II		18–35	M	L radius and ulna distal thirds	Simple oblique	Advanced	Fall on outstretched hand
Srubnaya	Barinovka I	K1, G2b	35–50	M	L first proximal foot phalanx distal	Simple oblique	Early	
Srubnaya	Nizhny Orleansky IV	K1, G2	50+	M	R tibia distal end	Compression	Advanced	
Srubnaya	Spiridonovka II	K11, G6	18–35	F	R femur shaft	Possible hairline	Advanced	
Srubnaya	Spiridonovka IV	K1, G10	35–50	F	L radius distal third	Simple oblique	Advanced	Fall on outstretched hand
Srubnaya	Spiridonovka IV	K2, G12	50+	M	R radius distal third	Simple oblique	Advanced	Fall on outstretched hand
Srubnaya	Uranbash	G88	18–35	F	R tibia midshaft	Simple oblique	Advanced	

Note: F = female; G = grave; K = kurgan; L = left; M = male; R = right; MT = metatarsal.

Table 8.28 Prevalence (Percentage) of the Different Fractured Long Bones Based on the Numbers of Right and Left Bones for Each Population Group

	Percentage (No./Total No.)			
	Yamnaya	Poltavka	Potapovka	Srubnaya
Radius (shaft)	4.3 (1/23)	2.6 (1/38)	4.8 (1/21)	1.4 (2/142)
Ulna (shaft)	(0/19)	2.8 (1/36)	5 (1/20)	(0/143)
Femur (shaft)	(0/20)	(0/41)	(0/25)	0.6 (1/175)
Tibia (shaft)	(0/23)	5.1 (2/39)	(0/23)	0.6 (1/174)
Tibia (distal end)	(0/20)	(0/39)	(0/22)	0.6 (1/164)

trend differed for the Srubnaya group, in which males (4.5 percent) and females (4.9 percent) appear to have been equally susceptible to such injuries.

Details of the fractured appendicular bones present in the populations are provided in Table 8.27. Most of the 13 affected individuals were male (76.9 percent; 10/13). The prevalence rate of each fractured long bone by population is provided in Table 8.28.

Again, the small sample sizes make it difficult to identify genuine trends, but the radius seems to have been the bone most susceptible to fracture in the Yamnaya (4.3 percent) and Srubnaya (1.4 percent) groups, while the ulna and radius were almost equally likely to be fractured in the Potapovka population. The trend was somewhat different for the Poltavka group (5.1 percent), in which the tibia was most susceptible to fracture.

Among all of the populations, the nature of the fractures to the forearm bones was mostly characteristic of falls on the outstretched hand, although in a number of cases, it was not possible to exclude the possibility that they had been caused by a direct blow to the arm (Hamblen and Simpson 2007:172; Resnick and Goergen 1995:2734). The 18- to 35-year-old Poltavka male recovered from the Lopatino I cemetery (K1, G1) also displayed myositis ossificans traumatica on his left femur (see below), which would tend to suggest that his forearm fracture had been attained a result of a fall rather than a direct blow.

A 50+-year-old Poltavka male (Tryasinovka, K2, G3) displayed a longstanding simple, oblique fracture to the distal end of his right tibia. A 35- to 50-year-old Poltavka male (Kalinovka, K1, G3) displayed a simple oblique fracture in the early to mid-stages of healing in a shaft fragment of one of his tibiae. The individual's right fourth metatarsal also appeared to have been fractured at the distal third of its shaft. An 18- to 35-year-old Srubnaya female (Uranbash, G88) displayed a long-standing simple, oblique fracture at the midshaft of her right tibia. There was only 50 percent apposition of the fracture parts, and the proximal

half was displaced anteriorly and slight medially. In addition, approximately 15 mm of overlap of fracture parts was apparent, and it is probable that the bone would have been notably shorter than its left counterpart.

In all three cases of fractured tibiae, the corresponding fibulae were not present, so it was not possible to know if the injury had affected only the tibia or both lower leg bones, although it is known that the latter injury is more common among modern populations (Hamblen and Simpson 2007:281). Fractures of the tibia and/or fibula shafts generally arise as a result of a direct blow to the leg, such as a kick (Hughes 1986:130, 133). Perhaps the tibia shaft injuries sustained by the two Poltavka individuals had been due to kicks from livestock, although there are, of course, many other possible ways that the bones could have been injured. A 50+-year-old Srubnaya male (Nizhny Orleansky IV, K1, G2) displayed a long-standing compression fracture of his right distal tibia. The fracture appears to have affected the posterolateral aspect of the articular surface where a series of small transverse fracture lines were apparent. The injury seems to have resulted in disruption to the associated soft tissue, and bone growths were evident in the region immediately superior to the fracture lines and on the posterior margin of the tibiofibular notch. This type of injury can be caused by a fall from a height (Hamblen and Simpson 2007:292). Among the Srubnaya population, an 18- to 35-year-old female

Table 8.29 Frequencies (Percentage) of Fractured Appendicular Bones as a Proportion of the Total Number of Adult Long Bones across the Different Time Periods

	Percentage (No./Total No.)		
Culture	Overall	Male	Female
Yamnaya	0.8 (1/128)	1.2 (1/82)	0 (0/46)
Poltavka	1.8 (4/228)	2.3 (4/172)	0 (0/56)
Potapovka	0.8 (1/125)	1.1 (1/91)	0 (0/34)
Srubnaya	0.5 (5/926)	0.4 (2/475)	0.7 (3/451)

(K11 G6), recovered from the Spiridonovka II cemetery, displayed evidence for a possible long-standing hairline fracture at the proximal end of her right femur.

Details of the frequencies of fractured appendicular bones, in terms of the overall numbers of long bones available for each period, are provided in Table 8.29. The frequencies of fractured appendicular bones as a proportion of the total numbers of adult long bones were notably low, ranging from 0.5 percent (5/926) for the Srubnaya group to 1.8 percent (4/228) for the Poltavka population. It is interesting that the Poltavka population group displayed the greatest prevalence of fractured appendicular bones as well as the highest prevalence of adults with appendicular fractures compared to the other populations. This finding may indicate that the Poltavka adults were genuinely more susceptible to the occurrence of appendicular fractures relative to the other groups. For the substantial Srubnaya corpus, it is clear that males (0.4 percent) and females (0.7 percent) were almost equally susceptible to non-violence-related fractures. Murphy (2003a:96) observed that fractures were present in 0.9 percent of all Uyuk culture and 0.8 percent of all Shurmak culture adult long bones from Iron Age Aymyrlyg, South Siberia. A survey of six British Medieval sites indicated that fracture prevalences ranged from 0.3 percent to 6.1 percent. The 6.1 percent frequency observed in one of these samples was notably higher than the prevalences observed in the other studies, and it has been suggested that the results reflect a small sample size (Roberts and Manchester 2005:99). The prevalences of fractures among the Volga populations, therefore, are well within the expected range for an archaeological population.

A small number of individuals displayed hand or foot fractures. Skeleton K1, G3, the 35- to 50-year-old Poltavka male recovered from the Kalinovka burial site, with a fractured tibia (see above) also had a fracture of the distal third of the shaft of the right fourth metatarsal. A 35- to 50-year-old male (Grachevka II, K2, G1) also recovered from the Poltavka group displayed a long-standing, simple, oblique fracture at the distal end of one of his proximal hand phalanges. A 35- to 50-year-old Srubnaya male (Barinovka, K1, G2b) displayed a simple oblique fracture at the distal end of his left first proximal foot phalanx that was in the early stages of healing.

Fractures of the Axial Skeleton
Fractures of the ribs and vertebrae occurred only in the Srubnaya population. Rib fractures arose among the Srubnaya adults with a prevalence of 1 percent (2/197). Most fractures of the ribs occur as a result of direct injury, such as a blow to the chest or a fall against a hard object (Hamblen and Simpson 2007:119). Skeleton K5, G2, an

18- to 35-year-old female recovered from the Kinel' I burial ground, displayed two fractured ribs. The left tenth and eleventh ribs displayed simple transverse fractures that occurred at the same regions of the midshafts and had probably been caused during a single incident. Both fractures were surrounded by extensive callus formation, suggesting they were in the early to mid-stages of healing. No other examples of trauma were apparent in the remains of the individual, making it likely that she had suffered from a direct blow or fall against a hard object.

Two Srubnaya adults displayed compression fractures of their thoracic or lumbar vertebral bodies. Most fractures of the vertebral bodies of the thoracic or lumbar vertebrae are caused by vertical forces acting through the long axis of the spinal column. The forces can act from above, as in situations where heavy weights fall on top of the individual, or from below as a result of a heavy fall on the feet or the buttocks (Hamblen and Simpson 2007:109). A compression fracture of the right side of TV12 was apparent in Skeleton K3, G17, a 35- to 50-year-old male, recovered from the Krasnosamarskoe IV burial ground. The individual also displayed osteochondritis dissecans (see below), which may be a further indicator of a heavy physical lifestyle. A compression fracture was also evidence in the LV5 of Skeleton K1, G22, a 35- to 50-year-old female, retrieved from the Spiridonovka IV cemetery. Spondylolysis was apparent in the LV4 (see below) of the individual, which may indicate that she had engaged in heavy physical activities. A total of 148 adult cervical, thoracic, and lumbar vertebrae were examined for compression fractures, 1.4 percent (2/148) of which displayed the injuries. Of the thoracic vertebrae examined, 0.6 percent (1/163) displayed the lesions, and of the lumbar vertebrae, 0.7 percent (1/143).

Skeleton K11, G13, an 18- to 35-year-old Srubnaya female recovered from the Spiridonovka II cemetery, displayed a hyperextension fracture at the anterior aspect of the superior body surface of LV4. An area of bone measuring 25.6 mm mediolaterally by 10 mm superoinferiorly had chipped off the superior surface to expose the spongy bone beneath. Marginal osteophytes were associated with the affected area.

Spondylolysis
Spondylolysis is a vertebral defect in which a lack of bony continuity occurs at the pars interarticularis, and the defective area is bridged by fibrous tissue (Adams and Hamblen 1990:190). The lesion occurs in adults of modern populations with a frequency of 5 to 6 percent (Schmorl and Junghanns 1971:88), although certain ethnic groups, such as the Japanese and Inuit, have a higher incidence of the defect. Up to 50 percent of Inuit may display spondylolysis,

a finding that has been explained as a consequence of their difficult and strenuous lifestyle (Merbs and Wilson 1960:160). The defect occurs with higher frequency among athletes, especially those involved in gymnastics, diving, weightlifting, pole vaulting, and American football, and the majority of cases in modern populations occur in males (Resnick et al. 1995:2597).

The etiology of spondylolysis is uncertain, with genetic or traumatic causes both considered as possible etiologies. It is generally accepted, however, that it is an acquired traumatic lesion that would have occurred at some stage between infancy and young adulthood. It has been suggested that it may arise as a result of a fatigue fracture as a consequence of repeated trauma, possibly due to bending and lifting in an upright position. An acute fracture at the pars interarticularis can also reflect a single incident of trauma, probably accounting for a proportion of the defects (Roberts and Manchester 2005:106). It is likely that, to a certain extent, genetic factors are also involved, as 25 percent of individuals in some families display the lesion. The defect may be asymptomatic, but lumbar back pain, tenderness, gait abnormality, and neurologic problems can occur (Resnick et al. 1995:2599). Details of the individuals with spondylolysis among the Volga populations are provided in Table 8.30.

The prevalence of spondylolysis ranged from 3.4 percent for Srubnaya LV4s to 11.1 percent for Srubnaya LV5s. Of the seven affected individuals four were female. Among the Srubnaya population the prevalence of spondylolysis amongst females was 11.8 percent (2/17) for LV5, while the frequency of occurrence in the LV5s of males was 10.5 percent (2/19). These results would tend to suggest that males and females were practically equally susceptible to the development of spondylolysis in Srubnaya times. Murphy (2003a:96), reported that the injury occurred with a frequency of 13 percent among Uyuk culture lumbar

spines and 5 percent among Shurmak culture lumbar spines at Aymyrlyg, South Siberia. In both populations females were more frequently affected than males. The occurrence of spondylolysis in a Poltavka female and three Srubnaya females suggests that both males and females in these cultures engaged in heavy physical activities which caused strain to the lower back.

Myositis Ossificans Traumatica
Myositis ossificans traumatica generally occurs as a sequela to trauma, and the sites most commonly affected are those most susceptible to trauma including the elbow, the thigh and the buttocks. Post-traumatic ossification of soft tissues generally arises after an incident of severe trauma, but it is also known to occur as a result of repetitive incidents of minor trauma which can be occupationally induced (Resnick and Niwayama 1995c:4577). Details of the cases of myositis ossificans traumatica among the Volga populations are provided in Table 8.31. The prevalence of the lesions by bone was generally low, ranging from 0.6 percent for Srubnaya proximal femora to 7.7 percent for Potapovka distal fibulae. Details of the frequencies of myositis ossificans traumatica, in terms of the overall numbers of long bones that were available for each period, are provided in Table 8.32.

Myositis ossificans traumatica occurred among the Volga populations at a low frequency, ranging from 0.1 percent for the Srubnaya group to 1.8 percent for Poltavka. The elevated Poltavka frequency repeats the pattern for fractures of the appendicular skeleton discussed earlier and would appear to confirm that the Poltavka adults were most susceptible to everyday injuries. This finding may suggest that the nature of their lifestyle made them more accident prone than individuals from the other periods, particularly Srubnaya times. In all populations, only males displayed myositis ossificans traumatica.

Table 8.30 Details of Spondylolysis in the Populations

Culture	Site	Context	Sex	Age, y	Vertebra	R	L	Other Trauma/ Vertebral DJD	Prevalence by Bone, Percentage (No./Total No.)
Yamnaya	Kutuluk I	K1, G1	M	18–35	LV5	+	+	o	10 (1/10)
Poltavka	Kalinovka	K1, G6	F	35–50	LV5	+	+	+	7.7 (1/13)
Srubnaya	Chisty Yar I	K2, G10	F	35–50	LV5	+	+	o	11.1 (4/36)
Srubnaya	Krasnosamarskoe IV	K3, G1	F	18–35	LV5	+	+	+	11.1 (4/36)
Srubnaya	Nizhny Orleansky	K1, G3	M	35–50	LV5	+	+	o	11.1 (4/36)
Srubnaya	Spiridonovka II	K1, G6	M	35–50	LV5	o	+	o	11.1 (4/36)
Srubnaya	Spiridonovka IV	K1, G22	F	35–50	LV4	+	+	+	3.4 (1/29)

Note: F = female; G = grave; K = kurgan; M = male; LV = lumbar vertebrae; L = left; R = right; DJD = degenerative joint disease; + = present; o = absent.

Table 8.31 Details of the Cases of Myositis Ossificans Traumatica among the Volga Populations

Culture	Site	Context	Age, y	Sex	Bone	Muscles Affected	Prevalence by Bone Part, Percentage (No./Total No.)
Yamnaya	Lopatino I	K31	35–50	M	L ulna proximal	Flexor digitorum superficialis, pronator teres, brachialis, supinator muscles	5 (1/20)
Poltavka	Lopatino I	K1, G1	18–35	M	R femur shaft	Vastus lateralis	2.4 (1/41)
Poltavka	Nikolaevka III	K1, G3	35–50	M	L femur distal	Tibial collateral ligament	2.6 (1/39)
Poltavka	Nizhny Orleansky I	K1, G4	35–50	M	R tibia and fibula proximal	Interosseous ligament	2.9 (1/35 tib); 3 (1/33 fib)
Potapovka	Potapovka I	K5, G3	35–50	M	R tibia and fibula distal	Tibial collateral ligament, interosseous ligament	4.5 (1/22 tib); 7.7 (1/13 fib)
Srubnaya	Barinovka I	K2, G15	35–50	M	R femur proximal	Iliofemoral ligament, gluteus minimus, vastus lateralis	0.6 (1/164)
Srubnaya	Spiridonovka IV	K2, G6	50+	M	L clavicle acromial	Trapezoid and conoid ligaments, deltoid	1.1 (1/93)

Note: Prevalence is calculated on right and left bones specific to the affected part. F = female; G = grave; K = kurgan; M = male; L = left; R = right.

Table 8.32 Frequencies (Percentage) of Myositis Ossificans Traumatica as a Proportion of the Total Number of Adult Long Bones across the Different Time Periods

Culture	Percentage (No./Total No.)		
	Overall	Male	Female
Yamnaya	0.8 (1/128)	1.2 (1/82)	0 (0/46)
Poltavka	1.8 (4/228)	1.7 (3/172)	0 (0/56)
Potapovka	1.6 (2/125)	1.1 (1/91)	0 (0/34)
Srubnaya	0.1 (1/926)	0.4 (2/475)	0 (0/451)

Ossified Hematomas

Muscle contusion can arise as a consequence of direct trauma made by a blunt implement, which may result in the rupture of capillaries and the occurrence of bleeding between the fibers of the damaged connective tissue. This type of injury is generally followed by edema and the development of an inflammatory mass (Resnick et al. 1995:2673), and the resultant soft tissue swelling may become replaced by a smooth bone swelling known as an ossified hematoma (Baker and Brothwell 1980:83).

Two Srubnaya adults and a Srubnaya nonadult displayed evidence of these injuries. Skeleton K1, G3, an 18- to 35-year-old male recovered from the Chisty Yar I burial ground, displayed an oval-shaped smooth bony nodule, which measured 12 mm anteroposteriorly by 5 mm mediolaterally, on the inferior margin of the mandibular

body in the region of the left second premolar and first molar. Skeleton K1, G7, an 18- to 35-year-old male retrieved from the Spiridonovka IV cemetery, displayed a smooth oval-shaped bony nodule, which measured 23.2 mm superoinferiorly by 4 mm anteroposteriorly, on the medial surface of the midshaft of the right tibia.

The injuries occurred on Srubnaya adult mandibles with a frequency of 1.3 percent (1/78) and on tibial midshafts at 0.6 percent (1/174). Skeleton K4, G4, Sk2, a 15- to 17-year-old possible female recovered from the Srubnaya Rozhdestvenno I burial ground, displayed a possible example of an ossified hematoma in the early stages of development. A smooth, raised area of bone was visible on the proximal third of the right tibia. The lesion was concentrated on the area immediately superior to the nutrient foramen on the lateral aspect of the posterior surface and was surrounded by finely pitted woven bone, which may indicate that it was still in the process of healing.

Os Acromiale

Os acromiale is an anomaly in which a persistent ossification center occurs at the most lateral part of the acromion of the scapula (McClure and Raney 1975:27). It has been suggested that in populations with a high prevalence of os acromiale, the anomaly may have been culturally, rather than genetically, induced. In the burials from the *Mary Rose*, a sixteenth-century AD warship that sank off the south coast of England, for example, the prevalence of os acromiale was 12.5 percent, and this was attributed to the long-term use of heavy longbows by professional archers on board the ship (Stirland 1991:44). Os acromiale generally occurs in 1 to 15 percent of shoulders (Resnick 1995b:2960).

Os acromiale was apparent in the right scapula of Skeleton K3, G1, an 18- to 35-year-old female, recovered from the Srubnaya Krasnosamarskoe IV burial ground. The lesion was only partial and had affected the superior half of the acromion. The left scapula was not available for analysis, so it is not possible to ascertain if the anomaly was unilateral or bilateral. A total of 27 Srubnaya adult acromions were present, and the lesion was found to have had a frequency of 3.7 percent (1/27). Since the individual recovered from Krasnosamarskoe IV displayed other indications of stress and strain to her skeleton in the form of Schmorl's nodes (see below) and spondylolysis (see above), it is considered probable that the os acromiale had also arisen for this reason. An underlying developmental weakness of the acromions cannot, however, be entirely excluded as a causative factor.

Osteochondritis Dissecans

Osteochondritis dissecans is a localized disorder that affects convex joint surfaces. An area of subchondral bone becomes avascular and, in conjunction with its associated articular cartilage, may slowly detach from the surrounding joint surface to form a loose body within the joint (Adams and Hamblen 1990:125). The joints most commonly affected by the disorder are the knees and elbows, although in some cases, the femoral heads and tali may display the lesions (Adams and Hamblen 1990:126). Males are more likely to be affected by the disorder than females, and the lesion is more likely to be unilateral than bilateral (Resnick et al. 1995:2616). In modern clinical cases, the disorder is generally presented in adolescents or young adults. During the early stages of necrosis, the individual may feel an aching sensation in the affected joint after use, and once the fragment completely separates from the articular surface, the symptoms include recurrent sudden locking of the joint followed by sharp pain and effusion of a clear fluid into the joint (Adams and Hamblen 1990:126).

Osteochondritis dissecans is generally considered the end result of an osteochondral fracture that was initially caused by shearing, rotatory, or tangentially aligned impaction forces (Resnick et al. 1995:2613). Wells (1974:367) recorded that the lesion occurred in the knee or foot in 95 percent of Romano-British and Anglo-Saxon populations. He observed that when using the feet for very heavy work—weight bearing, thrusting, and turning movements—that the principal line of force is directed through the big toe, the first cuneiform, the navicular, and the head and trochlear surface of the talus to the distal articular surface of the tibia, the line along which the majority of osteochondritic dissecans lesions are observed. This observation supports the theory that trauma or stress is a major cause of the lesion (Wells 1974:367), but modern studies have also indicated there is likely to be a genetic predisposition for the condition since it can occur throughout families, and an autosomal dominant mode of inheritance has been suggested. In addition, irregularities of ossification are considered a third possible etiology (Resnick et al. 1995:2611). Another theory suggests that the lesion occurs as a result of ischemia, in which the blood supply to the affected area is cut off, possibly as result of thrombosis of an end artery (Clanton and DeLee 1982:51).

Five Srubnaya adults displayed lesions that were possibly indicative of osteochondritis dissecans (Table 8.33). It is interesting to note that all five of the individuals with osteochondritis dissecans were male. In the four cases where it was possible to examine the corresponding right

Table 8.33 Details of Osteochondritis Dissecans in the Srubnaya Population

Site	Context	Sex	Age, y	Location	Bilateral/ Unilateral	Other Strains and Activity-Related Trauma
Krasnosamarskoe IV	K3, G17	M	35–50	Femur distal	Unilateral (L)	Compression fracture TV12 Pitting MT4s
Krasnosamarskoe IV	K3, G23	M	35–50	Tibia proximal	Unilateral (R)	Schmorl's nodes
Nizhny Orleansky II	K2, G1	M	35–50	Femur proximal		o
Spiridonovka II	K2, G37	M	18–35	Femur distal	Unilateral (R)	o
Spiridonovka II	K10, G7	M	18–35	Talus proximal	Unilateral (L)	Schmorl's nodes

Note: Vertebral osteophytosis and enthesopathies were not included in the "other strains and activity-related trauma" category. F = female; G = grave; K = kurgan; M = male; L = left; R = right; o = not present; TV = thoracic vertebra; MT = metatarsal.

Table 8.34 A Summary of the Prevalences of Osteochondritis Dissecans in the Affected Bones of the Srubnaya Population

Bone	No. Affected	No. Present	% Affected
Femur (proximal)	1	164	0.6
Femur (distal)	2	168	1.2
Tibia (proximal)	1	164	0.6
Talus (proximal)	1	45	2.2

Note: Both right and left bones are included.

and left bones, all lesions were found to be unilateral. Three of the individuals displayed other signs of stress and strain to their skeletons in the form of vertebral compression fractures and Schmorl's nodes. The occurrence of these lesions may indicate that the individuals had practiced active lifestyles that had resulted in considerable physical stress to their skeletons. A summary of the prevalences of osteochondritis dissecans for the affected bones of the Srubnaya adults is provided in Table 8.34. The summary indicates that osteochondritis dissecans occurred among the Srubnaya adults with low frequencies, which ranged from 0.6 percent to 2.2 percent.

Enthesophytes
Enthesophytes can occur at the sites of musculotendinous and ligamentous attachments, and they arise as a consequence of chronic repetitive irritation, bleeding and inflammation, periostitis, or microavulsions (Pavlov 1995:3246). Enthesophytes were apparent in the remains of three Srubnaya individuals. Skeleton K1, G1, Sk 2, an 18- to 35-year-old male recovered from the Ekaterinovka burial ground, displayed an enthesophyte at the proximal end of the left fibula. The lesion appeared to have affected the posterior talofibular ligament and measured approximately 10.5 mm superoinferiorly by 1.4 mm anteroposteriorly. An enthesophyte was evident at the proximal end, immediately inferior to the tibiofibular articular facet, of the right tibia of Skeleton K1 G2, an 18- to 35-year-old male retrieved from the Studenzy I cemetery. The lesion appeared to have been related to the tibialis posterior muscle and measured 10 mm mediolaterally by 8 mm anteroposteriorly. Postmortem damage had resulted in its superoinferior dimension remaining unknown. Skeleton K2, G4, a 35- to 50-year-old female retrieved from the

Table 8.35 Prevalences of Enthesophytes in the Srubnaya Population

Bone	No. Enthesophytes	No. Bones	% Enthesophytes
Ulna (proximal)	1	151	0.7
Tibia (proximal)	1	164	0.6
Fibula (proximal)	1	87	1.1

Studenzy I burial ground, displayed an enthesophyte on the medial surface of the distal third of the right ulna. The lesion measured approximately 11 mm superoinferiorly by 4.3 mm anteroposteriorly and appeared to have affected the pronator quadratus muscle. The prevalence of enthesophytes among the affected Srubnaya long bones is provided in Table 8.35. Enthesophytes were found to have occurred among the Srubnaya adult long bones in very low frequencies, which ranged from 0.6 percent to 1.1 percent.

Summary of Nonviolent Traumas
A wide variety of probable nonviolent injuries was apparent. The Srubnaya population displayed the greatest variety of injuries, including appendicular and axial fractures, spondylolysis, myositis ossificans traumatica, ossified hematomas, os acromiale, osteochondritis dissecans, and enthesophytes. Details of the crude prevalence rates of adults with one or more injuries considered likely to be related to lifestyle and activity rather than violence are provided in Table 8.36.

The crude prevalence rates are fairly similar, ranging from 14.3 percent for the Potapovka population to 25 percent for Yamnaya. For males, these injuries were most prevalent among the Yamnaya (33.3 percent) and Srubnaya (23.9 percent) populations. Only the Srubnaya population had sufficient sample sizes for both sexes, showing that males (23.9 percent) were more frequently affected by non-violence-related injuries, but females (13.1 percent) were not immune, and the difference was not statistically significant (χ^2 = 2.429; p = 0.119; df = 1). This finding suggests that both males and females engaged in physical activities that appear to have left them susceptible to injury.

Joint Disease
In human skeletal remains, it is possible only to identify degenerative processes that affected the bones and joints. The joint disease most common among archaeological population

Table 8.36 Crude Prevalence Rates (Percentage) of Non-Violence-Related Injuries Based on the Number of Individuals Present in Each Population Group

Culture	Percentage (No./Total No.)		
	Overall	Male	Female
Yamnaya	25 (4/16)	33.3 (4/12)	0 (0/4)
Poltavka	20.6 (7/34)	20.7 (6/29)	20 (1/5)
Potapovka	14.3 (2/14)	18.2 (2/11)	0 (0/3)
Srubnaya	18.6 (24/129)	23.9 (16/67)	13.1 (8/61)

Note: It was not possible to determine the sex of one Srubnaya individual or to examine the Khvalynsk group for trauma.

groups is osteoarthritis (Roberts and Manchester 2005:136). Primary osteoarthritis is directly related to the aging process and physiological wear and tear, while secondary osteoarthritis develops at an earlier age in structurally or functionally abnormal joints (Ortner 2003:546–547). By examining the distribution of degenerative changes in the joints of different social groups, culturally related differences may become apparent. If, for example, males and females were each principally engaged in separate specific occupational activities, a varying distribution pattern of degenerative changes may be apparent in their joints. Degenerative changes in the vertebrae are considered by many paleopathologists and clinicians to be related to functional stress. Consequently, studies have been undertaken to determine the relationship between degenerative changes in the spine and known culturally patterned activities in population groups (Lovell 1994:150). It is difficult to distinguish, however, between those extraspinal and spinal degenerative changes that are purely age related and those that may have been occupationally induced. It is considered that degenerative changes with an apparent specific distribution and high prevalence among the younger members of a population group may indicate that the lesions were indeed occupationally induced (Roberts and Manchester 2005:144).

Osteoarthritis is recognizable in skeletal material on the basis of several characteristic features, including the development of marginal osteophytes; subchondral bone reaction, which includes eburnation, sclerosis, and the development of cysts; porosity of the joint surfaces; and alterations in the contours of the joints (Rogers et al. 1987:185). Eburnation is considered the most pathognomonic indicator of osteoarthritis (Rogers and Waldron 1995:13), although it does not always need to be

Table 8.37 Crude Prevalence rates (Percentage) of Extraspinal Osteoarthritis Based on the Numbers of Individuals Present in Each Population Group

Culture	Overall	Male	Female
	Percentage (No./Total No.)		
Yamnaya	6.3 (1/16)	8.3 (1/12)	0 (0/4)
Poltavka	11.8 (4/34)	10.3 (3/29)	20 (1/5)
Potapovka	14.3 (2/14)	0 (0/11)	66.7 (2/3)
Srubnaya	16.3 (21/129)	22.4 (15/67)	9.8 (6/61)

Note: It was not possible to determine the sex of one Srubnaya or to examine the Khvalynsk group for osteoarthritis.

present in a joint to confirm that the individual suffered from osteoarthritis, and it is possible to make a diagnosis of osteoarthritis provided that at least two other characteristic degenerative changes can be recorded in the skeletal remains (Waldron and Rogers 1991:49).

Extraspinal Osteoarthritis

In modern clinical studies, osteoarthritis occurs in bones other than the spine more frequently in the lower limbs than the upper limbs (Jurmain 1980:148). The converse is generally true for archaeological populations, possibly indicating that the upper limbs were subject to greater functional stress in past groups compared to their modern counterparts (Jurmain 1980:148). In a study of a fourteenth-century population from London, for example, it was found that the shoulder (32.7 percent) was much more frequently affected by osteoarthritis than either the knee (4.1 percent) or the hip (3.1 percent) (Waldron 1992:236). Crude prevalence rates for extraspinal osteoarthritis in the middle Volga region are provided in Table 8.37.

Table 8.38 Prevalence Rates of Extraspinal Osteoarthritis

	Yamnaya	Poltavka	Potapovka	Srubnaya
	Percentage (No./Total No.) Affected			
Temporomandibular			10.5 (2/19)	5.9 (10/169)
Sternoclavicular		7.4 (2/27)		2 (2/98)
Acromioclavicular		14.8 (4/27)		7.5 (7/93)
Glenohumeral	5 (1/20)	11.1 (4/36)	14.3 (2/14)	9.1 (12/132)
Elbow		2.7 (1/37)	9.5 (2/21)	
Wrist		2.9 (1/34)		2.3 (3/128)
Sacroiliac				
Hip	7.7 (2/26)	8.1 (3/37)		3 (5/164)
Knee	4.5 (1/22)	2.6 (1/39)	9.1 (2/22)	4.2 (7/168)

Note: The number of joints is based on the part of the joint with the highest number of bones present and includes right and left sides.

Prevalences ranged from 6.3 percent for the Yamnaya group to 16.3 percent for Srubnaya. In the Srubnaya group, males (22.4 percent) displayed a higher level of extraspinal osteoarthritis than did females (9.8 percent), although the results were not statistically significant (χ^2 = 3.668; p = 0.056; df = 1). This situation may have arisen because more males survived into middle and old age. The extent of the difference, however, may also indicate that males engaged in physical activities that made them more susceptible to degeneration of the extraspinal joints. Details of the prevalences of osteoarthritis among the main extraspinal joints for the different populations are provided in Table 8.38 and Figure 8.5.

Extraspinal osteoarthritis occurred with a relatively low frequency, ranging from 0 percent to 14.8 percent. The glenohumeral (shoulder) and knee joints were the only joints to be affected across all periods, while no individuals displayed osteoarthritis of the sacroiliac joint. The glenohumeral joint was the most frequently affected joint for the Potapovka (14.3 percent) and Srubnaya (9.1 percent) groups, while the acromioclavicular (upper shoulder) joint (14.8 percent) followed by the glenohumeral joint (11.1 percent) were most frequently affected for the Poltavka population. The acromioclavicular joint is used to raise the arm above the head, so perhaps the Poltavka population performed this action particularly often. The hip was most frequently affected during the Yamnaya (7.7 percent) period. These differences in the pattern of affected joints may indicate that a change in activity had occurred between the Yamnaya and later periods,

with the principal stress shifting from the lower to the upper body. It should be noted, however, that the glenohumeral joint was also affected during the Yamnaya (5 percent) period, while the hip joints also displayed osteoarthritis during the Poltavka (8.1 percent) and Srubnaya (3 percent) periods. Murphy (1998:475) found that the shoulder was the most frequently involved extraspinal joint in both Iron Age groups from Aymyrlyg, Siberia, having a frequency of 3.7 percent among the Uyuk culture population and 9.2 percent among the Shurmak culture group.

Temporomandibular joints displayed osteoarthritis only in the Potapovka (10.5 percent) and the Srubnaya (5.9 percent) populations. It is not surprising that the Potapovka individuals displayed osteoarthritis of their temporomandibular joints since relatively high numbers of their teeth were very worn (25 percent). It is perhaps surprising, however, that the Poltavka individuals were not affected by osteoarthritis of the temporomandibular joints since this group displayed the highest frequencies of extensive dental attrition (26.2 percent). Furthermore, the Srubnaya population displayed relatively low levels of attrition (11 percent). One would have expected a better correlation between high frequencies of extensive tooth wear and osteoarthritis of the temporomandibular joints, but that expectation is not met here.

The large Srubnaya sample made it possible to examine extraspinal osteoarthritis in further detail. A total of 21 Srubnaya individuals displayed apparently primary

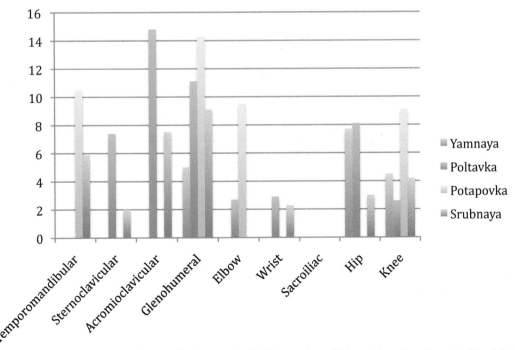

Figure 8.5 Prevalence rates (percentage) of extraspinal osteoarthritis (the number of joints is based on the part of the joint with the highest number of bones present and includes right and left sides).

Table 8.39 Details of the Prevalences (Percentage) of Osteoarthritis among the Main Extraspinal Joints for Srubnaya Males and Females

Joint	Percentage (No./Total No.) Affected		
	Overall	Male	Female
Temporomandibular	5.9 (10/169)	8.5 (8/94)	2.7 (2/75)
Sternoclavicular	2 (2/98)	0 (0/60)	5.3 (2/38)
Acromioclavicular	7.5 (7/93)	9.1 (5/55)	5.3 (2/38)
Glenohumeral	9.1 (12/132)	10 (7/70)	8.1 (5/62)
Elbow			
Wrist	2.3 (3/128)	4.3 (3/70)	0 (0/58)
Sacroiliac			
Hip	3 (5/164)	4.8 (4/83)	1.2 (1/81)
Knee	4.2 (7/168)	3.4 (3/88)	5 (4/80)

extraspinal osteoarthritis. Of the 20 individuals that could be assigned to specific age categories, only two had age at death values of 18 to 35 years (10 percent), while 10 (50 percent) had died at 35 to 50 years and 8 (40 percent) had died at the age of 50+ years. This finding would tend to suggest that extraspinal osteoarthritis in the Srubnaya population was largely related to advancing age. When the frequencies of extraspinal osteoarthritis are analyzed by sex, some interesting trends are apparent (Table 8.39; Figure 8.6).

For both males and females, the shoulder joint (glenohumeral) was most frequently affected. When it came to the lower limbs, however, the hip was more frequently affected in males, while the knee was slightly more frequently affected in females. Only males displayed osteoarthritis of the wrist. Notably higher frequencies of males displayed osteoarthritis of the temporomandibular joints. These findings would tend to suggest sex-related differentiation of physical activities in Srubnaya society.

Spinal Osteoarthritis

A summary of the prevalences of osteoarthritis of the vertebrae is provided in Table 8.40. The prevalences of spinal osteoarthritis among individuals with one or more vertebrae present were quite high, ranging from 43.7 percent for Srubnaya to 73.3 percent for Poltavka. Sex differences can be studied only in the large Srubnaya corpus, where males (47.4 percent) were more susceptible than females (39.4 percent), although the results were not statistically significant ($\chi^2 = 0.457$; $p = 0.499$; $df = 1$). The apophyseal joints were infrequently affected, ranging from 1.1 percent in the Potapovka group to 6.6 percent in the Poltavka group. The vertebral body surfaces were more frequently affected but still had low values ranging from 4.7 percent for Potapovka to 18.9 percent for Poltavka and 20 percent for Srubnaya. The prevalences of osteoarthritis of the apophyseal joints of the different vertebrae are provided in Table 8.41.

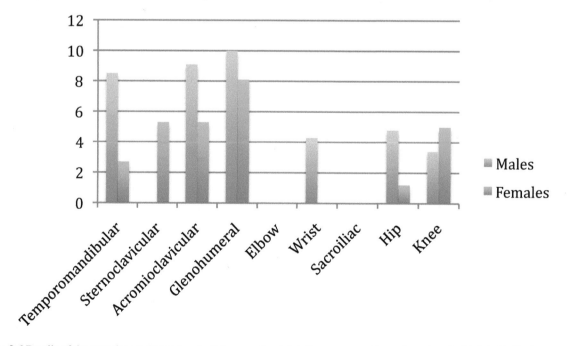

Figure 8.6 Details of the prevalences (percentage) of degenerative joint disease among the main extraspinal joints for Srubnaya males and females.

Table 8.40 Summary of the Prevalences (Percentage) of Spinal Osteoarthritis Based on the Number of Individuals, Apophyseal Joints (Excluding Costal and Transverse Facets), and Body Surfaces

Culture	Prevalence by Individuals, Percentage (No./Total No.) Affected			Prevalence by Joint Surface, Percentage (No./Total No.) Affected	
	Overall	Male	Female	Apophyseal	Bodies
Yamnaya	50 (6/12)	62.5 (5/8)	25 (1/4)	3.3 (15/458)	12.6 (28/223)
Poltavka	73.3 (11/15)	80 (8/10)	60 (3/5)	6.6 (72/1082)	18.9 (99/523)
Potapovka	66.7 (4/6)	60 (3/5)	100 (1/1)	1.1 (1/90)	4.7 (2/43)
Srubnaya	43.7 (31/71)	47.4 (18/38)	39.4 (13/33)	4.9 (85/1,732)	20 (171/856)

Table 8.41 Prevalence (Percentage) of Osteoarthritis in the Apophyseal Joints (Excluding Costal and Transverse Process Facets) of Each Vertebra

Apophyseal Joints	Percentage (No./Total No.) Affected		
	Yamnaya	Poltavka	Srubnaya
CV1		11.1 (4/36)	6.5 (3/46)
CV2		8.3 (4/48)	6.5 (6/92)
CV3		9.1 (4/44)	1.8 (1/56)
CV4		15 (6/40)	6.3 (4/64)
CV5		5.6 (2/36)	1.7 (1/60)
CV6		7.1 (2/28)	2.1 (1/48)
CV7			5.6 (2/36)
TV1		2.5 (1/40)	
TV2			
TV3		5.6 (2/36)	
TV4		6.8 (3/44)	1.9 (1/52)
TV5		7.5 (3/40)	
TV6	12.5 (2/16)	8.3 (4/48)	
TV7	18.8 (3/16)	6.3 (3/48)	1.9 (1/52)
TV8	25 (4/16)		3.3 (2/60)
TV9	12.5 (2/16)		1.7 (1/60)
TV10		10.4 (5/48)	1.8 (1/56)
TV11		13.6 (6/44)	3.8 (2/52)
TV12		5 (2/40)	5 (3/60)
LV1	3.6 (1/28)	8.3 (4/48)	
LV2		6.3 (3/48)	8 (9/112)
LV3		7.1 (4/56)	5.6 (7/124)
LV4		13.5 (7/52)	7.8 (9/116)
LV5	7.5 (3/40)	3.8 (2/52)	16 (23/144)
S1		3.3 (1/30)	7.5 (8/106)

Note: The Potapovka group is not included due to the very small numbers of vertebrae preserved. CV = cervical vertebra; TV = thoracic vertebra; LV = lumbar vertebra; S = sacral vertebra.

During the Yamnaya period, the mid-thoracic region (TV6–TV9) was most susceptible to osteoarthritis, while during Poltavka times, the lower thoracic and lumbar (TV10–LV4) and the upper cervical (CV1–CV6) were the regions of the spine most prone to degeneration. Among the Srubnaya group, the lumbar (LV2–S1) and the upper cervical (CV1–CV4) displayed the highest levels of osteoarthritis of the apophyseal joints. The lack of CV with osteoarthritis among the Yamnaya group was the most obvious difference between the three groups, and it may be an indication that these earlier individuals were not putting stress on their upper vertebrae to the same extent as the individuals of Poltavka and Srubnaya times. It is possible, however, that the Yamnaya results are anomalous due to the relatively small numbers of apophyseal joints preserved in this group. The occurrence of relatively high levels of osteoarthritis in the cervical vertebrae of the Poltavka and Srubnaya populations is interesting. Studies of other populations have interpreted this pattern of spinal osteoarthritis as an indication that they carried heavy loads on their heads (Larsen 1997:176). The prevalences of osteoarthritis of the body surfaces of the different vertebrae are provided in Table 8.42.

The occurrence of osteoarthritis of the cervical vertebral bodies for the Yamnaya group suggests that the lack of osteoarthritis in the corresponding apophyseal bodies is likely to be an anomaly due to sample size rather than due to differences in physical activity between the three groups. The small sample size makes it difficult to identify general trends for the Yamnaya period, but the lumbar bodies (LV3–LV5) would appear to be most susceptible to degeneration. During the Poltavka period, osteoarthritis most frequently affected the bodies of the lower cervical (CV4–CV6), mid to lower thoracic (TV7–TV10), and lower lumbar (LV3–S1) regions, while the lower lumbar (LV3–LV5) region was affected to the greatest extent among the Srubnaya individuals. The trends would tend to suggest that the vertebral bodies of the lower spine for all three cultures were most susceptible to stress and strain.

Table 8.42 Prevalence (Percentage) of Osteoarthritis in the Vertebral Body Surfaces

Body	Percentage (No./Total No.) Affected		
	Yamnaya	Poltavka	Srubnaya
CV2			4.3 (2/46)
CV3	25 (1/4)	13.6 (3/22)	3.4 (1/28)
CV4		25 (5/20)	9.4 (3/32)
CV5		27.8 (5/18)	6.7 (2/30)
CV6	25 (2/8)	20 (4/20)	12.5 (3/24)
CV7	25 (1/4)	7.1 (1/14)	5.6 (1/18)
TV1		15 (3/20)	
TV2			
TV3		11.1 (2/18)	7.1 (2/28)
TV4		13.6 (3/22)	3.8 (1/26)
TV5		15 (3/20)	16.7 (5/30)
TV6	25 (2/8)	12.5 (3/24)	15.4 (4/26)
TV7		20.8 (5/24)	26.9 (7/26)
TV8	12.5 (1/8)	25 (6/24)	16.7 (5/30)
TV9		25 (6/24)	23.3 (7/30)
TV10		29.2 (7/24)	25 (7/28)
TV11		9.1 (2/22)	19.2 (5/26)
TV12		10 (2/20)	23.3 (7/30)
LV1		25 (6/24)	25 (7/28)
LV2	12.5 (2/16)	12.5 (3/24)	25 (14/56)
LV3	28.6 (4/14)	28.6 (8/28)	40.3 (25/62)
LV4	35.7 (5/14)	26.9 (7/26)	34.5 (20/58)
LV5	45 (9/20)	38.5 (10/26)	41.7 (30/72)
S1	11.1 (1/9)	33.3 (5/15)	24.5 (13/53)

Note: The Potapovka group is not included due to the very small numbers of vertebrae preserved. CV = cervical vertebra; TV = thoracic vertebra; LV = lumbar vertebra; S = sacral vertebra.

Schmorl's Nodes

Schmorl's nodes are recognizable in the skeleton as indentations that occur on either the superior or inferior surfaces of the vertebral body and are most common in the lower thoracic and lumbar regions of the spine (Rogers and Waldron 1995:27). They arise as a result of intervertebral osteochondrosis in which the nucleus pulposus and the cartilaginous endplates of the vertebra simultaneously degenerate as part of the aging process (Resnick and Niwayama 1995d:1378). In addition, Schmorl's nodes can also occur as a result of other disease processes that disrupt the endplate or the subchondral bone, such as Scheuermann disease, infection, metabolic and endocrine disorders, neoplastic conditions, or trauma (Resnick and Niwayama 1995d:1421). Since there was no evidence of underlying disease among any of the individuals with Schmorl's nodes, it is probable that they arose mainly as a result of degenerative processes or trauma. A summary of the prevalences of Schmorl's nodes in the vertebrae is provided in Table 8.43.

The prevalence of individuals with Schmorl's nodes was quite high, ranging from 32.4 percent for the Srubnaya population group to 60 percent for the Poltavka adults. As was the case for osteoarthritis, it is difficult to be certain that the apparently higher prevalence for the Poltavka adults represents a real increase or is simply due to the small number of individuals included in the analysis. When the prevalences are calculated on the basis of the number of surfaces affected, the results are slightly different, with the Srubnaya (18.8 percent), Potapovka (14 percent), and Yamnaya (11.2 percent) groups having higher prevalence rates than the Poltavka (9 percent) population. The prevalence based on the number of bone surfaces is likely to be more reliable, suggesting that the Srubnaya group was most susceptible to the development of Schmorl's nodes. Murphy (1998:481) found that Schmorl's nodes occurred with frequency of 17.8 percent among the body surfaces of the Uyuk culture population and 13.1 percent among

Table 8.43 Summary of the Prevalences (Percentage) of Schmorl's Nodes Based on the Number of Individuals and Body Surfaces

Culture	Prevalence by Individuals, Percentage (No./Total No.) Affected			Prevalence by Body Surface, Percentage (No./Total No.) Affected
	Overall	Male	Female	
Yamnaya	41.7 (5/12)	50 (4/8)	25 (1/4)	11.2 (25/223)
Poltavka	60 (9/15)	80 (8/10)	20 (1/5)	9 (47/523)
Potapovka	33.3 (2/6)	20 (1/5)	100 (1/1)	14 (6/43)
Srubnaya	32.4 (23/71)	31.6 (12/38)	33.3 (11/33)	18.8 (161/856)

the Shurmak culture population from Iron Age Aymyrlyg, South Siberia.

Among the Srubnaya adults, males (31.6 percent) and females (33.3 percent) were almost equally susceptible to the development of Schmorl's nodes ($\chi^2 = 0.025$; $p = 0.875$; $df = 1$). Three Srubnaya males and seven females with age at death values of 18 to 35 years displayed Schmorl's nodes, a finding that indicates that both sexes were engaged in strenuous physical activities from a young age. The prevalences of Schmorl's nodes on the different vertebrae are provided in Table 8.44. In all three groups, the lower thoracic and lumbar spines were most susceptible to the development of Schmorl's nodes. A cluster of

Table 8.44 Prevalence (Percentage) of Schmorl's Nodes in the Vertebral Body Surfaces

Body Surfaces	Percentage (No./Total No.) Affected		
	Yamnaya	Poltavka	Srubnaya
CV2			
CV3			
CV4			
CV5			
CV6			
CV7			
TV1			
TV2			
TV3			
TV4			3.8 (1/26)
TV5			10 (3/30)
TV6	12.5 (1/8)	8.3 (2/24)	15.4 (4/26)
TV7	25 (2/8)	16.7 (4/24)	15.4 (4/26)
TV8	12.5 (1/8)	20.8 (5/24)	20 (6/30)
TV9	25 (2/8)	20.8 (5/24)	43.3 (13/30)
TV10	20 (2/10)	16.7 (4/24)	42.9 (12/28)
TV11	25 (2/8)	4.5 (1/22)	53.8 (14/26)
TV12	20 (2/10)	10 (2/20)	63.3 (19/30)
LV1	14.3 (2/14)	20.8 (5/24)	64.3 (18/28)
LV2	6.3 (1/16)	8.3 (2/24)	33.9 (19/56)
LV3	14.3 (2/14)	14.3 (4/28)	41.9 (26/62)
LV4	28.6 (4/14)	19.2 (5/26)	19 (11/58)
LV5	10 (2/20)	19.2 (5/26)	11.1 (8/72)
S1	11.1 (1/9)	20 (3/15)	5.7 (3/53)

Note: The Potapovka group is not included due to the very small numbers of vertebrae preserved. CV = cervical vertebra; TV = thoracic vertebra; LV = lumbar vertebra; S = sacral vertebra.

particularly high prevalences was evident for TV9 to LV3 of the Srubnaya population. The findings indicate that the lower spine was most susceptible to damage as a result of strenuous physical activities.

Violence and Society

Evidence for deliberate violence occurred in generally small levels among the population groups and comprised possible weapon injuries and fractured nasal bones.

Weapon Injuries

Since a variety of possible weapon injuries were observed, they will each be described in turn. Skeleton K3, G1, a 15- to 17-year-old Yamnaya male recovered from the Lopatino II cemetery, displayed an oval-shaped perforating injury on the posterior aspect of his right parietal. The perforation measured 38 mm anteroposteriorly by 6.5 mm mediolaterally at its anterior margin and 15 mm mediolaterally at its posterior margin. The anterior margin of the perforation had a beveled appearance, and a fracture line radiated from the lateral aspect of the anterior margin to the posterior part of the temporal bone. No evidence of healing was associated with the injury.

An 18- to 35-year-old male recovered from Yamnaya Flat Grave 5 at the Leshevskoe I burial site displayed a series of unusual weapon injuries that appeared to have been made during the perimortem period. A large chop mark was apparent on the lateral surface of the proximal end of the right femur, in the area immediately inferior to the greater trochanter (Figure 8.7). The injury appears to have been made with a fairly heavy blunt implement that was wielded with substantial force. The blow had resulted in the detachment of a triangular segment of bone, which would have measured approximately 35 mm anteroposteriorly by 51 mm superoinferiorly, and encompassed the entire mediolateral diameter of the bone in that region. The remaining underlying bone had a splintered appearance. The location of the injury indicates that it was dealt to the side of the individual.

Multiple injuries that can best be described as scrape or gouge marks, as a consequence of their broad and shallow nature, were apparent on the cranium (Figures 8.8 and 8.9) and are summarized in Table 8.45. A total of eight scrape or gouge marks were apparent on the individual's cranium. It is evident that the majority of marks were located on the posterior aspect of the cranium, particularly on the occipital. All of the scrape marks had a similar breadth of around 2 mm, which may indicate that they had been made using a single implement or by a single individual. In a number of cases, the marks had clearly been made

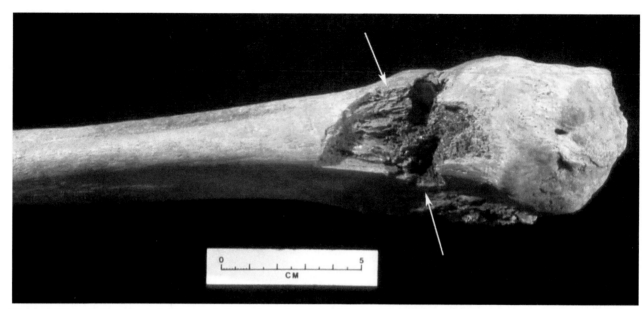

Figure 8.7 Lateral view of a probable case of slipped femoral capital epiphysis of the right femur apparent in an 18- to 35-year-old male of Yamnaya date recovered from Flat Grave 5 of the Leshevskoe I burial ground. A large chop mark was evident, which is considered to possibly be perimortem.

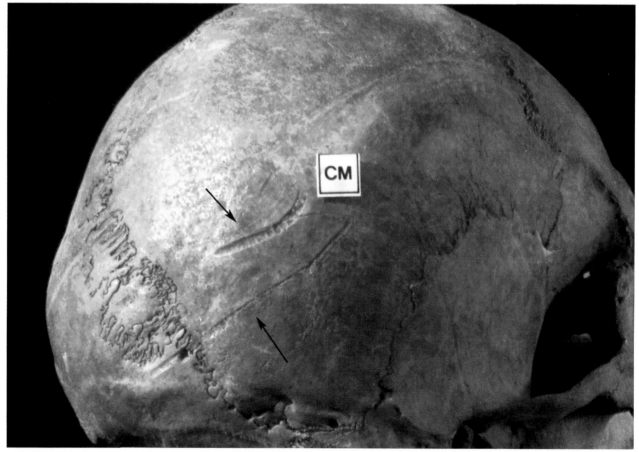

Figure 8.8 Perimortem gouge or scrape marks apparent on the posterolateral aspect of the right parietal and occipital of an 18- to 35-year-old male of Yamnaya date recovered from Flat Grave 5 of the Leshevskoe I burial ground. Note the serrated edge of the most superior mark.

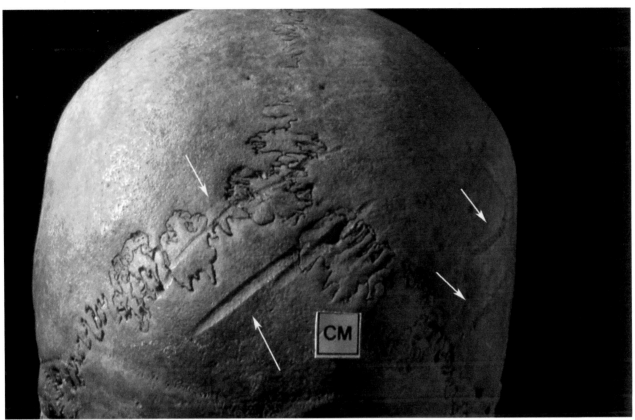

Figure 8.9 Perimortem gouge or scrape marks apparent on the posterolateral aspect of the right parietal and the superior aspect of the occipital of an 18- to 35-year-old male of Yamnaya date recovered from Flat Grave 5 of the Leshevskoe I burial ground.

Table 8.45 Yamnaya Individual—Details of the Cranial Injuries Apparent in the Individual Recovered from Flat Grave 5 of the Leshevskoe I Burial Ground

Bone	Location	Morphology	Dimensions
L parietal	Lateral	Transverse	36.4 mm SI × 2 mm AP
	Posterior	Transverse	20.1 mm ML × 1.7 mm SI
R parietal (Figure 8.8)	Posterior	Transverse, slightly curved	27.5 mm AP × 2 mm SI
R parietal-occipital (Figures 8.8 and 8.9)	Posterior (p) superolateral (o)	Oblique	79.6 mm AP × 2.3 mm SI
	Adjacent to lambda	Oblique	36.1 mm AP × 2.8 mm SI
	Adjacent to lambda	Oblique	32.5 mm AP × 2.6 mm SI
Occipital (Figure 8.9)	External occipital protuberance	Curved	29.4 mm ML × 2.1 mm SI
			28.6 mm AP × 2.1 mm SI
	L occipital condyle	Transverse	4.1 mm AP × 2 mm ML

Note: L = left; R = right; p = parietal; o = occipital; AP = anteroposterior; SI = superoinferior; ML = mediolateral.

using a serrated implement, which had the potential to leave a curved mark. The scrape marks do not appear to have been made for the purposes of scalping the individual since these marks are generally made in a very methodical manner, which follows the circumference of the cranium (see Murphy et al. 2002). The more random nature of the scrape marks in the case of the individual from Leshevskoe I may suggest that they had been employed for the purposes of removing tufts of hair from the individual, as opposed to his scalp. It can be speculated that this may have been a means of torture. The only injury that cannot be explained in this manner is the short mark that was apparent on the left occipital condyle. This injury may have been made during the decapitation of the individual, although it is curious that no further marks were evident on the occipital condyles or the cervical vertebrae.

Two transverse conjoined scrape marks were apparent on the medial surface of the proximal end of the distal third of the left femur. Both marks appeared to have emanated from the same point but became forked as they advanced toward the anterior surface of the shaft. They measured approximately 25 mm anteroposteriorly by 1.5 mm superoinferiorly. A further discrete transverse scrape mark was visible on the anterior surface of the distal aspect of the proximal half of the left femur. It measured approximately 10.5 mm anteroposteriorly by 1.5 mm superoinferiorly. In addition, further possible scrape marks were present on the anterior surface of the left femur, but these were notably less pronounced than the marks already described.

It can be postulated that the chop mark on the right proximal femur represented the initial injury to the individual since he would have been largely incapacitated by this blow. It would then have been possible for the assailants to undertake the gouging injuries on the individual's cranium and left femur. The individual also displayed probable slipped femoral capital epiphysis of his right femur and cleft neural arch defects (see above). In addition, it has been reported that he had been buried in a prone, contorted position in Grave 5, which was positioned adjacent to, but not beneath, a kurgan.

A single Poltavka individual displayed clear evidence for a depressed fracture of the cranium. The injury was apparent in the cranium of Skeleton K2, G3, a 50+-year-old male, recovered from the Tryasinovka burial ground. It had been made to the superior aspect of the parietals, approximately 25 mm posterior to the bregma, and comprised an oval-shaped perforation, which measured around 30 mm mediolaterally by 18 mm anteroposteriorly. The right side of the perforation had a beveled edge, and two fracture lines radiated from the right corner of the posterior margin of the perforation. The first fracture line ran parallel to the posterior margin in a lateral direction, while the second fracture line, which measured approximately 38 mm, radiated in a posterior direction until it reached the sagittal suture. A further fracture line ran in a posterior direction from the midpoint of the aforementioned line and ran toward the lambdoid suture. The morphology of the injury suggests that it had been made with a small, rounded object, presumably an axe. The occurrence of the large radiating fracture lines is an indication that the blow had been dealt with a substantial amount of force. The location of the beveled margin suggests that it had been dealt by someone standing to the left of the individual. The left side of the cranium was poorly preserved, but one of the broken margins of the left parietal, located just beneath the injury described above, was notably curved. It is considered possible that this curved edge may have been due to a second blow having been dealt to the cranium. No signs of healing were associated with either of the injuries, and it is probable that they had been responsible for the death of the individual. The individual also displayed a healed fracture of his right tibia (see above).

A single Potapovka individual—Skeleton K6, G6, an 18- to 35-year-old male, recovered from the Utyevka VI burial ground—displayed two possible cranial fractures. An oval-shaped depressed area, which measured approximately 10 mm anteroposteriorly by 16 mm mediolaterally, was situated on the superior aspect of the left side of the frontal bone, just anterior to the coronal suture. The oval-shaped area was surrounded by a pronounced sclerotic margin. It is possible that the lesion was a well-healed depressed fracture, which had been made with a small blunt implement. A linear indentation, of similar dimensions, was apparent just anterior to the oval-shaped depression and may represent a second healed injury. The ectocranial surfaces of the superior aspect of the frontal bone and the parietals had a generally irregular and porotic appearance. This finding may have been due to the occurrence of inflammatory or infectious activity on the cranial surface and could have been secondary to the possible injuries. It is difficult to be certain, however, that the lesions were traumatic in nature, and it is also possible that they had been due to some form of localized infection. Possible depressed fractures occurred with a prevalence of 8.3 percent (1/12) on the frontal bones of the Potapovka adults.

Four Srubnaya individuals displayed possible evidence for weapon injuries to their crania. A possible injury was evident at the midpoint of the frontal bone, immediately superior to the supraorbital ridges of Skeleton K2, G41, an 18- to 35-year-old male, recovered from the Barinovka I cemetery. The depression was sub-rectangular in shape and measured 14.1 mm mediolaterally by 3.6 mm superoinferiorly and had a depth of approximately 2 mm. No radiating fracture lines were apparent. The depressed area was not very distinct, and it is probable that the injury was in an advanced state of healing. The morphology of the injury would tend to suggest that it had been made with a small, sharp object, possibly a blade.

Skeleton K2, G13, a 35- to 50-year-old male, retrieved from the Srubnaya Chisty Yar I burial ground (Figure 8.10), displayed a very pronounced near-circular depressed area on the right side of the frontal bone, immediately anterior to

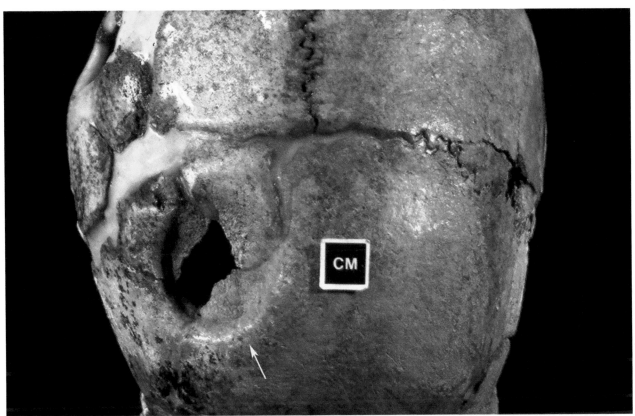

Figure 8.10 Probable longstanding depressed fracture on the right side of the frontal bone of Skeleton K2, G13, a 35- to 50-year-old male of Srubnaya date, recovered from the Chisty Yar I burial ground.

the coronal suture. Its external diameter was approximately 41 mm, while the internal diameter measured approximately 36.5 mm mediolaterally by 31 mm anteroposteriorly. It had a very pronounced sclerotic margin, which had a thickness of approximately 5 mm, and the depth of the depression was also around 5 mm. Bone was present in the interior of the depressed area, which appeared to derive from the inner vault table. No obvious fracture lines were visible around the margins, and they were very smooth, features that would tend to suggest the trauma was long-standing and well healed. A possible fracture line was apparent in the new bone formation within the interior of the injury. A line was visible on the endocranial surface, which demarcated the extent of the injury, and no beveling was evident. It is considered probable that the trauma represented a long-standing, healed blunt-force injury. The main indicator that the perforation may have represented a depressed fracture is the occurrence of the curved fracture line that affected the new bone formation in the interior of the circular area. If the depression had been due to blunt-force trauma, it is probable that it had been made using a rounded implement, with a diameter of around 40 mm, possibly a mace. The main differential diagnosis for the injury is that it was a

healed trepanation. The features compatible with this diagnosis include the regularity of the shape of the trauma, the development of new bone that is restricted to the inner vault table in the interior of the circular area, and the absence of beveling on the endocranial surface of the cranium. Numerous examples of antemortem trepanations are known from the paleopathological record for the Eurasian steppes (e.g., Mednikova 2001; Murphy 2003b), with the earliest possible cases dating to Epipaleolithic times (Lillie 2003).

Despite extensive surface erosion, a possible injury was apparent on the frontal bone of Skeleton K10, G7, an 18- to 35-year-old male, retrieved from the Spiridonovka II burial ground. An oval-shaped depression, which measured 12 mm mediolaterally by 4 mm anteroposteriorly, was situated on the superior aspect of the frontal anterior to the bregma by some 12.5 mm. No radiating fracture lines were visible, and the dimensions of the depressed area may indicate that it had been made by a sharp implement.

A possible healed depressed fracture was visible on the left temporal of Skeleton 2, a 50+-year-old male, recovered from the Poplavskoe cemetery. A ridge associated with a smooth indented area, which measured approximately 30 mm anteroposteriorly, was situated immediately beneath the superior margin of the temporal. A further possible fracture line, which measured 19 mm anteroposteriorly, was apparent just superior to the mastoid process. The fractured area would have affected a region that measured approximately 30 mm superoinferiorly and ran for the entire anteroposterior length of the temporal. It is considered probable that the injury would have been made with a blunt implement of similar dimensions. The individual also displayed fractured nasal bones (see below).

It was difficult to be certain of a definite etiology for any of the four Srubnaya cranial injuries. It is considered most probable, however, that the trauma represented two blade injuries and two blunt-force trauma injuries. The cranial vault injuries were found to have affected the frontal bone with a prevalence of 3.4 percent (3/89), while the right temporal displayed injuries with a frequency of 1.2 percent (1/86). The locations of the injuries—three on the frontal bone and one on the left temporal bone—is in keeping well the expected positions of injuries obtained during face-to-face interpersonal violence. All four of the injuries appeared to have been long-standing and in advanced states of healing.

Skeleton G52, a 6- to 7-year-old juvenile recovered from the Srubnaya Svezhensky burial ground, displayed a possible blade injury on his or her right scapula. A sharp injury, which measured 13.6 mm, ran in an anteroposterior direction through the central area of the spine. The margins of the injury were sharp, and the exposed bone was of similar color to the remainder of the bone, suggesting that it had occurred during the perimortem period. The cut appeared to have been made with an implement larger than a knife and was generally more extensive than cut marks considered indicative of defleshing or disarticulation apparent in other individuals (see below). If the trauma has been accurately identified as a blade injury, it is probable that it was dealt from behind the individual. No other traumatic lesions were apparent on the skeleton. Differential diagnosis should also include damage attained through the use of a sharpened shovel during the excavation process, although the exposed surface was the same color as the remainder of the bone and not paler.

Fractured Nasal Bones

Details of the individuals with fractured nasal bones are provided in Table 8.46. It was not possible to obtain a reliable prevalence rate of the injuries for the Yamnaya group since only five nasal bones were preserved. The injuries occurred with a frequency of 4.5 percent (6/134) for the Srubnaya adults. Fractured nasal bones are common in archaeological populations and probably arise as a conse-

Table 8.46 Details of Individuals with Fractured Nasal Bones in the Population Groups

Culture	Site	Context	Age, y	Sex	Right		Left	
					Type	Healing	Type	Healing
Yamnaya	Nizhny Orleansky I	K1, G5	35–50	M	Simple transverse	Advanced	Simple transverse	Advanced
Srubnaya	Chisty Yar I	K1, G2	35–50	F	Simple transverse	Unhealed	Simple transverse	Unhealed
Srubnaya	Poplavskoe	Sk2	50+	M	Simple oblique	Unhealed	Simple oblique	Unhealed
Srubnaya	Rozhdestvenno I	K5, G10	35–50	M	Simple oblique	Advanced	Simple oblique	Advanced

Note: F = female; G = grave; K = kurgan; M = male; Sk = skeleton.

Table 8.47 Crude Prevalence Rates (Percentage) of Probable Violence-Induced Trauma Based on the Numbers of Individuals Present in each Population Group

	Percentage (No./Total No.) Affected			
Culture	Overall Adult	Male	Female	Nonadult
Yamnaya	18.8 (3/16)	16.7 (2/12)	0 (0/4)	33.3 (1/3)
Poltavka	2.9 (1/34)	3.4 (1/29)	0 (0/5)	0 (0/7)
Potapovka	7.1 (1/14)	9.1 (1/11)	0 (0/3)	0 (0/4)
Srubnaya	3.9 (5/129)	5.9 (4/68)	1.7 (1/60)	1.6 (1/63)

Note: It was not possible to determine the sex of one Srubnaya adult or to examine the Khvalynsk group for trauma.

quence of fist-fighting (Roberts and Manchester 2005:109). It is interesting that both males and females displayed the injuries. In all cases, the fractures had affected both nasal bones. The individual recovered from Poplavskoe also displayed a possible depressed cranial fracture (see above). Murphy (2003a:97) reported that fractured nasal bones occurred with a frequency of 3.4 percent among the Uyuk culture population and 6 percent among their Shurmak culture counterparts from the Iron Age cemetery of Aymyrlyg, South Siberia.

Summary
Crude prevalence rates for probable violence-induced trauma are provided in Table 8.47. The lesions considered possibly indicative of deliberate violence comprised cranial and postcranial weapon injuries and fractured nasal bones. The adult crude prevalences ranged from 2.9 percent for the Poltavka population to 18.8 percent for the Yamnaya group. The small numbers of individuals in the majority of groups probably result in the inflation of trauma prevalence. A further problem with the analysis of cranial injuries is that extensive reconstruction of many of the crania with wax precluded a detailed analysis of certain broken edges. In the majority of groups, only males displayed possible violence-related injuries. Although males (5.9 percent) had the highest crude prevalence of possible violence-related injuries among the substantial Srubnaya population, females (1.7 percent) and nonadults (1.6 percent) were not immune to such injuries.

Funerary Processes
Ochre
Some 50 individuals from the Volga region had bones that were stained with ochre during funerary rites (Table 8.48). It is highly probable that the frequency of individuals with this staining has been underestimated due to taphonomic processes and postexcavation procedures, such as the cleaning of the skeletons. In the vast majority of cases, the ochre staining was red, although a 35- to 50-year-old Poltavka female (K2, G2) recovered during the excavations at Krasnosamarskoe IV was also associated with a black pigment. If the writers had not been involved in the excavation and postexcavation curation of this individual, it is highly probable that the association with the black pigment would have been missed since the staining could have been interpreted as a normal taphonomic process. It is feasible that other individuals included in the study group had also been associated with a black pigment, but this is now invisible on their skeletal remains. The following discussion is largely specific to the use of red ochre during the funerary ritual. None of the Khvalynsk individuals displayed evi-

dence for ochre staining, but it should be remembered that in the majority of cases, only the crania of these individuals were available for analysis, and there are several ochre-stained ritual deposits found above graves in this cemetery (Anthony 2007:184).

A detailed analysis of the distribution by skeletal element was not undertaken. In general terms, the results would tend to suggest that during Yamnaya and Poltavka times, the entire skeleton was covered with ochre, and deliberate concentrations appear to have been deposited on the skull or feet. No obvious trends are evident for the Potapovka adults, but the fact that nonadults of this culture displayed generalized ochre distribution may indicate that this may also have originally been the case for the adults. A slightly different pattern of staining may be evident for the Srubnaya group, although the results need to be interpreted with caution—it is difficult to be certain that the ochre staining on the bones accurately reflects its original deposition since taphonomic processes may have resulted in a lack of staining on certain bones. A number of skeletons displayed the generalized deposition observed for the previous cultures, but for five individuals, the ochre appeared to have been restricted to the skull. The prevalence rates of individuals with ochre are provided in Table 8.49.

There appears to have been a general decline in the use of ochre from the Yamnaya (73.7 percent) through to the Srubnaya (6.8 percent) periods. Due to the paucity of females in the earlier groups, it is difficult to ascertain any precise sex-specific trends, although adult males and females of all ages appear to have been accorded the funerary practice. Among the Srubnaya population, however, it is interesting to note that the prevalence of females (18 percent) with ochre staining was notably higher than for their male (3 percent) counterparts. It is possible that as the ritual declined, it remained largely associated with females.

Nonadults also appear to have been accorded this funerary rite, at least during the Yamnaya, Poltavka, and Potapovka periods. The affected individuals ranged from a perinatal infant through to a 15- to 17-year-old adolescent, suggesting that nonadults of all ages were accorded this funerary treatment. It is possible that social status, or perhaps manner of death, rather than age was a determining factor concerning who was buried with ochre. Despite the relatively large number of nonadults of Srubnaya date (*n* = 63), none displayed ochre staining. It is again possible that by the Srubnaya era, the ritual was in decline.

The association of ochre with a young adult female and a perinatal infant from Yamnaya contexts at the Leshevskoe burial ground (K1, G1a and b) is of interest. It is possible that these skeletons represent a mother and her baby who

Table 8.48 Details of the Individuals with Red Ochre Staining from the Different Cultures

Culture	Site	Context	Age, y	Sex	Bones Affected
Yamnaya	Kurmanaevka III	K3, G2	35–50	F	Entire skeleton
Yamnaya	Kutuluk I	K3, G1	35–50	M	Mandible, entire skeleton, esp. feet
Yamnaya	Kutuluk I	K3, G4	35–50	M	Skull, entire skeleton
Yamnaya	Kutuluk I	K4, G1	18–35	M	Skull, entire skeleton, esp. feet
Yamnaya	Kutuluk II	K1, G1	18–35	F	Entire skeleton
Yamnaya	Leshevskoe	K1, G1a	18–35	F	L forearm, lower legs
Yamnaya	Leshevskoe	K1, G1b	8–9 lunar months		R femur
Yamnaya	Leshevskoe I	Flat Grave 5	18–35	M	L distal femur
Yamnaya	Lopatino I	K22	18–35	M	Entire skeleton, esp. lower legs
Yamnaya	Lopatino I	K31	35–50	M	Entire skeleton
Yamnaya	Lopatino I	K32	Adult	M	Entire skeleton
Yamnaya	Lopatino II	K3, G1	15–17	M	Entire skeleton, esp. skull
Yamnaya	Nizhny Orleansky I	K1, G5	35–50	M	Entire skeleton, esp. skull
Yamnaya	Nizhny Orleansky I	K4, G2	18–35	M	Innominates (skeleton incomplete)
Poltavka	Grachevka	K1, G2	50+	M	Entire skeleton
Poltavka	Grachevka II	K2, G1	35–50	M	Entire postcranial skeleton, esp. feet
Poltavka	Kalach	K2, G2	35–50	F	R humerus
Poltavka	Kalinovka	K1, G4	50+	M	Entire skeleton
Poltavka	Krasnosamarskoe IV	K1, G3	18–35	F	Entire skeleton esp. R arm, skull, lower legs
Poltavka	Krasnosamarskoe IV (Figure 8.11)	K1, G4	0–0.5		Entire skeleton (heavy)
Poltavka	Krasnosamarskoe IV	K2, G2	35–50	F	Entire skeleton
Poltavka	Kryazh	K2, G1	18–35	M	Entire skeleton
Poltavka	Kutuluk III	K1 central	18–35	M	Entire skeleton, esp. feet
Poltavka	Lopatino I	K1, G1	18–35	M	Distal lower legs
Poltavka	Lopatino I	K30, G2	35–50	M	Facial area of skull
Poltavka	Lopatino I	K33	18–35	M	Facial area of skull and feet
Poltavka	Nikolaevka III	K3, G2	Adult	M	Entire skeleton
Poltavka	Nizhny Orleansky	K1, G4	35–50	M	Entire skeleton, esp. feet
Poltavka	Podlesnoe	K1, G6	18–35	M	Entire skeleton
Poltavka	Potapovka I	K5, G6	35–50	M	Feet
Poltavka	Tryasinovka	K2, G3	50+	M	Legs
Potapovka	Lopatino II	K1, G1, Sk 1	Adult	M	Distal lower legs
Potapovka	Lopatino II	K2, G3	50+	M	L side skull, legs, arms, torso
Potapovka	Potapovka I	K5, G4, Sk1	5.5–7.5		Entire skeleton
Potapovka	Potapovka I	K5, G11, Sk3	7.5–8.5		Entire skeleton
Potapovka	Utyevka II		18–35	M	R shoulder
Potapovka	Utyevka VI	K6, G5, Sk 1	18–35	F	L lower leg

Table 8.48 Details of the Individuals with Red Ochre Staining from the Different Cultures *(continued)*

Culture	Site	Context	Age, y	Sex	Bones Affected
Srubnaya	Barinovka I	K2, G28	18–35	F	Entire skeleton
Srubnaya	Chisty Yar I	K1, G1	35–50	F	L humerus, legs
Srubnaya	Chisty Yar I	K1, G2	35–50	F	R foot
Srubnaya	Chisty Yar I	K2, G10	35–50	F	Skull (?)
Srubnaya	Nizhny Orleansky II	K4, G9	18–35	F	Entire skeleton (?)
Srubnaya	Novoselki	K3, G7	18–35	F	Lower legs
Srubnaya	Rozhdestvenno I	K1, G3	35–50	M	Arms, legs
Srubnaya	Rozhdestvenno I	K5, G11	18–35	F	Entire skeleton
Srubnaya	Spiridonovka II	K10, G3	18–35	F	R side skull
Srubnaya	Spiridonovka II	K11, G8	18–35	F	L side skull
Srubnaya	Spiridonovka II	K11, G11	18–35	M	L side skull (?)
Srubnaya	Spiridonovka II	K14, G10	18–35	F	L side skull
Srubnaya	Uren II	K2, G2	50+	F	Entire skeleton

Note: F = female; G = grave; K = kurgan; L = left; M = male; R = right; Sk = skeleton.

Table 8.49 Prevalence Rates (Percentage) of Individuals Associated with Ochre

	Prevalence by Individuals, Percentage (No./Total No.)			
Culture	Overall	Male	Female	Nonadult
Yamnaya	73.7 (14/19)	75 (9/12)	75 (3/4)	66.7 (2/3)
Poltavka	41.5 (17/41)	44.8 (13/29)	75 (3/5)	14.3 (1/7)
Potapovka	33.3 (6/18)	27.3 (3/11)	33.3 (1/3)	50 (2/4)
Srubnaya	6.8 (13/192)	3 (2/67)	18 (11/61)	0 (0/63)

Note: It was not possible to reliably examine the Khvalynsk population for the occurrence of ochre.

had either died during or shortly after the baby's birth. A similar situation is evident for a pair of Poltavka burials from the Krasnosamarskoe IV burial ground. A young adult female recovered from the central burial of Kurgan 1 (G3) was covered in ochre. An adjacent burial of a young infant (G4; 0–0.5 years) was covered in notably heavy deposits of ochre (Figure 8.11). It is feasible that the individuals in the two burials were linked—perhaps again being a mother and infant. The association of ochre with death is obvious from its location within burials. The discovery of two possible mothers and young infants with deposits of the substance may also indicate that the red ochre was symbolic of life—perhaps blood. It may be the case that ochre was included within the burials as a symbol of the rebirth of the individuals in the afterlife.

Association with Copper/Bronze Artifacts
A total of 24 individuals from all periods displayed green discoloration that was due to their association with copper or bronze artifacts (Table 8.50). Only those metal objects that came in direct contact with bone are represented in this count. As such, it is quite probable that the actual frequencies of individuals buried with metal objects were higher. Nevertheless, since the same situation applies to all of the populations, it is still valid to determine if any trends are apparent.

All three of the Khvalynsk individuals exhibiting green staining probably were buried wearing earrings. Two of the individuals were males, suggesting that adults of both sexes wore copper ear ornaments. The single Yamnaya individual with green discoloration was a young adult male who seems to have worn an armlet at his left elbow. Three Poltavka individuals were affected—an infant who was buried wearing a pair of bracelets, a middle adult female who had green discoloration at her hip, and an old adult female who seems to have been buried with a pair of earrings, an armlet at her left elbow, and a pair of anklets. It is possible

Figure 8.11 In situ view of Skeleton K1, G4, a newborn to 0.5-year-old infant of Poltavka date, recovered from the Krasnosamarskoe IV burial ground. The entire skeleton was heavily covered with red ochre.

that the green discoloration at the hip of the middle adult female represented some form of belt attachment that may have been functional rather than decorative. The baby with bracelets is interesting since it indicates that young children could be buried with metal jewelry, which was presumably an indication of high status.

All six of the affected Potapovka individuals were from Kurgans 5 and 6 of the Utyevka VI burial ground, which are regarded as particularly high-status kurgans. A juvenile wore an armlet or bracelet (K5, G4, Sk1), while another wore an anklet (K5, G11, Sk3). One middle-aged adult female wore a pair of bracelets (K6, G1), while a young adult female seemed to have been associated with a headdress, a pair of bracelets, and an armlet (K6, G5, Sk1). A young adult male from the same burial wore an armlet (K6, G5, Sk2). Finally, a young adult male (K6, G2, Sk 1) wore an armlet and possibly a headdress or earring (Figure 8.12).

The Srubnaya findings appear to be more uniform, with all nine affected adults having been female. Six of these wore a single bracelet or a pair of bracelets, while a possible female adolescent from Spiridonovka II (K11, G15) wore at least one bracelet/armlet, and another adolescent of unidentifiable sex from the same burial ground (K1, G2,

Sk1) also wore a pair of bracelets. These 11 individuals derived from four sites and included adolescents as well as young, middle, and old adults, so it is possible that Srubnaya females in general wore bracelets. Two individuals were buried wearing one or more earrings, while a middle adult female from the Chisty Yar I cemetery (K1, G2) wore both a pair of earrings and a pair of bracelets.

The prevalence rates of individuals with green staining are provided in Table 8.51. The frequencies ranged from 4.9 percent for the Poltavka population to 33.3 percent for Potapovka. The high percentage for the Potapovka assemblage may have been largely due to the inclusion of the presumably high-status site at Utyevka VI. A definite decline in green discoloration occurred between Potapovka and the Srubnaya culture, when only 5.7 percent of individuals displayed staining.

Although most of the sample sizes are too small for the results to be considered definitive, females seemed to display higher levels of green discoloration than males. The only exception was in the Yamnaya population, in which the single affected individual was male. The definite female preponderance in the substantial Srubnaya group may indicate that this is a genuine trend throughout the different

Table 8.50 Details of the Individuals with Green Discoloration on Bones Indicative of Association with Metal Artifacts

Culture	Site	Context	Age, y	Sex	Bones Affected	Possible Object
Khvalynsk	Khvalynsk	G6	18–35	F	L mastoid and external auditory meatus	Earring
Khvalynsk	Khvalynsk	G13	18–35	M	R mastoid and mandible; L mastoid	Pair of earrings
Khvalynsk	Khvalynsk	G24	18–35	M	R and L mastoid and mandibular condyle	Pair of earrings
Yamnaya	Kutuluk I	K4, G1	18–35	M	L humerus distal; L ulna proximal	Armlet
Poltavka	Grachevka II	K3, G9a	50+	F	L mastoid; R temporal; L humerus distal	Pair of earrings; armlet
					L tibia distal; R calcaneus	Pair of anklets
Poltavka	Kalinovka	K1, G6	35–50	F	L femur proximal, anterior surface	Unid—object lying on hip
Potapovka	Utyevka VI	K5, G4, Sk 1	5.5–7.5		L ulna and radius midshaft	Armlet or bracelet
Potapovka	Utyevka VI	K5, G11, Sk 3	7.5–8.5		R tibia distal	Anklet
Potapovka	Utyevka VI	K6, G1	35–50	F	R and L ulna and radius distal	Pair of bracelets
Potapovka	Utyevka VI	K6, G2, Sk 1	18–35	M	L humerus proximal, posterior surface	Armlet
		(Figure 8.12)			L maxilla	Part of headdress
Potapovka	Utyevka VI	K6, G5, Sk 1	18–35	F	L humerus proximal, anterior surface	Armlet
					R and L ulna and radius distal	Pair of bracelets
					Skull esp. R external auditory meatus	Headdress
Potapovka	Utyevka VI	K6, G5, Sk 2	18–35	M	R humerus distal, anterior surface	Armlet
					R ulna and radius proximal	
Srubnaya	Chisty Yar I	K1, G2	35–50	F	R mandibular condyle; L mastoid process	Pair of earrings
					R and L ulna and radius distal	Pair of bracelets
Srubnaya	Chisty Yar I	K2, G10	35–50	F	L mastoid process	Earring
Srubnaya	Kinel' I	K5, G2	18–35	F	R mandibular condyle, mastoid, occipital	Pair of earrings
					Condyle; L mastoid process, asterion	
Srubnaya	Kinel' I	K6, G2	50+	F	R ulna and radius distal; L ulna distal	Pair of bracelets
Srubnaya	Nizhny Orleansky I	K5, G3	18–35	F	R ulna and radius distal	Pair of bracelets
Srubnaya	Spiridonovka II	K1, G2, Sk1	13–16		R radius distal; L ulna midshaft	Pair of bracelets
Srubnaya	Spiridonovka II	K11, G12	35–50	F	R and L radius distal	Pair of bracelets
Srubnaya	Spiridonovka II	K11, G15	12–16	F	L ulna and radius patches	1+ bracelet/armlet
Srubnaya	Spiridonovka IV	K1, G16	18–35	F	R ulna distal; L ulna and radius distal	Pair of bracelets
Srubnaya	Spiridonovka IV	K2, G1	35–50	F	R ulna distal	Bracelet
Srubnaya	Spiridonovka IV	K2, G13	18–35	F	R and L ulna and radius distal	Pair of bracelets

Note: F = female; G = grave; K = kurgan; L = left; M = male; R = right; Sk = skeleton.

Table 8.51 Prevalence Rates (Percentage) of Individuals with Green Discoloration Due to Their Association with Metal Objects

Culture	Prevalence by Individuals, Percentage (No./Total No.)			
	Overall	Male	Female	Nonadult
Khvalynsk	11.1 (3/27)	10 (2/20)	20 (1/5)	0 (0/2)
Yamnaya	5.3 (1/19)	8.3 (1/12)	0 (0/4)	0 (0/3)
Poltavka	4.9 (2/41)	0 (0/29)	40 (2/5)	14.3 (1/7)
Potapovka	33.3 (6/18)	18.2 (2/11)	66.7 (2/3)	50 (2/4)
Srubnaya	5.7 (11/192)	0 (0/67)	14.8 (9/61)	3.2 (2/63)

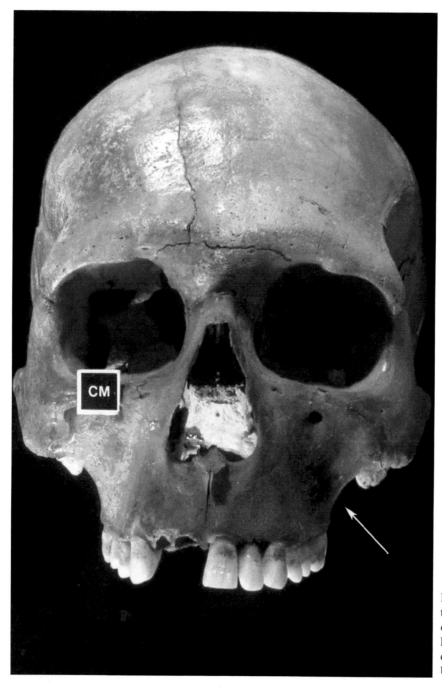

Figure 8.12 Green discoloration due to association with copper or bronze objects on the left maxilla of Skeleton K6, G2, Sk 1, an 18- to 35-year-old male of Potapovka date, retrieved from the Utyevka VI burial ground.

populations. Although the nonadult numbers are generally low, children and adolescents appear to have been buried wearing metal objects more frequently than adult males in the Poltavka, Potapovka, and Srubnaya population groups.

Defleshing and Disarticulation

Some 14 individuals displayed cut marks that were probably due to the disarticulation and/or defleshing of the body as part of a secondary burial process (Table 8.52). It is highly probable that the number of individuals processed in this manner is underestimated since not all bodies treated in this way will display the telltale cut marks. The skill of the processor, the size of the joint, and the state of decomposition of the remains are all factors that would have an impact on whether cut marks would be visible in the skeleton. This situation was made particularly clear during the excavations at Krasnosamarskoe IV when a bundle burial (K2, G1) of Poltavka date was discovered (Figure 8.13). Despite a thorough examination by the authors, no cut marks were observed on the remains, although it was clear that the individual had been fully disarticulated and buried within a small organic container that had since decomposed.

Two individuals derived from the Yamnaya culture displayed possible evidence of disemboweling and the detachment of the leg at the hip during disarticulation. Three Poltavka individuals displayed cut marks—one individual displayed possible evidence for disemboweling, the individual discussed above displayed evidence of having been entirely disarticulated, and cut marks on a third individual were indicative of the detachment of the lower leg at the knee during disarticulation. A total of nine individuals from the Srubnaya group displayed evidence of body processing. Of the 12 instances where different areas of the body had been disarticulated, the majority had involved disarticulation of the leg at the hip (33.4 percent; 4/12; Figure 8.14), followed in frequency by detachment of the lower leg from the upper leg at the knee (25 percent; 3/12) and evidence for the separation of the lower arm from the upper arm at the elbow (16.7 percent; 2/12; Figure 8.15). Single cases of the detachment of the arm from the shoulder (8.3 percent), separation of the wrist from the lower arm (8.3 percent), and removal of the foot from the lower leg (8.3 percent) were also observed.

The preponderance of disarticulations at the hips and knees would appear to indicate that the main objective

Figure 8.13 In situ view of the disarticulated bundle burial of Skeleton K2, G1, an 18- to 35-year-old male of Poltavka date, recovered from the Krasnosamarskoe IV burial ground.

Table 8.52 Details of Individuals with Evidence of Defleshing and/or Disarticulation as Part of the Funerary Process

Culture	Site	Context	Age, y	Sex	Bones Affected	Location	Dimensions	Possible Action
Yamnaya	Lopatino I	K22	18–35	M	LV2	Anterior surface	13 mm ML	Disemboweling
Yamnaya	Lopatino I	K29, G1	35–50	M	L femur	Superolateral aspect of head	17.6 mm SI	Disarticulation—detachment of leg
Poltavka	Nizhny Orleansky I	K1, G4	35–50	M	LV5	Anterior surface	18.2 mm ML	Disemboweling
Poltavka	Krasnosamarskoe IV (Figure 8.13)	K2, G1	18–35	M	All			No cut marks but body entirely disarticulated
Poltavka	Potapovka I	K5, G6	35–50	M	R tibia	Proximal, tibiofibular articular facet	24.4 mm AP	Disarticulation—detachment of lower leg
Srubnaya	Barinovka I (Figure 8.15)	K1, G2b	35–50	M	R humerus	Distal third, anterior surface	3–5 mm ML (x3)	Disarticulation—detachment of lower arm
						Capitulum, lateral margin	7 mm ML	
					L radius	Distal third, posterior surface	12.6 mm SM-IL	Disarticulation—detachment of hand
					R calcaneus	Superior surface	15 mm SP-IA	Disarticulation—detachment of foot
Srubnaya	Barinovka I	K2, G16	35–50	F	L humerus	Proximal, lesser tubercle	5.5 mm SI	Disarticulation—detachment of arm
					R tibia	Proximal, tibiofibular articular facet	7 mm SI	Disarticulation—detachment of lower leg
					L tibia	Proximal, medial condyle	3 mm SI	Disarticulation—detachment of lower leg
Srubnaya	Nizhny Orleansky	K1, G3	35–50	M	L femur	Head, anterior surface	18.3 mm and 7.9 mm SM-IL	Disarticulation—detachment of leg
						Midshaft, anterior surface	5 mm ML	Defleshing
Srubnaya	Nizhny Orleansky II	K4, G27	18–35	F	L femur	Lateral condyle, posterior surface	8 mm SL-IM	Disarticulation—detachment of lower leg
						Medial condyle, posterior surface	3 mm ML	Disarticulation—detachment of lower leg
Srubnaya	Nizhny Orleansky V	K5, G1	18–35	M	L radius	Head, posterior surface	11 mm ML	Disarticulation—detachment of lower arm
						Midshaft, medial surface	6 mm ML	Defleshing
						Midshaft, posterior surface	7.5 mm SM-IL	Defleshing
						Distal third, medial surface	4.6 mm AP (´2)	Defleshing

Table 8.52 Details of Individuals with Evidence of Defleshing and/or Disarticulation as Part of the Funerary Process *(continued)*

Culture	Site	Context	Age, y	Sex	Bones Affected	Location	Dimensions	Possible Action
Srubnaya	Spiridonovka II	K2, G37	18–35	M	L femur	Proximal third, AL margin	7.2 mm SL-IM	Disarticulation—detachment of leg
Srubnaya	Spiridonovka II (Figure 8.14)	K10, G7	18–35	M	R femur	Greater trochanter, lateral surface	26 mm AP	Disarticulation—detachment of leg
							12 mm SM-IL	Disarticulation—detachment of leg
							8.4 mm SL-IM	Disarticulation—detachment of leg
						Proximal third, lateral surface	3–6 mm ML (´3)	Disarticulation—detachment of leg
Srubnaya	Spiridonovka IV	K1, G10	35–50	F	R femur	Greater trochanter, AI surface	13 mm SP-IA	Disarticulation—detachment of leg
						Midshaft, lateral surface	4.2 mm AP	Defleshing
							7 mm SP-IA	Defleshing
Srubnaya	Spiridonovka IV	K2, G2	18–35	F	R tibia	Proximal, tibiofibular articular facet	15 mm SL-IM	Disarticulation—detachment of lower leg
							5.6 mm SL-IM	Disarticulation—detachment of lower leg

Note: F = female; G = grave; K = kurgan; L = left; M = male; R = right; Sk = skeleton; AL = antero-lateral; AI = antero-inferior; ML = medio-lateral; SI = supero-inferior; AP = antero-posterior; SM = supero-medial; IL = infero-lateral; IA = infero-anterior; SP = supero-posterior; IM = infero-medial; SL = supero-lateral.

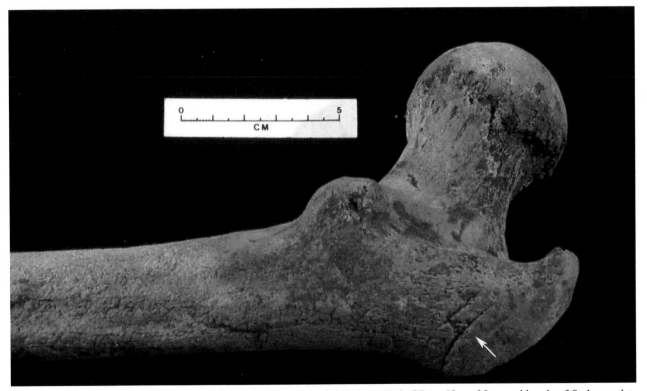

Figure 8.14 Disarticulation cut marks on the proximal right femur of Skeleton K10, G7, an 18- to 35-year-old male of Srubnaya date, recovered from the Spiridonovka II burial ground.

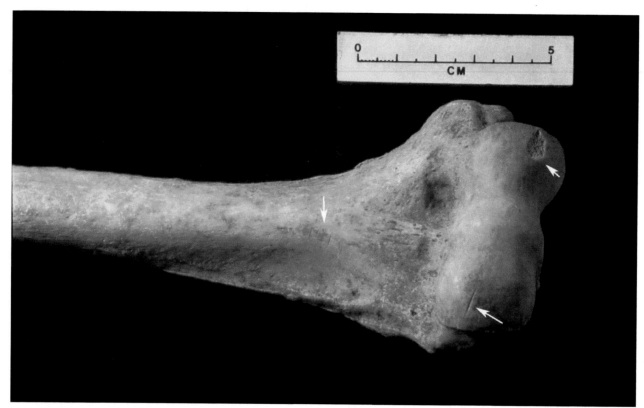

Figure 8.15 Disarticulation cut marks on the right distal humerus of Skeleton K1, G2b, a 35- to 50-year-old male of Srubnaya date, recovered from the Barinovka I burial ground.

of the procedure was to reduce the corpse to a more manageable size. Murphy (2000a) undertook a detailed analysis of the defleshing and disarticulation cut marks that were apparent among Iron Age Uyuk culture individuals recovered from the cemetery of Aymyrlyg, South Siberia. The results indicated that, similar to the Volga populations, the knee (26.1 percent) and the hip (23.9 percent) were the joints most frequently associated with disarticulation cut marks (*n* = 29). Three bones from the Srubnaya group— two femurs and a radius—also displayed evidence of having been defleshed and indicate that not only were some

Table 8.53 Prevalence Rates (Percentage) of Individuals with Evidence of Defleshing and/or Disarticulation

Culture	Prevalence by Individuals, Percentage (No./Total No.)			
	Overall	Male	Female	Nonadult
Yamnaya	10.5 (2/19)	16.7 (2/12)	0 (0/4)	0 (0/3)
Poltavka	7.3 (3/41)	10.3 (3/29)	0 (0/5)	0 (0/7)
Potapovka	0 (0/18)	0 (0/11)	0 (0/3)	0 (0/4)
Srubnaya	4.7 (9/192)	7.5 (5/67)	6.6 (4/61)	0 (0/63)

Note: It was not possible to analyze the Khvalynsk population for cut marks.

corpses reduced in size through disarticulation but that in some instances, efforts were made to skeletalize the bodies by removal of the flesh.

The prevalence rates of individuals with evidence of disarticulation and/or defleshing are provided in Table 8.53. They ranged from 0 percent for the Potapovka groups to 10.5 percent for the Yamnaya corpus. Apparently, only a small proportion of individuals from each period were treated in this manner. As discussed above, however, the disarticulation of a dead body does not necessarily involve cutting the bone, and the skill of the processor will also have an effect on whether the bones are marked with cuts. It is therefore highly probable that the number of Volga individuals whose bodies were disarticulated after death has been underestimated. Adult males displayed evidence for this form of body processing in all three affected populations, but only in the Srubnaya group were females treated in this manner. In this population, males (7.5 percent) and females (6.6 percent) exhibited similar frequencies. None of the nonadult individuals displayed evidence for cut marks, and this might be due to the fact that their bodies are smaller than those of adults and did not require processing. The generally smaller size of adult females compared to their male counterparts may also account for the lack of females with evidence of processing in the earlier populations. Alternatively, it is possible that pastoral strategies determined the prevalence of male, female, or nonadult disarticulations (see below).

Drawing on historical sources (e.g., the Chinese Annals) and archaeological and seasonality information derived from other excavations, including the Iron Age royal tombs at Pazyryk, South Siberia (Rudenko 1970), it has been postulated that the postmortem dismemberment apparent in the populations at Aymyrlyg, Siberia, was due to the semi-nomadic lifestyle of these societies (Murphy 2000a). It has been suggested that the distribution of large tribal burial grounds in Tuva, including that of Aymyrlyg, indicates that cyclic migration with fixed routes and set winter camp sites would have existed among the steppe-mountain pastoralist tribes (Vainshtein 1980:96). These regular repeated seasonal migrations would have been undertaken within the borders of a relatively well-defined territory (Mandelshtam 1992:193). Presumably, herds would have been pastured in the mountains during the summer and in the more low-lying land during the winter (Bokovenko 1995:255). Consequently, since Aymyrlyg is located in the valley of the Ulug-Khemski River, it is probable that the Uyuk culture and Shurmak culture groups would have been living in relatively close proximity to their cemetery during the winter months, the season when burial would have been most difficult because the ground was frozen.

Rudenko (1970) developed a model of seasonal interment for the burials at Pazyryk, which can help explain the presence of disarticulated bodies at the Aymyrlyg cemetery. Following this system, it is possible that burials would have occurred in autumn immediately before the ground became frozen or in spring as soon as the ground had sufficiently thawed. The corpses of individuals who had died during the winter period may have been temporarily preserved in the snow without need of artificial processing until the spring, when they would have been buried in a relatively undecomposed and intact condition. The cadavers of those who died during the later spring to early autumn months in the mountain areas would, however, have required some form of processing. It would have been both unhygienic and unpleasant for the remainder of the population if the corpses had been allowed to naturally decompose in the summer heat. It would, therefore, have been extremely practical for the bodies to have been defleshed and disarticulated and stored safely until the group returned to the main tribal cemetery at Aymyrlyg in the autumn (Murphy 2000a).

The Volga populations are extremely interesting because even as far back as Yamnaya times, they were actively disarticulating certain dead members of their society. Indeed, it would appear to be the case that throughout the Early, Middle, and Late Bronze Age periods that secondary burial was a necessary procedure for the Volga populations. Given the pastoralist nature of these Bronze Age populations, this finding is not unexpected. Frachetti (2008) has discussed the intricacies involved with the pastoral strategies used by particular groups, and his work has demonstrated the existence of considerable variation among steppe populations depending on the nature of social and environmental conditions.

The occasional disarticulation of the corpse appears to be a recurring trait of Eurasian pastoralism that has been largely ignored. Analysis of these secondary burial practices has the potential to add to the growing body of literature, which is providing a more nuanced understanding of the nature of steppe pastoralism. The necessity for such body processing has the potential to provide insights concerning the seasonality of pastoralism as well as the nature of the distances traveled by groups. The results of the current study perhaps indicate that the Yamnaya and Poltavka populations traveled further than the later Potapovka and Srubnaya groups and therefore needed to process a greater proportion of bodies. Perhaps only a few individuals, those with evidence of body processing, traveled the greatest distances. Although the numbers of females included in the study are admittedly small, it is interesting that only males in the Yamnaya and Poltavka groups had been afforded body processing. By Srubnaya times, examples of males and females with body processing were about equal. Perhaps a change had occurred that saw individuals of both sexes traveling greater distances. This finding is particularly curious in light of the results of the seasonality analysis of the settlement at Krasnosamarskoe, which indicated that the settlement was occupied all year round (Anthony et al. 2005:403). One might have envisioned that women and children would have remained at this settlement while males went to the pastures with their herds, but the occurrence of females with evidence of disarticulation would tend to suggest that this was not the case. The lack of nonadults with disarticulation cut marks may be an indicator that younger individuals were not required to travel as far as adults or, as discussed above, it may simply have been the case that these smaller bodies did not require processing to the same extent as their adult counterparts.

Conclusions

The Samara Valley Project applied a multidisciplinary approach to the study of the subsistence economy of the Late Bronze Age Srubnaya culture in the Samara River valley. A great increase in settlement sites occurred at this time. Analysis of 297 prehistoric human skeletons was undertaken to see if these changes in settlement pattern had affected the bodies of these ancient peoples. While many insights concerning the lives and deaths of the populations have been gained, a major limitation of the study has been the small sample size of most of the earlier population groups, which precluded a more detailed statistical analysis. In the following conclusion, the main trends across time are discussed, particularly within the context of the apparent economic changes that had occurred by Srubnaya times. Very few paleopathological studies of Eurasian steppe populations have been published to date, and it is hoped that the results of the current study will demonstrate the potential of this approach.

Developmental Defects

All of the population groups displayed a notable preponderance of defects of the blastemal desmocranium (33/297 individuals) or paraxial mesoderm (28/297). It is generally accepted that such similarities in developmental defects between skeletal populations are an indication of genetic relatedness (Barnes 1994:5). The middle Volga populations might have derived from similar gene pools, although this finding would need to be confirmed by analyses of larger populations from the region. The occurrence of individuals with the same developmental defects within cemeteries, such as the Potapovka cemetery of Utyevka VI and the Srubnaya cemetery of Spiridonovka IV, might be evidence for familial burials within some cemeteries.

All of the Bronze Age Volga populations displayed developmental defects of the appendicular skeleton, all of which involved the hip joints and would have caused the affected individuals to suffer from gait disturbances. An adult male recovered from the Yamnaya Leshevskoe I burial ground with slipped femoral epiphysis was of particular interest. This individual also displayed evidence that a heavy blow had been dealt to his right thigh, possibly with an axe, as well as a series of scrape or gouge marks on the posterior aspect of his cranium and on his left femur. The scrape marks on the cranium appeared to have been made with a serrated implement, and their random placement is not typical of scalping (see Murphy et al. 2002). It is possible that tufts of hair were removed from the individual, perhaps as some form of torture. The individual was reported to have been buried in a face-down prone position, suggesting that he had been accorded a nonnormative burial. Individuals with physical disabilities and nonnormative forms of burial have been recovered from around the world (see, e.g., Papadopoulos 2000;

Murphy 2008). Indeed, subtle differences in burial rites appear to have been afforded to a Potapovka adult male (Kurgan 1, Burial 8) and a Srubnaya adult male (Kurgan 2, Burial 6) with potential physical disabilities recovered from the Spiridonovka IV kurgan cemetery (Popova et al. 2011:300–301). It can be tentatively proposed that the apparent physical abuse and nonnormative burial of the man from Leshevskoe I may in some way have been related to his physical disability.

Health

Health is not only an important factor in the quality of life but also closely related to "demographic, social, economic, and political change and with the outcomes of wars and other conflicts" (Steckel and Rose 2002a:3). According to the World Health Organization (2006), health may be defined as "a state of complete physical, mental and social well-being and not merely the absence of disease or infirmity." Anthropological studies of war-torn populations have demonstrated a reduced state of well-being among the civilians caught up in such conflicts. As such, the evidence for violence is presented alongside the data for physiological stress (Figure 8.16).

When interpreting the indicators of physiological stress, it is important to remember the osteological paradox—a skeleton with no lesions may represent a healthy individual or, conversely, it may represent a person who was ill but whose immune system was too weak to react to the disease and who died before any changes had been caused to the skeleton (see Wood et al. 1992). Cribra orbitalia and enamel hypoplasia are both indicators of childhood physiological stress caused by nutritional deficiencies and childhood disease, whereas reactive new bone formation is indicative of the occurrence of an infection or inflammatory response during the time leading up to an individual's death (i.e., when he or she was an adult).

The results would tend to suggest that, with its low levels of cribra orbitalia, the Khvalynsk population was relatively healthy. This would correlate with a high prevalence of older adult males in the corpus (Murphy and Khokhlov 2004) and with the potentially high-status nature of the Khvalynsk II burial ground, as evidenced by the occurrence of a rich array of copper grave goods in the burials. The levels of enamel hypoplasia were relatively high, however, but given the other positive indicators of health, it is possible that this is just a sign that those individuals who had been subject to ill health as a child had the ability to recover, thereby enabling the hypoplastic defect to develop.

The standard of health appears to have dramatically declined between Khvalynsk (Eneolithic) and Yamnaya (EBA) times, when individuals had the highest levels of

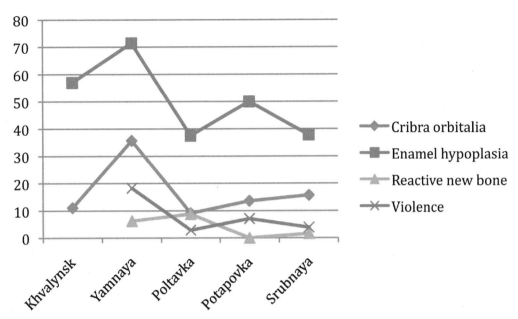

Figure 8.16 Summary of the prevalence rates (percentage) of cribra orbitalia (by bone), enamel hypoplasia (by individual), reactive new bone formation (crude), and violence (crude) for each culture based on the data contained in Tables 8.8, 8.11, 8.13, and 8.47. It was not possible to record the occurrence of reactive new bone formation or evidence for violence for the Khvalynsk group.

cribra orbitalia, enamel hypoplasia, and violence-related injuries. None of the Yamnaya adult males survived into older adulthood, which may be a further indicator of poor health (Murphy and Khokhlov 2004). The Yamnaya culture appears to have been associated with a time of great change in Eurasia, which saw major and sustained waves of migration and the first adoption of highly mobile pastoralism (Anthony 2007:304). Although warfare is not thought to have facilitated the spread of the Yamnaya horizon across the Pontic steppes (Anthony 2007:317), the results of the osteological analysis would tend to suggest that the Yamnaya people included in the current study were physiologically stressed and had a relatively high frequency of weapon injuries. It is possible that intensified social competition between pastoral nomadic groups (Anthony 2007:317) would also have been a source of physiological stress to the members of successful and less successful herding groups alike and that violence occurred at least sporadically.

Health appears to have again improved by Poltavka (MBA) times, during which the levels of cribra orbitalia, enamel hypoplasia, and violence-related injuries all markedly decreased. The average femoral length for Poltavka adult males had the greatest value of all Bronze Age populations, which again may be an indicator of good health. The highest levels of reactive new bone formation were apparent among the Poltavka population but, considering their low levels of other physiological stressors and tall stature, it is possible that this finding can be explained as evidence of an adult

population that had sufficient resilience to fight and survive infection, enabling lesions to develop in the skeleton. Both cribra orbitalia and enamel hypoplasia were lower in the MBA than in the Eneolithic, suggesting that the Poltavka population may have enjoyed an even higher level of good health than the Khvalynsk population, which included many high-status individuals.

Health appears to have deteriorated significantly from Poltavka (MBA) to Potapovka (final MBA) times. Levels of cribra orbitalia, enamel hypoplasia, and violence-related injuries rose, although they were still much lower than the high levels observed for the Yamnaya culture. Further evidence of stress was evidenced by notably high levels of death during young adulthood among the males. In addition, the average femoral length for adult males declined. Given the possible evidence for a slight Asian admixture in the Potapovka group (see Chapter 6), however, there is a possibility that the decline in stature was related to the changing genetics of the population. No individuals displayed evidence for reactive new bone formation, but in the context of poor health suggested by the other indicators of stress, it is possible that individuals who contracted an infection died quickly before any lesions had time to develop.

The Sintashta culture—and, by extension, the Potapovka culture—are generally associated with a major increase in demand for metal as well as being shaped by warfare (Anthony 2007:391–393). The archaeological evidence sug-

206 Eileen M. Murphy and Aleksandr A. Khokhlov

gests that a number of innovations occurred in Potapovka weaponry, and grave goods frequently comprise weapons as opposed to items of adornment (Anthony 2007:372). These included the development of the chariot as well as new types of projectile points, perhaps for use with spears and jave- lins, that might have been thrown from chariots (Anthony 2007:395). It has been suggested that Potapovka graves were sometimes deliberately dug through Poltavka graves, while some Sintashta settlements appear to have been developed on top of Poltavka settlements (Anthony 2007:386). If we accept this scenario, then it is possible that the Potapovka groups were deliberately destroying these sites as a way of asserting their authority over the herders of the region. As such, it is quite possible that a period of unrest and political tension was responsible for the general decrease in health status apparent among the Potapovka people.

The trends for the LBA Srubnaya culture are difficult to interpret. While the levels of enamel hypoplasia and violence-related trauma decreased from the preceding Potapovka era, the levels of cribra orbitalia rose slightly. The age at death profile for the adults was also somewhat conflicting since the majority of adult males survived until middle or old age, whereas the majority of females died as young adults (Murphy and Khokhlov 2004). Stature for both males and females underwent a dramatic decline during Srubnaya

times, which may again be indicative of poor health. Since the health indicators are so inconclusive, it is difficult to interpret the significance of the slight increase in prevalence of reactive new bone formation among the Srubnaya group. It would seem to be the case, however, that the Srubnaya people enjoyed a better standard of health than either the Yamnaya or Potapovka groups. Perhaps the increase in sedentarization resulted in an improvement in health.

Diet
As stated above, the principal goal of the Samara Valley Project was to document the nature of the subsistence economy of the LBA Srubnaya culture in the Samara Valley. The transition from the MBA to the LBA witnessed a great increase in settlement sites as the population of the region generally became more settled at the beginning of the Srubnaya period, around 1900 to 1700 BC. It has been proposed that this early Late Bronze Age sedentarization process was related to the adoption of agriculture, but the Samara Valley Project found no evidence for agriculture in Srubnaya settlements (see Anthony et al. 2005:408). One of the most interesting aspects of the human skeletal record is that it does not display any evidence for a significant change in diet between the Eneolithic and the Srubnaya periods.

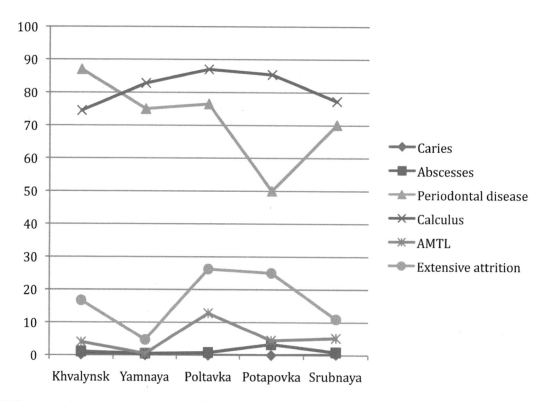

Figure 8.17 Summary of the dental paleopathological lesions among the Volga adults across the different time periods, based on Tables 8.18 to 8.21, 8.24, and 8.25. AMTL = antemortem tooth loss

The overall trends for caries, abscesses, periodontal disease, supragingival calculus, antemortem loss, and extensive tooth attrition did not differ greatly from the Khvalynsk to the Srubnaya cultures in the Volga region (Figure 8.17).

The dentitions of all groups were characterized by high levels (ca. 50–100 percent) of periodontal disease and calculus and generally low levels (0–30 percent) of extensive tooth attrition, antemortem loss, abscesses, and caries. Previous studies have indicated that, although there can be a variety of etiologies for the lesions, when studied at the population level, caries and calculus formation are particularly useful for paleodietary reconstruction. The precise nature of the relationship between diet and calculus formation is not fully understood, and high levels of calculus have been identified in populations that consumed diets rich in protein and high in carbohydrates (Lieverse 1999:226). When the frequencies of calculus and caries are compared, however, they can be used to assess the relative levels of proteins versus carbohydrates within a group's diet (Keenleyside 2008:265). Lillie (1996; 2000) found, for example, that Mesolithic and Neolithic populations in the Ukraine displayed no caries and high levels of dental calculus. He interpreted these findings as indicative of a protein-based diet that was low in carbohydrates and therefore compatible with the hunting-fishing-gathering and, for the Neolithic, pastoralist form of economy expected for these early populations. These trends are very similar to those derived

from the Volga populations, where caries are practically absent and the calculus levels are even higher. It can therefore be concluded that all of the Volga populations from the Eneolithic to Late Bronze Age times consumed a high-protein diet in which cereals were largely absent. This conclusion finds support both in the stable isotope analyses of the populations (see Chapter 7) and in paleoenvironmental studies of the region (see Chapter 5). It could be postulated that the dental paleopathological characteristics of these early Volga populations may reflect a largely pastoral economy. It is interesting to note that the dental paleopathological findings of the Volga populations, particularly in terms of caries prevalence, are very different from populations of Iron Age mobile pastoralists from the South Siberian steppe-lands where prevalences of 6.4 percent and 5.5 percent have been reported for the Uyuk culture and Hunno-Sarmatian Aymyrlyg, respectively, and a frequency of 1.9 percent was obtained for the Tagar culture Ai-Dai (Murphy 1998:498; Murphy et al. 2013:2551-2552). It is probable that crop-based agricultural products formed a major component of their diet.

Other features that warrant comment are the relatively low levels of periodontal disease recorded for the Potapovka group. This could be ascribed to the high number of young adults that occurred in this population (Murphy and Khokhlov 2004). Differing levels of extensive attrition were recorded, perhaps indicating that the Poltavka and Potapovka cultures had a greater tendency to eat coarse foodstuffs, which caused wear to their teeth. One would

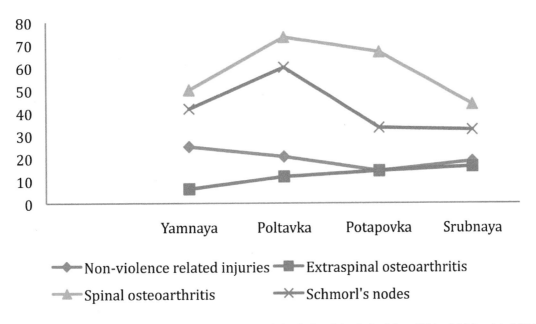

Figure 8.18 Summary prevalence rates of the potential indicators of physical activity derived from Tables 8.36 (crude), 8.37 (crude), 8.40 (individual), and 8.43 (individual).

imagine that the consumption of wild plants (see Chapter 5) and tough, possibly dried, meat would have the potential to cause extensive tooth wear. A more in-depth analysis of the patterns of attrition would be required, however, to enable the trends to be explored further.

Activity Patterns

Prevalence rates of the four main potential indicators of physical activity—non-violence-related injuries, spinal and extraspinal osteoarthritis, and Schmorl's nodes—are displayed in Figure 8.18.

No clear trends were apparent, and it would appear that each population engaged in physical activities that placed stress and strain on the body in different ways. The prevalence of non-violence-related injuries was highest during the Yamnaya period and appeared to decrease over time, only to rise for the Srubnaya population. The Poltavka group displayed the highest levels of spinal osteoarthritis and Schmorl's nodes, which may indicate that their daily activities had placed particular stress and strain on the spine, while the Srubnaya corpus of individuals displayed the least stressed spines but the highest levels of extraspinal osteoarthritis. The Yamnaya to Potapovka populations would have been more mobile and nomadic than the later Srubnaya people, who demonstrably lived more settled lives. The diversity of trends for the activity patterns would tend to suggest that, even though they were all pastoralists, the Yamnaya, Poltavka, and Potapovka groups engaged in a variety of different activities that focused strain and injury in different ways. This finding should not really be surprising, however, since recent research has demonstrated the existence of considerable variation in relation to the pastoral strategies that would have been used by steppe populations depending on the nature of social and environmental conditions (see Frachetti 2008).

The Srubnaya population displayed the least stressed spines, although they appeared to have been most susceptible to extraspinal osteoarthritis and displayed similar levels of non-violence-related injuries to the Middle Bronze Age populations. The more settled Srubnaya residence pattern apparently did not depend on agricultural work (see Chapter 5). It is known that seasonal mining activities were undertaken by the Srubnaya people, and a copper mine dating to this period has been partly excavated at Mikhailovka Ovsianka, 24 km to the south of the Samara River valley. Mining activities are generally thought to have increased in the Late Bronze Age across the western and central steppes in Srubnaya and Andronovo contexts. It is thought that there may have been a move from the exploitation of central metallurgical centers to a more widespread utiliza-

tion of resources (Anthony et al. 2005:414). It is possible that the change in activity patterns was somehow related to these activities. Although the prevalences were very low, only the Srubnaya population displayed rib and vertebrae fractures. Also of note was the relative diversity of injuries apparent among the Srubnaya people, including spondylolysis, ossified hematomas, myositis ossificans traumatica, os acromiale, osteochondritis dissecans, and enthesophytes. Perhaps this diversity of injuries is evidence that the Srubnaya individuals were engaging in a greater range of activities than preceding populations.

The occurrence of five cases of osteochondritis dissecans in five males is also of interest. Although there may be a genetic component, the lesion is generally considered the end result of an osteochondral fracture that was initially caused by shearing, rotatory, or tangentially aligned impaction forces (Resnick et al. 1995:2613). One could imagine that digging activities associated with mining could potentially have caused such twisting injuries. Another interesting characteristic of the Srubnaya activity patterns was the relatively high levels of extraspinal osteoarthritis. The Srubnaya population displayed the lowest levels of spinal osteoarthritis and Schmorl's nodes, however, and one would imagine that mining would potentially have caused major stress and strain to the spine. As such, it is possible that the interesting variety of injuries and relatively high levels of extraspinal osteoarthritis apparent in this group are not specifically related to mining but rather to a general change in activities associated with increasing sedentarization. Such activities may have included the construction of buildings. Perhaps the lower levels of lesions characteristic of spinal stress may be indicative of a decrease in herding activities, such as horseback riding and presumably the loading of wagons with supplies.

Another interesting aspect of the injury pattern among the Srubnaya individuals was the occurrence of a relatively high level of injury among female individuals (13.1 percent) as well as males (23.9 percent). Some of the affected women displayed lesions, including os acromiale and spondylolysis, thereby suggesting that Srubnaya males and females both engaged in arduous physical activities. It is a pity that the female sample sizes for the earlier populations were not larger since this would have enabled one to ascertain if the nature of female activities had changed with the increasing sedentarization of the Srubnaya period.

Since these results are based on fairly small sample sizes and are partly derived from crude prevalence rates, they can only be viewed in general terms. They do appear to be providing tantalizing glimpses of the occurrence of differing activities between the Bronze Age groups, however,

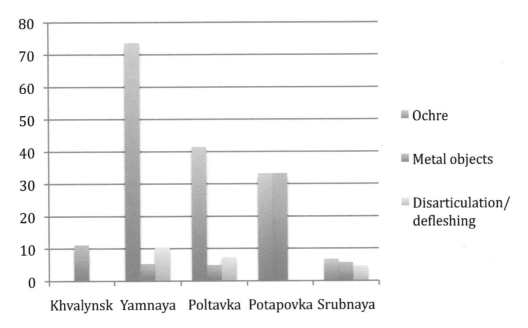

Figure 8.19 Summary of the prevalence rates for association with ochre and metal artifacts and evidence for disarticulation and/or defleshing based on the data contained in Tables 8.49, 8.51, and 8.53. It was only possible to examine the Khvalynsk group for their association with metal objects.

that may have been related to economic differences.

Funerary Processes

Three forms of funerary treatment were examined—the use of ochre in the burials, the presence of green discoloration on the skeletons as an indicator of the inclusion of metal objects, and the presence of cut marks due to disarticulation and/or defleshing (Figure 8.19).

When interpreting the data, it is important to bear in mind the problems associated with the small sample sizes of the earlier populations. All of the populations appear to have contained relatively low numbers of individuals with evidence of defleshing and/or disarticulation, although, as discussed earlier, it is highly probable that the frequencies of such individuals are underestimated. Nevertheless, it would appear that throughout the Early, Middle, and Late Bronze Ages, secondary burial was a necessary procedure. The disarticulation of the corpse appears to have been a recurring trait of Eurasian pastoralism that has been largely ignored. Perhaps this practice indicates that the Yamnaya and Potapovka populations were more mobile than the later Potapovka and Srubnaya groups and therefore needed to process a greater proportion of bodies. Although the numbers of females included in the study are admittedly small, it is interesting that only males in the Yamnaya and Poltavka groups had been afforded body processing. By Srubnaya times, both males and females exhibited body processing. Perhaps a change had occurred that saw individuals of both

sexes traveling greater distances, but this interpretation is complicated by the evidence for year-round settlements (Anthony et al. 2005:403). One might have envisioned that women and children would have remained in the settlement while males went to the pastures with their herds, but the occurrence of a few females with evidence of disarticulation would tend to suggest that this was not always the case.

The deposition of red ochre on the body appears to have been an important funerary rite for the Yamnaya population, but its use seems to have declined by Srubnaya times. The frequencies of disarticulation and defleshing also gradually decreased from the Yamnaya to Srubnaya times. Among the Srubnaya population, the prevalence of females (18 percent) with ochre staining was notably higher than for males (3 percent). It is possible that as this funerary ritual went into decline, it remained largely associated with females. Perhaps it was the females of society who were more inclined to keep tradition alive, while the males were more open to new ideas and belief systems. The occurrence of two apparently related female and infant burials colored with red ochre—one Yamnaya and the other Srubnaya— may further attest to the particular significance of ochre for women. Both infants were very young, and it is possible that they and their mothers had died during, or soon after, the birthing process. Perhaps red ochre was symbolic of life—perhaps blood—and was included within a funerary context as a symbol of the rebirth of the individuals in the afterlife.

All of the populations contained low numbers of individuals with green discoloration due to their association with metal artifacts, most of which appear to have been items of jewelry. A notably higher frequency of individuals with green staining was recorded for the Potapovka group. All of the affected individuals derived from a single kurgan—Kurgan 6 of the Utyevka VI burial ground—and, if we consider burial with jewelry to be a high-status characteristic, it is possible that this result was influenced by the fact that this was a particularly high-status kurgan. However, the increase in copper staining in the Potapovka sample correlates with a significant increase in the number of copper objects deposited in graves during the Potapovka period in general. At contemporary Sintashta settlement sites, located southeast of the Ural Mountains, copper working occurred in every excavated structure. The increase in copper-stained human bones complements the evidence for increased numbers of metal artifacts in Potapovka and Sintashta graves and for a great increase in metal production in Sintashta settlements of the same era (Anthony 2007:391). It is extremely interesting that despite this apparent wealth in metal, the Potapovka population had generally low levels of health, which may have been related to increasing levels of violence at this time (see above). This is in contrast to the Khvalynsk population, which was also associated with numerous copper grave goods but appeared to have enjoyed a relatively good standard of health.

Final Remarks

The results would tend to suggest that subtle differences in health, diet, lifestyle, levels of violence, and funerary practices were apparent among the Khvalynsk, Yamnaya, Poltavka, Potapovka, and Srubnaya populations. Perhaps most surprisingly, the dental paleopathological profile, with its very low levels of caries and high levels of calculus, did not provide evidence for the occurrence of a major economic change to correspond with the increased sedentarization of the Srubnaya culture. It would seem to be the case that all of the cultures included within the study were predominantly pastoralists. Evidence that the populations engaged in different forms of everyday physical activities was hinted in the distribution of osteoarthritis and non-violence-related injuries, although it was impossible to be more specific about the nature of the tasks in which each group was engaged.

Analysis of a suite of health indicators would tend to suggest that the standards of health were poorest during the Yamnaya and Potapovka times, while the Khvalynsk and Poltavka populations enjoyed the highest levels of good health. The occurrence of a physically disabled male with

an array of unusual signs of trauma, which may be indicative of torture, provides a glimpse into the darker side of life among the Yamnaya population. It is perhaps significant that this population appeared to have suffered from the poorest levels of health.

The osteological evidence has also provided insights concerning the funerary rituals afforded to individuals within each population. It would appear to be the case that certain individuals in all groups were buried with metal grave goods. The use of ochre and the practice of the disarticulation and defleshing of the body were used throughout the Bronze Age, although, as time advanced, they appear to have declined. Perhaps this apparent decline was related to the increasing sedentarization of the Srubnaya population. Within the Srubnaya sample, it is particularly interesting to note that although the frequencies were relatively low, cut marks were observed on both males and females. This may indicate that males and females were equally mobile at this time.

This study represents the first comprehensive paleopathological analysis undertaken on the prehistoric populations of the Volga region—a key location at the crossroads between Europe and Asia. While this general overview has provided significant insights concerning the people who lived and died in this region from Eneolithic to Late Bronze Age times, it is clear that a greater integration of site-specific mortuary data with osteological and paleopathological findings has the potential to provide an even richer understanding of these populations (see, e.g., Popova et al. 2011). The prehistoric Volga populations practiced a diverse array of complex burial rituals, and an integrated bioarchaeological approach has the potential to greatly enhance our understanding of the social aspects of the burial record. The adoption of such an approach has the potential to enable a truer understanding of what these populations valued, their relationships, and their belief systems—fundamental aspects of being human that lie at the heart of any society, past or present.

Notes
Figures, tables and photographs by E. Murphy.

References
Adams, J. C., and D. L. Hamblen
1990   *Outline of Orthopaedics.* 11th ed. Churchill Livingstone, London.
Anthony, D. W.
2007   *The Horse, the Wheel, and Language: How Bronze Age Riders from the Eurasian Steppes Shaped the Modern World.* Princeton University Press, Princeton, NJ.

2009   The Sintashta Genesis: The Roles of Climate Change, Warfare, and Long-Distance Trade. In *Social Complexity in Prehistoric Eurasia: Monuments, Metals and Mobility*, edited by B. K. Hanks and K. M. Linduff, pp. 47–73. Cambridge University Press, Cambridge.

Anthony, D. W., D. Brown, E. Brown, A. Goodman, A. Khokhlov, P. Kosintsev, P. Kuznetsov, O. Mochalov, E. Murphy, D. Peterson, A. Pike-Tay, L. Popova, A. Rosen, N. Russell, and A. Weisskopf

2005   The Samara Valley Project: Late Bronze Age Economy and Ritual in the Russian Steppes. *Eurasia Antiqua* 11:395–417.

Apley, A. G., and L. Solomon

1988   *Concise System of Orthopaedics and Fractures.* Butterworth-Heinemann, Oxford.

Aufderheide, A. C., and C. Rodríguez-Martín

1998   *The Cambridge Encyclopedia of Human Paleopathology.* Cambridge University Press, Cambridge.

Baker, J., and D. Brothwell

1980   *Animal Diseases in Archaeology.* Academic Press, London.

Barnes, E.

1994   *Developmental Defects of the Axial Skeleton in Paleopathology.* Colorado University Press, Niwot.

2008   Congenital Anomalies. In *Advances in Human Palaeopathology*, edited by R. Pinhasi and S. Mays, pp. 329–362. John Wiley and Sons, Chichester.

Berrizbeitia, E. L.

1989   Sex Determination with the Head of the Radius. *Journal of Forensic Sciences* 34:1206–1213.

Bokovenko, N. A.

1995   History of Studies and the Main Problems in the Archaeology of Southern Siberia during the Scythian Period. In *Nomads of the Eurasian Steppes in the Early Iron Age*, edited by J. Davis-Kimball, V. A. Bashilov, and L. T. Yablonsky, pp. 255–261. Zinat, Berkeley.

Brickley, M., and R. Ives

2008   *The Bioarchaeology of Metabolic Bone Disease.* Academic Press, London.

Brooks, S., and J. M. Suchey

1990   Skeletal Age Determination Based on the Os Pubis: A Comparison of the Acsádi-Nemeskéri and Suchey-Brooks Methods. *Human Evolution* 5:227–238.

Brothwell, D. R.

1981   *Digging Up Bones.* 3rd ed. British Museum and Cornell University Press, New York.

Buikstra, J., and D. H. Ubelaker (editors)

1994   *Standards for Data Collection from Human Skeletal Remains.* Fayetteville, Arkansas, Archaeological Survey Research Series No. 44.

Buzon, M. R., and M. A. Judd

2008 Investigating Health at Kerma: Sacrificial versus Nonsacrificial Individuals. *American Journal of Physical Anthropology* 136:93–99.

Carter, C. O.

1964   The Genetics of Common Malformations. In *Second International Conference on Congenital Malformations*, edited by M. Fishbein, pp. 306–313. The International Medical Congress, New York.

Chernykh, E. N.

2009   Formation of the Eurasian Steppe Belt Cultures: Viewed through the Lens of Archaeometallurgy and Radiocarbon Dating. In *Social Complexity in Prehistoric Eurasia: Monuments, Metals and Mobility*, edited by B. K. Hanks and K. M. Linduff, pp. 115–145. Cambridge University Press, Cambridge.

Clanton, T. D., and J. C. DeLee

1982   Osteochondritis Dissecans: History, Pathophysiology and Current Treatment Concepts. *Clinical Orthopaedics and Related Research* 167:50–64.

Dobney, K., and A. Goodman

1991   Epidemiological Studies of Dental Enamel Hypoplasias in Mexico and Bradford: Their Relevance to Archaeological Skeletal Studies. In *Health in Past Societies: Biocultural Interpretations of Human Skeletal Remains in Archaeological Contexts* (BAR International Series 567), edited by H. Bush and M. Zvelebil, pp. 81–100. Tempvs Repartvm, Oxford.

Epimakhov, A. V.

2009   Settlements and Cemeteries of the Bronze Age of the Urals: The Potential for Reconstructing Early Social Dynamics. In *Social Complexity in Prehistoric Eurasia: Monuments, Metals and Mobility*, edited by B. K. Hanks and K. M. Linduff, pp. 74–90. Cambridge University Press, Cambridge.

Feingold, M., and S. S. Gellis

1968   Ocular Abnormalities Associated with First and Second Arch Syndromes. *Survey of Ophthalmology* 14:30–42.

Feldesman, M. R., and R. L. Fountain

1996   'Race' Specificity and the Femur/Stature Ratio. *American Journal of Physical Anthropology* 100:207–224.

Ferembach, D., I. Schwidetzky, and M. Stloukal

1980   Recommendations for Age and Sex Diagnoses of Skeletons. *Journal of Human Evolution* 9:517–549.

Ferrer-Torrelles, M., and T. Ceballos

1982   Embryology of the Hip in Relation to Congenital Dislocation. In *Congenital Dislocation of the Hip*, edited by M. O. Tachdjian, pp. 1–25. Churchill Livingstone, London.

Finch, R. G., and P. Ball

1991   *Infection.* Blackwell Scientific, Oxford.

Frachetti, M. D.

2008   *Pastoralist Landscapes and Social Interaction in Bronze Age Eurasia*. University of California Press, Berkeley.

Goodman, A.

1991   Health, Adaptation, and Maladaptation in Past Societies. In *Health in Past Societies: Biocultural Interpretations of Human Skeletal Remains in Archaeological Contexts* (BAR International Series 567), edited by H. Bush and M. Zvelebil, pp. 31–38. Tempvs Repartvm, Oxford.

Goodman, A. H., and G. J. Armelagos

1988   Childhood Stress and Decreased Longevity in a Prehistoric Population. *American Anthropologist* 90:936–944.

Goodman, A. H., G. J. Armelagos, and J. C. Rose

1980   Enamel Hypoplasias as Indicators of Stress in Three Prehistoric Populations from Illinois. *Human Biology* 52:515–528.

Goodman, A. H., J. Lallo, G. J. Armelagos, and J. C. Rose

1984   Health Changes at Dickson Mounds, Illinois (AD 950–1300). In *Paleopathology at the Origins of Agriculture*, edited by M. N. Cohen and G. J. Armelagos, pp. 271–305.Academic Press, London.

Goodman, A. H., and D. L. Martin

2002   Reconstructing Health Profiles from Skeletal Remains. In *The Backbone of History: Health and Nutrition in the Western Hemisphere*, edited by R. H. Steckel and J. C. Rose, pp. 11–60. Cambridge University Press, Cambridge.

Goodman, A. H., R. B. Thomas, A. C. Swedlund, and G. J. Armelagos

1988   Biocultural Perspectives on Stress in Prehistoric, Historical, and Contemporary Population Research. *Yearbook of Physical Anthropology* 31:169–202.

Gruebel Lee, D. M.

1983   *Disorders of the Hip*. J. B. Lippincott, London.

Hamblen, D. L., and A. H. R. W. Simpson

2007   *Adams's Outline of Fractures*. 12th ed. Churchill Livingstone Elsevier, London.

Hillson, S. W.

1979   Diet and Dental Disease. *World Archaeology* 2:147–162.

1986   *Teeth (Cambridge Manuals in Archaeology)*. Cambridge University Press, Cambridge.

1996   *Dental Anthropology*. Cambridge University Press, Cambridge.

Hughes, S.

1986   *Aston's Short Textbook of Orthopaedics and Traumatology*. 3rd ed. Hodder and Stoughton, London.

Inman, V. T.

1963   Clubfoot and Other Bony Defects. In *Birth Defects*, edited by M. Fishbein, pp. 245–252. J. B. Lippincott, Philadelphia.

Işcan, M. Y., S. R. Loth, and R. K. Wright

1984   Age Estimation from the Rib by Phase Analysis: White Males. *Journal of Forensic Sciences* 29:1094–1104.

1985   Age Estimation from the Rib by Phase Analysis: White Females. *Journal of Forensic Sciences* 30:853–863.

Jurmain, R. D.

1980   The Pattern of Involvement of Appendicular Degenerative Joint Disease. *American Journal of Physical Anthropology* 53:143–150.

Keenleyside, A.

2008   Dental Pathology and Diet at Apollonia, a Greek Colony on the Black Sea. *International Journal of Osteoarchaeology* 18:262–279.

Krogman, W. M., and M. Y. Işcan

1986   *The Human Skeleton in Forensic Medicine*. 2nd ed. Charles C Thomas, Springfield.

Larsen, C. S.

1997   *Bioarchaeology: Interpreting Behavior from the Human Skeleton*. Cambridge University Press, Cambridge.

Leigh, R. W.

1925   Dental Pathology of Indian Tribes of Varied Environmental and Food Conditions. *American Journal of Physical Anthropology* 8:179–199.

Lettre, G., A. U. Jackson, C. Gieger, F. R. Schumacher, S. I. Berndt, S. Sanna, S. Eyheramendy, B. F. Voight, J. L. Butler, C. Guiducci, T. Illig, R. Hackett, I. M. Heid, K. B. Jacobs, V. Lyssenko, M. Uda, The Diabetes Genetics Initiative, FUSION, KORA, The Prostate, Lung Colorectal and Ovarian Cancer Screening Trial, The Nurses' Health Study, SardiNIA, M. Boehnke, S. J. Chanock, L. C. Groop, F. B. Hu, B. Isomaa, P. Kraft, L. Peltonen, S. Veikko, D. Schlessinger, D. J. Hunter, R. B. Hayes, G. R. Abecasis, H.-E.Wichmann, K. L. Mohlke, and J. N. Hirschhorn

2008   Identification of Ten Loci Associated with Height Highlights New Biological Pathways in Human Growth. *Nature Genetics* 40:584–591.

Lieverse, A. R.

1999   Diet and the Aetiology of Dental Calculus. *International Journal of Osteoarchaeology* 9:219–232.

Lillie, M. C.

1996   Mesolithic and Neolithic Populations of Ukraine: Indications of Diet from Dental Pathology. *Current Anthropology* 37:135–142.

2000   Stable Isotope Analysis and Dental Evidence of Diet at the Mesolithic-Neolithic Transition in Ukraine. *Journal of Archaeological Science* 27:965–972.

2003   Cranial Surgery: The Epipalaeolithic to Neolithic Populations of Ukraine. In *Trepanation: History, Discovery, Theory*, edited by R. Arnott, S. Finger, and C. U. M. Smith, pp. 175–188. Svets and Zeitlinger Publishers, Abingdon.

Lovejoy, C. O., R. S. Meindl, T. R. Pryzbeck, and R. P. Mensforth
1985   Chronological Metamorphosis of the Auricular Surface of the Ilium: A New Method for the Determination of Adult Skeletal Age at Death. *American Journal of Physical Anthropology* 68:15–28.

Lovell, N.
1994   Spinal Arthritis and Physical Stress at Bronze Age Harappa. *American Journal of Physical Anthropology* 93:149–164.

Lovell, N. C.
2000   Palaeopathological Description and Diagnosis. In *Biological Anthropology of the Human Skeleton*, edited by M. A. Katzenberg and S. R. Saunders, pp. 217–248. John Wiley and Sons, Chichester.

Lukacs, J. R.
1989   Dental Palaeopathology: Methods for Reconstructing Dietary Patterns. In *Reconstruction of Life from the Skeleton*, edited by M. Y. Işcan and K. A. R. Kennedy, 261–286. Alan Liss, New York.

Mandelshtam, A. M.
1992   Ranniye kochevniki Skifskova perioda na territorii Tuvi. In *Stepnaya Polosa Aziatskoi Chasti SSSR v Skifo-Sarmatskoye Vremya, Archeologiya SSSR*, edited by M. G. Moshkova, pp. 178–196. Nauka, Moskva.

McClure, J. G., and R. B. Raney
1975   Anomalies of the Scapula. *Clinical Orthopaedics and Related Research* 110:22–31.

McKern, T. W.
1970   Estimation of Skeletal Age: From Puberty to about 30 Years of Age. In *Personal Identification in Mass Disasters*, edited by T. D. Stewart, pp. 41–56. Smithsonian Institution, Washington, D.C.

Meiklejohn, C., C. T. Schentag, A. Venema, and P. Key
1984   Socioeconomic Change and Patterns of Pathology and Variation in the Mesolithic and Neolithic of Western Europe: Some Suggestions. In *Paleopathology at the Origins of Agriculture*, edited by M. N. Cohen and G. J. Armelagos, pp. 75–100. Academic Press, Orlando, Florida.

Mednikova, M. B.
2001   *Trepanatsii i drevnikh narodov Eurazii*. Scientific World, Moscow.

Merbs, C. F., and W. H. Wilson
1960   *Anomalies and Pathologies of the Sadlermuit Eskimo Vertebral Column*. Ottawa, National Museum of Canada Bulletin 180, Contribution to Anthropology Part 1:154–180.

Molnar, S.
1972   Tooth Wear and Culture: A Survey of Tooth Functions among Some Prehistoric Populations. *Current Anthropology* 13:511–526.

Moorrees, C. F. A., E. A. Fanning, and E. E. Hunt Jr.
1963   Formation and Resorption of Three Deciduous Teeth in children. *American Journal of Physical Anthropology* 21:205–213.

Murphy, E. M.
1998   An Osteological and Palaeopathological Study of the Scythian and Hunno-Sarmatian Period Populations from the Cemetery Complex of Aymyrlyg, Tuva, South Siberia. Unpublished Ph.D. dissertation, School of Archaeology and Palaeoecology, Queen's University Belfast.
2000a   Mummification and Body Processing: Evidence from the Iron Age in Southern Siberia. In *Kurgans, Ritual Sites, and Settlements: The Eurasian Bronze and Iron Age, Papers from the European Association of Archaeologists 4th and 5th Annual Meetings* (BAR International Series 890), edited by J. Davis-Kimball, E. Murphy, L. Koryakova, and L. Yablonsky, pp. 279–292. Archaeopress, Oxford.
2000b   Developmental Defects and Disability: The Evidence from the Iron Age Semi-Nomadic Peoples of Aymyrlyg, South Siberia. In *Madness, Disability and Social Exclusion* (One World Archaeology 40), edited by Jane Hubert, pp. 60–80. Routledge, London.
2003a   *Iron Age Archaeology and Trauma from Aymyrlyg, South Siberia* (BAR International Series 1152). Archaeopress, Oxford.
2003b   Trepanations and Perforated Crania from Iron Age South Siberia: An Exercise in differential diagnosis. In *Trepanation: History, Discovery, Theory*, edited by R. Arnott, S. Finger and C. U. M. Smith, pp. 209–221. Svets and Zeitlinger, Abingdon.

Murphy, E. M. (editor)
2008   *Deviant Burial in the Archaeological Record*. Oxbow, Oxford.

Murphy, E. M.
2012   A Bioarchaeological Study of Xiongnu Expansion in Iron Age Tuva, South Siberia. In *Regimes and Revolutions: Power, Violence, and Labor in Eurasia from the Ancient to the Modern*, edited by C. W. Hartley, B. Yazicioglu, and A. Smith, pp. 240–261. Cambridge University Press, Cambridge.

Murphy, E., and A. Khokhlov
2004   Osteological and Palaeopathological Analysis of Volga Populations from the Eneolithic to Srubnaya Periods. Unpublished report.

Murphy, E. M., Y. K. Chistov, R. Hopkins, P. Rutland, and G. M. Taylor
2009   Tuberculosis among Iron Age Individuals from Tyva, South Siberia: Palaeopathological and Biomolecular Findings. *Journal of Archaeological Science* 36:2029–2038.

Murphy, E. M., I. I. Gokhman, Y. K. Chistov, and L. L. Barkova
2002   A Review of the Evidence for Old World Scalping: New Cases from the Cemetery of Aymyrlyg, South Siberia. *American Journal of Archaeology* 106:1–10.

Murphy, E. M., R. Schulting, N. Beer, Y. Chistov, A. Kasparov, and M. Pshenitsyna
2013   Iron Age Pastoral Nomadism and Agriculture in the Eastern Eurasian Steppe: Implications from Dental Palaeopathology and Stable Carbon and Nitrogen Isotopes. *Journal of Archaeological Science* 40:2547–2560.

Ortner, D. J.
2003   *Identification of Pathological Conditions in Human Skeletal Remains.* 2nd ed. Smithsonian Institution Press, London.

Papadopoulos, J. K.
2000   Skeletons in Wells: Towards an Archaeology of Exclusion in the Ancient Greek World. In *Madness, Disability and Social Exclusion, One World Archaeology 40*, edited by J. Hubert. Routledge, London.

Pavlov, H.
1995   Physical Injury: Sports Related Abnormalities. In *Diagnosis of Bone and Joint Disorders*, Vol. 5, 3rd ed., edited by D. Resnick, pp. 3229–3263. W. B. Saunders, London.

Pearson, K.
1917–1919 *A Study of the Long Bones of the English Skeleton I: The Femur.* Company Research Memoirs Biometric Series X, University of London, Department of Applied Statistics, London.

Perry, M. A.
2007   Is Bioarchaeology a Handmaiden to History? Developing a Historical Bioarchaeology. *Journal of Anthropological Archaeology* 26:486–515.

Perzigian, A. J., P. A. Tench, and D. J. Braun
1984   Prehistoric Health in the Ohio River Valley. In *Paleopathology at the Origins of Agriculture*, edited by M. N. Cohen and G. J. Armelagos, pp. 347–366. Academic Press, London.

Pinhasi, R.
2008   Growth in Archaeological Populations. In *Advances in Human Palaeopathology*, edited by R. Pinhasi and S. Mays, pp. 363–380. John Wiley and Sons, Chichester.

Popova, L. M. S.
2009   Blurring the Boundaries: Foragers and Pastoralists in the Volga-Urals Region. In *Social Complexity in Prehistoric Eurasia: Monuments, Metals and Mobility*, edited by B. K. Hanks and K. M. Linduff, pp. 296–320. Cambridge University Press, Cambridge.

Popova, L. M., E. M. Murphy, and A. Khokhlov
2011   Standardization and Resistance: Changing Funerary Rites at Spiridonovka (Russia) during the Beginning of the Late Bronze Age. In *The Archaeology of Politics: The Materiality of Political Practice and Action in the Past*, edited by P. G. Johansen and A. M. Bauer, pp. 280–319. Cambridge Scholars Press, Cambridge.

Potter, E. L., and J. M. Craig
1975   *Pathology of the Fetus and the Infant.* 3rd ed. Year Book Medical Publishers, London.

Powell, M. L.
1985   The Analysis of Dental Wear and Caries for Dietary Reconstruction. In *The Analysis of Prehistoric Diets*, edited by R. I. Gilbert and J. H. Mielke, pp. 307–338. Academic Press, London.

Regöly-Mérei, G.
1967   Palaeopathological Examination of the Skeletal Finds of Naima Tolgoy and Hana. *Acta Archaeologica Academiae Scientiarum Hungaricae* 19:391–409.

Resnick, D.
1995a   Additional Congenital or Heritable Anomalies and Syndromes. In *Diagnosis of Bone and Joint Disorders*, Vol. 6, 3rd ed., edited by D. Resnick, pp. 4269–4330. W. B. Saunders, London.

1995b   Internal Derangement of Joints. In *Diagnosis of Bone and Joint Disorders*, Vol. 5, 3rd ed., edited by D. Resnick, pp. 2899–3228. W. B. Saunders, London.

Resnick, D., and T. G. Goergen
1995   Physical Injury: Extraspinal Sites. In *Diagnosis of Bone and Joint Disorders*, Vol. 5, 3rd ed., edited by D. Resnick, pp. 2693–2824. W. B. Saunders, London.

Resnick, D., and G. Niwayama
1995a   Osteomyelitis, Septic Arthritis and Soft Tissue Infection: Mechanisms and Situations. In *Diagnosis of Bone and Joint Disorders*, Vol. 4, 3rd ed., edited by D. Resnick, pp. 2325–2418. W. B. Saunders, London.

1995b   Osteoporosis. In *Diagnosis of Bone and Joint Disorders*, Vol. 4, 3rd ed., edited by D. Resnick, pp. 1783–1853. W. B. Saunders, London.

1995c   Soft Tissues. In *Diagnosis of Bone and Joint Disorders*, Vol. 6, 3rd ed., edited by D. Resnick, pp. 4491–4622. W. B. Saunders, London.

1995d   Degenerative Disease of the Spine. In *Diagnosis of Bone and Joint Disorders*, Vol. 3, 3rd ed., edited by D. Resnick, pp. 1372–1462. W. B. Saunders, London.

Resnick, D., T. G. Goergen, and G. Niwayama
1995   Physical Injury: Concepts and Terminology. In *Diagnosis of Bone and Joint Disorders*, Vol. 5, 3rd ed., edited by D. Resnick, pp. 2561–2692. W. B. Saunders, London.

Ribot, I., and C. Roberts
1996   A Study of Non-Specific Stress Indicators and Skeletal Growth in Two Mediaeval Subadult Populations. *Journal of Archaeological Science* 23:67–79.

Roberts, C., and K. Manchester
2005   *The Archaeology of Disease*. 3rd ed. Cornell University Press, New York.

Rogers, J., and T. Waldron
1995   *A Field Guide to Joint Disease in Archaeology*. John Wiley and Sons, Chichester.

Rogers, J., T. Waldron, P. Dieppe, and I. Watt
1987   Arthropathies in Palaeopathology: The Basis of Classification According to Most Probable Cause. *Journal of Archaeological Science* 14:179–193.

Roosevelt, A. C.
1984   Population, Health, and the Evolution of Subsistence: Conclusions from the Conference. In *Paleopathology at the Origins of Agriculture*, edited by M. N. Cohen and G. J. Armelagos, pp. 559–583. Academic Press, London.

Rudenko, S. I.
1970   *Frozen Tombs of Siberia: The Pazyryk Burials of Iron Age Horsemen*. J. M. Dent & Sons, London.

Rugg-Gunn, A. J.
1993   *Nutrition and Health*. Oxford University Press, Oxford.

Sartoris, D. J.
1995   Developmental Dysplasia of the Hip. In *Diagnosis of Bone and Joint Disorders*, Vol. 6, 3rd ed., edited by D. Resnick, pp. 4067–4094. W. B. Saunders, London.

Scheuer, J. L., J. H. Musgrave, and S. P. Evans
1980   The Estimation of Late Fetal and Perinatal Age from Limb Bone Length by Linear and Logarithmic Regression. *Annals of Human Biology* 7:257–265.

Schmorl, G., and H. Junghanns
1971   *The Human Spine in Health and Disease*. 2nd ed. Grune & Stratton, London.

Smith, B. H.
1991   Standards of Human Tooth Formation and Dental Age Assessment. In *Advances in Dental Anthropology*, edited by M. A. Kelley and C. S. Larsen, pp. 143–168. Wiley-Liss, New York.

Steckel, R. H.
1995   Stature and the Standard of Living. *Journal of Economic Literature* 33:1903–1940.

Steckel, R. H., and J. C. Rose
2002a   Patterns of Health in the Western Hemisphere. In *The Backbone of History: Health and Nutrition in the Western Hemisphere*, edited by R. H. Steckel and J. C. Rose, pp. 563–579. Cambridge University Press, Cambridge.

Steckel, R. H., and J. C. Rose (editors)
2002b   *The Backbone of History: Health and Nutrition in the Western Hemisphere*. Cambridge University Press, Cambridge.

Stewart, T. D.
1979   *Essentials of Forensic Anthropology*. Charles C Thomas, Springfield.

Stirland, A.
1991   Diagnosis of Occupationally Related Paleopathology: Can It Be Done? In *Human Paleopathology: Current Syntheses and Future Options*, edited by D. J. Ortner and A. C. Aufderheide, pp. 40–47. Smithsonian Institution Press, London.

Stuart-Macadam, P.
1985   Porotic Hyperostosis: Representative of a Childhood Condition. *American Journal of Physical Anthropology* 66:391–398.
1991   Anaemia in Roman Britain: Poundbury Camp. In *Health in Past Societies: Biocultural Interpretations of Human Skeletal Remains in Archaeological Contexts* (BAR International Series 567), edited by H. Bush and M. Zvelebil, pp. 101–113. Tempvs Repartvm, Oxford.

Suzuki, T.
1991   Paleopathological Study on Infectious Diseases in Japan. In *Human Paleopathology: Current Syntheses and Future Options*, edited by D. J. Ortner and A. C. Aufderheide, pp. 128–139. Smithsonian Institution Press, London.

Taylor, G. M., E. Murphy, R. Hopkins, P. Rutland, and Y. Chistov
2007   First Report of *Mycobacterium bovis* DNA in Human Remains from the Iron Age. *Microbiology* 153:1243–1249.

Torgersen, J.
1951   The Developmental Genetics and Evolutionary Meaning of the Metopic Suture. *American Journal of Physical Anthropology* 9:193–210.

Trotter, M., and G. C. Gleser
1958   A Re-evaluation of Estimation of Stature Taken during Life and of Long Bones after Death. *American Journal of Physical Anthropology* 16:79–123.

Ubelaker, D. H.
1989   *Human Skeletal Remains* (Manuals on Archaeology 2). 2nd ed. Smithsonian Institution, Washington, D.C.

Vainshtein, S. I.
1980   *Nomads of South Siberia: The Pastoral Economies of Tuva*. Cambridge University Press, Cambridge.

Waldron, T.
1992   Osteoarthritis in a Black Death Cemetery in London. *International Journal of Osteoarchaeology* 2:235–240.

216   Eileen M. Murphy and Aleksandr A. Khokhlov

Waldron, T., and J. Rogers
1991   Inter-Observer Variation in Coding Osteoarthritis in Human Skeletal Remains. *International Journal of Osteoarchaeology* 1:49–56.

Walker, P. L., R. R. Bathurst, R. Richman, T. Gjerdrum, and V. A. Andrushkp
2009   The Causes of Porotic Hyperostosis and Cribra Orbitalia: A Reappraisal of the Iron-Deficiency-Anemia Hypothesis. *American Journal of Physical Anthropology* 139:109–125.

Wells, C.
1974   Osteochondritis Dissecans in Ancient British Skeletal Material. *Medical History* 18:365–369.

Wells, C.
1975   Prehistoric and Historical Changes in Nutritional Diseases and Associated Conditions. *Progress in Food and Nutrition Science* 1:729–779.

Wood, J. W., G. R. Milner, H. C. Harpending, and K. M. Weiss
1992   The Osteological Paradox: Problems of Inferring Prehistoric Health from Skeletal Samples. *Current Anthropology* 33:343–358.

World Health Organization
2006   *Constitution of the World Health Organization, Supplement, Basic Documents*. 45th ed. World Health Organisation, Geneva.

Part IV

Excavation and Specialist Reports for the Krasnosamarskoe Kurgan Cemetery and Settlement and the Herding Camps in Peschanyi Dol

Chapter 9

The Geoarchaeology of the Krasnosamarskoe Sites

Arlene Miller Rosen

The Modern Landscape and Environment

The site of Krasnosamarskoe is situated in a semi-arid degraded steppic botanical zone with a continental climate, receiving about 300 to 400 mm of rainfall per year. The topography in the area is generally flat, although the microtopographic features of small hummocks, swales, and broad, shallow, ephemeral channels contribute to distinct differences in soil-vegetation associations. The area is drained through a combination of sheet-wash depositing silty sediments over all but the tops of low hummocks, slow flow through very shallow linear depressions, and flow through shallow meandering channels no more than 1 m in depth. The sediment load consists exclusively of fine material, with the coarsest deposits composed of sandy silt.

The two main types of soils in this area are referred to in the Russian literature as the *lugovo'e* or meadow soil and the *solenetz* or saline soil. The meadow soil, a variant of the true steppic *Chernozem* soils, is found on the tops of hummocks in well-drained locations. A deep, well-developed A horizon and many rodent burrows typify it, because the good drainage provides a drier habitat for small burrowing mammals than the water-saturated depressions. Table 9.1 presents a description of a typical profile of this soil. The *solenetz* soil is found in the poorly drained depressions. It is characterized by a very shallow A horizon poorer in organic colloids and is saturated with salts, including calcium carbonates, NaCl, as well as gypsum (see Table 9.2 for a description of the *solenetz* soil) (Igor Ivanov, personal communication, 1999).

Table 9.1 Sediment Description of a Typical *Lugovo'e* Meadow Soil at Krasnosamarskoe

Unit	Depth, cm	Color	Texture	Structure	Composition	Lower Boundary
1: A1 horizon	0–15/21	Black (10 YR 2/1, m)	Silt loam	Columnar	Some *krotovinas*	Graded and smooth
2: A2 horizon	15/21–68	Black (10 YR 2/1, m)	Clayey silt loam	Granular	Some *krotovinas*	Wavy and semi-abrupt
3: B horizon	68–88	Brown (10 YR 4/3, m)	Clayey loam	Small blocky (1.5 cm)		Wavy and smooth
4: Parent material	88–100	Brown (7.5 YR 4/4, m)	Clayey loam	Massive	Old flood plain silts	Not visible

Table 9.2 Description of a *Solenetz* Saline Soil

Unit	Depth, cm	Color	Texture	Structure	Composition	Lower Boundary
1: A horizon	0–16	Very dark brown (10 YR 2/2, moist)	Silt loam	Granular to columnar	Rootlets	Graded and irregular
2: B horizon	16–75	Strong brown (7.5 YR 3/4, moist)	Clayey silt loam	Small blocky structure (ca. 2-cm blocks)	Salt rich, NaCl and CaCO$_3$; Some *krotovinas*; thin fragments of floodwater silts at –30 cm	Smooth and graded
3: Parent material	75–107	Dark brown (7.5 YR 4/4, moist)	Clayey loam	Massive	Not visible	

These two main soil types are associated with distinct vegetation complexes. The meadow soils occur with the remnants of steppic grasses, which include *Stipa pennata* or feather grass, *Festuca sulcata*, and *Agropyron repens*, whereas the *solenetz* soils are found with *Artemisia* sp. According to a field survey conducted by Professor Matveeva, a botanist from Samara State University, in July 1999, the vegetation around the settlement site, located on the second terrace above the marshy floodplain, today shows mixed plant associations derived from pockets of both vegetation complexes. Typical of such second-terrace environments in the Samara Valley are clover (*Trifolium repens* with a small admixture of *Trifolium pratense*) and chicory (*Cichorium intybus*). Less dominant secondary plants found in 1999 in the steppe around the Krasnosamarskoe excavation site included *Plantago lanceolata*, an invasive weed resulting from overgrazing; *Festuca sulcata*, a grass of the dry steppe; *Medicago sativa*, or alfalfa, a common pasturage plant; *Achillea millefolium*, or yarrow, a popular medicinal herb; the purple flowers of *Veronica* sp.; *Galium verum*, or lady's bedstraw, another medicinal herb; and in low depressions with alkaline and saline soils, *Kochia prostrata*, *Alyssum desertorum*, and *Artemisia* sp.

Today, the three kurgans and the settlement site are situated between two ephemeral drainages, one to the north of the site and the other to the south. Both channels are seasonally active drainages that are shallow and muddy during the summer months. They drain into a manmade lake at the west edge of the settlement, and water from the lake fills the mouths of the two drainages, creating stagnant ponds with stands of *Phragmites* sp. (common reed), *Typha* sp.

(cattail rushes), *Juncus* sp., and *Cyperaceae* sedges, including *Cyperus* sp. and other genera. The southernmost drainage is incised into the landscape and displays no sections of former accumulations of alluvial sediment. This suggests that it is a relatively recent drainage channel, which might have occurred in association with the general downcutting of local streams and increased drainage density with the landscape degradation of the past several hundred years.

In contrast, the northernmost drainage does contain sections of older alluvial and marshy deposits, suggesting that this stream is older and existed here when the alluvial regime was depositional rather than erosional as is the modern situation. It also is deeper in the summer and is characterized by a number of cutoff meanders along its course, which supports the sediment evidence for a longer-lived drainage system. This stream appears to have a permanently moist channel bed, which suggests that it is fed by a low-yield spring or system of springs along its course. It is likely that this stream existed in this area during the Bronze and Iron Ages, and in periods with a moister climate or with less land degradation, the higher water table might have contributed to a permanent flow in this drainage. This would have provided one source of fresh water to the inhabitants of the site in the Bronze Age.

Reconstruction of Past Landscapes

The lake at the western edge of the settlement site was created in the 1970s for fish farming, but it was constructed over a former natural oxbow lake, originally formed from a cutoff meander of the Samara River. The location of this former lake is most likely to have been 120 m offshore from the current settlement site where a core taken in 1999 by Suzanne LeRoy (Figure 9.1) revealed around 1+ m of blue anaerobic and gleyed sediment at the bottom of the modern fishpond. Her core retrieved the basal section of blue gley sitting unconformably on a hard subsoil that was not penetrable by her coring equipment. A radiocarbon date (Table 9.3) on this basal blue gley soil (AA41034a) indicated that a shallow oxbow lake was present in the Early Holocene, before 9000 BC, and another date on a plant fragment embedded in the gley soil (AA41034b) showed that marsh plants were growing in the oxbow lake by 8700 to 8500 BC. Bulldozers were used to carve out a depression for the modern fishpond after its dams were built, and they might have removed the upper layers of gley, which might have originally been deeper. The same gleyed sediment was located within a section cut by shovel into the bank of the modern fishpond near the mouth of the northernmost stream, north of the settlement. This suggests that the eastern edge of the former lake at least spanned the area from the site to the north stream and that the north stream originally drained into a marshy oxbow lake.

The basal sediment unit, which underlies the kurgans and the settlement site consists of a former Pleistocene floodplain of the Samara River. This is the archaeologically sterile subsoil. This sediment unit is described here as the basal unit of all sections (see Tables 9.1, 9.2, 9.5, and 9.6) and is broadly characterized as a yellowish to reddish clayey loam. It contains no Late Pleistocene or Early Holocene paleosols, suggesting that this was an actively building Samara floodplain at least until Mid-Holocene times, with no long-term landscape stability, providing an opportunity for soil formation processes to dominate. These past floodplain loams grade into coarser sands as one approaches the channel of the Samara River.

Today, as in the past, the Samara River primarily carries coarse sands through this region. The finely laminated cross-bedding in the sands of the first terrace suggests a past flood regime characterized by strong steady flows, which deposited fine sands, silt and clays in the overbank deposits of the floodplain. Although the stream appears deeply incised during the summer, it is reported that the river still floods over its steep banks as a result of breached

Figure 9.1. Red pin marks Krasnosamarskoe settlement. The yellow pin near the settlement marks the lake core taken by Suzanne Leroy. The yellow pin on the Samara River is the location of Rosen's geological section (Samara Section 1) of the deeply incised Samara riverbed near Krasnosamarskoe (Table 9.4a,b). (Google Earth, Image © 2012 GeoEye)

Table 9.3 Environmental Dates from the Samara Riverbank and the Lake Bottom

Arizona Lab # and BP Date	Sample Site	Maximum Probability, cal BC	Next Highest Probability, cal BC	Next Highest Probability, Percentage
AA41033 8922 ± 59	Riverbank, old A horizon	8276–7844	8276–7938	92.30
AA41034a 9895 ± 58	Lake gley, basal sediment	9653–9255	9464–9255	84.10
AA41034b 9534 ± 95	Gley split, plants in sediment	9220–8638	9220–8692	91.10

ice dams in the spring. This modern flooding does not appear to greatly affect the immediate vicinity of the site, as testified by the soil development on the relatively stable landscape features, primarily the hummock tops with meadow soils. The current research has not yet determined the age of the final floodplain development in the vicinity of the site. This floodplain is a fine facies of the first Samara terrace. It would be important to know if floods were a regular seasonal feature in the vicinity of the site at the time of occupation. If so, then the site could only be occupied in the drier seasons of the year or during drier climatic periods when flooding was rare.

One promising geological section (Samara Section 1) was described on the side of the deeply incised Samara riverbed near Krasnosamarskoe (Table 9.4a,b). It appears to display a long history through the Late Pleistocene until the cessation of active floodplain aggradation and the beginning of the more recent phase of downcutting. The lowermost units of the section contain finely laminated, horizontally bedded medium sands representing ancient channel deposits of an alluviating stream. Within this is a thick deposit of heavily gleyed sandy silts probably representing a former cutoff channel and oxbow lake. These channel sands are truncated, and the later deposits are laminated silts, indicating that the active channel was farther from this location or that there was a reduction in flow. These silts are in turn truncated from a short downcutting phase, and floodplain deposits begin to accumulate. Within these clayey floodplain silts, there are the truncated $CaCO_3$ horizons of about six paleosols each separated by renewed floodplain alluviation. The last buried soil in the uppermost portion of the section has retained its A horizon and is located directly beneath the present-day soil. A radiocarbon date on this buried A horizon (Table 9.3, AA41033) provides us with a good estimation of the time when the major phase of floodplain alluviation ended here, around 8000 BC.

The paleolandscape of the site and its immediate surroundings appears to have been somewhat different from that of today. The gleyed sediments were discussed above

as evidence for the former existence of an oxbow lake near the site. It is unclear if this lake was actively flooded each year by the Samara overbank flow or if water draining from the north channel maintained the lake. The contemporaneity of the lake with the archaeological settlement still remains to be established, but the existence of lake fish bones suggests that it existed at the same time as the settlement (D. Anthony, personal communication, 1999).

We were also able to establish the existence of a former ephemeral stream channel to the south of the site. Alluvial flood sediments in the form of clasts of finely laminated silts appear in the fill of the three kurgans. Since these clasts occur only on the south side of each kurgan, we expected the ancient flood deposits to originate from that direction. A shovel test survey to the south of the kurgan resulted in an almost continuous line of small finds in the direction of the south channel. An approximately 5-m section of no finds interrupted this survey line. Based on these results, we put in two geological test pits in this archaeologically sterile section (GS-I and GS-II) and hit the remains of what was probably the original flood channel in both pits at a depth of approximately 35 to 45 cm (Figure 9.2). The sediment sequence from GS-II is described in Table 9.5. It is still unclear if these flood deposits were from a single event or a series of flood events, but it does not appear that the episode of flooding was long-lived. However, the appearance of these clasts of laminated silts primarily within the upper level of the kurgans suggests that the flood event(s) were contemporary with at least the later phase of kurgan construction. Since the secondary burials within the kurgan are dated to the Srubnaya period and therefore contemporary with the settlement, it is likely that the flood deposits used in the second kurgan phase are also contemporary with the settlement site.

Kurgans 1, 2, and 3 are dated to the Middle Bronze Age Poltavka period and therefore predate the settlement. Examination of Kurgans 1 and 3 indicated that they were founded on an old soil, which is truncated in some locations, as indicated by "shovel marks" within the A/B hori-

Table 9.4a Description of Alluvial Section on the Bank of the Samara River, "Samara 1": Middle of Section

Unit	Depth, cm	Texture	Structure	Composition	Depositional Environment	Lower Boundary
1: Upper soil A horizon	0–65	Loam	Granular structure		Floodplain	Irregular
2: Upper soil B horizon	65–85	Loam	Columnar structure		Floodplain	Irregular
3: Bca horizon	85–101	Loam	Massive	CaCO$_3$ nodules	Floodplain	
4: Parent material	101–135	Loam	Massive		Floodplain deposit	Smooth and abrupt
5: Paleosol Bca horizon	135–158	Loam	Massive	CaCO$_3$ nodules	Paleosol on floodplain deposit	Smooth and abrupt
6 through 12	158–165	Clayey loam	Massive	Sets of CaCO$_3$ nodules and gleyed deposits	Three sets of truncated Bca paleosol horizons separated by gleyed laminated silts from phases of water-saturated overbank deposits or oxbow lake deposits. Whole unit dips 10°N, 40°W	Smooth and abrupt
13	165–227	Well-sorted silt grading down to well-sorted fine sand	Horizontally bedded laminations	Iron stains and light gley with CaCO$_3$ fibrils	Levee silt deposits grading down to fluvial channel sands	Abrupt and smooth dipping down 26°N, 25°W
14	227–ca. 923	Very well-sorted medium sands	Horizontally bedded laminations; more rare cross-bedded sands	Occasional iron stains and thin gley beds; at −370 cm, there is a 70-cm-thick layer of heavily gleyed and iron stained sands	Fluvial channel sands and oxbow lake deposits	Not visible

Table 9.4b Description of Alluvial Section on the Bank of the Samara River, "Samara 1"; North Portion of Section

Unit	Depth, cm	Texture	Structure	Composition	Depositional Environment	Lower Boundary
1: Upper soil A horizon	0–55	Loam			Floodplain	
2: Upper soil B horizon	55–76	Loam			Floodplain	
4: Lower soil A horizon[a]	76–107	Loam	Blocky		Floodplain	Irregular
5: Lower soil B horizon	107–171	Loam	Massive		Floodplain	Abrupt and smooth

[a]Radiocarbon sample collected for dating of humus at −90 to −100 cm.

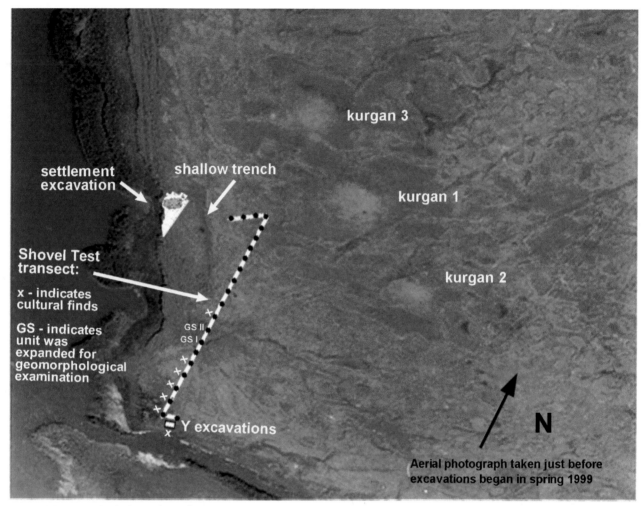

Figure 9.2 Two geological test pits (GS-I and GS-II) were dug in the archaeologically sterile section of the shovel test transect. In both pits, the remains of what was probably the original flood channel was found at a depth of approximately 35 to 45 cm. The sediment sequence from GS-II is described in Table 9.5. (Aerial photo by Boris Aguzarov)

zon. Prof. Ivanov (personal communication, 1999) has suggested that these truncated soils are of the meadow soil type rather than the *solenetz* type and point to a less degraded landscape than that of today with better drainage.

It is possible at this stage to suggest a hypothetical landscape setting at the time of the Poltavka occupation and later Srubnaya settlement. The absence of early *solenetz* soils suggests that the plain was less dissected than today and better drained, supporting an assemblage of steppic grasses. The existence of gleyed sediments from cores and dry-land sediment sections to the north of the site suggests that a narrow oxbow lake existed to the west of the Srubnaya settlement. A small spring-fed stream on the northern boundary of the Srubnaya deposits fed this lake. This stream also had marshy locations that would have been a source of reeds and rushes for basketry and matting. It is still unclear if the Samara Riv-

er floods extended to this location during seasonal flooding in the Bronze Age. If so, then they would have also contributed water and fish to this old lake. There was also a small ephemeral drainage to the south of the settlement that experienced major flood episodes during the course of a short period of time. These sediments were later excavated and used as fill within the kurgan.

Notes on Site Formation
Kurgan Formation
The kurgans were first constructed on meadow soils (see Table 9.6 for a description of the kurgan sediments). In some locations, these soils were undisturbed, and in others they were cut and the upper portion of the A horizon removed. After the grave was excavated, a fill was added to even out the surface, and blocks cut from the basal yellow clayey loam

Table 9.5 Description of *Solenetz* Soil Formed on Old Alluvial Channel from Geological Section GS-II

Unit	Depth, cm	Color	Texture	Structure	Composition	Lower Boundary
1: A horizon	0–15	Very dark brown (10 YR 2/2, m)	Moderately friable loam	Platey to columnar	Rootlets	Lower boundary irregular and slightly graded
2: B horizon	15–29	Brown (7.5 YR 5/4, m)	Very clayey loam; well compacted	Columnar structure	Occasional displaced clasts of laminated flood-water silts	Lower boundary graded
3: Parent material; ancient floodplain	29–70	Brown (7.5 YR 5/4, m)	Moderately friable clayey loam	Massive structure	3-cm × 6-cm clasts of laminated floodwater silts, which have been fragmented by postdepositional rodent activity	Lower boundary unseen
Laminated silts within Unit 3	29–49	White (10 YR 8/2, dry) to very pale brown (10 YR 7/3, dry) and light brownish gray (10 YR 6/2, moist)	Silt	Very fine horizontally bedded laminations (less than 0.5 mm in thickness)		

were placed on top. Finally, a larger mass of clayey fill was added to increase the height of the mound. This fill was taken from the A horizon of meadow soils in the vicinity of the site. A perimeter ditch was constructed around each kurgan. These ditches appear to have been left open for an unknown period of time after the construction of the kurgan.

At some point in time after the initial construction of Kurgan 3, the northernmost of the three kurgans, a flood occurred within the drainage channel south of the cemetery and extended up to the southern side of the kurgans but not as far as their north sides. In Kurgan 3, the ditch on the southern side of the kurgan filled with flood sediments. Sediment from this first flood does not appear within the ditch fill of Kurgan 1, located south of Kurgan 3. It is possible that Kurgan 1 predates this flood event, and the ditches had been naturally filled with colluvium before this flooding event occurred. Kurgan 1 does, however, show evidence of a flood event that deposited sediment against and on the mound on its south side. This sediment layer on top of Kurgan 1 is a sandy silt loam with much less clay than the flood deposit in the ditch of Kurgan 3. It also contains many clasts of laminated flood sediments, which are primarily located in this upper horizon. Some of these clasts are displaced by animal burrows, but in some locations, they appear as in situ flood deposits.

A different sequence is displayed in Kurgan 2, where there are displaced clasts of laminated flood silts found within the initial fill of the kurgan and an additional layer of in situ flood deposits over the surface. It therefore seems reasonable that Kurgan 2 was the last of the three to be constructed. The builders used the nearby alluvial sediments of a flood to construct the fill of the kurgan. Later, another flood occurred after its completion, covering part of the mound in laminated flood deposits.

After the passage of time, soil slumped into all of the ditch segments. After slumping, stabilization of the kurgan surface resulted in the formation of a second soil horizon on the surface of the kurgans.

Settlement Site

The Late Bronze Age (LBA) occupation at the site appears to have been founded on a gentle slope that dips down to the west toward the former lake. In addition to this, the A horizon of the former preoccupation soil was truncated and, in some excavation squares, was completely stripped away, perhaps in the construction of a pit-house. The main phase of LBA occupation occurs within the zone of –30 to –70 cm from modern ground surface. From the time of the LBA through the Iron Age, there was at least 40 cm of accumulated sediment. This post-LBA sediment accu-

Table 9.6 Description of Sediments from Section in Kurgan 1

Unit	Depth, cm	Color	Texture	Structure	Composition	Lower Boundary
1: Secondary kurgan fill	0–19	Very dark brown (10 YR 2/2, moist)	Sandy silt loam	Platey	Rootlets, occasional clasts of laminated flood silts anthropogenically transported with kurgan fill	Abrupt and smooth
2: A horizon of first kurgan surface	19–26/30	Very dark gray	Clayey loam	Granular	Rootlets	Graded and smooth
3: Transition zone	26/30–45	Very dark grayish brown (10 YR 3/2, m)	Clayey loam	Blocky	Fragments of orange clays brought from lower most unit by krotovinas	Irregular and graded
4: Primary kurgan fill	45–95	Very dark brown (10 YR 2/2, m)	Clayey silt loam	Blocky to columnar	8- to 15-cm krotovinas of orange clays brought from lower-most unit by krotovinas	Abrupt and irregular
5: Orange clay cover for Grave 3	95–107	Brown (7.5 YR 4/4, m)	Clayey loam	Massive structure	Blocks of parent material capping the gave	Abrupt and wavy

mulation could have been a function of the collapse and infilling of pit-houses and midden fills or a natural accumulation of sediments from either Samara River flooding or accumulated sheet wash from higher elevations. However, the sediments themselves suggest the first possibility due to the relatively rapid accumulation of sediment over a short period of time. After the Iron Age occupation, soil formation processes resumed on the stable land surface of the site. The natural sedimentation rate was very slow. The upper strata, dating back to 500 BC, were 25 cm thick, indicating an average accumulation of 1 cm per 100 years. Finally, post-depositional processes include much burrowing rodent activity, which significantly exceeds the amount viewed in any of the soil pits within natural sediments. Details of the settlement sediments are described in detail in Chapter 10.

Excavations at the LBA Settlement at Krasnosamarskoe

David W. Anthony • Dorcas R. Brown

Pavel F. Kuznetsov • Oleg D. Mochalov

Krasnosamarskoe means "little red Samara" (*krasno*, red; *samar*, root for Samara; *skoe*, diminutive) and is pronounced Kras-no-sa-MAR-sko-yeh. The "red" refers to the red sandy banks of the Samara River in this part of the river valley. The fields around the small village of Krasnosamarskoe contain numerous prehistoric kurgans, discussed in Chapter 17. During the 1995 survey, the Samara Valley Project (SVP) team visited the known kurgan cemeteries at Krasnosamarskoe I through IV to record their GPS positions. The unexcavated kurgans at Krasnosamarskoe IV were the last ones we recorded (Figure 2.1 [SVP #12] and Figure 17.2). The July day was hot, and some members of the SVP field team walked to a nearby manmade lake to cool our feet in the water. We discovered a dense accumulation of Srubnaya ceramic sherds, animal bones, bone tools, and even a lump of copper eroding out of the lake edge.

The lake was created in 1966 by building dams across a series of oxbow lakes and marshes in the Samara floodplain, after which the dammed ponds were topped off with water about a meter deep for a commercial carp fishery (Figure 10.1). The raised water level flooded a Srubnaya settlement located less than a meter above the original shoreline. Impressed by the density and diversity of Srubnaya artifacts at the site, we returned in 1998 to conduct a test excavation to see how much survived on land. Our tent camp was erected beside a wooden fishing lodge built in the 1970s for the weekend fishing excursions of the First Secretary of the Communist Party of the Samara oblast. It had a kitchen and a rustic dining room with a long table that eventually seated more than 20 at meals and served as the cataloguing table between meals, a large wooden *banya* (steam-bath) that could be fired up to produce hot water once a week (laundry/bath day), and electricity to power our computers and the pump used for the flotation barrel.

The 1998 test established that a substantial part of the Srubnaya structure was preserved under about 30 cm of surface sediments within easy walking distance of the fishing lodge. We returned in 1999 and 2001 for large-scale excavations (see Chapter 2 for a summary of the settlement excavations). Funding sources and important personnel are listed and thanked in the Acknowledgments.

General Description of the Settlement

The feature cut by the commercial fishpond was a Srubnaya structure about 8 × 12 m in preserved dimensions (originally longer, perhaps 8 × 16–20 m) with a post-supported roof constructed over a dug-out floor. The roof probably was made of *Phragmites* reed thatch, because after it collapsed, it created a black soil layer that contained dense, weathered *Phragmites* phytoliths, lying on top of the Srubnaya cultural deposit, sealing it (Figure 10.2, gray tone). The floor of the structure contained numerous pits, postholes, and artifacts. One deep pit (Pit 10) was a well. There were no built-up hearths or fireplaces in the excavated part of the structure, perhaps suggesting that it was not a residence but a thatched well-house or some other utility outbuilding with a well.

Figure 10.1 The Samara River and its oxbow lakes and marshes in the vicinity of Krasnosamarskoe. The dams built in 1966 are visible as straight lines across the lakes they created. (Google Earth, Image © 2013 DigitalGlobe)

Phragmites phytoliths were abundant also in the upper parts of pit features in the floor of the structure, possibly suggesting that the dug-out floor was covered with rushes (see feature descriptions below). In the center of the structure floor were refuse dumps where animal bones were discarded. Many of the animal bones came from feasting and sacrificial animals, as argued independently by the Russian archaeozoologist Kosintsev (Chapter 15) and by the U.S. team of Russell, Brown, and Brown (Chapter 16). Kosintsev counted a minimum number of individuals (MNI) of 51 dogs and seven wolves after examining 22,445 catalogued pieces of bone, of which 8,018 were identifiable to species. Dog and wolf bones composed 36 to 45 percent of the animal bones deposited at the site, depending on how they are counted (Chapter 14, "Materials and Methods"). It was unusual to find so many animal bones discarded inside rather than outside a Srubnaya structure, Kosintsev observed, and unique to find so many dog bones. The ritual and mythological implications of the winter-season dog and wolf sacrifices are explored at the end of Chapter 14.

The excavation also yielded 4,257 ceramic sherds, including large parts of eight pottery vessels that were either set in the floor or were broken in place. The floor layers contained a light scatter of other discarded objects, including a toothed shell stamp for pottery decoration, copper slag and molten copper in small bits, a bronze awl, a bone awl, two dozen handheld grinding stones, two spindle whorls, a rawhide thong-smoother, and eight well-used and polished cattle-knuckle (five) and sheep-knuckle (three) *astragali* dice (Figures 10.35–10.41).

Pit 10, a deep bag-shaped feature that contained preserved waterlogged wood and organics, was a Srubnaya well. Wooden artifacts recovered from the anaerobic mud at the bottom included long wooden poles or rods with notched ends, triangular chunks of wood-chopping debris removed by axe cuts, and pieces of chopped logs that had remained waterlogged since the Bronze Age, so must have been discarded into water. A notched log might have been related to the construction of the structure, because it was found beneath an organic-rich layer of sediment that devel-

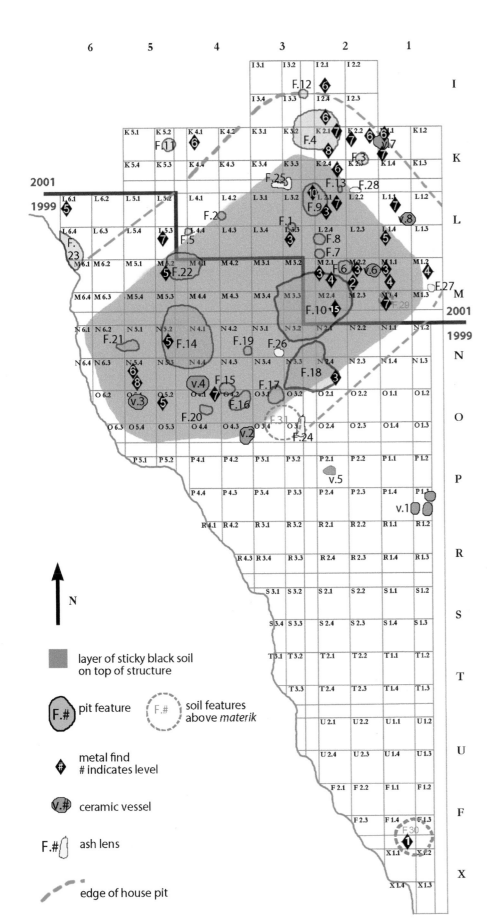

Figure 10.2 Plan of the excavated area at the Krasnosamarskoe settlement. Each square is 1 × 1 m; four of these make the four quadrants of each basic 2 x 2 meter unit.

oped during the use of the well, dated by three radiocarbon dates (see Radiocarbon Chronology below) to begin during the oldest phase of occupation and to continue through the entire occupation between around 1900 to 1700 BC. Pine pollen was greatly elevated, the highest count in any sample from the site, in the deepest and oldest sample from this band of organic sediment, and declined sharply just a few centimeters higher in the organic sediment. It is possible that deepest sediment in Pit 10 was exposed to a richer rain of pine pollen because the well was dug before the structure was roofed over. Perhaps a grove of pine trees stood not far away when the site was first chosen for a settlement.

The flooded and deflated part of the settlement was sampled by collecting pottery and animal bones underwater and mapping the edge of their distribution. The pond was only about 1.2 m deep at its center, so students could walk across it and fish with their toes for artifacts. The artifact deposit extended no more than 40 m offshore, indicating that the entire settlement was perhaps 60 m wide, sufficient space for just one or at most two additional buildings. If the excavated structure surviving on dry land was a utility outbuilding such as a well-house, then the artifacts from the

lake bottom probably represent the residence. The pottery types and radiocarbon dates from the lake bottom matched those from the excavated structure on land, so there is no doubt that they represent a single continuous settlement.

We cut back the eroded bank of the fishpond 100 m north and south of the excavated structure and found only isolated Srubnaya sherds in the exposed 200-m section. The settlement was spatially confined to the excavated area with the exception of a dump found 160 m south on the bank of a stream draining into the pond/marsh. It was tested with a 2-m × 4-m excavation unit and was designated Area Y (Я) (sometimes referred to as Ya in field notes). A line of test pits was dug at 10-m intervals from the Y excavation back toward the settlement. More than 20 m from the Y activity area, these pits showed no artifacts. The Y activity area was spatially isolated and discrete. The entire settlement was small, perhaps two buildings, with a separate activity area, probably a dump, 160 m to the south (Figure 10.5).

The excavated structure was occupied during three ceramic-typological phases: once in the Iron Age in Level 1 and during two ceramic-stylistic phases in the Late Bronze Age (LBA), Level 3 and deeper (Figure 10.3). There was

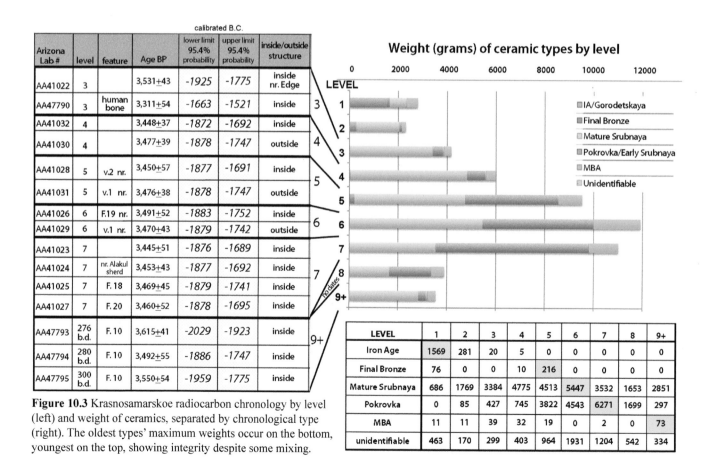

Figure 10.3 Krasnosamarskoe radiocarbon chronology by level (left) and weight of ceramics, separated by chronological type (right). The oldest types' maximum weights occur on the bottom, youngest on the top, showing integrity despite some mixing.

Arizona Lab #	level	feature	Age BP	calibrated B.C. lower limit 95.4% probability	calibrated B.C. upper limit 95.4% probability	inside/outside structure
AA41022	3		3,531±43	-1925	-1775	inside nr. Edge
AA47790	3	human bone	3,311±54	-1663	-1521	inside
AA41032	4		3,448±37	-1872	-1692	inside
AA41030	4		3,477±39	-1878	-1747	outside
AA41028	5	v.2 nr.	3,450±57	-1877	-1691	inside
AA41031	5	v.1 nr.	3,476±38	-1878	-1747	outside
AA41026	6	F.19 nr.	3,491±52	-1883	-1752	inside
AA41029	6	v.1 nr.	3,470±43	-1879	-1742	outside
AA41023	7		3,445±51	-1876	-1689	inside
AA41024	7	nr. Alakul sherd	3,453±43	-1877	-1692	inside
AA41025	7	F.18	3,469±45	-1879	-1741	inside
AA41027	7	F.20	3,460±52	-1878	-1695	inside
AA47793	276 b.d.	F.10	3,615±41	-2029	-1923	inside
AA47794	280 b.d.	F.10	3,492±55	-1886	-1747	inside
AA47795	300 b.d.	F.10	3,550±54	-1959	-1775	inside

Weight (grams) of ceramic types by level

IA/Gorodetskaya
Final Bronze
Mature Srubnaya
Pokrovka/Early Srubnaya
MBA
Unidentifiable

LEVEL	1	2	3	4	5	6	7	8	9+
Iron Age	1569	281	20	5	0	0	0	0	0
Final Bronze	76	0	0	10	216	0	0	0	0
Mature Srubnaya	686	1769	3384	4775	4513	5447	3532	1653	2851
Pokrovka	0	85	427	745	3822	4543	6271	1699	297
MBA	11	11	39	32	19	0	2	0	73
unidentifiable	463	170	299	403	964	1931	1204	542	334

a little activity on the site also during the Middle Bronze Age (MBA), represented by occasional sherds of two MBA types, but the activity could have been ritual in nature, related to the construction of the three MBA kurgans 60 m to the east (Chapter 17).

The Srubnaya occupation in Level 3 and deeper was represented by two ceramic types: Pokrovka (early Srubnaya) and developed or mature Srubnaya. Normally, these styles in pottery shape and decoration are interpreted as two successive chronological phases within the Srubnaya sequence, so sites containing both styles are seen as settlements that were reoccupied by chronologically separate groups at distinct points in time (Ostroshchenko 2003; Semenova 2001). At Krasnosamarskoe, radiocarbon dates between 1900 and 1700 BC have a distribution of means that suggests earlier and later phases rather than two separate occupations. The stratigraphic sequence of floor deposits within the excavated structure does not exhibit a break in occupation but rather shows a shift in frequency from the Pokrovka (early) style, which predominates in Level 7, to the developed Srubnaya (late) style, which predominates in Levels 3 to 6 (Figure 10.3). Both styles occurred together in every level but in differing proportions that ended with a clear preponderance of the developed Srubnaya (late) style. The presence of both styles at one site therefore does not by itself indicate two chronologically discrete occupations. At Krasnosamarskoe, the stratigraphy inside the structure appears to indicate a continuous occupation spanning the stylistic transition.

The final abandonment of the structure was represented archaeologically by the filling in of the well (Pit 10) with soils dug from the cultural deposits on the structure floor or just outside, sealing the well with sediments containing Pokrovka and developed Srubnaya sherds, mixed together with animal bone and other LBA artifacts. No later diagnostics were found in the well fill, so it was filled and sealed during the Srubnaya period.

Srubnaya Settlements in the Samara Oblast

During the 1,300 years of the Early Bronze Age (EBA) and MBA, around 3300 to 2000 BC, the Samara Valley was occupied by mobile pastoralists of the Yamnaya (EBA) and Poltavka (MBA) cultures. This was the first era of equestrian, wagon-aided pastoralism in the Pontic-Caspian steppes. No Yamnaya settlements have been found east of the Don River, although a few Yamnaya settlements can be found on the lower Don and Dnieper. In the middle Volga steppes, EBA/MBA mobile pastoralists apparently lived in temporary wagon camps. They left at least 60 kurgan cemeteries in the Samara oblast (Chapter 4), but no EBA settlements

are known, and only a few small scatters of ceramic sherds are assigned to the MBA Poltavka culture. Two of these Poltavka sherd scatters were discovered during the SVP. No EBA pottery was found at any site during the SVP. We do not know where the EBA population lived in the winter, when they must have been relatively sedentary.

At the opening of the LBA, Srubnaya settlement sites appeared, numbering more than 150 in the Samara oblast over the 700 years of the LBA, 1900 to 1200 BC (Figure 1.2). The shift happened during the brief transition between MBA II and the Pokrovka phase, probably beginning 1950 to 1850 BC.

Of the 150-plus Srubnaya settlement sites in the Samara oblast, 28 are located in the Samara River drainage (Chapter 4). Only six of these have been excavated sufficiently to reveal part of a structure, but settlement plans are not yet published from other Srubnaya settlements in the Samara Valley. Nearby, within the Samara oblast, settlement plans are published for a few Srubnaya sites. Most are small hamlets such as Krasnosamarskoe, with one or two residential houses and a utility structure (well-house or barn) like the one we excavated. At Kirovskoe, located in a small river valley in the drier steppes 80 km southwest of Krasnosamarskoe, two such small Srubnaya homesteads were discovered 500 m apart on the edge of an oxbow lake, perhaps representing sequential, shifting settlements on the same marshy lakeshore. A Srubnaya settlement at Shigonskoe, located in the forest-steppe zone on the north side of the Samarskaya Luka loop, was larger than most, with a handful of residential houses of varying orientations, with no street or plan. Almost all Srubnaya settlements in the Samara oblast were located on oxbow lakes and marshes near inflowing streams, like Krasnosamarskoe. Srubnaya settlements were not fortified, although in the Final Bronze Age, after 1200 BC, the Suskanskoe settlement seems to have been fortified with palisades, an indication of increasingly uncertain conditions at that time.

Sedova (2000) analyzed Srubnaya settlements in the Samara oblast. She thought that two to six Srubnaya settlement sites constituted a partly cooperating and partly cyclical settlement group, with some sites reoccupied sequentially. At the end of Chapter 2, we estimated herd sizes and pasture-carrying capacities for Spiridonovka, Krasnosamarskoe, and Barinovka, three Srubnaya settlements in the 30-km section of the Samara Valley around Krasnosamarskoe, assuming that an extended family consisting of one or two households occupied each site. We concluded that there was plenty of pasture available to continue pastoral production at this relatively low level of population on a sustainable basis. Labor would have been a more limiting economic factor than land or pasture in the LBA. Nevertheless, the LBA population could have been larger than that of the MBA simply because more cows were kept in the LBA than in the EBA/MBA (see Chapter 1). Modern cows produce five times more milk than sheep or goats, so more cows meant that more dairy food was available to the LBA population, which would have permitted a modest growth in population, perhaps necessary for the staffing of specialized mining settlements such as Gorny.

Residential and utility structures in Srubnaya settlements in the Samara oblast look similar in plan. Both were from 12 to 26 m long, with dug-out floors showing irregular clusters of postholes indicating clusters of timber roof posts, as at Krasnosamarskoe. A complete Srubnaya house excavated at Shelekhmet on the west side of the Volga in the Samarskaya Luka (Figure 10.4) measured 8 × 26 m with a floor dug 40 to 60 cm into the ground (Sedova 2000:215). Postholes following the line of the exterior walls are not present in Srubnaya structures. They seem to have had slanted A-frame roofs made of thatch, post-supported in the center, with eaves that rested on the ground on two sides (Figure 10.4, center). This design would have created a long, dark interior, 6 to 8 × 20+ m. The roof might have been gabled at side entrances to provide light to the interior. In the discussion of Feature 11 below, it is suggested that this posthole might indicate part of such a side entrance.

The roof of the structure at Krasnosamarskoe probably was made of thatch from *Phragmites* reeds, judging from the abundant weathered *Phragmites* phytoliths contained in the dark soil layer interpreted as roof fall. The edges of the roof probably did rest on the ground, excluding dogs and weather from the interior. Russell and the U.S. zoological team concluded that the animal bones found inside and outside the structure exhibited very different weathering and gnawing patterns, indicating that the inside of the structure was protected from weather and from dogs (Chapter 16).

Srubnaya residential houses contain hearths. Some hearths were large, 1 to 2 m in diameter, up to 40 cm deep, and stone lined, and some were small, 40 cm in diameter and shallow. At Kirovskoe, both residential houses contained dug-out hearths 10 to 120 cm in diameter and 25 cm deep (Sedova 2000:215). The absence of any hearth feature at Krasnosamarskoe led us to interpret the excavated structure as an outbuilding. It is of course possible that the structure contained a hearth at its southern end that was destroyed by lake erosion, but we did not find fire-cracked rock exposed there on the lake bottom. A stone-lined hearth existed somewhere on the site, because we found fire-cracked rock discarded in Pit 23, but it might have been a fire pit now buried beneath the lake bed. Small deposits of ash were found in several places within the excavated structure and are indicated on the site plan, but these ash lenses were part of trash discard and dump deposits rather than being primary sites of hearths or fires, as the soil was not baked and charcoal was present only in small flecks dispersed throughout the interior-structure soils.

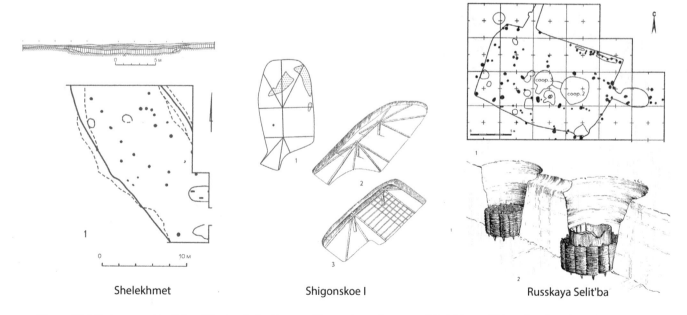

Shelekhmet   Shigonskoe I   Russkaya Selit'ba

Figure 10.4 Srubnaya residential architecture in the Samara oblast at the settlements of Shelekhmet, Shigonskoe 1, and Russkaya Selit'ba, where one structure contained two basket-lined wells (after Sedova 2000: Figures 14 & 15).

The existence of a well or wells inside the excavated structure does not distinguish it from residential structures, because wells have been found within both utility structures (lacking hearths) and residential houses (containing hearths) at other Srubnaya settlements. At the Final Bronze Age settlement of Russkaya Selit'ba there was one house that contained two basketry-lined wells (Kolev et al. 2000) to provide an indoor water supply (Figure 10.4, right). The excavated structure at Krasnosamarskoe is conditionally identified as a utility structure largely because it lacks a hearth, not because it contains a well (or perhaps two wells; see Features 10 and 14 discussion below). It was constructed in a typical Srubnaya fashion and was a typical size for either a house or a utility structure.

Contemporary Setting at Krasnosamarskoe

The site occupies the edge of first terrace above the Samara River floodplain, here elevated a meter or two above the natural level of the marshes. Extensive marshes of *Phragmites* and *Typha* (cattail) reeds and sedges cover

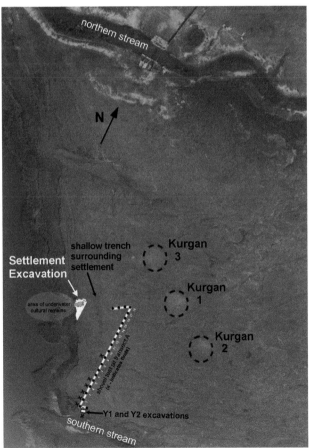

Figure 10.5 1998 aerial photo of Krasnosamarskoe with overlay indicating the archaeological operations at Krasnosamarskoe: the settlement (notice the crop mark indicating a surrounding trench), the underwater artifacts, the Y (or Ya) excavations, the test pit transect, and the three kurgans (the Srubnaya cemetery was in Kurgan 3). (photo by Boris Aguzarov)

the floodplain beside the site (Figure 10.1). The marshes are home to flocks of swans, geese, and ducks, and cattle graze in the shallows. The main channel of the Samara River is 3 to 4 km to the west, beyond the marshes and oxbow lakes that intervene. Two sluggish streams empty into the marshes north and south of the site (Figure 10.5). The northern stream seems to have been the larger of the two in the Bronze Age (Rosen, Chapter 9), although the southern stream is larger today. Gleys exposed in the subsoil around the northern stream mouth indicate that a stable wetland existed here, defining a mini-estuary, for millennia, probably during the LBA occupation.

To the east, moving away from the marshes, the ground rises very gently, rolling almost imperceptibly, toward a ridge top 9 km distant, beyond which is the Bolshoi Kinel' drainage, a right-hand tributary of the Samara. The plain between the site and the height-of-land 9 km to the east is intensely cultivated and plowed. Immediately around the site is a zone of pasture with access to the lakes for water for the cattle. The pasture is almost flat, dimpled with *solonchak*-filled spongy depressions, and the vegetation is a degraded and overgrazed steppe (see Chapter 12).

In July 1998, a single pedestrian herder, Aleksandr K'nyazev, assisted by two German Shepherd dogs, supervised 314 cattle in the lake-edge pastures in this area. He said that it was possible for him and his dogs (who did all of the work) to manage up to 500 cattle and that 800 to 1,000 cattle were managed by the collective farm or *kolkhoz* to which he belonged.

Summary of Field Operations

In 1999, approximately 100 people excavated the southern two-thirds of the settlement grid and all three kurgans in the adjoining cemetery (Krasnosamarskoe IV), as well as an activity area, Area Y, located on the lake edge 160 m south of the excavated structure. In 2001, approximately 30 people excavated the northern third of the settlement, finishing the excavation. Excavations were directed by the authors of this report, assisted by specialists listed below. A full list of important personnel and funders is in the Acknowledgments.

The primary excavation exposed 207 m² (Figure 10.2), within a triangular 26-m × 12-m grid along the lake edge; most of this area was excavated down to about 70 to 90 cm beneath the surface, where the *materik* subsoil was encountered. The structure occupied the northern part of the excavated grid, 8 × 12 m in preserved dimensions with a floor dug about 30 cm into the Bronze Age ground surface. More than 25,000 artifacts (Table 10.1) were processed in our field lab, over 80 percent of them bones and bone fragments. The artifacts found inside the structure imply activities from spinning thread and making rawhide to making pottery and smelting copper.

Area Y, a Srubnaya artifact concentration found 160 m south of the southern edge of the grid, was located on the north bank of the southern stream that flowed into the lake. This was tested with two 1-m × 2-m units (Figure 10.5: Y1 and Y2). The Srubnaya artifact types and radiocarbon dates were the same as the settlement, but the artifact density was much lower, indicating it was not another house site; rather, it was a related activity area or garbage dump.

Twenty-two 50-cm × 50-cm shovel test pits (STPs) were dug at 10-m intervals between Area Y and the settlement (Figure 10.5). Only three STPs (A1, A2, and A9) produced Srubnaya sherds and a few bone fragments. STPs A3, A4, and A5 each contained a few bone fragments but no ceramics. The other 16 STPs contained no cultural material. The activity at the site was concentrated around the excavated structure. (STPs A7 and A8 were expanded by Rosen to use as off-site noncultural soil columns for geomorphological study—see Rosen, Chapter 9.)

Recovery and Recording Methods

All soil was screened through ¼-inch (6.35-mm) mesh standing shaker screens. The use of shaker screens on 100 percent of the excavated soil was a new method in the excavation of an LBA settlement in the Samara oblast. As a result, our artifact counts in all categories, but particularly in bone fragments, were higher than expected, as Kosintsev noted in Chapter 15. Screening made the excavation proceed slower than normal for the Russian students, and bilingual paperwork was time-consuming for everyone. There was some resistance to the use of screens at first (see below).

The basic excavation unit in Russian archaeology was a 2-m × 2-m square. At Krasnosamarskoe, we broke these units into 1-m × 1-m quads recorded within each 2 × 2. The numbering of quads began in the upper left (northwest [NW]) corner with quad 1 (e.g., square P2/1 is the NW quad 1 in the 2 × 2 designated P2). The quads were numbered proceeding clockwise to the upper right (P2/2), lower right (P2/3), and lower left (P2/4). While it was standard practice in Russia to excavate in a grid of 2-m × 2-m squares, recording artifacts to 1-m squares was unusual.

Archaeological finds were recorded to a 1-m × 1-m square and a 10-cm arbitrary horizontal level within naturally or culturally defined strata—each find had a stratum, a level, and a square. Each 10-cm arbitrary level was excavated within naturally or culturally defined strata. If a natural stratum cut through a 10-cm level, that level was divided into its natural strata, and the artifacts from each stratum within the level were separated.

Digging in measured 10-cm levels also was unusual. Most Russian sites were excavated in *shtiks*, arbitrary levels about 20 cm deep, measured by a shovel length rather than a line level and tape. Traditionally, digging was done primarily by male students, and female students examined the backdirt to retrieve artifacts. Our shift to digging in measured 10-cm levels, with each 10 cm ending in a floor that was measured level with tapes and line levels, interacted with the use of shaker screens to cause a shift in gender roles among the Russian students.

Western students usually worked in pairs that shifted tasks between excavation and screening regardless of gender. But shaking a screen filled with dirt requires upper body strength and makes your legs very dirty, while digging in measured 10-cm levels requires precise excavation and periodic measurements. In the beginning, Russian women worked with the screens because they had been the ones who sorted the backdirt, but many found the screens awkward and annoying. The U.S. women on the team were not stronger, but they were accustomed to balancing the weight of a shaker screen because they had learned screening in U.S. field schools. Gradually, the screening and recovery of artifacts shifted among the Russian students to being a predominantly male task as male students came to the assistance of their female friends. Precise excavation in 10-cm levels was embraced by several Russian female students, although excavation remained a mixed-gender assignment. After more Russian men began to screen and more Russian women began to dig, some Russian women were among our most accurate and observant excavators. Sharpie graffiti appeared all over the screens, reinforcing their "ownership" by Russian males and emphatically domesticating the exotic (see Figure 18.11). In the second summer of fieldwork, the new methodologies were accepted, gender roles on the Russian side were more equally shared, and screens and measured 10-cm levels became part of the identity of the international crew. It was interesting to observe how material culture (shaker screens, line levels, and pocket-sized measuring tapes) prompted the Russian students to equalize traditionally gendered work assignments, but also the new items quickly were transformed and "owned" in new ways by their new users. U.S. students, perhaps more private property biased or perhaps entertaining different graffiti stereotypes, did not "tag" the excavation screens with Sharpies.

Every floor of every 10-cm level was photographed and recorded on field forms when all four quads in a 2 × 2 were taken down to the same 10-cm level. Profile sections were drawn after the 2 × 2 exposed the basal yellow clayey subsoil, or *materik*. Only pit features extending into the *materik* were counted as pit features (see Feature Descriptions below);

Table 10.1 Krasnosamarskoe 1998–2001 Material Culture by Level Whole Settlement Area

LEVEL	Iron Age/Gorodetskaya Ceramics			Final Bronze Ceramics			Developed Srubnaya Ceramics			Pokrovka Ceramics			MBA Ceramics			Unidentified Ceramics			Bones, Shell, Antler			Stone		Metal
	Count	Weight in grams (g)	% Weight of All Levels	Count	Weight (g)	% Weight of All Levels	Count	Weight (g)	% Weight of All Levels	Count	Weight (g)	% Weight of All Levels	Count	Weight (g)	% Weight of All Levels	Count	Weight (g)	% Weight of All Levels	Count	Weight (g)	% Weight of All Levels	Count	Weight (g)	Count
1	73	1,569	83.68	7	76	25.16	121	686	2.39	0	0		1	11	5.88	49	463	7.34	704	1,459	1.81	1	2	3
2	12	281	14.99				169	1,769	6.18	4	85	0.47	2	11	5.88	39	170	2.69	950	3,495	4.33	3	13	3
3	3	20	1.07				373	3,384	11.82	41	427	2.39	3	39	20.86	38	299	4.74	2,209	6,940	8.60	10	331	5
4	1	5	0.27	1	10	3.31	482	4,775	16.67	73	745	4.16	5	32	17.11	73	403	6.39	3,863	12,483	15.47	5	141	2
5				4	216	71.52	359	4,513	15.76	254	3,822	21.36	1	19	10.16	131	964	15.28	5124	1,9015	23.56	7	856	3
6							345	5,477	19.12	250	4,543	25.40				364	1,931	30.60	4,149	1,9038	23.59	14	388	10
7							224	3,532	12.33	299	6,271	35.06	1	2	1.07	75	1,204	19.08	2,065	9,283	11.50	8	652	6
8							120	1,653	5.77	68	1,699	9.50				24	542	8.59	1,122	5,487	6.80	3	652	2
9+							108	2,851	9.95	28	297	1.66	4	73	39.04	15	334	5.29	765	3,498	4.33	1	1	3
Total	89	1,875	100.01	12	302	99.99	2,301	28,640	99.99	1,017	1,7889	100.00	17	187	100.00	808	6,310	100.00	20,951	80,698	99.99	52	3,036	37

these were excavated and recorded, and sections were drawn. The 2 × 2 was then finished. Original field forms from 2001 are at Hartwick College, and digital copies are in Samara; original field forms from 1999 are in Samara, and digital copies are at Hartwick College.

Baulks were included in the 2-m × 2-m squares and were taken down at the end of the excavation season. Artifact recovery within the baulks probably was less complete and systematic than from the normally excavated soil.

Two-liter soil samples were collected for flotation from every level (except Level 1; see below) within each 2-m × 2-m unit and from every pit feature—274 samples in all. Flotation was conducted near the fishing lodge where electric power was available to run a pump (Figure 10.6a). It pulled

Figure 10.6 Flotation and soils. (a) Flotation tank with inflow hose on right and outflow spout on left. (b) Natural stratigraphy at Krasnosamarskoe. The top 15 to 30 cm is very hard black fine silt, with a columnar structure: the A1 horizon. The A2 horizon also is black but with more clay. Below that was a brown B horizon, also clayey and blocky, which extended down to about 80 cm, the transition to the yellowish clay subsoil or *materik*.

water from a fishing pond and pushed it into a refitted metal oil drum equipped with an input adapter in the middle of the side and a spout at the top. Window screen was slung across the top of the drum so that the screen bottom was about 15 cm underwater. Soil samples were poured into the water, onto the window screen. Water pressure from the hose created a slow constant upward flow. Floating items poured out the spout and were caught in a light cotton fabric (diaper cloth) suspended over a plastic bucket with the bottom cut out (Figure 10.6a). When all floating material had been captured in the diaper, it was tied up and hung to dry. The heavy fraction left behind in the window screen was saved separately.

Level 1 across the site was 20 cm deep rather than 10 cm. This was because the top 20 cm of soil, black clayey silt, was baked so hard by the sun that it came up as a single block, almost like concrete (Figure 10.6b). We did succeed in screening much of this soil, which turned into fine dust when broken. Because Level 1 was 20 cm deep, Level 2 ended at 30 cm rather than the expected 20 cm, and all level numbers were similarly offset: Level 3 was 30 to 40 cm below surface, and so on.

Artifacts of particular importance, including eight ceramic vessels crushed in situ, were point-plotted using measuring tapes and line levels. One dense scatter of discarded bone was point-plotted, as well as a few other artifact clusters. Most artifacts were assigned to a provenience within a 1-m × 1-m square and were bagged by the excavator or the screener. Bone was bagged separately from the other artifacts to protect it from getting scratched by harder artifacts.

Alla Semenova supervised all cataloguing. Students washed, dried, and rebagged all artifacts. They were then taken to the cataloguing tent where Semenova and her students numbered and catalogued each object. Semenova, an expert in ceramic styles and types, decided all typological assignments of ceramics. Brown and students entered the information from Semenova's cataloguing sheets into the digital database. All types, counts, and weights of artifacts reported in this chapter and presented in our tables and graphs are derived from this database. Brown also kept a field notebook that recorded artifact counts from the artifact bags for each finished level, so we had a field count to compare to the lab count. In a few cases, we know from her field records that some artifact bags were lost between the field and the cataloguing tent. Brown counted finds in the field but did not record weights or types, so we did not add missing objects back into the official catalog. In most cases, the loss was minor and did not significantly affect our results.

The single exception to this rule is small cuprous artifacts, particularly small fragments of ore, slag, or molten copper or bronze. We noticed in comparing our records that a significant number of these small, fragmentary objects, bagged by excavators in the field, did not make it into Semenova's catalogue. We were unaware of this problem in the field; probably student washers did not recognize these small objects as artifacts and discarded them. This would have been a significant loss of information, so we did add these small cuprous ore/slag artifacts that were recorded in our field records, but not in Semenova's catalogue, into our digital database. These metal objects are mapped on the site plan (Figure 10.2).

Specialist Analyses

Botanical studies were a primary focus for our project, so we collected samples to examine pollen, phytoliths, and macrobotanical remains. Forty-four soil samples for phytolith analysis were sent to Arlene Rosen and Alison Weisskopf of the University College of London (see Chapter 13). Rosen visited the field and conducted her own geomorphological soil tests in 1999 (see Chapter 9). Fifteen soil samples for pollen analysis were sent to Laura Popova of the University of Chicago (see Chapter 12). A total of 274 flotation samples to identify seeds and other macrobotanical remains were collected from the site: 159 from the 1999 excavations were sent to the Institute of the Ecology of Plants and Animals, Urals Branch of the Russian Academy of Sciences, Ekaterinburg, and 115 from the 2001 excavations were sent to Laura Popova (see Chapter 12).

Animal bones were studied by four archaeozoologists. Pavel Kosintsev of the Institute of the Ecology of Plants and Animals in Ekaterinburg, a senior scientist with many years of experience, was present in the field to examine the fauna each season and in the months following the end of fieldwork (see Chapter 15). Nerissa Russell of Cornell, who was then splitting her field time between Krasnosamarskoe and Catalhöyük, was assisted by Emmett and Audrey Brown, then grad students at the University of Alabama (see Chapter 16). In the end, Brown and Brown performed most of the identifications and cataloguing on the U.S. side, and Russell directed the analysis. Kosintsev identified a significantly larger percentage of bones than were identified by the U.S. archaeozoologists, and he actually seems to have examined a larger raw number of bones as well, although the total number of bones examined was close. Probably Kosintsev's long familiarity with the regional fauna and access to reference collections led to his ability to identify more bones to species, and storage problems between the end of fieldwork and a final cataloguing trip to Samara by Brown and Brown in 2002 might explain Brown and Brown seeing a slightly smaller raw number of bones. The U.S. team also used a protocol for identification that was different from Kosintsev's, so part of the difference was methodological. Kosintsev did not describe evidence concerning usage, pathologies, cooking, butchering, feasting, and so on and did not analyze the fauna by diagnostic zones, so for these kinds of analyses, we relied on the Western team in Chapter 16. Because Kosintsev identified many more specimens to species, we are using Kosintsev's counts for total numbers of specimens and MNI. The ratio of species is slanted even more strongly to dogs from the perspective of diagnostic zones.

Fifty-seven animal teeth were sent to Anne Pike-Tay and her students at Vassar College, of which 32 showed results for incremental banding analysis to determine age and season of death (see Chapter 14).

Ceramics from the 1999 season were analyzed by I. N. Vasilieva and N. P. Salugina, using methods developed by A. A. Bobrinskii in the ceramic ethno-archaeological laboratory that he created at Samara State University (Bobrinskii 1978; Bobrinskii and Vasilieva 1998; Vasilieva 2011). Their methods included a detailed microscopic examination of the ceramic paste for both natural and cultural inclusions, an analysis of construction methods, and visual observation of the firing characteristics.

Metals from the region were analyzed by David Peterson, then a grad student at the University of Chicago. Peterson, Popova and Christopher Gette were essential leaders of the settlement excavation, working closely with Brown and Anthony to define stratigraphic changes and monitor field finds. Peterson and Popova went on to conduct their own excavation at the Srubnaya mining site of Kibit, as an independent outgrowth of the SVP (see Chapter 11).

Ancient Environment

The origin of the oxbow lake adjacent to the site is dated by two radiocarbon dates (Table 9.3). The first was a date from basal blue gley soil (AA41034a) removed by a core drilled by Suzanne LeRoy. The dated gley was taken from the base of the gley stratum, just above the impenetrable natural clay subsoil or *materik* under the lake, at a point in the fishing pond 120 m west of the Krasnosamarskoe settlement. The basal gley, a soil that develops in anaerobic conditions under still water, was dated around 9000 BC. The other date was from a plant fragment embedded in the basal gley soil (AA41034b) showing that marsh plants were growing in the gley by 8700 to 8500 BC. We can safely conclude that the lakes and marshes were present in the Bronze Age, an important factor in attracting settlement because of their crucial roles as animal fodder and protection from the wind in winter (see Chapter 1).

The LBA environment is described in Chapter 12 by Popova and Chapter 13 by Weisskopf and Rosen. Based on the arboreal pollen from the LBA structure floor (see Tables 12.9 and 12.10), the forests in the vicinity of the settlement consisted of pine (*Pinus sylvestris*), oak (*Quercus robur*), hazel (*Corylus*), birch (*Betula*), poplar (*Populus*), and maple (*Acer*). Arboreal pollen was less than 2 percent of the total spore/pollen count, but this very low proportion of tree pollen was affected by the very high count of nonarboreal aquatic and wetland pollen grains, principally from *Typha* (cattail) and *Cyperaceae* (sedges). *Phragmites* reeds also were present, but this important marsh plant does not appear in pollen, only in phytoliths, which were dominated by *Phragmites* (see Chapter 13). The marsh signature was so overwhelming that it reduced the forest signature. Other pollen from the excavated structure demonstrates a powerful steppe signature with plants from the *Poaceae* (Grass), *Chenopodiaceae* (Goosefoot), and *Amaranthaceae* (Amaranth) families being the most commonly represented, with some mesic herbaceous plants as well. *Polygonum* (Knotweed), *Plantago* (Plantain), and *Artemisia* (Sage) were present in the surrounding grasslands, as well as small amounts of pollen from *Trifolium* (clover), indicating the high quality of the nearby pasture in the LBA.

In the LBA, Krasnosamarskoe was situated in an open grassy herbaceous steppe on the edge of a marshy *Typha* and *Phragmites* wetland, with some forests (pine-oak-hazel-birch-poplar-maple) present in the distance, but the immediate vicinity of the site was not forested. Some deciduous leaves seem to have been mixed in with the roof thatch (see Cultural Stratigraphy below), so there might have been a tree or two nearby, within leaf-blowing distance.

Seasons of Occupation

Pike-Tay's study of incremental banding on cattle teeth shows that older cattle at Krasnosamarskoe were culled from the herd in the spring before movement to the summer pastures, and younger animals were butchered in the fall, before the onset of winter. Such a culling pattern maximizes animal production in normal pastoral management (Chapter 14). She also determined that dogs were sacrificed in the winter in a series of winter ritual activities. The seasons of death for animals at Krasnosamarskoe included fall, winter, and spring (Table 14.1).

Pollen samples recovered from the structure floor contain pollen that is released from March through September (Chapter 12). Many of the seeds found in flotation samples, importantly *Chenopodium*, ripen in late summer and early fall. Most of the *Phragmites* phytoliths discussed in Chapter 13 came from winter-harvested reed, because the florescent parts were not present except in one or two samples (see Feature 11 below). Botanical evidence suggests activity during winter, spring, summer, and fall.

These faunal and floral indicators show that Krasnosamarskoe was occupied continuously through all seasons of the year. This is the first Srubnaya settlement in the middle Volga region that has been proven through faunal and floral studies to have been occupied permanently, although it is generally assumed that most Srubnaya settlements were occupied year-round.

Radiocarbon Chronology
(Figure 10.3, Figure 10.7, and Table 2.1)
Nineteen ^{14}C samples from the Bronze Age levels at the Krasnosamarskoe settlement yielded results at the University of Arizona accelerator mass spectrometry (AMS) laboratory. The oldest date at the site was from a sloping band of dark organic material that accumulated underwater at the bottom of the well, Pit 10 (Figure 10.8). Three dates from this organic layer were 3492 ± 55 BP (1961–1682 BC), 3550 ± 54 BP (2030–1745 BC), and 3615 ± 41 BP (2030–1745 BC), the latter the oldest date at the site. These three dates calibrate between 2030 and 1682 BC. The dates for this organic sediment in the well ranged slightly older than the principal cluster of dates for the occupation deposits on the structure floor above, but the ranges for the two sets of dates largely overlapped; it was only their means that were offset.

Nine of the dates from the excavated structure floor and fill deposits fell in a tight 32-year span in uncalibrated radiocarbon years between 3477 ± 39 BP (1878–1747 BC) and 3445 ± 51 BP (1876–1689 BC) (AA41023–25, 27–32). These dates represent the principal mature Srubnaya phase occupation. Calibrated, their range is much wider, indicating an occupation that occurred between around 1880 and 1700 BC, a little younger than the mean dates from the well.

The youngest date from the structure floor was on a human bone found in Square O5, Level 3, dated 3311 ± 54 BP (1663–1521 BC). The most recent dated Srubnaya grave in Kurgan 3, Grave 16, was older than this (3407 ± 46 BP, 1754–1632 BC), but it is nevertheless possible that this bone came from postoccupation funeral activities associated with later Srubnaya graves in the nearby kurgan after the settlement was abandoned.

Two dates from within the structure were somewhat older than the tight cluster of nine dates. The older of the two, 3531 ± 43 BP, from Square L5/2, Level 3 (30–40 cm) calibrated to 1974 to 1745 BC and is quite close in radiocarbon

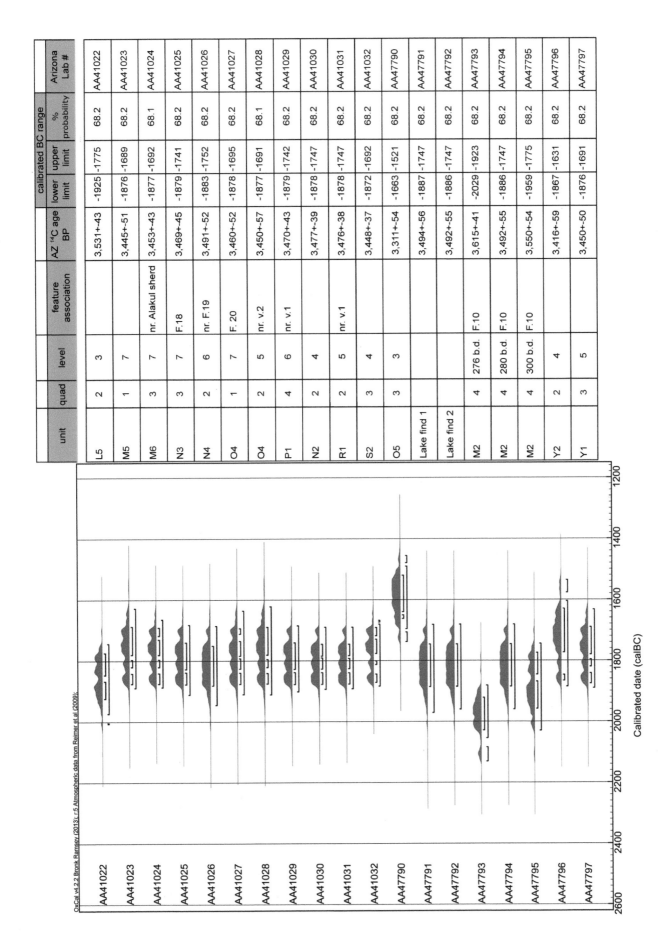

Figure 10.7 ^{14}C dates from the Krasnosamarskoe settlement.

years BP to one of the three dates (3550 ± 54 BP) from the well bottom. It is possible that the appearance in Level 3 of this older material was caused by the site occupants digging into the floor and casting it up to the ground surface at the edge of the structure. The other older date from within the structure, 3491 ± 52 BP, from N4/2, Level 6, is from a deep floor level and is identical with another date from the well bottom (3492 ± 55 BP) and with two dates from animal bones recovered from the lake bottom (the central figures for the four dates are 3491, 3492 twice, and 3494 BP). All of these dates probably reflect the early Srubnaya, principally "Pokrovka" phase of occupation, and calibrate to around 1960 to 1750 BC.

The two radiocarbon dates from Activity Area Y (Y1, Y2, in Figure 10.7) correspond with those from the developed Srubnaya occupation in the excavated structure.

Ceramic typology indicates that both the excavated and lake-collected parts of the settlement were occupied during the transition from the Pokrovka (early Srubnaya) phase to the developed Srubnaya phase, since pottery styles of both types (Ostroshchenko 2003; Semenova 2001) are found across the site. Radiocarbon dates from the well bottom, two from the structure fill and two from the lake bottom, just discussed, might derive from the "principally Pokrovka" phase, calibrated around 1960 to 1750 BC, and 11 dates from the structure floor and Area Y seem to represent the later "principally developed Srubnaya" phase, calibrated around 1880 to 1700 BC. There is a large overlap between these two groups of dates, with no obvious break or gap in the sequence.

The structure was built and occupied during the earliest centuries of the Srubnaya culture (1960–1700 BC), just after the transition from mobile pastoralism to settled life, and persisted during the time when the transition from the Pokrovka decorative style to the developed Srubnaya decorative style occurred.

Natural and Cultural Stratigraphy
The Natural Soil Profile
Rosen describes in Table 9.1 the typical natural stratigraphy for the meadow soils around the site. The top 15 to 30 cm is very hard black fine silt, with a columnar structure; this was the A1 horizon (Figure 10.6b). The top 20 cm was taken out as a single 0- to 20-cm level, as explained above under Recovery and Recording Methods. In unmodified natural profiles, there was an A2-horizon beneath the A1, also black in color but more granular in structure with more silt in the clay. This A2 could extend down to 40 to 50 cm. Below that was a brown B horizon, also clayey and

blocky, which extended down to about 80 cm, where the yellowish clay subsoil or *materik* was encountered. The 10 cm above the *materik* was the *do-materik*, a layer of mixed B and C soils with an orange-brown tint.

All of these soils contained clay and were baked by the sun, making them very tough to dig—easily the hardest dirt encountered by Anthony and Brown in their prior 30 years of archaeology. We actually broke the steel handle of a well-sharpened Marshalltown drop-forged trowel trying to excavate a particularly tough patch of baked clayey silt (Figure 10.8). A Russian short-handled shovel sharpened to a fine edge was a better floor-cleaning tool, used backhanded to shave the soil off in thin slices. Short-handled shovels were new to most of the Americans, and screens were new to most of the Russians; all of us adapted.

Both the natural and the cultural profiles were penetrated by many *krotovinas*, the tunnels left by burrowing rodents, or *susliks*. Rodent burrows crossed the site vertically, horizontally, and in every other direction. Many were the diameter of a human fist, large enough to convey important artifacts into new stratigraphic positions. The worst effect of the *krotovinas* was that they eventually blurred and homogenized soil color and texture distinctions, making cultural features such as pits, distinguished only by color and texture, difficult to perceive and define. In addition, the freeze-thaw cycle affected the upper soils, and this cycle also is a known taphonomic cause of artifact displacement. Together, rodent burrows and frost heaving undoubtedly displaced most of the artifacts we excavated either horizontally or vertically or both. However, the cultural stratigraphy survived all of these disturbances with surprising integrity (Figure 10.3).

Figure 10.8 The broken Marshalltown trowel, a clear testament to the hardness of the baked steppe soils.

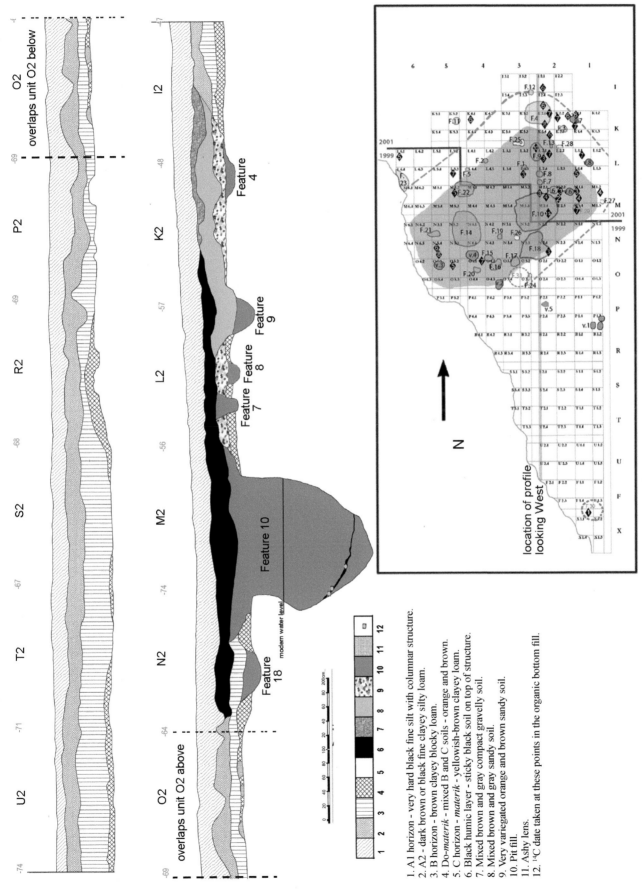

1. A1 horizon - very hard black fine silt with columnar structure.
2. A2 - dark brown or black fine clayey silty loam.
3. B horizon - brown clayey blocky loam.
4. Do-*materik* - mixed B and C soils - orange and brown.
5. C horizon - *materik* - yellowish-brown clayey loam.
6. Black humic layer - sticky black soil on top of structure.
7. Mixed brown and gray compact gravelly soil.
8. Mixed brown and gray sandy soil.
9. Very variegated orange and brown sandy soil.
10. Pit fill.
11. Ashy lens.
12. [14]C date taken at these points in the organic bottom fill.

Figure 10.9 North-South profile through the excavated structure, including Pit 10 (bottom) and the external occupation surface (top) at Krasnosamarskoe.

Table 10.2 Finds Inside the Krasnosamarskoe Settlement Structure

	Iron Age/Gorodetskaya Ceramics			Final Bronze Ceramics			Developed Srubnaya Ceramics			Poktrovka Ceramics			MBA Ceramics			Unidentified Ceramics			Bones, Shell, Antler			Stone		Metal
	Count	Weight (g)	% Weight of All Levels	Count	Weight (g)	% Weight of All Levels	Count	Weight (g)	% Weight of All Levels	Count	Weight (g)	% Weight of All Levels	Count	Weight (g)	% Weight of All Levels	Count	Weight (g)	% Weight of All Levels	Count	Weight (g)	% Weight of All Levels	Count	Weight	Count
Level 1	5	15	83.33				28	239	1.01							15	70	1.31	492	625	0.88	1	2	2
Level 2	1	3	16.67				101	910	3.84	2	11	0.08	2	11	8.60	25	63	1.18	735	2,254	3.15	3	13	3
Level 3							242	1,668	7.03	31	308	1.91	1	12	9.37	22	137	2.57	1,910	5,213	7.28	8	237	5
Level 4							380	3,612	15.23	56	498	3.01	5	32	25.00	57	212	3.97	3,533	10,516	14.68	4	138	2
Level 5				4	216	100	317	4,251	17.91	206	2,959	18.27				122	919	17.22	4,826	17,134	23.91	8	856	2
Level 6							336	5,415	22.83	229	4,286	26.45				362	1,926	36.09	3,965	18,371	25.64	14	389	10
Level 7							205	3,134	13.21	288	6,185	38.17				69	1,134	21.25	1,932	8,718	12.17	8	608	6
Level 8							119	1,643	6.93	64	1,662	10.26				24	542	10.16	1,095	5,350	7.47	3	652	2
Level 9+							108	2,851	12.01	28	297	1.84	4	73	57.03	15	334	6.26	765	3,498	4.81	1	1	3
Totals	6	18	100.00	4	216	1	1,836	23,723	100.00	904	16,206	0.9999	12	128	100.00	711	5,337	100.01	19,253	71,679	99.99	50	2,896	35

Table 10.3 Finds Outside the Krasnosamarskoe Settlement Structure

	Iron Age/Gorodetskaya Ceramics			Final Bronze Ceramics			Developed Srubnaya Ceramics			Pokrovka Ceramics			MBA Ceramics			Unidentified Ceramics			Bones, Shell, Antler			Stone		Metal
	Count	Weight (g)	% Weight of All Levels	Count	Weight (g)	% Weight of All Levels	Count	Weight (g)	% Weight of All Levels	Count	Weight (g)	% Weight of All Levels	Count	Weight (g)	% Weight of All Levels	Count	Weight (g)	% Weight of All Levels	Count	Weight (g)	% Weight of All Levels	Count	Weight	Count
Level 1	68	1554	83.68	7	76	88.37	93	447	9.09	0	0		1	11	18.64	34	393	40.39	212	834	9.25			1
Level 2	11	278	14.97				68	859	17.74	2	74	4.39				14	107	10.99	215	1,241	13.76			
Level 3	3	20	1.08				131	1,716	34.89	10	119	7.07	2	27	45.76	16	162	16.65	299	1,727	19.15	2	94	
Level 4	1	5	0.27	1	10	11.63	102	1,163	23.65	17	247	14.68				16	191	19.63	330	1,967	21.81	1	3	
Level 5							42	262	5.32	48	863	51.28	1	19	32.20	9	45	4.62	298	1,881	20.85	1	1	1
Level 6							9	62	1.26	21	257	15.27				2	5	0.51	184	667	7.39			
Level 7							19	398	8.09	11	86	5.11	1	2	3.39	6	70	7.17	133	565	6.26			
Level 8							1	10	0.20	4	37	2.20							27	137	1.52			
Total	83	1,857	100.00	8	86	100.00	465	4,917	100.24	113	1,683	100.00	5	59	99.99	97	973	99.96	1,698	9,019	99.99	4	98	2

Cultural Stratigraphy

Was stratigraphic mixing a serious problem? In Chapter 15, Kosintsev analyzes the 360 animal bones recovered from Level 1, the Iron Age stratum described below, and concludes that almost all had been displaced upward into the Iron Age stratum from the Bronze Age cultural deposit (probably by frost heaving, which tends to lift artifacts). While this sounds worrying, in fact even if *all* of the identifiable animal bones from Level 1 originated in the Bronze Age deposit below, then less than half of 1 percent of the animal bones in the Bronze Age deposit were displaced upward into Level 1. Some displacement occurred in every level, but most artifacts remain in rough stratigraphic sequence.

This sequence is shown by the following statistics: Pokrovka ceramic styles, the earliest phase of the Srubnaya culture, predominated (by sherd weight) in the deepest levels, Levels 7 and 8 in the floor deposit inside the structure (Figure 10.3, Tables 10.2 and 10.3) as well as in the deepest Level 5 outside the structure; mature or developed Srubnaya styles, thought to be later, predominated in the upper levels of the excavated structure, Levels 6 to 3, as well as in the upper levels outside the structure, Levels 4 to 3. A little activity happened on the site afterward, during the Final Bronze or Suskanskaya period, and these types are found in the upper levels, principally Levels 1 to 2. Iron Age artifacts also are found largely in Levels 1 to 2.

The expected stratigraphic sequence of ceramic types was retained in the cultural stratigraphy at Krasnosamarskoe with substantial integrity, despite frost heaving and burrowing rodents. As was noted above, the worst effect of the rodent burrows was to blur the edges of cultural features such as pits and floors. Some pit features remained fairly well defined at their edges, but others were seen only in profile, after they were partly excavated.

The Iron Age Cultural Component

Two cultural components were found within the primary excavated area at Krasnosamarskoe. The LBA occupation was, surprisingly, stratigraphically overlaid by a spatially scattered, low-density Iron Age occupation of the Gorodetskaya culture, apparently a specialized temporary iron-working facility. The Gorodetskaya pottery at Krasnosamarskoe consisted of 98 sherds from at least nine vessels (Figure 10.10).

The Gorodetskaya culture was an Iron Age culture of the forest-steppe and forest zone that occupied fortified towns (*gorodets*) built on hilltops, partly as protection against the steppe nomads of the Scythian-Sauromatian type. Gorodetskaya sites were distributed from the Oka and the upper Don to the west bank of the middle Volga between around 700 BC and 100 AD and are thought to represent a Uralic-speaking culture ancestral to the Mordvins (Vasiliev and Matveeva 1986:109–113). A large fortified Gorodetskaya settlement 7 ha in area was excavated near the town of Lbishche on the west side of the Volga in the Samarskaya Luka, about 100 km west of Krasnosamarskoe. The trading post at Krasnosamarskoe is apparently the easternmost Gorodetskaya site yet found and the only one in the steppe zone; it might have been created by ironworkers from Lbishche.

Two Iron Age features were excavated at Krasnosamarskoe. Feature 30 (originally Feature 1, later renumbered along with all of the features from 1999) was a circular pit containing a gray soil (Figure 10.2, bottom). Near the top was a spherical, spongy bloom of partially wrought iron about 8 cm in diameter, iron slag, and Gorodetskaya pottery (Figure 10.10). The bloom of iron was found in Level 1 of Square F1/3, 12 m south of the older Srubnaya structure. A very dark, dense concentration of charcoal was observed on the deflated bottom of the lake just 80 cm west of Feature 30. No Srubnaya pottery was found at this southern end of the grid, so this area was used only in the Iron Age. Feature 30, the iron bloom, and the apparent fireplace just west of it might represent iron brought to the site in a partly wrought state, ready to be forged and hammered into whatever was needed. The second Iron Age feature, Feature 31, also was a grayish-filled pit that contained iron slag, a concentration of charcoal, and Gorodetskaya pottery down to Level 4 in the center of Square O3, about 12 m north of the first one. Additional scatters of Gorodetskaya pottery were recovered in the upper three levels of Squares P1 and P2, as well as from the deflated lake bottom soils offshore. A Sauromatian arrowhead of a type generally dated to about the fifth to fourth century BC was found in Square L6, suggesting the presence of a Sauromatian arrow on the site, and perhaps of Sauromatians.

Two charred domesticated millet seeds (*Panicum miliaceum*) were found at Krasnosamarskoe, and both came from the Iron Age occupation (see Editor's Note, Chapter 12, and Table 12.14). One charred millet seed was found in Square F2, Level 4, fairly deep, but it was associated with Iron Age Feature 30 containing the iron bloom. No Srubnaya artifacts were found near this location, so this charred seed was associated with the Iron Age. The other charred millet seed was found in Level 1 in Square O2, near Iron Age Feature 31, where Gorodetskaya pottery and iron slag were found, and in this case in Level 1, the Iron Age level. The only charred domesticated cereals

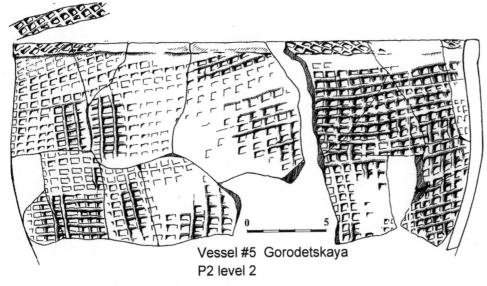

Vessel #5 Gorodetskaya
P2 level 2

Iron Bloom
F1.3 level 1

Sauromatian arrowhead
L6.1 level 5

Figure 10.10 Artifacts from the Iron Age Gorodetskaya culture component, 700 BC to 100 AD, including a collapsed pottery vessel (top), an iron bloom (bottom left), and a Sauromatian-style socketed arrowhead (bottom right).

found at the site were associated with the Iron Age component, a curious reversal of our expectations when the project began.

The animal bones from this Iron Age level are discussed briefly in Chapter 15 by Kosintsev, who concluded that almost all are derived from the Bronze Age layers by taphonomic processes. In Chapter 16, the U.S. archaeozoologists note that three of the four *roasted* sheep-goat specimens from the excavation are from Level 1 and Level 2 and were found outside the Bronze Age structure, spatially removed from the focus of LBA activities, so it is possible that these reflect an Iron Age episode in which a small number of sheep-goat were roasted. The sheep-goat bones found inside the LBA structure were rarely roasted.

A linear green crop mark bracketing the settlement area can be seen in aerial photographs of the site taken in 1998 (Figure 10.5). This subsurface ditch enclosing the site area probably was an Iron Age feature. It was tested by a 2-m × 2-m square in 1998 and was found to be a shallow subsurface depression with its deepest point at

28 cm below the modern surface—near the bottom of our Level 2, an Iron Age level. Its upper edge was at about 18 to 13 cm beneath the surface, within our Level 1. The ditch was a shallow linear trough only about 10 to 12 cm deep. No diagnostic artifacts were found in it. This linear feature was not deep enough to represent anything other than a drainage ditch around a campsite or possibly a symbolic boundary, perhaps designating a "safe" area for intercultural trade.

The Iron Age occupation at Krasnosamarskoe seems to have been a small, temporary trade emporium in the northern steppes where Gorodetskaya iron workers who lived in a town west of the Volga, possibly the large fortified town at Lbishche, traveled into the steppe borderlands to make and/or repair iron tools and fittings, possibly for nomadic customers represented by the Sauromatian arrowhead. They brought a little millet, perhaps roasted a sheep or goat, and abandoned or broke nine ceramic vessels between two pits that contained iron slag and a bloom of iron.

The spatial coincidence of so many liminal activities in this specific place is intriguing. Here we find, superimposed on the same spot, an Iron Age occupation presenting liminal cultural characteristics (a cultural border or frontier between Sauromatian nomads and settled farmers from a place like Lbishche), an LBA occupation presenting liminal ritual characteristics (dog and wolf sacrifices and boyhood rites of passage), and an MBA kurgan cemetery visited by both mobile nomads (Poltavka pottery) and settled herders from near Lbishche carrying Vol'sko-Lbishche culture pottery (see Ceramics below). Beginning in the MBA, this location seems to have been a place where liminal, border-testing activities occurred. Perhaps it had a sanctified or otherworldly reputation that made these border crossings and rituals appropriate for the place.

The LBA Cultural Component

The LBA cultural stratigraphy at Krasnosamarskoe contains important information about the sequence of activities at the site. Throughout this discussion, it will be important to distinguish between the stratigraphy inside the excavated structure, which had a dug-out floor that was gradually filled with thick cultural deposits, and the stratigraphy outside the structure, which exhibited thinner and shallower cultural layers (Figures 10.11–10.13).

Cultural Stratigraphy inside the Structure

We excavated an area of 118 m² inside the structure. The structure was covered by a humus layer about 15 to 20 cm deep, composed of very hard black fine silt with a columnar structure (Figure 10.6b); this was the A1 horizon. This top 20 cm was taken out as a single 0- to 20-cm level because of its hardness and blockiness, as explained above. All soils beneath that upper crust were excavated in 10-cm levels. Level 2 was between 20 and 30 cm deep, Level 3 was 30 to 40 cm, and so on.

Although 28 Srubnaya sherds were found in Level 1 (0–20 cm), most of the LBA artifacts found in the area defined by the structure were concentrated beneath Level 3 (30–40 cm). Most LBA ceramics, counting by weight, came from Levels 5 to 7, from 50 to 80 cm deep within the structure (Figure 10.12, Tables 10.2 and 10.3). The Bronze Age ground surface seems to have been in Level 3, around 30 to 40 cm beneath the modern surface. The floor of the excavated structure was about 40 cm deep, dug down to about 80 cm beneath the modern surface, where the *materik* subsoil was encountered. LBA pits were dug into this subsoil, and other pits were dug into the LBA ground surface outside the structure on both its northern and southern sides.

The LBA structure was sealed by a dark, leathery soil that was lens shaped, thicker in the middle of the structure and thinner at its edges, around 20 cm thick at the center, between 30 and 50 cm deep below surface, Levels 3 to 4. This black layer was interpreted as the remains of a thatched roof made of *Phragmites* reeds that had once covered the structure (tinted gray in Figure 10.2, black in Figure 10.9, and visible in profile, dipping down into the structure fill in Figure 10.14). According to Weisskopf and Rosen (Chapter 13), soil samples from this black layer (samples KS-02-03 and KS-02-05) contained many weathered, pitted *Phragmites* phytoliths, as well as a few other phytolith forms, suggesting that some tree leaves (pine and broadleaf) also were incorporated into the *Phragmites* thatch or blew in soon after the roof collapsed.

Beneath this leathery roof layer was a variegated brown soil, somewhat looser and sandier, with many lenses that constituted the cultural "floor" and "fill" deposits within the excavated structure (Figure 10.9). In the Russian interim reports, this was labeled Stratum 2 and was not differentiated (this was the stratigraphic designation Kosintsev used for the LBA occupation zone in Chapter 15). In this chapter, we follow the profiles as drawn in the field in 1999 and 2001, using Popova's and Brown's drawn profiles. According to these field drawings, the brown variegated soil was separated into two rather subtle sublayers. The top one (brown-gray) was more or less like the B horizon in Rosen's natural soil profile, and the lower one (brown-orange) was somewhat like the natural *do-materik* often encountered between the B and C horizons (Figure 10.9, Soils 8 and 9). So natural weathering in the past four millennia has probably affected the colors of these two layers in different ways, causing some of the observed contrast in color. However, the bottom layer (brown-orange) is of such variable thickness and variegated texture inside the structure that it cannot have entirely natural origins.

The top of this pair of brown soil deposits was a variegated mixture of brown and gray silty and sandy soils (Figure 10.9, Soil 8). It began at about 30 to 40 cm beneath the surface (Level 3) at the edges of the structure and dipped in the center of the structure, under the black leathery soil, down to about 50 to 60 cm beneath the surface, occupying Levels 3 to 5 over much of the interior.

Beneath that upper brown-gray soil was a very variegated brown and orange sandy soil that rested on the *materik* at about 80 to 90 cm, depending on location, and varied quite a lot in depth, dipping and rising (Figure 10.9, Soil 9 and parts of Soil 4). In most places, it bottomed out

KRASNOSAMARSKOE SETTLEMENT EXCAVATION						
UNITS OUTSIDE STRUCTURE			UNITS INSIDE STRUCTURE			
F 1.1	R 1.1	T 2.1	I 2.1	L 2.3	M 3.4	N 5.4
F 1.2	R 1.2	T 2.2	I 2.4	L 2.4	M 4.1	N 6.1
F 1.3	R 1.3	T 2.3	I 3.1	L 3.1	M 4.2	N 6.2
F 1.4	R 1.4	T 2.4	I 3.3	L 3.2	M 4.3	N 6.3
F 2.1	R 2.1	T 3.2	I 3.4	L 3.3	M 4.4	N 6.4
F 2.2	R 2.2	T 3.3	K 1.1	L 3.4	M 5.1	O 3.1
F 2.3	R 2.3	U 1.1	K 1.3	L 4.1	M 5.2	O 4.1
I 2.2	R 2.4	U 1.2	K 1.4	L 4.2	M 5.3	O 4.2
K 5.1	R 3.1	U 1.4	K 2.1	L 4.3	M 5.4	O 4.3
K 5.2	R 3.2	U 2.1	K 2.2	L 4.4	M 6.1	O 4.4
K 5.4	R 3.3	U 2.2	K 2.3	L 5.1	M 6.2	O 5.1
L 6.1	R 3.4	U 2.3	K 2.4	L 5.2	M 6.3	O 5.2
L 6.2	R 4.2	U 2.4	K 3.1	L 5.3	M 6.4	O 5.3
N 1.3	R 4.3	X 1.1	K 3.2	L 5.4	N 2.1	O 5.4
O 1.1	S 1.1	X 1.2	K 3.3	L 6.3	N 2.2	O 6.2
O 1.2	S 1.2	X 1.3	K 3.4	L 6.4	N 2.4	O 6.3
O 1.3	S 1.3	X 1.4	K 4.1	M 1.1	N 3.1	P 4.1
O 1.4	S 1.4	Ya1.1	K 4.2	M 1.2	N 3.2	P 5.2
O 2.3	S 2.1	Ya1.2	K 4.3	M 1.3	N 3.3	
P 1.1	S 2.2	Ya1.3	K 4.4	M 1.4	N 3.4	
P 1.2	S 2.3	Ya1.4	K 5.3	M 2.1	N 4.1	
P 1.3	S 2.4	Ya2.1	L 1.1	M 2.2	N 4.2	
P 1.4	S 3.1	Ya2.2	L 1.2	M 2.3	N 4.3	
P 2	S 3.2	Ya2.3	L 1.3	M 2.4	N 4.4	
P 3.2	T 1.2	Ya2.4	L 1.4	M 3.1	N 5.1	
P 3.3	T 1.3		L 2.1	M 3.2	N 5.2	
P 3.4	T 1.4		L 2.2	M 3.3	N 5.3	

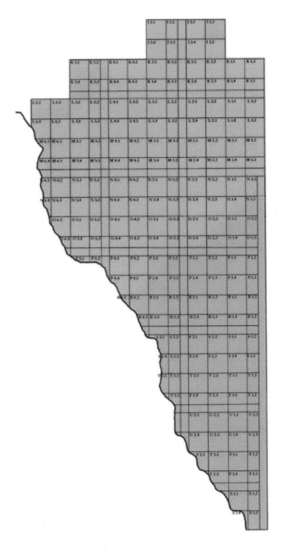

Figure 10.11 The excavation grid with inside-the-structure units distinguished from outside-the-structure units. Initially, we defined a third set of units as border units, but they were so similar in content to "inside" units that we combined them together.

in Level 7, 70 to 80 cm deep, and it could be just a lens or 20 to 30 cm thick. It occupied Levels 6 to 7 over much of the floor (dipping into upper Level 8 occasionally).

This basal brown-orange soil accumulated in place during the occupation of the structure. The evidence for this can be seen in the fact that the profile of the well, Pit 10, shows that the brown-orange soils were cut back by the site occupants from the original upper edge of the well (Figure 10.22), probably to keep the accumulating floor soil from falling into the well or from blocking the footing around the edge of the well. This cutting or clearing of the basal 20-cm brown-orange soil layer around the mouth of the well indicates that the lower 20 cm of the brown soil represents a "floor" deposit. After the well was filled, the fill deposit covered this horizontal area around the well

(Figure 10.9, Soil 10 inside Pit 10), but this fill deposit is postoccupation.

Also, cultural pits were dug into this lowest brown-orange deposit, and this shows that people lived on this surface. Pits 7 and 8 were dug into it at different times in a complex area between Pit 10 and Pit 9 (Figure 10.9). Between Pits 10 and 9 was an accumulation of soil, possibly upcast first from the well, Pit 10, and then from Pit 9 a few meters north. This pile of upcast soil made the floor higher in this area. It was cut into first by Pit 8 and then later, after more soil had accumulated, by Pit 7. These intercutting deposits and pits made the interior-structure stratigraphy between Pits 9 and 10 very complicated, but it also showed that the brown-orange floor deposits built up gradually and were cut into by stratigraphically successive features.

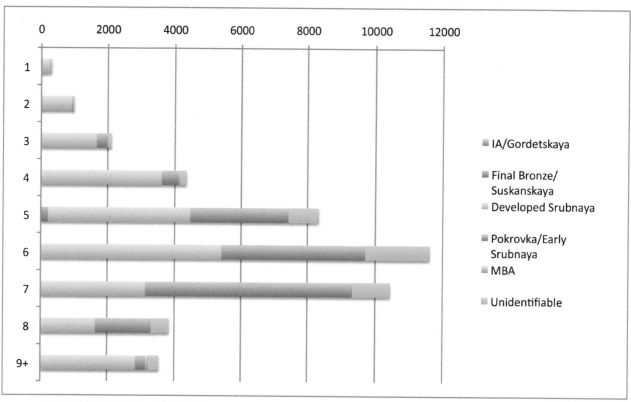

INSIDE STRUCTURE	LEVELS								
CERAMIC TYPES	1	2	3	4	5	6	7	8	9+
IA/Gordetskaya	15	3							
Final Bronze/Suskanskaya					216				
Developed Srubnaya	239	910	1668	3612	4251	5415	3134	1643	2851
Pokrovka/Early Srubnaya		11	308	498	2959	4286	6185	1662	297
MBA		11	12	32					73
Unidentifiable	70	63	137	212	919	1926	1134	542	334

Figure 10.12 Pottery styles by weight by level inside the structure. The stratigraphy is deeper inside than outside.

The upper 10 to 20 cm of brown-gray silty-sandy soils, Levels 4 to 5 over much of the structure, might have been shoveled in to fill the depression left by the abandoned structure (a "fill" deposit), or it might have originated like the lower 20 cm from occupation activities—more "floor" deposit. We were not able to resolve this uncertainty about the origin of the upper 10 to 20 cm of brown-gray variegated soils, a problem complicated by rodent burrows that cut across the entire deposit. It does seem that at least part of this upper brown-gray soil covered the filled-in Pit 10, which would make it a "fill" deposit associated with the abandonment of the site. But the brown-gray soil that actually sat directly over Pit 10 was moister than the surrounding soil because of water percolation upward in a soil column penetrating the *materik* and reaching below the water table. Therefore, in the horizontal stratigraphy over

the well, it was difficult to link the darker, moister over-the-well soils with a continuous horizontal covering stratum. Whether floor or fill, the upper brown-gray soil still contained many LBA artifacts and was largely an LBA deposit.

The well, Pit 10, has its own complex cultural stratigraphy, described in detail below under Feature Descriptions. The well contained an organic band of sediment at its bottom that accumulated under water while the well was in use, dated by three radiocarbon dates (see Radiocarbon Chronology above) to begin in the earliest phase of occupation, the "predominantly Pokrovka" or early Srubnaya phase, and to continue through the occupation. Above this organic layer are sediments containing wood fragments, including triangular chop-outs from logs, made with an axe, and at least two long poles with notched ends. Above them, and apparently above the LBA water surface, a notched log was set horizontally across the well, apparently as the edge of a step cut into the sediment on one side. When the site was abandoned, the well was filled with artifact-bearing sediments containing both Pokrovka and developed Srubnaya pottery, as well as other artifacts, presumably dug from the structure floor. The well was filled possibly to prevent animals and people from accidentally falling into the hole or possibly to keep spirits contained. No post-Srubnaya artifacts are found in the well fill deposit, so the filling-in activity was performed by Srubnaya people, presumably by the last occupants.

Cultural Stratigraphy outside the Structure

We excavated 89 m² of the occupation surface outside the structure (Figure 10.9, top). These were typically meadow soils as described by Arlene Rosen, Chapter 9 (Table 9.1).

Artifact density outside the structure was less than one-fourth that of inside the structure (compare Figures 10.12 and 10.13), and LBA artifact density declined with distance from the structure, showing that the structure itself was the focus of most LBA activity, with a few splotches of LBA activity outside near its south and north sides. Artifact densities also declined sharply above Level 3 and below Level 5 outside the structure, although there was still a substantial amount of LBA pottery, most of it in the early Pokrovka style, as deep as Level 5.

The upper edge of the dug-out floor of the structure, at the boundary between inside and outside, should tell us where the LBA ground surface was, and we could occasionally see this edge in Level 3, 30 to 40 cm deep, in some

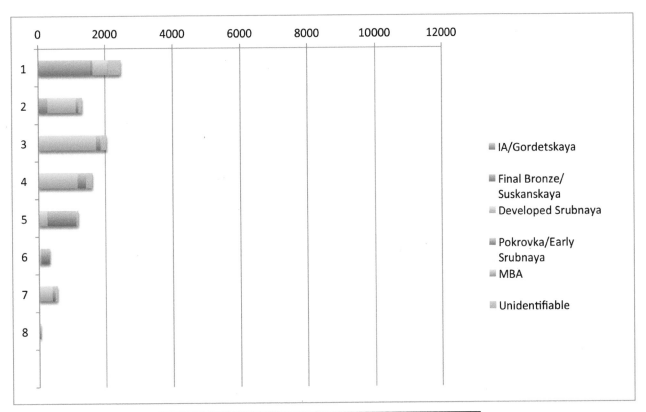

OUTSIDE STRUCTURE	LEVELS							
CERAMIC TYPES	1	2	3	4	5	6	7	8
IA/Gordetskaya	1554	278	20	5				
Final Bronze/Suskanskaya	76			10				
Developed Srubnaya	447	859	1716	1163	262	62	398	10
Pokrovka/Early Srubnaya		74	119	247	863	257	86	37
MBA	11		27		19		2	
Unidentifiable	393	107	162	191	45	5	70	

Figure 10.13 Pottery styles by weight by level outside the structure. Pokrovka styles are more frequent in deeper levels and decline with decreasing depth.

profiles of the structure edge. The edge of the dug-out probably was obscured in some places by the Srubnaya people digging up the floor to fill the well.

Stratigraphy of the Pokrovka and Developed Srubnaya Components

The Srubnaya culture is represented at Krasnosamarskoe by two ceramic types, differing largely in decoration and surface treatment of pots, designated Pokrovka (early phase) and developed or mature Srubnaya (late phase). Of the 3,194 sherds assigned to the Srubnaya component by lab director Alla Semenova, 2,198, or 69 percent, belonged to the developed Srubnaya phase, and 31 percent belonged to the Pokrovka phase (Figure 10.3). These styles are interpreted by Russian and Ukrainian experts as representing two successive chronological phases (Ostroshchenko 2003; Semenova 2001). A grave with a Pokrovka pot is considered older than a grave with a developed Srubnaya pot. An important extension of this assumption is that settlements containing both types, which many Srubnaya settlements do, are often assumed to contain at least two discrete and separate occupations. A model of Srubnaya settlement patterns has been constructed partly on the basis of this typological-chronological model, which suggested that settlements containing both types indicated a pattern of cyclical reoccupation of the same sites by chronologically discrete Srubnaya populations (Sedova 2000).

The stratigraphic sequences of floor deposits within the excavated structure at Krasnosamarskoe and in the occupation surface outside the structure both show a gradual shift in the frequency of these styles correlated with depth in measured 10-cm levels (compare Figures 10.12 and 10.13, totaled together in Figure 10.3). Sherds decorated in the Pokrovka style show the highest frequency in deeper levels (Level 5 outside the structure, Levels 7 and 8 inside the structure) and decline in frequency steadily through the upper levels, where developed Srubnaya sherds predominate (Levels 4–3 outside, 6–3 inside). Developed Srubnaya sherds were present with Pokrovka sherds in all levels but constituted an increasingly large proportion of the total as depth decreased. Both styles were used throughout the sequence but in differing proportions, suggesting that they probably were made by the same potters. This could not have been seen so clearly if we had not used 10-cm arbitrary levels and is one of the rewards for having recorded ceramic styles by 10-cm depth, using both sherd count and weight to quantify relative proportions of styles.

Pokrovka styles predominated in the Srubnaya graves in the associated cemetery (Chapter 17), as they do in most Srubnaya cemeteries in the region. Grave 16 contained a Pokrovka-style pot dated by radiocarbon to the later range of the Srubnaya occupation (3407 ± 46 BP, 1754–1632 BC), when developed Srubnaya ceramics were predominant in the nearby well-house or utility structure. The Pokrovka style perhaps began as an everyday secular style, then became associated with ancestors and funerals, and was retained as the preferred style for grave-gift pottery, explaining why the Pokrovka style predominates in most Srubnaya graves and cemeteries in the region while the developed Srubnaya style predominates in settlements (Chapter 4). Mochalov (2008:23), citing Kolev's excavation of the Srubnaya cemetery at S'yezzhee II (Kolev 2003), recognized that the two ceramic styles probably were used in the same chronological period, but at Krasnosamarskoe, there is good stratigraphic and radiocarbon evidence for their co-occurrence and for a shift in stylistic preference and function through a relatively brief period of time, perhaps less than a century.

The radiocarbon chronology (see section above) shows that the occupation at Krasnosamarskoe yielded some earlier dates clustered between 1960 and 1750 BC, but most of the dates were a little younger, clustered between 1880 and 1700 BC. The large overlap between the older and younger ends of the date sequence is supported by the stratigraphic observation that the well (Pit 10) remained open during the entire Srubnaya occupation, including "primarily Pokrovka" and "primarily developed Srubnaya" phases (see Pit 10, below), and was only closed and filled at the end of the occupation when the site was abandoned. Developed Srubnaya styles, however, overwhelmingly predominate in the pit feature fills, recorded as Level 9 and deeper (Figure 10.12), so it seems that most of the features and the floor deposits were created when the developed Srubnaya style predominated in settlements (also see Ceramics below).

Feature Descriptions

Identifying cultural pits can be tricky in steppe soils disturbed extensively by rodents. *Susliks*, however, prefer not to dig into the *materik* subsoil, which is very hard and clayey. Humans did often dig pits into the *materik* levels. Russian archaeologists therefore often ignore the many soil irregularities they encounter as they dig out a house floor, until they reach the *materik*. There they can easily distinguish a manmade pit that penetrated the *materik* from a rodent burrow. Only pits that penetrate into the *materik* get feature numbers. By then, the upper levels of the pit are gone, unless a profile is preserved in a sidewall or baulk. Pits that never reached the *materik* are not recognized.

Figure 10.14 Top: Central part of excavated structure—Units N2-4 and O2-4 with Features 10 (the well) and 14 through 20. Also with baulk profiles showing overlying sediments dipping down into the depression inside the house. Lower left: Plan showing the same area with adjoining units containing additional Features 21 and 22. Lower right: Photograph of the semi-circular line of pits between Pit 14 and Pit 10 (the well).

The American team had been trained differently, so wanted to assign feature numbers to pits as soon as a coherent stain was recognized in cultural sediments, well above the *materik*. This technical difference was difficult to negotiate. In the end, features were designated and numbered following the Russian methods, but Anthony and Brown kept a notational and photographic record of suspected features and pits in their field notes. We can add comments indicating that Feature X was initially noticed and photographed in Level Y (above the *materik*), and therefore the artifacts between Level Y and the *materik* in that square could have been associated with that feature. Some very obvious changes in soil color and texture turned out to be thin lenses that disappeared within one 10-cm level, and others were rodent borrows, so the U.S. desire to identify features quickly, particularly in these mixed sediments, would have introduced a lot of "noise" to the data recorded in daily field forms, feature photos, and bag tags, which would have contained feature numbers that were later withdrawn. There were advantages and disadvantages with both methods.

We are fairly certain that some cultural pits that existed on the site, particularly pits that did not penetrate the *materik*, were not recorded. Anthony suspects that a concentration of roasted dog skull fragments from Square N1/3 noted by Russell in the field were contained in an unrecorded pit just outside the structure, and we are pretty sure we observed a pit in Square P2 that was never recorded, also outside the structure. The occupation surface outside the structure on its southern side probably contained some shallow Srubnaya pits that do not appear on the site plan (Figure 10.2).

We recorded and drew 31 soil features we believe to be culturally created (Figure 10.2). However, not all of them are included in the detailed discussions below. Some were simply soil and ash stains with no discernable function. Some were pits cut into other pits so that it was especially difficult in Units N3, N4, O3, and O4 to decide how to distinguish them (Figure 10.14, lower right). Within this 4-m × 4-m square, a curving line of intersecting pits surrounded what looked like a platform with shallow postholes in its center. Two large, deep pits, possibly both wells, Features 10 and 14, were located on either side of this floor or platform, but it was very difficult to define the intersecting small pits between them. On our site plan (Figure 10.2), it appears that Features 15, 16, 17, 18, and 20 are separate and discrete, but they are really all part of an intersecting mass of pits that created a semi-circular ring between Pits 14 and 10 (Figure 10.14).

Feature 1 Unit L3/3, 80 to 90 cm: Posthole with Dark Fill and Ashy Lenses

I will use Feature 1 as an introduction to the features; therefore, it is a little longer than the other pit descriptions. Feature 1 was identified in Level 6 of Unit L3/2, but the top of the feature can be seen in the Level 5 floor photograph (Figure 10.15, right), so it began at about 50 cm deep. Its bottom was in Level 8, in the *materik*. It was a dark soil stain 22 cm in diameter and about 30 cm deep, very much resembling a classic posthole shape (Figures 10.15 and 10.16). It appeared to reveal tool marks inside. Ash was noted near the top of the feature, perhaps from burned grass matting. Feature 1 is surrounded by dense quantities of animal bones (visible in Figure 10.15), but this 1 × 1 m square represented a relative void within that concentration (plotted in Figure 16.1). Many dog bones were discarded a meter or more west of this post but not around its base, possibly to avoid undermining a support.

The phytolith sample (Figure 13.24) from inside Feature 1 contained a large number of tracheids, suggesting woody plants, possibly from the wooden post. It also contained many *Cyperaceae*, indicating sedge grass; a few *Phragmites* sp.; and many grasses. *Phragmites* phytoliths from reeds were more numerous at the top of the Feature 1 fill, and woody tracheid phytoliths that might be parts of the post were more numerous at the bottom of the posthole-shaped feature.

Feature 1 produced more pollen and a greater variety of pollen types than any other feature except the deepest samples in the well, Pit 10 (Table 12.1). The types included the same species in similar proportions that were encountered in almost all of the feature pollen samples, representing the shared background vegetation, but Feature 1 also contained some rare species, including pollen from a unique imported medicinal herb, *Seseli*.

In the shared background vegetation, the highest pollen count in Feature 1 and in all features was almost always from wild steppe grasses (*Poaceae*), followed by seedy weeds (*Chenopodium-Amaranthus*), which might have been exploited as seed food resources; with a strong marsh signature from *Typha* (cattails) and *Cyperaceae* (sedges, excellent forage for cattle); and accompanied by a range of herbs in flower, including *Urtica* (nettles), *Cichorium* (chicory, or wild endive, a salad herb), *Plantago* (plantains, leafy weeds), *Allium* (garlic), *Artemesia* (wormwood, a medicinal aromatic sage-like weedy herb), and *Polygynum* (another weed with edible seeds).

The most abundant tree pollen in Feature 1 and in all samples was *Pinus sylvestris* (Scots pine), which has relatively heavy pollen, most of which falls within 700

Figure 10.15 Feature 1 in Unit L3, a probable posthole. A particularly dense scatter of animal bones is exposed west of Feature 1 in L4, but it ends in L3. Feature 1 contained a rich array of pollen, including *Seseli*, a sedative herb.

m of the tree, but some of which (perhaps 5 percent) can be transported hundreds of kilometers by the wind. Like the other tested features, Feature 1 also contained a few grains of pollen from broad-leaf trees, including *Corylus* (hazel), *Betula* (birch), *Acer* (maple), *Populus* (poplar), and *Quercus* (oak). Stands of these trees might have been located many kilometers away—birch pollen in particular is very light and can travel a thousand kilometers on the wind—but pine trees probably grew closer to the site. Today there is a large patch of forest, 22 × 10 km in size, located 12 km southeast of Krasnosamarskoe, indicated in Figure 2.1 by a green shaded area. A pollen core taken inside a similar forest grove 70 km farther up the Samara Valley near Buzuluk showed that the Buzuluk forest has existed continuously since the Bronze Age, so it is possible that this nearer patch of forest (not cored for pollen) also was present in the Bronze Age. It could have been the source of much of the tree pollen recovered at the site.

Most interesting and unique to Feature 1 was a cluster of *Seseli* pollen (Table 12.7). Popova (Chapter 12) notes that *Seseli* did not grow locally and therefore was imported, probably from the chalky hills west of the Volga, 100 km or more to the west, where *Seseli* grows today. *Seseli* was known historically to treat mental disorders and had sedative qualities. It might have been used to calm the dogs during the winter ritual. The imported flowering herb must have been shaken or hung near this post.

The many traces of marsh sedges, grasses, and reeds could indicate that these materials covered the floor to provide a fresh walking surface. The abundance of pollen contained in this particular feature, more than in any other pit except the waterlogged well (Pit 10), suggests that a large number and variety of flowering plants were handled nearby, perhaps hung from the post that occupied Pit 1. These flowering plants included an imported bunch of *Seseli* that produced a cluster of pollen, perhaps brought here for use as a sedative.

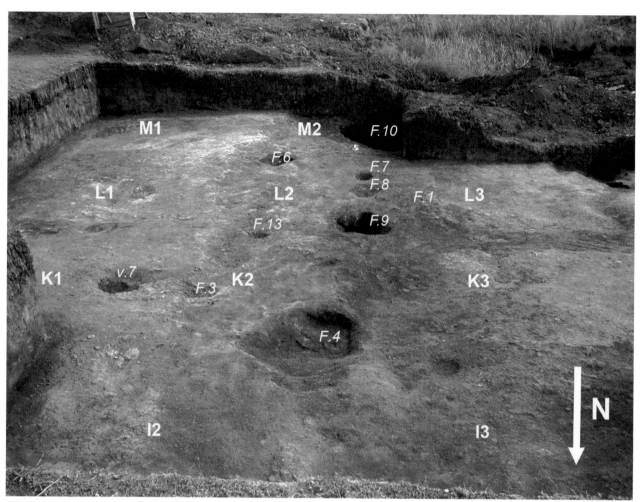

Figure 10.16 View south across the 2001 excavation area with the bases of pit features dug into the *materik* subsoil, including Features 1, 3, 4, 6 to 10, and 13, and the pit that contained Vessel 7, possibly a cheese strainer.

Feature 2 Unit L4/2: Posthole

Feature 2 resembles a posthole. It was located in Unit L4/1. It first appeared at the top of Level 5 (Figure 10.17). It was 20 cm in diameter and at least 22 cm deep, extending 12 cm into the *materik*. It is located near the northwestern side of the structure, near the base of the dug-out slope. It was surrounded by a dense layer of bone fragments, many bits of charcoal, red ochre, and burned, shattered ceramics. No botanical samples were taken.

Feature 3 Unit K2/2 and K2/3: Posthole

Feature 3 was a small posthole-shaped pit located in Unit K2 on the line between K2.2 and K2.3 at the northeastern end of the structure, in a location that would work structurally as a roof support position (Figure 10.18). When first noted in Level 6, it was 25 cm in diameter and about 13 cm deep. It was at the northern end of the structure where there were fewer artifacts than in the

center of the structure. Botanical samples were analyzed by Weisskopf and Rosen (Chapter 13) and Popova (Chapter 12). Weisskopf found a predominance of grasses among the phytoliths, and some phytoliths that might be from deciduous leaves, but no woody phytoliths that might suggest a post. Arboreal pollen was low, with pine dominant as always.

Quite interesting was *Galium* pollen found in this and three other features, one of them very nearby and similar in shape and appearance, Pit 12, and another on the south side of the structure, Feature 24. *Galium* is insect pollinated, not wind pollinated, so the actual flowering plant must have been carried into the structure during July or August, when it flowers. *Galium* (probably *Galium verum*, lady's bedstraw) can be used as a bedding straw; the coumarin scent of the flowers repels fleas. But *Galium* is also used with *Urtica* (nettles, also found in this feature) to make curdled milk products, importantly cheese, to which *Ga-*

Figure 10.17 Feature 2, a probable posthole in Unit L4 observed first in Level 6, beneath a dense scatter of animal bones.

lium also imparts a rich yellow color. Pit 3 was only 20 cm away from a crushed ceramic vessel (Vessel 7) with pierced walls, like a cheese strainer.

Feature 4 Units I3.3, I2.4, K3.2, and K2.1: Storage/Disposal Pit

Feature 4 was a large shallow pit in the northern corner of the structure. It was 80 cm across the top and 30 cm across the bottom in the *materik* level (Figures 10.16 and 10.9). It was dug 12 cm into the *materik*, but it was truncated on top by a layer of very variegated orange and brown soil. It contained at least 78 bone fragments weighing 321 g and 19 ceramic sherds weighing 614 g. Two sherds were Pokrovka; the rest were developed Srubnaya. There were also two pieces of copper ore in Levels 6 and 7.

Above Pit 4 (noted in Levels 5 and 6) was another pit (4a) dug into this variegated layer that contained an accumulation of bones (158 at 1,168 g), several of them burned, 19 developed Srubnaya ceramics (522 g), and a

stone arrow shaft straightener (Figure 10.40a). No botanical samples from these pits were analyzed.

Pits 4 and 4a appear to be disposal pits, one reexcavated into the other, containing general domestic and crafts waste, with some burned animal bone but not a particularly high concentration compared to other parts of the floor.

Feature 5 Unit L4/4: Posthole? Disposal Pit?

Feature 5 was noted in Level 8 of Unit L4/4 running into the baulk of L5/3. At the *materik* level, it was 30 cm across and about 10 cm deep. It contained very dark soil, two bone fragments, and a dog tooth. It was underneath several dense layers of fragmented animal bones and might be just a particularly deep gouge into the floor to make a shallow disposal pit for the animal bones above (Figure 10.19).

Feature 6 Units L2 and M2: Storage/Disposal Pit

Feature 6 was a medium-sized, irregularly shaped, and very deep pit, located on the boundary between Units L2 and

Figure 10.18 Features 3 and 4 in Units K1 and K2 at the base of Level 7, 80 cm deep. A good illustration of how rodent burrows complicated the definition of features, often more apparent in profile (inset of Pit 3) than in plan. Pit 3 was one of four features to contain *Galium* pollen.

M2, so it appeared in Units L2.4, L2.3, M2.1, and M.2. It was first acknowledged as a feature in Level 8, at the *materik* layer, but it can be seen clearly in excavation photos of the Level 6 floor and less clearly in Levels 5 and 4, so it was at least 50 to 60 cm deep and perhaps deeper (Figure 10.20). It was about 30 cm across and was dug 31 cm into the *materik*. The Level 10 fill included six bone fragments, five Srubnaya sherds, and some bits of ochre. A sample of soil yielded pollen varieties (Tables 12.5, 12.7, and 12.9) that contained the same range of background species found in most of the other features, described above for Feature 1. Most of the pollen was from wild grasses (*Poaceae*) and seed-bearing weeds (*Chenopodium-Amaranthus*), with some pine and a lot of cattail reeds and sedges.

This pit, like Pit 4, seems to have contained general domestic and crafts waste, with some burned animal bone but not a particularly high concentration compared to other parts of the floor.

Feature 7 Units L2/4 and M2/1: Post-Hole? Disposal Pit?

Pit 7 was a posthole-shaped pit when it was recognized in the *materik* (Figures 10.16 and 10.9). Pollen from Pit 7 was mostly like that from other pits: mainly grasses (*Poaceae*) and seedy weeds (*Chenopodium-Amaranthus*). *Urtica* (nettles) pollen occurred here in clusters, meaning that the plant was collected in flower, in the spring, and was introduced into this pit, perhaps by hanging a clump of nettles above the pit. Pine dominated the arboreal pollen, with a little oak, birch, maple, and poplar (Figure 12.9).

This was the only feature that contained *Lemna*, or duckweed pollen, from an aquatic plant that grows in shallow water and can be gathered in large quantities and dried for an excellent protein-rich cattle feed. Phytoliths of *Phragmites* reeds and *Cyperaceae* sedges were abundant, possibly with some phytoliths from oak leaves. Weisskopf noted that starches were present, which suggests plant food

Feature 5

Figure 10.19 Feature 5, a depression at the edge of Unit L4/4, might have been a shallow pit meant to contain the dense scatter of animal bones found above it in Unit L4.

waste was discarded here, adding weight to the interpretation that this was a disposal pit.

Feature 8 Unit L2/4: Storage/Disposal Pit with Chenopodium

Pit 8 was recognized at the *materik* and was a shallow pit about 30 cm across (Figures 10.9, 10.16). The phytoliths from Pit 8 were the normal grasses and sedges. But high levels of silica aggregates suggested burned vegetal matter and the deposition of ashes.

Pit 8 contained an exceptional abundance of pollen from *Chenopodium*. It was the only feature in which *Chenopodium* pollen was the majority of the pollen recovered, more than *Poacea*, which was the most common species in all samples except this one. A bunch of flowering *Chenopodium* plants must have been placed in the pit or hung over it. The concentration of *Chenopodium* in this single feature, located very close to other pit features such as Pit

7 that did not contain nearly so much *Chenopodium* pollen, suggests that it was intentionally manipulated inside the structure (Figure 10.21). This discovery is part of the argument indicating that *Chenopodium* was intentionally collected, carried into the structure, and consumed (see Pit 10) by the site occupants.

Pit 8 also was the only feature that contained pollen of the *Equisetum* genus, representing the horsetail plant. *Equisetum arvense*, or field horsetail, growing in moist meadow soils across the Northern Hemisphere, was used in Greece and Rome as an herbal remedy to stop bleeding, heal ulcers and wounds, and treat tuberculosis and kidney problems. It is a mild diuretic that increases urine output. It could have been brought into the structure as an herbal remedy. But the long stem is also edible in spring as a green, like asparagus, and the leaves are very high in silica, so are often used as a scouring or fine polishing agent.

Figure 10.20 Feature 6, a deep disposal pit containing general domestic and crafts waste, in Units L2 and M2. Inset photo by Boris Aguzarov, pictured here.

Feature 9 Units L2, L3, K2, and K3: Storage/Disposal Pit

The origin level of Pit 9 is uncertain; it was recognized in the *materik*, where it formed a broad depression almost 1 m across, containing many dog bones and Pokrovka-style pottery (Figures 10.9 and 10.16). Pit 9 contained relatively low counts of pollen and phytoliths, so perhaps was filled in quickly before pollen could accumulate in it. Both pollen and phytoliths indicate the standard background wild species growing in the site vicinity: marshy reeds and sedges, grasses, *Chenopodium-Amaranthus*, and a variety of herbs, including nettles, chicory, leafy plantains, *Artemesia*, and so on. Within the low overall pollen count, there was one unusual trait, a relatively high proportion of pollen from pine trees, the highest percentage of any of the features. But the absolute count of pine pollen was actually lower here than in several other pits, so it was not an unusual concentration of pine pollen but low counts of other species that explains the high pine percentage here.

Feature 10 Units M2, M3, N2, and N3: Well

Pit 10 was a well that was 290 cm deep, measured from the modern ground surface; it was 220 cm deep beneath the dug-out floor of the LBA structure (Figures 10.9, 10.14, and 10.22). It contained waterlogged wood, wooden artifacts, seeds, pollen, and animal bones that had been thrown into water and remained waterlogged in anaerobic sediments since the Bronze Age. It was therefore the most important feature found at Krasnosamarskoe, particularly for the recovery of botanical evidence, a principal goal of the project. Most of the artifacts found in Pit 10, however, were dumped into it when the well was filled at the end of the site's occupation. Perhaps the well was filled to prevent animals from falling into it after the site was abandoned. All of the artifacts in the well were from the Srubnaya culture, so it was filled during the Srubnaya period. Only the deepest deposits were associated with the actual use of the well, but the fill in the well contained valuable and exceptionally well-preserved information about the entire span of the Srubnaya occupation.

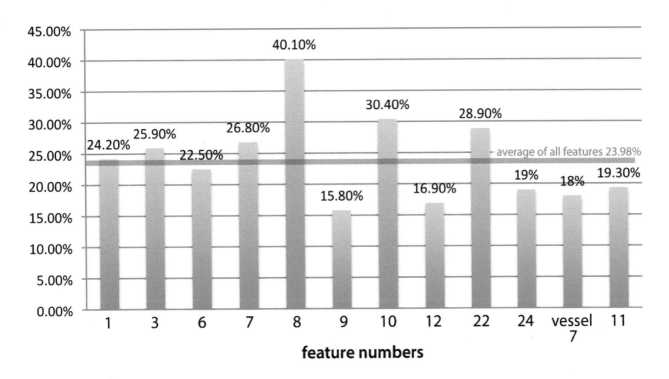

Krasnosamarskoe Settlement Chenopodium/Amaranthus
Pollen % in features

Figure 10.21 The anomalously high proportion of *Chenopodium* pollen in Pit 8 shows that this plant was manipulated in or near this pit much more than in any other pit in the structure, a possible indicator of intentional and selective use of this species.

In 1999, we excavated the edges of the opening of Pit 10 in Units M3, N3, and N2 (Figure 10.14). Only the upper levels were excavated. In 2001, the northern side of the same pit feature appeared as a patchy dark stain in Units M2/4 and M2/1 at a depth of 60 cm. Ten centimeters deeper, at 70 cm, the edge of a pit feature became clear, running northwest to southeast through both M2/1 and M2/4. Two baulks crossed just on top of Pit 10, and it was located on the boundary between the 1999 and 2001 excavation areas, so it could not be excavated completely until the baulks were removed and the fill over the 1999 excavation was shoveled back, a job that occurred in the final week of the 2001 season. We knew that it was a large pit feature but did not suspect that it would be so deep.

Laura Popova and Boris Aguzarov were trying to find the bottom of the pit feature when they began to expose a bell-shaped side wall in the *materik* that widened as the pit got deeper. Levels 7 and 8 of Pit 10, the top 20 cm dug into the *materik*, contained 658 g of ceramics, mostly Pokrovka, and dense animal bone, 1,462 g, much of it chopped and burned (Table 10.4). An ash lens at the base of Level 7, the upper fill, yielded a large proportion of fragmented silica and pitted phytoliths of burned wood, indicating wood ash; it also contained phytoliths of grass and *Phragmites* reeds, perhaps building or flooring materials for the structure.

With one week left in the 2001 season, a crew of four to six people began to work full-time in Pit 10 while everyone else backfilled the rest of the site (Figure 10.23). Below Level 8, the finds became much lighter, and we thought we were approaching the bottom, although a phytolith sample taken from 94 cm below the ground surface (b.s.) in the middle of this artifact-light zone later turned out to be the richest phytolith sample, with the highest abundance of phytoliths anywhere on the site. The phytoliths contained many *Phragmites* reed and grass forms.

At 150 cm below the modern ground surface, or 70 cm below the floor of the structure, the fill of Pit 10 became a gray waterlogged soil containing reddish bands of iron ore or ferric precipitate (Figure 10.24). This was the water table. Animal bones declined sharply in number below this

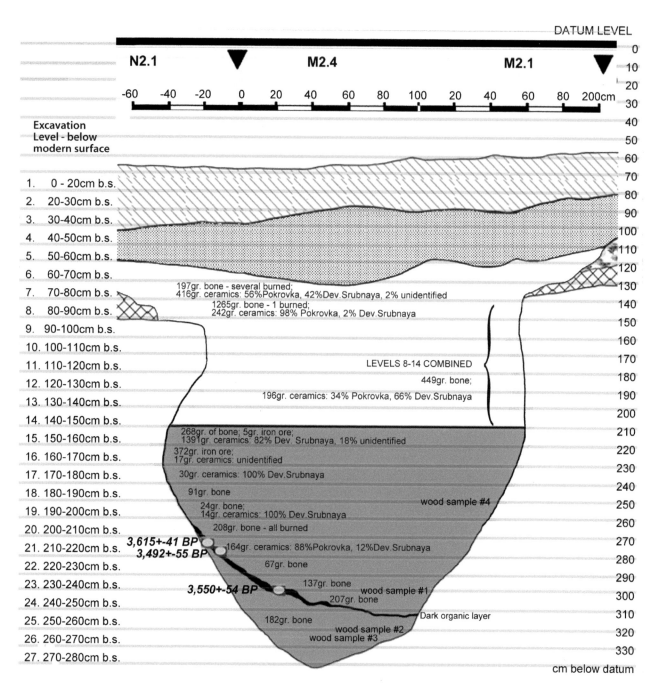

Figure 10.22 Profile of Pit 10: the well depth measurements on the right are below the primary site datum (b.d.), a reference point used in the field and therefore appearing in some field photographs. On the left, depth is converted to measurements below the ground surface (b.s.), a more convenient reference point when conceptualizing the structure and used throughout this report. The modern water table is tinted gray; the Bronze Age water table probably was below notched Log 4, at about 200 cm b.s. Dense deposits of seeds, including charred *Chenopodium*, appeared at about 210 cm b.s. and continued down to the bottom; the fill dumped into the upper part of the well contained relatively few seeds.

Table 10.4 Bone Finds in Pit 10 by Level

Depth in cm below modern surface (Taxon)	70–80	80–90	90–100	80–100	100–110	110–120	130–140	140–150	100–150	150–160	160–170	80–180	180–190	190–200	200–210	230–240	240–250	250–270	Taxon TOTALS
Indeterminate	42	25		1	19	17	18	8			4	1			1		1		137
Hare size to medium dog	1	1	2		5	8	8												25
Sheep-size (medium dog to medium sheep)	35	42	6	5	17	15	13	11		4			2	1	9				160
Pig size	1	1	2				1						1						6
Medium sheep to medium cattle								2							1				3
Cow size (cattle/red deer/horse)	13	34		3	11	9	8	11	1	2			3	1	12	4		2	114
Ovis/Capra/Capreolus		2	1																3
Ovis/Capra	1	11		3	2	1	1	1			1		1		1				23
Ovis	1	1				1	1							1					5
Capra						1													1
Bos sp.	7	11	2	4	9	5	1	5	2				1		4		1		52
Bos taurus		1	1											1					3
Sus scrofa	1		1																2
Equus caballus		1																	1
Equus sp.			1					1							2				4
Small mustelid	1																		1
Mustela																			
Canis sp.	13	1	11				5					1	1		1				33
Canis familiaris	6	11		5	6	10													38
Canis lupus																			
Rodent											1								
Citellus citellus (souslik)	1																		1
Homo																			
Medium bird							1												2
Large bird						1													
Turtle																			
Mussel								1											1
Snail								1											1
Total bones	123	142	27	21	69	68	57	40	3	6	6	2	9	4	31	4	2	2	616

Figure 10.23 Pit 10, the well, under excavation near the bottom of the feature. The modern ground surface, covered with backdirt, is visible in the lower left; the sandal and a muddy Khokhlov stand on the Bronze Age floor; and Kuznetsov (hat) and Mochalov (with shovel) stand ready to bring up buckets of mud from the bottom of the well.

level, but occasional bones and ceramic Srubnaya sherds continued to appear. We continued digging while beginning to bail water, as the nearby lake began to seep into the pit through the *materik* walls of the feature. The lead excavator was Dimitri (Dima) Kormilitsyn, a graduate student whose expertise in waterlogged excavations was recognized. We now realized that the pit was asymmetrical, sort of bag shaped, and undercut mainly on one side. At 190 cm b.s., Dima found several small pieces of preserved wood cut into small flat pieces 15 to 25 cm long and 5 to 8 cm wide. In the same level, he exposed a large, well-preserved, cut log lying horizontally at what appeared to be an internal ledge or step in the well (Figure 10.24, lower left). It was the largest piece of wood found, 98 cm long and 12 cm in diameter. It still had some bark, and the surface was blackened. One end was chopped into a point, and it had a notch

20 cm long cut in the middle, 57 to 77 cm from the pointed end. The notch faced the opening to the well as if to stabilize a cross-piece going down to the bottom.

Ceramic finds ended at 210 cm b.s., 20 cm below the horizontal log. They were primarily of Pokrovka type, but one sherd of developed Srubnaya style was found at this level also. Almost all of the sherds above that level (Figure 10.25) were identified as developed Srubnaya up to the depth of –90 cm, where the density increased and the ceramics were primarily Pokrovka. Pokrovka was not stratified under developed Srubnaya in Pit 10—instead, the two styles were mixed together or reversed their order from one arbitrary 10-cm level to the next. The sediments that filled the well were a jumbled mixture of the occupation deposits, presumably shoveled into the well from the floor or from the surrounding occupation surface.

One ceramic sherd was decorated with the impressed outline of an animal's head that resembles a horse (Figure 10.25). Representational images are very rare on Srubnaya pottery. Horse bones are unusually few in number at Krasnosamarskoe, compared to their average percentage in other Srubnaya settlements in the region (see Chapter 15), so we are uncertain why this image appeared here. Perhaps it refers not to actual horses but to a horse-related deity or symbol.

Wood finds in the middle part of the well were varied. Pieces of bark, twigs, chopped wood debitage, pole-like broken pieces, and three definite notched poles were found from 210 to 250 cm. At 210 to 220 cm b.s. (Figure 10.26), the wood was mostly bark (apparently oak and pine bark) and chopping debris. In the next level, 220 to 230 cm b.s. (Figure 10.27), there were somewhat larger pieces of cut wood, including axe-cut pointed log ends and a long thin pole with a notched end, an obviously modified wooden artifact. Broken pieces of the same diameter (2–3 cm) might have been part of a long handle for this pole or rod. Longer pieces of a similar carved pole and possibly another in the making were found in level 230 to 240 cm b.s. (Figure 10.28). An intact pole 57 cm long was found in situ at 242 cm b.s. at an upright angle, lying against the lower wall of the well (Figure 10.29). These poles or rods were intentionally modified, but their purpose is unknown. At 230 to 240 cm b.s., a different kind of carved and broken piece of wood appeared, 25 cm long and 8 cm wide, with a slightly concave flat side, making it look like a shovel or gouge (or drain spout?) exhibiting a broken half of a hole for some kind of hafting or attachment (Figure 10.29, top right).

Phytolith samples from this wood-rich part of the well (220 and 240 cm deep) produced many woody phytoliths, principally platey forms, possibly from bark. Also pres-

Figure 10.24 Uppermost wooden artifacts from Pit 10. Preserved wood began to appear in the waterlogged sediments filling the well at 190 to 200 cm b.s. Upper left: Horizontal notched Log 4, 98 cm long and 12 cm in diameter, found in a horizontal position possibly marking a ledge at 190 cm b.s., shown in situ on the lower left, a little more than a meter below the well opening in the floor. Bark survived on the horizontal notched log in places. One end was chopped to a point (see inset). The notch in the middle was about 20 cm long, turned toward the center of the well. Top right: Smaller pieces of wood emerging from the mud. Note reddish bands of precipitate iron in the wall. Bottom right: Roughly cut wooden planks from 190 cm b.s., the same level as the horizontal log.

ent were many Festucoid grasses, lovegrass or *Eragrosti*s types, and *Cyperaceae* sedge plants.

The base of the well exhibited a sloping band of organic sediment that developed during the use of the well. This band of organic-rich sediment marks a location at or near the bottom of the well during the occupation. The fill dumped into the well sits on top of the sediments at the bottom. The seed remains, discussed below, might be the best guide to where this transition occurred. Some animal bones (all cattle-sized ribs) were found in the same deep sediments that held 93 percent of the seeds.

Radiocarbon dates from this basal band of organic sediment were discussed above under "Radiocarbon Chronology" (Figure 10.22). The means of three dates from the organic sediment are slightly older than the mean dates from most of the floor deposits in the structure, but the date ranges from the well and the floor overlap substantially. The range for the well sediment is 2030 to 1682 BC; for the

structure floor and the lake finds, it is 1878 to 1689 BC. The earlier mean dates from the well suggest that the well might have been the oldest feature at the site, but it continued to be used throughout the occupation.

Pollen from the band of organic sediment was exceptionally well preserved and abundant (see Table 12.1). The concentration of pine and birch pollen is significantly higher in the deepest sample, taken from the deepest section of the organic sediment, 240 to 50 cm b.s., than it was in the sample from 20 cm above, near the top of the sloping band of organic sediment. From both samples, arboreal pollen made up a very small percentage of the total spore/pollen count, less than 2 percent (see Table 12.2), but this was partly because of the exceptionally high count of marsh-plant pollen in these sediments, depressing the percentage of arboreal pollen. *Pinus sylvestris* (Scots pine), *Betula* (birch), *Quercus robur* (oak), *Populus* (poplar), and *Tilia* (linden) were present, but in the deepest sample, pine and

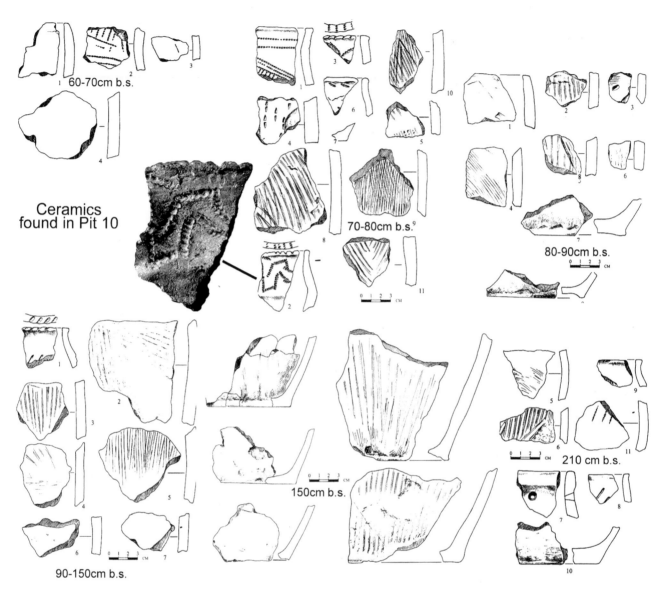

Figure 10.25 Ceramics found in Pit 10, grouped by level. Just a few sherds appeared below 150 cm b.s., lower right, but they included both Pokrovka and developed Srubnaya types.

birch occurred at their highest concentration found at the site. Possibly the deepest sample represents the more abundant pollen rain that occurred during construction, before the well-house was roofed over.

The other pollen from these organic sediment samples was much like the background pollen found in all of the features, with strong signatures from marsh, steppe, and flowering herb communities. The sample from 220 to 230 cm deep contained small amounts of pollen from *Trifolium* (clover), indicating the high quality of the nearby pasture, while the sample from the depth of 250 cm contained *Caryophyllaceae* (pink family) pollen, possibly *Gypsophila* (see Table 12.3). This is interesting, because *Gypsophila*

is a chalk-loving plant, like *Seseli*, and it has medicinal uses as a diuretic and expectorant and also as a treatment for mouth cancers. It flowers from June to August and might represent an imported medicinal herb collected during the summer months 150 km to the west, on the chalky west bank of the Volga, like the imported *Seseli* found in Feature 1 (see above).

Seeds were recovered from constant-volume 2-L soil samples taken from arbitrary levels throughout the well fill. Seeds found in each level can be more specific than pollen or phytoliths because seeds can be identified to species more frequently. Also, seeds of domesticated cereals are essential for studying the role of agriculture in a prehistoric

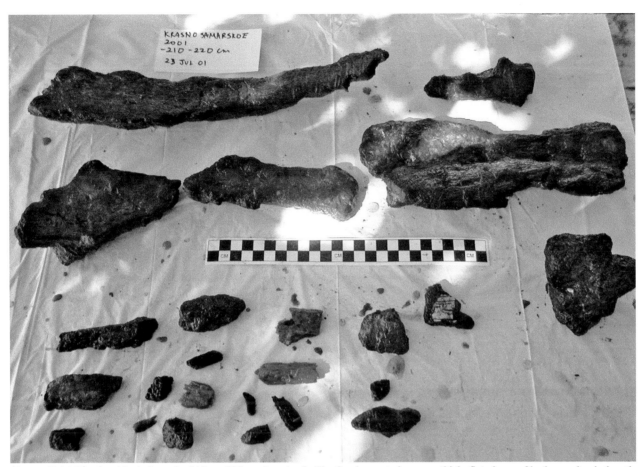

Figure 10.26 Wood and bark from the 210- to 220-cm b.s. depth. The five longest pieces are thick, flat pieces of bark, ranging in length from 10 to 31 cm. The smaller pieces are wood chips from various trees.

economy, so seed recovery was a major focus of the excavation. We were fortunate to find a feature that produced waterlogged seeds preserved in anaerobic conditions.

The upper part of the fill in the well contained relatively few seeds, and not one was charred. Below 190 cm b.s., or below the horizontally placed notched log, the seed count increased by 12 times, charred seeds appeared, and species diversity increased 5 times. Popova recovered 782 seeds from nine soil samples taken at various depths in the well (Table 12.13). The upper six sampled levels contained 80 seeds or 10 percent, and the bottom three levels contained 701 seeds or 90 percent of the seeds recovered. Six genera of plants were represented in the upper levels, and 31 (including those six) were present in the bottom three levels. The 701 seeds recovered from the bottom three levels probably can be related to the use of the well, like the sloping organic sediment that ran through the bottom two levels. The few seeds in the upper fill were included in the soil dumped into the well at abandonment. The discussion below relates to the 701

seeds found in the bottom levels, probably derived from the occupation and use of the structure.

Popova identified 31 genera of seeds in the basal three levels. Only three genera were charred: *Chenopodium* (306 charred seeds, 44 percent), *Polygynum* (74 charred seeds, 10 percent), and *Amaranthus* (11 charred seeds, 0.2 percent). These three edible species made up 54 percent of the seeds recovered from the basal three levels. The most common seed genus after these three was *Cyperus* sp., a common marsh-land sedge, with 47 seeds (6.6 percent), none charred. Additional seeds of *Chenopodium* and *Polygynum* were found in the fill sediments higher up in the well (80 *Chenopodium* seeds and 10 *Polygynum* seeds), but these were not charred and are interpreted here as accidental inclusions in fill sediments, fortuitously preserved by waterlogging. *Amaranthus* seeds were found only in the bottom three levels, and all were charred.

Seeds of *Chenopodium, Polygynum,* and *Amaranthus* were consumed, and the plants were temporarily domesticated by

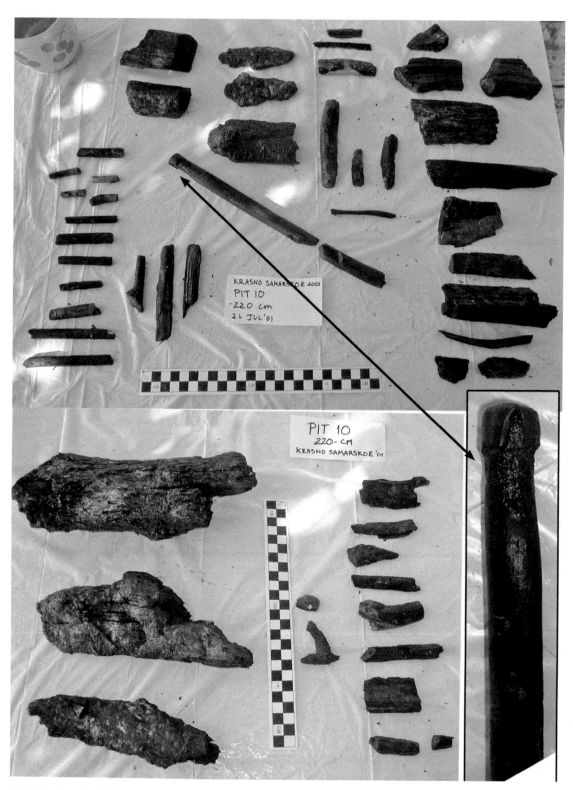

Figure 10.27 Wood and bark from the 220- to 230-cm b.s. depth. On the upper right are wedges of chopped wood debris. Top middle are two pieces of bark. To the left are twigs and sticks of various diameters and a stick with a carved notch at one end. Two or three additional pieces of this notched stick's handle could be represented among the other broken twigs and sticks. Bottom: Chopped pieces of logs and various twigs and chips. The top log is chopped diagonally at one end, broken at the other; the middle one is chopped diagonally twice across its center.

Figure 10.28 Wood and bark from the 230- to 240-cm b.s. depth, including another carved stick with a notched end, broken in three pieces that fit together, 48 cm long, possibly originally longer. Beside it is an unshaped stick with a naturally notched end, similar in size and shape to the notches cut on other sticks. On the upper right is a carved shovel-shaped tray, 25 cm long and 8 cm wide. The flat side is slightly concave and widens like a shovel or dispenser (or spout?) or some kind. The bottom side of the narrow end has a half-hole for the attachment of a sidepiece. Many twigs and sticks came from this level.

Native Americans in temperate North America before the domestication and diffusion of maize (Gremillion 2004). *Chenopodium album* seeds are as nutritious as rice or maize and have been found charred in large caches in Neolithic and Bronze Age sites in temperate Europe and even in the stomachs of "bog bodies" of the Iron Age, so they certainly were eaten in prehistoric Europe (Behre 2008). North American *Chenopodium belandieri* grows naturally in dense stands that can produce 500 to 1,000 kg of seeds per hectare, comparable to the yield of einkorn wheat (645–835 kg/ha) (Smith 1989:1569). Charring is required to remove the bitter pericarp from *Chenopodium* seeds prior to cooking them (López et al. 2011). Only the three most productive and nutritious wild seed–producing genera in Pit 10 were charred, suggesting that they were selectively collected and prepared for consumption. Feature 8, described earlier, contained a uniquely high concentration of *Chenopodium-Amaranthus* pollen (Figure 10.21), suggesting that *Chenopodium-Amaranthus* plants were selectively manipulated in that pit as well. The pollen of *Chenopodium-Amaranthus* and *Polygynum* was ubiquitous in pit features in the floor of the structure, showing that all three genera were growing in the vicinity when the site was occupied. Pit 10 at Krasnosamarskoe contains the best evidence in the steppes for the selective collection and charring of *Chenopodium*, *Amaranthus*, and *Polygynum* seeds during the Bronze Age. Shishlina (2008:Table 30) has found *Chenopodium* pollen in organic residues inside MBA Catacomb culture pots and in tooth tartar in MBA individuals in the Kalmyk steppes, north of the North Caucasus Mountains, but in both contexts, it was not absolutely clear that the inclusion of *Chenopodium* pollen was intentional or selective rather than accidental. At Krasnosamarskoe, we can say that the seeds of these three genera, but particularly *Chenopodium* and *Polygynum*, were selectively collected in significant quantities, much more than any other wild seed–producing plant, and were prepared for consumption by charring them, a treatment applied only to these genera.

The 28 wild, not-charred genera of seeds from the basal three levels constituted a rich array of marsh grasses and

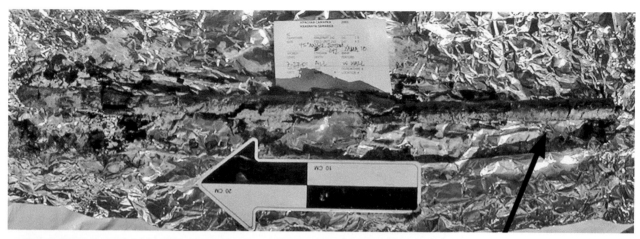

Figure 10.29 Wood from the 240- to 250-cm b.s. depth, an unbroken stick, 57 cm long and 2.5 cm diameter, found in situ lying at an angle against the sloping bottom. Its deep end was 242 cm below the modern surface, so its upper end protruded into the previous level but was concealed in mud. It is unaltered and retains its covering of bark.

sedges (*Carex, Cliocharis, Cyperus, Sparganium*), steppe grasses (bluegrass or *Poa*, wheatgrass or *Agropyron*, lovegrass or *Eragrostis*, ryegrass or *Lolium*, clover—both *Trifolium* and *Melilotis*), and herbs. The basal levels also yielded 6 seeds of *Galium*, lady's bedstraw, probably used to curdle milk for cheese making; 6 seeds of *Atriplex*, or orache, a very edible salad herb; and 22 seeds of *Rumex*, or sorrel, another commonly eaten herb. *Linaria*, or toadflax (five seeds), is a medicinal plant, as is *Arenaria*, or sandwort (one seed). None of these were charred. The seed remains as a whole indicate a rich pastureland, marsh, and a variety of wild green salad herbs that could have enriched the diet of the site occupants. It is notable that no seeds, pollen, or phytoliths of cultivated cereals were recovered from Pit 10 or from any other feature.

Bones from Pit 10 (Table 10.6) were well preserved but not numerous. Some have unusual markings, probably staining from minerals in the anaerobic mud, but some of the marks seem almost representational and intentional (Figure 10.30). Taking the Pit 10 fauna as a whole, 165 animal bones could be identified to species. Dogs were 43 percent of the total by number of identified specimens (NISP), cattle 33 percent, sheep-goat 19 percent, horse 3 percent, and pigs were represented by two bones, or 1 percent of the sample. These ratios were about what would be expected from floor deposits shoveled into the well after the dog sacrifices had occurred and been disposed of in the structure. Most of the animal bones were contained in the upper layers of the fill of Pit 10, consistent with a derivation from the floor deposits. However, the deepest animal bones

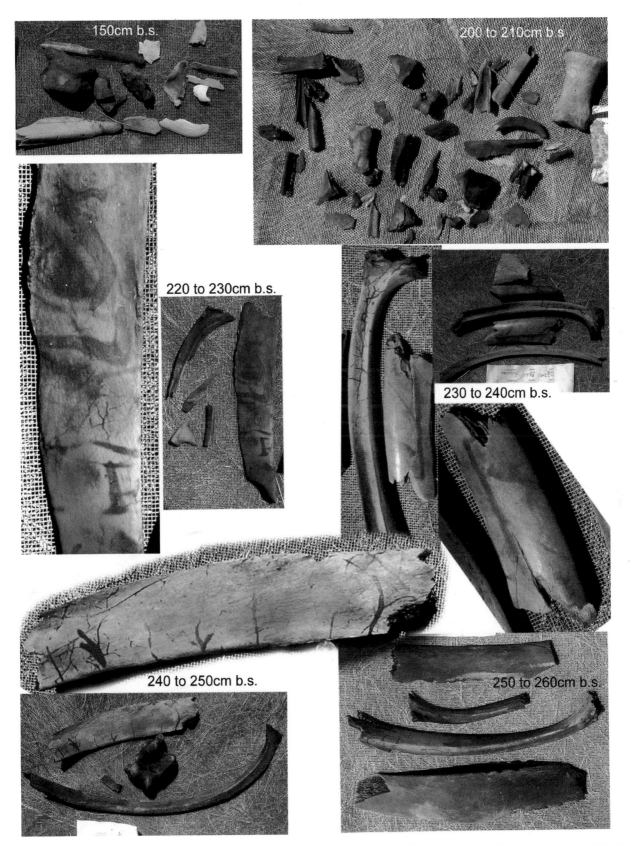

Figure 10.30 Animal bones found in Pit 10. Small pieces of chopped bone and some shell pieces were found in the upper levels. Mostly rib bones were found in lower levels. Many were partially or entirely burned. Several had unusual markings, most of them clearly natural but some seeming figural. One bone (230 to 240 cm) appears to have lines drawn with red ochre.

were seven large ribs from cattle, some of them marked in an interesting way. These seven cattle ribs were most likely dropped into the well during the occupation of the structure.

The deepest find from the very bottom of the gray mud that filled the well was a wooden log found at 270 cm b.s. (Figure 10.31), under the band of organic sediment. It was 57 cm long with three wedge-shaped axe cuts taken out of one side, $7 \times 7 \times 8$ cm in size. One side still had bark, and the whole piece was blackened. This log could have been construction debris, an extra length of a prenotched log meant for framing that was chopped off and accidentally

dropped into the newly dug well. It might have been part of the framing for the roof, notched to hold the cross-pieces on which thatch would be laid.

Feature 11 Unit K5/2: Posthole

Pit 11 was located outside, north of the structure. It was not covered by the black leathery soil representing the roof fall of *Phragmites* thatch that covered the pits inside the structure. Thatch is made from dead winter reeds, not from leafy summer reeds. Pit 11 was the only pit at the site that contained phytoliths from the green, leafy parts of *Phragmites*

wood sample #2
Pit 10: 262cm b.s..

reverse side

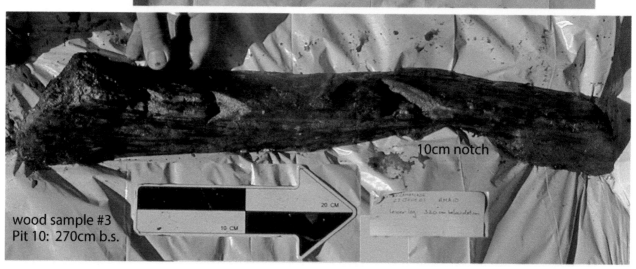

wood sample #3
Pit 10: 270cm b.s.

10cm notch

Figure 10.31 Wood from the 260- to 270-cm b.s. depth, consisting of two logs located under the dark organic layer that developed during the use of the well. Log sample 2 was found in the northwest quad of the well at 262 cm deep. It is 37 cm long, 8 cm wide, 4 cm thick, and cut like a thick plank. Log sample 3 was found at 270 cm deep, the deepest artifact recovered from the well. This log is 57 cm long and was trimmed by an axe, making it into a triangular wedge-shaped piece in section, measuring $7 \times 7 \times 8$ cm at one end. The 8-cm side retained bark. Parts of the external surface were charred by brief contact with fire, but the center of the piece retained a brown color. Three 45° notches were cut with an axe on one edge (intersecting with the bark side). The inside edge (no bark) has a wide notch at 10 cm in length, much like the 20-cm notch in the horizontal notched log. The triangular shape and notches suggest that the piece was trimmed and shaped to be part of a larger structure but was lost or discarded rather than being used for its intended purpose.

reeds, collected in the summer. Leafy green parts of reeds appeared outside the structure but not inside. The pit also contained many tracheids and platy forms, suggesting the presence of wood. Pit 11 contained the standard assortment of arboreal pollen (mainly pine, with a little poplar, birch, oak, and maple) and pollen from *Dianthus* flowers, which bloom from June to September.

It is possible, given the woody phytoliths in the pit, that this was a posthole for a gabled side entrance into the structure. Animal bones found in Square L4 seemed to be scattered into the structure down a slope with its high side on the northwest, as if they had been thrown down that slope, into the structure, from a spot near Pit 11—perhaps through this door.

Feature 12 Units I3/2 and I3/3: Posthole?

Pit 12 was small pit, possibly a posthole base, with a dark organic fill, located just inside the northern corner of the structure in a good structural position for a roof-post (Figures 10.2, 10.32). However, it contained very few woody phytolith types, so if a post was set here, it was removed, leaving

little woody material in the pit. The phytoliths from near the bottom of the pit fill were dominated by pitted, weathered *Phragmites* reeds and sedges, perhaps from the roof thatch, and amorphous silica, indicating burning, perhaps suggesting waste disposal. Pit 12 had a large quantity of pine pollen. Setting aside the well, Pit 10, a special case, Pit 12 had more pine pollen in absolute grain count (1,859) than any other pit except Pit 1, also a posthole-like pit with a dark fill. Pit 1 had the highest count of pine pollen outside the well (2,071).

Pit 12 also contained *Galium* (lady's bedstraw) pollen. *Galium* appears in only four features inside the structure (Pits 10, 12, and 3 and ashy-sandy Feature 24). Pit 12 and Pit 3 are close to each other. *Galium* is used for bedding (it repels fleas), and it is used medicinally as a diuretic, sedative, and a treatment for internal bleeding. It is also widely used, sometimes with nettles (*Urtica*, widespread in all features), as a cheese rennet to curdle milk in cheese making, and it gives a rich yellow color to the cheese. A ceramic vessel, Vessel 7, with holes pierced through its walls, like a cheese strainer, was found crushed in situ nearby.

Figure 10.32 Feature 12 was a small pit, possibly a posthole base, with a dark organic fill, located just inside the northern corner of the structure in a good structural position for a roof-post.

Feature 14 Units M3, M4, N3, and N4: Well?

Feature 14, found and partly excavated in 1999, was a large-diameter, deep pit containing dense concentrations of animal bones in its upper fill (Figure 10.14). In size, depth, and soil texture, it resembled the well, Pit 10, more than any other feature. East-west and north-south baulks in the excavation grid intersected on top of Pit 14, as they did over Pit 10, making excavations complicated and slow. On the last day of the 1999 season, excavation of this pit in Units N4/1 and N4/4 reached a depth of 150 cm, about 70 to 80 cm deep into the *materik*, without finding a bottom. We expected to finish excavating it the next field season. Unfortunately, when we returned to Krasnosamarskoe in 2001, advancing lake erosion had destroyed that part of the site. We suspect that the bottom was much deeper than 150 cm, perhaps deep enough to be a second well.

Pit 14 was nearly the same diameter as the well, Pit 10, and the soils above it were darkened in the same way that the soils above Pit 10 were darkened. This implies that water percolated up through the soft pit fill from the water table to nearly the modern surface, darkening the soil above the pit, as happened above Pit 10, where another column of absorbent fill went through the *materik*, "wicking" water up. The modern water table is encountered at around 150 cm, the depth of the deepest excavated level in Pit 14, so Pit 14 was deep enough to act as a sponge sitting in the water table, explaining the darkened soil above it. The early Srubnaya climate is thought to have been dry and cold, conditions argued in Chapter 1 to have partly caused the transition to sedentism, so the water table could have been lower in the LBA. Pit 10, the well, was deep enough to intersect even the LBA water table, but we do not know if Pit 14 was. If Pit 14 was a second well, an analogy can be found in the later site of Russkaya Selit'ba, a settlement of the Final Bronze Age, where one house contained two wells (Figure 10.4). Since Pit 10 remained open through the occupation of Krasnosamarskoe, this implies that Pit 10 and Pit 14 were open concurrently, for some period of time. We do not know why two wells would have been needed, but the space between them was densely covered with animal bones, including from dog sacrifices, so it might be that a ritual called for acts to be performed between two wells.

Pit 14 yielded no radiocarbon dates and no botanical studies. We presume that it was filled in during the abandonment of the site, when the well, Pit 10, was filled in or possibly before that event. The animal bones found in Pit 14 were fairly similar in species ratio to those found in Pit 10. (Tables 10.4–10.6). In both pits, dog bones were quite common, making up 43 percent of domesticated NISP in Pit 10 and 54 percent of domesticated NISP in Pit 14,

showing that the fill in both pits postdated the dog sacrifices. Pit 14 actually contained more animal bones, even though it was not dug as deeply as Pit 10. Pit 14 had 34 percent more animal bones than the equivalent levels of Pit 10. So the fill used to close Pit 14 was denser in the absolute number of animal bones than the fill used to close Pit 10, but the species ratios were about the same. Pit 10 was excavated to its bottom, however, and in the deepest three levels, not comparable to any data from Pit 14, cattle bones predominated.

We can't say exactly what Pit 14 was, unfortunately, but only Pit 10 was as wide and as deep and as darkly colored as Pit 14, so we suspect that Pit 14 was a second well.

Feature 18 Units N2/4 (and N2/1?), N3/2, and N3/3: Storage/Disposal Pit

Feature 18 was a broad, shallow pit visible in the field photograph (Figure 10.14) under the baulk and on both sides of it, largely in Squares N2/4 and N3/3 and in profile in Figure 10.9. It was initially visible in Level 4 and was better defined visually in Level 5, 50 to 60 cm. No samples were taken for botanical analysis.

There was an intense concentration of animal bones in these squares. Russell, Brown, and Brown (Chapter 16) observed a particular concentration of roasted and chopped dog remains, cranial and postcranial, in N2/1 and N2/4 in Level 6, representing at least three dogs; most of these might have been in Pit 18. Skeletochronological analysis of teeth from two cattle from Square N2, perhaps associated with Pit 18, show winter and end-of-winter season of slaughter for these two cattle. Almost all of the dogs and these two cattle were slaughtered in the same winter season, perhaps for the same ritual events, and their remains were then discarded in the same area, possibly in the same pit. The ceremonial slaughter of cattle could imply that large numbers of community members from beyond the single small household at Krasnosamarskoe shared in the feast, as would be expected for an age-set initiation ceremony (see the end of Chapter 14).

Feature 22 Unit L4/4: Disposal/Storage Pit?

Feature 22 was a broad, shallow pit scooped into the *materik* and filled with darker soil. Phytoliths (Figure 13.22) from near the base of the pit contained high levels of silica aggregates and many fragmented, heavily pitted phytoliths, suggesting a residue from burning, perhaps from burned reeds. *Phragmites* phytoliths were more abundant in this feature than in any other sample, suggesting that reeds were used to line the pit or perhaps served as flooring material above the pit.

Table 10.5 Bone Finds in Pit 14 by Level

Taxon	Depth in cm Below Modern Surface							Taxon Totals
	70–80	80–90	90–100	100–110	110–120	120–130	140–150	
Taxon								
Indeterminate			30	89		37	2	158
Hare size to medium dog			4	60		1		65
Sheep-size (medium dog to medium sheep)	42	17	66	39	35	43	5	247
Pig size	2		3	3	1	1		10
Medium sheep to medium cattle			26					26
Cow size (cattle/red deer/horse)	21	15		15	12	13	6	82
Ovis/Capra/Capreolus			8		1	3		12
Ovis/Capra	3	1		5	3	1	1	14
Ovis		1						1
Capra						3		3
Bos sp.	3	6	9	5	6	2	1	32
Bos taurus	2							2
Sus scrofa			2					2
Equus caballus								
Equus sp.								
Small mustelid								
Mustela						1		1
Canis sp.		1	1		6			8
Canis familiaris	6	1	16	29		16	1	69
Canis lupus		1						1
Rodent	1							1
Citellus citellus (souslik)								
Homo				1				1
Medium bird								
Large bird			1					1
Turtle					1			1
Mussel				1				1
Snail								
Total bones	80	43	166	247	65	121	16	738

Pollen from near the bottom of the pit represented the standard background vegetation seen in most of the examined features: primarily grasses (*Poaceae*) and seedy weeds (*Chenopodium-Amaranthus*), with a range of flowering herbs (nettles, plantains, chicory, garlic, wormwood) and a little tree pollen, dominated by *Pinus sylvestris*, as always, with a little birch, maple, juniper, poplar, and oak.

The only surprise in the pollen was a grain of *Gagea* pollen from a lily-like plant with an attractive yellow flower that normally blossoms early in the spring in damp woodland environments, thought to be many kilometers distant from Krasnosamarskoe. Of course, someone could easily have carried a bunch of *Gagea* flowers (yellow star of Bethlehem) to Krasnosamarskoe from a pine-oak-birch forest today located 12 km southeast of the site.

Feature 24 Units O3/2 and O3/3: Ash-Filled Pit

This feature was initially perceived (July 16, 1999) as a pit filled with ashy, sandy soil, partly concealed beneath the baulk between O3 and O2. It is drawn on the site plan as an ash lens, but it could have been a shallow pit filled with ashy soils.

No phytoliths were analyzed from this feature, but a pollen sample was analyzed. The pollen species and ratios were similar to the other features inside the

Table 10.6 Percentage of Domestic Animal NISP in All Levels of Pit 10 and Pit 14

Identified Domestic Animal Bones	Pit 10 -70 to -270 cm		Pit 14 -70 to -150 cm	
	NISP	%	NISP	%
Ovis/Capra/Capreolus	3		12	
Ovis/Capra	23		14	
Ovis	5		1	
Capra	1		3	
Ovis/Capra total	**32**	**19.39**	**30**	**20.83**
Bos sp.	52		32	
Bos taurus	3		2	
Bos total	**55**	**33.33**	**34**	**23.61**
Sus scrofa	**2**	**1.21**	**2**	**1.39**
Equus caballus	1			
Equus sp.	4			
Equus total	**5**	**3.03**		**0**
Canis sp.	33		8	
Canis familiaris	38		69	
Canis lupus			1	
Canis total	**71**	**43.03**	**78**	**54.17**

structure, with one exception: *Galium*. This was the third of three features (see Pit 1 and Pit 12) inside the structure that contained *Galium* pollen, possibly used for cheese making. One other unusual aspect of the pollen sample from this feature was that arboreal pollen was unusually low in quantity, and only two species of tree pollen were present (pine and poplar), an unusually low diversity of tree pollen. It seems that this location, just inside the structure on its south side, was shielded from arboreal pollen.

Feature 25 Unit K3/3: Ash Lens

This was the largest concentration of ash found inside the structure (Figure 10.33). It was larger in the photographs taken when it was fresh than it appears on the site plan, which was drawn after it had dried. Feature 25 (originally designated Feature 6 in the field) extended well into K3/3 and K3/4 when first seen. It was not associated with reddened or baked earth, so seems to represent a dump of ashes rather than a fireplace. There is a lot of fragmented amorphous silica in a sample examined for phytoliths, suggesting wood ash. A third of the phytoliths were woody types—tracheids, platey forms, and elongates—including *Quercus*-type phytoliths. The phytoliths in the sample also included *Cyperaceae* (sedges), festucoid grass leaves, and a very few panicoid grass forms. These could represent flooring materials.

Ash concentrations were noted in five places inside the structure (Figure 10.2) designated Features 24 to 28 (after the renumbering of features in 2001). None of these places exhibited baked earth or reddened soil. The only fire-cracked rock found at the site was in half-eroded Pit 23 outside the structure, so the ash deposits do not seem to be evidence for a hearth or fireplace inside the structure. Flecks of charcoal were scattered through almost all of the soils excavated inside the structure, so it seems that ashes, charcoal, and burned animal bones were discarded inside the structure together in a series of overlapping dumps.

Ashy lenses were noted within other pit features that also contained phytoliths from burned plants, confirming the visual identification of ashy soil lenses. These were Features 8, 10, 12, and 22. It therefore appears that ashes from burned vegetal matter, including wood, reeds, and grasses, were dumped in many separate places within the structure. Most of the pit features, however, did not contain ash or burned phytoliths, so the dumping of ashes was sporadic spatially. Charcoal flecks were much more widespread.

Summary

No fireplace or hearth was recognized, although several ash dumps were found, discussed under Feature 25 above. The well, Pit 10, was the most important feature from the perspective of the goals of the SVP, because it contained unusually well-preserved botanical evidence related to the role of agriculture in a permanent Srubnaya settlement. We found no agricultural seeds, phytoliths, or pollen in Pit 10 or any other Bronze Age archaeological context. Pit 10 did preserve evidence for the preferential collection and selective charring of wild *Chenopodium*, *Amaranthus*, and *Polygynum* seeds. Pit 8 also showed an unusual concentration of *Chenopodium* pollen, suggesting that the plant was manipulated near or in that pit but not in other pits, a possible indicator of intentional use. The elevated count of pollen from pine and birch trees in the deepest sample from Pit 10, but not in other samples, might suggest that a grove of pine and birch trees stood near the site when it was selected for a settlement, but these trees were cut down and/or the construction of the roof reduced the pollen count in all subsequent interior feature contexts. The well was filled with floor deposits containing Pokrovka and developed Srubnaya pottery and the remains of animal sacrifices, when the site was abandoned.

Several features yielded the botanical remains of medicinal plants that might have been selectively collected by the site occupants. *Seseli*, a sedative, was found only

Figure 10.33 Feature 25 was the largest concentration of ash found inside the structure. When fresh, it looked larger than it appears on the site plan, drawn after it had dried. It was not associated with reddened or baked earth, so seems to represent a dump of ashes rather than a fireplace.

in Pit 1. Pit 1 contained such an abundance and variety of pollen types that it suggests that flowering plants were stored or hung near or on the post that presumably stood in the posthole that defines Pit 1. *Gypsophilia*, found in Pit 10, like *Seseli*, grows on chalky or limestone soils not found around Krasnosamarskoe and is used as a diuretic and expectorant, as well as a treatment for mouth cancers. *Seseli* and *Gypsophilia* probably were imported from the chalky limestone hills on the west side of the Volga. *Artemesia*, or wormwood (pollen widespread in all features, used to flavor bitter drinks and as a flea repellent and antiseptic); *Linaria*, or toadflax (Pit 10, used as an antiseptic and to treat skin lesions); and *Arenaria*, or sandwort (Pit 10, used as a diuretic and laxative) also have medicinal uses. *Galium*, found in Features 3, 10, 12, and 24 at Krasnosamarskoe, appeared also in the pit features at the Srubnaya mining settlement of Gorny (Chernykh 2004). It had medicinal uses as a diuretic, lymphatic cleanser,

and treatment for skin lesions and stings. The intentional introduction of *Seseli* and perhaps of *Gypsophilia* from another region, probably from west of the Volga, suggests that herbal remedies were gathered in the excavated structure at Krasnosamarskoe. Combined with the repeated episodes of practiced ritual animal butchering that occurred at the site, the herbal evidence suggests that the residents of Krasnosamarskoe included a ritual/herbal specialist/ initiator-priest.

Galium also repelled fleas when used as bedding, and the flowers curdled milk in the cheese-making process and imparted a rich yellow color to the resulting cheese. Pits 3 and 12, containing *Galium* pollen, were very close to crushed Vessel 7, which had pierced sides, like a cheese strainer (Figure 10.34, bottom). We do not know why the occupants of Krasnosamarskoe collected *Galium*, but cheese making is suggested by its spatial proximity to a strainer.

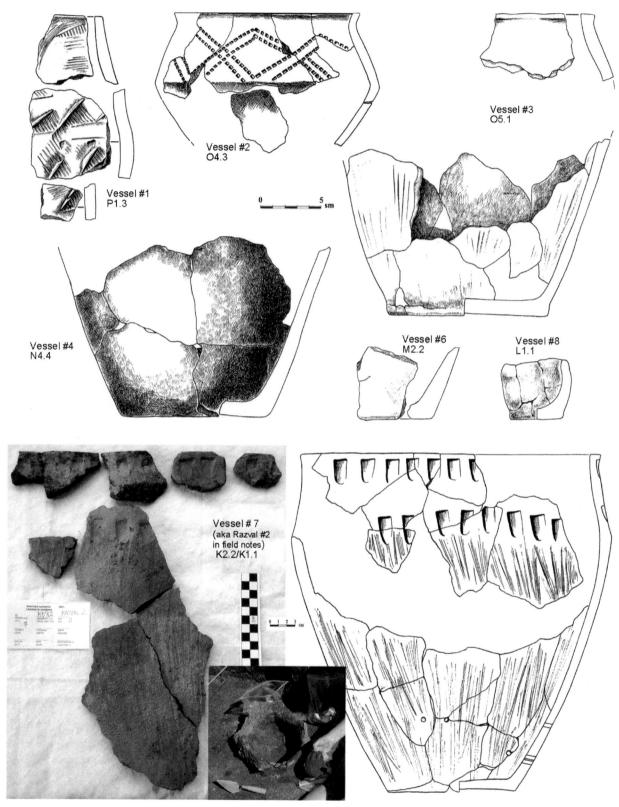

Figure 10.34 Semi-complete crushed Vessels 1 to 4 and 6 to 8. These artifactual features, broken in place, are marked with a "V" and number in the settlement plan. All of the LBA examples illustrated here were Pokrovka-type pots. The inset photo shows Vessel 7 in situ, with its lower portion, pierced with holes (drainage?) in several places, still intact, apparently set in a pit, possibly just outside the structure. Vessel 5 (Figure 10.10) was Iron Age Gorodetskaya.

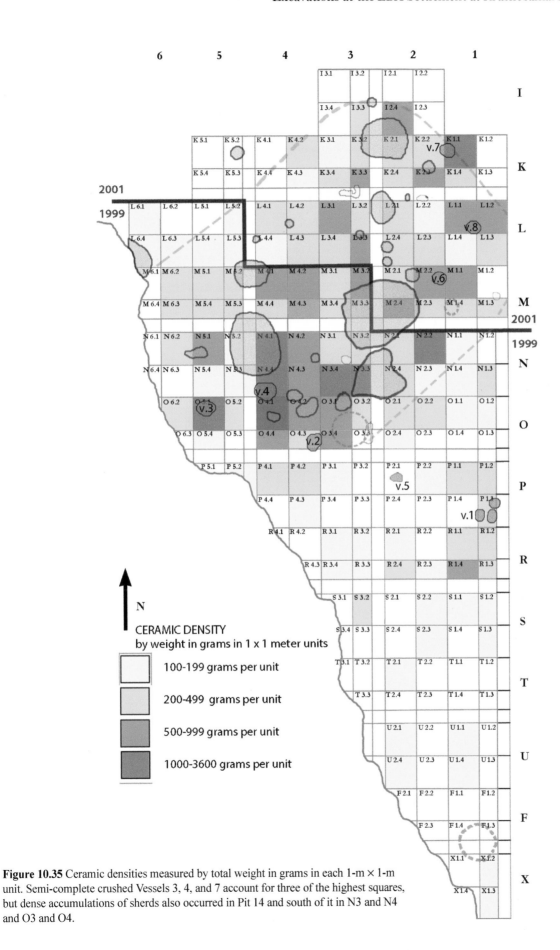

Figure 10.35 Ceramic densities measured by total weight in grams in each 1-m × 1-m unit. Semi-complete crushed Vessels 3, 4, and 7 account for three of the highest squares, but dense accumulations of sherds also occurred in Pit 14 and south of it in N3 and N4 and O3 and O4.

Ceramics

The Krasnosamarskoe settlement excavation produced 4,257 ceramic sherds. Of these, about 75 percent, or 3,194 sherds, were assigned by A. Semenova to Srubnaya types. The other sherds were unidentifiable (most of them) or belonged to the MBA or the Iron Age. Of the 3,194 sherds assigned to the Srubnaya period, 2,198, or 69 percent, belonged to the developed Srubnaya phase, and 32 percent belonged to the Pokrovka phase (Figure 10.3).

Ceramics sherds were scattered across the entire excavated site, but the greatest density was found inside the structure (Figure 10.35). Eight vessels were found crushed in place (Figure 10.34, indicated in Figure 10.35). Curiously, all of these vessels, except Iron Age Vessel 5, were of the Pokrovka style. The sherds of developed Srubnaya style were more dispersed. Perhaps the deepest levels containing primarily Pokrovka styles were protected from foot traffic and pit-digging disturbances that affected the shallower levels more strongly.

The ceramic fabrics were analyzed by I. N. Vasilieva and N. P. Salugina, using methods developed by A. A. Bobrinskii in the ceramic ethno-archaeological laboratory that he created at Samara State University (Bobrinskii 1978; Bobrinskii and Vasilieva 1998; Salugina 2011; Vasilieva 2011). Their methods included a detailed microscopic examination of the ceramic paste, an analysis of construction methods, and visual observation of the firing characteristics. The following section is based on our translation of their unpublished SVP report.

The Srubnaya Component

Vasilieva and Salugina analyzed 190 Srubnaya ceramic sherds from the Krasnosamarskoe settlement. This was about 6 percent of the Srubnaya-period sherds. The studied sherds were from the 1999 excavation or the southern two-thirds of the excavated structure. The results can be generalized to the entire site, since there was no difference in ceramics between the southern part of the structure and its northern part, excavated in 2001.

For the Srubnaya ceramic assemblage as a whole, 32 percent of the sherds were Pokrovka, and 69 percent were developed Srubnaya styles according to A. Semenova's catalogue (Figures 10.36 and 10.37). Vasilieva and Salugina did not specify the styles in their sample of Srubnaya pottery. All pots were flat-bottomed and handmade without a wheel. The clay for the bases of the pots was modeled on a form such as a textile-covered pot base, using a hammer to thin the clay, and the clay for the walls was similarly built up around a form by joining patches of clay and pressing it by hand in a continuous spiral around the form. The walls and the base were then joined, and the walls were thinned using a paddle-and-anvil technique. The entire surface, inside and out, was smoothed using fingers, cloth, or leather (variably) as smoothing devices.

Often no decoration was applied; Srubnaya pottery can be very plain. Only about 10 percent of the sherds we recovered were ornamented. Wall sherds made up 85 percent of the ceramic sherds, rims were about 10 percent, and bases were about 5 percent. When decoration was applied, it was incised or impressed, often in a simple geometric design such as a zigzag, using a pointed stick or bone; also some decoration was applied with a toothed shell stamp, and some decoration was impressed or scratched. Pokrovka pots were distinguished by all-over roughening of the exterior surface by scratching it with stiff grass or impressing it with the end of a wooden spatula.

Finished pots were air-dried and fired in an open fire above 650°C. The outer 1 mm of the surface is baked light brown or red-brown, but the core of the fabric is black. The reddish outer color of Srubnaya pottery distinguishes it from the brown-to-gray surfaces of EBA and MBA pottery. Some of the studied sherds showed spalling of the outer reddish layer and scorching of the spalled surface, indicating thermal shock associated with using the vessel over a fire.

The clays used were true clays, in contrast to the pond-bottom clayey silts that had often been used to make pottery in this region from the Neolithic through the Early Bronze Age. LBA pottery used better-selected clays than earlier pottery did, but the form-modeled and paddle-and-anvil manufacturing method was the same. The clays at Krasnosamarskoe tended to be on the "lean" side, with an admixture of sand amounting to 38 percent, typical for Srubnaya potters in this region, but about one-third of the examined sherds had a "fat" mixture with less than 30 percent sand.

The most common tempering material added to the clay by Srubnaya potters, appearing in 63 percent of examined Srubnaya sherds, was clay + grog, or crushed pottery sherds, some of which also contained grog, testifying to the stability of this tempering recipe. The second most common tempering recipe, appearing in 18 percent of sherds, was clay + grog + organic material (often grass fibers) + burned bone. The bone-temper recipe was most common in Level 6 and became less frequent in the upper levels. Three other less common tempering recipes were also noted: clay + grog + plant fibers, clay + grog + plant fibers + manure, and clay + grog + plant fibers + crushed shell. Srubnaya tempering materials were variations on a tradition of grog tempering, which seems to have changed in details during

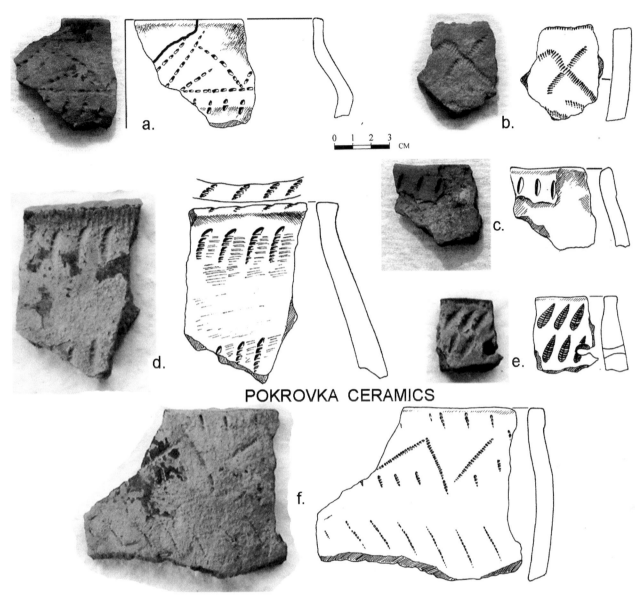

POKROVKA CERAMICS

Figure 10.36 Pokrovka-style ceramics: (*a*) R3/2 Level 3, (*b*) M3/1 Level 3, (*c*) P1/4 Level 6, (*d*) M1/1 Level 6, (*e*) L4/3 Level 6, and (*f*) L3/1 Level 6.

the occupation of the structure, possibly because of the presence and then the absence of a single potter.

An innovative and important aspect of the research carried out at the Bobrinskii ceramic laboratory in Samara was the identification of potting clay "Regions" or distinct clay sources. These have not been mapped against known clay deposits, so we do not know where each source was, but the separation of the clays used in ancient pots into distinct clay types indicating distinct clay sources provides a window on the variability of the clays used at any one site. The distinct sources are conceived of as spatially separate and are termed "Regions." Each region is defined by different

proportions of sand, silt, and clay and by different amounts and types of nonplastic *natural* inclusions such as different colors, sizes, and smoothness of sand grains; bog iron; oolite; fish scales; small shells naturally included in the clay; plants of various kinds naturally included; and other nonplastic contents. Within the defined "Regions," occasional sherds showed some slight variations that were referred to as "Places."

Vasilieva and Salugina detected clays from seven Regions in the 190 Srubnaya sherds analyzed from Krasnosamarskoe. Regions 1 and 5 included clays from two different Places. However, their Region 2 mixture appeared only in a few

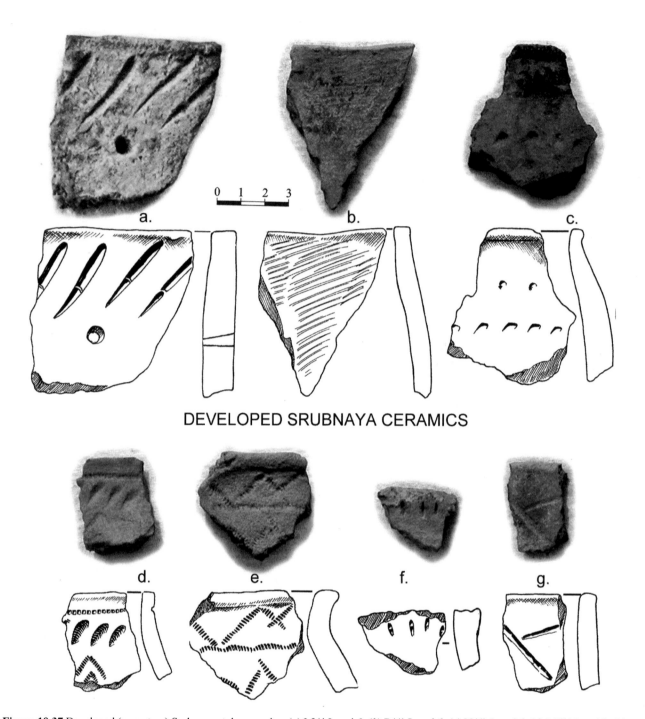

Figure 10.37 Developed (or mature) Srubnaya-style ceramics: (*a*) L3/4 Level 6, (*b*) P4/1 Level 6, (*c*) N4/2 Level 6, (*d*) M6/4 Level 3, (*e*) N3/1 Level 4, (*f*) M5/1 Level 6, and (*g*) N4/2 Level 6.

sherds found in upper levels and might be from the Final Bronze Age or some other non-Srubnaya origin. Also their Region 1/Place 2 clay type was found in just one sherd that also was different in temper from all the other sherds ascribed to Srubnaya, so they also doubted that this mixture truly belonged to the Srubnaya occupation. They were confident in ascribing just five clay sources, or Regions, to

the Srubnaya potters of Krasnosamarskoe.

These probably represent five clay sources located within a few kilometers of the site. This number defines a baseline of ceramic clay variability within a long-occupied Srubnaya settlement against which the clays used in the Peschanyi Dol short-term herding camps can be compared (see Chapter 18). Surprisingly, the herding camps, with a much smaller number of sherds, contained a much greater number of clay sources, almost three times the diversity seen at Krasnosamarskoe.

The MBA Component

Even very humble pottery scatters dated to the early period of mobile pastoralism in the EBA and MBA are interesting because of the almost total absence of settlement evidence from these periods. Just knowing the geographic location of an EBA/MBA sherd scatter allows us to put at least one temporary residence on the map. We found no EBA sherds at any location tested during the SVP.

MBA sherds came in two varieties (Figure 10.38). A local Samara oblast MBA archaeological culture known as the Vol'sko-Lbishche culture was defined based on a handful of settlement sites located on the forested west side of the Volga in the big bend of the Samara River, the Samarskaya Luka. Small assemblages of ceramics of Vol'sko-Lbishche type are found at three sites in the Samara Valley (Kirpichnie Sarai, Chelovech'ya Golova, and the Krasnosamarskoe settlement). These sites represent the easternmost extension of that culture. The second MBA variety is the much more widespread Poltavka culture of mobile pastoralists, the Volga-Ural equivalent of the well-known Catacomb culture of the Don-Manych and Ukrainian steppes. Poltavka is represented in the Samara Valley by 22 kurgan cemeteries, including the one we excavated at Krasnosamarskoe (Chapter 17) with no real settlement sites known and just a handful of sherd scatters that might represent temporary Poltavka camps. At Krasnosamarskoe, we found both Poltavka pottery and pottery of the Vol'sko-Lbishche culture together, possibly an MBA version of the liminal meeting place also represented by the Iron Age Gorodetskaya component at Krasnosamarskoe, which also perhaps was derived from a settlement near Lbishche in the Samaraskaya Luka (see "Cultural Stratigraphy," above, and "Iron Age Component," below).

Vasilieva and Salugina examined 17 MBA sherds, all of the MBA sherds excavated. However, they did not describe these sherds in their report. They did describe the MBA clays used at Peschanyi Dol (PD) 1, so the reader is directed there for a technical description of MBA pottery (Chapter 18). In general, MBA pottery was shell tempered, which distinguishes even small sherds from grog-tempered LBA pottery.

The catalogue shows that A. Semenova assigned 13 sherds to the MBA Poltavka type. Apparently, Vasilieva and Salugina found four shell-tempered sherds that Semenova missed. They were very small, so it was important that Krasnosamarskoe was excavated using screens. Small

shell-tempered, comb-stamped Poltavka ceramic sherds were found across the excavated grid. Most were concentrated within the area where the Srubnaya structure was later built, and they were undoubtedly disturbed and redeposited by the Srubnaya occupants, who left 187 potsherds for every one left by the Poltavka herders. But Poltavka sherds were found in squares outside the structure (K5, P2, S1) as well as inside (L3, N4, O2, O3), so they were scattered across the excavated area and probably continued at a very low density beyond it. The densest concentration (four sherds) was in Square N4, where it reached one sherd per 1 m². Across the entire excavation grid, Poltavka-type ceramic sherds occurred at a density of one sherd per 16 m². MBA settlement sites are not found because their artifact density is extremely low and therefore difficult to detect.

The small Poltavka ceramic assemblage at PD1 (see Chapter 18) also was scattered across the excavated area, at a density of about one sherd per 12 m², not much different from Krasnosamarskoe. At both sites, the density of MBA ceramic sherds was so low that they would not have been found if they had not been dropped in an area later used as a settlement by the Srubnaya culture. It is possible that the MBA activity at Krasnosamarskoe was related to the construction of the three MBA kurgans 65 m to the east, so it might not indicate a settlement but an MBA funeral camp, or a series of them.

Four sherds of pottery of the MBA Vol'sko-Lbishche culture were found in Squares N4, L3, and O1. In Squares N4 and L3, they were associated with Poltavka pottery sherds. The two types probably were dropped at the same time, during the same event. The two types could represent distinct ethnicities occupying territories on opposite sides of the Volga, or they could represent settled and pastoral components of the same ethnic group, with different pottery styles. Most local archaeologists believe that they were distinct groups who met occasionally in the Samara Valley. In that case, the funeral of one of the MBA Poltavka people buried at Krasnosamarskoe IV attracted foreign (?) Vol'sko-Lbishche visitors.

The Iron Age Gorodetskaya Component

Vasilieva and Salugina examined 14 sherds of 98 found, representing an estimated nine vessels of the Iron Age Gorodetskaya culture, probably dated between 500 BC and 100 CE. These vessels probably were carried to Krasnosamarskoe by Gorodetskaya people, who usually lived on the west side of the Volga, perhaps in the 7-ha Gorodetskaya settlement excavated near Lbishche on the south side of the Samaraskaya Luka, 100 km to the west (see "Cultural Stratigraphy" above). At Krasnosamarskoe, Gorodets-

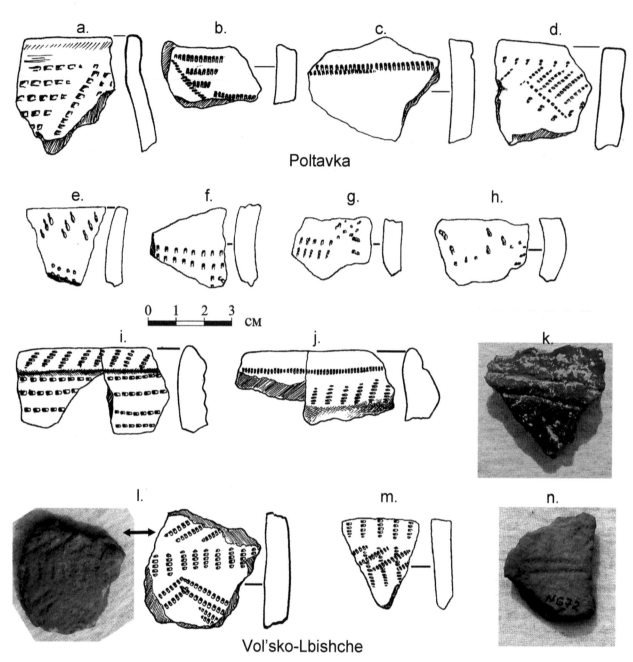

Figure 10.38 Middle Bronze Age ceramics. Poltavka and Vol'sko-Lbishche styles: (*a*) L3/3 Level 4, (*b*) L3/1 Level 4, (*c*) L3/3 Level 4, (*d*) K5/2 Level 3, (*e–h*) N4/1 Level 9, (*i*) O3/4 Level 3, (*j*) S1/3 Level 3, (*k*) O4/4 Level 7, (*l*) O1/3 Level 5, (*m*) N4/4 Level 4, and (*n*) P1/3 Level 3.

kaya sherds were concentrated southeast of a probable iron-working hearth (Feature 31) that contained charcoal and iron slag; the hearth feature was in Square O3, and the pottery was concentrated in P1 and P2. Another concentration of Gorodetskaya pottery was found around Feature 30 at the southern edge of the grid.

Gorodetskaya pots were handmade without a wheel (Figure 10.10). They were grog tempered, but unlike the

LBA grog temper, Iron Age grog pieces were coarse, up to 5 mm. The clays were categorized as coming from three distinct sources (Regions), one of which contained inclusions similar to those in one of the five LBA clay sources, but the other two were quite different, and the clays in all cases were red and ferruginous, and two clays contained mica. The outer surface of Gorodetskaya pottery was pale reddish brown, lighter in color than most Srubnaya pots, and was decorated with impressed checkerboards, visually quite distinctive (Figure 10.10, top).

A variety of secondary clues suggest that pottery was made near or in the Krasnosamarskoe settlement during the LBA occupation. We recovered a toothed shell stamp (Figure 10.41–j) that matched the tooth-impressed decoration on some Srubnaya pottery sherds and a bone tool used to polish the outer surface of ceramic pots, a cattle-rib pot polisher (figure 10.41l). Also, two unformed lumps of clay about 4 to 5 cm in length, accidentally (?) fired, were found in M4/1, Level 6, inside the structure, and in T3/2 Level 3, well south of the structure. Although we did not find a kiln or even a hearth, these artifacts suggest that clay lumps were manipulated at the site, and Srubnaya pottery vessels were smoothed with a pot polisher and decorated with a shell stamp.

Lithics

The Krasnosamarskoe settlement excavation yielded 46 culturally modified stone artifacts, including five pieces of fire-cracked quartzite rock (FCR) recovered from half-eroded Pit 23, north of the structure on the edge of the lake. This was the only FCR found at the site, a surprising gap in the excavated evidence. FCR indicates the presence of a rock-lined hearth somewhere nearby. In this case, the FCR was discarded into a pit, so the fire it was associated with could have been anywhere, probably under the lake.

No unutilized flakes or lithic debitage were found, although all excavated soil passed through ¼-inch mesh screens. No chipped stone tool repair or resharpening occurred in the excavation area at any time over what seems to have been many years, perhaps multiple generations, of occupation. It is remarkable to find absolutely no evidence of knapping activity in such an intensely used and lived-in place that contains abundant trash deposits. The absence of flakes does not testify to the absence of flint tools, as some chipped stone tools were recovered (see below), and utilized flakes were found, but they never were repaired or sharpened within the excavated area. If the site as a whole contained any chipping waste, it was confined to a location off our grid.

A possible explanation for the small number of chipped stone tools is the likely ubiquity of copper and bronze tools in a region so richly endowed with actively worked copper mines. It should be remembered that copper/bronze brackets were used to repair cracked ceramic vessels in the LBA in this region; we recovered a metal strip that probably was a repair bracket in Square L5/3, Level 7, on the floor of the structure (Figure 10.39f). Copper and bronze tools were not so common that they could be discarded or left behind, since we found only one finished bronze tool, an awl (Figure 10.39g), in the structure, but metal tools left their marks on many animal bones and probably were easily obtained.

The 41 non-FCR lithic artifacts included nine chipped stone items, six made of flint and three of quartzite. Three were finished tools (Figure 10.39). A quartzite scraper (Figure 10.39e), bifacially chipped on a flake, was found in Pit 18. A flint scraper (Figure 10.39d), bifacially chipped on a flake, was found in Pit 22. The only blade tool (Figure 10.39a), made on a section of a prismatic-sectioned blade, was a flint blade/end scraper 5 cm long, found in a dense animal bone deposit, including many dog bones, on the structure floor in Square L3/4. Very near it, in Square L4/3, was a large piece of a flat stone mortar, stained red by ochre. The blade and the ochre-grinding mortar might have been connected to the ritual behaviors associated with the dog bones. The other chipped-stone lithic items were fragments of broken bifacial tools or were utilized, edge-modified flakes.

Most of the lithic artifacts, 32 items, were handheld grinding stones (Figure 10.40) that showed abraded or polished facets that indicated they had been used in a variety of small-scale grinding or polishing tasks. They included one arrow straightener (Figure 10.40a) found in Square K2/1, Level 6, probably in Pit 4, in the northwestern corner of the structure, bearing a depressed straight channel abraded across its surface. A beaver-incisor sharpening tool (Figure 10.40b) was found in M1/4, Level 7, on the floor of the structure. The polished-abraded strip on its surface was the width of a beaver incisor, and beaver incisors were often sharpened and used as cutting tools in the LBA, although we did not find any beaver incisors at Krasnosamarskoe.

Most of the other 30 grinding stones had unknown functions, although some were quite well made. These included a 12-cm-long quartzite pestle (Figure 10.40d) in Square P4/2, Level 5, and another well-made round quartzite grinding stone (Figure 10.40c) in Square M1/1, in the upper part of the *materik*. Both were inside the structure.

If we exclude the FCR, fewer lithic artifacts were found at Krasnosamarskoe (41) than at the PD1 and PD2 herding camps combined (42), despite the fact that the area excavated at Krasnosamarskoe was 30 percent larger than PD1 and PD2 combined. The year-round settlement at Krasnosamarskoe had an artifact assemblage quite different from the seasonal camps at PD1 and 2, and chipped stone tools were not frequently made or used at the permanent settlement. Small polishing and grinding stones made on cobbles were common tools, however.

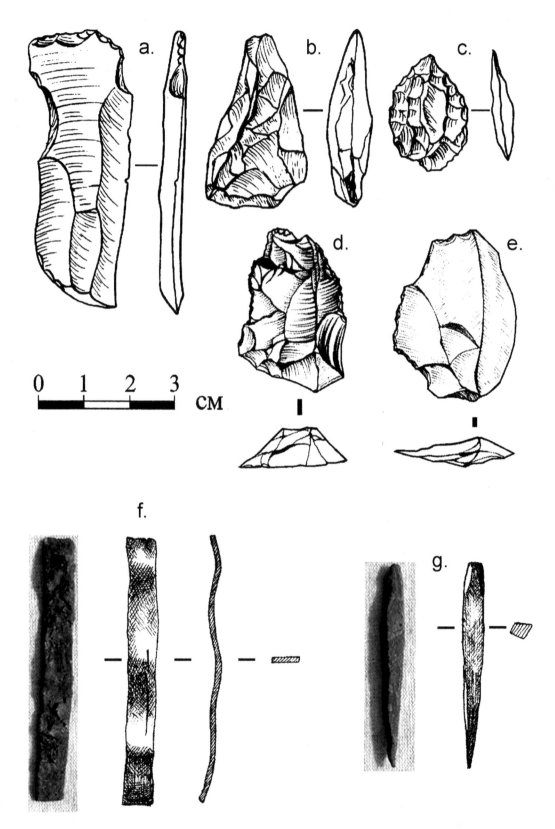

Figure 10.39 Chipped stone and metal artifacts: (*a*) L3/4 Level 4 flint knife/scraper, (*b*) M2/4 Levels 8 to 13 (upper Pit 10 well fill) midsection of quartzite bifacial tool, (*c*) L4/1 Level 5 quartzite bifacial flake tool, (*d*) M5/2 Level 7 flint scraper probably from Pit 22, (*e*) N3/3 Level 6 quartzite scraper in Pit 18, (*f*) L5/3 Level 7 metal strap or bracket fragment, and (*g*) N5/2 Level 5 bronze awl.

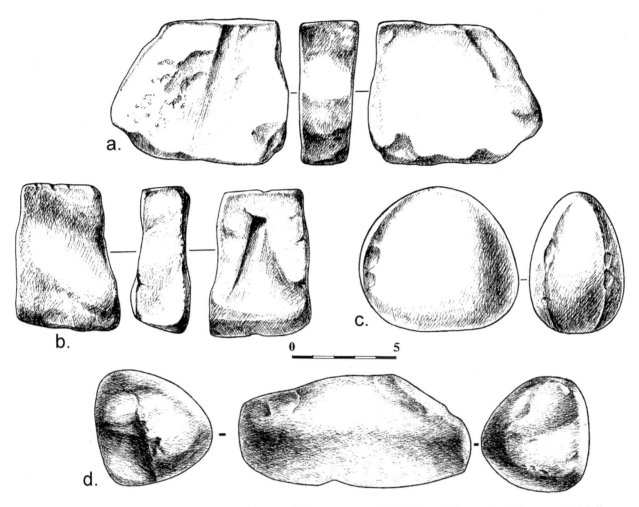

Figure 10.40 Ground stone artifacts: (*a*) K2/1 Level 6 arrow shaft straightener, (*b*) M1/4 Level 7 beaver tooth sharpener, (*c*) M1/1 *materik* level quartzite grinding stone or pestle, and (*d*) P4/2 Level 5 pounding and grinding stone or pestle.

Worked Bone Artifacts (Figure 10.41)

Most of the bone was not examined by a bone-tool expert for use wear or intentional working. What follows is a selected catalogue of worked bone objects from the excavated structure and from the lake bottom that were examined by Russell in 1999, augmented by a selection of objects that were obviously worked as determined by the authors of this chapter. The outstanding feature of the worked bone is that it is very diverse, including bone ornaments, eight dice, polishers and smoothers, perforators, a bone handle, a refined bone thimble-like object, and a bone spindle whorl. A variety of ordinary domestic crafts and tasks are implied.

Dice. Russell counted eight astragali used as knucklebones with very minimal modification. They were highly polished from use (Figure 10.41a). In one case, the use polish overlies dog gnaw marks and dismemberment cuts. Five were made

on cattle *astragali* and three on sheep-goat *astragali*. Found inside the structure in Squares O4, M4, M3, M1, and L2.

Dog canine pendant (Figure 10.41b). This dog canine tooth was broken longitudinally at its root before modification, probably during extraction from the jaw. A deep notch was cut into both sides across and over this break 5.5 mm from the base of the root, probably to facilitate tying a cord around the notch so the tooth could be suspended as a pendant. Otherwise, it was unmodified except for a little polish from use, indicating that it was used and worn. Found in O4/2.

Ornament (Figure 10.41c). This was a small, roughly rectangular pendant on a scapula blade. The edges and surfaces are thoroughly ground. One corner has a completed perforation with use wear; another corner has a partial drill hole that appears to be a false start. A bit of green stain from copper or bronze is visible around the partial perforation, suggesting it was drilled with a bronze tool; maybe it broke off in the hole and that is why they drilled the other corner. No stain is visible on the complete perforation. Found in M3/2, Level 5.

Flat pendant/scale mail? (Figure 10.41d). This flat, polished object probably was a pendant preform but conceivably could have been a piece of scale mail. It was made on a piece of scapula blade, shaped into rough teardrop form, ground on edges to make it flat and straight, and ground a little on both surfaces. The abrasive used was quite coarse, such as a piece of sandstone. (Perhaps one of the many small cobble polishing tools described above was used to abrade this object.) It was never pierced for attachment, so it looks unfinished. It was probably dropped outside the structure on its north side. Found in L6/3, Level 5.

Carved rim fragment. This is a small triangular fragment of a beautifully worked, thin, flat, polished piece of bone with a finely carved and polished rim, probably the edge of a handle, although it is too small to identify confidently. Traces of cancellous material remain on the inner side. The edge or rim decoration is so elegantly shaped that it looks like it was turned on a lathe, although faint traces of scraping and carving can barely be seen under the finely polished surface. The outer side is completely smoothed and deeply carved to raise a ridge circling the artifact in relief around 1.5 mm high, creating a beveled, rounded edge. The object from which this edge came appears to have been cylindrical, with a diameter smaller than a drinking cup, less than 10 cm. It could have been a fine bone handle or ring (like a napkin ring) or just a "tubular object." It is reminiscent of the edge of a pipe bowl, but there is no trace of burning, and pipes are unknown for the Srubnaya culture. Found in M4/1, Level 5.

Spindle whorl (Figure 10.41f). This roundish bone tool was an unfused femur caput with a cylindrical hole drilled through it approximately at the fovea. The area around fovea is ground flat and seems worn. The edges are trimmed somewhat to make them even. It looks like a spindle whorl, but it is asymmetrical. Would it work with the weight unevenly distributed? If it was another kind of weight, it is unclear why they would need to flatten the top. There are vertical striations inside the hole as if something hard moved up and down in it like a stick with bits of grit or sand, perhaps how the hole was made. Found in N6/2, Level 5.

Point (Figure 10.41g). A bone projectile point was found in O1/2, Levels 4 to 5. This is the only artifact from the LBA component that looks like a projectile point.

Awl (Figure 10.41h). This is a fairly casual but not totally expedient pointed tool. A segment of epiphysis probably formed the base in use but now is missing. It was made on a splinter of a proximal metacarpal (MP), with edges first scraped, probably with metal tool, then ground to form the tip. Slender-medium tip, reasonably sharp. Some rounding and polishing from use. Found in M6/3, Level 6.

Bone handle (Figure 10.41i). A highly polished bone handle with a single incised line around its socketed end was found on the lake bottom. It fits very well with the bronze awl found inside the excavated structure in N5/2, Level 5.

Shell with serrated edge (Figure 10.41j). Found inside the structure in Unit M4/2, Level 4, this small shell was carefully notched to create a tool for decorating pottery.

Bone polisher (Figure 10.41k). This polisher (for skins?) was made on a large long bone, from either *Bos* or *Equus*, and had an angled working surface heavily polished by use. It was found on the lake bottom, so could have been associated with the submerged part of the excavated structure, or it could have come from another structure.

Pottery polisher on a rib (Figure 10.41l). This was a fragment of an expedient pottery polisher on a rib, originally unsplit. Old breaks at both ends and splitting along the length postdate the use of the tool and may have happened in burning. Not a lot of use, but the outer surface and edges are covered with light polish and fine perpendicular striations, indicating a very fine temper in the pot. There is no sign of any deliberate modification to the shape of the bone. Found in L4/2, Level 4. A toothed shell tool apparently used as a pottery decorator stamp was found in M4/2, Level 4 (Figure 10.41). Together the shell stamp, the bone polisher, and several lumps of clay, accidentally (?) fired, suggest that pottery was made somewhere on the site.

Rawhide thong smoother (Figure 10.41m). A cow mandible heavily used as a thong smoother was found in L1/3, Level 6.

Conclusions

Krasnosamarskoe was one of the first Srubnaya settlements to be established during the "settling-down" process that was the focus of our field research. Radiocarbon dates indicate a beginning around 1900 BC, among the earliest dated Srubnaya settlements in the Samara oblast. Yet it looks like a settlement of a long-established sedentary culture, occupied permanently through all seasons of the year, and

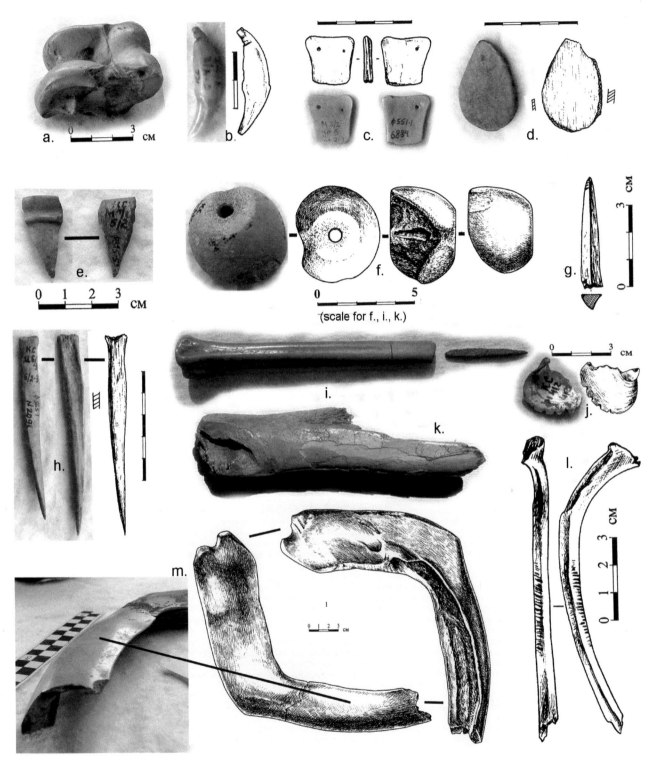

Figure 10.41 Worked bone artifacts: (*a*) L2/2 Level 5 polished astragali; (*b*) O4/2 Level 7 dog canine pendant; (*c*) M3/2 Level 9 rectangular pendant with perforation; (*d*) L6/3 Level 5 teardrop-shaped pendant; (*e*) M4/1 Level 5 finely carved and polished rim fragment of small bowl; (*f*) N6/2 Level 5 drilled femur caput possible spindle whorl; (*g*) O4/1 Level 4 projectile point; (*h*) M6/3 Level 6 awl; (*i*) Lake bottom—polished handle with incised line near socketed end. Metal awl in photo was not found with the handle but it fit perfectly and was found in the lake end of the structure. (*j*) M4/2 Level 4—shell with serrated edge used for decorating ceramics; (*k*) lake bottom—bone polisher with heavily polished working surface; (*l*) L4/1 Level 4—rib used as pottery polisher; (*m*) L1/3 Level 6—cow mandible heavily used as thong smoother. Polish can be seen in photo on left.

continuously for many years, as the stratified floor deposits indicate (see "Cultural Stratigraphy" above). Change sometimes happens so quickly that the "new normal" emerges almost overnight. That seems to have happened at the MBA II/LBA transition in the Samara Valley. But a simple artifact like the axe-notched log found at the bottom of Pit 10, perhaps the oldest and earliest artifact dropped at the site (Figure 10.31), raises questions about this transition. How did the local population learn the skills necessary to build their first log and thatch houses? If they had lived in tents and wagons earlier, how did they learn the rather complex craft of roof thatching? The notched log might have been prepared as an intended part of the roof, notched in three places on one side to hold the framework under the thatch. How did they learn to build houses in this way? From whom?

The excavated structure probably was an outbuilding rather than a residence. It had a thatched roof supported on irregularly spaced posts that collapsed over the structure and left a dark, *Phragmites*-phytolith-rich soil deposit. The dug-out floor accumulated layers of sediment into which pits were later dug, during what seems to have been a continuous span of occupation probably for less than a century, perhaps just two generations (there are only two clearly identified adult men and two adult women in the adjoining cemetery) sometime between 1900 and 1700 BC. The phytoliths of *Phragmites* reeds and *Cyperaceae* sedges were so ubiquitous even in deep pit features that it is possible the floor was covered with reeds and sedges.

An intensive program of paleobotanical recovery failed to find any phytoliths, pollen, or seeds of cultivated cereals at Krasnosamarskoe, a result repeated at the mining settlement of Gorny and at 12 other Srubnaya settlements cored for flotation in the Volga-Ural region (see Chapter 1). The occupants buried in the nearby cemetery had no caries in their teeth, a dental trait repeated across the Srubnaya populations studied in the region (Chapter 8). The Srubnaya people in the Volga-Ural region did not ordinarily cultivate or eat domesticated wheat, barley, or millet. Instead, the occupants of Krasnosamarskoe collected the seeds of three genera of wild "weeds"—*Chenopodium*, *Polygynum*, and *Amaranthus*—more than any other kind of seeds, and charred them, presumably to prepare them for consumption as dietary supplements (see Pit 10 discussion above). The selective charring of these three genera, a necessary step in removing the bitter pericarp, was intentional.

Krasnosamarskoe was the first Srubnaya settlement dug in 10-cm levels with screens, and the new methods paid off by demonstrating the stratigraphic co-occurrence of Pokrovka and developed Srubnaya styles in the same levels but in proportions that changed with 10-cm depth levels. It

seems likely that the accumulation of floor deposits and the sequence of pit features cut into successive levels reflect a continuous occupation, during which the Pokrovka style of ceramic decoration shifted from being an ordinary everyday ceramic style to being a style preferred for funeral deposits in graves, while the developed Srubnaya style became the more common style for everyday use. Since both styles appeared in the same house and in the same levels, it is probable that they were made by the same or by very closely related potters. What had been regarded as chrono-types were in reality contemporary types that varied for social and cultural reasons.

The household at Krasnosamarskoe was busy with a wide variety of domestic tasks. Although pottery making did not occur in the excavated structure, it seems to have happened somewhere on the site. At least a few lumps of raw clay were manipulated and discarded in the excavated area. We found a rib used as a pot polisher bearing typical pot-polishing microwear, and we also found a denticulate-edged shell with teeth the same size and spacing as the decorative impressions on some clay pots. Clay to make the pots was collected from five different clay sources presumably located within a few kilometers of the site.

Metalworking also occurred somewhere in or near the site. About 20 small bits of crushed sandstone-malachite copper ore were thinly scattered across the interior of the structure, as well as a few pieces of slag and a few unshaped droplets of copper. These three kinds of cuprous artifacts suggest that ore processing, smelting, and working with molten copper occurred somewhere on the site. The cuprous bits were in a complementary, largely nonoverlapping spatial distribution with the animal bones. The highest counts of animal bones occurred in squares located between Pits 10, 14, 18, and 22, in the center of the structure, and the discard of metallic objects occurred at either end of the structure, northeast and southwest of the central concentration of animal bones. Perhaps sacral animal remains and metalworking debris were disposed of separately, or perhaps coat-shaking metalworkers avoided walking over the central animal bone deposit.

A variety of bone tools and worked bone indicate domestic tasks such as polishing, smoothing, rawhide thong working, weaving, and puncturing. The awls, one bone and one bronze, and the thong and skin polishers suggest that hide working occurred at the site. A ceramic and a bone spindle whorl suggest thread making. The stone tools included many cobble tools used as smoothers, polishers, and grinders; very few chipped flint artifacts; and no flint debitage. Small polished bone ornaments were worn, and at least one dog canine pendant was used as an ornament, a specific personal display that must be interpreted in the context of the dog sacrifices that occurred here.

The winter-season dog and wolf sacrifices that were dumped into the structure were the biggest surprise found at the Krasnosamarskoe settlement. At least 51 dogs and at least seven wolves were burned or roasted, probably their flesh was eaten, and then their heads were chopped into the same 10 to 12 small squares by well-placed and accurate axe cuts, after which the burned and properly chopped pieces were discarded into the structure, possibly with the remains of winter-season cattle sacrifices, indicated by an overrepresentation of cattle head and distal forelimb elements, but not including the meaty rear limbs, discarded elsewhere. Dog bones accounted for 36 percent of the specimens (NISP) and 18 percent of individuals (MNI) from bones identified to species by Kosintsev (Chapter 15), as well as 40 percent of specimens (NISP) and 45 percent of diagnostic zones as counted by the U.S. archaeozoologists (Chapter 16). Because no other Srubnaya settlement shows evidence of a similar ceremony, we can be confident that dogs were not normally eaten. They were old dogs, unusually well cared for (few injuries), and the wear on their teeth suggests possibly a special diet. The violation of the Srubnaya rule against eating dogs was conducted during a winter rite of transformation that stressed transgressive behavior, liminality, and the suspension of established rules and identities. Krasnosamarskoe was a central location for the performance of this winter dog-and-wolf-sacrificing ritual. The cultural model behind the ritual can be found in Indo-European traditions related to the initiation into war bands of boys symbolized by dogs and wolves, who prepared to become wolf-like killers of men by killing and eating wild wolves and familiar old dogs, which might have been symbolic stand-ins for the humans they must be prepared to kill as warriors.

There are various clues suggesting that the residents of Krasnosamarskoe were unusual. The importing of *Seseli* and other medicinal herbs that probably grew only on chalk hills on the western side of the Volga suggests that they were herbalists. In addition, both of the adult males buried in the nearby Srubnaya cemetery (Chapter 17) had unusual knee and back injuries, and both were given unusual body treatments after they died. The adult females also had back injuries that were unusual among the Srubnaya women examined by Murphy in Chapter 8. Finally, 82 percent of the individuals buried in the cemetery were preadults, a uniquely high percentage for Srubnaya cemeteries in the region, possibly indicating that sick or injured children were brought there for healing. And, as just described, in this central place for the performance of winter-season dog sacrifices, someone wore a dog canine pendant as a personal ornament.

The settlement was occupied during the entire year and apparently for at least a couple of generations, so much of what we recovered represents ordinary everyday life. The dog ritual occurred only in the winter, probably over a series of winters. In between, we have the abundant pollen of summer flowers and herbs indicating a rich pasture of diverse grasses; a healthy array of marsh reeds, sedges, and other valuable water plants such as duckweed; and forests dominated by Scots pine that stood in the general vicinity. We were fortunate to shed light on both the quotidian daily economy and environment of a permanent Srubnaya settlement, as well as the performance of extraordinary rituals of transformation.

The chapters that follow discuss the metallurgy of the Bronze Age in the region as well as at Krasnosamarskoe (Chapter 11), the botanical remains from the settlement (Chapter 12), the fauna from the settlement (Chapters 14–16), the adjoining cemetery (Chapter 17), and the articulation of the pastoral economy of permanent settlements with the herding camps in Peschanyi Dol (Chapter 18).

Note

Figures and tables in this chapter were prepared by D. Brown, photographs were taken by D. Brown and D. Anthony unless otherwise noted in captions. All artifact drawings are by IHAV.

References

Behre, Karl-Ernst
2008   Collected Seeds and Fruit from Herbs as Prehistoric Food. *Vegetation History and Archaeobotany* 17:65–73.

Bobrinskii, A. A.
1978   *Goncharstvo Vostochnoi Evropy*. Istochniki i metody izucheniya. Nauka, Moscow.

Bobrinskii, A. A., and I. N. Vasilieva
1998   O nekotorykh osobennostiakh plasticheskogo syr'ya v istorii goncharstva. In *Problemy Drevnei Istorii Severnogo Prikaspiya*, edited by V. S. Gorbunov and G. I. Matveeva, pp. 193–217. Institut Istorii I Arkheologii Povolzh'ya, Samara.

Chernykh, E. N. (editor)
2004   *Kargaly, Tom III: Selishche Gornyi: Arkheologicheskie Materialyi: Tekhnologiya Gorno-Metallurgicheskogo Proizvodstva i Arkheobiologicheskie Issledovaniya*. Yazyki Slavyanskoi Kul'tury, Moskva.

Gremillion, Kristen
2004   Seed Processing and the Origins of Food Production in Eastern North America. *American Antiquity* 69:215–234.

Kolev, Y. I.
2003   Gruntovyi mogil'nik Srubnoi kul'tury S'yezzhee II (materialy raskopok). In *Material'naya Kul'tura Naseleniya basseina reki Samaray v Bronzovom Veke*, edited by Iu. I. Kolev, P. F. Kuznetsov, and O. D. Mochalov, p. 111. Samarskii Gosudarstvennyi Pedagogicheskii Universitet, Samara.

Kolev, Yu. I., A. E. Mamonov, and M. A. Turestskii (editors)
2000   *Istoria Samarskogo Povolzh'ye s drevneishikh vremen do nashikh dnei: bronzovii vek.* Tsentr Integratsiia, Samara.

López, Laura M., A. Capparelli, and A. E. Nielsen
2011   Traditional Post-Harvest Processing to Make Quinoa Grains (*Chenopodium quinoa* var. quinoa) Apt for Consumption in Northern Lipez (Potosí, Bolivia): Ethnoarchaeological and Archaeobotanical Analyses. *The Journal of Archaeological and Anthropological Sciences* 3:49–70.

Mochalov, Oleg D.
2008   *Keramika Pogrebal'nykh Pamiatnikov Epokhi Bronzy Lesostepi Volgo-Ural'skogo Mezhdurech'ya.* Samarskii Gosudarstvennyi Pedagogicheskii Universitet, Samara.

Ostroshchenko, V.
2003   The Economic Peculiarities of the Srubnaya Cultural-Historical Entity. In *Prehistoric Steppe Adaptation and the Horse*, edited by M. Levine, C. Renfrew, and K. Boyle, pp. 319–328. McDonald Institute, Cambridge.

Salugina, Natalya P.
2011   The Technology of the Yamnaya (Pit Grave) Ceramic Production and Its Relevance to the Population History of the Volga-Ural Region in the Early Bronze Age. *Archaeology Ethnology & Anthropology of Eurasia* 39(2): 82–94.

Sedova, M. S.
2000   Poseleniya Srubnoi kul'tury [Settlements of the Srubnaya culture]. In *Istoriya Samarskogo Povolzh'ya c Drevneishikh Vremen do Nashikh Dnei: Bronzovy Vek* [History of the Samara Region from the Most Ancient Times to the Modern Day. Bronze Age], edited by I. Y. Kolev, A. E. Mamonov, and M. A. Turetskii, pp. 209–241. Integratsiya, Samara.

Semenova, A. P.
2001   Osnovnye tendentsii razvitiya keramiki Pokrovskogo i razvitogo etapov Srubnoi kul'tury lesostepnogo Povolzh'ya (po dannym pograbal'nykh pamyatnikov). In *Bronzovyi Vek Vostochnoi Evropy: Kharakteristika Kul'tur, Khronologiya I Periodatsiya*, edited by Iu. I. Kolev, P. F. Kuznetsov, O. V. Kuzmina, A. P. Semenova, M. A. Turetskii, and B. A. Agapov, pp. 273–279. Samarskii Gosudarstvennyi Pedagogicheskii Universitet, Samara.

Shishlina, Natalia
2008   *Reconstruction of the Bronze Age of the Caspian Steppes.* Vol. 1876. British Archaeological Reports, Oxford.

Smith, Bruce
1989   Origins of Agriculture in Eastern North America. *Science* 246(4937):1566–1571.

Vasiliev, I. B., and G. I. Matveeva
1986   *U Istokov Istorii Samarskogo Povolzh'ya.* Kuibyshevskoe Knizhnoe Izdatel'svo, Kuibyshev.

Vasilieva, I. N.
2011   The Early Neolithic Pottery of the Volga-Ural Region (Based on the Materials of the Elshanka Culture). *Archaeology Ethnology & Anthropology of Eurasia* 39(2):70–81.

Chapter 11

Bronze Age Metallurgy
in the Middle Volga

David L. Peterson • Peter Northover • Chris Salter

Blanca Maldonado • David W. Anthony

etalwork first appeared in the middle Volga region during the Eneolithic period in the form of copper rings and bracelets from the Khvalynsk cemetery, circa 5000 to 4500 BC (Agapov et al. 1990; Chernykh 1992; Ryndina 1998). By the Bronze Age, metal became an important commodity that linked local producers and consumers to broad networks across Eurasia, portions of the Near East, and Central Asia. How was metal worked and used in the middle Volga during these periods? How did these local activities articulate with broader interactions as copper, bronze, and precious metals first emerged as an important focus of production and consumption?

The Samara Ancient Metals Project (the SAM project) was developed in association with the Samara Valley Project to examine these and other questions concerning the production, circulation, and consumption of metalwork during the Early to Late Bronze Age in the Samara oblast (province) of present-day Russia (Figure 11.1) (Peterson 2007, 2009, 2012; Peterson et al. 2006).[1]

This project began with a survey in the Kamyshla district of northeastern Samara, which uncovered evidence for copper mining in the fifteenth century BC. As a result, it is now the only area in Samara besides Mikhailovka-Ovsianka (Matveeva et al. 2004) where copper mining is known to have occurred during the Bronze Age. In addition, we performed chemical and microstructural analysis of third and second millennium BC metal artifacts that were collected through previous archaeological investigations, for

knowledge of the materials, practices, and interactions associated with early metal making in the middle Volga. This has been especially successful for the Middle Bronze Age II period of the Sintashta-Potapovka-Filitovka horizon (MBA II, circa 2100 to 1850 BC) to which most of the objects that we analyzed belong (Peterson 2009, 2012). Recently, there have been new findings for a small but important group of ornaments made with electrum (gold + silver) dating to the Early Srubnaya-Pokrovka stage of the Late Bronze Age, or LBA I, circa 1850 to 1700 BC (Lobell 2013; Peterson et al. 2012). These ornaments are from burials that are roughly contemporary with the primary occupation of the Krasnosamarskoe and Peschanyi Dol settlements and therefore have special relevance to the Samara Valley Project.

This chapter presents a summary of the results to date and offers provisional conclusions regarding the changing organization and role of the production and uses of metal by people in the middle Volga, as well as those in neighboring regions with whom they interacted during the Bronze Age. It does not replace the future publication of additional findings, especially of the ongoing investigation of LBA I gilding technologies. We begin with a brief overview of the study of early metallurgy in the middle Volga, followed by a summary of the results of the artifact analyses, and the evidence for metallurgical activities produced by the Samara Valley Project at Krasnosamarskoe and Peschanyi Dol and by the SAM project in Kamyshla. The results of the analyses and field investigations are contributing to the first account of

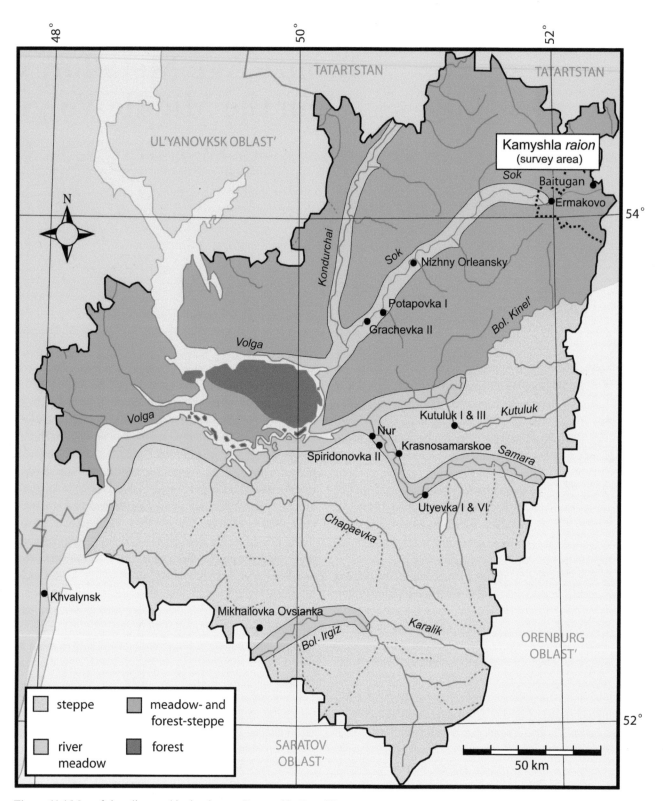

Figure 11.1 Map of sites discussed in the chapter. *Prepared by David Peterson*

the articulation of small-scale metalworking with the socio-economic structure of early mobile and sedentary herders and gatherers during the Bronze Age in the middle Volga.

Brief Overview of the Study of Early Copper and Bronze Metallurgy in the Middle Volga Region

Previously, analyses of prehistoric metalwork from the middle Volga have been published for Eneolithic copper objects from the Khvalynsk cemetery by Ryndina (1998) and Ryndina and Ravich (1987); for a variety of Bronze Age artifacts by Chernykh (1970, 1992), Korenevskii (1976, 1977, 1980), and Chernykh and Korenevskii (1976); and for materials from the Potapovka I kurgan cemetery by Agapov and Kuzminykh (1994). Metallurgy has had singular importance in scholarship on the prehistory of the region as a form of "productive economy" second only to agriculture and pastoralism. This orientation to metallurgy initially developed in Soviet archaeology and has had continuing importance (Vasil'ev et al. 2000). East of the Volga, there has been a tendency to accentuate evidence for large-scale mining and metal production in the South Ural Mountains region during the early to mid-second millennium BC, especially in the Kargaly district of the Orenburg oblast to the east of Samara (Chernykh 1997a, 1997b, 2002, 2004, 2005, 2007, 2008; Diaz del Río et al. 2006). This is for good reason, given the volume of early copper mining at Kargaly that we discuss later. However, evidence for mining and metal production at a smaller scale is far more widespread and includes the Late Bronze Age pastoralists that inhabited the landscapes investigated by the Samara Valley Project and the SAM project (Peterson 2007; Peterson et al. 2006).

Early steppe metallurgy occurred within a broader field of interregional interactions that were conducive to large-scale mining and metal production for limited periods in some areas (Kohl 2008). By the Middle Bronze Age, steppe metallurgists may have boosted their production to meet the demands of partners that included the oases polities of southern Central Asia, in networks that extended as far southwest as Mesopotamia (Anthony 2009). The appearance of imports such as lapis lazuli in steppe burials (Kuzmina 2007:118) and the potential contribution of Andronovo miners to the second millennium BC tin trade (Stöllner et al. 2011) offer tantalizing evidence of long-distance exchange with people who lived far to the south. This may have facilitated the transfer of advanced gilding techniques to metalworkers in the Eurasian steppes that are first known from Early Dynastic Ur (Hauptmann et al. 2010; La Niece 1995).

Although large-scale production may have occurred in some areas of the steppes by the second millennium BC, it still appears to have been the exception and not the rule. Even in the "global" circulation of finely crafted and ornamented tin bronze weaponry and other metalwork associated with the Seimo-Turbino phenomenon (Frachetti 2008), the output was relatively low and devoted to ceremonial use in burials and cenotaphs (Chernykh 1992; Chernykh and Kuz'minykh 1989; Parzinger 1997, 2002). Recently, research of early mining and metal production in Samara, Kargaly, and western Siberia has stressed community dynamics among early miners and metallurgists and the smaller scale of production that became increasingly common during the course of the Bronze Age (Diaz del Río et al. 2006; Hanks and Doonan 2009; Peterson 2009, 2012). This new perspective informs the discussion in this chapter, which addresses how smaller scales of metal making and metal use contributed to social integration (and sometimes conflict) in the middle Volga and the articulation of communities that used metal in broader networks extending as far as the Near East.

From the Eneolithic to the Bronze Age

Most of the current knowledge of metalworking before and during the Bronze Age in Samara has been gathered through the analysis of metal artifacts as opposed to other forms of evidence such as slags, crucibles, furnaces, and other features (but see Matveeva et al. 2004). Rings and bracelets from the Khvalynsk cemetery (ca. 5000–4500 BC) show that metalworking began in the middle Volga by the Eneolithic period, using copper imported over a distance of more than 2,000 km from the Carpathians and Balkans (Agapov et al. 1990; Chernykh 1992; Ryndina 1998; Ryndina and Ravich 1987). It is generally accepted that metalworking was practiced as far east as the middle Volga during the Eneolithic, based primarily on metallographic research on the techniques used to fabricate the earliest copper artifacts in the steppes. These differ from those that were used in Southeast Europe where the copper itself originated (Chernykh 1992; Ryndina 1998; Ryndina and Ravich 1987).

Early Bronze Age (EBA) Yamnaya pastoralists were the first to fully exploit the steppes and to integrate the production of copper and arsenical bronze metalwork into an increasingly mobile way of life (Anthony 1998:103). From the EBA through the beginning of the LBA, there is very little evidence for sedentism in the middle Volga. During these periods, the lives of the region's inhabitants appear to have been centered on mobile pastoralism, which has left minimal traces in the archaeological record. Small-scale metalworking and even mining and smelting may have taken place in campsites of EBA and MBA pastoralists similar to those investigated by the Samara Valley Project at Peschanyi Dol 2 (LBA I) that remain to be discovered.

By the early third millennium BC, Yamnaya communities are known to have effectively exploited copper deposits in Kargaly, which lies on the southern Ural periphery of the distribution of Yamnaya and Poltavka sites and at the northeastern limit of the EBA-MBA network that Chernykh has defined as the Circumpontic Metallurgical Province (Chernykh 1992; 2009; Peterson 2012). Based on the results of arc optical emission spectroscopy (OES) performed on metalwork from Yamnaya burials in the middle Volga, it has been argued that ore deposits from the Ural River to the Volga were already being exploited by this period (Anthony 1998:103; Chernykh 1992:85–86). The Samara Valley links the middle Volga to extensive ore deposits in the South Urals, including the Kargaly ore field. Volga-Ural cupric sandstone ore has been found in some Yamnaya kurgan burials, including Kurgan 2 at Utyevka I, which shows the cultural importance attached not only to metalwork but also to the raw materials involved in its fabrication. Perhaps the symbolic value of the ore was derived from transformative powers associated with turning stone into metal through the smelting process (Peterson 2009) and/or place-based associations linked to sources of ore (cf. discussions of "place value" in Papadopoulos and Urton 2012).

A burial in the Yamnaya cemetery at Utyevka I (Kurgan 1, Grave 1) also included two granulated golden rings and a copper pin with an iron head (Anthony 2007:Figure 13.9; Chernykh 1992:86; Vasil'iev 1980:38–42). These are remarkable in being among the earliest known granulated and iron artifacts in Eurasia, demonstrating the precocious metal making and metal use that middle Volga pastoralists engaged in even at the beginning of the Bronze Age. Most Yamnaya-Poltavka metalwork is in the form of copper implements (tanged knives and daggers, tetrahedral awls and chisels, adzes, and shaft-hole axes) that were used throughout the Circumpontic region during the third millennium BC. Some pieces were fashioned from arsenic bronze that may have been imported from the Caucasus, where large numbers of arsenical copper and arsenic bronze artifacts were produced at this time (Chernykh 1992:132–133). While arsenic bronze was undoubtedly used to enhance the appearance of metal ornaments from third millennium burials, its greater hardness compared to unalloyed copper would have also improved the performance of implements that were important to economic and ritual life. Many of these are woodworking tools that were needed to build the wagons that were crucial to mobile steppe pastoralism and became part of the kurgan burial rite by the end of the fourth millennium BC (Anthony 1998:103; Kuzmina 2000:119; Piggott 1983:58).

While there is little direct evidence for metal production (workshops, slags, crucibles) in the middle Volga region before the LBA, this does not mean it did not occur. Metallographic analysis of copper artifacts has shown that metalworking was practiced in the middle Volga by the middle of the fifth millennium BC, but since Ryndina (1998), little metallography has been performed to evaluate the possibility of local production where workshops and other evidence are absent. Later, we discuss metallographic evidence recently produced by the SAM project for local metalworking along the Sok and Samara river valleys during the MBA II period and what it tells us about the dynamics of early metal networks (Peterson 2012) in the region. Our findings suggest that metalworking probably continued to be practiced in the middle Volga after its introduction during the Eneolithic.

In the past, settlement archaeology focused on permanent hamlets and villages while the evidence indicates that Bronze Age pastoralists in the middle Volga lived and worked in small, temporary campsites and activity areas until the LBA. Without systematic recovery techniques, these kinds of sites have gone almost completely undetected. Numerous kurgan burials attest to the habitation of the Samara area in the EBA and MBA. The Samara Valley Project and the SAM project initiated the investigation of the small LBA campsites that served as satellites for larger, permanent settlements such as Krasnosamarskoe. Research on similar sites in earlier periods will be needed for an improved account of how activities like metallurgy were carried out earlier in the Bronze Age.

Metallurgy and Early Pastoralists

An important question that underlies research on ancient metallurgy is often left unaddressed: why was small-scale metal production so important to early steppe pastoralists in the middle Volga and elsewhere? Even where metallurgy was practiced on a small scale, the relationships fostered through the exchange of metal, metalwork, and even ore for animals and other goods (Chernykh 1997a) would have bolstered the sustainability of early pastoralist communities in the capricious Eurasian steppe environment. Small-scale production and exchange would have added much-needed diversity to interregional economies that might otherwise have been redundantly centered on pastoralism alone.

In pastoralist societies, the most important transactions are often social payments, such as bridewealth and bloodwealth, which are made with livestock. The initial adoption of domesticated cattle and pastoralism in the steppes may have accompanied the integration of steppe communities with early agriculturalists who used livestock for bridewealth (Russell

1998). Metal is likely to have been another key currency for social payments among groups in which even small exchanges may have had great impact. According to Barth (1961), a household of mid-twentieth-century Basseri nomads in Fars made up of a husband, one or more wives, and their children needed a herd of at least 60 sheep and goats to survive. In bad years, a herd was often quickly reduced by half or more, and it took years to recover. The availability of metal or metalwork to early pastoralist households for at least some social payments may have made it easier for them to maintain their herds year after year.

From its very earliest appearance during the Eneolithic in the middle Volga, metal was distributed and acquired through long-distance interactions. By the early second millennium BC, steppe communities were probably trading bronze and even tin in response to increasing demands to the south and west (Anthony 2009; Stöllner et al. 2011). This certainly had the potential to enrich groups and individuals, but the production and exchange of metal were unlikely to have grown as they did unless they enhanced the sustainability of broader communities through the greater economic diversity that they offered.

Microprobe and Metallographic Analysis of Bronze Age Metalwork
Objectives

Our laboratory investigation of the materials, techniques, and properties of Bronze Age artifacts from the middle Volga has centered on electron probe microanalysis with wavelength-dispersive spectrometry (EPMA-WDS, or WDS) and metallography. Scanning electron microscopy with energy-dispersive spectrometry (SEM-EDS) was used to a lesser extent for compositional and microstructural analysis in examining the surprisingly sophisticated technology used in making electrum foil–covered ornaments from LBA kurgan cemeteries in the middle Volga forest-steppe.

The objectives of the WDS analysis were to determine the raw material type for each object (metallurgical groups), to track changes through time in the materials selected for metalworking, and to obtain information on the raw materials that were used over the course of the Bronze Age. Long ago, Chernykh (1970) identified source groups used in Bronze Age Eurasian steppe metallurgy through spectral-chemical analysis using arc OES. These categories have continued to be used in steppe archaeology, especially in the Russian literature. Results of arc OES analysis performed by Agapov and Kuzminykh (1994) on a number of MBA II objects from Potapovka I are discussed below. We used a different technique for compositional analysis (WDS instead of arc OES), and it would have been inappropriate to use the present results to assign the samples to categories arrived at with a very different technique.

Arc OES was one of the first instrumental methods used in archaeometallurgy and summaries of the results, if not the data themselves, still circulate widely in archaeological literature. Pollard and his colleagues note problems with the use of these so-called legacy data that are not readily compared with the results of other techniques that have been more commonly used since the 1980s (Pollard et al. 2007:47–48). One problem with arc OES is that the amount of copper present in the artifacts was never measured. Even though the results are given as percentages, the values can be misleading because they have not been normalized to 100 percent according to the amount of copper present in the samples. The WDS analysis for this project did measure copper and normalize results. Another advantage of WDS is that unlike arc OES, samples are not consumed by the analysis and therefore it can be repeated. We repeated the analysis of each sample 5 to 10 times to ensure accuracy.

Arc OES data may remain viable for addressing archaeological questions in broad generalities (Pollard et al. 2007:64, 66) and therefore may be used to form hypotheses for continuing research. This is how we have used them here. Findings from our WDS analyses provide complementary evidence that by the MBA II in the middle Volga, copper and bronze metalwork was regularly recycled in making new pieces. This is important regarding the dynamics that surrounded Bronze Age metallurgy, since it implies a more varied supply chain than if only newly smelted metal had been used. Currently, the preferred technique for source analysis of prehistoric copper-based metalwork is lead isotope analysis (LIA), principally with tin bronze in which there is often a sufficient quantity of lead for the analysis to succeed. To date, LIA results have been published for only 16 tin bronzes and one tin bead from the Eurasian steppes, all from eastern Kazakhstan (Stöllner et al. 2011:247–248). Much work is needed in applying current sourcing techniques to evaluating hypotheses concerning sources of ancient copper and bronze in the Eurasian steppes, which were derived from arc OES results more than 40 years ago.

Methods

The analysis was performed on small samples (generally no more than 3 mm in length and width) that Peterson removed from the objects by hand with a jeweler's saw. These were mounted in a high-carbon bakelite thermosetting resin and ground and polished to a 1-μm diamond finish (the list of objects and their affiliations is presented in Table 11.1). WDS analysis was conducted at Oxford Materials by Northover and Salter, with Peterson as a visiting researcher. Maldonado prepared the samples and took micrographs of the etched sections (Peterson 2007, 2009).

Table 11.1 List of Sampled Objects

Sample	Site	Kurgan	Grave	Period/Affiliation	Object
DP88	Kutuluk I	4	1	EBA Yamnaya	Club (grip)
DP89	Kutuluk I	4	1	EBA Yamnaya	Club (grip)
DP9	Kutuluk III	1	2	E-MBA Yamnaya-Poltavka	Knife (blade)
DP10	Kutuluk III	1	2	E-MBA Yamnaya-Poltavka	Tetrahedral awl (tip)
DP47	Nur	2	4	MBA I Poltavka	Ring (1)
DP48	Nur	2	4	MBA I Poltavka	Ring (2)
DP49	Nur	2	4	MBA I Poltavka	Ring (3)
DP23	Potapovka I	1	4	MBA II Potapovka	Knife (blade)
DP24	Potapovka I	1	4	MBA II Potapovka	Knife (end)
DP61	Potapovka I	1	4	MBA II Potapovka	Knife (end)
DP32	Potapovka I	1	5	MBA II Potapovka	Knife (blade)
DP26	Potapovka I	2	1	MBA II Potapovka	Large hook
DP31	Potapovka I	2	1	MBA II Potapovka	Knife (blade)
DP84	Potapovka I	2	1	MBA II Potapovka	Awl (end)
DP87	Potapovka I	3	2	MBA II Potapovka	Awl (end)
DP22	Potapovka I	3	4	MBA II Potapovka	Hook (tip)
DP90	Potapovka I	3	4	MBA II Potapovka	Knife (knife)
DP64	Potapovka I	3	5	MBA II Potapovka	Blade (1) (grip)
DP65	Potapovka I	3	5	MBA II Potapovka	Blade (2) (grip)
DP66	Potapovka I	3	5	MBA II Potapovka	Large hook (1)
DP67	Potapovka I	3	5	MBA II Potapovka	Large hook (2)
DP86	Potapovka I	3	5	MBA II Potapovka	Awl (end)
DP95	Potapovka I	3	5	MBA II Potapovka	Ring
DP7	Potapovka I	3	8	MBA II Potapovka	Bracelet (1)
DP27	Potapovka I	3	8	MBA II Potapovka	Bracelet (2)
DP62	Potapovka I	3	8	MBA II Potapovka	Knife (2) (tang)
DP91	Potapovka I	3	8	MBA II Potapovka	Knife (1) (tang)
DP77	Potapovka I	5	4	MBA II Potapovka	Small adze
DP78	Potapovka I	5	4	MBA II Potapovka	Knife (blade)
DP30	Potapovka I	5	8	MBA II Potapovka	Knife (blade)
DP75	Potapovka I	5	8	MBA II Potapovka	Awl (end)
DP63	Potapovka I	5	11	MBA II Potapovka	Spatula (cuff)
DP76	Potapovka I	5	11	MBA II Potapovka	Awl (tip)
DP1	Potapovka I	5	13	MBA II Potapovka	Knife (blade)
DP20	Potapovka I	5	14	MBA II Potapovka	Hook (eye)
DP56	Potapovka I	5	14	MBA II Potapovka	Knife (1) (blade)
DP57	Potapovka I	5	14	MBA II Potapovka	Blade (2) (blade)
DP58	Potapovka I	5	14	MBA II Potapovka	Blade (3) (blade)
DP59	Potapovka I	5	14	MBA II Potapovka	Knife (4) (blade)
DP5	Utyevka VI	6	1	MBA II Potapovka	Bracelet
DP11	Utyevka VI	6	1	MBA II Potapovka	Knife (blade)
DP2	Utyevka VI	6	2	MBA II Potapovka	Bracelet
DP21	Utyevka VI	6	2	MBA II Potapovka	Hook (eye)
DP69	Utyevka VI	6	2	MBA II Potapovka	Knife (1) (blade)
DP70	Utyevka VI	6	2	MBA II Potapovka	Adze

Sample	Site	Kurgan	Grave	Period/Affiliation	Object
DP71	Utyevka VI	6	2	MBA II Potapovka	Knife (2) (blade)
DP72	Utyevka VI	6	2	MBA II Potapovka	Knife (3) (blade)
DP73	Utyevka VI	6	2	MBA II Potapovka	Awl (2) (end)
DP79	Utyevka VI	6	2	MBA II Potapovka	Awl (1) (end)
DP83	Utyevka VI	6	2	MBA II Potapovka	Needle (tip)
DP85	Utyevka VI	6	2	MBA II Potapovka	Awl (tip)
DP13	Utyevka VI	6	4	MBA II Potapovka	Knife (blade)
DP28	Utyevka VI	6	4	MBA II Potapovka	Spearhead (sleeve)
DP29	Utyevka VI	6	4	MBA II Potapovka	Flat axe (end)
DP50	Utyevka VI	6	4	MBA II Potapovka	Clamp (1)
DP51	Utyevka VI	6	4	MBA II Potapovka	Clamp (2)
DP52	Utyevka VI	6	4	MBA II Potapovka	Clamp (3)
DP53	Utyevka VI	6	4	MBA II Potapovka	Sheet ornament
DP74	Utyevka VI	6	5	MBA II Potapovka	Awl (tip)
DP8	Utyevka VI	6	6	MBA II Potapovka	Copper piece
DP12	Utyevka VI	6	6	MBA II Potapovka	Knife (1) (blade)
DP14	Utyevka VI	6	6	MBA II Potapovka	Sickle
DP15	Utyevka VI	6	6	MBA II Potapovka	Knife (2) (blade)
DP25	Utyevka VI	6	6	MBA II Potapovka	Chisel
DP68	Utyevka VI	6	6	MBA II Potapovka	Adze
DP6	Utyevka VI	6	11	MBA II Potapovka	Bracelet
DP80	Utyevka VI	6	11	MBA II Potapovka	Awl
DP81	Utyevka VI	6	11	MBA II Potapovka	Needle (1) (tip)
DP82	Utyevka VI	6	11	MBA II Potapovka	Needle (2) (tip)
DP18	Grachevka II	8	3	MBA II Potapovka	Knife (1) (blade)
DP19	Grachevka II	8	2	MBA II Potapovka	Knife (2) (end)
DP3	Grachevka II	8	8	MBA II Potapovka	Knife (1) (blade)
DP4	Grachevka II	8	8	MBA II Potapovka	Knife (2) (end)
DP60	Grachevka II	8	8	MBA II Potapovka	Knife (3) (tang)
DP40	Spiridonovka II	2	3	LBA Srubnaya	Bracelet
DP16	Spiridonovka II	2	14	LBA Srubnaya	Pendant (1)
DP17	Spiridonovka II	2	14	LBA Srubnaya	Pendant (2)
DP34	Spiridonovka II	2	14	LBA Srubnaya	Bracelet
DP41	Spiridonovka II	2	22	LBA Srubnaya	Sheet ornament
DP33	Spiridonovka II	2	29	LBA Srubnaya	Bracelet (1)
DP94	Spiridonovka II	2	29	LBA Srubnaya	Foil-covered pendant
DP45	Spiridonovka II	2	35	LBA Srubnaya	Pendant (1)
DP46	Spiridonovka II	2	35	LBA Srubnaya	Pendant (2)
DP54	Spiridonovka II	10	5	LBA Srubnaya	Sheet ornament (1)
DP55	Spiridonovka II	10	5	LBA Srubnaya	Sheet ornament (2)
DP44	Spiridonovka II	10	14	LBA Srubnaya	Needle (tip)
DP92	Nizhny Orleansky	3	8	LBA Srubnaya	Foil-covered pendant (1)
DP93	Nizhny Orleansky	3	8	LBA Srubnaya	Foil-covered pendant (2)

Note: EBA = Early Bronze Age; E-MBA = Early to Middle Bronze Age; MBA I = Middle Bronze Age; MBA II = Late Middle Bronze Age; LBA = Late Bronze Age.

Table 11. 2 EPMA-WDS Results

Sample	Fe	Co	Ni	Cu	Zn	As	Sb	Sn	Ag	Bi	Pb	Au	S	Al	Si	Mn
DP1	0.22	0.00	0.02	98.59	0.00	0.90	0.01	0.01	0.07	0.01	0.02	0.04	0.12	0.00	0.00	0.01
DP2	0.00	0.01	0.00	92.57	0.00	0.08	0.00	7.12	0.00	0.01	0.08	0.01	0.09	0.00	0.00	0.00
DP3	0.54	0.01	0.02	99.14	0.01	0.11	0.00	0.00	0.08	0.01	0.01	0.03	0.05	0.00	0.00	0.00
DP4	0.03	0.01	0.01	94.13	0.00	0.07	0.01	5.69	0.00	0.02	0.01	0.01	0.01	0.00	0.00	0.01
DP5	0.00	0.00	0.10	91.02	0.01	0.69	0.01	7.65	0.25	0.02	0.21	0.03	0.01	0.00	0.00	0.00
DP6	0.01	0.00	0.01	92.36	0.01	0.08	0.01	7.32	0.01	0.02	0.09	0.04	0.04	0.00	0.01	0.00
DP7	0.24	0.01	0.39	94.76	0.01	4.41	0.01	0.01	0.05	0.03	0.01	0.05	0.04	0.00	0.00	0.00
DP8	0.02	0.01	0.01	99.83	0.00	0.03	0.01	0.04	0.01	0.00	0.00	0.00	0.00	0.00	0.01	0.02
DP9	0.00	0.01	0.01	99.81	0.01	0.00	0.00	0.01	0.05	0.02	0.02	0.03	0.00	0.00	0.02	0.00
DP10	0.01	0.01	0.00	99.75	0.00	0.01	0.00	0.01	0.05	0.03	0.03	0.07	0.01	0.00	0.01	0.01
DP11	0.19	0.00	0.23	97.48	0.00	1.88	0.02	0.02	0.04	0.03	0.01	0.02	0.09	0.00	0.00	0.01
DP12	0.85	0.00	0.30	96.24	0.00	2.31	0.02	0.01	0.05	0.00	0.01	0.03	0.17	0.00	0.00	0.01
DP13	0.17	0.00	0.13	97.84	0.00	1.68	0.01	0.01	0.04	0.01	0.04	0.02	0.03	0.00	0.00	0.01
DP14	0.06	0.00	0.04	99.18	0.01	0.27	0.01	0.02	0.07	0.01	0.01	0.01	0.30	0.00	0.00	0.00
DP15	1.70	0.00	0.32	96.31	0.00	1.45	0.02	0.01	0.04	0.02	0.00	0.03	0.09	0.00	0.00	0.01
DP16	0.04	0.00	0.02	85.22	0.00	0.22	0.01	14.32	0.00	0.02	0.05	0.04	0.03	0.00	0.00	0.01
DP17	0.00	0.00	0.03	88.92	0.00	0.02	0.06	10.05	0.01	0.03	0.78	0.04	0.05	0.00	0.01	0.00
DP18	0.17	0.00	0.10	99.47	0.00	0.13	0.01	0.02	0.04	0.01	0.01	0.01	0.03	0.00	0.00	0.00
DP19	0.62	0.00	0.13	97.25	0.01	1.76	0.04	0.01	0.05	0.02	0.02	0.05	0.02	0.00	0.00	0.01
DP20	0.59	0.01	0.17	97.85	0.00	1.12	0.01	0.01	0.06	0.01	0.03	0.00	0.14	0.00	0.00	0.00
DP21	0.33	0.00	0.23	97.19	0.00	2.05	0.00	0.01	0.04	0.03	0.02	0.06	0.03	0.00	0.00	0.01
DP22	0.11	0.00	0.25	98.52	0.01	0.94	0.01	0.00	0.04	0.02	0.01	0.06	0.01	0.00	0.00	0.00
DP23	0.15	0.01	0.10	99.37	0.00	0.15	0.02	0.01	0.02	0.01	0.01	0.02	0.11	0.00	0.00	0.00
DP24	0.16	0.01	0.10	99.38	0.00	0.16	0.01	0.01	0.02	0.01	0.01	0.05	0.09	0.00	0.00	0.00
DP25	0.31	0.01	0.21	96.12	0.01	3.08	0.03	0.01	0.06	0.02	0.00	0.03	0.11	0.00	0.00	0.00
DP26	0.01	0.01	0.01	99.54	0.02	0.00	0.00	0.02	0.29	0.04	0.02	0.02	0.01	0.00	0.00	0.01
DP27	0.00	0.00	0.08	90.59	0.00	0.50	0.10	8.57	0.00	0.03	0.08	0.01	0.02	0.00	0.00	0.00
DP28	0.30	0.01	0.30	97.40	0.00	1.82	0.01	0.00	0.02	0.02	0.03	0.04	0.05	0.00	0.00	0.00
DP29	0.28	0.01	0.69	95.47	0.00	3.27	0.02	0.02	0.04	0.02	0.01	0.00	0.16	0.00	0.01	0.01
DP30	0.37	0.00	0.10	99.16	0.00	0.13	0.03	0.01	0.05	0.01	0.00	0.04	0.09	0.00	0.00	0.00
DP31	0.00	0.01	0.01	99.73	0.01	0.01	0.00	0.00	0.12	0.01	0.01	0.05	0.01	0.00	0.00	0.01
DP32	0.33	0.00	0.01	99.10	0.00	0.39	0.01	0.01	0.06	0.01	0.03	0.03	0.01	0.00	0.00	0.00
DP33	0.08	0.01	0.01	87.25	0.00	0.02	0.02	12.50	0.00	0.01	0.01	0.05	0.01	0.00	0.00	0.02
DP34	0.08	0.01	0.02	86.58	0.01	0.05	0.01	13.11	0.00	0.02	0.06	0.03	0.02	0.00	0.00	0.01
DP40	0.02	0.00	0.00	85.18	0.00	0.18	0.00	14.58	0.00	0.02	0.00	0.00	0.01	0.00	0.00	0.00
DP41	0.40	0.01	0.05	96.17	0.00	0.17	0.01	3.04	0.01	0.03	0.04	0.03	0.02	0.00	0.01	0.01
DP44	0.38	0.00	0.02	99.15	0.00	0.03	0.01	0.00	0.07	0.00	0.05	0.01	0.24	0.00	0.01	0.02
DP45	0.02	0.01	0.03	88.67	0.01	0.07	0.13	10.47	0.00	0.07	0.37	0.01	0.13	0.00	0.00	0.00
DP46	0.02	0.01	0.03	88.21	0.03	0.06	0.13	10.36	0.00	0.11	0.90	0.01	0.12	0.00	0.01	0.00
DP47	0.00	0.00	0.02	97.77	0.01	2.07	0.00	0.01	0.04	0.01	0.02	0.02	0.01	0.00	0.00	0.01
DP48	0.00	0.01	0.03	97.80	0.00	2.04	0.00	0.01	0.06	0.01	0.02	0.01	0.00	0.00	0.00	0.00
DP49	0.00	0.01	0.02	97.89	0.01	1.99	0.01	0.01	0.01	0.00	0.03	0.01	0.00	0.00	0.00	0.00
DP50	0.07	0.01	0.15	98.92	0.00	0.56	0.02	0.00	0.03	0.00	0.03	0.00	0.17	0.00	0.03	0.00
DP51	0.11	0.01	0.06	99.33	0.00	0.29	0.00	0.00	0.06	0.03	0.00	0.00	0.10	0.00	0.00	0.01
DP52	0.10	0.01	0.04	99.53	0.00	0.17	0.00	0.01	0.02	0.02	0.02	0.01	0.04	0.00	0.02	0.01
DP53	0.28	0.01	0.04	99.09	0.02	0.34	0.01	0.01	0.02	0.01	0.01	0.04	0.14	0.00	0.00	0.00
DP54	0.14	0.01	0.02	99.57	0.00	0.02	0.03	0.08	0.03	0.03	0.03	0.01	0.03	0.02	0.00	0.01

Sample	Fe	Co	Ni	Cu	Zn	As	Sb	Sn	Ag	Bi	Pb	Au	S	Al	Si	Mn
DP55	0.16	0.01	0.02	99.59	0.00	0.03	0.02	0.06	0.02	0.01	0.05	0.02	0.01	0.00	0.01	0.01
DP56	0.54	0.01	0.26	96.21	0.00	2.65	0.01	0.00	0.02	0.02	0.03	0.03	0.04	0.00	0.17	0.01
DP57	0.00	0.00	0.00	99.81	0.00	0.01	0.01	0.01	0.09	0.01	0.01	0.01	0.00	0.00	0.00	0.00
DP58	0.00	0.00	0.01	99.79	0.00	0.01	0.00	0.01	0.10	0.02	0.02	0.02	0.01	0.00	0.00	0.00
DP59	0.01	0.01	0.01	99.79	0.01	0.00	0.01	0.01	0.07	0.03	0.03	0.02	0.00	0.00	0.00	0.00
DP60	0.18	0.00	0.08	98.87	0.01	0.56	0.01	0.01	0.06	0.03	0.02	0.06	0.09	0.00	0.00	0.01
DP61	0.52	0.00	0.03	99.08	0.00	0.15	0.01	0.01	0.06	0.01	0.01	0.01	0.10	0.00	0.00	0.00
DP62	0.49	0.00	0.04	99.10	0.01	0.15	0.03	0.01	0.04	0.02	0.01	0.03	0.06	0.00	0.00	0.01
DP63	0.31	0.01	0.20	96.89	0.01	2.32	0.00	0.01	0.05	0.02	0.02	0.05	0.09	0.00	0.01	0.01
DP64	0.22	0.00	0.22	96.82	0.01	2.51	0.00	0.01	0.08	0.04	0.02	0.00	0.05	0.00	0.01	0.00
DP65	0.86	0.00	0.20	98.70	0.01	0.09	0.00	0.01	0.02	0.01	0.00	0.00	0.07	0.00	0.01	0.00
DP66	0.92	0.01	0.21	98.55	0.00	0.08	0.01	0.01	0.02	0.04	0.01	0.01	0.12	0.00	0.00	0.00
DP67	0.00	0.00	0.04	99.50	0.00	0.18	0.00	0.01	0.17	0.01	0.01	0.04	0.02	0.00	0.00	0.01
DP68	0.33	0.01	0.26	97.78	0.00	1.42	0.01	0.01	0.06	0.02	0.03	0.02	0.04	0.00	0.00	0.01
DP69	0.40	0.00	0.04	99.13	0.00	0.10	0.00	0.00	0.14	0.00	0.03	0.05	0.08	0.01	0.00	0.01
DP70	0.22	0.01	0.04	99.41	0.00	0.12	0.01	0.00	0.02	0.01	0.00	0.02	0.13	0.00	0.00	0.00
DP71	0.09	0.01	0.02	98.80	0.00	0.26	0.00	0.00	0.11	0.03	0.02	0.03	0.62	0.00	0.01	0.00
DP72	0.01	0.01	0.00	99.69	0.00	0.06	0.02	0.01	0.10	0.03	0.04	0.03	0.00	0.00	0.00	0.01
DP73	0.26	0.01	0.31	97.46	0.00	1.69	0.01	0.01	0.06	0.01	0.01	0.02	0.16	0.00	0.00	0.01
DP74	0.11	0.01	0.16	98.21	0.00	1.36	0.01	0.01	0.05	0.02	0.02	0.01	0.02	0.00	0.00	0.01
DP75	0.06	0.00	0.07	98.54	0.02	0.65	0.00	0.01	0.10	0.00	0.00	0.03	0.49	0.00	0.02	0.00
DP76	0.01	0.01	0.01	99.74	0.00	0.05	0.02	0.00	0.11	0.03	0.00	0.01	0.01	0.00	0.01	0.01
DP77	0.08	0.00	0.16	98.87	0.00	0.64	0.01	0.01	0.03	0.01	0.02	0.03	0.13	0.00	0.00	0.01
DP78	0.35	0.02	0.13	99.03	0.00	0.32	0.01	0.00	0.01	0.01	0.03	0.02	0.06	0.00	0.01	0.00
DP79	0.13	0.01	0.31	95.34	0.01	3.98	0.00	0.08	0.05	0.01	0.00	0.02	0.04	0.00	0.00	0.00
DP80	0.35	0.01	0.19	97.27	0.02	1.97	0.02	0.01	0.06	0.02	0.00	0.04	0.03	0.00	0.00	0.00
DP81	0.23	0.01	0.01	99.60	0.00	0.03	0.01	0.01	0.01	0.01	0.02	0.03	0.01	0.00	0.01	0.00
DP82	0.74	0.00	0.24	96.84	0.00	1.96	0.01	0.08	0.05	0.01	0.01	0.02	0.03	0.00	0.00	0.00
DP83	1.33	0.01	0.14	97.53	0.00	0.91	0.01	0.00	0.03	0.01	0.00	0.00	0.02	0.00	0.00	0.01
DP84	0.01	0.00	0.00	99.84	0.00	0.01	0.00	0.00	0.08	0.02	0.01	0.01	0.01	0.00	0.00	0.00
DP85	0.21	0.01	0.36	94.69	0.00	4.52	0.01	0.01	0.05	0.04	0.01	0.02	0.06	0.00	0.00	0.00
DP86	0.02	0.01	0.02	99.79	0.00	0.01	0.01	0.01	0.08	0.01	0.01	0.03	0.01	0.00	0.00	0.01
DP87	0.35	0.01	0.01	98.55	0.00	0.15	0.01	0.01	0.06	0.00	0.01	0.04	0.79	0.00	0.00	0.01
DP88	0.01	0.00	0.01	99.75	0.00	0.01	0.01	0.00	0.12	0.02	0.00	0.03	0.01	0.00	0.01	0.00
DP89	0.01	0.00	0.02	99.76	0.00	0.01	0.01	0.01	0.12	0.02	0.01	0.02	0.01	0.00	0.01	0.00
DP90	0.42	0.00	0.28	84.83	0.01	13.89	0.05	0.01	0.35	0.01	0.01	0.03	0.10	0.00	0.01	0.01
DP91	0.15	0.01	0.38	96.70	0.01	2.48	0.07	0.01	0.07	0.00	0.03	0.03	0.06	0.00	0.01	0.00
DP92/core	0.25	0.02	0.01	99.32	0.00	0.00	0.00	0.30	0.04	0.01	0.00	0.00	0.02	0.00	0.01	0.02
DP92/foil	0.01	0.02	0.01	1.53	0.00	0.00	0.02	0.00	68.83	0.26	0.02	29.29	0.00	0.00	0.01	0.00
DP93	0.01	0.00	0.00	1.75	0.00	0.01	0.00	0.00	76.09	0.18	0.01	21.86	0.03	0.00	0.02	0.04
DP93/inner	0.00	0.01	0.02	1.33	0.00	0.02	0.04	0.00	78.33	0.00	0.12	20.12	0.00	0.00	0.01	0.00
DP93/mid	0.01	0.00	0.01	1.94	0.00	0.00	0.03	0.00	57.21	0.00	0.00	40.76	0.01	0.00	0.01	0.02
DP93/outer	0.00	0.00	0.01	1.97	0.00	0.01	0.00	0.00	67.18	0.00	0.02	30.79	0.00	0.00	0.01	0.02
DP94	0.13	0.00	0.02	60.71	0.01	0.02	0.01	0.01	36.25	0.08	0.02	2.72	0.01	0.00	0.01	0.00
DP94/outer	0.00	0.00	0.00	2.27	0.00	0.00	0.00	0.00	24.40	0.00	0.00	73.29	0.00	0.00	0.02	0.01
DP94/inner	0.08	0.00	0.01	1.62	0.07	0.00	0.00	0.00	94.62	0.05	0.00	3.55	0.01	0.00	0.00	0.00
DP95	0.01	0.01	0.03	0.59	0.01	0.24	0.00	0.00	98.95	0.10	0.02	0.03	0.02	0.00	0.00	0.01

The conditions of the WDS analysis were similar to those that Northover reports for the analysis of nonferrous metalwork from the Iron Age cemetery at Pottenbrunn (Northover 2002:251). The instrument used was a Cameca SU30, operated with an accelerating voltage of 25 kV, beam current of 30 nA, and X-ray take-off angle of 62°. Sixteen elements were analyzed as listed in Table 11.2, with a count time of 10 seconds per element. The detection limits for most elements were between 100 to 200 parts per million (ppm); the principal exceptions were limits of 300 to 400 ppm for gold in bronze and about 200 ppm for arsenic due to the interference between the principal spectral lines of lead and arsenic. The experiment therefore relied on alternative spectral lines for these elements. The relative weakness of the $K\alpha$ line used for arsenic resulted in the slight degradation in performance for that element, a small concession that was needed to include both arsenic and lead in the study since both are commonly present in ancient copper and bronze metalwork.

Five to 10 areas of 50×30 µm were analyzed in each sample. The mean composition of each sample is listed in Table 11.2, in which the values have been normalized to 100 percent with concentrations given in proportion to the weight of the sample (weight percent, or wt%). The variation in values for analyses of individual elements in the same samples was relatively small, about 1 percent for major elements and reaching about 10 percent for impurities analyzed in concentrations as low as 0.02 wt%.

Ninety-five objects were examined in all. We found that 7 of 95 were too corroded for effective analysis, bringing the total number that were analyzed down to 88 (Tables 11.1 and 11.2). The artifacts include a variety of tools, weapons, fasteners, and ornaments dating from the early third to early second millennium BC (Table 11.1). The major metal groups identified were copper (45 samples), arsenical copper or arsenic bronze (26), and tin bronze (13) (Table 11.3). In addition, one ring was made of unalloyed silver (99 wt% Ag), and three spiral pendants were composed of a copper core covered over with a very thin foil of electrum (no greater than 0.1 mm thick).

The copper alloys in the assemblage have been identified by the presence of arsenic or tin in levels greater than 1 wt% (Table 11.3). Whether arsenic bronze (copper + arsenic) was intentionally produced is often a question, since it may have been made intentionally by mixing arsenic minerals with copper and intentionally or unintentionally by smelting with high arsenic copper ores. For this reason, some researchers are reluctant to refer to this mixture as bronze and prefer the term *arsenical copper*. In Eurasian steppe archaeology, it is traditionally referred to as arsenic bronze, which is how it is referred to here. This does not preclude the possibility that some of it was made without the knowledge that the use of high arsenic ores would result in a material different from unalloyed copper.

Copper and Arsenic Bronze Objects from the EBA to LBA

Only six of the artifacts that were examined are from EBA-MBA Yamnaya or Yamnaya-Poltavka burials. These are the earliest items in the analyzed assemblage. They include the large copper staff from Kurgan 4, Grave 1 (male) at Kutuluk I (Yamnaya); a tanged, leaf-shaped copper knife and tetrahedral awl from Kurgan 1, Grave 3 (male) at Kutuluk III (Yamnaya-Poltavka); and three rings from Kurgan 2, Grave 4 (female) at Nur (Yamnaya-Poltavka) (Figures 11.2–11.4). The MBA I Poltavka period (ca. 2800–2100 BC) postdates the EBA Yamnaya (ca. 3300–2800 BC), and a Poltavka presence is often identifiable only through intrusive, secondary burials in Yamnaya kurgans. The chief distinction between Yamnaya and Yamnaya-Poltavka is the presence of Yamnaya or Poltavka ceramics, respectively. Steppe archaeologists therefore frequently use the ambiguous Yamnaya-Poltavka designation, as is used here for the rings from the woman's burial at Nur.

A Yamnaya object that appears to be of especially high social significance is the unique copper club from Grave 1, Kurgan 4 at Kutuluk I (Figure 11.2), the burial of an adult male dating to circa 2930 BC (Anthony 1998:103–104; Kuznetsov 2005), which has no known analogies in the steppes. It is 48 cm long and is made of 770 g of unalloyed copper and is by far the largest copper artifact known from the EBA in the Eurasian steppes. It was found cradled like a scepter in the left arm of the deceased, perhaps as a symbol of authority and status (Anthony 2008:Figure 13.8). It is very highly polished without visible use-wear, which also supports the interpretation of a symbolic and not a utilitarian function. There are a few worn-down, pearl-sized beads in the grip area, a characteristic shared by some shaft-hole axes of the period (Chernykh 1992:Figure 28.24). Similar "pearls" on some Yamnaya ceramics from the broader Volga-Ural region (Yamnaya ceramic Type A) are interpreted as skeuomorphs of rivets that occur in sheet-cauldrons of this period from the North Caucasus (Mochalov 2008). Riveted daggers also appear in the

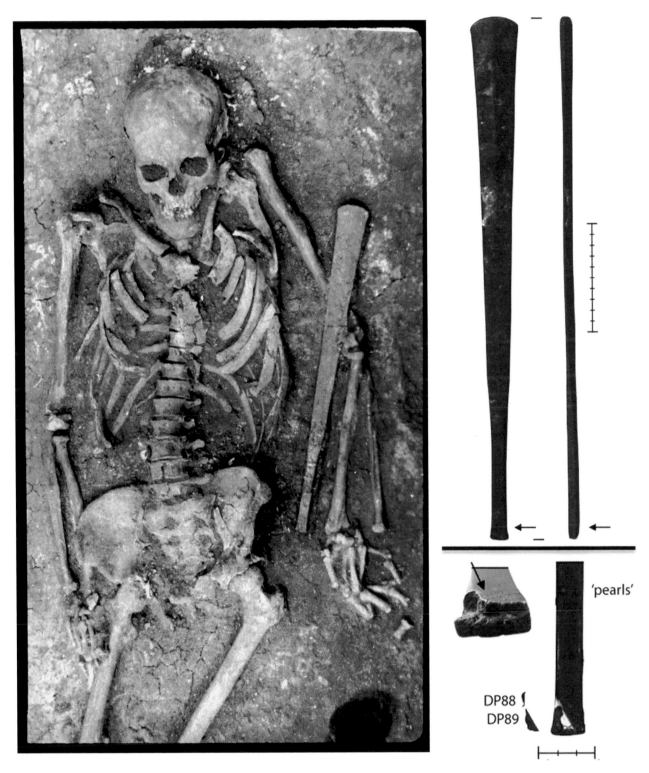

Figure 11.2 Kutuluk I, Kurgan 4, Grave 1. Copper club dimensions: 48.5 × 4.85 × 1.36 cm; weight 767 g. Bottom right image shows details of the grip. The right side shows the grip after removal of samples DP88 and DP89, also note the "pearls" at the top; the left side shows an end-on view of the base of the club. *Prepared by David Peterson*

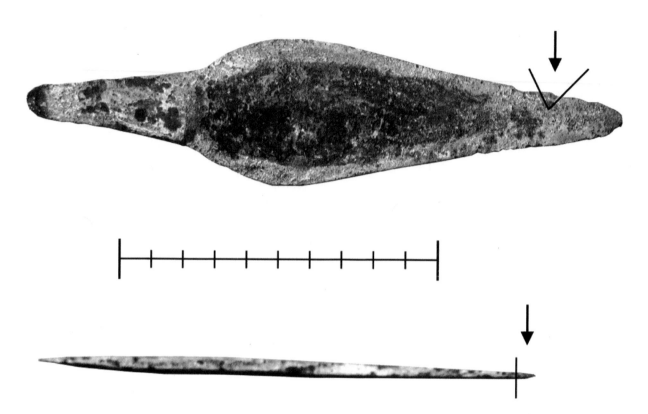

Figure 11.3 Above: The copper blade from Kutuluk III, Kurgan 1, Grave 2—dimensions: 18.0 × 4.4 × .35 cm; weight 69.4 g. Below: The copper awl from Kutuluk III, Kurgan 1, Grave 2 (tetrahedral section)—dimensions: 15.0 × 44 × .44 cm; weight 11.8 g. *Prepared by David Peterson*

Black Sea region at this time (Anthony 1996, 2008:317). Along with its unique form and the large amount of copper devoted to it, the faux rivets on the handle may have been meant to create an association with elite riveted metalwork from the Caucasus or Black Sea regions.

Based on the hypothesis that the people whose remains constitute the Yamnaya horizon had an Indo-Iranian language and culture, the excavator of the Kutuluk I burial, Pavel Kuznetzov (2005), has argued that the club is an Indo-Iranian symbol of power, emphasizing parallels between its shape and material and descriptions of the weapon of Indra in the Rig Veda, the *vajra*. There are signs of wear indicating the handle once had a covering, and in addition to its size and form, the bottom of the handle grip shows that it was cast in two pieces. One of the cast sections is shorter than the other, a flaw that would have been hidden by the original covering. The rest of the surface is seamless and has been carefully polished. This object is unique for the EBA. It is the among the innovations in metallurgy that appear in middle Volga Yamnaya assemblages, along with the granulated golden rings and iron-headed copper pin

from Utyevka I (Anthony 2007:Figure 13.9; Chernykh 1992:86; Vasil'iev 1980:38–42).

Altogether, there are 26 arsenic bronzes in the assemblage. The three rings from the woman's burial at Nur are rare examples of Yamnaya-Poltavka ornaments made of arsenic bronze, each with arsenic content from 1.5 to 2.5 wt%. Nineteen of the arsenic bronzes are from MBA II Potapovka period burials (ca. 2200–1800 BC) in the Potapovka I and Utyevka VI kurgan cemeteries (Vasil'iev et al. 1992, 1994). Arsenic reaches its highest level at 14 wt% in a knife from Kurgan 3, Grave 4 at Potapovka I. The remaining four arsenic bronzes that were analyzed are from LBA kurgan burials.

In a large assemblage of copper and arsenic bronze artifacts like this, there is usually a hiatus in arsenic values between those for bronzes and those for unalloyed copper. In contrast, in these results there is a nearly log-normal curve in the distribution of arsenic values in the assemblage as a whole, which joins the arsenic values for unalloyed copper and bronze in a continuous sequence, while the frequency becomes greater as the level of arsenic diminishes in unalloyed copper (Figure

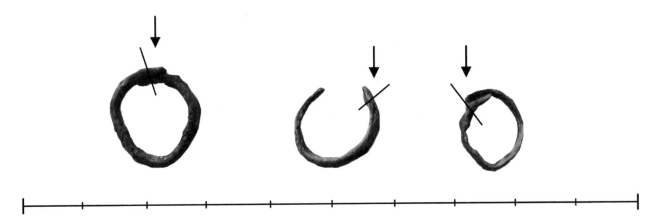

Figure 11.4 Arsenic bronze rings from Nur, Kurgan 2, Grave 4. Above left is Ring 1, (DP47): overall diameter 15.1 mm, width 4.2 mm, thickness 1.1 mm; weight 1.0 g. Ring 2, DP48 (above middle): overall diameter 14.8 mm, width 4.0 mm, thickness 1.1 mm; weight 0.6 g. Ring 3, DP49 (above right): overall diameter 13.1 mm, width 3.6 mm, thickness 0.9 mm; weight 1.0 g. Lines and arrows indicate where analyzed samples were removed. *Prepared by David Peterson*

11.5). This suggests frequent recycling and repeated mixture of copper and bronze with higher and lower levels of arsenic over an extended period, causing the concentration of arsenic in the overall pool of available metal to diminish to a very low level (Peterson 2007, 2009:198). This is especially true for the MBA II objects from the Potapovka I and Utyevka VI cemeteries, which account for 62 of 88 tested items, or over 70 percent of the analyzed assemblage.

Tin Bronzes from the MBA II and LBA

There are fewer tin bronzes than arsenic bronzes in the assemblage, only 17 in all. Five of the 17 tin bronzes are bracelets from MBA II Potapovka horizon burials; another is a knife from a Potapovka burial in Kurgan 8, Grave 8 at Grachevka II; and the other 11 are LBA ornaments (Tables 11.1–11.3).

Compared to the concentrations of arsenic in the samples that were analyzed, there is a sharper division between alloy levels of tin (greater than 1 wt%) and lower concentrations of tin in which it occurs only as an impurity. The level of tin in the tin bronzes varies from 3 to 15 wt% (Figure 11.6). This broad range of tin values in bronzes may be another indication of recycling practices in the MBA and LBA. However, tin bronze appears to have been recycled less frequently than arsenic bronze, creating a more disparate range of tin values as opposed to the nearly log-normal curve for arsenic concentrations. The lack of tin–arsenic bronze in the assemblage may indicate that metalworkers avoided mixing arsenic bronze and tin bronze together, another sign of a difference in the recycling practices for these two materials.

Copper Sources and Geographic Divisions in Metalworking

The WDS analysis provided little information about copper sources. This is not surprising given the evidence for recycling in the arsenic and tin values for these samples. Recycling tends to mix metal from different sources together, so that it is no longer possible to identify the particular sources that contributed the metal that made the individual artifacts. However, as discussed below, values for iron and antimony in the metalwork from Potapovka I and Utyevka VI have other implications for geographic divisions in metalworking during the MBA II period in the middle Volga. Previously, Agapov and Kuzminykh (1994) performed arc OES analysis of metalwork from Potapovka I to specific source groups. Due to the great difference between WDS and arc OES results, including the measurement of copper and normalization of the results with WDS but not arc OES, we do not attempt to resolve the results of the two methods. However, Agapov and Kuzminykh's arc OES results for Potapovka I are summarized below, with a brief explanation of the source groups to which they have assigned the objects.

Multivariate analysis of WDS values for elements besides copper showed the strongest correlation in concentrations of nickel and arsenic, which was quite weak (0.55). The scatterplot of values for nickel and arsenic shows groupings that vary between periods, and it appears that by the MBA II period, metalworkers were drawing from a greater variety of sources than earlier in the Bronze Age (Figure 11.7). Just what those sources were is not clear. Determining this would require

Table 11.3 Metal Groups Based on WDS Results for Major Elements

Sample	Object	Cu	As	Sn	Ag	Au	Metal Group
DP1	Knife	98.59	0.90	0.01	0.07	0.04	Cu
DP2	Bracelet	92.57	0.08	7.12	0.00	0.01	Cu+Sn
DP3	Knife	99.14	0.11	0.00	0.08	0.03	Cu
DP4	Knife	94.13	0.07	5.69	0.00	0.01	Cu+Sn
DP5	Bracelet	91.02	0.69	7.65	0.25	0.03	Cu+Sn
DP6	Bracelet	92.36	0.08	7.32	0.01	0.04	Cu+Sn
DP7	Bracelet	94.76	4.41	0.01	0.05	0.05	Cu+As
DP8	Cu piece	99.83	0.03	0.04	0.01	0.00	Cu
DP9	Knife	99.81	0.00	0.01	0.05	0.03	Cu
DP10	Tetrahedral awl	99.75	0.01	0.01	0.05	0.07	Cu
DP11	Knife	97.48	1.88	0.02	0.04	0.02	Cu+As
DP12	Knife	96.24	2.31	0.01	0.05	0.03	Cu+As
DP13	Knife	97.84	1.68	0.01	0.04	0.02	Cu+As
DP14	Sickle	99.18	0.27	0.02	0.07	0.01	Cu
DP15	Knife	96.31	1.45	0.01	0.04	0.03	Cu+As
DP16	Pendant	85.22	0.22	14.32	0.00	0.04	Cu+Sn
DP17	Pendant	88.92	0.02	10.05	0.01	0.04	Cu+Sn
DP18	Knife	99.47	0.13	0.02	0.04	0.01	Cu
DP19	Knife	97.25	1.76	0.01	0.05	0.05	Cu+As
DP20	Hook	97.85	1.12	0.01	0.06	0.00	Cu+As
DP21	Hook	97.19	2.05	0.01	0.04	0.06	Cu+As
DP22	Hook	98.52	0.94	0.00	0.04	0.06	Cu
DP23	Knife	99.37	0.15	0.01	0.02	0.02	Cu
DP24	Knife	99.38	0.16	0.01	0.02	0.05	Cu
DP25	Chisel	96.12	3.08	0.01	0.06	0.03	Cu+As
DP26	Mounted hook	99.54	0.00	0.02	0.29	0.02	Cu
DP27	Bracelet	90.59	0.50	8.57	0.00	0.01	Cu+Sn
DP28	Spearhead	97.40	1.82	0.00	0.02	0.04	Cu+As
DP29	Flat axe	95.47	3.27	0.02	0.04	0.00	Cu+As
DP30	Knife	99.16	0.13	0.01	0.05	0.04	Cu
DP31	Knife	99.73	0.01	0.00	0.12	0.05	Cu
DP32	Knife	99.10	0.39	0.01	0.06	0.03	Cu
DP33	Bracelet	87.25	0.02	12.50	0.00	0.05	Cu+Sn
DP34	Bracelet	86.58	0.05	13.11	0.00	0.03	Cu+Sn
DP40	Bracelet	85.18	0.18	14.58	0.00	0.00	Cu+Sn
DP41	Sheet ornament	96.17	0.17	3.04	0.01	0.03	Cu+Sn
DP44	Needle	99.15	0.03	0.00	0.07	0.01	Cu
DP45	Pendant	88.67	0.07	10.47	0.00	0.01	Cu+Sn
DP46	Bracelet	88.21	0.06	10.36	0.00	0.01	Cu+Sn
DP47	Ring	97.77	2.07	0.01	0.04	0.02	Cu+As
DP48	Ring	97.80	2.04	0.01	0.06	0.01	Cu+As
DP49	Ring	97.89	1.99	0.01	0.01	0.01	Cu+As
DP50	Clamp	98.92	0.56	0.00	0.03	0.00	Cu
DP51	Clamp	99.33	0.29	0.00	0.06	0.00	Cu
DP52	Clamp	99.53	0.17	0.01	0.02	0.01	Cu
DP53	Sheet ornament	99.09	0.34	0.01	0.02	0.04	Cu
DP54	Sheet ornament	99.57	0.02	0.08	0.03	0.03	Cu
DP55	Sheet ornament	99.59	0.03	0.06	0.02	0.02	Cu

Sample	Object	Cu	As	Sn	Ag	Au	Metal Group
DP56	Knife	96.21	2.65	0.00	0.02	0.03	Cu+As
DP57	Blade	99.81	0.01	0.01	0.09	0.01	Cu
DP58	Blade	99.79	0.01	0.01	0.10	0.02	Cu
DP59	Knife	99.79	0.00	0.01	0.07	0.02	Cu
DP60	Knife	98.87	0.56	0.01	0.06	0.06	Cu
DP61	Blade	99.08	0.15	0.01	0.06	0.01	Cu
DP62	Knife	99.10	0.15	0.01	0.04	0.03	Cu
DP63	Spatula	96.89	2.32	0.01	0.05	0.05	Cu+As
DP64	Blade	96.82	2.51	0.01	0.08	0.00	Cu+As
DP65	Blade	98.70	0.09	0.01	0.02	0.00	Cu
DP66	Mounted hook	98.55	0.08	0.01	0.02	0.01	Cu
DP67	Mounted hook	99.50	0.18	0.01	0.17	0.04	Cu
DP68	Flat axe	97.78	1.42	0.01	0.06	0.02	Cu+As
DP69	Knife	99.13	0.10	0.00	0.14	0.05	Cu
DP70	Flat axe	99.41	0.12	0.00	0.02	0.02	Cu
DP71	Knife	98.80	0.26	0.00	0.11	0.03	Cu
DP72	Knife	99.69	0.06	0.01	0.10	0.03	Cu
DP73	Awl	97.46	1.69	0.01	0.06	0.02	Cu+As
DP74	Awl	98.21	1.36	0.01	0.05	0.01	Cu+As
DP75	Awl	98.54	0.65	0.01	0.10	0.03	Cu
DP76	Awl	99.74	0.05	0.00	0.11	0.01	Cu
DP77	Mini flat-axe	98.87	0.64	0.01	0.03	0.03	Cu
DP78	Knife	99.03	0.32	0.00	0.01	0.02	Cu
DP79	Awl	95.34	3.98	0.08	0.05	0.02	Cu+As
DP80	Awl	97.27	1.97	0.01	0.06	0.04	Cu+As
DP81	Needle	99.60	0.03	0.01	0.01	0.03	Cu
DP82	Needle	96.84	1.96	0.08	0.05	0.02	Cu+As
DP83	Needle	97.53	0.91	0.00	0.03	0.00	Cu(+Fe)
DP84	Awl	99.84	0.01	0.00	0.08	0.01	Cu
DP85	Awl	94.69	4.52	0.01	0.05	0.02	Cu+As
DP86	Awl	99.79	0.01	0.01	0.08	0.03	Cu
DP87	Awl	98.55	0.15	0.01	0.06	0.04	Cu
DP88	Staff	99.75	0.01	0.00	0.12	0.03	Cu
DP89	Staff	99.76	0.01	0.01	0.12	0.02	Cu
DP90	Blade	84.83	13.89	0.01	0.35	0.03	Cu+As
DP91	Knife	96.70	2.48	0.01	0.07	0.03	Cu+As
DP92/core	Pendant	99.32	0.00	0.30	0.04	0.00	Cu
DP92/foil	Pendant	1.53	0.00	0.00	68.83	29.29	Au+Ag[+Cu]
DP93	Pendant	1.75	0.01	0.00	76.09	21.86	Au+Ag[+Cu]
DP93/inner	Pendant	1.33	0.02	0.00	78.33	20.12	Au+Ag[+Cu]
DP93/mid	Pendant	1.94	0.00	0.00	57.21	40.76	Au+Ag[+Cu]
DP93/outer	Pendant	1.97	0.01	0.00	67.18	30.79	Au+Ag[+Cu]
DP94	Pendant	60.71	0.02	0.01	36.25	2.72	Au+Ag[+Cu]
DP94/inner	Pendant	2.27	0.00	0.00	24.40	73.29	Au+Ag[+Cu]
DP94/outer	Pendant	1.62	0.00	0.00	94.62	3.55	Au+Ag[+Cu]
DP95	Ring	0.59	0.24	0.00	98.95	0.03	Ag

Note: Cu = copper; Cu+Sn = tin bronze; Cu+As = arsenic bronze; Au+Ag = electrum; Ag = silver.

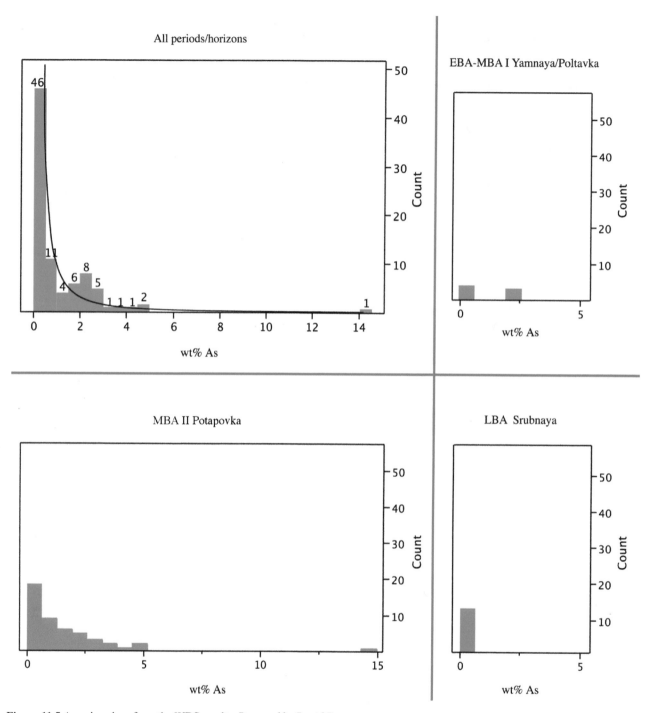

Figure 11.5 Arsenic values from the WDS results. *Prepared by David Peterson*

sampling and analysis of ores from major deposits with an effective technique of source discrimination, such as lead isotope analysis, as well as its application to the artifact samples. Using LIA to match objects to sources would also require that the samples were made up of copper and bronze from discrete sources and that recycled metal from different sources was not mixed together in the same artifacts.

LIA was not pursued due to the indications of recycling in the WDS data, with the possibility of the mixture of metals from different sources in individual artifacts.[2]

Nonetheless, an interesting pattern appears in the bivariate plot of iron and antimony concentrations from the WDS results for the metalwork from the Potapovka I and Utyevka VI kurgan cemeteries (MBA II). There is

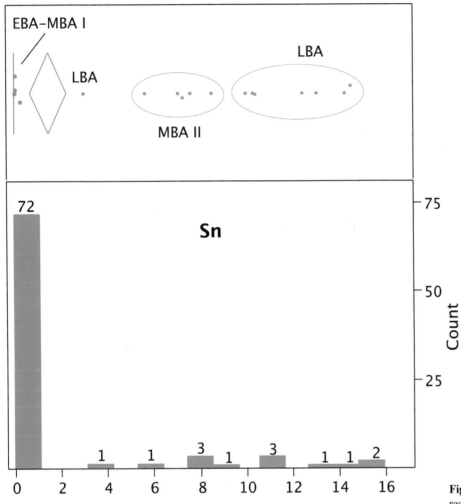

Figure 11.6 Tin values from the WDS results. *Prepared by David Peterson*

a tendency toward higher iron and lower antimony in the samples from Potapovka I and higher antimony and lower iron in those from Utyevka VI (Figure 11.8). These differences in iron and antimony content may indicate that people who made these objects drew from separate, local pools of recycled metal. They may have lived in separate communities of mobile pastoralists, one that dwelled in the Sok River valley and the other in the Samara Valley in which the Potapovka I and Utyevka VI cemeteries are respectively situated (Peterson 2009). As Figure 11.8 shows, there is some overlap in the iron and antimony values in both sets of artifacts. This may mean that they drew from the same variety of sources with different frequency or that metalworkers in the Potapovka area occasionally got metal from the Utyevka area and added it to their own local supply, or vice versa.

Agapov and Kuzminykh (1994) performed arc OES analyses of 48 objects from the Potapovka I. They identified

31 objects made of unalloyed copper (~65 percent of the assemblage), 13 made of arsenic bronze (~27 percent), and four made of tin bronze (~8 percent). They assigned the 48 objects to five chemical groups previously defined by Chernykh (1970), which are summarized in English by Peterson (2007:253–265). These groups are Elenovka-Ushkatta (EU), a small group of sources between the Ural and Tobol Rivers in western Kazakhstan (two objects from Potapovka I); Tashkazgan (TK), a high-arsenic copper ore deposit east of the confluence of the Ural and Belaya Rivers, which was a key source of arsenic bronze (19 objects); sources in the Volga-Kama (VK) (9 objects), which in Agapov and Kuzminykh's estimation supplied all of the tin bronze among the 48 objects they tested from Potapovka I ($n = 4$); copper sandstones (MP) like those encountered in Kamyshla that are discussed below (8 objects); and unidentified source(s) in the Volga-Ural (VU) that were used to make 3 objects.[3] Another seven objects were identified as

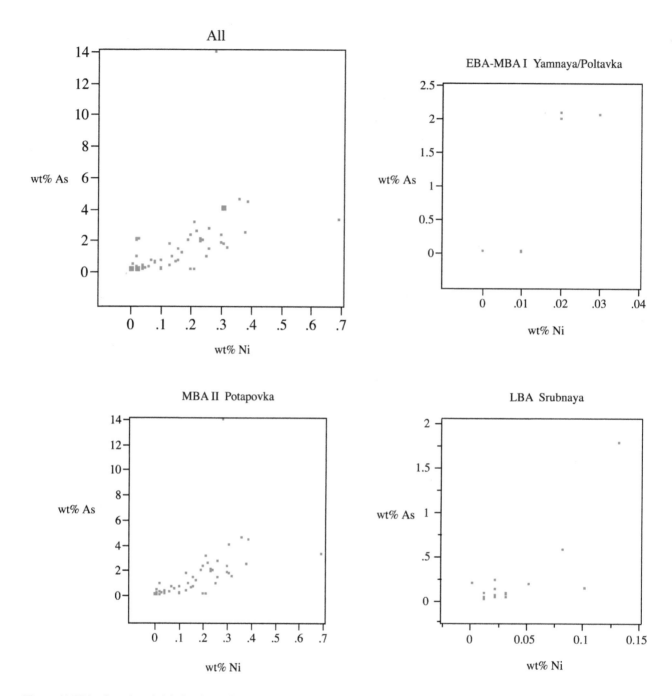

Figure 11.7 Bivariate plot of nickel and arsenic values from the WDS results. *Prepared by David Peterson*

probably made using ores from these sources—three with ore from the MP group, two from VU, one from EU, and one using ore from TK. They do not discuss why some artifacts may be confidently assigned to specific source groups, while others may not.

It is notable that VK is the sole source for tin bronze that they identify as having been used to make the Potapovka metalwork. TK and VK are the main source groups they identify for high arsenic copper and arsenic bronze; Chernykh (1970) distinguished TK from VK metal by the higher levels of iron in VK copper and bronze compared to TK. The VU and MP groups both encompass the kinds of ores found in the Kargaly district. However, MP cupric sandstones occur elsewhere in the steppes besides the Volga-Ural, including the Don Basin, and it has not been possible to discriminate the sandstone ores from

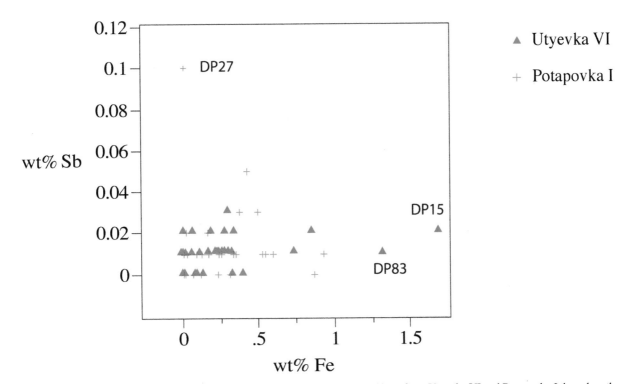

Figure 11.8 Bivariate plot of iron and antimony values in copper and bronze artifacts from Utyevka VI and Potapovka I, based on the WDS results. *Prepared by David Peterson*

different regions by arc OES analysis (Chernykh 1970, 1992). Agapov and Kuzminykh assign about two-thirds of the arsenic bronzes in the assemblage that they tested to Tashkazgan (*n* = 9) and about one-third to the Volga-Kama (*n* = 4).

Previous arc OES analyses do not directly address which source(s) of tin were used for tin bronze, even if the tin was mixed with copper from the Volga-Kama as Agapov and Kuzminykh concluded. It has become increasingly apparent that the Kalba-Narym formation in eastern Kazakhstan is host to one of the oldest known tin mining centers in the world. Its proximity to the Volga-Ural steppes makes Kalba-Narym a chief candidate as the source of the tin found in bronze from the MBA II and LBA in Samara. Chernikov (1949) was the first to suspect Kalba-Narym's importance as an early tin-mining region; he identified at least six deposits that were worked in the remote past, perhaps by LBA Andronovo miners (Chernikov 1949; Stöllner et al. 2011:Figure 2). Recently, evidence of early tin mining in Kalba-Narym has been greatly augmented by the investigation of four Andronovo tin mining complexes by the Deutsches Bergbau-Museum's (DBM's) Kazakhstan project (Stöllner et al. 2011). At one of these, Askaraly II, the project encountered a cemetery and settlement (Mastau Baj) affiliated with the Andronovo-Federovka culture; the

settlement not only contained hammer stones like the mines in the area but also a casting spoon and crucible fragments used in tin metallurgy (Stöllner et al. 2011:235–245). The DBM team performed LIA on 16 tin and tin bronze artifacts from the surrounding region. The results indicate that the geological age of the lead in the artifacts from Kazakhstan matches the Cambrian and early Paleozoic age of the Kalba-Narym formation (Stöllner et al. 2011:247–247, Figure 18). Sources in eastern Kazakhstan probably contributed much if not all of the tin used during the Bronze Age in the middle Volga, but it remains to be shown whether the isotopic profiles of middle Volga tin bronzes match those of the Kalba-Narym deposits or of deposits in other areas (Bulgaria, Anatolia, and the Aegean) in which LIA has been performed on ores, ancient slags, and metalwork (Pernicka 1995; Pernicka et al. 2003).

Metallographic Results and Work Patterns in MBA II Objects

Metallographic examination of the samples was facilitated by micrographs taken of the etched surfaces of each at 75× to 750 magnification, to observe microstructures that are diagnostic of particular working techniques and the combinations in which they were applied in fabricating the objects, the *chaîne opératoire* (Gosselain 1992;

Soressi and Geneste 2011) of early metalworking in the middle Volga. The metallographic observations are summarized in the Appendix (end of chapter).

Metallography is a means of identifying the techniques used to make ancient metalwork that are not accessible through compositional analysis alone (Northover 1989; Scott 1991) and is the method that Ryndina (1998) and Ryndina and Ravich (1987) used to show that metalworking was already practiced in the middle Volga no later than 4500 BC. However, metallographic data are complex and are therefore summarized here in terms of patterns in the combinations of metalworking techniques used to make the objects, which we refer to as work patterns. In this way it was possible to group the samples into four basic work patterns (WPs) (Peterson 2007, 2009; Figure 11.9):

1. WP 1: objects that were cast, then lightly cold-worked (rare, encountered in only one sample or ~1 percent of the assemblage)
2. WP 2: objects that were cast, then cold-worked, annealed (heated to a temperature below the melting point of the metal but high enough and for a duration long enough to recrystallize it, thereby restoring its malleability for further cold-working), and cold-worked after they had been annealed (42 samples or ~52 percent of the assemblage)
3. WP 3: objects that went through the same three steps as WP 2 but in the end were more heavily cold-worked than WP 2, resulting in crystal grains that appear flat or "feathered" (34 samples or ~41 percent of the total)
4. WP 4: objects with a structure of small crystals in comparison to the others, possibly as a result of numerous alternating bouts of cold-work and annealing (infrequent, only four samples or ~5 percent of the assemblage)

The sole example of WP 1 is a knife from Grave 8 at the Grachevka II cemetery (Figure 11.10), associated with the MBA II Potapovka horizon (ca. 2100–1800 BC). This knife is made of a medium tin bronze (5.7 wt% Sn) that is now highly corroded. The form is a one-sided blade with a straight back, which is unusual for the MBA II in Samara. This form also occurs during the same period in Sintashta graves in western Siberia (Gening et al. 1992:Figure 153.20) but is more typical of the LBA in the eastern Urals (Chernykh 1992:Figure 82.14, 82.16). This was the only sample in the assemblage that showed no sign of appreciable working or annealing and may be a ceremonial object or an unworked "blank." It should be noted that through their placement in burials, all of the objects discussed here are ceremonial. However, the Grachevka knife may be more strictly ceremonial in the sense that in addition to being a funerary object, it was not worked in a way that would have made it effective for practical use.

In addition to the tin-bronze knife, four more samples from knives were examined from Grachevka II, three copper and one arsenic bronze. All were worked with WP 2 except for one of the copper knives, which was fabricated with WP 3.

There were 21 samples (~26 percent of the assemblage) that showed residual coring or retention of a "ghost" of the as-cast structure before the object was worked and annealed, indicating that these objects were not annealed to the point that complete recrystallization occurred. Twelve of the samples with residual coring are unalloyed copper, six are arsenic bronze, and only two are tin bronze (Peterson 2007:Table 7.5). Out of a combined total of 44 objects made of arsenic or tin bronze, only ~18 percent (n = 8) show such coring; in comparison, ~27 percent (n = 12) exhibit this characteristic in the unalloyed copper artifacts.

The variation in the occurrence of residual coring in copper and bronze objects suggests that the metalworkers that made them took greater care in annealing bronze than copper, even though it took more effort to do so. The typical bronze must be heated up to 500°C for one hour for complete recrystallization to occur. In contrast, the temperature for annealing unalloyed copper in one hour is only about 200°C (Scott 1991:7). From a production standpoint, there is no obvious cost savings in annealing bronze more thoroughly than copper. This tendency in annealing practices may have been associated with the relative importance placed on the materials themselves and the artifacts made with them, in which greater care was taken in working bronze than copper.

The MBA II objects that were analyzed include the majority of the metalwork from Potapovka I and Utyevka VI. Samples from a combined total of 60 artifacts were examined from these cemeteries. Fifty-six were fashioned with WP 2 and WP 3 and only four with WP 4 (~5 percent). Samples from nearly the same number of objects were examined from Potapovka I (n = 29) and Utyevka VI (n = 30), but there is a notable difference in the frequency of WP 2 and WP 3 (Figure 11.11). The number of samples from Potapovka I that were made with WP 2 is 18, while only 9 were made with WP 3. The opposite is true for Utyevka VI, where the majority of objects were made using WP 3 (n = 19) and fewer with WP 2 (n = 10).

As shown above, metalworkers shared a *chaîne opératoire* and performed the same basic sequence of operations in making the metalwork from both cemeteries. The work patterns differ chiefly in the final stage of cold-working,

1. Cored dendritic crystals of an as-cast copper or bronze, as shown in 1, below.

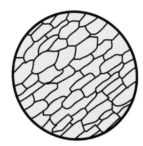

2. Deformed equiaxed grains resulting from annealing followed by cold working, as shown in 2, below.

3. Twinned grains produced by annealing a previously recrystallized and cold worked copper or bronze, as shown in 3, below.

4. Deformed grains with bent twins and strain lines, from heavily cold working a previously cold worked and annealed copper or bronze, as shown in 4, below.

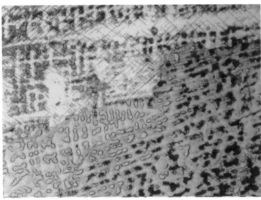

1. WP 1, as-cast (tin bronze knife, Grachevka II, kurgan 8, grave 8, 300x).

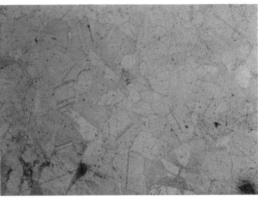

2. WP 2, annealed and light-to-moderately cold worked (tin bronze pendant, Spiridonovka II, kurgan 2, grave 14, 300x).

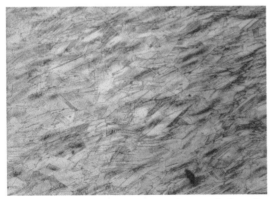

3. WP 3, annealed, cold worked, annealed, and heavily cold worked (arsenic bronze knife, Utevka VI, kurgan 6, grave 4, 300x).

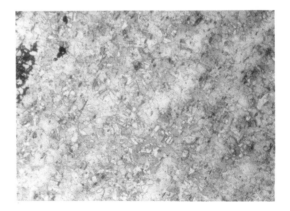

4. WP 4, small grains from multiple bouts of heavy working and annealing (tin bronze knife, Potapovka I, kurgan 1, grave 4, 300x).

Figure 11.9 Work patterns in Bronze Age metalwork from the middle Volga based on metallographic observations. *Prepared by David Peterson*

Figure 11.10 The tin bronze blade from Grachevka II, Kurgan 8, Grave 8—dimensions: 9.2 × 2.9 × .30 cm; weight 20.8 g. *Prepared by David Peterson*

which was performed more heavily in finishing the objects from Utyevka VI than Potapovka I. The preference for heavy final cold-working among the metalworkers that made the Utyevka VI assemblage suggests that the metalwork from the two cemeteries was made by different groups of artisans. The differences in the networks involved in acquiring raw materials for the objects from these sites were accompanied by this variation in metalworking practices. The metallographic results support the hypothesis of local metalworking proposed earlier from the results of the WDS analysis. Perhaps the people who made these

pieces belonged to separate bands of herders in the areas in which the cemeteries are respectively situated, with those who made the metalwork from Potapovka I dwelling in the Sok Valley and those who made the pieces from Utyevka VI in the Samara Valley.

There are more than twice as many arsenic bronzes among the metalwork from Utyevka VI ($n = 15$) than Potapovka I ($n = 7$). Arsenic bronze is more malleable than unalloyed copper and therefore more conducive to heavy cold-working, which appears more frequently in the pieces from Utyevka VI than Potapovka I. Utyevka VI is

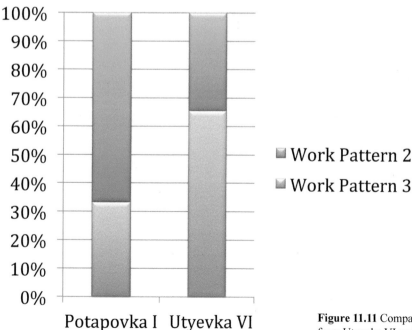

Figure 11.11 Comparison of work patterns present in metalwork from Utyevka VI and Potapovka I. *Prepared by David Peterson*

near the Samara River, which begins in the South Urals near Kargaly, the largest mining and metallurgical center in operation during the Bronze Age in the Volga-Ural steppes. Kargaly lies between Utyevka and Tashkazgan, which Agapov and Kuzminykh (1994) identified as the key source of arsenic bronze during the MBA II period in the middle Volga. In Chapter 1, Anthony argues that raw materials for metalworking, including arsenic bronze, may have been shipped by raft down the Samara River from the South Urals to the middle Volga. If so, it is possible that arsenic bronze or high-arsenic ores from Tashkazgan may have been imported first to Kargaly, then shipped down the Samara River to the area around Utyevka. Perhaps only a portion were ported later by horse, by cart, or on foot to the vicinity of Potapovka I along the Sok River to the north of Utyevka VI. If metalworkers in the Utyevka area had greater access to arsenic bronze than those who dwelled near Potapovka I, it would help to explain why more than twice as many arsenic bronzes occur in Utyevka VI than in Potapovka I. It might also explain why there is a tendency for heavier final cold-working at Utyevka VI, since it is easier to cold-work arsenic bronze than unalloyed copper even if greater effort is needed to anneal arsenic bronze in the process.

Gilding Practices in LBA Srubnaya Ornaments

Three spiral ornaments with copper cores covered with gold-colored foil were recovered from burials in the Nizhny Orleansky and Spiridonovka II kurgan cemeteries. Like Krasnosamarskoe and Peschanyi Dol 1 and 2, these graves date to the LBA I period (Figure 11.12).

Spiridonovka II is reputed to be the richest Srubnaya cemetery in the Volga-Ural region, with good reason. Kurgan 1, located just a few meters northeast of the Kurgan 2 grave described here, contained four rich Srubnaya graves among a total of 13 that were excavated. Grave 1 in Kurgan 1 contained weapons (a dagger and a set of 12 lanceolate projectile points) and a bone clasp or belt ornament. Grave 2 contained faience beads that were probably imported from south of the steppes and numerous bronze bracelets, beads, and pendants, including a pair of long, dangling earrings made of leaf-like sets of pendants arranged in three rows. Grave 7 contained a bronze bracelet, ring, and bead, while Grave 13 contained 16 tubular bronze beads and eight bronze medallions.

While the bronze ornaments from Kurgan 1 at Spiridonovka II were not analyzed, samples from one gold-covered pendant from Kurgan 2 at Spiridonovka II and two more from another early Srubnaya cemetery

at Nizhny Orleansky were obtained for WDS analysis. Analysis of a section through the objects, which is rarely done with Bronze Age gold ornaments from the Eurasian steppes, was performed at Oxford Materials. This showed that the very thin foil covering each object (less than 0.1 mm thick) was made of a mixture of silver and gold known as electrum. Variable enrichment of gold and silver occurs through the section of the foil on each object, which is noteworthy given the high intersolubility of gold and silver.

The pendants from Nizhny Orleansky are from Kurgan 3, Grave 8 (Table 11.1). In the first pendant examined from Nizhny Orleansky (DP92; Figure 11.12, top left), the WDS analysis found that the core was composed of 99 wt% copper. Multiple analyses were not performed along the section of the foil around it. Analyses were done near the inner surface, the center, and the outer surface of the foil in the second pendant from this grave (DP93; Figure 11.12, top center). Gold content varied from about 20 to 40 wt% and was lowest on the inside, highest in the middle, and about 30 wt% near the outside or about the same as the first pendant (Table 11.2). This variation in concentrations of gold was interesting but not remarkable.

The gold foil–covered pendant from Spiridonovka II is from Kurgan 2, Grave 29. Aleksandr Khokhlov determined that this is the burial of a child about 12 years of age, probably a girl. A high proportion of graves in the Spiridonovka II cemetery are of children, and this is a particularly ostentatious example. The 12-year-old was also buried with a copper-bronze bracelet (DP35 in Table 11.1), but it was too corroded for effective analysis. Out of the three ornaments that were analyzed, WDS revealed that the greatest variation in concentrations of silver and gold occur in the foil covering this pendant. It contained 73 wt% gold and 24 wt% silver at the outer surface but was composed of about 95 wt% silver and 4 wt% gold further inside the section.[4] These WDS results suggested that the outer surface of the foil might have been artificially enriched to create the appearance of gold. This is the first time evidence of such enrichment had been found in Early Srubnaya gold work. One of the reasons may be that this is one of the few times that a sample from a gold artifact dating to the Bronze Age from the Eurasian steppes has been analyzed in section.

When it was first detected by WDS, it appeared that the variable concentration of silver and gold through the foil on the Spiridonovka II pendant might have been the product of diffusion bonding (Peterson 2007; Peterson and Khatchadourian 2006). According to Oddy (2000:4–5), diffusion bonding appeared in the Old World by 1200 BC. That is only a few centuries after the Spiridonovka II pendant, which might have been an early example. However,

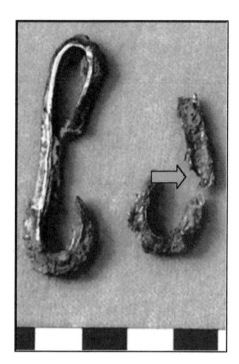
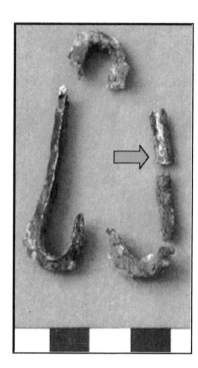

Figure 11.12 Top: Pendants from Nizhny Orleansky, Kurgan 3, Grave 8 (left and center) and Spiridonovka II, Kurgan 2, Grave 29. The arrows indicate areas sampled for analysis. Bottom: The Spiridonovka II pendant. One of the two loops was broken from the pendant before it was buried. The analyzed section was removed from the fragment to the right. *Prepared by David Peterson*

through subsequent examination, it appeared instead that it might have been fabricated using depletion gilding. Depletion gilding was developed before diffusion bonding and has been identified before the first millennium BC in only a few objects from the Royal Cemetery of the Ur I dynasty, circa 2600 BC (Hauptmann et al. 2010; La Niece 1995).

Recently, the samples from the Spiridonovka II and Nizhny Orleansky ornaments were reexamined at Idaho State University by Peterson, Dr. John Dudgeon, and Monica Tromp, using scanning electron microscopy with energy dispersive spectrometry (SEM-EDS) at the CAMAS laboratory (Lobell 2013; Peterson et al. 2012). For all three pendants, the dimensions of the samples in section were about 3.75 × 3.75 mm. Using EDS element mapping, spectral data were collected for each pixel point in the scanned areas, for quantification and imaging of the relative proportion of elements at any point. This made it possible to visualize the concentrations of gold in the foils on each pendant.

Surface enrichment of gold is clearly present in the pendant from Spiridonovka II (Figure 11.13). The thickness of the foil that covered the Spiridonovka pendant was about 50 μm. The foil was placed over an unalloyed copper core. EDS showed that the uncorroded remains of the core are composed of 99.79 percent copper and 0.21 percent iron. The EDS element mapping revealed that the foil shows significant enrichment of gold and depletion of silver from the surface to a depth of 5 μm.

It is unlikely that the surface enrichment of the Spiridonovka II ornament is due to postdepositional corrosion (Scott 1983). Scanning electron microscopy revealed that while the interior edge of the foil has been eaten away where it has been in contact with the heavily corroded copper core, the surface face is coherent. The surface is not heavily cracked or pitted and appears to be more compressed than the interior crystals in the foil (Figure 11.13), which may be the result of burnishing after depletion gilding had been performed. Silver depletion and gold enrichment are not present along the corroded interior surface of the foil as might be expected if postdepositional corrosion was the cause. The surface enrichment was more likely caused by technical manipulation, probably as a result of depletion gilding through

Gold-enriched surface zone (65.64 wt% gold, 28.34 wt% silver)

Silver-rich foil (90.47 wt% silver, 5.57 wt% gold)

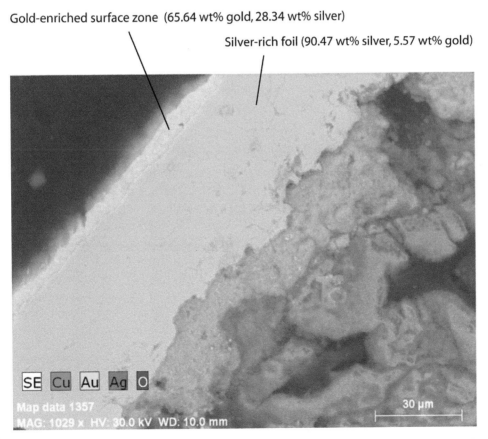

Figure 11.13 SEM-EDS element map of the Spiridonovka II girl's pendant. The gold-enriched zone (represented in yellow) extends to a depth of 5 μm from the surface. The foil covering the pendant is 50 m thick, including the gold-enriched surface zone. Except for the gold-enriched surface, the foil is composed mostly of silver (represented in pink). *Prepared by David Peterson*

a process of either cementation or cold corrosion as described by Lechtman (1973 and elsewhere) and summarized by La Niece (1995). The lack of a more gradual gradient at the transition between the gold-enriched surface and interior of the foil suggests that gold enrichment in the foil on this pendant was the result of a cold corrosion process.

The pattern of gold enrichment in the foil on the two Nizhny Orleansky pendants is much different than the one from Spiridonovka II. The gold-enriched zone in the foil on the Nizhny Orleansky pendants is in the interior of the foil and not at the outer surface and would not have been visible like the gold-enriched surface of the pendant from Spiridonovka II. The foils on the Nizhny Orleansky pendants contain less than 50 wt% gold and are higher in silver content than in gold. There is no substantive literature on the decoration of Bronze Age ornaments with silver foil to compare with these. Could they represent a failed attempt at depletion gilding?

Recently, Dr. Zihua Zhu at the Environmental Molecular Science Laboratory in Richland, Washington, worked with Peterson on nanoscale secondary ion mass spectrometry (nano-SIMS) analysis of the interface between gold- and silver-rich layers in the foils covering these pendants. The results support the previous findings and will be the topic of an upcoming publication devoted to the evidence for depletion gilding in these ornaments.

LBA Copper Production in the Samara Oblast

Metal occurred at all of the LBA sites investigated by the Samara Valley Project (SVP). The Kamyshla survey that was carried out as the first stage of the SAM project obtained evidence for LBA copper mining in the Ural foothills near the northeastern border of the Samara oblast (Peterson 2007; Peterson et al. 2006). We consider this evidence below against the background of the much more intensive LBA mining in the Kargaly ore field, which, as noted above, was well situated for the export of arsenic bronze or high-arsenic ore from Tashkazgan to the middle Volga.

The Samara Valley Project

The Peschanyi Dol (PD) 1 site produced one small scrap of a bent fragment of copper-bronze sheet metal. It was in a secondary erosion deposit in slopewash derived from a Srubnaya activity area that occurred somewhere uphill from the excavation in the north portion of PD1.

The PD2 site produced a small bubbly lump of melted copper-bronze. It was relatively dense, with the green patina of copper oxide, and was probably the by-product of an activity such as casting or forging. This is surprising to find at a herding camp. Perhaps bits of copper were routinely carried for remelting and casting, small exchanges, or even as charms. One small lump may have been dropped and lost at PD2. A single event of metalworking could have been carried out at PD2, and this may be a by-product.

At Krasnosamarskoe, more metallic and metalliferous artifacts were found totaling 31 pieces (Table 11.4 and Figure 11.14). These included small crushed fragments of ore (azurite and sandstone ore with what Russians describe as an "iron hat" of red ferric minerals); a few scraps of broken copper implements, including two awl fragments and a copper staple of the type used to repair Srubnaya pottery vessels; and about a dozen bubbly cuprous objects. These were not available for analysis. These may be slag or drops of casting spill, possibly from recycling objects like the broken awls and staple. The staple was previously analyzed by SEM-EDS and is composed of unalloyed copper (Anthony et al. 2005). The inventory of metallic objects from Krasnosamarskoe (Table 11.4) indicates that all phases of metallurgy, from ore crushing to smelting and metalworking, occurred somewhere at the site.

If any of these activities actually occurred in the excavated structure at Krasnosamarskoe, we would expect to see more evidence for that activity. For example, if ore crushing occurred in the structure, we would expect to see many more pieces and larger and more varied sizes. It seems more probable that these small bits came from an activity area elsewhere at the site, perhaps now under the lake or near Area Y, where all phases of metalworking may have been performed. The metallic objects are small enough that many could have been accidentally carried to the structure in shoes or clothing, or perhaps they were included in trash intentionally dumped in refuse pits in the structure. In either case, it is interesting that the metallic bits were distributed in a complementary, largely nonoverlapping spatial distribution at either end of the main concentration of animal bones. The central animal bone deposit, located between Pits 10, 14, 18, and 22, was in the center of the structure. The discard of metallic objects occurred at either end of the structure, northeast and southwest of the central concentration of animal bones. Whether discard was accidental or intentional is not clear. Perhaps the symbolic associations of the sacral animal remains and metalworking required that they be disposed of separately, or perhaps coat-shaking metalworkers avoided walking over the central animal bone deposit.

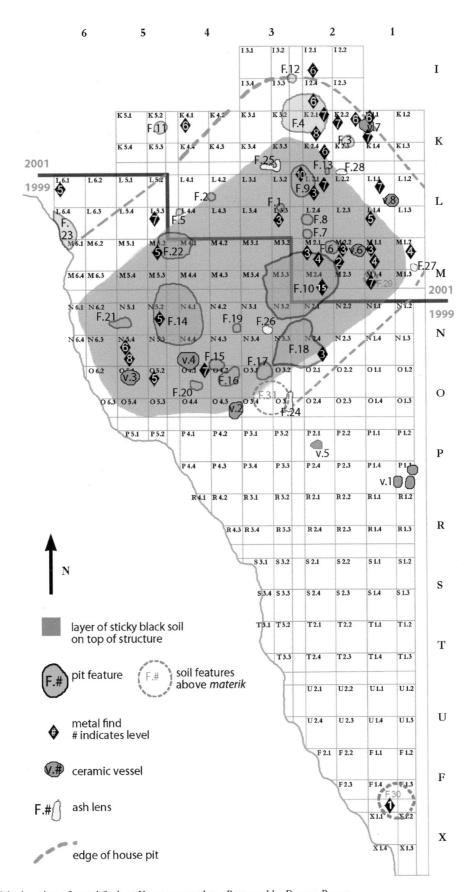

Figure 11.14 Plan of the location of metal finds at Krasnosamarskoe. *Prepared by Dorcas Brown*

Table 11.4 Metal Finds Recovered from Krasnosamarskoe by Unit and Level

Number	Year	Excavation Unit	Level	Description
1	1999	F1.3	1	Gorodetskaya iron bloom
2	2001	I 2.1	6	Copper ore
3	2001	I2.4	6	Copper/bronze fragment
4	2001	K 2	8	Copper ore
5	2001	K 2.3	6	Copper ore
6	2001	K 2.4	6	Bronze awl
7	2001	K1?	*Materik*	Azurite
8	2001	K2.1	7	Copper ore
9	2001	K2.2	6	Copper/bronze slag
10	2001	K2.2	7	Copper ore
11	2001	K2.2	7	Copper/bronze slag
12	2001	K4.1	6	Copper/bronze awl fragment
13	2001	L 2	1	Copper ore
14	2001	L1.1	7	Azurite
15	2001	L1.4	5	Copper/bronze slag
16	2001	L2.1	3	Copper/bronze slag
17	2001	L2.1	7	Azurite
18	2001	L2.1	10	Copper/bronze slag
19	2001	L2.3	1	Iron slag?
20	2001	L3.3	3	Copper ore
21	1999	L5.3	7	Copper/bronze staple
22	1999	L6.1	5	Bronze Sauromatian arrowhead
23	2001	M 2.4	15	Iron ore in Pit 10 at 150 cm b.s.
24	2001	M1.2	4	Copper/bronze slag
25	2001	M1.4	7	Copper ore
26	2001	M2.1	3	Copper/bronze slag
27	2001	M2.1	4	Copper/bronze slag
28	2001	M2.2	2	Copper/bronze slag
29	2001	M2.2	3	Copper/bronze slag
30	1999	N2.4	3	Iron fragment
31	1999	N5.2	5	Bronze awl
32	1999	N5.4	6	Copper/bronze fragment
33	1999	N5.4	8	Copper ore
34	1999	O3-4/N3-4	2	Iron fragments
35	1999	O4.1	7	Copper ore with iron "hat"
36	2000	PD1 B4.1	4	Copper/bronze fragment
37	2000	PD1 ZH30.4	3	Copper/bronze fragment

The Samara Ancient Metals Project

In addition to what is known from Krasnosamarskoe and Peschanyi Dol, in the summer of 2001, a crew of staff and students from Samara State University, Samara State Pedagogical University, Institute for the History and Archaeology of the Volga (IHAV), and the University of Chicago conducted a field survey under the direction of Peterson, Pavel Kuznetsov, and Oleg Mochalov near the upper Sok River in the Kamyshla *raion* (district) of northeastern Samara (Figure 11.1). In the eighteenth century, early researchers identified ancient workings in this area, near the modern villages of Staroe Ermakovo, Chuvashkii Baitugan, and Novoe Usmanovo (Lepekhin 1795; Pallas 1773). Geologists now count it as one of only two copper ore–bearing regions in Samara (N. Nebritov, personal communication, 2001).

The survey covered 9 km² and combined surface reconnaissance and shovel testing in an effort to locate the kind of small, ephemeral sites that are characteristic of the Bronze Age in the western steppes, which had been successfully identified at Peschanyi Dol through shovel testing. Areas containing artifacts or archaeological features were designated archaeological sites, and in each of these, units ranging from 1 to 16 m² were excavated. Nine new archaeological sites were identified, three quarries and six habitations associated through ceramic evidence with the Srubnaya horizon. This is the first recorded evidence of Bronze Age settlement in Kamyshla, in the upper Sok River region to the northeast of Potapovka and Nizhny Orleansky (Figure 11.15). One of these, Kibit I, was the site of a Srubnaya longhouse with a sunken floor. It contained mid-second millennium BC Srubnaya potsherds and has been assigned by two accelerator mass spectrometry (AMS) dates to circa 1488–1442 BC.[5]

Besides Kibit I, the most important sites encountered in the survey and test excavations were the quarries. Three quarries were identified: Baitugan I and II and Novoe Usmanovo I. Each of the quarries contained layers of sedimentary cupric sandstone ore, of the type that Chernykh (1970:34) has associated with the MP source group. Deposits of this sandstone ore are known along the Volga, Ural, and Belaya Rivers (Peterson 2007:253–265). These quarries did not contain diagnostic artifacts or carbon samples that could be used for dating.

The investigation of Kibit I during the Kamyshla survey indicates that mining and metallurgy were practiced there during the fifteenth century BC. Kibit I is located on a promontory 300 m north of the Sok River between the modern villages of Novoe Usmanovo and Chuvashkii Baitugan. An area of 16 m² was excavated during the survey, uncovering 481 Srubnaya potsherds and the corner of a Late Bronze Age house floor, including a posthole (Figure 11.16). Also found were a very corroded piece of copper and a 3-cm chunk of copper ore (Peterson 2007:209–214). The subsequent excavation of Kibit I by Popova, Kuznetsov, and Mochalov uncovered a greater extent of the Srubnaya longhouse as well as more metallurgical evidence—most important, a high volume of crushed ore within the dwelling. A stream flowed through it during one stage of its occupation. Popova (2006) interprets this as a structure designed to sort crushed ores in preparation for smelting.

Also recovered were a small assemblage of slags and related materials that provide additional evidence for metal making within and near the settlement sites. These include some with a green, glassy matrix formed by the reduction of copper ore by a nontapping process, also found in Kargaly (see Diaz del Río et al. 2006). These are from an artifact scatter 2 km north of Kibit I. Subsequent shovel testing revealed no buried site in the area; these may have been redeposited by stream activity in the past and may postdate the Bronze Age.

Kargaly and Connections with the Middle Volga

During the Bronze Age, metal production occurred at a far larger scale than Samara in Kargaly, where there are over 30,000 surface workings and an unknown number of subsurface mines of copper sandstone and shale ore deposits. These are concentrated in a 500-km² area on the watershed between the Ural and Samara River drainages, 60 km northwest of the city of Orenburg. How many actually date to the Bronze Age is unclear. Kargaly was one of the chief sources of Russian copper in the eighteenth and nineteenth centuries, and many of the workings must date to that late period. However, some 20 Srubnaya settlement sites and four kurgan cemeteries dating from the late fourth to early second millennium BC have been investigated there, uncovering plentiful evidence for metal production in the earliest stages of its occupation (Chernykh 1997, 2002; Kohl 2007:170; Koryakova and Epimakhov 2007:32–33).

The exploitation of Kargaly ores probably began by the early third millennium BC, as shown by the use of sandstone ore and unalloyed copper tools as grave goods in Yamnaya kurgan burials in the southern Urals and adjacent areas, including Samara. While it has not been possible to differentiate between sandstone ores like those from Kargaly from deposits of similar ores

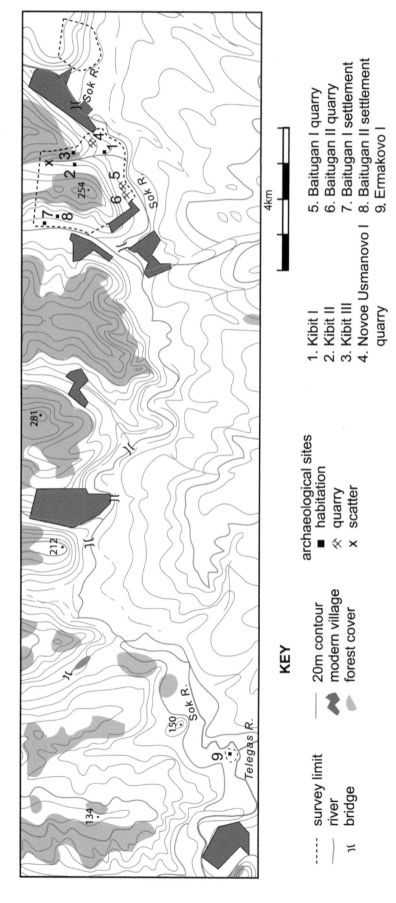

KEY

		archaeological sites
----- survey limit	—— 20m contour	■ habitation
—— river	modern village	⚒ quarry
)(bridge	forest cover	x scatter

1. Kibit I
2. Kibit II
3. Kibit III
4. Novoe Usmanovo I quarry

5. Baitugan I quarry
6. Baitugan II quarry
7. Baitugan I settlement
8. Baitugan II settlement
9. Ermakovo I

Figure 11.15 The sites identified in Kamyshla. *Prepared by David Peterson*

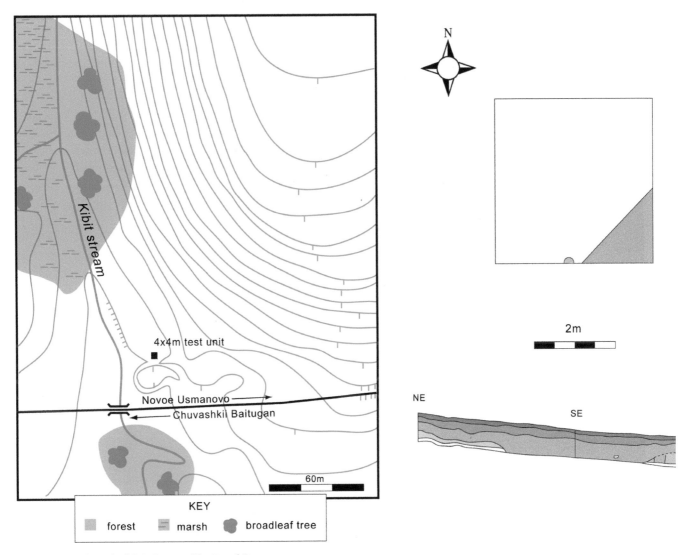

Figure 11.16 Plan of Kibit I. *Prepared by David Peterson*

throughout the steppes (Chernykh 1970, 1992), given the sheer extent of mining in Kargaly, there is a high probability that many copper and bronze objects from third and second millennium burials in the Volga-Ural were fabricated with copper smelted from Kargaly ores. Palynological analyses have also shown that significant deforestation began there near the Srubnaya mining settlement at Gorny by the early third millennium BC (Diaz del Río et al. 2006). Mining and smelting require large volumes of charcoal fuel, and the initiation of large-scale smelting in the EBA would have contributed greatly to deforestation.

Exploitation of the Kargaly deposits during the second millennium BC is best known through the excavation of the Gorny settlement (Chernykh 1997, 2002). The latest

level of occupation at Gorny (1650–1330 BC) contained a remarkable concentration of evidence for intensive copper-based metallurgy over a 200-m² area, including house remains, smelting yards, ore processing areas, and waste pits. A palynological study of tree cover in Kargaly during this period has shown that it was closely similar to the present day, drawing into question previous estimates of scale of production during the LBA, which would have required more fuel than is presently available. This and the relatively small amount of slag recovered may indicate that the people at Kargaly were principally involved in mining and the partial reduction of copper ore, which was traded to outlying communities that finished smelting it into metallic copper (Diaz del Río et al. 2006). An immense quantity of animal bone has been recovered from Gorny, some 2.3 million pieces in all. Of these, 99.8 percent are domesticated species, including cattle, sheep, goat, and pig (Antipina 2004). Large grazing areas would have been required to support them, probably beyond what is available in the vicinity of the site. Herders in the Samara Valley may have brought livestock to settlements of miners and metallurgists like Gorny to exchange for partially reduced ore, enabling miners to live and work in Kargaly year round (Chernykh 1997:69–71; Kohl 2007:174–176).

It is striking that two principal focuses of production throughout the Bronze Age in the middle Volga were herding and copper-based metallurgy. While explanations for this have often centered on communities' need for metal for tools and defense, local and interregional exchange also motivated these practices. As noted earlier, social payments such as bridewealth and bloodwealth may have been among the most important of these exchanges. In some instances, the availability of a greater variety of exchangeable goods than livestock alone would have contributed to the sustainability of early steppe communities by providing a commodity besides cattle for interregional exchange, enabling pastoralists to maintain larger herds. In other cases, it may have given people with fewer head of livestock access to them or to pastoralist goods such as dairy, meat, and skins that normally required a sufficiently large herd of their own.

The Kargaly district was an important player in these relationships in the third and second millennium BC. Its proximity to the middle Volga and links to the Samara Valley indicate that it was the likely home of exchange partners for pastoralists that lived in the area of present-day Samara during the occupations of Krasnosamarskoe and the Peschanyi Dol sites. As noted earlier, its location near the source of the Samara River and the potential for communication and exchange with the middle Volga may have made Kargaly an important node in the distribution of metal (copper, bronze, silver, and gold) to the west. The wealth of the Spiridonovka II cemetery and the ability of the community that used it to attract that wealth were probably associated with the rich pasture that surrounded it and the capacity to raise surplus livestock to exchange with distant communities, such as those in Kargaly.

Summary and Conclusions

Ore, slag and other metallurgical by-products, and small fragmentary objects at the sites investigated by the Samara Valley Project and the Samara Ancient Metals

Project show a pattern of widespread, small-scale, dispersed production of copper and bronze during the Late Bronze Age in the western steppes. This adds significantly to the previous focus on the metallurgy of this period as a large-scale, centralized industry and improves the present knowledge of the varying scales and regional contexts of metal production in prehistoric Eurasia.

LBA metallurgy in the middle Volga was built on a foundation of local metalworking from the Eneolithic to MBA II that included the influx of new materials and techniques through contacts with mining and metal-producing communities in Kargaly and elsewhere. Kargaly was clearly an important mining center in the South Urals to the east of Samara and a hub in the distribution of copper, bronze, and precious metals in a network (or networks) that included the middle Volga. Metal was also produced at two small sources of copper ore known in the Samara oblast. The first, Mikhailovka-Ovsianka, was worked by the fourteenth century BC (Matveeva et al. 2004). The second was identified by the SAM project in the Kamyshla *raion* (Baitugan and Novoe Usmanovo) and was used by the fifteenth century BC. Metalworking was carried out at settlements such as Krasnosamarskoe, the dwelling at Kibit I, and even small, ephemeral herding camps such as Peschanyi Dol 2. Settlement evidence is currently lacking for earlier stages of the Bronze Age. During the EBA to MBA II, metalworking was probably carried out in small herding camps like those at Peschanyi Dol that remain to be discovered. The surveys of Peschanyi Dol and Kamyshla demonstrate successful methods for future investigations of such sites.

During the period of the Yamnaya and Yamnaya-Poltavka cultures, people in the middle Volga used large, unalloyed copper objects that were fabricated by casting, annealing, and moderate final cold-working. By about the third quarter of the third millennium BC, heavier, final cold-working was practiced with the adoption of arsenic bronze, which is more easily worked than unalloyed copper. Heavier cold-work produces harder implements, while arsenic bronze is more easily cast, has a lighter color than unalloyed copper, and has advantages for making ornaments as well.[6] Tin bronze appeared in middle Volga metal assemblages by the beginning of the second millennium BC. While previous researchers attributed this to imports from the Volga-Kama region, the nearest known sources of tin in the ancient steppes are in eastern Kazakhstan, which must have supplied much of the tin used in making bronze from Samara.

Concentrations of arsenic and tin in the objects that were analyzed indicate that copper and bronze were frequently recycled. Early metalworkers in the middle Volga were not simply dependent on a constant flow of raw materials from the South Urals, Volga-Kama, or elsewhere. Instead, a pool of existing metal appears to have been maintained locally, to which new materials were added from time to time. The composition of the objects also provides evidence of geographic divisions in metalworking. The majority are from the Potapovka I and Utyevka VI cemeteries, the two most heavily investigated sites of the MBA II Potapovka horizon (Kuznetsov and Semenova 2000; Vasiliev et al. 1992; Vasiliev et al. 1994). Differences in minor elements (iron and antimony) suggest that the assemblages from these cemeteries were made by different groups of metalworkers. Potapovka I and Utyevka VI are some 80 km apart; metalworkers may have belonged to different pastoralist bands that lived in the Sok and Samara River valleys in which the cemeteries are respectively situated and maintained their own pools of raw materials.

The SAM project initiated the investigation of the chaîne opératoire of prehistoric metalworking in the Eurasian steppes, identifying variations in these practices in the MBA II period that may be attributed to local tendencies, the materials used in metalworking, or both.[7] Metallographic evidence adds further support to the hypothesis of a geographic division in MBA II metalworking. There is a notable difference in final cold-working in the metalwork from Potapovka I and the metalwork from Utyevka VI in which heavier final cold-working was practiced. The majority of arsenic bronze metalwork in the middle Volga during this period is from Utyevka VI. Although it must be annealed at a higher temperature than unalloyed copper, arsenic bronze is easier to cold-work than copper. This may in part account for the greater frequency of heavy final cold-working in the metalwork from Utyevka VI, and the differences in the composition and fabrication of metal artifacts from Potapovka I and Utyevka VI may owe to the greater accessibility of arsenic bronze to metalworkers in the vicinity of Utyevka. Utyevka VI is located along the Samara River downstream from Kargaly and was a closer neighbor to metal suppliers in the South Urals than Potapovka I. The position of Potapovka I and Utyevka VI in an MBA II metal network may also help to explain the differences in materials and practices in the metalwork from these cemeteries, providing a view of network dynamics not previously available through the Metallurgical Province model.

What was the socioeconomic status of metalworkers during the Bronze Age in the middle Volga? The demands and limits of pastoralism make it both a labor-intensive and extensive form of subsistence. In the 1950s, South Iranian nomads of the Kamseh federation were short on the resources needed to support specialized labor or collective projects (Barth 1961:101–102, 113). Instead of being full-time specialists that a pastoralist band may have lacked the resources to support, metalworkers during the MBA II in the middle Volga may have been closely integrated members of leading households in their respective communities, which had the resources to support small-scale metalworking and to organize construction of the kurgan burials in which the metalwork was found. However, the success of these households is not easily encompassed by a simple metric such as size and wealth, since large herds could be quickly devastated by the frequent droughts that occur in the steppes, epidemics, and competition over rangeland in seasonal migrations. Membership in metal networks (Peterson 2012) may have offered a variety of opportunities to enhance the position and influence of their members, while the long-term sustainability of households and bands was improved by local and distant alliances like those that surrounded the production and exchange of metalwork.

During the LBA in the South Urals, large-scale mining operations may have provided copper to trade for rare and complex ornaments made with electrum foil. Some may have been given as gifts or exchanged with herders in the rich grasslands of the Samara River valley, who had greater stores of traditional wealth in livestock. The foil-covered ornament from the child's burial at Spiridonovka II (Kurgan 2, Grave 29) provides evidence that some artisans had knowledge of depletion gilding techniques for the enrichment of gold on the outer surface of ornaments. Until now, evidence of such techniques before the first millennium BC was known only in the jewelry from the Royal Cemetery of Ur. These techniques may have been far more widespread than presently known and part of a longer history that culminated in the gold refinement used to make the earliest coinage in Lydia (ca. 600 BC). Kurgan 1 at Spiridonovka II contained rich graves equipped with sets of weapons, many bronze ornaments, and faience beads. This may be further indication of participation in trade networks that reached as far as Mesopotamia and facilitated the transfer of advanced gilding techniques to metalworkers in the Eurasian steppes.

Acknowledgments

In addition to the individuals and organizations acknowledged within the chapter, we wish to thank the students of the History Department of Samara State Pedagogical University and colleagues with the Institute for the History and Archaeology of the Volga (IHAV), Samara State Pedagogical University, and Samara State University, especially Aleksandr Khokhlov, Boris Aguzarov, Dmitri Kormilitsyn, Ala Semenova, and Nikolai Nebritov, for their efforts on the Kamyshla survey. Emmett Brown and Audrey Brown prepared a faunal report (Peterson et al. 2006), and Laura Popova organized flotation. Special thanks to Zagafar for his warmth, hospitality, logistical support, and permission to conduct the survey and test excavations in the vicinity of Baitugan. We are grateful for the advice and assistance of Michael Dietler, Igor Vasiliev, Adam T. Smith, Kathleen Morrison, K. Aslihan Yener, and Nicholas Kouchoukos. As a member of the Making of Ancient Eurasia Project (co-directed by Adam T. Smith and William Ellingson), Peterson conducted preliminary analyses of the Spiridonovka II and Nizhny Orleansky pendants with the assistance of Lori Khatchadourian at Argonne National Laboratory's Electron Microscopy Center. A later stage of research on the pendants was performed at the Environmental Molecular Science Laboratory (EMSL), a national scientific user facility sponsored by the Department of Energy's Office of Biological and Environmental Research and located at Pacific Northwest National Laboratory.

The Wenner-Gren Foundation generously funded research for the SAM project through Individual Research Grant 6760. This material is based on work supported by the National Science Foundation under Grant No. 0431940. Any opinions, findings, conclusions, or recommendations expressed in this material are those of the authors and do not necessarily reflect the views of the National Science Foundation. The Russian Academy of Sciences provided financial support to our colleague Pavel Kuznetsov for the Kamyshla survey in 2001.

Appendix: Summary of Metallographic Observations

Key:

Structure
Microstructures indicative of the manner in which the object was worked:
As-cast = cored dendritic structure (not annealed)
cw = cold-worked
recryst. = recrystallized (annealed)

partial recryst. = incomplete recrystallization due to insufficient annealing time, and/or annealing temperature, or both

Coring
Special pattern of secondary phasing in which the latter solidifies around the core phase of the material, especially in alloys, due to differences in cooling rates in which the latter have a higher melting/solidification temperature than the secondary phase(s); also as a residual structure of the original casting due to incomplete recrystallization or lack of homogenization

Slip traces
Indicates the presence of slip lines, representative of intensive cold-working

Final cold-work
Estimate of relative degree of final cold hammering, based on the deformation of crystals, slip lines, and inclusions, used in assigning the objects to work pattern groups.

Work pattern (WP)
Patterns in the fabrication of objects, based chiefly on manner on combination of techniques with degree of final cold-working: WP 1: objects that were cast and only very lightly cold-worked; WP 2: objects that were cast, cold-worked, annealed, and moderately cold-worked again; WP 3: objects that went through steps similar to WP 2 but at the end were heavily cold-worked to the point of heavy cold-work reduction; WP 4: objects with a structure of small crystals in comparison to the others, probably as a result of more alternating bouts of cold-work and annealing than WP 2 or WP 3.

Corrosion
i.g. = intergranular, corrosion following crystal boundaries
t.g. = transgranular, corrosion along slip traces or of whole crystals
i.d. = interdendritic, corrosion between arms of unannealed or residual cast dendrite crystals
Porosity = small zones of oxidation, often bubble-like in appearance and filled with copper oxide, formed by the take-up of oxygen during casting
Pitting = heavy oxidation that has eaten away portions of the metal

Sample/ Object	Period	Material	Structure	Coring	Slip Traces	Final Cold-Work	Corrosion	Work Pattern, Comments
DP 1 Knife	MBA II	Cu	Recryst./cw	None apparent	Some, bent	Moderate-heavy	Porosity	WP2
DP 2 Bracelet	MBA II	Cu+Sn	Recryst./cw	None apparent	Duplex	Moderate-heavy	i.g., t.g., porosity	WP4 very small grains
DP 3 Knife	MBA II	Cu	Recryst./cw	None apparent	Some	Heavy	i.g., t.g., porosity	WP3
DP 4 Knife	MBA II	Cu+Sn	As-cast	Yes	Duplex	Light	i.d.	WP1
DP 5 Bracelet	MBA II	Cu+Sn	Recryst./cw	None	Some, bent	Moderate	i.g.	WP2
DP 6 Bracelet	MBA II	Cu+Sn	Recryst./cw	None	Gradient, duplex	Moderate	i.g., t.g., porosity	WP2
DP 7 Bracelet	MBA II	Cu+As						WP not identified
DP 8 Copper piece	MBA II	Cu	Recryst./cw	None	Duplex, bent	Very heavy+	i.g., t.g., porosity, pitting	WP3 ~95 percent or more cw reduction; linear bands of corrosion as a result of folding
DP 9 Awl	EBA-MBA I	Cu	Recryst./cw	Residual	Some, bent	Moderate	i.d., t.g., pitting	WP2 earlier recryst/cw shown by i.d. coring
DP 10 Knife	EBA-MBA I	Cu						
DP 11 Knife	MBA II	Cu+As	Recryst./cw	None	Duplex, bent	Very heavy	i.g.?	WP3 ~95 percent or more cw reduction
DP 12 Knife	MBA II	Cu+As	Recryst./cw	None	Gradient; duplex, bent	Heavy	Light (i.g., t.g., porosity)	WP3
DP 13 Knife	MBA II	Cu+As	Recryst./cw	Residual	Duplex, bent	Very heavy	Light (i.g., t.g., porosity)	WP3 ~95 percent or more cw reduction; earlier recryst/cw indicated by traces of flattened cored dendrites
DP 14 Sickle	MBA II	Cu	Recryst./cw	None	Bent	Very heavy	Porosity; see comments	WP3 ~99 percent cw reduction; linear bands of corrosion as a result of folding
DP 15 Knife	MBA II	Cu+As	Recryst./cw	None	Duplex, flattened	Very heavy	i.g., porosity	WP3 High Fe indicates metal is newly smelted; almost 100 percent cw reduction visible in parts
DP 16 Pendant	LBA	Cu+Sn	Recryst./cw	None	Some	Light	Porosity	WP2
DP 17 Pendant	LBA	Cu+Sn	Recryst./cw	None	Duplex	Light	Porosity	WP2
DP 12 Knife	MBA II	Cu+As	Recryst./cw	None	Gradient; duplex, bent	Heavy	Light (i.g., t.g., porosity)	WP3
DP 18 Knife	MBA II	Cu	Recryst./cw	None	None apparent	Moderate	Porosity	WP2

Sample/ Object	Period	Material	Structure	Coring	Slip Traces	Final Cold-Work	Corrosion	Work Pattern, Comments
DP 19 Knife	MBA II	Cu+As	Recryst./cw	Residual	Gradient	Light	Porosity, pitting	WP2
DP 20 Fish hook	MBA II	Cu+As	Recryst./cw	None	Bent	Heavy	i.g., porosity, pitting (see comments)	WP3 ~95 percent cw reduction; linear bands of corrosion as a result of folding
DP 21 Fish hook	MBA II	Cu+As	Recryst./cw	None	Duplex, bent	Heavy	i.g., t.g., porosity, pitting (see comments)	WP3 Linear bands of corrosion as the result of folding
DP 22 Fish hook	MBA II	Cu	Recryst./cw	Residual	Slight	Light	Porosity	WP2
DP 23 Knife (blade)	MBA II	Cu	Recryst./cw	None	None apparent	Light-moderate	Porosity	WP2 Same object as DP24
DP 24 Knife (butt)	MBA II	Cu	Recryst./cw	None	Some	Very heavy	Porosity	WP3 Same object as DP23
DP 25 Chisel	MBA II	Cu+As	Recryst./cw	Residual	None apparent	Light	Porosity	WP2
DP 26 Massive hook	MBA II	Cu	Recryst.	None	None apparent	None apparent	Porosity	WP2
DP 27 Bracelet	MBA II	Cu+Sn	Recryst./cw	Residual	Duplex, bent	Moderate-heavy	i.g., t.g., pitting	WP3 Some small grains; linear bands of corrosion as a result of folding
DP 28 Spear-head	MBA II	Cu+As	Recryst./cw	None	Residual	Light	Porosity, t.g., heavy pitting	WP2
DP 29 Adze	MBA II	Cu+As	Recryst./cw	Residual	Duplex, bent	Moderate-heavy	Porosity	WP3
DP 30 Knife	MBA II	Cu	Recryst./cw	Residual	Light	Moderate	Porosity	WP3
DP 31 Knife	MBA II	Cu	Recryst./cw	None	Residual	Light	Porosity, pitting	WP2
DP 32 Knife	MBA II	Cu	Recryst./cw	Residual	Bent	Moderate-heavy	i.g., t.g., porosity	WP3
DP 33 Bracelet	LBA	Cu+Sn	Recryst./cw	None	Duplex	Moderate-heavy	i.g., t.g., pitting	WP2
DP 34 Bracelet	LBA	Cu+Sn	Recryst./cw	None	Duplex	Moderate-heavy	i.g., t.g., porosity, pitting	WP2
DP 40 Bracelet	LBA	Cu+Sn	Recryst./cw	None	Duplex, bent	Moderate-heavy	i.g., t.g., porosity, pitting	WP2
DP 45 Pendant	LBA	Cu+Sn	Recryst./cw	None	None apparent	Light	i.g., t.g., porosity	WP2
DP 46 Pendant	LBA	Cu+Sn	Recryst./cw	None	Few	Light	i.g., t.g., porosity, pitting	WP2
DP 47 Ring	MBA I	Cu+As	Recryst.	None	None apparent	None apparent	i.g., t.g., pitting	WP2
DP 48 Ring	MBA I	Cu+As	Recryst./cw	None	Some, bent	Light-moderate	i.g., t.g., porosity, pitting	WP2

Sample/Object	Period	Material	Structure	Coring	Slip Traces	Final Cold-Work	Corrosion	Work Pattern, Comments
DP 49 Ring	MBA I	Cu+As	Recryst./cw	None	Bent	Moderate-heavy	i.g., t.g., porosity, pitting	WP2
DP 50 Clamp	MBA II	Cu	Recryst./cw	None	Some, bent	Moderate-heavy	Porosity	WP3
DP 41 Sheet ornament	LBA	Cu+Sn	Recryst./cw	Residual	Slight	Moderate	i.g., t.g., porosity, pitting	WP4 Small grains
DP 44 Needle	LBA	Cu	Recryst./cw	None	None apparent	Light	i.g., porosity, pitting	WP2
DP 51 Clamp	MBA II	Cu	Recryst./cw	None	None apparent	Light	i.g., t.g., porosity	WP2
DP 52 Clamp	MBA II	Cu	Recryst./cw	None	None apparent	Light	i.g., porosity	WP2
DP 53 Sheet ornament	MBA II	Cu	Recryst./cw	None	Slight?	Light	Porosity, pitting	WP2
DP 54 Sheet ornament	LBA	Cu	Recryst./cw	None	None apparent	Light	i.g., t.g., porosity, pitting	WP2 Corroded at crack
DP 55 Sheet ornament	LBA	Cu	Recryst./cw	None	None	Light	i.g., t.g., porosity, pitting	WP2 Corroded at crack
DP 56 Knife	MBA II	Cu+As	Recryst./cw	None	Duplex, bent	Heavy	i.g., porosity	WP3
DP 57 Blade	MBA II	Cu	Recryst./cw	None	?Slight	Light-moderate	Porosity	WP2
DP 58 Blade	MBA II	Cu	Recryst./cw	None	?Slight	Light-moderate	Porosity, t.g., pitting	WP2
DP 59 Knife	MBA II	Cu	Recryst./cw	None	None	?Light	t.g., i.g., porosity, pitting	WP2
DP 60 Knife	MBA II	Cu	Recryst./cw	Residual	Duplex, flattened	Very heavy	Porosity, pitting	WP3
DP 61 Blade	MBA II	Cu	Partial recryst./?cw	Residual	Few, bent	?Moderate	i.g., t.g., porosity, pitting; ?i.d.	WP2
DP 62 Knife	MBA II	Cu	Recryst./cw	Residual	None apparent	Moderate	i.g., t.g., porosity	WP2
DP 63 Spatula	MBA II	Cu+As	Recryst./cw	None	?Slight (750×)	Light	i.g., t.g.	WP2
DP 64 Blade	MBA II	Cu+As	Recryst./cw	None	None apparent	Moderate	i.g., t.g., porosity, pitting	WP2
DP 65 Blade	MBA II	Cu	Recryst./cw	Residual	None	Light-moderate	High porosity	WP2
DP 66 Massive hook	MBA II	Cu	Recryst./cw	Residual	None	Light-moderate	High porosity	WP2
DP 67 Massive hook	MBA II	Cu	Recryst./cw	None	Slight, bent	Heavy (300×)	Porosity, t.g., heavy pitting	WP3
DP 68 Adze	MBA II	Cu+As	Recryst./cw	None	Slight	Moderate	i.g., t.g.	WP2

Sample/ Object	Period	Material	Structure	Coring	Slip Traces	Final Cold-Work	Corrosion	Work Pattern, Comments
DP 69 Knife	MBA II	Cu	Recryst./cw	Light residual	Some, flattened	Very heavy	i.g., porosity; ?i.d.	WP3 ~99 percent cw reduction; linear bands of corrosion may be the result of folding
DP 70 Adze	MBA II	Cu	Recryst./cw	None	None	Heavy	i.g., porosity	WP3
DP 71 Knife	MBA II	Cu	Recryst./cw	None	Duplex	Heavy	Porosity	WP3
DP 72 Knife	MBA II	Cu	Recryst./cw	Residual	Some, bent	?Heavy	Heavy pitting, ?i.g.	WP3
DP 73 Awl	MBA II	Cu+As	Recryst./cw	None	Bent	?Heavy	i.g., t.g., porosity, pitting	WP3
DP 74 Awl	MBA II	Cu+As	Recryst./cw	Residual	Few, duplex	Heavy	i.d.?, porosity, pitting	WP3
DP 75 Awl	MBA II	Cu	Recryst./cw	Residual	Few, bent	Moderate	i.g., t.g.	WP3
DP 76 Awl	MBA II	Cu	Recryst./cw	None	Few, bent	?Heavy	i.g., t.g., porosity, pitting	WP3
DP 77 Adze	MBA II	Cu	Recryst./cw	None	Few, duplex	Heavy	i.g., t.g. (at surface), porosity	WP3
DP 78 Knife	MBA II	Cu	Recryst./cw	None	Some, bent	Very heavy	Porosity	WP3
DP 79 Awl	MBA II	Cu+As	Recryst./cw	None	Duplex, slightly bent	Heavy	i.g., t.g., porosity, pitting	WP3
DP 80 Awl	MBA II	Cu+As	Recryst./cw	None	Duplex	Heavy	i.g., t.g., porosity, pitting	WP3
DP 81 Awl	MBA II	Cu	Partial recryst./cw	None	None apparent	Light	i.g., porosity, pitting	WP2
DP 82 Needle	MBA II	Cu+As	Recryst./cw	None	Few, bent	Moderate-heavy	i.g., t.g., porosity, pitting	WP3
DP 83 Needle	MBA II	Cu(+Fe)	Recryst./cw	None	Bent, dislocations	Very heavy	i.g., t.g., porosity, ?i.d.	WP4 High Fe indicates metal is newly smelted, not recycled; very small grains; almost complete work reduction in parts
DP 85 Awl	MBA II	Cu+As	Recryst./cw	None	Duplex, bent	Very heavy	Porosity, i.g.	WP4 Small grains
DP 86 Awl	MBA II	Cu					Porosity, heavy pitting	WP not identified
DP 87 Awl	MBA II	Cu	Recryst./cw	None	None apparent	Light	Porosity, pitting	WP3
DP 88 Staff	EBA	Cu	Partial recryst./cw	Residual	Very slight	Moderate	Porosity	WP2
DP 89 Staff	EBA	Cu	Partial recryst./cw	Residual	None apparent	Light-moderate	Porosity,	WP2
DP 90 Blade	MBA II	Cu+As	Partial recryst.	Residual	None	?Light	Porosity, i.d., i.g.	WP2
DP 91 Knife	MBA II	Cu+As	Partial recryst./cw	Yes	Bent	Heavy	Porosity, i.d., i.g.	WP3

Sample/Object	Period	Material	Structure	Coring	Slip Traces	Final Cold-Work	Corrosion	Work Pattern, Comments
DP 94 Pendant (core)	LBA	Cu+Ag+	Recryst./cw	None	None apparent	Moderate	i.g., t.g., pitting, ?porosity	WP2
DP 95 Ring	MBA II	Ag	Recryst./cw	Faint?	None	Parts		

Notes

1 The SAM project was formerly known as the Samara Bronze Age Metals Project. The name was later changed to accommodate other periods into the investigation.

2 Some geochemists prefer to reserve LIA for copper and bronze artifacts dating no later than the EBA, because they believe they are less likely to have been made with recycled metal than objects from later periods like those from Potapovka I (Kh. Meliksetian, personal communication, 2012).

3 The original Russian map of these sources by Chernykh (1970) is reproduced in English by Koryakova and Epimakhov (2007:Figure 1.1).

4 There was also about 2 wt% Cu at the outer surface and a little less than 2 wt% Cu in the inner section.

5 AA65309: 3438 ± 39 BP, AA65310: 3392 ± 38 BP.

6 In some instances like the EBA to MBA in Daghestan, arsenic bronze was reserved for ornaments and diverted from use in tools and weapons (Peterson 2003, 2012).

7 Although unfamiliar with the concept of *chaîne opératoire*, Ryndina and Ravich (1987) and Ryndina (1998) used metallography earlier to produce the same kind of evidence that we did for the SAM project. They were trailblazers in this respect and part of the inspiration for our use of metallography and investigation of the *chaîne opératoire*.

References

Agapov, S., and S. Kuzminykh
1994 Metall Potapovskogo mogil'nika v sisteme Evraziiskoi Metallurgicheskoi Provintsii (Appendix 1). In *Potaposkii kurgani mogil'nik.* Samarskii Universiteta, edited by I. B. Vasil'ev, P. F. Kuznetsov, and A. P. Semenova, pp. 167–173. Samara.

Agapov, S. A., I. B. Vasiliev, and V. I. Pestrikova
1990 *Khavalynskii eneoloticheskii mogil'nik.* Saratov University, Kuibyshev.

Anthony, D.
1996 V. G. Childe's World System and the Daggers of the Early Bronze Age. In *Craft Specialization and Social Evolution: In Memory of V. Gordon Childe,* edited by B. Wailes, pp. 47–66. University Museum Monograph No. 93. University of Pennsylvania, Philadelphia.

1998 The Opening of the Eurasian Steppe at 2000 BCE. In *The Bronze Age and Early Iron Age Peoples of Eastern Central Asia: Vol. 1. Archaeology, Migration and Nomadism, Linguistics,* edited by V. Mair, pp. 94–113. Institute for the Study of Man, Washington, D.C.

2007 *The Horse, the Wheel, and Language: How Bronze Age Riders from the Eurasian Steppes Shaped the Modern World.* Princeton University Press, Princeton, NJ.

Anthony, D., D. Brown, E. Brown, A. Goodman, A. Kokhlov, P. Kuznetsov, P. Kosintsev, O. Mochalov, E. Murphy, D. Peterson, A. Pike-Tay, L. Popova, A. Rosen, N. Russell, and A. Weisskopf
2005 The Samara Valley Project: Late Bronze Age Economy and Ritual in the Russian Steppes. *Eurasia Antiqua* 11:395–417.

Antipina, E. E.
2004 Arkheozoologicheskie materialy. In *Kargaly III,* edited by E. N. Chernykh, pp. 182–239. Iazyki slavianskoi kul'tury, Moscow.

Barth, F.
1961 *Nomads of South Persia: The Basseri Tribe of the Khamseh Confederacy.* Little, Brown, Boston.

Chernikov, S. S.
1949 *Drevnyaya metallurgiya i gornoe delo zapadnogo Altaya.* Alma-Ata.

Chernykh, E. N.
1970 *Drevneishaya metallurgiya Ural I Povolzhya.* Nauka, Moscow.
1992 *Ancient Metallurgy in the USSR.* Cambridge University Press, Cambridge.
1997a *Kargaly. Zabytii mir.* Iazyki slavianskoi kul'tury, Moscow.
1997b Kargaly-krupneishii gornometallurgicheskii tsentr Severnoi Evraziyi. *Rossiiskaya arkheologiya* 1:21–36.

Chernykh, E. N. (editor)
2002 *Kargaly II.* Iazyki slavianskoi kul'tury, Moscow.
2004 *Kargaly III.* Iazyki slavianskoi kul'tury, Moscow.
2005 *Kargaly IV.* Iazyki slavianskoi kul'tury, Moscow.
2007 *Kargaly: fenomen i paradoksy razvitiia.* Iazyki slavianskoi kul'tury, Moscow.

2008   The "Steppe Belt" of Early Stockbreeding Cultures in Eurasia during the Early Metal Age. *Trabajos de Prehistoria* 65(2): 73–93.

Chernykh, E. N., and S. N. Korenevskii

1976   O metallicheskikh predmetakh c Tsareva Kurgana bliz g. Kuibysheva. In *Vostochnaya Evropa v epokhu kamnaya i bronzy*, pp. 201–208. Nauka, Moscow.

Chernykh, E. N., and S. V. Kuz'minykh

1989   *Drevniaia metallurgiia Severnoi Evrazii (seiminsko-turbinskii fenomen)*. Nauka, Moscow.

Diaz del Río, P., P. L. García, J. A. López Sáez, M. I. Martina Navarette, A. L. Rodrígues Alcalde, S. Rovira-Llorens, J. M. Vicent García, and I. de Zavala Morencos

2006   Understanding the Productive Economy during the Bronze Age through Archaeometallurgical and Paleo-Environmental Research at Kargaly. In *Beyond the Steppe and the Sown: Proceedings of the 2002 University of Chicago Conference on Eurasian Archaeology*, edited by D. Peterson, L. Popova, and A. Smith, pp. 343–357. Brill, Leiden.

Frachetti, M.

2008   *Pastoralist Landscapes and Social Interaction in Bronze Age Eurasia*. University of California Press, Berkeley.

Gening, V. F., G. B. Zdanovich, and V. V. Gening

1992   *Sintashta*. Chelyabinsk.

Gosselain, O.

1992   Technology and Style: Potters and Pottery among Bafia of Cameroon. *Man* 27(3):559–586.

Hanks, B., and R. Doonan

2009   From Scale to Practice: A New Agenda for the Study of Early Metallurgy on the Eurasian Steppe. *Journal of World Prehistory* 22:329–356.

Hauptmann, A., S. Klein, M. Prange, and R. Zettler

2010   Gold from the Royal Tombs of Ur, 2600 BC: Gilding Techniques, Tumbaga Alloys, Depletion Gilding—On the Use of a Hand-Held XRF Spectrometer. *Metalla Sonderheft* 3:57–59.

Kohl, P.

2008   *The Making of Bronze Age Eurasia*. Cambridge University Press, Cambridge.

Koryakova, L., and A. V. Epimakhov

2007   *The Urals and Western Siberia in the Bronze and Iron Ages*. Cambridge University Press, Cambridge.

Korenevskii, S. N.

1976   O metallicheskikh toparakh Severnogo Prichernomorya, Srednogo i Nizhnego Povolzhya epokhi srednei bronzy. *Sovietskaya arkheologiya* 4:16–31.

1977   O drevnem metalle basseina r. Samary. In *Srednevolzhskaya akheologicheskaya ekspeditsiya*, edited by G. I. Matveeva, pp. 44–46. Kuibyshev State University, Kuibyshev.

1980   O metallicheskikh veshchakh i Utyevskogo mogil'nika. In *Arkheologiya Vostochno-Evropeiskoi lesostepi*, edited by A. D. Pryakhin, pp. 59–66. Voronezhkogo Universiteta, Voronezh.

Kuzmina, E. E.

2000   The Eurasian Steppes: The Transition from Early Urbanism to Nomadism. In *Kurgans, Ritual Sites, and Settlements: Eurasian Bronze and Iron Age*, edited by J. Davis-Kimball, E. I. Murphy, L. Koryakova, and L.T. Yablonsky, pp. 118–125. BAR International Series No. 890. British Archaeological Reports, Oxford.

2007   *The Prehistory of the Silk Road*. University of Pennsylvania Press, Philadelphia.

Kuznetsov, P.F.

2005   An Indo-Iranian Symbol of Power in the Earliest Steppe Kurgans. *Journal of Indo-European Studies* 33(3–4): 325–338.

Kuznetsov, P. F., and A. P. Semenova

2000   Pamyatniki potapovskogo tipa. In *Istoriya Samarskogo Povolzh'ya c drevneishikh vremen do nashikh dnei: bronzovyi vek*, edited by Yu. I. Kol'ev, A. E. Mamonov, and M. A. Turetskii, pp. 122–151. Izdatel'stvo Samarskogo nauchnogo tsentra, Samara.

La Niece, S.

1995   Depletion Gilding from Third Millennium BC Ur. *Iraq* 57:41–47.

Lechtman, H.

1973   The Gilding of Metals in Pre-Columbian Peru. In *Application of Science in Examination of Works of Art*, edited by W. Young, pp. 38–52. Museum of Fine Arts, Boston.

Lepekhin, I.

1795   *Dnevhye zapiski putshestviya po raznym provintsiyam Rossiiskovo gosudarstva*. St. Petersburg.

Lobell, J.

2013   Ancient Alchemy? *Archaeology Magazine* January–February:14.

Matveeva, G. I., Yu. I. Kolev, and A. I. Korelev

2004   Gorno-metallurgicheskii kompleks bronzovogo veka y c. Mikhailo-Ovsyanka na yuge Samarskoi oblasti (perv'ie rezultaty I problemy issledocaniya). *Voprosy arkheologii Urala I Povolzh'ya* 2:69–88.

Mochalov, O. D.

2008   *Ceramics from Burial Sites in the Forest-steppe of the Volga-Urals Interstream Area*. Samara.

Northover, J. P.

2002   Analysis of Non-ferrous Metalwork from the Iron Age Cemetery at Pottenbrun, NÖ. In *Das eisenzeitliche gräberfeld von Pottenbrun*, edited by P. C. Ramsl, pp. 251–263. Forschungsansätze zu wirtschaftlichen Grundlagen und sozialen Strukturen der latènezeitlichen Bevölkerung des Traisentales, Niederösterreich, Fundberichte aus Österreich, Vienna.

Northover, P.
1989   Non-ferrous Metallurgy in Archaeology. In *Scientific Analysis in Archaeology*, edited by J. Henderson, pp. 213–236. UCLA Institute of Archaeology, Los Angeles.

Oddy, A.
2000   A History of Gilding with Particular Reference to Statuary. In *Gilded Metals: History, Technology and Conservation*, edited by T. Drayman-Weisser, pp. 1–19. Archetype Publications and American Institute for Conservation of Historic Artistic Works, London.

Pallas, P. S.
1773   *Putshestvie po raznym provintsiyam Rossiiskoi imperii.* St. Petersburg.

Papadopoulos, J., and G. Urton (editors)
2012   *The Construction of Value in the Ancient World.* Cotsen Institute, UCLA, Los Angeles.

Parzinger, H.
1997   Sejma-Turbino und die Anfänge des sibirischen Tierstils. *Eurasia Antiqua* 3:223–247.
2002   Das Zinn in der Bronzezeit Eurasiens. In *Anatolian Metal II*, edited by Ü. Yalçın, pp. 159–177. *Der Anschnitt* 15.
2008   The Scythians: Nomadic Horsemen of the Eurasian Steppe. In *Preservation of the Frozen Tombs of the Altai Mountains,* pp. 19–24. UNESCO, Ateliers Industria, Paris.

Pernicka, E.
1995   Gewinnung und Verbreitung der Metalla im prähistorischer Zeit. *Jahrbuch des Römisch-Germanischen Zentralmuseums Mainz* 37(1): 21–129.

Pernicka, E., C. Eibner, Ö. Öztunali, and G. A. Wagner
2003   Early Bronze Age Metallurgy in the Northeast Aegean. In *Troia and the Troad*, edited by G. A. Wagner, E. Pernicka, and H. P. Uepermann, pp. 143–172. Springer, Berlin.

Peterson, D.
2003   Ancient Metallurgy in the Mountain Kingdom: The Technology and Value of Early Bronze Age Metalwork from Velikent, Dagestan. In *Archaeology in the Borderlands: Investigations in Caucasia and Beyond*, edited by K. S. Rubinson and A. T. Smith, pp. 22–37. Cotsen Institute, UCLA, Los Angeles.
2007   Changing Technologies and Transformations of Value in the Middle Volga and Northeastern Caucasus, ca. 3000–1500 BCE. Ph.D. dissertation, University of Chicago, Chicago. University Microfilms, Ann Arbor.
2009   Production and Social Complexity: Bronze Age Metalworking in the Middle Volga. In *Social Complexity in Prehistoric Eurasia: Monuments, Metal, and Mobility*, edited by B. Hanks and K. Linduff, pp. 222–261. Cambridge University Press, Cambridge.
2012   Forging Social Networks: Metallurgy and the Politics of Value in Bronze Age Eurasia. In *The Archaeology of Power and Politics in Eurasia: Regimes and Revolutions*, edited by C. W. Hartley, G. B. Yazıcıoğlu, and A. T. Smith, pp. 283–301. Cambridge University Press, New York.

Peterson, D., and L. Khatchadourian
2006   FESEM-EDS Analysis of Ancient Eurasian Goldwork: An Early Example of Gilding by Diffusion Bonding. Presented at the Users Meetings for DOE/BES User Facilities at Argonne National Lab, Lemont, Illinois.

Peterson, D., P. Kuznetsov, J. Dudgeon, M. Tromp, B. Paige, and O. Mochalov
2012   Wrapped by the Sharp-Beaked Hounds of Zeus: Gilding Techniques in Late Bronze Age Pendants from the Middle Volga. Presented at the 77th Annual Meeting of the Society for American Archaeology, Memphis, Tennessee.

Peterson, D., P. Kuznetsov, and O. Mochalov
2006   The Samara Bronze Age Metals Project: Investigating Changing Technologies and Transformations of Value in the Western Eurasian Steppes. In *Beyond the Steppe and the Sown: Proceedings of the 2002 University of Chicago Conference on Eurasian Archaeology*, edited by D. Peterson, L. Popova, and A. Smith, pp. 322–342. Leiden, Brill.

Piggott, S.
1983   *The Earliest Wheeled Transport.* Cornell University Press, Ithaca, New York.

Pollard, M., C. Batt, B. Stearn, and S. Young
2007   *Analytical Chemistry in Archaeology.* Cambridge University Press, New York.

Popova, L. M.
2006   Political Pastures: Navigating the Steppe in the Middle Volga Region (Russia) during the Bronze Age. Unpublished Ph.D. dissertation, University of Chicago, Chicago.

Popova, L. M., E. M. Murphy, and A. A. Khokhlov
2011   Standardization and Resistance: Changing Funerary Rites at Spiridonovka (Russia) during the Beginning of the Late Bronze Age. In *The Archaeology of Politics: The Materiality of Political Practice and Action in the Past*, edited by P. Johansen and A. Bauer, pp. 280–319. Cambridge Scholars Press, Cambridge.

Russell, N.
1998   Cattle as Wealth in Prehistoric Europe: Where's the Beef? In *The Archaeology of Value*, edited by D. Bailey, pp. 42–54. BAR International Series No. 730. British Archaeological Reports, Oxford.

332   David L. Peterson • Peter Northover • Chris Salter • Blanca Maldonado • David W. Anthony

Ryndina, N. V.

1998   *Drevneisheye metalloobrabatyvayushcheye proizodstvo Yugo-Vostochnoi Evropy.* Moscow State University, Moscow.

Ryndina, N. V., and I. Ravich

1987   Khimiko-tekhnologicheskoe Izuchenie mednykh izdelii Khvalynsknogo mogil'nika. In *Metody estestvennykh nauk v arkheologii,* pp. 6–13. Editorial USSR, Moscow.

Scott, D.

1983   The Deterioration of Gold Alloys and Some Aspects of the Conservation. *Studies in Conservation* 28:194–203.

Scott, D.

1991   *Metallography and Microstructures of Ancient and Historic Metals.* Getty Museum, Malibu, California.

Soressi, M., and J.-M. Geneste

2011   The History and Efficacy of the *Chaîne Opératoire* Approach to Lithic Analysis: Studying Techniques to Reveal Past Societies in an Evolutionary Perspective. *PaleoAnthropology* 2011:334–350.

Stöllner, T., Z. Samaschev, S. Berdenov, J. Cierny, M. Doll, J. Garner, A. Gontscharov, A. Gorelik, A. Hauptmann, R. Herd, G. Kusch, V. Merz, T. Riese, B. Sikorski, and B. Zickgraf

2011   Tin from Kazakhstan–Steppe Tin for the West. In *Anatolian Metal V*, edited by Ü. Yalçın, pp. 231–251. *Der Anschnitt* 24, Bochum.

Vasil'ev, I. B.

1980   Mogil'nik Yamno-Poltavinskovo vremeni u s. Utëvka v srednem Povolzhe. In *Arkheologiya vostochnoevropeishkoi lesostepi*, pp. 32–58. Voronezhkogo Universiteta, Voronezh.

Vasil'ev, I. B., P. F. Kuznetsov, and A. P. Semenova

1992   Pogrebenia znati epokhi bronzy v srednem Povolzh'e. *Arkheologicheskie vesti* 1:52–63.

Vasil'ev, I. B., P. F. Kuznetsov, and A. P. Semenova

1994   *Potaposkii kurgani mogil'nik.* Samarskii Universiteta, Samara.

Vasiliev, I. B., P. F. Kuznetsov, and M. A. Turetskii

2000   Yamnaya i Poltavkinskaya kul'tura. In *Istoriya samarskogo povol'zha s drevneishikh vremen do nashikh dnei: Bronzovyi vek,* edited by Yu. Kolev, A. Mammonov, and M. Turyetskii, pp. 6–64. Samarskogo Nauchnogo Tsentra RAN, Samara.

Chapter 12

Floral Data Analysis: Report on the Pollen and Macrobotanical Remains from the Krasnosamarskoe Settlement

Laura M. Popova

major research goal of the Samara Valley Project was to better understand the shift in settlement strategies that mark the transition from the Middle to Late Bronze Age (Chapter 2). While archaeologists have located only a handful of ephemeral settlement sites associated with the Early and Middle Bronze Age in the Volga-Ural region, suggesting highly dispersed temporary communities, hundreds of Late Bronze Age settlements have been discovered (Kolev et al. 2000). The most impressive of these settlements consist of several large structures, roughly rectangular in plan, and are often semi-subterranean (Chernykh 1992). Krasnosamarskoe was one of these new kinds of settlements. It is argued that the catalyst for this growth was a subtle change in climate from arid to slightly more humid, which allowed formerly mobile pastoralists to settle and establish a new type of economy grounded in stockbreeding and farming (Sedova 2000:219; Vasiliev and Matveeva 1986:89–90). The presence of sickles, mortars, and pestles at settlement sites seemed to confirm this theory of the introduction of farming during the Late Bronze Age (see Vasiliev and Matveeva 1986).

Before the Samara Valley Project, there had been only a handful of studies in the region that confirmed the agricultural aspect of this economy. Based on impressions of grain on ceramics sherds, Pashkevich (1984, 1997, 2003) demonstrated that people in the Northern Pontic region cultivated several kinds of wheat, barley, hemp, and millet during the Early, Middle, and Late Bronze Ages. Spiridonova (1989)

and Kremenetski (1995) suggested, through pollen analysis, that cultivation was practiced in the Late Bronze Age in the regions west of the Volga. Lastly, Lebedeva (1996:53) conducted research in which she sampled 38 archaeological sites ranging in date from the Eneolithic to the Iron Age for macrobotanical remains. She concluded, based on this study, that the evidence of cultivation was very weak in the territory east of the Dnieper up to the Ural Mountains during the Bronze Age. On the basis of the strength of this research, Chernykh (1997) later suggested that in the regions east of the Volga River, people relied on little or no cultivated grains during the Late Bronze Age and were thus labeled "settled stock-breeders."

The Samara Valley Project considerably expanded the initial paleobotanical research in the region by combining macrobotanical, palynological, and phytolith analysis of systematically collected samples from Late Bronze Age Krasnosamarskoe, a settlement of the Srubnaya culture dated 1900 to 1700 BC. The purpose of the study was to better understand how Late Bronze Age pastoralists used the botanical resources available to them. More recently, paleobotanical techniques have been incorporated on several more Eurasian archaeology projects (e.g., Chang et al. 2002; Chang et al. 2003; Frachetti et al. 2010; Honeychurch and Amartushin 2007; Pashkevich 2003; Rosen et al. 2000; Shishlina 2000; Shishlina et al. 2008), further expanding our knowledge of what botanical resources pastoralists used in the past. This recent literature suggests that there is a good deal of variability in how pastoralists from region to region chose to tackle the challenges of maintaining their livestock and meeting their own nutritional needs.

In this chapter, I discuss the macrobotanical and palynological data from Krasnosamarskoe. The phytolith data will be discussed in Chapter 13. It is important to unite these different types of botanical analyses, because they make it possible to answer different questions or to answer certain questions more completely. For example, palynological analysis of sediment samples from archaeological contexts can provide a localized picture of the vegetation surrounding the settlement, help answer questions of seasonality, and sometimes point to the specialized use of particular plants. On the other hand, using the macrobotanical data, it is possible to address questions of diet, assess whether the inhabitants of this settlement relied on cultivated grain, and determine the activities that took place in and around the structure.

Palynological Methods

Eighty sediment samples were extracted from the settlement at Krasnosamarskoe for phytolith analysis, and 13 of these were selected for pollen analysis. All of the samples came from the structure floor or from a feature. Although some archaeological palynologists (e.g., Dimbleby 1985) caution against taking spot samples from archaeological contexts, many palynological studies of archaeological contexts have produced clear interpretations of localized pollen dispersal within and between structures using this strategy (Cummings 1998; Dean 1998; Fish 1998; Morrison and Truran 1998). Pollen deposited in the course of processing, cooking, craft manufacture, and storage is mixed on floors by walking, sweeping, and other activities. Over time, some of this pollen becomes compacted into floor sediments, incorporating a "time-averaged" record of resource use. In many ways, the pollen associated with the occupation at Krasnosamarskoe was ideally preserved. As Rosen points out in Chapter 9, the dug-out floor of the structure was filled in quickly upon abandonment. The cultural layers were covered in fine clayey sediment that essentially locked the pollen in place. The sediment retained water well, which was good for the preservation of the pollen, although it is likely this hindered the preservation of macrobotanical remains.

All sediment samples were chemically prepared using the standard techniques of quaternary analysis (Faegri and Iversen 1989; see Popova 2006:Appendix A for a full discussion of the processing technique used). One tablet of *Lycopodium* spores (13,111) was added to each sample at the start of the preparation to allow pollen concentrations

to be assessed. Samples were examined by traversing each microscope slide until at least 300 pollen grains had been counted (Maher 1972). Pollen grains found were identified; the presence of charcoal fragments and any possible parasite eggs was noted.

Macrobotanical Methods

At Krasnosamarskoe, a composite sampling method was used in collecting samples for flotation. During the excavations, flotation samples were collected from each level of each 2-m × 2-m unit until 2 L had been amassed. All features (storage pits, ashy features, trash pits) were sampled, as well as the soil around the features for comparison. Pearsall (2000) argues that for most situations, composite sampling is sufficient to capture most actions and places within a locus. The samples from Krasnosamarskoe were floated using a SMAP (or Shell Mound Archaeological Project) flotation machine set up in the field, as described in Pearsall (2000:29–33) and Watson (1976:79–80). This type of flotation system uses a rigid barrel that catches the heavy flotation fraction, while the flotation material is carried over a sluiceway and is caught in geological sieves. Flotation samples from Krasnosamarskoe were sorted at the Paleoecology Laboratory at the University of Chicago with the help of undergraduate volunteers. The sorting strategy followed procedures established by Pearsall (2000). The light fraction was weighed and the sample was divided into two splits with a 2-mm geological sieve. All charred material was removed from the >2-mm fraction, identified and put into containers. For the <2-mm split, an illuminated dissection microscope was used to sort and identify charred seeds, which were stored in gelatin capsules. A comparative collection of seeds from the region as well as published seed identification manuals (Corner 1976; Delorit 1970; Martin and Barkley 1961) were used for identification.

Current Botanical Resources around Krasnosamarskoe

The region surrounding the village of Krasnosamarskoe is currently used as pasture. The heavy usage of the land has transformed the steppe into a mosaic of resilient plants able to withstand the constant grazing. It has been suggested that in the past, the second terrace was a typical meadow-steppe environment in which *Festuca sulcata* was the dominant grass species (Lavrenko et al. 1991). It is the mosaic of soils and salt concentrations in the region that creates these patches of plants on the second terrace where the Late Bronze Age structure was located (see Chapter 9 for a more detailed discussion of the surrounding landscape). Currently, a human-made lake stands at the edge of the excavation site, destroying part of the settlement site, although in the past, there was a smaller oxbow lake or marshy depression farther away from structure. This old oxbow lake was located on the first terrace and will be discussed later in more detail. Typical plants currently on the second terrace are *Trifolium repens* and *pratense* (clover), *Cichorium intybus* (chicory with blue flower), *Plantago lanceolata*, *Medicago* sp. (lucerna), *Archillea millifolium* (yarrow), *Veronica* sp., *Artemisia* sp., *Kochia prostrata*, *Galium verum*, *Festuca sulcata*, *Alyssum desertorum*, and *Agropyron repens* (couch grass). The prevalence of *A. desertorum* demonstrates that the pastures in the region are heavily used. In recent years, the pastures have been further denuded as livestock owners are forced to take cattle out to pasture before the end of the spring floods, due to a rise in the cost of fodder. The animals slog through the mud, further causing more fragile steppe plants to be replaced by hardy plants such as *P. lanceolata* and *A. desertorum* and leading to a decline in the overall diversity of plants around Krasnosamarskoe.

Local Vegetation during the Late Bronze Age

Krasnosamarskoe was occupied in the early Late Bronze Age, between 1900 and 1700 BC (see Chapter 2). One feature is particularly important for botanical studies: Pit 10, probably a well (see Figures 12.1 and 10.22). During the 2001 field season, this feature was completely excavated, uncovering a bell-shaped pit with an opening 1.8 m in diameter and 2.1 m at the widest part of the pit. At the base of the pit on the south side was a small step, while the north side was scooped out. The bottom of the pit was 2 m below the Bronze Age land surface. The fill of the pit contained Pokrovka (Early Srubnaya) and mature Srubnaya ceramic fragments. The bottom 70 cm of the pit (2–2.7 m deep) was filled with rich organic debris and well-preserved wooden artifacts.

There were likely many uses for this particular pit, but it seems likely that it was a well at some point, since it was obviously filled with water before it was backfilled. The consistently waterlogged conditions of the well created a situation in which there was incredible preservation of botanical remains. Given the density of pollen found in this context, it appears that it was left open to the elements at some point and thus acted as a local pollen trap that was later sealed. As a result, it is possible to use the pollen data from the samples from the well to describe the local vegetation during the time of the occupation. The spot samples from the well were extracted at the depths of 240 cm and 260 cm below the modern ground surface in the thick organic layers.

Pollen from the samples from this context was exceptionally well preserved and abundant, with the pollen concentrations being 299,513 pollen grains/mL of sediment at the depth of 240 cm and 588,740 pollen grains/mL of sediment at the depth of 260 cm (see Table 12.1). Overall, the makeup of the pollen assemblage from both samples is very similar. From both samples, arboreal pollen made up a very small percentage of the total spore/pollen count, less than 2 percent (see Table 12.2). *Pinus sylvestris* (Scotch pine), *Betula* (birch), *Quercus robur* (oak), *Populus* (poplar), and *Tilia* (linden) were all encountered. This is probably partially caused by the relatively high number of aquatic and wetland pollen grains in the sample. However, the concentration of pine pollen is significantly higher in the sample from 260 cm below datum than in the higher sample.

Other pollen from these samples demonstrates a powerful steppe 'signature' with plants from the *Poaceae* (Grass), *Chenopodiaceae* (Goosefoot) and *Amaranthaceae* (Amaranth) families being the most commonly represented, with some mesic herbaceous plants as well. *Polygonum* (Knotweed) was encountered in both samples. *Plantago* (Plantain) made up about 5 percent of the total pollen and spore count in both samples, and *Artemisia* (Sage) made up about 4 percent. Both samples also had small amounts of pollen from *Urtica* (Nettle) and *Asteraceae* (Composites). However, the sample from 240cm depth contained small amounts of pollen from *Trifolium* (clover) and *Ranunculus* (buttercup), while the sample from the depth of 260cm contained *Caryophyllaceae* (pink family) pollen, possibly *Gypsophila* (see table 12.3).

This meadow steppe environment contained a localized concentration of marshy, wet plants that probably formed at the edge of an oxbow lake, as indicated by some of the pollen found in these samples. Pollen from *Typha* (cattail) and *Cyperaceae* (sedges) are the most common from both well samples (see Table 12.4). *Typha* pollen is abundant in both samples but slightly more so in the sample from the 260-cm depth below datum. This result could be due to the fact that there is a higher overall pollen concentration in the lower sample (see Table 12.1). The concentration of *Cyperaceae* pollen was less in the sample from 240 cm below datum, but it was still abundant in both samples. It is likely that the high concentrations of *Typha* and *Cyperaceae* pollen, plus the presence of *Equisetum* (horsetail) spores, indicate the close proximity of the marshland to the settlement.

By linking the background pollen from the samples from the settlement with the marsh core collected at Sharlyk, it is possible to reconstruct what the landscape at Krasnosamarskoe looked like during the occupation (see Chapter 5). Although forests expanded in the middle Volga

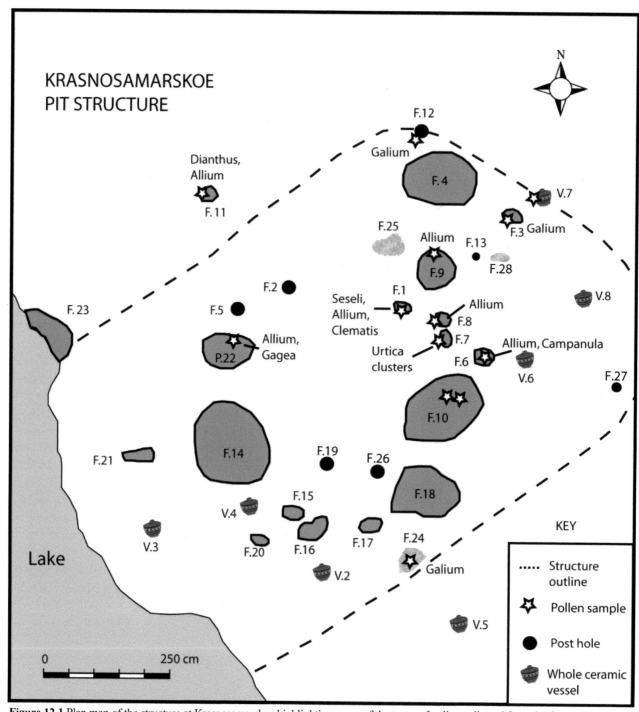

Figure 12.1 Plan map of the structure at Krasnosamarskoe highlighting some of the types of pollen collected from the floor.

region during the Late Bronze Age, the arboreal pollen signature for this time period from the Sharlyk swamp shows that the size of forests in this region remained relatively stable (see Kremenetski et al. 1999). This signature suggests that human settlements in this region were actively harvesting wood resources from the nearby oasis forests (mapped in Figure 2.1). Based on the arboreal pollen from the structure floor (see Tables 12.9 and 12.10), the forests in the region around the settlement consisted of pine (*Pinus sylvestris*), oak (*Quercus robur*), hazel (*Corylus*), birch (*Betula*), *Populus*, and maple (*Acer*). From the Sharlyk core, it is clear that human activity in part is responsible for changing the composition local forests. *Pinus* and *Betula* remain the dominant arboreal species in the region, but

Table 12.1 Overall Pollen Concentrations from All Samples

Location: Krasnosamarskoe	Overall Pollen Concentration
L3/2, Feature 1, 80–90 cm depth[a]	30,991 pollen grains/mL of sediment
M2/2, Feature 6, 80–90 cm depth	13,887 pollen grains/mL of sediment
O3/2, Feature 24, 70–72 cm depth	18,887 pollen grains/mL of sediment
L2/4, Feature 7, 80+ cm depth[a]	9,732 pollen grains/mL of sediment
L2/4, Feature 8, 80–90 cm depth[a]	13,917 pollen grains/mL of sediment
K2/L2, Feature 9, 90–110 cm depth[a]	10,148 pollen grains/mL of sediment
M2/4, Feature 10, 240 cm depth, early LBA[a]	299,513 pollen grains/mL of sediment
M2/4, Feature 10, 260 cm depth, early LBA	588,740 pollen grains/mL of sediment
K5/2, Feature 11, 80–90 cm depth[a]	9,969 pollen grains/mL of sediment
I3/3, Feature 12, 80–90 cm depth[a]	15,857 pollen grains/mL of sediment
K2/3, Feature 3, 80+ cm depth[a]	7,374 pollen grains/mL of sediment
L4/4, Feature 22, 80–90 cm depth[a]	10,506 pollen grains/mL of sediment
K1/K2, Vessel 7, 60–80 cm depth fill[a]	16,244 pollen grains/mL of sediment
Kurgan 1, Grave 3, bottom of shaft, MBA	9,556 pollen grains/mL of sediment

a Indicates that phytolith data are available for this sample (see Chapter 13). All samples are from the developed Late Bronze Age (LBA) time period unless otherwise noted. MBA = Middle Bronze Age.

Table 12.2 Count, Percent, and Concentration of Arboreal Pollen from Feature 10

Arboreal Pollen Location	TAXA	Count	Percent	Concentration grains/mL soil
240cm Depth	Pinus sylvestris	2	0.4	1,064
	Betula	2	0.4	1.064
	Quercus robur	1	0.2	532
	Populus	1	0.2	532
	Tilia	1	0.2	532
	Acer	1	0.2	532
260cm Depth	Pinus sylvestris	5	1.0	5,911
	Betula	2	0.4	2,364
	Quercus robur	1	0.2	1,182
	Populus	1	0.2	1,182
	Acer	1	0.2	1,182

Table 12.3 Count, Percent, and Concentration of Nonarboreal Pollen and Spores (Herbs/Shrubs) from Feature 10

NA, Herbs Location	TAXA	Count	Percent	Concentration Grains/mL Soil
240 cm depth	POACEAE	176	31.3	93,631
	CHENO-AM	174	30.9	92,567
	Plantago	28	5.0	14,896
	Artemisia	22	3.9	11,704
	Polygonum	6	1.2	3,724
	Trifolium	5	0.9	2,660
	ASTERACEAE (HS)	3	0.5	1,596
	Urtica	3	0.5	1,596
	Ranunculus	1	0.2	532
	APIACEAE	1	0.2	532
260 cm depth	POACEAE	168	33.7	198,611
	CHENO-AM	147	29.5	173,785
	Plantago	25	5.0	29,555
	Artemisia	18	3.6	21,280
	Polygonum	9	1.8	10,640
	Urtica	4	0.8	4,729
	ASTERACEAE (HS)	1	0.2	1,182
	Gypsophila	1	0.2	1,182

during this time period, *Corylus* and *Salix* pollen increased, while the percentage of *Alnus* and *Populus* pollen declined. The decrease in *Alnus* pollen could be the result of alder exploitation during the Late Bronze Age, since this type of wood makes good steady burning charcoal. There was also an expansion of shrubs and herbs that favor forests with

Table 12.4 Count, Percent, and Concentration of Nonarboreal (NA) Pollen and Spores (Wetlands) from Feature 10 Samples

NA, Wetlands Location	TAXA	Count	Percent	Concentration Grains/mL Soil
240 cm depth	*Typha*	67	11.9	35,644
	CYPERACEAE	21	3.7	11,172
	Equisetum	4	0.7	2,128
260 cm depth	*Typha*	51	10.2	60,293
	CYPERACEAE	22	4.4	26,009

light cover, including *Ribes*, Rubiaceae, and Rosaceae, suggesting that the forests were being thinned out. The increase in *Corylus* (hazelnut) pollen during this time period could also be linked to human activity, with the inhabitants of the region actively protecting these particular trees for their food potential.

Moreover, based on the analysis of pollen from sediment samples collected from the structure floor (see Tables 12.5 and 12.6), it seems that there was a marsh near the settlement consisting of sedges (*Cyperaceae*) and knotweeds (*Polygonum*), as well as some cattail (*Typha*). (*Phragmites* reeds are also documented by phytoliths.) However, as a regional trend, the percentage of aquatic pollen in the total pollen sum for this time period at Sharlyk declined, so there might have been some natural reduction of wetlands (see Chapter 5).

The land surrounding the settlement was primarily a grassland (*Poaceae* pollen was dominant), with a significant presence of goosefoot (*Chenopodiaceae*) and amaranth (*Amaranthaceae*) family plants. It is clear that this area around the structure was being used for grazing based on the elevated percentages of *Asteraceae*, *Cichorium* type, *Rumex*, and *Plantago* pollen in the Sharlyk swamp core for this period. However, it seems that the level of grazing was just as intensive in the Middle Bronze Age (see Chapter 4), and in both periods, it was not intensive enough to seriously alter the overall composition of steppe vegetation.

Seasonality

Determining the seasonality of occupation is essential for understanding the ways in which the excavated structure at Krasnosamarskoe was used. Archaeologists of the region assumed that Late Bronze Age wooden pit structures were occupied year round due to the heavy artifact density at these particular sites and also because they believed that farming was an important element in the LBA economy, and cultivated fields would require constant attention throughout the year (Sedova 2000; Vasiliev and Matveeva 1986). Various lines of evidence demonstrate that Krasnosamarskoe was

Table 12.5 Count, Percent, and Concentration of Nonarboreal (NA) Pollen (Wetlands) Found in Samples from Inside Structure

NA Pollen, Wetlands Location	TAXA	Count	Percent	Concentration Grains/mL Soil
L3/2, Feature 1	*Typha*	7	1.6	500
	CYPERACEAE	7	1.6	500
M2/2, Feature 6	*Typha*	15	4.6	641
	CYPERACEAE	7	2.2	299
O3/2, Feature 24	*Typha*	7	1.7	315
	CYPERACEAE	18	6.0	1,133
L2/4, Feature 7	*Typha*	8	2.3	227
	Lemna	1	0.3	28
	CYPERACEAE	3	0.9	85
L2/4, Feature 8	*Typha*	9	2.8	383
	CYPERACEAE	5	1.5	213
	Equisetum	5	1.5	213
K2/L2, Feature 9	*Typha*	11	3.3	338
	CYPERACEAE	4	1.2	123
I3/3, Feature 12	*Typha*	5	1.6	258
	CYPERACEAE	19	6.2	981
K2/3, Feature 3	*Typha* (cluster)	20	5.7	420
	CYPERACEAE	7	2.0	147
L4/4, Feature 22	*Typha* (cluster)	5	1.5	155
	CYPERACEAE	5	1.5	155
K1/K2, Vessel 7	*Typha*	5	1.7	271

Table 12.6 Count, Percent, and Concentration of Nonarboreal (NA) Pollen (Wetlands) Found in Sample Outside the Structure

NA Pollen, Wetlands Location	TAXA	Count	Percent	Concentration Grains/mL Soil
K5/2, Feature 11	*Typha*	12	3.5	350
	CYPERACEAE	22	7.3	1,300

used year-round. Faunal seasonal indicators were studied by looking at seasonal incremental banding of cementum on the roots of animal teeth (see Chapter 14). It was determined that cattle and sheep/goat teeth deposited in pits in the structure floor came from every season of the year. An equal number of cattle were butchered in the winter and summer months.

The abundant plant phytoliths studied by Weisskopf (2003) from inside the structure did not include dendritic long cells and thus husks were underrepresented (see also Chapter 13). This indicates that most of the plants from the Poaceae family, principally reeds (*Phragmites*) as well as sedges (*Cyperaceae*), were harvested in the fall or winter.

This makes sense for a lot of reasons. First, reeds used for roof thatching are normally harvested in the fall or winter after the first frost has stripped away the leaves and florescent parts; thatchers only need and use the reeds (Anthony et al. 2005). It also makes sense to let the reeds grow through the spring and summer, since cattle and other domesticated animals like to graze on the leaves. Sometimes marshland is slightly drained to encourage the growth of *Phragmites*, which prefers to grow where the water level fluctuates from 15 cm below soil surface to 15 cm above (Duke 1979).

It seems likely that during the spring and summer, the people who lived in this settlement collected wood and fodder for the winter, as well as food and medicinal plants. There was no forest in the immediate vicinity of the settlement, so it would have taken time to collect all the wood necessary to winter in such a location. From the features within the structure, we have very light pollen signatures from plants that bloom during the spring and summer in forested region such as *Gagea* (flowers March through May), a flower that must have been brought from a forest in the region, and *Campanula* (flowers June to August), a flower that grows in both shade and sunny grasslands. Pollen from these plants was always found in contexts where there was more diversity in arboreal pollen compared with other features without these types of plants (see Tables 12.7 and 12.9). The sediment sample from Feature 11, which is located outside the structure, similarly contained a very diverse assortment of arboreal pollen (see Tables 12.8 and 12.10).

There were also traces of pollen of the *Cichorium*-type pollen and nettle (*Urtica*). These plants seem to have been common weeds in the region since they are in almost all samples (see Tables 12.7 and 12.8). However, it is possible these plants were collected, since a cluster of nettle pollen was uncovered in Feature 7, while a cluster of *Cichorium*-type pollen was found in Feature 3. Chicory and nettle bloom in the spring and summer. Also, one pit feature in the structure, Feature 11, contained leaf phytoliths from *Phragmites* reeds harvested in the summer, perhaps for food (Weisskopf 2003). It is still common practice in the villages of Russia to harvest the rhizomes and roots of *Phragmites* and process them into starch (Duke 1979). Various lines of evidence corroborate the interpretation that the Krasnosamarskoe settlement was used during the whole year.

Plant Use Based on the Pollen Data

The pollen data confirm that the people who lived at Krasnosamarskoe during the Late Bronze Age were not farmers, since *Cerealia*-type pollen was not uncovered in

the sediment samples from the structure floor and was present only in the Sharlyk swamp core in the final phase corresponding with the modern period (see Chapter 5). Based on the macrobotanical data, it seems likely that *Chenopodium* and perhaps also *Polygonum* seeds were collected during the Late Bronze Age. It was clear that *Chenopodiaceae/Amaranthaceae* (Cheno-Am) were growing near the settlement. The pollen signature from Feature 8 suggests that *Chenopodium* or *Amaranthus* was collected in that location more than any other. In all the other samples from the occupation, the steppe signature was dominated by *Poaceae* pollen, which is to be expected in a steppe environment. However, in Feature 8, there was almost twice as much *Chenopodiaceae* and *Amaranthaceae* pollen compared to *Poaceae* pollen. The uses of *Chenopodium* will be discussed later.

In addition, pollen from *Allium* (garlic), which is an insect-pollinated plant, was found primarily in features that were deep within the structure and also in Feature 12, which was probably a trash midden based on Weisskopf's (2003) analysis. *Allium* was clearly collected and used within the structure. Besides being used as a flavoring to other foods, garlic can be used to repel insects and moles (Riotte 1998).

Although *Urtica* (nettle) pollen was found in almost all samples, indicating that it was growing nearby, it still seems likely the people who lived at Krasnosamarskoe in the Late Bronze Age at least occasionally collected it. Nettle has countless uses. Young leaves of nettle can be cooked and make a very nutritious addition to other foods as nettle is high in minerals and vitamins (Kunkel 1984). Moreover, a strong flax-like fiber is obtained from the stems and can be used for making string and cloth (Grieve 1984; Uphof 1959; Usher 1974). For this purpose, nettle is harvested when the plant begins to die down in early autumn. A beautiful and permanent green dye can also be obtained from a decoction of the leaves and stems of nettle (Grieve 1984). In Feature 7, there were clusters of *Urtica* pollen, which means that *Urtica* was collected while it was still in flower and deposited into this feature (see Table 12.7). Weisskopf (2003) has noted that there were starches present in Feature 7, perhaps indicating food waste.

Moreover, the presence of clusters of *Galium* (lady's bedstraw) pollen in sediment samples from features found around the inner edges of the structure (primarily in the northeast) and not in other samples is telling (see Figure 12.1). *Galium verum* currently grows on the second terrace at Krasnosamarskoe, and it is possible that *Galium* grew in the vicinity of the structure during the occupation. Nevertheless, the fact that most of the pollen is concentrated in one part of the structure seems to suggest that it was collected and used or dried inside the northern

Table 12.7 Count, Percent, and Concentration of Nonarboreal (NA) Pollen (Herbs/Shrubs) from Contexts inside the Structure

NA Pollen, Herbs Location	TAXA	Count	Percent	Concentration Grains/mL Soil
L3/2, Feature 1	POACEAE	182	41.9	12,996
	CHENO-AM	105	24.2	7,498
	ASTERACEAE (HS)	16	3.7	1,143
	Seseli (cluster)	11	2.5	785
	Urtica	9	2.1	643
	Plantago	5	1.2	357
	Cichorium type	4	0.9	286
	ASTERACEAE (LS)	4	0.9	286
	Polygonum	4	0.9	286
	Artemisia	3	0.7	428
	Allium	2	0.5	286
	Ranunculus	2	0.5	286
	Trifolium	1	0.2	71
	Clematis	1	0.2	71
M2/2, Feature 6	POACEAE	151	46.5	6,452
	CHENO-AM	73	22.5	3,119
	ASTERACEAE (HS)	10	3.1	427
	Cichorium type	6	1.8	256
	Plantago	5	1.5	214
	Urtica	5	1.5	214
	ASTERACEAE (LS)	4	1.2	171
	Campanula	2	0.6	85
	Polygonum	1	0.3	43
	Allium	1	0.3	43
O3/2, Feature 24	POACEAE	154	52.7	9,947
	CHENO-AM	57	19.0	3,589
	Plantago	7	2.3	441
	Urtica	4	1.3	252
	Polygonum	3	1.0	189
	CRUCIFERAE	3	1.0	189
	Artemisia	1	0.3	63
	ASTERACEAE (HS)	1	0.3	63
	Galium	1	0.3	63
L2/4, Feature 7	POACEAE	146	42.6	4,143
	CHENO-AM	92	26.8	2,610
	ASTERACEAE (HS)	14	4.1	397
	Urtica (cluster)	13	3.8	369
	Cichorium type	4	1.2	113
	Plantago	3	0.9	85
	Artemisia	2	0.6	57
	ASTERACEAE (LS)	2	0.6	57
	Ranunculus	2	0.6	57
L2/4, Feature 8	CHENO-AM	131	40.1	5,575
	POACEAE	96	29.4	4,086
	ASTERACEAE (HS)	10	3.1	426
	Plantago	7	2.1	298
	Cichorium type	3	0.9	128
	Urtica	2	0.6	85
	ASTERACEAE (LS)	1	0.3	43
	Polygonum	1	0.3	43
	Allium	1	0.3	43
	Rumex	1	0.3	43

NA Pollen, Herbs Location	TAXA	Count	Percent	Concentration Grains/mL Soil
K2/L2, Feature 9	POACEAE	151	45.8	4,643
	CHENO-AM	52	15.8	1,599
	ASTERACEAE (HS)	15	4.5	461
	Urtica	8	2.4	246
	Plantago	7	2.1	215
	Cichorium type	6	1.8	185
	Allium	3	0.9	92
	ASTERACEAE (LS)	2	0.6	62
	Artemisia	2	0.6	62
	Polygonum	1	0.3	31
I3/3, Feature 12	POACEAE	129	42.0	6,662
	CHENO-AM	52	16.9	2,686
	Plantago	9	2.9	465
	ASTERACEAE (HS)	5	1.6	258
	Cichorium type	4	1.3	207
	CRUCIFERAE	4	1.2	207
	Urtica	3	1.0	155
	ASTERACEAE (LS)	2	0.7	103
	Polygonum	1	0.3	52
	APIACEAE	1	0.3	52
	Galium	1	0.3	52
	Trifolium	1	0.3	52
K2/3, Feature 3	POACEAE	138	39.3	2,899
	CHENO-AM	91	25.9	1,912
	Cichorium type (cluster)	10	2.8	210
	Urtica	10	2.8	210
	ASTERACEAE (HS)	6	1.7	126
	Plantago (cluster)	3	0.9	63
	Polygonum	2	0.6	42
	Artemisia	1	0.3	21
	Galium	1	0.3	21
L4/4, Feature 22	POACEAE	128	37.8	3,967
	CHENO-AM	98	28.9	3,037
	Cichorium type	10	2.9	310
	ASTERACEAE (HS)	9	2.7	279
	Plantago	5	1.5	155
	Polygonum (cluster)	5	1.5	155
	Urtica	5	1.5	155
	Allium	2	0.6	62
	ASTERACEAE (LS)	2	0.6	62
	Artemisia	1	0.3	31
	Gagea	1	0.3	31
K1/K2, Vessel 7	POACEAE	140	47.3	7,689
	CHENO-AM	52	18.0	2,924
	Plantago	15	5.0	812
	ASTERACEAE (HS)	6	2.0	325
	Cichorium type	3	1.0	162
	ASTERACEAE (LS)	2	0.7	108
	Ranunculus	1	0.3	54
	CRUCIFERAE	1	0.3	54

Table 12.8 Count, Percent, and Concentration of Nonarboreal (NA) Pollen (Herbs/Shrubs) from Contexts outside the Structure

NA Pollen, Herbs Location	TAXA	Count	Percent	Concentration Grains/mL Soil
K5/2, Feature 11	POACEAE	143	41.8	4,169
	CHENO-AM	66	19.3	1,924
	ASTERACEAE (HS)	19	5.6	554
	CYPERACEAE	9	2.6	262
	Urtica	9	2.6	262
	Cichorium type	4	1.2	58
	Plantago	2	0.6	58
	Artemisia	2	0.6	58
	Dianthus	2	0.6	58
	Allium	2	0.6	58
	ASTERACEAE (LS)	1	0.3	29

corner of the structure. For most uses, *Galium* is collected while flowering and dried for later use. *Galium* has been used as bedding, but it was more commonly used in the past for curdling milk products. In some places, *Galium* is mixed with stinging nettle for this purpose (Chiej 1984; Facciola 1998; Phillips and Foy 1990). Perhaps spring was an important time for making curdled milk products at Krasnosamarskoe. One bottom-perforated ceramic vessel, usually interpreted as a vessel for making cheese, was found in the same located in association with clusters of *Galium* pollen in the northeastern section of the structure (Figure 10.34). It would be interesting to see if this pattern of *Galium* pollen along the edges of structures is found in other Late Bronze Age structures in the region.

One of the most unexpected pollen signatures uncovered in the settlement samples was from Feature 1, a posthole-shaped pit. In addition to the background pollen signature found in all samples, I counted several clusters of *Seseli* (or mooncarrot) pollen. This plant is in flower from July to August, and the seeds ripen from August to September. The flowers are hermaphrodite (have both male and female organs) and are pollinated by insects, so clusters of pollen from this plant indicate that the plant was collected when it was flowering. *Seseli* can grow in sandy, loamy, or clayey soils so long as there is good drainage. In the Samara region, however, *Seseli* grows best on chalk hills. It cannot currently be found anywhere near Krasnosamarskoe. What would have been the reason to collect *Seseli*? *Seseli* is cited in early Greek writings as a component of incense, and in India, *Seseli* is used to this day in veterinary medicine and to treat mental disorders. According to Ambasta (1986:570), the fruits of *Seseli* are used as a stimulant, whereas the roots

and aerial parts yield volatile oils that cause a fall in blood pressure, vasoconstriction, and stimulation of respiration, having a tranquilizing effect on humans and animals. Given that this pollen signature was found in connection to the remains of ritually butchered dogs perhaps gives some credence to the idea that *Seseli* was used to sedate the dogs before they were killed (see Chapters 14 and 16). This would have been an especially necessary precaution if these were guard dogs that were trained to be vicious.

Plant Use Based on the Macrobotanical Data

Surrounded by rich meadow steppe, Krasnosamarskoe could in theory have supported cultivated cereals during the Late Bronze Age—wheat grows throughout the region today. However, intensive sampling for macrobotanical remains at Krasnosamarskoe failed to uncover a single cultivated grain associated with the Late Bronze Age occupation. (Two charred millet seeds were associated with the Iron Age occupation; see Chapter 10, "Cultural Stratigraphy.") In general, the preservation of macrobotanical remains from the features was poor, except for the waterlogged Pit 10 (Table 12.11). It is not surprising that so few macrobotanical remains were recovered, since there was no hearth and only a few small ash dumps associated with the occupation in the structure, which apparently was not used for cooking. The seeds recovered indicate that some of the same "weeds" grew in the region throughout the Bronze Age that grow there today (Table 12.12), including sedges (*Cyperus*), knotweed (*Polygonum*), bluegrass (*Poa annua*), chicory with blue flowers (*Cichorium intybus*), goosefoot (*Chenopodium* sp.), and mustard (*Brassica*).

Table 12.9 Arboreal Pollen from Contexts inside the Structure

Arboreal Pollen Location	TAXA	Count	Percent	Concentration Grains/mL Soil
L3/2, Feature 1	*Pinus sylvestris*	29	6.7	2,071
	Corylus	5	1.2	357
	Acer	5	1.2	357
	Betula	4	0.9	286
	Populus	2	0.5	143
	Quercus robur	1	0.2	71
M2/2, Feature 6	*Pinus sylvestris*	22	6.8	940
	Quercus robur	2	0.6	85
	Populus	2	0.6	85
	Betula	1	0.3	43
	Acer	1	0.3	43
O3/2, Feature 24	*Pinus sylvestris*	8	2.7	504
	Populus	2	0.7	126
L2/4, Feature 7	*Pinus sylvestris*	30	8.7	851
	Quercus robur	2	0.6	57
	Betula	2	0.6	57
	Acer	2	0.6	57
	Populus	1	0.3	28
L2/4, Feature 8	*Pinus sylvestris*	22	6.7	936
	Betula	8	2.4	340
	Quercus robur	4	1.2	170
	Populus	4	1.2	170
	Acer	4	1.2	170
	Corylus	2	0.6	85
K2/L2, Feature 9	*Pinus sylvestris*	52	15.8	1,599
	Populus	2	0.6	62
	Betula	1	0.3	31
	Acer	1	0.3	31
I3/3, Feature 12	*Pinus sylvestris*	36	11.7	1,859
	Quercus robur	2	0.7	103
	Populus	2	0.7	103
	Betula	1	0.3	52
K2/3, Feature 3	*Pinus sylvestris*	41	11.7	861
	Acer	3	0.9	63
	Betula	1	0.3	21
L4/4, Feature 22	*Pinus sylvestris*	24	7.1	744
	Betula	5	1.5	155
	Acer	3	0.9	93
	Juniperus	1	0.3	31
	Populus	1	0.3	31
	Quercus robur	1	0.3	31
K1/K2, Vessel 7	*Pinus sylvestris*	24	8.0	1,300
	Populus	1	0.3	54
	Acer	1	0.3	54

344 Laura M. Popova

Table 12.10 Arboreal Pollen from Contexts outside the Structure

Arboreal Pollen Location	TAXA	Count	Percent	Concentration rains/mL Soil
K5/2, Feature 11	*Pinus sylvestris*	36	10.5	1,049
	Populus	3	0.9	87
	Betula	2	0.6	58
	Quercus robur	1	0.3	29
	Acer	1	0.3	29

Table 12.11 Density of Macrobotanical Remains at Krasnosamarskoe, Comparing Pit 10 and All Other Features

Site	Sediment Volume (L)	Seeds (*n*)	Seed Density (Seeds/L)	Genera
Pit 10	23.5	1,100	46.8	37
Other features	203.5	32	0.2	12

Table 12.12. List of the Count for Each Taxa Represented by Macrobotanical Remains at Krasnosamarskoe for the Features Excluding Pit 10

Feature	Taxa	Count
Late Bronze Age floor deposits	*Amaranthus retroflexus*	1
	Brassica sp.	4
	Chenopodium album	3
	Cichorium intybus	1
	Cyperus sp.	2
	Eleocharis sp.	1
	Polygonum sp.	5
	Rumex hydrolapathum	1

The macrobotanical remains associated with Pit 10 were better preserved because they were preserved in the waterlogged well (see Table 12.13). Still, it seems likely that most of the botanical species found with Pit 10 were not deliberately deposited into the well but rather were growing wild in the environment and were introduced into the well accidentally. The macrobotanical, pollen, and phytolith data all provide clear evidence that the bottom of the pit developed a layer of organic debris 30 to 40 cm thick, part of which was driven up the sidewall when the well was backfilled during the site abandonment process. Radiocarbon samples from this sediment show that it developed throughout the period when the site was occupied.

The macrobotanical samples from Pit 10 consisted of a mix of charred and uncharred seeds representing both steppe and wetland taxa as well as charcoal. The charred seeds (*Chenopodium album*, *Polygonum* sp., and *Amaranthus*) perhaps indicate food preparation. The rest of the seeds came from the surrounding territory and thus give a more nuanced picture of the specific plants that were growing in the immediate vicinity. For example, it seems that *Cyperus glaber*, *Cyperus fuscus*, *Carex*, and *Polygonum hydropiper* were growing in the marsh and that the surrounding steppe featured *Medicago* sp., *Brassica campestris*, *Digitaria*, and *Kochia*.

An analysis of the macrobotanical remains uncovered from Pit 10 can provide an interesting glimpse into subsistence activities at Krasnosamarskoe. Given that relatively large numbers of charred *Chenopodium* and *Polygonum* seeds that were uncovered in the well ($n = 306$ and $n = 74$, respectively), it seems likely that people or animals were consuming these highly edible seeds. It is also possible that dung was used as fuel and these seeds were charred in that way. However, Weisskopf (2003) determined from phytoliths that wood, not dung, was the primary fuel at the Krasnosamarskoe. Also, the three genera of charred seeds are known for their human dietary usage, while 28 other genera of seeds also found in Pit 10 were not charred, and these genera included seeds of pasture plants such as clover, ryegrass, bluegrass, and sedges, which would have been eaten by dung-producing grazing animals and should have been charred if dung burning was the cause of seed charring.

Table 12.13. List of the Count for Each Taxa Represented by Macrobotanical Remains from Feature 10

Taxa	Levels 8–10	Level 12	Level 16	Level 17	Level 18	Level 19	Level 20	Level 24	Level 26
Achillea sp.								2	
Agropyron sp.								6	
Agrostis sp.								3	
Amaranthus sp.							8[a]	3[a]	
Arenaria sp.								1	
Astragalus sp.							1		
Atriplex sp.					4		3	16	
Brassica sp.								1	
Carex sp.								7	
Chenopodium sp.	1	1	8	21	21	7	139[a]	120[a]	47[a]
Cichorium intybus								27	1
Cyperus sp.							3	42	2
Digitaria sp.								5	
Eleocharis sp.								12	1
Eragrostis sp.							1		4
Erodium sp.								1	
Galium sp.								6	
Glyceria sp.								1	
Hieracium sp.								6	
Hypericum sp.								1	
Kochia sp.								3	
Linaria sp.								5	
Lolium perenne								5	
Medicago sp.								18	
Melilotus sp.								8	
Phragmites australis								1	
Poa sp.					1			14	2
Polygonum sp.			1	2	4	3	21[a]	48[a]	5[a]
Rumex sp.				1	2	1	4	13	5
Scirpus sp.				2					
Setaria sp.								1	
Solanum sp.								1	
Sparganium erectum								46	
Stipa sp.								5	
Trifolium sp.								1	
Unidentifiable							4	21	1

Note: Two liters of sediment were sampled from each level recorded above.

a Indicates that the seeds were charred.

Therefore, at this point, it seems at least plausible that *Chenopodium* and *Polygonum* made up a portion of the diet of the Late Bronze Age inhabitants of this region. These nutritious seeds were easily obtained from wild plants. Modern wild *Chenopodium belandieri* grows in dense stands that can produce seed yields in the range of 500 to 1,000 kg of seeds per hectare, about the same as einkorn wheat, which yields 645 to 835 kg/ha (Smith 1989:1569). In places where flotation of sediment samples has become standard practice, *Chenopodium* and *Amaranthus* seeds are commonly uncovered. For example, flotation has been used extensively at the Bronze Age sites recently excavated in the Kalmyk steppes, and they have uncovered *Amaranthus* seeds in Middle Bronze Age graves (Shishlina et al. 2002). It is equally possible that *Chenopodium* was collected as fodder to feed livestock over the lean winter months. Kott (1955) has suggested that it was common practice in some areas of the Soviet Union to regularly use *Chenopodium* as fodder. Its history as food for animals can be seen in some of the common names for *Chenopodium* such as fat-hen and pigweed. It seems very possible that it could double as both food for humans and animals.

Conclusions

It is clear at this point that grains (whether wild or cultivated) were not a major component of the day-to-day diet of Late Bronze Age pastoralists in the middle Volga region. This theory is supported by the absence of dental caries in the human remains associated with the Late Bronze Age population of Krasnosamarskoe (see Chapter 8). In addition, the stable isotope analysis of Late Bronze Age populations in the Samara Valley indicated that people in the region did not rely principally on grain for their sustenance (see Chapter 7). It would be a mistake, however, to ignore the way in which foraging for wild grains and useful plants helped Bronze Age pastoralists thrive. Eating foraged grains when times were lean would enable a family to keep themselves and their livestock alive until the spring. Carefully collected specialized plants could have been important for ritual functions and for use as medicines. Finally, plants can be used to make a living space more comfortable. For example, dried *Gallium* could be used to make sleeping mats softer or could be used to block out a draft. *Phragmites* reeds could be collected to make a strong roof to keep out the winter snow. We still have much to learn about how plants were used by Bronze Age pastoralists of the European steppe. We can only find out more by continuing to systematically sample archaeological sites for macrobotanical, palynological, and phytolith analyses.

Editors' Note

Macrobotanical remains from the LBA settlement at Krasnosamarskoe were collected through the flotation of settlement sediments and the collection of floating materials in a diaper cloth. Of the 274 flotation samples collected and catalogued from the Krasnosamarskoe settlement site, 159 were sent for identification to the Institute of the Ecology of Plants and Animals, Urals Branch of the Russian Academy of Sciences, Ekaterinburg, and 115 were sent to Laura Popova at the University of Chicago. Popova's report is above. In Table 12.14, we present the results of the Ekaterinburg analysis. It does not add anything to what Popova observed in her samples with one important exception: two charred domesticated millet seeds were found in the Ekaterinburg floats.

One charred millet seed was found in Square F2, Level 4. Square F2 was at the extreme southern end of the excavation grid, where there was an Iron Age hearth in Levels 1 and 2 containing an iron bloom, iron slag, and Iron Age Gorodetskaya culture pottery (see Chapter 10). No Srubnaya artifacts were found anywhere near this southern end of the grid, so this charred seed was associated with the Iron Age, not Bronze Age, activity at the site.

The other charred millet seed was found in Level 1 in Square O2, again in an area where Gorodetskaya pottery and iron slag were found, and in this case in Level 1, the Iron Age level. The only domesticated cereals found at the site were associated with the Iron Age component.

Notes

All figures and tables in this chapter were prepared by L. Popova.

References

Ambasta, S. P. (editor)
1986   *The Useful Plants of India.* Council of Scientific and Industrial Research, New Delhi.

Anthony, David W., D. Brown, E. Brown, A. Goodman, A. Khokhlov, P. Kosintsev, P. Kuznetsov, O. Mochalov, E. Murphy, D. Peterson, A. Pike-Tay, L. Popova, A. Rosen, N. Russell, and Alison Weisskopf
2005   The Samara Valley Project: Late Bronze Age Economy and Ritual in the Russian Steppes. *Eurasia Antiqua* 11:395–417.

Chang, Claudia, Norbert Benecke, Fedor P. Grigoriev, Arlene M. Rosen, and Perry A. Tourtellotte
2003   Iron Age Society and Chronology in South-east Kazakhstan. *Antiquity* 77(296):298–312.

Chang, Claudia, P. Tourtellotte, K. M. Baipakov, and F. P. Grigoriev
2002   *The Evolution of Steppe Communities from Bronze Age through Medieval Periods in Southeastern Kazakhstan (Zhetysu).* Sweet Briar College, Sweet Briar, Virginia.

Table 12.14 Macrobotanical Remains from 1999 Excavations, Sorted and Analyzed at the Institute of Ecology of Plants and Animals, Russian Academy of Sciences, Ekaterinburg, Russia

Chronological Period	Unit	Level	Stratum	Macrobotanical Remains
Early Srubnaya	O3	7	2–3	*Chenopodium glaucum L.*, 1 seed
Srubnaya	O2	6	2	*Chenopodium* sp., 1 seed (disturbed)
Srubnaya	O4	6	2	*Salix* sp. (willow), 1 box
Developed Srubnaya	O4	5	2	*Polygonum lapathifolium L.*, 1 seed
Iron Age ceramics (Gorodetskaya) are found as deep as Level 4 in Units P1 and P2. There are several Iron Age artifacts across the length of the excavation, including an iron smelting hearth in this unit.	F2	4	2	*Panicum miliaceum L.* (millet to sow), 1 seed
Developed Srubnaya	N3	4	2	Asteraceae gen. indet., 1 seed
Developed Srubnaya	M5	3	2	*Polygonum arviculare L.*, 1 seed; Poacea gen. indet. (herb), 1 seed; *Poa trivialis L.*, 1 seed
Developed Srubnaya	S2	3	1	*Setaria* sp., 1 seed
Bronze Sauromatian Arrowhead found in Level 5	L6	2	2	Atriplex cg. Hastata L., 1 seed; *Chenopodium glaucum L.*, 1 seed; *Elytrigia repens* (*L.*) Nevski, 1 seed
IA/Srubnaya	N4	2	1	*Lavatera thuringiaca L.*, 1 seed
IA/Srubnaya	O2	2	2	*Atriplex* sp. (*meved*) ,1 seed
Iron slag found in this feature	O3	2	Old F.2 (1999 season)	*Lavatera thuringiaca L.*, 1 seed
IA/Srubnaya	P4	2	2	*Polygonum patulum L.*, 2 seeds
Iron Age	U2	2	1	Scirpus tabernaemontni C.C.Gmel (reed), 1 seed
Iron Age	O2	1	1	*Panicum miliaceum L.* (millet to sow), 1 seed; Scirpus tabernaemontni C.C.Gmel, 2 seeds; *Elytrigia repens* (*L.*) Nevski, 2 seeds; *Setaria* sp., 1 seed; *Amaranthus retraflexus L.*, 2 seeds; Polygonum patulum Bieb., 1 seed; *Lycopus exaltatus L.*, 1 seed; *Potentilla anserina L.*, 1.5 seed; *Atriplex* spp. (*A. hastata L.*, 16 seeds + *A. patula L.*, 2 fruits *A. tatarica L.*) with seeds; Caryophyllaceae gen. indet., 1 seed

Chernykh, E. N.
1992 *Ancient Metallurgy in the USSR: The Early Metal Age.* Translated by S. Wright. Cambridge University Press, Cambridge.
1997 *Kargaly. Zabytii mir.* NOX, Moscow.
Chiej, R.
1984 *The Macdonald Encyclopedia of Medicinal Plants.* Macdonald and Co, London.
Corner, E. J. H.
1976 *The Seeds of Dicotyledons.* Cambridge University Press, Cambridge.

Cummings, L. S.
1998 Sampling Prehistoric Structures for Pollen and Starch Granules. In *New Developments in Palynomorph Sampling, Extraction, and Analysis*, edited by V. M. Bryant and J. H. Wrenn, pp. 35–52. American Association of Stratigraphic Palynologists Foundation, Dallas, Texas.
Dean, G.
1998 Finding a Needle in a Palynological Haystack: A Comparison of Methods. In *New Developments in Palynomorph Sampling, Extraction, and Analysis*, edited by V. M. Bryant and J. H. Wrenn, pp. 53–60. American

Association of Stratigraphic Palynologists Foundation, Dallas, Texas.

Delorit, R. J.

1970   *An Illustrated Taxonomy Manual of Weed Seeds.* Agronomy, River Falls, Wisconsin.

Dimbleby, G. W.

1985   *The Palynology of Archaeological Sites.* Academic Press, London.

Duke, J. A.

1979   Ecosystematic Data on Economic Plants. *Quarterly Journal of Crude Drug Research* 17(3–4):91–110.

Facciola, S.

1998   *Cornucopia II: A Source Book of Edible Plants.* Kampong, Vista, CA.

Faegri, K., and J. Iversen

1989   *Textbook of Pollen Analysis.* 4th ed. Revised by K. Faegri, P. E. Kaland, and K. Krzywinski. John Wiley & Sons, Chichester.

Fish, S. K.

1998   A Pollen Perspective on Variability and Stability in Tonto Basin Subsistence. In *Environment and Subsistence in the Classic Period Tonto Basin: The Roosevelt Archaeology Studies, 1989 to 1998,* edited by K. A. Spielmann, pp. 49–69. Roosevelt Monograph Series 10. Anthropological Field Studies 39. Office of Cultural Resource Management, Department of Anthropology, Arizona State University, Tempe.

Frachetti, M. D., R. N. Spengler, G. J. Fritz, and A. N. Mar'yashev

2010   Earliest Direct Evidence for Broomcorn Millet and Wheat in the Central Eurasian Steppe Region. *Antiquity* 84:993–1010.

Greive, M.

1984   *A Modern Herbal.* Penguin, New York.

Honeychurch, William, and Chunag Amartushin

2007   Hinterlands, Urban Centers, and Mobile Settings: The "New" Old World Archaeology from the Eurasian Steppe. *Asian Perspectives* 46(1):36–64.

Kolev, Yu. I., A. E. Mamonov, and M. A. Turestskii (editors)

2000   *Istoria Samarskogo Povolzh'ye s drevneishikh vremen do nashikh dnei: bronzovii vek.* Tsentr Integratsiia, Samara.

Kott, S. A.

1955   Sornyi rasteniia i bor'ba s nimi.. 2nd ed. Moscow: Selkhozgiz.

Kremenetski, C. V.

1995   Holocene Vegetation and Climate History of Southwestern Ukraine. *Review of Paleobotany and Palynology* 85:289–301.

Kremenetski, C. V., T. Bittger, F. W. Junge, and A. G. Tarasov

1999   Late and Postglacial Environment of the Buzuluk Area, Middle Volga Region, Russia. *Quaternary Science Reviews* 18:1185–1203.

Kunkel, G.

1984   *Plants for Human Consumption.* Koeltz Scientific Books, Koenigsten.

Lavrenko, E. M., Z. V. Karamysheva, and R. I. Nikulina

1991   *Stepi Evrazii.* Nauka, Leningrad.

Lebedeva, E. Y.

1996   O zemledelii v stepe i lesostepe Vostochnoi Evropy v epokhu bronzy. *XIII Uralskoe arkheologicheskoe soveshchanie* I:53–55.

Maher, L. J., Jr.

1972   Nomograms for Computing 95% Limits of Pollen Data. *Review of Paleobotany and Palynology* 13:85–93.

Martin, A. C., and W. D. Barkley

1961   *Seed Identification Manual.* University of California Press, Berkeley.

Morrison, K. D., and A. E. Truran

1998   Spatial Patterning of Soil Chemistry, Sediment, and Pollen from Plaza Surfaces at L.A. 162 (Paa-ko), New Mexico. Poster presented at the Sixty-first Annual Meeting of the Society for American Archaeology, New Orleans, Louisiana.

Pashkevich, Galina A.

1984   Palaeoethnobotanical Examination of Archaeological Sites in the Lower Dnieper Region, Dated to the Last Centuries BC and the First Centuries AD. In *Plants and Ancient Man: Studies in Palaeoethnobotany,* edited by W. van Zeist and W. A. Casparie, pp. 277–292. A. A. Balkema, Boston.

1997   Zemledeliye u plemen sabatinovskoi kul'tury po dannim paleobotanicheskikh issledovanii. In *Sabatinovskaya i srubnaya kul'tury: problemy vzaimosvyazey vosto-ka i zapada v epokhu pozdney bronzy,* edited by V. N. Klyushintsev, pp. 59–61. Institut Archeologii NAN Ukrainy, Kiev.

2003   Paleoethnobotanical Evidence of Agriculture in the Steppe and Forest-Steppe of East Europe in the Late Neolithic and Bronze Age. In *Prehistoric Steppe Adaptation and the Horse,* edited by M. Levine, C. Renfrew and K. Boyle, pp. 287–297. McDonald, London.

Pearsall, Deborah M.

2000   *Paleoethnobotany: A Handbook of Procedures.* 2nd ed. Academic Press, San Diego.

Phillips, R., and N. Foy

1990   *Herbs.* Pan Books, London.

Popova, Laura M.

2006   Political Pastures: Navigating the Steppe in the Middle Volga Region (Russia) during the Bronze Age. Unpublished Ph.D. dissertation, Department of Anthropology, University of Chicago.

Riotte, L.
1998   *Carrots Love Tomatoes: Secrets of Companion Planting for Successful Gardening.* 2nd ed. Storey, North Adams, Massachusetts.

Rosen, A. M., C. Chang, and F. P. Grigoriev
2000   Paleoenvironments and Economy of Iron Age Saka-Wusun Agro-Pastoralists in Southeastern Kazakhstan. *Antiquity* 74:611–623.

Sedova, M. S.
2000   Poselenia srubnoi kul'turi. In *Istoria Samarskovo Povolzh'ye s drevneishikh vremen do nashikh dnei: bronzovii vek,* edited by Yu. I. Kolev, A. E. Mamonov, and M. A. Turetskii, pp. 209–255. Tsentr Integratsiia, Samara.

Shishlina, N. I.
2000   *Sesonni economicheskii tsikl naseleniia Severa-Zapadnovo Prikaspiya v bronzovom veke.* Vipusk 120. Trydi Gosydarstvennovo Istoricheskovo Muzeya, Moscow.

Shishlina, N. I., M. A. Novikova, and A. G. Devyatov
2002   Seeds in the Funeral Ritual of Bronze Age Nomads. Paper presented at the Eighth European Association of Archaeology Annual Meeting, Thessaloniki, Greece.

Shishlina, Natalya I., E. I. Gak, and A. V. Borisov
2008   Nomadic Sites of the South Yergueni Hills on the Eurasian Steppe: Models of Seasonal Occupation and Production. In *The Archaeology of Mobility: Old World and New World Nomadism,* edited by H. Barnard and W. Wendrich, pp. 230–249. Cotsen Institute of Archaeology, University of California Los Angeles.

Smith, B.
1989   Origins of Agriculture in Eastern North America. *Science* 246(4937):1566–1571.

Spiridonova, E. A.
1989   Rezultati izucheniya kulturnogo sloya mosolovskogo poseleniya epokhi poznei bronzi metodom sporo-piltsebogo analiza. In *Poseleniya srubnoi obshosti,* edited by A. D. Pryakhin, 100–105. University of Voronezh, Voronezh.

Uphof, J. C. Th.
1959   *Dictionary of Economic Plants.* 2nd Ed. Stechert-Hafner; Codicote, Herts., Wheldon & Wesley, New York.

Usher, G.
1974   *A Dictionary of Plants Used by Man.* Hafner, New York.

Vasiliev, I. B., and G. I. Matveeva
1986   *Istokov istorii Samarskogo Povolzh'ya.* Kuibyshevskoe Knizhnoe Izdatel'stvo, Kuibyshev.

Watson, Patty Jo
1976   In Pursuit of Prehistoric Subsistence: A Comparative Account of Some Contemporary Flotation Techniques. *Midcontinental Journal of Archaeology* 1:77–100.

Weisskopf, A.
2003   A Study of the Phytoliths from the Late Bronze Age Site of Krasno Samarskoe (*sic*), Samara Valley, Russia and the Information that They Provide on Agro-Pastoral Economies and Environment. Unpublished thesis, University College London, Institute of Archaeology.

Chapter 13

Phytoliths from the Krasnosamarskoe Settlement and Its Environment

Alison Weisskopf • Arlene Miller Rosen

We present here an analysis of phytoliths collected from the Late Bronze Age (LBA) settlement of Krasnosamarskoe in the Samara River valley in the northern Russian steppes. This chapter should ideally be read in conjunction with Chapter 12 by Popova, which describes the pollen and macrobotanical evidence from the same settlement, occasionally with complementary results that must be combined to obtain a full picture of the ancient environment. For example, *Typha* (also known as bulrush or cattail) pollen was abundant and ubiquitous at Krasnosamarskoe, clearly attesting to its importance in the local vegetation, but *Typha* does not produce identifiable phytoliths, so in the phytolith window, *Typha* was almost absent. The opposite was true for *Phragmites* (Cav) Trin.x Streud reeds, which were abundant in phytoliths but low in pollen. To perceive that the ancient environment contained abundant stands of both kinds of reeds, the phytolith and pollen evidence must be considered together.

Phytoliths are microscopic silica bodies formed in plants from the monosilicic acid that is taken up in ground water. They are also known as plant opals or plant silica bodies. As the plant grows, the silica is absorbed into its tissues and forms phytoliths, made of opaline silica ($SiO_2.nH_2O$) (Piperno and Pearsall 1993:9). In many (although not all) taxa, mainly monocotyledons such as grasses and sedges, they take on the distinctive forms of the plant cells. After the organic material has died and decayed, the inorganic phytoliths remain, so are an invaluable source of information for the archaeologist. They can be used to suggest past environments, subsistence patterns, diet, building materials, medicines, and much else.

While many plant taxa (e.g., grasses and sedges) generate abundant phytoliths, some groups such as most dicotyledons do not produce any (Piperno and Pearsall 1993:9). Many phytoliths can be identified to genus and in rare cases some even to species (Piperno and Pearsall 1993:9). The different parts of the plant, such as leaf, stem, and husk, produce distinctive phytolith types (Figure 13.1), enabling us to make inferences about details such as seasonality or which parts of the plant were being used. The aim here is to identify key distinctive shapes of phytoliths from the samples we have extracted.

Twenty phytolith samples were analyzed, including 19 from the settlement site of Krasnosamarskoe (all from the LBA) and one from an alluvial deposit on the bank of the Samara River. Phytoliths were also extracted from modern plants to use as comparative reference material. The sediment and modern plant samples were processed counted and analyzed.

Method

We used Rosen's method for phytolith extraction (Rosen 1993). The size of the aliquot was 750 to 800 mg of sediment from each sample. Ten percent HCl was used to remove the pedogenic carbonates, and then 15 mL of Calgon (sodium hexamaphosphate) was added. The

Single-cell

Figure 13.1 Common phytolith morphotypes (from Weisskopf 2014).

sand- and silt-sized particles, including the phytoliths, will sink to the bottom of an 8-cm column of water in an hour, leaving the clays in suspension. These are poured off and the process is continued until the suspension is clear. The samples were then ashed in a muffle furnace at 500°C for 2 hours and 30 minutes. When cool, the samples were washed and dried again at just under 50°C. The dried phytoliths were weighed to obtain a total phytolith weight, and around 2 mg of phytoliths per sample were mounted in Entellan.

The modern reference plant samples were separated into three parts, leaf, culm, and husk, including spikelet where available, and ashed before mounting in Entellan. A Leica petrological microscope was used at 40× magnification to count the phytoliths.

Reference Samples

Reference samples were prepared of *Typha* and *Ephedra* as well as the following grasses: *Avena L.*, *Bromus Scop.*, *Eragrostis*, *Phragmites*, and *Stipa* (Figure 13.2).

Figure 13.2 Reference Samples

Taxon	Abundance	Diagnostic	Photo
Avena sterilis husk	Abundant	Diagnostic	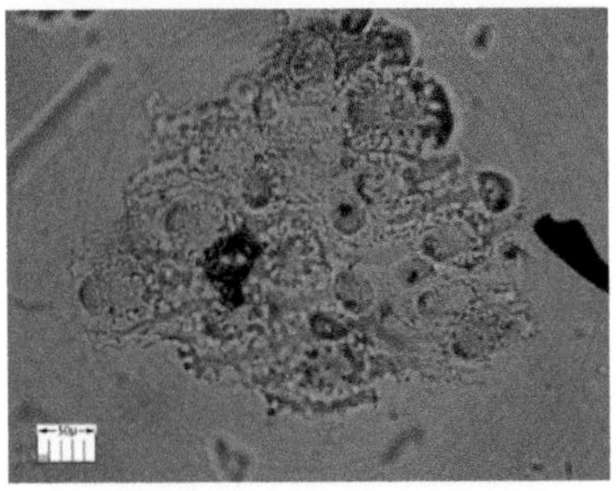
Bromus sterilis inflorescence and awn	Common	Diagnostic	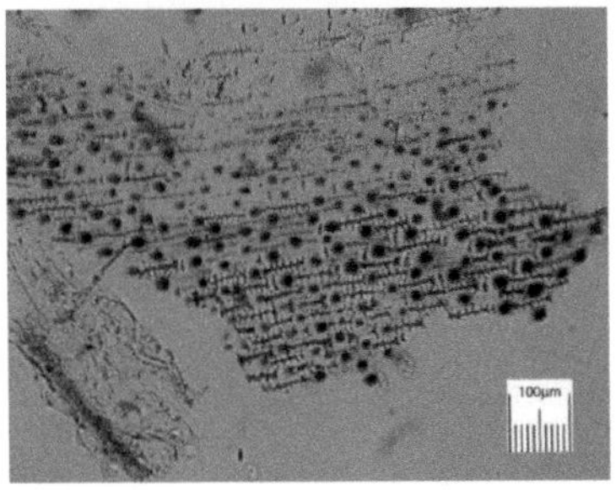
Ephedra	Sparse	Not diagnostic	
Eragrostis minor culm	Abundant	Diagnostic to subfamily Short saddles	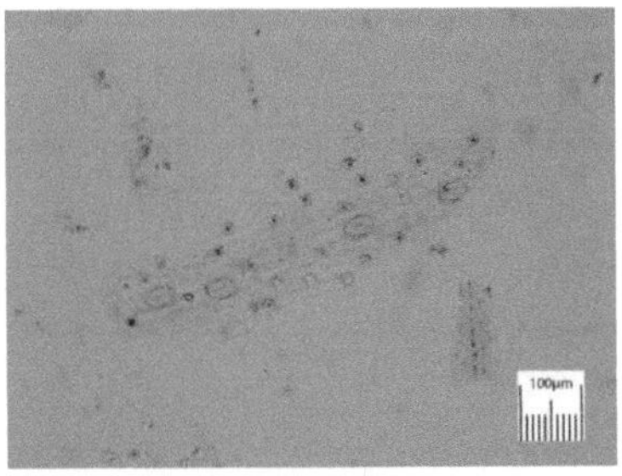
Phragmites australis leaf	Abundant	Diagnostic to genera Long saddles Chunky bulliforms Distinctive keystones (not in photo)	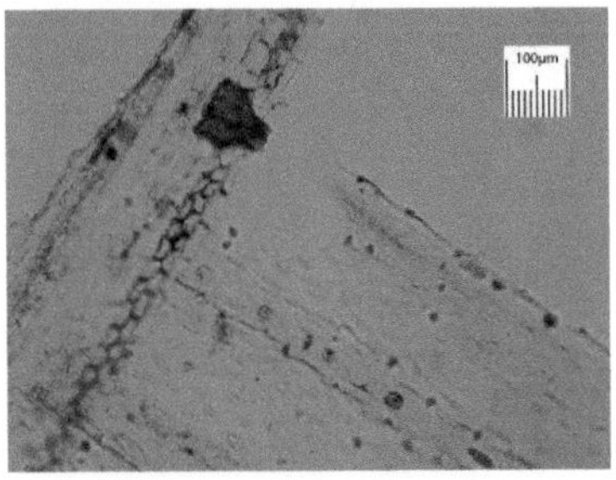
Stipa tirsa leaf	Common	Diagnostic Stipa-type rondels— round with dot	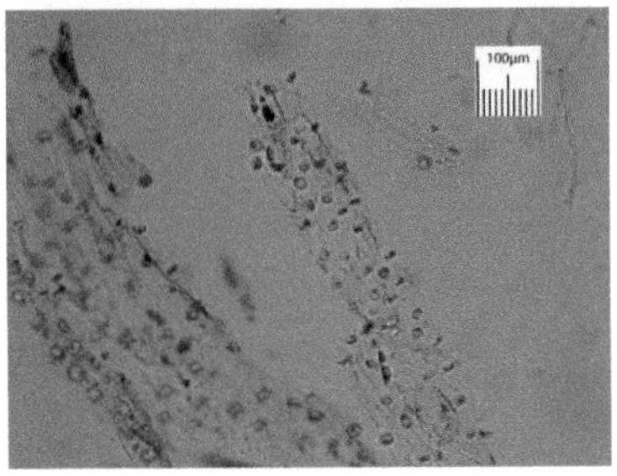
Typha	Sparse	Not diagnostic	

Typha

Typha (cattail or bulrush) produced very few phytoliths despite being a wetland monocotyledon, where one would expect high numbers of phytoliths. The pollen analysis (Popova 2002:5–6) reported abundant *Typha latifolia*, which was consistent with the location of the site on the edge of a marsh or oxbow lake where *Typha* grows today. However, there were very few phytoliths in any of the samples and disappointingly none diagnostic. It would seem that *Typha* is much more abundant in pollen than in phytoliths at this site. It should be noted that Kealhofer and Piperno (1998) also did not find phytoliths of *Typha* in an expected location in Southeast Asia.

Ephedra

Samples were prepared from *Ephedra* stem and leaves, which were very woody. The results were not diagnostic. However, there were starches.

Eragrostis

Eragrostis produced identifiable phytoliths in the husks, long cells with shallow dendritic edges, and papillae. Saddle-shaped short cells were produced in the leaves, which is what would be expected from a member of the Chloridoid subfamily (Twiss 1992). *Eragrostis* is a disturbance indicator, a pioneer that prefers sunny moist conditions such as sandy soils at the edge of marshes. It is a useful early spring forage plant (Hershdorfer 2009).

Phragmites

Phragmites produced long, almost oval-shaped saddle morphotypes in the leaves, as well as large bulliforms, although the diagnostic keystones reported by Lu and Liu (2000) were not present.

Quantification

Separate counts were made of single-cell versus multicell phytoliths. The senior author counted around 400 single cells per sample and any multicells that were within these fields, then scanned the rest of the slide for the remaining additional multicells. Once recorded, the counts were extrapolated up to number per gram density (absolute count), and percentage (relative count) per sample of phytolith morphotypes was calculated.

Reference slides prepared for this project were consulted, in addition to digital photographs of slides prepared by Emma Harvey and Arlene Rosen. Published photographs and drawings of silica skeletons (Greiss 1957; Rosen 1992:Figures 7.1–7.14; Rosen 1993:169), dicotyledons (Bozarth 1992:Figures 10.1–10.8), grass silica bodies (Mulholland

and Rapp 1992:Figures 4.1–4.15), Cyperaceae (Ollendorf 1992:Figures 5.1–5.5; Metcalfe 1969), cereals (Ball et al. 2001:Figures 1a–4b; Kaplan et al. 1992:Figures 8.1–8.37), Wang and Lu's (1992) general photographic references, the descriptions and drawings in Metcalfe's (1960) *Anatomy of the Monocotyledons I. Gramineae* and the web pages at www.missouri.edu/~phyto/index.shtml were all used.

Some nonquantified traits were noted but could not be included in counts. Heavy pitting on phytoliths can suggest they were windblown so possibly intrusive (Powers et al. 1989), so their presence has been noted. Some samples contained a background of amorphous silica, which was weighed, but again could not contribute to the count of morphotypes. The same applies to silica aggregates, which can be indicative of wood ash and contribute to weight but cannot contribute to morphotype counts.

Overall Density in Archaeological Samples

All the samples (Table 13.1) contained phytoliths. The 8000 BC off-site sample (KS-02-11) had far fewer than those from Krasnosamarskoe. There is a general paucity of silica skeletons, which can be abundant in monocotyledons (grasses, sedges, and rushes) (Rosen 1992:129). These should be frequent in this area, and the plants they come from are represented in the single-cell forms. The lack of silica skeletons may be connected to less evapo-transpiration in the moist environment of the region.

The weight percent density chart (Figure 13.3) shows that the density of phytoliths in the 8000 BC off-site sample (KS-02-11) was very low compared with the samples from the occupation site. Two samples, both pit fills, contained far higher densities of phytoliths than the others. This is mostly due to large concentrations of rondel forms and short cells from Festucoid grass leaves in these two samples. The KS-02-18 sample was taken from Pit 22, 80 to 90 cm deep, and KS-02-19 came from Pit 10, 94 cm deep (Table 13.1).

The chart in Figure 13.4 shows the number of identifiable phytoliths per gram of sediment and presents a slightly different picture from the weight percent. Sample KS-02-15 was particularly elevated in number compared to its comparatively low weight. Weight is elevated by the amorphous silica and silica aggregate present in some samples, which is impossible to count but nevertheless affects the weight.

Phytolith Counts and Types for Each Sample

Following are the results obtained from individual samples presented in numerical order by sample number. Rondels, short cells mainly from Festucoid grass leaves, made up

Table 13.1 Krasnosamarskoe Phytolith Samples Grouped by Feature

Feature Name	Weisskopf Sample #	Location	cm Depth below Surface	Feature Descriptions
Offsite control sample	KS-02-11	Samara riverbank	Buried A horizon	Control sample
Sticky black soil	KS-02-05	L4/1	30–40	Black soil layer on top of structure
Sticky black soil	KS-02-03	L2/4	40–50	Black soil layer on top of structure
v.7	KS-02-13	K2/2	60–70	Contents of ceramic Vessel 7
F.1	KS-02-20	L3/2	70–80	Pit 1
F.1	KS-02-16	L3/3	80–90	Gray ashy soil within Pit 1
F.3	KS-02-06	K2/3	80–90	Pit 3
F.7	KS-02-09	L2/4	80–90	Pit 7
F.8	KS-02-17	L2/4	80–90	Pit 8
F.9	KS-02-12	K2/L2	50–110	Pit 9
F.10	KS-02-02	M2/3	80	Pit 10—well
F.10	KS-02-19	M2/4	94	Pit 10–well
F.10	KS-02-10	M2	200–210	Pit 10—well
F.10	KS-02-01	M2	220	Pit 10—well
F.10	KS-02-07	M2	240	Pit 10—well
F.11	KS-02-15	K5/2	80–90	Pit 11
F.12	KS-02-14	I3/3	80–90	Pit 12
F.22	KS-02-18	L4/4	80–90	Pit 22
F.25	KS-02-04	K3/3	70–80	Ash feature 25
F.25	KS-02-08	K3/4	80	Ash feature 25

the greatest proportion of single-cell phytoliths across most samples. Smooth long cells were also predominant. This indicates the typical northern latitude steppe signature of grasses. The exception is the 8000 BC off-site sample taken from the bank of the Samara River, which contained both rondels and long cells but consisted mostly of phytoliths from dicotyledons, indicating a forested environment.

KS-02-01: Unit M2, 220 cm b.s. Pit 10, Well—Wet Sample with Preserved Organics

This sample (Figure 13.5) comes from Pit 10, a well, inside the structure. The other organic remains from Pit 10 contained a considerable amount of wood, including identifiable birch bark. The phytolith sample includes morphotypes from dicotyledons that have platey forms, often produced in bark. Birch is a dicotyledonous tree (so are oak and maple). The platey forms, possibly from bark, make

up 4.29 percent of the single cells. There are also "jigsaw puzzles," morphotypes found in dicotyledon leaves, as opposed to bark, so leaves might have been present as well. There are some possible *Pinus* forms (a gymnosperm) that fell outside the count. Phytoliths from grasses are more frequent. The highest densities are long smooth cells from grass leaves and rondels, which are found in many Festucoid grasses. *Eragrostis*-type saddles are present (Wang and Lu 1992:3), as are cones and rods from *Cyperaceae*, marshy sedge plants, very desirable as cattle pasturage. There are very few multicell forms in this sample (719 per gram sediment), and none of these were identifiable beyond grass leaf/culm.

KS-02-02: Unit M2/3, 80 cm b.s. Pit 10, Well, Small Ash Lens

This sample (Figure 13.6) was taken from an ash lens excavated in the middle fill of the well, Pit 10. The morphotype

Weight % per gram DENSITY

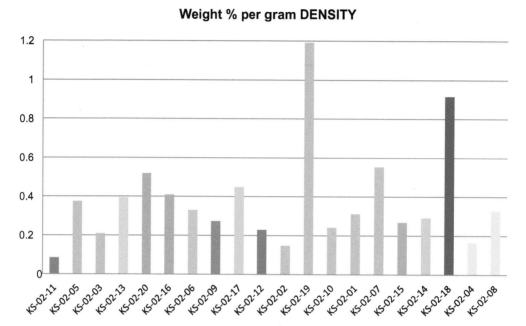

Figure 13.3 Phytolith weight percent per gram sediment per sample.

NUMBER per gram DENSITY

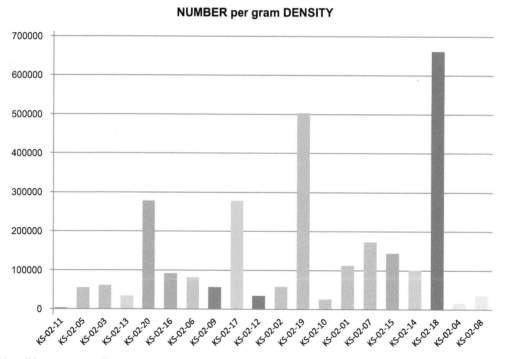

Figure 13.4 Phytoliths per gram sediment.

with the highest density in this sample is the rondel, a short cell found in grass leaves, mainly Festucoid (Pooid) but sometimes in other subfamilies. As in most other samples, the majority of morphotypes are from grass leaves, although this sample contains some phytoliths

from grass inflorescences, long dendritic cells and papillae, *Cyperaceae*, and rods and cones. There are possible *Avena* sp. (wild oat) rondels. *Avena* is a disturbance species (Keller 1927). The sample produced many long saddles indicative of *Phragmites* sp. Forms produced in

KS-02-01 M2 Pit 10, well, waterlogged organics

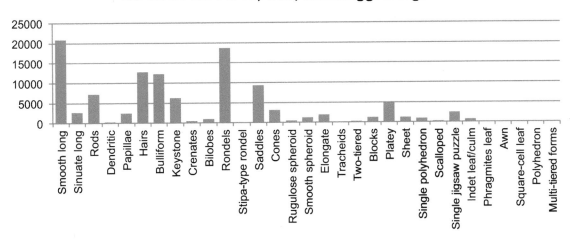

Figure 13.5 KS-02-01: Unit M2, 220 cm b.s., Pit 10 well—wet with preserved organics. Artifact density: 1,200 to 3,500; phytolith density: 112,433 per gram sediment.

KS-02-02 M3/2 Pit 10, well, ash lens

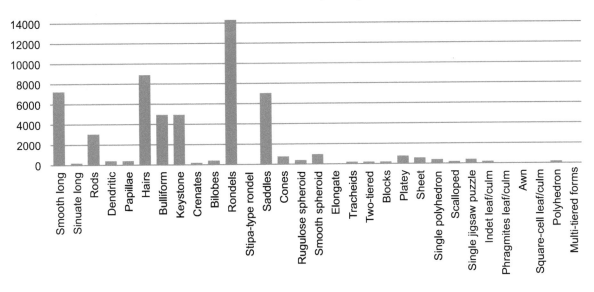

Figure 13.6 KS-02-02: Unit M3/2, 80 cm b.s., Pit 10, well—small ash lens in pit fill. Artifact density: 1,200 to 3,500; phytolith density: 57,276 per gram sediment.

dicotyledons are also present from dicotyledon leaves, jigsaw puzzles, and polyhedrons. Polyhedrons are often indicative of plants that prefer a humid environment. Multicells are sparse, and only indeterminate leaf/culm and polyhedrons are present. The majority of the phytoliths are pitted, and there is a large proportion of fragmented silica suggesting burning, which is not surprising as this is an ash sample.

KS-02-03: Unit L2/4, 40 to 50 cm b.s., Leathery Black Soil Sample from Inside Structure

This sample (Figure 13.7) was taken from a thick black, leathery soil that overlay the center of the structure, marked with a gray tone on the Krasnosamarskoe site plan (Figure 10.2). This soil was very noticeable by color and texture, and it was superimposed over the LBA occupation levels, although its lower portion, from which this sample was taken, contained many LBA artifacts. The location of this sample, taken from L2/4, was in the center of the structure, where the black layer was thickest, near the northeastern end of the structure. During the excavation, this dark layer was interpreted as the possible remains of an organic roof, collapsed over and sealing the LBA occupation. The phytoliths in this sample are very pitted and include a lot of *Phragmites* reeds with the florescent parts but also including other leafy greens. *Phragmites* are commonly used for thatching (Smith et al. 1999), supporting the premise that this dark soil represents roofing material. The highest density of phytoliths in this sample is the rondel morphotype, frequently found in grass leaves, followed by long smooth cells, also found in grass leaves. There are also relatively high levels of keystones and bulliforms pointing to a predominance of leaves from hydrophilic grasses, suggesting a damp environment (Bowdery 2007). The long saddles in these forms suggest *Phragmites* sp. Papillae and dendritic cells from grass inflorescences are present in low levels. Dicotyledon phytoliths are sparse but include scalloped, polyhedron, and jigsaw puzzle–shaped morphotypes found in arboreal leaves.

KS-02-04: Unit K3/3, 70 to 80 cm b.s., Feature 25 Ash Lens

In this sample (Figure 13.8), taken from an ash lens in the excavated structure, the largest proportion of diagnostic single-cell morphotypes are platey forms (19 percent). These are usually arboreal, from bark (Bozarth 1992:198). Other forms from dicotyledons were present, including elongate, smooth spheroids, and single polyhedrons. There are bulliform types, from grass leaves. *Phragmites* make distinctive fan-shaped bulliforms and long saddle phytoliths (Lu and Liu 2000), and both were present in low numbers, alongside low levels of forms from *Cyperaceae*. As in the other ash lenses, there is a great deal of fragmented silica aggregate. Starches and possible spherulites from sheep and cattle stomachs are also present in this sample. Multicells from reed grasses are also present. This was a very diverse sample of ash, with many different kinds of burned materials.

KS-02-05: Unit L4/1, 30 to 40 cm b.s., Sticky Black Soil on Top of Structure

This sample (Figure 13.9) came from the upper part of the black leathery soil interpreted as a collapsed organic roof, examined also by the KS-02-03 sample discussed above. As in the deeper context (KS-02-03), the phytoliths in this sample are very pitted, and there are few dicotyledons. Twelve percent of the sample consists of keystones, many *Phragmites* type, and long *Phragmites*-type saddles are present. There are some large bulliforms and elongates that may be *Pinus* (Wang and Lu 1992:1). The majority of morphotypes are from grasses. There were no multicells in this sample.

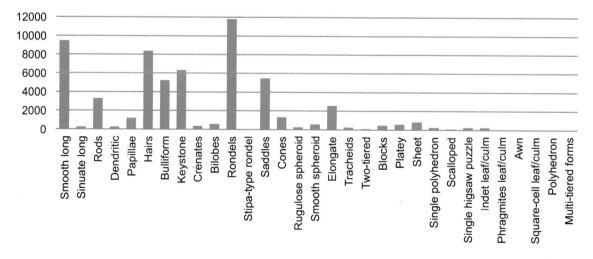

Figure 13.7 KS-02-03: Unit L2/4, 40 to 50 cm b.s., sticky black soil on top of structure. Artifact density: 550 to 1,200: phytolith density: 60,523 per gram sediment.

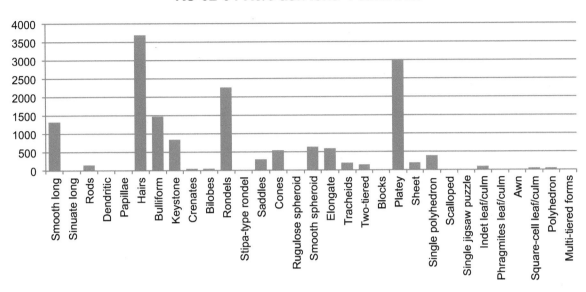

Figure 13.8 KS-02-04: Unit K3/3, 70 to 80 cm b.s., Feature 25 ash lens. Artifact density: 550 to 1,200; phytolith density: 15,997 per gram sediment.

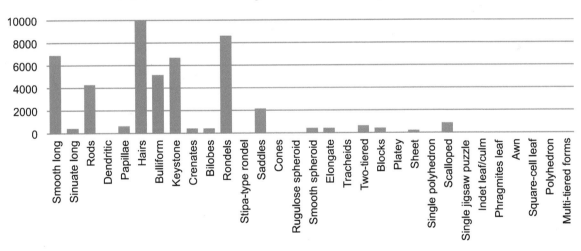

Figure 13.9 KS-02-05: Unit L4/1, 30 to 40 cm b.s., sticky black soil on top of structure. Artifact density: 1,200 to 3,500; phytolith density: 54,807 per gram sediment.

KS-02-06: Unit K2/3, 80 to 90 cm b.s., Pit 3

Nearly a quarter (24 percent) of the phytoliths in this sample (Figure 13.10) are long cells, and 23 percent are rondels, which means there is a very large proportion of grass leaf phytoliths. There are very few dicot morphotypes and hardly any platey forms, which suggests little wood, although the only multicells are polyhedrons, which are commonly found in dicotyledon leaves. The majority of dicotyledon forms are scalloped, which can sometimes be found in cucurbit rind (Piperno 2006) but are also found in dicotyledon leaves (Bozarth 1992). This pit is from the northern corner of the outside edge of the structure and contained relatively few artifacts. The predominance of grasses and lack of other morphotypes types suggests it was not a midden.

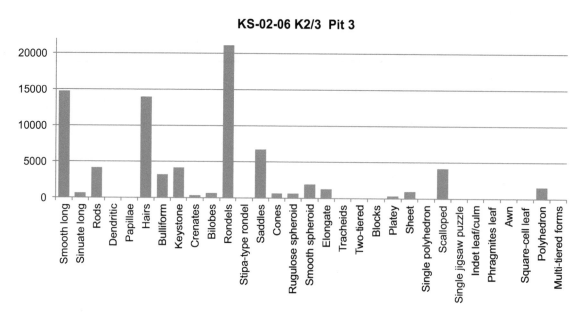

Figure 13.10 KS-02-06: Unit K2/3, 80 to 90 cm b.s., Pit 3. Artifact density: 550 to 1,200/1,200 to 3,500; phytolith density: 81,060 per gram sediment.

KS-02-07: Unit M2, 240 cm b.s., Pit 10, Well, Ash Lens

This sample (Figure 13.11) was taken from a layer of gray ash found deep in the fill in Pit 10, the well. It contains a wide variety of morphotypes, suggesting many different species of plant, although again the sample is dominated by rondels (33 percent of single cells). There is at least one *Cyperaceae* silica skeleton (recorded outside the counts). It also has more saddles than any other sample (15.5 percent or 25,999 per gram); most of these are *Phragmites* type. The vast majority of the phytoliths are from grasses with only a small number of dicotyledons. There are three types of multicelled forms: indeterminate leaf stem, square cells, and multitiered forms (both can indicate hydrophyllic plants). Among the grasses were *Eragrostis*, *Tristeum* Pers. (oat grass) type, and *Festuca* type (Wang and Lu 1992:3). Many of the silica bodies are pitted, which can be caused by dissolution while in the ground or indicate they were blown in from outside.

KS-02-08: Unit K3/4, 80 cm b.s., Feature 25, Ash Lens

There is a lot of fragmented amorphous silica in this sample (Figure 13.12), suggesting wood ash (Albert 2001). Thirty-two percent of the phytoliths are dicotyledons, most of them tracheids, platey forms, and elongates. *Quercus*-type phytoliths are present but very pitted like many of the phytoliths

in this sample. This may be due to intrusion or taphonomic processes. *Cyperaceae* silica skeletons are present as well as rods and cones. The highest proportions of morphotypes are from Festucoid grass leaves. There are a number of short cells from Chloridoids and very low levels of Panicoid grasses, which prefer warmer, drier environments.

KS-02-09: Unit L2/4, 80 to 90 cm b.s., Pit 7, Fill

This sample (Figure 13.13) contains a mixture of grasses and dicotyledons. Starches are evident, which might suggest food waste. As in the majority of samples, *Phragmites* is well represented, including some multicells. There are phytoliths from *Cyperaceae* as well as a relatively large proportion of polyhedral multicells, suggesting dicot leaves, possibly oak (*Quercus L.*).

KS-02-10: Unit M2, 200-210 cm b.s. Pit 10

This sample (Figure 13.14) contains scant small phytoliths, mostly grasses, some dicotyledons, and a few multicells. Apart from some papillae, small hairs found on husks, the grass phytoliths are all from leaves and stems. There are a few Panicoid grasses, but most are Festucoid. The most common form from dicotyledon is platey (usually from bark), and there are a few polyhedrons and scalloped morphotypes. The only multicells are square cells from grass leaves.

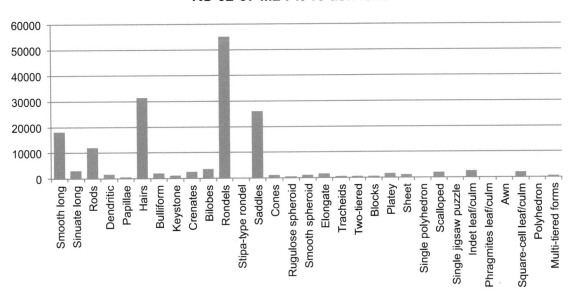

Figure 13.11 KS-02-07: Unit M2, 240 cm b.s., Pit 10, ash lens. Artifact density: 1,200 to 3,500; phytolith density: 172,780 per gram sediment.

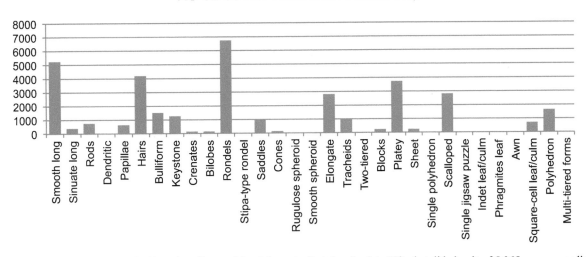

Figure 13.12 KS-02-08: Unit K3/4, 80 cm b.s., Feature 25, ash lens. Artifact density: 1 to 550; phytolith density: 35,065 per gram sediment.

KS-02-11: Off-Site Natural Alluvial Buried A Horizon

Sample KS-02-11 (Figure 13.15) was an off-site sample taken from a buried A horizon about 1 m beneath the modern ground surface in an exposed riverbank section of the Samara River. A soil date yielded an age of about 8000 BC (Anthony et al. 2005). Phytoliths were very sparse in comparison to the on-site samples, with the lowest phytolith weight. The low counts probably reflect the gallery forests in this riverside ecotone. Markedly different from the other samples, this sample contains 57 percent dicotyledon phytoliths; 41 percent are platey forms, often found in bark, so suggests typical arboreal types. Grasses produce many more silicate bodies than trees and herbaceous plants, so this is a very strong indication that the area was forested at that time. The proportions here indicate an area of trees or shrubs with little open space for grass to thrive. Phytoliths from *Cyperaceae* are present as well as polyhedral forms

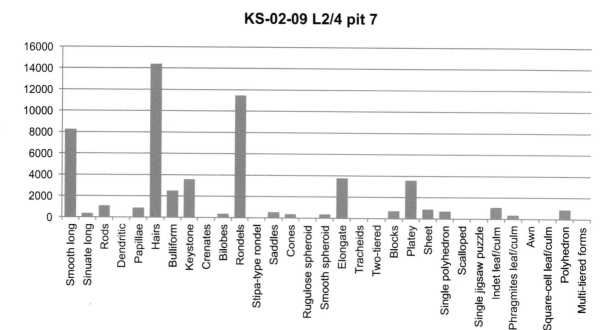

Figure 13.13 KS-02-09: Unit L2/4, 80 to 92 cm b.s., Pit 7, fill. Artifact density: 550 to 1,200; phytolith density: 56,112 per gram sediment.

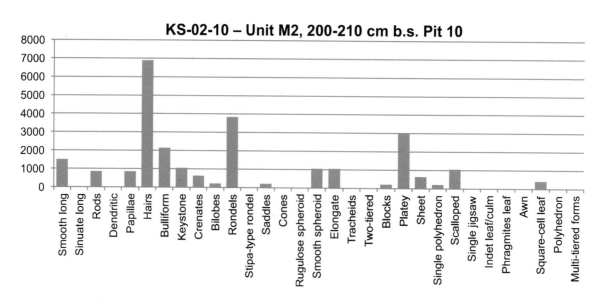

Figure 13.14 KS-02-10: Unit M2, 200 to 210 cm b.s., Pit 10. Artifact density: 1,200 to 3,500; phytolith density: 25,891 per gram sediment.

from dicotyledon leaves, often indicating humid surroundings (Tsartsidou et al. 2007). Among the grassy forms present, there were no bilobes or saddles, suggesting that the climate was not warm enough to support C_4 Panicoid-type grasses. The climate was probably wetter and cooler than today.

KS-02-12: Unit K2/4, 50 to 110 cm b.s., Pit 9

The density of phytoliths in this sample (Figure 13.16) is low. This sample contains square stem cells often associated with water-loving reedy plants as well as rods and cones from *Cyperaceae*. As in the majority of samples, the most

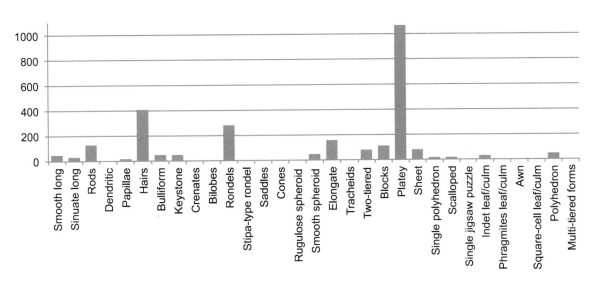

KS-02-11 Buried A horizon 8000 BC

Figure 13.15 KS-02-11: off-site natural buried A horizon dated to 8000 BC. Artifact density: 0; phytolith density: 2,655 per gram sediment.

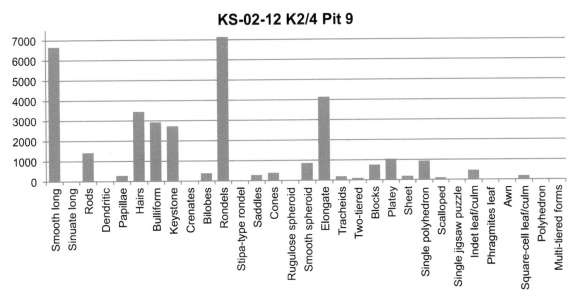

KS-02-12 K2/4 Pit 9

Figure 13.16 KS-02-12: Unit K2/4, 50 to 110 cm b.s., Pit 9. Artifact density: 550 to 1,200; phytolith density: 34,520 per gram sediment.

frequent morphotype is the rondel. There is a relatively high proportion of elongate-type phytoliths from dicotyledon leaves (12.19 percent) in this sample. Bulliforms and keystones are well represented. There are mainly long smooth cells and rondels, including *Stipa*-type rondels. Many phytoliths are fragmented and pitted.

KS-02-13: Unit K2/2, 60 to 70 cm b.s., Crushed Ceramic Vessel 7

This sample (Figure 13.17) was taken from inside a Srubnaya ceramic vessel (*razval*, or crushed ceramic vessel, Vessel 7) that was found standing vertically, with the upper walls broken and crushed into the vessel interior, as if it had been set in a hole in the ground with just the upper walls exposed, at the northeastern end of the excavated structure. No feature was detected—no hole could be seen around it—but the soils in this square were churned by rodent burrows that could have homogenized the distinctive fill within the hole with the surrounding soils. Nevertheless, a hole seems to have held the lower part of the vessel in place while the upper part broke inward. The vessel is interpreted as a Srubnaya pot installed in the floor as a permanent receptacle at the edge of the structure. What was it used for? There are a lot of fragmented amorphous silica and silica aggregates in the sample. These suggest burning. Charcoal also was found in this sample (Popova 2002:9 and Chapter 12, this volume), confirming that charred material was placed in the vessel. The structure overall does not seem to have been burned, as there is only a scatter of charcoal in the excavated soils inside the structure, so the concentration of burned material inside the vessel might have been placed or dumped there. The pollen sample taken from the vessel showed the presence of small amounts of *Apiaceae* (carrot) and *Legumes* (Popova 2002:6). Among the phytoliths, there are similar proportions of rondels from Festucoid grass leaves and platey form phytoliths from dicotyledons, probably tree bark. There are starches surviving among the phytoliths, despite the fact that phytolith processing often destroys starches, so a larger quantity of starches might have been present. The receptacle might have contained food waste mixed with ash and charcoal.

KS-02-14: Unit I3/3, 80 to 90 cm b.s., Pit 12

This sample (Figure 13.18) came from a small pit, possibly a posthole base, with a dark organic fill. Over half the phytoliths are either long smooth cells or rondels from a variety of grasses. *Phragmites* keystones and saddles are present as well as *Cyperaceae*. Dicotyledon forms are scarce, and there are very low proportions of multicells, so if a wooden post had been set here, it was removed, and little to no trace of woody material was left in the pit. There is a lot of amorphous silica and dense pitting, suggesting weathered *Phragmites* reeds and burned organics.

KS-02-15: Unit K5/2, 80 to 90 cm b.s., Pit 11

This sample (Figure 13.19) was unusual because it had relatively large proportions of multicelled *Phragmites* leaf, the only sample that produced any. The pit is outside the structure and also contained the usual relatively high levels of long smooth cells and rondels. There are also tracheids found in the vascular parts of plants and platey forms, both suggestive of wood. Many of the phytoliths are small, unidentifiable to form, and pitted.

KS-02-16: Unit L3/3, 80 to 90 cm b.s., Pit 1 Ashy Soil

This sample (Figure 13.20) contained a wide variety of phytolith types. The highest percentage was 19 percent

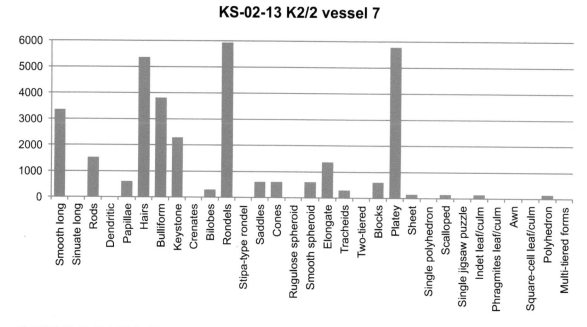

Figure 13.17 KS-02-13: Unit K2/2, 60 to 70 cm b.s., crushed ceramic Vessel 7. Artifact density: 550 to 1,200; phytolith density: 33,676 per gram sediment.

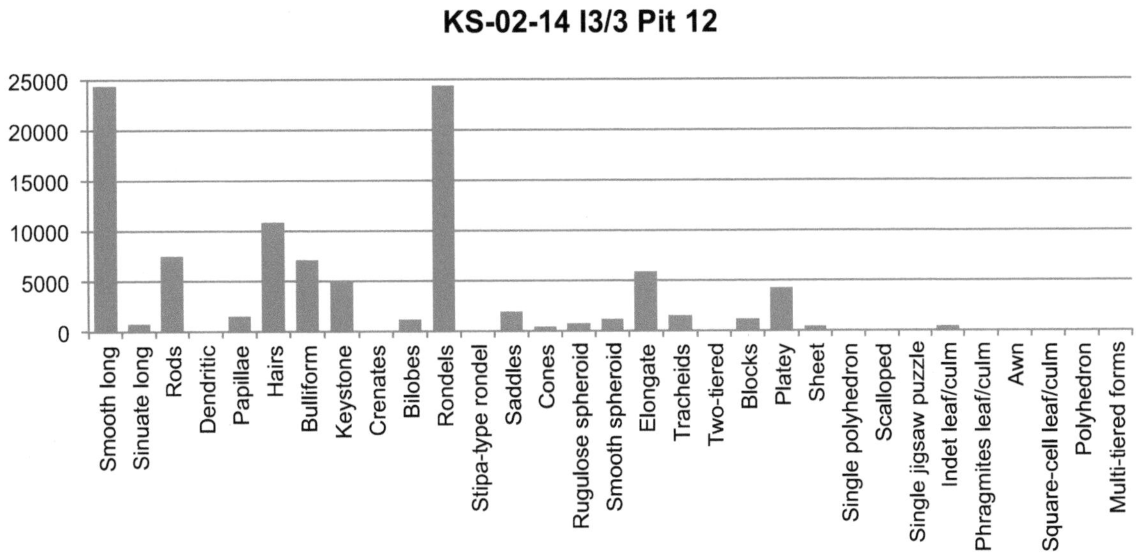

KS-02-14 I3/3 Pit 12

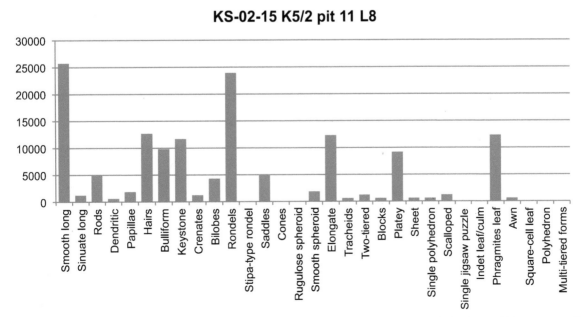

Figure 13.18 KS-02-14: Unit I3/3, 80 to 90 cm b.s., Pit 12. Artifact density: 1 to 550: phytolith density: 101,005 per gram sediment.

long rods from *Cyperaceae.* Also from *Cyperaceae,* cone-shaped morphotypes occurred at the highest percentage in this sample. Given the context of ashy soil at the top of a pit opening, this could suggest the remnants of rush matting. There were a marked number of bulliforms and many different grass types, including *Phragmites.* Many dicotyledon types were present, although the densities were lower than those of the grasses. Grasses produce many more phytoliths than dicotyledons, so this does not necessarily represent the proportion of plants present. There is a wide

variety of phytolith types, particularly dicotyledons, suggesting this may have been an area where some kind of processing activity took place, for example, food preparation.

KS-02-17: Unit L2/4, 80 to 90 cm b.s., Pit 8

Grass leaves are well represented in this sample (Figure 13.21). There are many different rondel types and long smooth cells. *Cyperaceae* are also present (rods and cones). There are few silica skeletons, just low levels of

KS-02-15 K5/2 pit 11 L8

Figure 13.19 KS-02-15: Unit K5/2, 80 to 90 cm b.s., Pit 11. Artifact density: 550 to 1,200; phytolith density: 14,400 per gram sediment.

KS-02-16 L3/3 ashy soil Pit 1

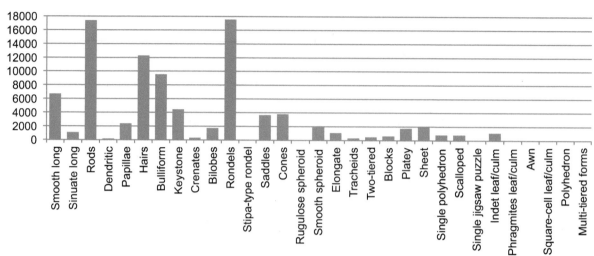

Figure 13.20 KS-02-16: Unit L3/3, 80 to 90 cm b.s., Pit 1, ashy soil. Artifact density: 550 to 1,200; phytolith density: 92,094 per gram sediment.

KS-02-17 L2/4   Pit 8

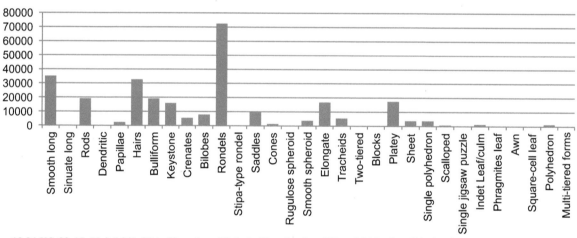

Figure 13.21 KS-02-17: Unit L2/4, 80 to 90 cm b.s., Pit 8. Artifact density: 550 to 1,200; phytolith density: 277,977 per gram sediment.

indeterminate leaf and a few polyhedrons. Once again, there are high levels of silica aggregates, suggesting burning.

KS-02-18: Unit L4/4, 80 to 90 cm b.s., Pit 22

This sample (Figure 13.22) contained high levels of silica aggregates and many broken, fragmented phytoliths with a large incidence of pitting. This could suggest burning. This sample contains the most multicelled forms among all the samples tested. The multicells are mostly *Phragmites*. It is possible that reeds were used to line the pit.

KS-02-19: Unit M2/4, 94 cm b.s., Pit 10

This sample (Figure 13.23) from the upper fill of the Srubnaya well has stem and *Phragmites* multicells. This is the richest sample, with the highest abundance of phytoliths, and contains a wide variety. The phytoliths were 1.91 percent of the sediment, many more than any other sample (see density chart). The range of phytolith types is broad. There are a few *Bromus*-type long cells (Wang and Lu 1992:5). *Bromus* includes grasses that are both desirable and undesirable, depending on the species, for animal forage. *Bromus riparius*, or meadow grass, is a *Bromus*

KS-02-18   L4/4   Pit 22

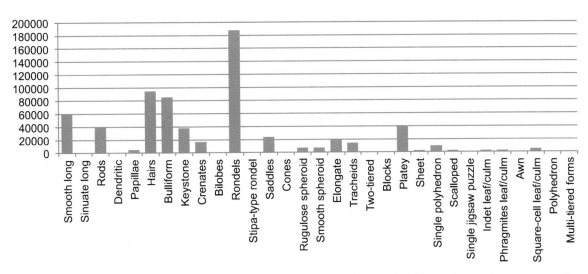

Figure 13.22 KS-02-18: Unit L4/4, 80 to 90 cm b.s., Pit 22. Artifact density: 1,200 to 3,500; phytolith density: 661,965 per gram sediment.

KS-02-19 M2/4   Pit 10

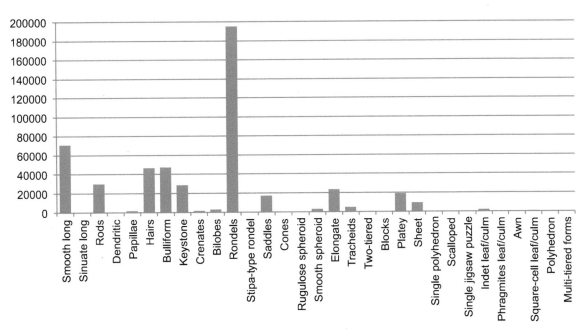

Figure 13.23 KS-02-19: Unit M2/4, 94 cm b.s., Pit 10. Artifact density: 1,200 to 3,500; phytolith density: 503,691 per gram sediment.

species native to the Russian steppes and is highly desirable for cattle forage, but we cannot be certain about the species represented in sample KS-02-19.

KS-02-20: Unit L3/2, 70 to 80 cm b.s., Pit 1

This sample (Figure 13.24) contained a large number of tracheids. This suggests woody stems. Keystones and

saddles are more infrequent, indicating fewer *Phragmites* sp. There are abundant long cells and rondels, so grasses are well represented.

Correspondence Analysis

Relative percentages of the phytoliths in each sample were calculated, single and multicells separately, and these were used in the correspondence analysis.

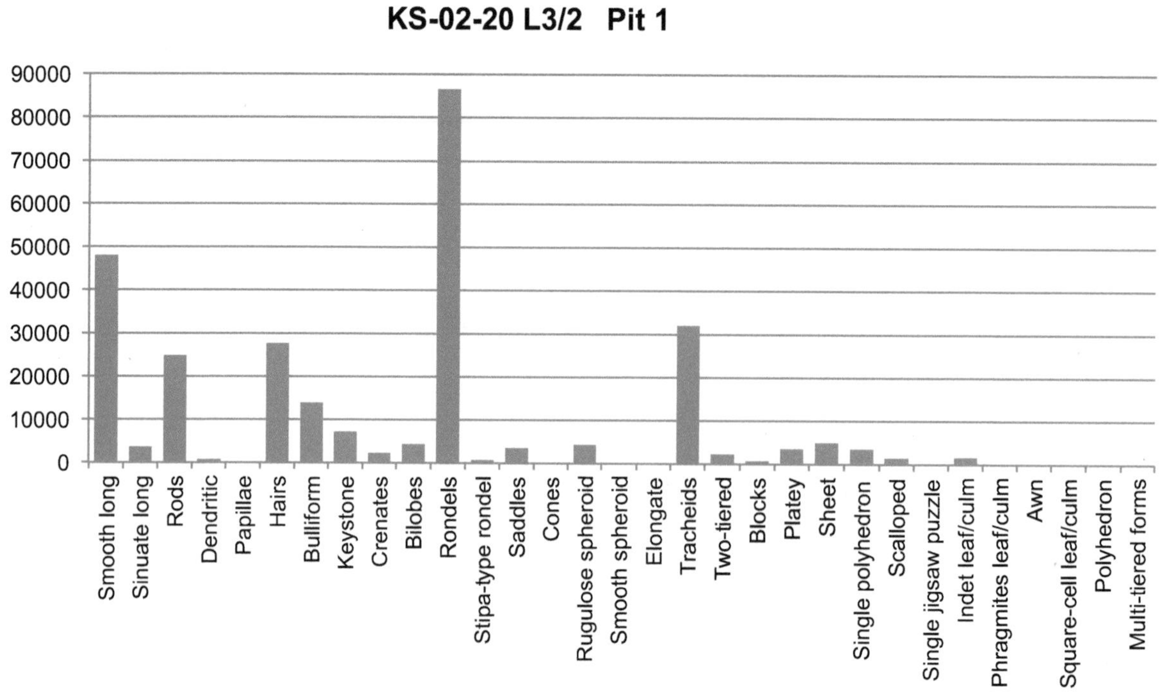

KS-02-20 L3/2   Pit 1

Figure 13.24 KS-02-20: Unit L3/2, 70 to 80 cm b.s., Pit 1. Artifact density: 550 to 1,200; phytolith density: 278,169 per gram sediment.

In Figure 13.25, the samples have been classified into five groups: grass, sedge (*Cyperaceae*), water loving or hydrophilic, dicot leaf, and dicot. Weight percent density is shown along Axis 1. The densest samples (KS19 and 18) are separated along this axis. These samples also contain low levels of dicot leaf. The samples with higher levels of water-loving morphotypes fall into the upper half of the chart, while those with higher concentrations of dicot leaves are in the lower. *Cyperaceae* sits in the middle.

Discussion
General Trends
All the samples had abundant short cells, but there were very few multicells, except in sample KS-02-18. Rondels, short single-cell phytoliths mainly from Festucoid grass leaves, made up the greatest proportion of phytoliths across most samples. The low number of multicells means that in most samples, it is difficult to identify phytoliths to genus. Why so few multicells? It could be because of the microenvironment of plant growth. Multicells are often produced with high evapo-transpiration, and the environment may have been too cool and damp.

There are barely any dendritic long cells, so husks are very underrepresented, suggesting the samples were not deposited in the spring or summer when the plants are in seed. The phytoliths generally did not include hulls or florescent

parts, which suggests that if plants were harvested, it would have been in the fall or winter when the parts of the plant that produce dendritic phytoliths have been shed.

Most of the identifiable multicell phytoliths came from *Phragmites* reeds or from *Cyperaceae* (sedges), which are marsh plants. *Phragmites* (common reed), a perennial reed grass (Uphof 1959; Fitter et al. 2002:102), has two species. *Phragmites australis* is the one found in Eurasia today and was likely to have been present in the LBA. There are *Phragmites*-type keystones in many of the samples, and *Phragmites* leaf/stem are the most predominant of the few multicells. *Phragmites* lives through the winter as hard canes and is common in marshes and swamps so would have thrived in the environment of the oxbow lake (Fitter et al. 2002:102). *Phragmites* could have been used for thatch as a roofing material or for matting or containers. *Phragmites* reeds used for roof thatching are normally harvested in the fall or winter after the first frost has stripped away the leaves and florescent parts, because thatchers use only the reeds. It is possible that most of the *Phragmites* reeds at Krasnosamarskoe were used for roof thatching, since almost all were fall/winter harvested; no inflorescences were found. It is possible that the phytoliths from inside the structure were dominated by the remains of a collapsed thatched roof (Anthony et al. 2005). *Phragmites* stems are also used for fencing in animal pens and for fuel, and the young shoots are eaten by cattle.

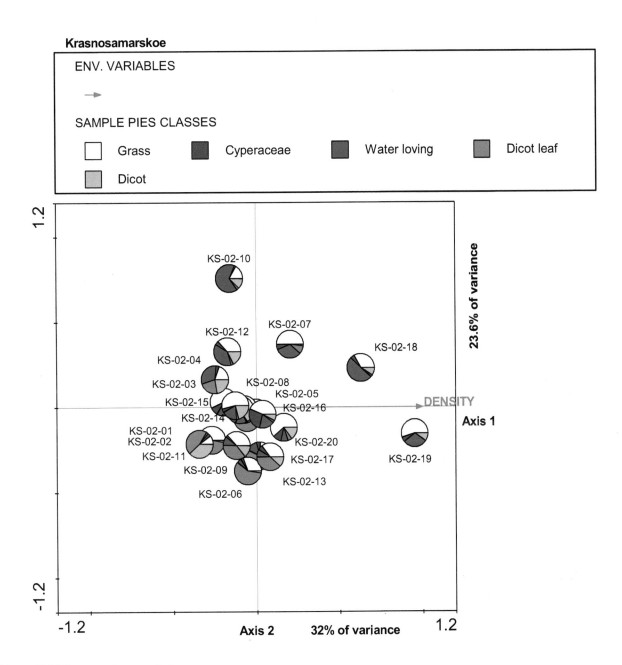

Figure 13.25 Correspondence analysis.

Pit 11, an apparent posthole located just outside the excavated structure on its north side, was the only sampled pit that contained leaf phytoliths from *Phragmites* reeds, perhaps because this posthole was outside the structure so was open to the external environment.

All samples contain some *Cyperaceae*, although often in small quantities, indicative of the marshy surroundings. There are larger proportions of leaves than nutlets; 14 samples contain both. Ethnographically, *Cyperaceae* is used for basketry, matting, and even knitting hats; the early autumn harvest produces the best-quality material.

Agriculture

There is no evidence from the phytoliths for agriculture or even the consumption or processing of domesticated crops. No weed grasses, such as *Lolium*, that are associated with crops are apparent. The presence of grasses that thrive in disturbed soil such as *Eragrostis* are probably the result of the ground being churned up by browsing animals. Neither the pollen (Popova 2002) nor macro remains (Anthony et al. 2005) reveal domesticated crops. The lack of agricultural evidence adds weight to the argument that the early Srubnaya people occupying Krasnosamarskoe were not influenced in their subsistence economics by agricultural communities in the Caucasus or southeast Europe, the occasionally cultivating pastoralists in the steppe river valleys north of the Black Sea (Motuzaite-Matuzeviciute 2012), or the possible millet-using pastoralists of the Tien Shan piedmont in eastern Kazakhstan (Spengler et al. 2014). Infertile soil, high winds, and the high probability of drought for between 3.5 and 6.5 of every 10 years do not make agriculture on the steppes an attractive prospect (Khazanov 1984:45). Climatic cooling may have encouraged settlement in marshy river valleys such as the Samara. Also, the Srubnaya people occupied a boundary zone that allowed gathering foods from steppe, woodland, and marshlands.

Available Food

Although cultivated grain has been found in kurgan burials in the Dniester River steppes west of the Black Sea, it has not been found in kurgan graves east of the Don River, despite Shishlina's systematic efforts to identify botanical remains in Bronze Age kurgan graves in the Manych steppes west of the Caspian Sea, using flotation, palynology, and phytolith analysis in human dental tartar (Shishlina 2008). Nor was grain present in Srubnaya graves or settlements east of the Don, between the Don and Volga-Ural Rivers, as far as present knowledge goes. Srubnaya people in the Don-Ural region could have obtained grain through trade and exchange pathways, but it does not seem to have constituted a significant portion of their diet.

If they were not growing crops, what were they eating? It is possible to base a large proportion of the diet on meat and milk (Khazanov 1984:39). Many pastoralists base a large part of their diet on milk in the summer and meat in the winter. But carbohydrates are also necessary for good health (Chang and Tourtellotte 1998:266–267). The carbonized seed evidence discussed by Popova in Chapter 12 suggests that they were gathering food resources from local wild plants. The vegetation local to the site contained many edible plants that could provide necessary nutritional supplements. *Cichorium intybus* (chicory) was present in Pit 13 and Vessel 7 (Popova 2002:8). It can be boiled and eaten or roasted to make a drink (Mabey 1989:144). The other contents of Vessel 7 included carrot, legumes, chicory, and starches. It would be interesting to test the residues in the ceramic vessels for traces of adipose fats for meat or lipids to discover if milk was being heated to high temperatures consistent with heat treatment, indicative of processing food such as cheese or yogurt (Dudd et al. 1999:147–180). *Gallium verum* L., which Popova (2002:8) found in both Pits 6 and 13, can be used for curdling milk to make junkets and cheese (Mabey 1989:119).

Phragmites is very common in the local environment and contains high levels of sugar. Native North Americans and contemporary rural Russians used its gum as sweets. They also dried and ground the reeds to make flour, which swells and browns near fire and can be eaten like toasted marshmallows (Mabey 1989:153). The young sprouts can also be eaten (Zeven and de Wet 1982:153). Wild oat (*Avena*) was present among the phytoliths, and *Typha*, although not clear in the phytoliths, was well represented in the pollen; both can provide starchy carbohydrates.

Finally, the carbonized seeds of *Chenopodium album*, *Amaranthus* sp., and *Polygynum* sp. found in the waterlogged sediments at the bottom of Pit 10, also described by Popova, suggest that the seeds of these three genera were selected for charring, while seeds belonging to 28 other genera were not charred. Charring is a common first step in removing the bitter pericarp from *Chenopodium* seeds, so can be seen as a step in food preparation. Wild *Chenopodium* plants can form stands that produce as much seed weight per hectare as cultivated einkorn wheat, so have a large potential as a source of food.

Pastoral Pursuits

Krasnosamarskoe is too far from a biotope where C_4 grasses thrive to make a worthwhile analysis of the proportions of C_3 versus C_4 grasses in order to detect transhumance. Any saddle forms are likely to be from *Phragmites* or local micro-climates. There is no direct evidence of fodder, but the majority of grasses in the samples were common livestock forage (e.g., *Festuca*) and disturbance grasses (e.g., *Eragrostis*), suggesting suitable pasture for livestock nearby.

Environmental Setting

The riverbank geomorphological sample dated 8000 BC (see Chapter 9) showed a heavily wooded natural landscape, probably with larger floodplain gallery forests than those that survive today. This fits well with the chronologically corresponding data from Buzuluk forest, 60 km upstream on the Samara River, where a pine forest was thriving at that time (Kremenetski et al. 1999:1201). The climate seems to have been cooler, and there were fewer species such as *Artemisia*, which prefer a drier environment (Kremenetski et al. 1999:1201). In contrast, by the LBA, the Buzuluk forest had receded.

At the LBA Krasnosamarskoe settlement, the samples are full of steppe grasses such as *Festuca* and *Stipa*. Both types are good forage grasses, so suitable for pasturing herds. *Festuca* is from temperate or other cool regions (Keller 1927:206). The large quantities of *Phragmites* demonstrates the proximity of water and marshland, highlighting the availability of fishing and fowling, as does the presence of *Cyperaceae*, which can also indicate infertile soil (Fitter et al. 1984:13).

The ashy deposits all contained abundant amorphous silica fragments, pointing to wood ash. This suggests there was enough wood available within easy reach of the settlement to make burning dung unnecessary.

Seasonality

Phytoliths from inflorescent parts are uncommon (except in Pit 11), which by itself could suggest that the structure was not occupied during the summer. However, incremental banding on animal teeth showing fall, winter, and spring kills and pollen from plants blooming in spring, summer, and fall show that the structure was used during all seasons of the year (Chapters 12 and 14). Several different kinds of analysis are needed to build a full picture of any site.

Conclusion

The phytoliths from Krasnosamarskoe have provided information that is both interesting and useful to the main aims of the project. It would seem that the site was on open steppe but near enough trees to use various species for fuel. The surroundings were marshy, and reeds were readily available to use for matting, baskets, and roofing material. Although there is no evidence of agriculture, the local environment could have supplied an assortment of edible wild plants. The strong focus on a pastoral lifestyle raises questions about food procurement and contact or interdependence with agricultural societies. The phytoliths, pollen, macro remains, and other environmental data, taken together, add a new and necessary dimension to the economic and environmental data from Krasnosamarskoe during the Late Bronze Age.

Note

Figures and tables in this chapter were prepared by A. Weisskopf.

References

Albert, R. M., and S. Weiner
2001   Study of Phytoliths in Prehistoric Ash Layers from Kebara and Tabun Caves Using a Quantitative Approach. In *Phytoliths: Applications in Earth Sciences and Human History*, edited by F. C. J. D. Meunier, pp. 251–266. Balkema, Lisse.
Anthony, D. W., D. R. Brown, E. Brown, A. Goodman, A. A. Khokhlov, P. A. Kosintsev, P. F. Kuznetsov, O. Mochalov, E. M. Murphy, D. Peterson, A. Pike-Tay, L. Popova, A. M. Rosen, N. Russell, and A. Weisskopf
2005   The Samara Valley Project Late Bronze Age Economy and Ritual in the Russian Steppes. *Eurasia Antiqua* 11:395–417.
Ball, T. B., J. S. Gardner, and N. Anderson
2001   An Approach to Identifying Inflorescence Phytoliths from Selected Species of Wheat and Barley. In *Phytoliths: Applications in Earth Sciences and Human History*, edited by J. D. Meunier and F. Colon, pp. 289–302. Balkema, Exton, Pennsylvania.
Bowdery, D.
2007   Phytolith Analysis, Sheep, Diet and Fecal Material at Ambathala Pastoral Station (Queensland, Australia). In *Plants, People and Places: Recent Studies in Phytolith Analysis*, edited by M. Madella and D. Zurro, pp. 134–150. Oxbow, Oxford.
Bozarth, S. R.
1992   Classification of Opal Phytoliths Formed in Selected Dicotyledons Native to the Great Plains. In *Phytolith Systematics*, edited by G. Rapp and S. Mullholland, pp. 193–214. Premium, New York.
Chang, C., and P. A. Tourtellotte
1998   The Role of Agro-Pastoralism in the Evolution of Steppe Culture in the Semirechye Area of Southern Kazakhstan during the Saka/Wusun Period (600 BCE–400 CE). *The Bronze Age and Early Iron Age Peoples of Eastern Central Asia* 1:264–279.
Dudd, S. N., R. P. Evershed, and A. M. Gibson
1999   Evidence for Varying Patterns of Exploitation of Animal Products in Different Prehistoric Pottery Traditions Based on Lipids Preserved in Surface and Absorbed Residues. *Journal of Archaeological Science* 26(12):1473–1482.
Fitter, R., A. Fitter, and A. Farrer
2002   *Grasses, Sedges, Rushes and Ferns of Britain and Northern Europe*. Collins, London.
Greiss, E. A. M.
1957   *Anatomical Identification of Some Egyptian Plant Materials*. Le C. Tsoumas, Cairo.
Hershdorfer, M.
2009   Plant Guide for Plains Lovegrass (*Eragrostis intermedia* A.S. Hitchc.). USDA Natural Resources Conservation Service, Tucson Plant Materials Center, Tucson, Arizona.
Kaplan, L., M. B. Smith, and L. A. Sneddon
1992   Cereal Grain Phytoliths of Southwest Asia and Europe. In *Phytolith Systematics*, edited by G. R. J. Rapp and S. C. Mulholland, pp. 149–174. Plenum, New York.
Kealhofer, L., and D. R. Piperno
1998   *Opal Phytoliths in Southeast Asian and Thai Flora. Smithsonian Contributions to Botany.* Smithsonian Institution Press, Washington, D.C.
Keller, B.
1927   The Distribution of Vegetation on the Plains of European Russia. *Journal of Ecology* 15:209–229.

Khazanov, A. M.

1984   *Nomads and the Outside World.* 2nd ed. University of Wisconsin Press, Madison

Kremenetski, C. V., T. Böttiger, F. W. Junge, and A. G. Tarasov

1999   Late- and Postglacial Environment of the Buzuluk Area Middle Volga Region, Russia. *Quaternary Science Reviews* 18:1185–1203.

Lu, H., and K. Liu

2000   *Illustrations of Phytoliths from Grasses in China and the USA.* Institute of Geology and Geophysics, Chinese Academy of Sciences, Beijing.

Mabey, R.

1989   *Food for Free.* Collins, London.

Metcalfe, C. R.

1960   *Anatomy of the Monocotyledons I. Gramineae.* Oxford University Press, London.

1969   Anatomy as an Aid to Classifying the Cyperaceae. *American Journal of Botany* 56(7):782–790.

Motuzaite-Matuzeviciute, Giedre

2012   The Earliest Appearance of Domesticated Plant Species and Their Origins on the Western Fringes of the Eurasian Steppe. *Documenta Praehistorica* 39:1–21.

Mullholland, S. C., and G. Rapp, Jr.

1992   Morphological Classification of Grass Silica Bodies. In *Phytolith Systematics*, edited by G. R. J. Rapp and S. C. Mulholland, pp. 68–90. Plenum, New York.

Ollendorf, A. L.

1992   Towards a Classification Scheme of Sedge (Cyperaceae) Phytoliths. In *Phytolith Systematics: Emerging Issues*, edited by G. J. Rapp and S. C. Mulholland, pp. 91–111. Plenum, New York.

Piperno, D.

2006   *Phytoliths: A Comprehensive Guide for Archaeologists and Palaeoecologists.* Altamira, Oxford.

Piperno, D. R., and D. R. Pearsall

1993   The Nature and Status of Phytolith Analysis. In *Current Research in Phytolith Analysis: Applications in Archaeology and Palaeoecology*, edited by D. R. Pearsall and D. R. Piperno, pp. 9–20. MASCA, Philadelphia.

Popova, L. M.

2002   Meadow-Steppe and Marsh: The Late Bronze Age Environment at Krasnosamarskoe and Pollen Analysis. Paper presented at the meetings of the European Association of Archaeologists, Thessaloniki, Greece.

Powers, A. H., J. Padmore, and D. D. Gilbertson

1989   Studies of Late Prehistoric and Modern Opal Phytoliths from Coastal Sand Dunes and Machair in Northwest Britain. *Journal of Archaeological Science* 16: 27–45.

Rosen, A.

1992   Preliminary Identification of Silica Skeletons from Near Eastern Archeological Sites: An Anatomical Approach. In *Phytolith Systematics*, edited by G. R. J. Rapp and S. C. Mulholland, pp. 129–148. Plenum, New York.

1993   Phytolith Evidence for Early Cereal Exploitation in the Levant. In *Current Research in Phytolith Analysis: Applications in Archaeology and Palaeoecology*, edited by D. R. Pearsall and D. Piperno, pp. 161–171. MASCA Research Papers in Science and Archaeology, Philadelphia.

Shishlina, N. I.

2008   *Reconstruction of the Bronze Age of the Caspian Steppes: Life Styles and Life Ways of Pastoral Nomads.* British Archaeological Reports, Oxford.

Smith, D., J. Letts, and A. Cox

1999   Coleoptera from Late Medieval Smoke-Blackened Thatch (SBT): Their Archaeological Implications. *Environmental Archaeology* 4(1):9–17.

Spengler, R., M. Frachetti, P. Doumani, L. Rouse, B. Cerasetti, E. Bullion, and A. Mar'yashev

2014   Early Agriculture and Crop Transmission among Bronze Age Mobile Pastoralists of Central Eurasia. *Proceedings of the Royal Society. B Biological Sciences* 281(1783):20133382.

Tsartsidou, G., S. Lev-Yadun, R.-M. Albert, A. Miller-Rosen, N. Efstratiou, and S. Weiner

2007   The Phytolith Archaeological Record: Strengths and Weaknesses Evaluated Based on a Quantitative Modern Reference Collection from Greece. *Journal of Archaeological Science* 34(8):1262–1275.

Twiss, P. C.

1992   World Distribution of C_3 and C_4 Phytoliths. In *Phytolith Systematics*, edited by G. Rapp and S. Mullholland, pp. 113–128. Premium, New York.

Uphof, J. C. T.

1959   *Dictionary of Economic Plants.* HR Engleman, Weinheim.

Wang, Y., and H. Lu

1992   *The Study of Phytolith and Its Application.* China Ocean Press, Beijing.

Weisskopf, A. R.

2014   *Millets, Rice and Farmers Phytoliths as indicators of agricultural and social change in Neolithic and Bronze Age Central China.* British Archaeological Reports, Oxford.

Zeven, A. C., and J. M. De Wet

1982   *Dictionary of Cultivated Plants and Their Regions of Diversity.* 2nd ed. Centre for Agricultural Publishing and Documentation, Wageningen.

Chapter 14

Dog Days of Winter: Seasonal Activities in a Srubnaya Landscape

Anne Pike-Tay • David W. Anthony

The Late Bronze Age Srubnaya culture (c. 1900–1200 cal BC) was descended from a long tradition of pastoral economies beginning in the Neolithic in the European steppes, west of the Ural Mountains (Chapter 1). But these economies differed through time in the management of domesticated animals. Reconstruction of land-use patterns, settlement systems, and subsistence strategies in the Samara Valley region requires, among many other things, assessment of the nature of stock management. Stockbreeding types vary from small-scale, intensive, mixed farming with stock keeping as the activity of a household or an individual (Bar-Yosef and Khazanov 1992; Halstead 1996) to a central emphasis on livestock by whole communities, with regions of higher seasonal extremes necessitating higher mobility (e.g., Halstead 1996; Jarman et al. 1982). To determine where the Srubnaya economy should be placed within this range of possible economic organizations, the seasonal mobility or stability of the Srubnaya household must be assessed, which is one goal of the present study. In addition, we should assess the degree to which livestock were exploited for their secondary products (wool, milk, traction) for community use and as exchange items (Sherratt 1981). Finally, animals hold symbolic as well as economic value, but this component of the zooarchaeological record of the Bronze Age steppes can be as elusive as it is compelling. In this study, however, we describe unique evidence for the symbolic importance of a seasonal ceremony involving dogs and wolves. This find is unique in the LBA archaeological record of the Russian steppes.

As discussed in Chapters 1 and 2 of this volume, the Samara Valley Project (SVP) was designed to answer questions regarding the Srubnaya subsistence economy, including whether or not LBA sites were permanent agricultural centers occupied year round, seasonally occupied herding centers, or something in between. The degree of sedentism inherent to these various settlement choices would have very different implications for productivity of the local landscape and the social geography of the people inhabiting it. In this study, we tried to understand the seasonal circulation of people and animals between four places: the settlement at Krasnosamarskoe and close-by kurgan cemetery at Krasnosamarskoe IV, two small probable herding camps in a tributary stream valley of Peschanyi Dol, and Mikhailovka Ovsianka, a copper mine in the steppes south of the Samara Valley. It has become clear that the settlement of Krasnosamarskoe has a ceremonial component that is at least as interesting as its secular aspect.

In this chapter, we review the season-of-death and age at death results of the skeletochronological (growth-increment) analysis completed by Pike-Tay of the large mammals from the above locations to answer the basic question of whether they were permanently or seasonally occupied. Incidental to this inquiry, light is shed on the circulation of livestock and people between herding camps and settlements as well as on the unique character of ritual activity surrounding dogs at the site of Krasnosamarskoe.

Materials and Methods
Sites Sampled
Krasnosamarskoe
The settlement at Krasnosamarskoe was built at the edge of an abandoned channel of the Samara River. The site overlooked an old oxbow lake bordered by marshes. Strongly clustered radiocarbon dates suggest that it was occupied for a short time during the interval 1900 to 1700 BC. As noted by Anthony and colleagues in this volume, the central focus of the 210-m² excavation was a large multipurpose structure, 8 × 12 m. The unexpected evidence for dog-related ceremonial activity detailed by Kosintsev and Russell et al. (this volume) was found inside this structure. One well and a possible second one were also discovered within the structure, which produced an unparalleled trove of LBA wooden artifacts, as well as animal bones and early Srubnaya ceramics. Animal bones, including dog bones, were distributed across the floor of the structure. From Square L5 to M5, the bones could be seen to be sloping downward, as if discarded on the sloping interior northwestern wall of the dug-out structure. Dog bones occurred in particularly dense clusters from around Vessel 3 at the southwestern end of the structure to Pit 9 at the northwestern end (Figure 10.2).

Kosintsev's counts of taxa (Chapter 15) and Russell, Brown, and Brown's analyses of taxa and usage (Chapter 16) show that the large faunal assemblage from Krasnosamarskoe is composed primarily of dogs and cattle, with their proportions depending on how they are counted. In the larger sample identified by Kosintsev, he counted 7,958 bones of domesticated animals identified to species, representing a minimum number of individuals (MNI) of 368. Of these, a minimum of 51 dogs were present, representing 18 percent of the MNI but fully 36 percent of the number of identifiable specimens (NISP). The proportion of dog bones counted by pieces, or NISP, was so much higher because the dog bones were fragmented and chopped much more intensely than the bones of any other animal. Kosintsev's sample contained 38 percent cattle counted by MNI, much more than dogs, and 35 percent cattle counted by NISP. Russell et al. identified a smaller proportion of bones and, in that smaller sample, counted 40 percent dogs by NISP (1,518 identifiable dog bones), quite similar to Kosintsev's 36 percent dogs by NISP (2,755 identifiable dog bones). However, when analyzed by diagnostic zones, the proportion of dogs counted by Russell et al. rose even higher, to 45 percent. Clearly, dog bones composed either the largest or second largest percentage of the animal bones at Krasnosamarskoe. No other Srubnaya settlement has more than 3 percent dog bones, and most

have only 1 to 2 percent. Krasnosamarskoe has a unique faunal profile.

In addition to an MNI of 51 domestic dogs, Kosintsev found remains of 7 MNI (18 NISP) wolves and 6 more canids between the size of dogs and wolves, together totaling a minimum of 64 individuals. Kosintsev noted that the wolf bones were also fragmented, cut, and split like the dog bones, and Russell et al. agreed that at least one wolf was roasted and its skull was chopped just like the dogs. Hunting was not a common activity at Krasnosamarskoe, with just a few bones of roe deer and elk. More wolves were hunted or trapped than any other wild animal at the site, indicating an unusual attention to wolves, balancing in the wild the attention given to dogs in the domestic world.

Two components of the faunal assemblage stand out just looking at the numbers of bones: horse, by its near absence, unusual in a Srubnaya settlement assemblage, as well as dog and wolf, by their very high occurrence (Tables 15.24 and 16.1). Kosintsev and Russell et al. agree that this surprising pattern may be due to the status of Krasnosamarskoe as a ceremonial site.

Peschanyi Dol
Inferences from topographic location and historic use as summer pastures led our project members to hypothesize that the tributary stream sites of Peschanyi Dol 1 and 2, some 25 km from Krasnosamarskoe, are small-scale warm-season herding camps (see Chapter 18). Remains of caprines and cattle, as well as only one dog specimen, comprise the bulk of the relatively small faunal assemblage from the two locations (Table 15.39).

Mikhailovka Ovsianka
In the open steppe country 60 km south of the Samara Valley is the LBA Srubnaya copper mining site and settlement of Mikhailovka Ovsianka. This is the final site to be examined here for direct seasonal information.

Methods: Skeletochronology
Investigations into season of site use and human mobility have been increasingly aided by skeletochronological or growth-increment studies of archaeofaunas. Recent skeletochronological studies of major prey species from Middle, Upper, and Epipalaeolithic sites (e.g., *Rangifer*, *Cervus*, *Equus*, *Capreolus*, *Gazella*, *Bos*, and *Macropus* [especially Bennett's wallaby]) have been successful in assessing variability in hunter-gatherer subsistence, site seasonality, and degree of mobility in Western Eurasia and Tasmania (e.g., Burke 1993, 1995; Burke and Pike-Tay 1997; Lieberman 1993a; Miracle and O'Brien 1998; Pike-Tay

1991a, 1993, 2000; Pike-Tay and Bricker 1993; Pike-Tay and Cosgrove 2002; Pike-Tay et al. 1999; Stutz 1997; Stutz et al. 1995). Skeletochronological research is also relevant to the archaeology of societies involved in animal husbandry. Seasonal variation in the availability of food for stock affects such decisions as timing of the slaughter and whether to move herds to pasture or to stay put and fodder them. Each of the latter solutions results in different settlement patterns and differently affects the overall productivity of the local environment. Seasonal data along with mortality data are needed to investigate culling strategies and livestock productivity (see, e.g., Halstead 1998; Sherratt 1981).

Skeletochronology can provide *direct* indications of both season of death and age at death of individual animals. Site topographic location, reconstructions of demography and settlement patterns, functional analyses of tool assemblages, geochemical and geomorphological studies, coprolite analysis, and ethnographic analogy have all fueled *indirect* seasonal inferences of site seasonality (cf. Monks 1981), which are most useful in building hypotheses that can be tested with *direct* methods (Pike-Tay 1991a). Direct methods of estimating seasonality rely on the presence-absences of fauna (including insect) and floral remains as well as the state and composition of seasonally indicative organic remains (Monks 1981). Before proceeding to the skeletochronological analysis of cattle, ovicaprid, and canid samples from the Samara Valley study region, we review the two major categories of direct methods employed by the current study: (1) population structure and (2) the record of cyclical, developmental physiological events found on organic remains. (For a comprehensive review of methods used in seasonal determinations, including particular applications, see Monks [1981]; Pike-Tay [1991a]; and Pike-Tay and Cosgrove [2002].)

Population Structure

Hunting strategies and culling/domestic herd management practices have long been inferred from population structure data (e.g., Davis 1983; Klein 1982, 1987, 1989; Greenfield 1991; Halstead 1998; Koike and Ohtaishi 1985, 1987; Lyman 1987; Payne 1973, 1987; Spinage 1967; Stiner 1990; contributions to Lubinski 1997, 2000; Lubinski and O'Brien 2001; Stiner 1991; and Weinstock 2000). Age profiles of archaeofaunal assemblages are compared to theoretical "catastrophic," "attritional," "prime-age dominated," and "hunting pressure" patterns for the investigation of scavenger-hunter-gatherer studies, as well as to variations on Payne's (1973) "milk," "meat," and "wool" patterns for the study of animal husbandry. Integral to the application of this method is the fact that the age

and sex composition of hunter-gatherer prey species and of domestic stock vary seasonally.

Differential preservation (e.g., loss of immature and fetal bones), differential transport and processing according to anatomical part, and culinary practices are some of the taphonomic and cultural variables that can affect the harvest profile. In terms of gaining seasonal information from the age data, the range of temporal variation in the occurrence of some of the physiological and attritional markers of aging, such as dental eruption and attrition, crown height wear, and epiphyseal closure, is often too wide for a seasonal determination. Although younger animals provide reliable seasonal data if tooth eruption is assessed as eruption schedules are fairly standardized, tooth wear does not occur at an even pace, and the age at which ossification occurs varies among the skeletal elements. Therefore, seasonality determinations based on population structure alone are not always reliable or comprehensive.

Cyclical, Developmental Physiological Events

The development of bony tissue often leaves annual, seasonal, or diurnally paced growth marks. Such developmental marks are found in the incremental growth structures of a wide range of fish, molluscs, reptiles, and marine and terrestrial mammals. Skeletochronology or sclerochronology measures the incremental structures, the "distinctive, self-contained additions to the previous growth of an organism" (Monks 1981:193), for information regarding environment, seasonality, and/or mortality profiles.

The processes of skeletal biomineralization responsible for these incremental structures across a wide range of taxa have been reviewed (see Bandel [1990a, 1990b] and Claasen [1998][1] for the mechanisms of shell formation and gastropod shell structure, Carter [1990] for the microstructure of the Bivalvia, and Francillon-Vieillot et al. [1990], Carlson [1990], Lieberman [1993b], and Klevezal [1996] for the microstructure and mineralization of vertebrate skeletal tissues, including dental structures). The work of Klevezal (e.g., 1980, 1996) and colleagues, especially Klevezal and Kleinenberg (1969 [1967]), constitutes the longstanding major scientific reference for investigations into the incremental structures of mammalian bone and teeth. "Adhesion lines," the most common incremental structures in bone, form during winter in many high-latitude and temperate-zone mammals and are often most visible in the mandible (cf. Francillon-Vieillot et al. 1990; Klevezal and Mina 1973; Klevezal et al. 1985; Pike-Tay and Cosgrove 2002). However, the potential of the incremental structures of bone (as opposed to those of teeth) for the archaeological assessment of age or season of death has not yet been fully explored.

Skeletochronology of Mammalian Teeth

The assessment of season of capture and age at death from the recording structures of mammalian teeth is the method employed in the current study of the Samara Valley settlements' fauna. The mineralized tissues of the teeth of most high-latitude and temperate-zone mammals record a yearly cycle with one wide (growth) zone, temporally corresponding to the warmer seasons, in addition to one narrow annulus (slow growth) and/or a "line of arrested growth" (LAG), temporally corresponding to "winter" and observable in the dental cementum and/or dentine (cf. Castanet 1981; Francillon-Vieillot et al. 1990; Klevezal 1996; Lieberman 1993a, 1993b; Mina and Klevezal 1970; Pike-Tay 1995; Pike-Tay and Cosgrove 2002). Wildlife biologists have long used these annular increments to age individual animals (e.g., Grue and Jensen 1979; Klevezal 1996; Klevezal and Kleinenberg 1969 [1967]; Laws 1952; Morris 1972; Spinage 1973).

The optical and physical expressions of the growth increments in dental cementum result from differing patterns of collagen fiber organization and of cell content/degree of mineralization (Castanet 1981; Francillon-Vieillot et al. 1990; Klevezal 1996; Lieberman 1993a, 1993b). Differentiation of growth layers in dental cementum results from seasonal rhythms of cementoblast activity as well as from occlusal strain (Lieberman 1993a, 1993b). Controlled experiments with goats point to at least two major causal factors in the formation of dental cementum increments: (1) nutritional quality of diet, which accounts for the width of the growth band, and (2) food hardness, which affects occlusal strain, resulting in fibrillar angle changes in the extrinsic and intrinsic collagen fibers (responsible for the different optical qualities of the *growth zone* and *annulus* under the microscope) (Lieberman 1993a, 1993b). Pike-Tay's (1995) and Weinand's (1997) studies of well-documented *Rangifer* and *Odocoileus* herds, whose forage quality and coarseness varied seasonally, respectively support Lieberman's conclusions. As seasonal differences in the forage characteristics of herbivore diets affect the microstructure of the animals' teeth, skeletochronology provides zooarchaeology with a valuable tool in the reconstruction of site seasonality and prehistoric subsistence strategies.

Skeletochronology of the Samara Valley Sample

The techniques for dental growth mark analysis of the Samara Valley cattle, ovicaprid, and canid teeth follow the protocol described in Pike-Tay (1995), including (1) the preparation and use of radial "dry" thin sections (ca. 30 μ) taken at the mesial-distal midline of the tooth, (2) measuring the areas of acellular cementum where the apposition of growth increments is most regular (which is near the root-enamel junction on the teeth of cervids, large bovids, and ovicaprids but differs in location on some carnivore and macropod teeth: Pike-Tay and Cosgrove 2002), and (3) the use of computerized image analysis of digitized scans of slides under polarized transmitted light (magnification 40×, 100×, and 250×) to measure consecutive growth zone widths at two or three cementum transects per tooth.

Aging of the individual animals by dental annuli counts also followed the protocol outlined in the Pike-Tay (1995) study, where the eruption schedule of each tooth is taken into account. In other words, since first "winter" annulus forms during the first winter of life with ovicaprids of known age studied to date by the author, to assess the correct age in years, the number of annuli counted on the incisors or M1 is a direct measure of age; 1 year is added to M2; and 2 years are added to P2, P3, P4, and M3 (cf. Grue and Jensen 1979; Miller 1974; Mitchell 1963; Pike-Tay 1991a, 1991b). Thus far, a total of 88 cattle, sheep/goat, and dog teeth have undergone dental cementum growth-increment analysis.

Skeletochronology Results: Cattle and Sheep/Goat

Of the total sample, 13 cow and one sheep/goat tooth from Krasnosamarskoe provided results. One cow tooth and one sheep/goat tooth from the copper mining site of Mikhailovka Ovsianka could also be successfully analyzed.

Unfortunately, the teeth from Peschanyi Dol were too fragmentary and friable to furnish seasonal data. The poor preservation of these teeth, though, is informative in that it demonstrates the difference in archaeological context between these probable herding camps and the settlement, between weathered surface deposits and well-preserved pit refuse, which is consistent with the identification of the Peschanyi Dol sites as short-term herding camps. Of course, that same poor preservation leaves us without direct indicators of the season of occupation at these herding camps.

The sample from Krasnosamarskoe shows a year-round slaughter pattern for cattle (Table 14.1). However, it is important to note that faunal analysis by Kosintsev and Russell et al. (Chapters 15 and 16) find the body part distribution of cattle to be skewed toward an overrepresentation of heads and feet (in contrast to the presence of whole skeletons of sheep/goat and dogs from nonfeasting contexts). They suggest two alternative explanations for this pattern: the first a result of ritual activity and the second due to transport of hides (attached to skulls and feet) to the site from cattle that were slaughtered elsewhere. If Russell et al.'s second hypothesis is correct, the year-round pattern picked up by skeletochronological analysis does not reflect the season(s) when cattle were pastured *away* from Krasnosamarskoe. It may mean that cattle hides, along with skulls bearing the teeth analyzed here, were returned to the main settlement regardless of the location of their (summer?) pastures. We will return to this question below.

The age structure of the sample of Krasnosamarskoe's cattle and ovicaprids according to dental annuli counts is shown in Table 14.2.

The majority of older cattle were slaughtered in the spring or summer, and the younger ones were killed in the fall. The one sheep/goat tooth that was well enough preserved to be analyzed was that of a 3-year-old individual with a fall season of death. Of the dental specimens from Area Y, a 2-m × 4-m unit at Krasnosamarskoe located 160 m south of the main settlement, three cattle teeth were well enough preserved to be analyzed and are included in the total count in Table 14.2 and Table 14.3. Area Y contained a large amount of animal bone and ceramics, and radiocarbon dates show it to be contemporary with the Krasnosamarskoe main structure. The three teeth from this site, representing two to three individual adult cattle, all show a late fall season of death.

In sum, the nearly year-round butchery of the cattle (even if off-site, with hides being brought back) leads us to the conclusion that some if not all of the inhabitants of Krasnosamarskoe occupied the settlement year-round.

Table 14.1 Krasnosamarskoe Seasonal Indicators

Season of Death	Species			
	Deer	Dog	Cattle	Sheep/Goat
Late fall or winter	1	8	2	0
Winter	0	3	1	0
Late winter/early spring	0	3	2	0
Spring	0	0	1	0
Summer	0	0	3	0
Late summer/early fall	0	1	2	0
Fall	0	0	2	1

Table 14.2 Bos and Sheep-Goat Ages for Krasnosamarskoe and Mikhailovka Ovsianka

Age	Krasnosamarskoe	Mikhailovka Ovsianka
Juvenile (0–2 y)	0	0
Subadult (2.5–5 y)	1	1
Prime adult (6–9 y)	4	0
Post prime (10+ y)	4	1

Table 14.3 Bos and Sheep-Goat Seasonality for Krasnosamarskoe and Mikhailovka Ovsianka

Season of Death	Krasnosamarskoe	Mikhailovka Ovsianka
Late winter/early spring	2	0
Spring	1	0
Late spring/early summer	1	0
Summer	2	0
Late summer/early fall	2	0
Fall	3	0
Late fall/early winter	2	2
Winter	1	0

Two teeth from the copper mining site of Mikhailovka Ovsianka, 60 km south of Krasnosamarskoe, could be analyzed. A prime adult cow and a subadult sheep/goat both show a late fall time of slaughter (Table 14.3). This is surprising, as the site's location in very open steppe country would have left it open to the cold autumn weather. However, it may be possible that the late season of use was connected with evidence of large fires and ore-roasting pits at the site, which might have made for uncomfortable work in the hot summer months.

Discussion of Cattle and Ovicaprid Results

If these sites were indeed part of the same settlement system, the evidence for fall slaughter of ovicaprids and year-round killing of cattle at Krasnosamarskoe, the possible satellite/ seasonal-pasture locations in Peschanyi Dol, and the fall-slaughtered cattle at Mikhailovka Ovsianka are consistent with a seasonal strategy of culling stock according to age and probably according to sex. Research on early pastoralism has suggested that differential slaughter patterns between cattle and sheep/goat species were related to herd management practices (Greenfield 1991; Sherratt 1981). In our combined sample from Krasnosamarskoe and Mikhailovka Ovsianka, the two sheep/goat teeth analyzed showing fall slaughter were from two 2- to 3-year-old animals, while the cattle consisted of a subadult and two prime-aged adults being killed in the fall, while the older, postprime animals were primarily slaughtered in the spring. These lines of evidence fit the pattern of pastoral movement identified by other zooarchaeological studies in which older animals were culled from the herd in the spring before movement to the summer pasture, and younger animals were butchered in the fall, before the onset of winter (Greenfield 1991:180–181). Such patterns fit with both the maximization of animal products (e.g., returns gained in the slaughtering of juveniles and subadults), which would have peaked in terms of their body weight; at the same time, negative impact on available pasture would be minimized as a result of herd culling.

Skeletochronology Results of the Dogs

The dog remains were restricted to the site of Krasnosamarskoe. The final cementum growth stages observed for 24 of the 25 dog teeth analyzed provided evidence for primarily cold-season deaths (Table 14.4). The deaths ranged from late fall or early winter to late winter or early spring. It is possible that the 24 cold-season dog deaths occurred in three clusters: early winter, midwinter, and late winter.

As with the bovine and caprine samples, ages of the individual dogs were determined by factoring the age at eruption of the tooth with the number of winter annuli. Table 14.5 shows the age profile of the dogs analyzed. Results show that the majority of the dogs were older adults, in the 6- to 12-year-old range, although a small number of younger dogs were present across the site. Due to taphonomic factors, some specimens were too damaged to undergo skeletochronological analysis, although the majority of the recovered assemblage provided useful information.

A clear picture arises from the canid evidence when we combine the skeletochronology for dogs with the faunal analysis of cattle described here and in Chapters 15 and 16. It appears that dogs were killed, butchered, roasted, and eaten in a manner similar to cattle but not exactly the same. Important differences were that most dogs were very old, and they were chopped into small pieces in a ritual context (see Russell, Brown, and Brown's description of ritual chopping of dog heads, Chapter 16), and finally their deaths clustered in the early through late winter months. Kosintsev (Chapter 15) and Russell et al. (Chapter 16) both suggested that the dog sacrifice may have been attended by the sacrifice of cattle, which probably were consumed in feasts. The ceremonial slaughter of the cattle implies that large numbers of community members from beyond the single small household at Krasnosamarskoe shared in the feast.

Skeletochronological analysis of teeth from two cattle from Square N2, perhaps associated with Pit 18 (these are included in the totals in Table 14.1), show winter and end-of-winter season of slaughter for these two cattle. Russell et al. note in Chapter 16 that there was a particular cluster of roasted and chopped dog skulls from at least three dogs in the same square, N2, probably also associated with Pit 18, supporting the possibility that dogs and cattle were slaughtered in the same winter-season ritual events, and their remains were then discarded in the same pits.

Kosintsev (Chapter 15) observes that the cattle and ovicaprid bones he examined at Krasnosamarskoe, in contrast to the dog bones, were skewed toward an overrepresentation of heads and distal limbs, and he suggested that a percentage of these individuals might have been discarded in the form of skins with the head and hooves attached, a common symbolic offering representing the gods' portion of a sacrifice. Head-and-hoof deposits are well-known remains of ritual activity across the Eurasian steppes (Piggott 1962), beginning in the Eneolithic at the cemetery of S'yezzhee (Vasiliev and Matveeva 1979), not far from Krasnosamarskoe but two and a half millennia earlier. Usually, they are found archaeologically in cemeteries, not in settlements. If head-and-hoof offerings explain the overrepresentation of head and lower limb elements among the cattle and ovicaprids at Krasnosamarskoe, this is perhaps the first detection of head-and-hoof offerings in a settlement.

Russell et al. (Chapter 16) also noted that many cattle bones were roasted like the dogs and seemed to represent feasting food but that the hindlimb elements, the best meaty parts, seem to have been discarded elsewhere. The cattle and sheep bones in the excavated structure were biased toward the front limbs (for initiates?), with hindlimbs (for adults?) discarded in another place. Almost all of the horse bones were from the feet, but inside the structure were the remains of a horse skull that was roasted, and the mandible was chopped in a way similar to some of the dog mandibles.

Table 14.4 Krasnosamarskoe Dogs: Season of Death

Season of Death	
Late fall or winter	8
Winter	3
End of winter/early spring	3
Spring	0
Summer	0
Summer/fall	1

Table 14.5 Dog Ages

Age	No. of Specimens
Juvenile (0–3 y)	0
Young adult (4–5 y)	3
Prime adult (6–9 y)	10
Older adult (10+ y)	2

Discussion of Skeletochronology of the Dogs and Conclusions

The seasonal data indicating a winter sacrifice of dogs (and cattle) should be considered in light of the other indications of ritual activity. As Russell et al. noted, the standardized and nonfunctional chopping of the dogs' heads into 10 to 12 equal-sized pieces with an axe implies not just a ritual but one conducted by a practiced ritual butcher. Russell et al. also observed other unusual things about the dogs: older dogs were overrepresented and were clearly selected for sacrifice, some as old as 10 to 12 years; they were unusually well cared for (few injuries); and the wear on their teeth suggests that they might have eaten a special diet. Most of them probably had lived elsewhere, since the level of carnivore gnawing on the other animal bones at Krasnosamarskoe is quite low. They were roasted and almost certainly eaten, but fire was also applied sometimes to their paws, which cannot be eaten and, oddly, also to some cattle hooves, suggesting that lower legs of both cattle and dogs might have been scorched by fire at some point in the ceremony. Wolves also were included in the ceremony, possibly wolves that were intentionally hunted or trapped just for this purpose, and they were roasted like the dogs, and at least one wolf skull was chopped like the dog skulls. Dogs and wolves were equated in this way.

Kosintsev noted, and Russell et al. agree, that the body part distribution of the dogs indicates that the whole body of the dog was used and discarded at Krasnosamarskoe. Heads are somewhat overrepresented, so might have played a special role, but the discarded dog bones include vertebrae, ribs, and proximal limb bones, suggesting that the whole body was roasted, and defleshing cut-marks suggest fileting for food. Because neither dogs nor wolves were normally eaten in Srubnaya society, as the Srubnaya settlement fauna reviewed by Kosintsev shows (Table 15.24), the ritual consumption of dogs and wolves in the winter ceremonies conducted at Krasnosamarskoe, particularly of dogs that were old and familiar, would have been a difficult emotional challenge and probably was conducted in a liminal psychological state during a rite of transformation that stressed liminality and initiation into a new status. At such a moment, a normally forbidden act is accepted as proof of the transformational power of the event and even becomes a metaphor for a future blessed by the appropriate divine powers.

What was the meaning of this winter-season dog and wolf sacrifice? What cultural model might explain it?

Dogs and wolves are strongly associated in Indo-European mythology and literary traditions with death and war. A multiheaded dog guarded the entrance to the Underworld in Greek, Latin, and Indic traditions. Dogs were symbols of death across the ancient Indo-European world. Because of their strong association with death, dogs were connected with war and war-bands. In particular, wolves and dogs were the principal symbols of youthful war-bands composed of boys who had been initiated into a liminal introductory period of warrior status. Youthful war-bands, symbolized by wolves and dogs, operated on the edges of society   stayed together for a number of years, and were disbanded when their members reached a certain age and rejoined society as men. They can be found in mythological and legendary traditions in Germanic (where they are called *Männerbünde*, a label often applied to all similar Indo-European institutions), Celtic (*fían*), Italic (*Luperci, sodales*), Greek (*korios, ephebes*), and Indo-Iranian, particularly Vedic (*Vrātyas*), sources.

The Indo-European distribution of this institution of dog-and-wolf-related youthful war-bands was explored by Wikander (1938) and reexamined by (Bremer 1982:141), Falk (1986), McCone (1987), and Lincoln (1991a, 1991b). Their studies were reviewed at length and elaborated by Kershaw (2000) and later by Spiedel (2002). The subject was examined in a volume edited by Das and Meiser (2002) and critically reviewed by Zimmer (2004), and the institution was reconsidered most recently by Mallory (2007). According to Das and Meiser (2002) and Mallory (2007), youthful war-bands shared many features across the Indo-European ancient world: they were composed of boys of about the same age who fought together as an age set or cohort; in some versions of the institution, they came from elite families (Latin, Germanic, Vedic); their activities were principally raiding for cattle and women but could also include learning poetry and athletics; they lived "in the wild," apart from their families, without possessions; they wore animal skins, appeared as if they were wolves or dogs, and bore names containing the word *wolf* or *dog* (Celtic, Greek, Germanic, Roman, Indic, Iranian); and they were noted for sexual promiscuity, thievery, and attracting outlaws to their camps. Occasionally, their raids resulted in the founding of a new settlement, and it has even be argued that the legends of Romulus (two brothers raised as wolves) and the first kings of Rome (who took in thieves and landless young men) suggest that youthful war-bands played a role in the founding legends of that city (Bremer 1982:136–137). Both Bremer (1982) and Zimmer (2004) suggested that the term *Männerbünde*, which refers to Germanic war-bands of several different kinds, should be reserved for adult male war-bands and a new term, *Jungmannschaft*, should be applied specifically to the initiatory youthful war-band. Zimmer (2004) felt that the comparative material was sufficiently compelling to *postulate* the existence of Indo-European youthful war-bands but not sufficient to *prove* their existence, a precariously balanced interpretation published before the archaeological evidence from Krasnosamarskoe was known.

The Indo-Iranian myths and texts related to youthful war-bands might be most relevant to the ritual at Krasnosamarskoe. The dominant theory of Indic and Iranian origins is that these languages and people were derived from steppe populations that spread into Iran and South Asia from the north (Kuzmina 2007; Parpola 2012; Witzel 1995, 2003; but see also Lamberg-Karlovsky 2002). Iranian languages were spoken across the steppes, including the Volga-Ural region, by the Scythian-Sauromatian-Saka circa 500 BC. If most Russian archaeologists are correct in seeing continuity between late Srubnaya and Scythian populations, as reviewed in Chapter 1, then the Indo-Iranian traditions should be those that offer the most parallels with Krasnosamarskoe.

Kershaw (2000) reviewed the Indo-Iranian evidence for youthful war-bands. In the Vedic tradition, there was a winter ceremony of initiation into youthful war-bands that also included the eating of dogs. The Vedic texts refer to a group of outsiders called Śvapaca. This roughly translates to "dog-cooker," but it can also been understood as "nourished by dogs," "suckled by dogs," or "children of dogs" (White 1991:72). The dog sacrifice and consumption at Krasnosamarskoe can accurately be described using the same terms. Among the Śvapaca were people called Vrātyas or "dog-priests" (White 1991:96). They lived apart from normal society and performed a winter ceremony called Ekāstakā at the winter solstice, when Indra, the god of war, was born with his band of Maruts (Kershaw 2000:233–234). The ceremony occurred during the approximately 12 days between the end of the solar year (the winter solstice) and the end of the associated lunar cycle, to restore vitality and balance to the natural world (Falk 1986; Heesterman 1962; Kershaw 2000:201–256; White 1991:Chapter 5). Heesterman (1962) recognized that the dog-priests called Vrātyas and their winter sacrifices represented an archaic aspect of Indic ritual that was phased out and demonized with the rise of the Brahmin caste, a process that had started already when the *Rig Veda* was compiled between around 1500 and 1200 BC. Vrāta was used in the *Rig Veda* to refer to the Maruts, the troop of young war and storm gods associated with Rudra and Indra, the gods of wildness and war. Falk (1986) elaborated the connection between the Vrātyas and the Maruts and argued that one function of the Vrātyas was to initiate boys at midwinter into youthful war-bands that were described as violent, thieving, and promiscuous, like Rudra's Maruts. While living in the wild with their age-brothers, they became like wolves or dogs, but after a number of years of raiding, they returned to society and married. In the *Rig Veda*, Indra himself received a sacrifice of 100 black dogs (White 1991:93).

Several researchers (Falk 1986:37–56; Heesterman 1962; White 1991:95–100) have suggested that the Vedic midwinter sacrifice by dog-priests had parallels in the Roman *Lupercalia*, with its midwinter sacrifice of a dog, and the Scandinavian Twelve Nights of Christmas, originally a pagan festival during which the hunter-god Odin roared through the forests with his wolves or hounds, exactly like Rudra in midwinter in the Vedic tradition. The Roman *Lupercalia* required a winter-season dog or wolf sacrifice, the skin of which was carried or worn by the adolescent sons of the aristocrats, who ran around the walls of Rome, symbolically protecting the community, while striking women with goat skins to encourage conception and pregnancy (Harrison 1991 [1903]:51–54). Although the *Lupercalia* was no longer understood by its participants by the time it was described, it contained elements that connected it to the old institution of youthful war-bands that seems to have faded away with the rise of the state: adolescent sons of the elite, dressed in dog or wolf skins, ran around at the border of the community and were associated with sexual fecundity and generation.

The Greek *ephebes* were young men who lived on the border, dressed in skins, and fought on the frontier (Cebrián 2010:351–352). In Archaic Greek initiation rituals, boys moved from the city center to a temple dedicated to coming-of-age deities, often Apollo or Artemis, on the frontier, where they took part in rites that manifested a temporary inversion of values and then returned to the center (de Polignac 1995:60). One last analogy should be mentioned: the Celtic sources describe the *fían* as "landless, unmarried, unsettled, and young men given to hunting, warfare, and sexual license in the wilds outside the *túath* [the tribe or people] . . . for which it might perform elementary police or military services where relations were not strained" (West 2007:49). The legendary Irish warrior hero Cuchulainn, when just a boy, killed a giant dog that belonged to a warrior named Cullan and served Cullan as its replacement, thereby earning his name, which meant Cullan's Hound; at the other end of his life as a famous warrior, he was tricked into eating dog meat, thereby breaking a taboo that led to a loss of strength that allowed his enemies to kill him in battle. Dogs, death, warriors, and youths are woven together in many Indo-European traditions and probably provide the cultural model that explains the dog and wolf sacrifices at Krasnosamarskoe.

Between 1900 and 1700 BC, Krasnosamarskoe probably was a central place for the performance of a winter ritual connected to boys' initiations, a place where boys became warriors who would eventually feed the dogs of death. Dogs and wolves were sacrificed and eaten, and cattle and sheep were feasted upon. No other Srubnaya settlement contains such evidence. Boys from other settlements who participated in this ritual trudged through the winter frosts to Krasnosamarskoe to do so. This suggests that seasonal rituals were regionally organized around specific places in the LBA in the Samara Valley. Perhaps other Srubnaya seasonal rituals were conducted at other settlements.

Rites of passage are not often preserved recognizably in archaeological contexts, so are comparatively neglected in the archaeological study of ancient religion and ritual (Garwood 2011). The principal indicator that a rite of passage occurred at Krasnosamarskoe is the occurrence of a tabooed behavior—eating dogs and wolves—that was repeated regularly and included highly repetitive, ritualized butchering, during a season that focused on the winter solstice. Rites of passage typically are highly gendered, as they are one of the principal means by which gender roles are publicly affirmed. The connection of dogs and wolves with initiatory male war-bands in Indo-European mythology permits us to suggest that the rites of passage conducted at Krasnosamarskoe were a public moral discourse on the ideal life path for at least some young males, symbolized by becoming a wolf and feeding the dogs of war.

Acknowledgments

Anne Pike-Tay thanks David Anthony and Dorcas Brown for the invitation to work on the Samara Valley fauna. She is also grateful to Nerissa Russell for the providing valuable help and context for the dental samples. Finally, she thanks Vassar students Molly Trauten, Anne Tiballi, and Emily Zucker for their laboratory assistance.

Notes

1 Claasen (1993, 1998) provides an in-depth literature review and critically compares methods of assessing seasonality in archaeological shells, including isotopic and incremental-growth structure analysis.

References

Bandel, K.

1990a Cephalopod Shell Structure and General Mechanisms of Shell Formation. In *Skeletal Biomineralization: Patterns, Processes and Evolutionary Trends*, Vol. I, edited by J. Carter, pp. 97–116. Van Nostrand Reinhold, New York.

1990b Shell Structure of the Gastropoda Excluding Archaeogastropoda. In *Skeletal Biomineralization: Patterns, Processes and Evolutionary Trends*, Vol. I, edited by J. Carter, pp. 117–134. Van Nostrand Reinhold, New York.

Bartosiewicz, L.

1996 Bronze Age Animal Keeping in Northwestern Transnubia, Hungary. *Pápai Múzeum Ertesító* 6:31–42.

Bar-Yosef, O., and A. Khazanov (editors)

1992 *Pastoralism in the Levant.* Prehistory Press, Madison.

Bremer, J.

1982 The suodales of Poplios Valesios. *Zeitschrift für Papyrologie und Epigraphik* 47:133–147.

Burke, A. M.

1993 Observation of Incremental Growth Structures in Dental Cementum Using the Scanning Electron Microscope. *Archaeozoologia* 5(2):41–54.

1995 *Prey Movements and Settlement Patterns during the Upper Paleolithic in Southwestern France.* British Archaeological Reports International Series S619, Tempus Reparatum, Oxford.

Burke, A. M., and A. Pike-Tay

1997 Reconstructing "l'Age du Renne." In *Caribou/Reindeer Hunters of the Northern Hemisphere*, edited by L. Jackson and P. Thacker. World Archaeology, Aldershott, Brookfield.

Carlson, S.

1990 Vertebrate Dental Structures. In *Skeletal Biomineralization: Patterns, Processes and Evolutionary Trends*, Vol. I, edited by J. Carter, pp. 531–556. Van Nostrand Reinhold, New York.

Carter, J.

1990 Shell Microstructural Data for the Bivalvia. In *Skeletal Biomineralization: Patterns, Processes and Evolutionary Trends*, Vol. I, edited by J. Carter, pp. 297–411. Van Nostrand Reinhold, New York.

Castanet, J.

1981 Nouvelles données sur les lignes cimentantes de l'os. *Archives Biologiques* (Bruxelles) 92:1–24.

Cebrián, Reyes B.

2010 Some Greek Evidence for I-E Youth Contingents of Shape-Shifters. *Journal of Indo-European Studies* 38(3–4):343–357.

Claasen, C.

1993   Problems and Choices in Shell Seasonality Studies and Their Impact on Results. *Archaeozoologica* 5(2):55–76.

1998   *Shells (Cambridge Manuals in Archaeology).* Cambridge University Press, Cambridge.

Das, R. P., and G. Meiser (editors)

2002   *Geregeltes Ungestüm. Brüderschaften und Jugendbünde bei altindogermanischen Völkern.* Hempen, Bremen.

Davis, S.

1983   The Age Profiles of Gazelles Predated by Ancient Man in Israel: Possible Evidence for a Shift from Seasonality to Sedentism in the Natufian. *Paléorient* F:55–62.

de Polignac, François

1995   *Cults, Territory and the Origins of the Greek City-State.* University of Chicago Press, Chicago.

Falk, H.

1986   *Bruderschaft und Würfelspiel.* Hedwige Falk, Freiburg.

Francillon-Vieillot, H., V. de Buffrénil, J. Castanet, J. Gé raudie, F. J. Meunier, J. Y. Sire, L. Zylberberg, and A. de Ricqlès

1990   Microstructure and Mineralization of Vertebrate Skeletal Tissues. In *Skeletal Biomineralization: Patterns, Processes and Evolutionary Trends*, Vol. I, edited by J. Carter, pp. 471–530. Van Nostrand Reinhold, New York.

Garwood, Paul

2011   Rites of Passage. In *The Oxford Handbook of the Archaeology of Ritual and Religion*, edited by Timothy Insoll. Oxford University Press, Oxford.

Greenfield, H.

1991   Fauna from the Late Neolithic of the Central Balkans: Issues in Subsistence and Land Use. *Journal of Field Archaeology* 18(2):161–186.

Grue, H., and B. Jensen

1979   Review of the Formation of Incremental Lines in Tooth Cementum of Terrestrial Animals. *Danish Review of Game Biology* 11(3):3–48.

Halstead, P.

1996   Pastoralism or Household Herding? Problems of Scale and Specialization in Early Greek Animal Husbandry. *World Archaeology* 28(1):20–42.

1998   Mortality Models and Milking: Problems of Uniformitarianism, Optimality and Equifinality Reconsidered. *Anthropozoologica* 27:211–234.

Harrison, J. E.

1991   [1903]. *Prolegomena to the Study of Greek Religion.* Reprint, Princeton University Press, Princeton, New Jersey.

Heesterman, J.

1962   Vrâtyas and Sacrifice. *Indo-Iranian Journal* 6:3–37.

Jarman, M. R., G. N. Bailey, and H. N. Jarman (editors)

1982   *Early European Agriculture.* Cambridge University Press, Cambridge.

Kershaw, Kris

2000   *The One-Eyed God: Odin and the (Indo-) Germanic Männerbünde.* Journal of Indo-European Studies, Monograph No. 36. Institute for the Study of Man, Washington, D.C.

Klein, R. G.

1982   Age (Mortality) Profiles as a Means of Distinguishing Hunted Species from Scavenged Ones in Stone Age Archaeological Sites. *Paleobiology* 8:151–158.

1987   Reconstructing How Early People Exploited Animals: Problems and Prospects. In *The Evolution of Human Hunting*, edited by M. Nitecki and D. Nitecki, pp. 11–45. Plenum, New York.

1989   Why Does Skeletal Part Representation Differ between Smaller and Larger Bovids at Klasies River Mouth and Other Archaeological Sites? *Journal of Archaeological Science* 16:363–381.

Klevezal, G.

1980   Layers in the Hard Tissues of Mammals as a Record of Growths of Individuals. *Report of the International Whaling Commission* Special Issue 3:161–164.

1996   *Recording Structures of Mammals: Determination of Age and Reconstruction of Life History.* A. A. Balkema, Rotterdam.

Klevezal, G., and S. Kleinenberg

1969   [1967]. *Age Determination of Mammals from Annual Layers in Teeth and Bones of Mammals.* Translated from Russian by the Israel Program for Scientific Translations, Jerusalem.

Klevezal, G., and M. Mina

1973   Factors Determining the Pattern of Annual Layers in the Dental Tissues and Bones of Mammals. *Zhurnal Obschei Biologii* 34(4):594–605.

Klevezal, G., M. Pucek, and E. Malafeeva

1985   Differentiation of Seasonal Generations of Field Voles on Bone Adhesion Lines. *Acta Theriologica* 30(23):349–358.

Koike, H., and N. Ohtaishi

1985   Prehistoric Hunting Pressure Estimated by the Age Composition of Excavated Sika Deer (*Cervus nippon*) Using the Annual Layer of Tooth Cement. *Journal of Archaeological Science* 12:443–456.

1987   Estimation of Prehistoric Hunting Rates Based on the Composition of Sika Deer. *Journal of Archaeological Science* 14:251–269.

Kuzmina, Elana E.

2007   *The Origin of the Indo-Iranians.* Brill, Leiden.

Lamberg-Karlovsky, C. C.

2002   Archaeology and Language: The Indo-Iranians. *Current Anthropology* 43(1):63–88.

Laws, R. M.
1952   A New Method of Age Determination for Mammals. *Nature* 169:972–973.

Lieberman, D.
1993a   Mobility and Strain: The Biology of Cementogenesis and Its Application to the Evolution of Hunter-Gatherer Seasonal Mobility in the Southern Levant during the Late Quaternary. Unpublished Ph.D. dissertation, Harvard University.
1993b   Life History Variables Preserved in Dental Cementum Microstructure. *Science* 261:1162–1164.

Lincoln, Bruce
1991a   Homeric *Lyssa*; "Wolfish Rage." In *Death, War, and Sacrifice, Studies in Ideology and Practice*, pp. 131–137. University of Chicago Press, Chicago.
        1991b Warriors and Non-Herdsmen: A Reply to Mary Boyce. In *Death, War, and Sacrifice, Studies in Ideology and Practice*, pp. 147–166. University of Chicago Press, Chicago.

Lubinski, P.
1997   Pronghorn Intensification in the Wyoming Basin: A Study of Mortality Patterns and Prehistoric Hunting Strategies. Unpublished Ph.D. dissertation, University of Wisconsin, Madison.
2000   A Comparison of Methods for Evaluating Ungulate Mortality Distributions. In *Assessing Season of Capture, Age and Sex of Archaeofaunas*, edited by A. Pike-Tay, pp. 121–134. Archaeozoologia XI, Grenoble, France.

Lubinski, P., and C. O'Brien
2001   Observations on Seasonality and Mortality from a Recent Catastrophic Death Assemblage. *Journal of Archaeological Science* 28:833–842.

Lyman, R. L.
1987   On the Analysis of Vertebrate Mortality Profiles: Sample Size, Mortality Type, and Hunting Pressure. *American Antiquity* 52:125–142.

Mallory, J. P.
2007   Indo-European Warfare. In *War and Sacrifice: Studies in the Archaeology of Conflict*, edited by Tony Pollard and Iain Banks, pp. 77–98. Brill, Leiden.

McCone, Kim
1987   Hund, Wolf, und Krieger bei den Indogermanen. In *Studien zum Indogermanischen Wortschatz*, edited by W. Meid, pp. 101–154. Institut für Sprachwissenschaft der Universität Innsbruck, Innsbruck.

Miller, F. L.
1974   *Biology of the Kaminuriak Population of Barren-Ground Caribou. Part 2: Dentition as an Indicator of Age and Sex; Composition and Socialization of the Population.* Canadian Wildlife Service, Ottawa.

Mina, M., and G. Klevezal
1970   The Principles of Investigating Recording Structures. *Uspekhy Sovremennoi Biologii* 7(3):341–352. (In Russian)

Miracle, P., and C. O'Brien
1998   Seasonality of Resource Use and Site Occupation at Badanj, Bosnia-Herzegovina: Subsistence Stress in an Increasingly Seasonal Environment? In *Seasonality and Sedentism: Archaeological Perspectives from Old and New World Sites*, edited by T. Rocek and O. Bar-Yosef, pp. 41–74. Peabody Museum of Archaeology and Ethnology, Harvard University, Cambridge, Massachusetts.

Mitchell, B.
1963   Determination of Age in Scottish Red Deer from Growth Layers in Dental Cementum. *Nature* 198:350–351.

Monks, G.
1981   Seasonality Studies. In *Advances in Archaeological Method and Theory*, Vol. 4, edited by M. Schiffer. Academic Press, New York.

Morris, P. A.
1972   A Review of Mammalian Age Determination Methods. *Mammal Review* 2:69–104.

Parpola, A.
2012   Formation of the Indo-European and Uralic (Finno-Ugric) Language Families in the Light of Archaeology: Revised and Integrated 'Total' Correlations. *Suomalais-Ugrilaisen Seuran Toimituksia* 266:119–184.

Payne, S.
1973   Kill-Off Patterns in Sheep and Goats: The Mandibles from Asvan Kale. *Anatolian Studies* 23:281–303.
1987   Reference Codes for Wear States in the Mandibular Cheek Teeth of Sheep and Goats. *Journal of Archaeological Science* 14:609–614.

Piggott, Stuart
1962   Heads and Hoofs. *Antiquity* 36(142):110–118.

Pike-Tay, A.
1991a   *Red Deer Hunting in the Upper Paleolithic of Southwest France: A Study in Seasonality.* British Archaeological Reports International Series S569, Tempus Reparatum, Oxford.
1991b   L'Analyse du cement dentaire chez les cerfs: l'application en Préhistoire. *Paléo* 3:149–166.
1993   Hunting in the Upper Périgordian: A Matter of Strategy or Expedience? In *Before Lascaux: The Complex Record of the Early Upper Paleolithic*, edited by H. Knecht, A. Pike-Tay, and R. White, pp. 85–100. CRC Press, Boca Raton, Florida.
1995   Variability and Synchrony of Seasonal Indicators in Dental Cementum Microstructure of the Kaminuriak *Rangifer* Population. *Archaeofauna* 4:273–284.

2000   Seasonality Studies of Archaeofaunas within a Multiscalar Framework: A Case study from Cantabrian Spain. In *Animal Bones, Human Societies*, edited by P. Rowley-Conwy. Oxbow, Oxford.

Pike-Tay, A., and H. M. Bricker
1993   Hunting in the Gravettian: An Examination of Evidence from Southwestern France. In *Hunting and Animal Exploitation in the Later Paleolithic and Mesolithic of Eurasia*, edited by G. Larsen Peterkin, H. M. Bricker, and P. Mellars, pp. 127–143. Archaeological Papers of the American Anthropological Association, No. 4., Wiley-Blackwell, New York.

Pike-Tay, A., V. Cabrera Valdés, and F. Bernaldo de Quirós
1999   Seasonal Variations of the Middle-Upper Paleolithic Transition at El Castillo, Cueva Morín and El Pendo (Cantabria, Spain). *Journal of Human Evolution* 36:283–317.

Pike-Tay, A., and R. Cosgrove
2002   From Reindeer to Wallaby: Recovering Patterns of Seasonality, Mobility, and Prey Selection in the Palaeolithic Old World. *Journal of Archaeological Method and Theory* 9(2):101–146.

Sherratt, A.
1981   Plough and Pastoralism: Aspects of the Secondary Products Revolution. In *Pattern of the Past: Studies in Honour of David Clarke*, edited by I. Hodder, G. Isaac, and N. Hammond, pp. 261–305. Cambridge University Press, Cambridge.

Spiedel, Michael P.
2002   Berserks: A History of Indo-European "Mad-Warriors." *Journal of World History* 13(2):253–290.

Spinage, C. A.
1967   Ageing the Uganda Defassa Waterbuck. *East African Wildlife Journal* 5:1–17.
1973   A Review of Age Determination of Mammals by Means of Teeth, with Especial Reference to Africa. *East African Wildlife Journal* 11:165–187.

Stiner, M. C.
1990   The Use of Mortality Patterns in Archaeological Studies of Hominid Predatory Adaptations. *Journal of Anthropological Archaeology* 9:305–351.

Stiner, M. C. (editor)
1991   *Human Predators and Prey Mortality*. Westview, Boulder, Colorado.

Stutz, A.
1997   Seasonality of Magdalenian Cave Occupations in the Mosan Basin: Cementum Increment Data from Bois Laiterie, Chaleux, and the Trou da Somme. In *La Grotte du Bois Laiterie*, edited by M. Otte and L. Straus, pp. 197–204. E.R.A.U.L. 80, Liège.

Stutz, A., D. Lieberman, and A. Spiess
1995   Toward a Reconstruction of Subsistence Economy in the Upper Pleistocene Mosan Basin: Cementum Increment Evidence. In *Le Trou Magrite, Fouilles 1991–1992*, edited by M. Otte and L. Straus, pp. 167–187. E.R.A.U.L. 69, Liège.

Vasiliev, I. B., and G. I. Matveeva
1979   Mogil'nik u s. S'yezhee na R. Samare. *Sovietskaya Arkheologiia* 4:147–166.

Weinand, D.
1997   Increment Studies of White-Tailed Deer (*Odocoileus virginianus*) from Coastal Georgia. Unpublished master's thesis, University of Georgia, Athens.

Weinstock, J.
2000   Demography through Osteometry: Sex Ratios of Reindeer and Hunting Strategies in the Late Glacial Site of Stellmoor, Northern Germany. In *Assessing Season of Capture, Age and Sex of Archaeofaunas*, edited by A. Pike-Tay. Archaeozoologia XI, Grenoble, France.

West, M. L.
2007   *Indo-European Poetry and Myth*. Oxford University Press, Oxford.

White, D. G.
1991   *Myths of the Dog-Man*. University of Chicago Press, Chicago.

Wikander, Stig
1938   *Der arische Männerbund*. Håkan Ohlssons Buchdruckerei, Lund.

Witzel, Michael
1995   Rigvedic History: Poets, Chieftains, and Polities. In *The Indo-Aryans of Ancient South Asia: Language, Material Culture and Ethnicity*, edited by George Erdosy, pp. 307–352. Walter de Gruyter, Berlin.
2003   Sintashta, BMAC and the Indo-Iranians: A Query. In *Linguistic Evidence for Cultural Exchange in Prehistoric Western Central Asia*. Sino-Platonic Papers, Philadelphia.

Zimmer, Stefan
2004   Review of Das, R.P. and G. Meiser (eds), Geregeltes Ungestüm. Brüderschaften und Jugendbünde bei altindogermanischen Völkern, Bremen. *Journal of Indo-European Studies* 32:207–216.

Chapter 15

Archaeozoological Report on the Animal Bones from the Krasnosamarskoe Settlement

Pavel A. Kosintsev

The animal bones found at the Krasnosamarskoe settlement in the Samara oblast during the joint U.S.-Russian excavations in 1999 and 2001 constitute the subject of this report. The Krasnosamarskoe settlement contained two occupations, one during the Late Bronze Age (LBA) pertaining to the Srubnaya culture and another, much lighter occupation in the Iron Age, pertaining to the Gorodetskaya culture. Occasional artifacts of other archaeological cultures were extremely few. The prehistoric animal bones derived from this site amounted to 8,480 bones or bone fragments that were identifiable to species and 13,965 pieces that were identifiable only as mammal, for a total of 22,445 specimens analyzed. Of these, 7,655 bones and bone fragments could be identified as representing the domesticated animals deposited by ancient human activity.

The animal bones were found distributed vertically in definite clusters and also were concentrated in particular horizontal areas extremely unevenly. Vertically, all of the site soils were separated into three principal strata by color and consistency and then into transitional zones between them. There was a very dark brown upper stratum, Stratum 1, that was quite hard and broke into large blocks, but when the blocks were shattered, the soil had a very fine dusty consistency. Stratum 1 contained principally Iron Age artifacts. Stratum 2 was brown and compact but not so blocky and contained the principal Late Bronze Age occupation. Stratum 3 represented the *materik*, or natural subsoil, pen-

etrated by rodent burrows and Bronze Age pits. The greatest number of bones was found in Stratum 2, the central zone of Late Bronze Age occupation deposits. Stratum 3, the subsoil or *materik*, contained notably fewer bones, as expected. The transitional stratum, 2 to 3, also contained relatively few bones. A secondary concentration of bones was found in the Iron Age Stratum 1. This was separated from the LBA deposit by a transitional soil zone, Strata 1 to 2, that contained significantly fewer bones than the cultural layers above and below (Table 15.1—all tables are at the end of this chapter.) Horizontally, bone finds were concentrated in the squares that revealed the Bronze Age structure. Squares excavated outside the structure (on the lines designated P, R, S, T, U, F, and X) contained relatively few bones.

The bone remains from the excavations were separated by the year they were recovered (1999, 2001) and defined and described in accordance with the instructions on the label; that is, horizontally, they were assigned to each 1-m × 1-m quarter of each 2-m × 2-m square, and vertically, they were assigned to a stratum. Arbitrary 10-cm levels also were recorded, but in this report, only the strata, visible by color and consistency and to a more mixed extent by artifact types, are used in the analysis of animal bones. For some tables, the faunal remains from different strata were recombined. All bones from the cultural layers for which the stratum was recorded were assigned one of the following stratum numbers: 1, 1 to 2, 2, 2 to 3, 3, or 1 to 3.

Each bone was characterized by the following parameters: species, element of the skeleton, whole or fragmented bone, portion of the bone (diaphysis, epiphysis, or fragments thereof), age-specific features (rooted or not rooted epiphyses, the change of teeth in the jaws), cutmarks of human tools, toothmarks of predators, and the traces of fire or other external influences.

The bones of birds and fish were identified at the Institute of Plant and Animal Ecology, Ural Branch of RAS Nekrasov AE. The bones of mammals not identified to species were assigned to *Mammalia* indet. or, in the case of rodents, to *Microtinae gen.* Bones not definable beyond "bird" were assigned to *Aves* indet., those of undefined amphibians to the *Amphibia* indet., those of unidentified fish to *Pisces* indet., and those of unidentified shellfish to *Mollusca* indet.

The bones excavated in 2001 and not assigned to specific species of mammals ("*Mammalia* indet.") were divided into three groups. Separation was carried out on the basis of visual assessment of wall thickness of the bones and their overall massiveness. The bones with thick walls and more massive size were assigned to the group "large," the size of cattle and horses. Bones with thin walls or less massive were assigned to the group "medium," the size of ovicaprids, pigs, and dogs. Small fragments that were difficult to attribute unambiguously to one of the groups were assigned to a third group, "large or medium."

The estimation of the degree of fragmentation of the bones from the excavations in 1999 and 2001 was calculated by stratum. The amount of *mammalia* indet. and the number of specimens assignable to cattle, sheep and goats, horses, pigs, and dogs were determined from each stratum. The percent of *mammalia* indet. also was determined within the indeterminate bone remains overall. For the excavation in 2001, the degree of fragmentation also was assessed as the ratio of groups "large," "medium," and "large or medium" in each layer.

The age structure was determined for pigs, cattle, and small ruminants according to the eruption and wear of teeth separately for the upper and lower jaws (Silver 1969). Both the whole jaw and fragments thereof were used. In the latter case were taken only those instances where it was possible to unambiguously determine the state of dentition. The age structure of horses could be defined only by isolated teeth and so is not statistically reliable. The degree of wear on the crowns of the teeth was examined for four age groups: young (up to 2 years), semi-mature (2–5 years), adults (5 to around 15 years), and old (older than 15 years).

Measurement of bones in cattle, sheep and goats, horses, pigs, dogs, and other species was carried out by the method of A. von den Driesch (1976). Only the phalanges I of cattle, sheep and phalanges I and II of the horses could be measured. Sagittal length (LA) was measured by the method of Eisenmann et al. (1988). Data on the size of the bones from the excavations of 1999 and 2001 were combined into one sample.

The withers height of cattle was determined by the coefficients proposed by V. I. Tsalkin (1970) on the talus. The withers height of sheep was determined by the length of the talus (Teichert 1975).

A Comment on the Fauna from Stratum 1

The Stratum 1 animal bones merit a brief analysis just because a small number of artifacts of the early Iron Age were deposited in this stratum, so the animal bones found in this stratum could relate to the early Iron Age. Alternatively, they could be derived from the LBA strata through rodent activity. A comparison of the species composition between Strata 1 and 2 to 3 will show if the composition of the bones from Stratum 1 was different from the composition of bones from Strata 2 and 3, in which case the bones of the early Iron Age could be different from the Late Bronze Age and should be analyzed separately. As will be clear, it is quite probable that the animal bones found in Stratum 1 were derived from Strata 2 to 3.

Stratum 1 contained only about 360 definable animal bones, and in every respect, they repeated the faunal patterns of Strata 2 and 3 (Table 15.1). Here, as in the Bronze Age levels, many dog bones were found. In the Stratum 1 material excavated in 1999, dogs accounted for 34 percent of the fauna; in 2001, they accounted for 21 percent. Stratum 1 contained few horse bones, an unusual trait that also characterized the Bronze Age sample. In Stratum 1, pig bones were absent; in Strata 2 and 3 also, they were very rare. The percentage of mammal bones unidentifiable to species was similar to the indeterminate mammals in Strata 2 and 3. Thus, the ratio of species in 1 is the same as in 2 and 3.

If we compare the composition of species from Stratum 1 with the documented faunal profiles of early Iron Age settlements in the middle Volga region (Tsalkin 1966), we see a pronounced difference from what we should expect. In early Iron Age settlements, on average, the bones of dogs should be less than 1 percent. Horse bones should be more than 30 percent. Pigs are more than 10 percent. As can be seen from these data, the composition of remains from Stratum 1 is very different from the composition of fauna in early Iron Age settlements in the middle Volga. The species composition corresponds to the species composition of

Strata 2 and 3. Therefore, Stratum 1 can contain only a very small number of animal bones dated to the early Iron Age, not enough to have any impact on the overall species composition. Almost all of the animal bones found in Stratum 1 were derived from Strata 2 and 3 through the burrowing activities of rodents and perhaps from Iron Age human activities. Therefore, the materials of Stratum 1 are hereafter considered together with the fauna of the Late Bronze Age occupation.[1]

Material from the Excavations of 1999

In 1999, 138 m² were excavated at the Krasnosamarskoe settlement to a depth of about 1 m. The largest concentrations of the bones were found in Units N2, N3, N4, M3, M4, M5, L5, O4, and, to a lesser degree, in L6, M6, O2, and O3. The excavated soils contained 6,108 bones that were identified to species. Of these, 6,040 bones were identified mammalian species, including both ancient bones deposited by human activity and modern bones deposited by burrowing animals. Of these, 5,645 bones represented ancient domesticated animals: cattle, ovicaprids, pigs, horses, and dogs; 48 bones represented ancient wild animals: elk, roe deer, and wolf. In addition, 10,882 bone fragments from 1999 were assigned to "Mammalia indet."

Cattle—Bos taurus L.

Cattle represented the second largest number of bones and bone fragments (1,816), after dogs (1,963), which were in first place (Table 15.1). But by minimum number of individuals or MNI (69), cattle were the largest number, many more than dogs (26). The bones of dogs were much more fragmented. Cattle bones also were highly fragmented compared to other LBA sites in the region, although this could be because screens were used at Krasnosamarskoe and not at other sites.

The 1999 sample of cattle bones contains all the bones of the skeleton (Table 15.2). Body parts are dominated by remains of the head. The bones of the skull, lower jaw, and isolated teeth totaled about half of all the bones of cattle—42 percent (Table 15.3). If we exclude isolated teeth, the most numerous body parts are the bones of the skull and distal extremities, each of which accounts for up to 28 percent or together 56 percent of all cattle bones recovered. Other body parts were evidenced much less: proximal extremities (19 percent) and trunk bones (16 percent). Least of all were carpal and tarsal bones, which together accounted for 8 percent (Table 15.3).

Large fragments of the skull were found, including fragments of adults, with no horns. There are a number of entire skulls from individuals under the age of 6 months. There

are no traces of the formation of horns. All this suggests that the vast majority of the herd was polled or bred for a hornless state. Of other features of craniology, nothing definite can be said.

The age structure defined by the upper jaw (Table 15.4) and mandible (Table 15.5) is different. This is probably due to small sample sizes. Nevertheless, in general, one can observe a very high proportion of juveniles under the age of 1.5 years. Counting the upper jaw, they make up 52 percent, and counting the lower jaw, 59 percent. Very little slaughter occurred at the ages between 1.5 and 2.5 years. Counting the upper jaw, only an additional 12 percent of individuals were added that were between 1.5 and 2.5 years of age, and by the lower jaw, none or 0 percent were added that were in this age range. That is, the proportion of individuals under the age of 2.5 years is 64 percent for the upper jaw and 59 percent for the lower jaw. The average proportion of individuals under the age of 2.5 years for the upper and lower jaws is 62 percent. The proportion of individuals older than 2.5 years is a significant amount—36 percent and 41 percent, respectively. The average proportion of individuals older than 2.5 years for the upper and lower jaws is 38 percent.

The data on age at death for cattle slaughtered at Krasnosamarskoe are not very common in the Late Bronze Age. Therefore, it was desirable to obtain information from an independent source about the age structure of the slaughtered animals. All isolated milk teeth (D2-4, P2-4, M1-3, d2-4, p2-4, and m1-3) were divided into two groups. The first group consisted of all milk teeth D2-4 and d2-4; unworn permanent teeth P2-4, p2-4, M3, and m3; and little worn M1-2 and m1-2. The second group included P2-4, M3, and m3 with the first signs of wear and M1-2 and m1-2 with moderate and high wear. Thus, the first group belonged to individuals who had M3 and m3 not erupted, which indicates an age younger than 2.5 years. The second group belonged to individuals who had erupted M3 and m3 (i.e., were older than 2.5 years). The number of teeth is 125 in the first group and 66 in the second group. The ratio of these groups is 65 percent and 35 percent. This ratio is very close to the ratio of these age groups obtained by analysis of the upper and lower jaws, 62 percent and 38 percent. The results obtained by two methods coincided. This suggests that in the studied material, the juveniles are about two-thirds, while the adults are around one-third. Six bones derived from embryos.

Most of the bones and teeth of the youngest individuals (up to 1.5 years) were excavated from a horizontally defined space, defined by Squares N/3 and N/4. A smaller fraction was concentrated in the Squares M/3, M/4, M/5, N

2, O/2, O/3, and O/4. Almost all are concentrated in Layer 2 or on the boundary of Layers 2 and 3. It can be assumed that they form a single complex. This complex is strongly defined by the young age of the slaughtered calves and yearlings. If these very young animals are excluded, then adults significantly dominate the remaining assemblage, but the sample size is dramatically reduced, making it impossible to derive reliable conclusions about structure of the remaining older age categories.

Small Stock—*Ovis aries L. et Capra hircus L.*

The vast majority of the bones of sheep and goats are not defined to the species because of the strong fragmentation of the specimens (Table 15.1). Among the determinable bone remains, sheep account for 71 percent and goats for 29 percent. The composition of skeletal elements is given for both species. The sample has all the elements of the skeleton (Table 15.6). At first, like the cattle, the bones in the ovicaprid category seem to be dominated by the remnants of heads. The bones of the skull, lower jaw, and isolated teeth totaled 32 percent (Table 15.3). But if we exclude isolated teeth, the different parts of the body are approximately the same: 21 percent of the bones derive from the head, 24 percent from the trunk, 27 percent from proximal limb bones, and 23 percent from distal extremities. Least of all were carpal and tarsal bones, which together accounted for 4 percent.

The age structure defined by the upper (Table 15.7) and lower (Table 15.8) jaws differs markedly. This is due to small sample sizes. The main distinction of the assemblage is the absence of jaws of animals younger than 3 months. Averaging the age data from the upper and lower jaws, 24 percent of the individuals were butchered between 3 and 12 months, 16 percent were aged 12 to 24 months, and 60 percent were over the age of 24 months. Thus, more than half of the butchered individuals were adults. Among the ovicaprid remains were 12 bones from embryos, and 2 bones were probably from a newborn animal.

Sheep—*Ovis aries L.*

The remains of sheep definitely dominate the determinable sheep and goat bones. Sheep are two times more frequent than the remains of goats (Table 15.1). There is only one piece of sheep horn, which may indicate a high percentage of hornless animals in the herd, since there are many other ovicaprid bones.

Goat—*Capra hircus L.*

Goat bones were two times less than sheep bones (Table 15.1). Probably, in the actual herds, the proportion of goats

to sheep was similar: at least a factor of two smaller. Among the remains of goats, there are 13 fragments of horns. Judging by their size, they all belong to females. Probably most of the goats had horns. Whole goat bones are absent.

Horse—*Equus caballus L.*

Very few horse bones were found in the excavated area of the Krasnosamarskoe settlement (Table 15.1). Together with the high frequency of very young cattle and dogs, this was another unusual aspect of the faunal profile at this settlement, distinguishing it from other Srubnaya settlements in the region. Not all the parts of the horse skeleton were found. Bones that were not found included the ulna, tibia, and metacarpal bones (Table 15.9). The most frequent horse remains were isolated teeth. In Stratum 1, the Iron Age occupation, were the remains of a young horse (under 2 years old), one adult (5–15 years) and two old (15 years) individuals. In Strata 2 and 3, the Late Bronze Age, were the remains of three young horses or colts, four semi-mature (2–5 years), two adults, and two older individuals. The age composition of the horse herd cannot be determined from the slaughtered animals because of the small sample size.

Pig—*Sus scrofa domestica L.*

Pig bones were not found in Stratum 1, attributed to the Iron Age (Table 15.1). In the Late Bronze Age, strata pig bones occurred but were few. Among these are all parts of the body but not all skeletal elements (Table 15.10). The ages as defined by the lower jaw dentition were as follows: five individuals (12–18 months) had m2 but not m3, and one individual (over 18 months) had m3. Three fragments of the upper jaw indicate the same ages—two individuals from 12 to 18 months and one individual older than 18 months.

Dog—*Canis familiaris L.*

The dog remains from Krasnosamarskoe are unique compared with Late Bronze Age settlements in the region and probably have no parallel in any Srubnaya culture settlement anywhere. A very large amount of dog bones (1,963 fragments, from MNI 26 dogs) were found in the excavated area in 1999, so dog was actually the single most frequent species among all of the animal bones (Table 15.1). The bones include all elements of the skeleton (Table 15.11). They are dominated by fragments of the skull, vertebrae, ribs, and metapodia (Table 15.12). Nearly all the epiphyses of the bones are fused or adnate, and some teeth are heavily worn. This indicates that the bones belonged mostly to adults and older dogs. The most frequently represented body parts were the head (23 percent of all dog bones), the trunk (25 percent), and the proximal limbs (23 percent). The distal limb bones were slightly fewer (17 percent). Isolated teeth and carpal and tarsal bones together amounted to just 6 percent of the dog bones found (Table 15.12).

Even in a bone assemblage containing many fragmented bones, the bones of the dog were more fragmented than other species. This is shown by the fact that, by the number of identified bone fragments, dog bones were the most numerous of any species found in the 1999 excavation, while, by the MNI, cattle (minimum 69 individuals) were much more frequent than dogs (26). The dogs were cut and chopped like no other species. Whole bones were rare and included only the phalanges, carpals, tarsals, sesamoid bones, and metapodia. The dog heads typically were split into several parts: the nose was cut off just in front of the eyes, and another cut was made behind the eyes. The trunk of the body was chopped into many pieces. This is reflected in the high percentage of bone fragments derived from the skull and the proximal limb bones (Table 15.12).

The sizes of dogs have not been studied for this report. However, it is evident from the general range of bone sizes that the dogs were of average and below-average size. Large dogs were not present.

In addition to bones, coprolites of dogs were found in Stratum 2, where two specimens were recovered, and in Stratum 3, where three specimens were found, perhaps derived from trash pits. One has a length of 43 mm and a diameter of 22 mm.

Eurasian Elk—*Alces alces L.*
This large forest animal was represented by 12 bones (Table 15.1): fragments of the humerus, femur, radius, and metacarpal bones. Whole bones were the first phalanx and six carpal bones. All bones are gray in color. In Stratum 2, the lower end of the radius and six carpal bones were found. Probably, there was a joint of the lower limb, including the end of ulna with the carpal bones. The width of the lower end of radius is 69.8 mm.

Roe Deer—*Capreolus pygargus Pall*
This small forest dweller was represented by 11 bones (Table 15.1): fragments of the femur, tibia, metapodia, and second phalanges, as well as two whole carpal bones. All bones are gray in color. The width of the lower end of tibia is 30.0 mm.

Wolf—*Canis lupus L.*
The wolf was represented by 16 bones (Table 15.1): fragments of the skull, jaw, elbow, shoulder, pelvis, and metapodia, as well as whole bones—heel and ankle bones. All bones are gray in color. The bones were fragmented, cut, and split like the dog bones.

Dog/Wolf—*Canis* sp.
This group includes canid bone fragments the size of a wolf or large dog but not clearly belonging to one category or the other and gray in color.

Fox—*Vulpes vulpes L.*
We found a whole rib. The color is light gray.

Steppe Polecat—*Putorius eversmanni Lesson*
This ferret-like animal was represented by six bones (Table 15.1): three whole lower jaws and pelvic, shoulder, and thigh bones. The bones are light gray or white.

Hare—*Lepus* sp.
It is difficult to reliably determine which of the two species these bones belong to: hare (*Lepus timidus L.*) or European hare (*Lepus europaeus Pallas*). Hare is represented by a whole rib, vertebrae, radius, tibia, and metapodia. The bones are light gray or white. Among them are two bones of newborn animals.

Pika—*Ochotona pusilla Pallas*
One whole tibia of this mouse-sized animal was recovered. The bone is white.

Russet Ground Squirrel—*Spermophillus major Pallas*
This species was represented by fragments of skulls, mandibles, and bones of the postcranial skeleton. In Stratum 2 was an almost complete skeleton. The bones are light gray and white.

Steppe Marmot—*Marmota bobak Muller*
This burrowing rodent was represented by eight bones (Table 15.1): fragments of the skull, mandible, clavicle, pelvis, elbow, and shin bones. The lower jaw was broken off at the ascending ramus. The bones are light gray and white.

Jerboa—*Allactaga major Kerr*
This species was represented by fragments of the mandible, tibia, and metapodia. The bones are white.

Hamster—*Cricetus cricetus L.*
This species was represented by fragments of skulls, mandibles, and the postcranial skeleton. The bones are light gray and white.

Northern Mole Vole—*Ellobius talpinus Pallas*
This species was represented by the skull and lower jaw. The bones are white.

Water Voles—*Arvicola terrestris L.*
This species was represented by the skull and lower jaw. The bones are white.

Voles—*Microtinae* gen.
This group included the bones of the postcranial skeleton derived from rodents the size of voles. The bones are light gray and white.

Mammals Unidentifiable—*Mammalia* indet.
This group included bone fragments that are not defined to the species level. All belong to animals dog-sized and larger. The bones are gray.

Birds—*Aves*
Many of the bones are not definable to species (Table 15.13). Among the unidentifiable remains of birds are six pieces of eggshell. The bones are light gray and white.

Amphibians—*Amphibia*
Some bones of the postcranial skeleton, probably of the species and genera of *Anura*, were found. The bones are light gray and white.

Fish—*Pisces*
Only two fish bones are definable to species: one from Stratum 1 and one from Stratum 2. Both belong to the gold or silver carp—*Carassius carassius*. Carp are raised commercially in the manmade lakes adjacent to the excavated site. The bones are light gray.

Mollusks—*Mollusca*
All the finds are fragments of the shells of bivalves *Bivalvia*. From the edge of Horizon 7 is an entire fossil seashell.

Human—*Homo sapiens L.*
Human remains were represented by teeth, a lower jaw fragment, and isolated bones of the postcranial skeleton. The bones are light gray.

Taphonomy of the Bone Complex
The color of bones and their degree of fragmentation show that all the bones can be divided into two parts. The first part consists of bones of domestic animals, elk, roe deer, wolves, humans, and "*mammalia* indet." All are gray in color, and all are highly fragmented. The second part consists of the bones of other mammals, birds, amphibians, and fish. All have a light gray or white color, and most are whole or broken just in small parts.

The second part includes species that live in burrows: fox, polecat, pika, marmot, ground squirrel, hamster, Northern mole vole, and jerboa. Visible burrow features of various sizes and dimensions crossed the excavated area both vertically and horizontally; these noncultural burrows were in fact more visible and numerous than cultural features in the site. Probably these bones are the remains of animals that died in burrows or that were the prey of burrow dwellers. A few bones of hare, water vole, birds, amphibians, and fish are likely to represent the remains of meals eaten by the fox and steppe polecat.

The first set of bones formed as a result of human activity. They consisted principally of domestic animals, including dogs, cattle, sheep, goats, pigs, and horses. These animals were accompanied by occasional scattered finds of wild animals, including elk, roe deer, and wolves, and by a few human bones. The kurgan cemetery of Krasnosamarskoe IV, less than 100 m distant from the excavated settlement, was used for human burials before and during the period the settlement was occupied, and it is likely that the human bones that appeared within the settlement were connected in some way to the funeral activities that took place at the cemetery. Below we will analyze the first set, the bones deposited by ancient human activity. But first we must describe the bones from the excavations of 2001.

Material from the Excavations of 2001
The area excavated in 2001 was located to the north of the area excavated in 1999 but was only about one-third the size of the 1999 excavation. In 2001, 52 m² of soil were excavated to a depth of about 1 m. The new squares exhibited extensions of the same cultural layers studied in 1999. Because the 2001 excavation was in the center of an LBA structure, many pit features were also excavated, and one of them, Pit 10, apparently a well, extended an additional 1 m into the subsoil. Cultural pits numbered 1, 4, 9, and 10 contained animal bones. Each pit contained only a few bones, so the bones of all the pits have been combined into one sample, labeled "pits."

Cattle—*Bos taurus L.*
In the area excavated in 2001, cattle represented the largest number of identified bones and bone fragments (845), more than dogs (807) (Table 15.16). The bones include all elements of the skeleton (Table 15.17). The bones are highly fragmented. The most frequent body parts deposited were derived from the head and distal extremities (Table 15.3). Not counting isolated teeth, bones from cattle head parts amounted to 28 to 33 percent of all cattle bones deposited in different horizontal parts of the site. The percentage of

bones derived from the trunk, proximal limbs, and isolated teeth are about the same, 13 to 16 percent, and the small bones amounted to only 6 percent. Distal limb bones, however, composed 25 to 28 percent of the bones deposited. The most frequent body parts deposited were heads and distal limbs, both of which are relatively meatless parts of the body.

One piece of cow horn was found in Stratum 3 in 2001. Large fragments of the skulls of adult cattle were not found, but whole skull bones of individuals aged under 6 months were recovered. On these bones were no traces of the formation of horns. This suggests that the majority of the herd was polled, or bred for the hornless phenotype.

The age structure defined by the upper (Table 15.4) and lower (Table 15.5) teeth differs. This is probably due to small sample sizes. Nevertheless, the general observation can be made that there is a high proportion of juveniles under the age of 1.5 years. They make up 48 percent of the sample using the upper teeth and 41 percent using the lower teeth. Combining all teeth, the juveniles under 1.5 years are 44 percent of the animals deposited. Individuals slaughtered between the ages of 1.5 and 2.5 years compose 28 percent of the sample using the upper teeth and 18 percent using the lower teeth. The average frequency for this age range is 23 percent. Individuals older than 2.5 years are a little more numerous. Using the upper teeth, they are 24 percent; using the lower teeth, 41 percent. The average frequency of older animals is 32 percent of those deposited. Also, five bones from fetuses were recovered and three bones from newborn calves. The outstanding feature of the age structure is the very high frequency of calves under 1.5 years of age, which composed almost half (44 percent) of the cattle.

Small Stock—*Capra et Ovis*

The bones included all elements of the skeleton (Table 15.18). Because of the strong fragmentation, the majority of the bones of sheep and goats (511 bone fragments) cannot be defined to the species level (Table 15.16). Among those identifiable to species (only 55 bones total), the remains of sheep account for 71 percent and the bones of goats 29 percent.

Unlike cattle, all parts of the ovicaprid bodies are nearly equally represented. The head, the proximal limbs, and distal limbs are 22 percent, 24 percent, and 19 percent, respectively (Table 15.3). Bones derived from the trunk and isolated teeth are slightly less: 15 percent for the trunk and only 5 percent for the small bones.

The age structure defined by the upper (Table 15.7) and lower (Table 15.8) teeth differs. Probably this is due to the small sample size. Teeth from individuals aged younger than 3 months were not observed in the sample. On average, according to the definition of upper and lower teeth, at the age of 3 to 12 months, 28 percent of individuals deposited in this sample were killed; at the age of 12 to 24 months, 24 percent of individuals were killed; and over the age of 24 months, 48 percent of individuals. Thus, about half of the killed animals were adults. Also, the 2001 excavation yielded five bones of embryos and one bone, probably from a newborn animal.

Sheep—*Ovis aries L.*

Among the bones identifiable as to species, the remains of sheep (55 bones) dominate those of goats in a consistent and significant manner. Sheep were deposited more than goats by a factor of two to one (Table 15.16). Fragments of the horns are missing, which may indicate a high percentage of hornless animals in the herd.

Goat—*Capra hircus L.*

Identifiable goat bones (23 bones) were half as frequent as those of sheep (Table 15.16). Probably the living herds were composed principally of sheep. Among the remains of goats were four horn pieces. Judging by their size, they all belong to females. Probably most of the goats had horns. Whole bones were absent.

Horse—*Equus caballus L.*

Very little remains of horses were found, only 38 bones (Table 15.16), and among them not all skeletal elements were represented (Table 15.19). Most pieces were isolated teeth. The slaughtered animals included the remains of a young horse (under 2 years), a semi-mature individual (2–5 years), and two adults (5–15 years). Individuals of all age groups are documented, but the small sample size does not allow reliable conclusions about their age structure.

Pig—*Sus scrofa domestica L.*

Remains of the pig amounted to 28 specimens. None were found in Stratum 1, the Iron Age deposit (Table 15.16). Among these are all elements of the skeleton (Table 15.20). According to mandibular and maxillar teeth, one pig was aged 5 to 12 months, nine were aged 12 to 18 months, and two were aged older than 18 months. Young individuals dominated the assemblage.

Dog—*Canis familiaris L.*

A very large number of dog remains (807 fragments, from MNI 21 dogs) were found in 2001 (Table 15.16), including all elements of the skeleton (Table 15.21). The most frequent bones were derived from the skull, vertebrae, ribs, and metapodia. The parts of the body represented by the most bones were the head, trunk, and proximal extremities. Their share is 24 to 26 percent (Table 15.12). Distal lower extremities were fewer: 17 percent. Isolated teeth and the small bones were much less, only 6 percent.

Nearly all the epiphyses of the bones are adnate (fused), and some teeth are heavily worn. This indicates that the bones belonged mostly to adults and older individuals.

The dog remains were very strongly cut, chopped, and fragmented. Whole bones were limited to the phalanges, carpals, tarsals, sesamoid bones, and metapodia. The head was split into three parts by a cut in front of the eyes and another behind the eyes. The trunk was cut into many pieces. The tarsal and carpal bones of the legs were cleaved into several parts.

The size of the dogs has not been studied. On the basis of visual assessment of the size of the bones, it can be said that the dogs were predominantly middle and small sizes. In addition to the bone fragments were three dog coprolites.

Eurasian Elk—*Alces alces L.*
One whole second phalanx with an adnate epiphysis was found, as well as a whole patella of gray color. The latter was chewed by a large carnivore.

Wolf—*Canis lupus L.*
The glenoid cavity of a scapula and a fragment of the radius of an adult wolf were found; they are gray in color.

Fox—*Vulpes vulpes L.*
A whole lower jaw and a radius with fused epiphyses were found. They are a light color.

Steppe Polecat—*Mustela eversmanni L.*
A whole right half of the pelvic bone of an adult was found, of a light color.

Steppe Marmot—*Marmota bobak Muller*
The 2001 excavation produced fragments of a skull, mandible, clavicle, pelvis, elbow, and carpal bones. All bones can be divided into two groups: gray and light gray. This suggests that the bones of the first group were in a layer much older than the bones of the second group.

Russet Ground Squirrel—*Spermophillus major Pallas*
The fauna included five fragments of the skull, 13 jaw fragments, an entire clavicle, scapula, two fragments of the pelvis, scapula, and two cannon bones. They all have a light color.

Jerboa—*Allactaga major Kerr*
We found two shin bones from adults, of a light color.

Northern Mole Vole—*Ellobius talpinus Pallas*
We found two lower jaws of adults, light colored.

Hamster—*Cricetus cricetus L.*
The sample contained an upper and lower jaw, a whole femur, and tibia bones of a light color.

Mammals Unidentifiable—*Mammalia* indet.
This group includes the bones of mammals not determinable to species. They were divided into three groups: large (horse or cattle sized), medium (the size of sheep, goats, dogs, pigs), and large-medium for fragments so small that size cannot be determined (Table 15.16). All the bones are a gray color.

Birds—*Aves* indet.
We found nine fragments of bird bone, but none can be assigned to a specific species (Table 15.16). Two belong to a very large bird, the size of a swan or a crane. The bones are white or light gray.

Amphibians—*Amphibia* indet.
We found two bones of amphibians related to *Anura*. The bones are light gray.

Fish—*Pisces* indet.
We found three fragments of bones belonging to individuals of small size. The bones are light gray.

Mollusks—*Mollusca* indet.
We found two fragments of bivalve mollusk shells.

Taphonomy of the Bone Complex from 2001
All of the bones are assignable to two taphonomic complexes. The first set was formed as a result of human activity and includes the bones of domestic animals, elk, wolf, and "*Mammalia* indet." The second set was formed as a result of natural animal deaths (deaths in the burrows and burrowing predators, food waste) and includes the bones of the fox, polecat, rodents, birds, amphibians, and fish. In what follows, we consider only the first taphonomic complex.

Distribution of Bone Remains in the Cultural Layer, 2001
Analysis of species composition shows that in all the strata and the combined "pits," the remains of domestic animals composed 99 percent of the finds. The remains of

wild animals were very few in all levels and in the pits (Table 15.16). Analysis of the stratigraphic distribution of domestic animals indicates that in Layers 2, 2 to 3, and 3, their ratio can be considered the same (Table 15.22). Cattle ranged from 36 to 39 percent, ovicaprids from 19 to 26 percent, pigs and horses from 1 to 2 percent, and dogs from 35 to 40 percent in the different strata. One peculiarity of the "pits" was an increase in horse bones, which in this context reached 6 percent of the sample.

Fragmentation of the Bones, 2001

The degree of fragmentation of the bones in strata and pits was evaluated by two parameters: the ratio of large, medium, and large or medium bones (Table 15.23) in the indeterminate bones (*Mammalia* indet.) and the proportion of indeterminate bone (*Mammalia* indet.) of all the bones (Table 15.15). In general, the large, medium, and large or medium bones were distributed fairly evenly in the strata and in the pits (Table 15.23). The bones of medium-sized animals were slightly less than the bones from animals of large size, and least of all were the small fragments. However, the data indicate that, within the category of highly fragmented bone (indeterminate), there was a smaller proportion of very small fragments in the cultural pits (1 percent) in comparison with Strata 2 and 3 (7–12 percent). Analysis of the degree of fragmentation of the bones shows the fragmentation of the bones in Layers 2 and 3 can be considered the same.

Bones too fragmented to be identified as to species (indeterminate) varied from 39 to 47 percent of the total analyzed bone sample in Strata 2 and 3 (Table 15.15), but in the pits, these very small fragments of mammal bone were only 13 percent of the total sample. The degree of fragmentation in the pits on both measures is less than in the occupation strata. According to the degree of bone fragmentation, Stratum 1 was again the most fragmented (Tables 15.15 and 15.23). In this top stratum, we found a large proportion of very small fragments (40 percent) and relatively small proportion of identified bone (28 percent). It is in our opinion these anomalous numbers were due to the small amount of material from this layer (Table 15.16).

The analysis of bone fragmentation in strata and pits allows the following conclusions. The bone assemblage of Strata 2, 2 to 3, and 3 forms a single complex, created and affected by similar processes. The bone assemblage from Stratum 1 differs, but these differences we believe are random and are associated with a very small sample size. The bone assemblage from the pits is markedly different. The bones in the pits are less fragmented and include more horses. This suggests that the process of formation was different from the processes of formation of the occupation strata.

Comparison of Bone Assemblages from the Excavations of 1999 and 2001

The bone assemblages from 1999 and 2001 were compared to determine their degree of homogeneity. Uniformity was evaluated on the following parameters: species composition, the ratio of domestic animals, the ratio of parts of the skeleton in different species of animals, the age composition of cattle and ovicaprids, and the proportion of fragmented bones ("*Mammalia* indet.").

Comparison of species composition from 1999 and 2001 shows that they differ only in minor species. Both complexes were dominated by the bones of the same domestic animals and "*Mammalia* indet." The bones of wild animals were less than 1 percent. Thus, the species composition and structure of the bone assemblages from the two seasons of excavation are almost identical.

Comparison of the frequency of domestic animals in the two parts of the site excavated in 1999 and 2001 shows that the proportion of cattle does not vary by more than 6 percent, the proportion of ovicaprids differs by no more than 4 percent, the proportion of pigs differs by no more than 2 percent, the proportion of horses differs by no more than 1 percent, and the proportion of dogs differs by no more than 2 percent (Table 15.14). It is obvious that the proportion of domestic animals recovered in 1999 and 2001 hardly differs.

The parts of the skeleton in the assemblages of 1999 and 2001 differ by no more than 5 percent for cattle (Table 15.3). Parts of the skeleton of ovicaprids differ by no more than 6 percent (Table 15.3). Parts of the skeleton for dogs differ by no more than 3 percent (Table 15.12). As can be seen from the above data, the parts of the skeleton found in different years are very similar.

In contrast, the age composition of cattle from maxillary teeth was different in 1999 and 2001. Age class proportions differ by more than twofold (Table 15.4). Also, a different age distribution for cattle is confirmed, but to a lesser degree, by the mandibular teeth (Table 15.5). It is possible that the cattle slaughtered in the southern (1999) and northern (2001) parts of the settlement were selected from different age groups. The age composition of sheep and goats determined by maxillary and mandibular teeth also is slightly different in the complexes of different years (Table 15.7). The largest differences are observed in the age class "more than 24 months" (Tables 15.7 and 15.8). The age structure of the dogs in 1999 and 2001 is not significantly different.

The proportion of bone fragments assigned to "*Mammalia* indet." in different years is similar (Table 15.15). Fragmentation is less in the deeper strata and increased near the surface. The percentage of all analyzed bones attributed to "*Mammalia* indet." is 81 percent in Stratum 1, the Iron Age stratum, and declines significantly to 69 percent in Stratum 2 and 64 percent in Stratum 3. The degree of fragmentation of the bones in Strata 2 and 3 can be considered equal. The decrease in the degree of fragmentation with depth probably reflects a greater mechanical effect on the bone in the upper layer.

Analysis of the stratigraphic distribution of all domestic animals (Table 15.14) shows that Strata 2, 2 to 3, and 3 can be considered almost equal. Cattle range from 33 to 39 percent, ovicaprids range from 19 to 29 percent, pigs and horses are 1 to 3 percent, and dogs range from 34 to 40 percent.

Comparison of bone complexes from the excavations of 1999 and 2001 showed that all indicators, except for the age composition of cattle and ovicaprids, differ only slightly. In our opinion, this indicates that they are samples from the same complex.

Summary of Species, 1999 and 2001 Combined

In the two excavation seasons combined, archaeologists recovered 7,958 remains of domesticated animals identified to species, representing an MNI of 368 individuals.

Cattle—*Bos taurus L.*

The remains of cattle constitute 35 percent of all bone and tooth remains of domestic animals (Table 15.24). Counting by MNI, cattle are more dominant, composing 38 percent of all domestic animals (Table 15.38). Cattle bones are the most numerous among the remains of domestic ungulates, constituting 54 percent (not counting dogs) of their remains (Table 15.24). The most frequently deposited body parts of cattle are the head—42 percent of all cattle remains—and the distal extremities—29 percent (Table 15.25). The bones of the trunk and proximal leg compose respectively 13 percent and 16 percent of the recovered cattle bones (Table 15.25). The remains of cattle are dominated by meatless parts of the body (head, the distal part of legs), amounting to 71 percent of all remains. Meaty parts of the body account for only 29 percent of all remains.

The age structure for butchered cattle is seen in the combined evidence from the upper and lower teeth (Table 15.26). The greatest number of specimens (32 percent) were from cattle slaughtered between the ages of 6 and 18 months and, in contrast, from animals older than 30 months (36 percent). Individuals under 6 months were 18 percent, and those between 18 and 30 months were only 14 percent. Thus, two-thirds of the cattle slaughtered at Krasnosamarskoe were juveniles under the age of 2.5 years, among

which animals 1.5 years old and younger were half of those slaughtered. This age structure might indicate that cattle were used mainly for meat and less for milk, or it might indicate a ritual purpose for the cattle.

The dimensions of cattle bones are shown in Table 15.27. There are two whole metapodia: a metacarpal and a metatarsal. The metacarpal has a length of 180.5 mm, the width of the shaft is 33.6 mm, and the width of the top end is 58.0 mm. The index of the width of its shaft is 18.6 percent. The metatarsal has a length of 215.5 mm, the width of the proximal end is 46.0 mm, the width of the diaphysis is 1.25 mm, and the width is 54.2 mm for the distal end. The index of the width of its shaft is 11.7 percent. The size and proportions of these two bones indicate that they came from cows (Tsalkin 1960). The length of the talus can indicate the approximate height at the withers of cattle (Tsalkin 1970). Withers height range from 108 to 138 cm, with an average of 119 cm (Table 15.27).

Small Stock—*Ovis aries L. et Capra hircus L.*

The remains of sheep and goats make up 25 percent of the remains of domestic animals including the dog bones and 39 percent of the domestic animals excluding the dog bones (Table 15.24). By MNI, the proportion of sheepgoat is less, about 25 percent of the domestic animals (Table 15.38). Among the bones identifiable to species, sheep bones accounted for 71 percent and goat bones 29 percent. It should be noted that this general ratio, about two sheep to one goat, was repeated in the different parts of the site studied in 1999 and 2001. Among all ovicaprid remains, the most frequently deposited body parts (Table 15.28) were the head, 35 percent of all ovicaprid remains, and the bones of the proximal and distal limbs, 25 percent each of the remains. The bones of the trunk amounted to only 15 percent. The ovicaprid remains were dominated by the meatless parts of the carcass (the head, the distal part of legs), amounting to 60 percent of all remains. This bias toward the head and distal limb bones is not so great among ovicaprids as among cattle (71 percent) (Table 15.25), but nevertheless it is a notable feature of the ovicaprid remains.

The age structure is seen in the combined sample of the upper and lower teeth from the excavations of 1999 and 2001 (Table 15.29). The most numerous age category was adults aged over 24 months, which amounted to 53 percent of the remains. Young and semi-mature specimens between 3 and 24 months composed 47 percent. Very young individuals younger than 3 months are missing. This age structure may indicate that small ruminants were used for meat and wool. Goats could have been used to produce milk.

Sheep—*Ovis aries L.*

Bones that are suitable for measurements are few (Table 15.30). Based on the length of the talus, one can determine the approximate height at the withers of small ruminants (Teichert 1975). Withers height ranges from 65 to 81 cm, averaging 73 cm.

Goat—*Capra hircus L.*

Bones that are suitable for measurements are very few (Table 15.31). The dimensions are small, indicating that the goats were smaller than the sheep.

Horse—*Equus caballus L.*

Very few remains of the horse were found in the excavated area (Table 15.24). They constitute 1.5 percent of the remains of domesticated animals and 3 percent of domestic ungulates (Table 15.24). Not all the elements of the skeleton are represented (Tables 15.9 and 15.19). The teeth indicate that the dead animals included all age classes. These included four specimens from horses under 2 years old, four from semi-mature horses (2–5 years), three from adults (5–15 years), and four from old horses (15 years or more). The small sample size does not permit any firm conclusions on the age structure of the horses whose remains appeared in the settlement.

Pig—*Sus scrofa domestica L.*

Pigs were present, but very few appeared in the excavated bone sample (Table 15.24). All elements of the skeleton are represented (Tables 15.10 and 15.20). The ages of the slaughtered animals were defined by the presence of m1 and no m2 (one specimen, 5–12 months) and the presence of m2 but no m3 (two specimens, 12–18 months).

Dog—*Canis familiaris L.*

Dog remains composed a very large proportion of the identified bones and teeth, accounting for more than 36 percent of domesticated specimens (Table 15.24). However, if the MNI is counted, dogs composed a much smaller proportion, only 18 percent of all domesticated animals. While this is still a uniquely large proportion of dogs for this period, it shows that the dog remains were selected for intense chopping and splitting, to a greater extent than any other species, that increased the absolute quantity of dog fragments in relation to other species. The outstanding feature of the dog remains, besides their sheer quantity, is their very strong fragmentation. Whole bones include only phalanges, carpals, tarsals, sesamoids, and metapodia. The head was split into at least three parts: the nose was chopped off in front of the eyes and the skull behind the eyes. The trunk was cut into many pieces. The tubular bones of the legs were cleaved into several parts.

The dog materials include all elements of the skeleton (Tables 15.11 and 15.21). Fragments of the skull account for 29 percent, trunk bones are 25 percent, the proximal limbs compose 24 percent, and the distal limbs are 22 percent (Table 15.12). Nearly all the epiphyses of the bones are adnate (fused), and some teeth are heavily worn. This indicates that the bones belonged mostly to adults and older individuals.

The size of the dogs has not been studied. On the basis of visual assessment of the size of the bones, it can be said that the dogs were medium and medium to small sized. Five dog coprolites also were found.

Wild Animals

The wild animals that are most likely to be ancient and related to human activities include only a few species: elk, roe deer, wolves, and perhaps some bones of hares and birds. They compose a very small proportion of the site fauna—less than 1 percent (Table 15.24). It is obvious that the hunt had very little importance in the economy of the LBA population.

Season of Habitation

Among the remains of cattle and ovicaprids were the bones of fetuses and newborns, as well as the bones of cattle under the age of 6 months. Most varieties of cattle and ovicaprids are born in the late spring. Therefore, the presence of fetuses, newborns, and calves under 6 months indicates their deaths in the period from spring through the summer and into the early winter. At least in these seasons, the Krasnosamarskoe settlement was inhabited by people. It is possible that they lived there the rest of the year, but other chapters address this question.

Comparison with the Fauna of Other LBA Sites in the Volga Region of Samara Oblast

In the same region as Krasnosamarskoe, archaeologists have investigated several other settlements of the Late Bronze Age. In the 1950s, two large LBA settlements were studied: Moechnoe Ozero I and Suskanskoe I. The latter site became the regional type site for a chronological phase termed the Final Bronze Age, occupied probably centuries later than the early LBA occupation at Krasnosamarskoe. The archaeozoological collections from these and other settlements were studied by V. I. Tsalkin (1958). Later, Tsalkin summarized the faunal materials from 26 LBA settlements in the middle Volga region (Tsalkin 1972a, 1972b, 1972c). In the 1990s, the LBA settlements at Lebyazhinka V, Sachkovo, and Poplavskoe were investigated archaeologically. Their archaeozoological collections were investigated by the author (Kosintsev 2003). The number of animal bones catalogued from Poplavskoe is quite small, but it is included because this Srubnaya settlement was located near Krasnosamarskoe. Below I compare the characteristics of the archaeozoological assemblages of these settlements with the settlement of the Krasnosamarskoe.

Cattle—*Bos taurus*

The body parts of cattle at Krasnosamarskoe match most closely the parts of cattle recovered at the LBA settlement of Sachkovo (Table 15.25). Both settlements contain numerous bones derived from the head, constituting 42 percent and 43 percent of the body parts for cattle at each site. This high frequency of head parts differs markedly from the body part distributions of cattle in other LBA settlements (Table 15.25). However, Krasnosamarskoe has significantly fewer bones of the proximal limbs, the meatiest bones on the body, than Sachkovo or any other LBA settlement.

The age composition of the cattle from Krasnosamarskoe also is closest to the age structure of the cattle from Sachkovo (Table 15.26). In both populations are very high proportions of bones of young animals. In Krasnosamarskoe, individuals under the age of 18 months were 50 percent; for the settlement at Sachkovo, 49 percent. At other LBA settlements, cattle in this young category composed 15 to 27 percent of those slaughtered. Adult cattle at Krasnosamarskoe are 36 percent of the sample, while at Sachkovo they are 32 percent, and at other LBA settlements, adult cattle range from 52 to 58 percent.

Sample sizes are small for most cattle bones at the Krasnosamarskoe settlement (Table 15.27) and did not allow a statistical comparison of sizes with bone samples from other settlements (Table 15.32). Statistically, you can compare the length of the m3, the lateral length of the talus, and the sagittal length of phalanx I. Comparison by *t* test showed significant differences in the length of the m3 and the lateral length of the talus between the settlements of Krasnosamarskoe, Lebyazhinka V, Sachkovo, and Tsalkin's LBA of the Samara Volga region. The sagittal length of the phalanges from Krasnosamarskoe are not different from Sachkovo but are significantly different from Lebyazhinka V (at 1 percent significance level, p = 0.99). Dimensions of the other bones from Krasnosamarskoe are within the range of variability for other settlements of the middle Volga region (Table 15.32). The withers height of the cattle from Krasnosamarskoe is 119 cm (Table 15.27), which is not different from the withers height of cattle at the other settlements in the Samara Volga region (Table 15.32).

Small Stock—*Ovis aries L. et Capra hircus L.*

The body parts of the Krasnosamarskoe ovicaprids show the closest similarity to the body parts of ovicaprids at Sachkovo (Table 15.28). In both populations, in contrast to other sites, there were relatively few proximal limbs, the meaty parts, which were 25 percent and 31 percent, respectively. At other LBA settlements, these body parts are 44 to 45 percent of ovicaprid skeletal samples. The proportions of bones from the head and trunk at Krasnosamarskoe also are closest to Sachkovo. However, the proportion of distal limb bones in the ovicaprid bones from Krasnosamarskoe (25 percent) is significantly greater than in all other settlements, where it is no more than 15 percent.

The age composition of the ovicaprids from Krasnosamarskoe is similar to other middle Volga LBA sites (Table 15.29). In all sites, adult ovicaprids account for about 50 percent. The most similar age composition to Krasnosamarskoe is again Sachkovo, where remains of animals younger than 3 months were found.

Sample sizes of most bones of sheep and goats from the settlement Krasnosamarskoe are small (Tables 15.30 and 15.31) and did not allow a statistical comparison with samples from other settlements. Statistically, you can only compare the length of the lateral talus (Tables 15.33 and 15.34). Comparison by *t* test showed no significant differences in the length of the lateral talus between the samples of sheep from Krasnosamarskoe, Lebyazhinka V, Sachkovo, and Tsalkin's 26 LBA sites. The dimensions of the other sheep bones from Krasnosamarskoe (Table 15.30) are comparable to Tsalkin's LBA sites (Table 15.33). The average withers height of the Krasnosamarskoe sheep is 73 cm (Table 15.30), which is not different from the withers height of sheep from other settlements in the Volga region of the Samara oblast (Table 15.33). For goats, comparison by *t* test showed no significant differences in the length of the lateral talus between the goats of Krasnosamarskoe (Table 15.31), Lebyazhinka V, and Sachkovo (Table 15.34).

Other species from Krasnosamarskoe, such as horses (*Equus caballus*) and pigs (*Sus scrofa domestica*), did not include enough bones for size analysis (Tables 15.35 and 15.37). One can only note that the sizes of the horse bones from Krasnosamarskoe are in the range of Tsalkin's LBA sites (Table 15.36). Dog (*Canis familiaris*) is not preserved enough for morphological comparisons between the LBA settlements of the middle Volga (Table 15.24).

Comparison of the proportions of animals at Krasnosamarskoe and at other LBA settlements of the Volga region in the Samara oblast shows significant differences between them (Table 15.24). Krasnosamarskoe stands out because it contains, uniquely, a very large number of dog bones, 10 times greater than in other LBA settlements. Even if the dogs are put aside, and only the domesticated ungulates are compared, Krasnosamarskoe is markedly different from other settlements of the LBA in the middle Volga region. Krasnosamarskoe had a higher proportion of bones of sheep and goats and a much smaller proportion of horses. Horses were three to five times lower at Krasnosamarskoe than in other LBA settlements. Pigs varied from 2 to 7 percent. The proportion of wild animals is very small, as in other LB A settlements in the middle Volga region.

The unusual proportions of dogs and domestic ungulates at Krasnosamarskoe cannot be attributed to biases in the excavation and collection procedures of bones. If the high proportion of ovicaprids at Krasnosamarskoe were attributed to the excavation or collection procedures (e.g., to the use of screens in the excavation at Krasnosamarskoe), then it would be quite unlikely that the proportion of horses would be less than in other LBA settlements by at least three times, and the proportion of cattle bones would be less than other LBA settlements by almost two times. Cattle remains at Krasnosamarskoe constitute 30 to 35 percent of the bones, a low proportion not documented in any other LBA settlement of the middle Volga, Don, or Ural regions (Kosintsev 2001, 2003; Petrenko 1984). It must be noted that, if the dog bones are put aside, then the proportion of cattle among the remaining domesticated animals at Krasnosamarskoe is over 50 percent, like other LBA settlements (Table 15.24). However, it seems that the high proportion of sheep and goats and the low percentage of horses at Krasnosamarskoe cannot be adjusted in a similar manner, and thus these statistics are related to the specifics of the studied part of the settlement at Krasnosamarskoe.

Conclusion

Analysis of the composition and structure of bones excavated in 1999 and 2001 at the Krasnosamarskoe settlement showed that they constitute a single assemblage and can be considered together. A comparison of the bone assemblage of Krasnosamarskoe and other LBA settlements in the Volga region of the Samara oblast showed significant differences.

The bone complex from Krasnosamarskoe is primarily characterized by a very large number of dog bones, which have a very high degree of fragmentation. The proportion of sheep and goats is also unusually high and that of the horse is low. The remains of cattle are different from most other settlements of this time in that a larger share of the remains are from the bones of the head, and a larger proportion are juveniles, than is usually found. The remains of sheep and goats are different from most other settlements of this time in that a larger share of the bones are distal parts of legs and a smaller share of the bones are of the proximal legs. The bone assemblage structure of Krasnosamarskoe has some similarities to the structure of the Sachkovo settlement but also is noticeably different.

Withers height for the cattle and sheep from Krasnosamarskoe did not differ from cattle and sheep from other LBA settlements in the Volga region of Samara.

Comparative analysis allows the following conclusions:

The cattle and sheep from the Krasnosamarskoe settlement were the same size as the domesticated stock at other LBA settlements. This suggests that in the investigated part of the Krasnosamarskoe settlement, the cattle and sheep were randomly selected from a flock without selection for a specific breed or size.

However, there was a selection of animals by age. Young cattle, particularly those aged under 6 months and 6 to 18 months, were selected for slaughter in greater numbers than in the LBA settlements on the middle Volga compiled by Tsalkin or at Lebyazhinka V, while the LBA settlement at Sachkovo exhibited a similar abundance of young cattle. Perhaps a specific activity or ritual that required the use of young calves was conducted at Sachkovo and Krasnosamarskoe.   The body parts of the cattle and the ovicaprids at Krasnosamarskoe also were selected in a manner that was markedly different from most other settlements, again with some similarities with Sachkovo but also with notable differences in the parts selected. Thus, cattle heads were more frequently deposited at both Sachkovo and Krasnosamarskoe than at other LBA sites, but at Krasnosamarskoe, the cattle heads were combined with unusually frequent distal limb fragments, a selection that emphasized the more meatless parts of the body, while at Sachkovo, the proximal limbs, the meaty parts of the cattle, appeared more frequently. The ovicaprids at Krasnosamarskoe included many more distal limb elements than at any other LBA site, again possibly displaying a selection before the bones were deposited for the more meatless parts of the body. The partition of slaughtered animals in the studied part of the settlement differed from the body parts found in other LBA settlements. Krasnosamarskoe exhibits more heads and distal extremities and fewer proximal limb bones than is normally found in LBA settlements in the region.

It might be noted that the deposit of "head-and-hoof" sacrifices, including just the head and distal limbs of the sacrificed animal, probably attached to the hide, is well known as a funerary ritual conducted in cemeteries in the middle Volga region from the Eneolithic through the Iron Age. Animal sacrifices of this type, in which the animal's hide with head and hooves attached was offered as a symbol of the whole animal, have not been documented previously in settlements. Perhaps ritual activities occurred at Krasnosamarskoe that involved a similar symbolic offering.

The remains of the dogs at Krasnosamarskoe obviously reflect a ritual usage. Unlike the cattle and sheep, the whole body of the dog was deposited, usually old dogs, in great numbers, including at least 51 individuals by MNI. All of the dog remains were subjected to intense chopping and segmenting that produced many more pieces per individual than was produced from cattle or sheep, probably as a part of a dog-specific ritual. Also specific, redundant cuts were used to segment the dogs' heads, probably another part of the ritual. Other features of the bone assemblage related to the cattle and sheep, noted above, may also be associated with ritual and symbolic activities. Thus, the analysis of the animal bones from the excavations of the settlement of Krasnosamarskoe indicates that the excavation uncovered the part of the site where rituals occurred or where the remains of ritual activities were discarded.

Peschanyi Dol 1

The cultural layer at PD1 produced an assemblage of 319 mammal bones (Table 15.38). The degree of fragmentation and the color of the bones divide them into two groups.

The first group includes all traces of rodents (42 bones). They are represented by large fragments of skulls, mandibles, and the entire postcranial skeleton bones. The color of the bones is white or light gray. All belong to the species living in burrows. Obviously, the first group belongs to the animals that died in burrows probably of natural causes. Their bones entered the cultural layer later, after people had abandoned the site.

The second group includes all the remaining bones (277 specimens). All belong to an animal the size of a dog and larger. The vast majority of them (212) are fragments indeterminate to species. Their color is gray or brownish-gray. The bones of this group belong to domesticated animals and roe deer (Table 15.38). The second group had accumulated as a result of human activity. Among them are three carbonized and five calcified bones.

Cattle—*Bos taurus*

Cattle bones were the second most frequent species found, with 25 identifiable specimens. Among the remains of this species are all parts of the skeleton—the head, trunk, and proximal and distal parts of the legs. The most abundant specimens are isolated teeth and fragments thereof. Among them are baby teeth and permanent teeth in varying degrees of wear, some very heavily worn, probably of old animals.

Small Stock—*Ovis aries, Capra hircus*

Sheep-goat bones were the most frequently found species at this site (34 identifiable specimens). Among the remains of this species are all parts of the skeleton—the head, trunk, and proximal and distal parts of the legs. There are a few whole bones, including isolated teeth, carpal bones, and phalanx II. The most abundant specimens are isolated teeth and fragments thereof. Among them are baby teeth and permanent teeth in varying degrees of wear.

Unidentified Mammals—*Mammalia* indet.

This category contained by far the majority of the bone specimens analyzed, with 212 specimens. All are represented by small fragments of bone.

Others

Horse (*Equus caballus*), swine (*Sus scrofa domestica*), dog (*Canis familiaris*), and roe deer (*Capreolus pygargus*) are represented by scattered isolated bones (Table 15.38). The species composition corresponds to the skeletal remains of LBA settlements from the middle Volga Srubnaya culture, although the frequency of sheep-goat is higher at this site than is normal (Kosintsev 2003). No bones were suitable for measurement. Comparative analysis cannot be conducted because of the very small sample size.

Peschanyi Dol 2

The cultural layer produced a very small amount of bones—63 pieces (Table 15.38). According to the degree of fragmentation and color, these are well divided into two groups.

The first group includes all traces of rodents (seven bones). They are represented by large fragments of skulls, mandibles, and the entire postcranial skeleton. The color of the bones is white or light gray. All definable bones belong to species living in burrows. Obviously, the first group belongs to the animals that died in burrows from natural causes. Their bones entered the cultural layer later, after people abandoned the site.

The second group includes all the other bones (55 specimens). All belong to animals the size of dogs and larger. The majority (30) is indeterminate as to species. The color of the bones is gray or brownish-gray. Definable bones of this group belong to domesticated animals only (Table 15.38). The second group accumulated as a result of human activity.

Among the bones are three specimens from cattle (*Bos taurus*), 12 from sheep and goats (*Ovis aries, Capra hircus*), and 10 from horses (*Equus caballus*) (Table 15.38). Unidentified mammal bone is represented by 30 small fragments. No further analysis is possible because of the very small sample size.

Tables

Table 15.1 Species Present in the Fauna Excavated in 1999, NISP/MNI

Species	Strata						Totals
	1	1–2	2	2–3	3	1–3	
Cattle—*Bos taurus*	81/6	17/2	1,110/29	230/14	137/7	241/11	1,816/69
Goat and sheep—*Capra* et *Ovis*	76/3	10/2	686/13	157/5	72/4	145/5	1,415/48
Sheep—*Ovis aries*	11/2	7/2	114/7	23/3	19/3	17/3	191/20
Goat—*Capra hircus*	4/1	1/1	51/5	10/2	3/1	9/2	78/12
Pig—*Sus scrofa domestica*	—	1/1	60/4	11/2	12/2	11/2	95/11
Horse—*Equus caballus*	17/4	—	46/6	6/2	6/1	12/3	87/16
Dog—*Canis familiaris*	98/2	29/1	1,209/12	222/4	168/3	237/4	1,963/26
Eurasian elk—*Alces alces*	2/1	—	8/2	—	2/1	—	12/4
Roe deer—*Capreolus pygargus*	1/1	—	8/2	—	—	2/1	10/4
Wolf—*Canis lupus*	—	—	12/3	2/1	—	2/1	16/5
Dog—*Canis* sp.	2	—	3	—	1	—	6
Fox—*Vulpes vulpes*	1/1	—	—	—	—	—	
Steppe polecat–*Mustela eversmannii*	—	—	4/2	—	2/1	—	
Hare—*Lepus* sp.	—		3	—	2	1	
Pika—*Ochotona pusilla*	—		—	1/1	—	—	
Russet ground squirrel– *Spermophillus major*	10	1	107	33	7	11	
Steppe marmot—*Marmota bobak*	1/1	1/1	5/2	1/1	—	—	
Jerboa—*Allactaga major*	—	—	4/2	3/1	1/1	—	
Hamster—*Cricetus cricetus*	3/2	1/1	54/9	11/4	—	9/3	
Northern mole vole—*Ellobius talpinus*	1/1	1/1	8/4	—	—	—	
Water vole—*Arvicola terrestris*	2/1	—	4/2	—	—	—	
Human—*Homo sapiens*	—	3	6	—	2	—	
Vole—*Microtinae* gen.	10	—	24	11	—	3	
Unident. mammal—*Mammalia* indet.	1,197	347	7,193	1,051	744	350	
Bird—*Aves*	5	1	22	7	2	4	
Amphibian—*Amphibia*	—	—	6	4	1	1	
Fish—*Pisces*	2	—	2	—	1	1	
Shellfish—*Mollusca*	1	—	6	—	2	—	

Table 15.2 Skeletal Elements of Cattle (*Bos taurus*) in 1999

Bones	Strata					
	1	*1–2*	*2*	*2–3*	*3*	*1–3*
Horn	—	—	—	—	—	—
Skull—brain	3	—	87	17	17	24
Skull—face	3	—	73	18	5	7
Mandible	8	—	97	17	9	32
Teeth	29	8	199	45	27	34
Vertebrae	3	1	54	8	4	7
Rib	1	—	108	19	14	24
Scapula	—	—	24	4	5	—
Pelvis	1	—	23	3	—	6
Humerus	1	—	20	7	—	9
Radius	—	—	34	5	3	9
Ulna	1	—	26	4	2	7
Femur	—	—	19	3	—	5
Tibia	2	1	45	4	2	9
Calcaneus	3	—	9	2	1	1
Talus	1	—	14	2	6	4
Carpi, tarsi, sesamoidea	3	2	36	13	5	12
Metacarpalia III + IV	1	1	34	9	6	20
Metatarsalia III + IV	8	2	86	10	9	16
Metapodia	2	1	19	9	5	3
Phalanx I	7	1	61	17	8	6
Phalanx II	3	—	27	6	4	5
Phalanx III	1	—	15	8	5	1

Table 15.3 Body Parts (Percent) of Cattle (*Bos taurus*) and Ovicaprid (*Ovis aries, Capra hircus*) in 1999 and 2001 (with Isolated Teeth/without)

Skeletal Unit	Cattle		Ovicaprid	
	1999	*2001*	*1999*	*2001*
Head—skull and mandible	23/28[a]	27/33	18/21	22/25
Isolated teeth	19/—	17/—	14/—	15/—
Trunk—vertebrae, ribs	13/16	13/16	20/24	15/18
Proximal limb (scapula, pelvis, humerus, femur, radius, ulna)	16/19	15/18	23/27	24/28
Carpalia, tarsalia, sesamoidea	6/8	6/7	4/4	5/7
Distal limb (metapodia, phalanges 1–3)	23/28	21/25	20/23	19/22
NISP	1,816/1,474	845/703	1,415/1,210	511/436

[a]First number—ratio including isolated teeth. Second number—ratio not counting isolated teeth.

Table 15.4 Age Structure of Cattle (*Bos taurus*) from Maxilla in 1999 and 2001

Age (Months)	1999		2001		1999–2001	
	Count	Percent	Count	Percent	Count	Percent
< 6	12	36	7	17	19	25
6–18	5	16	13	31	18	24
18–30	4	12	12	28	16	21
>30	12	36	10	24	22	30
Total	33	100	42	100	75	100

Table 15.5 Age Structure of Cattle (*Bos taurus*) from Mandible in 1999 and 2001

Age (Months)	1999		2001		1999–2001	
	Count	Percent	Count	Percent	Count	Percent
<6	6	13	3	8	9	11
6–18	21	46	13	33	34	40
18–30	0	0	7	18	7	8
>30	19	41	16	41	35	41
Total	46	100	39	100	85	100

Table 15.6 Skeletal Elements Ovicaprid (*Ovis aries, Capra hircus*) in 1999

Bones	Strata					
	1	1/2	2	2/3	3	1/3
Horn	—	—	8	1	2	2
Skull—brain	4	—	42	15	4	8
Skull—face	1	—	54	7	7	11
Mandible	5	1	55	11	4	13
Teeth	24	3	129	19	16	14
Vertebrae	6	—	44	7	4	10
Rib	8	1	128	37	13	30
Scapula	—	2	6	1	—	4
Pelvis	2	1	9	1	1	4
Humerus	5	—	34	11	6	5
Radius	2	—	57	16	2	14
Ulna	1	—	23	4	4	5
Femur	4	—	19	7	3	2
Tibia	6	2	41	10	2	11
Calcaneus	—	—	3	2	—	—
Talus	2	—	15	4	1	2
Carpi, tarsi, sesamoidea	1	—	20	3	—	3
Metacarpalia III + IV	5	4	42	3	2	11
Metatarsalia III + IV	9	2	66	19	11	10
Metapodia	—	—	12	4	2	1
Phalanx I	2	1	28	5	7	10
Phalanx II	2	1	8	3	1	—
Phalanx III	2	—	8	—	2	1

Table 15.7 Age Structure of Ovicaprid (*Ovis aries, Capra hircus*) Maxilla in 1999 and 2001

Age (Months)	1999		2001		1999–2001	
	Count	Percent	Count	Percent	Count	Percent
<3	0	0	0	0	0	0
3–12	5	18	5	23	10	20
12–24	3	11	4	18	7	14
>24	20	71	13	59	33	66
Total	28	100	22	100	50	100

Table 15.8 Age Structure of Ovicaprid (*Ovis aries, Capra hircus*) Mandible in 1999 and 2001

Age (Months)	1999		2001		1999–2001	
	Count	Percent	Count	Percent	Count	Percent
<3	0	0	0	0	0	0
3–12	10	30	12	34	22	32
12–24	7	20	10	29	17	25
>24	17	50	13	37	30	43
Total	34	100	35	100	69	100

Table 15.9 Skeletal Elements Horse (*Equus caballus*) in 1999

Bones	Strata				
	1	2	2–3	3	1–3
Skull—brain	—	2	—	—	—
Skull—face	1	3	1	—	—
Mandible	—	4	1	1	—
Teeth	7	11	2	1	4
Vertebrae	2	2	—	—	—
Rib	—	8	—	1	2
Scapula	1	—	—	—	—
Pelvis	—	2	—	1	—
Humerus	—	—	1		—
Radius	1	1	—	—	—
Femur	—	1	—	1	—
Calcaneus	—	—	—	—	1
Talus	2	—	—	—	2
Carpi, tarsi, sesamoidea	1	3	—	—	—
Metatarsalia III	1	4	1	—	1
Metapodia	—	—	—	—	1
Phalanx I	—	4	—	—	1
Phalanx II	1	1	—	1	—

Table 15.10 Skeletal Elements Pig (*Sus scrofa domestica*) in 1999

Bones	Strata				
	1–2	2	2–3	3	1–3
Skull—brain	1	5	—	—	—
Skull—face	—	5	1	2	—
Mandible	—	5	—	1	—
Teeth	—	6	—	3	3
Vertebrae	—	—	—	—	3
Rib	—	7	1	—	1
Scapula	—	1	1	—	—
Pelvis	—	1	—	—	—
Humerus	—	3	1	—	—
Radius	—	3	—	—	2
Ulna	—	1	—	—	1
Femur	—	6	—	—	1
Tibia	—	2	2	—	—
Talus	—	2	—	1	—
Carpi, tarsi, sesamoidea	—	2	—	—	—
Metacarpalia	—	2	—	—	—
Metatarsalia	—	1	—	—	—
Metapodia	—	3	2	1	—
Phalanx I	—	3	3	3	—
Phalanx II	—	2	—	1	—

Table 15.11 Skeletal Elements Dog (*Canis familiaris*) in 1999

Bones	Strata					
	1	1–2	2	2–3	3	1–3
Skull—brain	8	3	107	20	12	18
Skull—face	5	3	99	14	15	17
Mandible	1	1	91	13	11	22
Teeth	13	3	67	10	13	5
Vertebrae	12	5	165	35	26	30
Rib	3	4	115	24	25	37
Scapula	—	—	1	—	—	1
Pelvis	—	—	11	3	—	4
Humerus	—	—	13	—	2	4
Radius	2	2	21	13	—	10
Ulna	4	1	42	10	4	11
Femur	1	—	41	9	4	2
Tibia	3	—	48	8	9	15
Calcaneus	1	2	54	11	10	17
Talus	1	1	41	3	7	7
Carpi, tarsi, sesamoidea	2	—	13	2	3	1
Metacarpalia	—	—	8	1	3	2
Metatarsalia	8	1	49	7	9	7
Metapodia	14	3	117	18	5	21
Phalanx I	6	—	69	16	6	4
Phalanx II	10	—	26	4	1	2
Phalanx III	4	—	11	1	3	—

Table 15.12 Body Parts (Percent) of Dog (*Canis familiaris*) in 1999 and 2001 (with Isolated Teeth/without)

Skeletal unit	1999	2001
Head—skull and mandible	23/25[a]	25/26
Isolated teeth	6/—	4/—
Trunk—vertebrae, ribs	25/26	24/25
Proximal limb (scapula, pelvis, humerus, femur, radius, ulna)	23/24	26/27
Carpalia, tarsalia, sesamoidea	6/6	4/4
Distal limb (metapodia, phalanges 1–3)	17/18	17/18
NISP	1,963/1,852	807/776

[a]First number—ratio including isolated teeth. Second number—ratio not counting isolated teeth.

Table 15.13 Bird (*Aves*) Species in 1999

Types of Bird	Strata					
	1	1–2	2	2–3	3	1–3
Mute swan—*Cygnus olor*	1	—	—	—	—	—
White-fronted goose—*Anas albifrons*	—	—	—	—	—	1
Corn crake—*Crex crex*	—	—	1	—	—	—
Hooked crow—*Corvus cornix*	—	—	5	—	—	—
Swan/goose–*Cygnus ex gr. olor—cygnus*	—	—	—	—	—	1
Goose—*Anser* sp.	—	—	2	—	—	—
Duck—*Anas* sp.	—	—	2	—	1	—
Sandpiper—*Charadrii* sp.	—	—	1	—	—	—
Passerine—*Passeriformes* gen.	—	—	—	—	—	1
Unidentified bird	4	1	11	7	1	1

Table 15.14 Percent of All Domesticated Animals for Each Domestic Species in 1999 and 2001

Species	Strata					
	2		2–3		3	
	1999	2001	1999	2001	1999	2001
Cattle—*Bos taurus*	34	37	35	37	33	39
Goat/sheep—*Capra et Ovis*	26	26	29	26	23	19
Pig—*Sus scrofa domestica*	2	1	2	1	3	1
Horse—*Equus caballus*	1	1	1	1	1	1
Dog—*Canis familiaris*	37	35	34	35	40	40
NISP	3,276	764	669	472	417	653

Table 15.15 Percent of Indeterminate Mammal (Mammalia indet.) Bones in 1999 and 2001

Year	Strata					
	1	1–2	2	2–3	3	1–3+ Pits[a]
1999, percent	81	84	69	61	64	13
NISP	1,197	347	7,193	1,051	744	319
2001, percent	72	—	61	55	57	53
NISP	133	—	1,184	539	877	319
						T3052

[a]1–3 = unstratified material from 1999 + "pits" = features excavated in 2001.

Table 15.16 Species Present in the Fauna Excavated in 2001, NISP/MNI

Species	Strata						
	1	1–2	2	2–3	3	Pits	Totals
Cattle—*Bos taurus*	23/3	4/1	271/14	190/10	257/12	100/7	845/47
Goat and sheep—*Capra* et *Ovis*	15/4	4/2	181/9	95/6	94/5	44/3	511/50
Sheep—*Ovis aries*	2/1	—	16/6	14/6	16/7	7/4	55/24
Goat—*Capra hircus*	—	—	4/2	7/3	8/4	4/2	25/11
Pig—*Sus scrofa domestica*	—	—	5/1	5/1	14/2	4/1	28/5
Horse—*Equus caballus*	—	—	10/2	7/2	5/1	16/2	38/7
Dog—*Canis familiaris*	11/2	3/1	277/7	154/5	259/6	103/4	807/25
Eurasian elk—*Alces alces*	—	—	1/1	—	1/1	—	
Wolf—*Canis lupus*	—	—	1/1	—	1/1	—	
Fox—*Vulpes vulpes*	—	—	1/1	—	1/1	—	
Steppe polecat—*Mustela eversmanni*	—	—	—	1/1	—	—	
Steppe marmot—*Marmota bobak*	—	—	7/2	—	2/1	—	
Russet ground squirrel	—	—	11/4	4/2	10/3	—	
Jerboa—*Allactaga major*	—	—	1/1	—	1/1	—	
Northern mole vole—*Ellobius talpinus*	—	—	2/1	—	—	—	
Hamster—*Cricetus cricetus*	—	—	1/1	3/2	—	—	
Indeterminate large mammal	37	8	454	165	334	148	
Indeterminate average mammal	42	12	589	310	481	168	
Indeterminate average to large mammal	54	11	141	64	62	3	
Total *Mammalia* indet.	133	31	1,184	539	877	319	
Bird—*Aves* indet.	—	—	2	—	4	3	
Amphibian—*Amphibia* indet.	—	—	—	—	2	—	
Fish—*Pisces* indet.	—	—	—	—	3	—	
Shellfish—*Mollusca* indet.	—	—	—	—	—	2	

Table 15.17 Skeletal Elements of Cattle (*Bos taurus*) in 2001

Bones	Strata					
	1	1–2	2	2–3	3	Pits
Horn	—	—	—	—	1	—
Skull—brain	—	1	28	20	21	9
Skull—face	2	—	13	24	24	10
Mandible	3	1	25	17	24	9
Teeth	9	2	51	26	38	16
Vertebrae	1	—	10	8	13	5
Rib	2	—	22	19	18	16
Scapula	—	—	7	3	8	1
Pelvis	—	—	6	5	7	—
Humerus	—	—	2	2	5	—
Radius	—	—	5	10	9	2
Ulna	—	—	11	1	1	1
Femur	—	—	5	—	6	1
Tibia	1	—	9	5	9	2
Calcaneus	—	—	1	3	1	1
Talus	—	—	4	1	2	4
Carpi, tarsi, sesamoidea	2	—	12	4	15	4
Metacarpalia III + IV	1	—	14	11	12	3
Metatarsalia III + IV	2	—	19	14	19	6
Metapodia	—	—	2	3	4	2
Phalanx I	—	—	13	6	11	5
Phalanx II	—	—	9	6	6	1
Phalanx III	—	—	3	1	3	2

Table 15.18 Skeletal Element of Ovicaprids (*Ovis aries, Capra hircus*) in 2001

Bones	Strata					
	1	*1–2*	*2*	*2–3*	*3*	*Pits*
Horn	—	—	—	5	—	—
Skull—brain	—	1	8	11	3	1
Skull—face	—	—	11	4	6	3
Mandible	2	—	25	13	10	7
Teeth	4	—	29	20	17	5
Vertebrae	—	—	4	4	4	2
Rib	—	—	20	11	23	12
Scapula	—	—	3	—	5	1
Pelvis	2	—	3	3	2	—
Humerus	1	—	7	4	5	5
Radius	1	—	14	6	5	1
Ulna	—	—	6	2	2	—
Femur	—	—	8	1	4	3
Tibia	2	1	9	5	5	4
Calcaneus	—	—	—	—	—	—
Talus	—	—	4	2	9	5
Carpi, tarsi, sesamoidea	1	—	5	1	2	—
Metacarpalia III + IV	3	1	9	10	4	2
Metatarsalia III + IV	1	1	14	9	7	2
Metapodia	—	—	9	3	2	—
Phalanx I	—	—	4	1	2	2
Phalanx II	—	—	2	1	2	—
Phalanx III	—	—	1	—	1	—

Table 15.19 Skeletal Element of Horse (*Equus caballus*) in 2001

Bones	Strata				
	1	*2*	*2–3*	*3*	*Pits*
Skull—face	—	1	2	1	1
Mandible	—	—	—	1	1
Teeth	—	1	—	—	3
Rib	1	2	4	1	5
Scapula	—	—	—	—	2
Pelvis	—	—	—	1	—
Humerus	—	1	1	—	—
Tibia	—	1	—	—	—
Calcaneus	—	1	—	—	—
Carpi, tarsi, sesamoidea	—	1	—	—	1
Metapodia	—	1	—	—	1
Phalanx I	—	—	—	—	1
Phalanx II	—	1	—	1	1

Table 15.20 Skeletal Elements of Pig (*Sus scrofa domestica*) in 2001

Bones	Strata				
	1	*2*	*2–3*	*3*	*Pits*
Skull—brain	—	1	—	3	—
Skull—face	—	—	—	1	—
Mandible	—	—	3	4	—
Teeth	—	1	1	1	—
Vertebrae	—	—	—	1	—
Pelvis	—	—	—	—	1
Humerus	—	—	1	1	—
Femur	—	1	—	—	—
Tibia	—	1	—	1	1
Carpi, tarsi, sesamoidea	—	—	—	—	1
Metapodia	—	—	—	—	1
Phalanx I	—	—	—	2	—

Table 15.21 Skeletal Elements of Dog (*Canis familiaris*) in 2001

Bones	Strata					
	1	*1–2*	*2*	*2–3*	*3*	*Pits*
Skull—brain	—	—	22	16	27	9
Skull—face	—	—	22	10	24	5
Mandible	1	—	23	11	18	10
Teeth	2	—	11	6	8	4
Vertebrae	2	1	38	26	29	19
Rib	—	—	29	13	18	17
Sternum	—	—	1	—	—	—
Baculum	—	—	—	—	—	—
Scapula	—	—	6	4	7	—
Pelvis	—	—	2	3	4	1
Humerus	—	—	7	9	10	3
Radius	—	—	8	4	13	3
Ulna	—	—	11	3	9	1
Femur	—	—	14	11	11	8
Tibia	—	—	14	10	15	7
Fibula	—	—	3	4	6	1
Calcaneus	—	—	2	—	3	—
Talus	—	—	1	—	—	1
Carpi, tarsi, sesamoidea	2	1	7	5	12	1
Metapodia	2	—	38	9	28	7
Phalanx I	2	1	12	6	8	1
Phalanx II	—	—	5	3	9	3
Phalanx III	—	—	1	1	—	2

Table 15.22 Percent of All Domesticated Animal Bones, by Species, 2001

Species	Strata				
	1	*2*	*2–3*	*3*	*Pits*
Cattle—*Bos taurus*	56/43	57/37	56/37	64/39	58/36
Goat/sheep—*Capra* et *Ovis*	44/33	40/26	40/26	31/19	31/20
Pig—*Sus scrofa domestica*	0/0	2/1	2/1	1/1	9/6
Horse—*Equus caballus*	0/0	1/1	2/1	4/2	2/1
Dog—*Canis familiaris*	—/24	—/35	—/35	—/40	—/37
NISP	53/42	487/764	318/472	394/653	175/278

Note: First number excludes dogs; second number includes dogs.

Table 15.23 Percent of Indeterminate Mammal (*Mammalia indet.*) Bones 2001

Group	Strata				
	1	2	2–3	3	Pits
Indeterminate large mammal	28	38	31	38	46
Indeterminate average mammal	32	50	58	55	53
Indeterminate average to large size mammal	40	12	11	7	1
NISP	133	1,184	539	877	319
					Total NISP 3,052

Table 15.24 Comparison of Percentages of Domesticated Animal Bones in Srubnaya Settlements in the Middle Volga Region (Krasnosamarskoe, Site 1, without/with Dogs)

	Settlement Site[a]						
	1	2	3	4	5	6	7
Species							
Cattle—*Bos taurus*	54/35	52	53	62	67	52	60
Goat/sheep—*Capra* et *Ovis*	39/25	25	23	20	18	28	27
Horse—*Equus caballus*	3/1.5	15	15	12	9	16	10
Pig—*Sus scrofa domestica*	3/1.5	5	7	4	4	2	2
Dog—*Canis familiaris*	—/36	3	0.3	0.1	0.5	0.5	0.7
Wild animals	0.7/0.7	0.05	1	1	0.7	0.3	1.3
NISP	4,885/7,655	3,795	4,692	4,767	3,183	1,767	502

Note: First number excludes dogs; second number includes dogs.
[a] 1 = Krasnosamarskoe; 2 = Sachkovo; 3 = Moechnoe Ozero 1; 4 = Lebyazhinka V, Layers 4–6; 5 = Lebyazhinka V, Layers 1–3; 6 = Suskanskoe I; 7 = Poplavskoe.

Table 15.25 Body Parts (Percent) of Cattle (*Bos taurus*) in Srubnaya Settlements in the Middle Volga Region

Skeletal Unit	Krasnosamarskoe	Sachkovo	Lebyazhinka V	Tsalkin Compilation[a]
Head—skull and mandible	42	43	24	22
Trunk—vertebrae, ribs	13	12	18	16
Proximal limb (scapula, pelvis, humerus, femur, radius, ulna)	16	23	31	31
Distal limb (metapodia, phalanges 1–3)	29	22	27	31
NISP	2,661	1,041	2,239	3,865

[a] V. I. Tsalkin (1972), including 26 LBA mid-Volga settlements.

Table 15.26 Age Structure (Percent) of Cattle (*Bos taurus*) in Srubnaya Settlements in the Middle Volga Region

Age (Months)	Krasnosamarskoe	Sachkovo	Sites Compiled by Tsalkin (1972)	Lebyazhinka V	
				Layers 1–3	Layers 4–6
<6	18	22	9	6	11
6–18	32	27	18	9	11
18–30	14	19	21	27	23
>30	36	32	52	58	54
NISP	160	200	?	127	107

Table 15.27 Measurements of Cattle (*Bos taurus*) Bones from Krasnosamarskoe Settlement

	n	*lim*	*M ± m*	*δ*
Maxilla				
Length P2–P4 (No. 22)	2	48.5–51.7	50.1	
Length M1–M3 (No. 21)	1		72	
Length M3 (L)	9	27.0–29.9	28.7	
Width M3 (B)	8	20.7–24.0	22	
Mandibula				
Length p2–p4 (No. 9)	1		56.4	
Length m3 (L)	10	34.3–38.8	36.6 ± 0.60	1.71
Width m3 (B)	12	14.9–17.4	16.1 ± 0.21	0.79
Scapula				
Height joint with tubercle (GLP)	4	53.5–60.9	58.4	
Height of the joint (LG)	5	48.4–53.9	51	
Width of the joint (BG)	4	40.0–48.3	44	
Height of cervical (SLl)	1		37.7	
Radius				
Width of upper end (Bp)	1		75.5	
Width of top joint (BFp)	1		70	
Talus				
Length of the lateral (GLl)	22	58.3–74.0	63.9 ± 0.62	2.94
Length of the medial (GLm)	22	53.9–66.3	59.3 ± 0.75	3.31
Width of distal end (Bd)	21	36.0–44.9	40.6 ± 0.60	2.6
Diameter of the lateral (Dl)	22	32.3–38.6	35.2 ± 0.40	1.91
Metacarpalia III+IV				
Length (GL)	1		180.5	
Width of upper end (Bp)	1		58	
Width of shaft (SD)	1		33.6	
Width of lower end (Bd)	2	59.0–64.0	61.5	
Metatarsalia III+IV				
Length (GL)	1		215	
Width of upper end (Bp)	2	46.0–47.0	46.5	
Width of shaft (SD)	1		25.1	
Width of lower end (Bd)	1		54.2	
Phalanx I				
Sagittal length (LA)	18	47.7–57.2	50.7 ± 0.56	2.4
Width of upper end (Bp)	19	22.7–34.4	28.4 ± 0.49	2.31
Minimum width of shaft (SD)	17	21.0–25.4	23.0 ± 0.30	1.42
Width of lower end (Bd)	18	24.3–31.3	27.2 ± 0.44	2.04
Diameter of lower end (Dd)	12	19.4–24.3	21.1 ± 0.43	1.49
Phalanx II				
Length (GL)	18	31.6–41.2	36.2 ± 1.01	3.51
Width of upper end (Bp)	18	25.2–34.6	28.3 ± 0.89	3.03
Minimum width of shaft (SD)	20	18.9–29.9	22.2 ± 0.81	3.2
Width of lower end (Bd)	15	20.8–32.4	24.4 ± 1.30	3.99
Diameter of lower end (Dd)	7	23.9–33.6	27.9	
Height at the withers, см	22	108–138	119	

Note: Abbreviations for signs from von den Driesch (1976).

Table 15.28 Body Parts (Percent) Ovicaprid (*Ovis aries, Capra hircus*) in Srubnaya Settlements in the Middle Volga Region

Skeletal Unit	Krasnosamarskoe	Sachkovo	Lebyazhinka V	Tsalkin (1972) Compilation
Head—skull and mandible	35	33	25	36
Trunk—vertebrae, ribs	15	21	16	8
Proximal limb (scapula, pelvis, humerus, femur, radius, ulna)	25	31	45	44
Distal limb (metapodia, phalanges 1–3)	25	15	15	12
NISP	1,846	619	943	1,886

Table 15.29 Age Structure (Percent) of Ovicaprid (*Ovis aries, Capra hircus*) in Srubnaya Settlements in the Middle Volga Region

Stage of Tooth Eruption	Krasnosamarskoe	Sachkovo	Lebyazhinka V Layers 1–3	Lebyazhinka V Layers 4–6
M1 not present <3 months	0	0	1	2
M1 present, M2 not present; young; 3–12 months	27	19	17	28
M2 present, M3 not present; semi-mature; 12–24 months	20	28	32	26
M3 present; adult; > 24 months	53	53	50	44
NISP	119	127	109	54

Table 15.30 Measurements of Sheep (*Ovis aries*) Bones from Krasnosamarskoe Settlement

Element Measurement	n	lim	M ± m	δ
Maxilla				
Length P2–P4 (No. 23)	1		26.1	
Length M1–M3 (No.22)	1		49.9	
Length M3 (L)	14	19.2–25.8	21.5 ± 0.48	1.7
Width M3 (B)	12	12.5–16.1	13.8 ± 0.32	1.1
Mandibula				
Length p2–m3 (No. 7)	3	72.0–78.8	74.9	
Length p2–p4 (No. 9)	9	22.5–26.3	25.1	
Length m1–m3 (No. 8)	7	51.5–59.5	56.9	
Height before p2 (No. 15c)	2	19.9–20.0	20	
Height before m1 (No. 15b)	1		26.1	
Length m3 (L)	8	24.0–27.0	25	
Width m3 (B)	8	8.8–9.9	9.2	
Scapula				
Height of cervical (SLl)	3	19.6–24.2	21.9	
Humerus				
Width of lower end (BT)	9	29.7–35.5	33.2	
Diameter of lower end (Dd)	4	31.0–33.5	32	
Radius				
Width of upper end (Bp)	2	34.9–35.8	35.4	
Width of top of joint (BFp)	2	30.7–33.0	31.9	
Tibia				
Width of lower end (Bd)	4	29.7–33.9	31.6	
Talus				
Length of lateral (GLl)	23	28.7–35.9	32.4 ± 0.58	2.67
Length of medial (GLm)	24	27.2–34.4	31.2 ± 0.48	2.56
Width of distal end (Bd)	23	18.4–22.6	21.0 ± 0.27	1.58
Diameter of lateral (Dl)	23	15.7–19.7	18.1 ± 0.26	1.43
Metacarpalia III + IV				
Width of upper end (Bp)	3	24.5–28.3	26.2	
Diameter of upper end (Dp)	3	16.5–20.4	18.7	
Width of lower end (Bd)	3	27.4–30.8	28.6	
Metatarsalia III + IV				
Width of upper end (Bp)	5	22.5–24.6	23.8	
Phalanx I				
Sagittal length (LA)	5	33.9–37.7	36	
Width of upper end (Bp)	5	12.6–14.5	13.7	
Minimum width of shaft (SD)	4	10.6–11.8	11.3	
Width of lower end (Bd)	10	11.9–14.2	12.9	
Diameter of lower end (Dd)	8	10.9–12.9	11.8	
Phalanx II				
Width of upper end (Bp)	3	11.8–12.9	12.5	
Minimum width of shaft (SD)	4	9.0–11.5	9.9	
Width of lower end (Bd)	2	10.0–11.9	11	
Height at withers, cm	23	65–81	73	

Table 15.31 Measurements of Goat (*Capra hircus*) Bones from Krasnosamarskoe Settlement

Element Measurement	n	lim	M ± m	δ
Horn—Cornu				
Length of horncore—front margin	1		141	
Length of horncore—falling margin	2	100–121	110.5	
Greatest diameter of horncore base (No. 41)	3	30.0–44.5	35.6	
Least diameter of horncore base (No. 42)	2	22.0–28.1	25.1	
Maxilla				
Length M3 (L)	2	17.6–20.2	18.9	
Width M3 (B)	2	12.2–13.9	13.1	
Mandibula				
Length p2–p4 (No. 9)	2	22.5–24.6	22.5	
Length m3 (L)	1		18.9	
Width m3 (B)	1		23.6	
Radius				
Width of upper end (Bp)	1		30	
Width of top of joint (BFp)	1		28.5	
Talus				
Length of lateral (GLl)	14	27.0–31.4	29.1 ± 0.43	1.41
Length of medial (GLm)	14	25.8–29.6	27.4 ± 0.32	1.22
Width of distal end (Bd)	13	17.1–21.0	18.70.31	1.23
Diameter of lateral (Dl)	14	14.1–16.2	15.2 ± 0.21	0.62
Metacarpalia III + IV				
Width of upper end (Bp)	1		18.6	
Metatarsalia III + IV				
Width of upper end (Bd)	1		24.7	
Phalanx I				
Sagittal length (LA)	3	32.0–35.1	34	
Width of upper end (Bp)	3	11.1–13.0	11.9	
Minimum width of shaft (SD)	3	9.0–10.7	9.8	
Width of upper end (Bd)	3	10.5–13.4	11.9	

Table 15.32 Measurements of Cattle (*Bos taurus*) Bones in Other LBA Sites in the Middle Volga Region

Element Measurement	n	lim	M ± m	δ
Lebyazhinka V (Kosintsev 2003)				
Maxilla				
Length M3 (L)	52	24.4–33.2	29.6 ± 0.25	1.6
Mandibula				
Length m3 (L)	31	33.1–41.2	37.2 ± 0.32	1.8
Tibia				
Width of lower end (Bd)	10	57.3–71.9	62.3 ± 1.48	4.69
Talus				
Length of lateral (GLl)	126	55.0–73.7	65.2 ± 0.45	3.51
Width of distal end (Bd)	126	35.0–50.9	42.0 ± 0.31	3.43
Metacarpalia III + IV				
Width of upper end (Bp)	18	49.9–65.9	58.5 ± 1.26	5.33
Width of lower end (Bd)	21	51.9–72.7	61.0 ± 1.39	6.34
Metatarsalia III + IV				
Width of upper end (Bp)	26	39.0–56.3	48.3 ± 0.69	3.53
Width of lower end (Bd)	23	50.0–71.0	57.7 ± 1.31	6.3
Phalanx I				
Sagittal length (LA)	73	45.2–63.5	53.4 ± 0.81	3.36
Height at withers, см	126	102–137	120	
Sachkovo (Kosintsev 2003)				
Maxilla				
Length M3 (L)		25.7–30.9	28.8 ± 0.33	1.41
Mandibula				
Length m3 (L)	13	31.9–37.9	36.2 ± 0.52	1.86
Talus				
Length of lateral (GLl)	37	56.1–76.7	64.0 ± 0.66	4.02
Width of distal end (Bd)	35	34.9–49.7	41.0 ± 067	3.54
Phalanx I				
Sagittal length (LA)	18	44.7–54.8	50.0 ± 0.64	2.53
Height at withers, cm	37	104–143	119	
Samara oblast sites (Tsalkin 1958)				
Talus				
Length of lateral (GLl)	111	59.0–75.0	65.1 ± 0.38	3.98
Height at withers, cm	111	110–140	121	

Table 15.33 Measurements of Sheep (*Ovis aries*) Bones in Other LBA Sites in the Middle Volga Region

Element Measurement	n	lim	M ± m	δ
Lebyazhinka V (Kosintsev 2003)				
Humerus				
Width of lower end (BT)	25	33.0–38.8	36.2 ± 0.45	1.6
Talus				
Length of lateral (GLl)	53	28.9–35.8	32.9 ± 0.26	1.86
Width of distal end (Bd)	70	16.7–24.7	20.9 ± 0.19	1.61
Phalanx I				
Sagittal length (LA)	16	31.9–43.0	38.0 ± 0.79	3.16
Height at withers, cm	53	66–81	75	
Sachkovo (Kosintsev 2003)				
Talus				
Length of lateral (GLl)	29	30.0–35.4	31.9 ± 0.27	1.44
Width of distal end (Bd)	29	18.7–23.6	20.6 ± 0.20	1.17
Height at withers, см	29	68–80	72	
Samara oblast sites (Tsalkin 1958)				
Talus				
Length of lateral (GLl)	20	31.0–37.0	33.3	
Height at withers, cm	20	70–84	75	

Table 15.34 Measurements of Goats (*Capra hircus*) Bones in Other LBA Sites in the Middle Volga Region

Element Measurement	n	lim	M ± m	δ
Lebyazhinka V (Kosintsev 2003)				
Talus				
Length of lateral (GLl)	11	26.1–30.1	28.5 ± 0.41	1.37
Width of distal end (Bd)	11	13.7–20.6	18.0 ± 0.57	1.88
Sachkovo (Kosintsev 2003)				
Talus				
Length of lateral (GLl)	35	25.7–30.9	28.9 ± 0.25	1.5
Width of distal end (Bd)	35	16.3–20.3	18.2 ± 0.17	1.02

Table 15.35 Measurements of Horse (*Equus caballus*) Bones from Krasnosamarskoe Settlement

Element Measurement	n	lim	M
Mandibula			
Length m3	1	—	33.5
Width m3	1	—	12.5
Tibia			
Width of lower end (Bd)	1	—	69.3
Talus			
Maximum height (GH)	2	60.0–63.0	61.5
Length of medial crest (LmT)	2	59.0–65.4	62.2
Breadth (GB)	2	61.6–64.5	63.1
Width of the distal joint (BFd)	2	50.4–56.3	53.4
Height of distal joint (HFd)	2	36.5–39.3	37.9
Metatarsalia III			
Width of lower joint (Bd)	1	—	47.7
Phalanx I anterior			
Sagittal length (LA)	2	77.5–77.8	77.7
Width of shaft (SD)	2	33.3–37.5	35.4
Width of upper end (Bp)	2	51.3–53.5	52.4
Width of top joint (BFp)	2	49.0–49.6	49.3
Diameter of upper end (Dp)	2	34.5–34.9	34.5
Width of lower end (Bd)	2	42.3–46.7	46.5
Width of lower joint (BFd)	2	42.5–43.0	42.8
Phalanx I posterior			
Sagittal length (LA)	2	76.5–78.4	77.5
Width of shaft (SD)	2	32.1–36.4	34.3
Width of upper end (Bp)	2	56.7–58.0	57.4
Width of top joint (BFp)	2	52.5–54.6	53.6
Diameter of upper end (Dp)	2	38.5–40.0	39.3
Width of lower end (Bd)	2	43.9–45.6	44.8
Width of lower joint (BFd)	2	42.9–45.1	44
Diameter of lower joint (DFd)	2	24.1–26.5	25.3
Phalanx II anterior			
Sagittal length (LA)	3	36.6–40.5	39.1
Width of shaft (SD)	3	46.7–50.2	48.9
Width of upper end (Bp)	3	52.8–59.5	57.2
Width of top joint (BFp)	3	46.0–53.2	50.4
Diameter of upper end (Dp)	3	31.9–36.6	35
Width of lower end (Bd)	3	52.6–54.5	53.7
Phalanx II posterior			
Sagittal length (LA)	4	37.8–40.0	38.7
Width of shaft (SD)	4	42.1–45.9	43.7
Width of upper end (Bp)	4	51.4–54.3	52.4
Width of top joint (BFp)	4	44.2–47.5	45.9
Diameter of upper end (Dp)	4	32.6–34.5	33.2
Width of lower end (Bd)	4	46.5–52.0	49

Table 15.36 Measurements of Horse (*Equus caballus*) Bones in Other LBA Sites of the Middle Volga Region

Element Measurement	All Sites Kosintsev 2003, *n*	*lim*	*M ± m*	*δ*
Talus				
Maximum height (GH)	24	55.4–65.8	60.3 ± 0.60	2.86
Metatarsalia III				
Width of lower joint (Bd)	10	47.8–55.5	51.2 ± 0.91	2.88
Phalanx I anterior				
Sagittal length (LA)	13	72.2–95.0	83.2 ± 1.53	5.51
Width of shaft (SD)	16	32.8–41.7	36.5 ± 0.72	2.89
Phalanx I posterior				
Sagittal length (LA)	22	72.3–83.9	78.6 ± 0.69	3.25
Width of shaft (SD)	20	32.1–38.1	35.1 ± 0.41	1.84
Phalanx II anterior				
Sagittal length (LA)	18	34.3–40.7	37.8 ± 0.46	1.98
Width of shaft (SD)	18	40.8–49.7	45.9 ± 0.57	2.4
Phalanx II posterior				
Sagittal length (LA)	18	37.5–42.5	39.9 ± 0.36	1.52
Width of shaft (SD)	18	39.8–46.9	43.4 ± 0.43	1.81
	All sites Tsalkin 1972, *n*			
Talus				
Maximum height (GH)	27	56.0–66.0	60.8 ± 0.49	2.56

Table 15.37 Measurements of Pig (*Sus scrofa domestica*) Bones from Krasnosamarskoe Settlement

Element Measurement	*n*	*lim*	*M*
Scapula			
Height joint with tubercle (GLP)	1		41
Height of the joint (LG)	1		33.4
Width of joint (BG)	1		28.2
Height of cervical (SLC)	2	17.4–23.9	20.7
Metacarpalia III			
Width of upper end	2	14.5–15.1	14.8
Metatarsalia III			
Width of upper end	1		19.4
Talus			
Length of the lateral (GLl)	2	47.8–48.2	48
Length of the medial (GLm)	2	43.7–43.8	43.8
Width of the distal end (Bd)	2	27.0–27.4	27.2
Diameter of lateral (Dl)	3	24.4–25.0	24.7

Table 15.38 Species Identified at Peschanyi Dol 1 and 2

Species	Site	
	PD1	PD2
Cattle—*Bos taurus*	25/3	3/1
Goat and sheep—*Capra* et *Ovis*	26/3	12/2
Sheep—*Ovis aries*	6/2	—
Goat—*Capra hircus*	2/1	—
Pig—*Sus scrofa domestica*	1/1	—
Horse—*Equus caballus*	3/1	10/2
Dog—*Canis familiaris*	1/1	—
Roe deer—*Capreolus pygargus*	1/1	—
Steppe marmot—*Marmota bobak*	4/1	1/1
Gopher—*Spermophilus major*	2/1	2/2
Jerboa—*Allactaga major*	2/2	—
Hamster—*Cricetus cricetus*	5/3	2/1
Mole—*Ellobius talpinus*	8/2	—
Water vole—*Arvicola terrestris*	2/2	—
Steppe lemming—*Lagurus lagurus*	1/1	—
Vole—*Microtinae* gen.	18	2
Unidentifiable mammal bones—*Mammalia* indet.	212	30
Fish—*Pisces* indet.	—	1

Notes

1   Editor's note: In Chapter 16 by Russell, Brown, and Brown, it is noted that three of the four *roasted* sheep-goat specimens are from Level 1 and Level 2 outside the Bronze Age structure, so it is possible that these reflect Iron Age roasting of a small number of sheep-goat, a way of preparing sheep-goat not typical of the Bronze Age.

References

Driesch, A. von den

1976   *A Guide to the Measurement of Animals Bones from Archaeological Sites.* Peabody Museum Bulletin 1. Harvard University, Cambridge, Massachusetts.

Eisenmann, V., M. T. Alberdi, C. De Giuli, and U. Staesche

1988   *Studying Fossil Horses.* Vol. 1. Brill, Leiden.

Kosintsev, P. A.

2001   Komplex kostnykh ostatkov domashnikh zhivotnykh iz poselenij i mogilnikov epokhi bronzy Volgo-Uraliya i Zauraliya. In *Bronzovyj vek Vostochnoj Evropy: kharakteristika kultur, khronologiya i periodizatsiya*, edited by Yu. I. Kolev, pp. 363–367. "NTZ," Samara.

2003   Zhivotnovodstvo u naseleniya Samarskogo Povolzhiya v epokhu pozdnej bronzy. In *Materialnaya kultura naseleniya bassejna reki Samary v bronzovom veke*, edited by Yu. I. Kolev, P. F. Kuznetsov, O. D. Mochalov, pp. 126–146. Izdatelstvo SGPU, Samara.

Petrenko, A. G.

1984   *Drevnee I srednevekovoe zhivotnovodstvo Povolzhiya I Preduraliya.* Izdatelstvo "Nauka," Moskow.

Silver, J. A.

1969   The Ageing of Domestic Animals. In *Science and Archaeology: A Survey of Progress and Research*, edited by D. Brothwell and E. Higgs, pp. 283–302. Thames & Hudson, New York.

Teichert, M.

1975   Osteometrische Untersuchungen zur Berechnung der Wiederristhöhe bei Schaffen. In *Archaeozoological Studies*, edited by A. T. Clason, pp. 51–69. Elsevier, Amsterdam.

Tsalkin, V. I.

1958   Fauna iz raskopok archaeologicheskikh pamyatnikov Srednego Povolzhya. In *Trudy Kujbyshevskoj archaeologicheskoj expeditsyi*, edited by A. P. Smirnov, pp. 221–281. Izdatelstvo Akademii nauk SSSR, Moscow. (Materialy I issledovaniya po archaeologii SSSR. No. 61)

1960   Izmenchivost metapodij I ee znachenie dlya izucheniya krupnogo rigatogo skota drevnosti. *Bulleten Moskovskogo obshchestva ispytatelej prirody.* 65(1):109–126.

1966   Drevnee zhivotnovodstvo plemen Vostochnoj Evropy I Srednej Azii. *Materialy I issledovaniya po archaeologii SSSR* 135. "Nauka," Moskow.

1970   Drevneishie domashnie zhivotnye Vostochnoj Evropy. *Materialy I issledovaniya po archaeologii SSSR* 161. "Nauka," Moskow.

1972a Domashnie zhivotnye Vostochnoj Evropy v epokhu pozdnej bronzy. Soobshchenie 1. *Bulleten Moskovskogo obshchestva ispytatelej prirody.* T. LXXVII(1):46–65.

1972b Domashnie zhivotnye Vostochnoj Evropy v epokhu pozdnej bronzy. Soobshchenie 2. *Bulleten Moskovskogo obshchestva ispytatelej prirody.* T. LXXVII(2):42–50.

1972c Domashnie zhivotnye Vostochnoj Evropy v epokhu pozdnej bronzy. Soobshchenie 1. *Bulleten Moskovskogo obshchestva ispytatelej prirody.* T. LXXVII(3):61–72.

Chapter 16

Human-Animal Relations at Krasnosamarskoe

Nerissa Russell • Audrey Brown • Emmett Brown

W e discuss here the animal bones recovered from Operation 2 (the excavated structure and surroundings) at the Krasnosamarskoe IV settlement. Our focus is on Late Bronze Age human-animal relations at the site, particularly in relation to dogs and cattle. While we attempted to record the same material treated by Pavel Kosintsev in Chapter 15, limitations on time, the vagaries of storage, and differences in method have yielded slightly different totals, although in general congruence with Kosintsev's results. Thus, we recorded 20,161 specimens from the settlement excavation, Operation 2, of which 3,765 are identified to taxon (Table 16.1). Quantification is a vexing issue in zooarchaeology and all measures imperfect (e.g., Brewer 1992; Domínguez-Rodrigo 2012; Grayson 1978; Lyman 2008; Meadow 1999; O'Connor 2001). For estimating relative proportions of taxa, we prefer diagnostic zones (Bogucki 1982; Watson 1979). Diagnostic zones (DZ) solve many, although not all, of the problems of NISP (number of identified specimens) by regularizing for differing numbers of bones among taxa and partly controlling for fragmentation. They also avoid the worst problems of MNI (minimum number of individuals), which tend to overrepresent rare species and are not additive (meaning that results will vary dramatically depending on the units within which the MNI is calculated).

Taxa

The Krasnosamarskoe assemblage (Table 16.1) is dominated by sheep/goat, cattle, and dogs, and we will focus our discussion on these taxa. By our calculations, dog is the most frequent taxon both by NISP and by DZ. Comparing our counts to those in Chapter 15, it appears that Kosintsev was able to identify more cattle and sheep/goat, while we conservatively placed these specimens in size classes. In any case, it is clear that this is not an ordinary faunal assemblage. The amount and the treatment of the dog remains are highly unusual not only for the Late Bronze Age of the Eurasian steppe but also for prehistoric assemblages in general. Bartosiewicz (1990) found a positive correlation between the proportion of dogs and the proportion of wild fauna at Neolithic sites in the Near East and Europe, suggesting that dogs are more abundant when they are used in hunting. However, the very low levels of wild taxa at Krasnosamarskoe argue against extensive use of hunting dogs. We will use contextual analysis and other lines of evidence to explore the roles of dogs and other animals at Krasnosamarskoe in life and death.

As noted in Chapter 15, the taxonomic proportions do not differ significantly for pit and nonpit material. However, there are significant differences between material from outside the structure and the considerably more abundant animal bone within it (Figure 16.1). Excavation suggested two phases in the use of this structure, but they were not clearly separated. We have approximated these phases by designating Levels 3 to 5 as upper structure and Levels 6 and below as lower structure. Although there is more dog in the upper structure and more cattle in the lower (Figure 16.2), these

Table 16.1 Identified Macro-Mammalian Bones from Operation 2 by Number of Identified Specimens (NISP) and Diagnostic Zones (DZ)

Taxon	NISP	NISP (Percent)	DZ	DZ (Percent)
Sheep/goat (*Ovis/Capra*)	910	24.2	206.5	23.4
Cattle (*Bos taurus*)	1,164	30.9	215.5	24.5
Elk (*Alces alces*)	5	0.1	1.5	0.2
Pig (*Sus scrofa*)	72	1.9	16	1.8
Horse (*Equus caballus*)	50	1.3	12	1.4
Small carnivore	4	0.1	3	0.3
Medium carnivore	8	0.2	2.6	0.3
Small mustelid	1	0.0	1	0.1
Polecat (*Mustela eversmanni*)	6	0.2	6	0.7
Dog (*Canis familiaris*)	1,518	40.3	398.2	45.2
Wolf (*Canis lupus*)	11	0.3	11	1.2
Fox (*Vulpes vulpes*)	5	0.1	5	0.6
Human (*Homo sapiens*)	11	0.3	3	0.3
Total	3,765		881.3	

differences are not statistically significant. Both upper and lower levels of the structure differ significantly from material outside the structure, based on a chi-square test (Table 16. 2). Sheep/goat is proportionally less frequent inside the structure than outside it, while cattle are more frequent in the lower levels, and dog is more frequent inside the structure (Figure 16.3) but especially in the upper levels. This suggests that the meals associated with the indoor deposits differed in nature from those whose remains were deposited outside, as well as a change in emphasis between the two phases of deposition.

Body Parts

To facilitate comparison and control to some degree for fragmentation, we also use diagnostic zones to compare body part distributions, grouped into body areas. These areas are the head (measured here by mandibles and maxillae, the only cranial DZ), axial (vertebrae and pelvis), forelimb (scapula, humerus, radius, ulna), hindlimb (femur, patella, tibia, fibula/lateral malleolus), and feet (carpals and tarsals, metapodials, phalanges). The axial, forelimb, and hindlimb portions bear most of the meat, while heads and especially feet are often primary butchery waste or left attached to the skin. Since diagnostic zones are not evenly distributed through these body areas, we provide the distribution in a whole animal for comparison (Figure 16.4).

At Krasnosamarskoe in general, horses are represented solely by feet in terms of diagnostic zones; among the fragments that did not contain DZ, nearly all are feet or cranial, although there is one specimen each of scapula and humerus. Horses are also quite scarce, and we may only be catching remains of skins or butchery waste of horses sacrificed as part of funerary rites at the nearby kurgans. Horse bones are not more weathered than other taxa, though, so

Table 16.2 Proportions of Major Taxa outside Structure vs. Upper and Lower Structure, by Diagnostic Zones

Taxon	Nonstructure, *n* (Percent)	Upper Structure, *n* (Percent)	Lower Structure, *n* (Percent)
Sheep/goat (*Ovis/Capra*)	59.5 (35)	66.5 (26)	80.5 (21)
Cattle (*Bos taurus*)	36 (21)	56 (22)	123.5 (32)
Dog (*Canis familiaris*)	76.8 (45)	134.8 (52)	186.6 (48)
Total	172.3	257.3	390.6
Chi-square		0.0098	0.0000000002
p		0.995	1.0

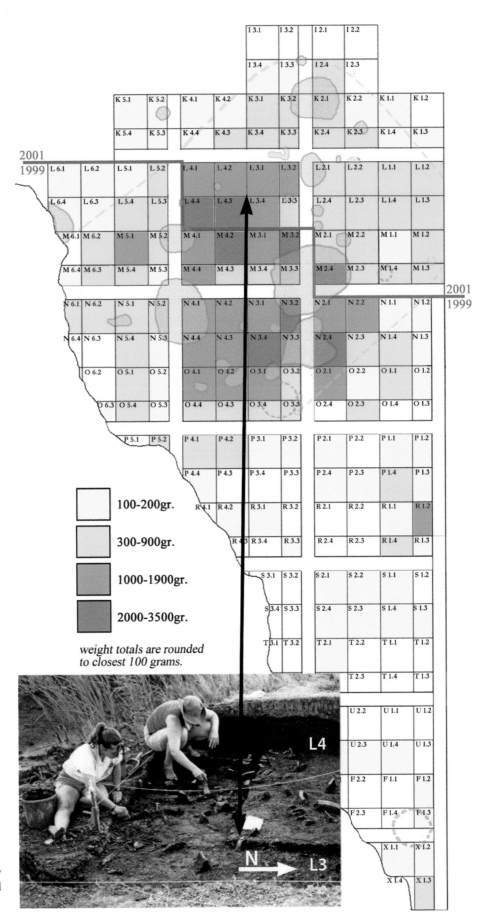

Figure 16.1 Animal bone density by weight. Photo of Units L3 and L4 with animal bones in situ.

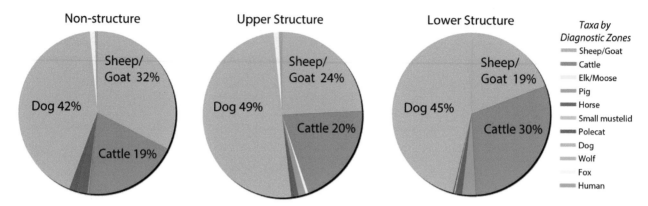

Figure 16.2 Distribution of taxa outside the structure and in the upper and lower levels of the structure.

these are not, for the most part, remains of skins exposed on the kurgans. Moreover, the kurgan burials did not contain special deposits of horse remains as seen at other contemporary sites, so there is no direct evidence of horse sacrifice. There is little sign that horses were consumed at the Krasnosamarskoe settlement.

The sample size for the pigs is rather small, with only a single specimen with a diagnostic zone outside the structure (so the feet-only pattern there is not meaningful). While numbers inside the structure are still low, it may be of interest that pigs follow cattle in an overrepresentation of feet in the lower structure.

Sheep and goat approximate an unbiased distribution outside the structure, and inside it show an excess of head remains. Forelimbs are more common than hindlimbs in all three contexts.

Cattle are only slightly biased to heads and feet outside the structure but more so inside, especially in the lower levels where cattle are more frequent. Inside the structure, forelimbs are again more common than hindlimbs.

Outside the structure, the dog body part distribution is quite similar to that of cattle. Inside the structure, particularly in the lower levels, meaty parts and especially heads are overrepresented. Forelimbs again predominate over hindlimbs but less so than for the cattle and sheep/goat.

In sum, focusing on the three major taxa, both meaty parts (which might be expected to be discarded after consumption) and butchery waste (which might be discarded earlier) are present in all three contexts. However, sheep/goat have somewhat more butchery waste inside, as do cattle in the lower levels of the structure, while dogs have more meaty parts inside. The bias to forelimbs is interesting and does not appear to be taphonomic. While four of six forelimb DZ are dense areas compared to three of six in the hindlimb, the softer hindlimb DZ such as the patella are well represented.

This pattern raises the possibility of a meat-sharing system that distributed some hindlimbs to other structures, perhaps as a tithe to a leader. However, as the putative other structures were inaccessible or destroyed under the pond, we can only guess what happened to the hindlimbs. The body part distributions are sufficiently even as to indicate that slaughter of the major taxa occurred locally.

Processing

Table 16.3 summarizes butchery traces (cuts and chops, as well as abrasion to prepare for marrow fracture) for the various taxa. It tabulates occurrences of butchery actions rather than individual marks or blows, so that several cut-marks from around a joint to dismember it count as one, while different kinds of traces on the same specimen (e.g., skinning marks in one area, dismemberment in another) are counted in each category. Specimens that could only be placed in size classes are included, since filleting (to remove raw meat from the bone) and consumption (to remove cooked meat) marks are disproportionately found on fragments that cannot be assigned to more precise taxa, since they tend to occur on shafts. Note that all the size categories are somewhat fuzzy and that "sheep size" will include sheep, goat, dog, and wolf, and "cow size" will include cattle, horse, and elk/moose, although the proportions of identified specimens suggest that these will be overwhelmingly cattle.

Even allowing for most of the filleting and consumption marks being relegated to size categories, dismemberment cuts clearly predominate, as is usual except where obsidian is used in butchery (Dewbury and Russell 2007). These are cuts that result from breaking down the carcass into smaller segments (Binford 1981). The sheep/goat and cattle have similar proportions of dismemberment cuts (even though these proportions are somewhat inflated because most filleting and consumption marks are attributed only to size

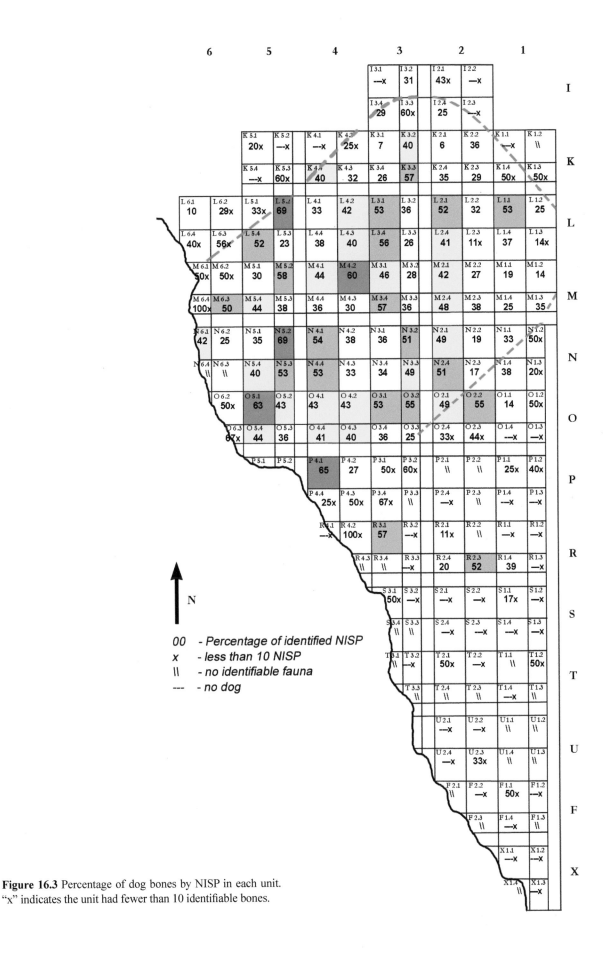

Figure 16.3 Percentage of dog bones by NISP in each unit.
"x" indicates the unit had fewer than 10 identifiable bones.

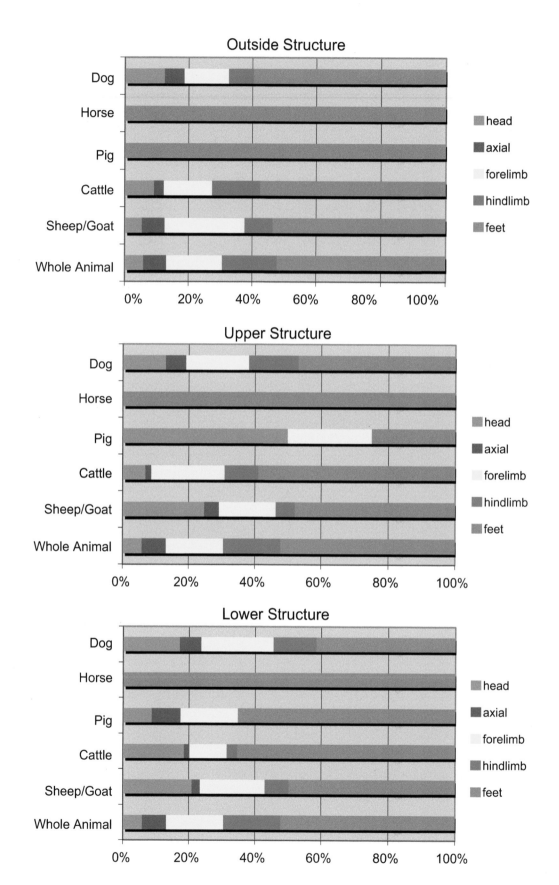

Figure 16.4 Body part distributions for major taxa outside the structure and in the upper and lower levels of the structure, with distribution in intact animal for comparison.

categories). The proportion in dogs is lower, although still the largest category. However, the ratio of dismemberment to skinning cuts is similar for sheep/goat, cattle, and dogs, suggesting that the difference for dogs is not that there are fewer dismemberment cuts but more chopped cranial specimens.

The most interesting feature of butchering and processing at Krasnosamarskoe is the phenomenon tallied in Table 16.3 as segmenting of skulls and mandibles. The chopped mandibles in this category may not all be part of the same phenomenon as the chopped skulls. All the cattle specimens in this category are mandibles: two have their condylar processes chopped off and in one case trimmed further for reasons that are unclear; the third was chopped through the alveolus of the first molar. Of the three dog mandibular specimens, one was similarly chopped across the horizontal ramus to produce a 3-cm section, the second was chopped behind the tooth row to remove the back of the mandible, and the third was chopped lengthwise below the teeth as well as crosswise through the alveoli of the canine and fourth premolar. The remaining dog specimens, as well as the sheep-size specimen (quite likely also dog) and one wolf specimen, are pieces of skull that have been neatly chopped into geometric pieces with axes or cleavers (Figure 16.5). For the dogs, the largest dimension of these

pieces varies from 2 to 10 cm, with most in the 3- to 7-cm range (Figure 16.6). These chops were executed with considerable precision and tend to follow a standard pattern, although there is some variation. Figure 16.7 illustrates many of these chop locations (some additional ones on the palate cannot be shown in this view); heavy lines indicate repeated locations.

Many of these specimens show light burning on exposed areas from roasting; the others may have been roasted as well but were covered in skin and flesh that protected them from the flames. Thus, this treatment follows cooking and is probably a preparation for consumption. The amount of flesh on the skull is fairly slight, and these chops are far in excess of what is needed to access the brain—many of them target the muzzle, in any case. They are perhaps instead meant to provide many small pieces of the head so that all participants may partake, largely symbolically, in the shared substance of the animal. While axe blows are used along with knife cuts to dismember carcasses and access marrow, this kind of segmentation is seen postcranially in only a few instances. One dog axis (second vertebra) was chopped with multiple blows into small pieces, while a single chop removed the proximal articulation of a dog

Table 16.3 Cut/Chop Types by Taxon, with Row Percentages in Parentheses

Taxon	Skinning	Dismemberment	Fillet	Tendon Removal	Hoof Removal	Consumption	Marrow Fracture	Open Muzzle	Segment Skull/ Mandible	Segment Other
Sheep size	2 (5)	15 (37)	19 (46)	0	0	4 (10)	0	0	1 (2)	0
Pig size	1 (33)	0	2 (67)	0	0	0	0	0	0	0
Cow size	5 (15)	14 (41)	13 (38)	0	0	2 (6)	0	0	0	0
Sheep/ goat	2 (7)	21 (78)	1 (4)	1 (4)	0	0	1 (4)	1 (4)	0	0
Cattle	5 (9)	42 (74)	1 (2)	1 (2)	1 (2)	1 (2)	1 (2)	1 (2)	3 (5)	1 (2)
Horse	1 (25)	1 (25)	0	1 (25)	0	0	0	0	1 (25)	0
Pig	0	3 (100)	0	0	0	0	0	0	0	0
Dog	4 (4)	60 (53)	10 (9)	0	0	1 (1)	2 (2)	0	35 (31)	2 (2)
Wolf	0	1 (50)	0	0	0	0	0	0	1 (50)	0
Small carnivore	1 (50)	1 (50)	0	0	0	0	0	0	0	0
Rodent	0	0	1 (100)	0	0	0	0	0	0	0
Bird	0	1 (100)	0	0	0	0	0	0	0	0

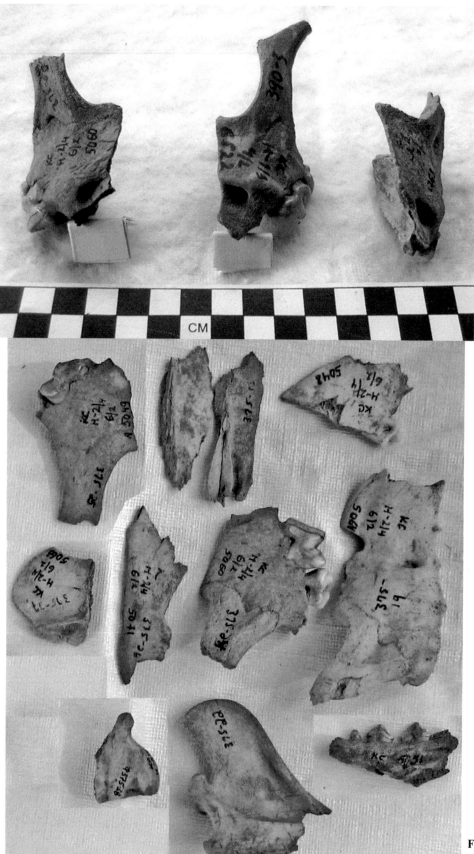

Figure 16.5 Chopped dog skull pieces.

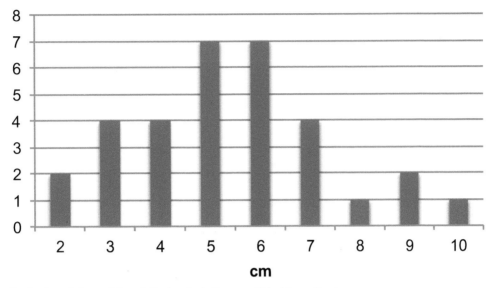

Figure 16.6 Size distribution of chopped dog skulls (not including mandibles) in centimeters.

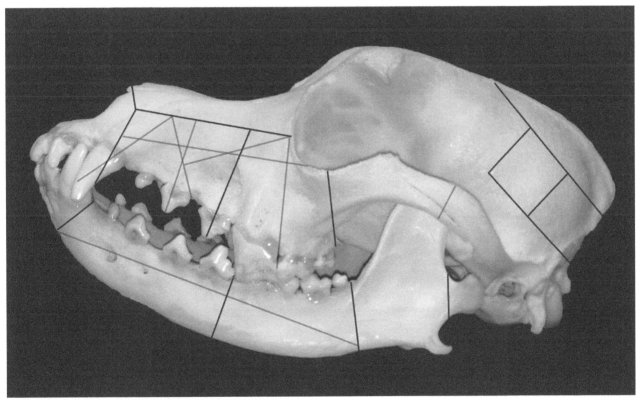

Figure 16.7 Location of chops on dog skulls.

tibia. A cattle pelvis was chopped through the acetabulum and pubis shaft to yield a 5-cm fragment. It is not clear whether these postcranial instances are part of the same phenomenon or ordinary butchery taken a bit further than usual. Many vertebrae were chopped in half lengthwise to separate the two sides of the body and sometimes crosswise to segment the spine (Figure 16.8).

Dog postcranial remains, like those of other taxa, show butcher marks indicating that they were consumed. The geometric segmentation of the skull is, however, largely

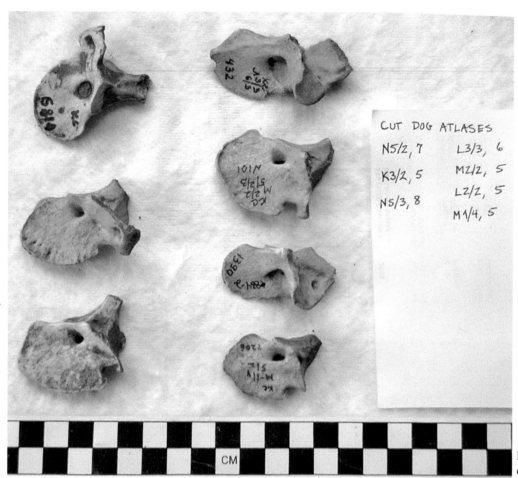

Figure 16.8 Dog atlases chopped longitudinally.

reserved for dogs and at least one wolf. As noted, a few cattle and dog mandibles were chopped up in similar ways. One horse skull fragment shows multiple chops in the maxillary area that has removed the premolars with their alveoli; this is fairly similar to a recurring segment of chopped dog maxillae.

Not all dogs are treated in this way. A minority of skull fragments shows chop marks (Figure 16.9), and while some may have lost chopped edges through postdepositional fracture, the fragment size range is similar to that of the chopped fragments, so most of these were probably not chopped but broken with a blunt instrument or postdepositionally. The chopped dog skull segments are limited to Levels 3 to 9, peaking in Level 6. Spatially, they are found inside the structure or, in Levels 3 and 4, just outside it. The wolf (Level 6) and horse (Level 5) chopped skull pieces were also found inside the structure. While Level 6 has some clusters of chopped pieces, they occur in many different places within the structure in Levels 3 to 9.

Discoloration from burning is apparent on 1,226 specimens from Operation 2. These range from slight toasting through carbonization to calcination, with most in the carbonized-calcined range. The majority of this burning is clearly postconsumption, as bones fell or were thrown into fires, or fires burned in deposits containing bones. Boiling does not discolor bones, and this is probably how most of the meat was cooked at Krasnosamarskoe. Some bones show a pattern of burning that is likely to result from roasting, however: light-medium burning at the ends of bones or other areas exposed as the flesh shrinks back during roasting (Gifford-Gonzalez 1989). Roasting traces will only occur where bone or teeth are exposed and only if kept for long enough over a hot fire; thus, many bones from roasted joints will not exhibit diagnostic burning, so roasting burns underestimate the prevalence of roasting. Roasting is often, although certainly not always, associated with feasting, as it is a good way to cook large amounts of meat and somewhat more wasteful than boiling due to loss of fat (Lévi-Strauss 1965; Twiss 2008).

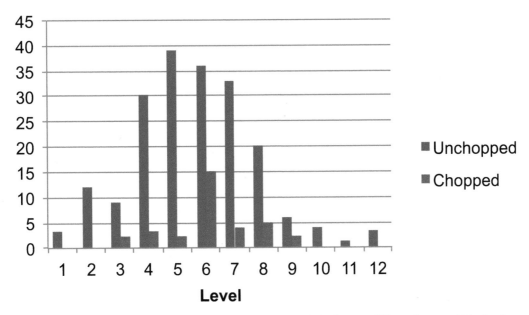

Figure 16.9 Distribution of unchopped and chopped dog skull fragments (not including mandibles or loose teeth) by level.

In total, 4 sheep/goat specimens, 13 cattle specimens, 1 horse specimen, 24 dog specimens, and 1 sheep size (probably sheep/goat or dog) rib show possible roasting traces (Figure 16.10). Given the relative proportions of these taxa (Table 16.1), cattle and especially dogs are overrepresented compared to sheep/goat. In all taxa, roasting is most common for the heads (where it is primarily indicated by light burning of the teeth), but except for horses, postcranial roasting also occurs. Oddly, the feet of cattle and dogs were sometimes roasted (or the burning pattern is spurious in these instances), although they lack flesh. As noted above, many, but not all, of the roasted dog heads were then chopped into small, neat segments.

Roasting occurs throughout Levels 1 to 10; below Level 2, all the roasted specimens derive from inside the structure (as does most of the animal bone). Three of the four roasted sheep/goat specimens are from Levels 1 and 2, so the roasted specimens inside the structure are mainly cattle and dog. Rates of roasting (roasted specimens/NISP) increase slightly for cattle from the lower to the upper structure, while the roasting rate for dog is considerably higher in the lower than the upper structure (Figure 16.11). Of the chopped segments of dog skull where roasting might be observable (mandibles, maxillae, and premaxillae), 10 of 23 show signs of roasting (again, we cannot be sure that the others were not roasted or roasted with the mandible still articulated). There is a particular concentration of roasted and chopped dog remains, cranial and postcranial, in N2/1 and N2/4 in Level 6, representing at least three dogs.

Exposure to Scavenging

A small proportion of the bones show signs of gnawing or digestion. Rodents gnawed 61 bones, while 187 were gnawed by carnivores, most likely dogs. Signs of digestion are evident on 41 specimens; since these are in the 1- to 3-cm range, and mostly 2 to 3 cm (Figure 16.12), they probably derive from dog feces. Dogs typically swallow bones up to about 3 cm, while humans do not usually swallow pieces larger than 1 cm (Esteban Nadal et al. 2010; Horwitz 1990; Payne and Munson 1985; Solomon and David 1990).

Gnawing and digestion occur on a range of taxa and body parts but at low rates. Either not very many dogs lived on site, or animal waste was gathered up and buried relatively quickly, limiting their access. Both gnawing and digestion are proportionally more frequent outside than inside the structure. Outside the structure, 2 percent of bones bear gnaw marks, while only 1 percent do inside the structure, both upper and lower levels. Digested bones form 0.4 percent of the specimens outside the structure, but 0.1 percent in the upper levels and 0.2 percent in the lower levels inside. Dogs apparently had lesser access to material inside the structure.

Mortality Profiles

Kosintsev has discussed mortality profiles for most of the major taxa in Chapter 15. Dog age distributions are difficult to construct with precision because the permanent teeth erupt at a fairly young age, and tooth wear is negligible except in very old animals. We resort to a rough division into

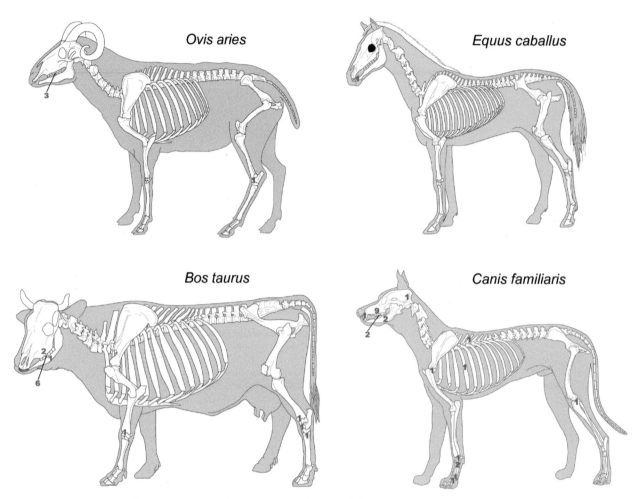

Figure 16.10 Placement of roasting traces on sheep/goat, cattle, horse, and dog.

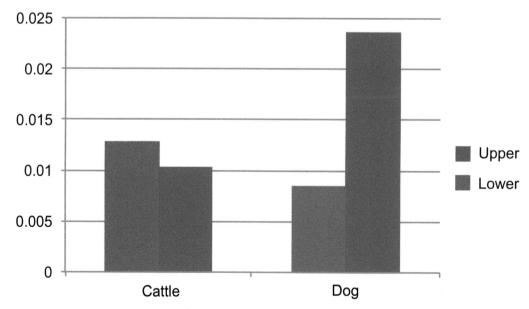

Figure 16.11 Rates of roasting per NISP for cattle and dog in the structure.

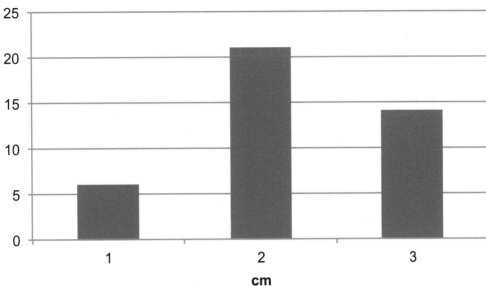

Figure 16.12 Size range of digested bones.

age stages based on a combination of postcranial (epiphyseal fusion) and cranial (tooth eruption and wear) data (Figure 16.13; see also Chapter 14). The age distribution is notably tilted to adult and indeed elderly dogs (the senile category includes those with heavy tooth wear or highly developed muscle attachments). This is particularly unusual for dogs, which give birth to litters at fairly frequent intervals, so that populations are usually dominated by immature animals. The dog mortality profile at Krasnosamarskoe is unlikely to represent a full population; rather, mature or even elderly animals were selected for slaughter.

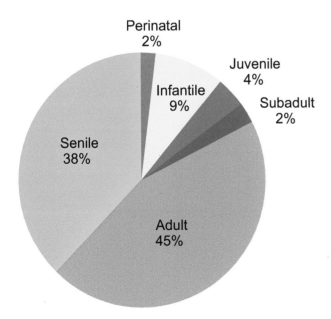

Figure 16.13 Dog age stages.

In the teeth with dentine exposure, the dentine often bears gritty striations not usually seen in dogs. These animals may have been fed a special diet, perhaps heavy in bread (if made with stone-ground flour). This wear is seen on several of the roasted and chopped specimens.

Pathologies

The pathological specimens from Krasnosamarskoe are summarized in Table 16.4. The congenital anomalies include extra foramina in vertebrae and a pit in the articular surface of a rib, as well as fused premolars in a dog. A few vertebrae are asymmetrical, probably a developmental issue. One cattle upper permanent premolar erupted at an angle, pointing up into the palate: it may have been deflected by an impacted deciduous tooth, although if so, this deciduous tooth was no longer present; alternatively, early loss of the deciduous tooth may have caused the adjacent teeth to move in and block eruption of the permanent tooth; or an injury to the developing permanent premolar may have displaced it (Miles and Grigson 1990). Both cattle and dogs show healed alveoli where teeth were lost in life. The lost cattle tooth was a lower second premolar. The lost dog teeth were all upper, one a first molar and the other two first premolars. Both lost premolars occurred in chopped segments of dog skull; one had been broken in life and retains a root and a bit of the crown. The anomalous tooth wear in several animals likely also reflects tooth loss, leading to uneven wear in the occluding teeth. These lost teeth may be the result of trauma or of nutritional deficiencies. Nutritional problems are also likely to be the ultimate cause of the two caries in sheep/goat premolars, as well as abscesses in a sheep/goat and a cattle mandible.

Table 16.4 Pathologies

	Sheep Size	Pig Size	Cow Size	Sheep/Goat	Cattle	Horse	Dog
Congenital anomaly			3				1
Vertebral asymmetry	2		2				
Caries				2			
Anomalous tooth wear				2	2	1	
Tooth loss in life					1		3
Malocclusion					1		
Healed fracture/injury	1	1		1			2
Abscess/infection			2	1	1		
Exostosis			4	1	5	1	8
Osteoarthritis			1		1	2	2

A few injuries appear to result from trauma. A sheep-size rib is swollen at the distal end, probably reflecting healing of an injury to its juncture with the costal cartilage. A pig-size rib has a healed fracture, as does a sheep/goat jugal process on the temporal, and a dog metatarsal. A dog tibia has what appears to be an ossified hematoma (resulting from a blow to the bone that causes a bubble of blood below the periosteum, which is later replaced with bone); it is placed unusually, however, on the lateral posterior of the proximal shaft (Figure 16.14). Signs of infection (osteomyelitis or a similar condition) on two cow-size long bone shaft fragments probably resulted from trauma that broke the skin, permitting infection.

Exostosis is extra bone growth around joints or muscle attachments. When not associated with infections, it is generally the result of stress on the joint. It develops with age and may simply indicate an older animal but, like osteoarthritis, tends to reflect activity. In particular, animals ridden or used in traction may show patterns of exostosis and arthritis. Cow-size specimens show exostosis in the glenoid of the temporal, a scapula, a caudal vertebra, and a long bone fragment, while another long bone fragment exhibits osteoarthritis. One sheep acetabulum has some exostosis that is likely a sign of age. Cattle specimens include an arthritic proximal femur (Figure 16.15) and an acetabulum with exostosis, as well as three first phalanges (two of them articulated; Figure 16.16) and two second phalanges

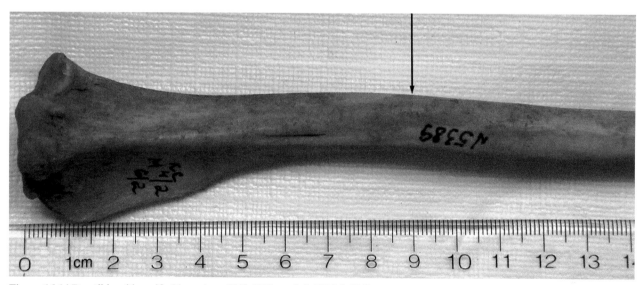

Figure 16.14 Dog tibia with ossified hematoma (443-17 Russell #, 5389 field #).

with stage 2 exostosis (De Cupere et al. 2000). Sometimes termed *spavin*, exostosis in the phalanges has been associated with use in traction (Baker 1984; Bartosiewicz et al. 1997; De Cupere et al. 2000), as has exostosis and arthritis in the hip (Groot 2005). However, with this relatively small sample, the evidence is only suggestive, since similar alterations have been observed in wild cattle (Johannsen 2005). Similarly, two horse first phalanges are arthritic (Figure 16.17), and a second phalanx (Figure 16.18) has exostosis.

Since this is 3 of only 10 first and second phalanges (four first, six second) from the site, it may indicate use in traction or riding. The dogs exhibit osteoarthritis in a metacarpal and a scapula, as well as exostosis in a scapula, three metacarpals/metatarsals, two phalanges, and two cervical vertebrae. These rather abundant signs of joint stress probably mostly reflect the advanced age of many dogs at the site but may also show high activity levels, possibly including carrying loads.

Figure 16.15 Cattle femur with osteoarthritis on caput (668-1 Russell #).

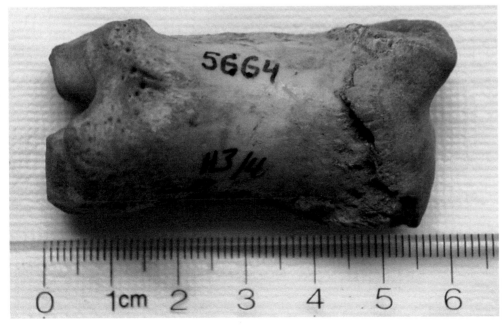

Figure 16.16 Cattle posterior first phalanx with exostosis (418-16 Russell #).

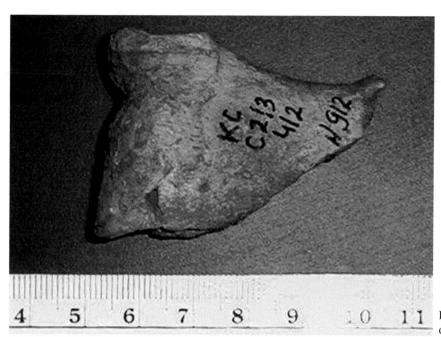

Figure 16.17 Horse first phalanx with osteoarthritis (257-4 Russell #).

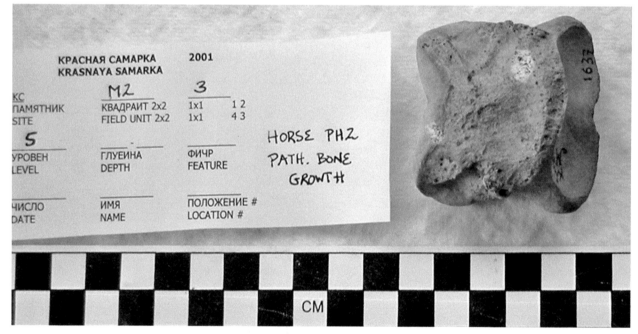

Figure 16.18 Horse second phalanx with exostosis (781-6 Russell #).

Discussion

We may now draw on the several lines of evidence outlined above to consider the roles played by the major taxa at Krasnosamarskoe. As discussed in Chapter 15, the sheep/goat mortality profile suggests that wool production was one reason for keeping them. The butchery and fragmentation of the remains show that they were also eaten. This consumption seems to have occurred in a somewhat different context from the cattle and dogs, however. Caprine remains are more common outside the structure than in it. In contrast to the dogs and, in the upper levels of the structure, cattle, meaty remains of sheep/goat are underrepresented inside the structure compared to outside. Their heads may have been taken inside the structure, however.

The deposits inside the structure do not necessarily relate directly to its use; rather, they appear to include both pre- and postconsumption animal remains that were gathered up and dumped there. The two instances of refitting unfused epiphyses separated during cooking but deposited together suggest considerable integrity to at least some of these deposits. The waste from all phases of particular events was apparently gathered up for disposal. These events are likely to have been feasts (large-scale meals), as the large amount of waste generated is more bothersome than that from daily meals (Davenport 1986). The lower levels of gnawing and digestion inside the structure also indicate that material was collected relatively quickly for deposition inside, while dogs maintained greater access to outdoor food remains. In addition to the nuisance value of the large amounts of waste generated by a feast, remains of ceremonial meals may retain power that needs to be contained or that can be harnessed to animate or consecrate a place (Zedeño 2013).

Thus, the lower quantities of caprine material inside the structure suggest that they were not favored for feasting but may have been consumed more often in smaller-scale, daily meals that were disposed of more casually. It is unclear why their heads were brought indoors; they were fragmented and show no signs of being displayed or specially deposited. The low levels of roasting and lack of stylized chopping also indicate that sheep/goat played a lesser role in feasting and ritual. Their wool, however, was no doubt highly valued; textiles are often prized objects of exchange.

While a family can consume a sheep or goat on its own, cattle are too large for a few people to consume before the meat spoils. Cattle are therefore more likely to be preserved for storage, shared out, or consumed in feasting contexts. In addition, domestic cattle generally hold higher value than sheep and goats. Not only do they provide more meat (and potentially milk), but they also may be prized for their labor and frequently serve as key units of wealth for many transactions (Russell 1998). There are signs that they were consumed in feasts at Krasnosamarskoe. Cattle are more common in the lower levels of the structure than outside or the upper levels, and cattle remains show traces of roasting at a rate second only to dogs; both these are likely indications of use in feasting. Two finds of articulating cattle pieces cooked separately but deposited together also suggest the sort of collection of pre- and postconsumption waste for careful deposition that is likely to mark feasting events.

As discussed in Chapter 15, the cattle mortality profile, if it accurately reflects culling practices (i.e., if the Krasnosamarskoe assemblage is a representative sample of all cattle slaughtered from the herd), suggests use for meat (juveniles) and perhaps traction (adults). It is also possible

that dairy was a major factor, if the presence of calves was necessary to stimulate let-down, so that calves were slaughtered at the end of lactation rather than the beginning (Gillis et al. 2013; McCormick 1992). The use of cattle in feasting, and thus potentially in a ritual context, however, implies that there may also have been selection of particular age and sex (and color, etc.) categories. If cattle functioned as wealth, there would also be a motivation to keep as many as possible to adulthood to increase the herd. Pathological specimens suggest that some cattle may have been used in traction, which would both encourage retention of adult males and add value.

The frequency and treatment of dogs stand out as unusual both in comparison to other sites and in comparison to other taxa at Krasnosamarskoe. By our count, they are the most frequent taxon; Kosintsev's (Chapter 15) calculations put them in a close second to cattle. They receive different treatment, with the highest incidence of roasting and the peculiar segmentation of many of their skulls. Their mortality profile is heavily skewed to old adults, in contrast to usual dog mortality patterns and to other taxa.

Dogs can play a remarkably broad range of roles in human society (Russell 2012): food, pet, beast of burden, hunting or herding aid, and many others. There is every indication that most or all dogs at Krasnosamarskoe ended their lives as food, many of them in a ritual context. The presence of gnawed and digested bones on the site shows that dogs lived there, but the levels are quite low, which stands in contrast to the extraordinary proportion of dog remains. It is therefore likely that many of these dogs spent most of their lives elsewhere. This makes their use in hunting a possibility despite the very low levels of wild fauna at Krasnosamarskoe, although many other functions are equally plausible. Traumatic injuries during life are few and trauma to the head absent, in contrast to many ancient dog assemblages (Bartelle et al. 2010; Binois et al. 2013; Lawler et al. 2013; Park 1987; Russell 1993); this indicates that they were well treated and perhaps argues against extensive use in large game hunting or warfare. Treasured hunting dogs are often treated as valued persons and may receive burial treatment similar to humans (Bulmer 1976; Koster 2009; Lupo 2011; White 1972); we do not see any dogs treated that way at Krasnosamarskoe. Specialized herding dogs that help control the flock are a late development, starting in the Middle Ages (Planhol 1969). But dogs may have been used much earlier to help guard the flocks from predators such as wolves, as well as to guard human houses and settlements. In a pastoral society such as Krasnosamarskoe, this is quite likely but certainly would not require more dogs than sheep.

If dogs were raised for their meat, we would expect a mortality profile dominated by younger animals (Powers and Powers 1984; Wing 1978). The Krasnosamarskoe dogs lived full lives before they were eaten, shown by the tooth sectioning study (Chapter 14) as well as our rough age stage analysis. Many of them, at least, were consumed in a ritual context, as indicated by the concentration of dog bones in general and meaty parts in particular inside the structure, the high rate of roasting, and the careful segmentation of many of their skulls. The unusual tooth wear that many exhibit, together with the low rates of gnawing and digestion in the Krasnosamarskoe animal bone assemblage, suggests that they did not feed themselves by scavenging waste around the camp. Rather, they may have been kept confined and fed a special diet high in ground plant foods for a considerable period before their slaughter—to fatten them or perhaps to purify them.

The whole dog was eaten, but special attention was given to the head, which was often roasted and then carefully chopped into fairly small, more or less standardized portions. These portions would have had very little flesh. This focus on the head suggests a notion of a soul or essence of the animal lodged there; its careful division would permit many of those present to partake of this essence. Tooth sectioning (Chapter 14) indicates that most dogs died in winter. Possibly this is because their skins were sought and the fur would be in the best condition at this time, but the ritualized context of consumption, special diet, and narrow season imply that dogs were sacrificed and consumed in a particular ceremony. The single horse maxilla with similar chopping may mean that horses were sometimes treated the same way, but we do not see the rest of the body consumed as dogs were. At least one wolf was also treated in the same way as the dogs (although with no indication of special diet). This may show that the special significance of dogs for this ceremony rested in their being fierce and carnivorous or in being a species that was not normally eaten, making this occasion powerful in its transgression. The sharing of substance implied by the skull segmentation would permit all participants to absorb this power. If dogs were not ordinarily eaten, their meat is likely to have been regarded with considerable disgust (Whitehead 2000); recognizable pieces of the skull would be particularly evocative. These powerful emotions would amplify the experience of the ceremony.

Dogs are often seen as liminal creatures: on the border between human and animal, wild and domestic, and life and death (Gottlieb 1986; Leach 1964; Mason and Snyder 2006; Ojoade 1990; Schwabe 1994; Sharp 1976; Tambiah

1969; Trantalidou 2006). Their consumption thus mediates among opposed spheres. In Native American groups on the North American Great Plains, warriors consumed dogs at special ceremonies. "Dog killing and eating was then another means of ritual mediation between the 'craziness' of warriors and the normal social conduct. As a wild animal that overcomes its fear of fire acquires power over it, so the fierce warrior who manages to control his own destructive powers can conform to the ideal behavior pattern enforced by the social ethics of his own society" (Comba 1991:47).

Winter would be an odd time to reserve for burials in the nearby kurgans, since the ground would be frozen. But the presence of the ancestors may have been important to the sanctity of the ceremony. While there is a particular concentration in Level 6, dog bones are found in large numbers throughout the sequence, with roasted and chopped dog bones through most of it. Thus, this was not a single event but one repeated in multiple years.

Conclusion

With only a part of the settlement accessible for excavation, it is unclear whether Krasnosamarskoe as a whole was a special-purpose settlement or whether the structure we excavated was associated with special ceremonies in an otherwise residential site. The inside/outside distinctions indicate that sheep and goats figured in more ordinary meals, while cattle were more often consumed at feasts. In addition, special seasonal ceremonies featured the sacrifice and ritualized consumption of dogs. The seasonal restriction and particular attention to carefully dividing the head suggest a powerfully emotive experience centered on the sharing of normally taboo substance.

Another pattern that is difficult to interpret with only one structure is the apparent movement of hindlimbs out of the area excavated. This phenomenon is seen in all the domestic taxa except the dog (or only weakly). This consistent deficit suggests that hindlimbs may have been owed to a leader or person of special status either at Krasnosamarskoe or elsewhere.

While the flooding of part of the site impedes our full understanding, the animal remains at Krasnosamarskoe clearly show that this settlement hosted not only feasts that featured primarily cattle but also periodic winter ceremonies to which dogs from a larger area were brought for sacrifice and ritual consumption, possibly after a period of captive feeding. The participants also likely came from beyond Krasnosamarskoe itself, to commune with the ancestors buried in the kurgans and join in intense ceremonies.

Addendum: Area Y Fauna

Area Y to the south of the main excavations yielded a low density of animal bone (124 specimens). The surface condition of the bone varies among the deposits and in some cases is quite variable within an excavation unit, suggesting redeposition of material from multiple sources. Some material was quite rapidly buried, most seems to have been buried after a brief period of exposure, and some was quite weathered.

Only 28 specimens are identifiable beyond size categories; one of these is an intact marmot tibia that may be intrusive, although it does not appear very recent. A few smaller rodent bones are likely intrusive. Otherwise, the identified taxa are cattle, sheep, goat, and dog (Table 16.5). The two dog specimens are a phalanx and a skull fragment; the body part representation for other taxa appears fairly evenly distributed through the body, given the small sample. The bones are processed and appear to be postconsumption discard.

With such a small sample size, we should be cautious in interpretation. Nevertheless, it is interesting that sheep/goat seem somewhat more frequent here than elsewhere on site and dog much less so. We do not see any of the careful chopping on these remains, which appear to derive from daily meals.

Table 16.5 Identified Macro-Mammalian Bones from Area Y by Number of Identified Specimens (NISP) and Diagnostic Zones (DZ)

Taxon	NISP	NISP (Percent)	DZ	DZ (Percent)
Sheep/goat (*Ovis/Capra*)	13	48.1	2.5	53.2
Cattle (*Bos taurus*)	12	44.4	2.0	42.6
Dog (*Canis familiaris*)	2	7.4	.2	4.3
Total	27		4.7	

Note

All figures and tables in this chapter were prepared by N. Russell except figures 16.1, 3, 5 (top photo), 8, 15, and 18, which were prepared by D. Brown.

References

Baker, John R.
1984   The Study of Animal Diseases with Regard to Agricultural Practices and Man's Attitudes to His Animals. In *Animals and Archaeology: 4. Husbandry in Europe*, edited by C. Grigson and J. Clutton-Brock, pp. 253–257. British Archaeological Reports, International Series, Oxford.

Bartelle, Barney G., René L. Vellanoweth, Elizabeth S. Netherton, Nicholas W. Poister, William E. Kendig, Amira F. Ainis, Ryan J. Glenn, Johanna V. Marty, Lisa Thomas-Barnett, and Steven J. Schwartz
2010   Trauma and Pathology of a Buried Dog from San Nicolas Island, California, U.S.A. *Journal of Archaeological Science* 37(11):2721–2734.

Bartosiewicz, László
1990   Species Interferences and the Interpretation of Neolithic Animal Exploitation. *Acta Archaeologica Academiae Scientiarum Hungaricae* 42:287–292.

Bartosiewicz, László, Wim Van Neer, and An Lentacker
1997   *Draught Cattle: Their Osteological Identification and History*. Annales Sciences Zoologiques, No. 281. Musée Royale de l'Afrique Centrale, Tervuren.

Binford, Lewis R.
1981   *Bones: Ancient Men and Modern Myths*. Academic Press, New York.

Binois, Annelise, Christophe Wardius, Pierre Rio, Anne Bridault, and Christophe Petit
2013   A Dog's Life: Multiple Trauma and Potential Abuse in a Medieval Dog from Guimps (Charente, France). *International Journal of Paleopathology* 3(1):39–47.

Bogucki, Peter I.
1982   *Early Neolithic Subsistence and Settlement in the Polish Lowlands*. British Archaeological Reports, International Series, No. 150. British Archaeological Reports, Oxford.

Brewer, Douglas J.
1992   Zooarchaeology: Method, Theory, and Goals. In *Archaeological Method and Theory*, Vol. 4, edited by M. B. Schiffer, pp. 195–244. University of Arizona Press, Tucson.

Bulmer, Ralph
1976   Selectivity in Hunting and in Disposal of Animal Bone by the Kalam of the New Guinea Highlands. In *Problems in Economic and Social Archaeology*, edited by G. d. G. Sieveking, I. H. Longworth, and K. E. Wilson, pp. 169–186. Duckworth, London.

Comba, Enrico
1991   Wolf Warriors and Dog Feasts: Animal Metaphors in Plains Military Societies. *European Review of Native American Studies* 5(2):41–48.

Davenport, William H.

1986   Two Kinds of Value in the Eastern Solomon Islands. In *The Social Life of Things: Commodities in Cultural Perspective*, edited by A. Appadurai, pp. 95–109. Cambridge University Press, Cambridge.

De Cupere, Beatrice, An Lentacker, Wim Van Neer, Marc Waelkens, and Laurent Verslype

2000   Osteological Evidence for the Draught Exploitation of Cattle: First Applications of a New Methodology. *International Journal of Osteoarchaeology* 10(4):286–309.

Dewbury, Adam G., and Nerissa Russell

2007   Relative Frequency of Butchering Cutmarks Produced by Obsidian and Flint: An Experimental Approach. *Journal of Archaeological Science* 34(3):354–357.

Domínguez-Rodrigo, Manuel

2012   Critical Review of the MNI (Minimum Number of Individuals) as a Zooarchaeological Unit of Quantification. *Archaeological and Anthropological Sciences* 4(1):47–59.

Esteban Nadal, Montserrat, Isabel Cáceres, and Philippe Fosse

2010   Characterization of a Current Coprogenic Sample Originated by *Canis lupus* as a Tool for Identifying a Taphonomic Agent. *Journal of Archaeological Science* 37(12):2959–2970.

Gifford-Gonzalez, Diane P.

1989   Ethnographic Analogues for Interpreting Modified Bones: Some Cases from East Africa. In *Bone Modification*, edited by R. Bonnichsen and M. H. Sorg, pp. 179–246. Center for the Study of the First Americans, Orono, Maine.

Gillis, Rosalind, Stéphanie Bréhard, Adrian Bălășescu, Joël Ughetto-Monfrin, Dragomir N. Popovici, Jean-Denis Vigne, and Marie Balasse

2013   Sophisticated Cattle Dairy Husbandry at Bordușani-Popină (Romania, Fifth Millennium BC): The Evidence from Complementary Analysis of Mortality Profiles and Stable Isotopes. *World Archaeology* 45(3):447–472.

Gottlieb, Alma

1986   Dog: Ally or Traitor? Mythology, Cosmology, and Society among the Beng of Ivory Coast. *American Ethnologist* 13(3):477–488.

Grayson, Donald K.

1978   Minimum Numbers and Sample Size in Vertebrate Faunal Analysis. *American Antiquity* 43(1):53–65.

Groot, Maaike

2005   Palaeopathological Evidence for Draught Cattle on a Roman Site in the Netherlands. In *Diet and Health in Past Animal Populations: Current Research and Future Directions*, edited by J. J. Davies, M. Fabiš, I. L. Mainland, M. P. Richards, and R. M. Thomas, pp. 52–57. Oxbow, Oxford.

Horwitz, Liora R. K.

1990   The Origin of Partially Digested Bones Recovered from Archaeological Contexts in Israel. *Paléorient* 16(1):97–106.

Johannsen, Niels N.

2005   Palaeopathology and Neolithic Cattle Traction: Methodological Issues and Archaeological Perspectives. In *Diet and Health in Past Animal Populations: Current Research and Future Directions*, edited by J. J. Davies, M. Fabiš, I. L. Mainland, M. P. Richards, and R. M. Thomas, pp. 39–51. Oxbow, Oxford.

Koster, Jeremy M.

2009   Hunting Dogs in the Lowland Neotropics. *Journal of Anthropological Research* 65(4):575–610.

Lawler, Dennis F., D. A. Rubin, Richard H. Evans, C. F. Hildebolt, K. E. Smith, Christopher C. Widga, T. J. Martin, M. Siegel, Jill E. Sackman, G. K. Smith, and T. K. Patel

2013   Differential Diagnosis of an Unusual Shoulder Articular Lesion in an Ancient Domestic Dog (*Canis lupus familiaris* L., 1758). *International Journal of Paleopathology* 3(4):282–287.

Leach, Edmund R.

1964   Anthropological Aspects of language: Animal Categories and Verbal Abuse. In *New Directions in the Study of Language*, edited by E. H. Lenneberg, pp. 23–63. MIT Press, Cambridge, Massachusetts.

Lévi-Strauss, Claude

1965   Le triangle culinaire. *L'Arc* 26:19–29.

Lupo, Karen D.

2011   A Dog Is for Hunting. In *Ethnozooarchaeology: The Present and Past of Human-Animal Relationships*, edited by U. Albarella and A. Trentacoste, pp. 4–12. Oxbow, Oxford.

Lyman, R. Lee

2008   *Quantitative Paleozoology*. Cambridge University Press, Cambridge.

Mason, Michael A., and Lynn M. Snyder

2006   What Do Dogs Mean? What Do Dogs Do? Symbolism, Instrumentality, and Ritual in Afro-Cuban Religion. In *Dogs and People in Social, Working, Economic or Symbolic Interaction*, edited by L. M. Snyder and E. A. Moore, pp. 49–61. Oxbow, Oxford.

McCormick, Finbar

1992   Early Faunal Evidence for Dairying. *Oxford Journal of Archaeology* 11(2):201–209.

Meadow, Richard H.

1999   Animal Remains—Quantification. In *Archaeological Method and Theory: An Encyclopedia*, edited by L. Ellis. Garland, New York.

Miles, A. E. W., and Caroline Grigson
1990   *Colyer's Variations and Diseases of the Teeth of Animals.* Cambridge University Press, Cambridge.

O'Connor, Terence P.
2001   Animal Bone Quantification. In *Handbook of Archaeological Sciences*, edited by D. R. Brothwell and A. M. Pollard, pp. 703–710. John Wiley & Sons, London.

Ojoade, J. Olowo
1990   Nigerian Cultural Attitudes to the Dog. In *Signifying Animals: Human Meaning in the Natural World*, edited by R. Willis, pp. 215–221. Unwin Hyman, London.

Park, Robert W.
1987   Dog Remains from Devon Island, N.W.T.: Archaeological and Osteological Evidence for Domestic Dog Use in the Thule Culture. *Arctic* 40(3):184–190.

Payne, Sebastian, and Patrick J. Munson
1985   Ruby and How Many Squirrels? The Destruction of Bones by Dogs. In *Palaeobiological Investigations: Research Design, Methods and Data Analysis*, edited by N. R. J. Fieller, D. D. Gilbertson, and N. G. A. Ralph, pp. 31–39. British Archaeological Reports, International Series, Oxford.

Planhol, Xavier de
1969   Le chien de berger: Développement et signification géographique d'une technique pastorale. *Bulletin de l'Association des Géographes Français* 370:355–368.

Powers, William K., and Marla M. N. Powers
1984   Metaphysical Aspects of an Oglala Food System. In *Food in the Social Order: Studies of Food and Festivities in Three American Communities*, edited by M. Douglas, pp. 40–96. Russell Sage Foundation, New York.

Russell, Nerissa
1993   Hunting, Herding and Feasting: Human Use of Animals in Neolithic Southeast Europe. Unpublished Ph.D. dissertation, University of California, Berkeley.

1998   Cattle as Wealth in Neolithic Europe: Where's the Beef? In *The Archaeology of Value: Essays on Prestige and the Processes of Valuation*, edited by D. W. Bailey, pp. 42–54. British Archaeological Reports, International Series. British Archaeological Reports, Oxford.

2012   *Social Zooarchaeology: Humans and Animals in Prehistory.* Cambridge University Press, New York.

Schwabe, Calvin W.
1994   Animals in the Ancient World. In *Animals and Human Society: Changing Perspectives*, edited by A. Manning and J. A. Serpell, pp. 36–58. Routledge, London.

Sharp, Henry S.
1976   Man: Wolf: Woman: Dog. *Arctic Anthropology* 13:25–34.

Solomon, Su, and Bruno David
1990   Middle Range Theory and Actualistic Studies: Bones and Dingoes in Australian Archaeology. In *Problem Solving in Taphonomy: Archaeological and Palaeontological Studies from Europe, Africa and Oceania*, edited by S. Solomon, I. Davidson, and D. Watson, pp. 233–255. University of Queensland Anthropology Museum, Tempus, St. Lucia.

Tambiah, Stanley J.
1969   Animals Are Good to Think and Good to Prohibit. *Ethnology* 8:423–459.

Trantalidou, Katerina
2006   Companions from the Oldest Times: Dogs in Ancient Greek Literature, Iconography and Osteological Testimony. In *Dogs and People in Social, Working, Economic or Symbolic Interaction*, edited by L. M. Snyder and E. A. Moore, pp. 96–120. Oxbow, Oxford.

Twiss, Katheryn C.
2008   Transformations in an Early Agricultural Society: Feasting in the Southern Levantine Pre-Pottery Neolithic. *Journal of Anthropological Archaeology* 27(4):418–442.

Watson, John P. N.
1979   The Estimation of the Relative Frequencies of Mammalian Species: Khirokitia 1972. *Journal of Archaeological Science* 6(2):127–137.

White, Isobel M.
1972   Hunting Dogs at Yalata. *Mankind* 8(3):201–205.

Whitehead, Harriet
2000   *Food Rules: Hunting, Sharing, and Tabooing Game in Papua New Guinea.* University of Michigan Press, Ann Arbor.

Wing, Elizabeth S.
1978   Use of Dogs for Food: An Adaptation to the Coastal Environment. In *Prehistoric Coastal Adaptations: The Economy and Ecology of Maritime Middle America*, edited by B. L. Stark and B. Voorhies, pp. 29–41. Academic Press, New York.

Zedeño, María Nieves
2013   Methodological and Analytical Challenges in Relational Archaeologies: A View from the Hunting Ground. In *Relational Archaeologies: Humans, Animals, Things*, edited by C. Watts, pp. 117–134. Routledge, London.

Chapter 17

The Bronze Age Kurgan Cemetery at Krasnosamarskoe IV

Pavel F. Kuznetsov • Oleg D. Mochalov • David W. Anthony

The Samara River valley contains more Bronze Age kurgans than any other tributary of the Volga in the middle Volga region. Kurgan cemeteries were constructed in this region continuously throughout the Bronze Age for two and a half thousand years, from the start of the Early Bronze Age (EBA), around 3300 BC, to the end of the Final Bronze Age (FBA), around 800 BC. Many years of excavations have shown that there was a definite preference in the positioning of Bronze Age kurgan groups. Topographically, the earlier kurgans are always situated on the low, level fields of the first terrace above the Samara floodplain and in the floodplain meadows themselves. Two notable clusters of EBA and Middle Bronze Age (MBA) kurgans, built by mobile pastoralists, appear around the villages of Utyevka and Krasnosamarskoe. There are about a hundred kurgans near Utyevka and nearly 50 near Krasnosamarskoe. Both villages are near places where wide marshes and oxbow lakes (abandoned river channels) are found on both sides of the main river channel, which according to geomorphological studies (Chapter 9) probably has not moved significantly since the Bronze Age. According to the data we have acquired, in the Krasnosamarskoe region (Figure 17.1), at least six kurgan cemeteries and 29 kurgans are at least partly dated by radiocarbon combined with typological assessment. All the Krasnosamarskoe kurgans are situated north of the village, on the first floodplain terrace, near the northeastern shores of oxbow lakes and marshes. Artificial fishponds

today fill the old oxbow lake near the cemetery designated Krasnosamarskoe IV, excavated by the Samara Valley Project (SVP) joint Russian-American team in 1999.

Krasnosamarskoe IV was mapped during a survey by Vasiliev and Kuznetsov in 1987 (Vasiliev and Kuznetsov 1988). They discovered four cemeteries, each containing three to six kurgans spaced 30 to 70 m apart, separated from each other by distances of 1.5 to 2 km between cemeteries, designated Krasnosamarskoe I through IV, numbered from south to north. Krasnosamarskoe I was a cluster of four kurgans, II also contained four kurgans, III had six kurgans, and IV, the northernmost, originally was designated as containing three kurgans. After the SVP began, additional kurgans were recognized within 1 km of the central three and were added to Krasnosamarskoe IV (Figure 17.2). The original three kurgans now compose the northern kurgan group, and the southern cluster of four kurgans, located 570 m to the south, on the opposite side of a seasonal stream, constitutes the southern group within Krasnosamarskoe IV. All seven kurgans in the two clusters are aligned on the same northwest-southeast axis. The northern cluster of three kurgans, situated near the Krasnosamarskoe settlement, was excavated in its entirety in 1999 as a part of the SVP. The southern group was partly investigated in the years after the SVP by Kuznetsov and Mochalov. The northern and southern kurgan groups are sufficiently far apart so that they "feel" separate from each other, as if they occupy different places in the landscape.

444 Pavel F. Kuznetsov • Oleg D. Mochalov • David W. Anthony

Figure 17.1 Krasnosamarskoe kurgan cemeteries I to VI. (Google Earth, Image © 2012 GeoEye)

Indeed, the southern group of kurgans was not noticed in 1987 or 1995, when archaeologists made multiple visits to map and photograph the northern group. The southern group was obscured and damaged by a modern cattle pen, but even without that, it occupied a separate space.

After the SVP concluded, one additional kurgan cemetery and a large isolated kurgan located north and northwest of Krasnosamarskoe IV were given numbers. These are designated Krasnosamarskoe V and VI.

The oldest kurgans in two of these six cemeteries were identified in archaeological excavations directed by Vasiliev and Kuznetsov (1988). At Krasnosamarskoe I and III, respectively about 4.5 and 1.5 km southeast

of Krasnosamarskoe IV, both kurgan groups were constructed in the MBA by the Poltavka culture. Their modest graves contained Poltavka pottery, a stone pestle, a bifacial flint tool, a copper awl, and a bone ring. The broad marshes and flat steppe pastures in this part of the Samara Valley seem to have been favored locations for Poltavka pastoral groups.

The excavations at Krasnosamarskoe IV in 1999 demonstrated that the three kurgans in the northern cluster (Figure 17.3) also were erected by Poltavka pastoralists. Radiocarbon dates were obtained for seven MBA graves in these three kurgans (Table 2.1). Overlapping dates for the three central graves show that all three kurgans were

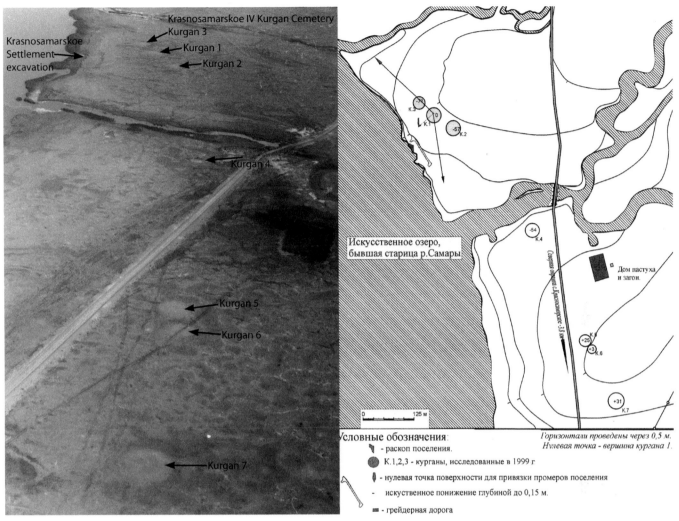

Figure 17.2 Left: Aerial photo (by Boris Aguzarov) Krasnosamarskoe (KS) IV Kurgans 1 to 7 and settlement location. Right: Contour drawing of Krasnosamarskoe IV site.

raised in a surprisingly limited, brief period of activity at the earliest EBA/MBA transition around 2900 to 2800 BC. They were between 20 and 40 m in diameter, and according to the soil expert I. V. Ivanov, the original height of all three kurgans was 2 to 3 m. Although the other Krasnosamarskoe kurgan cemeteries are not dated by radiocarbon, it would seem from these early dates at Krasnosamarskoe IV that I to III probably were created later in the MBA. Modest funerary gifts, typical of the Poltavka culture, were contained in the MBA graves in Krasnosamarskoe IV north.

The central graves in all of the Poltavka cemeteries around Krasnosamarskoe shared common traits. They were dug into clay with steps or ledges, wide at the top, and narrowing leading down to the grave floor. The bottom of the burial pit and parts of the body were covered with red ochre. At Krasnosamarskoe IV, the deepest graves, including the central Poltavka graves in all three kurgans,

were flooded by the rising water table associated with the construction of fishponds nearby. For this reason, some of the grave floor deposits of ochre or organic materials were dissolved in water.

All three kurgans at Krasnosamarskoe IV north were surrounded by deep circular ditches, dug into the clay subsoil (*materik*). The ditches were not continuous but segmented, interrupted by pathways allowing passage into the area where the grave was dug in the center, and where the mound was raised. In the fill of the ditches, there were ceramic sherds and small bones or isolated teeth of sheep, horse, and cattle, probably the remains of sacrificial meals associated with the funeral of the person buried in the central grave. According to zoological studies (Kosintsev and Roslyakova 1999:50), sheep-goat bones predominate in these ditch deposits generally in the region. It is thought that generally, these ceremonies occurred after the kurgan

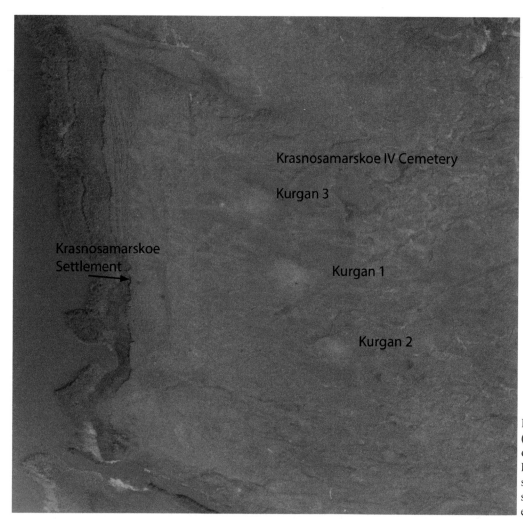

Figure 17.3 Aerial photo (by Boris Aguzarov) of Krasnosamarskoe Kurgans 1 to 3 and settlement site taken spring 1999, just before excavations began.

was raised. Erosion into the ditch and reconstruction show that the Krasnosamarskoe IV kurgans were revisited, and one kurgan was later heightened.

Kurgan 3 was reused as a cemetery in the LBA by a Srubnaya population, probably derived from the Srubnaya settlement 65 m to the south. According to eight radiocarbon dates from LBA graves, the Srubnaya cemetery was used between 1900 and 1600 BC, similar to the dating of the settlement but perhaps continuing for a brief period after the settlement was abandoned. During the LBA, 27 individuals were buried in 22 graves located on the northern side of Kurgan 3, the opposite side from the settlement. After the LBA, these three kurgans became a silent monument, visible to all who lived in the area, but no additional human graves were placed there.

Method of Excavation

All three kurgans in the northern group were excavated in 6 weeks during the summer of 1999. The large volume of soil in a kurgan requires that a bulldozer is used to cut strips or trenches across the mound, leaving a baulk of 1 m width standing between each excavated trench (Figure 17.4). The largest kurgan, Kurgan 1, required five bulldozer strips or trenches. For each trench, the bulldozer operator set his blade to remove between 15 and 20 cm of soil and proceeded to cut a path slowly across the mound. Archaeologists followed the bulldozer on foot, watching for features or graves. When a grave was revealed, the bulldozer stopped and the grave was excavated by hand. When the bulldozer reached the ancient surface beneath the mound, a team of archaeologists continued to excavate by hand, exposing the ditch and any graves dug into the subsoil. After all graves and ditches were excavated, measured, and drawn, the profiles exposed in the baulks were measured, drawn, and photographed, and finally the baulks were taken down by hand. Occasionally, small bundled graves were found in the baulks. These methods were standard for kurgan excavations in Russia.

Figure 17.4 Top: Bulldozer beginning excavation of Kurgan 1. Bottom: Bulldozer-exposed strips.

MBA Kurgans and Graves at Krasnosamarskoe IV

Kurgan 1 (Figure 17.5) was the largest of the three in this cemetery. Its preserved height was 1.1 m and its diameter 40 m. The kurgan was entirely excavated. It contained four graves, all dated to the MBA: the central grave of an adult female (3), a peripheral grave of an infant dug into the original surface at the same time as the central grave (4), and the grave of an adult male in the upper part of the mound over the central grave (1), again dated to the same time as the central grave, all around 2800 BC. An additional grave (2) was inserted into the upper part of the mound many centuries afterward, around 2300 BC, and perhaps at this time the original mound was repaired, the ditch was cleared, and soil was added to the mound. The ditch around the mound contained occasional sheep bones, horse teeth, a fragment of a flat stone mortar, MBA ceramic sherds, and a flint scraper (Figure 17.6).

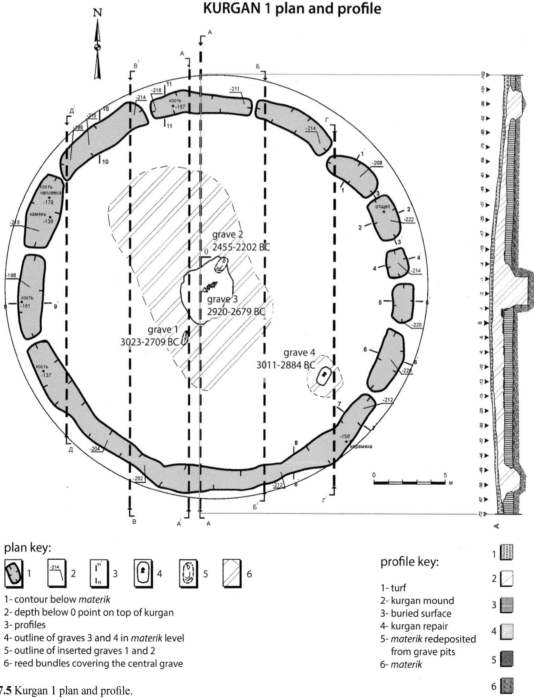

KURGAN 1 plan and profile

grave 2
2455-2202 BC

grave 3
2920-2679 BC

grave 1
3023-2709 BC

grave 4
3011-2884 BC

plan key:

1- contour below *materik*
2- depth below 0 point on top of kurgan
3- profiles
4- outline of graves 3 and 4 in *materik* level
5- outline of inserted graves 1 and 2
6- reed bundles covering the central grave

profile key:

1- turf
2- kurgan mound
3- buried surface
4- kurgan repair
5- *materik* redeposited
   from grave pits
6- *materik*

Figure 17.5 Kurgan 1 plan and profile.

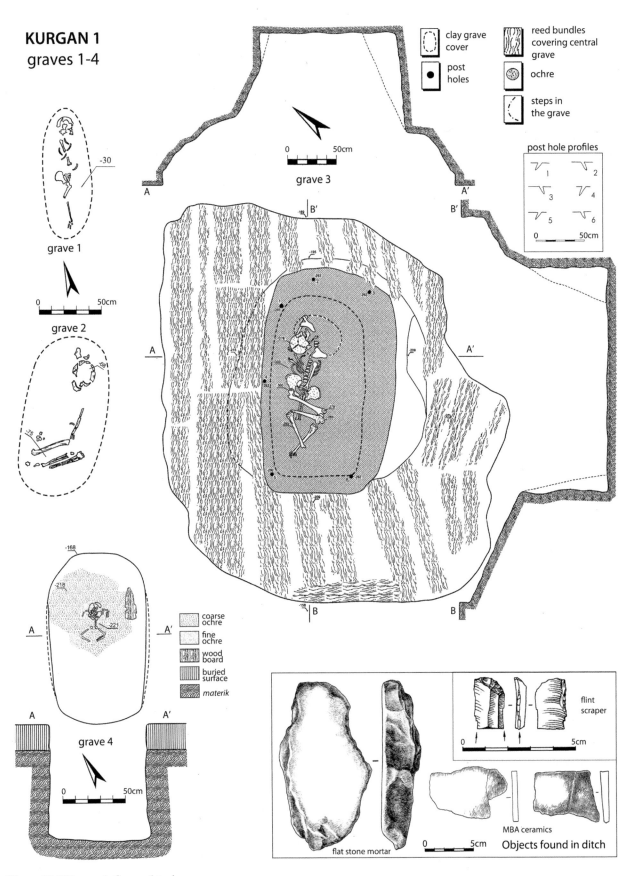

Figure 17.6 Kurgan 1, Graves 1 to 4.

Grave 3 was the central grave under Kurgan 1, designated K1/3 (Figure 17.7). A large rectangular step or depression was dug about 30 cm deep into the original ground surface around the grave opening, and the grave covering or roof was laid down over the grave inside this rectangular ledge. The covering or roof looked from its well-preserved remains to be composed of bundles of reeds, packed together side-by-side—perhaps the reed bundles were tied together, or perhaps they were just laid beside each other. The length of each bundle varied from 0.5 to 2.21 m, and the diameter of each bundle varied from 10 to 25 cm. The reed bundles were packed together side-by-side, in the shape of a large rectangle (4.1 × 3.55 m) covering the pit and the ledge dug into the ground around it. The eventual collapse of the section of this organic grave cover that composed the roof over the grave was clearly seen in the pit profile. The reed bundles were laid parallel to the long sides of the burial pit. On the southern part of the reed roof was a circular spot of red ochre 3.5 cm in diameter, with intense red spots around it 1 cm in diameter. Under the layer of reed bundles was a layer of pure yellow clay about 10 to 15 cm thick, very visible below the remains of the reeds at the grave edge, as well as within the grave, where the clay and reed cover collapsed against the walls of the grave pit. Probably the clay was originally applied to a wooden grave cover, but its remains were not separable from the grave fill.

The central Grave 3 was aligned on a northeast-southwest axis. The grave pit was oval in shape, 3.98 × 3.07 m at the top and 2.29 × 1.74 m at the bottom. It was dug to a maximum depth of 1.55 m beneath the ancient ground surface. Toward the bottom of the pit, there were wide inclined steps that reduced the size of the floor. The floor contained six holes for wooden posts, seen at a depth of 1.47 m below the old surface along the pit edges. Three posts were located along the northwest wall, two along the east wall, and one in the northeast corner. The posts were set 3 to 4 cm deep in the clay and were 8 to 10 cm in diameter. The posts supported the grave pit cover.

Figure 17.7 Kurgan 1, Grave 3, central grave, MBA Poltavka culture, showing remains of bundled reed cover above the grave. The raised water table under the nearby manmade fishpond flooded the floors of the deepest graves (photo by Christopher Gette).

The skeleton was that of a robust adult female, 17 to 20 years old, about 160 cm in height, positioned on her back, lying on a mat of grass or reeds. Her head was oriented to the northeast. The skull was shifted to the right side of the chest, neck up. The reason for this shift was a ledge of artificial clay with a diameter 45.5 × 55 cm in plan and 4.3 cm high—probably a kind of clay pillow for the elevation of the head and shoulders. Her legs were bent at the knees and placed vertically but then fell upon each other to the left. Her forearms might have been tucked under her hips, possibly tightly swaddled. The skull, pelvis, and knees were thickly painted with red ochre.

Under the spine was a layer of organic matter covering an area up to 1.52 cm over the bottom of the pit, probably rotted grass, black in color, with a thickness of 0.2 to 0.5 cm. Under that, the bottom of the pit was coated with specially brought clay, up to 5 cm thick. No artifacts accompanied the burial. A radiocarbon date on bone from this burial (AA37033, 4241 ± 70 BP) calibrated to 2920 to 2679 BC, an early MBA date.

Grave 4 (Figure 17.6), a peripheral grave associated with central Grave 3, contained an infant, possibly newborn, heavily covered with dense red ochre. The infant, possibly the child of the 17-to 20-year-old female in the central grave, was oriented northeast, laid on its back, with its knees raised, like the female in Grave 3, but later its knees collapsed apart. Its elbows were spread apart, parallel with its shoulders, and its hands pointed down at right angles. A fragment of burned wood 22 cm long and 4 to 10 cm wide was placed on the grave floor beside the infant, possibly a cradle board. The infant grave was located 11.8 m southeast of the central grave and was dug to a depth of 70 cm beneath the ancient surface. The pit was wider at the bottom than at the top, unlike the central grave pit.

Grave 1 (Figure 17.6) was located in the upper part of the mound, a few meters south of the mound center. A shallow grave, subject to weathering, was only partly preserved. It contained the fragmentary bones of a male aged 30 to 40 years. A radiocarbon date (AA 37031, 4284 ± 79 BP) gave a calibrated range of 3023 to 2709 BC, probably contemporary with K1/3 and K1/4, about 2800 BC.

Grave 2 (Figure 17.6), a male aged 35 to 45 years, was added to the mound much later. It was placed near the center of the mound, in an ovoid pit inserted into the mound soil. It was difficult to see how the body was arranged as most of the bones were decayed, but it might have been placed in a contracted position, unlike the older graves. A radiocarbon date (AA37032, 3837 ± 62 BP) calibrated to 2455 to 2202 BC, or about 2300 BC, perhaps 500 years after the initial construction of the kurgan, near the end of the MBA. No artifacts were found.

Kurgan 2 (Figures 17.8, 17.9, 17.10)

Kurgan 2 was 35 m in diameter and was preserved to a height of 67 cm (Figure 17.8). It had an unusual subrectangular shape, unlike most EBA or MBA burial mounds, which are almost always circular. The original kurgan was surrounded with a subrectangular ditch. When it subsided, the ditch was filled with eroded mound soil. The rectangular mound shape was preserved after it slumped over the ditch, which was not cleared or redug.

In Kurgan 2, there were three graves, all dated to the MBA (Figure 17.9). The central grave (2) was Poltavka in age and origin, like the central grave of Kurgan 1, but with a simpler construction. Grave 3 was a very interesting and unusual Catacomb grave, dug just outside the ditch of the kurgan. Normally, this kind of grave, typical of the lower Don–North Caucasus steppes, would be considered culturally distinct from Poltavka, but the radiocarbon dates and stratigraphy in Mound 2 suggest that the peripheral Catacomb grave and the central Poltavka grave could have been contemporary. A large sherd of pottery of North Caucasian Novotitorovskaya culture type, distinct from local Poltavka pottery types, was found in the mound fill. The Novotitorovskaya culture was a variant of late Yamnaya limited to the Kuban River region in the North Caucasus steppes, that interacted with the early Catacomb culture in the lower Don-Kalmyk steppes; elements of both cultures appeared in Kurgan 2. Kurgan 2 therefore shows long-distance contacts between local Poltavka and immigrant people from the North Caucasus steppes, 600 km to the south. Grave 1 was a secondary bundle of bones added into the eroded skirt of the mound near the end of the MBA, about 2100 BC.

Grave 2 was the principal grave located under the center of the mound (Figure 17.9). The grave pit was 1.46 m deep beneath the ancient surface. On the ground around the burial pit were traces of the remains of an organic covering, dark gray with a whitish tinge. Organic fibers up to 2 cm thick could be seen in the organic layer, probably the remains of reeds. In this case, they seemed to be reed mats rather than the log-like reed bundles used under Kurgan 1. The reed covering left a substantial organic layer 30 cm deep. The dimensions of the organic grave cover were 2.48 × 2.04 m, smaller than the organic cover in Kurgan 1. Beneath this layer was a second organic layer, dark gray, covering the burial pit, possibly a skin or hide.

The grave pit was oriented northeast-southwest, like the central grave under Kurgan 1. The dimensions at the top were 2.48 × 2.25 m. The walls narrowed toward the bottom, and at a depth of 53 cm beneath the opening, along the north wall, a ledge or step was made, and along the south wall at 62 cm beneath the opening, a matching ledge was

452   Pavel F. Kuznetsov • Oleg D. Mochalov • David W. Anthony

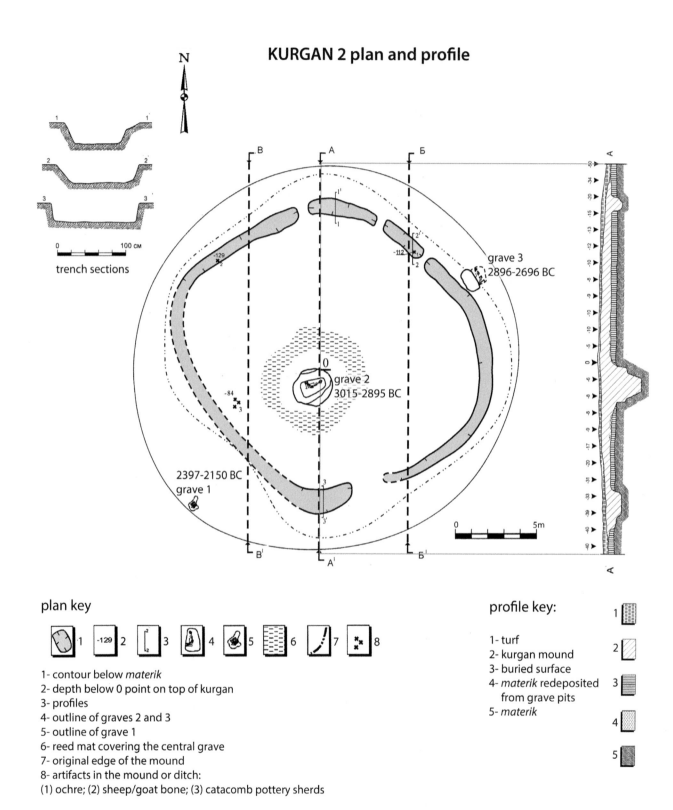

Figure 17.8 Kurgan 2 plan and profile.

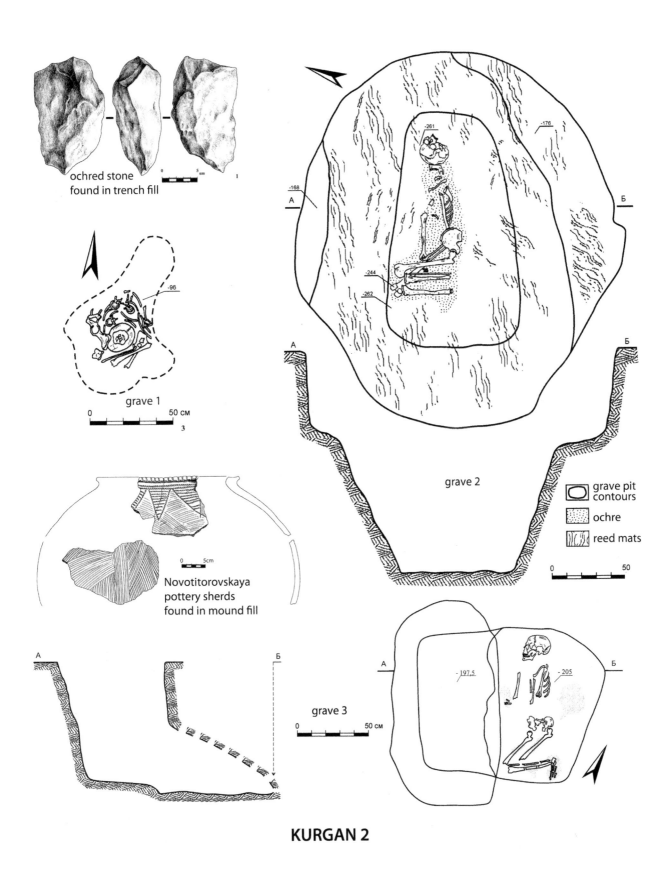

ochred stone
found in trench fill

grave 1

Novotitorovskaya
pottery sherds
found in mound fill

grave 2

grave 3

grave pit contours
ochre
reed mats

KURGAN 2

Figure 17.9 Kurgan 2, Graves 1 to 3.

made. At a depth of 80 cm, just above the grave floor, was a thick organic layer of dark gray, almost black material, possibly part of the original roof. The floor measured 1.56 m in length and between 45 cm and 92 cm in width. Across the bottom of the burial pit were traces of a litter made of black organic material (possibly grass). The litter thickness was about half a centimeter.

On the floor, on the litter, was an adult female 40 to 45 years old, lying on her right side with knees flexed—a different position than the principal grave in Kurgan 1. Her head was oriented to the east-northeast. Her skull was removed and placed upside down on her shoulders, with the mandible removed and placed near the back of the skull. The right arm, bent at the elbow, pointed toward the abdomen, with the wrist under the pelvic bone. The humerus of the left arm was pressed against the ribs. The position of the skeleton suggests that it was buried tightly swaddled, perhaps after partial decomposition of the body and separation of the head. The entire skeleton, except for the skull, was covered with intense red and black ochre. No artifacts were preserved. A radiocarbon date (AA37036, 4327 ± 59) calibrated to a range of 3015 to 2895 BC. Her craniofacial type, as reported by Khokhlov below, was more similar to MBA North Caucasian populations than to Samara MBA populations.

Grave 3 was placed in a Catacomb-style grave, in a side chamber, dug just beyond the ditch around the mound (Figure 17.9, bottom). Catacomb-style graves were typical of the Don–North Caucasus Catacomb culture. Although some Catacomb-style grave pits are found in a few MBA kurgans in the Samara oblast, the occurrence of a Catacomb-style grave is a surprise. The body was contracted on its right side and oriented to the northwest. The deceased was a female, 12 to 15 years old. Her feet were intensely colored with red ochre and her hands also, but less ochre was deposited by the hands. Oddly, her incisors were shovel shaped. No artifacts were placed in the grave chamber, but a pot of North Caucasian Novotitorovskaya culture type was included in the mound fill on the opposite side of the mound from Grave 3 (Figure 17.10c). In the mound fill near this exotic sherd were some bones of a sheep and a stone mortar used to grind red ochre, probably related to the rituals associated with the funeral.

The radiocarbon date from Grave 3 (AA37037, 4207 ± 52 BP) calibrated to 2886 to 2694 BC, just after the single delta range for central Grave 2. However, the North Caucasian–type sherd in the mound fill suggests that a North Caucasian element accompanied the construction of the mound over the central grave, so the statistical separation between their radiocarbon dates is weighed against stratigraphic evidence suggesting that the Catacomb grave might have

accompanied the construction of the mound. Radiocarbon dating of Catacomb and Yamnaya graves in Ukraine showed that the Catacomb culture generally began earlier than most archaeologists had thought, by about 2900 to 3000 BC, and was contemporary with Yamnaya pit-graves for several centuries in the first half of the third millennium BC (Telegin et al. 2003). The date for Grave 3 at Krasnosamarskoe IV makes it a very early Catacomb culture grave but within the range for the earliest Catacomb graves in Ukraine. Grave 3 and the pottery in the mound soil suggest contact and exchange (perhaps even exchange of marriage-aged girls?) between the Samara Valley and the North Caucasian steppes around 2950 to 2750 BC.

Grave 1 was a secondary bundle burial of the disarticulated bones of a male, 17 to 25 years old (Figure 17.10b), placed in the edge of the mound many centuries after the first two graves. The body must have been disarticulated in some other place. For example, the Zoroastrians used well-known Towers of Silence, specially built houses of the dead. Being situated on natural hills, they looked like kurgans. After the tissue was eaten by animals and birds, special priests took the preserved bones and buried them. Something similar might have happened to Grave 1. A radiocarbon date (AA37035, 3820 ± 52 BP) calibrated to 2397 to 2150 BC, perhaps 700 years after the initial two graves. No artifacts were found.

MBA Graves in Kurgan 3 (Figure 17.12)

Kurgan 3 was 27 m in diameter and was preserved to a height of 42 cm. It was entirely excavated. It contained 25 MBA and LBA graves and one sacrificial deposit (Figure 17.11). The MBA kurgan was constructed over Grave 9, the central grave, and a peripheral sacrificial deposit, Grave 8/Sacrificial Deposit 1, created by people of the Poltavka culture.

The MBA usage of Kurgan 3 is dated by radiocarbon to about 2800 BC, contemporary with the central graves in the other two kurgans.

Grave 9 (Figure 17.12) was the central MBA grave under Kurgan 3. It contained an adult male aged 17 to 25 years who seems to have died of a systemic infection that caused thick plaques of periosteal reactive gray woven bone over much of his body, from his mandible to his metatarsals. He was buried contracted on his right side, similar to the pose of the female in the central grave of Kurgan 2, but the Grave 9 male was more strongly contracted. The grave pit was 1.15 m deep beneath the ancient surface. On the ancient surface around the grave opening were the remains of an organic cover, dark gray with a whitish tinge. Reeds up to 2 cm in diameter could be seen in the decayed organic matter, which probably represented reed mats lying on a

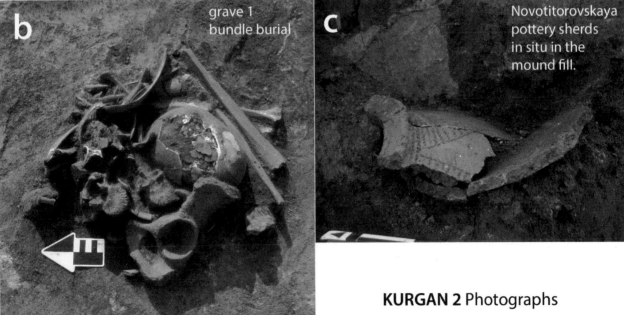

Figure 17.10 Kurgan 2 photographs: (*a*) measuring and mapping square trench around the kurgan; (*b*) Grave 1, a bundle burial (photo by Christopher Gette); (*c*) Novotitorovskaya-type ceramic found in kurgan fill.

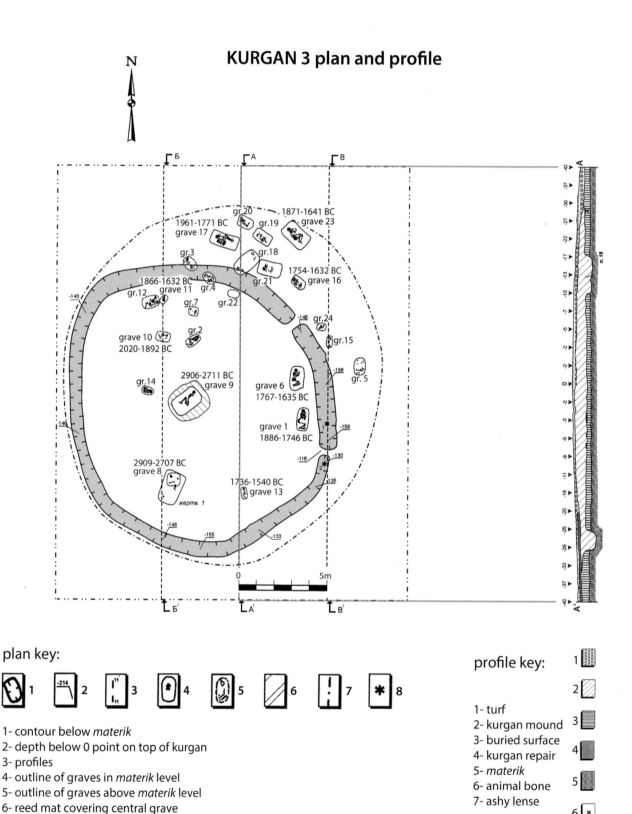

KURGAN 3 plan and profile

plan key:

1- contour below *materik*
2- depth below 0 point on top of kurgan
3- profiles
4- outline of graves in *materik* level
5- outline of graves above *materik* level
6- reed mat covering central grave
7- original edge of mound
8- bones in the bottom of the ditch:
  (1) ram and human; (2) animal rib

profile key:

1- turf
2- kurgan mound
3- buried surface
4- kurgan repair
5- *materik*
6- animal bone
7- ashy lense

Figure 17.11 Kurgan 3 plan and profile.

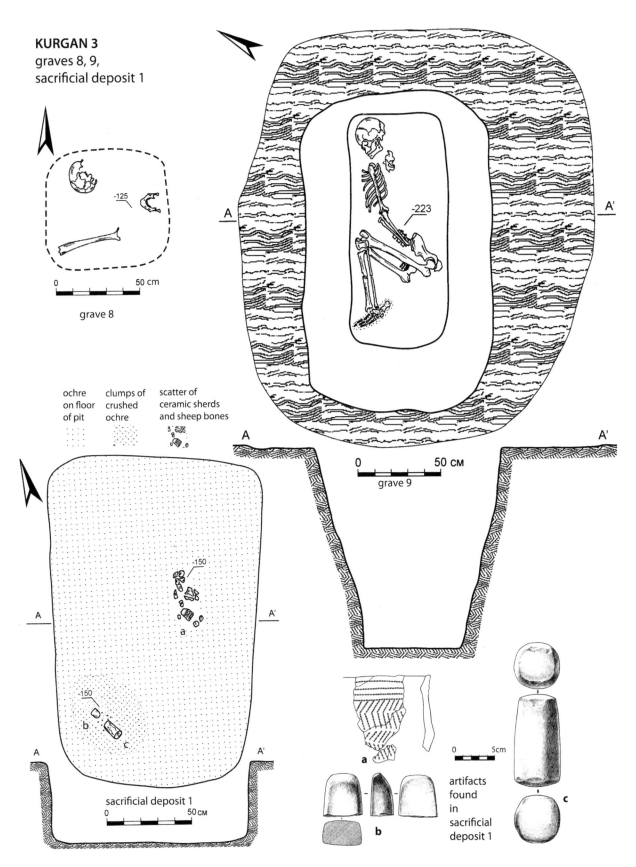

KURGAN 3
graves 8, 9,
sacrificial deposit 1

grave 8

-125

0   50 cm

-223

ochre
on floor
of pit

clumps of
crushed
ochre

scatter of
ceramic sherds
and sheep bones

0   50 см

grave 9

-150

-150

a

b

c

sacrificial deposit 1

0   50 см

a

b

0   5cm

c

artifacts
found
in
sacrificial
deposit 1

Figure 17.12 Kurgan 3, Graves 8, 9 and Sacrificial Deposit 1.

ledge around the burial, forming a rectangular grave cover measuring 2.44 × 2.15 m. The grave pit had rounded corners. The pit sides were aligned northeast-southwest, like all of the central Poltavka grave pits. Around the grave pit were ledges, and the walls sloped toward a narrower bottom. The top of the pit measured 1.87 × 1.15 m; the floor measured 1.37 × 0.59 m. The skeleton was oriented northeast, contracted, with the arms straight against the sides of the body. Judging by the position, the body was tightly swaddled. The feet were evenly covered with red ochre. Under the body was an organic dark gray fibrous layer a few millimeters thick, probably grass. No artifacts were found in the grave. A radiocarbon date (AA37041, 4236 ± 47 BP) calibrated to 2909 to 2711 BC, or about 2800 BC.

Grave 8/Sacrificial Deposit 1 (Figure 17.12) was in a shallow pit dug into the ancient surface and accompanied Grave 9 before the mound was built. Sacrificial Deposit 1, the deepest and first inclusion in this feature, contained fragments of a typical Poltavka pot and two polished stone tools, a cylindrical pestle, and a flat axe-shaped tool, not sharpened, perhaps used as a polisher. Both had traces of use-polish. Probably they were used for grinding ochre. An even layer of red ochre was all over the bottom of the pit. Some bones from a sheep or goat also were included in this deposit. After the animal bones, tools, and the potsherd were placed in the red ochre, the pit was partly filled with dirt. Then, in its upper levels, Grave 8 was created. It was a secondary burial of the skull and femur of an adult male, aged 35 to 45 years. The surfaces of the bones were eroded, perhaps from exposure prior to burial. Apparently, the bones of this person were retrieved from where they were exposed to be buried under Kurgan 3 at Krasnosamarskoe IV, with the sick young man in central Grave 9. A radiocarbon date (AA37040, 4239 ± 49 BP) calibrated to 2909 to 2707 BC, or about 2800 BC, contemporary with the central grave.

Overview of the MBA Cemetery at Krasnosamarskoe IV

The three northern mounds in the Krasnosamarskoe IV kurgan cemetery were created at the beginning of the MBA by mobile pastoralists of the Poltavka culture. The radiocarbon dates for all three MBA central graves largely overlap, suggesting a relatively brief period of mound construction and ritual activity around 2900 to 2700 BC, followed by many centuries with no observable activity at the site.

The brevity of the MBA mortuary activity at Krasnosamarskoe IV is interesting because the three kurgans vary in important details of mortuary ritual and physical type. Kurgan 2 was given an unusual shape, subrectangular rather than circular (Kuznetsov 2003:48). The central

burials in Grave 2 of Kurgan 2 (designated K2/2) and in Grave 9 of Kurgan 3 (K3/9) were posed on their right sides, contracted, but the central burial in K1/3 was posed on her back with knees raised and her head on a clay pillow, an archaic pose typical of the EBA Yamnaya culture.

The adult females buried in the central graves, K1/3 and K2/2, also were unusual. About 80 percent of the central graves in Poltavka kurgans in the region contain adult males (see Chapter 6). The circumstances that permitted a female to be buried in the central grave occurred in 20 percent of EBA/MBA kurgans in the middle Volga region, not an insignificant frequency, but at Krasnosamarskoe, this occurred in two-thirds of the cases. Therefore, it is interesting that the woman (40–45 years) in K2/2 was at first classified as a male because her bones show such thick cross sections and articular surfaces and such high-relief muscle attachments, but her pelvis showed without doubt that this individual was a female, indicating a very strong, robust woman. In K1/3, the woman in the central grave was younger, aged 17 to 20 years, and somewhat less robust but as tall as the woman in K2/2 (about 160 cm) and quite strong. According to Khokhlov, such hyperdeveloped, robust women are found particularly among the females in the Yamnaya-Poltavka osteological series of the EBA-MBA. It seems that not only the appearance but also the behavior of these women were similar to that of a man in terms of muscular activity. Their stature and muscular activity apparently played a role in their selection for kurgan burial, an honor that was denied to most of the population.

The male aged 17 to 20 years in the central grave in K3/9, unlike the two females, died of an obvious cause, a systemic infection reflected in fibrous bone tissue over his entire skeleton. He was taller than the women (171.8 cm, about 5'7"), and his musculature was also highly developed, like the female in K2/2.

The craniofacial types of the male and two females in the central graves also differed, according to Khokhlov. The male in K3/9 and the hyperrobust female in K2/2 both had brachycephalic skulls of the north Europoid type, unusual for the Poltavka population in the Volga-Ural region but more common among MBA Catacomb populations in the lower Don-Caspian region. The other central burial, the young female in K1/3, had a narrower face and dolichocranial skull, a type well represented among Poltavka skulls in the middle Volga region.

The peripheral graves associated with the central MBA graves also were quite different: in Kurgan 1, the peripheral deposits were an infant heavily covered with red ochre and a young man placed in the mound soil above the central grave; in Kurgan 2, the peripheral grave was a Catacomb culture grave dug outside the demarcating ditch accompanying a very robust Poltavka adult woman aged 40 to 45 years; and in Kurgan 3 was a pit containing ochre-stained sheep bones, tools, and the secondary bundle burial of a disarticulated adult man aged 35 to 45 years, accompanying the central grave of a young Poltavka man, aged 17 to 25 years. Red ochre was a unifying trait. The central grave pits were dug in similar shapes, with steps for access and ledges around the grave for grave covers made of reeds and perhaps hides and grass. Categories such as "central grave" and "peripheral grave" were observed in all three MBA kurgans, but the occupants of those categories varied in many ways over a short period of time in one place, possibly within a related group of people.

LBA Cemetery in Kurgan 3

Kurgan 3 produced 22 Srubnaya graves containing 27 individuals, probably the people who occupied the Srubnaya settlement just 65 m to the southwest (Figures 17.11 and 17.13). The bones of four individuals were added to these graves as grave gifts or heirlooms. Eight of the Srubnaya graves were dated by radiocarbon, and the dates conformed to the dates from the settlement, falling between about 1900 and 1600 BC. All the graves were positioned in the northern or eastern quadrant of the mound, avoiding the center of the kurgan and also avoiding the side of the kurgan that faced the settlement. Twelve graves contained 13 whole or fragmentary Srubnaya ceramic vessels; other objects in the LBA graves included a stone pestle, a stone polisher, and a pair of ceramic disk–shaped spindle whorls. None of the graves contained metal objects or any indication of wealth.

Five Srubnaya adults were buried at Krasnosamarskoe, although one (K3/5) was represented by only a few bones, 10 to 20 percent of the body. The other four were two adult males in K3/17 and K3/23 (both aged 35–45 years) and two adult females (aged 17–25 and 45+ years) in K3/1 and K3/13. The other 22 individuals buried at Krasnosamarskoe were subadults, from infants to adolescents, who made up 82 percent of the buried population. Most of these, 15 of the

Figure 17.13 Kurgan 3 excavations were very complex with 24 graves.

22 (68 percent), were 7 years old or younger at death. Only 2 of these 22 individuals were in the 15 to 17 age category, an age at which they might have behaved as adults despite their subadult biological development, so the preponderance of children is notable, an unusually high percentage for a Srubnaya cemetery (see overview and Table 17.1).

Isolated long bones of humans were included in four graves, apparently as intentional grave gifts. The curated bones were a femur and humerus from two infants (added to Graves 2 and 16), a 4-year-old's femur (added to Grave 18), and an adult tibia (added to Grave 4). The bones of these four individuals might have been retained from individuals buried in earlier graves in the same cemetery; for example, the adult tibia included with the 5- to 7-year-old in Grave 4 might have come from the partial adult skeleton in Grave 5, which is quite incomplete and has only one tibia. Or it might have been curated and carried into the cemetery from elsewhere, from an older home. Because of that uncertainty, these four single-bone individuals are not included in the cemetery totals as *additional* individuals; if they were, the total would rise from 25 to 29 individuals. Perhaps some of the human bones found in the settlement nearby represent the curation of family bones within the residential area.

Grave 1 (Figure 17.14) contained the complete skeleton of a female aged 17 to 25 years, in a contracted position on her left side, with her head to the north-northeast. Her estimated height was 163 cm, or about 5′4″. Cribra orbitalia in her left orbit indicated probable dietary deficiencies, which could have been caused by parasites rather than actual food deficits. She had suffered various small injuries to her back, evident in spondylolysis, os acromilae, and Schmorl's nodes on the vertebrae and scapula. A radiocarbon date (AA37038, 3490 ± 57 BP) calibrated to 1886 to 1746 BC.

Grave 2 (Figure 17.14) contained 70 to 80 percent of the bones of an adolescent aged 12 to 14 years, in a contracted position on the left side, head to the northeast. The left humerus of an infant was recovered from the grave, apparently placed next to the deceased. Hypoplastic grooves suggest numerous incidents of physiological stress between the ages of 2 and 5 years, and short long bones in comparison to the age determined by the teeth indicate that the individual might have been very small for his or her age.

Grave 3 (Figure 17.14) contained two children aged 6 to 7 years, one on its left side and the other on its right side. Both were tightly contracted. One skeleton was highly fragmented, perhaps a secondary burial.

Grave 4 (Figure 17.14) contained 40 to 50 percent of the bones of a child aged 5 to 7 years, in a contracted position on its left side, head to the northwest. Parts of an adult tibia and fibula were associated with the skeleton.

Grave 5 (Figure 17.14) contained only 10 to 20 percent of the skeleton of an adult; neither age nor sex were determinable. The individual suffered from degenerative joint disease in the left knee, and an enthesopathy on the left patella suggested a rheumatic disease.

Grave 6 (Figure 17.14) contained the complete skeleton of an adolescent aged 15 to 17 years, in a contracted position on the left side with the head to the north-northeast. The phalanges of an elk or red deer lay near the feet. A radiocarbon date (AA37039, 3411 ± 46 BP) calibrated to 1767 to 1635 BC.

Grave 7 (Figure 17.14) contained only 10 to 20 percent of the bones of two children aged 5 to 7 years; both were quite fragmentary, with only 10 to 20 percent of the skeleton present. One small unornamented ceramic sherd, grog tempered, was contained in the grave.

Grave 8 and Grave 9 dated to the MBA and were discussed above.

Grave 10 (Figure 17.14) contained a few bones of a child aged 5 to 7 years, in a contracted position on its left side. The skull was not preserved (possibly destroyed by the bulldozer). It was oriented east-southeast. A radiocarbon date (AA37042, 3594 ± 45) calibrated to 2020 to 1892 BC.

Grave 11 (Figure 17.15) contained 30 to 40 percent of the bones of a child 6 to 8 years old. The grave contained two small ceramic cups of developed Srubnaya type (Figure 17.18). A radiocarbon date (AA37043, 3416 ± 57 BP) calibrated to 1866 to 1632 BC.

Grave 12 (Figure 17.15) contained 50 to 60 percent of the bones of two juvenile children, one 8 to 10 years old and the other 7 to 9 years old. The older child had hypoplastic grooves suggesting physiological stress on at least four occasions between the ages of 2 and 4 years. The younger child had cribra orbitalia, possibly indicating anemia in an individual of this age, in the left orbit but not in the right orbit. The grave contained one horse tooth and some cattle bones.

Grave 13 (Figure 17.15) contained 30 to 40 percent of the bones of an adult female, 45+ years old, with a height of only 146.5 cm (4′9″), in a contracted position on her right side, head to the northwest. This was probably a secondary burial of disarticulated bones exhibiting eroded surfaces from exposure. She had osteophytosis on her right scapula and on the proximal ulna, as well as on several cervical vertebrae; she also exhibited hypoplastic grooves on her teeth that indicated an episode of physiological stress at the age of 5 to 5.5 years.

Grave 14 (Figure 17.15) contained 50 to 60 percent of the bones of an adolescent male, 15 to 17 years old, in a contracted position on his right side, head to the east. It is

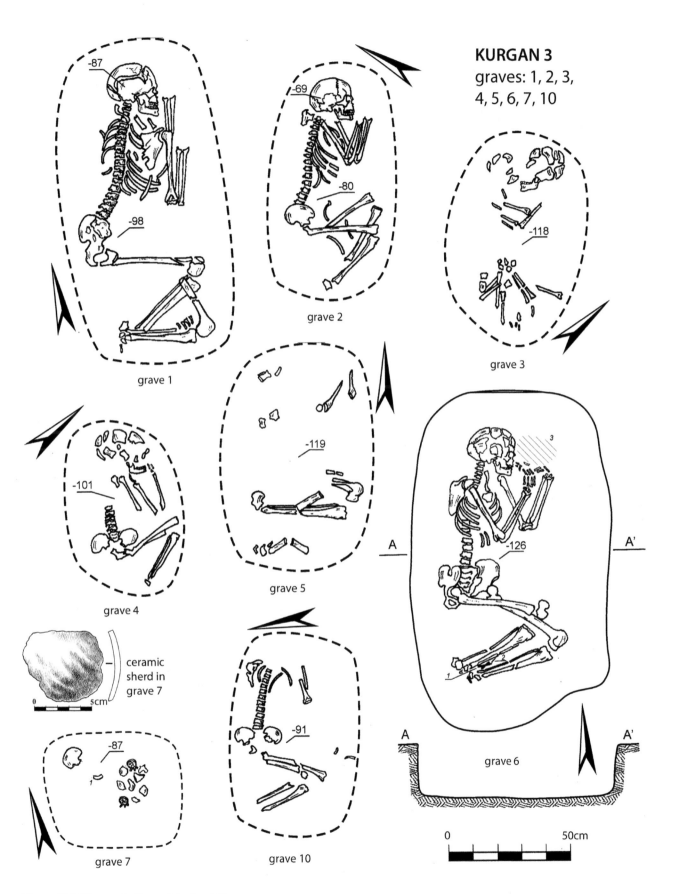

KURGAN 3
graves: 1, 2, 3,
4, 5, 6, 7, 10

grave 1

grave 2

grave 3

grave 4

grave 5

ceramic
sherd in
grave 7

grave 6

grave 7

grave 10

Figure 17.14 Kurgan 3, Graves 1 to 7 and 10.

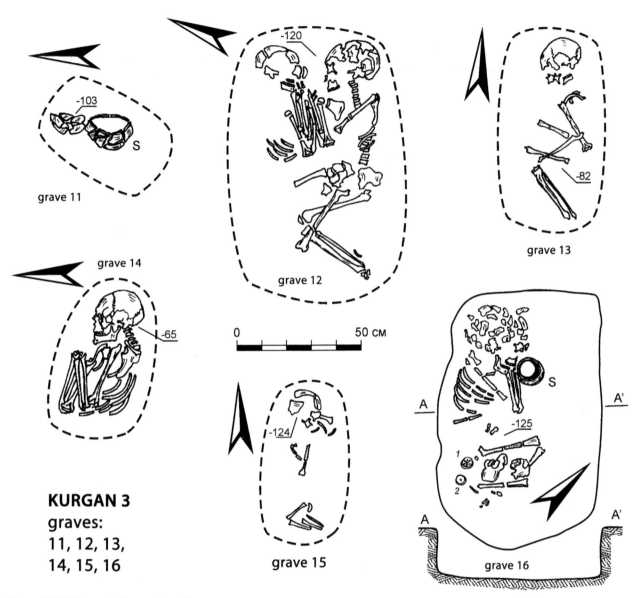

KURGAN 3
graves:
11, 12, 13,
14, 15, 16

grave 11

grave 12

grave 13

grave 14

grave 15

grave 16

Figure 17.15 Kurgan 3, Graves 11 to 16.

likely that more bones were originally present, as the lower part of the skeleton was destroyed by the bulldozer.

Grave 15 (Figure 17.15) contained 40 to 50 percent of the bones of an infant 1.5 to 2.5 years old, in a contracted position on its left side.

Grave 16 (Figure 17.15) contained 50 to 60 percent of the bones of a juvenile 7 to 8 years old, in a contracted position on its left side. The left femur of an infant, aged newborn to 6 months, was recovered with the skeleton. Cribra orbitalia was present in the left orbit. The grave also contained two clay disk spindle whorls and a small ceramic cup of Pokrovka (early Srubnaya) type (Figure 17.18). A radiocarbon date (AA37045, 3407 ± 46 BP) calibrated to 1754 to 1632 BC.

Grave 17 (Figures 17.16 and 17.17) contained the complete skeleton of an adult male aged 35 to 45 years, with a height of 167 cm (5'6"), in a contracted position on his left side, head to the northwest. Prior to his death, he sustained a twisting injury to his left knee, evidenced by osteochondritis dissecans on the medial condyle of his distal femur, and other strains on both lower legs (enthesopathies on his tibiae and humeri), as well as on his feet (enthesopathies and pitting on his metatarsals). He also sustained a compression fracture in the twelfth thoracic vertebrae of his mid-lower back, in addition to other spinal injuries (osteophytosis on four thoracic vertebrae). He often assumed a squatting posture, as squatting facets were well worn laterally on both

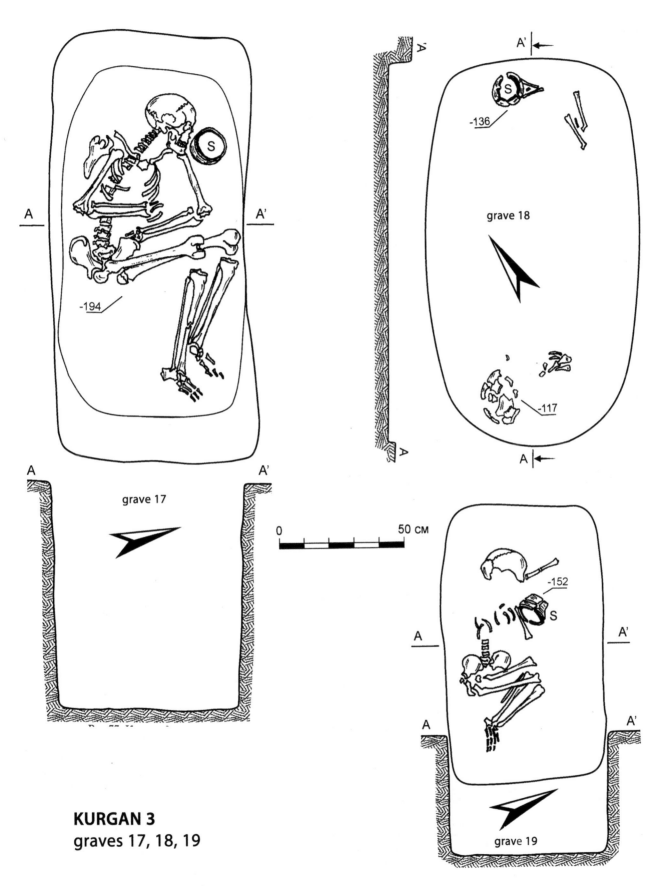

KURGAN 3
graves 17, 18, 19

Figure 17.16 Kurgan 3, Graves 17 to 19.

tibiae. He also exhibited cribra orbitalia in both orbits, perhaps from a vitamin deficiency, and hypoplastic grooves indicate two episodes of physiological stress between the ages 2 to 4.5 years. He had chop marks on the head of his left femur and on his right ankle, probably indicating that some leg joints were cut after death to compress the knees against the body to reduce the size of the body for storage or transport. The time interval between death and burial must have been short, since the complete skeleton was preserved for burial and the flesh held the skeleton in anatomical order. The legs were relaxed when the body was placed in the grave, so the disarticulation of the hip was not needed for the final burial posture but must have been dictated by the location of his death some distance away, requiring transport of the bundled corpse. A small ceramic cup, 11.7 cm in diameter, decorated with a toothed stamp, of Pokrovka (early Srubnaya) type, was placed by the head of the male (Figure 17.19). A radiocarbon date (AA37046, 3545 ± 65 BP) calibrated to 1961 to 1771 BC.

Grave 18 (Figure 17.16) contained 30 to 40 percent of the bones of a child aged 1.5 to 3.5 years. The grave also contained fragments of animal bone and the femur of a child 4 years of age, as well as two pottery sherds from Pokrovka-style cups (Figure 17.19).

Grave 19 (Figure 17.16) contained 30 to 40 percent of the bones of a child 4.5 to 6.5 years old, in a contracted position on the left side, oriented to the northwest. The child was buried with a ceramic cup 10.4 cm in diameter, decorated with a toothed stamp in a zigzag motif typical of Pokrovka style (Figure 17.19).

Grave 20 (Figure 17.18) contained 40 to 50 percent of the bones of a child 3 to 4 years old, in a contracted position on the left side, oriented northwest. The child had a ceramic cup almost exactly like the one in Grave 19, with a 10.7-cm diameter, decorated the same way (Figure 17.19). This child exhibited cribra orbitalia, indicating anemia or vitamin deficiency, and had hypoplastic grooves in its teeth, indicating a dietary stress that occurred at 3.5 to 4 years, close to when the child died.

Figure 17.17 Kurgan 3, Grave 17. As in 17.07, the floors of the deepest graves were flooded by the 1-m rise in the water table when local fishponds were filled (photo by Christopher Gette).

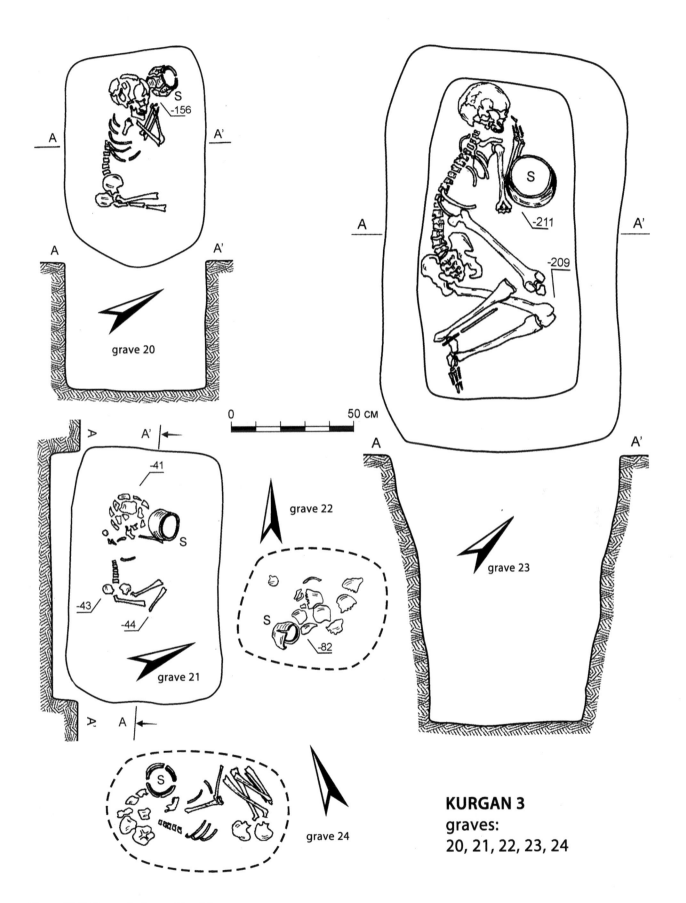

Figure 17.18 Kurgan 3, Graves 20 to 24.

Grave 21 (Figure 17.18) contained 50 to 60 percent of the bones of a child aged 3 to 4 years, in a contracted position on the left side, oriented west-northwest. The child had a ceramic cup similar to those in Graves 19 and 20, but slightly bigger, 11.7 cm in diameter, and decorated with incised zigzag lines rather than a toothed stamp (Figure 17.19).

Grave 22 (Figure 17.18) contained 60 to 70 percent of the bones of a child aged 5 to 6 years, disarticulated and bundled before burial. Rodent gnawing was visible on numerous bones, so the disarticulation might have occurred through exposure, leaving the remains vulnerable to rodents for some period of time before they were collected for burial. The child was buried with an unornamented ceramic cup 10.8 cm in diameter and 6.8 cm high (Figure 17.19).

Grave 23 (Figure 17.18) contained 70 to 80 percent of the bones of an adult male, 35 to 45 years old, with a height of 164.5 cm (5'5"), in a contracted position on his left side, head to the northwest. He had suffered a twisting injury to his right knee, evident in osteochondritis dissecans on the proximal condyle of the tibia, with a matching osteophytosis on the right distal femur and patella. He also had osteophytosis on his thoracic and cervical vertebrae in his upper back and Schmorl's nodes on thoracic and lumbar vertebrae in his lower back, possibly involving a herniation of vertebral disks. Like the male in Grave 17, his strains extended to his feet, where his inflamed Achilles tendons were evident in enthesopathies on his calcanei. Chop marks on the head of his proximal right femur indicate that his hip joint was loosened to permit his knees to be pressed against his body for storage or transport prior to burial, like the adult male in Grave 17. Like that male, he was buried while his flesh still maintained his skeleton in anatomical order, and his legs were relaxed and placed in a natural position in the grave. He was buried with an unornamented ceramic cup of Pokrovka (early Srubnaya) type, only a few sherds of which survived (Figure 17.19). A radiocarbon date (AA37047, 3425 ± 52 BP) calibrated to 1871 to 1641 BC.

Grave 24 (Figure 17.18) contained the partial remains of a newborn infant, buried with an unornamented ceramic cup 10.3 cm in diameter (Figure 17.19).

Overview of the LBA Cemetery

The LBA Srubnaya cemetery of 22 graves and 27 individuals (Table 17.1), inserted into the northeastern face of Kurgan 3, revealed many interesting details of life during the period 1900 to 1700 BC.

The Adults: Pathologies and Postmortem Treatment

Only two adult men, aged 35 to 45 years, were buried among the 22 Srubnaya graves (Graves 23 and 17). In Grave 5, a partial adult that could not be sexed, could have been a third man. Both of the definite men had their femur heads chopped in a way that suggested to Murphy that the hip joints were cut and loosened to forcibly compress the legs against the body for storage or transport. This might suggest that both men died elsewhere, not in the Krasnosamarskoe settlement, and were brought back home for burial.

This treatment occurred in only 5 of the 67 Srubnaya males (7.5 percent of Srubnaya males) that Murphy examined from across the middle Volga region in Chapter 8, but both males from Krasnosamarskoe are included in this small group. An alternative explanation, that hip-cutting was performed on people who died in the winter to store the body until warm weather thawed the ground for burial, should have occurred in many more individuals, so is unlikely to explain the adult males at Krasnosamarskoe.

Both of the relatively complete adult males also were unusually short, according to Khokhlov, but Murphy's measurements suggest a taller stature for both. K3/17 was estimated by Khokhlov at 163.8 cm height, and K1/23 was 162.7 cm (about 5'4"). Both had unusually short arms and legs in relation to the width of bone articular surfaces and cross sections, indicating that they had similar body proportions: short-limbed and short-statured, with thick bones and a strong musculature.

Both men had twisting injuries to their knees, and it is interesting that the partial Grave 5 adult also had a knee injury. Both men had injuries to their feet, and one had pronounced squatting facets. The two definite men also both exhibited numerous pathologies on their vertebrae (osteophytosis and Schmorl's nodes) suggesting back strain and, in Grave 17, a vertebral compression fracture. Murphy noted in Chapter 8 that the settled Srubnaya population generally showed fewer back injuries than did the mobile pastoralists of the EBA and MBA, but both men from Krasnosamarskoe IV had multiple back injuries. They died at similar ages (35–45 years) with similar pathologies. But probably they were not related genetically. One (K3/17) had a dolichocranial skull shape and a narrow face, like most of the Srubnaya population in the region, and the other (K3/23) had a broad face and brachycranial skull, unusual for the region.

Murphy suggested that this suite of injuries might suggest participation in heavy mining work, but if that was the case, then the men did not bring their work home—there is only a light scatter of copper ore and no observable wealth in the settlement. A second possibility, considering that chariots were driven (and sometimes

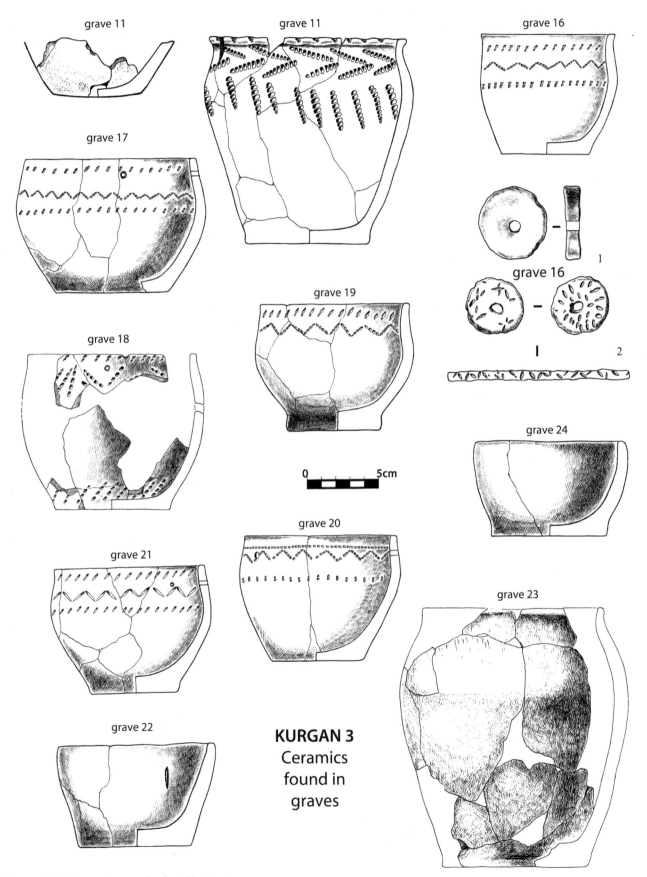

grave 11

grave 11

grave 16

grave 17

grave 19

grave 16

1

2

grave 18

grave 24

grave 21

grave 20

grave 23

grave 22

0   5cm

KURGAN 3
Ceramics
found in
graves

Figure 17.19 Kurgan 3, ceramics found in graves.

Table 17.1 Krasnosamarskoe IV, Kurgan 3, Srubnaya Individuals' Ages

Grave No.	Age (y)	Age Group	Sex	Percent of Skeleton
3	6–7		Unknown	100
3	6–7		Unknown	100
4	5–7		Unknown	40–50
7	5–7		Unknown	10–20
7	5–7		Unknown	10–20
10	5–7		Unknown	10–20
15	1.5–2.5		Unknown	40–50
16	0–0.5	*Younger than 7 years. 15/27, 55.55 percent*	Unknown	1 femur
18	1.5–3.5		Unknown	30–40
18	4		Unknown	1 femur
19	4.5–6.5		Unknown	30–40
20	3–4		Unknown	40–50
21	3–4		Unknown	50–60
22	5–6		Unknown	60–70
24	0–0.5		Unknown	Partial
2	12–14		Unknown	70–80
11	6–8		Unknown	30–40
12	8–10	*7–14 years, 5/27, 18.52 percent*	Unknown	50–60
12	7–9		Unknown	50–60
16	7–8		Unknown	50–60
6	15–17	*15–17 years, 2/27, 7 percent*	Unknown	100
14	15–17		Male	50–60
1	17–25		Female	100
5	Adult		Unknown	10–20
13	45+	*Older than 17 years, Adults. 5/27, 18.52 percent*	Female	30–40
17	35–45		Male	100
23	35–45		Male	70–80

were buried in graves) throughout the Srubnaya period, is that the short, powerful build was preferred for chariot driving, since short legs would lower the driver's center of gravity in a vehicle that would have bounced dangerously while racing over uneven ground. Jumping in and out of a moving chariot could cause knee and foot injuries. But the number of horses at Krasnosamarskoe was unusually low compared to other Srubnaya settlements in the region (Chapter 15), and no chariot-related artifacts such as antler cheekpieces or bone whip handles were found. A third possibility, more in keeping with the ritual activities that occurred in the settlement, is that the men were shamanic dancers who frequently engaged in leaping and

twisting movements. The third possibility conforms most closely to the archaeological evidence at the site.

There were also only two adult women in the cemetery, K3/13, aged 45+ years, and K3/1, aged 17 to 25 years. The older woman in K3/13 also seems to have died elsewhere, like the adult males, but in this case, her bones showed signs of exposure to weathering and were completely disarticulated, as if transported in a bundle. Both women also had back injuries, including vertebral spondylolysis, Schmorl's nodes, and osteophytosis of the vertebrae. Again, in general, the Srubnaya population of the middle Volga region had relatively few back injuries, but at Krasnosamarskoe, the adults of both sexes seem to have engaged in behaviors that demanded unusual strains on their backs and, for the men, unusual twisting strains on their knees and on their feet.

According to Khokhlov, the craniofacial structures of the two adult women cannot be compared since the exposure of the bones of K3/13 resulted in the loss of many of her facial bones. The other adult female in K3/1 exhibited a sub-dolichocranial skull shape, according to Khokhlov's report, and a small face that is horizontally flattened in the lower part with low and abruptly protruding nasal bones and a narrow chin. This complex of traits and some other features suggested to Khokhlov that this woman had distant ancestry among ancient Uralic populations of the forest zone, probably through the Sintashta-Potapovka population of the preceding MBA II era. This female's skull and face were not similar to most of the other Srubnaya individuals in the cemetery; she might have married into this group.

The Subadults: Why So Many?

The other 17 graves contained 22 preadult individuals: 3 adolescents, 12 to 17 years; 4 between 7 and 12 years; and 15 infants or children younger than 7 years, including three paired child burials (Table 17.1). The 4:1 ratio of immature to adult deaths is unique for Srubnaya cemeteries in the region. Indications of dietary stress such as cribra orbitalia and hypoplastic grooves on teeth were not seen on most of the children; they were more common in juveniles and adults. Only one individual, an adolescent aged 12 to 14 years buried in Grave 2, was obviously unhealthy—his or her stature was very small and stunted. All of these young individuals died of either disease or injury, but direct evidence of either was relatively rare.

The large percentage of children (82 percent of the Srubnaya individuals) at Krasnosamarskoe IV was not typical for the neighboring three Srubnaya communities. Of 21 excavated Srubnaya graves at Barinovka, 21 km to the south, near a Srubnaya settlement, there were only 10 graves (48 percent) of juveniles and infants (Khokhlov 2002). At Spiridonovka II, 14 km to the northwest, downstream from Krasnosamarskoe IV, a kurgan cemetery near a Srubnaya settlement contained only four infants and juveniles, or 17 percent of the 23 Srubnaya graves (Khokhlov 1999a). Another Srubnaya cemetery was found on the other end of the modern village of Spiridonovka, at Spiridonovka IV, with two kurgans containing 24 Srubnaya graves in one and 15 in the other. They contained 40 to 50 percent infants and juveniles (Khokhlov 1999b). These are the closest three Srubnaya cemeteries to Krasnosamarskoe with described ages, and like Krasnosamarskoe, two of the other three are near small Srubnaya settlements. While the number of Srubnaya culture graves was similar (15–24) in all four

kurgan cemeteries, the proportion of infants and juveniles at Krasnosamarskoe (82 percent) was unusually high.

There is another Srubnaya cemetery that should be compared, located near S'yezzhee and designated S'yezzhee II, 30 km upstream from Krasnosamarskoe, past Utyevka. It had no kurgans and was therefore discovered by accident. It was unique in the region, being composed of flat graves with no preserved mound. It is also the largest Srubnaya cemetery yet found in the area, with 71 aged and sexed Srubnaya graves (Kolev 2003). While there are other Srubnaya flat-grave cemeteries in other regions of the Srubnaya culture on the lower Volga, they are rare and generally considered to represent a late period in the evolution of Srubnaya mortuary rituals (Kolev 2003:109), unlike the Krasnosamarskoe settlement and cemetery, which are early Srubnaya. However, Kolev recovered both Pokrovka (early Srubnaya) and developed Srubnaya pottery types from the flat S'yezzhee II cemetery and in fact argued that they represented partly contemporary, partly successive pottery styles, a position adopted in this report as well (see Chapter 10). In any case, at this unusual flat cemetery at S'yezzhee II, the proportion of infants and children was 60 percent, or 43 of 71 graves. This percentage of children and juveniles is closer to Krasnosamarskoe but still is significantly lower than 82 percent.

We do not know why so many children were buried at Krasnosamarskoe. Perhaps, if the people who lived here were regarded as ritual specialists and herbalists, people from around the region brought their sick children for treatment, and those who died were buried in Kurgan 3 with the family who actually lived here.

Pokrovka and Developed Srubnaya Ceramics in Dated Graves

Pokrovka (early Srubnaya)–style pots predominate very strongly in Srubnaya culture graves in the Samara Valley, as noted in Chapter 4 and by Mochalov (2008). This odd predominance of the early phase style in Srubnaya mortuary pottery was repeated at Krasnosamarskoe IV, where six graves contained Pokrovka-style and four contained developed Srubnaya-style ceramics. From the perspective of chronology, it is interesting that three of the six graves containing Pokrovka-style ceramics were dated by radiocarbon, and the dates ranged across the entire occupation period, 1900 to 1700 BC (Table 17.2). One date from Grave 16 containing an "early" Pokrovka-style pot was calibrated to 1754 to 1632 BC, certainly one of the later dates for the Srubnaya occupation at Krasnosamarskoe. This shows that the Pokrovka style was not, strictly speaking, limited to the early period of the Srubnaya culture.

Table 17.2 Dated Graves at Krasnosamarskoe IV with Typed Ceramics

Ceramic Style	Grave No.	Calibrated Date	BP Date	^{14}C Sample No.
Developed Srubnaya	11	1866–1632 BC	3416 ± 57 BP	AA37043
Pokrovka	16	1754–1632 BC	3407 ± 46 BP	AA37045
Pokrovka	17	1961–1771 BC	3545 ± 65 BP	AA37046
Pokrovka	23	1871–1641 BC	342 5 ±52 BP	AA37047

Grave 17 is among the earliest Srubnaya graves at the site and contains a Pokrovka-style pot, but Grave 16 is among the latest Srubnaya graves at the site and still has a Pokrovka-style pot. Pokrovka and developed Srubnaya styles were made and used at the same time. As Kolev argued at S'yezzhee II (Kolev 2003), the two styles were only partly successive/chronological; they were also partly contemporary. An isolated grave, not dated by radiocarbon, cannot be dated to an older period just because it contains a Pokrovka pot.

Notes

Figures and tables in this chapter were prepared by D. Brown, photographs were taken by D. Brown and D. Anthony unless otherwise noted in captions. All drawings are by IHAV.

References

Khokhlov, Aleksandr A.

1999a   Kraniologicheskie materialy Spiridonovskogo II mogil-nika (kurgan 1). In *Okhrana i Izuchenie Pamyatnikov Istorii i Kul'tury v Samarskoi Oblasti*, Vol. 1, edited by I. N. Vasil'eva and M. A. Turetskii, pp. 93–97. Samarskii Oblastnoi Istoriko-Kraevedcheskii Muzei im. P.V. Alabina, Samara.

1999b   Antropologicheskiya kurganov 1 i 2 mogil'nika Spiridonovka IV. In *Voposy Arkheologii Povolzh'ya*, edited by R. S. Bagautdinov and L. V. Kuznetsova, pp. 2227–2230. Samarskii Gosudarstvennyi Pedagogicheskii Universitet, Samara.

2002   Paleoantropologiya mogil'nika Srubnoi kul'tury Barinovka I. In *Voprosy Arkhelologii Povolzh'ya*, edited by A. A. Vybornov, V. N. Myshkin, and M. A. Turetskii, pp. 134–144. Samarskii Gosudarstvennyi Pedagogicheskii Universitet, Samara.

Kolev, Y. I.

2003   Gruntovyi mogil'nik Srubnoi kul'tury S'yezzhee II (materialy raskopok). In *Material'naya Kul'tura Naseleniya basseina reki Samaray v Bronzovom Veke*, edited by Iu. I. Kolev, P. F. Kuznetsov, and O. D. Mochalov, p. 111. Samarskii Gosudarstvennyi Pedagogicheskii Universitet, Samara.

Kosintsev, P. A., and N. V. Roslyakova

1999   Ostatki zhivotnykh is Kalinovskogo mogil'nika. In *Okhrana i Izuchenie Pamyatnikov Istorii i Kul'tury v Samarskoi Oblasti*, Vol. 1, edited by I. N. Vasil'eva and M. A. Turetskii, pp. 48–58. Samarskii Oblastnoi Istoriko-Kraevedcheskii Muzei im. P.V. Alabina, Samara.

Kuznetsov, P. F.

2003   Osobennosti kurgannykh obryadov naseleniya Samarskoi doliny v pervoi polovinie Bronzogo Veka. In *Material'naya Kul'tura Naseleniya basseina reki Samary v Bronzovom Veke*, edited by Iu. I. Kolev, P. F. Kuznetsov, and O. D. Mochalov, pp. 43–51. Samarskii Gosudarstvennyi Pedagogicheskii Universitet, Samara.

Mochalov, Oleg D.

2008   *Keramika Pogrebal'nykh Pamiatnikov Epokhi Bronzy Lesostepi Volgo-Ural'skogo Mezhdurech'ya*. Samarskii Gosudarstvennyi Pedagogicheskii Universitet, Samara.

Telegin, D. Y., Sergei Z. Pustalov, and N. N. Kovalyukh

2003   Relative and Absolute Chronology of Yamnaya and Catacomb Monuments: The Issue of Co-existence. *Baltic-Pontic Studies* 12:132–184.

Vasiliev, I. B., and Pavel Kuznetsov

1988   Poltavkinskie mogil'niki u s. Krasnosamarskoe v lesostep-nom zavolzh'e. In *Issledovanie Pamyatnikov Arkheologii Vostochnoi Evropy*, edited by A. T. Siniuk, pp. 39–59. Voronezhskii Gosudarstvennyi Pedagogicheskii Institut, Voronezh.

Chapter 18

Bronze Age Herding Camps:
Survey and Excavations in Peschanyi Dol

David W. Anthony • Dorcas R. Brown
Pavel F. Kuznetsov • Oleg D. Mochalov

Peschanyi Dol means Sandy Valley ("dol" is cognate with English "dale"). The soils we encountered in the middle and upper valleys were not sandy, so it is likely that the folk name derives from the sandy soils around the mouth of the Peschanyi Dol stream where it joins the red, sandy banks of the Samara River (Figure 18.1).

Peschanyi Dol was carved by what today is a small, sluggish stream that rises in springs near Filipovka and meanders through patches of marsh (mainly *Typha* or sedges, some *Phragmites* or cattail) before disappearing into oxbow lakes and thickets in the Samara River floodplain (Figure 18.1). The stream is 16 km long and flows northward on the southern or "steppe side" of the Samara River. It is 20 km upstream from the Late Bronze Age (LBA) Krasnosamarskoe settlement and 2.5 km upstream from the LBA Barinovka settlement (Figure 18.2). A strip of marshes, oxbow lakes, and bushy thickets adjoins the Samara River at the mouth of Peschanyi Dol, accessible today only to ducks and roe deer. Above that is a grassy meadow 2.7 km wide (Figure 18.3 and 18.6), deeply carved into the surrounding terrain, sheltered by steep, grassy bluffs on the west, crowning at 68 meters above sea level (MASL) and a lower, gentler upland (actually an eroded river levee) on the east, rising to 50 MASL, embracing a meadow that dips to 39 MASL at its junction with the Samara River marshes. The elevations on both sides of the floodplain meadow are crowned by kurgan cemeteries. In the middle part of

the valley, south of the floodplain meadow, stream-bottom marshes about half a kilometer wide continue for about 6 km. The upper part of the valley, where it narrows significantly, ends at a spring near Filipovka. The watershed south of Filipovka, at an elevation of 146 MASL, separates the Samara drainage from the much smaller Chapaevka River in the steppes to the south. Unexcavated kurgans crown the watershed ridge top. The stream valley is bracketed by kurgan cemeteries.

There had never been a project aimed specifically at finding low-density (and therefore low-reward), ephemeral pastoral Bronze Age camps in the middle Volga region. The longer labor per artifact at any low-density site and the expectation that the artifacts themselves might be quite humble, possibly so humble as to be uninformative, made this kind of archaeology difficult to justify. But no tributary stream valley had ever been systematically surveyed in the Samara Valley. This was the first systematic archaeological exploration of these very common environments and was justified locally simply on those grounds. Also, to understand how the Srubnaya pastoral economy operated across a seasonally varied landscape, we had to find Srubnaya herding camps. They were a necessary part of the complete Srubnaya settlement system that we were trying to map.

We expected that Bronze Age herding camps would be more easily found in a stream valley like Peschanyi Dol that would constrain and concentrate campsites than in the cultivated fields on the north side of the river, where the

Figure 18.1 The lower Peschanyi Dol valley looking southwest across the floodplain marshes. The dirt road in the middle distance exposes sandy red soil.

Samara Valley was very broad and almost flat, presenting few constraining topographic features. Also the narrow stream valley was not suitable for agriculture, so sites located there might be stratigraphically intact, while any ephemeral camps in the flatter part of the valley would be plowed and disturbed in intensely cultivated fields. Finally, the Srubnaya settlement found in 1995 at Barinovka, near the mouth of Peschanyi Dol, would have generated herding camps, and we hoped to find them in Peschanyi Dol.

If the Srubnaya herding system was simple, then each settlement took its herds to the nearest pastures, and camps in Peschanyi Dol would be generated exclusively by the nearest settlement, identified by the local clays in its pottery. Local clays are a part of the local geomorphology, not affected by culture or chronology. So, regardless of cultural identities, as long as ceramics were produced internally as a part of household production, the local clays around the mouth of Peschanyi Dol should have been used to make pottery by whomever lived in permanent settlements there. If the herding system was simple, these same clays would appear in herding camps. If the herding system was more complex, then settlements in various places, near and far, distributed their herds through negotiated agreements across a larger landscape, and the camps in Peschanyi Dol (PD) would be generated by settlements in various places with diverse, heterogeneous clays. Those diverse clays would then appear in the pottery in the herding camps. Homogeneity or diversity in the clays used for the Srubnaya

pottery that was deposited in the PD camps would tell us which of these patterns operated during the early LBA.

Clays from different natural sources were differentiated into distinct groups (called "regions") by Vasil'eva and Salugina, specialists at the Bobrinskii Laboratory in experimental ceramic analysis in Samara. "Regions" were defined by the number and nature of nonplastic natural inclusions in the clay, including the grain characteristics and proportions of sand, as well as the presence and density of plant fibers, different kinds of shells, microfauna, iron micro-nodules, and so on. Intentionally added, culturally selected tempering materials were also analyzed, and these helped to sort the sherds also into different production recipes (see "Ceramics" sections in this chapter).

We succeeded in finding ephemeral seasonal camps of Srubnaya and other cultures in Peschanyi Dol, sites that were invisible on the surface, during the subsurface testing program of 1996. We returned to excavate two of these, PD1 and PD2, in 2000. Test excavations also undertaken in 1996 at the Srubnaya settlement at Barinovka (see Chapter 2) showed that it was too disturbed to merit further excavation. Disappointed at first, we changed the target for a permanent settlement excavation from Barinovka to the Srubnaya settlement at Krasnosamarskoe, 20 km downstream. Regardless of which Srubnaya settlement generated the Srubnaya herding camps in Peschanyi Dol, the excavations in 2000 showed that PD1 and PD2 were *not* generated solely by the nearest Srubnaya settlement. The

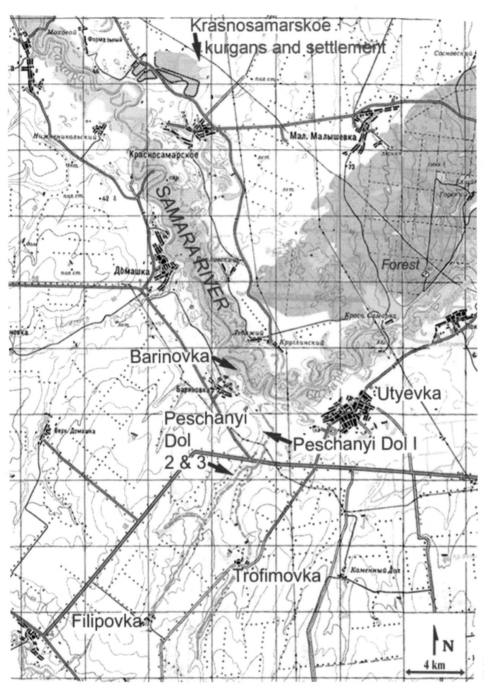

Figure 18.2 Peschanyi Dol, Barinovka, and Krasnosamarskoe.

clays in the Srubnaya pottery in the herding camps were surprisingly heterogeneous in their natural inclusions (regions), although Srubnaya ceramic production methods were fairly homogeneous (minor variations on a shared grog-tempered recipe). Ceramic vessels were carried to the same Peschanyi Dol herding camps from various Srubnaya settlements, and at the camps, pottery from diverse sources was discarded into the same pit. The two excavated Srubnaya herding camps at PD1 and PD2 shared about half

of their clay sources, so people from the same Srubnaya "region" circulated between the excavated camps, sharing them with other people whose pottery was found at only one camp and not the other (the other half of the pottery at each camp). Comparing the diversity of clays at PD1 and PD2 to the diversity of clays in the much larger ceramic sample from Krasnosamarskoe, the PD camps exhibit three to four times the diversity seen in the settlement, implying that three to four settlements cooperated to use Peschanyi

Dol as a shared seasonal pasture. Interestingly, this is exactly how modern Russian villages in the area manage their cattle today.

Modern and Ancient Cattle Herding in Peschanyi Dol

The Peschanyi Dol valley can be divided into three parts, according to the amount of summer-season marsh pasture available: the marshy floodplain 2.7 km wide at its widest point (Figure 18.3); the middle valley, with a floodplain .5 to .75 km wide, with continuous and significant marshes; and the narrow upper valley, with a strip of forest beside the stream, opening occasionally into just a few patches of marsh. The ecological patches utilized by the modern herder are in the lower and middle valleys. Locations near where he remained grazing his cattle for the longest time in the summers of 1996 and 2000, especially within view of PD1 and PD2, were the places where we found the largest Srubnaya campsites.

Cattle herders today regularly use Peschanyi Dol as a summer pasture (Figure 18.3). It is convenient for summer herding because it keeps the animals separated from the agricultural fields around the villages on the Samara floodplain during the growing season. Also, and more important for the agriculture-free Bronze Age, flies are less bothersome at higher elevations above the floodplain. In 1996 and 2000, Peschanyi Dol was a summer grazing location for about 600 head of cattle, we were told by the herder who watched them. The cattle were collected from three modern villages within 6 to 8 km that pooled their cattle under the management of one herder. This could have happened also in the LBA. We frequently encountered the herder riding on horseback accompanied by two German Shepherd dogs, the species used by all of the cattle herders we observed in both Russia and Kazakhstan. We never saw all 600 head at one time. Usually, the herder was seen managing herds of 200 to 300 cattle. Cattle can be grazed up one side of the valley and down the other, he told us, all summer.

Modern cattle remained in the *floodplain meadows* near PD1 in late June and early July (Figure 18.3). Cattle grazed in the background of almost every photograph taken of our excavations at PD1, the largest-area Srubnaya herders' camp we found. A metal trailer used by the herder was stationed permanently quite near PD1.

Figure 18.3 Excavations at PD1 in 2000, looking southeast and upstream across the floodplain meadow, dotted with distant cattle. The entrance to the narrower middle valley is in the gap between the trees on the middle horizon.

Figure 18.4 The Peschanyi Dol valley with locations of selected test sites (Locations) and archaeological sites discovered (PDs 1 to 6). (Google Earth; Image © 2015 CNES/Artrium; © 2015 Google; Image Landsat; Image © 2015 DigitalGlobe)

Modern cattle were moved to the *middle valley*, above the floodplain, near our sites PD2 and PD3 in July and early August. Here, 2 to 2.5 km in distance and about 5 m in elevation above PD1, the marshy bottomland is still about .5 km wide (Figure 18.11). PD2 had lower artifact densities than PD1 (Figure 2.7), and PD3 was lower than PD2.

Upstream from PD2 and PD3, the intensity of LBA usage dropped off sharply. About 6 km upstream from the Samara River is a dam, built across the valley to make a small reservoir, 2.5 km long. We dug many shovel tests at intuitively "good" spots between PD2 and the dam, a distance of 1.6 km, but found just one small Srubnaya sherd scatter, with two pottery sherds, at PD6. Similar two-sherd scatters were found above the dam near the modern herder's metal-fenced corral, located about 8.3 km from the Samara River. Here a smaller tributary stream joined Peschanyi Dol from the west through a narrow defile that was unusually thickly wooded, containing a gallery forest 50 m wide of oak and birch trees, a useful resource for firewood in a steppe area almost devoid of forest. Within a kilometer of the modern herder's corral where the two valleys joined, we found a very low-density Srubnaya site at PD4 and an Iron Age scatter at PD5. Above this point was the transition to the *upper valley*, much narrower and steeper sided, where the stream bottom and its associated strip of vegetation is only 30 to 50 m wide. Neither the modern herder nor Bronze Age herders seem to have used this steepest and narrowest part of the valley.

The behavior of modern cattle herders in Peschanyi Dol seems to match the spatial distribution and intensity of activities in LBA herding camps. The big sites (PD1 and PD2) correspond to the places most frequently used by the modern herder, who sometimes occupied a trailer or caravan not far from PD1. PD3 is an intermediate-sized site, while the two-sherd sites (PD4–PD6) are in an area used only occasionally by the herder today (but equipped with a permanent corral, usually empty, used when shifting cattle into or out of the valley). Our excavations in 2000 at Location 13 at the top of the valley, not used by the modern herder, produced no prehistoric artifacts. The pattern of pastoral usage in the valley seems to be constrained by animals, ecology, and topography in similar ways, whether in the Bronze Age or today. Cows still prefer the same summer foods, marsh grasses and sedges, which grow more or less in the same places at the same seasons.

The 1996 and 2000 Surveys of Peschanyi Dol

In 1996, a team consisting of the coauthors of this volume, university students from Samara, and U.S. archaeologists Petar Glumac, Charles McNutt, and Chris Gette conducted a semi-systematic archaeological survey in the Peschanyi Dol valley, supported by a grant from the National Geographic Society. We began the survey with considerable worry about whether we would find anything. No artifacts were visible on the surface. Ephemeral Bronze Age herding camps had not been found before. Systematic shovel testing was a U.S. technique borrowed from Cultural Resource Management archaeology, not proven in the steppes.

We first selected 12 locations for testing. Most were good places to camp on level terraces near the stream with a view across meadow marshes (Figure 18.4). Locations 4, 7, and 8 were in more elevated topographic positions overlooking a forested ravine (Locations 4, 8) and the junction of that ravine with the main stream valley (Location 7), where the modern herder's corral is located. In addition, in 2000, we returned to Peschanyi Dol and tested around a thirteenth location overlooking the springs at the origin of the valley near Filipovka and a fourteenth location near the modern dam.

Each location was tested by excavating 50-cm × 50-cm shovel test pits (STPs) across the selected location on a grid at 15-m intervals (Figure 18.5). If an artifact was found, the testing interval was decreased to 3 m around the positive STP.

We dug 81 shovel test pits plus two 1-m × 2-m squares (at PD1) at 14 locations, or an average of six subsurface tests per location. We found 65 catalogued artifacts, or less than one artifact per STP. These came from six sites, designated PD1 to PD6, that produced between 2 and 34 ceramic and lithic artifacts. Eight of the 14 locations tested with STPs in 1996 and 2000 yielded no typologically datable ceramics or lithics. Six locations, all within 8.5 km of the Samara River, produced prehistoric ceramic sherds at depths of 10 to 40 cm beneath the modern surface. LBA Srubnaya pottery was discovered at five of the six sites and was by far the most common type of pottery found.

The two sites with by far the most cultural material, PD1 and PD2, were closest to the Samara River (2.5 and 4.5 km) and overlooked broad meadows (Figure 18.3 and background in Figure 18.11). PD2 was about the same artifact density as PD1, if measured in artifacts per meter squared, but because of the deep *chernozem* at PD2, we had to dig much deeper below the cultural levels to reach the sterile subsoil or *materik*, so measured in artifacts per excavated cubic meters of soil, PD2 had a much lower artifact density than did PD1. The difference in cubic meters was, in short, caused largely by different soil types at the two sites. There was a sharp falloff to PD3, which was so light in density that we abandoned a planned excavation there in 2000. No sites were found beyond 8.5 km up the

Figure 18.5 PD1 in 1996 looking west from a high point in the meadow. Two shovel-testing crews work with shaker screens 15 m apart. The crew on the right found artifacts and switched to trowels.

16-km-long valley, but access was steep and difficult in the upper valley, so survey there was spotty and superficial. Nevertheless, it appears from the down-trending artifact densities (Figure 2.7) that herding camp usage fell off sharply between 3 and 5 km upstream from the Samara River. The floodplain-oriented herding camps suggest that Srubnaya herds tended to be concentrated in a localized set of pastures near the floodplain, rather than being taken seasonally to distant pastures by more mobile herders.

PD1 also contained a few MBA sherds. The MBA artifacts, although numbering less than 1 percent of the LBA artifacts, are nevertheless significant because settlements from the Early Bronze Age (EBA)/Middle Bronze Age (MBA) era of mobile pastoralism are almost unknown. Only one of the other five PD sites (PD3) had a single shell-tempered sherd that might be EBA/MBA, but the sherd was too small to constitute conclusive evidence of EBA/MBA occupation. No EBA pottery was found.

Tested Locations (Figure 18.4)

The 12 locations in the lower half of the Peschanyi Dol valley selected for subsurface shovel testing in 1996 were principally on low, level terraces directly overlooking the PD stream and its marshy bottomlands. A few (4, 7, and 8) were in higher locations, with a good view over the valley and near gentle fans or slopes that provided easy access to animals grazing in the valley. Two additional locations, 13 and 14, were tested in 2000.

Location 1: 52 53 21.22 N, 50 52 02/2 E

Our first testing site was on a level terrace overlooking the lower Peschanyi Dol floodplain, sheltered by a ridge to the west. Bunch grass, artemesia, chicory, lavender, other flowering herbs, and wild cannabis were recorded growing in the area. Nine 50-cm × 50-cm STPs were opened on a 15-m grid extending 30 m back from the terrace edge. Mottled black and brown fine sandy silts were encountered. No cultural material was found. Our first attempt at using shovel testing to find ephemeral Bronze Age camps failed.

Location 2 (PD1): 52 53 32 N, 50 51 10 E

This testing site was on a level terrace at an elevation of about 43 MASL, overlooking the lower Peschanyi Dol floodplain about 500 m north of Location 1. The terrace ended in an eroded bank that dropped down about 2.5 m to the floodplain. Weathered, burned animal bones were seen protruding from the eroded bank. The bank was shoveled back, and two ceramic sherds were found. Two large units, 1 × 2 m, were excavated on the terrace above this location 15 m apart. The northernmost unit was then expanded to a 2-m × 2-m square. These units produced 31 MBA and LBA ceramic sherds weighing 74 g, 39 pieces (30 g) of animal bone and a horse tooth, and a retouched lunate flint blade from depths of 20 to 50 cm beneath the modern surface. One small pit feature, possibly a posthole, was found in Unit 2, the southernmost unit. Two hundred meters to the north, near the dirt road running along this part of the valley, a flint blade and a scraper were found on the surface. This location became PD1 in all notes and Samara Valley Project (SVP) 70 in the database.

Location 3 (PD2): 52 52 30 N, 50 51 03 E

For this testing site, we moved 2 km upstream in Peschanyi Dol, crossing the modern highway that skirts the floodplain. About .75 km south of the highway, we found a level terrace on a projecting thumb of land about 50 m wide at an elevation of 49 MASL, overlooking the marsh meadows in the middle Peschanyi Dol valley. Here eight STPs were dug, and cultural materials were found in three, near the base of the promontory and on its south side. In the top 10 cm, in black humus, were four Medieval potsherds. A flint blade retouched on both ends, 12 pieces of animal bone, and five Srubnaya potsherds were found between 20 and 40 cm, and occasional animal bones of unknown age were found down to 60 cm. This location became PD2 in all notes and SVP 71 in the database.

Location 4: 52 50 56 N, 50 47 46 E

This testing site was located 4.7 km southwest of Location 3 (PD2) on a high bluff overlooking the middle Peschanyi Dol valley at the point where a densely wooded tributary stream cuts into the Peschanyi Dol valley from the west. This stream junction defines the end of the middle valley and the beginning of the narrow upper stream valley. The site was chosen for its commanding view over both forest and valley resources and because a Srubnaya sherd had been found on the surface during a walkover surface survey in 1995. The site was intensively surface-collected again in 1996, yielding nothing. Three STPs yielded nothing but scattered bone fragments. Because we could not replicate the surface find of the Srubnaya sherd, we could not be certain that any datable prehistoric human activity had actually occurred in this place, so no PD number was assigned. The test location became SVP 72.

Location 5 (PD3): 52 52 24 N, 50 50 50 E

This testing site was located on a level terrace on a projecting thumb of land 300 m southwest of Location 3 (PD2), overlooking the meadows of the middle Peschanyi Dol valley. Thirteen STPs were excavated on a line slightly east of north-south down the center of the promontory at 15-m intervals. Only Units 1 and 2, at the tip of the promontory, yielded cultural materials. Four additional STPs were dug at 3-m intervals from Unit 2 and four more STPs around Unit 1. Those units on the west side of the line between Unit 1 and Unit 2 and on the line itself yielded additional cultural materials. Units placed north, south, and east of the line were culturally sterile. The five STPs that produced artifacts together yielded 15 ceramic sherds weighing 86 g

at depths from 10 to 40 cm. Five sherds were found in and around Unit 1 and 10 sherds in and around Unit 2. Most were identified as Srubnaya. One sherd, from the 20- to 30-cm level in Unit 2d, was identified as possibly EBA/MBA based on the shell temper. Unit 2c also contained a little burned animal bone. This location became site PD3 and SVP 73 in the database.

Location 6: 52 52 14 N, 50 50 47 E

This testing site was located in the center of the Peschanyi Dol valley about 420 m southeast of Location 5 (PD3). In the middle Peschanyi Dol valley, there are actually two streams running parallel on opposite sides of the valley, with a raised dry-level terrace between them. This raised central terrace looked like a good place to watch a herd grazing anywhere in the valley bottoms on either side. Six STPs placed at 15-m intervals along the west edge of the terrace produced one sheep molar and no cultural materials.

Location 7 (PD4): 52 50 44 N, 50 48 47 E

This testing site was located in a strategic location at the southernmost point of the middle Peschanyi Dol valley, not far from Location 4. A permanent shepherd's corral was located near here, although we never saw cattle in it, and there were never any fresh signs of usage by cattle (such as manure) in it during July 1996. Nevertheless, the permanent corral and the churned earth indicated that this was a place used regularly by modern herders, and its topographic situation, on a gentle open slope descending to the junction of Peschanyi Dol with a narrow wooded valley on the west, made it seem an ideal place to examine. We found very little cultural material, however. We excavated 19 STPs at relatively close intervals of 10 m. One unit halfway up the slope yielded two Iron Age sherds. This location became PD4 and SVP 74 in the database.

Location 8 (PD5): 52 50 53.45 N, 50 50 18 E

This testing site again seemed to be in a perfect location. It was on an elevated plateau 390 m northwest of Location 7 (PD4), overlooking the wooded side valley near its confluence with Peschanyi Dol (Figure 18.7). The pleasant shaded forest in this side valley would have been a valued resource, if it existed in the Bronze Age, and the plateau was just a few steps from the steep edge of the valley in a protected and convenient situation. Six STPs were excavated at 15-m intervals here. Two STPs produced one small ceramic sherd each that might be Srubnaya, but their cultural designation was uncertain. Another produced a modern piece of pottery. With two probable LBA sherds, this location became PD5 and SVP 75 in the database.

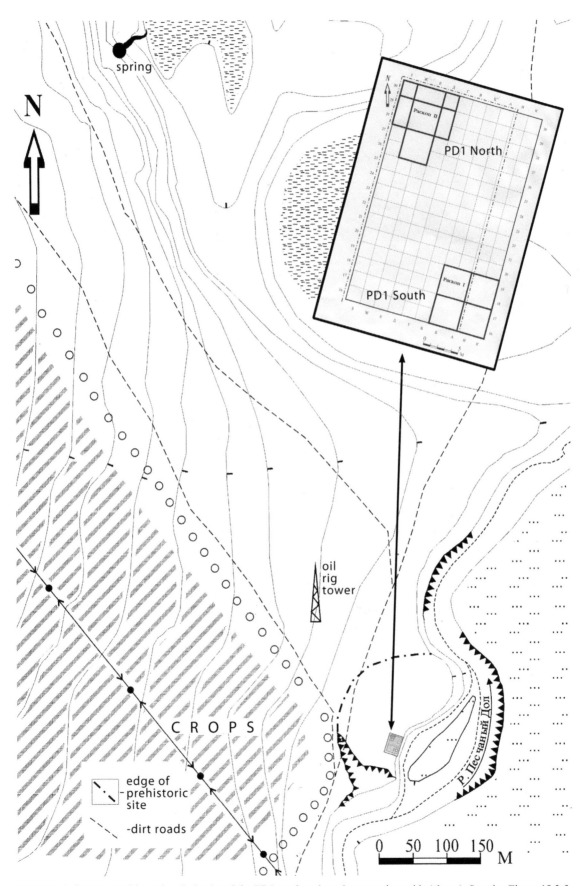

Figure 18.6 PD1 in its topographic setting (below) and the PD1 north and south excavation grids (above). See also Figure 18.3 for a view from the oil rig tower.

Figure 18.7 PD5 in 1996, looking northwest over the wooded side valley. Crews are 15 m apart.

Location 9: 52 51 59 N, 50 50 18 E

This testing site, together with Locations 10 to 12, consti-tuted a cluster of testing locations in the middle Peschanyi Dol valley not far below the modern dam. The undulating edge of the first terrace above the marshy stream bottom seemed to present many level terraces overlooking good grazing, so we tested this part of the middle valley in-tensely. None of the tested locations yielded any artifacts. Location 9 was measured with a GPS, and Locations 10 to 12 were measured from Location 9. At Location 9, five STPs produced no cultural materials. This location has no SVP number.

Location 10: No GPS

This testing site was 150 m west of Location 9. Five STPs produced no cultural materials.

Location 11: No GPS

This testing site was on a low knoll overlooking Location 9. Four STPs produced no cultural materials.

Location 12: No GPS

This testing site was on a level terrace 20 m from the edge of the floodplain, downstream from Location 9. Five STPs produced no cultural materials.

Location 13

In addition to the 12 locations surveyed in 1996, in 2000 we dug nine STPs above the spring at Filipovka at the top of the valley in an effort to discover any traces of settlement associ-ated with the source spring. The STPs were located on a level terrace between a line of kurgans on the watershed ridgetop and the break in the slope down into the bowl-like spring where the stream originated. None of the units in the water-shed grassland above the Filipovka spring yielded artifacts.

Location 14 (PD6)

Also in 2000, we conducted a limited additional survey in the middle Peschanyi Dol valley just below the modern dam. Four STPs produced two Srubnaya sherds. This be-came PD6 in the database.

The 2000 Excavations at PD1 and PD2: Overview

We returned to PD 1 and PD2 in July and August 2000 with a team consisting of the authors of this report, University of Chicago graduate students David Peterson and Laura Popova (then Soikkelli), University of Pennsylvania graduate student Anne Martin-Matthewson, and University of Alabama graduate student Emmett Brown, with about 60 Russian students and staff, including students from what was then Samara State Pedagogical University and high school students from local schools. The high school students came with a school bus and driver that were the backbone of daily logistics between our tent camp on the Samara River and the PD excavation sites. Hartwick College undergraduates Russell Becker, Alex J. Noury, Eric Regnell, and Ben White-Hamerslough assisted, and Russian university students Dmitry Kormilitsyn and Anatoly Pozhidaev were essential crew chiefs in the field. Our co-directors were Pavel Kuznetsov and Oleg Mochalov, then with the Institute for the History and Archaeology of the Volga, Samara State Pedagogical University, and our lab director again was A. Semenova. The 2000 season was partly supported by a grant from the National Science Foundation.

Our initial goal in 2000 was to excavate three of the Bronze Age herding camps discovered in 1996. PD3, however, apparently contained almost no more artifacts than the 15 Srubnaya sherds we had found in 1996 and was abandoned. We excavated the other two, PD1 and PD2. We screened 216 tons of earth in 5 weeks, according to the calculations of I. Ivanov, our Russian geomorphologist, or about 10.5 tons per working day.

All excavated soil passed through quarter-inch mesh hardware-cloth screen imported from the United States and built into portable wooden shaker screens. We recorded 10-cm arbitrary levels within strata defined by color and texture. Constant-volume soil samples were taken for flotation from each level of each 2-m × 2-m unit. Our Russian colleagues did the theodolite work and electronic resistivity remote sensing; Anthony and Brown managed the GPS, digital imaging, and database management.

The 2000 season was difficult: temperatures above 40°C; camping with no electricity, running water, or buildings; all bathing and laundry done in the river; and a 20-minute walk to Barinovka, a small rural village, to get to our "office," where we did our data entry in a room rented in a pigeon-infested, slowly collapsing building that also contained the Barinovka village post office. The women who operated the small rural store across from the post office sold a lot of cold beer and instant coffee that summer and temporarily became barbers for the entire crew.

Excavations at PD1

PD1 was a Srubnaya site located on an erosional fan formed by soil washing down into the valley from the enclosing hills above and to the west, creating a low terrace that overlooked the 2.7-km-wide floodplain meadow at the mouth of the Peschanyi Dol valley (Figures 18.3, 18.5, 18.6). The prehistoric soils that formed the terrace contained coarse sand lenses that reflect occasional colluvial aggradation events, interfingered with alluvial silts and clays from flooding from the floodplain, sitting on a very ancient yellow clay subsoil, or *materik*. The edge of the terrace was scalloped into a series of bays and promontories by the wandering stream. PD1 was located in a sheltered bay between two promontories overlooking seasonally marshy low spots in the stream valley. Two separate excavation blocks, each 64 m^2 in size, designated PD1 north and PD1 south, were measured and gridded to investigate two parts of the terrace. PD1 north was meant to investigate a subsurface anomaly detected during an initial electrical resistivity survey. PD1 south was meant to open up the exact location where artifacts were found in test excavations in 1996.

The soils at the two sites were quite different. The PD1 north excavation showed that the subsurface anomaly detected in the electrical resistivity survey was not a cultural feature but an ancient erosional gulley that once cut through the terrace to the north of the prehistoric site. The ancient erosional gulley contained eroded sediments with MBA, LBA, and Medieval materials in secondary contexts. Only a few squares on the southern margin of the erosional gulley (rows 26, 27, and some of 28, numbered on the right side of the grid in Figure 18.8) encountered stable landforms with intact cultural deposits in primary context. The artifacts in the erosion gulley at PD1 north testify to the presence of Medieval, LBA, and MBA sites somewhere uphill and to the west of PD1. Materials of the same eras also appeared at PD1 south in primary context.

Our most important results came from PD1 south. At PD1 south, the artifacts were in primary context, but there was very little stratigraphic separation between cultural components. Two Medieval sherds were found in Level 2 (10–20 cm deep), beneath some Srubnaya sherds and above others. Occasional Mesolithic flint microliths were found in Level 3 (20–30 cm), below many LBA Srubnaya artifacts but in the same level with others. One MBA sherd also was found in Level 3, but again Srubnaya sherds were found in the same level. Like all of the steppe soils excavated at every site in the SVP, the soils at PD1 were extensively churned by burrowing rodents (*susliks*), so stratigraphic separation between chronologically separate components was observed as a statistical tendency rather than an absolute distinction between levels. Pit features could be seen only in a smudged and indistinct way and usually only in profile, after they had been excavated, because rodent burrows created such varied soil colors and textures in any horizontal floor. However, since 99 percent of the 343 ceramic sherds catalogued from PD1 north and south had color, paste, and decoration typical of the Srubnaya culture, with only seven sherds dated to the Medieval and MBA periods, PD1 as a whole can be interpreted as a Srubnaya site with very faint traces of occupation in the Mesolithic, MBA, and Medieval eras.

PD1 North

Electrical resistivity remote sensing was undertaken at the PD1 site prior to the excavation season in 2000, directed by I. V. Zhurbin. Subsurface pit features might be revealed by their anomalous electrical conductivity. The electrical sensors revealed no anomalies around PD1 south, where the 1996 survey had found Srubnaya sherds in test pits, but discovered a large electrical subsurface anomaly 15 to 20 m to the north, which was designated PD1 north. This anomaly seemed to derive from a large subsurface pit-like feature, suspected at first to be a house pit, northwest of the location tested with STPs in 1995. This feature was excavated in 2000 (Figure 18.8).

Unfortunately, the subsurface feature detected at PD1 north turned out to be a natural erosion gulley with a narrow, water-eroded base and broad, flat slopes, filled with flood and sheet wash deposits. It contained obvious gulley-and-fill soils, with alternating coarse and fine micro-layers clearly deposited by water, visible in profile in the walls of the excavation square illustrated in Figure 18.8. The gulley contained LBA and Medieval artifacts, out of context and mixed, including a fragment of folded bronze sheet metal (Figure 18.10:31), derived from unknown sites probably located uphill.

On the southern end of the PD1 north excavation, four MBA sherds were found in Square E27 (Figure 18.8), on a level, stable landform overlooking the northern erosion gulley, possibly in primary context, representing the faint traces of an MBA camp (Figure 18.10:14–17). A very distinctive MBA-style barbed flint arrowhead was found in E29, downslope from E27, possibly derived from E27 (Figure 18.10:18). These few, highly fragmented artifacts suggest the presence of an MBA camp at PD1 north and, as will be seen below, extending between PD1 north and PD1 south, but its material signature was very faint. The MBA camp left less than 1 percent of the artifacts deposited during the LBA usage of the same site. This difference implies a functionally different kind of site usage/activity

at the MBA and LBA herding camps, probably with larger and/or more frequently repeated camping groups at PD1 during the LBA.

PD1 South

PD1 south was a 64-m² unit (8 × 8 m) near the edge of the terrace where the 1996 testing had found Srubnaya sherds (Figures 18.3, 18.5, 18.6, 18.9). All soils were passed through ¼-inch mesh screens, and 2-L samples were taken from each 10-cm level of each 2 × 2 for flotation. Within 2 × 2s, finds were recorded to each 1-m × 1-m quad. Quad 1 is the northwest or upper left quad, and Quads 2 to 4 are numbered clockwise.

The soils were salinized silty-clayey-loesses, weathered in place, with a gray-brown A horizon, a thin B horizon, and a yellowish clayey *materik*, or C horizon. Burrowing rodents had tunneled through and mottled the site soils, occasionally digging into the *materik*, making it difficult to see and distinguish cultural features.

Most of the artifacts were concentrated in an area of about 4 × 3 m in the northeastern corner of the 8-m × 8-m excavation (I18,19; K18,19), but there was at least one other, lighter artifact concentration in the southern part (Figure 18.9). The eastern side of the excavation, nearer the edge of the terrace overlooking the floodplain, generally had higher artifact densities than the western side.

Radiocarbon dates (Table 18.1) from the southern concentration (A16) and from the northern concentration (I18, K18) within PD1 south are almost the same and overlap a slightly older date from the northeastern corner, suggesting occupations within a narrow chronological range, the same time period as Krasnosamarskoe, 1900 to 1700 BC.

One posthole-like feature and one irregular pit feature were recorded at PD1 south (Figure 18.9, top). The pit feature, possibly two intercut pits, was visible in profile in K18 and K17, and its fill was recorded as being sandier and looser than the surrounding compact soil. Many animal bones and ceramic sherds came from these squares, probably from the pit fill. No ash or charcoal concentrations were detected, and no hearth was found, but one 1 × 1 square (B17/Quad 4) contained an area of fire-reddened soil and lumps of vitrified sediment, perhaps heated beneath a surface fire, and B17/1 also produced fire-cracked jasper pebbles. A few other fire-cracked jasper pebbles were found in K19 and I19, in the northeastern artifact cluster. These might be the faint traces of surface fires.

Within the northeastern artifact cluster, one 1-m × 1-m square (K18/Quad 1) contained twice the weight of artifacts seen in any adjacent 1-m × 1-m square and four times more than the adjacent squares to the south (Figure 18.9). Since

Figure 18.8 PD1 north plan and profile on the Zh transect. Photo of the E-Zh/28-29 4 × 4 with the erosional gulley in its northwest corner.

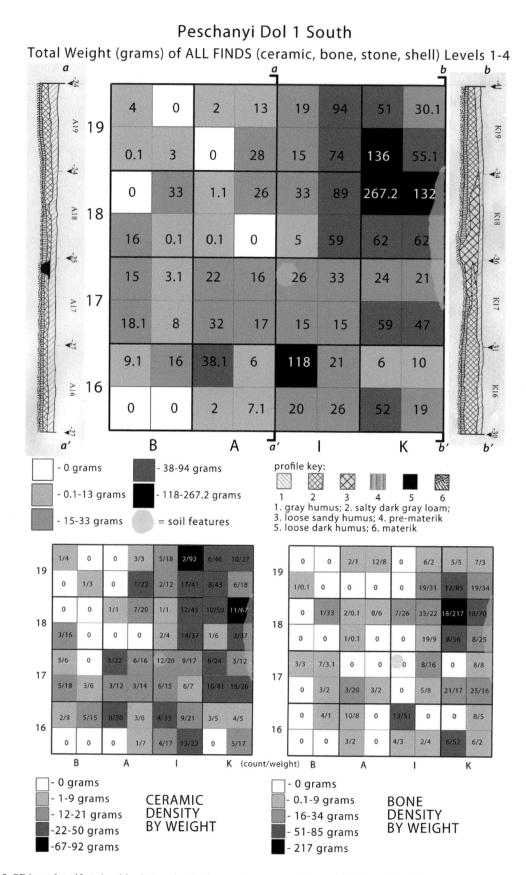

Figure 18.9. PD1 south artifact densities in Levels 1 to 4, per meters squared, by weight. Top: All artifacts. Bottom: Just ceramic and bone. Profiles on the indicated transects are at the top, with a posthole on the left and a broad trash pit on the right profile.

Table 18.1 Radiocarbon Dates from PD1

Lab Number	Unit/Quad/Level	Material	Age BP	Calibrated BC (OxCal 12/2012)
AA47798	A 16/3/3	Bone	3480 ± 52	1942–1682 cal BC, 95.4 percent probability
AA47799	I 18/2/2	Bone	3565 ± 55	2037–1748 cal BC, 94.3 percent probability
AA47800	K 18/1/2	Bone	3440 ± 56	1899–1615 cal BC, 95.4 percent probability

most of this artifact mass consisted of animal bones, it is deemed possible that we encountered a disposal pit in this square. An irregular broad pit was evident in the sidewall of K18, although the soils were so disturbed by rodents that this feature was not clearly defined in plan. This could have been a primary disposal area within one camp or more likely a long-term disposal area through multiple occupations at the site. The weathered and carnivore-chewed surfaces of the animal bone (see below) dictate against disposal in a filled-in pit feature, but an open pit could have been used for garbage disposal during successive LBA occupations.

The overlapping but separate centers of artifact density within the excavation could be the result of an overlapping series of seasonal camps, none of which contained much in the way of permanent facilities. Campfires seem to have been made on the open ground, and shelters might have been tents with perhaps a supporting post (I-17/1).

One MBA sherd was found in Square I-19/3, Level 3. It was the only MBA sherd found at PD1 south and could represent a very low-density continuation of the MBA site found 16 m to the north, in Square E27 at PD1 north (Figure 18.8). If the five MBA sherds and the arrowhead in PD1 south and north are derived from the same episodes of MBA occupation, then the MBA camp extended over an area of at least 16 to 18 m, but with a density of just one to four artifacts per 2-m × 2-m square, providing an insight into why MBA settlements are so infrequently found. Although we were looking specifically for ephemeral sites, this one was so ephemeral that we probably would have missed it if a denser LBA camp had not been established at the same place.

The artifacts recovered at PD1 south and north together included 343 ceramic sherds, weighing 1,446 g; 395 animal bone fragments, weighing 1,160 g; and 29 stone tools, weighing 43.5 g. One piece of cuprous material, possibly slag, but probably a burned fragment of copper ore, was found in Square K19. Most of the artifacts were found between 10 and 40 cm deep. The fact that ceramics outweighed animal bone immediately identified this site as functionally different from the permanent settlement at Krasnosamarskoe, where animal bones outweighed all other artifacts.

PD1 Ceramics

The ceramics at PD1 were analyzed by I. N. Vasil'eva and N. P. Salugina, using methods developed by A. A. Bobrinskii in the ceramic ethno-archaeological laboratory that he created at Samara State University (Bobrinskii 1978; Bobrinskii and Vasil'eva 1998; Vasil'eva 2011). Their methods included a detailed microscopic examination of the ceramic paste, an analysis of construction methods, and visual observation of the firing characteristics. The following section is based on their unpublished SVP report.

Vasil'eva and Salugina analyzed 42 ceramic sherds from PD1. The pottery was highly fragmented, the individual sherds were quite small, and they included relatively few rims or bases, so construction methods were not observable except in a few cases. Two sherds were from wheel-made Medieval pots, probably dated to the Golden Horde period of the twelfth and thirteenth centuries AD. The remaining 40 sherds were handmade Bronze Age sherds fired in open fires. Five sherds were datable by type and fabric to the MBA (this was all of the MBA ceramics found), and 35 conformed to the LBA Srubnaya type (this was a 10 percent sample of the LBA ceramics).

The five MBA sherds (Figure 18.10:14–17) were surprisingly heterogeneous in paste and composition. Potting clays from three different clay sources ("regions") were used to make the five MBA sherds. In addition to the differences observed in the compositions of potting clays, the intentionally added tempers also were variable. Three different tempering recipes were identified in five sherds: (1) clay, grog (old sherds), and organics that left voids in the paste; (2) clay, crushed snail shell (up to 2 mm), and organics, leaving voids; and (3) clay, grog, burned bone, and the manure of ruminants, leaving chewed plant fibers up to 7 mm long. The second tempering recipe, with added snail shell, was most common, found in three sherds. The vessels were fired in similar ways, with a light brown color on both the inside and outside surfaces and a core that was almost black. The surface was decorated with comb-impressions. The varied potting clays and tempering recipes in five sherds indicate that the MBA occupation was not a single event but the residue of multiple different camps by different groups with different potting clays, and each broken pot was widely scattered.

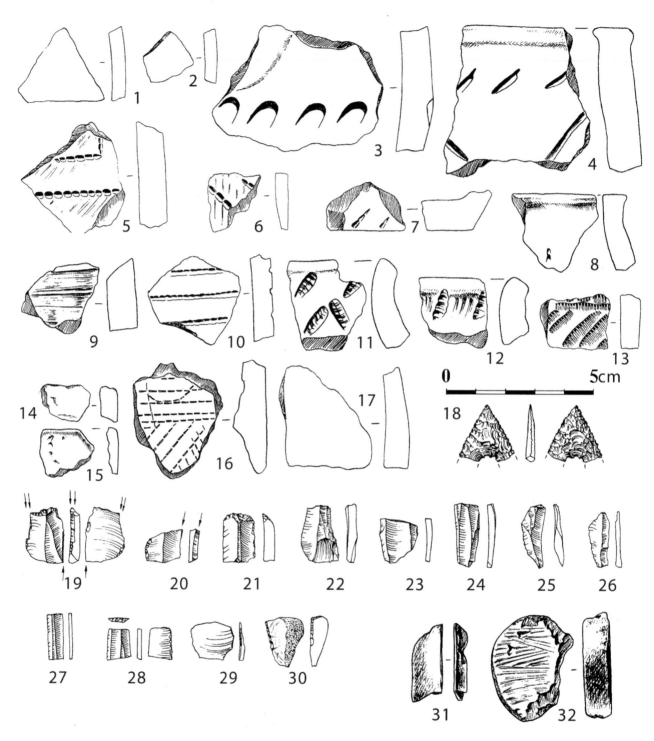

Figure 18.10 Artifacts from PD1, with excavation square/quadrant and catalogue number. Medieval sherds: 1. I18/1 #404; 2. D29/1 #403; Srubnaya sherds: 3. K18/1 #254; 4. K18/3 #325; 5. I16/1 #215; 6. B17/1 #118; 7. I17/2 #202; 8. D29/4 #94; 9. I18/3 #321; 10. K17/1 #382; 11. I16/3 #299; 12. I17/1 #165; 13. Zh28/1 #55; Middle Bronze Age sherds: 14. E27/2 #390; 15. I19/3 #360; 16. E27/2 #388; 17. E27/2 #387; 18. E29/3 #66—MBA barbed flint point; 19. Z30.3 #136—retouched flint fragment; 20. Z29/3 #141—gray banded flint blade, one edge worked; 21. A16/3 #77—flint end scraper; 22. D30/1 #409—flake fragment; 23. Zh28/2 #85—gray flint blade midsection; 24. D29/1 #410—gray streaked flint micro—blade; 25. D29/4 #149—gray and black flint flake possibly retouched; 26. Zh30/2 #97—cream color flint blade fragment; 27. B16/1 #65—gray and white striped flint micro-blade; 28. K19/4 #240—cream flint blade midsection; 29. Zh29 #238—gray flint flake, proximal; 30. K19/3 #160—flint cortical flake worked edge; 31. Zh30/4 #235—bronze fragment; 32. E28/2 #98—clay disk.

The 35 LBA Srubnaya sherds examined from PD1 were even more heterogeneous. Vasil'eva and Salugina were surprised to find 15 different kinds of clay, extracted from distinct clay deposits, which they refer to as "regions," and within those 15 distinct clay extraction regions, some exhibited slight variations that they refer to as "places." The LBA pottery vessels carried into PD1 therefore were made of clay gathered from at least 15 different "regions," presumably reflecting distinct clay deposits, and no single LBA pot is represented by more than three sherds, implying that the sherds were scattered widely.

The 15 clay-type "regions" were defined by different proportions of silt and clay (from silt to silty clay to clay) and by different amounts and types of nonplastic natural inclusions such as different kinds and sizes of sand grains, bog iron, oolite, fish scales, shells, plants of various kinds, and other nonplastic contents (Table 18.2 at end of chapter). The 15 different potting clays recognized in this way occurred in just 35 Srubnaya sherds examined from PD1, in only 10 percent of the ceramics. For comparison, the clays used to make the much larger volume of Srubnaya ceramics (190 sherds studied by Vasil'eva and Salugina) at the permanent settlement of Krasnosamarskoe, where there were two ceramic types, came from five "regions," probably five clay deposits within walking distance of Krasnosamarskoe. The Srubnaya pottery carried into PD1 was made from three times the number of clay sources seen in the much larger sample of pottery from the two-phase settlement at Krasnosamarskoe and therefore probably came from at least three such Srubnaya settlements. Vasil'eva and Salugina were surprised by the number of "regions" they encountered in this small collection of sherds from a single site. The great variety of clay sources, they said, indicates that pots were taken to PD1 by different groups of Srubnaya people from a large territory.

These varied clays were then combined with tempering materials using six different tempering recipes. (Five tempering recipes were recognized at the Krasnosamarskoe settlement.) All tempering methods included grog but with different additional materials added, presumably by different potters. Shell was not added to any of the tempering recipes, but organics represented by voids, manure, and burned bone were combined with grog temper in six different ways. These were local variations on a shared custom of grog tempering by potters from different Srubnaya settlements.

PD1 was used between 1900 and 1700 BC by Srubnaya herders whose pottery was made in multiple different places. It was not used simply by the nearest Srubnaya settlement. Either cattle from many different localities with different potting clays were pooled in the valley, and the herders who watched the pooled cattle alternated between settlements, or different Srubnaya settlements with different potting clays used the valley sequentially, perhaps in different years. The second possibility, sequential usage by independent Srubnaya groups, does not explain why independent herders camped in the same place and even used the same trash pit if they were, in this hypothesis, independent of each other. Also, if they were independent users, an additional complexity is raised: how was access to PD pastures scheduled and negotiated between independent herding groups? The first alternative fits better with the archaeological evidence for various kinds of regional organization (see below), and it describes how cattle are managed in the region today, with three nearby modern villages pooling their cattle in Peschanyi Dol under a shared herder.

PD1 Lithics

At PD1 north and south together, we found 29 stone artifacts, flakes included, weighing 43.5 g (Figure 18.10:19–30). Five of these were narrow flint microliths on prismatic blades and probably represent the residue of camps dated to the Mesolithic or Early Neolithic, before domesticated animals were adopted in the Volga-Ural steppes (Figure 18.10:24–28). Two microliths were found in PD1 south in Squares B16 and K19, and three were found in PD1 north in secondary eroded deposits. The other stone tools probably were associated with the Bronze Age occupations at PD1. A unifacial endscraper was found in PD1 south, and a few broken prismatic blade midsections were recovered from both PD1 north and south. Most of the stone tools were opportunistic modified flakes.

Jasper pebbles and cobbles seem to be incorporated in the natural sediments, because many unmodified jasper pebbles, some water-worn, were recovered from the excavated soils. Some of these were fire-cracked and therefore testify to the presence of campfires on the site, which were otherwise difficult to detect archaeologically. But only seven of the modified stone tools were made on these local jasper pebbles (Figure 18.10:30). With less than five unmodified flakes found, no tool manufacture happened at the site, and tool maintenance or sharpening was a rare activity. Flakes with minimally retouched edges, regarded as opportunistic tools, and broken prismatic blade sections were the most common stone tool categories. Most of the tools were made of flint that was carried into the site. The flint was varied in colors: solid gray, white or cream-colored, gray and black banded, and gray and white streaked. A gray flint broken barbed projectile point with a notch in the center of the base and two flaring barbs was the only bifacial tool; it conformed to a classic type for the MBA Poltavka culture. It was found near the small cluster of MBA sherds at PD1 north.

PD1 Fauna

The excavations at PD1 yielded 65 mammalian animal bones identifiable to species, derived primarily from domesticated animals, probably ancient (Table 15.38). An additional 42 animal bones identifiable to species but derived from burrowing rodents and voles probably were modern. Unidentifiable mammalian bone fragments totaled 212. In the first group, animals that probably were ancient, sheep/goat was the dominant taxon, with 52.3 percent of identifiable specimens; cattle were 38.5 percent; horse were 4.6 percent; and there was 1.5 percent each of pig, dog, and roe deer. The sheep-dominant fauna was quite different from the standard faunal profile of permanent Srubnaya settlements, which were usually dominated by cattle.

Flotation also yielded a few small bones. Among these were a fragment of the epiphysis of a cattle tibia; a human phalange; four dog canines, one burned in a fire; a dog carpal; and a dog phalange. The dog remains are interesting, in light of the dog rituals documented at Krasnosamarskoe. Perhaps the Srubnaya herders at PD1 wore dog canines as ornaments. The single human finger-bone was either the result of an accident or was carried loose into the camp. The second possibility reminds us that the structure at Krasnosamarskoe also contained a few curated human bones, and four of the Srubnaya graves in the Krasnosamarskoe IV cemetery contained a curated bone from another human. Apparently human bones (family members?) were occasionally recovered and carried around or curated by some Srubnaya individuals.

The preservation of dental roots, necessary for incremental banding studies of seasonality, was poor, so we could not recover data on the season of occupation. The poor condition of the animal bone at the PD herding camps was a direct result of the temporary kind of occupation these sites represented. Russell (Chapter 16) observed that the condition of the bone surfaces indicates that the PD animal bones were burned in open fires and discarded on the open ground. Some were chewed by carnivores, digested, excreted, and weathered. The chewing marks of dog-sized carnivores and actual dog bones at PD1 south indicate that dogs were present in the herding camps and that animal bones from human food were not protected from dogs. The concentration of discarded bones in a single 2-m × 2-m square (K18 and part of K19) suggests that the pit feature seen in these squares was a target zone for bone discard, used repeatedly by different campers.

Excavations at PD2

PD2 was about 2.3 km upstream and southwest of PD1, in the middle valley, on a low, level promontory overlooking *Typha* and *Phragmites* meadows, here about .75 km wide (Figure 18.11). The stream had eroded the edge of the first terrace, cutting it into a series of peninsulas and bays, and PD2 was on a peninsula. We found very little Srubnaya occupation above PD2, although many places seemed to be good locations.

The soils at PD2 were quite different from those at PD1. Instead of an erosional fan developing into salty *solenetz* soils, as at PD1, we found at PD2 a very dark brown or black chernozem more than 1 m deep (Figure 18.11). The deep chernozem that has developed and survived here indicates that this promontory is an extremely stable landform and has been under steppe grass cover continuously since the Bronze Age. Artifacts drifted down through the chernozem to the bottom of that soil horizon, down to 1 m (10 levels), but more than half of the artifacts were found between 20 and 40 cm (two levels), probably the approximate depth of the LBA surface.

The excavated area at PD2 was 32 m², half the size of the excavation at PD1 south. Most of the artifacts were concentrated in an area of 3 × 3 m in the northwestern corner of the excavation (Figure 18.12), less than half the size of the principal concentration at PD1, but a light scatter extended over the entire excavation area. The combined weight of ceramic, bone, and stone artifacts per excavated meter squared was about the same at PD2 as at PD1, but because of the deeper *materik* and deeper excavation at PD2, the artifact weight per cubic meter was much less at PD2.

At PD2, we found two particularly interesting artifacts, given the small size of the Srubnaya occupation and the absence of even the simplest facility such as a stone setting for a fire. One was a typical Srubnaya-type stone mortar about 10 × 5 cm, found in A3/Quad 1, Level 3 (Figure 18.13:6). It was either a reused fragment of a larger mortar of a more typical Srubnaya size or an intentionally small hand mortar. Mortars usually are interpreted as grain grinders in Srubnaya settlements, tools used to make flour. At this small camp, herders might have used the mortar for grinding pigments (?) or something else.

More surprising was a small (1 cm long) bubbly lump of reheated copper found in B4/Quad 1, Level 4, an artifact usually interpreted as a residue of metalworking. Similar copper bits from Krasnosamarskoe and PD2 are relatively dense and have the green patina of oxidized copper, so probably were by-products of an activity such as casting or forging rather than smelting. Copper and cuprous mineral ore were being carried around in small chunks and worked in a very dispersed manner at the Krasnosamarskoe settlement and even at herding camp PD2.

Figure 18.11 Excavations at PD2 in 2000 looking east across the Peschanyi Dol valley. Note the dark chernozem soil and the screens tagged with graffiti reading "Gray Legion of Death" in English.

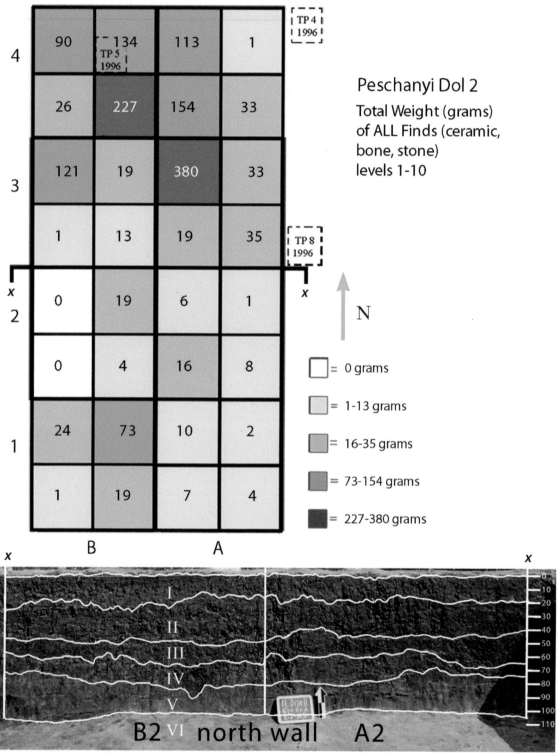

Figure 18.12 Plan and profile of PD2.

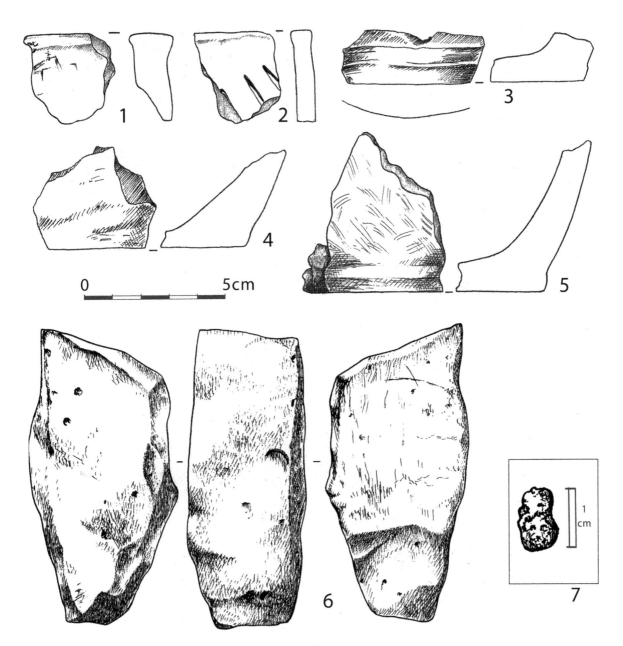

Figure 18.13 Artifacts from PD2, including a mortar and copper casting waste.

One radiocarbon date (AA47801) was obtained on animal bone from Square A3/3, Level 4, at PD2. It was Medieval: 5141 ± 42, or 1315 to 1450 AD (Table 2.1), associated with the Medieval pottery found at PD2 (see "Ceramics" below). Animal bones were much lower in count and weight at PD2 than at PD1, and they obviously included Medieval as well as Srubnaya food waste. However, because the potting clays and the styles of Srubnaya pottery were largely the same between PD1 and PD2, we assume that they were occupied by overlapping groups.

At PD2, we recovered 183 ceramic sherds weighing 931 g, 13 stone tools weighing 415 g, and 133 animal bone fragments weighing 246 g (Figure 18.14). PD2 had about one-third the number of animal bones and about half the weight per meter squared of animal bone compared to PD1. This reduction in animal bones between PD1 and PD2 is important, as it indicates that food was consumed more frequently at PD1 than at PD2. Ceramics outweighed bone at PD2, a signature trait of these ephemeral camps, where there was relatively little food preparation for few people, and stone tools constituted a distinctly high percentage of the artifacts.

PD2 Ceramics

Diagnostic ceramic sherds at PD2 were derived primarily from the LBA Srubnaya culture with two sherds assigned to the Golden Horde period (thirteenth to fourteenth centuries AD) and one sherd probably an early Russian product of the fourteenth to fifteenth centuries, according to Vasil'eva and Salugina's unpublished technical report. The only radiocarbon date from PD2 was associated with these occupations. The ceramic fragments at PD2 averaged a little bigger in size than at PD1; large base fragments of ceramic pots were preserved at PD2 better than at PD1.

Vasil'eva and Salugina analyzed 39 sherds (a 22 percent sample) of the LBA Srubnaya culture at PD2. Twelve different "regions" or clay types were present in these 39 sherds. Of these 12 clay sources, 9 were the same as at PD1. Three of the clays were from new sources, not represented at PD1. These naturally different clays were combined with tempering materials in five different grog-tempering recipes, again like those at PD1. These were clay and grog; clay and organics, leaving voids; clay, grog, and organic voids; clay, grog, and manure; and clay, grog, and burned bone. The great majority were tempered with two of these recipes: (1) clay, grog, and organic voids and (2) clay, grog, and manure. All other tempering recipes were seen only in single sherds. The pots were made in forms using a paddle-and-anvil technique for the bases and strap molding inside a hollow form to build up the walls, leaving occasional traces of the form against the outer surfaces of the recovered sherds. The pots were fired in an open fire at temperatures higher than 650 to 700°C. The inner and outer surfaces of the sherds were light brown or red-brown, and the core was black.

Vasil'eva and Salugina concluded that the Srubnaya pottery at PD1 and PD2 was morphologically, stylistically, and technically quite similar, and half the clays came from the same deposits. They felt that it was safe to assume that the people living at PD1 and PD2 were "relatives or had some familiar intimate relations." Nine of the clay sources documented at PD1 and PD2 were the same; PD1 contained another six clay types not seen at PD2, and PD2 contained three clay types not seen at PD1. Together, the two camps contained pottery made from 18 distinct clay deposits, half of them shared. Vasil'eva and Salugina decided that the pots that produced these sherds were taken to Peschanyi Dol "by different Srubnaya groups from different territories during a definite simultaneous period of time."

PD2 Lithics

At PD2, we recovered 13 stone artifacts weighing 415 g. The very small number of flakes indicates that stone tool manufacture did not occur here. Lithic tool maintenance and sharpening also were not activities conducted at either PD site. A white flint side scraper was the only chipped stone tool identified. Four white flint and gray flint flakes or broken flake fragments were recovered. Six quartzite flakes were recovered at PD2, and this lithic material was used most commonly in the Eneolithic by the Khvalynsk culture. A quartzite Khvalynsk-style side scraper was found near PD1, eroding from the terrace bank. So it is possible that there are faint traces of an Eneolithic camp at PD2. The small stone hand mortar found in A3/1, Level 3, has already been described. There was also a quartzite cobble with a pecked channel across one face, possibly an arrow straightener (?).

PD2 Animal Bones

At PD2, we recovered 133 pieces of bone weighing 246 g. As at PD1, sheep-goat was the numerically dominant taxon. In second place was horse, unlike PD1. No dog bones were found (Table 15.38). But very few bones at PD2 were identifiable to species, so we cannot trust the species ratios. Really, the outstanding aspect of the animal bone is its extremely fragmented state, and the very few number of bones overall, about one-third the number of bones and half the bone weight per meter squared seen at PD1. This decline in food remains from PD1 to PD2 is significant. Overall artifact counts per meter squared were about the same at PD1 and PD2, but animal bone declined significantly at PD2, indicating that less eating was done there. This drop in animal bone was a leading indicator of the decline in all classes of artifacts that characterized sites located upstream from PD2.

The Peschanyi Dol Herding Camps: Conclusions

We were able to find ephemeral camps by using systematic shovel testing in Peschanyi Dol in five places where no artifacts or other traces of prehistoric occupation were visible on the surface, in addition to one place (PD1) where surface artifacts were found. We found ephemeral components from the Mesolithic/Neolithic, MBA, LBA, Golden Horde era, and early Russian periods. Electrical resistivity sensing was successful at PD1 north in locating a large subsurface anomaly. This turned out to be natural (an erosion gulley) rather than cultural, but the scattered artifacts associated with it were still interesting because they included the faint traces of an MBA camp.

The little data we recovered from the MBA occupation at PD1 suggest that the MBA usage of this site was almost 100 times lighter in artifact deposition than the LBA usage. This probably means that the LBA usage was more frequent and regular over multiple years. The LBA settling-down process does seem to have made pasture usage more intensive and regular near the LBA settlements in the Samara River valley. We know from the absence of settlement evidence that MBA herding was more mobile, and we know from the tightly clustered dates at the MBA Krasnosamarskoe IV cemetery that it was used for a brief period only, around 2900 to 2800 BC, and then was abandoned and not used again for many centuries. It is odd to think that such brief and passing settlements, with one to four MBA artifacts per 2 × 2 m at PD1, could have been created by people with substantial wealth. But the richest Poltavka kurgan grave in the western steppes, Utyevka I, is located just 5 km east of the mouth of Peschanyi Dol (SVP site 32, Figure 2.1). The central grave contained two gold earrings decorated with granulation, the oldest example of granulation in the steppes, as well as a copper pin with a decorative iron head forged onto one end, the only example of the decorative use of iron (Anthony 2007:335). The Poltavka pottery styles in the grave suggest a date probably in the middle of the third millennium BC, although this is very close in date to the earliest known examples of granulation in Early Dynastic Mesopotamia and Troy II. This precocious set of ornaments was carried around in a wagon, which could have stopped briefly at the PD1 north site.

The count of LBA artifacts per meter squared was about the same at PD2 and PD1 (Figure 2.7). Krasnosamarskoe had much higher artifact counts, and the percentages of stone, bone, and ceramics were quite different.

The PD camps were fundamentally different from the Krasnosamarskoe settlement in basic artifact inventories (Figure 18.14). Both PD1 and PD2 had a high percentage of lithics and a relatively low percentage of animal bone by count, while the permanent settlement yielded more animal bone by count than ceramic sherds and a very low proportion of lithics. Also, at Krasnosamarskoe, animal bones were discarded into formal facilities (pits), where they were protected from scavengers and the weather, while at the PD herding camps, bones were discarded on the surface and were gnawed by carnivores and weathered. These differences in artifact inventories and in deposition indicate that the PD sites were functionally discrete from the Krasnosamarskoe settlement, not just smaller versions of it.

Animal bones declined significantly even between PD1 and PD2, suggesting that more food was eaten at PD1 than at PD2. Farther upstream, perhaps meals were not prepared at camps, which were more like short-term day stations. A ceramic spindle whorl of Srubnaya type was found at PD1 north, in a secondary context in an erosion deposit (Figure 18.10.32); perhaps this object suggests visits by females to the herders at PD1 (to bring food?).

The function of the PD sites is suggested by the close correlation between places used in the summer by modern herders and the PD sites. The modern herder used the meadows around PD1 and PD2 for the longest observed time when we were watching him in July and early August 2000. PD1 and PD2 are 2.5 and 4.7 km from the Samara River. Just 300 m upstream from PD2, beginning at PD3, artifact densities fell off sharply, suggesting less frequent or shorter visits in the upper part of the middle valley. Many of our testing locations were situated in the middle valley above PD3, and they contained no cultural artifacts. This is also a part of the modern valley where we never saw the herder lingering with his herd. Our LBA sites resumed very near where the modern herder has a permanent corral, at PD4 to 6. These are very low-density, low-artifact count sites, but two of the three have Srubnaya pottery. The modern herder does not use the upper valley, above this location, and our excavations in the upper valley, concentrated around the source spring at Filipovka, also yielded no artifacts. The LBA pastoral usage of Peschanyi Dol seems to mirror the pattern of modern pastoral usage.

The floodplain orientation of the LBA herding camps in the Peschanyi Dol valley provides support for Sedova's suggestion that Srubnaya herding patterns in the middle Volga region were localized around permanent settlements (Sedova 2000:211). The PD herding camps used most frequently and/or intensively by LBA herders were those closest to the floodplain.

Together, the 81 Srubnaya pottery sherds from PD1 and PD2 examined by Vasil'eva and Salugina derived from 18 distinct clay deposits, more than three times more diversity in clays than appeared in the 190 Srubnaya sherds examined from the settlement of Krasnosamarskoe (five sources), although the Krasnosamarskoe sample was two times larger than PD1 and 2 combined. If other permanent Srubnaya settlements were like Krasnosamarskoe in ceramic source diversity, then at least three to four settlements used the PD camps. PD1 contained six unique clay types not seen at PD2, and PD2 contained three unique clay types not seen at PD1, but the sharing of half of the clay types suggests that herders from a single settlement used both camps, moving from one to the other.

The simplest herding system would have been for each LBA settlement to use the *closest* seasonal pastures, a system of sedentary, independent local herding. What we found suggests a more complex, negotiated, and cooperative herding system. The seasonal meadows in Peschanyi Dol were used by diverse Srubnaya settlements, necessarily located at various distances from Peschanyi Dol. The use of one meadow by different settlements at different distances implies that cattle were driven to *selected* pastures rather than the *nearest* pasture. This suggests some degree of cooperation between

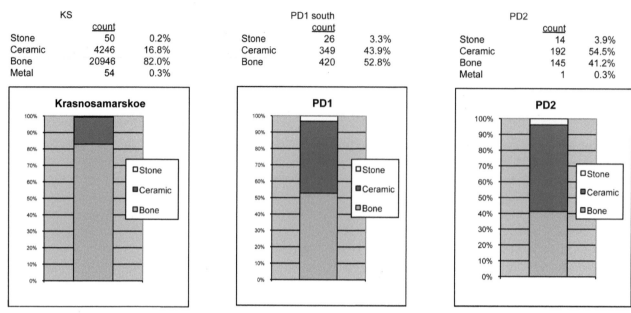

KS	count	
Stone	50	0.2%
Ceramic	4246	16.8%
Bone	20946	82.0%
Metal	54	0.3%

PD1 south	count	
Stone	26	3.3%
Ceramic	349	43.9%
Bone	420	52.8%

PD2	count	
Stone	14	3.9%
Ceramic	192	54.5%
Bone	145	41.2%
Metal	1	0.3%

Figure 18.14 Percentage of stone, ceramic, and bone finds by count at three sites.

contemporary settlements in scheduling access to the pastures in Peschanyi Dol. The contemporaneity of the sites in the cooperative system is suggested by close similarities in Srubnaya ceramic styles and in tempering recipes of clays at PD1 and PD2; by radiocarbon dates showing occupation at PD1 in a narrow chronological range, similar to Krasnosamarskoe, around 1900 to 1700 BC; and finally by the spatial overlap of distinct Srubnaya occupations using different clays from different sources but camping in the same spot and using the same open trash pit at PD1. Pots made from the same clays were broken at PD1 and at PD2, suggesting that then, as now, the same herder was present at PD1 and PD2, moving between them with his herd, but the surprising heterogeneity of the Srubnaya potting clays at each camp site suggests that the home base of the herder (and therefore the clay source) shifted as different Srubnaya settlements took turns caring for their combined herds.

Cooperative herding arrangements are not the only archaeological evidence for cooperative agreements and even forms of specialization between Srubnaya settlements across this region. The provisioning of beef cattle to the Srubnaya copper miners at Gorny was another indicator of region-wide integration, in this case to organize and support copper mining. The cattle at Gorny were taken from a narrow age range (2–4 years old) not representative of a natural herd (Antipina, Lebedeva, and Chernykh 2002), and the cattle bones were cut and sawed in standardized ways (Morales and Antipina 2003:344). A third indicator of regional integration was the ritual specialization at

Krasnosamarskoe and its stature as the only place in the region where the dog sacrifice/initiation was performed. This suggests a ritual affiliation for the performance of winter initiation ceremonies. The evidence from potting clays suggesting that multiple Srubnaya communities cooperated in sending their herds and herders (and pots) seasonally to Peschanyi Dol fits this larger pattern of regional integration.

Together, three indicators of region-wide organization can be seen in the archaeological evidence: for copper mining (Gorny), ritual ceremonies (Krasnosamarskoe), and summer herding (Peschanyi Dol). The different organizational scales and responsibilities implied by these very different activities suggest a heterarchical, multiscalar form of tribal integration and political decision making—in an economy without agriculture. Heterarchical political institutions of community management and social affiliation operated at different scales and at different seasons—at a local scale for herding and perhaps for ritual gatherings, perhaps at a larger scale for the management of mining at Gorny and at other sites such as Mikhailovka Ovsianka, and for patron-client relationships between people like those at Krasnosamarskoe and the local elites at Spiridonovka (discussed in the conclusion of Chapter 2 and in Chapter 11). It is rare that the overlapping integrative and affiliative institutions that define tribal social organization can be seen in archaeological data, but it is one of the benefits of a multidisciplinary research strategy that these different kinds and levels of LBA regional tribal integration have become visible through multiple distinct windows of evidence.

Table 18.2 Peschanyi Dol 1 Ceramic Sources

R	P	DESCRIPTION
1	1	Silty clay containing sand fine (0.1–0.3 mm), unsmoothed, quartzite, transparent and frosted sand, with oolite bog iron of 1 to 3 mm; single inclusions of shell of freshwater mollusks, the size of the unsmoothed pieces is less than 0.5 to 2 mm and also single plant traces of 1 to 3 mm.
1	2	Silty clay of the same quality and contents, differs through the degree of the contents of sand. The contents of sand are average.
2	1	Silty clay containing iron and fine (0.1–0.2 mm), unsmoothed, mostly quartzite transparent and colored sand, friable inclusions of bog iron of oval shape and bright red color 0.5 to 1 mm; with small concentration of shell (10–15 inclusions for 1 cm²), the size of the pieces is less than 1 mm, and there are single fish scales up to 3 mm; single crushed plant remains (detritus) and string-like water plants or plants growing near the water.
3	1	Silty clay containing iron and fine (0.1–0.2 mm), unsmoothed, and semi-smoothed sand (colored, transparent and frosted quartzite, flattened black); with oolite bog iron of 1 to 2 mm; small concentration of shell less than 1 mm and up to 3 mm; dense clay blocks up to 1 mm, single plant traces up to 1 mm.
3	2	Silty clay of the same quality and contents as Place 1, but it contains less sand and the quality of sand is similar to the previous but the size of single inclusions is up to 0.5 mm; the size of the bog iron is up to 4 mm.
4	1	Silty clay, enriched with iron, containing fine (0.1–0.5 mm), unsmoothed colored, and transparent quartzite and semi-smoothed black sand, with iron represented by friable oval red-brown inclusions up to 5 mm and oolite bog iron of 1 mm, with small concentration of shell of less than 3 mm, dense clay blocks of 1 mm; single prints of plants up to 1 to 2 mm.
4	2	Silty clay of the same quality and contents but contains less sand.
5	1	Clay, containing dust-like and fine (less than 0.1 mm) quartzite unsmoothed sand; oolite bog iron of 1 to 2 mm, white friable carbonate inclusions of less than 0.1 mm.
6	1	Clay, containing fine, quartzite transparent and colored, unsmoothed and semi-smoothed sand, of 0.1 to 1 mm; with iron inclusions of oval soft brown pieces.
7	1	Clay slightly enriched with sand. It is dust-like (up to 0.2 mm), quartzite unsmoothed and semi-smoothed; with oolite bog iron of 1 mm; rounded dense blocks of pure clay of 1 mm.
8	1	Clay slightly enriched with sand and iron. The sand is fine sand from 0.1 to 0.3 mm, colored, frosted, and black unsmoothed and quartzite semi-smoothed; oval iron inclusions are of brown color and 1.5 mm and bright red ochre inclusions of 1 mm; rounded clay blocks of 1 mm.
9	1	Clay, slightly enriched with sand and iron. The sand is fine unsmoothed, quartzite, transparent, and frosted of 0.1 to 0.2 mm; friable iron inclusions of red color up to 0.5 mm and ochre bright red inclusions up to 0.5 mm; clay blocks up to 1 mm, some contents of shell of 3 mm and single prints of crushed plants.
10	1	Clay with iron, slightly enriched with sand. The sand is fine (0.1–0.2 mm, single samples 0.5 mm), colored unsmoothed and semi-smoothed; with oolite bog iron of 1 mm.
10	2	Clay of the same contents but with medium concentration of sand.
11	1	Clay with iron, slightly enriched with sand, which is colored unsmoothed and semi-smoothed of 0.5 mm; with iron inclusions having the shape of friable oval spherulites of 6 mm and amorphous red-brown inclusions of 0.5 mm.
11	2	Clay of the same contents but with medium concentrations of sand.
12	1	Clay with iron of medium plastic quality containing a great quantity of dust-like sand and quartzite unsmoothed sand of 0.1 to 0.2 mm; mica; ochre red-brown amorphous inclusions of 0.5 mm.
13	1	Silty clay with iron, enriched with average quantity of sand, which is dust-like (up to 0.3 mm), unsmoothed, and semi-smoothed transparent and frosted quartzite sand; oolite bog iron of 2 mm and ochre amorphous inclusions of bright red color of 0.5 mm, single inclusions of shell up to 2 mm.
13	2	Clay of the same contents but with less sand.
14	1	Clay with iron, slightly enriched with sand, which is dust-like of 0.2 mm, with single pieces of 0.5 mm, of different colors, unsmoothed and semi-smoothed, also containing amorphous iron inclusions of bright red color of 1.5 mm and oval friable ones of brown color of 0.5 mm.
15	1	Silty clay enriched with average quantity of sand and iron. The sand is quartzite and colored, unsmoothed and semi-smoothed of 0.1 to 0.2 mm, with single pieces of 0.5 mm; the iron inclusions are of amorphous shape and red-brown color of 0.5-mm dense clay blocks of 1 to 2 mm; small quantity of shell of 2 mm; with single traces of crushed plants and unsmoothed lens-like inclusions of slate clay (shale) of 4 mm.
15	2	Same silty clay with less sand.

Note: R = region; P = place.

Note

Figures and ables in this chapter were prepared by D. Brown, photographs were taken by D. Brown and D. Anthony. All drawings are by IHAV.

References

Antipina, E. E., E. Iu. Lebedeva, and E.N. Chernykh
2002   Skotovodstvo i zemledelie na Gornom? In *Drevneishie Etapy Gornogo Dela i Metallurgii v Severnoi Evrazii: Karagalinsky Kompleks, Materialy Simpoziuma*, pp. 27–28. IARAN, Moskva.

Bobrinskii, A. A.
1978   *Goncharstvo Vostochnoi Evropy*. Istochniki i metody izucheniya. Nauka, Moscow.

Bobrinskii, A. A., and I. N. Vasil'eva
1998   O nekotorykh osobennostiakh plasticheskogo syr'ya v istorii goncharstva. In *Problemy Drevnei Istorii Severnogo Prikaspiya*, edited by V. S. Gorbunov and G. I. Matveeva, pp. 193–217. Institut Istorii I Arkheologii Povolzh'ya, Samara.

Morales Muniz, Arturo, and Ekaterina Antipina
2003   Srubnaya Faunas and Beyond: A Critical Assessment of the Archaeozoological Information from the East European Steppe. In *Prehistoric Steppe Adaptation and the Horse*, edited by M. Levine, C. Renfrew, and K. Boyle, pp. 329–351. McDonald Institute, Cambridge.

Sedova, M. S.
2000   Poseleniya Srubnoi kul'tury [Settlements of the Srubnaya culture]. In *Istoriya Samarskogo Povolzh'ya c Drevneishikh Vremen do Nashikh Dnei: Bronzovy Vek* [History of the Samara Region from the Most Ancient Times to the Modern Day: Bronze Age], edited by I. Y. Kolev, A. E. Mamonov, and M. A. Turetskii, pp. 209–241. Integratsiya, Samara.

Vasil'eva, I. N.
2011   The Early Neolithic Pottery of the Volga-Ural Region (Based on the Materials of the Elshanka Culture). *Archaeology Ethnology & Anthropology of Eurasia* 39(2):70–81.

Index

Note: Page numbers in **bold italics** indicate illustrations or tables.

Abashevo, *16,* 74–75, *75,* 76–77

Acer, 98, 238, 253, 336, *337, 343, 344*

Achillea, 345

Achillea millefolium, 220, 335

activity patterns, in bioarchaeology, *175,* 175–187, *176, 178–187, 207,* 208–209

adhesion lines, 375

adzes, *79,* 86, 294, *296, 297, 326, 327, 328*

Afanasievo, 23

affiliation, 9, 10, 28, 58, 494

ages, in demographics, *106,* 107, *111, 115,* 116–118, *117, 118*

agriculture, 4, 10. *See also* herding camps; plant use; pollen studies
dependency theory and, 5, 20–24, *22*
economy and, 86–87
in floral analysis, 344–346
in Iron Age pastoral nomadism transition, 26–28, *27*
pastoralism and, 5–6, 10, 20
phytoliths and, 369–370
pollen studies and, 333
Srubnaya, 15–17

agropastoralism, 15–19, 27. *See also* agriculture; pastoralism

Agropyron, 268, *345*

Agropyron repens, 220, 335

Agrostis, 345

Alakul, 12, 13, *78,* 80, *81,* 122, *142*

Alandskoe, 143

Alces alces, 389, 392, *405*

Alexseevsky, 150

Allactaga major Kerr, 389, 392, *399, 405, 419*

Allium, 252, 339, *340, 341, 342*

alluvial section, *223*

Alnus, 95, 96, 97, 98, 99

Althaea officinalis, 24

Alyssum desertorum, 220, 335

Amaranthaceae, 96, 97, 99, 238, 338, 339

Amaranthus, 6, 9, 20, 23, 25, 52, 143, 252, 256, 265, 267, 273, 274, 339, 344, *345,* 346, 370

Amaranthus retroflexus, 344, 347

amphibians, 392, *399, 405*

Andreevka, *38,* 74

Andreevskaya Dune, *38,* 77

Andronovo, 5, 14, 22, 72, 77, 80, 88, 208, 293, 309. *See also* Srubnaya-Andronovo horizon

animal(s). *See also* archaeozoology; herding camps; human-animal relations; ritualistic behavior, with dogs; *specific animals*
mortality profiles, 431–433, *432, 433*
pathologies, 433–435, *434–436*
sacrifice, 7, 8, 9, 10, 14, 22, 52, 53, 86, 289, 378, 379, 380, 397–398, 422
in skeletochronology, 374–375, 376–381, *377, 378*

anklets, 195–196, *197*

Apiaceae, 337, 364

appendicular skeleton, in bioarchaeology, 158–169, *159, 162–167, 175,* 175–177

archaeozoology. *See also* human-animal relations
amphibians in, 392, *399, 405*
animal sacrifice and, 397–398
birds in, 390, 392, *399, 404, 405*
bone fragmentation in, 393
cattle in, 387–388, 394, 396, 398, *399, 400, 404, 405, 406, 409, 410, 411, 415, 419*
in cultural layer, 392–393
deer in, 389, 398, *399, 419*

dogs in, 388–389, 391–392, 395, 398, *399, 403, 404, 405, 409, 410, 419*
elk in, 392, *399, 405*
fish in, 390, 392, *399, 405, 419*
fox in, 389, 392, *399, 405*
goats in, 388, 391, 394, 395, 396–397, 398, *399, 400, 401, 402, 404, 405, 407, 409, 410, 412, 414, 419*
gopher in, *419*
hamster in, 392, *399, 405, 419*
hare in, 389, *399*
horses in, 388, 391, 395, 398, *399, 402, 404, 405, 408, 409, 410, 417, 418, 419*
Iron Age, 386–387
jerboa in, 389, 392, *405, 419*
lemming in, *419*
marmots in, 389, 392, *405, 419*
methodology with, 385–386
mole vole in, 389, *419*
mollusks in, 390, *399, 405*
in other sites, comparison with, 395–397
at Peschanyi Dol, 398, *419*
pigs in, 388, 391, 395, 398, *399, 403, 404, 405, 408, 410, 418, 419*
pika in, 389, *399*
polecat in, *399, 405*
in prior excavations, 393–394
seasonality and, 395
sheep in, 388, 391, 394, 395, 396–397, 398, *399, 400, 401, 402, 404, 405, 407, 409, 410, 412, 413, 416, 419*
squirrels in, 389, 392, *399, 405*
stratigraphy in, 385
taphonomy in, 390–392
voles in, 389–390, *399, 405, 419*
wolves in, 389, 392, *399, 405*
Arenaria, 268, 275, *345*
Arkaim, 143
armlet, in burials, 195, 196, *197*
arrowhead
    bronze, 8, 27, 244, 245, *245, 318, 347*
    flint, 482, 485
arrow straightener, 255, 283, *285*, 492
Artemisia, 96, 97, 98, 99, 220, 238, 252, 335, *337, 340, 341, 342*
artifact density, 45, 77
artifacts, 85–86. *See also* ceramics; metal artifacts; *specific artifacts*
    funerary processes and, 195–199, *196–198, 209*, 210
    at Krasnosamarskoe, *235, 242, 243*
Arvicola terrestris, 390, *399, 419*
ash-filled pit, at Krasnosamarskoe, 273–274
ash lens, at Krasnosamarskoe, 274, *275*

Asteraceae, 96, 97, 100, 335, *337*, 338, *340, 341, 347*
astragali, bone, *84*, 228, 285, *287*
Astragalus, 345
Atasu, 13, 19, 122
Atriplex, 268, *345, 347*
Atriplex hastata, 347
Atriplex patula, 347
Atriplex tatarica, 347
Avena, 356, 370
Avena sterilis, 353
Aves, 390, *399, 404, 405. See also* bird(s)
awl
    bone, 51, *79*, 286, *287*, 288
    bronze, 51, *79, 84*, 228, 283, *284, 287*, 288, *318*
    copper, 54, 85, 294, *296, 297*, 300, *302, 304, 305*, 316, *325, 328*, 444
axe
    bronze, 75
    copper, 85, *304, 305*
axial skeleton, in bioarchaeology, *153–155*, 153–158, *157, 158*, 177
Aymyrlyg, 160, 163, 165, 170, 171, *171*, 177, 207
azurite, 45, *48*, 316, *318*

Bactria-Margiana Archaeological Complex (BMAC), 14
Barinovka, *5*, 8, *38*, 41, *56, 73*, 74, 76, 77, *78–79, 473*
    in bioarchaeology, *150, 154*, 168, *173, 175, 179, 195, 200, 202*
    cemetery at, 49, 55, *84*, 469
    excavation at, 48–50, *49*
    isotope analysis at, *135*
    mining at, 87
barley, 6, 17, 27, 333
Bashkirs, 66, 67, 68, 69, 70
bead(s), 10
    bone, *84*
    bronze, 58, 313
    carnelian, 85
    copper, 107
    dog tooth, *79*
    faience, 58, *84*, 140, 313, 323
    nastovix, *84*
    silver, *84*, 85
    stone, *79*
    tin, 295
beaver incisors, 283
beaver tooth sharpener, *285*
Begash Ia, 14, 17, 143
Belogor'e, 130, *133*
Belogorka, *78–79*, 80

Belosersky, *38, 78–79*

Betula, 95, 96, 97, 98, 99, 238, 253, 263, 335, 336, *337, 343, 344*

bifacial tool, quartzite, *284*

bioarchaeology. *See also* crania

    activity patterns in, *175,* 175–187, *176, 178–187, 207,* 208–209

    appendicular skeleton in, 158–169, *159, 162–167, 175,* 175–177

    axial skeleton in, *153–155,* 153–158, *157, 158,* 177

    blastemal desmocranium in, 153–156, *154–155*

    cribra orbitalia in, 164–165, *165,* 204–205, *205*

    defleshing in, *199–202,* 199–203

    dental abscesses in, 170–171, *171, 206*

    dental attrition in, *174,* 174–175, *206*

    dental calculus in, *172,* 172–173, *173, 206,* 207

    dental caries in, 170, *170, 171, 206*

    dental enamel hypoplasia in, *165,* 165–166, 204

    dental health in, *169–174,* 169–175

    developmental defects in, *153–155,* 153–162, *157–159,* 204

    diet in, *169–174,* 169–175, 206–208

    disarticulation in, *199–202,* 199–203, 209

    enthesophytes in, 181, *181*

    femoral dysplasia in, 161–162

    first branchial arch in, 158

    fractures in, *175,* 175–177, *192,* 192–193, 208

    funerary processes in, 193–203, *194–203, 209,* 209–210

    growth in, *162,* 162–163, *163*

    health in, *162–167,* 162–169

    hip dysplasia and dislocation in, 160–161

    infectious disease in, *166,* 166–168, *167*

    joint disease in, 181–187, *182–187*

    materials in, 151

    methods in, 151–152

    myositis ossificans traumatica in, 178–179, *179*

    nasal fractures in, *192,* 192–193

    non-violent trauma in, *175,* 175–181, *176, 178–181*

    ochre staining in, 193–195, *194–195, 196, 209*

    os acromiale in, 179–180

    ossified hematomas in, 179

    osteoarthritis in, 181–185, *182–185, 207*

    osteochondritis dissecans in, *180,* 180–181, *181*

    osteoporosis in, 168–169

    paraxial mesoderm in, 156

    periodontal disease in, 171–172, *172,* 207

    periods in, *150*

    population profiles in, 152, *152*

    porotic hyperostosis in, 164–165, *165*

    Schmorl's nodes in, *180, 186,* 186–187, *187, 207,* 208

    sites in, *150*

    slipped femoral capital epiphysis in, 158–160, *159, 188,* 204

    spondylolysis in, 177–178, *178*

    stature in, *162,* 162–163, *163*

    sternum in, 156–158, *157–158*

    tooth loss in, 173–174, *175*

    violence in, 187–193, *188, 189, 191, 192,* 208

    weapon injuries in, 187–192, *188, 189, 191*

bird(s), *261, 273,* 386, 390, 392, *399, 404, 427*

blade. *See also* knife

    bronze, 17, 310, *312*

    copper, *302, 305, 326, 327, 328*

    flint, *84,* 283, 477, 478, *486,* 487

blastemal desmocranium, 153–156, *154–155*

Bobrovka, *38, 74, 75,* 85

bone artifacts, 285–289, *287*

bone astragali, *84,* 228, 285, *287*

bone awl, 51, *79,* 286, *287*

bone beads, *84*

bone bridle cheekpiece, 86

bone dice, 285, *287. See also* bone astragali

bone handle, 286, *287*

bone ornament, 285–286

bone pendant, 285, 286, *287*

bone points, 85, 286, *287*

bone polisher, 286, *287*

bone rim fragment, 286, *287*

bone rings, 54, *286,* 444

bones. *See* archaeozoology; bioarchaeology; isotope analysis; taphonomy

bone spindle, 86

bone spindle whorl, 285, 286, *287,* 288

bone tools, 85

Bor, 80

Bos, 261, 273, 274, 374

Bos taurus, 273, 274, 387–388, 390–391, 394, 396, 398, *399, 400, 401, 405, 406, 409, 410, 411, 415, 419. See also* cows

boys, initiation of, 9, 53–54, 289, 379, 380. *See also* ritualistic behavior, with dogs

bracelet(s), *84,* 196, *197, 296*

    bronze, 58, *84,* 85, 195, 313

    in burials, 196

    copper, 291, *304, 325, 326*

bracket fragment, *284*

Brassica, 98, 342, *344, 345*

Brassica campestris, 344

bread, 6, 17, 20, 23, 26, 27, 28, 433

bridle cheekpiece, bone, 86

Bromus, 366–367

Bromus riparius, 366

Bromus sterilis, 353

bronze arrowhead, 8, 27, 244, *245, 318, 347*

bronze awl, 51, *79, 84,* 228, 283, *284, 287,* 288, *318*

bronze axe, 75

bronze bead, 58, 313

bronze blade, 17, 310, *312*

bronze bracelet, 58, *84,* 85, 195, 313

bronze funerary artifacts, 195–199, *196–198*

bronze knife, 79, *84,* 85, 302, 303, 310

bronze needle, *79, 84*

bronze rings, 58, 302, *303,* 313

bronze sickles, *79,* 86, 87

bronze spearhead, 75

Bulgar Khanate, 66

bundle burials, 454

Burdyginski, 82

burial mounds, 54, 80, 149–151, 224–225, *226. See also*
    cemetery(ies)
  in Early and Middle Bronze Age, 3–4
  in Samara oblast, *5*
  Yamnaya, 72

buried soil studies, 91–92

burrows, rodent, 40, 49

calculus, dental, *172,* 172–173, *173, 206,* 207

Campanula, 98

Canis, 261, 273, 274, 389, *399*

Canis familiaris, 261, 273, 274, 388–389, 395, 398, *399, 403, 404,*
    405, 409, 410, 419. See also dogs

Canis lupus, 261, 273, 274, 389, 392, *399. See also* wolves

Capra, 261, 273, 274, 391, *404, 405, 409, 410. See also* goat

Capra hircus, 388, 391, 394, 395, 396–397, 398, *399, 400, 401,*
    402, 407, 414, 419

Capreolus, 273, 274, 374

Capreolus pygargus Pall, 389, 398, *399, 419*

Caprifoliaceae, 99

Carex, 268, 344, *345*

carnelian bead, 85

Carpinus betulus, 95, 99

Caryophyllaceae, 264, 335

Catacomb culture, *16,* 23, 26, 74, 81–82, 116, 141, 143, 267, 281,
    450, 453, 457, 458–459

cattle. *See* cows

Caucasus, 11, 23, 24, 26, 68, 74, 85, 88, 115, 116, 120, 122, 136,
    137, 141, *141,* 142, *142,* 294, 302, 370, 450, 453

cavalry, 20, 69

cemetery(ies), 80–81, *81. See also* burial mounds
  Abashevo, 81–82
  ages in, *478*
  artifacts in, 85–86
  Barinovka, 41, 49, 55, 469
  bones as grave gifts in, 459, 460

bundle burials in, 454, *455,* 459

Catacomb culture, 81–82, 450, 453, 458–459

at Chelovech'ya Golova, 80

chronology of, 444

common traits of graves at, 445

cranial studies and, 109–122, *112, 112–113*

ditches in, 445–446

Early Bronze Age, 81

elite graves in, 58

excavation of, 446, *447*

infants in, 448, 451

at Khvalynsk, 72, 106–107

at Krasnosamarskoe, 54–55, *55, 81,* 82, *84,* 114, 250, *444, 445,*
    446, 448–450, 448–470, *452, 453, 455–457, 459, 461–*
    465, 467, 468, 470

at Kutuluk, 72

Late Bronze Age, 82, *83, 84,* 85, 459–470, *461–465, 467, 468,*
    470

litters in, 454

Middle Bronze Age, 81–82, 458–459

at Nikiforovskoe, 80

at Nizhny Orleansky, 72

pathologies in, 466–469

at Pershin, 80–81, *81, 84*

Pokrovka, 469–470, *470*

Poltavka, 445, 458

postmortem treatment in, 466–469

Potapovka, 81–82, 149

radiocarbon dating at, 451

reeds in, *448, 449,* 450, *450,* 451, *452, 453,* 454, *456,* 459

separateness of, 443–444

settlement patterns and, 57

at Spiridonovka, 49, 58, 82, *84,* 121, 469

Srubnaya, 446, 459, 466, 469–470, *470*

subadults in, 451, 460, 462, 464, 466, 469

at S'yezzhee, 72, 80, 82, *84,* 469

at Uranbash, 80–81, *81*

at Utyevka, 75, 76, 80, *81,* 82, *84,* 294, 493

Yamnaya, 81, 149, 458

Centurea, 96

ceramics, 85–86. *See also* clays
  Alakul-type, 12, 13, *78,* 80
  at Barinovka, 49
  clays in, 44, 279–280
  Fedorovo, 13
  Gorodetskaya, 281–283
  in graves, 54–55, 56–57, *452, 455, 457,* 459, 462, 464, *465,* 466,
    467, 469–470, *470*
  at herding camps, 25, 280–281
  in herding camps, 477, 478, 480

Iron Age, 281–283
at Krasnosamarskoe, 51, 54–55, 74, *230*, 231, *235, 242, 243*, 244, *249*, 250, 259, *260*, 262, *264*, 271, *276, 277*, 278–283, *279, 280, 282, 317, 336, 455, 467*
Middle Bronze Age, 281, *282, 486*
at Peschanyi Dol, 25, 43–44, *44*, 280–281, 477, 478, 480, 481, 482, *484*, 485–487, *486, 490*, 491–492, 493, *494, 495*
Pokrovka, 231, *235, 242, 243*, 244, *249*, 250, 278, *279*
Srubnaya, 231, *242, 243, 249*, 250, 278–281, *280, 486*, 487, 492
Vol'sko-Lbishche, 77
Cerealia, 99, 339
Cervus, 374
chariots, 86, 466, 468
cheese, *254*, 254–255, 268, 271, 274, 275, 342
Chekalino, *132*
Chelovech'ya Golova, *38*, 40, *75*, 77, 281
artifacts at, 85
cemetery at, 80
Chenopodiaceae, 96, 97, 238, 335, *337*, 338, 339, *340, 341, 342*
Chenopodium, 6, 9, 17, 20, 23, 25–26, 52, 252, 256, 257, *259*, 265, 273, 274, 342, *345*, 346, *347*, 370
Chenopodium album, 27, 267, 344, *344*
Chenopodium belandieri, 267, 346
Chenopodium glaucum, 347
Chernaja Rechka, *38, 84*
Chernorechensky, *38, 78–79*
chisels, *79*, 86, 294, *297, 304, 326*
Chisty Yar, *38*, 82, *84, 150, 154, 157, 178,* 190–191, *191, 192, 195, 197*
chronology. *See also* radiocarbon dating
of cemeteries, 444–445, *445*
demographics and, *106*
of Late Bronze Age, 12, *12*
Cichorium, 97, 98, 252, 338, 339, *340, 341*
Cichorium intybus, 335, 342, *344, 345,* 370
Circumpontic Metallurgical Province, 294
Citellus citellus, 261, 273
clamp, copper, *304, 327*
clay loom weights, 86
clays, 44, 279–280, 472, 473, *495*
Clematis, 340
climate
pastoralism and, 21, 28
in soil studies, 91
Cliocharis, 268
clubs, *296*, 300, *301*, 302
Convolvulus, 98
cooperation, 9–10, 28, 58, 493–494
cooper dagger, 85
copper alloys, 300

copper awl, 54, 85, 294, *296, 297*, 300, *302, 304, 305*, 316, *325, 328*, 444
copper axe, 85, *304, 305*
copper beads, 107
copper blade, *302, 305, 326, 327, 328*
copper bracelet, 291, *304, 325, 326*
copper chisel, *304, 326*
copper clamp, *304, 327*
copper club, 300, *301*
copper funerary artifacts, 195–199, *196–198*
copper hook, *304, 305, 326, 327*
copper knife, 85, 300, *304, 305, 325, 326, 327, 328*
copper mace, 72, 85
copper mining. *See also* metallurgy; mining
at Gorny, 9–10, 18, 24, 26, *38*, 45
at Mikhailovka Ovsianka, 45–48, *46–48*
Srubnaya, 18–19, 24–25
copper needle, *304, 305, 327, 328*
copper ornament, *304, 327*
copper pendant, *304, 305*, 313, *325, 326, 329*
copper pin, 294
copper production, 316–322, *317, 318, 320, 321. See also* metallurgy
copper rings, 300, *304, 305, 326, 327, 329*
copper sickle, *304, 325*
copper sources, 303, 306–309, *306–309*
copper spatula, *296, 305, 327*
copper spearhead, *304, 326*
copper staff, 300, *305, 328*
copper staple, 316, *318*
Corylus, 95, 97, 98, 99, 238, 253, 336, 338, *343*
Cossacks, 67–68
Country of Towns, 143
cows
in archaeozoology, 387–388, 394, 396, 398, *399, 400, 401, 404, 406, 409, 410, 411, 415, 419*
and dairy in diet, 4
in diet, 378–379
in economy, 86
hauling by, evidence of, 19
herding, 474–476 (*See also* herding camps)
in human-animal relations, *422*, 424, *424, 426*, 427, *427*, 429, *432, 434*, 434–435, *435*, 437, 438
in isotope analysis, 138, *138*, 141, *142*
at Krasnosamarskoe, *261, 273*
in modern times, *69*
in pastoralism conceptions, *22*, 22–23
at Peschanyi Dol, 488
in seasonality study, 376–377, *377*
taphonomy, 390–391

crania, 109–122, *112, 112–113*. *See also* bioarchaeology

cribra orbitalia, 163–164, *164*, 204–205, *205*, 460, 464

Cricetus cricetus, 389, 392, *399, 405, 419*

cultures, Bronze Age, in Samara Valley, 72–76, *73–75*

cup, ceramic, 462, 464, *465*, 466, *467*

curdled milk products, 342

Cyperaceae, 94, 97, 220, 238, 252, 256, 263, 274, 288, 335, 338, *338, 342*, 356, 358, 361, 362, 364, 365, 368

Cyperus, 220, 265, 268, 342, *344, 345*

Cyperus fuscus, 344

Cyperus glaber, 344

dagger, copper, 85. *See also* knife

dairy, 4. *See also* cheese; milk

deer, *138, 142*, 389, 398, *399, 419*

defleshing, in bioarchaeology, *199–202*, 199–203

demographics

    by age class, *106*

    ages in, *106*, 107, *111, 115*, 116–118, *117, 118*

    by chronological period, *106*

    Early Bronze Age, 109–114

    Final Bronze Age, 116–119, 122

    gender in, *106*, 107, *108, 109*

    Late Bronze Age, *119–121*, 119–122

    life expectancy in, 107

    Middle Bronze Age, 114–116

dental abscesses, 170–171, *171, 206*

dental attrition, *174*, 174–175, *206*

dental calculus, *172*, 172–173, *173, 206*, 207

dental caries, 26, 56, 170, *170, 171, 206*

dental enamel hypoplasia, *165*, 165–166, 204

dental health, *169–174*, 169–175

dental loss, antemortem, 173–174, *175*

dependency theory, 5, 20–24, *22*

depletion gilding, 58

developmental defects, in bioarchaeology, *153–155*, 153–162, *157–159*, 204

Dianthus, 271, *342*

dice, bone, 285, *287*. *See also* astragali, bone

Dickson Mounds, 167

diet. *See also* human-animal relations

    in bioarchaeology, *169–174*, 169–175, 206–208

    bread in, 6, 17, 20, 23, 26, 27, 28, 433

    cattle in, 378–379

    cheese in, *254*, 254–255, 268, 271, 274, 275

    dairy in, 4

    dogs in, 9, 378

    fish in, 130, *138*, 139

    grains in, 6, 9, 26, 370

    isotope analysis and, 127–144, *131–139, 141, 142*

    phytoliths and, 370

    seeds in, 267, 344, 346

    teeth and, 26

    wolves in, 9

Digitaria, 344, *345*

disarticulation, in bioarchaeology, *199–202*, 199–203, 209

disposal pits, at Krasnosamarskoe, *241, 254*, 255–258, *257, 258*, 272–273

dog canine pendant, 285, *287*

dogs, 9, 53, *138, 142*, 143, *261, 273*, 283, 289, 342

    in archaeozoology, 386, 388–389, 391–392, 395, 398, *399, 403, 404, 405, 409, 410*

    in human-animal relations, 421–422, *422, 424, 425, 426, 427, 427, 428, 429*, 429–430, *430, 431, 432, 433, 434*, 435, 437–438, *439*

    at Peschanyi Dol, 488

    ritualistic behavior with, 7, 8, 9–10, 50, 52, 53–54, 55, 58, 143, 228, 238, 246, 253, 275, 283, 289, 342, 373, 378, 379–381, 398, *429*, 429–430, *430, 431*, 438, 494

    in seasonality study, *378*, 378–381

Domashka, *84*

dye, 339. *See also* ochre staining

Dzhezkazgan, 19

Early Bronze Age (EBA), 3–4, 6, 8, 10, 12, 17, 18, 21, 26, 54, 81, 85, 109–114, 232, 293–294

earrings

    bronze, 85

    in burials, 58, 195, 196, *197*, 313, 493

ecological setting, 63–65, *64*. *See also* environment; landscape

economic adaptations, 86

economy, 4–5, 68–69. *See also* trade

Ekaterinovka, *133, 150, 157*

electrum ornaments, 291

electrum pendant, 300, 313–315, *314, 315*

Eleocharis, *344, 345*

elite family, of region, 58

elk, 389, 392, *399, 405, 422, 424*

Ellobius talpinus Pallas, 389, *399, 405, 419*

Elytrigia repens, *347*

Eneolithic, 7, 22, 23, 40, 71, 72, 80, 86, 94, *94*, 95, 105–111, *106, 108, 112, 113*, 122, 130–131, *131, 132, 136, 137, 138*, 138–139, *139*, 140–141, *142*, 144, *150*, 204, 291, 293, 492

enthesophytes, 181, *181*

environment. *See also* ecological setting; landscape

    at Krasnosamarskoe, 237–238, 334–335

    local, 37–40, *38–40*

    model, *219*, 219–220, *220*

phytoliths and, 370–371

Ephedra, 354

Ephimovka, *74, 75, 81, 84*

Equisetum, 94, 96, 99, 257, *338*

Equisetum arvense, 257

Equus, 261, 273, 274, 374. *See also* horse(s)

Equus caballus, 261, 273, 274, 388, 391, 395, 398, *399, 402, 404, 408, 409, 410, 417, 418, 419*

Eragrostis, 263, 268, *345,* 354, 355, 360, 370

Eragrostis minor, 353

Erodium, 345

Esox lucius, 131

ethnicity, of Srubnaya, 15

Europeoid, 109, 111, 114–116, 118–119

excavation

at Barinovka, 48–50, *49*

of cemeteries, 446, *447*

of herding camps, 476–477

at Krasnosamarskoe, 50–54, *51–53, 229,* 233–237, *235, 236, 251,* 446, *447*

at Mikhailovka Ovsianka, 45–48, *46–48*

at Peschanyi Dol, 42–45, *43,* 481–492, *483–486, 489–491*

exostosis, 434–435, *435*

facial reconstructions, *110*

Fatyanovo, *16*

Fedorovo, 13, 14

femoral capital epiphysis, in bioarchaeology, 158–160, *159, 188,* 204

femoral dysplasia, proximal, 161–162

Festuca, 360, 370

Festuca sulcata, 220, 334, 335

Final Bronze Age (FBA), 5, 10, 17, 28, 77, 80, 116–119, 122

Finno-Ugric language, 15

fire-cracked quartzite rock (FCR), 283. *See also* quartzite

first branchial arch, in bioarchaeology, 158

fish, 130, *138,* 139, *142,* 392, *399, 405, 419. See also* bird(s)

flake fragment, *486*

flint arrowhead, 482, 485

flint artifacts, 85, *284, 486*

flint blade, *84,* 283, 477, 478, *486,* 487

flint scraper, *79,* 477–478, *486,* 492

floral data analysis

local vegetation in, Late Bronze Age, 335–338, *336–338*

macrobotanical methods in, 334

palynological methods in, 334

phytoliths and, 338–339, 344

plant use in, 339–346, *340–345*

seasonality in, 338–339

forests, 40, *41*

fox, 389, 392, *399, 405, 422, 424*

fractures, in bioarchaeology, *175,* 175–177, *192,* 192–193, 208

Fraxinus, 95

funerary processes, in bioarchaeology, 193–203, *194–203, 209,* 209–210. *See also* cemetery(ies)

Gagea, 273

Galium, 254, 268, 271, 274, 275, 339, *340, 341,* 342, *345*

Galium verum, 220, 254–255, 335, 339, 370

Garin-Bor, 15, 114

Gazella, 374

gender

in demographics, *106,* 107, *108, 109*

in isotope analysis, *139*

geoarchaeology

kurgan formation in, 224–225, *226*

modern landscape in, *219,* 219–220, *220*

reconstruction of past landscape in, 220–224, *221–224*

settlement site in, 225–226

gilding, 58, 313–316, *314, 315*

Glyceria, 345

goat, 22, *22, 69,* 138, *138, 142,* 245

in archaeozoology, 388, 391, 394, 395, 396–397, 398, *399, 400, 401, 402, 404, 405, 407, 409, 410, 412, 414, 419*

in human-animal relations, *422, 424, 426, 427,* 431, *434,* 437, *439*

at Peschanyi Dol, 492

in seasonality study, 376–378, *377*

Golden Horde, 27, 43, 65, 66–67, 99, 485, 492

gold ornament, 85

gold pendant, 313, 316

gold rings, 85, 294

gopher, *419*

Gorny, 9–10, 18, 24, 26, *38,* 45, 58, 86, 87, 232, 275, 288, *321,* 494

Gorodetskaya, 76, *242, 243,* 244, 245, *245, 249,* 281–283

Grachevka, *46, 74, 134,* 303, 310, *312*

in bioarchaeology, *150,* 168, *173, 175, 194, 197*

cemetery at, *81,* 310

Grachev Sad, *73, 75,* 76, *78–79*

grains, 6, 9, 26, 52, 333, 370. *See also* agriculture; phytoliths; pollen studies

graves. *See* cemetery(ies)

grinding stones, 17, *79,* 228, 283, *285,* 457

ground graves, 80. *See also* cemetery(ies)

growth, in bioarchaeology, *162,* 162–163, *163*

gum disease, 171–172, *172, 206,* 207

Gvardeitsi, *38,* 40, *81, 84, 133*

Gypsophila, 264, 275, 335, *337*
hammer
    in metallurgy, 87
    stone, *79,* 86
hamster, 392, *399, 405, 419*
handle, bone, 286, *287*
hare, *261, 273,* 389, *399*
health, in bioarchaeology, *162–167,* 162–169
hematoma, ossified, 179
hemp, 68, 333
herbal remedies, 257, 275, 468
herding, 9–10, 57
    cattle, modern and ancient, 474–476
    modern, *69*
herding camps, 3, 6, 8, 9–10, 17, 41, 42, 44, *44,* 50, 56, *56,* 58,
        283. *See also* Peschanyi Dol
    cattle in, 474–476
    ceramics at, 25, 280–281, 477, 478, 480
    clays at, 472, 473
    cooperation and, 493–494
    excavation of, 476–477
    lithics at, 283, 477, 478, *486,* 487
    locations, *475,* 477–480, *479, 480*
    metallurgy and, 58, 316, 322
    seasonality and, 373, 374
    settlements vs., 45
    skeletochronology and, 376
Hieracium, 345
hip dysplasia and dislocation, 160–161
historic setting, 63–65, *64*
hooks, 86, *304, 305, 326, 327*
Hordeum vulgare, 27
horse(s), *22,* 67, *69*
    in archaeozoology, 386, 388, 395, 398, *399, 402, 404, 405,*
        408, 409, 410, 417, 418
    economic role of, 86
    in graves, 448
    in human-animal relations, 422, *422,* 424, *424, 426, 427, 432,*
        434, 436
    in isotope analysis, *138, 142*
    taphonomy, 391
horse burials, 75
Hsiung-Nu, 5, 170
human-animal relations. *See also* archaeozoology; diet
    birds in, *427*
    body parts in, 422–424, *426*
    cattle in, *422,* 424, *424, 426,* 427, *427,* 429, *432, 434,* 434–
        435, *435,* 437, 438
    dogs in, 421–422, *422, 424, 425, 426,* 427, *427, 428, 429,*
        429–430, *430, 431, 432, 433, 434,* 435, 437–438, *439*

    elk in, *422, 424*
    fox in, *422, 424*
    goat in, *422, 424, 427,* 431, *434,* 437, *439*
    horse in, *422, 424, 426, 427, 432, 434, 436*
    mortality profiles in, 431–433, *432, 433*
    pathologies in study of, 433–435, *434–436*
    pig in, *422,* 424, *424, 426, 427, 434*
    polecat in, *422*
    processing in study of, 424, 427, *427–432,* 429–431
    scavenging and, 431
    sheep in, *422, 424, 426, 427,* 431, *432, 434,* 437, *439*
    taxa in, 421–422, *422–425*
    wolves in, *422, 424, 427*
human remains. *See* bioarchaeology; cemetery(ies); crania
Hunnic, 27
Hypericum, 99

Indo-Iranian, 15
infant graves, 448, 451
infectious disease, in bioarchaeology, *166,* 166–168, *167,* 454
Iron Age, 5, 10, 20, 26–28, *27,* 65, 98, 160, 163, 165, 170, 174,
        177, 207, 230, *235,* 244–246, *246,* 281–283, 386–387
iron head pin, 85, 294
Ishkinovka, *133*
isotope analysis
    carbon in, 127–129
    materials in, 130
    methods in, 130
    nitrogen in, 127–129
    results, 130–140, *131–139*
    sites in, *128*
Ivanokva, 22, *75,* 76, 77, *78–79,* 80, 87

jerboa, 389, 392, *399, 405, 419*
joint disease, in bioarchaeology, 181–187, *182–187*
Juncus, 220

Kalach, *150, 194*
Kalinovka, *150, 157, 158,* 168, *175, 178, 194*
Kalmyks, 3, 67, 68, 267, 346, 450
Kamyshla, 291, 307, *320,* 322, 324
Kargaly, 18, 19, 58, 72, 87, 293, 294, 308, 319–322
Karnab, 19
Kemi-Oba, 115
Khvalynsk, 22, *46,* 72, *132, 133,* 138, 139, 195, *209,* 293, 492
Khvalynsk-Eneolithic, 105–109, *106–109*
Kibit, 8, 17, 18–19, 20, 25, 58, 319, *321*

Kinel', *84, 150, 154, 157, 197*

Kinzelsky, *84*

Kirovskoe, 231, 232

Kirpichni Sarai, 72, *73, 75,* 76, *78–79,* 87, 281

Kirsanovka, *84*

knife, *84, 296, 297. See also* blade
  bronze, 79, *84,* 85, 302, 303, 310
  copper, 85, 300, *304, 305, 325, 326, 327, 328*
  copper/bronze, 85
  flint, *284*
  tin, 303, 310, *312*

Kochia, 344, 345

Kochia prostrata, 220, 335

Konovalovka, *73,* 77

Krasnosamarskoe, *5,* 8–9, 10, 12, 17, 18, 19, 20, 25–26, *38, 39,* 41, *56, 73, 75,* 77, *78–79, 228, 233, 473. See also* cemetery(ies)
  animal remains at, 52–53, *261, 269, 273, 274,* 288, *410*
  artifact density at, 45
  ash-filled pit at, 273–274
  ash lens at, 274, *275*
  in bioarchaeology, *150,* 151, *154,* 164, 166, 168, *173, 178, 180,* 193, *194, 196,* 199, *200*
  bone artifacts at, 285–289, *287*
  botanical resources in, current, 334–335
  cemeteries at, 54–55, *55, 81,* 82, *84,* 114, 250, *445, 446, 448– 450,* 448–470, *452, 453, 455–457, 459, 461–465, 467, 468, 470 (See also* cemetery(ies))
  ceramics at, 51, 54–55, 74, *230,* 231, *235, 242, 243,* 244, *249,* 250, 259, *260,* 262, *264,* 271, *276, 277,* 278–283, *279, 280, 282, 317, 336, 455, 467*
  chronology of, 77
  contemporary setting at, 233, *233*
  disarticulation at, 199, *199*
  disposal pits at, *241, 254,* 255–258, *257, 258,* 272–273
  dogs at, 143
  environment at, ancient, 237–238, 335–338, *336–338*
  environment at, current, 334–335
  excavation at, 50–54, *51–53, 229,* 233–237, *235, 236, 251,* 446, *447*
  feature descriptions at, 250–275, *251, 253–271, 273–277*
  field operations at, 233–234
  Gorodetskaya at, 244, *245*
  houses at, 80
  human remains at, 54–55
  Iron Age at, 244–246, *246*
  Late Bronze Age at, 246–250, *247–249*
  lithics at, 283, *284, 285*
  material culture at, *235*
  metallurgy, 316, *317, 318*
  modern landscape and environment at, *219,* 219–220
  ochre staining at, 193, *196*
  paleobotanical research at, 333–334
  Peschanyi Dol vs., 493
  postholes at, 252–255, *253–257,* 256–257, 270–271, *271, 336*
  previous investigations at, 72
  radiocarbon dating at, *46, 47,* 51, 238–240, *239,* 250, 263, 444– 445, *445,* 451, 462, 464
  reconnaissance at, 50
  rites of passage at, 53–54
  seasonality at, 374, 377, *377*
  settlement at, 227–231, *228–230*
  soil profile at, 240, *241*
  storage pit at, *241, 254,* 255–256, 257, 258, 272–273
  stratigraphy at, *240–243,* 240–250, *245, 247–249,* 250
  structure at, 50–51, 97, 232, *232,* 233–234, 246–249, *247, 248,* 258–270, *260–270,* 288, 338, *340–343,* 357–358, *358, 422*
  vegetation at, 335–338, *336–338*
  well at, 258–270, *260–270,* 272, *273, 274,* 335, *336, 345*
  wooden artifacts at, 262, *263, 267, 270*

Kristianskii, *38*

Krutyenkova, *150,* 168

Kryazh, *150, 157, 194*

Kuibyshev Expedition, 72

kurgans. *See* burial mounds

Kurmanaevka, *46, 74, 133, 150, 194*

Kutuluk, *46,* 72, *74,* 76, 85, *133, 134, 150, 154, 178, 194, 197, 296,* 300, *301, 302*

Lagurus lagurus, 419

landscape. *See also* environment
  modern, *219,* 219–220, *220*
  reconstruction of past, 220–224, *221–224*

language map, *11*

languages, 11, 15, 63

Late Bronze Age (LBA)
  cemeteries, 82, *83, 84,* 85, 459–470, *461–465, 467, 468, 470*
  dating of, 12
  demographics, *119–121,* 119–122
  end of, 19–20
  at Krasnosamarskoe, 246–250, *247–249*
  local vegetation in, 335–338, *336–338*
  settlements in, 3, 4, 77–80, *78–79*
  "settling down" in, 4–5, 24–28

Lavatera thuringiaca, 347

Lebyazhinka, 130, *132,* 139, 144, 395, 396, *410*

Legumes, 364

lemming, *419*

Lepus, 389, *399*

Leshevskoe, *38, 74, 78–79, 84,* 160
  in bioarchaeology, *150, 157,* 158–159, *159, 188, 189, 194*
  cemetery at, 80
life expectancy, 107, 110
Liliaceae, 98
Linaria, 268, *345*
Linearbandkeramik (LBK), 25
lithics, 283, *284, 285,* 477, 478, *486,* 487, 492. *See also entries at*
  stone
local environment, 37–40, *38–40. See also* ecological setting
Lolium, 268
Lolium perenne, 345
loom weights, clay, 86
Lopatino, *46, 133, 134,* 140, *150, 154, 157, 158,* 167, *173, 175,*
  179, 187, *194, 200*
Luzhki, *46, 133*

Maasai, 27
mace, 72, 85
macrobotanical methods, 334
Macropus, 374
magnetic properties, of soil, 91–92
Maikop, 115
maize, 25, 127, 267
Maksimovka, *38, 73,* 77, *78–79,* 98
malachite, 18, 45, *48,* 288
Mari, *11,* 66
marmot, 389, 392, *405, 419*
Marmota bobak Muller, 389, 392, *399, 405, 419*
marshes, 24
Mary Rose, 179–180
meadow soil, 219, *219*
Medicago, 335, 344, *345*
Medicago sativa, 220
medicine, 257, 342, 346
Medvedka, *74, 81*
Melilotus, 268, *345*
metal artifacts, 85–86, *235, 242, 243. See also entries at* bronze,
  copper
metallurgy, 87–88
  copper production, 316–322, *317, 318, 320, 321*
  copper sources in, 303, 306–309, *306–309*
  Early Bronze Age, 293–294
  emergence of, 291
  gilding in, 313–316, *314, 315*
  Late Bronze Age, 316–322, *317, 318, 320, 321*
  map of sites in, *292*
  microprobe and metallographic analysis of, 295–313, *296–299,*
    301–309, 311, 312

  overview of, 293–295
  pastoralism and, 294–295
  work patterns in, 310, *311, 312*
metal strap, *284*
Microtinae, 390, *399, 419*
Middle Bronze Age (MBA), 3–4, 6, 8, 10, 12, 13, 14, 15, *16,* 17,
  21, 41, 54, 57, 74, *75,* 76–77, 81–82, 114–116, 232, 281,
  282, 293, 454, 458–459, 477, *486*
Mikhailovka Ovsianka, *5,* 18, 24, 45–48, *46, 46–48,* 58, 208, 291,
  322, 374, 377, *377*
milk, 4, 28, 52, 65, 67, 68, 129, 143, 232, 254, 268, 271, 275, 342,
  370, 394, 437
millet, 6, 17, 26, 27, 127, 143, 244, 333
mining, 87–88. *See also* metallurgy
  copper, 18–19, 24–25, 291
  tin, 19
  trade and, 57–58
Mnogovalikovaya, 24
modern landscape and environment, *219,* 219–220, *220*
Moechnoe Ozero, 395, *410*
mole vole, 389, *399, 405, 419*
Mollusca, 390, 392, *399, 405*
mollusks, 390, 392, *399, 405*
Monasheskii Khutor, 72, *73, 78–79*
Mongolia, 23–24
Mordvin, *11*
mortality profiles, animal, 431–433, *432, 433*
mortar, 17, 20, *79,* 87, 283, 333, 448, 454, 488, *491,* 492
mortuary. *See* cemetery(ies); funerary processes
Murzikha, 130, *132, 150*
mussel, *261, 273*
Mustela, 261, 273, 405
Mustela eversmannii, 399
mustelid, *261, 273*
myositis ossificans traumatica, 178–179, *179*

Nadezhdinka, *135, 150, 157*
nasal fractures, in bioarchaeology, *192,* 192–193
needle, *297*
  bronze, *79, 84*
  copper, *304, 305, 327, 328*
Nemchanka, *73,* 77
Neprik, *84,* 85
Nikiforovskoe Lesnichestvo, *75,* 80, 82, 85, 88
Nikolaevka, *38, 75,* 82, *134, 154,* 164, *179, 194*
Nikol'skoe-Mariupol, 22, 106
Nizhne Nikol'skoe, *38*
Nizhny Orleansky, *46,* 72, *155, 157, 158,* 164, *173, 175,* 176, *178,*
  179, 180, 192, 194, 195, 197, 200, 297, 313, *314,* 316, 319

Nogai Horde, 66–67
nomadism, 4–6, 20–21, 26–28, *27*
North Caucasus-Caspian steppes, 23
North Caucasus Mountains, 11, 23, 26, 74, 85, 110, 116, 122, 136, 137, *138,* 141, *141,* 142, *142,* 267, 300, 450, 453
North Caucasus steppes, 115, 116, 120, 122, 450, 453
Noua-Sabatinovka, 16
Novoberezovskii, *84*
Novonikol'skoe I, 13
Novoorlovsky, *150, 155*
Novoselki, *135, 150,* 161, *195*
Novotitorovskaya, 107, 116, 450, 453, *454*
Nur, *38, 46, 73, 75,* 77, *78–79,* 87, *133, 296, 303*

obligation, 9–10, 58
Ochotona pusilla Pallas, 389, *399*
ochre staining, 193–195, *194–195, 196,* 209, *209,* 451, *453,* 454, *457,* 459
Odonochnii, *38*
Oirats, 67
ornament
    bone, 285–286
    copper, *304, 327*
    electrum, 291
    gold, 85
os acromiale, 179–180
ossified hematomas, 179
osteoarthritis, 181–185, *182–185, 207*
osteochondritis dissecans, *180,* 180–181, *181*
osteoporosis, in bioarchaeology, 168–169
Ovis, 261, 273, 274, 404, 405, 409, 410, 412. See also sheep
Ovis aries, 388, 391, 394, 395, 396–397, 398, *399, 400, 401, 402, 407, 413, 416, 419*

paleosols, 91–92
palynological studies, 92, 334. *See also* floral data analysis; phytoliths; pollen studies
Panicum, 127
Panicum miliaceum, 17, 26, 27, 244, *347*
paraxial mesoderm, in bioarchaeology, 156
pastoral dependency, 5, 20–24, *22. See also* agriculture
pastoralism, 55–58, *56. See also* herding camps
    agriculture and, 5–6, 10, 20
    bread and, 6
    climate and, 21, 28
    in Iron Age vs. Bronze Age, 27–28
    of Maasai, 27
    metallurgy and, 294–295

phytoliths and, 370
    in Vola-Ural steppes, 24–28
pastoral nomadism, 4–6, 20–21, 26–28, *27*
Pavlovka, 13
Pazyryk, 203
pendant
    bone, 286, *287*
    copper, *304, 305,* 313, *325, 326, 329*
    dog canine, 285, *287*
    electrum, 300, 313–315, *314, 315*
    gold, 313, 316
periodontal disease, 171–172, *172, 206,* 207
Permian, *11*
Pershin, *74,* 80–81, *81, 84*
Perthes disease, 160
Peschanyi Dol, 25, *38,* 41–42, *73, 78–79,* 319, 322, *472, 473, 475, 489. See also* herding camps
    archaeozoology at, 398, *419*
    artifact density at, 45, 77
    ceramics at, 25, 43–44, *44,* 280–281, 477, 478, 480, 481, 482, *484,* 485–487, *486, 490,* 491–492, 493, *494, 495*
    copper at, 488, *491*
    excavations, 42–45, *43,* 481–492, *483–486, 489–491*
    fauna at, 488, *490,* 492, 493
    herding camps at, 3, 6, 8, 9–10, 17, 25, 41, 42, 44, *44,* 45, 50, 56, *56,* 58, 280–281, 283, 316, 322, 373, 374, 376, 471–494, *472–475, 477, 479, 480, 483–486, 489–491, 494, 495*
    Krasnosamarskoe vs., 493
    lithics at, 283, 477, 478, *486,* 487, 492
    metallurgy, 316–322, *317, 318, 320, 321*
    modern environment at, 471
    radiocarbon dating at, *46, 485,* 491
    seasonality at, 374, 376, 377
    stone artifacts at, 488, *490, 491, 494*
    survey, 42–45, *44*
pestle
    quartzite, 283, *285*
    stone, 54, *79, 84,* 85, 86
Petrovka, 13, 14, 122
Phragmites, 24, 43, 51, 94, 220, 227, 232, 233, 238, 246, 252, 256, 259, 270–271, 272, 288, 338, 339, 354, 356, 358, 360, 364, 365, 366, 367, 368, 370–371
Phragmites australis, 345, 353
phytoliths, 351, *352*
    agriculture and, 369–370
    in alluvial horizon, 361, *363*
    in ash ens at Krasnosamarskoe, 274, 355–357, *357,* 360, *361*
    in ash lens at Krasnosamarskoe, 358, *359*
    in ceramic vessel, 363–364, *364*

in correspondence analysis, 367–368, *369*

counts, 354–368, *355–368*

density, in samples, 354, *356*

environmental setting and, 370–371

floral data analysis and, 338–339, 344

food availability and, 370

general trends with, 368–369

methodology with, 351–352

morphotypes of, *352*

pastoralism and, 370

in posthole at Krasnosamarskoe, 252, 254, 256, 270–271, 359, *360, 364, 365*

quantification of, 354

reference samples, 352, *353*

in roof structure, 227, 288, 358

seasonality and, 238, 371

in storage pit at Krasnosamarskoe, 257, 258, 272, 362–363, *363*

in structure at Krasnosamarskoe, 52, 232, 246, 357–358, *358, 359*

in well at Krasnosamarskoe, 259, 262–263, 355, *357,* 360, *361, 362*

pig, *138, 261, 273*

in archaeozoology, 386, 388, 391, 395, 398, *399, 403, 404, 405, 408, 409, 410, 418, 419*

in human-animal relations, *422,* 424, *424, 426, 427, 434*

pika, 389, *399*

pike, 131

pin, iron head, 85, 294

Pinus, 95, 96, 97, 98, 99, 358

Pinus sylvestris, 238, 252–253, 263, 273, 335, 336, *337, 343, 344*

Plantago, 96, 97, 98, 238, 252, 335, *337,* 338, *340, 341, 342*

Plantago lanceolata, 220, 335

plants. *See* floral data analysis; grains; phytoliths; pollen studies; *specific plants*

plant use, 339–346, *340–345*

plaque, dental, *172,* 172–173, *173, 206,* 207

Poa, 345

Poa annua, 342

Poaceae, 96, 238, 252, 256, 257, 273, 335, *337, 340, 341, 342*

Poa trivialis, 347

Podlesnoe, *38, 150, 194*

points

bone, 85, 286, *287*

flint, 85

Pokrovka, *38, 42,* 54, 56, *74, 78–79, 84,* 120

cemeteries, 469–470, *470*

ceramics, 231, *235, 242, 243,* 244, *249,* 250, 278, *279*

houses at, 80

Pokrovka phase, 77–*78–79*

polecat, *399, 405, 422*

polisher, bone, 286, *287*

pollen studies, 92–100, *94, 95,* 333. *See also* floral data analysis; phytoliths

Poltavka, *16,* 23, 54, 74, *75,* 76–77, *152,* 281, *282*

cemeteries, 445, 458

funerary processes of, *194,* 199, *199, 202, 209*

metallurgy, *296*

Polygonum, 6, 9, 20, 52, 238, 252, 265, 267, 274, 335, *337, 340, 341,* 342, 344, *344, 345,* 346, 370

Polygonum aviculare, 347

Polygonum hydropiper, 344

Polygonum lapathifolium, 347

Polygonum patulum, 347

Polypodiaceae, 96, 99

Pontic-Caspian steppes, *4,* 11

Poplavskoe, *56, 73, 78–79,* 80, *155,* 156, *173, 192, 410*

population growth, 4

population structure, in seasonality analysis, 375

Populus, 96, 97, 99, 238, 253, 263, 335, 336, *337, 343, 344*

porotic hyperostosis, 164–165, *165*

postholes, at Krasnosamarskoe, 252–255, *253–257,* 256–257, 270–271, *271, 336*

Potapovka, 14, *46,* 72, 75, *75,* 76–77, 85, 116–119, 118, 122, 293, 307, 308, *308, 309,* 310, *312,* 319, 323

in bioarchaeology, *179, 194*

cemeteries, 81–82, 149

demographics, *106, 108, 112–113,* 116–120, *117, 118, 120,* 121, 122, *122*

funerary processes of, *194, 200, 202, 209*

isotope analysis at, *133, 134*

metallurgy, *296,* 303

radiocarbon dating at, *46*

Potapovka MBA II, 7

Potentilla anserina, 347

pottery. *See* ceramics

pottery polisher, 286

quartzite bifacial tool, *284*

quartzite pestle, 283, *285*

quartzite scraper, *79,* 283

Quercus, 99, 253, 274, 360

Quercus robur, 95, 96, 98, 238, 263, 335, 336, *337, 343, 344*

radiocarbon dating, *46–47*

at cemeteries, 451

at Krasnosamarskoe, 51, 238–240, *239,* 250, 263, 444–445, *445,* 451, 462, 464

in Late Bronze Age chronology, 12, *12*

at Leshevskoe, 160
   at Peschanyi Dol, 44, *485,* 491
   in pollen studies, 96
rainfall, 92, 129, 219. *See also* climate
Rangifer, 374
Ranunculus, 335, *337, 340, 341*
rawhide thong smoother, 286, *287*
reeds, in graves, *448, 449,* 450, *450,* 451, *452, 453,* 454, *456,*
      459
Ribes, 338
Rig Veda, 15, 302, 378, 380
rim fragment, bone, 286, *287*
rings, *296*
   bone, 54, *286,* 444
   bronze, 58, 302, *303,* 313
   copper, 300, *304, 305, 326, 327, 329*
   gold, 85, 294
   silver, 300, *329*
rites of passage, 9, 53–54, 289, 342, 378, 379, 380
ritual, skull scraping, 109
ritualistic behavior, with dogs, 7, 8, 9–10, 50, 52, 53–54, 55, 58,
      143, 228, 238, 246, 253, 275, 283, 289, 342, 373, 378,
      379–381, 398, 438, 494
rodent burrows, 40, 49, *261, 273*
Rosaceae, 338
Rozhdestvenno, *134, 135, 155, 157, 192, 195*
Rubiaceae, 338
Rumex, 96, 97, 268, 338, *340, 345*
Rumex hydrolapathum, 344
Russkaya Sel'itba, *5,* 17, *73, 232*

Sachkovo, 395, 396, 397, *410*
sacrifice, animal, 7, 8, 9, 10, 14, 22, 52, 53, 86, 289, 378, 379,
      380, 397–398, 422. *See also* ritualistic behavior, with dogs
Sagittaria, 98
Saka, 5, 6, 15, 20, 26, 27, 380
saline soil, 219, *219, 220*
Salix, 97, 98, *347*
Samara Ancient Metals Project (SAM), 291, 319
Samara *oblast, 4, 5,* 7, *64,* 68–69, *69*
Samara Valley, 7, 10–11, 37–40, *38–40,* 63–64
Samara Valley cultures, 72–76, *73–75*
Samara Valley Project (SVP), 3–4, 6, 7–10, 37
Samara Valley sites, 76–85, *78–79, 81, 83, 84*
Samarskaya Luka, 3, 64, 66, 68, 69, 77, 231, 232, 244, 281
Sarazm, 14, 17
Sarmatians, 15, 65–66, 69, 98
Sauromatians, 8, 27, 65–66, 244, 245, *245,* 246, *318, 347,* 380
scale mail, 286

scavenging, 431
Schmorl's nodes, *180, 186,* 186–187, *187, 207,* 208, 466
Scirpus, 345
Scirpus tabernaemontni, 347
scraper, *84*
   flint, *79, 284,* 477–478, *486,* 492
   quartzite, *79,* 283
Scythian, 5, 15, 19, 20, 63, 65, *135,* 160, *171,* 244, 380
Scythian-Saka, 5, 6, 27
Scythian-Sauromatian-Saka, 380
seasonality
   archaeozoology and, 395
   cattle in study of, 376–377, *377*
   development and physiology in, 375
   dogs in study of, *378,* 378–381
   in floral data analysis, 338–339
   goats in study of, 376–378, *377*
   at Krasnosamarskoe, 374, 377, *377*
   methodology in study of, 374–375
   at Mikhailovka Ovsianka, 374, 377, *377*
   at Peschanyi Dol, 374, 376, 377
   phytoliths and, 238, 371
   population structure in study of, 375
   sheep in study of, 376–378, *377*
   sites sampled in study of, 374
   skeletochronology in, 374–375, 376–381, *377, 378*
   teeth, mammalian, in study of, 376–377, *377*
Secaria, 127
seeds, in diet, 267, 344, 346
Semenovka, *38*
Seseli, 55, 253, 264, 274–275, 289, *340,* 342
Setaria, 345, 347
settlement patterns, 52, 56–57
"settling down," 4–5, 24–28
Sharlyk swamp, 92–94, *93,* 339
sheep, 22, *22,* 22–23, *69,* 136–137, 138, *138,* 141, *142,* 245, *261,*
      273
   in archaeozoology, 388, 391, 394, 395, 396–397, 398, *399,*
      400, 401, 402, 404, 405, 407, 409, 410, 412, 413, 416,
      419
   in graves, 448, *452,* 454, 458, 459
   in human-animal relations, *422, 424, 426, 427,* 431, *432, 434,*
      437, *439*
   at Peschanyi Dol, 488, 492
   in seasonality study, 376–378, *377*
Shelekhmet, 232, *232*
shell(s)
   buckle, *84*
   in ceramics, 281, 477, 478, 485, *495*
   in graves, *84,* 85

at Krasnosamarskoe, *235, 242, 243, 269,* 278, 288
   mollusk, 390, 392, *399*
   stamp, 228, 278, 283, 286, *287*
Shigonskoe, 231, *232*
Shirakinskii, *38, 78–79*
Shirochenka, *38, 75, 84,* 85
Shumaevo, 72
Shurmak, 163, 164, 165, 170, 171, *171,* 172, 174, 177, 178, 183, 187, 193, 203
sickles, 17, 68, *79,* 86, 87, *297, 304, 325,* 333
silver bead, *84,* 85
silver ring, 300, *329*
Sintashta, 7, 13–14, 24, 75, 116–119, 118, 149, 205–206, 310
Sintashta-Potapovka-Filitovka horizon, 291
sites, 76–85, *78–79, 81, 83, 84*
skeletal analysis, 151. *See also* bioarchaeology; crania; isotope analysis
skeletochronology, 374–375, 376–381, *377, 378*
slipped femoral capital epiphysis, in bioarchaeology, 158–160, *159, 188,* 204
snail, *261, 273,* 485
soil studies, 91–92, 219, *219,* 219–220, *220*
Solanum, 345
Sorochinsky, *78–79,* 87
Sparganium, 268, *345*
spatula, copper, *296, 305, 327*
spearheads, 28, 75, *297, 304, 326*
Spermophilus major Palls, 389, 392, *399, 419*
spindle, *79*
   bone, 86
spindle whorl, 51, 54, 228
   bone, 285, 286, *287,* 288
   ceramic, 458, 461, 493
   clay, 462
Spiridonovka, 19, *38, 56, 73, 74, 78–79, 84*
   artifacts at, 85
   in bioarchaeology, *155, 157,* 161, 164, 166, *173, 175,* 177, *178, 179, 180, 195,* 196, *197, 201,* 204
   cemetery at, 55, 58, *81,* 82, 121, 469
   isotope analysis at, *134, 135, 137,* 139–140
   metallurgy, *297,* 313–316, *315,* 323
   radiocarbon dating at, *46*
spondylolysis, 177–178, *178*
squirrel, 389, 392, *399, 405*
Srubnaya, 5, 8, 9, 10, 12, 14
   Abashevo and, 77
   agropastoralism, 15–17
   cattle in pastoralism of, 22
   cemeteries, 446, 459, 466, 469–470, *470*
   ceramics, 231, *242, 243, 249,* 250, 278–281, *280,* 487, 492

copper mining and trade, 18–19, 24–25
ethnicity, 15
funerary processes of, 193, *200, 202, 209*
gilding, 313–316, *314, 315*
metallurgy, 313–316, *314, 315*
pastoralism, 55–58, *56*
   in Samara oblast, 231–233, *232*
settlements, 231–233, *232*
Srubnaya-Andronovo horizon, 5, *12,* 12–24, *13, 16, 22*
staff, copper, 300, *305, 328*
staple, copper, 316, *318*
stature, in bioarchaeology, *162,* 162–163, *163*
sternum, in bioarchaeology, 156–158, *157–158*
Stipa, 345, 363
Stipa pennata, 220
Stipa tirsa, 353
stone artifacts, *235,* 283, *284, 285, 490, 494*
stone beads, *79*
stone hammer, *79,* 86
stone mortar, 17, 20, *79,* 87, 283, 448, 454, 488, *491,* 492
stone pestle, 54, *79, 84,* 85, 86, 444
storage pit, at Krasnosamarskoe, *241, 254,* 255–256, 257, 258, 272–273
structure, at Krasnosamarskoe, 50–51, 232, *232,* 233–234, 246–249, *247, 248,* 258–270, *260–270,* 288, 338, *340–343,* 357–358, *358, 422*
Studenzy, *155, 157,* 158, *158, 173*
Sukhorechenskoe, 87
survey area, 37–40, *38–40*
Suskanskaya, 76, *249*
Suskanskoe, 19, 138, 231, 395, *410*
suslik burrows, 40, 49
Sus scrofa, 261, 273, 274, 388, 391, 395, 398, *399, 403, 404, 405, 408, 409, 410, 418, 419. See also* pig
Sverdlovo, *74, 81,* 82, *84*
Svezhensky, *155,* 156, *157,* 164, *173*
S'yezzhee, *38, 56,* 72, *73, 75, 78–79,* 80, 82, *84,* 469

Tanabergin, *46,* 130, *134*
taphonomy, 390–392
Tasbas, 14, 17, 20
Tashkazgan, 307, 309, 313, 316
teeth. *See* dental
thong smoother, 286, *287*
Tilia, 95, 98, 263, 335, *337*
timber, 18
Timber Grave, 5, 12, 119, 149
tin beads, 295
tin bronzes, 303

tin knife, 303, 310, *312*

tin mining, 19

Tokskoe, 17, *78–79,* 87

trade, 57–58

   copper, 18–19

   mining and, 57–58

   Srubnaya, 18–19

   warfare and, 14

trauma, in bioarchaeology

   non-violent, *175,* 175–181, *176, 178–181, 207*

   violent, 187–193, *188, 189, 191, 192*

Trifolium, 238, 268, 335, *337, 341, 345*

Trifolium pratense, 220, 335

Trifolium repens, 220, 335

Tripol'ye, 23

Tristeum, 360

Triticum aestivum, 26

Triticum dicoccum, 26

Troy, 19, 493

Tryasinovka, *150, 175,* 176, 190, *194*

turtle, *261, 273*

Typha, 24, 43, 98, 220, 233, 238, 252, 335, 338, *338,* 354, 370

Ulmus, 95, 99

Ur, 293, 315, 323

Uranbash, *74,* 80–81, *81, 150, 175,* 176

Uren, *150, 157, 195*

Urtica, 254–255, 256, 271, 335, *337,* 339, *340, 341, 342*

Uste' Reki Kinel', *75*

Ust-Kamenogorsk, 19

Utyevka, *5,* 23, *38,* 40, *56,* 72, *74, 75,* 77, *78–79, 84*

   artifacts at, 85

   in bioarchaeology, *154,* 156, *157, 173, 175, 194,* 196, *197*

   cemetery at, 75, 76, 80, *81,* 82, 294, 493

   isotope analysis at, *134*

   metallurgy at, 294, *296, 297, 309,* 310, 312, *312,* 312–313, 323

   mining at, 87

   radiocarbon dating at, *46*

Uvarovka, *84, 135*

Uyuk, 163, 164, 165, 172, 174, 178, 183, 186, 193, 202, 203, 207

Varfolomievka, 22

Veronica, 220, 335

Vilovatoye, *38,* 40, *73, 75,* 76, 77, *84*

violence, in bioarchaeology, 187–193, *188, 189, 191, 192,* 208

voles, 389–390, *399, 405, 419*

Volosovo, 15, *16,* 106, 114

Vol'sko-Lbishche group, 74, *75,* 76–77, *78,* 82, 85, 96, 116, 119, 244, 245, 246, 281, *282*

Vulpes vulpes, 389, 392, *399*

wagons, 4, 14, 19, 22–23, 28, 58, 65, 72, 76, 86, 87, 231, 294, 493

war-bands, 379–380

warfare, 14, 19, 20, 205, 380, 437

water voles, 390, *399, 419*

weapon injuries, in bioarchaeology, 187–192, **188,** *189, 191*

well, at Krasnosamarskoe, 258–270, *260–270,* 272, *273, 274,* 335, *336, 345*

wheat, 17, 26, 333

wolves, 9, 53, 289, 379, 389, 392, *399, 405, 422, 424, 427*

wooden artifacts, at Krasnosamarskoe, 262, *263, 267, 270*

Yamnaya, 6, 18, 22, 23, *42,* 43, 72

   artifacts, 85

   cemeteries, 81, 149, 458

   in demographics, *106, 108,* 109–116, *111, 112–113,* 118, 122, *122*

   funerary processes of, 193–195, *194,* 199, *200, 202, 209*

   metallurgy, *296,* 300, *308*

Zakhar-Kal'ma, *38,* 71, *73,* 77, *78–79*

Zalivnaya, *38, 78–79*

Zea mays, 127

UCLA COTSEN INSTITUTE OF ARCHAEOLOGY PRESS

MONUMENTA ARCHAEOLOGICA

Volume 38   *The Archaeology of Grotta Scaloria: Ritual in Neolithic Southeast Italy,* edited by Ernestine S. Elster, Eugenia Isetti, John Robb, and Antonella Traverso

Volume 37   *A Bronze Age Landscape in the Russian Steppes: The Samara Valley Project,* edited by David W. Anthony, Dorcas R. Brown, Aleksandr A. Khokhlov, Pavel F. Kuznetsov, and Oleg D. Mochalov

Volume 36   *Rural Archaeology in Early Urban Northern Mesopotamia: Excavations at Tell al-Raqa'i,* edited by Glenn M. Schwartz

Volume 35   *New Insights into the Iron Age Archaeology of Edom, Southern Jordan,* by Thomas E. Levy, Mohammad Najjar, and Erez Ben-Yosef

Volume 34   *The Excavation of the Prehistoric Burial Tumulus at Lofkënd, Albania,* by John K. Papadopoulos, Sarah P. Morris, Lorenc Bejko, and Lynne A. Schepartz

Volume 33   *Formative Lifeways in Central Tlaxcala: Volume 1: Excavations, Ceramics, and Chronology,* edited by Richard G. Lesure

Volume 32   *Integrating Çatalhöyük: The 2000-2008 Seasons (Çatal Research Project Volume 10),* edited by Ian Hodder

Volume 31   *Substantive Technologies at Çatalhöyük: Reports from the 2000-2008 Seasons (Çatal Research Project Volume 9),* edited by Ian Hodder

Volume 30   *Humans and Landscapes of Çatalhöyük* (Çatal Research Project Volume 8), edited by Ian Hodder

Volume 29   *Çatalhöyük Excavations: The 2000-2008 Seasons (Çatal Research Project Volume 7),* edited by Ian Hodder

Volume 28   *Light and Shadow: Isolation and Interaction in the Shala Valley of Northern Albania,* edited by Michael L. Galaty, Ols Lafe, Wayne E. Lee, and Zamir Tafilica

Volume 27   *Last House on the Hill: BACH Area Reports from Çatalhöyük, Turkey,* edited by Ruth Tringham and Mirjana Stevanović

Volume 26   *The History and Archaeology of Jaffa I,* edited by Martin Peilstöcker and Aaron A. Burke

Volume 24   *The Early Iron Age Cemetery at Torone,* by John K. Papadopoulos

Volume 23   *The Plain of Phaistos: Cycles of Social Complexity in the Mesara Region of Crete,* by L. Vance Watrous, Despoina Hadzi-Vallianou, and Harriet Blitzer

Volume 22   *K'axob: Ritual, Work, and Family in an Ancient Maya Village,* edited by Patricia A. McAnany

Volume 21   *The Sydney Cyprus Survey Project: Social Approaches to Regional Archaeological Survey,* by Michael Given and A. Bernard Knapp

Volume 20   *Prehistoric Sitagroi: Excavations in Northeast Greece 1968–1970. Volume 2. Final Report,* edited by Ernestine S. Elster and Colin Renfrew

Volume 19   *Archaeology of Solvieux, An Upper Paleolithic Open Air Site in France,* by James Sackett

Volume 18   *Down by the Station: Los Angeles Chinatown, 1880–1933,* by Roberta S. Greenwood

Volume 17   *Rock Art of Easter Island: Symbols of Power, Prayers to the Gods,* by Georgia Lee

Volume 16   *Landscape Archaeology as Long-Term History: Northern Keos in the Cycladic Islands,* by J. E. Cherry, J. L. Davis, and E. Mantzourani

Volume 15   *Selevac: A Neolithic Village in Yugoslavia,* edited by Ruth Tringham and Dusan Krstic

Volume 14   *Achilleion: A Neolithic Settlement in Thessaly, Greece, 6400–5600 B.C.,* by Marija Gimbutas, Shan Winn, and Daniel Shimabuku

Volume 13   *Excavations at Sitagroi: A Prehistoric Village in Northeast Greece. Volume 1. By Colin Renfrew, Marija Gimbutas, and Ernestine S. Elster

Volume 12   *Petroglyphs in the Guianas and Adjacent Areas of Brazil and Venezuela: An Inventory with a Comprehensive Bibliography of South American and Antillean Petroglyphs,* by C. N. Dubelaar

Volume 11	*Chinese Archaeological Abstracts 4*, edited by Albert E. Dien, Jeffrey K. Riegel, and Nancy T. Price
Volume 10	*Chinese Archaeological Abstracts 3*, edited by Albert E. Dien, Jeffrey K. Riegel, and Nancy T. Price
Volume 9	*Chinese Archaeological Abstracts 2*, edited by Albert E. Dien, Jeffrey K. Riegel, and Nancy T. Price
Volume 8	*Kolmakovskiy Redoubt: The Ethnoarchaeology of a Russian Fort in Alaska*, by Wendell Oswalt
Volume 7	*Prehistoric Trails of the Atacama: Archaeology of Northern Chile*, by Clement Meighan and D. L. True
Volume 6	*Chinese Archaeological Abstracts*, by Richard C. Rudolph
Volume 5	*The Stone and Plaster Sculpture: Excavations at Dura Europos*, by Susan B. Downey
Volume 4	*The Transition to Mycenaean*, by Sarah and Jeremy Rutter
Volume 3	*The Marine Thiasos in Greek Sculpture*, by Steven Lattimore
Volume 2	*The Archaeology of Amapa, Nayarit*, edited by Clement W. Meighan
Volume 1	*Neolithic Macedonia as Reflected by Excavations at Anza, Southeast Yugoslavia*, edited by Marija Gimbutas